DAVID A. ASTON, MANFRED BIETAK · TELL EL-DAB^{c}A VIII

For Larry Stager, great friend and great archaeologist
by Manfred
25th April 2012

ÖSTERREICHISCHE AKADEMIE DER WISSENSCHAFTEN
DENKSCHRIFTEN DER GESAMTAKADEMIE, BAND LXVI

UNTERSUCHUNGEN DER ZWEIGSTELLE KAIRO DES ÖSTERREICHISCHEN ARCHÄOLOGISCHEN INSTITUTES

HERAUSGEGEBEN IN VERBINDUNG MIT DER KOMMISSION FÜR ÄGYPTEN UND LEVANTE DER ÖSTERREICHISCHEN AKADEMIE DER WISSENSCHAFTEN VON MANFRED BIETAK

BAND XII

Verlag der
Österreichischen Akademie
der Wissenschaften

Wien 2012

ÖSTERREICHISCHE AKADEMIE DER WISSENSCHAFTEN

DENKSCHRIFTEN DER GESAMTAKADEMIE, BAND LXVI

Ausgrabungen in Tell el-Dab^{c}a

Manfred Bietak (Hrsg.)

TELL EL-DAB^{C}A VIII

THE CLASSIFICATION AND CHRONOLOGY OF TELL EL-YAHUDIYA WARE

DAVID A. ASTON, MANFRED BIETAK

With contributions by Aren Maeir, Robert Mullins, Lawrence E. Stager, Ross Voss, Hanan Charaf, Mary Ownby and Rolf Rottländer

Verlag der Österreichischen Akademie der Wissenschaften

Wien 2012

Vorgelegt von w. M. MANFRED BIETAK in der Sitzung am 12. Dezember 2008

Gedruckt mit Unterstützung

der Historisch-Kulturwissenschaftlichen Fakultät der Universität Wien

des Spezialforschungsbereiches SCIEM 2000

British Library Cataloguing in Publication data.
A Catalogue record of this book is available from the British Library.

Die verwendete Papiersorte ist aus chlorfrei gebleichtem Zellstoff hergestellt, frei von säurebildenden Bestandteilen und alterungsbeständig.

ISBN 978-3-7001-6590-3

Grafik, Satz, Layout: Angela Schwab
Druck: Wograndl Druck GmbH, 7210 Mattersburg

Printed and bound in the EU

http://hw.oeaw.ac.at/6590-3
http://verlag.oeaw.ac.at

Contents

List of Figures

Figures for Part V

Ashkelon

Beth Shan

Arqa

List of Plates of Tell el-Yahudiya Ware found in Tell el-Dab^ca

Photographic Plates

List of Bibliographical Abbreviations

Bibliographical abbreviations follow those of the *Lexikon der Ägyptologie* with the addition of:

AP	Bietak M., *Avaris and Piramesse. Archaeological Exploration in the Eastern Nile Delta*, ²Oxford, 1986.
PuF	Bietak M. and Hein I., *Pharaonen und Fremde. Dynastien im Dunkel*, Exhibition Catalogue, Vienna, 1994.
PEQFS	*Palestine Exploration Fund Quarterly Statement*, London
TD V	Bietak M., *Tell el-Dabᶜa V: Ein Friedhofsbezirk der Mittleren Bronzezeitkultur mit Totentempel und Siedlungsschichten Teil I*, Vienna, 1991.
TD X	Fuscaldo P., *Tell el-Dabᶜa X. The Palace District of Avaris: The Pottery of the Hyksos Period and the New Kingdom (Areas H/III and H/VI), Part I, Locus 66*, Vienna, 2000.
TD XI	Hein I. and Jánosi P., *Tell el-Dabᶜa XI. Areal A/V, Siedlungsrelikte der späten Hyksoszeit*, Vienna, 2004.
TD XII	Aston, D.A., *Tell el-Dabᶜa XII: A Corpus of Late Middle Kingdom and Second Intermediate Period Pottery*, Vienna, 2004.
TD XVI	Forstner-Müller I., *Tell el-Dabᶜa XVI. Die Gräber des Areal A/II von Tell el-Dabᶜa* Vienna, 2008.
TD XVII	Müller V., *Tell el-Dabᶜa XVII. Opferdeponierungen in der Hyksoshauptstadt Auaris (Tell el-Dabᶜa) vom späten Mittleren Reich bis zum frühen Neues Reich*, Vienna, 2008.
TD XVIII	Schiestl R., *Tell el-Dabᶜa XVIII. Die Palastnekropole von Tell el-Dabᶜa. Die Gräber des Areals F/I der Straten d/2 und d/1*, Vienna, 2009.
TD XIX	Bader B., *Tell el-Dabᶜa XIX. Auaris und Memphis im Mittleren Reich und in der Hyksoszeit. Vergleichsanalyse der materiellen Kultur*, Vienna, 2009.

Pottery Abbreviations

Bd Base diameter
D Rim dameter
Md Maximum body diameter
Nd Neck dameter

Pht preserved height
Ht Height
Wd Wall thickness
VI Vessel index

Preface

In some ways it is perhaps strange to devote an entire Tell el-Dab^ca volume to one particular family of pottery, rather than including it with the other ceramic finds already published by one of the authors. There are several reasons, however, for devoting a monograph to Tell el-Yahudiya Ware. Tell el-Yahudiya Ware – generally in the form of brown or black polished juglets with punctured decoration – is widely distributed throughout the eastern Mediterranean. Thus if it would be possible to produce a chronologically workable typology for this ware, which is confined to the first half of the Second Millenium BC, then it can be seen as an important tool in establishing datum lines between different sites. Through a careful analysis of previous research in the study of this ware, and the cataloguing of more than 650 pieces found in controlled stratigraphic excavations at Tell el-Dab^ca, we believe we are now at a stage to produce such a chronologically workable typology, and, as such, we feel more than justified in devoting an entire monograph to the Tell el-Yahudiya Ware found at Tell el-Dab^ca. Besides the chronological importance of this family of pottery the identification of its clays and the dissemination of Tell el Yahudiya Ware from the Levant to Cyprus and Egypt and from Egypt to the Levant, Cyprus, the Aegean and to Nubia as far as Kerma in the Sudan opens a field of reconstructing trade and cultural relationship.

We have divided this book into four parts as the material seems to dictate. Firstly we review previous research in the topic (Part One), which clearly indicated that a new classification of this ware was sorely needed. In response to this need, we have established a new classification of Tell el-Yahudiya ware, based on fabric, form and shape attributes, style of decoration and distribution patterns (Part Two). As a result of this analysis, it can be seen that, following the first appearance of such pottery in the northern Levant during the Middle Bronze IIA period, Tell el-Yahudiya Ware developed along distinctive lines. Firstly the earliest vessels – the Primeval group – evolved into a northern and a southern group, differentiated by styles of their decoration. For the sake of argument, and based on the findspots of these pots, these groups may be termed Levantine and Early Palestinian respectively. Whilst the Palestinian group continued to evolve through Middle and subsequently Late Palestinian styles, the northern group split into a Levantine (Syrian) group, and an Egyptian one, the latter presumably arising out of attempts by potters in Egypt, possibly of Near Eastern origin, to copy Levantine imports. At first the true Levantine vessels and their Egyptian copies were very similar and the term Levanto-Egyptian can truly be applied to these pots. During the later Middle Bronze Age, however, Syrian and Egyptian types developed along their own distinctive paths so that typically Late Egyptian forms differ markedly from their Late Syrian contemporaries. In Part Two we have deliberately included full-page maps in the expectation that new examples of these type groups will continue to be discovered in future excavations. Users of this monograph will therefore be able to add these new vessels to the respective maps thus keeping this book up-to-date. The Tell el-Yahudiya Ware from Tell el-Dab^ca, is then catalogued according to this new typology (Part Three), and thence chronological implications are drawn from this material (Part Four).

We have also been fortunate to have received contributions from Lawrence Stager and Ross Voss, Aren Maier and Robert Mullins, and Hanan Charaf and Mary Ownby, on Tell el-Yahudiya vessels from Ashkelon, Beth Shan and Tell Arqa. These we have gathered as Part Five, a view from the north, followed by a short appendix, an analysis of contents of Tell el-Yahudiya and other vessels from Tell el-Dab^ca, which was undertaken in 1986 by R. Rottländer, but has not yet been published.

Finally it remains for us to thank Paul Åström (†) for permission to reproduce various drawings from Maureen Kaplan's The Origin and Distribution of Tell el Yahudiyeh Ware, and the Austrian Academy for permission to reproduce Part One which, in an earlier version, was previously published in M. Bietak and E. Czerny (eds.), The Bronze Age in the Lebanon, Vienna, 2007, 165–194: To all of the colleagues who have shown us various jugs over the years, and freely discussed their findings with us we are very grateful. To mention them all by name would be to give a complete compendium of everyone who has worked in the Levant over the past forty years. They know who they are, and we hope this book will be a token of our gratitude.

David A. Aston
Manfred Bietak
Vienna, December 2010

I. The Typology, Origin and Distribution of Tell el-Yahudiya Ware: New Evidence, New Interpretations

Introduction

Black-polished white-incised juglets were first collected and excavated by E. Naville, F.Ll. Griffith and W.M.F. Petrie in Khatana (i.e. Tell el-Dab^{c}a) and Tell el-Yahudiya in the Eastern Delta, and subsequently at other places near the Fayoum entrance and in Middle Egypt.[1] Since most of them were found at Tell el-Yahudiya this site gave its name to this particular type of pottery. These juglets belong to a distinct group made of a variety of fabrics from the 18th to the 16th century BC., all sharing a red or brown to black burnished surface with white incised decoration. The principal shape of these wares is a juglet with many variations in form and vessel attributes. The distribution of such vessels extends throughout the Eastern Mediterranean,[2] from Cyprus, Coastal Syria-Palestine as far inland as the Jordan Valley, Egypt, including the Red Sea coast and Dakhleh Oasis, and the Northern Sudan as far south as Kerma, with an isolated piece reported from Thera.[3] Although various writers have sometimes included monochrome red- and black-burnished jugs,[4] or even painted jugs[5] under the heading of Tell el-Yahudiya Ware, Tell el-Yahudiya Ware as used in this monograph refers specifically to only those vessels which have white incised decoration.

Generally seen as a container for precious oils, this ware group can, by virtue of its distinctive shape and decoration, be accurately traced, and thus forms a valuable source for the study of changing trade relationships between Egypt, the Sudan, Cyprus and Syria-Palestine during the Middle Bronze Age/Second Intermediate Period. (c.1770–1530 BC.).

The point of origin of Tell el-Yahudiya ware has, at various times been assigned to Egypt,[6] Nubia[7] and Cyprus,[8] though the most favoured location has been Syria-Palestine.[9] Attempts at classification were made with divisions into Syrian and Palestinian groups being noted,[10] whilst G.A. Reisner and R.S. Merrillees recognised the possibilities of chronological differentiation.[11]

Previous research

Apart from a few minor observations on Tell el-Yahudiya ware by, among others, Petrie who originally thought it derived from Italian inspiration,[12] a view he later changed to being brought into Egypt by the Hyksos as a result of his own excavations at Tell el-Yahudiya,[13] the first serious study of this particular style of pottery was undertaken by Junker in 1921.

---

1 Naville, *The Shrine of Saft el-Henneh*, 1887, 21–23; Griffith, *The Antiquities of Tell el-Yahudiya* 1890, 40, pl. XI, a–b; Petrie, *Hyksos and Israelite Cities*, 1906, 14, F. – For further references of early finds of Tell el-Yahudiya ware, see Reisner, *Excavations at Kerma IV–V*, 1923, 386 n.1.

2 A useful compilation, of vessels known before 1980, is to be found in M. Kaplan, *The Origin and Distribution of Tell el-Yahudiyeh Ware*, 1980.

3 Åström, Three Tell el-Yahudiyeh Juglets in the Thera Museum, in: *Acts of the Ist International Scientific Congress on the Volcano of Thera*, 1971, 415–421.

4 Åström, Three Tell el-Yahudiyeh Juglets in the Thera Museum, 415–421; Bietak, *LÄ* VI, 1986, 347.

5 Junker, *Der Nubische Ursprung der sogennanten Tell el-Jahudiye Vasen*, 1921, 44–55, fig. 1; Bietak, *LÄ* VI, 1986, 347.

6 Naville, *The Mound of the Jew*, 1890, 9; Macalister, *The Excavations at Gezer*, 1912, 160ff; Reisner, *Excavations at Kerma IV–V*, 385–388.

7 Junker, *Tell el-Jahudiye Vasen*, 93; Kaplan, *The Origin and Distribution of Tell el-Yahudiyeh Ware*, 1980, 121–122.

8 Petrie, *Kahun, Gurob and Hawara*, 1890, 25; Idem, *Hyksos and Israelite Cities*, 12: Meyer, 1912, 287.

9 Petrie, *Hyksos and Israelite Cities*, 15: Dussaud, *Syria* 9, 1928, 147–150; Van Seters, *The Hyksos: A New Investigation*, 1966, 49–51; Amiran, *Ancient Pottery of the Holy Land*, 1969, 120.

10 Junker, *Tell el-Jahudiye Vasen*, Åström, *The Middle Cypriote Bronze Age* ; Van Seters, *The Hyksos*.

11 Merrillees, *Levant* 6, 1974, 193–195; idem, *Trade and Transcendance in the Bronze Age Levant*, 1974, 73; idem, *Levant* 10, 1978, 75–98, with the two groups Merrillees designated as El-Lisht ware (late Middle Kingdom) and Tell el-Yahudiya ware (Second Intermediate Period). Reisner had already recognised that there were two distinct chronological groups, which he referred to as group i and group ii; *Excavations at Kerma IV–V*, 388.

12 Petrie, *JHS* 11, 1890, 276; idem, *Kahun, Gurob and Hawara*, 10; idem, *Illahun, Kahun and Gurob*, 1891, 26, 42.

Junker 1921

Junker divided the ware into five main types, with several subtypes, based on body shape (Fig. 1):[14]

> Typ a: Birnenförmiger Rumpf, das breitere Ende oben. Hierbei lassen sich wieder drei Unterabteilungen feststellen:
>
> 1. eine gedrungenere Form mit breiter und flächer Schultur, die Seiten jedoch ziemlich jäh abfallend
> 2. eine schlankere Form mit mehr abfallenden Schulturn
> 3. eine ovale Form, meist schlank.
>
> Typ b: Birnenförmig, das dicke Ende am Boden, mit folgenden Unterabteilungen:
>
> 1. sich nach oben stark verjüngend:
> 2. kugeliger
> 3. mit weniger gewölbten Seiten, die Verbindung mit Typ d herstellend.
>
> Typ c: Die breiteste Stelle befindet sich ungefähr in der Mitte des Rumpfes; von dort verläuft die Linie nach oben und unten in gleichem Winkel. Diese Mittelkante ist entweder:
>
> 1. breiter und rundlich und der Übergang nach Hals und Fuß vollzieht sich in etwas gebogener Linie:
> 2. oder sie zeigt eine schärfere Kante, der Winkel ist kleiner und die Linien nach oben und unten sind weniger geschwungen.
>
> Typ d: Der Rumpf ist zylindrisch, die Schulter ziemlich flach, der Boden flach oder leise gewölbt.
>
> 1. Breiter niedriger Typ
> 2. Schlanker Typ
> 3. Einige Beispiele sind nicht mehr eigentlich zylindrisch, sondern zeigen eine Verbreiterung des Rumpes nach dem Boden zu
> 4. Andere verengen sich nach der Aufsatzfläche zu.
>
> Typ e: Hohe konische Form, ohne Schultur zum Hals übergehend.

Of these types, Type e does not exist – Junker's conical form derives from an incorrect drawing, which in reality, is nothing more than a beaker typical of Nubian ceramic traditions, which has been wrongly reconstructed.[15] Junker went on to describe the necks, rims, handles and bases of all the vessels then known to him, followed by descriptions of the material, technique and decorative patterns.[16] He also concluded that Tell el-Yahudiya Ware was Nubian in origin from whence it was exported to Egypt, Cyprus and Palestine.[17]

Unfortunately, owing to Junker's over-fussy classification, his erroneous Type e, and his attribution of the ware to Nubia, his study did not find much favour amongst his colleagues, being systematically criticised by Bonnet,[18] and fell further out of fashion when Reisner, two years later, and Dussaud, three years after him, produced somewhat more convincing arguments for an Egyptian or Syrian origin for Tell el-Yahudiya ware.

Reisner 1923

In 1923 Reisner attributed an Egyptian origin to Tell el-Yahudiya ware, indicating that the clay of which they were made was only ordinary alluvial mud, such as is found all along the Nile Valley from Khartoum to Alexandria,[19] and divided it into only two major types depending on whether or not the punctured decoration occurred within lines of delineation.[20] However by tabulating the two groups he indicated that group i "contained pattern", ie. within lines of delineation occurs at Kerma, Abydos, Hu, Rifeh, Kahun, and rarely in the Delta. They are generally found as isolated examples in graves, and are generally variations of two distinct forms, (a), a shouldered jug with handle (or twin handle) and small ring bases; and (b) an ovoid jug with handle and round base. They are generally associated in cemeteries with red polished jugs of the same shape. At Kerma, Abydos and Hu such vessels are associated with Kerma-Ware beakers and ordinary Egyptian pottery. At Rifeh such vessels were associated only with Egyptian pottery.

On the other hand he pointed out that jugs of group ii, "uncontained pattern" occur at Hu, Rifeh, Giza, Abydos and prevails in the Delta. They occur in groups of three or four in each of many graves at Tell el-Yahudiya. They usually comprise variations of three

[13] Petrie, *Hyksos and Israelite Cities*, 10.

[14] Junker, *Tell el-Jahudiye Vasen*, 2–5, fig. 1.

[15] As pointed out by Kaplan, *The Origin and Distribution of Tell el-Yahudiyeh Ware*, 1980, 6 n.5. A drawing of this vessel with its section was to appear two years after Junker's book was published. – Reisner, *Excavations at Kerma IV–V*, 382, fig. 263.

[16] Junker, *Tell el-Jahudiye Vasen*, 5–38.

[17] Junker, *Tell el-Jahudiye Vasen*, 93, 113–130.

[18] Bonnet, *ZÄS* 59, 1924, 119–130.

[19] Reisner, *Excavations at Kerma IV–V*, 388.

[20] Reisner, *Excavations at Kerma IV–V*, 385–388.

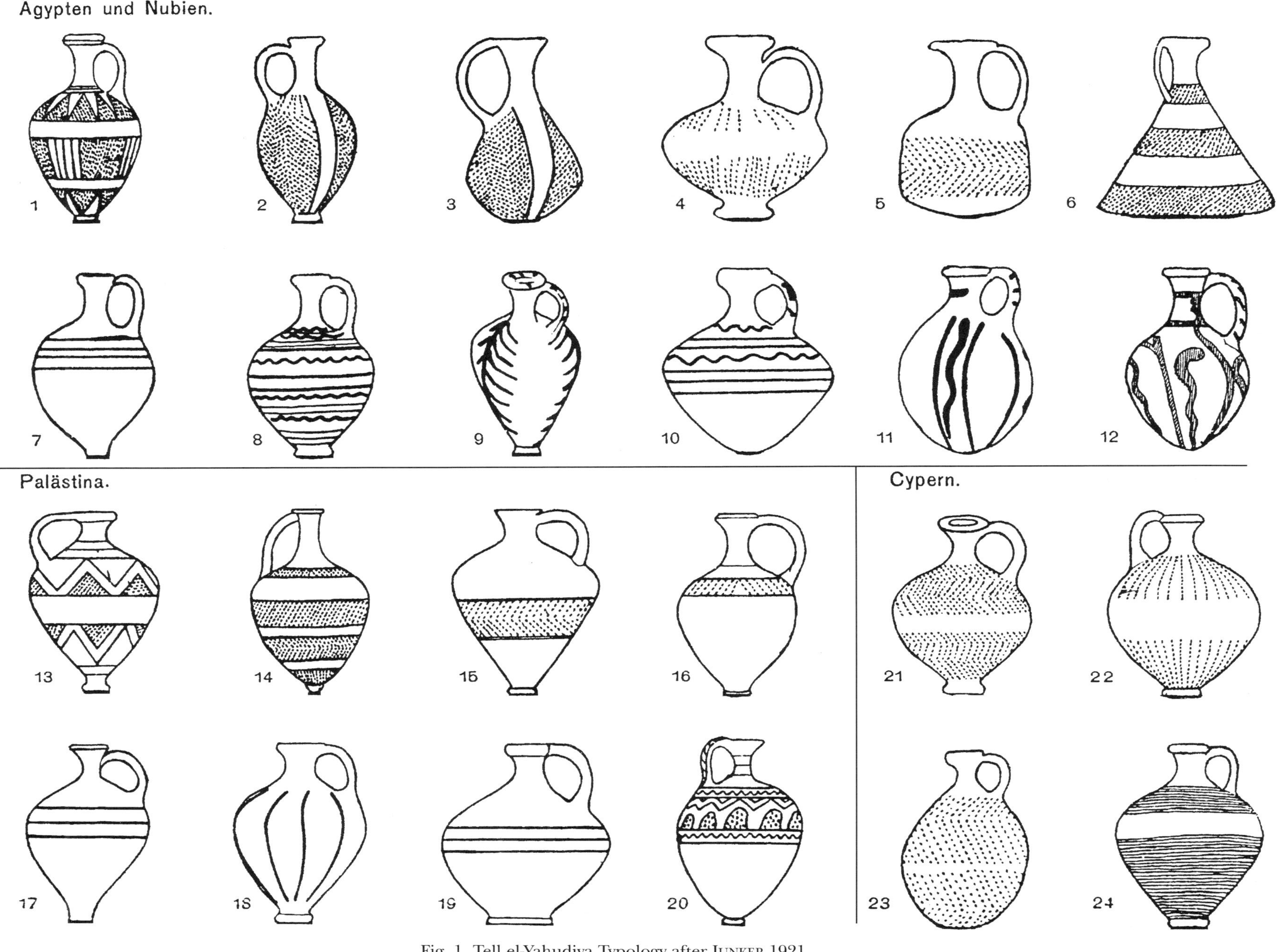

Fig. 1 Tell el-Yahudiya Typology after Junker 1921

forms, (a) ovoid or shouldered with a ring base; (b) ovoid with round bases and (c) straight-sided with convex bases. They are often found with red-, black- or buff-polished jugs. At Hu and Rifeh they were found in cemeteries with Tell el-Yahudiya jugs of group i, Kerma pottery, and Pan-Grave pottery, whilst at Tell el-Yahudiya they are associated with ordinary Egyptian pottery of the Second Intermediate Period. Reisner thus concluded that:

> "It is clear by the association that the following chronological order may be set forth as fixed
> (a) The Kerma jugs, the Abydos jugs recorded by Mace and Peet and the Kahun jugs recorded by Petrie. Dyns. XIII–XIV.
> (b) The Hu jugs recorded by Mace from the 'pan grave' and Second Intermediate Period cemetery (Y and YS) where the two groups of jugs occur in the same cemetery. The same conditions apply at Rifeh.
> (c) The earlier Delta jugs as indicated by Petrie (HIC pl. vii, graves 2, 407 and 3), continuing into the Hyksos period.
> (d) The later Delta jugs as indicated by Petrie. Here also belongs the Abydos jug recorded by Garstang and perhaps the Giza jug (undated)."

It should be noted that differences in form and pattern

> "prove that the two groups of jugs (i and ii) were made by two different sets of potters. The conclusions as to the chronology of the Kerma and the Delta examples shows that one of these sets of men lived earlier than the other. Yet examples of both groups of jugs were recorded from the same cemeteries at Hu and Rifeh, so that the second set of potters must have been in immediate chronological succession to the first. Moreover the later set of potters must have had direct knowledge of the products or methods of the first in order to imitate them so closely. The most plausible solutions which occur to me are as follows:
> (a) Both sets of potters lived at the same place and the makers of the Delta pots (group i) were the successors of the other set (group ii).
> (b) The earlier set of potters lived at one place and their products having been introduced were taken up and imitated by another set of potters (those of the Delta jugs) who continued to work after the cessation of the older workshop.
>
> Now the distribution of the two groups of jugs is entirely different. The rarity and the widely separated proveniences of the earlier group (which includes the Kerma jugs) indicate its distribution from a common centre of manufacture as a container of some valuable substances. In any case here was the one place where the jugs were abundant and apparently cheap. It is, therefore, to be concluded that the centre of manufacture was not far from Tell el-Yahudieh. I am of the opinion, until some site is found in or out of Egypt where these [Tell el-Yahudieh] jugs occur in greater abundance, that Tell el-Yahudieh is the place marked out by the facts as the centre of their manufacture.
>
> The next question is whether the earlier jugs were made also in the Delta in the period immediately preceding that of the Tell el-Yahudieh jugs, and distributed from there as containers of perfume or something similar. A few examples of the earlier jugs occur at that place [1]. The distribution in graves elsewhere is that of practicable containers of valuable substances. No place is marked by the occurrence of the examples as a centre of distribution of the later jugs.
>
> At both Hu and Abydos Tell el-Yahudieh jugs are associated with beakers which are identical with the Kerma beakers and which were undoubtedly exported from Kerma. Thus a certain plausibility is created for the theory that Kerma was the centre of distribution of this vessel. But the infrequence of its occurrence at Kerma and our ignorance of a substance requiring such a container which might have been exported from there, makes me hesitate to reach this conclusion."[21]
>
> [1] Petrie, *Hyksos and Israelite Cities*, pl. vii.25, pl. viia.75 and 83.

Bonnet, 1924

In systematically criticising Junker, point for point, Bonnet came to the conclusion that Tell el-Yahudiya Ware must have come from the Near East, and following Petrie, was brought into Egypt by the Hyksos.[22]

[21] Reisner, *Excavations at Kerma IV–V*, 387–388. Note, however, that the graves in which these vessels were found may have been those of Nubian archers in the employ of the Hyksos kings.

[22] Bonnet, *ZÄS* 59, 1924, 119–130.

DUSSAUD, 1928

In 1928 Dussaud unconsciously reconfirmed the points made by Bonnet, whose article was seemingly unknown to him, and, based on the shape of Tell el-Yahudiya jugs, suggested that the ware actually originated in Syria-Palestine.[23]

OTTO, 1938

In 1938 Heinz Otto published a long, and almost forgotten, article on Middle Bronze Age pottery from Syria-Palestine, which included a discussion of Tell el-Yahudiya pottery,[24] though it would appear that he was unaware of Reisner's study:

> "Diese Kännchen aus schwarzem bis grauschwarz-braunem, seltener rotem Ton treten in dreierlei Gestalt auf, denen allen der hohe Hals mit der dicken Lippe und der kräftig geschwungene, meist doppelteilige Henkel gemeinsam ist. Die typischste Gestalt ist die ei- oder birnenförmige auf gut durchgebildetem Standring; die Höhe schwankt zwischen 10 und 18 cm. Diesem Kännchen ist das mit zylindrischem Körper eng verwandt, wobei der Durchmesser halb, aber auch doppelt so groß wie die Höhe sein kann, die durchschnittlich 15 cm beträgt. Das sackförmige Kännchen stellt vielleicht nur eine Mischung und Entartung dieser beiden dar [Fig. 2.1–5].
>
> Bezeichnend für die gesamte Gattung sind die eingeritzten geometrischen Ornamente, die in weiß ausgelegt waren und nur in seltenen Fällen, wie bei der Schale aus dem Krug mit der Kinderleiche in Megiddo, auch auf andere Formen übergreifen. In sehr wenigen späteren Fällen ist das Ornament auch aufgemalt; in Byblos wird das geometrische Muster durch ein pflanzliches abgelöst.
>
> Nicht nur in Ägypten, sondern auch in Syrien und Palästina stehen neben den Kännchen mit Ritzmustern solche ohne Ornament, deren Oberfläche rot, braun, oder schwarz überzogen und meist sorgfältig poliert ist (Fig. 2.16–31.)
>
> Bei den beutelförmigen, seltener bei den eiförmigen Typen ist durch am Boden des Gefäßes zusammenlaufende eingeritzte Bänder eine vertikale Teilung vorgenommen, wogegen die zylindrischen Typen meistens ein breites um den Bauch laufendes Ritzband besitzen. Die eiförmigem Exemplare weisen eine Gliederung um die größte dicht unter der Schultur liegende Gefäßweite durch einen eingeritzten Streifen auf, der sich mitunter über dem Fuß wiederholt. Der Hals bleibt stets frei. Das Ornament besteht aus gepunkteten Zickzack- oder Grätenmustern. In vereinzelten Fällen (*tell el-jehudije* Grab 37) treten auch einfache horizontale Ritzbänder in zwei Gruppen unter dem Bauch auf.
>
> Die Verzierungen durch geritzte und mit andersfarbigem Ton ausgelegte Muster, einer Art Tauschierung in Ton, erscheinen ja nicht nur in ganzen Mittelmeergebiet – charakteristisch ist ihre Verbindung mit eben dieser Gefäßform und dem doppelteiligen Henkel. Für die Ermittelung des Ursprungsgebietes dieser Gattung scheinen folgende Tatsachen sehr wichtig zu sein.
>
> Die vollendetste Form mit dem reichsten und vielgestaltigsten Ornament findet sich in Syrien. Die Dekorationsart durch Ritzungen und Stichelungen ist in Syrien und Palästina schon in der FBZ IV in Gebrauch. Zudem ist die Form henkellos, d.h. als Flasche, in Syrien nichts Neues und findet sich um 2000 v. Chr. nicht selten (Katna usw.).
>
> Zur Zeit der 12. Dynastie, der "Hyksoszeit" und noch im Neuen Reich liegt das Hauptverbreitungsgebiet der Gattung auf kanaanäischem Boden und in der kanaanäischen Einflußzone: Unterägypten, Palästina, Syrien und östliches Cypern. In Oberägypten kommt die Ware an zwei Orten vor: Kerma und Buhen. Besonders Buhen enthält schöne und zahlreiche Exemplare, die durch ägyptische Mitfunde in die 12. Dynastie datiert werden.
>
> Die eingehende Untersuchungs Junkers über den Ursprung der *tell el-jehudije*-Ware, die mit aller Entschiedenheit sich für nubische Herkunft ausspricht, wurde von Bonnet in allen wesentlichen Punkten widerlegt. Gegen den nubischen Ursprung spricht die nicht zu klärende Frage, wie es möglich war, daß die keramische Ware eines selbst von den Ägyptern gering geachteten Volkes einen so riesigen Export auf über tausend Kilometer Entfernung erfahren haben soll. Anderseits ist es ganz unwahrscheinlich, daß nubische Töpfereien z.B. in *ras schamra* bestanden und Syrien, Cypern und Palästina mit ihrer Keramik versorgten oder daß die Keramik von nubischen Söldnern über so weite Strecken und in so großer

[23] DUSSAUD, *Syria* 9, 1928, 147–150.

[24] OTTO, *ZDPV* 61, 1938, 168–174.

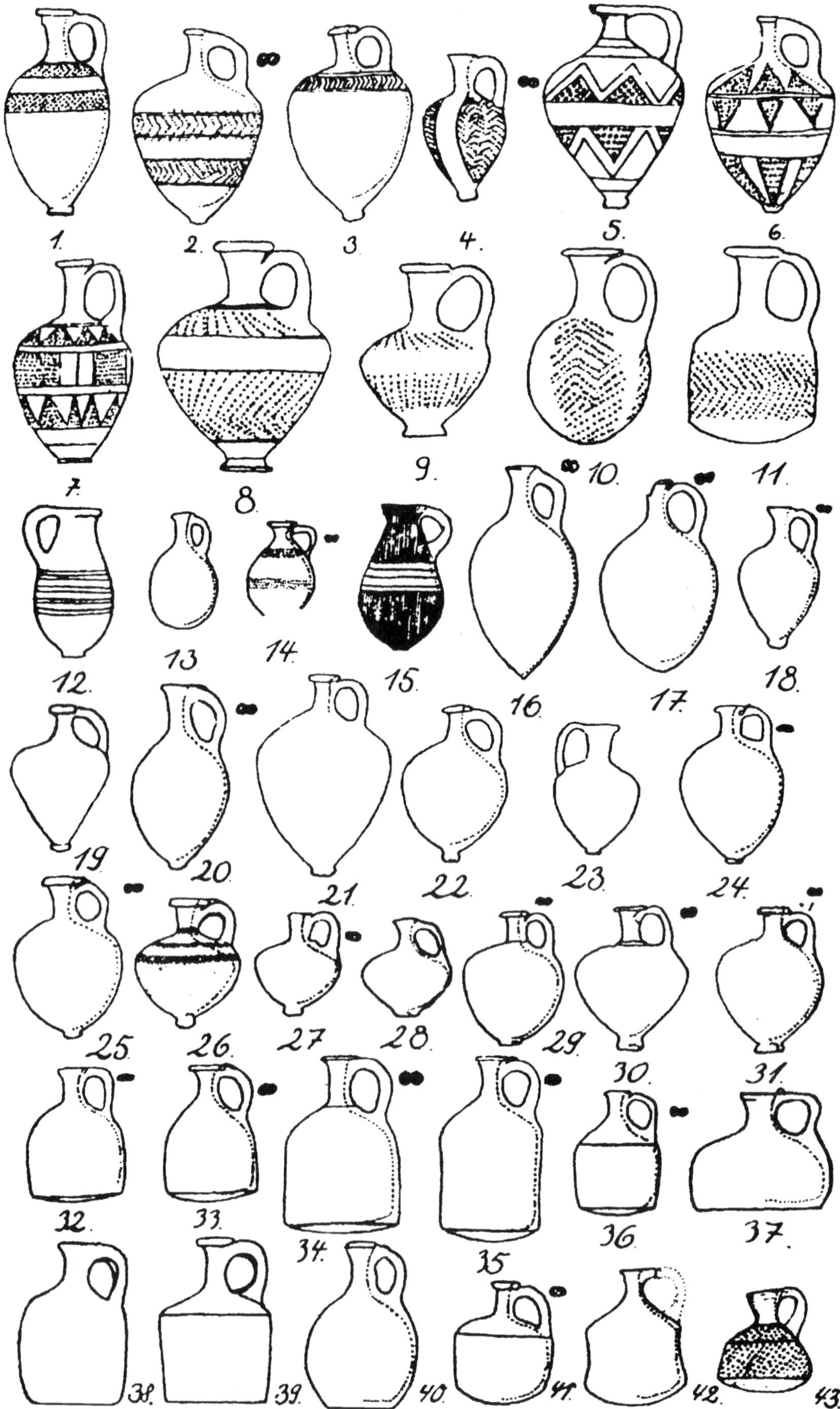

Fig. 2 Tell el-Yahudiya Typology after Otto 1938

Zahl an vielen Orten verbreitet wurde. Hinzuzufügen wäre noch, daß die nubische Keramik einen ganz andersartigen Charakter aufweist, zu dem die Kännchen in keiner Weise passen. Auffallend ist auch, daß die nubische Tonware dieser Zeit die Scheibe nicht kennt, dagegen alle Kännchen scheibengedreht sind.

Neben den oben genannten drei Hauptformen stehen nun aber doch eine ganze Anzahl Varianten. Grab 2 von *tell el-jehudije*, das wegen eines MR-Skarabäus als das älteste angesehen wird, enthält die drei Hauptformen nebeneinander (Fig. 2.9–11). Auffallend ist jedoch, daß der eiförmige Typ hier ebensowenig wie in Grab 407 in seiner vollendeten Form vertreten ist, diese erscheint in dem nach seinen Skarabäen wesentlich jüngeren Grabe 3."

Man wäre nun geneigt, in den Kännchen mit dem scharfen Umbruch der Schultur (Fig. 2.9) den ersten Typ der *tell el-jehudije*-Gattung zu sehen, der sich unter Angleichung an die Formwandlung der unten zu besprechenden knickkurvigen Schalen und Näpfe allmählich zu der schön geschwungenen typischen eiförmigen" Gestalt der *tell el-jehudije* Kännchen entwickelt hätte. Spräche der schöne MR-Skarabäus für diese Annahme, so widersetzt sich dem zunächst die Tatsache. daß die gleichen geknickten Fläschenformen auch in dem sicher jüngeren Grab 3 in *tell el-jehudije* vertreten sind. Hinzu kommt, daß die gleiche stark gebauchte und geknickte Form auch bei Kännchen mit poliertem Überzug auftritt, deren Knopfbasis schon zur Verbreiterung und Ringbasis neigt (Fig. 2.27, 28). Am stärksten spricht jedoch gegen eine so frühe Einordnung des Grabes 2 das eiformige bemalte Kännchen, das in dieser Form von *tell 'addschul* bis hinauf nach Syrien frühestens dem Ausgang der MBZ II angehört. Indem wir das angeblich älteste Grab der "Hyksos" in *tell el-jehudije* in die MBZ II verweisen, müssen wir die anderen ihren Skarabäen nach, unter denen die für den Übergang zur SBZ so charakteristischen Skarabäen mit konzentrischen Ringen vertreten sind, in den gleichen Zusammenhang einordnen.

.....

Auch das zylinderförmige Kännchen erscheint in drei Varianten, von denen jedoch nur die erste und letzte wirkliche Entwicklungsstufen darstellen dürften (Fig. 2.32ff). Neben dem wohlgerundeten Typ auf leicht gerundeter Basis steht ein anderer auf flachem Boden, dessen Linienführung schwer nach unten gezogen ist, so daß die Gefäße fast einen in sich zusammengesunkenen Eindruck machen (Fig. xx.37) Diese zweite Form erfährt keine Weiterentwicklung, wogegen die erste im weiteren Verlauf durch scharfe Knickun an Schulter und Bodensatz zu einer streng gegliederten Form geführt wird. (Fig. 2.39, 41, 43), ein anderer aber gleichzeitiger Zweig der Entwicklung führt zu einer Überhöhung des Gefäßkörpers, so daß die ursprüngliche Form dahin abgeändert wird, daß nun die Breite geringer ist als die Höhe im Gegensatz zu den früheren Typen (Fig. 2.35). Zahlreiche Zwischenformen vervollständigen das Bild.

.....

Es ist unverkennbar, daß der *tell el-jehudije*-Typ die einheimischen roten Kännchen in ihrer Formung stark beeinflußt hat und daß man versuchte, diese elegante Ware nachzubilden. Die Nachahmungen der *tell el-jehudije*-Ware erfahren in der MBZ I ihre Blüte und bilden in dieser Epoche die erste große Gruppe. Die schön geschwungenen eiförmigen Körper mit hohem Hals und runder wulstiger Lippe und der charakteristischen Knopfbasis weisen nun immer den zweifachen Henkel der *tell el-jehudije*-Kännchen auf; auch der schwarze polierte Überzug wird von dorther übernommen, besitzt aber bei weitem nicht immer Stich- und Ritzmuster. Wie sehr das Bodenständige erhalten bleibt, zeigt der in zahllosen Fällen auftretende dicke, rote, polierte Überzug der diese Kännchen eben doch an jene der Übergangszeit (FBZ IV) anschließt. Neben diesem roten Überzug ist noch brauner und vereinzelt (Gezer Grab 1) sogar grünlicher Überzug verwendet."

Engberg 1939

By the time Engberg wrote his *The Hyksos Reconsidered*, which was published in 1939, and hence could not have taken Otto's ideas into consideration, the hypotheses of Junker and Reisner had been overcome to such a degree that the Levantine, and by extension, Hyksos origin of this ware had become so entrenched in Egyptological thinking, that Engberg included it in his discussion of that ethnic group.[25] He characterised the ware as "piriform in shape, with a long constricted neck. The handle, which is characteristically double

---

[25] Engberg, *The Hyksos Reconsidered*, 1939, 25–28, 50–51.

(ie. figure of eight in cross-section), extends from the shoulder to the rim. The base is often finished with a button effect, and the polished surface is usually deep black or bright orange. If black the surface is often punctured in various designs which are fitted with a white pigment."[26] As a result of his association of the ware with the Hyksos, Engberg postulated that the Hyksos were already present in Egypt in the Twelfth and Thirteenth Dynasties, though he saw them as peaceful intruders at that time.[27]

Säve-Söderbergh 1951

By 1951, Säve-Söderbergh, however, referring to the article of Otto, with additional references to von Bissing[28] and Stock,[29] was arguing against a link with the Hyksos:

> "It is again and again stated that the so-called Tell el-Yahudiyah ware should be regarded as Hyksos products and, as the American scholar Engberg puts it, be 'an invaluable aid in the detection of the Hyksos occupation of a site'. This is in my opinion wholly unwarranted. First of all it is a very dangerous method to deduce ethnic movements from the presence of a certain type of ceramic ware only, if there is not at the same time important change in burial customs, and it can often be proved that a change in the archaeological material is simply due to trade.
>
> Moreover, the typical Tell el-Yahudiyah jugs are gradually developed in Palestine and Syria, and their appearance there marks a no sudden change in the ceramic tradition. In Egyptian territory they were introduced long before the arrival of the Hyksos, and are found in tombs in Lower Nubia dating from a time when the Hyksos had hardly even reached Middle Egypt. The most that can be said about the connexion between the Hyksos and the Tell el-Yahudiyah jugs is that the Hyksos perhaps liked them, and that possibly greater quantities were imported when the Hyksos rulers controlled the trade than when it was handled by a more conservative Egyptian government. It should also be stressed that these jugs were used in Egypt after the unpopular Hyksos had been expelled."[30]

Åström 1957

Åström, though concerned primarily with the vessels found in Cyprus, was the first to produce a detailed typology for Tell el-Yahudiya ware and divided it into a number of different types, viz: [31]

Type a (swollen piriform with a more or less carinated body) which at that time was represented in Cyprus at Kalopsidha,[32] Klavdhia,[33] Enkomi,[34] and Milia;[35] in Nubia, at Buhen[36] and Aniba:[37] in Egypt at Hu,[38] Abydos,[39] Deir Rifeh,[40] Giza[41] and Tell el-Yahudiya;[42] in Palestine at Tell el-Ajjul,[43] Jericho,[44] and Megiddo,[45] and in Syria at Ras Shamra,[46] and Tell Nebi Mend.[47]

Type b (with oval to globular body) represented in Cyprus at Kalopsidha[48] and Enkomi;[49] found in Egypt at the Fayoum[50] and Tell el-Yahudiya;[51] in Palestine at Tell el-Ajjul,[52] Tell Beit Mirsim[53] and Gezer;[54] in Syria at Rhozlâniyé[55] and Majdalouna,[56] with two others of unknown provenance.

---

[26] Engberg, *The Hyksos Reconsidered*, 18.

[27] Engberg, *The Hyksos Reconsidered*, 29–30, 33.

[28] von. Bissing, *AFO* 14, 1944, 85–86.

[29] Stock, *Studien zur Geschichte und Archäologie der 13 bis 17 Dynastie Ägyptens*, 1942, 72.

[30] Säve-Söderbergh, *JEA* 37, 1951, 57. Cf. also his earlier study, *Ägypten und Nubien*, 1941, 125.

[31] Åström, *The Middle Cypriote Bronze Age*, 1957, 130–132, 233–239, pl. xxx.20–24.

[32] Myres, *JHS* 17, 1897, 140, fig. 4.23–24, 141, fig. 5.6; Corpus Vasorum Antiquorum, Gt. Britain I, Brit. Mus. I IIC.a, pl. 3.37.

[33] Corpus Vasorum Antiquorum, Gt. Britain I, Brit. Mus. I IIC.a, pl. 3.38.

[34] Schaeffer, *Missions en Chypre*, 1936, 72, fig. 30.2., pl. xxxi.d

[35] Westholm, *QDAP* 8, 1939, 4, pl. 1.

[36] Randall-MacIver and Woolley, *Buhen*, 1911, pl. 49:10595, tomb J21; pl. 49:10621, tomb J41; pl. 92:10869, tomb K44.

[37] Steindorff, *Aniba*, 1937, II, pl. 86.45a1, 45b1, 45b2.

[38] Petrie, *Diospolis Parva*, pl. xxxvi.186–7.

[39] Randall-MacIver and Mace, *El Amrah and Abydos*, pl. liv.13. Peet and Loat, *Cemeteries of Abydos III*, 1914, pl. xii.4; Peet, *Cemeteries of Abydos II*, 1913, 68.

[40] Petrie, *Gizeh and Rifeh*, 1907, pl. xxiii.29; xxvi.94

[41] Hassan, *Excavations at Giza II*, 1936, pl. xxxv.2

[42] Naville, *The Mound of the Jew*, pl. xii.3; Petrie, *Hyksos and Israelite Cities*, pl. vii.3, 11–12, 23–25, pl. viii.38, 50, 52, viiia.72.

[43] Petrie, *Ancient Gaza III*, 1933, pl. xxxviii.60M9.1, with grooves on the shoulder.

[44] Kenyon, *PEQ*, 1952, pl. xxii, fig. 1

[45] Guy and Engberg, *Megiddo Tombs*, 1938, pl. 23:27, 30; Loud, *Megiddo II*, 1948, pls. 24:32, 122:17

[46] Schaeffer, *Syria* 17, 1936, 131, fig. 18D, 144.

[47] Pézard, *Qadesh: Mission Archéologique à Tell Nebi Mend*, 1931, 73, fig. 8:2.

[48] Myres, *JHS* 17, 1897, 141, fig. 5.7.

[49] Schaeffer, *Missions en Chypre*, 72, fig. 30.4., pl. xxxi.c

[50] Weigall, *ASAE* 9, 1908, 110 fig. 5.

[51] Petrie, *Hyksos and Israelite Cities*, pl. viii.49, viiia.71.

[52] Petrie, *Ancient Gaza II*, 1932, pl. xxxiv.60M5.

[53] Albright, *Tell Beit Mirsim Ia*, 1933, 78, pl. 9.4.

[54] Macalister, *Gezer*, III, pl. lx.12.

[55] Von der Osten, *Tell es-Salihiyeh*, 1956, 14, 77, 86.

[56] Chehab, *BMB* 4, 1940, 4, fig. 3a.

Type c (with ovoid body) found in Cyprus at Milia;[57] in Nubia at Buhen[58] and Aniba;[59] in Egypt at Deir Rifeh,[60] Giza,[61] and Tell el-Yahudiya;[62] in Palestine at Jericho[63] and Megiddo,[64] in Syria at Byblos[65] and Kafr ed-Djarra,[66] with an unprovenenaced vessel, Sydney Nicholson Museum 52.404, assigned to the Lebanon.

Type d (ovoid with high more or less marked shoulder) found in Cyprus at Milia;[67] in Nubia at Kerma,[68] Buhen[69] and Aniba;[70] in Egypt at Edfu,[71] Hu,[72] Abydos,[73] Harageh,[74] Kahun,[75] Tell el-Yahudiya[76] and Khatana (Tell el-Dabᶜa);[77] in Palestine at Tell el-Ajjul,[78] Beth Shemesh,[79] Gezer,[80] Jericho,[81] Tel Aviv,[82] Tell Taᶜanek ,[83] Afula,[84] and Megiddo;[85] in Syria at Sin el-Fil,[86] Byblos,[87] and Ras Shamra.[88]

Type e (barrel-shaped body) recorded in Cyprus at Enkomi[89] and Galinoporni;[90] in Egypt at Mostagedda,[91] Deir Rifeh,[92] Sedment,[93] Tell el-Yahudiya,[94] Saft el Henneh,[95] and Khatana (Tell el-Dabᶜa);[96] in Palestine at Tell el-Ajjul,[97] Beth Shemesh,[98] Jericho,[99] and Megiddo.[100]

Type f (sack-shaped body with a curved base) found at Enkomi[101] in Cyprus; Aniba[102] in Nubia; Abydos,[103] Deir Rifeh,[104] Harageh,[105] Tell el-Yahudiya,[106] in Egypt, and at Tell el-Ajjul in Palestine.[107]

Type g (fish-shaped) which then occurred only at Tell el-Yahudiya,[108] and from Cyprus, site unknown.[109]

In addition Åström was aware of other types which he termed conical,[110] biconical,[111] inverted piriform[112] or quadrilobal,[113] together with jars,[114] a rhyton,[115] and

[57] WESTHOLM. *QDAP* 8, 1939, 4, 11, pls. I, VI.

[58] RANDALL-MACIVER and WOOLLEY, *Buhen*, pl. 49:10527, 10617, 10540.

[59] STEINDORFF, *Aniba*, II, pl. 86.45b4.

[60] PETRIE, *Gizeh and Rifeh*, pl. xxvi.92*.

[61] HASSAN, *Excavations at Giza II*, pl. xxxv.1.

[62] NAVILLE, *The Mound of the Jew*, pl. xi.1 (four); PETRIE, *Hyksos and Israelite Cities*, pl. viiia.78, 83.

[63] GARSTANG, *LAAA* 19, 1932, pl. xli.1: G.K. HARDING, PEF 6, 1953, 17, no. 63, 21 fig. 7, pl. II.

[64] LOUD, *Megiddo II*, pls. 24:31, 32:26.

[65] MONTET, *Byblos et l'Égypte*, 1929, 244 no. 915, pl. cxlviii.

[66] CONTENAU, *Syria* 1, 1920, 127, fig. 33e, pl. xi.

[67] ÅSTRÖM, *The Middle Cypriote Bronze Age*, fig. xxx.23.

[68] REISNER, *BMFA* 13, 1915, 77, fig. 9; IDEM, *Excavations at Kerma IV–V*, 383, figs. 264.23–25, 386 pls. 70.3, 76.6.

[69] RANDALL-MACIVER and WOOLLEY, *Buhen*, pl. 49:10765, tomb K9; pl. 92:10876, tomb K45.

[70] STEINDORFF, *Aniba* II, pl. 86.45b5.

[71] Cairo JE 46743, unpublished.

[72] PETRIE, *Diospolis Parva*, pl. xxxvi.188.

[73] PEET, *Cemeteries of Abydos II*, pl. xiii.8.

[74] ENGELBACH, *Harageh*, 1923, pl. xli.99F, 99J.

[75] PETRIE, *Kahun, Gurob and Hawara*, pl. xxvii.202*

[76] NAVILLE, *The Mound of the Jew*, pl. xi.2; PETRIE, *Hyksos and Israelite Cities*, pl. viiia.86, 87.

[77] HALL, *The Oldest Civilization of Greece*, 1901, 68, fig. 29 no.2.

[78] PETRIE, *Ancient Gaza II*, pl. xxxiv.60Mb, III, pl. xxxviii.60M5.

[79] GRANT, *Beth Shemesh*, 1929, 151:236, 156 tomb 2: GRANT and WRIGHT, *Ains Shems V*, 1939, 108.

[80] MACALISTER, *Gezer*, III, pl. xxiii.16, cave 15 I: pl. cliii.8–10.

[81] GARSTANG, *LAAA* 19, 1932, pls. xxx.6; 20, xxxix.1: 20, IDEM, *LAAA* 20, 1933, pls. xvii.4–5, xx.9–10.

[82] KAPLAN, *Atiqot* 1, 1955, 10, fig. 3.4.

[83] SELLIN, Tell Taᶜanek, 1904, 52, fig. 57.

[84] SUKENIK, *JPOS* 41, 1948, pl. xiv.18.

[85] GUY and ENGBERG, *Megiddo Tombs*, pl. 23.23; LOUD, *Megiddo II*, pls. 32.31–32*, 113.14.

[86] CHEHAB, *Mélanges syriens*, 1939, 805, fig. 5 a–c.

[87] MONTET, *Byblos et l'Égypte*,, 244 no. 914, 917, pl. cxlvi: DUNAND, *Fouilles de Byblos*, I, 1937–39, 236 no. 3489, pl. clxiii; *Fouilles de Byblos*, II, 1958, 198 no. 8521, fig. 205*.

[88] SCHAEFFER, *Syria* 14, 1933, 110; IDEM, *Ugaritica* I, 1939, figs. 16, 17, 53, pl. xiii.2; II, pls. xl, xliii.

[89] SCHAEFFER, *Missions en Chypre*, 72, fig. 30.7, pl. xxxi.b.

[90] ÅSTRÖM, *The Middle Cypriote Bronze Age*, 131.

[91] BRUNTON, *Mostagedda*, 1937, pls. lxxii.60, lxxiv, group 3146.

[92] PETRIE, *Gizeh and Rifeh*, pl. xxiii.28.

[93] PETRIE and BRUNTON, *Sedment II*, 1924, pl. xlv.64, grooved variety.

[94] NAVILLE, *The Mound of the Jew*, pl. xi.6; PETRIE, *Hyksos and Israelite Cities*, pls. vii.5, 26, viiia.66.

[95] PETRIE, *Hyksos and Israelite Cities*, pl. xxxixB.3.

[96] NAVILLE, *Mound of the Jew*, pl. xix.6; HALL, *The Oldest Civilization of Greece*, 68, fig. 29 no.3.

[97] PETRIE, *Ancient Gaza I*, 1930, pl. xlix.08, grooved variety, III, pl. xxxix:74015.

[98] GRANT, *Beth Shemesh*, 119, 127:770, 134: IDEM, *Rumeilah*, 1934, frontispiece.

[99] GARSTANG, *LAAA* 20, 1933, 10, fig. 4.2; IDEM, *LAAA* 21, 1934, pl. xvii.19.

[100] GUY and ENGBERG, *Megiddo Tombs*, pl. 28.40.

[101] MYRES, *JHS* 17, 1897, 145 n.2; Corpus Vasorum Antiquorum, Gt. Britain I, Brit. Mus. I IIC.a, pl. 3.40, 43.

[102] STEINDORFF, *Aniba*, II, pl. 81.36b4, grooved variety, pl. 86.45b2.

[103] GARSTANG, *El Arabeh*, 1901, pl. xvii.

[104] PETRIE, *Gizeh and Rifeh*, pl. xxiii.38.

[105] ENGELBACH, 1923, pls. xli.99D, xlv.99M.

[106] NAVILLE, *The Mound of the Jew*, pl. xi.5; PETRIE, *Hyksos and Israelite Cities*, pls. vii.4, 35, pl. viii.39–41, 48, viiia.76, 77, 84, 85.

[107] PETRIE, *Ancient Gaza II*, pl. xxxv.90, grooved variety, *Ancient Gaza IV*, 1934, pl. lv.68j.

[108] PETRIE, *Hyksos and Israelite Cities*, pl. viiia.64–65.

[109] MYRES, *Cessnola Collection*, 1914, 42, fig. 384.

[110] REISNER, *BMFA* 13, 1915, p. 77., IDEM, *Excavations at Kerma IV–V*, 382, fig. 263.18, 385 pl. 70.3.

[111] NAVILLE, *The Mound of the Jew*, pl. XI.4; PETRIE, *Hyksos and Israelite Cities*, 1906, pl. vii.22.

[112] RANDALL-MACIVER and WOOLLEY, *Buhen*, pl. 49.10831.

[113] PETRIE, *Hyksos and Israelite Cities*, 1906, pl. viiia.64–65; ORY J., *QDAP* 13, 1948, 82 fig. 20.

[114] PEET, *The Cemeteries of Abydos II*, pls. xiii.8, xxxix.o4; SCHAEFFER, *Syria* 19, 1938, 248f, fig. 36g, 249, fig. 38.

[115] GARSTANG, *LAAA* 19, 1932, pls. xlii, xliii.

a hawk-shaped jar,[116] but because such types had, at least until then, not been found on Cyprus, he did not include such vessels into his general classification. He rounded off his typology with references to unclassifiable sherds or unillustrated pots recorded from Buhen,[117] Aswan,[118] Hu,[119] Abydos,[120] Deir Rifeh,[121] Gurob,[122] Harageh,[123] Kahun,[124] Lisht,[125] Giza,[126] Tell el-Yahudiya,[127] Khatana (Tell el-Dabᶜa),[128] Tell el-Ajjul,[129] Tell Beit Mirsim,[130] Beth-Zur,[131] Ashklon,[132] Bethlehem,[133] Jericho,[134] Naᶜan,[135] Tell Jerisheh,[136] Ras el-ᶜAin (Tel Aphek),[137] Balata,[138] Afula,[139] Megiddo,[140] Nahariya,[141] Byblos,[142] Hama,[143] Aleppo,[144] and Tell Judeideh.[145]

Thus Åström was able to show that Tell el-Yahudiya ware had a wide distribution range from Kerma in the Sudan to Tell Judeidah in the plain of Antioch. He also pointed out that all the types found in Cyprus find ready parallels at Tell el-Yahudiya, and thus both that site and those in Cyprus must be contemporary. In origin he believed that the ware was probably manufactured at several sites, and concluded that:[146]

> "Tell el-Yahudiyeh ware occurs at the end of the Second Intermediate Period and at the beginning of the Eighteenth Dynasty. For an earlier dating of the ware we have some evidence, which at the best only gives *termini post quem*. In view of the homogeneous character of the ware, which remained practically unchanged, while it was popular, [8] it is not likely to have been in use for more than about a century. It is highly improbable that the ware was current in the XIIth Dynasty and nothing warrants such a date. [9] It is not contrary to the evidence if we place the beginning of the ware at c.1700 BC. or later [10]: indeed the finds from Buhen and Khatana indicate this date. The ware was in vogue in Cyprus for a short period at the end of the M.C.III and the beginning of the L.C.I. [11]; by comparison with the finds at Tell el-Yahudiya and occurrences during the XVIIIth Dynasty it is evident that this period should coincide with the last phase of the Hyksos Age and the beginning of the XVIIIth Dynasty. An early style of Tell el-Yahudiya Ware, with regular panels of punctured triangles is reflected in Cypriote Black Slip III Ware which hardly antedates the middle of M.C.III."
>
> [8] A certain development in decoration and shape can of course be traced. The regular ornamentation with punctured triangles is, for instance, no doubt earlier than the decoration with punctured zigzags. See Reisner, *Exc. At Kerma IV–V*, pp. 386ff.
>
> [9] A XIIth Dynasty date for the ware has been rejected by e.g. Peet, *The Cemeteries of Abydos* II p. 68: Dunand, *Fouilles de Byblos* I p. 237: Fimmen, *Die Kretische-Mykenische Kultur* (second ed.), p. 159; Guiges in *Bull. Mus. Beyrouth* I, 1937, pp. 49ff; Säve-Söderbergh, *Ägypten und Nubien*, pp. 124ff; Fitzgerald in *Palest. Expl. Quart.*, 1949, pp. 152 f.; cf. Kantor in Ehrich (ed.), *Relative Chronologies in Old World Archaeology*, p. 12. The absence of Tell el-Yahudiya Ware in the Royal tombs at Byblos is an *argumentum ex silentio* that the ware is later than the XIIth Dynasty.

---

116 Hall, *The Oldest Civilization of Greece*, 69, fig. 30 (London BM 17046).

117 Randall-MacIver and Woolley, *Buhen*, pl. 49, upper half.

118 Junker, *Tell el-Jahudiye Vasen*, 3, 25, 58, 133.

119 Petrie, *Diospolis Parva*, pl. xl group 43.

120 Peet and Loat, *Cemeteries of Abydos III*, pl. lviii.6.

121 Petrie, *Gizeh and Rifeh*, pl. xxiii.30, 31, 37, xxvi, (90), 93.

122 Loat, *Gurob*, 1905, pl. iii.108.

123 Engelbach, *Harageh*, pls. x.15, lxii.530, tomb 644.

124 Petrie, *Illahun, Kahun and Gurob*, pl. I.17, 20, 21. JHS 11, 1890, pl. xiv.9 where the sherds are reconstructed into an ovoid jug.

125 Mace, *BMMA* Nov. 1921, pt ii 17f.

126 Reisner, *Excavations at Kerma IV–V*, 386 n.1k

127 Petrie, *Hyksos and Israelite Cities*, pl. viiia.68–70, 73–75, 78–82.

128 Naville, *Saft el-Henneh*; idem, *The Mound of the Jew*, 56; Myres, *JHS* 17, 1897, 145 n.6.

129 Petrie, *City of Shepherd Kings*, 1952, pl. xxvii.60N3.

130 Albright, *Tell Beit Mirsim I*, 1932, 16, pl. 6.54, 50; 25 pl. 10.21, 25, pl. 13.1–2, 4, 24–26*.

131 Myres, *JHS* 17, 1897, 3. (London BM 1876/2/82/2, two examples).

132 Albright, *BASOR* 6, 1922, 14f.; Pythian-Adams, *PEFQSS* 1923, 79, pl. I.16, 18.

133 Welch, *ABSA* 6, 1900, 119.

134 Sellin and Watzinger, *Jericho*, 1913, 130, fig. 142.

135 Notes and News. *IEJ* **2**, 1952, 142.

136 Albright, *Tell Beit Mirsim I*, 25.

137 Ory, *QDAP* 6, 1937, pl. xxxiv.11, 12.

138 Iliffe, *QDAP* 5, 1936, 126.

139 Sukenik, *JPOS* 41, pl. xiv.10; Notes and News, *IEJ* 1 1951, 249; Perrot, *Syria* 29, 1952, 298..

140 Loud, *Megiddo II*, pls. 121.5.

141 Ben-Dor, *QDAP* 14, 1950, fig. 26d, pl. ix.27–28.

142 Montet, *Byblos et l'Égypte*, 244 no. 916, pl. cxlviii: Dunand, *Fouilles à Byblos* I, 181 no. 2854, fig. 169; II, pl. ccxi.13199.

143 Ingholt, *Hama*, 1940, 56, 65.

144 Engberg, *The Hyksos Reconsidered*, 18, n.4.

145 McEwan, AJA 41, 1937, 9ff.

146 Åström. *The Middle Cypriote Bronze Age*,, 239, with footnote 12 omitted. Footnote 11 refers the reader back to p. 197 n.6, and this is quoted above. The tomb there referred to has since been published by Merrillees, *Trade and Transcendance*, 43–77.

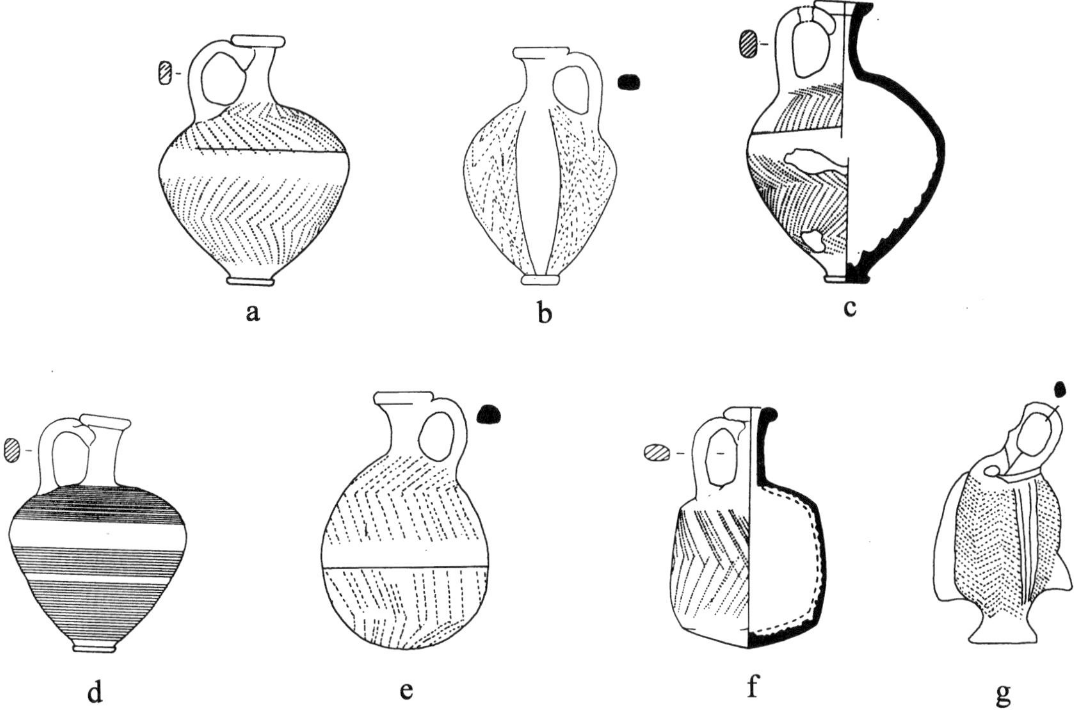

Fig. 3 Tell el-Yahudiya Typology after Åström 1957

[10] Miss Tufnell has suggested to Mr. Stewart that Tell el-Yahudiya Ware falls into two groups of which the latest is that found at Tell el-Yahudiya itself. The earliest probably does not antedate 1680 BC. and may be later.

[11] [When this book had been set up, Dr. Karageorghis sent me photographs of the contents of Arpera Mosphilos Tomb IA. The Tomb contains three Tell el-Yahudiya juglets with ovoid bodies and high, marked shoulders; they are decorated in the early, elaborate style. These jugs are earlier than the specimens recorded in the corpus above and probably belong to the middle of M.C. III].

Amiran 1957, 1963/69

In 1957, Ruth Amiran published an article on the Tell el-Yahudiya pottery found in Syria, in which she indicated that both Syria and Lower Egypt were only peripheral areas, and that the true centre of production should be sought in Palestine,[147] a point which she further emphasised in 1963/69,[148] when she wrote:

"The distinctive Tell el-Yahudiyeh Ware is characterized by the punctured design arranged in geometric patterns. Two important points should be noted: first, this type of decoration has been found, up to the present only on juglets (with the exception of the two small carinated bowls from Megiddo [6]). Secondly, the Tell el-Yahudiya juglets are similar in form to the two main juglet types of the period and their variants, which usually have a burnished slip. Both facts have a bearing on the problem of the geographic and ethnic origin of this ware, named after Tell el-Yahudiya in the Nile Delta where Petrie first uncovered such juglets. [7]

MB IIA and B–C: Two main types of punctured decoration can be distinguished as well as some unusual forms:

a) The piriform juglets: Oval to start with the juglet becomes gradually more piriform and the shoulder more strongly marked, evolving into the typical MB II B–C juglet, one of whose hallmarks is the pronounced shoulder. At the same time, a number of features, such as the tendency towards squat shapes point to a certain degeneration of the type. The rim is another feature which differentiates between MB II A and B juglets: the earlier forms have a profiled rim appearing in many variations, and especially a ridge below the rim just like the ordinary juglets; in the later juglets

[147] Amiran, *IEJ* 7, 1957, 96.

[148] Amiran, *Ancient Pottery of the Holy Land*, original Hebrew edition, 1963, English translation, 1969.

the predominating rim is everted, usually rounded and thickened, and a handle attached just below the rim is one of the marked features of MB II B–C pottery.
b) The cylindrical juglet: Such juglets are found already in MB II A, but it is difficult to differentiate between such early specimens and similar, though later, juglets.
Decoration: The clay of the Tell el-Yahudiyeh juglets is usually grey or light brown, with numerous grits. The burnished slip is grey, brownish black, or yellowish. The decoration consists entirely of punctures made in the clay after slip and burnish had been applied and filled with white chalk, which often is still preserved.

Two main types of punctured decoration can be distinguished; designs delineated by grooves, and areas without delineation filled with straight, diagonal, or zig-zag lines of punctures. In both types horizontal designs are more common, but vertical designs, usually segment-shaped, are also fairly frequent. The predominant motifs are triangles, squares, and rhomboids, and only three instances of concentric circles are known. In all three the concentric circles are contained in a plain horizontal band enclosed by puncture-filled bands.
Distribution: The thirty-three specimens [illustrated by Amiran] show that Tell el-Yahudiyeh ware has been found on the coast of northern Canaan, in all of southern Canaan (Palestine), in eastern Cyprus, and in Egypt, from the Delta to Nubia. It should be noted that, up to the present [1963], the ware has not been found in inland Syria i.e. on the upper Orontes and farther east.
Date: As we have seen above, the Tell el-Yahudiyeh ware first appears in MB II A, and the examples known, though few are dated with a fair measure of certainty by their context. The cylindrical juglet also makes its appearance already at this early stage. The two small carinated bowls are also dated to the MB II A. Interestingly enough, bowls disappear from the repertoire of this ware in MB II B–C. The evidence from Egypt and Phoenicia also points to the first appearance of this ware in the earlier part of the Middle Bronze Age. At Kahun, [8] fragments of Tell el-Yahudiyeh juglets were found together with other Canaanite vessels characteristic of MB II A. At Sin el-Fil, [9] the context in which two juglets were found, includes vessels which can be dated to MB II A. However the Tell el-Yahudiyeh Ware reaches the peak of its popularity in MB II B, and is found very frequently on sites of that period. In LB I, the last descendants of this ware still occur.
Origin: The form of the Tell el-Yahudiyeh juglet is firmly rooted in Canaanite ceramic tradition, and can be traced back through earlier periods to such prototypes as, for instance, the juglets from Tomb A at Jericho.

Of particular significance is the potters kiln excavated at Afula,[149] where both complete vessels and numerous fragments of Tell el-Yahudiyeh Ware were found, including many fragments of unbaked juglets. Thus it appears that the ware was manufactured in Canaan and exported from there to Egypt and Cyprus.[150]

[6] G. SCHUMACHER, *Tell el-Muteseillim*, I, Leipzig, 1908, figs. 41–42.

[7] W.M.F. PETRIE, Hyksos and Israelite Cities, London, 1906.

[8] C.F.A. SCHAEFFER, Stratigraphie comparée et chronologie de l'Asie Occidentale, Oxford, 1948, fig. 53.

[9] Ibid., fig. 73.

Whilst she thus added to the chronological development of the ware, her conclusions regarding its origin echoed those already voiced by Otto several years before, though strangely she seemed unaware of this earlier study.[151]

VAN SETERS, 1966

Van Seters apparently overlooked Åström's study, and ignoring the remarks of Säve-Söderbergh, simply followed in the footsteps of Engberg, in attributing the ware to the Hyksos, but, going on from Reisner, made the distinction between a Syrian type which was usually piriform with a button or ring base and a delineated pattern of triangles and diamonds, considering all other shapes and decorative styles to be Palestinian, writing:

> "The place of the Tell el-Yahudiyeh ware in the ceramic typology of the Levant and in Egyptian chronology is now fairly clear. It belongs to MB II B–C, which corresponds to the Second Intermediate Period. Some scholars have proposed that

[149] See now ZEVULUN, *EI* 21, 1990, 174–190.
[150] AMIRAN, *Ancient Pottery of the Holy Land*, 118–120.
[151] At least there is no mention of it in the quoted works.

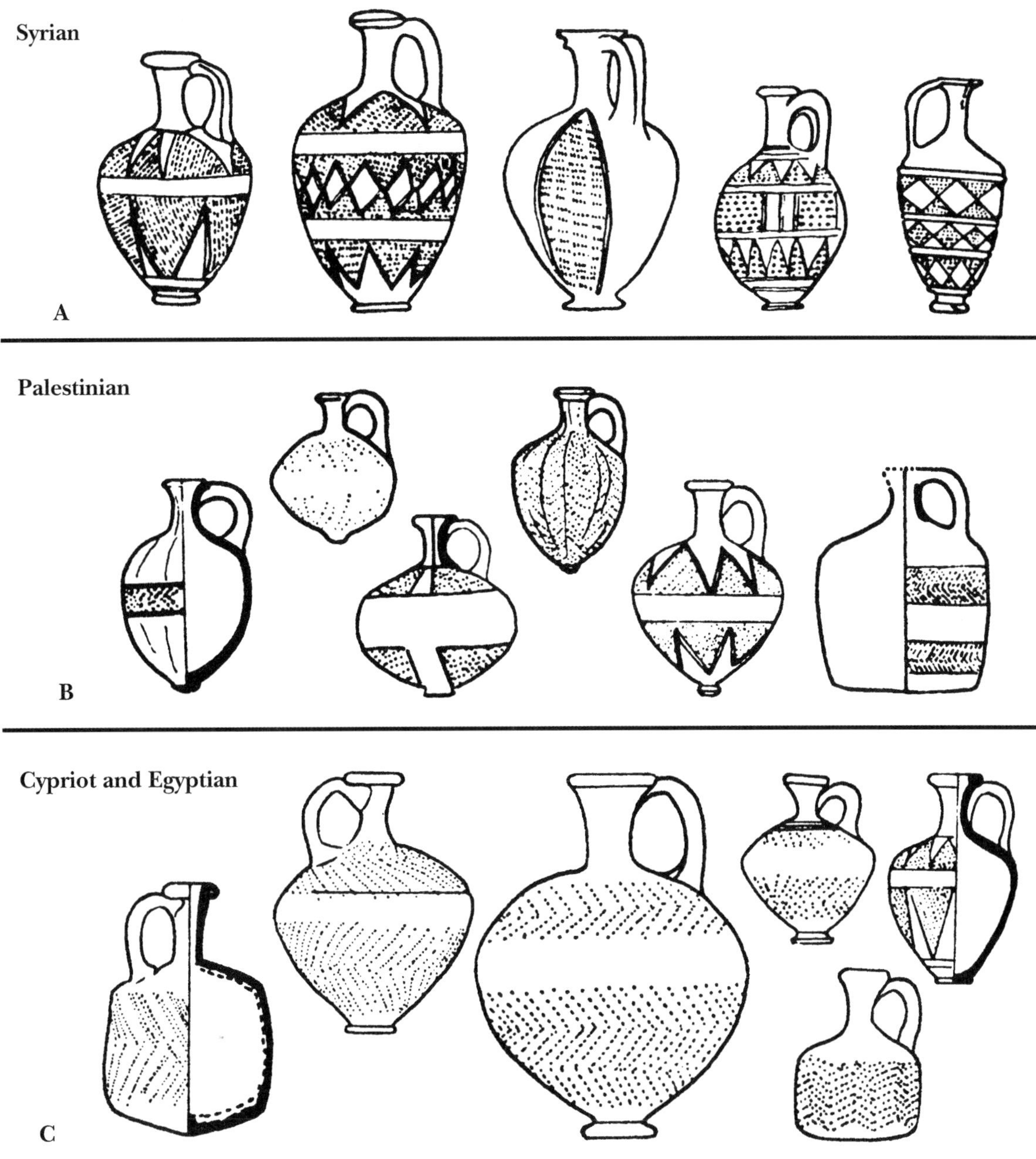

Fig. 4 Tell el-Yahudiya Typology after VAN SETERS 1966

Tell el-Yahudiyeh ware occurs in Egypt in the Twelfth Dynasty, but the evidence for this is entirely faulty, and the occurrences are actually to be dated later. It is nevertheless possible to arrive at a closer dating within the Second Intermediate Period by differentiating between two styles. The first may be called Syrian; the form of the juglet, piriform with high round shoulders and disc or ring base, is characteristic of coastal Syria in this period. The pattern is contained within lines and consists of a picked design in triangular or diamond zones [Group A]. The second style is Palestinian, and may best be regarded as a degenerate form of the Syrian style. The juglet shapes may be squat piriform, cylindrical with convex bottom, or baggy. The patterns are usually not concentrated in lines, but they may be in simple, parallel horizontal zones. The picking is done in chevron or zig-zag patterning [Group B].

The distribution of these two styles is significant. The Syrian type is found in coastal Syria throughout the whole period. It also occurs in Palestine, particularly at Megiddo, but usually in an imitated form, where the juglets are more globular and the base is button-shaped. The Syrian types are also found in Egypt at Khata^{c}na in the Delta, at Kahun in Middle Egypt, and at Buhen and Kerma in Nubia. The Palestinian style is found in Egypt primarily in the Delta at Khataᶜna and Tell el-Yahudiya, with perhaps a few pieces in Middle Egypt, but none in Nubia. This style is also found in Cyprus at Enkomi [Group C]."[152]

Whilst Van Seters' groups A and B seem clear, his group C is, as described, non-existent, since it is only a combination of vessels of Groups A and B which have, by chance, been found in Egypt and Cyprus. From his accompanying figure, reproduced here as Fig. 4, it is clear, however, that the vessels of Group C all have different decorative schemes to his illustrated vessels of Groups A and B. Since his attribution of Syrian and Palestinian types derive mainly from the places where most vessels were found, ie. Syrian types come mostly from the northern Levant, and Palestinian types from the southern Levant, the logical next step would be that the juglets of group C, which in terms of their decoration are neither truly Syrian nor Palestinian, should also have been manufactured in the areas where they were found. That is to say that the vessels of Group C ought to be both Cypriot and Egyptian. However Van Seters did not go so far owing to his belief that the ware must be associated with the Hyksos, and thus entirely non-Egyptian.

Merrillees, 1974

In a series of articles Merrillees concentrated on Van Seters' Syrian type which he demonstrated was earlier, than for example, the types discussed by Åström, and proposed to name this earlier variant by the name of another Egyptian site which had produced a substantial number of these vases, El-Lisht; most of which pieces had, at that time, not been published.[153] Merrillees then proceeded to provide a catalogue of 27 pieces of so-called El-Lisht ware from Lisht, and a further 83 pieces from elsewhere which were then known to him in 1974, with a further eight pieces in 1978.[154] His 1974 study led him to the following conclusions:[155]

> "Nearly all the specimens listed above belong to the piriform juglet type which, after passing through a transitional phase, represented in large part by Van Seters' group B (Van Seters 1966, p. 50 Fig. 9, p. 51) and by the finds from ᶜAfula in Palestine (Åström, 1957, 236 n. 13, 237; Amiran, 1970, pl. 36.3, p. 116, p. 118 Photos 115–118, p. 121 Photo 124, p. 120), became one of the distinctive forms of the later, Tell el-Yahudiya Ware (Åström, 1957, pp. 233f.; Åström, 1971, pp. 419ff.). Other features which differentiate the El-Lisht juglets from their immediate and ultimate successors are their generally large size, base ring, everted rim, multiple stranded handle, fine manufacture, highly burnished brown or black slipped surface, and elaborate decorative designs. The incised ornamental patterns on these pots fall into two main categories, one naturalistic and the other abstract, mostly geometrical.
>
> The overall date of the El-Lisht Ware has yet to be firmly established. Egyptian evidence suggests that the style had a chronological range from the XIIIth Dynasty, which probably saw its floruit, to half way through the Hyksos period, about the middle of the 17th century BC. Circumstantial indications from Syria and Palestine tend to confirm this dating."

Merrillees went on to suggest that El-Lisht Ware was probably more common in Cyprus than the number of extant examples would tend to indicate since the type was extensively copied in Black Slip III ware, particularly in Åström's jug type II,[156] and that, moreover the decoration on the vessels found in the tomb at Arpera can be closely matched in Black Slip III vessels from Pendayia Mandres Tomb 1.[157] However this connection with Black Slip III is probably mistaken since Merrillees wished to date the Arpera tomb to a late stage of Middle Cypriot III as the material found in it looks forward to Late Cypriote IA. He thus places it at the transition between Middle Cypriot III/Late Cypriot IA, c.1650 BC. on his 1974 dates. However, as Kaplan points out, nothing in the tomb group is so late,[158] and Åström's date in the middle of Middle Cypriot III seems more appropriate, a date, which on the Tell el-Dabᶜa evidence (see below), would be more likely. As such the Arpera material ought to predate Black Slip III.

---

[152] Van Seters, *The Hyksos*, 50–51.
[153] Merrillees, *Trade and Transcendance*, 59.
[154] Merrillees, *Levant* 10, 1978, 76–84.
[155] Merrillees, *Trade and Transcendance*, 73.
[156] Åström, *The Middle Cypriote Bronze Age*, 105–107, 226, 239, fig. xxx.11–14.
[157] Karageorghis, *Nouveaux documents pour l'étude du bronze récente à Chypre*, 1965, 30, fig. 10.4, 12, 33, 39, 47, 48, 100, 101, 110, pp. 48ff.
[158] Kaplan, *Tell el-Yahudiyeh Ware*, 76.

Williams, 1975

Following Merrillees' 1974 publication, Williams enthusiastically adopted the chronological divisions put forward by Merrilleees in his unpublished Ph.D thesis,[159] but referred to Merrillees' El-Lisht ware as Early Tell el-Yahudiya Ware, and Merrillees' Tell el-Yahudiya Ware as Late Tell el-Yahudiya Ware. Based on the then published finds from Tell el-Dab^ca, he also added a Transitional Tell el-Yahudiya Ware, (Fig. 5) which is different to, and should not be confused with, Merrillees' Transitional Tell el-Yahudiya Ware of 1978. However, Williams then went on to discuss the dating of Tell el-Yahudiya pottery by reference to the published finds from Kerma, since for him this provided the only instance that "contained unequivocal historical evidence for the date."[160] This led him to suppose that his Early and Transitional Tell el-Yahudiya Ware should be dated to the late Seventeenth Century BC., and his Late Tell el-Yahudiya Ware to the early Sixteenth Century BC., and that all groups should date to the Hyksos period. Since he then used these dates, which are now known to be incorrect, to date all other Second Intermediate Period assemblages which contained Tell el-Yahudiya pottery, Williams' thesis, which is an otherwise very valuable gathering of material, has been generally ignored by the academic community.

Amiran, 1975

In 1975 Ruth Amiran returned to the topic of Tell el-Yahudiya vessels and offered some notes on the decorative styles of the ware, making a broad division into two classes, geometric and figurative:

> "The main element of the geometric pattern is the 'punctured field', be it the triangle, the lozenge or the oblong, and very rarely the circle. There would be some logic in a definition that the puncturing is actually the 'creator' of the pattern by filling in alternate fields, thus developing the style from the linnear to the two-dimensional. However, it seems that the puncturing should rather be considered only as the main means of making up the pattern and that the 'punctured field' is its essence. In the geometric class we can distinguish two orders: the horizontal and the vertical. Being natural to the tectonics of pottery making, the horizontal order is common to most decorative styles. In our style the order is composed of a number of horizontal bands of the forms just ennumerated, each containing punctured fields. On the other hand it is of interest to seek the origin of the vertical order of our style, in which the whole surface is divided into alternately punctured and plain vertical areas. .... We can ... suggest that the 'gaps' in the vertical order are part of the idea behind the pattern itself and are meant to enhance the impression of the deep shadowy 'folds' in the fruit-like vessels.[161] Thus the origin of the vertical order should be sought in the fruit-like juglets.
>
> Another aspect relevant to the understanding of the significance of the whole Tell el-Yahudiya class of juglet should be pointed out. Botanical identification of the fruit imitated here would supply information far beyond the mere history of the shape. It would constitute the key to the cultural understanding of the whole class. The exclusiveness of the application of this style to one class of containers on the one hand and its great diffusion throughout the whole of the Levant, from Alalakh and Cyprus to Kerma and all the regions in between on the other permit us to assume that the commodity "packed" in these juglets (seeds or powder or liquid?) has something to do with the style of decoration and with the fruit some of these juglets imitate. Unfortunately this identification still eludes us.
>
> The figurative class ... with depictions of figures on juglets of this style is very fragmentary and raises the cardinal question of whether it deserves (or permits) designation as a class or whether these are merely sporadic, whimsical creations."[162]

Merrillees 1978, 1980

In 1978, Merrillees, unconsciously reflecting some of the ideas put forward by Otto some forty years earlier (whose article seems also to have been curiously overlooked by him),[163] further defined the differences between his El-Lisht and Tell el-Yahudiya Wares thus:

[159] Williams, Archaeology and Historical Problems of the Second Intermediate Period, unpublished Ph.D Dissertation, University of Chicago, 1975, 83–97.

[160] Williams, Archaeology and Historical Problems of the Second Intermediate Period, 95.

[161] That is, what are now commonly called quadrilobal jugs.

[162] Amiran, *Israel Museum News* 10, 1975, 41.

[163] At least there are no references to Otto's article in Merrillees' basic works on the subject.

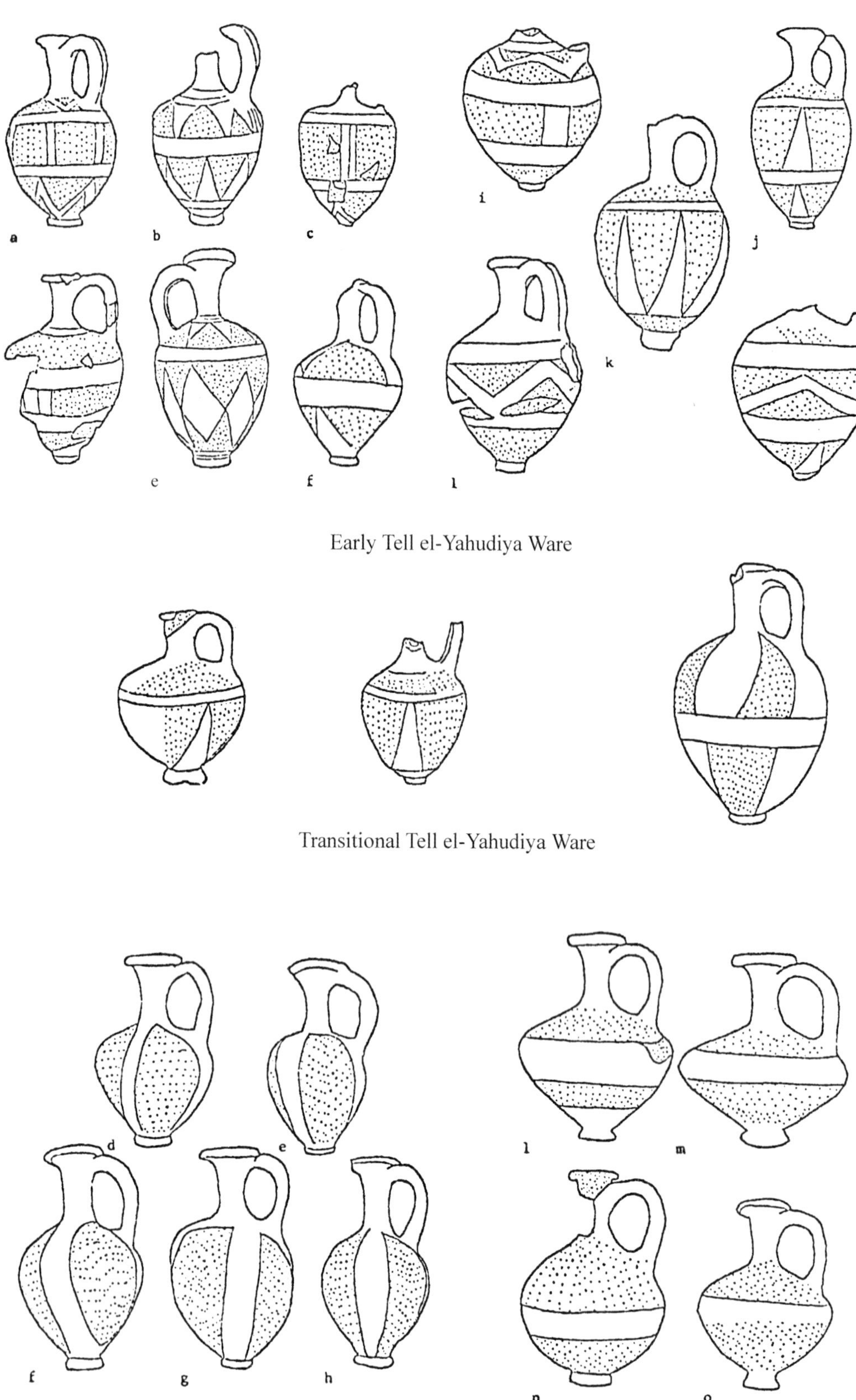

Late Tell el-Yahudiya Ware

Fig. 5 Tell el-Yahudiya Ware after WILLIAMS 1975

"Typologically the el-Lisht and Tell el-Yahudiya jugs, which make up the bulk of their respective Wares, can be readily differentiated on the basis of several criteria. In the first place the majority of el-Lisht jugs are on an average larger in all respects than the mass of closed Tell el-Yahudiya vases. While the former are generally more than 10 cm. tall, ... the latter are mostly less than 10 cm. in height. ... Secondly the range of shapes represented in both Wares offers significant contrasts. To the el-Lisht Ware belong only two main types, the jug and duck or goose vase. ... On the other hand Tell el-Yahudiya Ware embraces a wide variety of shapes including bird and fish shaped containers. The morphology of the vases attributable to the el-Lisht and Tell el-Yahudiya Wares shows certain differences in common features that enable the styles to be identified. Probably the most noteworthy variation between the Wares is the shape of the handle, which in the case of el-Lisht jugs is composed of two or more loops, whereas that on their Tell el-Yahudiya descendants is typically in the form of the strap. There are, however, other diagnostic features of use for classificatory purposes. The bodies of the el-Lisht jugs are usually ovoid with broad, low flat base or base-rings. Their typological successors have less elongated, squatter, piriform bodies and characteristic button base. The necks of the jugs in both Wares are usually extremely constricted but rims do appear to have had some typological and chronological significance. El-Lisht Ware characteristically sports an unusual everted, upright, circular rim, turned over and inset, often giving the appearance of a hollow tyre. This kind occurs in Egypt to the almost complete exclusion of the everted, circular open funnel-shaped rim which is attested predominantly in Syria, where it is closely related to the contemporaneous plain jugs of Black and Red Burnished Ware, and in Cyprus. This inset rim does not recur in Tell el-Yahudiya Ware, where the geographical dimension to the distribution of rim forms appears to have less significance. Attested in this Ware all over the Levant are the solid tyre-shaped rim and the everted, circular, thickened rim, the former presumably a successor of the earlier, hollow form, the latter keeping in step with the evolution of contemporaneous Syro-Palestinan juglets.

Technically speaking certain divergences in the ways in which the fabrics of el-Lisht and Tell el-Yahudiya Wares were treated and finished can be detected in specimens of both types. The walls of the former are usually thinner and more finely made. .... the sections of el-Lisht vases are almost always brown or buff while those of the Tell el-Yahudiya containers are seldom anything but grey. Whereas the exterior surfaces of Tell el-Yahudiya vases are invariably black with varying degrees of lustre, el-Lisht Ware generally has a brown and tan as well as black exterior surfaces, which are almost always evenly burnished to a very high finish. There is overall a marked difference in qualities between the two styles, the el-Lisht Ware on the whole being much finer than its successor.

The techniques of incised decoration also reveal important divergences, for the el-Lisht Ware favoured the use of rectilinear or curvilinear elements to form a design into which the punctures were fitted. In the later Tell el-Yahudiya Ware, however, straight lines served almost always to divide up the field rather than create individual patterns, and curved lines are entirely absent. The incised stippling now stands decoratively in its own right, as witnessed by the transitional vases.

The ornamental layouts are themselves particularly instructive, as the naturalistic and geometric motifs that characterise the el-Lisht Ware have disappeared from Tell el-Yahudiya repertory. Birds, fish, quadrupeds, even apparently humans, feather patterns, palm trees, lotus flowers, rectangles, triangles, and interlocking spirals are all included in the field on el-Lisht jugs, whereas the Tell el-Yahudiya Ware has abandoned these elements. The division of the field into horizontal or vertical bands is a feature of both styles, but the arrangement of the various motifs in the earlier is much more formalized than in its successor. Both show a strong attachment to symmetry, which does not, however, detract from the individuality and even idiosyncracy of the particularly decorative layouts in the el-Lisht Ware. The pricked filling of the el-Lisht motifs is replaced in the Tell el-Yahudiya Ware by stippled designs on their own, such as multiple straight lines, chevrons and zigzags, which give the latter a more stereotyped and massproduced air than their precursors."[164]

---

[164] Merrillees, *Levant* 10, 89–91

Merrillees, however, slightly clouded the issue by introducing a transitional el-Lisht/Tell el-Yahudiya Ware, different to the Transitional Tell el-Yahudiya Ware introduced by Williams three years before, to which he attributed eight vessels which came from the area of Syria/Lebanon. (Fig. 6).[165] This transitional ware was classified by the fact that:

"... the shape, finish and decoration of the juglets which hark back typologically and stylistically to the el-Lisht Ware but at the same time look forward to the more common and standardized Tell el-Yahudiya Ware. Their bodies look mid-way between the tall ovoid shape of the earlier, and the more bulbous piriform shape of the later examples of this fabric, and they all have double loop handles but peg or button bases. In height they average between 10 to 14 cm., taller than the majority of Tell el-Yahudiya juglets but shorter than the bulk of el-Lisht jugs. Their fabrics in section resemble both the El-Lisht and Tell el-Yahudiya Wares, particularly in colour, as both brown and grey firings are attested. Their exterior surfaces though nearly always black, are usually highly burnished, and the incised decoration, though simplified in the Tell el-Yahudiya style, shows a more rigorous attachment to precision and symmetry.

A note of caution, however, must be sounded in making this ascription too categorical. Just as the rim types seem to reveal as much a difference in ceramic traditions between Egypt and the Asiatic mainland as a typological and hence chronological development, so certain of the features on the putative el-Lisht/Tell el-Yahudiya vases may reflect more the continuance of morphological and technical customs in an indigeneous industry than an intermediate stage of manufacture. It could be, for instance, that the specimens under review were being made in Syria, more particularly Phoenicia, contemporaneously with the Tell el-Yahudiya Ware proper of Egypt and Palestine which is barely attested in this region."[166]

By 1980, Merrillees had so crystallised his ideas on El-Lisht and Tell el-Yahudiya juglets that, although he saw both types as part of a single evolving tradition which also produced specimens 'transitional' stylistically between the two types, he was able to write:[167]

"A convenient source of reference is the chart published in J. Van Seters, The Hyksos [here Fig. 4]. The juglets to which the term El-Lisht ware is applied consist of his type A, plus the top right hand specimen of type C, and perhaps the specimen second from the right in type B. These juglets are frequently larger in size than the later ones, and display a disc or ring-shaped base, everted rim, multiple stranded handle, and incised designs. These latter fall into two main categories: one naturalistic, the other consisting of square or triangular areas framed with incised borders, and filled with punctured stippling. They also possess a highly burnished black or brown slipped surface. G.A. Reisner long ago regarded the fabric as 'only ordinary alluvial mud, such as is found all along the Nile Valley from Khartoum to Alexandria,[239] and whilst the type was ultimately derived from the Syro-Palestinian ceramic repertory, the black burnished fabric had a long though limited history in Egypt, and the quantities of the juglets found in Egypt make it likely that they are, for the most part a local and imitative, or partly imitative, product. A similar fabric seems occasionally to have been used in Egypt around these times to create other shapes as well. One example is a remarkable carinated bowl with incised spiral patterns found at Kerma, with a hieroglyphic group incised on it as well. Traces of red and yellow pigment are said to survive in the incisions, as well as the usual white.

The advantage of separating the two classes of juglets by terminology is that the Hyksos association of the term 'Tell el-Yahudiya' are not automatically present, even though faint, when the earlier class is considered. The el-Harageh evidence then falls into place very satisfactorily. Two sherds were found in the domestic debris, one of them in house group 530. More importantly two tombs contained them amongst other material which places them securely within the el-Harageh Middle Kingdom sequence though apparently towards the latter end, thus presumably in the

[165] Merrillees, *Levant* 10, 84–87.

[166] Merrillees, *Levant* 10, 91–92. Cf. idem, *Levant* 6 (1974), 193–195.

[167] Kemp and Merrillees, *Minoan Pottery*, 91–8, with the original footnotes omitted except where additional discussion is included.

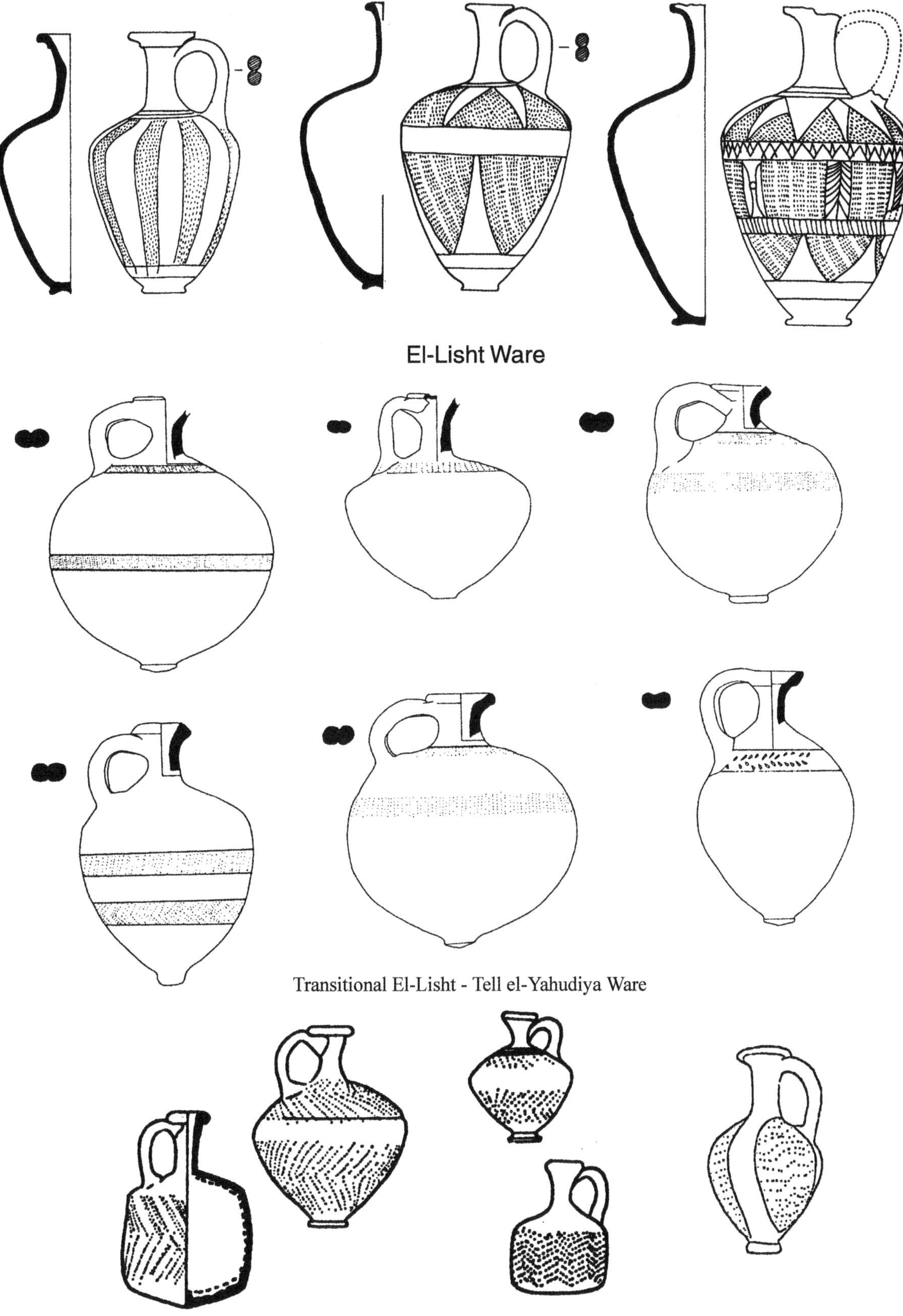

Fig. 6 Tell el-Yahudiya Typology after MERRILLEES 1978, 1980

Thirteenth Dynasty.[168] It is interesting to note that one of them, from tomb 354, seems to be a transitional type.

Tell ed-Dab^ca provides important corroboration here. Juglets which are essentially of el-Lisht ware type, though usually of brown or grey-brown appearance, presumably a local trait, occurred in the lower strata, including at least two from level G, dated by M. Bietak to the Thirteenth Dynasty. [243] All of the illustrated juglets of this type assigned to levels F and E/2 were recovered from tombs, not all of which could be placed in their exact stratigraphic horizon...[169]

In this connection it should be noted that el-Lisht ware appears to have been entirely lacking from the excavated parts of Tell el-Yahudiya itself. The same distinction can also be made for the pan-grave cemeteries from Upper Egypt, where mostly Tell el-Yahudiya rather than el-Lisht ware juglets are part of the ceramic repertoire. These facts seem to suggest that el-Lisht ware had its floruit before the middle of the 17th century BC., thus during the Thirteenth Dynasty, after which Tell el-Yahudiya ware proper came into vogue and remained the more popular until the end of the Hyksos Period. [252] The fact that el-Lisht ware juglets do not occur in the court burials of the period, such as the tomb of King Awibre Hor at Dahshur, is probably of no chronological consequence. The very same reluctance to include Minoan and imitation Minoan pottery in tomb groups is very evident from el-Harageh, and although terribly robbed, no trace of anything exotic including el-Lisht juglets was found in the various cemeteries around Kahun itself.

To establish an initial date for el-Lisht ware is a much more difficult proposition, rendered almost intractable by the state of the extant evidence, not least in Egypt from the evident reluctance to include such material in burial groups. A comparison of the distribution patterns of both these types of juglet when viewed against the contemporary historical background in Egypt, Palestine and Syria, reveals what might be interpreted as a correlation between geographical and political aspects, and a contrast overall between the el-Lisht and Tell el-Yahudiya wares, with implications for their chronological ranges. Thus el-Lisht ware juglets occur in western Asia mainly, it would seem in regions where there is other evidence for relations with Egypt, that is the Syrian coast. [253] One might read into this, as others have done, that the bulk of this ware should antedate the presumed eclipse of the Thirteenth Dynasty in the Delta.

[239] Reisner, *Kerma IV–V*, 388. This impression seems to have been confirmed by scientific analysis for it is reported that neutron activation analysis of Tell el-Yahudiya ware from Egypt, Cyprus and the Levant shows that most of it was produced in Egypt. This was reported by Artzy, in a paper entitled 'Ceramic chronologies and provenience studies in the Bronze Age eastern Mediterranean' read at the 1976 annual meeting of the American Oriental Society held in Philadelphia, and cited by Weinstein, *JARCE* 14 (1977), 115, n.11; cf. also Bimson, *Redating the Exodus and Conquest*, 169, 266 note 9.

[243] Bietak, *MDAIK* 26 (1970) 39, and 19, 23–24 for dates.[170]

[252] Cf. Åström, *The Middle Cypriote Bronze Age*, 239, note 10; Merrillees, *The Cypriote Bronze Age Pottery found in Egypt*, 96f., Bourriau, *JNES* 28, (1969), 131; Merrillees, *Australian J. Biblical Archaeology* 1 no. 3 (1970), 16, 23–24; Ward, *Egypt and the East Mediterranean World*, 79, note 323; Merrillees, *Levant* 10 (1978), 92–96. After the completion of our text Dorothea Arnold published an el-Lisht sherd and what is perhaps the neck of a Tell el-Yahudiya ware juglet from the new German excavations around the pyramid of Amenemhet III at Dahshur. Both come from strata belonging to the Early Eighteenth Dynasty. See Arnold, *MDAIK* 33 (1977) 21–24. As the manuscript was going to press there appeared in print, Bimson, Redating the Exodus and Conquest. This contains brief but polemical discussions of various aspects of East Mediterranean archaeology. (....in which....) pp. 165–170, a case is made that Tell el-Yahudiya ware juglets were present in significant quantities or as a significant product in post-Hyksos Period times, indeed with some later than the early Eighteenth Dynasty. Now it is indeed true that a few can be found in what are evidently very early New Kingdom contexts, one from Medinet el Ghurab [Kemp and Merrillees, Minoan Pottery 56], and others have been referred to by Merrillees on occasions, e.g. The Cypriote Bronze Age Pottery found in Egypt, 97. For the later extension of their period of use Bimson cites Abydos tomb D 114 of Peet, which contained scarabs bearing the name Men-kheper-ra (Tuthmosis III). However the contents of this tomb clearly cover an extended period of time, back into the early Eighteenth Dynasty, see Merrillees, *op. cit.* 115–116.

Negbi 1978

In 1978, Ora Negbi published an article detailing the Tell el-Yahudiya vessels found at Toumba tou

---

[168] See Kemp and Merrillees, *Minoan Pottery*, 1980, 33–36.

[169] The remainder of this paragraph is omitted since it refers to the dating of the Tell el-Dab^ca sequences as given in the preliminary reports, from *MDAIK* 23 and 26, which have since been revised. The revised dating does not affect Merrillees' argument.

[170] Note these dates have since been revised.

Skourou.[171] In discussing five vessels she concludes that all of them were made in Cyprus. Whilst this may be true for the two handmade and clumsy copies, P963 and P1027, this is not the case with the other three which can be seen as normal vessels of what we shall later term the Levanto-Egyptian Tell el-Yahudiya ware.[172] In regard to the proposed Cypriote origin of these vessels it may be significant that a group of 21, admittedly slightly later Tell el-Yahudiya vessels found on Cyprus were specifically analysed by means of NAA by Artzy and Asaro in order to determine their place of origin. The results showed that of the 21 pots, 8 were made in the Egyptian Delta, 8 others probably originated in Egypt and the other 5 may be of Egyptian origin.[173]

Kaplan 1980

The last comprehensive monograph, and the first since Junker, was written by Maureen Kaplan, and is still the standard reference work on the subject.[174] It also comprised the first attempt to find a systematic classification of this pottery group based on a chemical as well as a typological analysis. The typological approach, using a combination of body shapes and attributes, followed in the footsteps of Åström, but being concerned with all Tell el-Yahudiya jugs, rather than those found only in Cyprus, was, of course, more substantial. As a result she distinguished six main families, Cylindrical, Globular, Quadrilobal, Piriform, Biconical and Ovoid, with other minor families, Miniature, Grooved, Bird-shaped, Ichthyomorphic, Vessels with Naturalistic Designs, and finally a group of Typological Variations to cover everything which could not be readily fitted into any of the others. With the exception of the Globular and Quadrilobal groups, her main groups were subdivided to produce the following basic typology:[175]

"*Cylindrical 1:* These juglets are small with a size range of 7.6 to 12.6 cms. in height. The bases tend to be rounded, sometimes showing no angle of carination as the vertical plane of the body is reached. The transition from the shoulder to the body of the vessel is also less angular than in Cylindrical 2 vessels. There is no difference in the rim types between the two cylindrical types, both have rolled-over or slightly everted rims. The handle is formed by a single strand of clay, and the decoration is restricted to the vertical plane of the body, which is covered with chevrons or rows of punctures.

Cylindrical 2: The size ranges in height from 9.7 to 15.4 cm., and are noticeably larger then Cylindrical 1. The transitions from the shoulder to the body and from the body to the base are very angular. Bases tend to be flat or very gently curved, and the handle is consistently double-stranded.

Globular: The rim is primarily rolled over, though some straight and slightly everted rims are found. The handle is single, and there is a general progression from globular to squat globular forms, but it is a general progression and does not warrant constituting into two subdivisions. The most common decoration is three or four vertical gores of herringbone incision. Other minor variations in decoration include two bands of triangles, two broad bands of chevrons and random lines of pricking.

Quadrilobal: In body proportion these are similar to the globular type, but what sets them apart is that the body is indented in such a manner as to form four lobes.

Piriform 1: This is the type Merrillees terms El-Lisht ware. The vessels fall into two size groups averaging 12.2 and 15.8 cms. in height. The base may vary from a ring to indented button [note what Kaplan calls a button is referred to as a disc by us]. The handle is almost always multiple stranded; double handles are the most common. The rim is usually inverted. The bodies are often burnished all over, in contrast to other types where the burnishing occurs only on the unincised areas. The most frequent comb size has between three and seven teeth. The decoration comes in several variations: three or four bands filled with triangles and rectangles, three bands of rectangles, and two bands of standing and pendant triangles. There seems to be no preference for combining any one style with a particular vessel size, handle or base type.

[171] O. Negbi, Cypriot Imitations of Tell el-Yahudiya Ware, *AJA* 78, (1982), 137–149.

[172] Cf. below page 142.

[173] M. Artzy and F. Asaro, Origin of Tell el-Yahudiyah Ware found in Cyprus, *RDAC*, 1979 139.

[174] Kaplan, *Tell el-Yahudiya Ware*,. See also M. Kaplan, G. Harbottle and E. Sayre, Multi-disciplinary Analysis of Tell el Yahudieh Ware, *Archaeometry* 24, 1982, 127–142; and iidem, Tell el-Yahudiya Ware: A Re-evaluation, in: P.M. Rice (ed.), *Pots and Potters: Current Approaches in Ceramic Archaeology*, Los Angeles, 1984, 227–241.

[175] Kaplan, *Tell el-Yahudiyeh Ware*, 15–39, figs. 4–131.

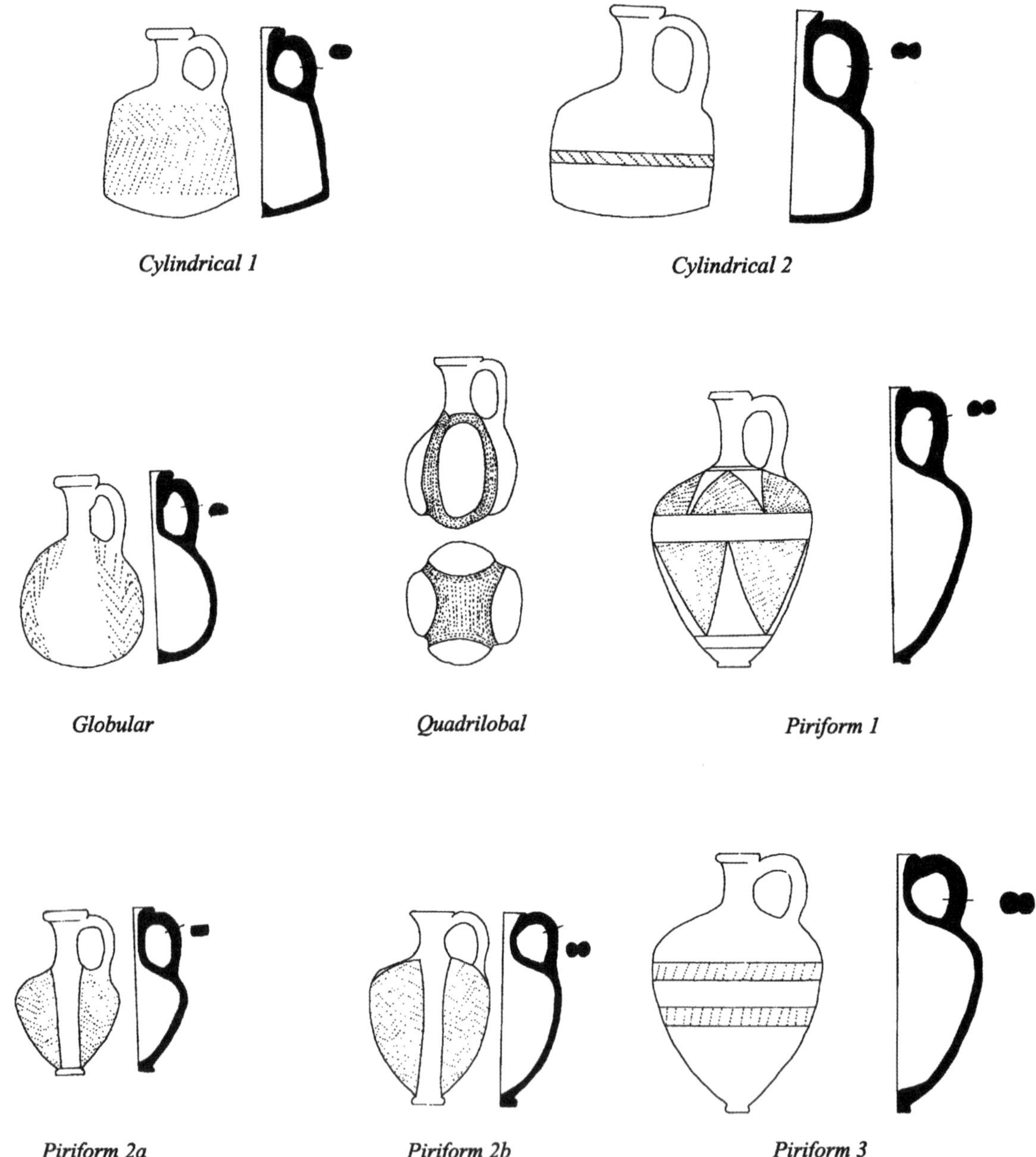

Fig. 7 Tell el-Yahudiya Typology after KAPLAN 1980

Piriform 2a: This type of vessel never has an inverted rim, but almost always has a rolled over rim. The handle is always single and may have either a ring or button [disc] base. The decoration invariably consists of three or four gores filled with a herringbone pattern of incised dots. The comb used for the incisions had eight or more points, and the area of incision is usually delineated. The vessel is burnished only on the unincised areas which may have resulted in the obliteration of some of the lines of delineation.

Piriform 2b: This is similar to type 2a, but with a few important differences. The rim seems to have been either drawn up and trimmed without being rolled over on itself, or else it was rolled over and pressed thin. The handle is always double. The button base is quite pronounced and often protrudes to a point.

Piriform 3: The third and final group of piriform jugs is more heterogeneous in form and possibly also in decoration, though there are some unifying factors. The decoration is horizontally orientated, and invariably covers less than half the available body area. The decoration usually consists of one or two narrow delinated bands filled with chevrons, herringbone patterns, triangles or vertical lines, though there are exceptions. The vessels tend to come in two sizes, the smaller averaging 12.0 cms. in height, and the larger 15.9 cms. The larger vessels also tend to have proportionally shorter necks. The rims may be rolled or everted. The handle is usually bipartite though single and triple stranded examples can be found. The base is always a [disc] or button base.

Biconical 1: The height of these vessels varies between 7.8 and 16.0 cms. The rim is always rolled over, the handle single and the base is always a button [disc] though it may be slightly indented [ring]. The decoration invariably covers most of the body, leaving only a narrow burnished band around the girth of the vessel. The upper and lower broad bands are usually filled with horizontal chevrons, a herringbone pattern or oblique lines. The areas of incision are consistently delineated, and the incision is done with a comb having eight or more points.

Biconical 2: This encompasses two different types, the first being similar to the Biconical 1 type but having three zones of decoration, and the other being similar to Biconical 1 but having a multi-stranded handle.

Ovoid 1: Ovoid 1 jugs are large with multiple handles and button [disc] bases. The bodies are almost spherical. The rim is everted. Decoration usually consists of two or three narrow delineated bands of straight or oblique lines.

Ovoid 2: In these the rim is never rolled but varies from inverted to straight to slightly everted. The handle is rarely single, it is usually double. Button bases are usually smaller and thinner than those seen on other Ovoid types. Decoration is usually several bands of oblique lines or dots, though the horizontal bands may also be filled with triangles, chevrons or circles.

Ovoid 3: These are distinguished by the sharp angle between the shoulder and body, otherwise they are similar to Ovoid 2.

Ovoid 4: These are related to Piriform 1 vessels but their bodies are slightly wider, and the maximum point is lower. The rim is inverted, the handle triple-stranded and the base is either a ring or a button [disc]. The decoration is in four horizontal rows.

Ovoid 5: These vessels are distinguished from all others of the Ovoid group by the use of circles and spirals as their primary geometric patterns."

Kaplan, whilst discussing the dating of her types, did not attempt a full scale chronological discussion which is necessary to understand the development of this type of pottery, though she did give some date suggestions. Hence she assigned Cylindrical 1 from the Hyksos Period (Tell el-Dab^{c}a stratum E/1) to the Eighteenth Dynasty; Cylindrical 2 to the MBIIB; (Wheel-made) Globular from the late Thirteenth (Tell el-Dab^{c}a stratum E/2) to the Eighteenth Dynasty; Piriform 1 she assigned to the late Twelfth and Thirteenth Dynasties in Egypt, from the transitional MBIIA/B to early MBIIB in the Levant, and to MC III in Cyprus; Piriform 2a from Tell el-Dab^{c}a stratum E/2 to D/2; Piriform 2b she assigned from the transitional MB IIA/B to late MB IIB, the same date range she gives to Piriform 3. She dated Biconical 1 from some point in the first half of the Second Intermediate Period down to the early Eighteenth Dynasty, whereas her Ovoid types range from the transitional MB IIA/B to mid to late MB IIB, with Ovoid 5 being confined to the MB IIA or transitional MB IIA/B.

The major new point of her work, however was the NAA analysis of many of these jugs and Kaplan was thus able to show that certain types were manufactured only in certain areas,[176] hence her Cylindrical 1, Globular, Quadrilobal, Biconical 1 and Grooved ware were undoubtedly made in Egypt, whilst her Cylindrical 2, Piriform 2a, Piriform 3 and Ovoid vessels were Levantine productions. Her Piriform 1, however, was made both in Egypt and the Levant.

However, Kaplan's typological classification is not consistent since the shapes within her typological groups do not always follow her own typology, and thus her chronological conclusions are in need of revision. As a result Kaplan's conclusions have received a somewhat mixed reception from the academic community.[177]

[176] Kaplan, *Tell el-Yahudiyeh Ware*, 60–66; M. Kaplan, G. Harbottle and E. Sayre, Multi-disciplinary Analysis of Tell el Yahudieh Ware, *Archaeometry* 24, 1982, 129–133; and idem, Tell el-Yahudiyeh Ware: A Re-evaluation, in: P.M. Rice (ed.), *Pots and Potters: Current Approaches in Ceramic Archaeology*, Los Angeles, 1984, 232–234.

[177] They were accepted by Bourriau, *Umm el Ga'ab. Pottery from the Nile Valley*, 1981, 41–42, but criticised by, most notably, Weinstein, *AJA* 86, 1982, 450–52; Merrillees, Late Cypriote Pottery from Byblos "Necropole K" *RDAC* 1983, 188–189; Bietak, Archäologischer Befund und Historische Interpretation am Beispiel der Tell el-Yahudiya-Ware, in: S. Schoske (ed.), *Akten des Vierten Internationalen Ägyptologen Kongreßes, München 1985*, 1989, 7–34.

Fig. 8 Tell el-Yahudiya Typology after Kaplan 1980

The main conclusions of Kaplan's study can be summarised in the following manner:[178]

1) There are several areas of manufacture of Tell el-Yahudiya ware of which Egypt and the Levant are the most important centres, with Ras Shamra and Nubia as minor ones.

2) There are two major families of Tell el-Yahudiya ware: Egyptian and Levantine.

3) The shape of the Tell el-Yahudiya ware is Levantine in origin, but the firing techniques and the incised decoration are foreign to the Levant.[179] Kaplan suggests Nubia as the place of origin for this

[178] Kaplan, *Tell el-Yahudiyeh Ware*, 121–123.

[179] Note, however, Amiran, *Ancient Pottery of the Holy Land*, 120, pl. 20/28, photo 73; and Åström, *The Middle Cypriote Bronze Age*, 11–18, fig. 30.6.

decoration since this technique was endemic within the A-group, C-group and Kerma cultures.

4) The combined evidence of chemical and chronological analysis seems to indicate that the Tell el-Yahudiya ware was first produced in Egypt, and that the earliest examples in the Levant are of Egyptian origin. The earliest vessels manufactured in the Levant only appeared during the MBIIA–B transitional period.

5) Whilst vague about the area of production of the early Tell el-Yahudiya ware (her Piriform 1 = Merrillees' Lisht ware), she considers the Delta the likely manufacturing area of the later Egyptian types (her Piriform 2a, Biconical, Globular and Quadrilobal jugs).

6) In stratum G at Tell el-Dab^c^a, Kaplan states that Tell el-Yahudiya ware occurs in an Egyptian, rather than a MB IIA context and is absent from the earliest foreign burials of stratum F.[180] Since this ware shows a great efflorescence of new forms from stratum E/1 onwards, she speculates that the Hyksos, who apparently borrowed Egyptian nomenclature, titles, art work and scarabs, may also have borrowed this pottery type as well.

Strangely her point 4 would tend to negate her point 3, since if the decoration is, with Kaplan, stylistically Nubian then why, with her, were the earliest Tell el-Yahudiya vessels produced in Egypt and not Nubia ?

Kaplan, Harbottle and Sayre, 1984

In 1984 there appeared a paper with the enigmatic name, 'Tell el Yahudiyeh Ware: A re-evaluation';[181] however, in essence that paper simply republished the typology and conclusions already formulated by Kaplan in 1980.

Bietak 1986, 1989

From stratified excavations at Tell el-Dab^c^a it was soon obvious that Kaplan's conclusions 3, 4 and 6 were in need of revision, and first steps in this direction were made by Bietak in two articles written in the early 1980's.[182] In the first article to be published, in 1986, he divided Tell el-Yahudiya ware into the following groups:

1. *Die palästinensische Gruppe*: Krüge, häufig mit ovoider Form, meist hellrot bis hellbraun, manchmal auch schwarzpolierte Oberfläche (meist ohne Hämatitzusatz). Charakteristisch sind schmale horizontale ungegliederte Musterstreifen, die matt belassen und mit Kammstich – oder Einzelstichmuster gefüllt sind. Die Krüge des Frühstadiums besitzen meist drei bis fünf solcher Musterstreifen, manchmal ist die unterste oder oberste Zone in Dreiecke gegliedert. ... Andere Beispiele haben zwischen den Streifen Zonen aus Kreisen.

Die frühesten Exemplare wurden bisher in ^c^Afula gefunden; sie haben einen gekröpften Hals und sind zeitgleich mit Stratum G in Tell ed-Dab^c^a. ... In der späteren Phase haben diese Krüge nur mehr 1–2 Streifen.

Es gibt noch weitere Subgruppen in Palästina wie Krüge mit zwei Zonen, meist aus inkrustierten Dreiecken auf der Schulter. Dieser Typ dürfte im Inland bei Jericho, ^c^Ain Samiyeh und Malacha beheimatet sein. Ungeklärt ist die Herkunft der kugeligen bis eiförmigen Krüge mit einfacher Strichverzierung mit Dreieckseffekt in Tell ed-Dab^c^a.

2. *Die syrisch-ägyptische Gruppe* (z.T. identisch mit der Lischt Ware von R. Merrillees). Diese bestheht aus einer lückenlosen Serie von Krügen, deren waagrechte Musterzonen von vier (oder mehr) bis auf zwei Zonen abnimmt, die dann in direkter Fortsetzung in einer rein äg. Gruppe ihren Weitergang findet. Auch in der Größe nimmt die T. kontinuerlich ab, von Formen mit einer Höhe von über 25 cm bis zu Formen mit einer Größe um 10 cm. Vereinfachungen sind auch in der typologischen Entwicklung der Henkel (von dreigeteilten bis zu einfachen Bandhenkeln) und bei den Bodenformen (vom Ringboden bis zum einfachem Bandknopf) feststellbar. Die normale Form der syrisch-ägyptischen Gruppe ist der birnenförmige Krug mit hochgelagertem Schwerpunkt und entspricht größenteils Kaplans Form piriform 1 und ovoid 4.

---

[180] This statement is incorrect, though at the time Kaplan wrote her book, very little material from this stratum had been published.

[181] M. Kaplan, G. Harbottle and E.V. Sayre, in: P.M. Rice (ed.), *Pots and Potters: Current Approaches in Ceramic Technology*, 1984, 227–241.

[182] Bietak, *LÄ* VI, 1986, idem, Archäologischer Befund und Historische Interpretation am Beispiel der Tell el-Yahudiya-Ware, in: S. Schoske (ed.), *Akten des Vieren Internationalen Ägyptolgen Kongresses, München 1985*, 1989, 7–34. The latter was delivered as a lecture at the Fourth International Congress of Egyptologists, Munich, in 1985, but only appeared in print in 1989.

a) Vier Musterzonen oder mehr aus stehenden oder hängenden Dreiecken, Rechtecken, Zick-zack-Musterzonen. Die Musterfelder sind auf mattem Grund belassen und mit Einzel- oder Gabelstich gefüllt. Die Henkel sind zwei- oder dreigeteilt, die Innenlippe und der Ringboden typisch, die Politur ist meist dunkelbraun bis schwarz. ...

b) Drei Musterzonen, ähnlich wie a). Höhe immer noch um 20 cm, aber auch in Kleinformen mit etwa 12 cm, dunkelbraun- bis schwarzpolierte Oberfläche, normalerweise zweigeteilte Henkel; die nach innen gelagerte Lippe kommt noch vor. ....

c) Zwei Musterzonen, aus vier bis fünf oder mehr stehenden und hängenden Dreiecken, mit Kammstichreihen gefüllt, zweigeteilter Henkel, meist noch Standring, Innenlippe kommt vereinzelt noch vor, dunkelbraun- bis grauschwarzpoliert, meist äg. Herkunft. ....

3. *Ägyptische Gruppe*: Entwickelt sich direkt aus der syrisch-ägyptischen Gruppe. Weitere Vereinfachungen der Musterzonen in vertikaler oder horizontale Ebene.

a) Fünf oder mehr senkrechte Musterstreifen kommen meist noch mit der späten syrisch-ägyptischen Gruppe c gemeinsam vor, manchmal sogar noch mit archaisierenden Tendenzen wie Innenlippe und Standring. Die Krüge a-d sind birnenförmig (piriform 2a nach Kaplan). Die ovoiden Krüge mit senkrechten Musterstreifen gehören zu den Sonderformen der palästinensischen Gruppe.

b–d) Normalerweise vier, drei oder zwei matte Segmentmusterfelder mit Kammstichmuster gefüllt, dunkelgrau- bis schwarzpolierte Oberfläche, meist Bandhenkel und Standknopf. Eine Sondergruppe bilden Krüge mit 3 oder 4 Segmentmusterfeldern und zweigeteiltem Henkel (Kaplan piriform 2b). Sie sind, soweit beprobt, meist aus palästinensischen Tonen hergestellt und kommen vorweigend in Südpalästina, dem von den Hyksos beherrschten Bereich vor. ....

e) Breite bis doppelkonische Formen mit ringförmigen Musterstreifen je über und unter dem Bauch, Standknopf. Kleinformen vorherrschend. Ausschließlich äg. Fabrikation. ....

f) Horizontal gekämmte Krüge kommen nur im Delta und in Zypern vor.

Darüber hinaus gibt es sackförmige Krüge (Kaplan: globular) mit meist 3 Segmentfeldern sowie Krüge mit viergeteilter Wandung und zylindrische Formen mit viergeteilter Wandung und zylindrische Formen mit Kammstich rundumher. Sie sind alle, soweit nachgerüft, rein äg. Provenienz.

4. *Sonderformen:* a) Es gibt sowohl in der ägyptische-phönikischen Gruppe als auch in der ägyptischen Gruppe Keramik mit figural eingeritzten Verzierungen, vor allem Lotusblumen, Wellenbändern, Vögeln, Fischen und andere Tieren. Soweit nachprüfbar, ist diese verzierte Keramik vor allem Krüge, in Ägypten entstanden. Diesbezüglich ist auch das Lotusmuster ein Hinweis. Eine Ausnahme bildet der anthropoide Krug mit figuralem Dekor aus Jericho.

b) Tierkörper-, Fruchtkörper- und anthropoide Gefäße: Aus der ägyptischen Gruppe sind Krüge in Fisch, Falken und Entenform bekannt, aus dem Bereich von Palästina Gefäße in Fisch-, Eichel- und Ziegeneuterform sowie in anthropoider Form."[183]

A further two types, Types 5 and 6 were also listed by Bietak in 1986; Type 5 comprising so-called Painted Tell el-Yahudiya ware, and type 6, red and black burnished juglets, both of which are not considered in this monograph.

In a later article published in 1989, but also originally written in 1985, Bietak concentrated on vessels with incised patterns; his former types 5 and 6 no longer being considered. In essence this was a revised classification, Fig. 9, which also forms the basis of this monograph. There he divided Tell el-Yahudiya Ware into the following groups:[184]

"Urgruppe ([Kaplan] Ovoid 1). Als sogenannte Urgruppe wurden jene Krüge angesehen, die typologisch die ältesten Mermale (Mittlere Bronzezeit = MB II/A) aufweisen wie Kragenhals, fallende zwei- oder mehrfach geteilte Henkel und ovoider Körper. Sie kommen in Byblos, ᶜAfula und Tell el-Dabᶜa vor. In Tell el-Dabᶜa ist dieser Krug von der gesamten Tell el-Yahudiya Ware der lteste und in Str. d/1 = etwa 1. Hälfte 18. Jhdt. v. Chr. zu datieren. ... Der makroskopischen Untersuchung nach

[183] Bietak, *LÄ* VI, 335–347.

[184] Bietak, Archäologischer Befund, 9–17.

scheint diesere Krug aus syrisch-palästinensischem Redfield clay angefertigt worden zu sein.

Die Krüge in ᶜAfula sind aus Levante-Ton, vermutlich lokaler Provenienz, hergestellt, und es ist bemerkenwert, daß die ältesten Tell el-Yahudiya-Krüge offenbar aus dem Bereich Galiläa-Phönizien stammen.

Die inkrustierten Muster dieser ältesten Gruppe der Tell el-Yahudiya-Ware weisen sowohl horizontale als auch vertikale ungegliederte Bänder auf, wobei die ersteren auch für die frühe palästinensische Gruppe ([Kaplan] Ovoid 2) charakteristisch sind. Sie haben auch horizontale aus Rechtecken und Dreiecken gegliederte Bänder, wie sie für die Syrische-ägyptische Gruppe typische sind. Die Ornamentierung ist noch nicht nach einem fixen Schema festgelegt, und es scheint, als ob diese Gruppe sowohl für die Entwicklung der frühen palästinensischen als auch für die Syrisch-ägyptische Gruppe verantwortlich war.

Die frühe palästinensische Gruppe (vor allem [Kaplan] Ovoid 2, aber auch 3 und 4) ist fast ausschließlich in Palästina mit dem Schwerpunkt im Norden zu finden und ist aus palästinensischen Tonen (vor allem Redfield clay) hergestellt. Ihre Verbreitung scheint die Bildung einer eigenen Provinz Palästina innerhalb der MB-Kultur zur Zeit des Überganges von MB II/A zu II/B anzudeuten. ... Die Krüge vom Typ [Kaplan] Ovoid 4 sind als Sondergruppe anzusehen. Sie haben ein Dreiecks oder Schachbrettmuster, einen breiten Standknopf und eine einfache ausgezogene Mündung. Sie kommen nur im Bereiche von Jericho-Malacha vor. Die frühe palästinensische Gruppe der MB II/B–C weiter, vor allem [Kaplan] Piriform 3. Die genannte Subgruppe [Kaplan] Ovoid 4 entwickelt sich direkt in die ebenfalls lokale Subgruppe piriform 4 weiter.[185]

Die syrisch-ägyptische Gruppe ([Kaplan] Piriform 1) läßt sich nach dem Befund von Tell el-Dabᶜa in folgende chronologische relevanten Gruppen teilen: Piriform 1 a (mit vier und mehr Musterzonen übereinander), piriform 1 b (mit drei Musterzonen) und piriform 1 c (mit zwei Musterzonen übereinander). Die zuerstgennante ist die älteste, ... sie kommt noch in Nordpalästina (ᶜAfula, Megiddo) vor, wo sie aus limestone hill clay, also aus lokalem Ton hergestellt ist. Sie kommt auch in Byblos und in Tell el-Dabᶜa vor. Hier scheint sie aus lokalem Nilton hergestellt worden zu sein. Die Verbreitung dieser Gattung erreicht im Süden die Gegend des Fayoums, vermutlich den Bereich der Residenz des Mittleren Reiches bei Lischt. In Tell el-Dabᶜa kommt diese Gruppe ausschließlich in Str. G im Zusammenhang mit Gräbern der späten Mittleren Bronzezeit II/A vor. Auch in ᶜAfula ist der Fundzusammenhang der gleichen Chronologiestufe zuzuweisen. ...

Die piriform 1 b-Krüge kommen in Tell el-Dabᶜa in Str. F und in kleineren Formen in Str. E/3 vor. Sie zeigen nun eine fast ausschließliche Verbreitung in Phönizien und Ägypten und z.T. auch in Zypern. ... Der Raum von Palästina ist aus dieser Verbreitung ausgespart ...

Die piriform 1 c-Krüge zeigen in ihrer Verzierung eine weitere Vereinfachung in nur zwei Zonen, meist aus stehenden und hängenden Trapezen auf Schulter und dem unteren Körperbereich. Sie kommen in Tell el-Dabᶜa in den Schichten F, E/3 und vereinzelt bis E/2 vor. Ihre frühesten Repräsentanten haben noch alte Attribute wie nach innen umgeschlagene Lippe, während späte piriform 1 b-Krüge nach außen umgeschlagene Lippen haben können. Alle besitzen jedoch gewöhnlich einen zweigeteilten Henkel.

Die piriform 1 c-Krüge haben die weiteste Verbreitung; sie kommen sowohl in Phönizien als auch wieder in Palästina vor. Während sie in Nubien gut vertreten sind und jetzt erst Kerma erfassen, beginnt sich das Vorkommen der Tell el-Yahudiya-Ware in Oberägypten zu verdünnen, wenn man von archaischen Typen mit Innenlippe in Abydos und möglicherweise in Karnak absieht ...

Es gibt auch piriform 1-Krüge mit figuraler Verzierung. Die Motive sind sowohl ägaische wie springende Delphine oder Fische und Spiralmäander; Lotusblumen und Vögel lassen auf ägyptischen Einfluß schließen. Der ägaische Einfluß ist aber schon bei den Piriform 1 a-Krügen nachweisbar und konnte auch als Hinweis auf die Herkunft dieser Dekorationstechnik der weißen Inkrustation aufzufassen sein. ...

[185] The so-called Piriform 4 type was never described, but from the accompanying illustration, Piriform 4 is to be seen as Piriform jugs with double handles and two rows of hanging or pendant traingles on the shoulder. See further below p. 67, Type Group B2.2–B2.3.

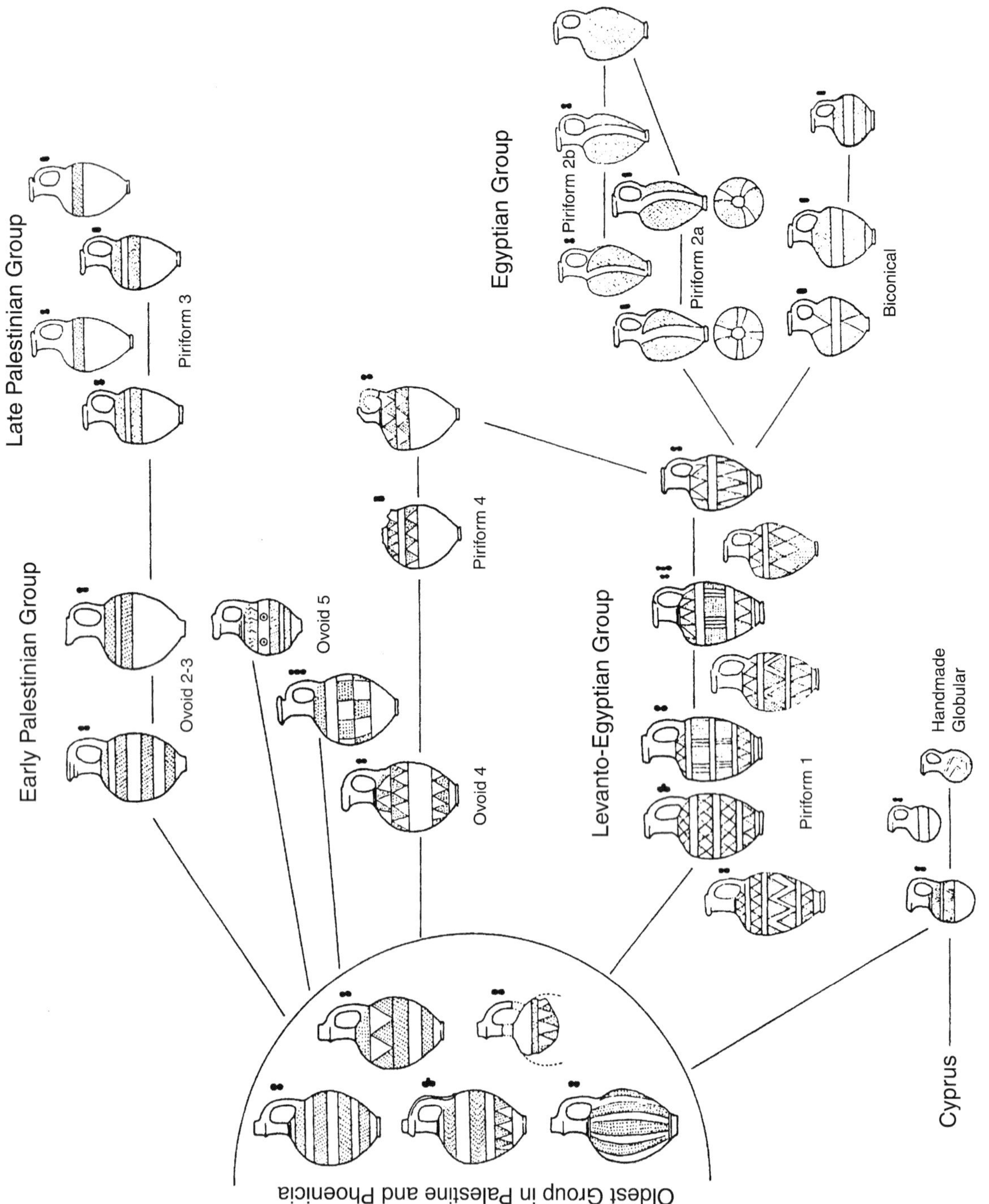

Fig. 9 Tell el-Yahudiya Typology after Bietak 1985

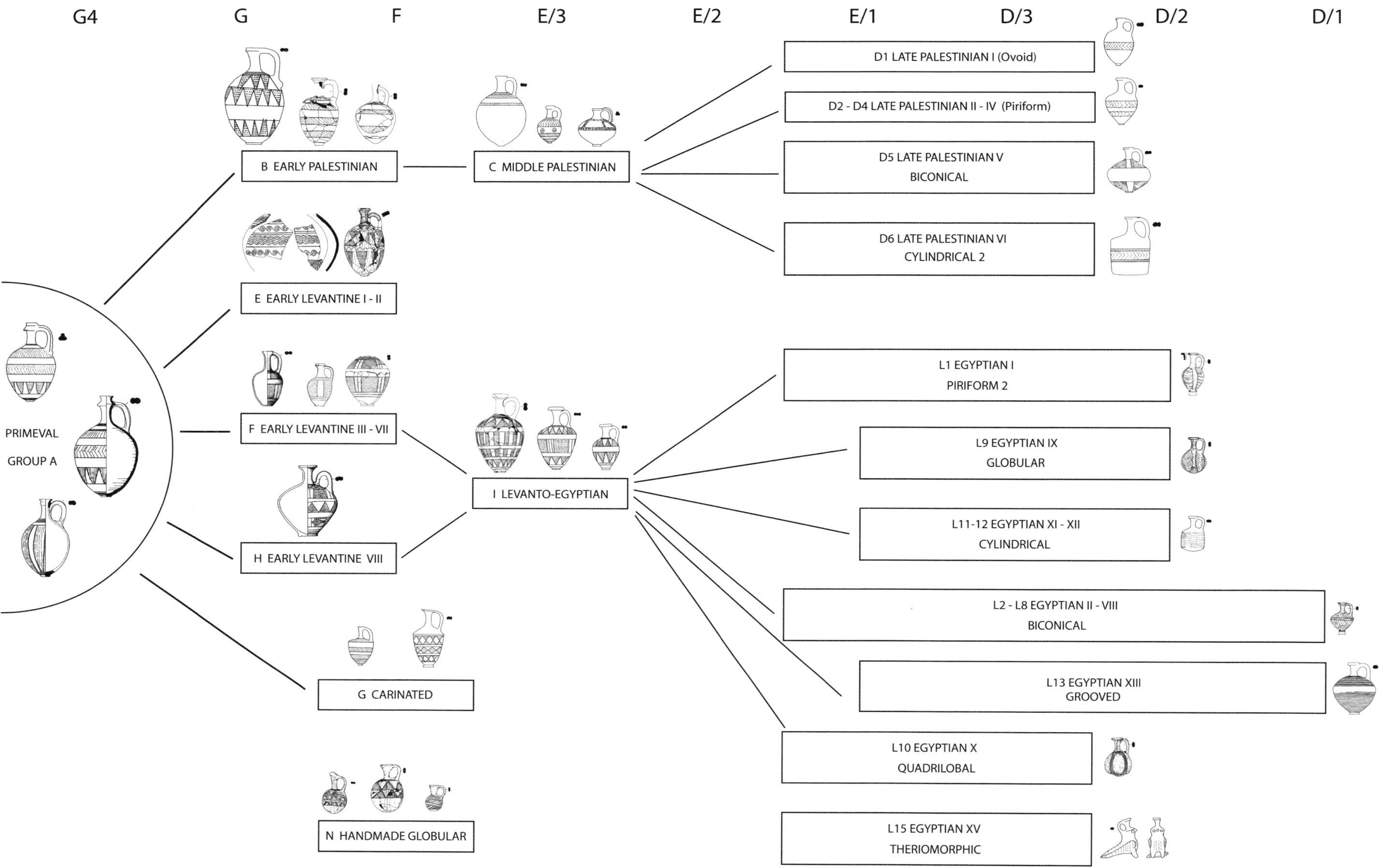

Fig. 10 Tell el-Yahudiya Typology after Bietak and Aston 2010

Ägyptische Motive wie Lotusblumen sind auf der Tell el-Yahudiya-Ware erst auf piriform 1 b und c-Krügen nachweisbar. ... Es gibt aber auch in der Levante Tell el-Yahudiya-Krüge mit mesopotamischen Motiven in der Verzierung wie Ziegenböcke, die von einem Baum fressen.

Die ägyptische Gruppe zeigen sich zweierlei Trends in der Vereinfachung der Ornamentik. Bei den doppelkonischen Krügen ist die Vereinfachung in grobe stehende und hängende Dreiecke uns schließlich in zwei ringförmige Musterzonen ober- und unterhalb des Bauchumbruches feststellbar. Bei den [Kaplan] piriform 2-Krügen gibt es die Vereinfachung in senkrechte segmentförmige Musterstreifen, anfangs in 5 (selten), dann in 4 und 3 Streifen, später nur mehr in drei Streifen. Die gleiche Verzierung tragen auch die kugeligen Krüge. Zur ägyptischen Gruppe zählen aber auch zylindrische Krüge mit umlaufender Verzierung oder Dreiecksmuster sowie viergeteilte Krüge.

Die Piriform 2-Krüge kann man nach Kaplan in piriform 2 a-Krüge mit Bandhenkel und nach außen umgeschlagener Mündung und in piriform 2 b-Krüge mit zweigeteiltem Henkel und nach außen ausgezogener (nicht umgeschlagener) Mündung einteilen. Letzere Art ist Südpalästinensischer Provenienz. Sie ist jedoch stilistisch mit den piriform 2 a-Krügen, die in Ägypten allein produziert, als Einheit zu betrachten ...

Die bikonischen Krüge sind in S-Palästina, besonders in O-Delta, vereinzelt in Oberägypten und besonders stark in Nubien, allerdings nicht in Kerma vertreten. ...

Verteilungskarten der kugeligen, der zylindrischen, der gereiften und der viergeteilten Ägyptischen Gruppe der Tell el-Yahudiya-Ware werden hier aus Raumgründen nicht vorgelegt. Sie zeigen eine besondere Konzentration im O-Delta und sind für Export weniger verwendet worden. Sie worden wohl ausnahmslos aus ägyptischen (Nil-)Tonen hergestellt....

Die späte palästinensische Gruppe. Von dieser sind die piriform 3-Krüge nach der Terminologie von M. Kaplan eine Weiterentwicklung der ovoid 2-Krüge.

Dieser Typ wie auch die anderen Typen der späten palästinensischen Gruppe, vor allem die [Kaplan] zylindrischen 2-Krüge kommen in ihrer Verbreitung ausschließlich in Palästina vor, wobei sich eine Konzentration im Inlandsbereich und eine Verdünnung nach S-Palästina und der Küste zu zeigt."

Over the past two decades since Bietak's articles were written, much new evidence has been assembled from the excavations at Tell el-Dab^{c}a making a reassessment of several aspects of the typology, origin and distribution of Tell el-Yahudiya ware desirable.[186] At Tell el-Dab^{c}a more than 600 Tell el-Yahudiya juglets have been found (cf. Part Three); most of them in clear stratified contexts.[187] Additionally more vessels have been discovered at Tell Sakka,[188] Ebla,[189] Tell el-Ghassil,[190] Jatt,[191] Tell ^{c}Ain ^{c}Abdah,[192] Gebel Zeit,[193] Tell el-Maskhuta,[194] Mendes,[195] Memphis,[196] Karnak,[197] Qaret el Tub, Bahriya,[198] with many others

[186] As indeed has been pointed out by W.A. Ward and W.G. Dever, *Studies on Scarab Seals III*, 1994, 82–86.

[187] A small group of these have been published in Bietak, *TDV* passim, Bietak and Hein, *PuF*, Fuscaldo, *TD X*, passim, Hein and Jánosi, *TD XI*, passim, and Forstner-Müller, *Ä&L* 11, 2001, 197–220: Eadem, *TD XVI*, passim.

[188] A.F. Taraqji, Nouvelles découvertes sur les relations avec l'Égypte à Tel Sakka et à Keswé dans la region de Damas, *BSFE* 144, 1999, 41, fig. 12.

[189] L. Nigro, The Smith and the King of Ebla, in: M. Bietak, *SCIEM II*, 2003, 398–349.

[190] C. Doumet-Serhal, Le Bronze Moyen IIB/C et le Bronze Récent I au Liban: L'evidence de Tell el Ghassil, *Berytus* 42, 1995–96, 54.

[191] E. Yanni, A Late Bronze Age Tomb at Jatt, *^{c}Atiqot* 39, 2000, 69, fig. 6 no. 61.

[192] Unpublished. We are grateful to Peter Fischer for copies of drawings of these vessels.

[193] Exhibition catalogue, *25 ans de découvertes archéologiques sur les chantiers de l'IFAO, 1981–2006*, (Cairo, 2007), 56 nos. 37–38.

[194] Holladay, *Cities of the Delta III. Tell el-Maskhuta* 1982, pl 1; idem, The Eastern Nile Delta During the Hyksos and Pre-Hyksos Periods: Toward a Systematic/Socioeconomic Understanding, in: E.D. Oren (ed.), *The Hyksos, New Historical and Archaeological Perspectives,* (University Museum Monograph 96), Philadelphia, 1997, 183–252.

[195] Cf. Do. Arnold, Zur Keramik aus den Taltempelbereich der Pyramide Amenemhets III. in Dahschur, *MDAIK* 33, 1977, 22–24, pl. 4; Castel, Gout and Soukassian, 1994, 44–57; Redford, *FS Simpson*, 1996, 682. Reference to sherds from Mendes, unpublished.

[196] B. Bader, TD *XIX* 383–387, 497–498. Unfortunately most of these are too fragmentary to be ascribed to specific types.

[197] Lauffray, 1979, 205, photo 176, erroneously referred to as Pangrave pottery); Debono *Karnak VII*, 1982, 377–386; Idem, Rapport de cloture sur les resultants et études des objets du sondage à l'est du lac sacré de Karnak, *Cahiers de Karnak VIII*, 1987, 121–122.

[198] Colon, Laisney, Marchand, Qaret el Tub: Un fort romain et une nécropole pharaonique, *BIFAO* 100, 2000, 186.

now known in inland Syria,[199] whilst a number of completely new types have come to light in recent years. The latter include a remarkable two-necked jug from the area of Turan,[200] and an evidently Egyptian fly-shaped jug[201] whilst many more open forms have been excavated at Ashkelon[202] to mention just a few. Many more unpublished vessels from the Eastern Delta are stored in SCA magazines at Zagazig.[203]

These Tell el-Dab^c^a juglets, excavated in a finely differentiated stratigraphic sequence in contexts with other finds provide an important new source of information, and bring a well controlled chronological order into a series covering about 200 years of development, and it is perhaps time to combine this largely untapped body of evidence with that already published by Kaplan, to produce a new typology. The wealth of material from Tell el-Dab^c^a makes it essential to introduce new groups, such as the Globular Handmade Group, which are absent from Kaplan's typology. The combed sub-group of Egyptian Tell el-Yahudiya ware (Kaplan's grooved ware) should perhaps also be given more weight than she allowed since it is chronologically significant. Indeed, when the vessels from Tell el-Dab^c^a are arranged in stratigraphic order, it quickly becomes apparent that the ornamental aspect of classification is often more meaningful than one based entirely on shape. A new typology is thus provided in Part Two of this monograph.

---

[199] L. Nigro, personal communication, and cf. TARAQJI, *BSFE* 144, 1999, 41, fig. 12.

[200] O. MISCH-BRANDL, 1997, 47.

[201] Hildesheim 6350, SEIDEL, 1993, 49.

[202] We are grateful to L. Stager for showing us this material, and see below pages 559–575.

[203] Most notably material from Tell Farasha, and, probably, Tell el-Sahaba. For some vessels from the Wadi Tumilat see REDMOUNT, 1989, 626.

II. Typology

In postulating a new typological system, let us first consider some new discoveries from Tell el-Dab^ca. Excavations have now shown that Tell el-Yahudiya ware already occurs here as early as Phase G/4 (= str. d/1) and G/3–1 (= str. c), the early Thirteenth Dynasty. These are evident MBIIA contexts influenced by contemporary Egyptian material culture. Within Phases G/1–3, we find MBIIA house burials with the body in a contracted position, fully equipped with MB style offerings. Therefore at the (Egyptian) site where the Tell el-Yahudiya ware has made its most abundant and earliest appearance so far, it was found in a Middle Bronze context. Although the MB culture in the Delta exhibits strong Egyptian influence, offering deposits,[204] burial customs,[205] tomb structures,[206] temple buildings,[207] and to some extent, domestic architecture,[208] but most noticeably in the physical anthropological features of the inhabitants,[209] it is obvious thfat Tell el-Dabca was populated by carriers of a Syro-Palestinian MB IIA–B culture. In addition to Tell el-Dabca there is also some indication that the abundant early Tell el-Yahudiya finds (and imported Canaanite amphorae) from Lisht, and Illahun can be explained by the presence of Canaanites at these sites,[210] since there exists documentary proof in the form of the Illahun papyri[211] for the presence of Asiatics in the Thirteenth Dynasty royal residence.

These earliest examples of Tell el-Yahudiya ware were produced in a technique unknown in Egypt before the first appearance of the ware. The vessels were fashioned on a fast wheel[212] with wheel-formed ring or disc bases; sometimes the vessels were reopened at the bottom and then closed on the wheel. This sophisticated technique was a two-step procedure. First the vessel was formed and only after it had dried to the leather-hard stage was the base produced. Such techniques are well known in MB IIA Syria-Palestine where they were utilised for the production of plain red-polished jugs and bowls. Both the fast wheel and the adoption of these base production techniques were gradually adopted by the Egyptians during the course of the late Middle Kingdom and Second Intermediate Period,[213] being utilised first for open forms, and only later for

---

[204] M. Bietak, *Avaris and Piramesse, Proceedings of the British Academy* 65, 1979, 284–287; idem, *Eretz Israel*, 21, 1990, 10–17*, M. Bietak and I. Hein, *Pharaonen und Fremde*, 1994, 46; V. Müller, Offering Deposits at Tell el-Dabca, in: C.J. Eyre, (ed.), *Proceedings of the Seventh International Congress of Egyptologists,* (OLA 82) Leuven, 1998, 793–803, eadem, Bestand und Deutung der Opferdepots bei Tempeln in Wohnhausbereichen und Gräbern der Zweiten Zwischenzeit in Tell el-Dabca, in: H. Willems (ed.), *Social Aspects of Funerary Culture in the Egyptian Old and Middle Kingdoms,* (OLA 103), Leuven, 2001, 175–204; eadem, Offering Practices in the Temple Courts of Tell el-Dabca and the Levant, in: M. Bietak, (ed.), *The Middle Bronze Age in the Levant*, Vienna, 2002, 269–295; eadem, *TD XVII*, 2008.

[205] E.C.M. van den Brink, *Tombs and Burial Customs at Tell el-Dabca*, 1982.

[206] *Ibid*, 93–95; I. Forstner-Müller, *TD XVI*, 2008.

[207] M. Bietak, *Avaris and Piramesse, Proceedings of the British Academy* 65, 1979, 247–258, figs. 8–10; idem, Near Eastern Sanctuaries in the Eastern Nile Delta, *BAAL Hors Série VI*, Beirut, 2010, 209–28.

[208] D. Eigner, *Landliche Architektur und Siedlungsformen im Ägypten der Gegenwart,* Vienna, 1984, fig. 1.

[209] E.M. Winkler and H. Wilfing, *TD VI*, 1991, 120, 139.

[210] M. Bietak and I. Hein, *Pharaonen und Fremde*, 1994, 41–43; Do. Arnold, F. Arnold and S. Allen, *Ä&L* 5, 1995, 13–32.

[211] W.F. Albright, *JAOS* 74, 1954, 222–233; G. Posener, Les Asiatiques en Égypte sous les XIIe et XIIIe dynasties, *Syria* 34 (1957), 145–163; U. Luft, Asiatics in Illahun, A Preliminary Report, in: *Atti VI Congresso Internazionale di Egittologia* II, Turin, 1993, 291–7; S.G.J. Quirke *The administration of Egypt in the Late Middle Kingdom: The Hieratic Documents,* 1990; T. Schneider, *Ausländer in Ägypten während des Mittleren Reiches und der Hyksoszeit* 2 vols, 1998–2003.

[212] The fast wheel has the effect of a strong centrifugal force which produces a fine ribbing on the insides of the vessels. This effect is often omitted from archaeological drawings of Tell el-Yahudiya jugs since the neck is too narrow to see the profile. Only broken vessels disclose these tell-tale lines.

[213] Do. Arnold, *MDAIK* 32, 1976, 29–34, pls. 8–11; eadem, Techniques and Traditions of Manufacture in the Pottery of Ancient Egypt, Fascicle 1 in Do. Arnold and J. Bourriau (eds.), *An Introduction to Ancient Egyptian Pottery,* Mainz, 1993, 56–62.

restricted vessels. The surface preparation involving heavy burnishing and firing under oxidising and reducing conditions was also a Levantine tradition during the MB IIA before the first development of Tell el-Yahudiya ware. Thus in terms of production, Tell el-Yahudiya ware must have first developed not in Egypt, as Kaplan suggests, but in the Levant, as stated by, among others, Otto and Säve-Söderbergh (cf. above pages 29–32).

Kaplan's classification of the Tell el Yahudiya ware according to geometrical shapes, Ovoid, Piriform, Biconical, Globular, Cylindrical, Quadrilobal, Bird-shaped, and Ichthyomorphic cannot be rigidly enforced.[214] The differentiation between Ovoid and Piriform is not convincing.[215] Not all ovoid jugs are ovoid; not all biconical jugs are biconical; rather it is a combination of features, particularly decorative styles which show which jugs belong together, and this is evident in our classification, where some apparently piriform vessels are classed with the biconical vessels since their styles of decoration are more conducive of such a placement, as for example the group L.7.1. Nevertheless in the following, Kaplan's designations, as further modified by Bietak, will be kept (in parentheses) in order to build on some common ground, though it will become clear that a refinement of such designations becomes indispensable. Based on the Tell el-Dab^ca material it also becomes essential to introduce new groups, such as the Globular Handmade Group (below Groups N.1–10) which are absent from Kaplan's typology. The combed sub-group of Egyptian Tell el-Yahudiya ware (Kaplan's grooved ware) is also given more weight in this study since, as will be seen, it is chronologically significant. Indeed, when the vessels from Tell el-Dab^ca are arranged in stratigraphic order, it quickly becomes apparent that the ornamental aspect of classification is often more meaningful than one based entirely on shape.

In postulating an integrative classification system such as that suggested on the following pages, one has to consider firstly the genetic mainstreams in the development of the Tell el-Yahudiya ware, hereafter Branches A B–D, E, F, H–I, K and L, and secondly those shapes which form consistent groups that lie outside of the main development, hereafter Branches G, J, and M–Q. After the earliest examples, here termed the Primeval Group (A), two main lines of development can be noticed – a Palestinian Branch (B-D), and a Levanto-Egyptian one (E–I). Within the Levanto-Egyptian realm are a series of vessels decorated with faunal and floral motifs, and these will be termed Branch J. Additionally a third line of development, Branch, N, which differs from the others in being handmade, and may thus owe its origins to Cypriot ceramics, although vessels belonging to this group are so far known only from Egypt, can also be recognised. The Palestinian vessels can also be differentiated into two clear chronological groupings, an Early Palestinian Group (B), and a Late Palestinian Group (D), with a small number of transitional vessels which fall between both groups (C). The northern types can be divided into early Levantine Groups (E-H) which evolve into a Levanto-Egyptian Group (I), which itself develops into a Late Egyptian Group (L). The primeval group is primarily of Levantine origin, with at least one kiln site known at ^cAfula,[216] whilst Branches B-D are primarily of Palestinian origin. Branches E-H are again primarily of Levantine origin but the later vessels within this grouping (Branch I) were often faithfully copied in Egypt, from whence the ware developed along peculiarly Egyptian lines (Branch L). it is quite possible that one or more other minor groupings may become evident in the future, particularly within Lebanon and inland Syria, where one might expect to find a late Syrian Group (Branch K), but the published material is, as yet, still insufficient to determine. In addition a number of late forms from southern Palestine and northern Egypt show a hybrid mix of Late Palestinian and Egyptian influences, and these, worthy of separate note, are collected as Group M. A series of jars, as opposed to jugs are here ascribed to a group O. Finally the open forms are gathered together as Group P, whilst a possible ringstand is attributed its own group, Q.

Whilst the above system works well in principle, a number of problems of classification arise in determining distinct types within the Primeval Group (A) and the early vessels of Groups B and E because, at this stage in the development of Tell el-Yahudiya ware, it is not a mass-produced product: the jugs

[214] M. KAPLAN, *Tell el-Yahudiyeh Ware*, 60–65. She also recognises a grooved variety, and vessels with naturalistic designs, but this terminology, being based on decorative techniques is inconsequent with her geometric types.

[215] Cf. also W.A. WARD and W.G. DEVER, *Studies on Scarab Seals III*, 1994, 84.

[216] U. ZEVULUN, *EI* 21, 1990, 174–90.

being made individually by very few potters with almost every jug displaying its own peculiar features – witness the variety of different types found in the kiln site at ᶜAfula.[217] It is only shortly before the onset of the Hyksos Period that this kind of pottery shows signs of mass production and standardisation, a trend which can be observed both in Palestine (Branch D) and in Egypt (Branch I).

Branch A: The Primeval Group of Tell el-Yahudiya Ware (Kaplan's Ovoid 2 = Bietak's Ovoid 1)

Type Groups A.1.1–A.1.2 (Figs. 11, 12, 15)

From a typological point of view the most archaic attributes on Tell el-Yahudiya jugs can be observed on those found at ᶜAfula. In general they are brown, rather than black, have an ovoid body, a small slightly set-off base, a long narrow neck with a ridged swelling under the rim, incisions at the base of the neck and often just above the base, and tripartite (type A.1.1) or bipartite (type A.1.2) handles, which typically slope outwards on their upper part and join the body near the base of the neck. Similar vessels in plain red or brown burnished wares are common in the late MBIIA period.[218] The decoration shows a variety of patterns which cover the entire body. Every jug has a unique pattern which is usually in three horizontal zones.

Type Groups A.1.3–A.1.4 (Figs. 13–15)

Type groups A.1.3–4 are also ovoid, but instead of a ridged swelling under the neck, these vessels have a kettle rim (type A.1.3) or a candlestick rim, (type A.1.4). Otherwise they are similar to those of types A.1.1–2, in being brown, rather than black, have an ovoid body, a small slightly set-off base, incisions at the base of the neck, and sometimes, but not always, just above the base, and bipartite handles. Vessels of type A.1.3 are known from ᶜAfula[219] and Ginosar,[220] whilst type A.1.4 is, at present, only attested at ᶜAfula.[221] The decoration of these two groups comprises, for the most part, vertical bands filled with indentations, but there also exist jugs with three, four or five horizontal zones of oblique lines or chevron decoration, a decorative motif which becomes very popular on vessels of the early Palestinian group (below Branch B). Yet others have standing or pendant triangles which become popular on vessels of the Levanto-Egyptian group, (below Branch I).

With the exception of the ᶜAfula vessels, the find circumstances of all other primeval Ovoid jugs (= Kaplan Ovoid 2/Bietak Ovoid 1) from the Levant is not known, and are thus not definitely datable. However the earliest Tell el-Yahudiya jug so far found at Tell el-Dabᶜa belongs in this primeval Ovoid group. This jug represented through a fragment of a brown burnished vessel, TD 5971E,[222] is made of a particularly fine fabric, and has an extremely thin wall, incised with a vertical grooved decoration outlining segments. It originates from the late Twelfth Dynasty, Phase H = d/2. Chronologically the next jug found at Tell el-Dabᶜa, TD 4211, has a ridged neck in the ᶜAfula style and, according to neutron activation analysis was made of a Levantine clay. The fragment was retrieved from a palatial mansion of Phase d/1 = G/4, which, according to pottery seriation, is dated approximately to the beginning of the Thirteenth Dynasty, before the middle of the 18th century BC. This Tell el-Dabᶜa example is very similar to a fragment found at Byblos,[223] on which the position of the handle attachment on the shoulder close to the neck is in close agreement with the piece from Tell el-Dabᶜa. Unfortunately no analysis of the clay from which the Byblite jug was manufactured has been undertaken, but from the published description it is unlikely to be Nile clay. This Byblos vessel also relates to TD 5250A, another shoulder fragment from Tell el-Dabᶜa, with a handle attached near to the base of the neck. It was found in a Phase G/1–3 dump which thus provides a *terminus ad quem*, and could thus also derive from Phase G/4 (beginning of the Thirteenth Dynasty). NAA analysis indicates that it is not of Egyptian manufacture, though its exact origin could not be determined.[224]

[217] Kaplan, *Tell el-Yahudieh Ware*, figs. 111b, 112b; U. Zevulun, Tell el-Yahudiyah Juglets from a Potter's Refuse Pit at Afula, *EI* 21, 1990, 174–90.

[218] Cf. Beck, The Pottery of the MBIIA at Tel Aphek, *TA* 2, 1975, 45–75, Eadem, Area A. Middle Bronze IIA Pottery 173–238 and The Middle Bronze Age IIA Pottery Repertoire. A Comparative Study, 239–254, in: M. Kochavi, P. Beck, E. Yadin, (eds.), *Aphek-Antipatris I. Excavation of Areas A and B. The 1972–1976 Seasons*, 2000.

[219] Kaplan, *Tell el-Yahudieh Ware*, figs. 109b–110b; Zevulun, *EI* 21, 1990, 174–190.

[220] Kaplan, *Tell el-Yahudieh Ware*, figs. 111a, 112a.

[221] Zevulun, *EI* 21, 1990, 174–190.

[222] P. McGovern, *The Foreign Relations of the Hyksos*, Oxford, 2000, 154 no. MB024.

[223] Beirut, American University 4906, 4908, Merrillees, *Levant* 10, 1978, figs. 1, 2.

[224] P. McGovern, *The Foreign Relations of the Hyksos*, Oxford, 2000, 152 no. JH911

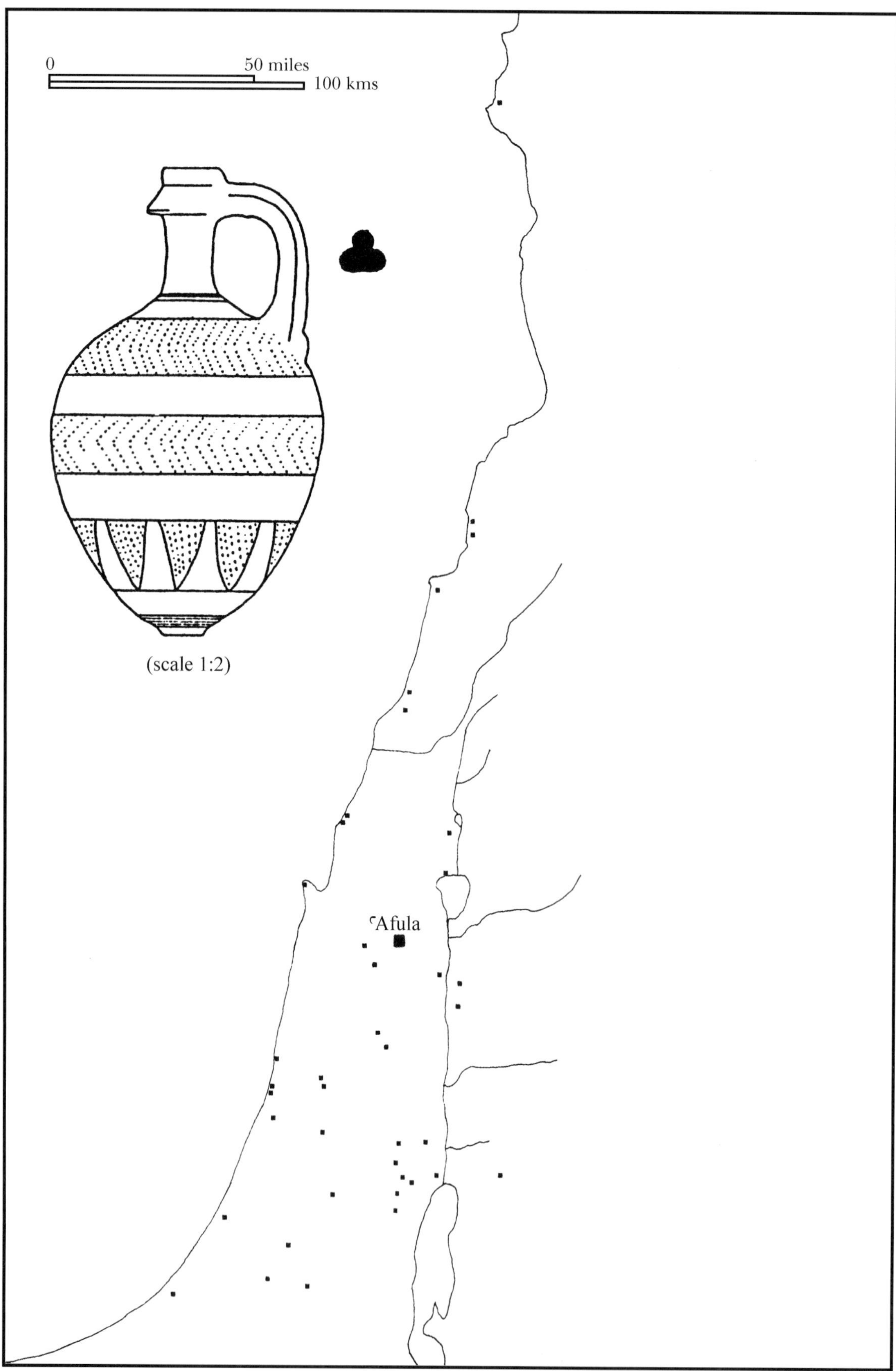

Fig. 11 Distribution and Shape Class of Type Group A.1.1

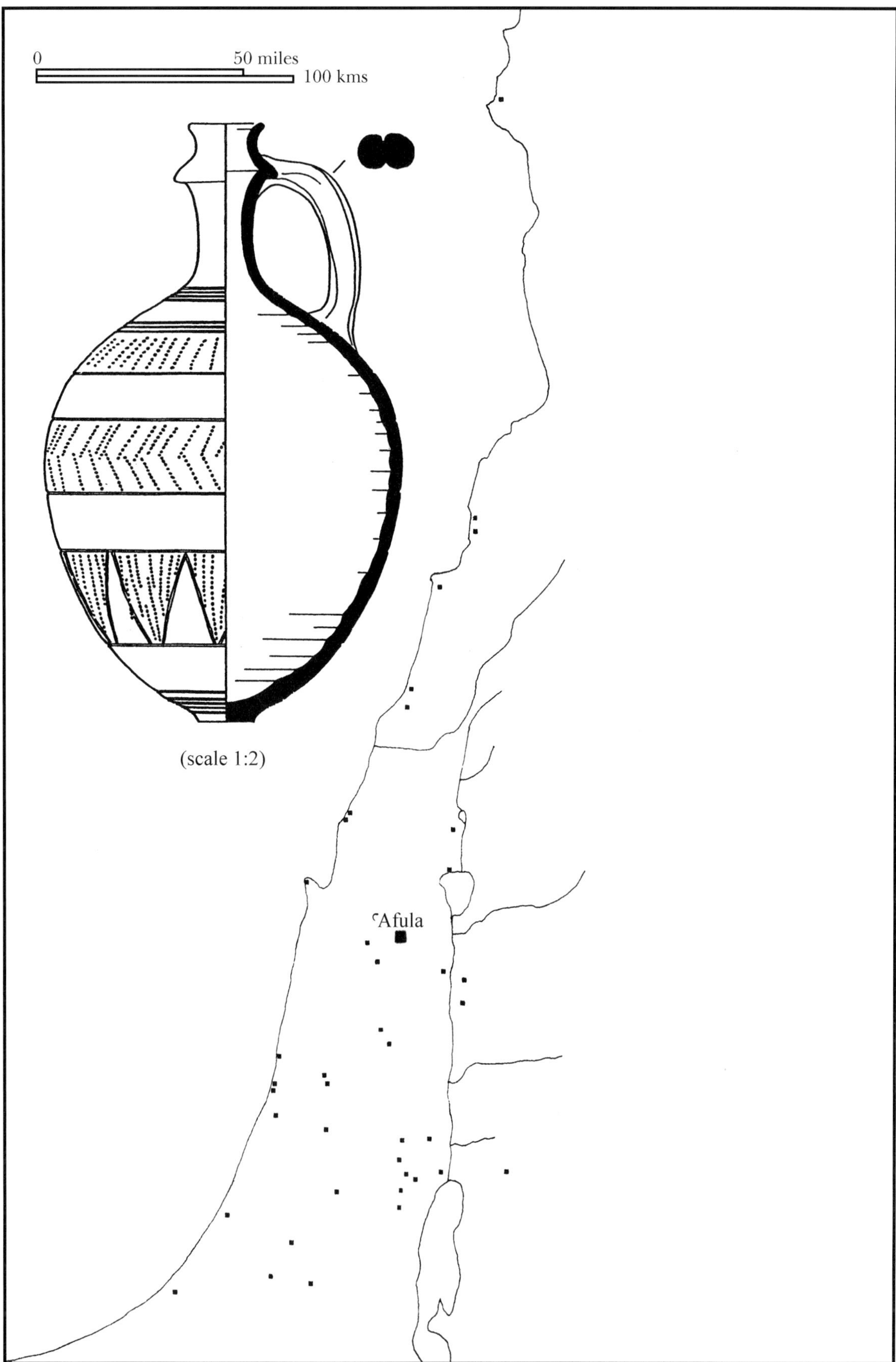

Fig. 12 Distribution and Shape Class of Type Group A.1.2

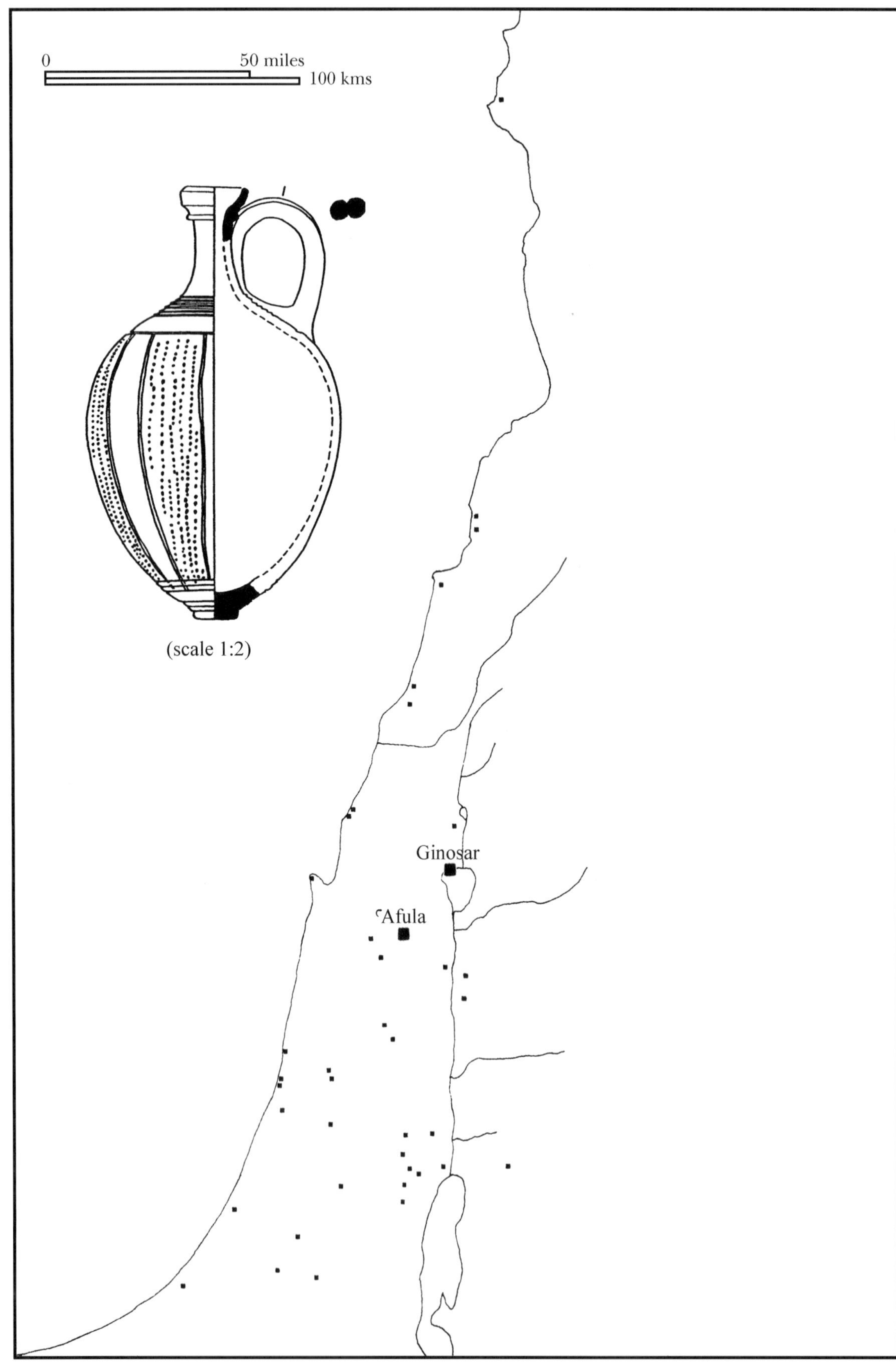

Fig. 13 Distribution and Shape Class of Type Group A.1.3

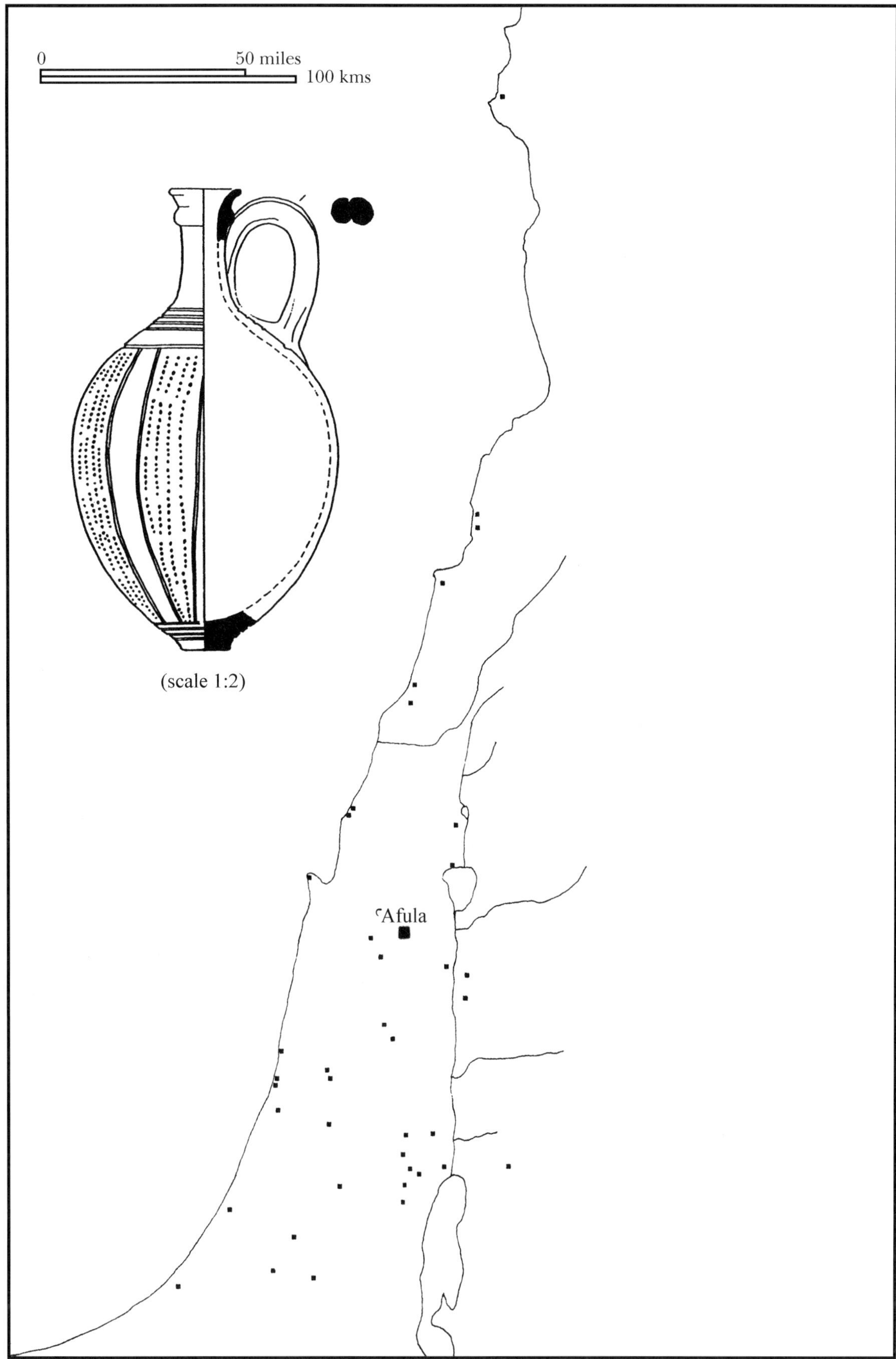

Fig. 14 Distribution and Shape Class of Type Group A.1.4

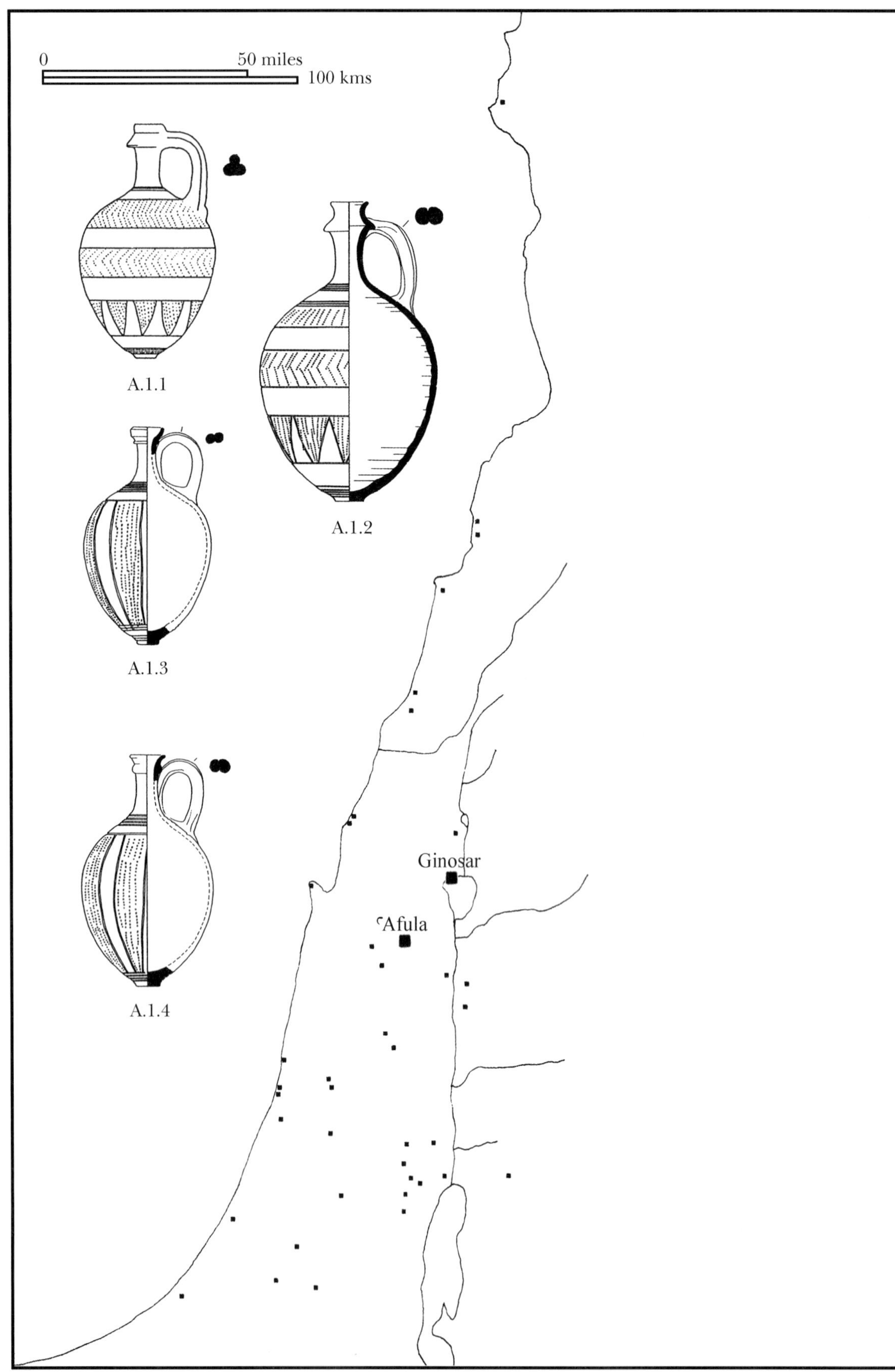

Fig. 15 Combined Distribution of Type Group A.1

It is surely no coincidence that all three Tell el Dabᶜa pieces mentioned above have been found in very early strata at Tell el-Dabᶜa. All three are foreign imports and all share an ovoid shape. To sum up then this group has the most archaic attributes with most of the known examples coming from ᶜAfula, two or three fragmentary examples from Tell el-Dabᶜa, one from Byblos and perhaps one other from Ginosar.[225] These similarities indicate close ties between the Eastern Delta and the area around Byblos, coastal Lebanon and coastal Galilee. Most probably, therefore, this is where the prototypes of true Tell el-Yahudiya ware were first manufactured.

A.2. Double-Necked Ovoid Vessels

Type Group A.2 (Fig. 16)

Clearly related to the Ovoid 1 group is an unusual ovoid vessel from Turan with two necks. This vessel, Jerusalem, Israel Antiquities Authority 75–72[226] was found in a tomb containing the remains of at least seven individuals, along with typical MB IIB pottery. This vessel has a neck in the normal position and another where one would expect the handle. From the top of both necks a bridge links the two together thus forming a handle. The usual neck has a spout in the form of a capride. Although in a poor state of preservation five bands of decoration can be distinguished. At the base of the neck are a series of upward pointing triangles. Beneath this is a band of vertical dots, and then running around the major point of the vessel is a large frieze of diamonds with intervening vertical bands. Below this main frieze is a band of pendant triangles and, just above the base, another frieze of upward pointing triangles.

From the original Tell el-Yahudiya vessels, the technology spread both northwards into the Levant, and southwards into Palestine. Vessels from both areas can generally be told apart, not only by their findspots, but also by their styles of decoration. The northern, or Levantine, group generally favouring pendant and standing triangles, whilst the southern, or Palestinian, group tended, with the exception of some of the Early Palestinian vessels, to favour a chequer board or banded decoration. Whilst the Palestinian and Levantine vessels are contemporary with one another, this study will proceed along geographical lines, so that the Southern or Palestinian group will be considered first. This is itself divided chronologically into Early (below branch B), Middle (below branch C) and Late (below branch D). The Palestinian branch is then followed by a treatment of the Levantine material. Here the early Levantine types (below branches E–H) were not only produced in what is today Lebanon and northern Israel, but were slavishly copied in Egypt, hence the term Levanto-Egyptian is utilised for the later vessels of the early Levantine branch (below branch I) of Tell el-Yahudiya ware. Eventually, within Egypt proper, the Levanto-Egyptian style developed into its own localised Late Egyptian style (below branch L) contemporary with the Late Palestinian types. Presumably a Late Levantine or Syrian style also developed out of the original Levanto-Egyptian repertoire, but unfortunately the archaeological record for the later Middle Bronze Age in inland Syria is still much of a blank.

Branch B: The Early Palestinian Group

The Early Palestinian Group covers the period from the latest phase of the MB IIA, the transitional MB IIA–B and the early MB IIB period, being approximately coeval with the advanced Thirteenth Dynasty in Egypt. This Early Palestinian Group comprises not only ovoid shapes, but also plump piriform to biconical and normal piriform shapes. As a whole this group is mainly found in what is today northern Israel, with others coming from southern Lebanon and Transjordan, and, as is to be expected, all are made of Levantine clays. Into the early Palestinian Group fall Kaplan's Ovoid 3–5, but the internal division of the ovoid group by Kaplan is unfortunately illogical and therefore not entirely successful – her Ovoid 3 and 4 types are lacking any similarities to an ovoid concept. Her Ovoid 3 have a distinctly carinated shoulder, whereas her Ovoid 4 should clearly be related to her Piriform 1 group, as she herself admits. Consequently we offer here a new classification of the Early Palestinian Group in keeping with previous evaluations of Tell el-Yahudiya ware, but with somewhat different qualifying attributes. Characteristic of the Early Palestinian I group is the ovoid shape, pointed or broad button bases, everted sharp trimmed rims, bipartite or tripartite handles sloping

[225] Epstein, *Atiqot* 7, 1974, 27, fig. 8/19; Kaplan, *Tell el-Yahudiyeh Ware*, fig. 111a.

[226] W. Seipel (ed.), *Land der Bibel. Schätze aus dem Israel Miseum, Jerusalem*, Exhibition catalogue, Vienna, 1997, 47 no. 58.

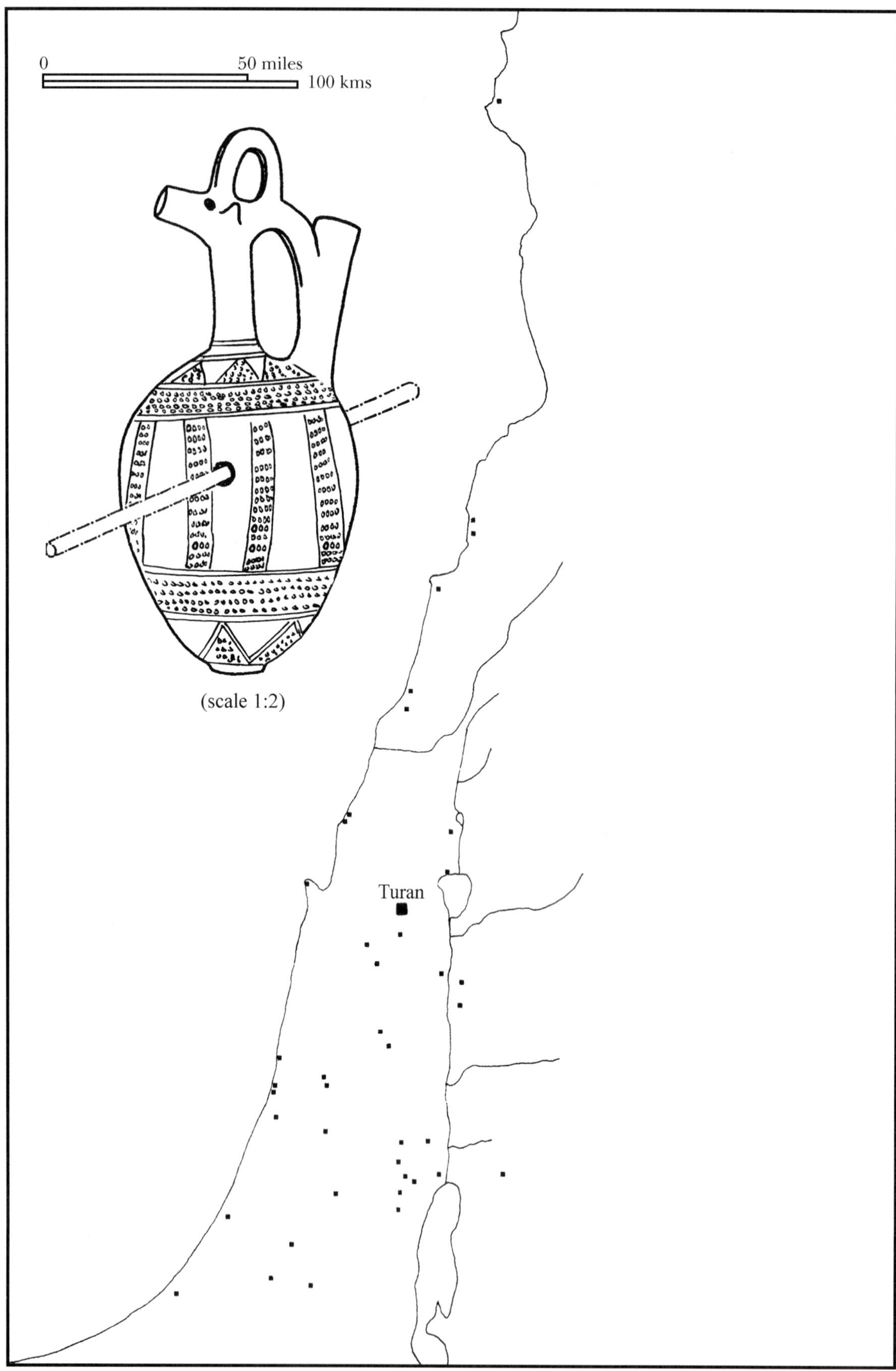

Fig. 16 Distribution and Shape Class of Type Group A.2

outwards and a triangle or chequerboard design covering the major part of the body.[227] This group is somewhat localised occurring in a very restricted area around Gibeon (?), Jericho and Malacha and is in need of a more detailed study. It coexists with, or develops probably by intermediate steps into, the B.3 group which has a similar local restriction. Unclassified but clearly belonging to this Early Palestinian branch is Toronto ROM GA 1276 from Jericho.

B.1. Early Palestinian I

Type Group B.1 (Fig. 17)

Type Group B.1 is defined solely on the basis of the fragmentary vessel from tomb 22 at Gibeon.[228] The shape of this jug is unclear: it was reconstructed by Pritchard as a biconical vessel, but it could equally well have originally been ovoid with an offset disc rather than a ring base. The candlestick rim and tripartite handle, placed on the shoulder near to the neck, are certainly archaic features, and the handle with its elegantly modelled snake finds an exact parallel on a 'fruit-like juglet' (which, incidentally has a ring base), provisionally dated to the MB IIA period.[229] In any case the Gibeon vessel is, at present, a unique piece which anticipates the development of the Piriform 4 vessels of the Early Palestinian Group.

B.2. Early Palestinian II

Type Group B.2.1 (Bietak's Ovoid 4) (Figs. 18, 22)

Group B.2.1 is actually more the result of guesswork owing to the vagaries of the archaeological record. It is transitional from the Primeval Group and seems to be very similar, but is not placed in that group since no neck with a ledged swelling nor any handles or bases are preserved to justify such a placement. It is also likely that the contexts in which sherds of this provisional group are found are not as early as those of the primeval Ovoid grouping. Of the possible examples of this type group, one is a complete vessel of unknown provenance[230] with a kettle rim, incisions at the base of the neck, an offset disc base, a bipartite handle sloping outwards on its upper attachment. Its decoration consists of two friezes of pendant triangles below the neck and one of standing triangles near the base. One is a body sherd of so-called Red Field clay from Khirbet Qurdaneh which preserves a horizontal band with pendant triangles similar to those of the Ovoid 1 group from Tell el-Dab^ca and Byblos, and seems to be ovoid in shape.[231] A jug from Shiqmona is definitely ovoid, has a narrow neck and a pattern which is normally associated with the Piriform 1 jugs of the Levanto-Egyptian group (below L.1), consisting of standing and pendant triangles and two grooves around the base of the neck. Such patterns could also be expected in the Primeval Group or its direct derivations. The tomb in which this fragment was found has both MB IIA and MBIIB forms indicative either of a transitional MBIIA-B time period, or that the tomb was in use for a long period of time.[232] Also to be attributed to this group is perhaps an incomplete vessel from tomb B51 at Jericho.[233]

Type Groups B.2.2–B.2.3 (Bietak's Piriform 4) (Figs. 19, 20, 22)

Again a small, local, and not very homogeneous group from the area around Jericho and should be seen in close association with the previous groups. Without doubt these jugs were locally made.[234] The necks are narrow and the incised decoration is restricted to two zones of standing or pendant triangles on the shoulder. They are all filled with coarse indentations. The grey to black burnishing is all over, including the ornamentation zones, or, in one case, entirely absent. The offset disc base is small, either rounded or disc shaped. The only preserved rim is everted and sharply trimmed. Kaplan classified these among her Piriform 3 Group, with which they have little in common. One of the jugs is ovoid (type B.2.2) and one is piriform (type B.2.3).

Type Group B.2.4 (Figs. 21, 22)

Group B.2.4 is represented by a single example from Malacha which is ovoid in shape, has a distinctly

---

[227] KAPLAN, *Tell el-Yahudiyeh Ware,* fig. 114. To which examples add Toronto ROM GA 1276 from Jericho.

[228] PRITCHARD, *Gibeon,* 1963, 38–40, pl. 30.9; KAPLAN, *Tell el-Yahudiyeh Ware,* fig. 131a.

[229] AMIRAN, *Israel Museum News* 10, 1975, 40–45.

[230] Jerusalem, Hebrew University 1964, KAPLAN, *Tell el-Yahudiyeh Ware,* fig. 114b.

[231] KAPLAN, *Tell el-Yahudiyeh Ware,* fig. 84a.

[232] KAPLAN, *Tell el-Yahudiyeh Ware,* fig. 83c. The tomb is still unpublished. We are grateful to the late Aharon Kempinski for information about the contents of this tomb.

[233] Birmingham 568'58. KENYON, *Excavations at Jericho II,* 343–344, fig. 168.27.

[234] KAPLAN, *Tell el-Yahudiyeh Ware,* fig. 78, 231 samples J4, J25.

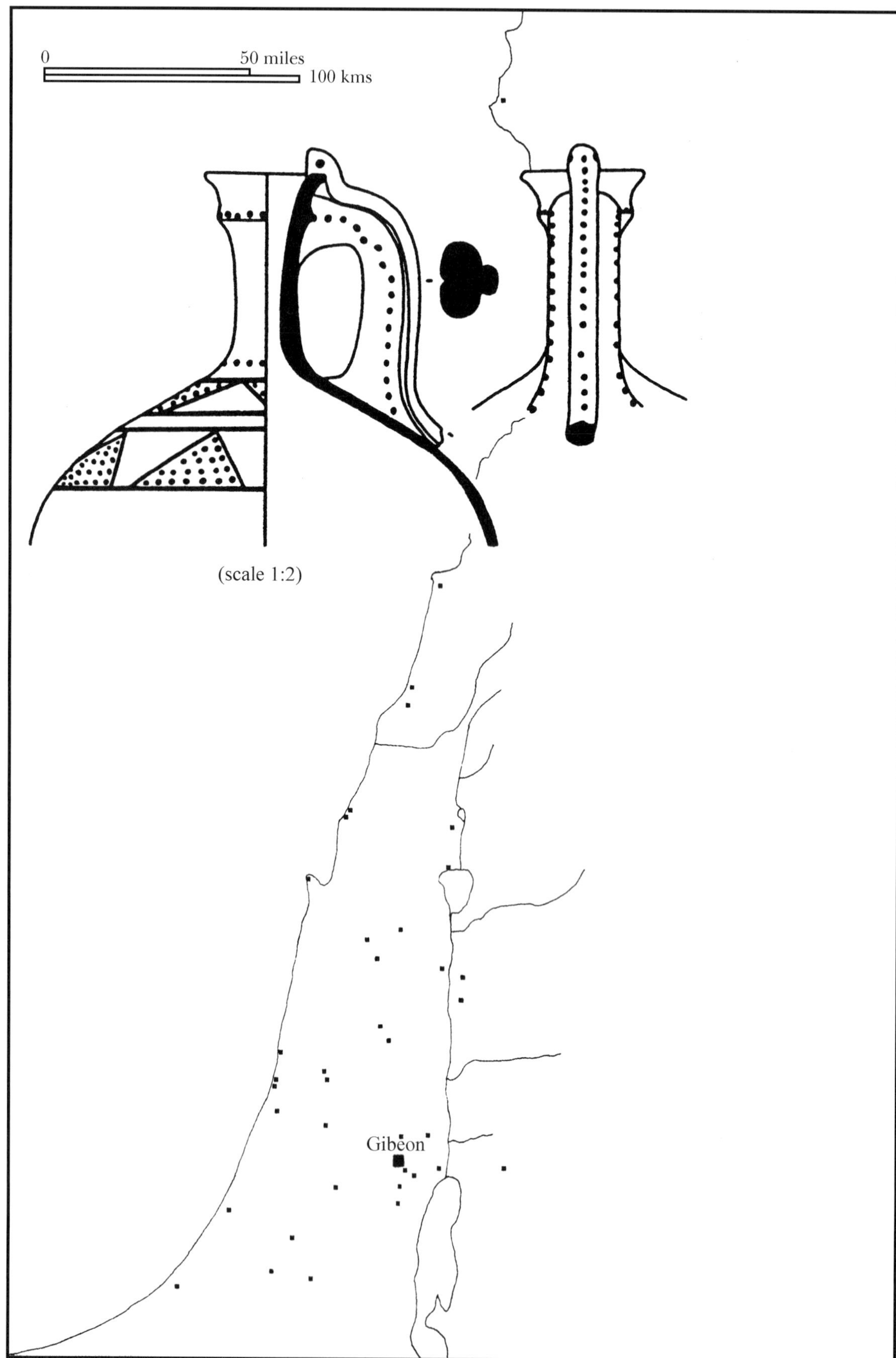

Fig. 17 Distribution and Shape Class of Type Group B.1

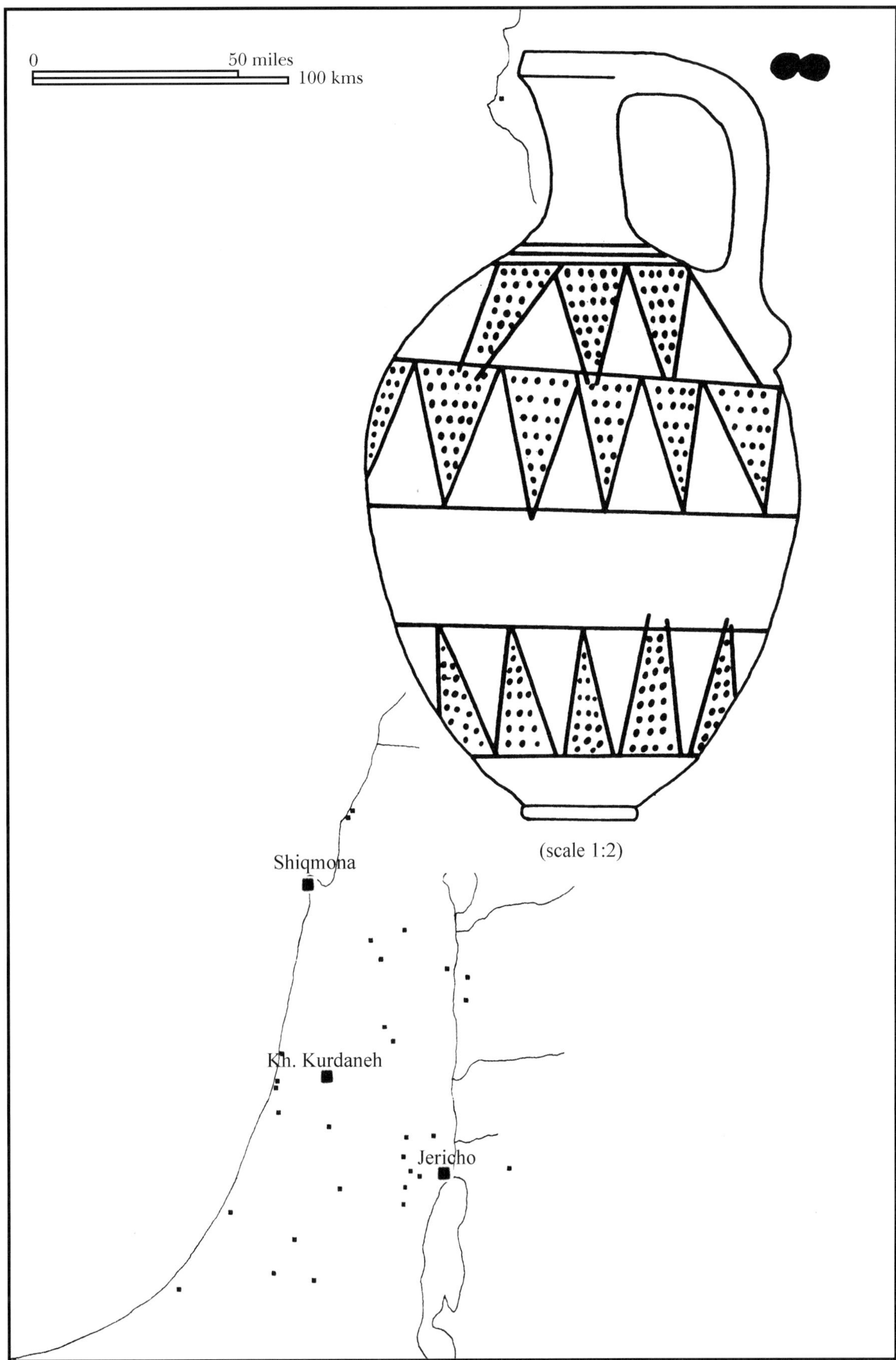

Fig. 18 Distribution and Shape Class of Type Group B.2.1

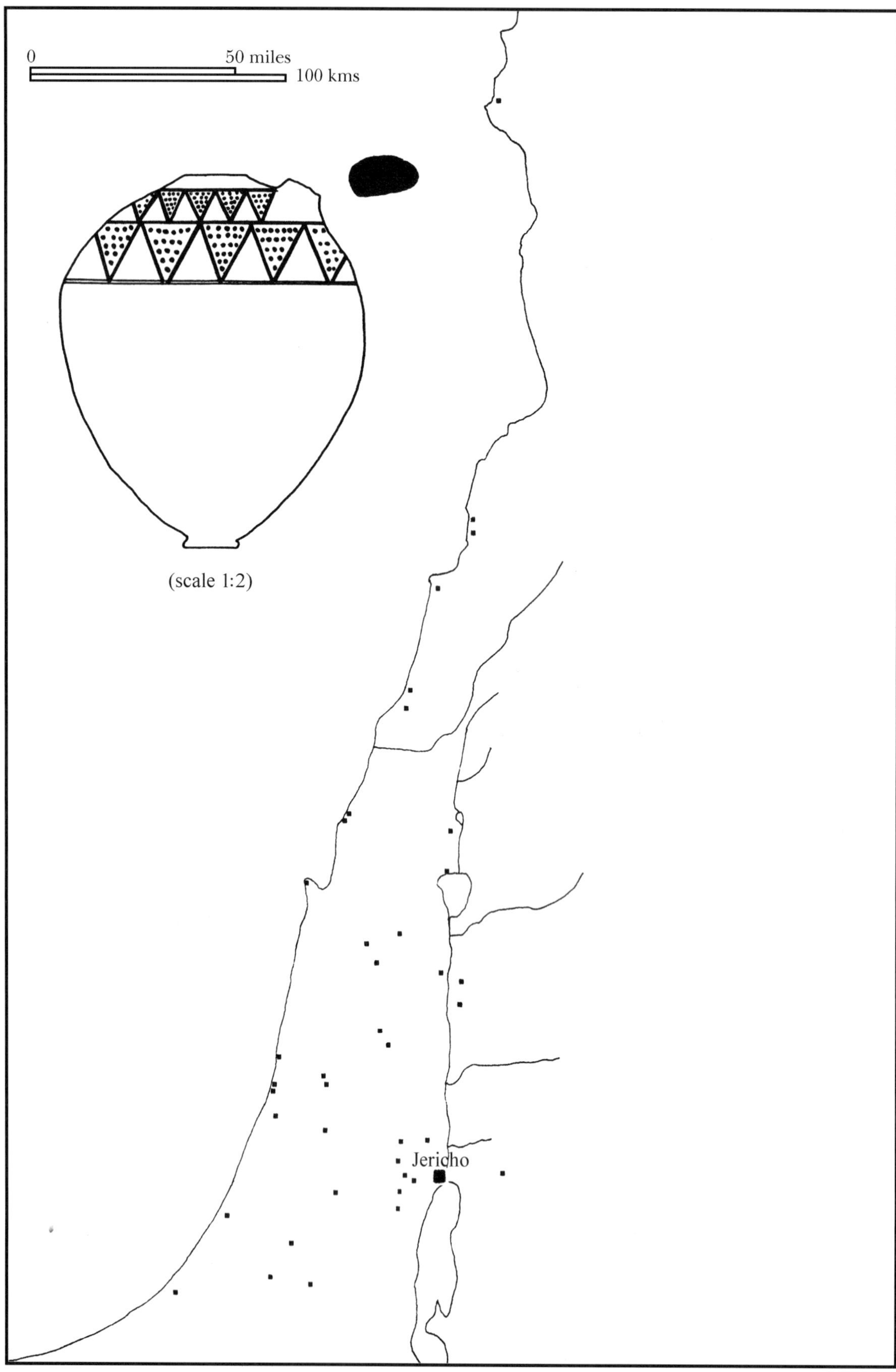

Fig. 19 Distribution and Shape Class of Type Group B.2.2

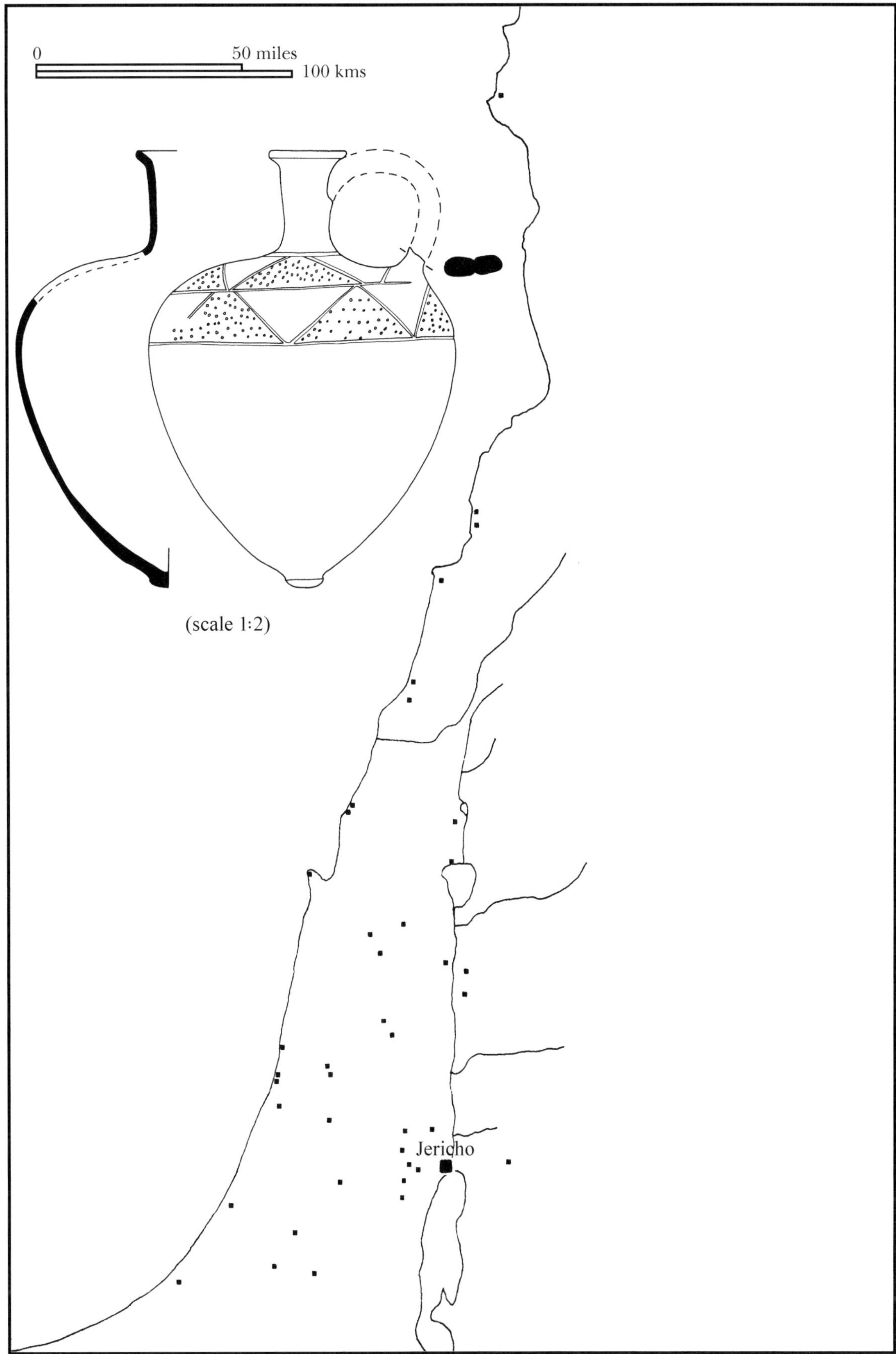

Fig. 20 Distribution and Shape Class of Type Group B.2.3

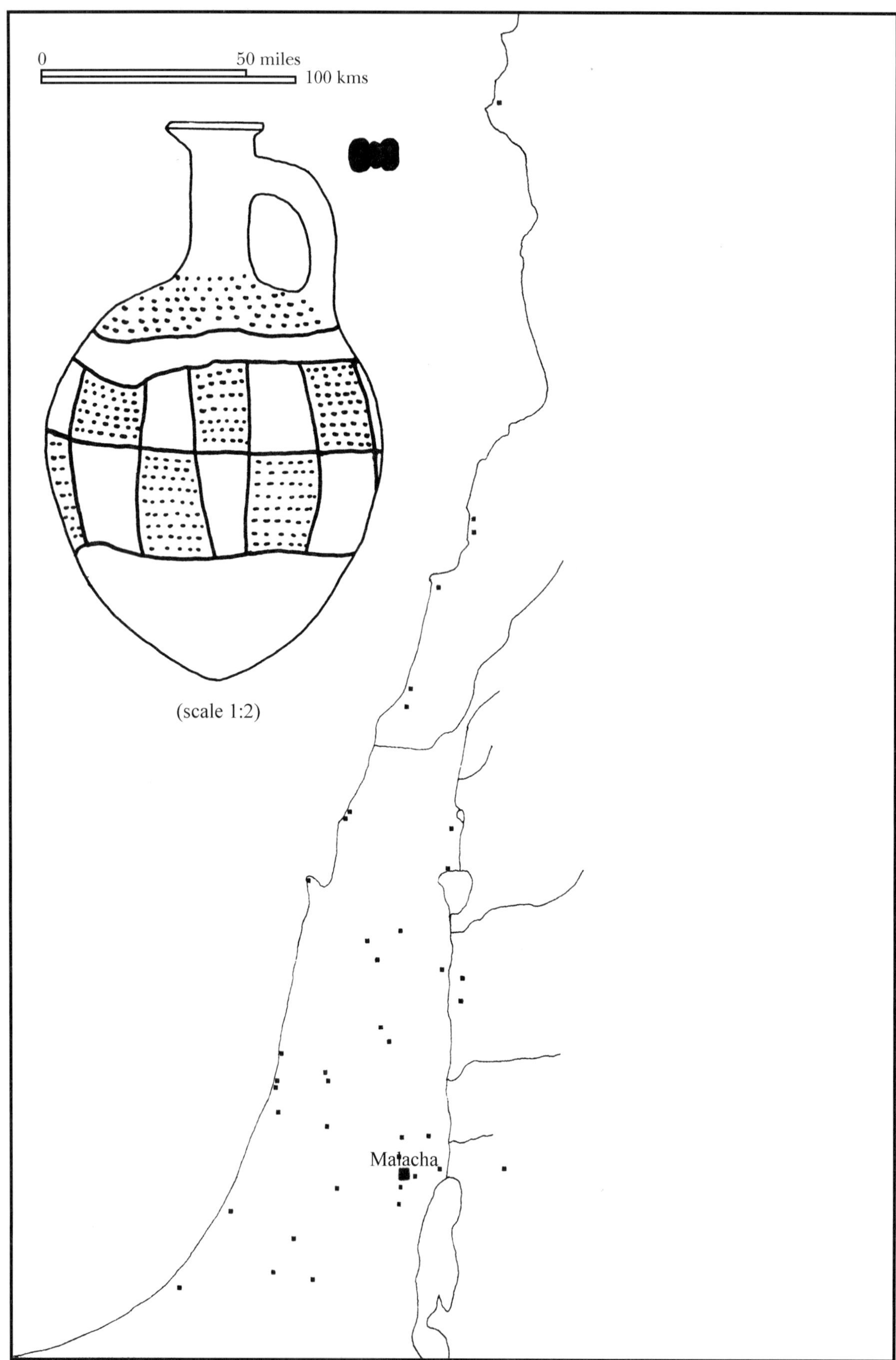

Fig. 21 Distribution and Shape Class of Type Group B.2.4

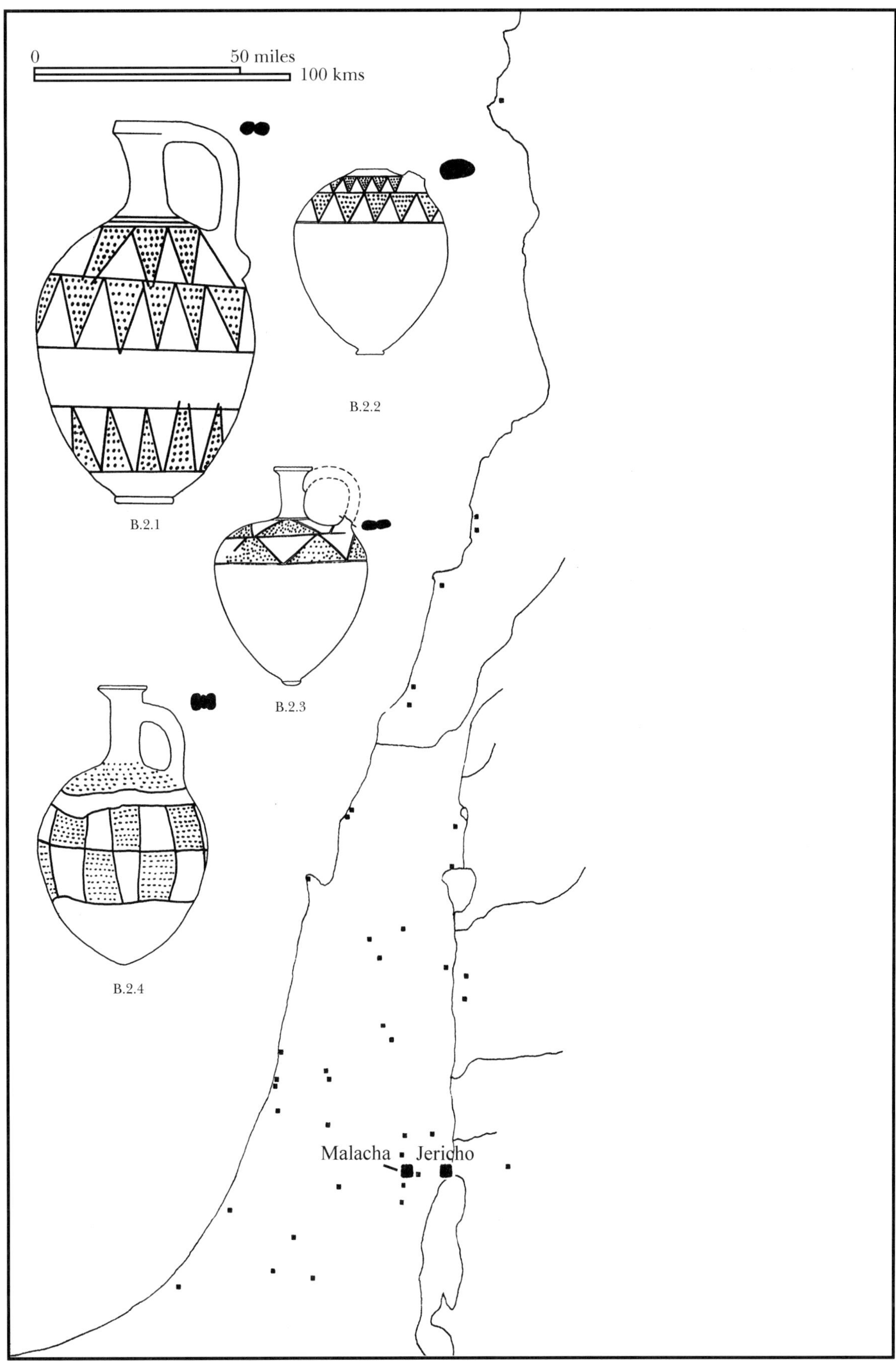

Fig. 22 Combined Distribution of Type Group B.2

everted rim, no incisions at the base of the neck, a tripartite handle sloping outwards, a pointed base, and a chessboard design covering the major part of the body.[235]

B.3. Early Palestinian III

Early Palestinian III vessels comprise a series of ovoid jugs (Bietak's Ovoid 2) with direct rims, and usually have three or four horizontal ornament bands.

Type Group B.3.1 (Figs. 23, 26)

It came as something of a surprise to find a juglet (TD 7505A) with three horizontal ornament bands, produced of Levantine clay (IV-2-b), in a transitional MBIIA-B context at Tell el-Dabᶜa.[236] No NAA sample has yet been taken but the visual examination with a microscope was absolutely clear in this respect. This jug has a straight direct rim without lip. The handle is bipartite and sloping outwards at the upper attachment of the handle whereas the lower joint of the handle is near the base of the neck, similar to the typical pieces of the Primeval Group. The small base is slightly set off and convex. The burnishing in between the decoration zones is brown. A very similar piece, made of Red Field clay comes from Chamber II of tomb JR 59 in El-Jisr, not far from Tel Aviv.[237] It perfectly matches the cited Tell el-Dabᶜa jug, except that it has a pointed base, and was classified by Kaplan as an Ovoid 2. Looking at both examples the shoulder seems flat enough to classify them as plump piriform.

Type Groups B.3.2–B.3.3 (Figs. 24–26)

This group develops from the primeval Ovoid group and has four or more horizontal zones with incised decoration, consisting normally of comb imprints. Subdivisions into triangles or other geometric motifs are missing, additional zigzag filling of a void band is known in at least one example from Ginosar.[238] Only one of these vessels, again from Ginosar, has a rim preserved which is direct and straight without lip.[239] The handles are rounded strap ones, (– an unusual feature considering the date of these vessels –) and the bases are either small offset discs (B.2.2) or rounded bases (B.2.3). Both B.2.2 and B.2.3 are only known in Levantine clays with a grey to black burnish between the ornamentation zones. There are two deviating examples from northern Israel; one from Ginosar tomb 3, the other, known only through a body sherd, from Hazor, with impressed concentric circles, probably representing eyes, on a void band[240] which show their relationship to the small piriform jugs from southern Lebanon (below type group C.3). A small vessel from Gezer[241] is perhaps also to be associated with group B.2.3. It shares the rounded base and round handle, but has only three, rather than four horizontal bands of decoration. Incomplete vessels from Ginosar[242] and Megiddo should perhaps also be attributed to these groups.[243]

B.4. Early Palestinian IV

Type Group B.4 (Fig. 27)

Another interesting type group which along with groups B.3.2–B.3.3 shares the four horizontal ornamental bands, is known through two brown burnished jugs, Tell el-Dabᶜa TD 2518 and TD 2519, found in an early Phase F, (transitional MB IIA/B), tomb, but these may be old vessels originating from Phase G/1–3. They deviate from the normal Ovoid 2 type, not only by their piriform shape, but also by other attributes such as a candlestick rim, high bipartite handle and a small offset disc base. An original NAA analysis of one of these vessels by Kaplan indicates a Levantine Red Field clay origin for these vessels,[244] but a more recent analysis by McGovern indicates a production area in the Nile Valley.[245] Since this style of decoration is decidedly not Egyptian, it would seem likely that a Levantine origin for these vessels is

---

235 Kaplan, *Tell el-Yahudiyeh Ware,* fig. 114a.

236 From A/IV-h/6, tomb no. 13, Str. G or F, not yet finally assessed.

237 Jerusalem 42.271, Ory 1946, 38–39, pl. 12.50: Kaplan, *Tell el-Yahudiyeh Ware,* fig. 113d, 232, JS1.

238 Jerusalem 56.724. Epstein, *Atiqot* 7, 1974, 27, fig. 8.18; Kaplan, *Tell el-Yahudiyeh Ware,* fig. 113b.

239 Jerusalem 56.721. Epstein, *Atiqot* 7, 1974, 27, fig. 8.16; Kaplan, *Tell el-Yahudiyeh Ware,* fig. 113c.

240 Ginosar = Jerusalem 56.724. Epstein, *Atiqot* 7, 1974, 27, fig. 8.18; Kaplan, *Tell el-Yahudiyeh Ware,* fig. 113b: Hazor = Jerusalem 55.104. Amiran, *Ancient Pottery of the Holy Land,* 1969, 119 photo, 121. Kaplan, *Tell el-Yahudiyeh Ware,* fig. 133c.

241 Tel Aviv Haaretz Museum 55060. Kaplan, *Tell el-Yahudiyeh Ware,* fig. 115a.

242 Jerusalem 56.720. Epstein, *Atiqot* 7, 1974, 27, fig. 8.17; Kaplan, *Tell el-Yahudiyeh Ware,* fig. 112a.

243 Kaplan, *Tell el-Yahudiyeh Ware,* fig. 113a.

244 Kaplan, *Tell el-Yahudiyeh Ware,* 232 TD3.

245 P. McGovern, *The Foreign Relations of the Hyksos,* Oxford, 2000, 129 no. JH322.

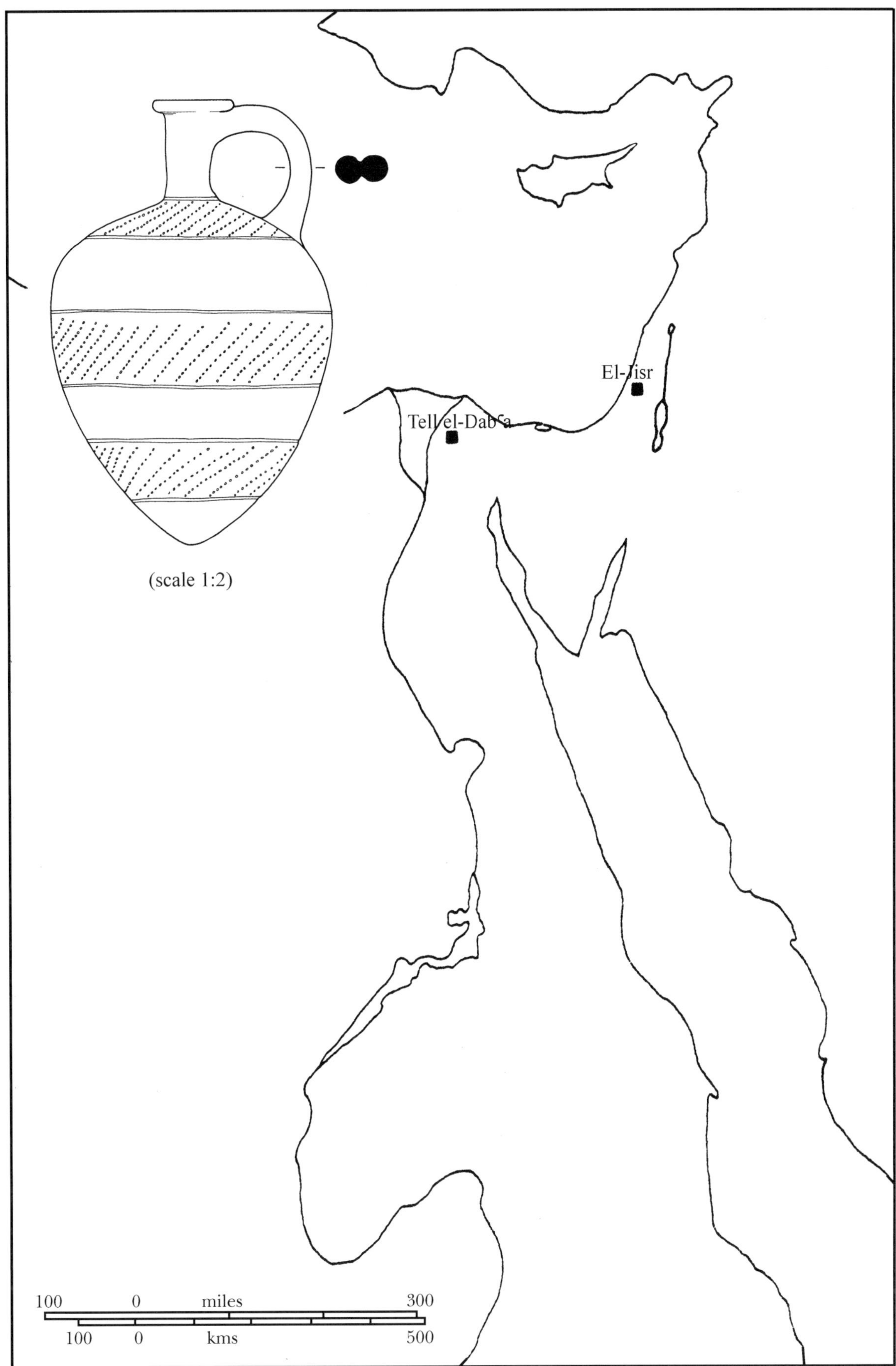

Fig. 23 Distribution and Shape Class of Type Group B.3.1

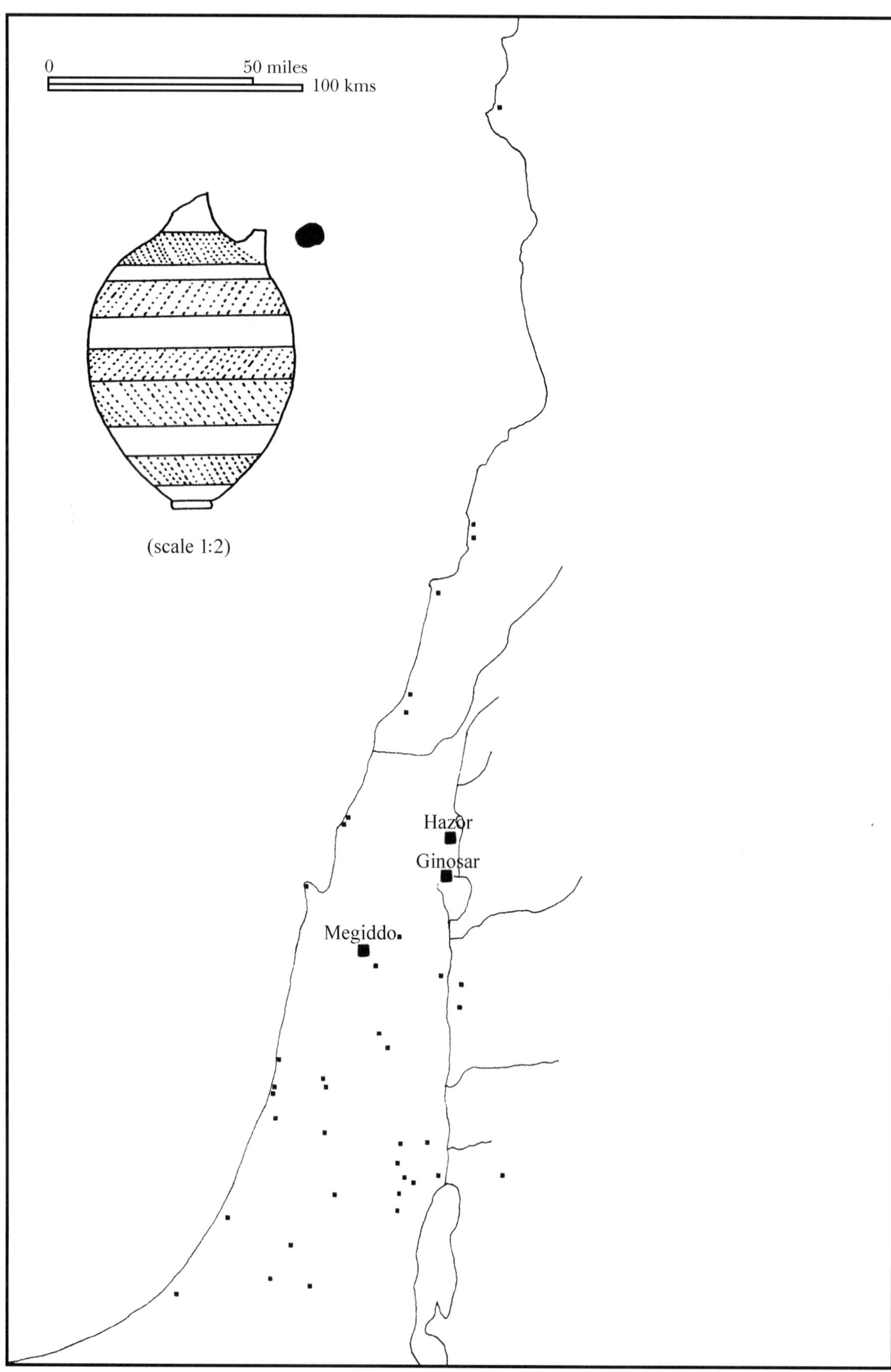

Fig. 24 Distribution and Shape Class of Type Group B.3.2

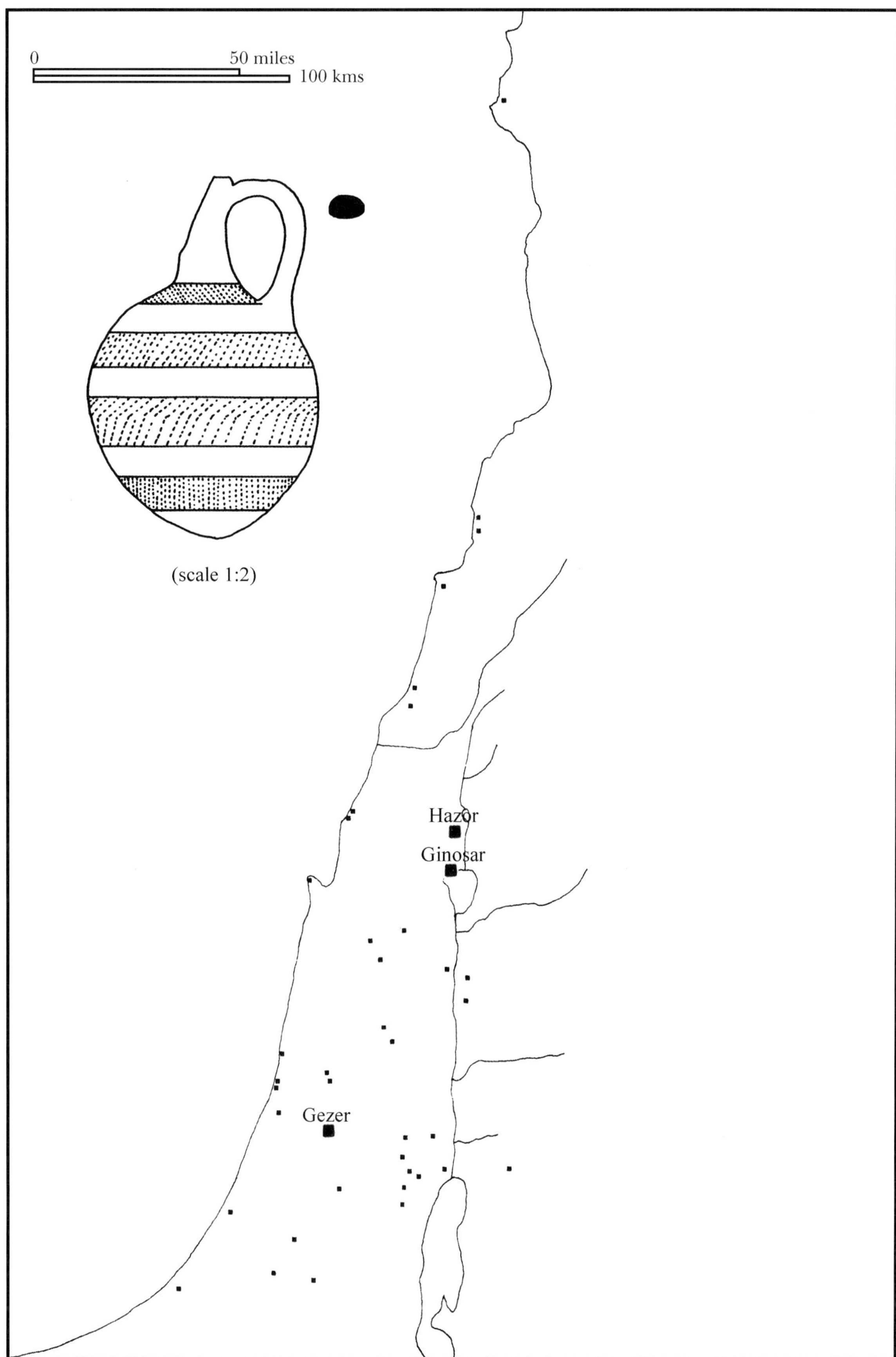

Fig. 25 Distribution and Shape Class of Type Group B.3.3

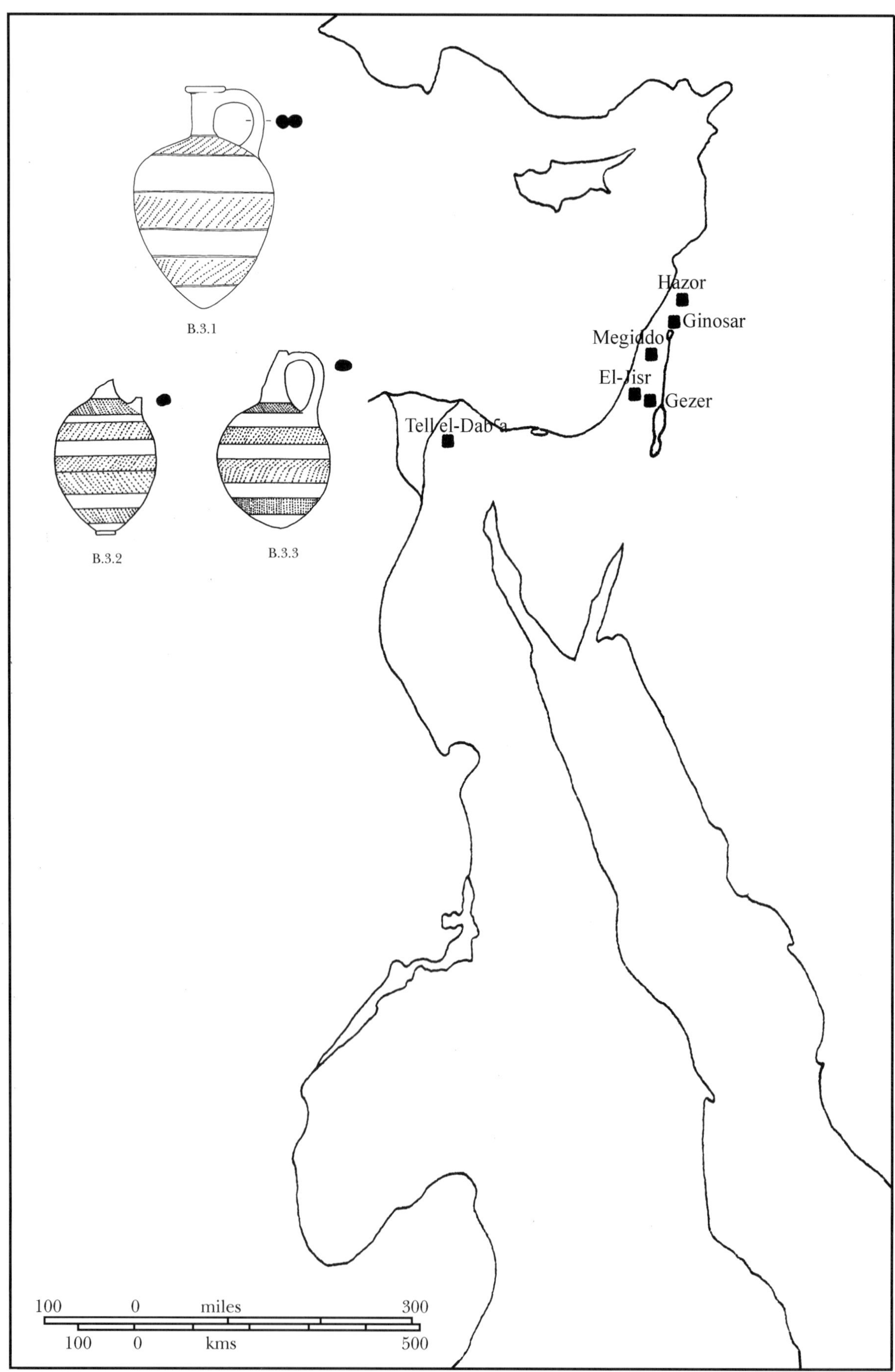

Fig. 26 Combined Distribution of Type Group B.3

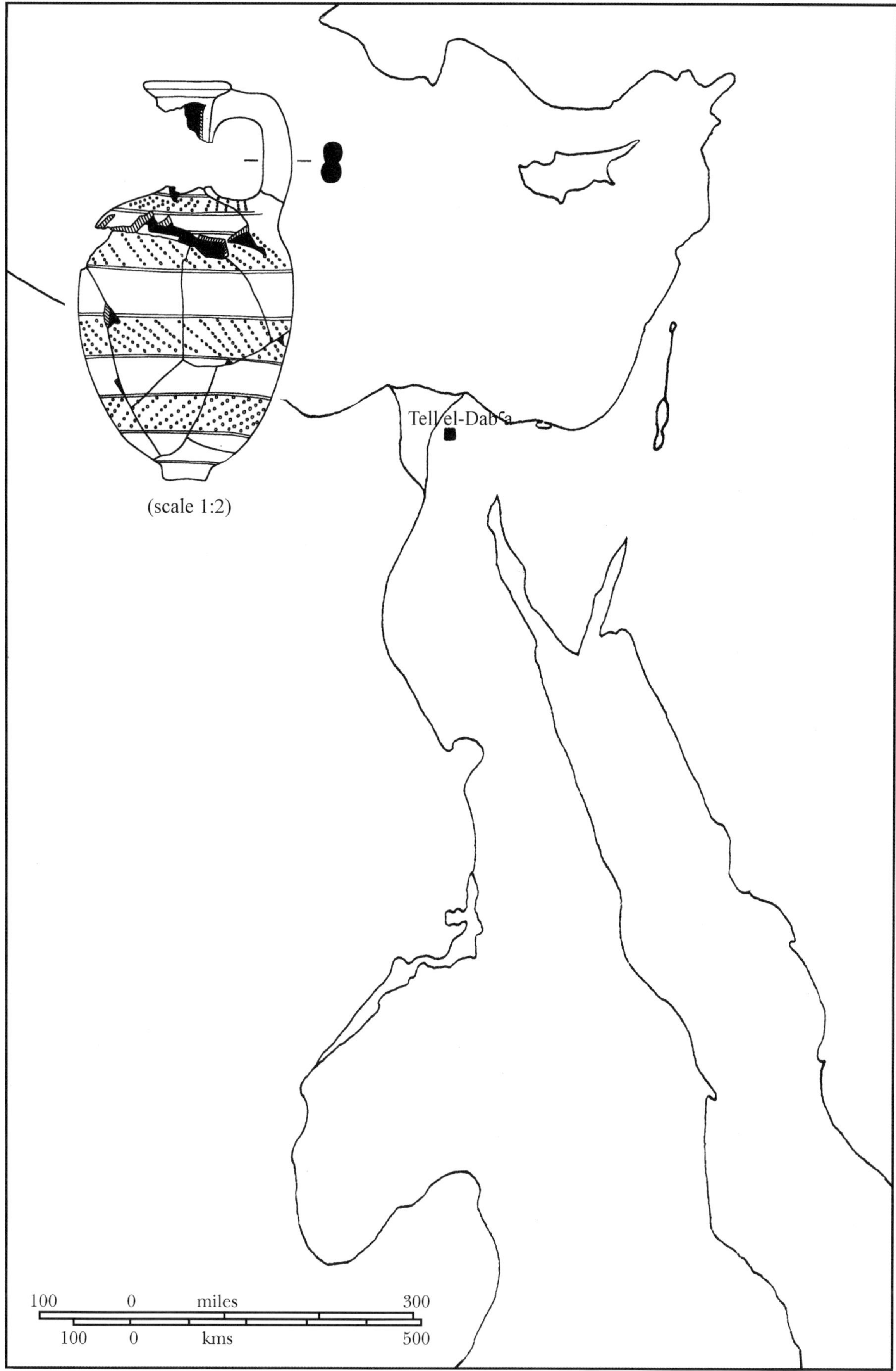

Fig. 27 Distribution and Shape Class of Type Group B.4

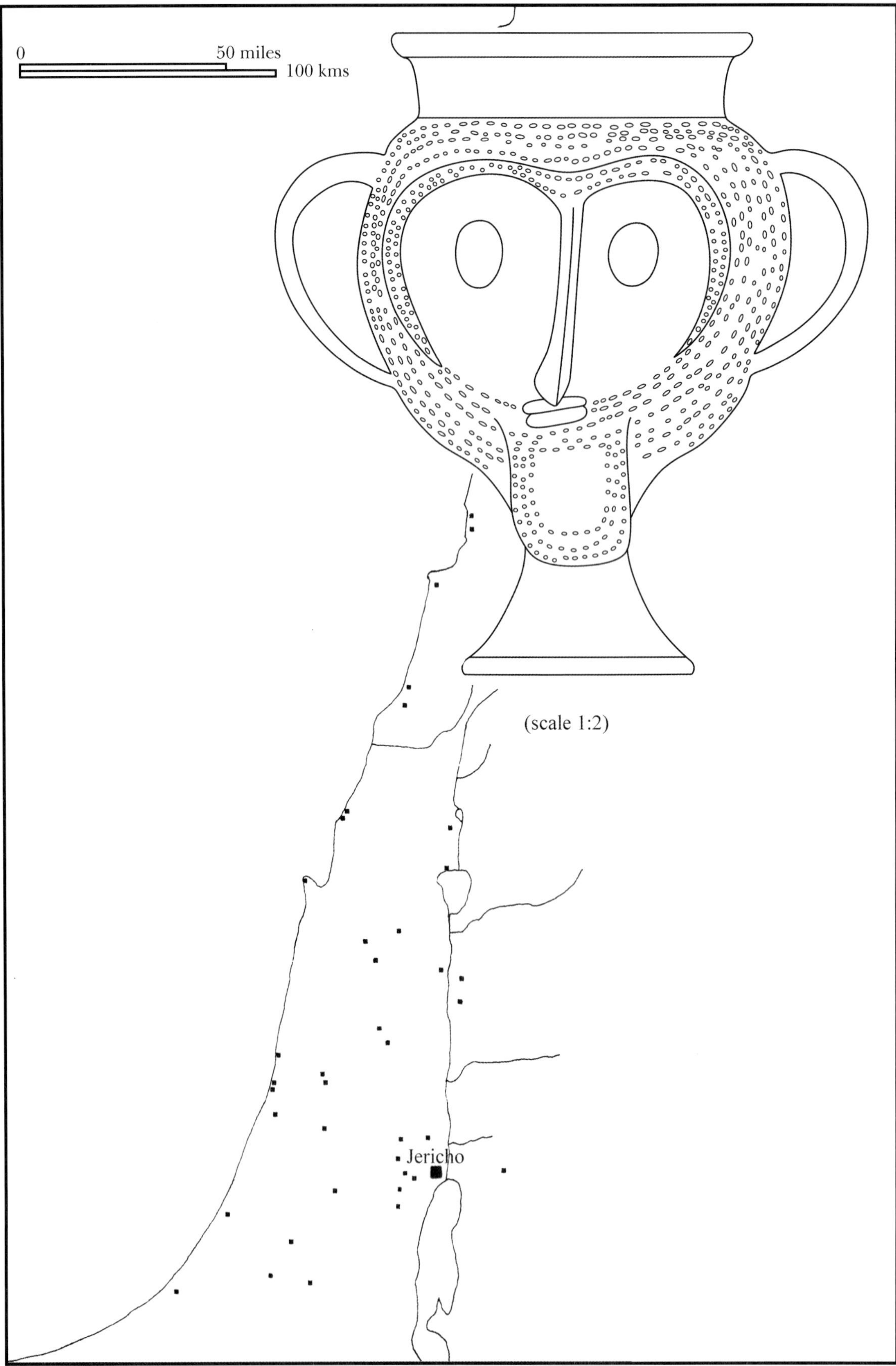

Fig. 28 Distribution and Shape Class of Type Group B.5.1

the more correct, and one can only assume that McGovern accidentally misplaced his records.

B.5. Early Palestinian V ("Palestinian Figural Vases")

The figural group; Early Palestinian V, consists of a few anthropomorphic, faunal and fruit-shaped jugs or vessels: each is an individual production, and their function is most likely cultic. Although a few faunal jugs are found in this Early Palestinian group, one can suggest that, as a general rule, anthropomorphic and fruit shaped vessels mostly belong with the early Palestinian Group, whilst the faunal shaped vessels generally belong in the Late Egyptian group and date to the early Hyksos Period (cf. below Group L.15).

Type Group B.5.1 Male Heads (Fig. 28)

A pedestal jar with the representation of a male head with prominent eyebrows and beard in typical Tell el-Yahudiya style, was found in tomb 9 at Jericho.[246] The surface of the unincised areas were beige burnished. No doubt this object served a cultic purpose.

Type Group B.5.2 Ducks (Fig. 29)

Early Palestinian bird-shaped askoi are known from at least two complete examples, which differ distinctly from the bird-shaped vessels of the later Egyptian group (below groups L.15.1–2). The first from tomb 5137 in Megiddo[247] has an elongated body, a bipartite handle, and the lip is placed directly on the top of the head. The second, from Golan (?),[248] is similar but the spout is formed by the beak of the bird, and the decoration is more advanced. A group of, unfortunately fragmentary, bowls with duck head handles decorated in Tell el-Yahudiya technique are also known from Byblos.[249] A sherd from Beth Shan has also been considered as coming from such a vessel.[250]

Type Group B.5.3 Falcons (Fig. 30)

This group is represented by at least one incomplete example from Ashkelon.[251] That vessel was found in an early Middle Bronze IIB tomb, and as far as it is preserved shows a seated falcon with double handle. The wings are decorated with comb impressions whilst a lotus flower is drawn on its breast.

Type Group B.5.4 Fishes (Fig. 31)

From a tomb at Tel Poleg comes a hollow figurine of a heavily burnished fish with open mouth.[252] The scales are indicated by white incised indentations, and the fins by plastic applications and incisions. Contrary to the relatively frequent fish-shaped Tell el-Yahudiya jugs of the late Egyptian Group, this figure has no attributes of a jug, and is again a unique production which may have served some cultic purpose.

Type Group B.5.5 Acorns (Fig. 32)

Probably the original model for the Tell el-Yahudiya jug was a fruit with segmented anatomy.[253] The same is true with the Late Cypriot Base Ring ware which was fashioned after poppies in order to signal the contents to customers.[254] It is therefore not surprising that among the Tell el-Yahudiya corpus there exist jugs which clearly show the shape of fruits, in this case, acorns, from Ginosar,[255] Megiddo[256] and Gibeon.[257] The base of the fruit-shaped body issues into the orifice and the strap handle. There are other jugs where the acorn model is less obvious but still recognisable.

---

[246] Jerusalem, Rockefeller Museum 32.1366. GARSTANG *LAAA* 19, 1932, 45–46, fig. 9; KAPLAN, *Tell el-Yahudiyeh Ware*, fig. 131b.

[247] Jerusalem, Rockefeller Museum 39.596. GLANVILLE, Egyptian Theriomorphic vessels in the British Museum, *JEA* 12, 1926, 61, 68–69, pl. 13.5: LOUD *Megiddo II*, 185, pl. 247.1

[248] Jerusalem Israel Museum, 82.2.197 - O. TALLAY, in: *A Man and his Land, Highlights from the Moshe Dayan Collection*, Jerusalem, 1986, 51; W. SEIPEL (ed.), *Land der Bibel. Schätze aus dem Israel Museum, Jerusalem*, Exhibition catalogue, Vienna, 1997, 48 no. 59; L. NIGRO, The Smith and the King of Ebla, in: M. BIETAK (ed.), *The Synchronisation of Civilizations in the Eastern Mediterranean in the Second Millenium BC II*, 2003, 355, fig. 18.

[249] R. DUNAND, *Fouilles de Byblos, I*, 1937–39, pl. clxxvi, in particular no. 11314.

[250] Cf. A. MAEIR and R. MULLINS, below page 584.

[251] L. STAGER, The MBIIA Ceramic Sequence at Tel Ashkelon and its Implications for the "Port Power" Model of Trade in M. BIETAK (ed.), *The Middle Bronze Age in the Levant*, Vienna, 2002, 358 fig. 16, below page 567.

[252] Jerusalem, Israel Museum 68.32.150. R. GOPHNA, Ichythomorphic Vessel from Tel Poleg, Museum *Haaretz Bulletin*, 11, 1969, 43–45, pl. 1.9; K. PRAG, A Tell el-Yahudiyeh Ware Fish Vase: An Additional Note, *Levant* 6, 1974, 192; KAPLAN, *Tell el-Yahudiyeh Ware*, fig. 131b; W. SIEPEL (ed.), *Land der Bibel. Schätze aus dem Israel Museum, Jerusalem*, Exhibition catalogue, Vienna, 1997, 46 no. 56.

[253] AMIRAN, *IMN* 10, 1975, 40–48.

[254] MERRILLEES, *Antiquity* 36, 1962, 287–92, *Trade and Transcendance*, 32–40

[255] Jerusalem, Rockefeller Museum 56.1402. EPSTEIN, *Atiqot* 7, 1974, 27, fig. 4.8; KAPLAN, *Tell el-Yahudiyeh Ware*, fig. 130a.

[256] Jerusalem, Rockefeller Museum 38.990. SHIPTON, *Megiddo Pottery*, 1939, pl. 9.9; LOUD, *Megiddo II*, 180, pls. 19.27, 119.14; KAPLAN, *Tell el-Yahudiyeh Ware*, fig. 129f.

[257] Jerusalem, Rockefeller Museum 45.127. AMIRAN, *Ancient Pottery of the Holy Land*, 1969, 119, pl. 36.17, photo 120; KAPLAN, *Tell el-Yahudiyeh Ware*, fig. 129e.

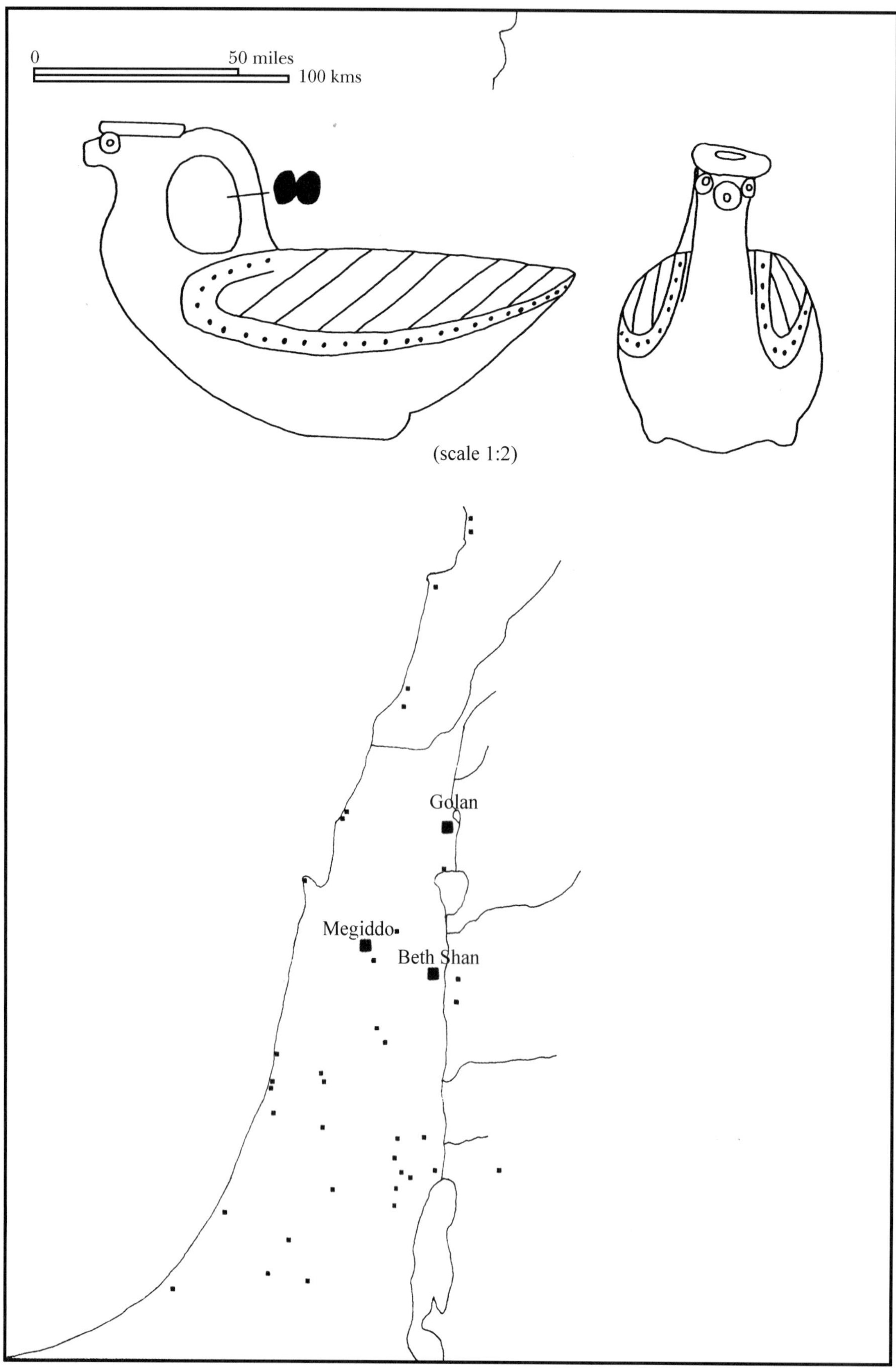

Fig. 29 Distribution and Shape Class of Type Group B.5.2

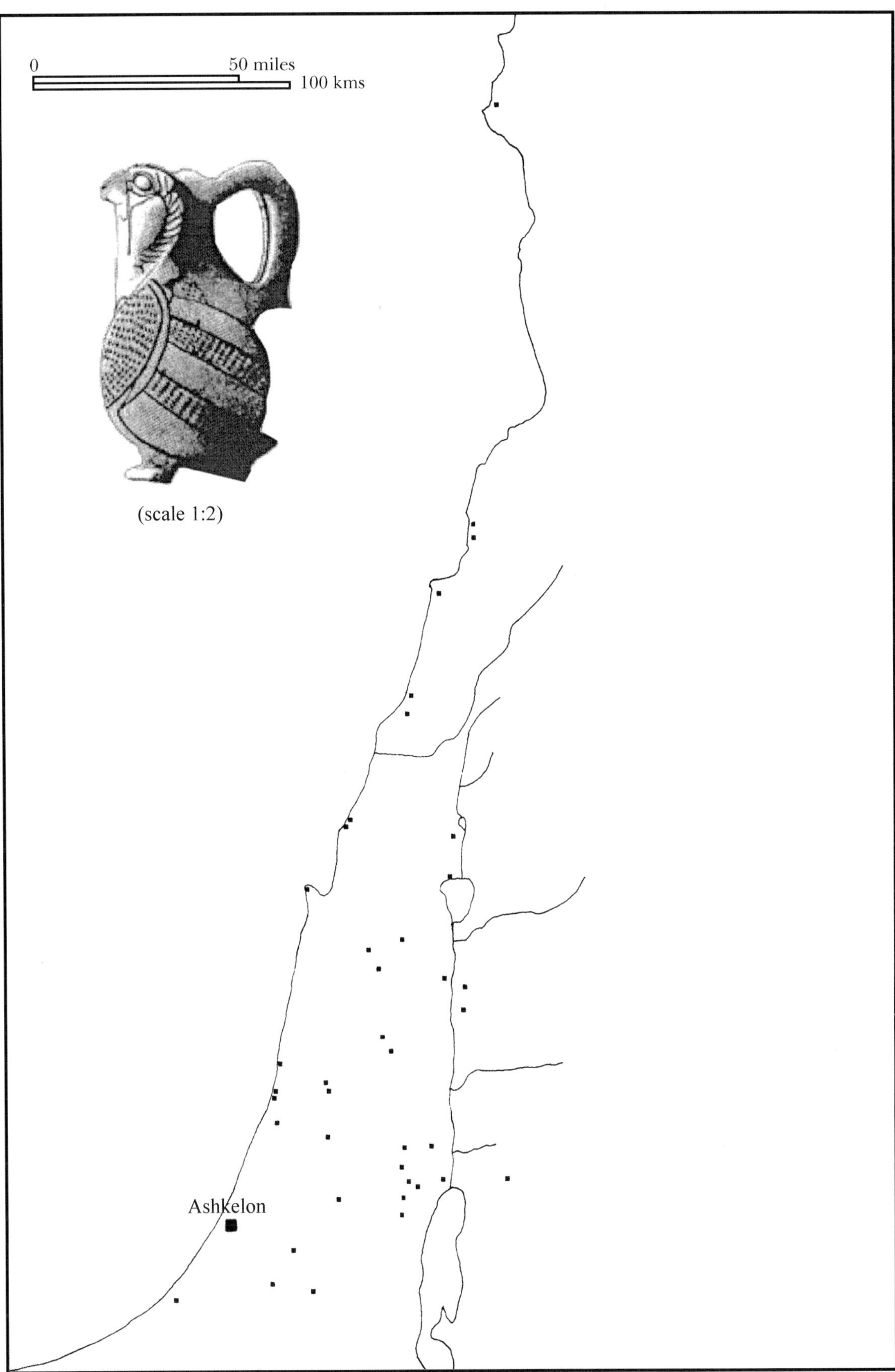

Fig. 30 Distribution and Shape Class of Type Group B.5.3

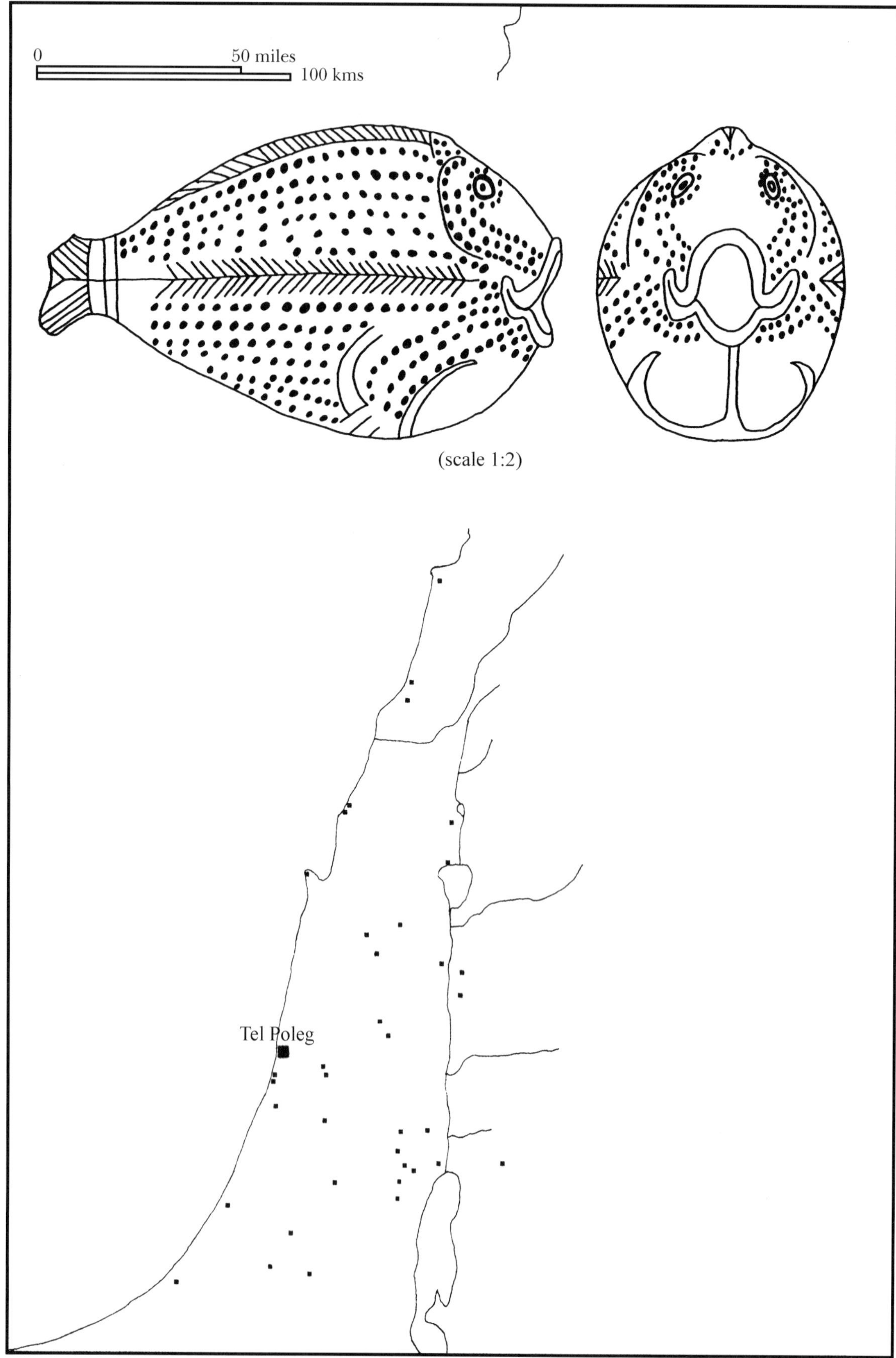

Fig. 31 Distribution and Shape Class of Type Group B.5.4

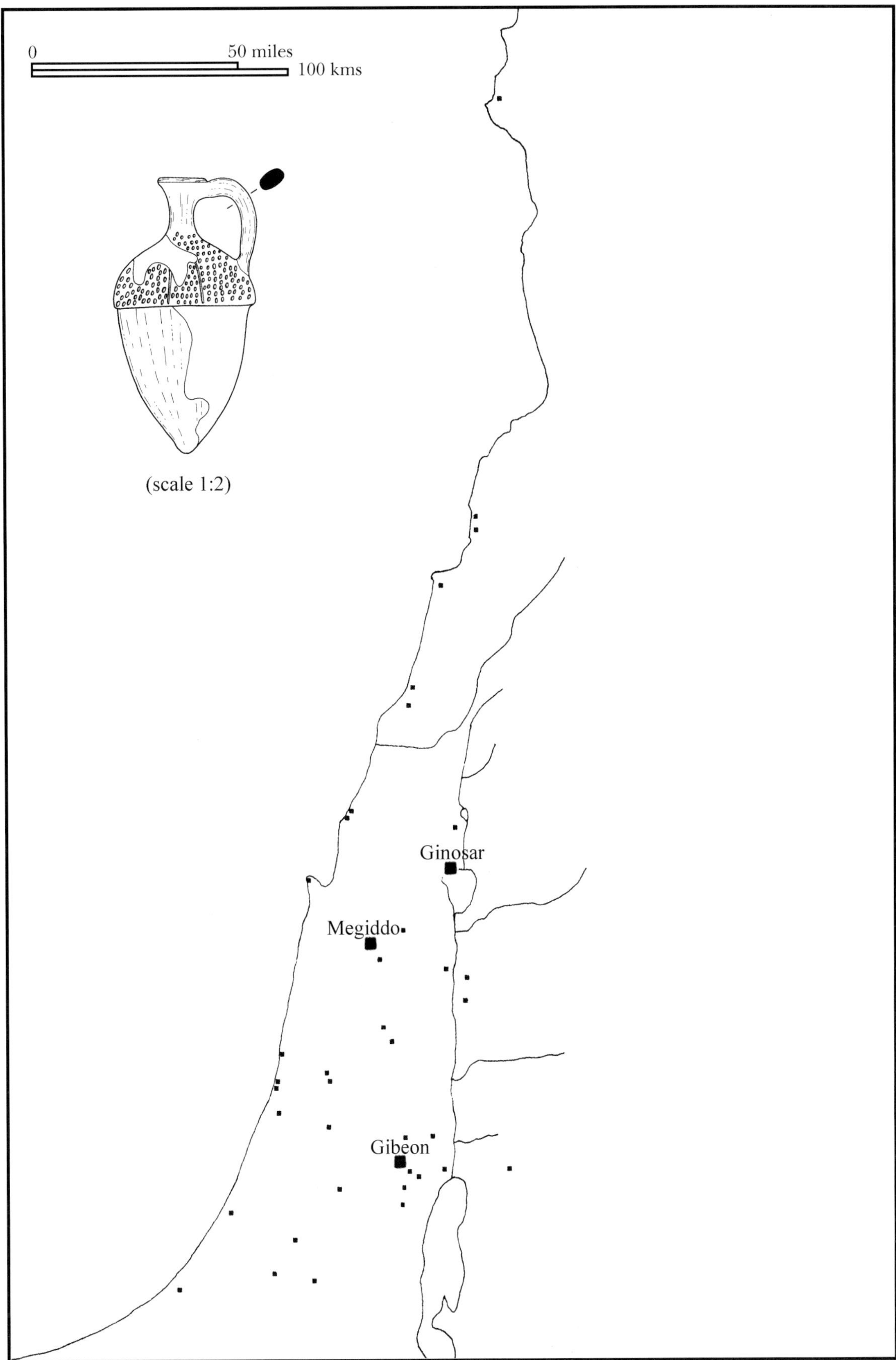

Fig. 32 Distribution and Shape Class of Type Group B.5.5

B.6. Early Palestinian VI

Group B.6 Jugs with Human Heads

Type Group B.6.1 Female-Headed (Fig. 33)

Type group B.6.1 comprises a small group, of which the only complete example comes from Jericho.[258] That vessel is essentially piriform in shape, and the body bears two zones of designs. The lower body is decorated with designs representing a human figure and the fauna of the land (goat), sea (fish) and air (bird) along with a plant and some indication of landscape, whilst the upper body bears standing triangles and two more birds. The neck of the jug issues into a female head with braids wound around it. The tripartite handle is attached to the back of the head. The jug is about 19 cm. high and has remains of a reddish brown burnishing. The remains of a similar jug were found in a disturbed context at Tell el-Dab^{c}a (see below page 341).

Closely related, in terms of decoration, to the complete B.6.1 vessel, and thus possibly of the same type, is an incomplete globular vessel, now in the Israel Museum, Jerusalem.[259] Broken off at the base of the neck the vessel is essentially globular in shape and once had a bipartite handle, now missing. Around the body is a hunting scene with a hunter, dressed in a short kilt and holding a bow and arrow, and three rams. The man and animals being decorated with white punctuated dots in typical Tell el-Yahudiya style.

B.7 Early Palestinian VII

Group B.7 Cylindrical Jugs (Fig. 34)

A clear, but incomplete, cylindrical jug, and a sherd of what may be a second example have been found in Phases 13 and 12 at Ashkelon.

Branch C: The Middle Palestinian Group

The Middle and Late Palestinian Groups are represented by a number of vessels found in Syria and Palestine. The following type groups may be distinguished:

C.1. Middle Palestinian I (Kaplan's Ovoid 1)

The Middle Palestinian I group comprises a series of divergent vessels, Merrillees' Transitional and Kaplan's Ovoid 1, distributed between Jericho,[260] Gezer[261] and Ginosar,[262] with others of unknown provenance.[263] The common features of these vessels are a brown or grey burnished slip, a plump body, either plump ovoid (C.1.1–C.1.3), piriform (C.1.4) or rounded biconical (C.1.5–C.1.6), with thick walls, a height between 14 and 22 cms., and everted rims which are sharply trimmed but usually without a lip. The handle can be tripartite (C.1.1), but is usually bipartite (C.1.2–C.1.6), and the base is a small slightly set off disc. Two or three narrow ornamented horizontal bands are mainly on the shoulder. They are filled with vertical comb imprints but never show a herringbone design.

Type Group C.1.1 (Figs. 35, 41)

Type group C.1.1 consists of plump ovoid vessels with an everted rim, a tripartite handle, and is identified through the presence of a vessel of unknown provenance now in Tel Aviv.[264] That vessel has three bands of punctuated decoration, one at the base of the neck, one at the base of the handle and one on the shoulder.

Type Group C.1.2 (Figs. 36, 41)

Group C.1.2 comprise plump ovoid vessels with an everted rim, short neck, bipartite handle, an offset disc base and two bands of decoration on the upper and lower bodies. A good example with a grey burnished slip comes from Jericho tomb P17.[265]

Type Group C.1.3 (Figs. 37, 41)

Group C.1.3, another plump ovoid shape, is known through a single example from Tell el-Ashari (Syria), which consists of an ovoid vessel with candlestick rim,

---

[258] Amman, National Museum J.5173. Åström, *Alasia* I, 1971, 13, Merrillees *Levant* 10, 1978, 83, Kaplan, *Tell el-Yahudiyeh Ware,* fig. 131c.

[259] Jerusalem, Israel Museum 71.67.225. W. Siepel (ed.), *Land der Bibel. Schätze aus dem Israel Miseum, Jerusalem,* Exhibition catalogue, Vienna, 1997, 47 no. 58.

[260] National Museum, Amman, J.6950. Kenyon, *Jericho II,* 1964, 358–368.

[261] Rockefeller Museum, Jerusalem V.347. Macalister, *Gezer* I, 301–302, III, pl. 60.12.

[262] Jerusalem 56.717. Epstein, *Atiqot* 7, 1974, 27, fig. 8.20.

[263] Kaplan, *Tell el-Yahudiyeh Ware,* figs. 74b, 108a.

[264] Tel Aviv 54860, Åström, Three Tell el-Yahudieh Juglets in the Thera Museum, 1971, 420; Kaplan, *Tell el-Yahudiyeh Ware,* fig. 108a.

[265] Amman National Museum J.6950, Kenyon, *Excavations at Jericho II,* 362, fig. 177.6; Kaplan, *Tell el-Yahudiyeh Ware,* fig. 107b.

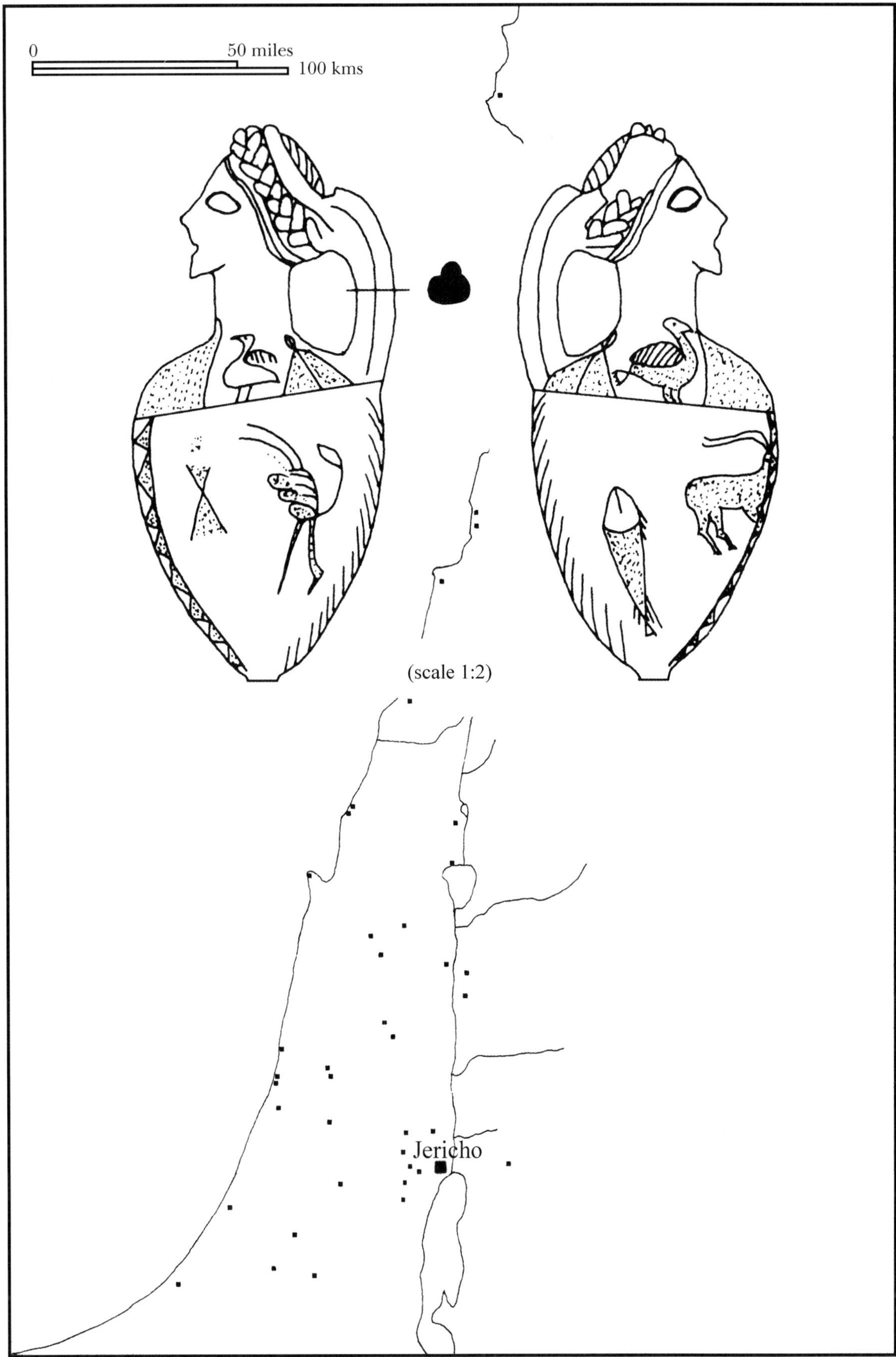

Fig. 33 Distribution and Shape Class of Type Group B.6.1

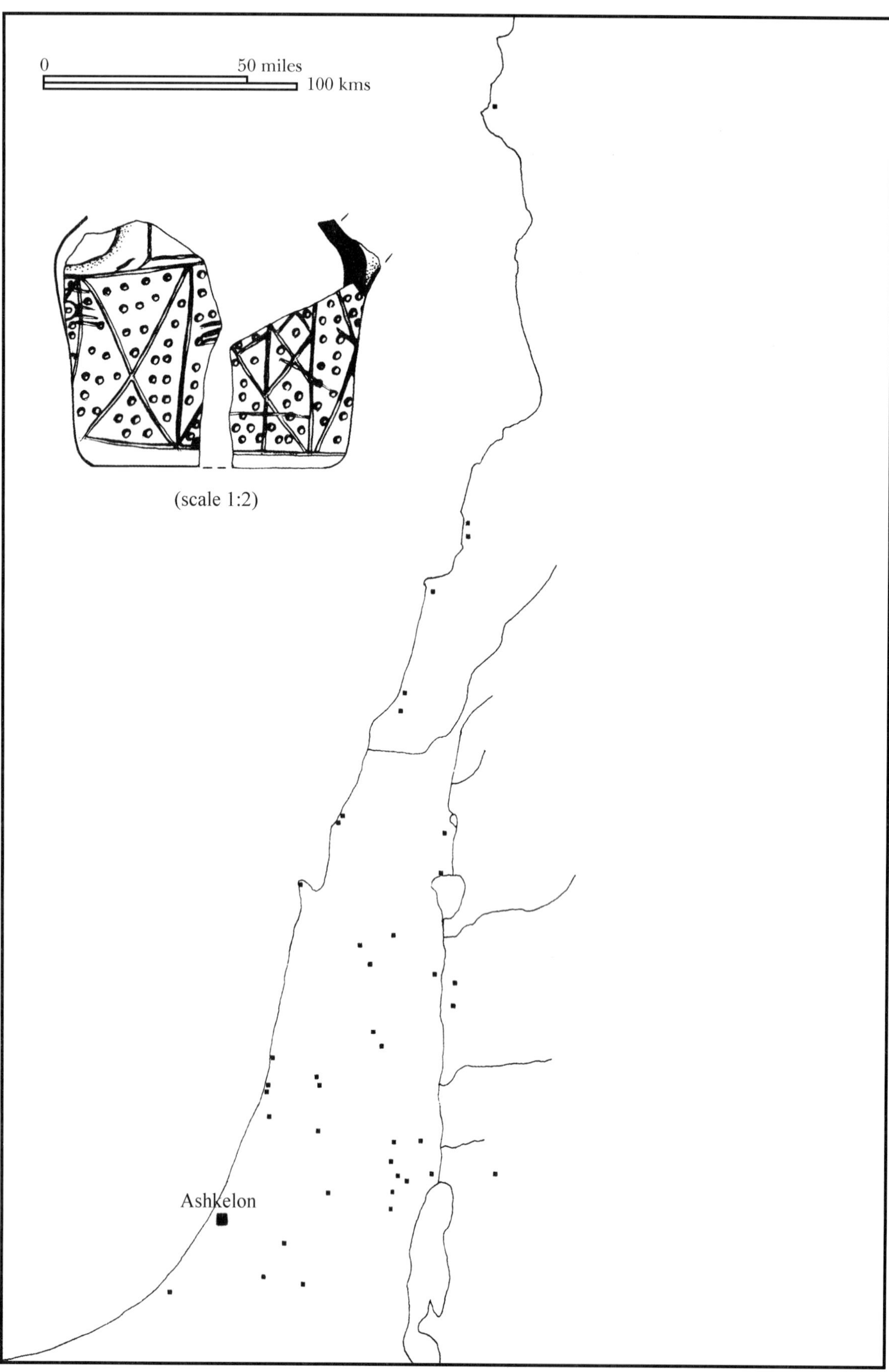

Fig. 34 Distribution and Shape Class of Type Group B.7

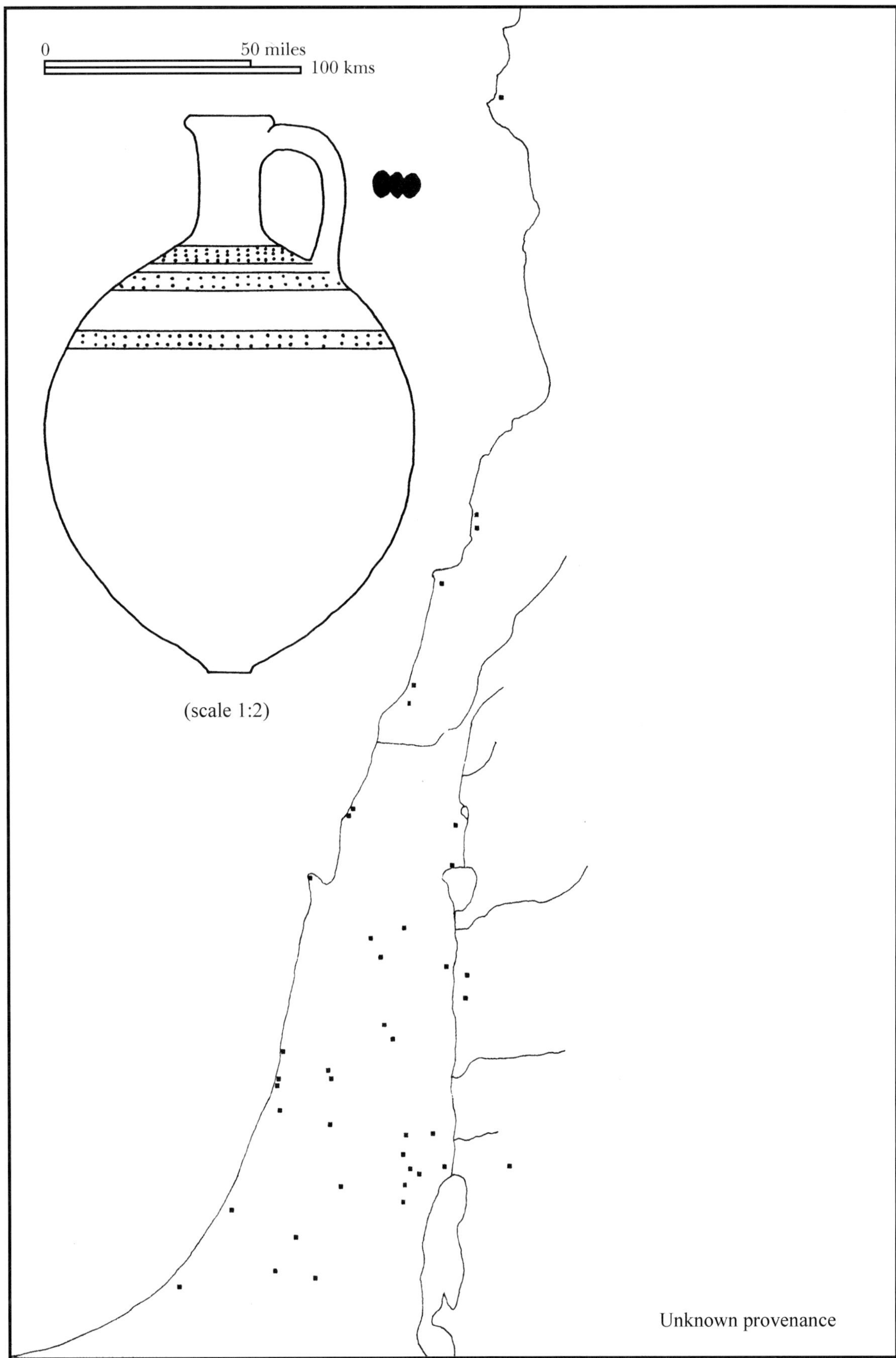

Fig. 35 Distribution and Shape Class of Type Group C.1.1

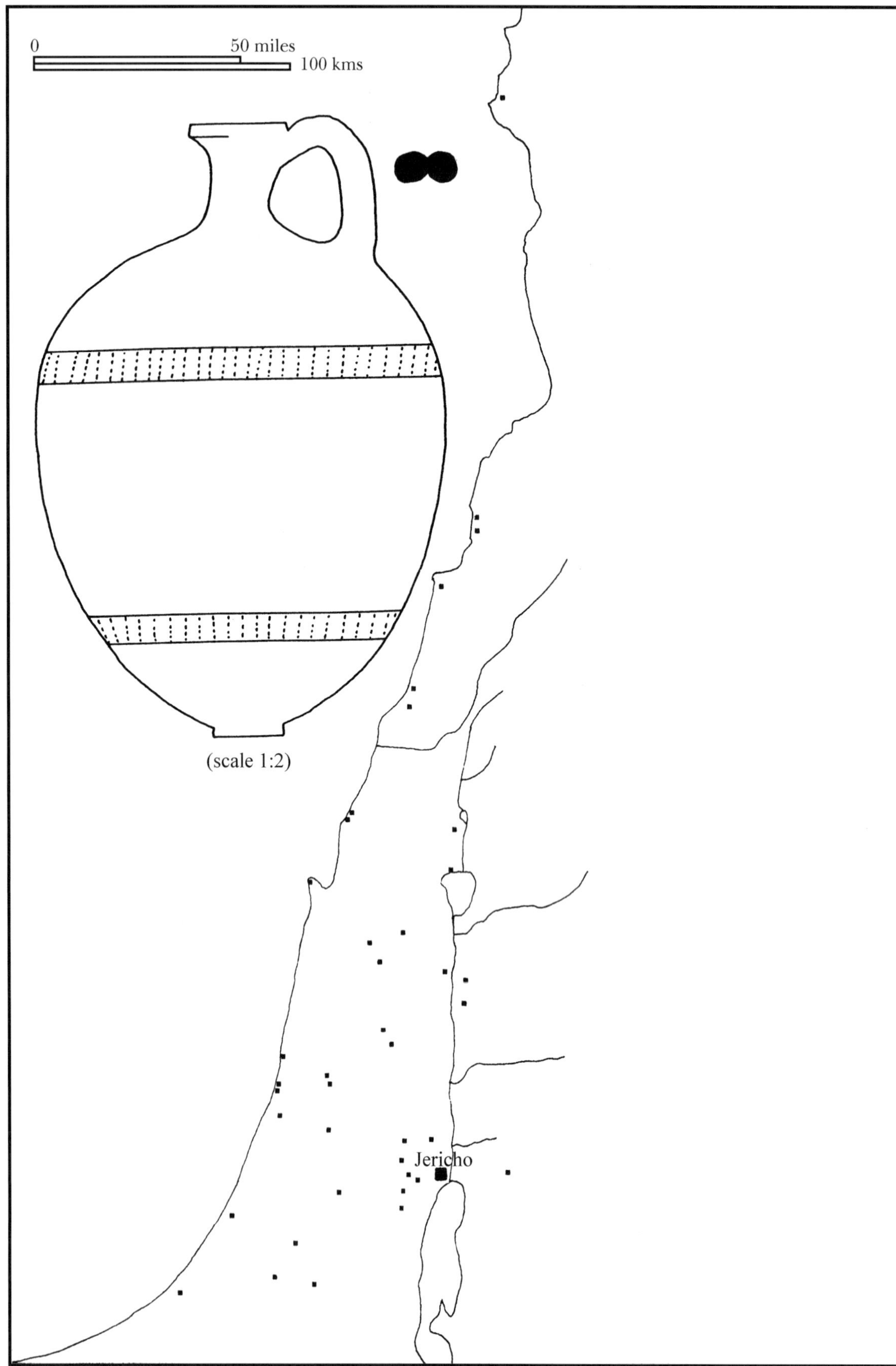

Fig. 36 Distribution and Shape Class of Type Group C.1.2

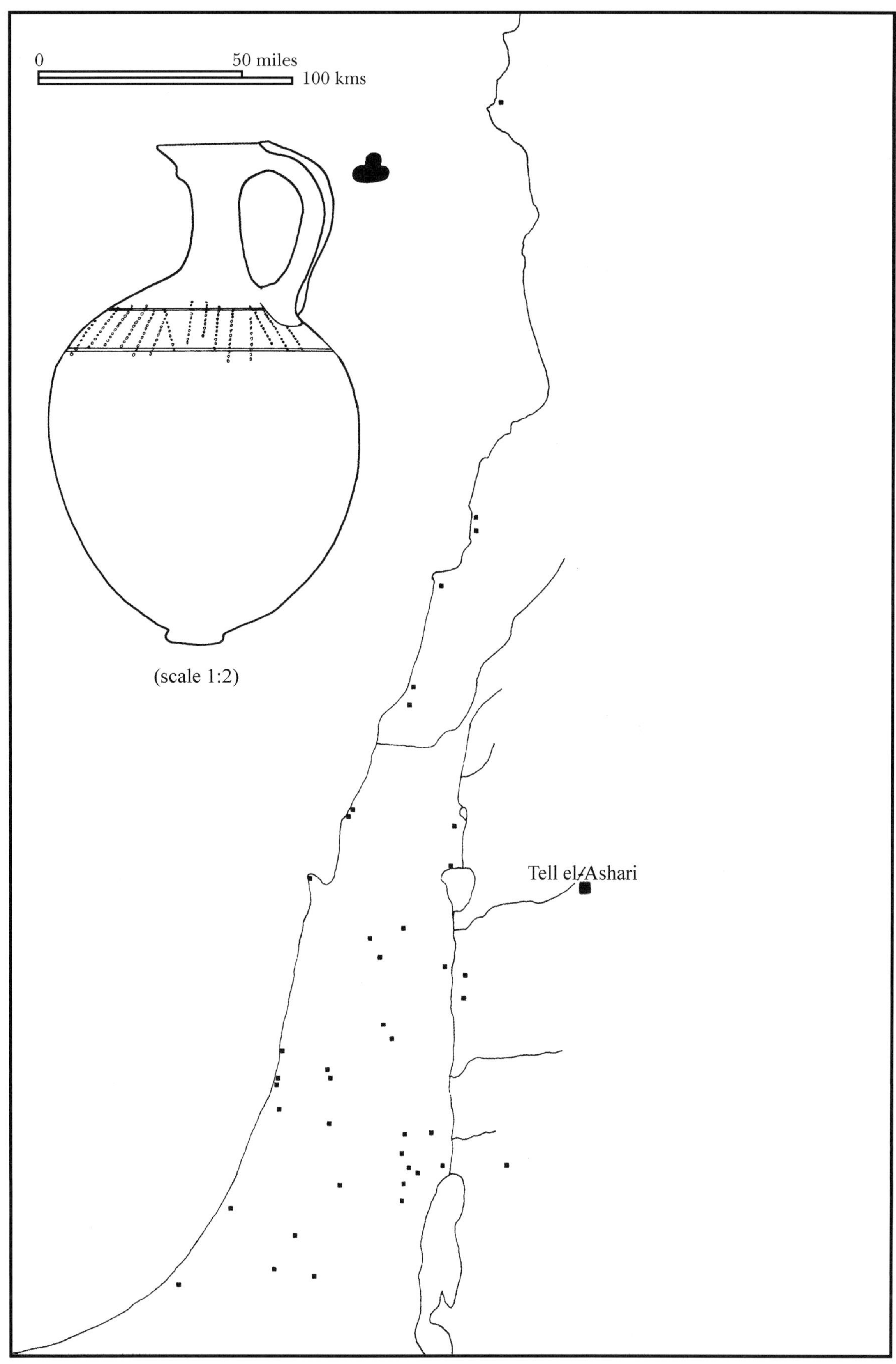

Fig. 37 Distribution and Shape Class of Type Group C.1.3

a tripartite handle, an offset disc base and a single band of decoration running around the shoulder.[266]

Type Group C.1.4 (Fig. 38, 41)

These vessels have a rolled rim, bipartite handles, an offset disc base, a distinctly piriform body and one thin ornament band on the shoulder with simple indentations and no herringbone designs. Examples are known from Hazor,[267] and Megiddo tomb 3175.[268] These jugs vary in size between 12 and 18 cm.

Type Group C.1.5 (Fig. 39, 41)

Vessels of group C.1.5 tend to be similar to group C.1.2 but are distinctly plump biconical in shape. Several examples are known, with complete vessels having been found at Ginosar,[269] Gezer,[270] and in Jordan.[271] To this group may perhaps be added a weathered example from Jericho tomb A.134,[272] and a fragmentary piece from Tell el-Sakka, Syria.[273]

Type Group C.1.6 (Figs. 40, 41)

Vessels of type group C.1.6 are somewhat smaller than other jugs of the C.1 group. They have everted rolled rims, a bipartite handle, an offset disc base and one band of decoration below the handle. A good example of such a vessel comes from Amman.[274]

C.2. Middle Palestinian II

Type Group C.2 (Fig. 42)

Middle Palestinian biconical Tell el-Yahudiya jugs are rare, although among the plain burnished jugs this shape is not infrequent. There is a good example from Tell Ta^canek made of Limestone Hill clay, with an everted sharp trimmed rim, a bipartite handle and an offset disc base.[275] The form and its attributes has parallels among light brown polished juglets of Phase E/3 at Tell el-Dab^ca.[276] On the upper part of the jug are two horizontal undelineated bands which are joined together with (probably) six vertical bands all consisting of comb imprints in a right angle towards the band directions. Other incomplete biconical vessels with bipartite handles and offset disc bases are also known from Mtouné, (Syria), and Dhibin (Syria), where they have one or two zones of decoration on the shoulder. These decorative zones comprise either bands of vertical comb imprints, or chevrons.[277]

C.3. Middle Palestinian III (Kaplan's Ovoid 5)

Type Group C.3 (Fig. 43)

From Southern Lebanon, in the area of Majdalouna[278] and Sin el-Fil,[279] come a series of small juglets with several ornamentation bands with concentric circles (eyes) between them (= Kaplan's Ovoid 5 type), similar to two juglets of the Early Palestinian B.3.2–3 groups from Ginosar and Hazor. This type group could also belong to the Late Palestinian Group. The rim of the Majdalouna juglet looks rolled, at the base there is a small rounded button. The base of the neck is surrounded by three horizontal grooves on the shoulder.

Branch D: The Late Palestinian Group

The time range of the Late Palestinian Group is MB IIB–C. The majority of the MB IIB jugs are now Piriform, but during the MB IIC the cylindrical shape becomes very popular. Ovoid and Biconical jugs are now rare. There is an increased standardisation but still each jug is an individual production. In general, as in Egypt at this time, there is a tendency for the

---

[266] Al-Maqdissi, *Syria* 70, 1993, 473 fig. 5.2; Braemer and Al-Maqdissi, in: Maqdissi, Matoïan, Nicolle, *Céramique de l'age du bronze en Syrie, I.*, 50, fig. xxB.112.

[267] Israel Museum. Jerusalem 67.1171. Yadin *et al*, *Hazor I*, 1958, 133, pl. 121.2, Kaplan, *Tell el-Yahudiyeh Ware*, fig. 67a.

[268] Loud, *Megiddo II*, 175 pl. 32.26, pl. 125.3; Kaplan, *Tell el-Yahudiyeh Ware*, fig. 75c.

[269] Epstein, 1974, 27, fig. 8.20; Kaplan, *Tell el-Yahudiyeh Ware*, fig. 107a.

[270] Macalister, *The Excavation of Gezer, 1902–1905 and 1907–1909*, 1912, I, 301–302, III pl. 60.12; Kaplan, *Tell el-Yahudiyeh Ware*, fig. 108b.

[271] U. Mo. Museum of Art and Archaeology 66.335, Columbia, Missouri, Kaplan, *Tell el-Yahudiyeh Ware*, fig. 74b.

[272] National Museum, Amman, J.5831 – Kenyon, Excavations at Jericho II, 371 fig. 183.7; Kaplan, *Tell el-Yahudiyeh Ware*, fig. 109a.

[273] Unpublished. We are grateful to Peter Fischer for showing us a drawing of this fragment.

[274] National Museum, Amman, J.1545. Harding, *PEFA* 6, 1953, 14–18, pl. 2.63.

[275] Kaplan, *Tell el-Yahudiyeh Ware*, fig. 105a, 232 sample TT1.

[276] Bietak, *TDV*, 1991, 83, fig. 44.3.

[277] al-Maqdissi, *AAAS* 39, 1989, 71, fig. 6.5–6; Idem, *Syria* 70, 1993, 470 fig. 45a; Braemer and al-Maqdissi, in: Maqdissi, Matoïan, Nicolle, *Céramique de l'age du bronze en Syrie, I.*, 50, fig. xxB.113–15, 117.

[278] Chehab, *BMB* 4, 1940, 48, fig. 3a; Kaplan, *Tell el-Yahudiyeh Ware*, fig. 115e.

[279] Chehab, *Mélanges Syriens*, 1939, 806 fig. 3b; Kaplan, *Tell el-Yahudiyeh Ware*, fig. 115f.

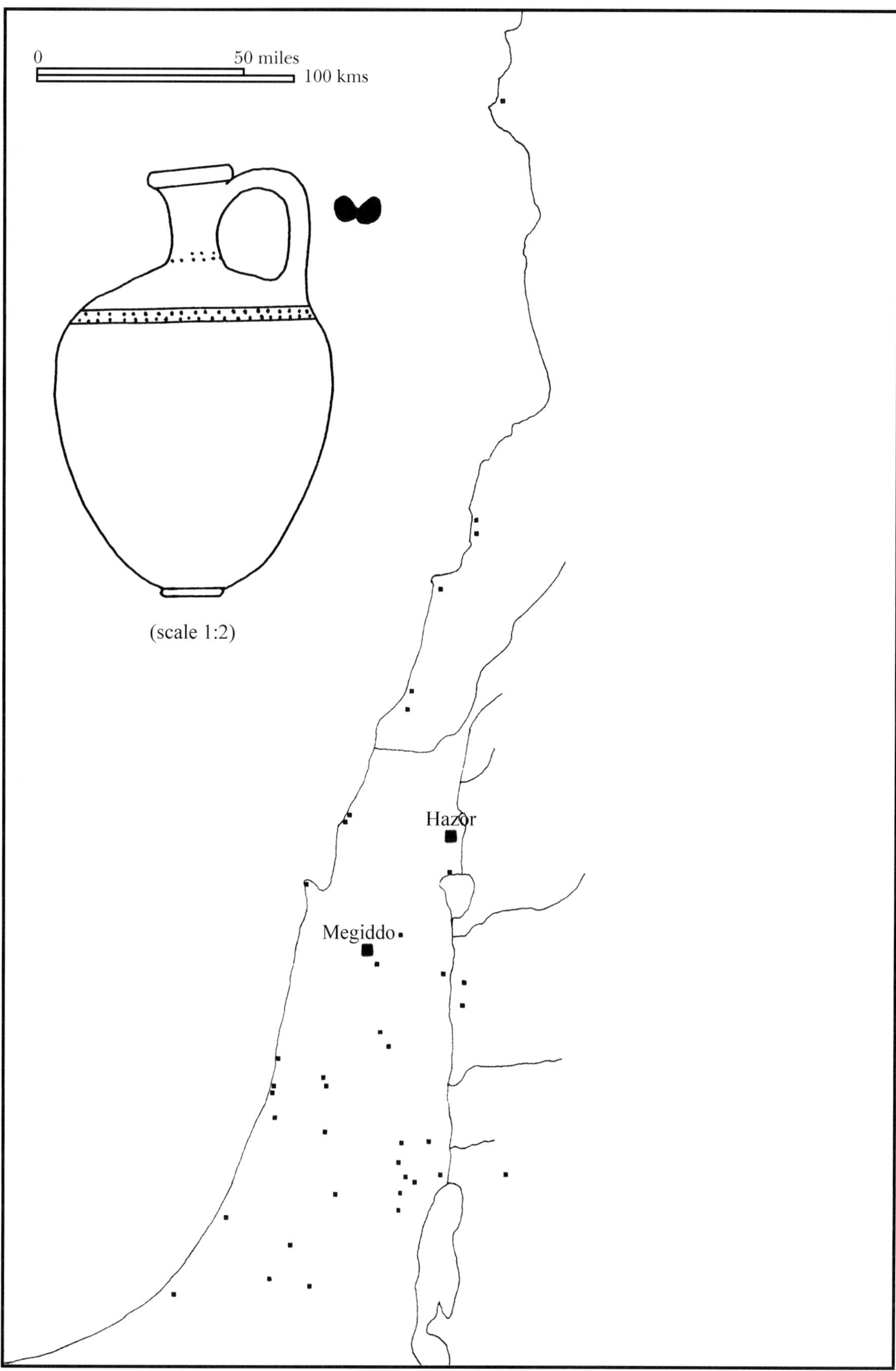

Fig. 38 Distribution and Shape Class of Type Group C.1.4

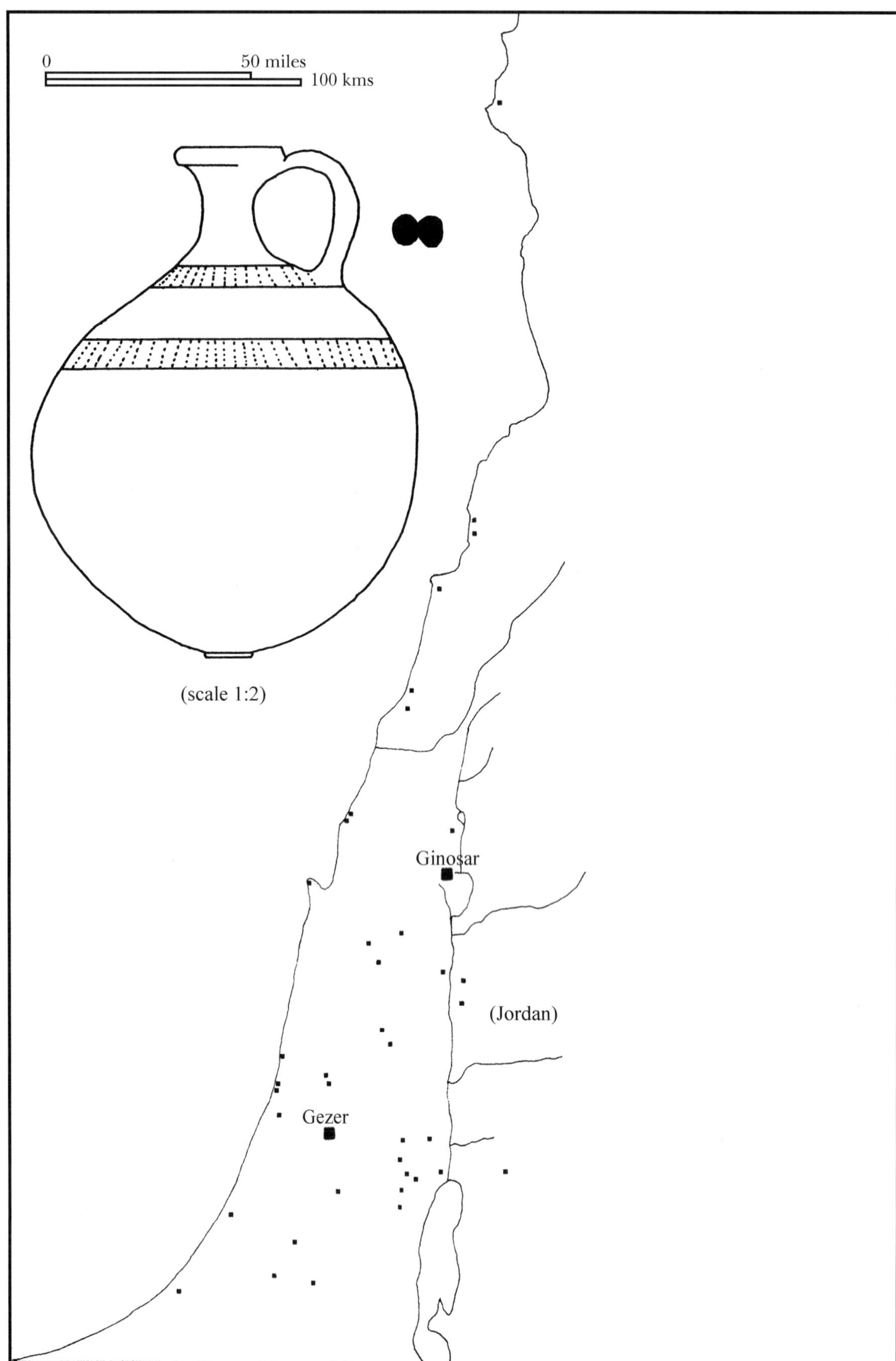

Fig. 39 Distribution and Shape Class of Type Group C.1.5

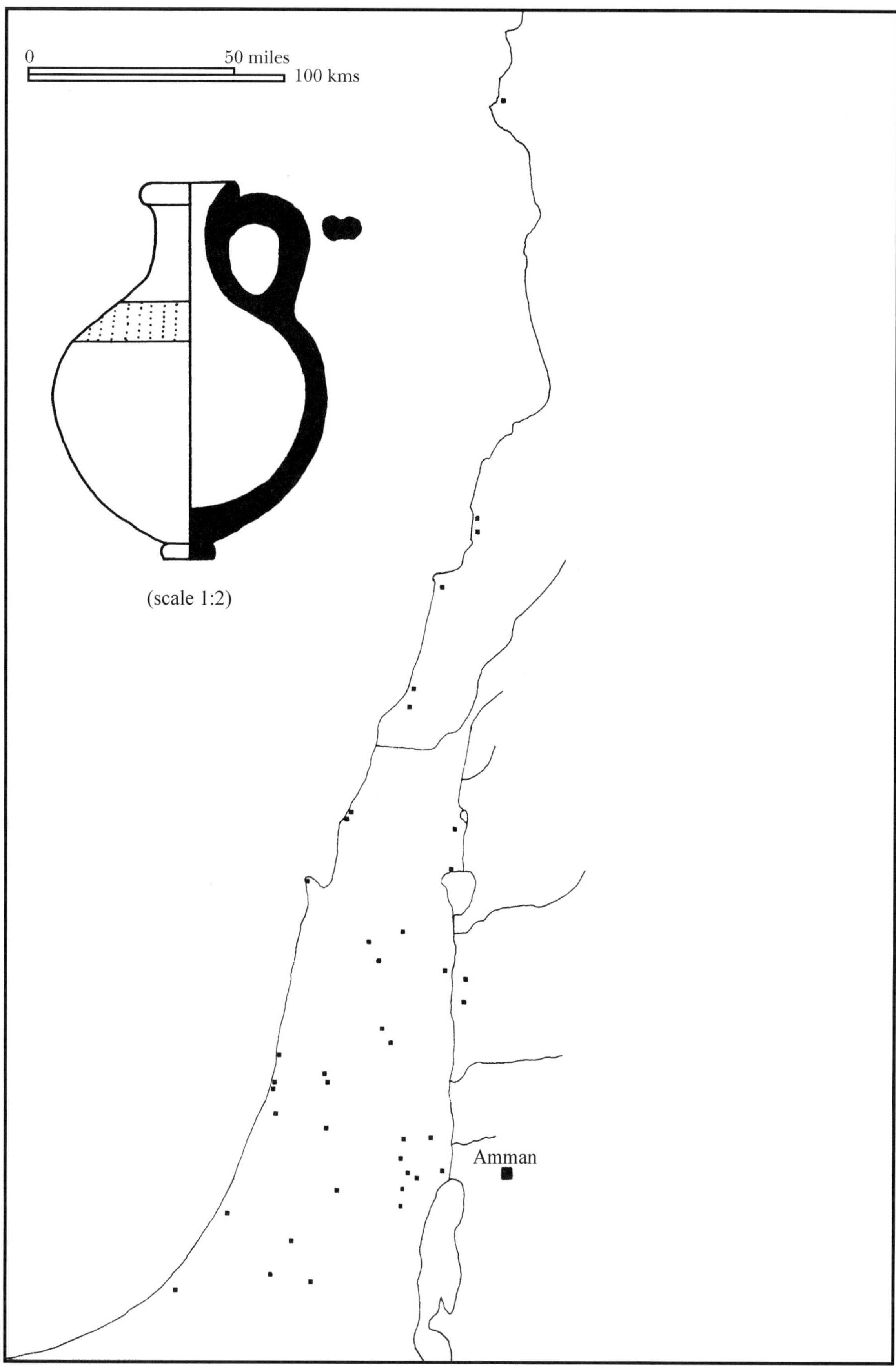

Fig. 40 Distribution and Shape Class of Type Group C.1.6

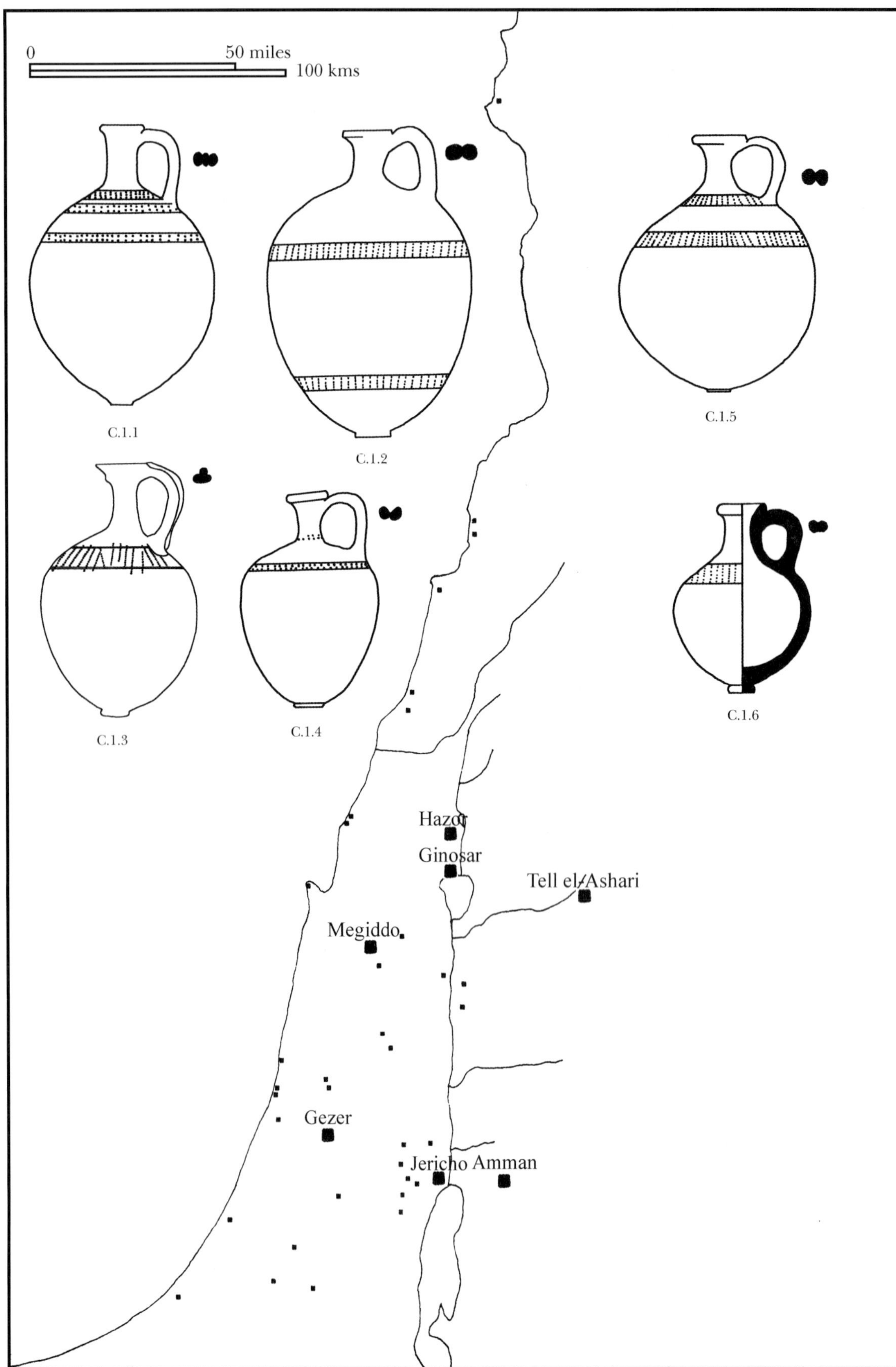

Fig. 41 Combined Distribution of Type Group C.1

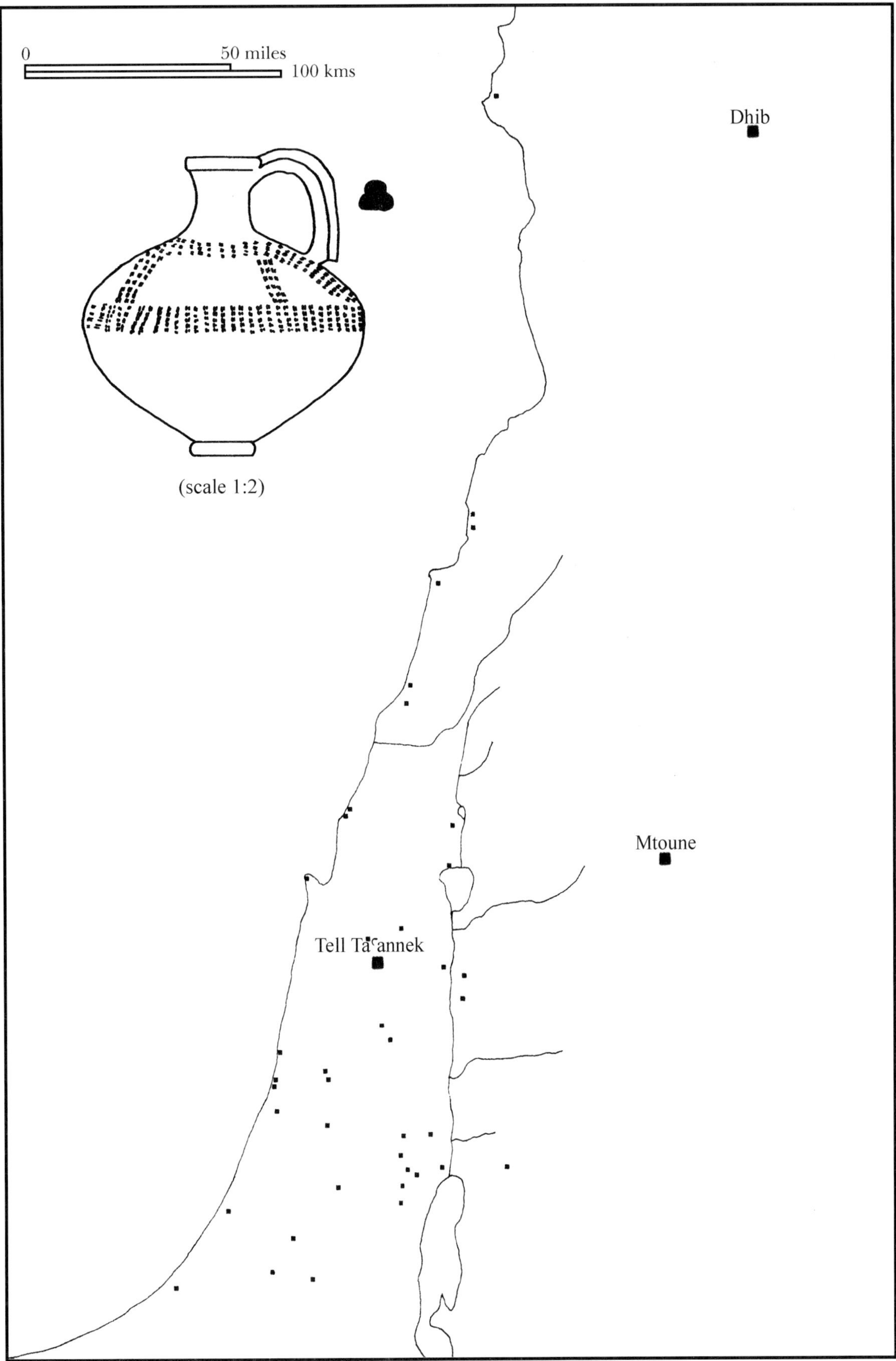

Fig. 42 Distribution and Shape Class of Type Group C.2

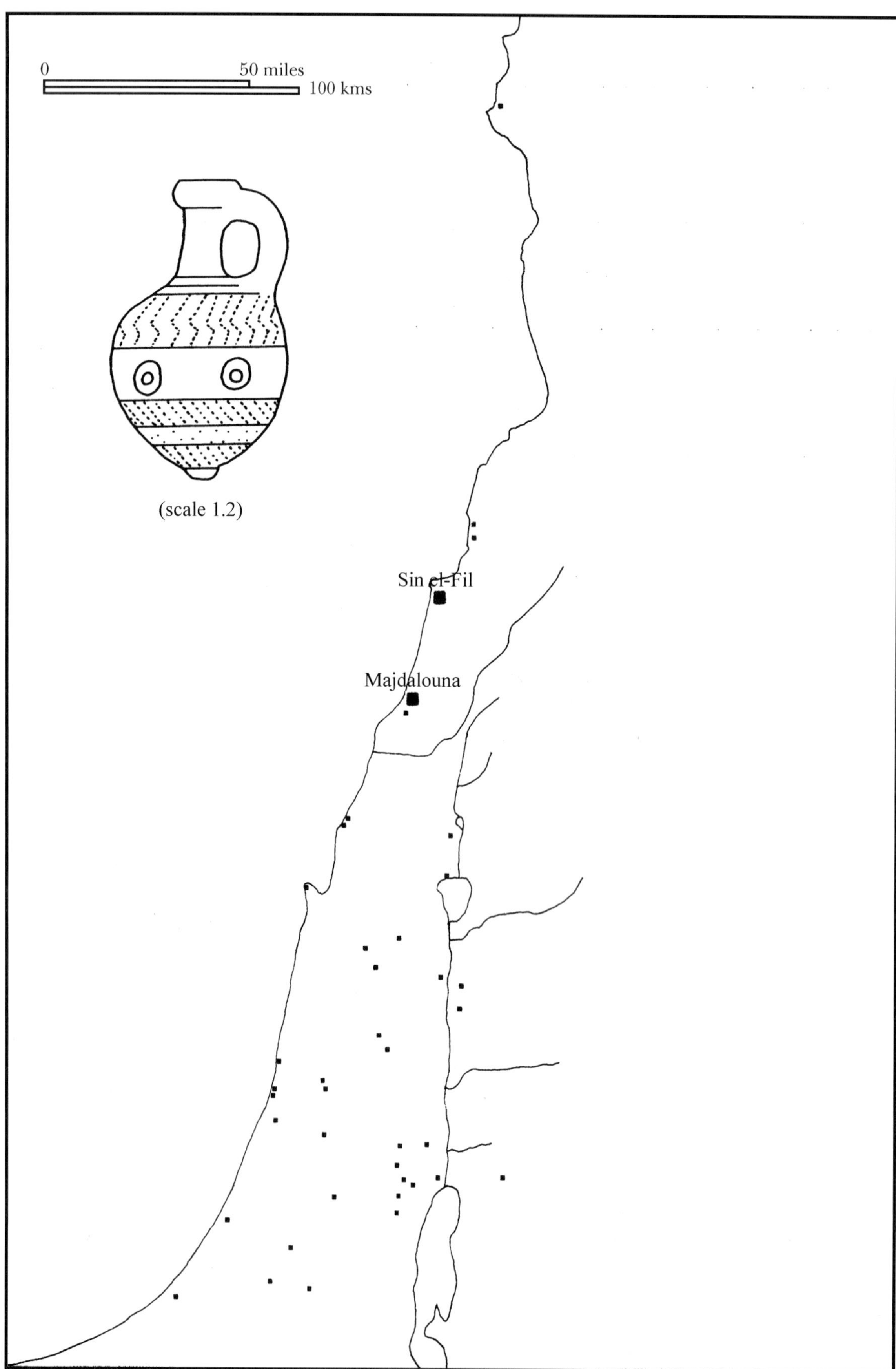

Fig. 43 Distribution and Shape Class of Type Group C.3

jugs found in tombs to be smaller in size than previously. The burnished surface is now either grey to black or reddish brown. All known examples are produced from Palestinian clays.[280]

Since not much is known about the development of Tell el-Yahudiya Ware in the northern Levant during the later MB IIB–C periods, the few pieces known to us are included with the Late Palestinian group simply for convenience. There is, however, increasing evidence to show that Tell el-Yahudiya production in Inner Syria developed along its own independent lines, but a study of Syrian Tell el-Yahudiya Ware has not yet been systematically undertaken. However vessels found at Damascus, Hauran, Jebel el-Arab, Tell Sakka, Julan and the Suweida region all point to a local Syrian manufacture.[281]

D.1. Late Palestinian I

Type Group D.1.1 (Fig. 44)

Vessels of type group D.1.1 are clearly related to the Middle Palestinian I group, but these vessels have everted rims, bipartite handles and offset disc bases. Running around the midpoint is a delineated band of vertical chevrons. Examples of vessels of type group D.1, which are distinctly ovoid are known from Megiddo,[282] Lachish tomb 145[283] and Jericho.[284]

Late Palestinian II–IV (Kaplan's Piriform 3)

The Late Palestinian groups II–IV can be equated with Kaplan's Piriform 3 types, and are here divided by their handle forms, bipartite in the cases of Late Palestinian II and III, and strap in the case of Late Palestinian IV. Late Palestinian II and III are separated from one another by the base forms, which comprise ring or disc bases in the case of Late Palestinian II, and button bases in Late Palestinian III.

D.2. Late Palestinian II

Type Group D.2.1 (Figs. 45, 49)

This group consists, at least at present, of only one example from Beth Shemesh.[285] It is the only jug from the so-called Piriform 3 jugs of Kaplan which has a ledged candlestick rim. Such rims occur in Tell el-Dab^ca in Strata F-E/3 (transitional MBIIA-B – early MBIIB). The unique character of this jug can also be deduced by the fact that it is not burnished. The handle is bipartite and the base button is an offset disc. There are two bands of ornament on the shoulder with vertical comb imprints.

Type Group D.2.2 (Figs. 46, 49)

Type group D.2.2 can be seen as a continuation of group C.1.3, and most have a plump piriform shape, a rolled rim, bipartite handle, in contrast to the small Piriform 3 jugs, group D.4, which invariably have a strap handle, and offset disc base. The height ranges from between 14 to 18 cm. Vessels from Jericho[286] tend to have single bands of delineated chevrons on the shoulder, whilst vessels from Malacha[287] have single horizontal bands on the lower body, filled with chevrons. Another vessel from Silat edh-Dhahar has two bands of chevrons at the base of the neck, and below the handle.[288] Another incomplete jug from Jericho is presumably also to be included in this group through the similarities in the decoration to the Silat edh-Dhahar vessel.[289] To this group should

---

280 KAPLAN, *Tell el-Yahudiyeh Ware*, 229, 231.

281 TARAQJI A.F., Nouvelles découvertes sur les relations avec l'Égypte à Tel Sakka et à Keswé dans la region de Damas, *BSFE* 144, (1999), 27–43; NIGRO L., The MB Pottery Horizon of Tell Mardikh/Ancient Ebla, in: M. BIETAK (ed.), *The Middle Bronze Age in the Levant*, Vienna, 2002, 297–328. IDEM, The Smith and the King of Ebla. Tell el-Yahudiyeh ware, Metallic Wares and the Ceramic technology of Middle Bronze Syria, in: M. BIETAK (ed.), *The Synchronisation of Civilisations in the Eastern Mediterranean in the Second Millennium II*, Vienna, 2003, 345–363.

282 LOUD, *Megiddo II*, 1948, pl. 32.32; Kaplan, *Tell el-Yahudiyeh Ware*, fig. 64f.

283 O. TUFNELL, *Lachish IV*, 1958, 189, 230, pl. 77.727; KAPLAN, *Tell el-Yahudiyeh Ware*, fig. 63c.

284 Leeds City Museum J.33.20.d.14 - KAPLAN, *Tell el-Yahudiyeh Ware*, fig. 63d.

285 Philadelphia UM 61-14-112; GRANT, *AASOR* 9, 1928, 7: IDEM, *Beth Shemesh*, 151 no. 236, 156; KAPLAN, *Tell el-Yahudiyeh Ware*, fig. 74a.

286 Paris Louvre AO 15676. GARSTANG, 1933, 21–27, pl. 17.5. KAPLAN, *Tell el-Yahudiyeh Ware*, fig. 73a Paris Louvre AO 17084. KAPLAN, *Tell el-Yahudiyeh Ware*, fig. 71b: Emory Univeresity Museum J 11194, KENYON, *Jericho II*, 1964, 303–312, fig. 147.8, KAPLAN, *Tell el-Yahudiyeh Ware*, fig. 68b. Jerusalem Rockefeller Museum 32.1091, KAPLAN, *Tell el-Yahudiyeh Ware*, fig. 68a. Jerusalem Rockefeller Museum 32.1194, Kaplan, *Tell el-Yahudiyeh Ware*, fig. 80a; Birmingham City Museum, KAPLAN, *Tell el-Yahudiyeh Ware*, fig. 80b.

287 Jerusalem Clarke Collection 2728. KAPLAN, *Tell el-Yahudiyeh Ware*, fig. 81c.

288 Jerusalem. Museum of the Flagellation. KAPLAN, *Tell el-Yahudiyeh Ware*, fig. 79b.

289 Jerusalem, Rockefeller Museum 32.1194. GARSTANG, Jericho. City and Necropolis (II), *LAAA* 20, 1933, 27–36; KAPLAN, *Tell el-Yahudiyeh Ware*, fig. 80a.

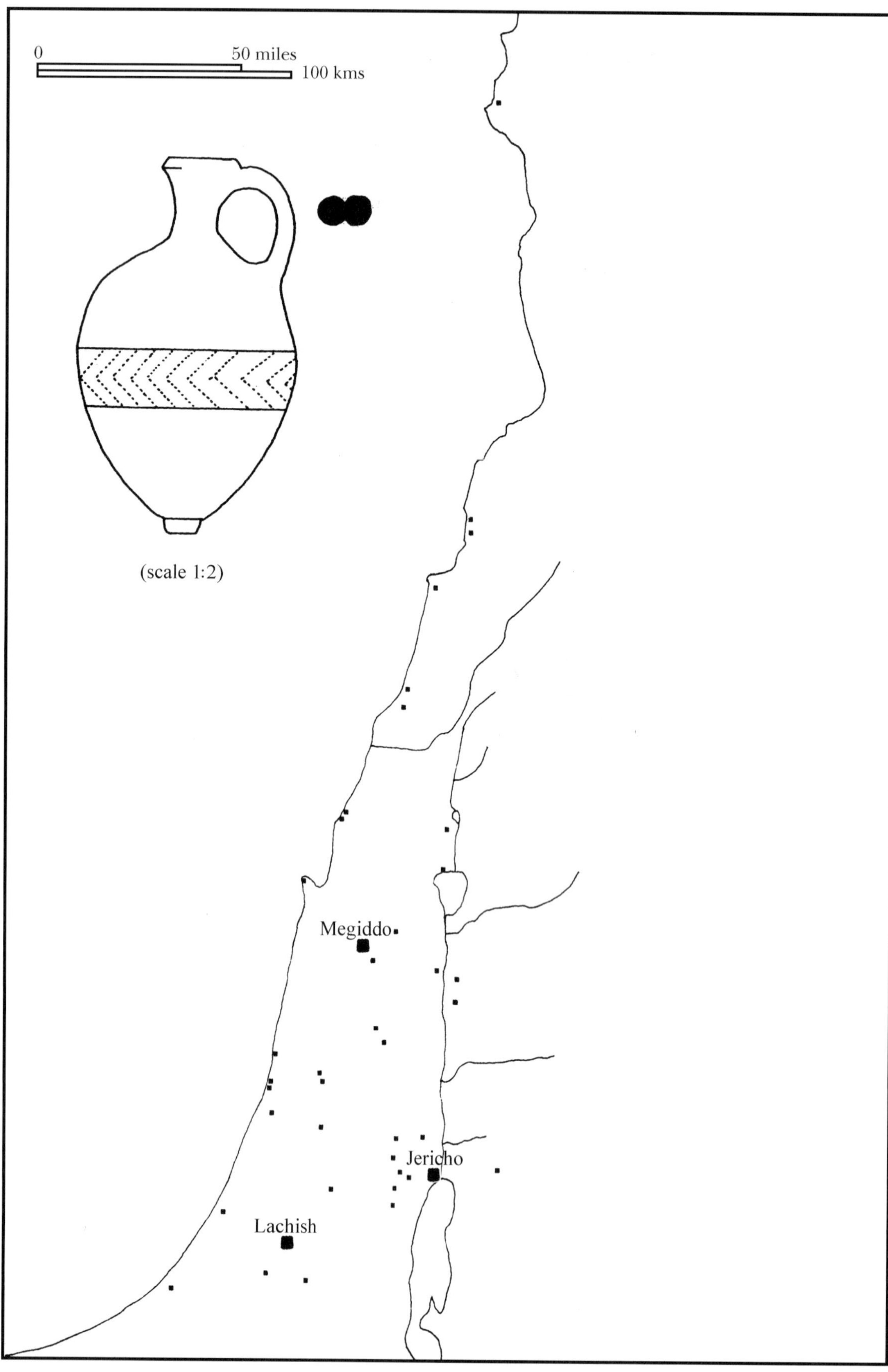

Fig. 44 Distribution and Shape Class of Type Group D.1

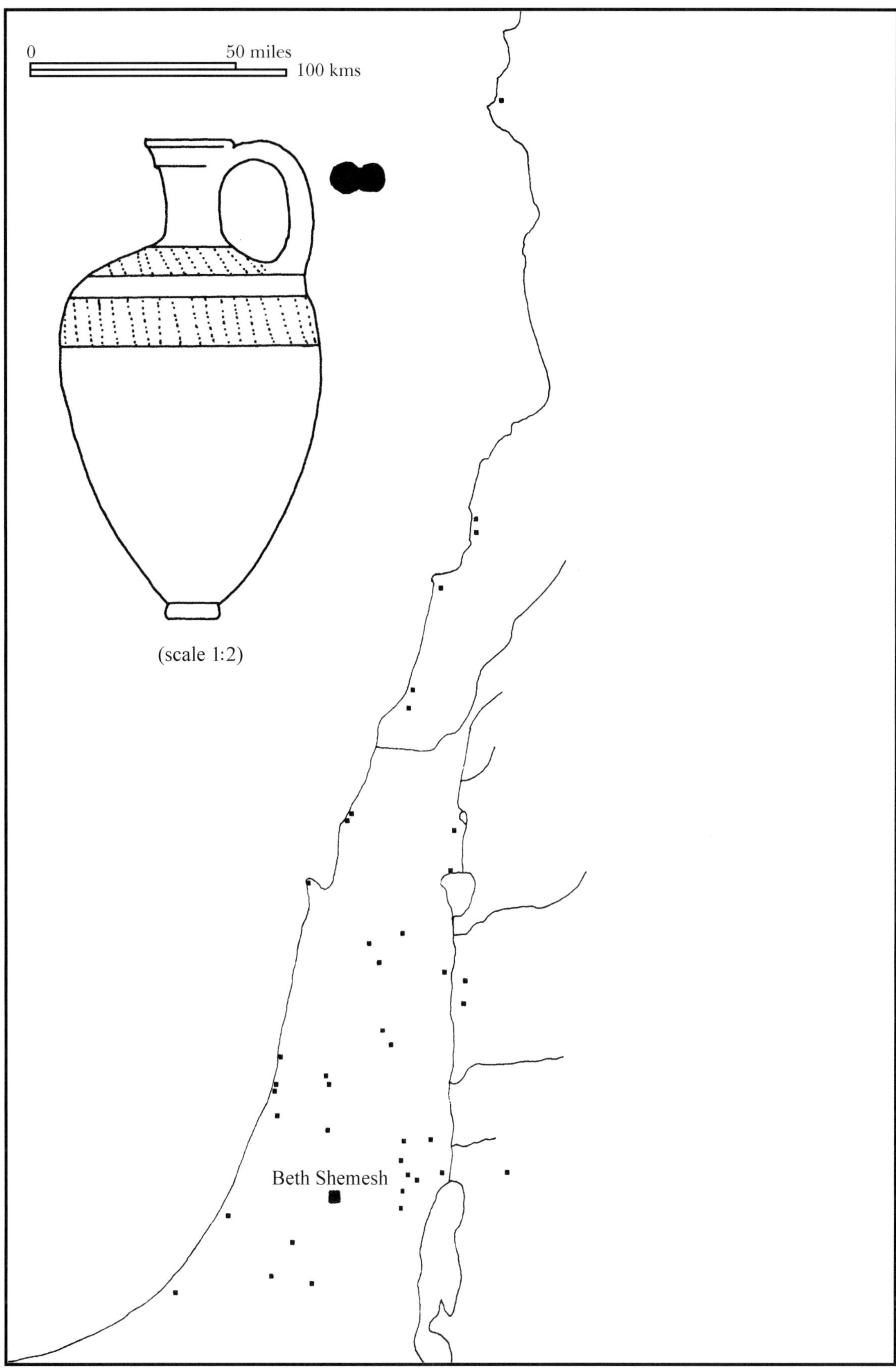

Fig. 45 Distribution and Shape Class of Type Group D.2.1

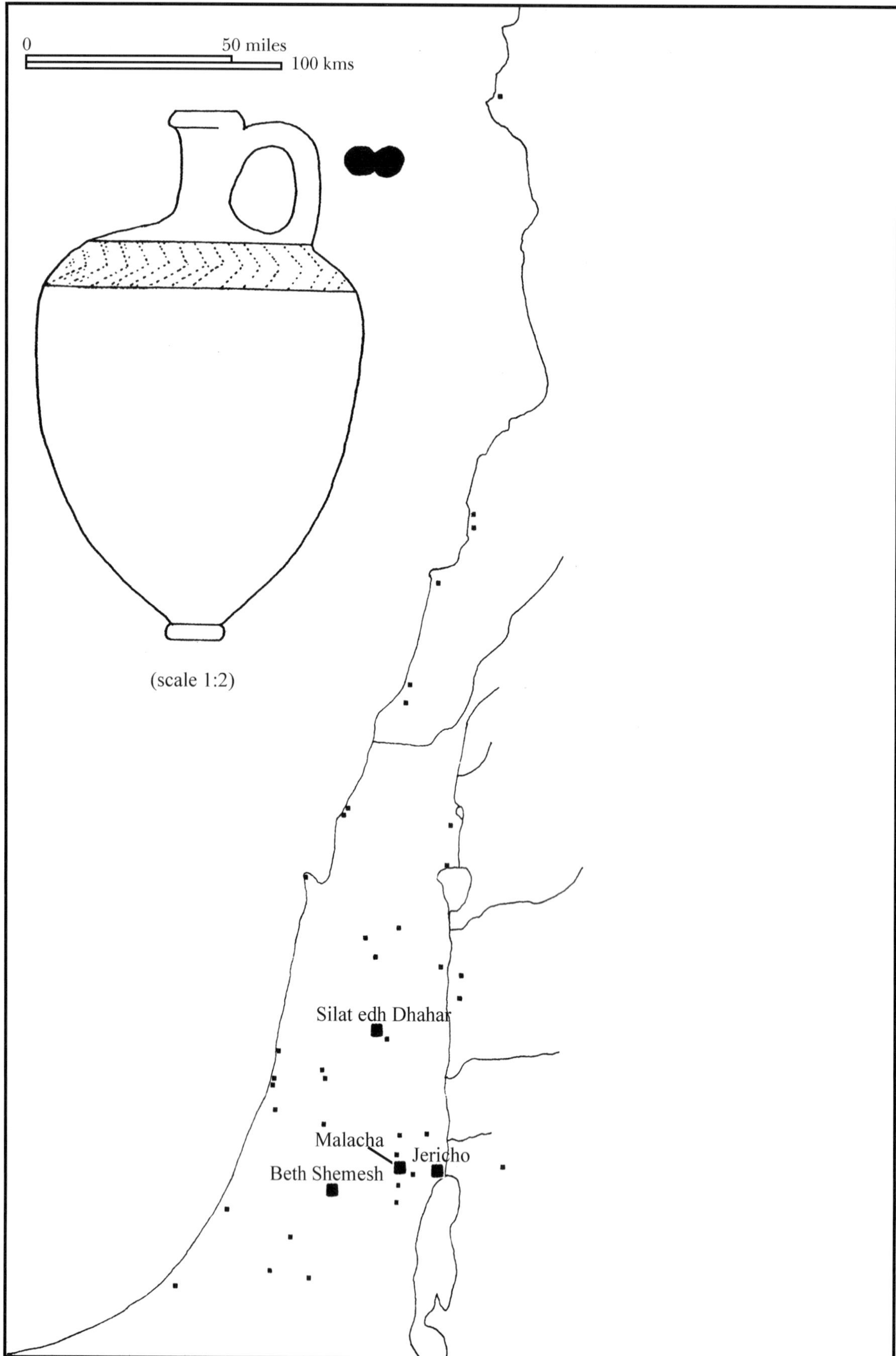

Fig. 46 Distribution and Shape Class of Type Group D.2.2

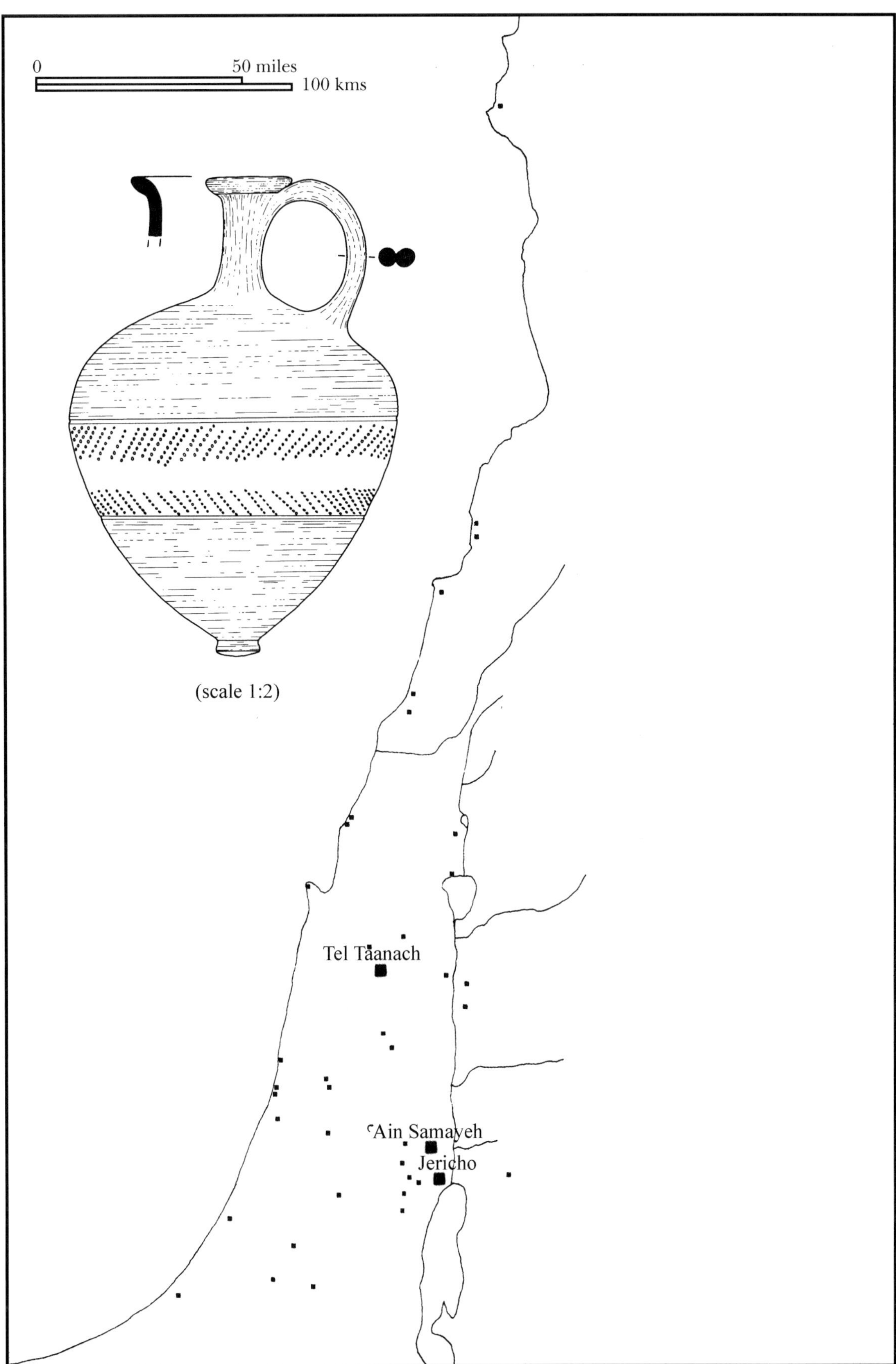

Fig. 47 Distribution and Shape Class of Type Group D.2.3

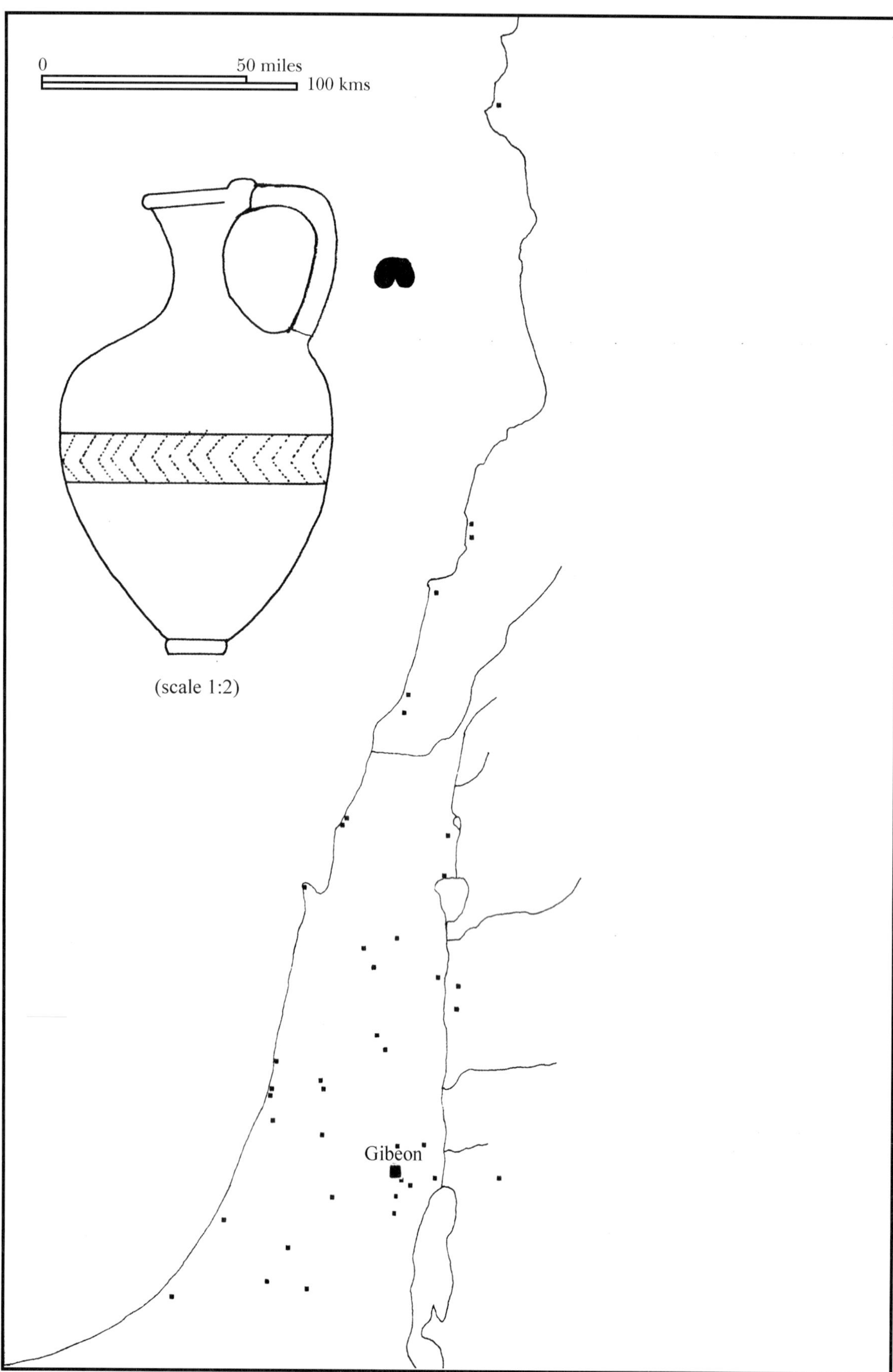

Fig. 48 Distribution and Shape Class of Type Group D.2.4

perhaps also be added a vessel from Jericho with two delineated bands of vertical rows of indentations,[290] and perhaps an incomplete pot from Beth Shemish.[291]

Type Group D.2.3 (Figs. 47, 49)

A number of jugs from ᶜAin Samayeh,[292] Jericho,[293] and Tell Taᶜannek,[294] are clearly associated with group D.2 through their size (c. 16 cm. tall). They have bipartite or even tripartite handles, a rounded base button and one or two horizontal ornament bands filled with an indented herringbone pattern on the lower body.

Type Group D.2.4 (Figs. 48, 49)

Small Piriform jugs with rolled rims, double handles and ring bases are known from Gibeon being decorated with a single band of chevrons.[295]

D.3. Late Palestinian III

Type Group D.3.1 (Figs. 50, 52))

Closely associated with the vessels of group D.2.1 is a vessel from Gezer[296] with a bipartite handle, but this time with a distinct button base. It is decorated with two horizontal bands of incised dots made with an eight-toothed comb. Perhaps to this group should also be attributed a jug from Gibeon, though it only has one band of decoration.[297]

Type Group D.3.2 (Figs. 51, 52))

Group D.3.2 consists of small piriform jugs with direct rims, double handles and offset button bases, known from Jericho.[298]

D.4. Late Palestinian IV

Type group D.4, comprise those of Kaplan's Piriform 3 jugs with single strap handles. Within group D.4 are the small Piriform 3 Tell el-Yahudiya jugs, types D.4.2–3, which comprise the largest group of Tell el Yahudiya vessels known from Palestine in the MB IIB–C period. In size they range between 10 and 14 cms. tall, and almost all are piriform with a tendency towards a flat shoulder. Most of these jugs have a strap handle. The ornament zones are generally on the lower body, though there are exceptions. Through differences in rim types, handles, bases, and decoration at least three subgroups can be distinguished. Single jugs with exceptional designs may enlarge this group in future when the discovery of more such examples would constitute specific sub-groups. Overall they can be divided into the following types: The decoration on all types generally comprises one or two horizontal bands of chevrons or, in rare cases, vertical rows of dots.

Type Group D.4.1 (Figs. 53, 57)

Type Group D.4.1 consists of at least two large vessels, both from Jericho, which are somewhat similar to type group D.1, but have single strap handles, rather than the more usual bipartite ones. Both have rolled rims, disc bases and a single vertical herringbone band located on the lower body.[299]

Type Group D.4.2 (Figs. 54, 57)

Type group D.4.2 comprises small piriform jugs with rolled rims, strap handles and offset disc bases, known from Gezer[300] Abu Dis,[301] Jericho,[302]

---

[290] Paris Louvre AO 17084. Kaplan, *Tell el-Yahudiyeh Ware,* fig. 71b.

[291] Grant, 1929, 127 no. 672; Kaplan, *Tell el-Yahudiyeh Ware,* fig. 75b.

[292] Kaplan, *Tell el-Yahudiyeh Ware,* fig. 70b (private collection), and 71a, (Harvard Semitic Museum, 907.76.32).

[293] Birmingham City Museum 568.58a. Kenyon, *Jericho II,* 332–357, fig. 168.26: St Andrews, Kenyon, *Jericho II,* fig. 122.6; Kaplan, *Tell el-Yahudiyeh Ware,* fig. 64e: Oxford Ashmolean 1955.531, Kenyon, *Jericho II,* 448–465, fig. 235.9: Jerusalem Rockefeller Museum 32.1216, Garstang, 1933, 27–36; Kaplan, *Tell el-Yahudiyeh Ware,* fig. 72b.

[294] Sellin, *Tell Taᶜanek,* 1904, 52 fig. 57, Kaplan, *Tell el-Yahudiyeh Ware,* fig. 66b.

[295] Philadelphia UM 62–30–260, Pritchard *Gibeon,* 58–60, figs. 61.20, 97.8, Kaplan, *Tell el-Yahudiyeh Ware,* fig. 67b.

[296] Jerusalem H.U. 61. Kaplan, *Tell el-Yahudiyeh Ware,* fig. 80c.

[297] Jerusalem Rockefeller Museum 45.129; Kaplan, *Tell el-Yahudiyeh Ware,* fig. 66f.

[298] Jericho tomb D6. Melbourne, Aust Inst Arch, Kenyon, *Jericho II,* 274–276, fig. 131.7; Kaplan, *Tell el-Yahudiyeh Ware,* fig. 66a.

[299] Amman J.7035, Kenyon, *Jericho II,* 358–368, fig. 177.5; Kaplan, *Tell el-Yahudiyeh Ware,* fig. 72a: Toronto ROM 955.166.17. Kenyon, Jericho II, 410–420, fig. 214.6; Kaplan, *Tell el-Yahudiyeh Ware,* fig. 65b: Kenyon, Jericho II, 410–420, fig. 214.8; Kaplan, *Tell el-Yahudiyeh Ware,* fig. 65c.

[300] Macalister, *Gezer,* 1912, III pl. 153.8; Kaplan, *Tell el-Yahudiyeh Ware,* fig. 66c.

[301] Jerusalem, Rockefeller Museum, 38.1876. Kaplan, *Tell el-Yahudiyeh Ware,* fig. 63b.

[302] Cambridge Mus. of Arch. and Anth. 54.253B. Kenyon, *Jericho I,* 1960, 418–425, fig. 175.17; Kaplan, *Tell el-Yahudiyeh Ware,* fig. 63a: Jerusalem Rockefeller Museum 33.1073, Kaplan, *Tell el-Yahudiyeh Ware,* fig. 63e; Toronto ROM 955.166.67, Kenyon, *Jericho II,* 410–420, fig. 214.7; Kaplan, *Tell el-Yahudiyeh Ware,* fig. 65a: Manchester UM 9805, Kaplan, *Tell el-Yahudiyeh Ware,* fig. 69b; Oxford Ashmolean 1955.531, Kenyon *Jericho II,* 448–465, fig. 235.9; Kaplan, *Tell el-Yahudiyeh Ware,* fig. 64d: others: Kenyon, *Jericho II,* 410–420, fig. 214.8; Kaplan, *Tell el-Yahudiyeh Ware,* figs. 64c, 65d, 66d.

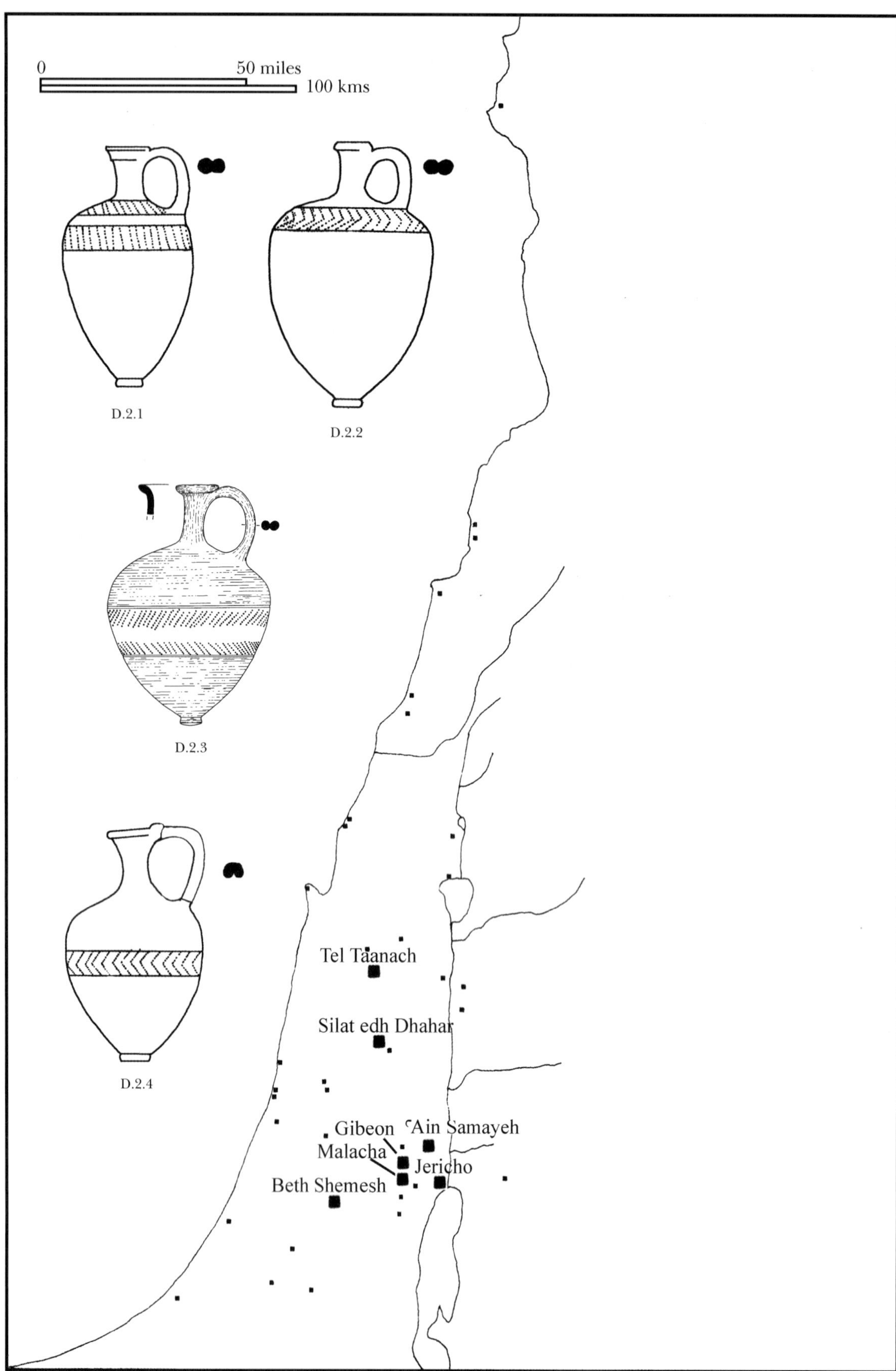

Fig. 49 Combined Distribution of Type Group D.2

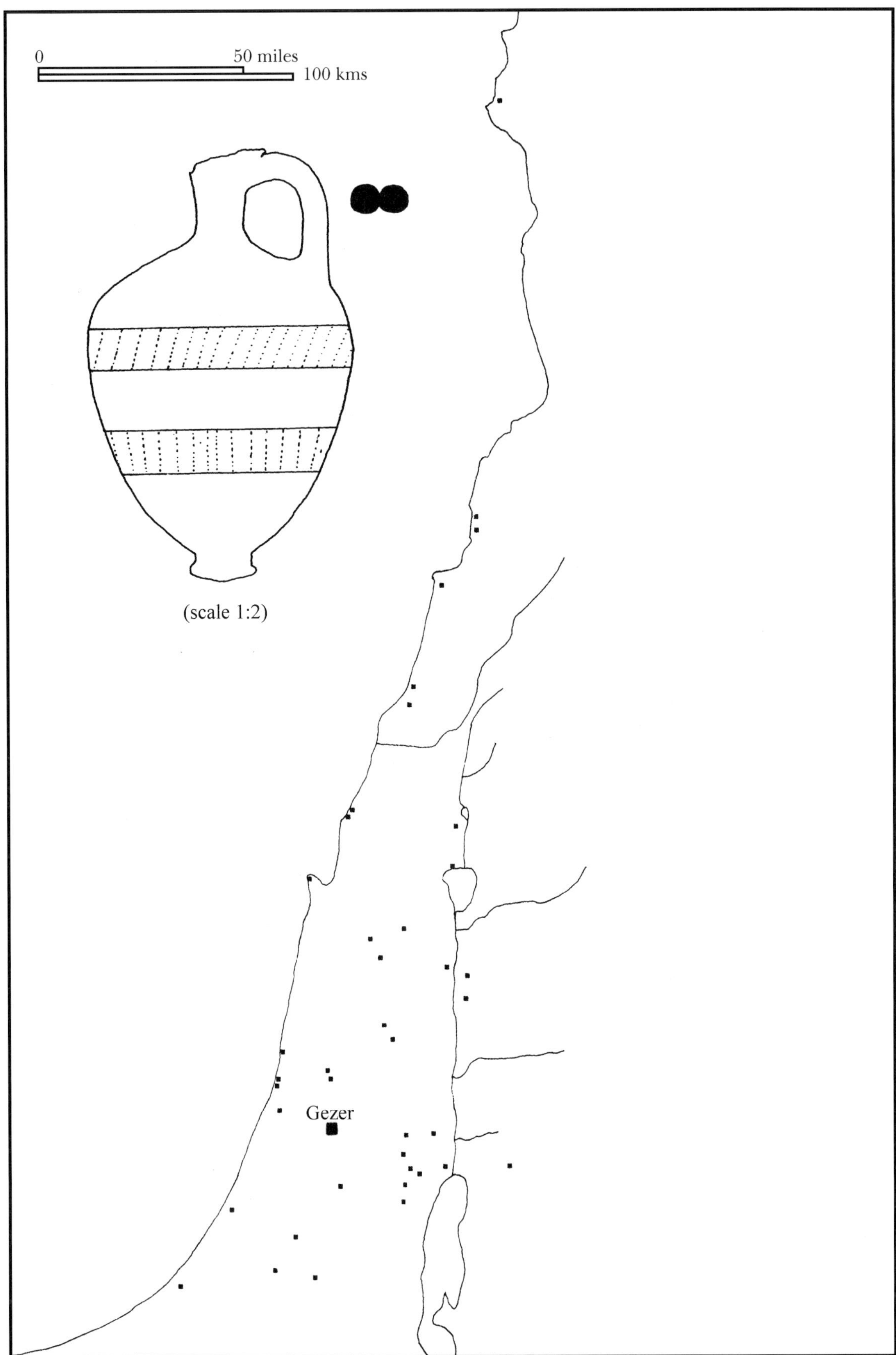

Fig. 50 Distribution and Shape Class of Type Group D.3.1

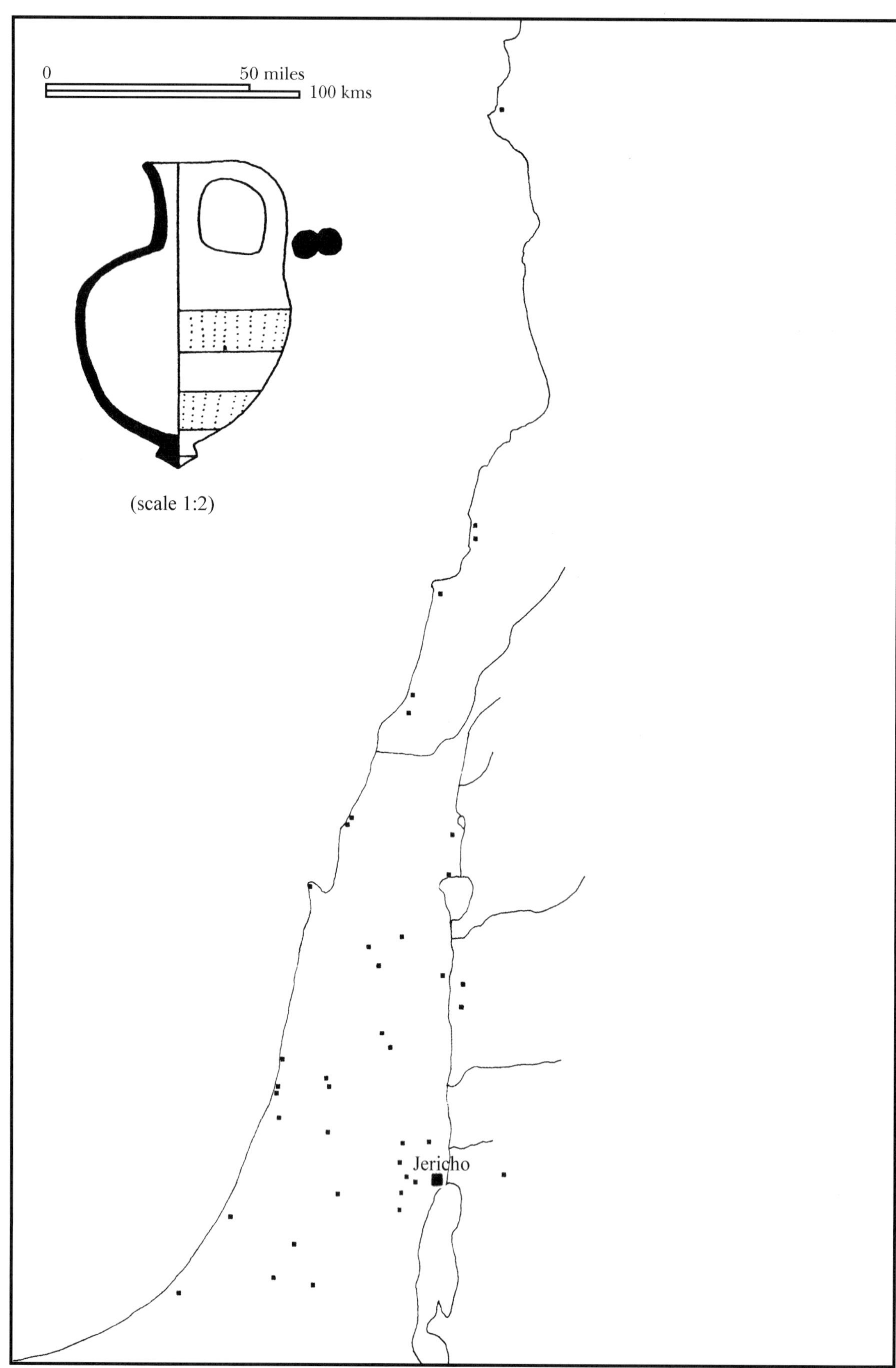

Fig. 51 Distribution and Shape Class of Type Group D.3.2

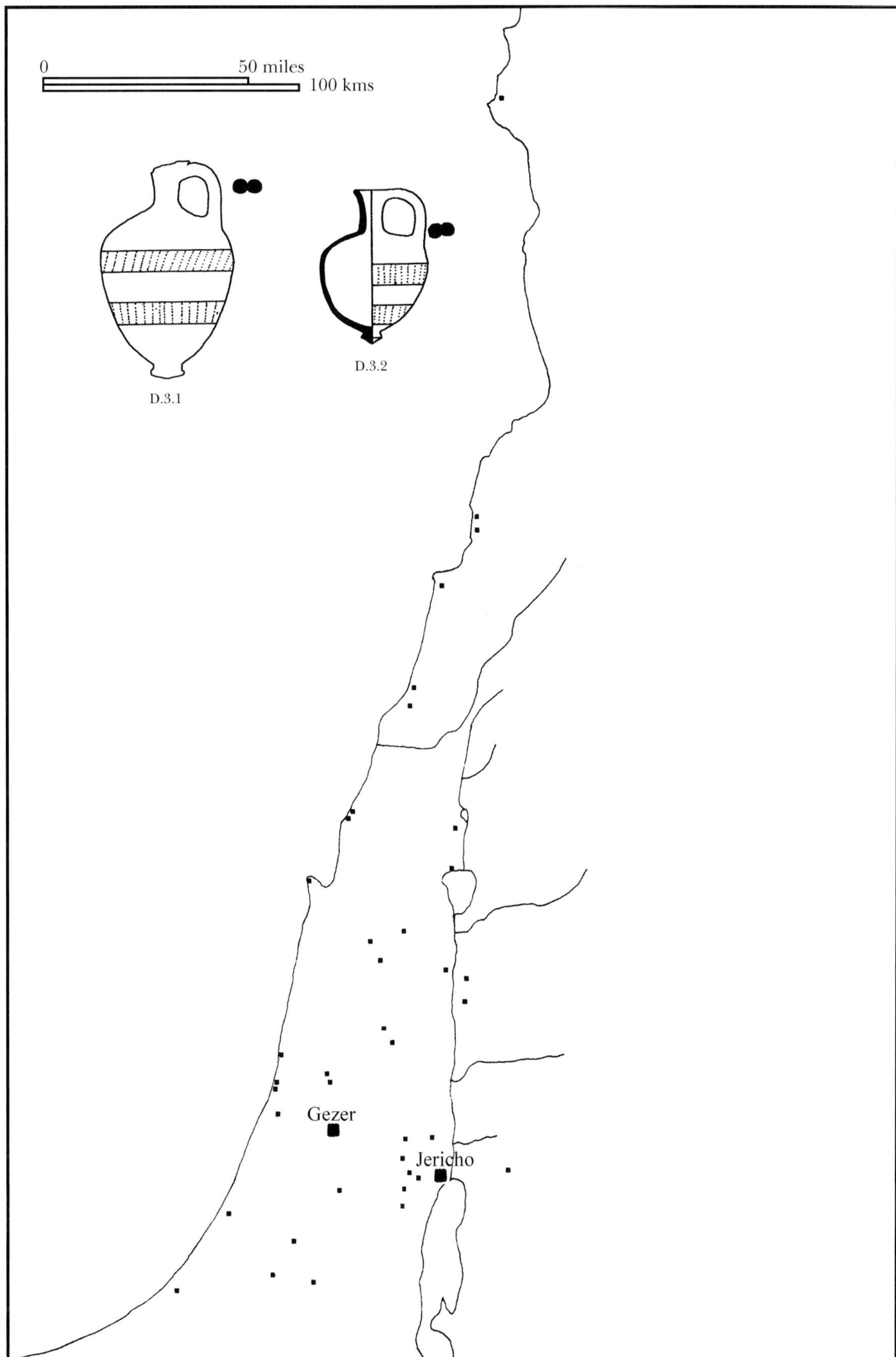

Fig. 52 Combined Distribution of Type Group D.3

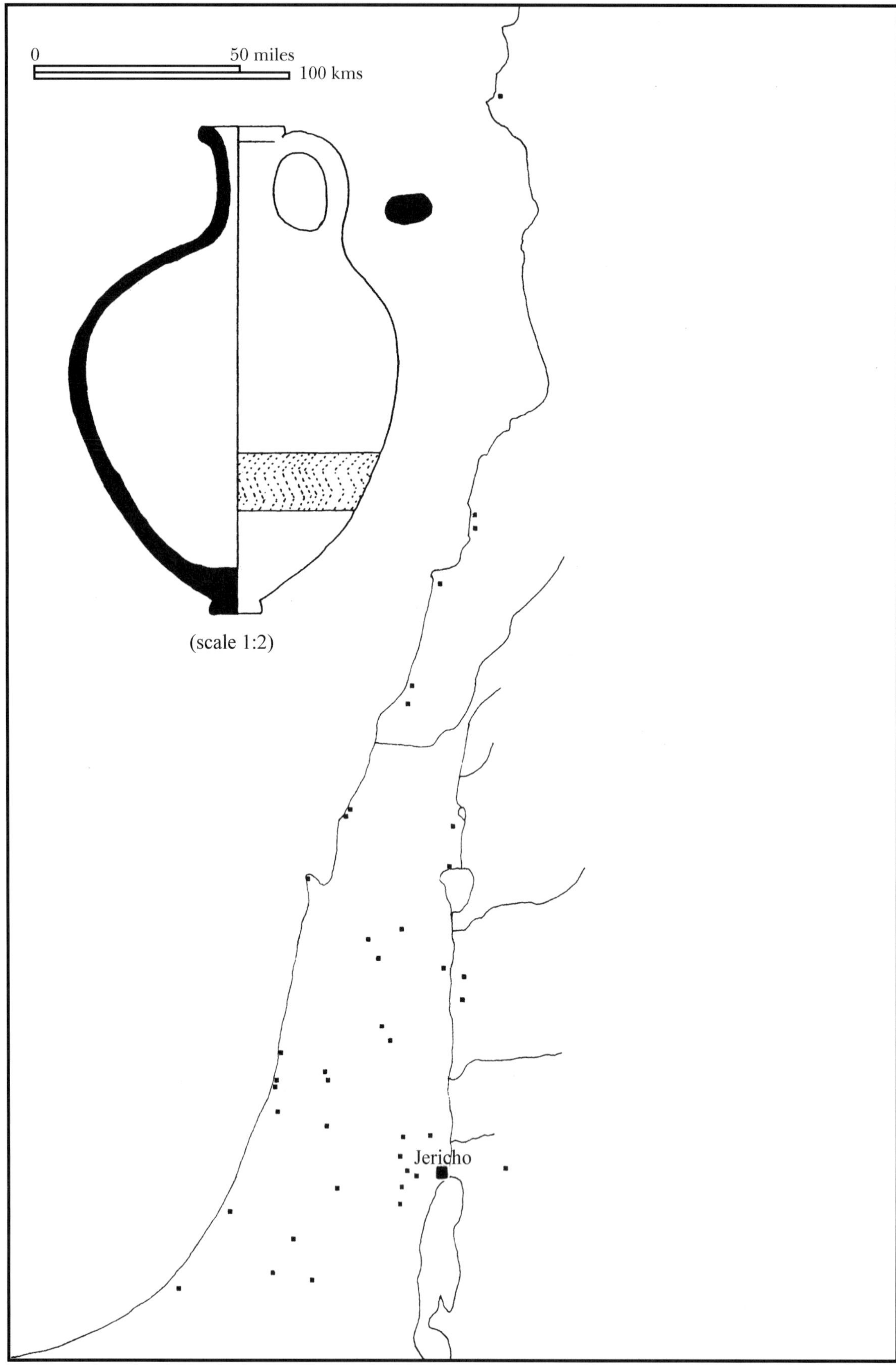

Fig. 53 Distribution and Shape Class of Type Group D.4.1

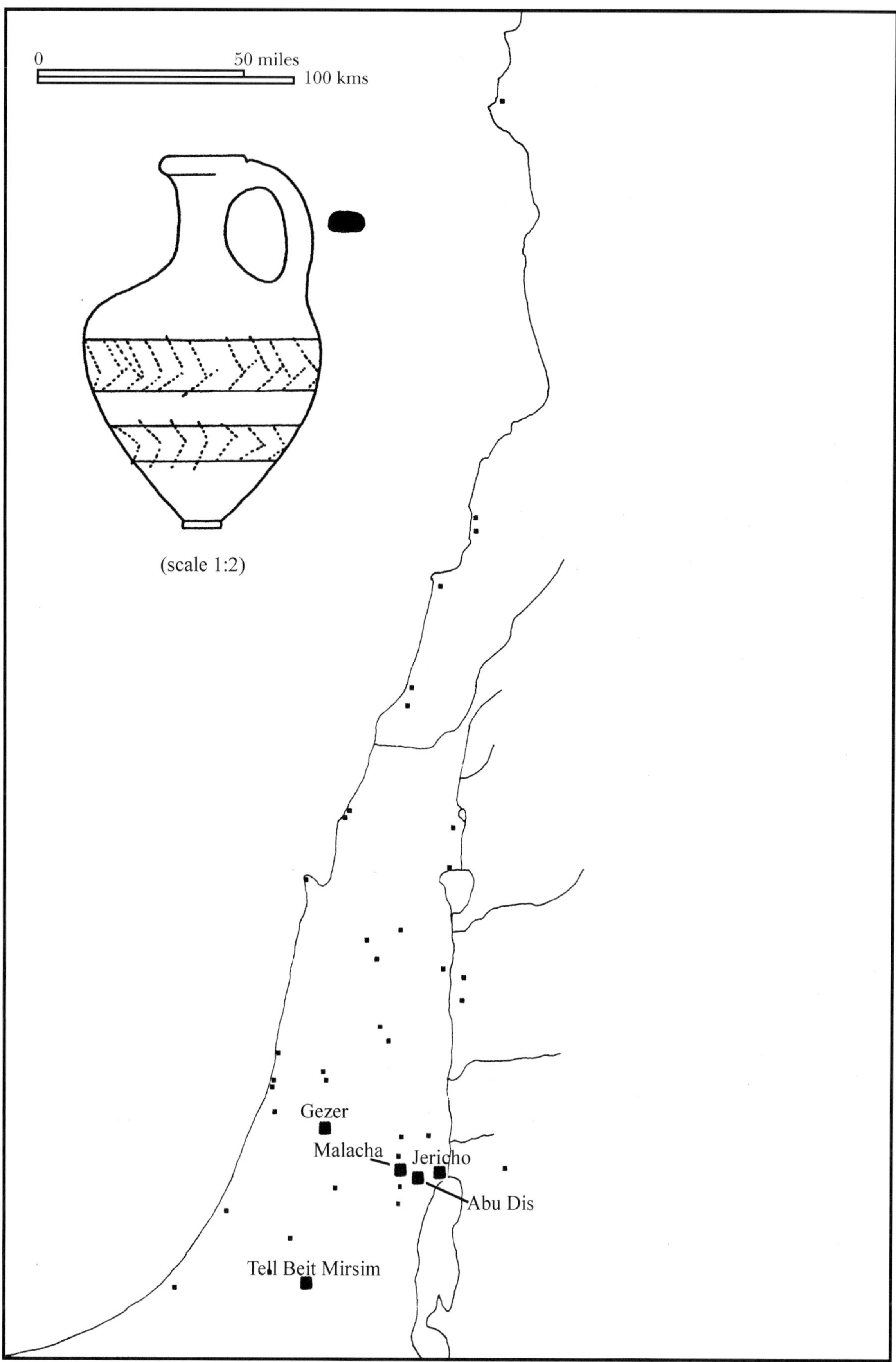

Fig. 54 Distribution and Shape Class of Type Group D.4.2

Malacha,[303] and Tell Beit Mirsim,[304] and are decorated with one or two bands of chevrons, which sometimes extend beyond the delineated bands. An apparent vessel of this type was exported to Cyprus, where it was found in a tomb at Milia.[305] A variant vessel from Jericho tomb J20 has two bands of oblique lines instead of the more normal chevrons.[306]

Type Group D.4.3 (Figs. 55, 57)

The group comprises small piriform jugs with rolled rims, strap handles and offset button bases, known from Jericho.[307] To this group can also be added vessels now in Haifa[308] and Tel Aviv.[309] The decoration usually comprises one or two bands of delineated chevrons.

Type Group D.4.4 (Figs. 56, 57)

Type group D.4.4 is represented by a single example from Megiddo.[310] This jug has a rolled rim, a rounded strap handle, piriform body and offset disc base. The decoration comprises two bands of chevrons and a lowermost band of oblique lines.

D.5. Late Palestinian V

In contrast to the piriform shapes of the Late Palestinian II–IV groups, jugs attributed to the Late Palestinian V group are distinctly biconical.

Type Group D.5.1 (Figs. 58, 63)

Late Palestinian biconical jugs of group D.5.1 have an everted rim, bipartite handle, and disc base. Examples are known from ᶜAin Samayeh[311] Jericho[312] and Amman.[313] The decoration compises one or two horizontal bands of herringbones, chevrons or oblique lines.

Type Group D.5.2 (Figs. 59, 63)

Late Palestinian biconical jugs of group D.5.2 are similar to D.5.1 but have candlestick rims and button bases. A complete example of such a vessel is known from Jericho tomb D.22,[314] whilst incomplete examples which may belong with this group are also known from Jericho[315] and Tell Beit Mirsim.[316] The lower zone of decoration on this type and that found on type D.5.4 may have been influenced by contemporary Egyptian vessels of group L.2.

Type Group D.5.3 (Figs. 60, 63)

Type Group D.5.3 is represented by examples from Tell Sakka which have rolled rims, bipartite handles and ring bases (?).[317] The decoration is confined to the shoulder area consisting of two horizontal bands with comb decoration, linked by oblique bands, also with infilled comb decoration.

Type Group D.5.4 (Figs. 61, 63)

Type Group D.5.4 is known through an example found at Lachish in tomb 1552[318] made of Red Field clay.[319] Such vessels have kettle rims, bipartite handles, a plump biconical body and a slightly offset disc base. The decoration consists of an upper band of standing, and a lower band of pendant triangles

---

303 Jerusalem, YMCA 2713; Kaplan, *Tell el-Yahudiyeh Ware,* fig. 81a.

304 W.F. Albright, *Tell Beit Mirsim I: The Bronze Age Pottery of the First Three Campagins,* 1933, pl. 9.4; S. Ben Arieh, *Bronze and Iron Age Tombs at Tell Beit Mirsim,* 2004, 14, 43 fig. 2.10.51.

305 Westholm, Some Late Cypriote Tombs at Milia, *QDAP* 8, 1939, 11, pl. 6.2, Kaplan, *Tell el-Yahudiyeh Ware,* fig. 81b

306 Kenyon *Jericho II,* 410–420, fig. 214.9; Kaplan, *Tell el-Yahudiyeh Ware,* fig. 65d.

307 Oxford Ashmolean 1952.592. Kenyon, *Jericho I,* 342–351, fig. 136.23; Kaplan, *Tell el-Yahudiyeh Ware,* fig. 63f: Amman no number, Kaplan, *Tell el-Yahudiyeh Ware,* fig. 64a; Kenyon, *Jericho I,* 407–410, fig. 168.9; Kaplan, *Tell el-Yahudiyeh Ware,* fig. 64b.

308 Haifa 3120. Kaplan, *Tell el-Yahudiyeh Ware,* fig. 69a.

309 Tel Aviv Haᶜaretz Mus. 54660. Kaplan, *Tell el-Yahudiyeh Ware,* fig. 69c.

310 Jerusalem Rockefeller Museum I.3120. Guy, Megiddo Tombs, 1938 pl. 23.27, Kaplan, *Tell el-Yahudiyeh Ware,* fig. 104b.

311 Kaplan, *Tell el-Yahudiyeh Ware,* fig. 70b: Harvard Semitic Museum 907.76.32, Kaplan, *Tell el-Yahudiyeh Ware,* fig. 71a.

312 Tomb B51, Birmingham City museum 568.58a, Kenyon, *Jericho II,* 332–357, fig. 168.26 = Kaplan, *Tell el-Yahudiyeh Ware,* fig. 73b.

313 Amman National Museum J.1545, Kaplan, *Tell el-Yahudiyeh Ware,* fig. 75a.

314 Birmingham J.32.22.d.36, Garstang 1932, 51–54, pl. 41.1; Kaplan, *Tell el-Yahudiyeh Ware,* fig. 76a.

315 Kenyon, *Excavations at Jericho II,* 331 fig. 162.3.

316 S. Ben Arieh, *Bronze and Iron Age Tombs at Tell Beit Mirsim,* 2004, 14, 43 fig. 2.10.50

317 A.F. Taraqji, Nouvelles découvertes sur les relations avec l'Égypte à Tel Sakka et à Keswé dans la region de Damas, *BSFE* 144, 1999, 41, fig. 12.

318 London, Institute of Archaeology 1552.2173, Tufnell, *Lachish II,* 1958, 272, pl. 50.15, pl. 77.728: Kaplan, *Tell el-Yahudiyeh Ware,* fig. 104c.

319 London, Institute of Archaeology. Tufnell, *Lachish IV,* 1958, 272, pl. 50.15, pl. 77.728. NAA analysis, Kaplan, *Tell el-Yahudiyeh Ware,* 232, sample L4.

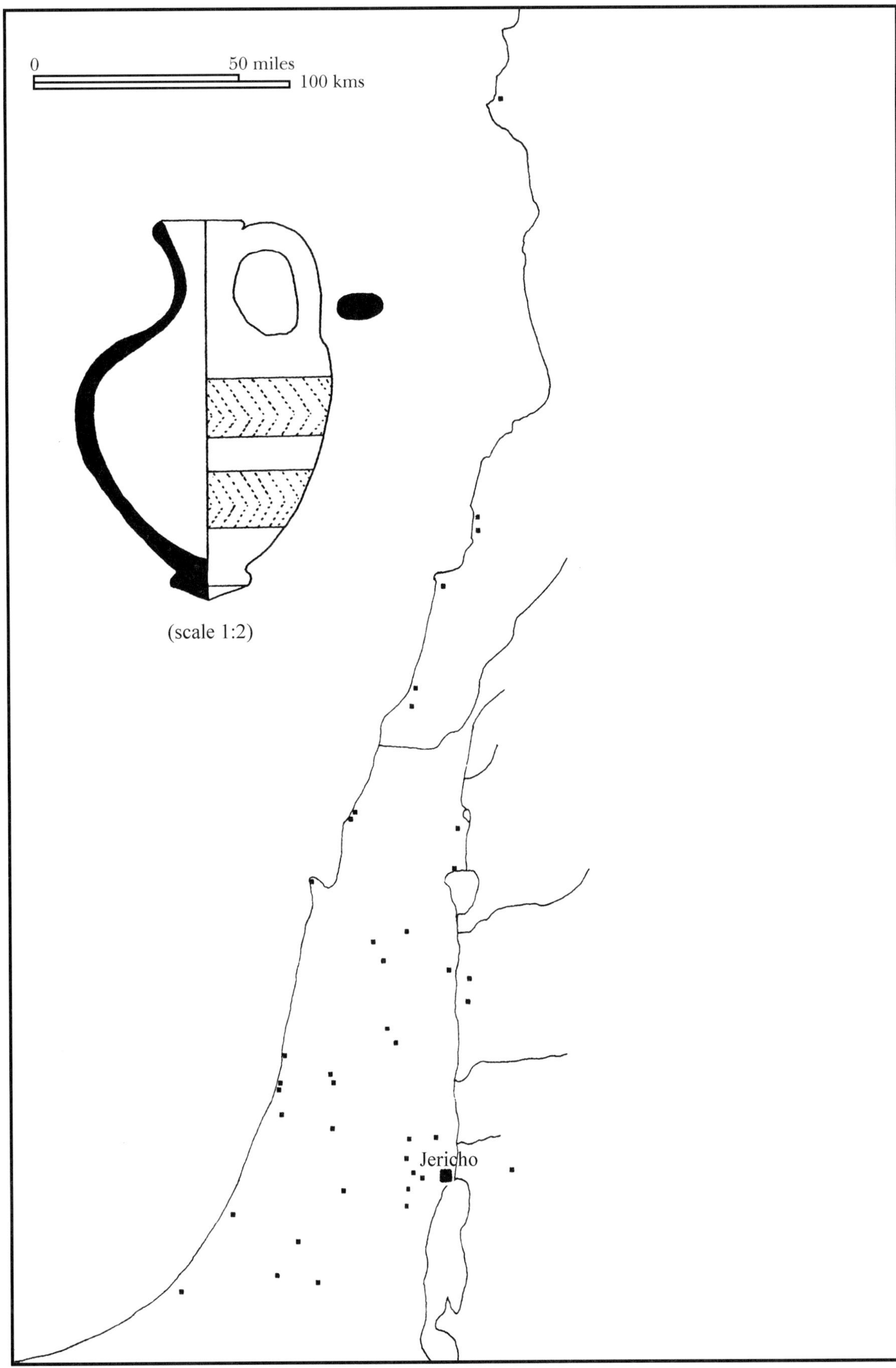

Fig. 55 Distribution and Shape Class of Type Group D.4.3

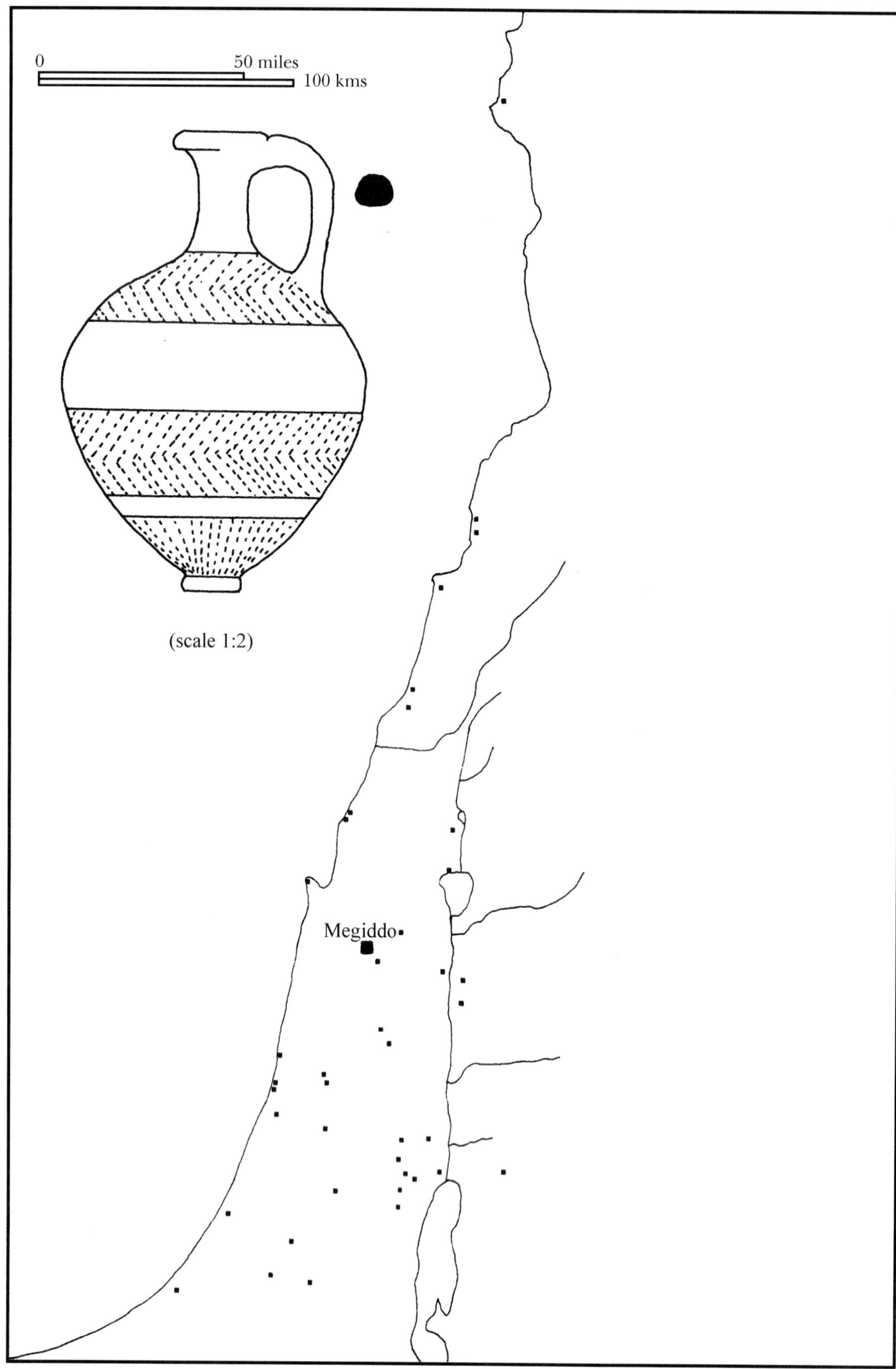

Fig. 56 Distribution and Shape Class of Type Group D.4.4

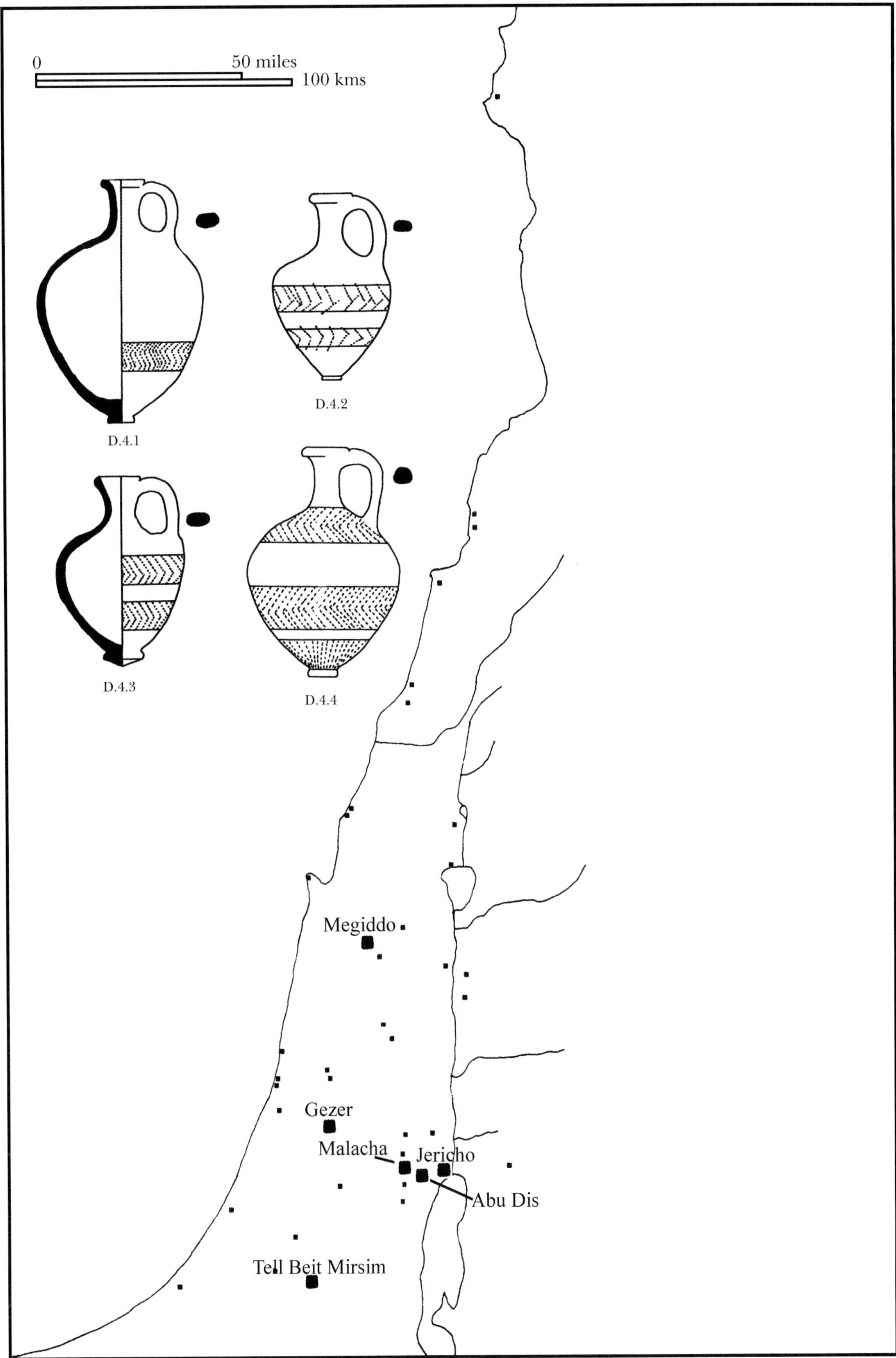

Fig. 57 Combined Distribution of Type Group D.4

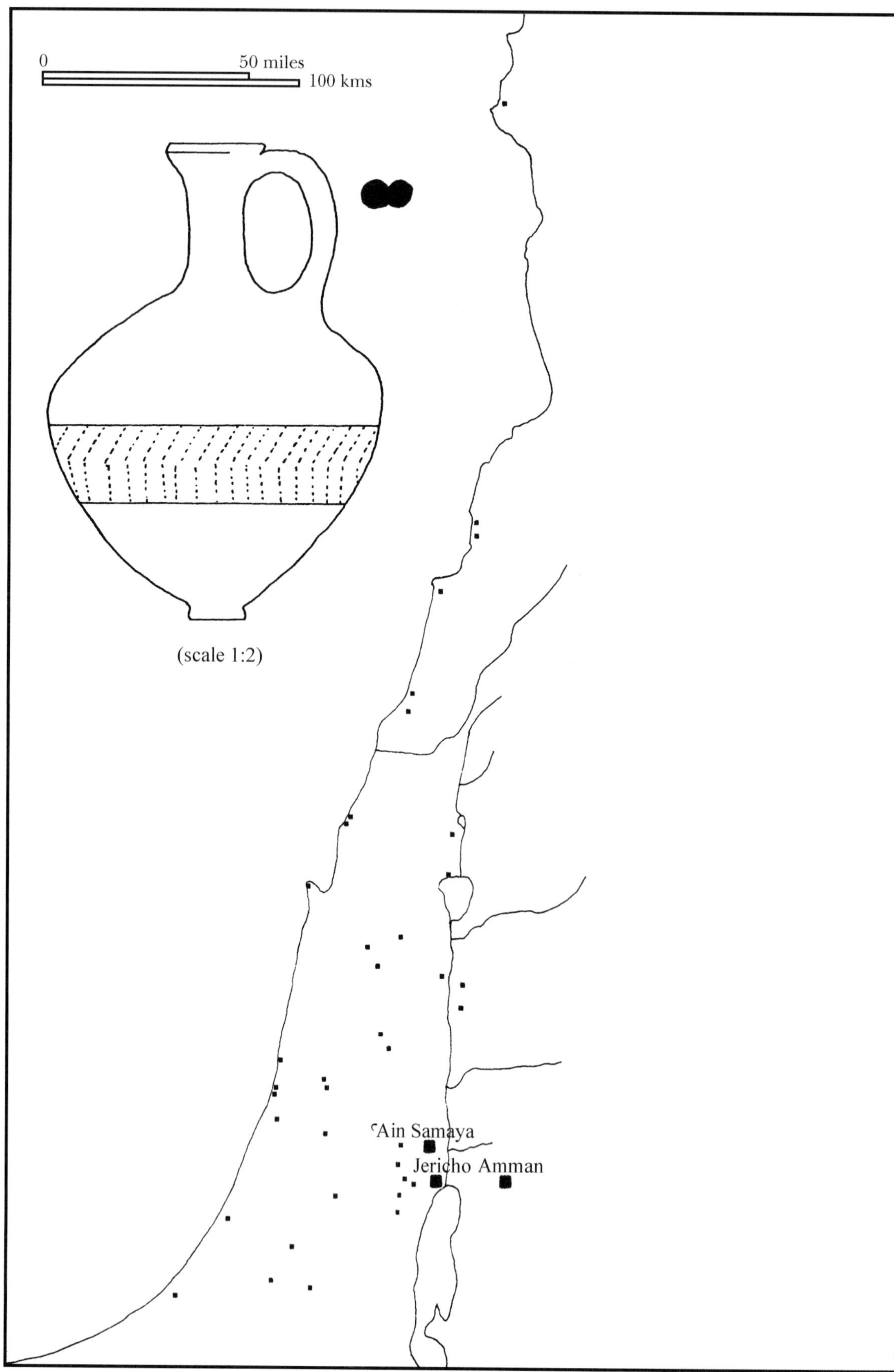

Fig. 58 Distribution and Shape Class of Type Group D.5.1

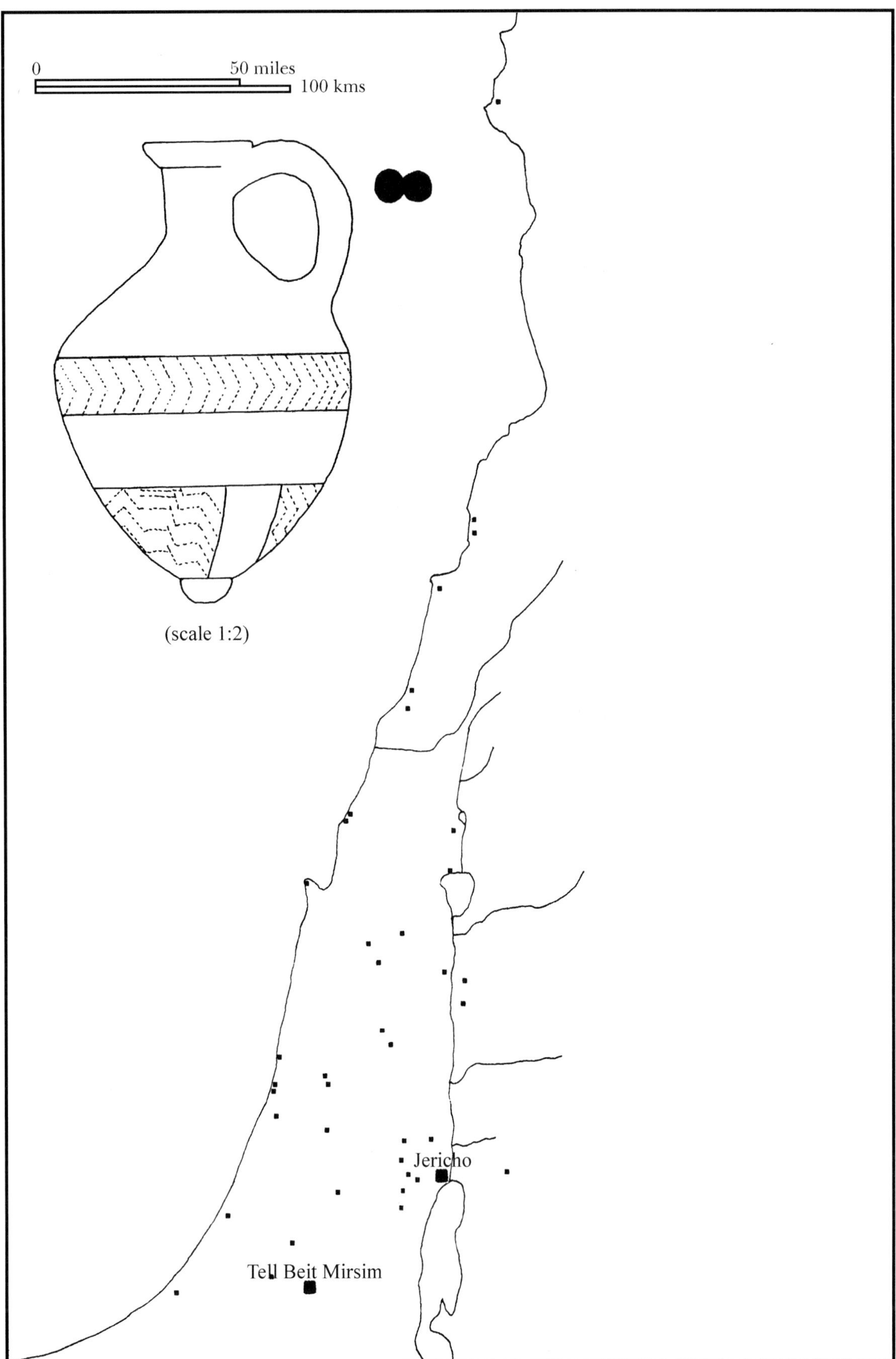

Fig. 59 Distribution and Shape Class of Type Group D.5.2

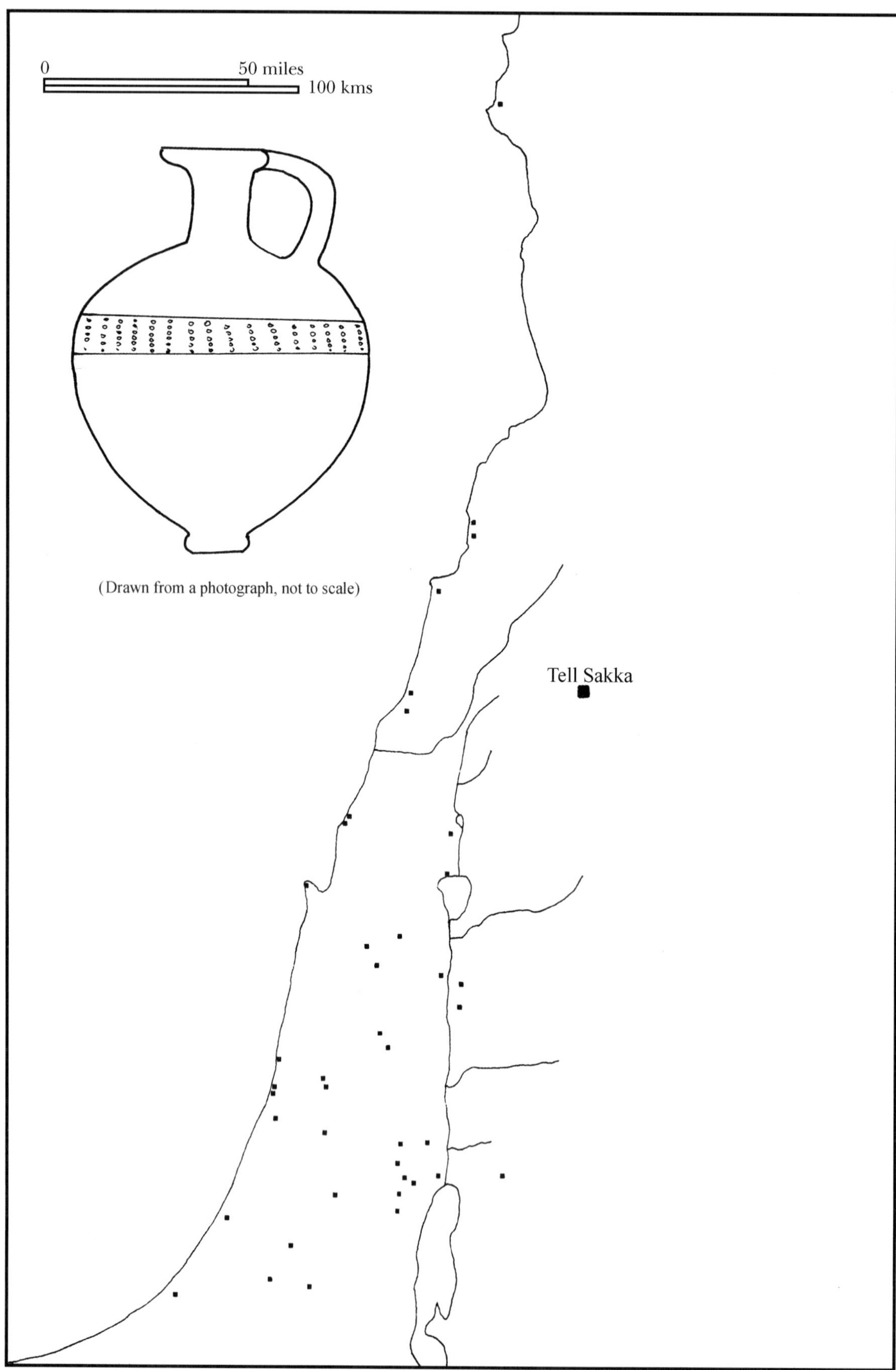

Fig. 60 Distribution and Shape Class of Type Group D.5.3

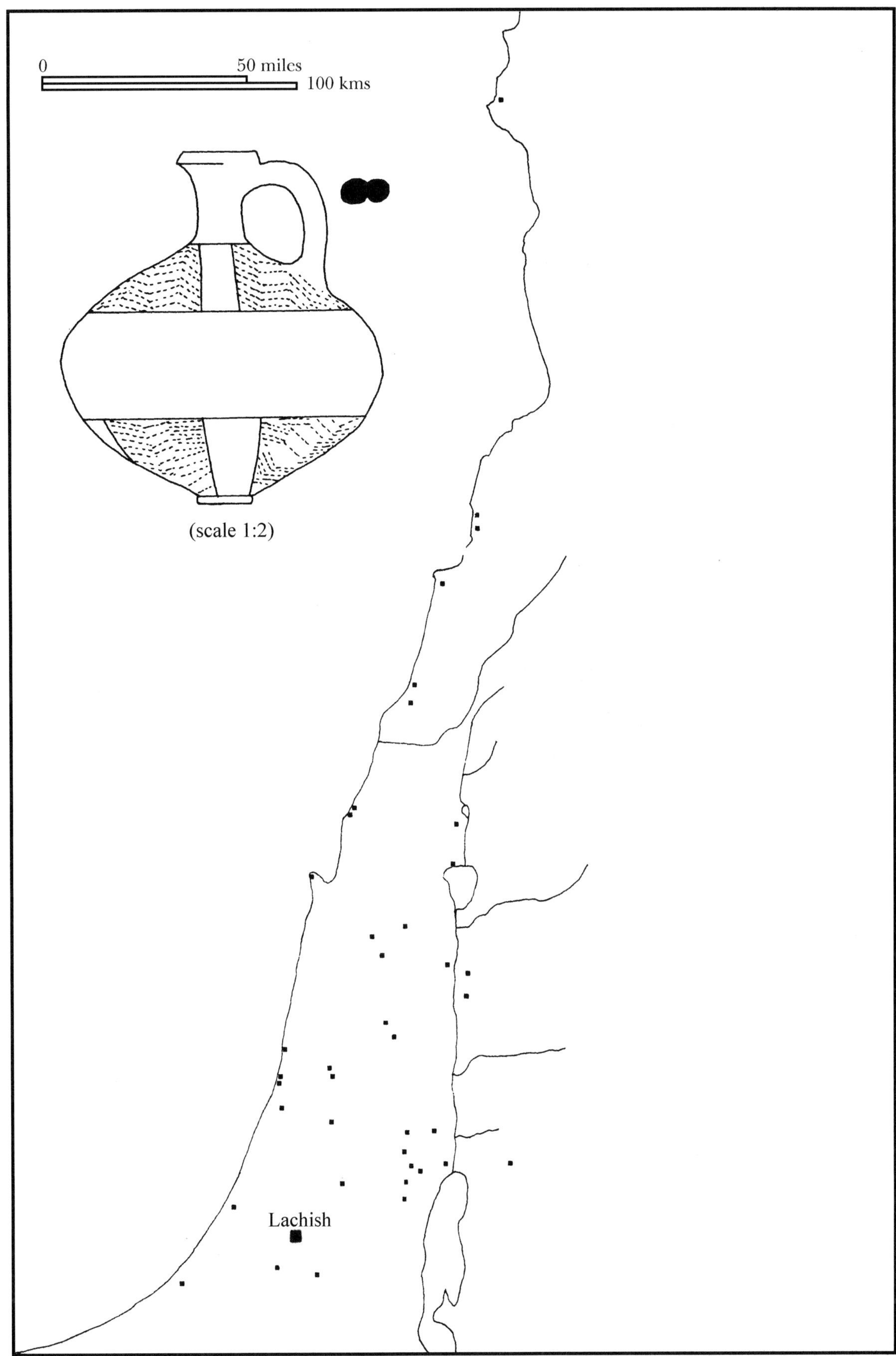

Fig. 61 Distribution and Shape Class of Type Group D.5.4

enclosing a herringbone pattern made with a multi-toothed comb, separated by a wide reserved band. This type is clearly influenced by contemporary Late Egyptian V biconical vessels.

Type Group D.5.5 (Figs. 62, 63)

Type group D.5.5 is known from a single example from Burial Feature 106 at Pella. It comprises a globular vessel with candlestick rim, double handle and ring base. One band of vertical chevrons runs around the shoulder of the vessel.[320] It is possibly a MB IIB development of type group C.2.

D.6. Late Palestinian VI

To the Late Palestinian VI group belong jugs which are distinctly cylindrical.

Type Group D.6.1 (Figs. 64, 68)

Vessels of type group D.6.1 are known only through an example found at Jatt in a tomb ascribed to the Late Bronze I.[321] Whilst the vessel could have been an old one at the time of deposition, all the other pottery found in the tomb seems to be of LB I date thus it is probable that this Tell el-Yahudiya vessel is one of the latest made. It is dark grey with a grey core and has a wet smoothed surface, similar to the 'gray cylindrical juglets' common in LB I assemblages. The decoration consists of two ridges at the base of the neck and an additional horizontal incised circle around the shoulder, between which are punctured radial lines. Below is a decorative panel with vertical and diagonal punctured lines filled with white pigment. The vessel has an everted rim, bipartite handle, a collar at the base of the neck, a rounded shoulder and a slightly bevelled base. Around the base of the neck is a delineated band of lines made with a four-toothed comb, whilst around the body runs an unframed band of straight lines and upright chevrons, also made with the same four-toothed comb. Petrographic analysis suggests the vessel was made either in Cyprus or northern Syria.[322]

Type Group D.6.2 (Figs. 65, 68)

Vessels of group D.6.2 are represented by an example from Beth Shemesh tomb 770.[323] It consists of a squat cylindrical jug with thickened (?) rim, strap handle and bevelled base. The decoration comprises two delineated bands of oblique dots made with an eight (?) toothed comb.

Type Group D.6.3 (Kaplan's Cylindrical 2) (Figs. 66, 68)

Juglets of group D.6.3 (Kaplan's Cylindrical 2) have a cylindrical body, a broad flat base, a sloping shoulder, a bipartite handle and a rolled lip, and thus differ from contemporary Egyptian cylindrical jugs, below group L.12 (Kaplan's Cylindrical 1), which have, as a rule, strap handles and a rounded base. In addition the ornament patterns differ. Those of the Late Palestinian Group have, like the other vessels of the Late Palestinian Group, one or two ornament bands filled with oblique comb imprints or such indentations in a herringbone pattern. Cylindrical 2 vessels are relatively well known with examples being found at Megiddo,[324] Beth Shemesh,[325] Lachish[326] Jericho,[327] and Tell el-Ajjul,[328] with at least two others of unknown provenience.[329]

Type Group D.6.4 (Figs. 67, 68)

Late Palestinian Cylindrical Tell el Yahudiya jugs with double handles, and rounded, as oppposed to a flat base, are known from an example found at Tell

---

[320] S. BOURKE, R. SPARKS and M. SCHROEDER, Pella in the Middle Bronze Age, in: P.M. FISCHER (ed.), *The Chronology of the Jordan Valley during the Middle and Late Bronze Ages: Pella, Tell Abu al-Kharaz, and Tell Deir 'Alla*, Vienna, 2006, 48–49, figs. 41–42.

[321] E. YANNI, A Late Bronze Age Tomb at Jatt, *'Atiqot* 40, 2000, 69, no. 61.

[322] Y. GORAN, in: E. YANNI, A Late Bronze Age Tomb at Jatt, *'Atiqot* 40, 2000, 52–53.

[323] Philadelphia University Museum 61-14-58. GRANT, 1929, 70, 119, fig. 127: KAPLAN, *Tell el-Yahudiyeh Ware*, fig. 8d.

[324] Jerusalem, Rockefeller Museum 34.1725. GUY, *Megiddo Tombs*, 1938, pl. 28.40; KAPLAN, *Tell el-Yahudiyeh Ware*, fig. 76a.

[325] Philadelphia UM 61-14-58. GRANT, *Beth Shemesh*, 1929, fig. 127 no. 770.

[326] Jerusalem, Rockefeller Museum 34.2979, TUFNELL, *Lachish IV*, pl. 77.750, KAPLAN, *Tell el-Yahudiyeh Ware*, fig. 9b.

[327] Jerusalem, Rockefeller Museum I.10089, GARSTANG 1934, pl. 17.19, 32.1764, KAPLAN, *Tell el-Yahudiyeh Ware*, fig. 9a, 33.1221, GARSTANG, 1933, fig. 4.2; Jerusalem Rockefeller Museum 32.1764, Kaplan, *Tell el-Yahudiyeh Ware*, fig. 9a: Jerusalem Rockefeller Museum 33.1221, KAPLAN, *Tell el-Yahudiyeh Ware*, fig. 10a: Amman J.5839, KENYON, *Jericho II*, 368–§72, fig. 138.9, KAPLAN, *Tell el-Yahudiyeh Ware*, fig. 8f; St. Andrews University, KAPLAN, *Tell el-Yahudiyeh Ware*, fig. 11a; others, KENYON, *Jericho II*, 438–446, fig. 231.17, KAPLAN, *Tell el-Yahudiyeh Ware*, fig. 11b.

[328] PETRIE, Ancient Gaza III, pls. 39.74015', 39.74015", KAPLAN, *Tell el-Yahudiyeh Ware*, figs. 12 a–b.

[329] Tel Aviv Haᶜaretz Museum 51460, KAPLAN, *Tell el-Yahudiyeh Ware*, fig. 10b; BRAEMER and AL-MAQDISSI, in: MAQDISSI, MATOÏAN, NICOLLE, *Céramique de l'age du bronze en Syrie I*, 50, fig. xxB.118.

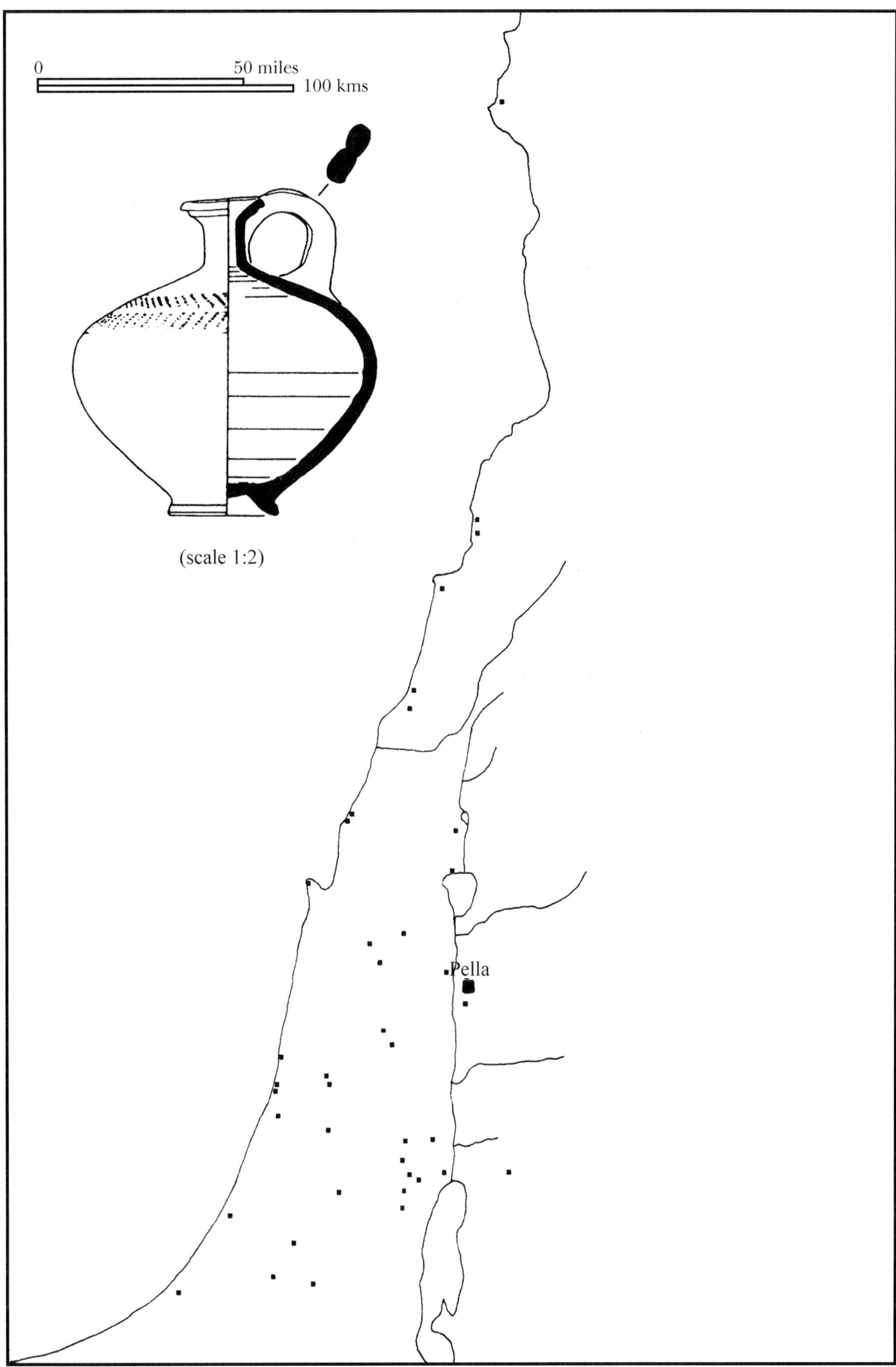

Fig. 62 Distribution and Shape class of Type Group D.5.5

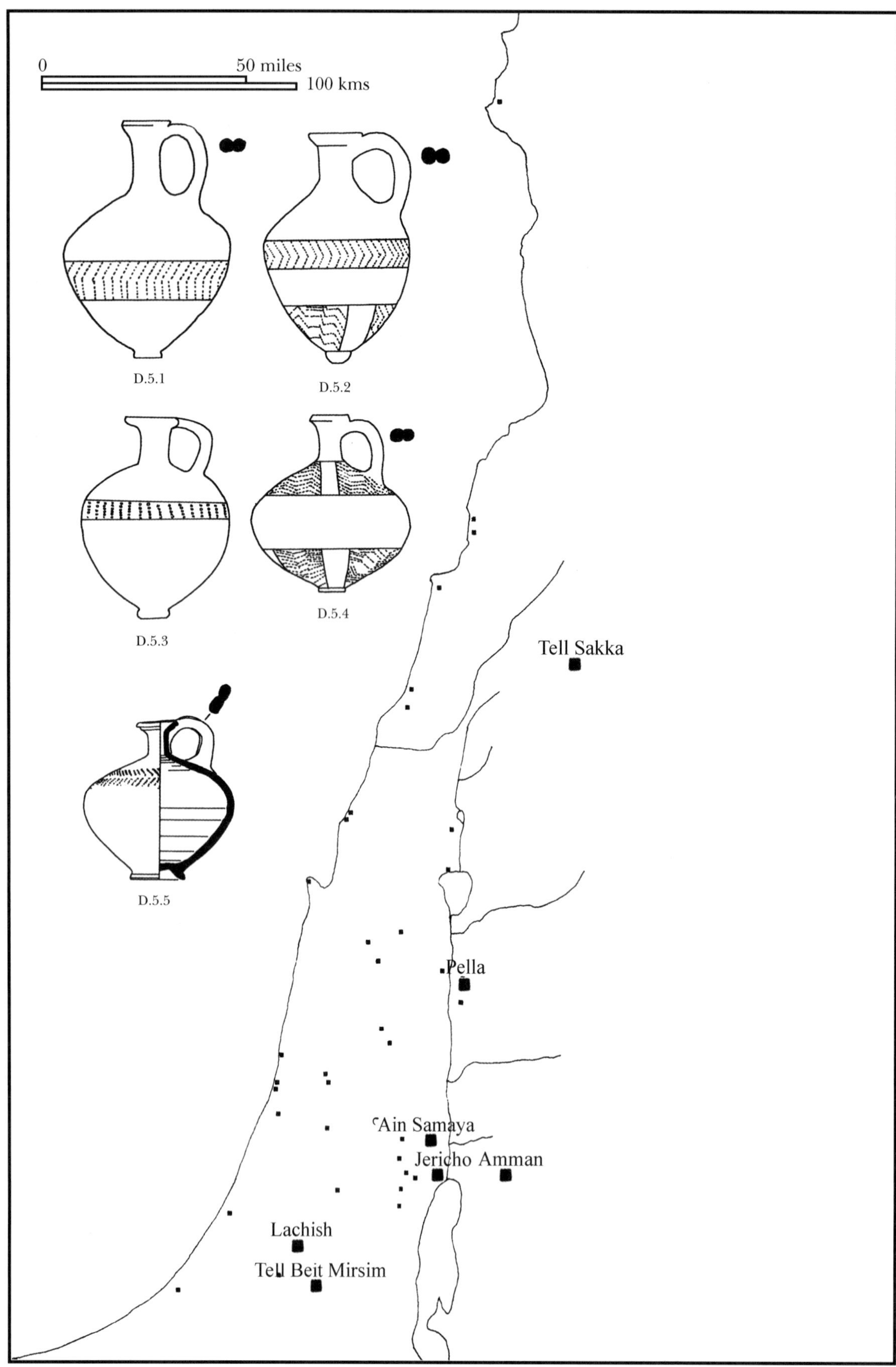

Fig. 63 Combined Distribution of Type Group D.5

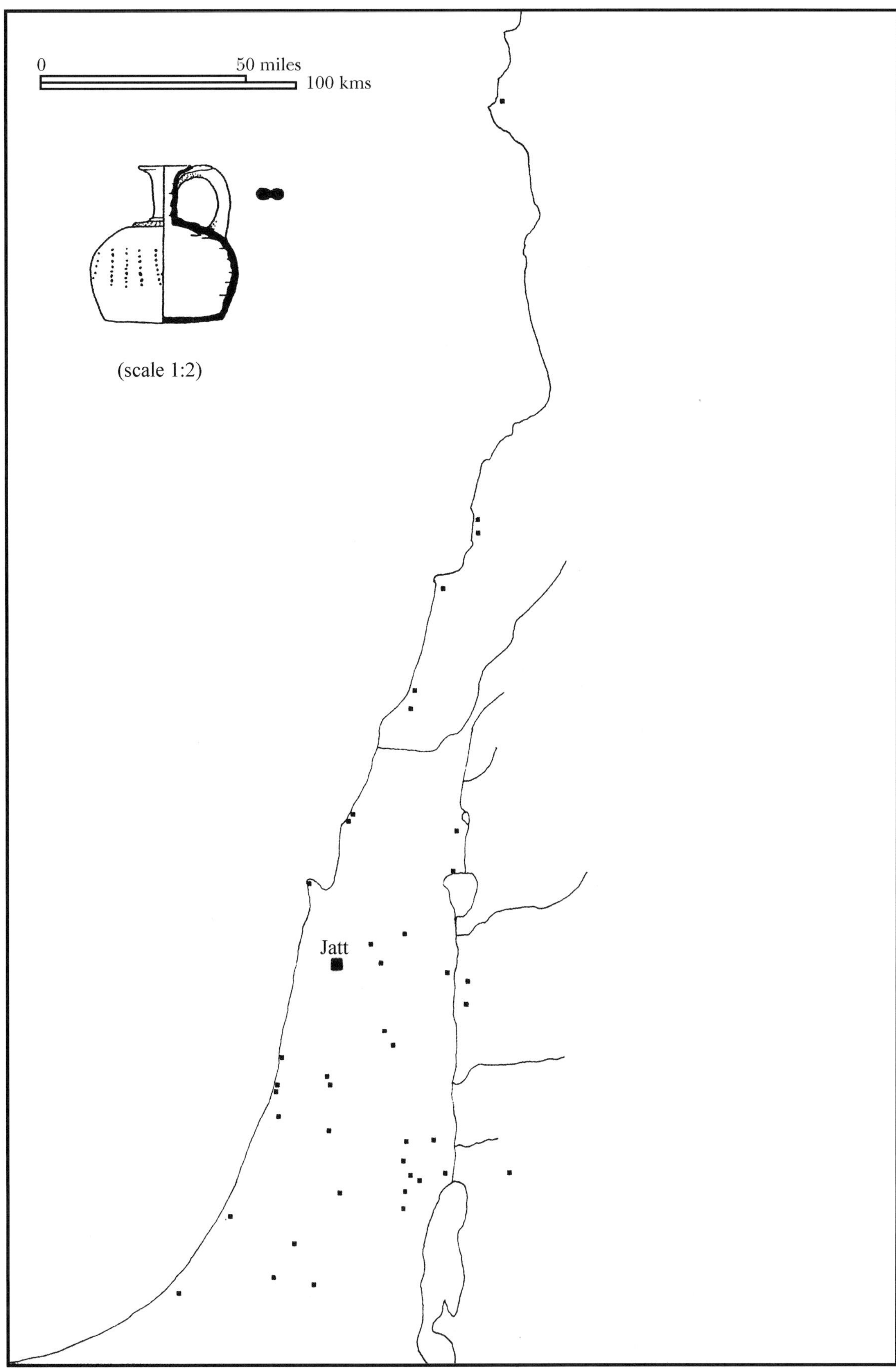

Fig. 64 Distribution and Shape Class of Type Group D.6.1

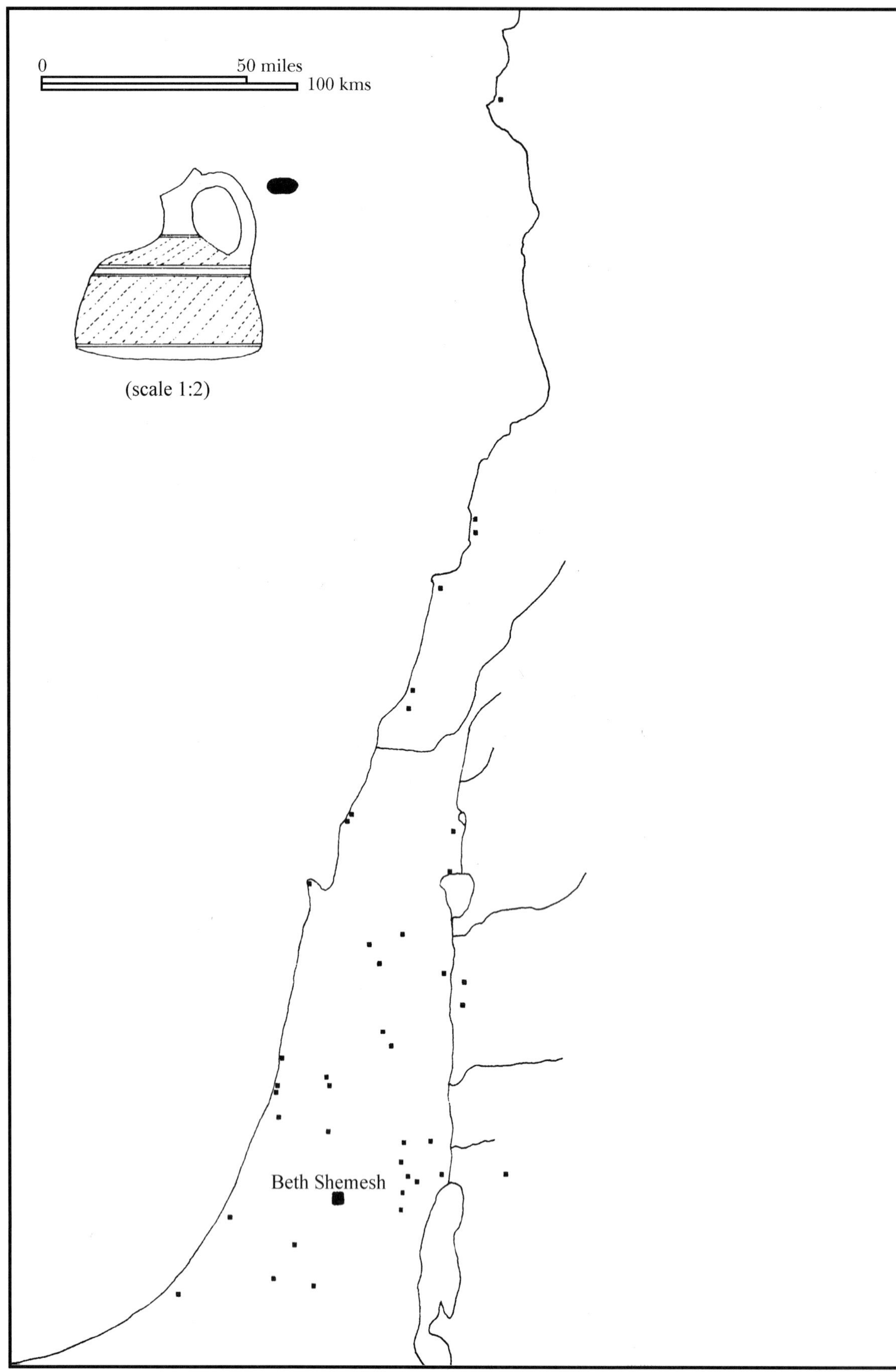

Fig. 65 Distribution and Shape Class of Type Group D.6.2

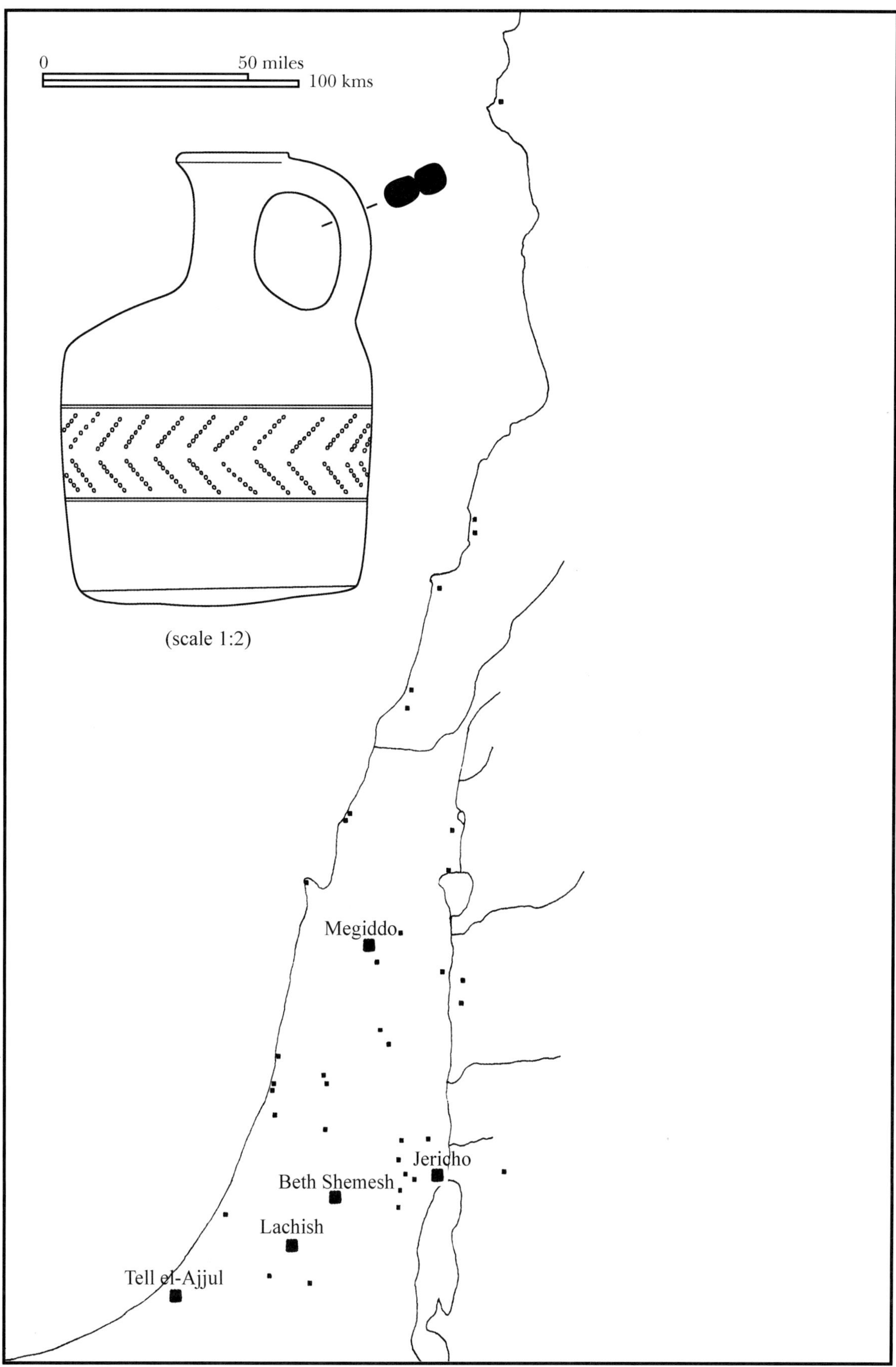

Fig. 66 Distribution and Shape Class of Type Group D.6.3

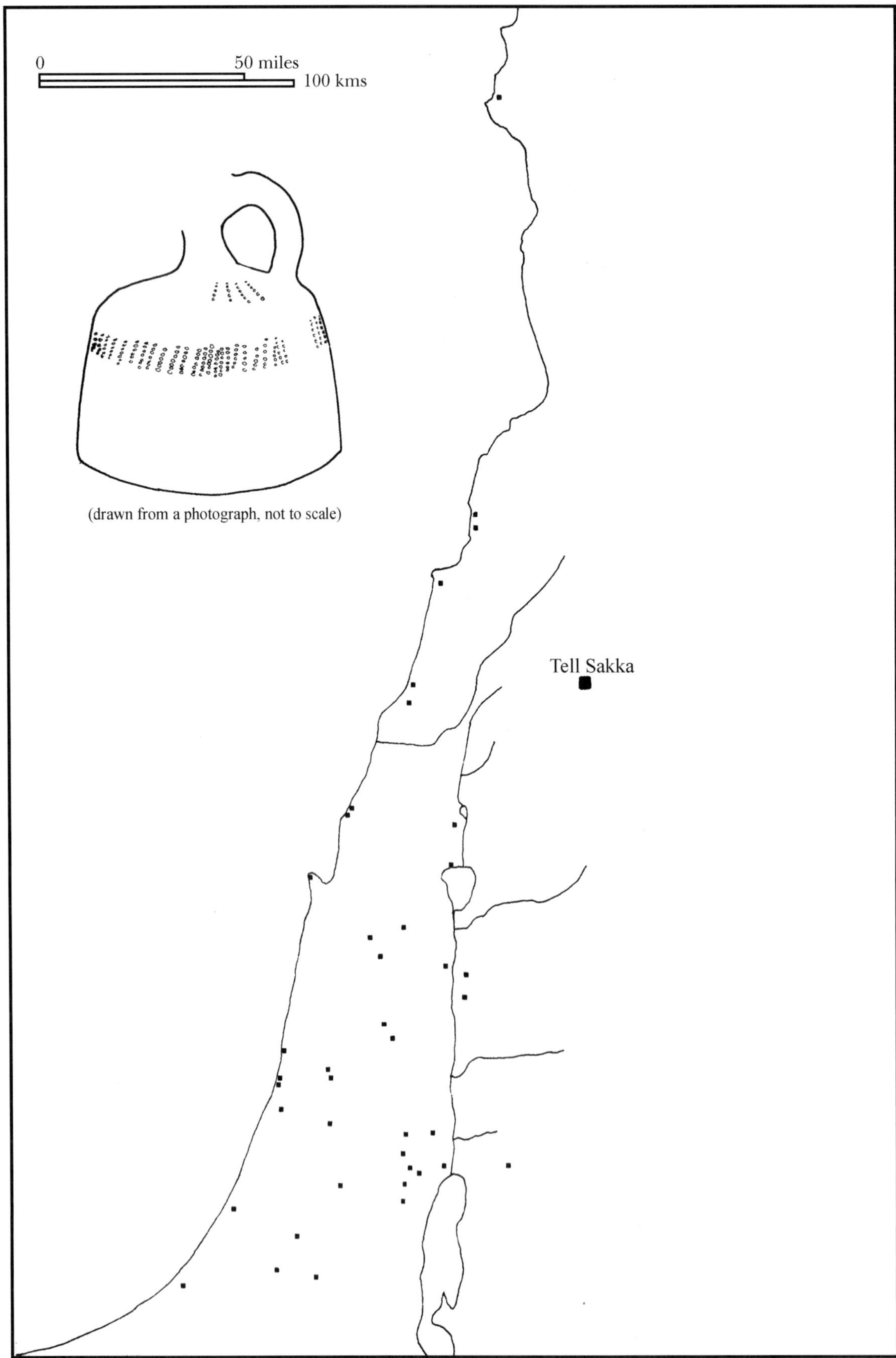

Fig. 67 Distribution and Shape Class of Type Group D.6.4

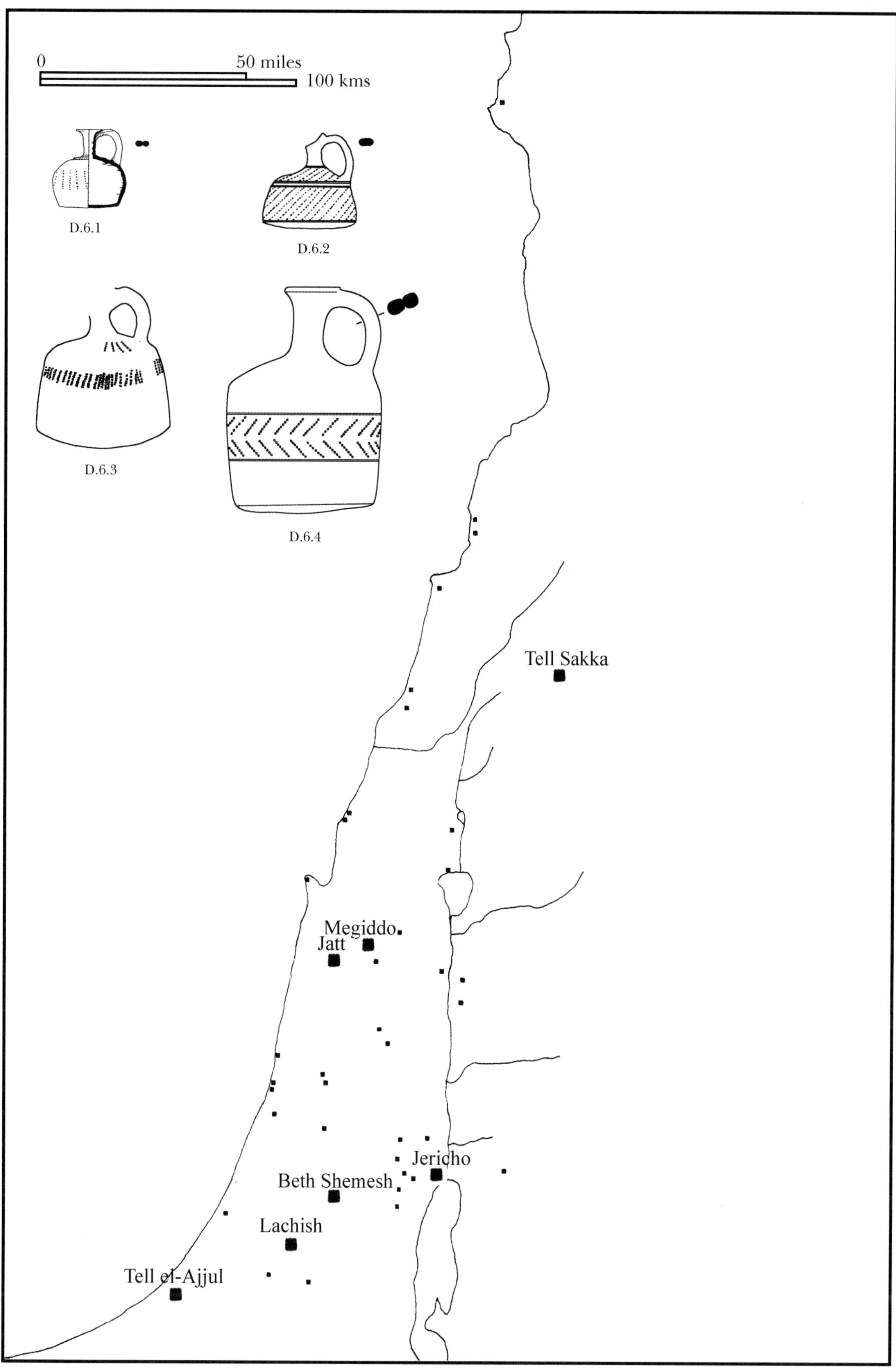

Fig. 68 Combined Distribution of Type Group D.6

Sakka.[330] It is decorated with two bands of oblique lines, one on the shoulder, and one on the upper body.

D.7. Late Palestinian VII (Fig. 69)

Late Palestinian VII comprises vessels which are clearly models. One incomplete example of a model biconical vessel was found at Beth Shan.[331] As preserved the vessel has a round handle and a button base. Running round the shoulder of the jug is one undelineated band of chevrons

Branches E–H: Early Levantine

Whilst the Early Palestinian group is easily recognizable, the vagaries of archaeological chance are such that the MB IIA Early Levantine group is not so well known. However to this group may be attributed a few individually produced vessels, mostly unpublished, which are ovoid, biconical or piriform. They tend to have four horizontal zones of decoration comprising triangles, rectangles, spirals and wavy lines but no chequer board or horizontal band patterns such as are found on contemporary Early Palestinian vessels.

E.1. Early Levantine I

Type Group E.1 (Biconical) (Fig. 70)

Type group E.1 is known through two fragmentary examples, one from Ashkelon[332] and an import at Tell el-Daba. The latter, TD 5588, an incomplete large biconical jug with a maximum body diameter of 25 cm., was found in Phase d/1 (= G/4), which dates to the beginning of the Thirteenth Dynasty. This is a red slipped vessel, made of Levantine clay, and decorated with five or more horizontal zones comprising three zones of wavy bands filled with six-toothed comb imprints alternating with two zones of running spirals.

E.2–3. Early Levantine II

Type Group E.2 (Ovoid) (Fig. 71)

Type Group E.2 is at present represented by one vessel of Levantine clay from Tell el-Dabᶜa, (TD 3139) found in a Phase F grave. This has a kettle rim, a distinct swelling of the neck, a triple loop handle, which comes from the base of the handle to the base of the shoulder, and a button base. The decoration consists of four zones of pendant or standing triangles with an incised wavy line in the reserved zones between the first and second, and between the third and fourth decorative zones.

Branch F

Branch F comprises a small group of early Levantine vessels which are characterised by their bands of decoration in the form of squares. Although some examples have been found in Egypt they clearly originate from the northern Levant. The following groups may be differentiated:

F.1. Early Levantine III

Type Group F.1 (Fig. 72)

Type group F.1 comprises small piriform, almost ovoid jugs, between 8 and 9 cm. tall, known from Byblos, with one (incomplete) example being found at Tell el-Dabᶜa (TD 6173). They have a rolled rim, double handle, button base and have one zone of large rectangles around the major part of the body.[333]

F.2. Early Levantine IV

Type Group F.2 (Fig. 73)

Type Group F.2 comprise jugs with a direct everted rim, a bipartite handle joining at the rim, incisions at the base of the neck, and a flat base. An example of such a vessel comes from a Middle Bronze IIA burial at Ebla.[334] The decoration consists of two zones of infilled rectangles.

F.3. Early Levantine V

Type Group F.3 (Fig. 74)

Type group F.3 probably has kettle rims, double handles joining at the neck below the rim, incisions at the neck, and ring bases, with three zones of decoration. Examples of such are known from Tell el-Dabᶜa, Kafr ed-Djarra,[335]

---

330 Taraqji, *Syria* 70, 1993, 456.

331 Jerusalem, Rockefeller Museum 34.1332, Kaplan, *Tell el-Yahudiyeh Ware*, fig. 117c and cf. below page 585.

332 See contribution by L. Stager and R. Voss, below 560.

333 Beirut 8521. Dunand, *Fouilles de Byblos* II, 198, fig. 205 no. 8521. The attributes are not shown in the published drawing but a double handle and button base are assumed through a comparison with the Tell el-Dabᶜa examples.

334 Burial D.3712, L. Nigro, The Smith and the King of Ebla. Tell el-Yahudiyeh ware, Metallic Wares and the Ceramic technology of Middle Bronze Syria, in: M. Bietak (ed.), *The Synchronisation of Civilisations in the Eastern Mediterranean in the Second Millennium II*, 2003, 349.

335 Paris Louvre AO 7497. Contenau, *Syria* 1, 1920, 127–128, pl. 11, Kaplan, *Tell el-Yahudiyeh Ware*, fig. 30a.

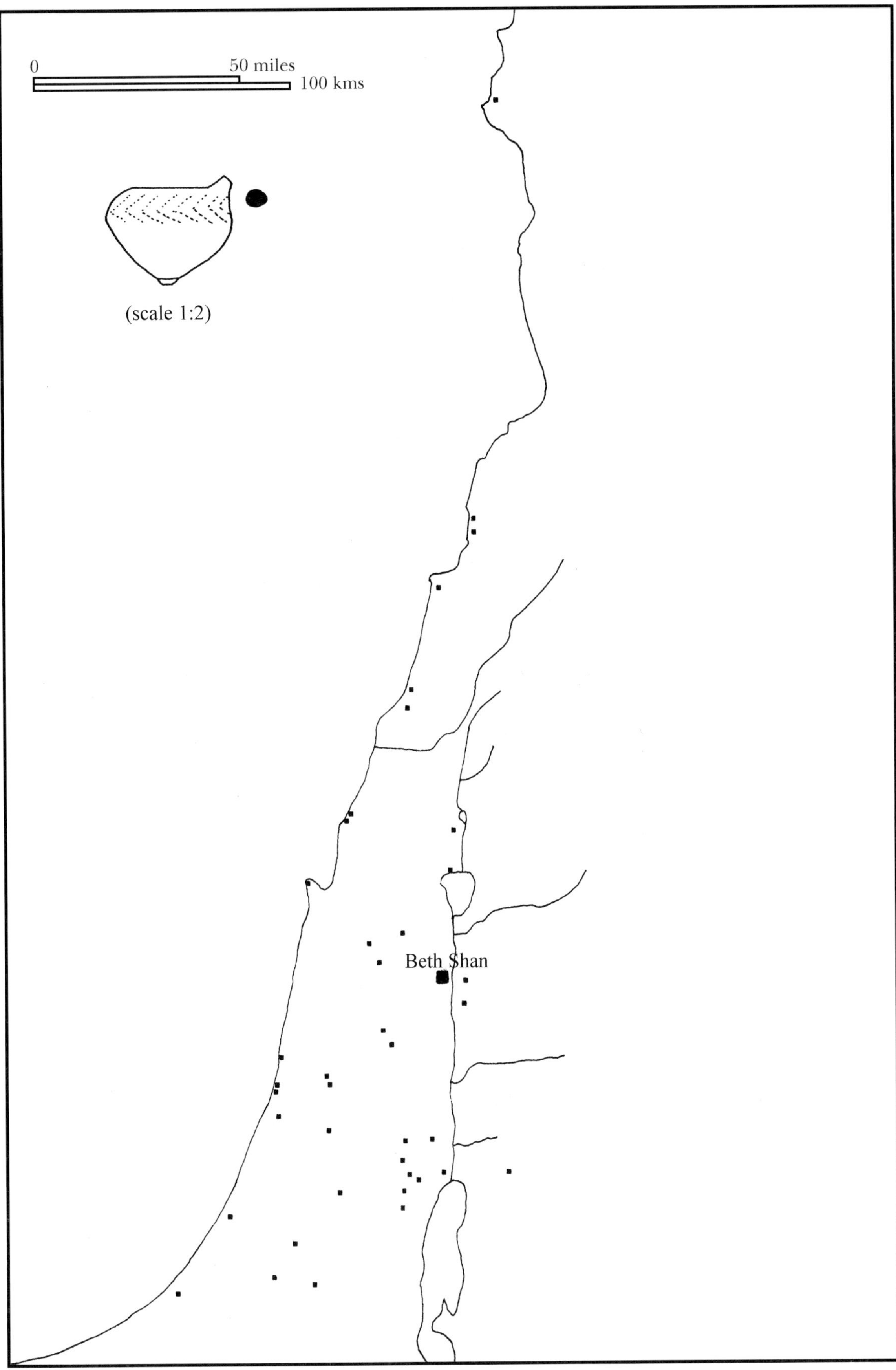

Fig. 69 Distribution and Shape Class of Type Group D.7

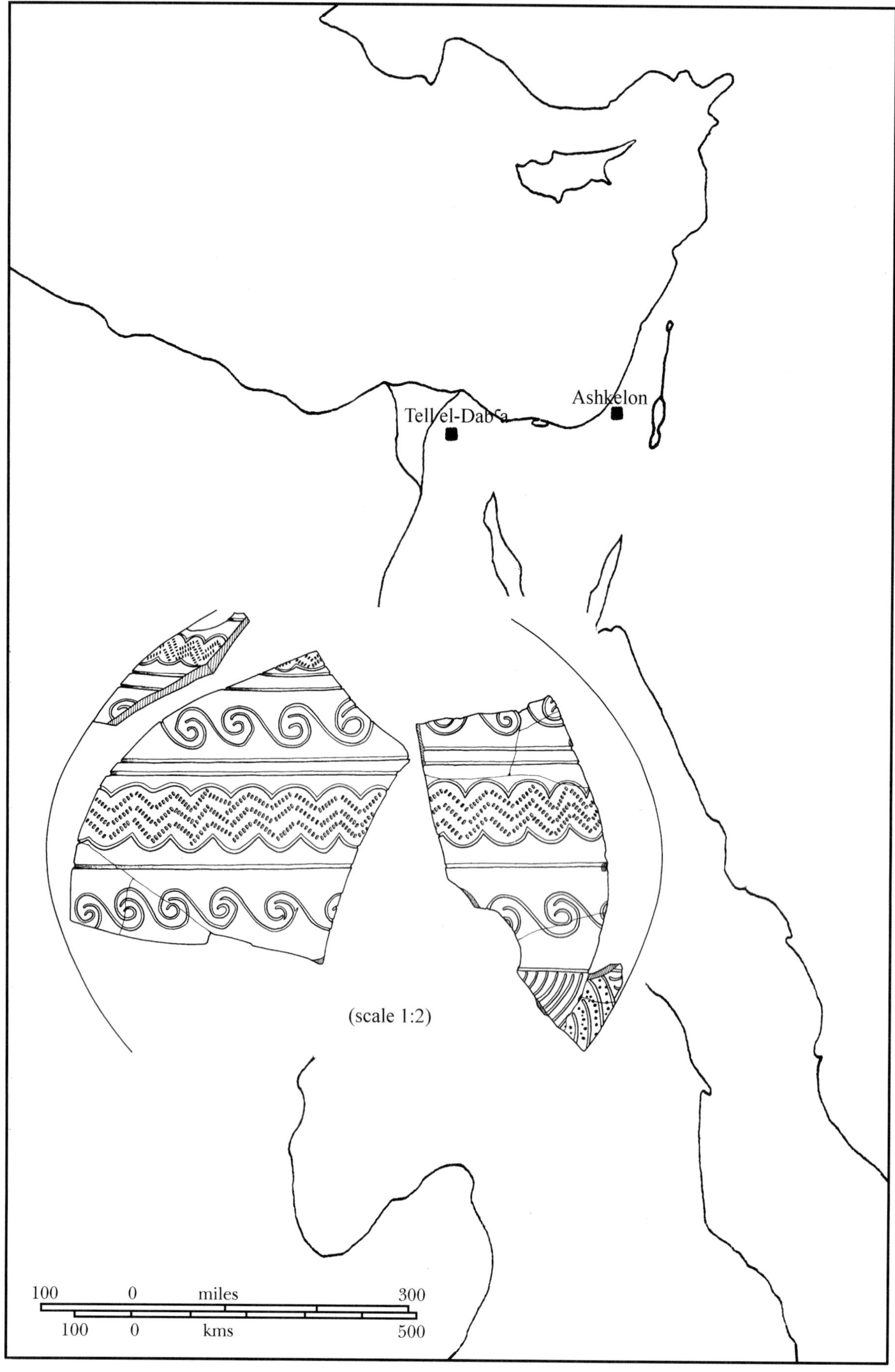

Fig. 70 Distribution and Shape Class of Type Group E.1

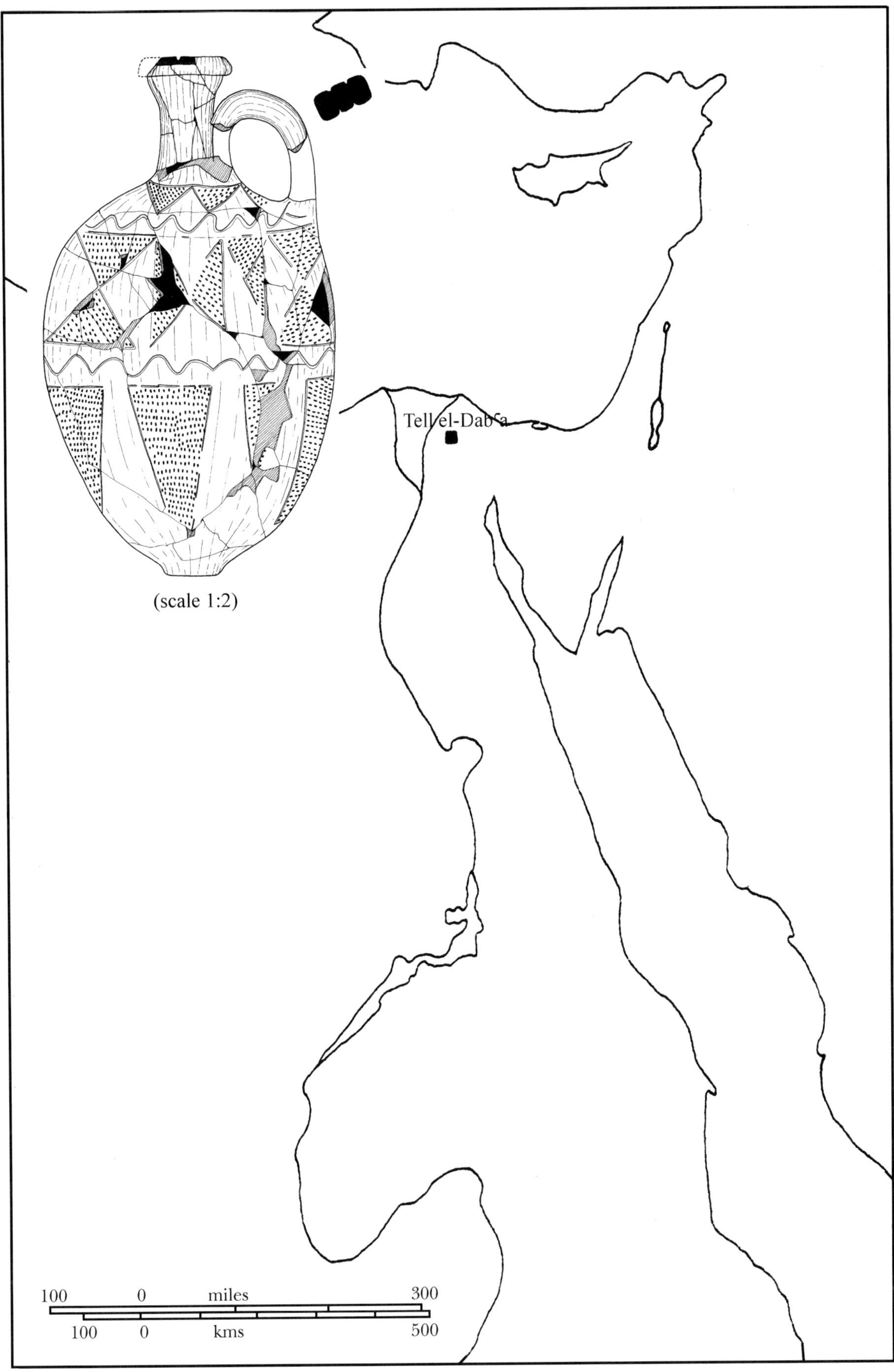

Fig. 71 Distribution and Shape Class of Type Group E.2

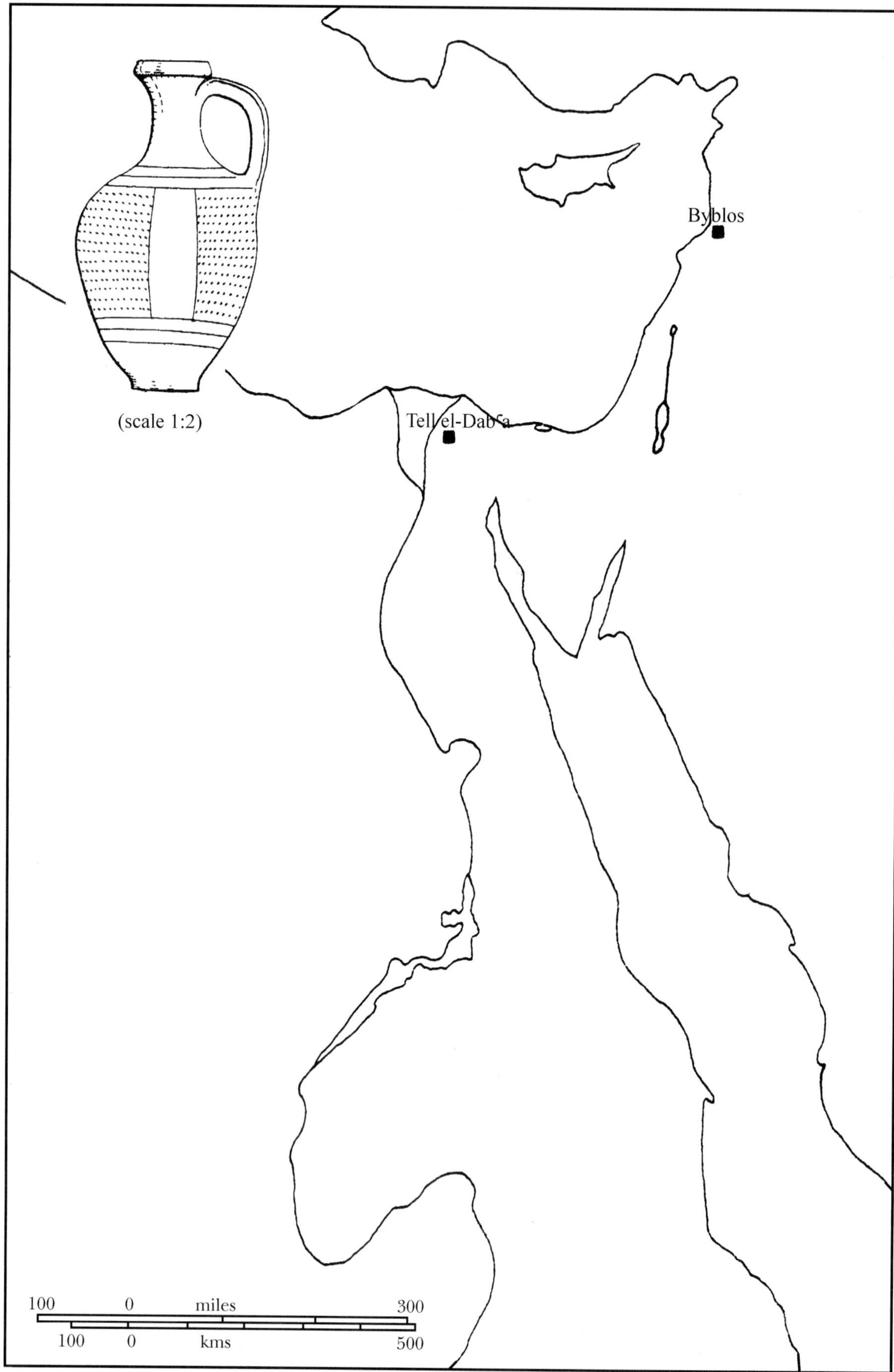

Fig. 72 Distribution and Shape Class of Type Group F.1

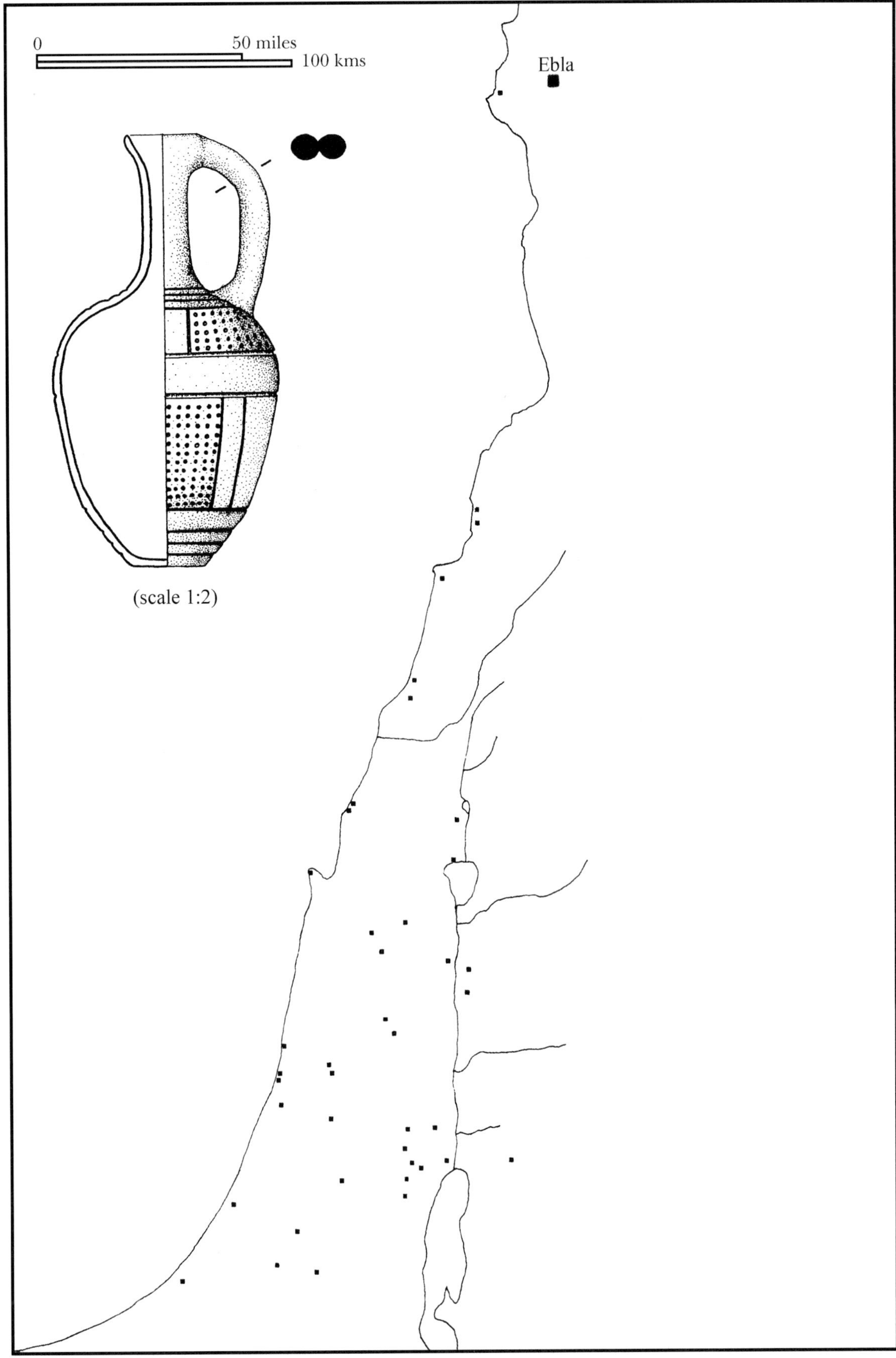

Fig. 73 Distribution and Shape Class of Type Group F.2

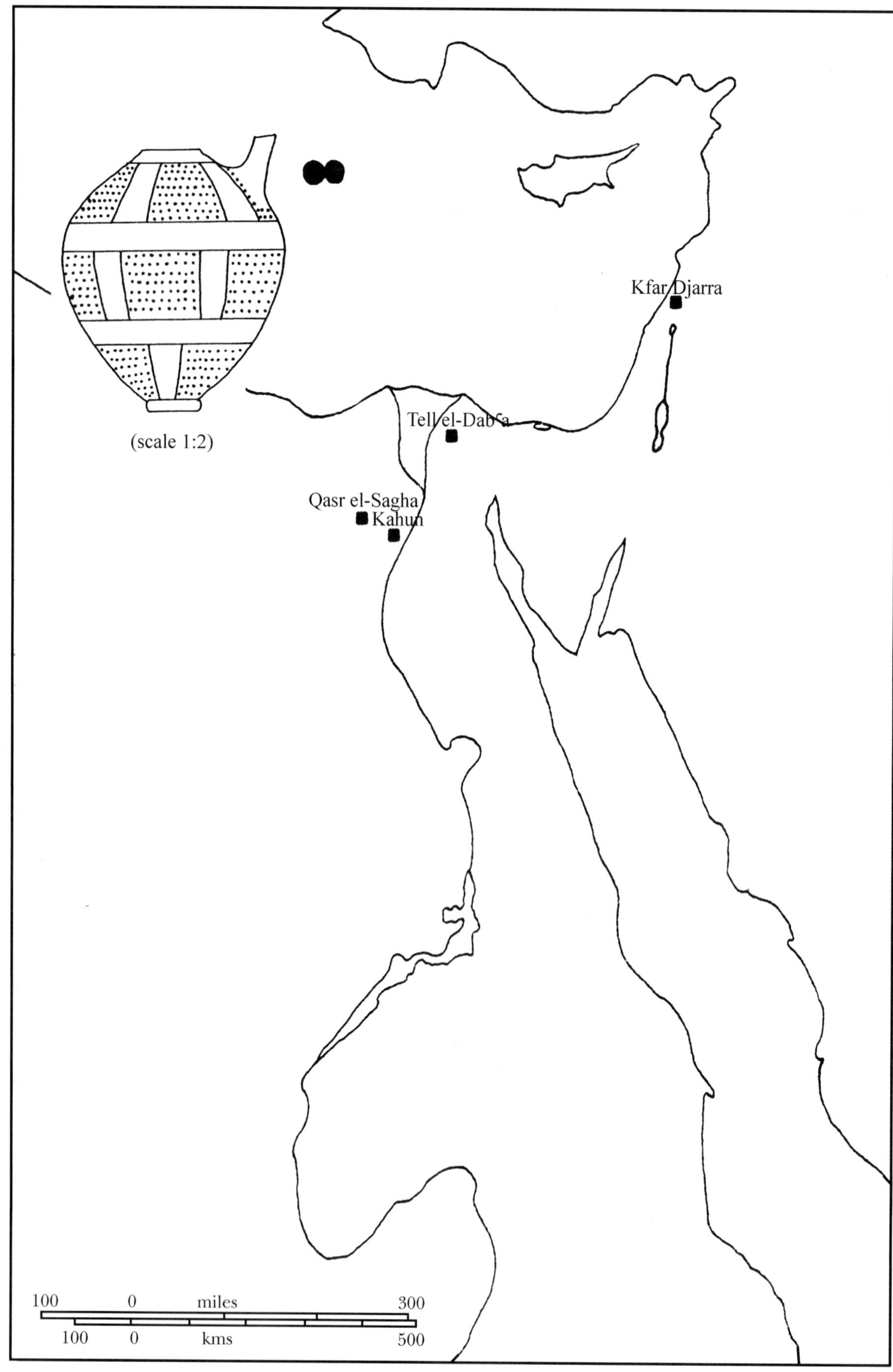

Fig. 74 Distribution and Shape Class of Type Group F.3

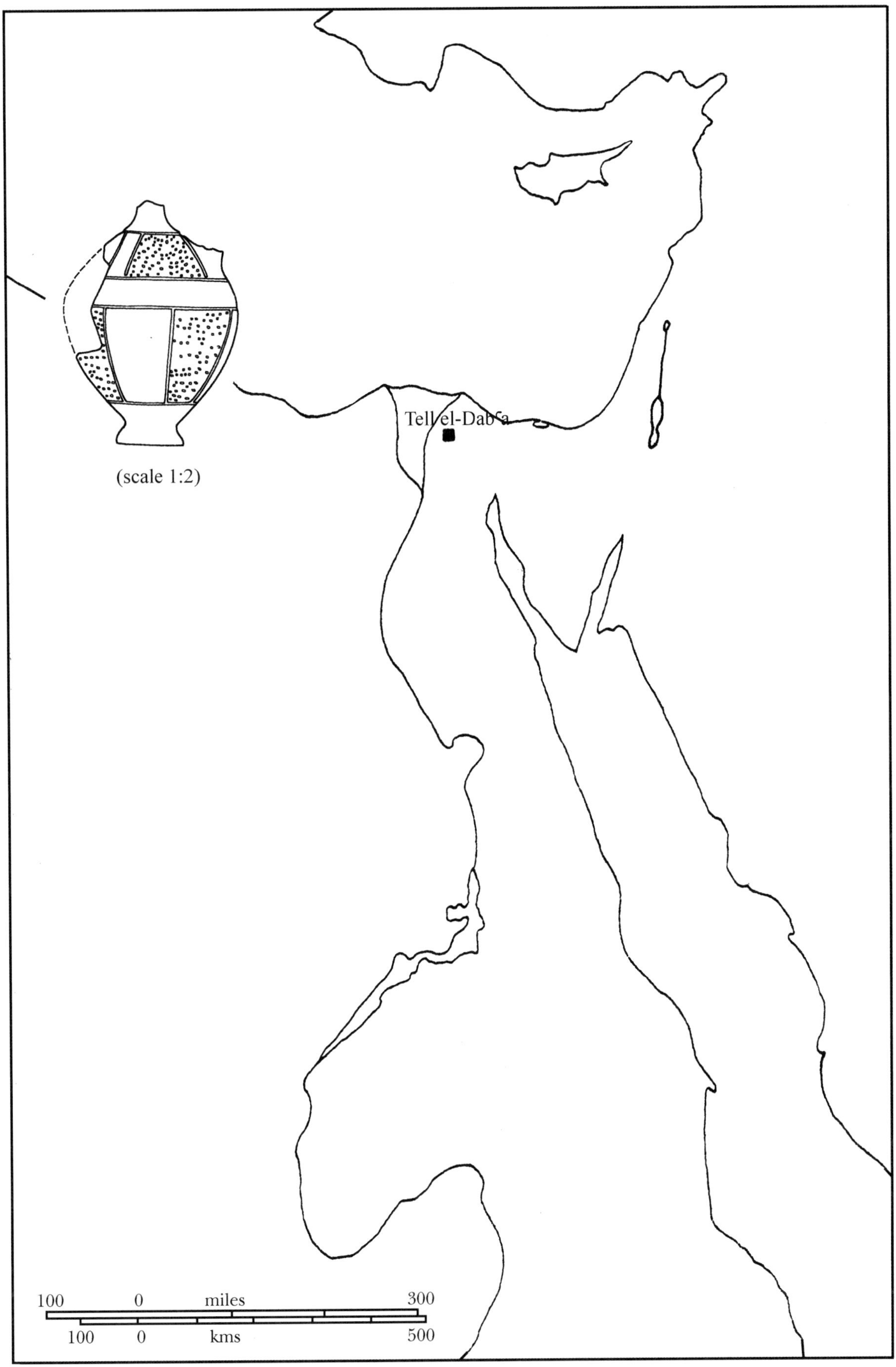

Fig. 75 Distribution and Shape Class of Type Group F.4

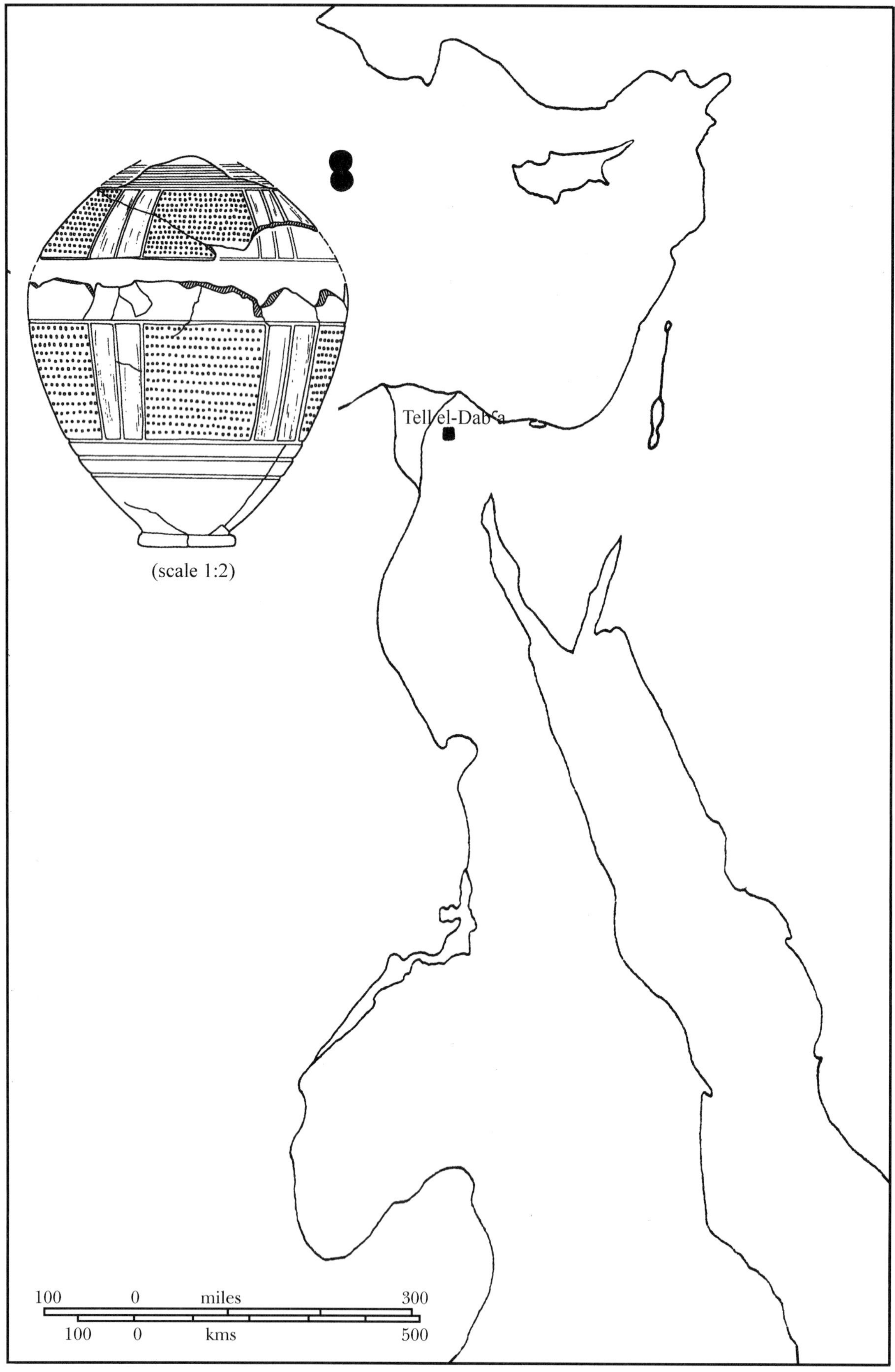

Fig. 76 Distribution and Shape class of type Group F.5

Kahun[336] and possibly Qasr el-Sagha.[337] A large, incomplete vessel now in the Medelhavsmuseet, Stockholm, would appear to also be of this type, but the lower zone seems to be incomplete.[338]

F.4. Early Levantine VI (Fig. 75)

Tell el-Yahudiya jugs of group F.4 are piriform in shape, have double handles, incisions at the base of the neck, ring bases, and only two decorative zones, one on the upper body and one on the lower body, and presumably kettle rims. The type group is known from an example fround at Tell el-Dabᶜa, TD 2068, which bears two zones of rectangles separated by reserved zones.

F.5. Early Levantine VII

Type Group F.5 (Fig. 76)

Tell el-Yahudiya jugs of group F.5 are piriform in shape, have kettle rims, double handles incisions at the base of the neck, ring bases, and, like group F.4 only two decorative zones, one on the upper body and one on the lower body. The best example of such a vessel known to us is an incomplete example from Tell el-Dabᶜa (TD 4501).

Branch G: Carinated Jugs

Also attributable to the Early Levantine group are a number of distinctly carinated vessels with kettle rims, tripartite handles, ring bases and three or four decorative zones.

G.1. Carinated I

Type Group G.1 (Fig. 77)

Group G.1 is represented by a single example from Gezer Cave 15 I,[339] the present location of which is unknown. As drawn in the original publication, the vessel has a direct rim, a carinated shoulder and a ring (?) base. The decoration consists of four delineated horizontal bands of oblique lines made with a five-toothed comb.

G.2. Carinated II (Kaplan's Ovoid 3)

Type Group G.2 (Fig. 78)

Vessels of group G.2 have kettle rims, tripartite handles, ring bases and three decorative zones consisting of joined pendant and standing triangles. As such their style of decoration anticipates the decorative scheme which becomes very popular in the Levanto-Egyptian branch, branch I below. They were subsumed into Kaplan's Ovoid 3 group, but are evidently the forerunners of the Piriform 1 jugs of the Levanto-Egyptian I.1 group. At present vessels of group G.2 are only known from Ras Shamra.[340]

Branch H: Early Levantine VIII ("Compact Piriform")

Type Groups H.1.1–H.1.2 (Figs. 79, 80)

Type Group H.1.1 is known through a complete orange burnished example of unknown provenance now in the Louvre.[341] This vessel has a candlestick rim, incisions at the base of the neck, a tripatite handle which runs from the base of the neck to half way down the shoulder, a compact piriform to biconical body, a low ring base, and has four bands of decoration. Below the neck is a wavy zigzag line above a frieze of rectangles, whist on the lower body is a frieze of standing triangles and a lower band with possible floral motifs. To this group, as subgroup H.1.2 should perhaps also be assigned the fragmentary jug Tell el-Dabᶜa TD 1734 which would also appear to have four zones of decoration, an upper large one of rectangles, followed by a band of pendant triangles, a band of swimming fish and a lower zone of connected standing and pendant triangles. This group is clearly related to the Levanto-Egyptian I.1 (Piriform 1a) group, but the examples of this group found thus far

---

[336] London BM EA 50754. Petrie, *Illahun, Kahun and Gurob,* 10, Merrillees, *Trade and Transcendance,* 64, fig. 56, Kaplan, *Tell el-Yahudiyeh Ware,* fig. 28a. A variant of this consisting of two zones of squares and one zone of incised lines (?) is found on a Nile clay jug now in Stockholm (MM E.391). Kaplan *Tell el-Yahudiyeh Ware,* fig. 28a.

[337] Sliwa, Die Siedlung des Mittleren Reiches bei Qasr el-Sagha, *MDAIK* 48, 1992, 188, Abb 8.1.

[338] Kaplan, *Tell el-Yahudiyeh Ware,* fig. 28b.

[339] Macalister, *Gezer,* 1912, I, 89–93, III pls. 22.12, 23.16; Kaplan, *Tell el-Yahudiyeh Ware,* fig. 115d.

[340] Paris Louvre AO 20379. Schaeffer, *Syria* 19, 1938, 244, 249, figs. 36h, 38; idem, *Ugaritica I,* 60–67, fig. 53h, pl. 18.2; Kaplan, *Tell el-Yahudiyeh Ware,* fig. 115c.

[341] Paris Louvre AO. 29886. L. Nigro, The Smith and the King of Ebla. Tell el-Yahudiyeh ware, Metallic Wares and the Ceramic technology of Middle Bronze Syria, in: M. Bietak (ed.), *The Synchronisation of Civilisations in the Eastern Mediterranean in the Second Millennium II,* 2003, 359.

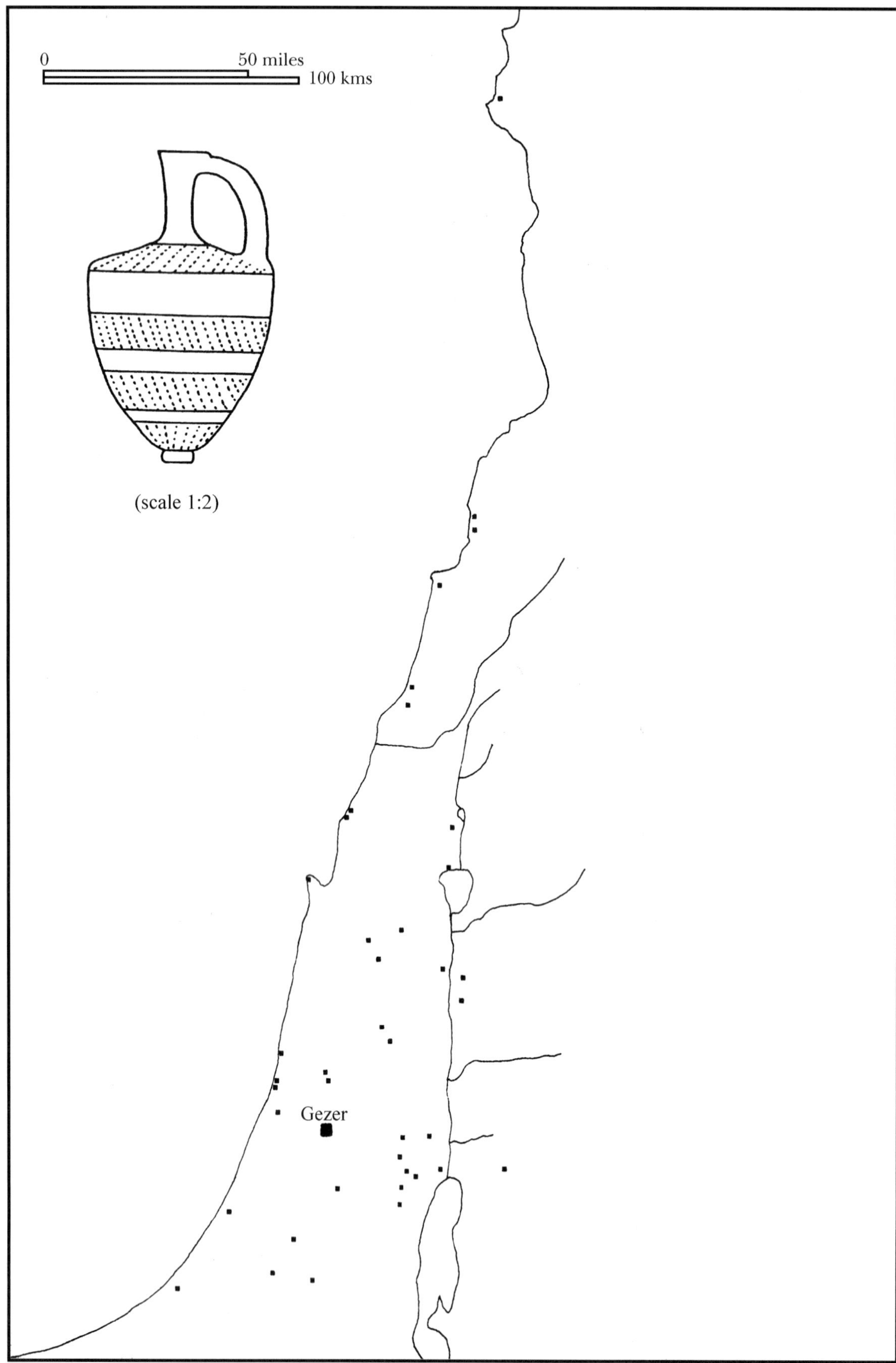

Fig. 77 Distribution and Shape Class of Type Group G.1

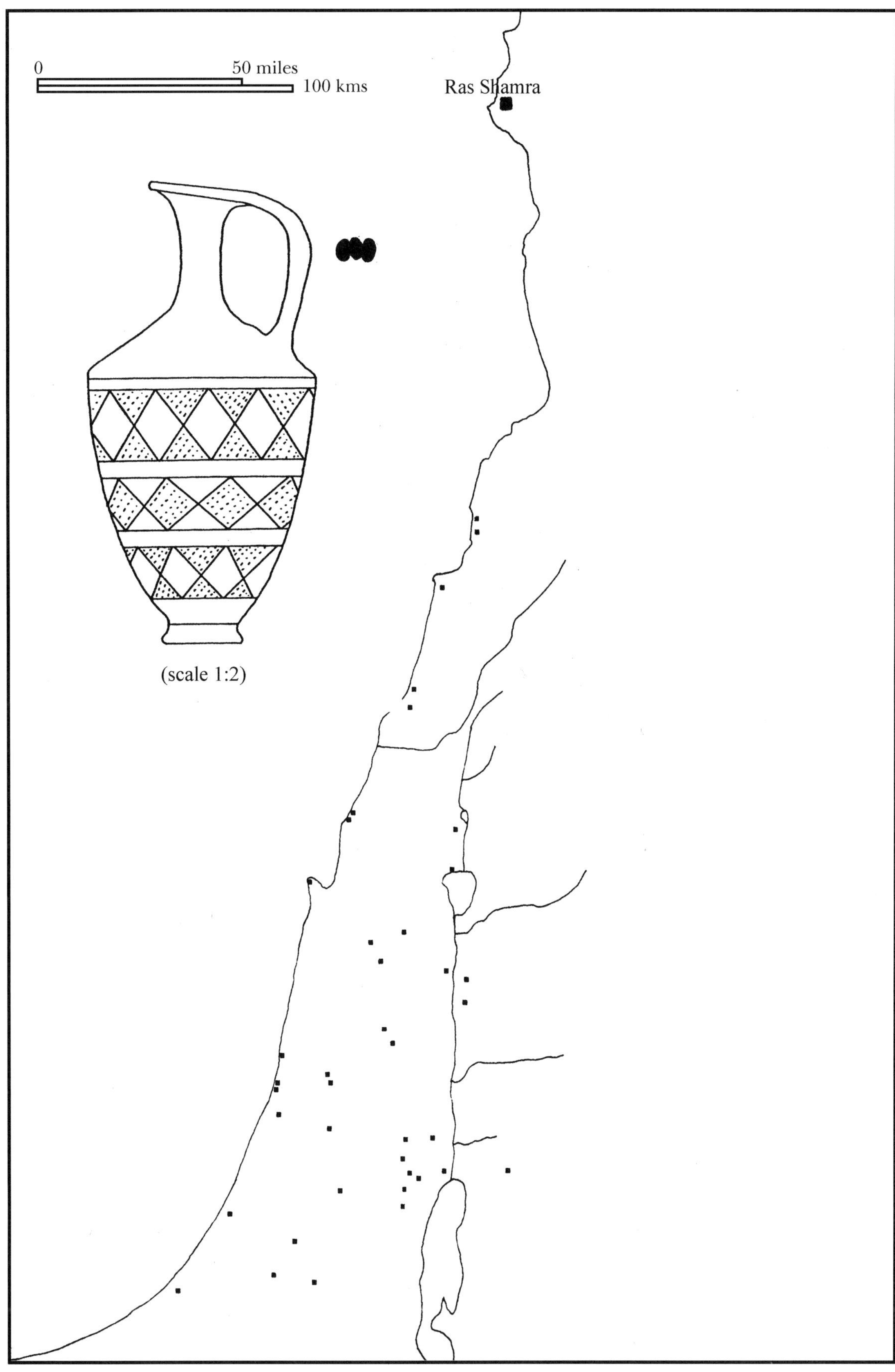

Fig. 78 Distribution and Shape Class of Type Group G.2

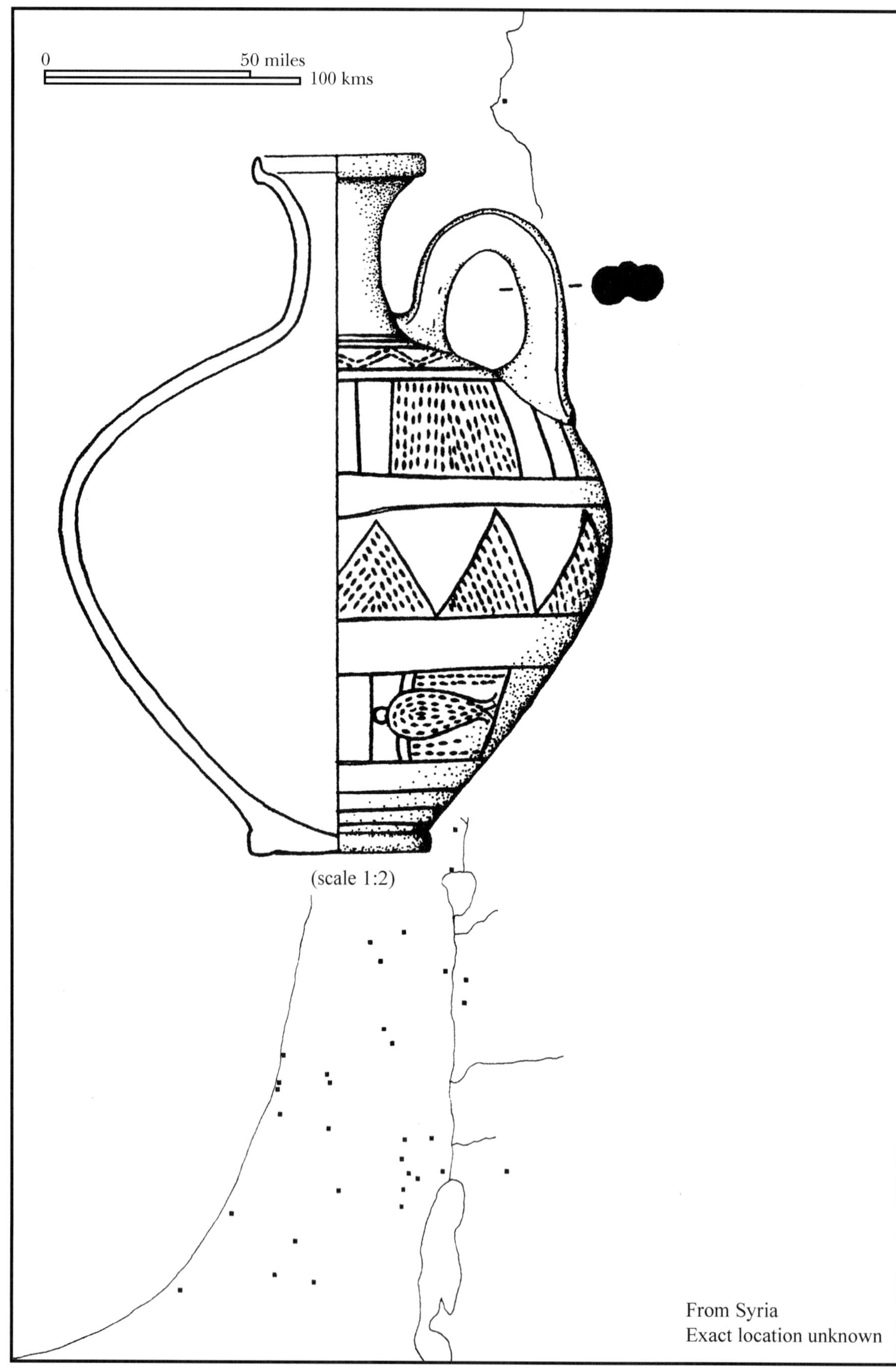

Fig. 79 Distribution and Shape Class of Type Group H.1.1

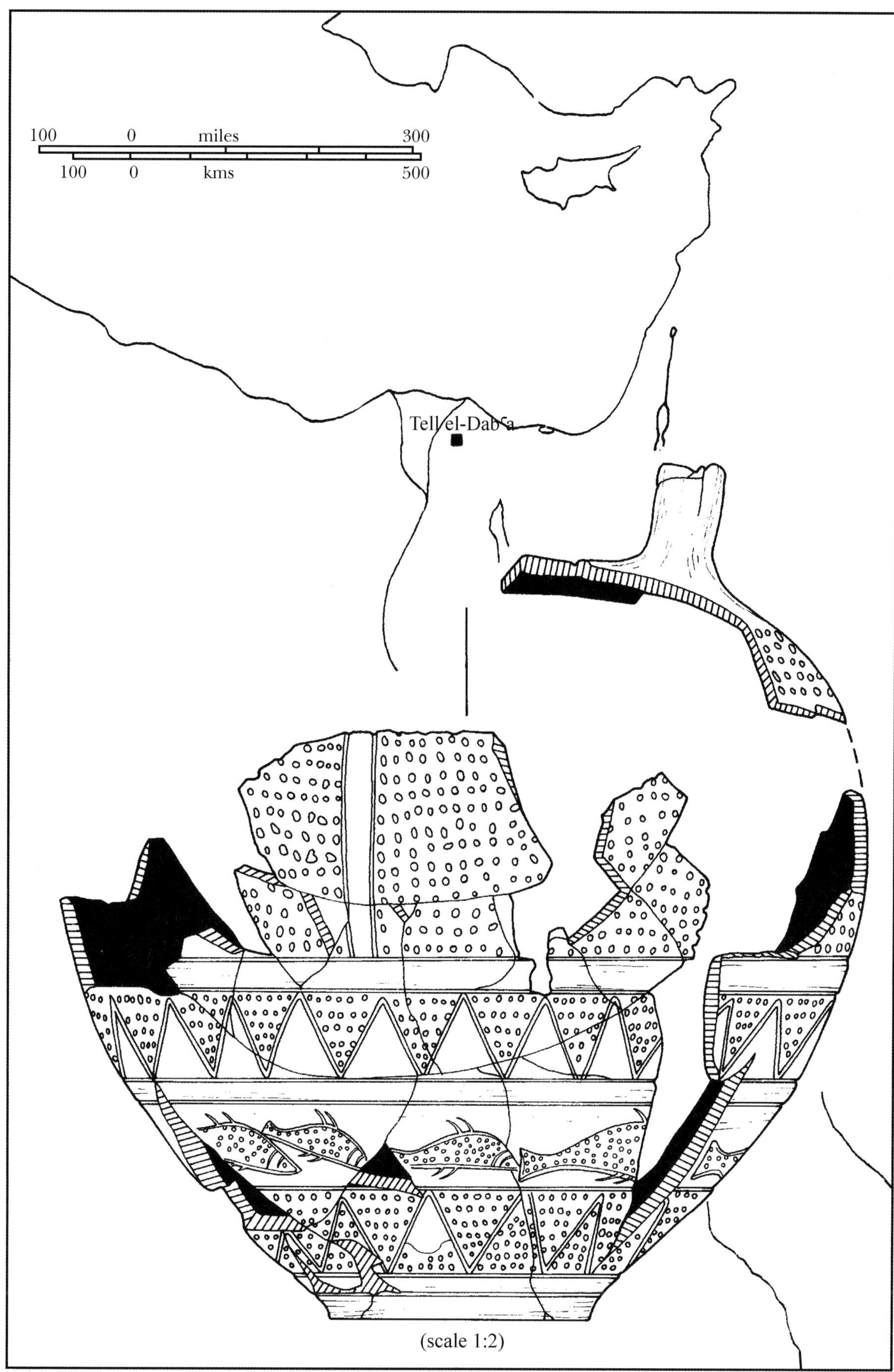

Fig. 80 Distribution and Shape Class of Type Group H.1.2

are the largest of the Tell el-Yahudiya ware, reaching a height of over 30 cm.

Branch I: The Levanto-Egyptian Group of Tell el-Yahudiya Ware

Trade connections between the Levant and Egypt during the early Thirteenth Dynasty led to the importation, and copying, of Early Levantine Tell el-Yahudiya Ware. At first the true Levantine vessels and their Egyptian copies were very similar and the term Levanto-Egyptian can be applied to these early examples. The classic type of Levanto-Egyptian Tell el-Yahudiya Ware contemporary with the late MB IIA in the Levant and the late Thirteenth Dynasty in Egypt, invariably has a piriform shape (Kaplan's Piriform 1, Merillees' El-Lisht Ware). Such Piriform 1 jugs may have ring bases, convex or concave button bases, bipartite or tripartite, sometimes five-stranded handles, and, usually, an inverted kettle rim; however towards the end of the Thirteenth Dynasty, strap handles and rolled rims appear, which then become typical for the Piriform 2a juglets of the Hyksos Period (cf. below). Whilst Kaplan places the emphasis of her classification system on form, stratigraphic excavations at Tell el-Dab^{c}a show that the ornamental schemes found on these Piriform 1 jugs, can often be more meaningful as a classification tool. Over time not only do these jugs tend to become smaller but there is also a trend in the reduction of four to two, and in some cases, one decorative zone. The earliest vessels, those with four zones of decoration may be termed Piriform 1a. They are produced of Levantine clays and seem to originate from the central Levant between Byblos and Kabri, and are closely related to the Early Levantine group. Jugs with three zones of decoration are specified as Piriform 1b, those with two zones, Piriform 1c, and those with only one zone, Piriform 1d. As in the Early Levantine vessels, Piriform 1a jugs tend to have unique decorative patterns, though by the time Piriform 1b vessels evolved, the decorative schemes have also become more standardised. The Piriform 1c with two zones of decoration are even more standardised, with decoration consisting almost exclusively of an upper zone of standing triangles and a lower one of pendant triangles. If the two zones consist of rectangles they originate, as a rule, from the Levant, most probably from the area around Byblos. Piriform 1d vessels are rare, but those with standing rectangles come from the Levant, whilst those with five to seven vertical decorative stripes or lozenges tend to be produced of Nile clay and are the forerunners of the Piriform 2a jugs (cf. below, Late Egyptian L.1).

I.1. Levanto-Egyptian I (Bietak's Piriform 1a)

The Pirifom 1a jugs are subdivided into five groups dependent on the handle attributes; the first two have handles which are placed on the shoulder, and the following three have handles which rise from the shoulder to the rim. In this latter category those jugs with tripartite (or more) handles forming the first subgroup and those with bipartite handles, the second. It is also noticeable that the jugs of group I.1.1 and I.1.2 are somewhat large, and both this and their handle placement relate them to the "Compact Piriform" group H. Jugs of group I.1 are made only from Levantine clays, but are placed under the Levanto-Egyptian group since in their typological and chronological development they evolve into similar forms made in both the Levant and in Egypt.

Type Group I.1.1 (Figs. 81, 86)

Type group I.1.1 is represented by an incompete jug from Tell Arqa Level 14, made in a grey ware, that originated in coastal Lebanon, probably in or around the area of Tripoli, which has fired black, and was burnished to a high lustre.[342] It is ovoid to piriform in shape with a double loop arched handle positioned on the shoulder. This is a shape similar to other local vessels from Arqa found in the same level.[343] It has an inverted triangle decoration on its lower part; the preserved parts of the vessel show a series of pendant triangles framed by an incised line on the shoulder, whilst parts of squares and pendant triangles are also preserved from lower down the jug. It is possible that the entire jug would have had another row of standing triangles touching the tips of the inverted one as on jugs from tombs at Sin el-Fil[344] and Ugarit,[345] or separated by a horizontal band as found on a juglet from a MB IIA fill at Yoqne^{c}am.[346]

[342] See below contribution by H. Charaf, 596.

[343] J. Ph. Thalmann, *Tell Arqa – I. Les niveaux de l'âge de Bronze,* 2006, pl. 85:17.

[344] M. Chehab, Tombe phénicienne de Sin el-Fil, in: *Mélanges offerts à M. R. Dussaud,* Vol. II, Paris, 1939: 806, fig. 5:b.

[345] R. Amiran, *Ancient Pottery of the Holy Land,* 1969, pl. 36:26.

[346] A. Livneh, The Pottery of the Middle Bronze Age, in: A. Ben-Tor, D. Ben-Ami and A. Livneh (eds.), *Yoqn'eam III. The Middle and Late Bronze Ages.* Jerusalem, 2005, fig. II.34:13, Stratum XXIV.

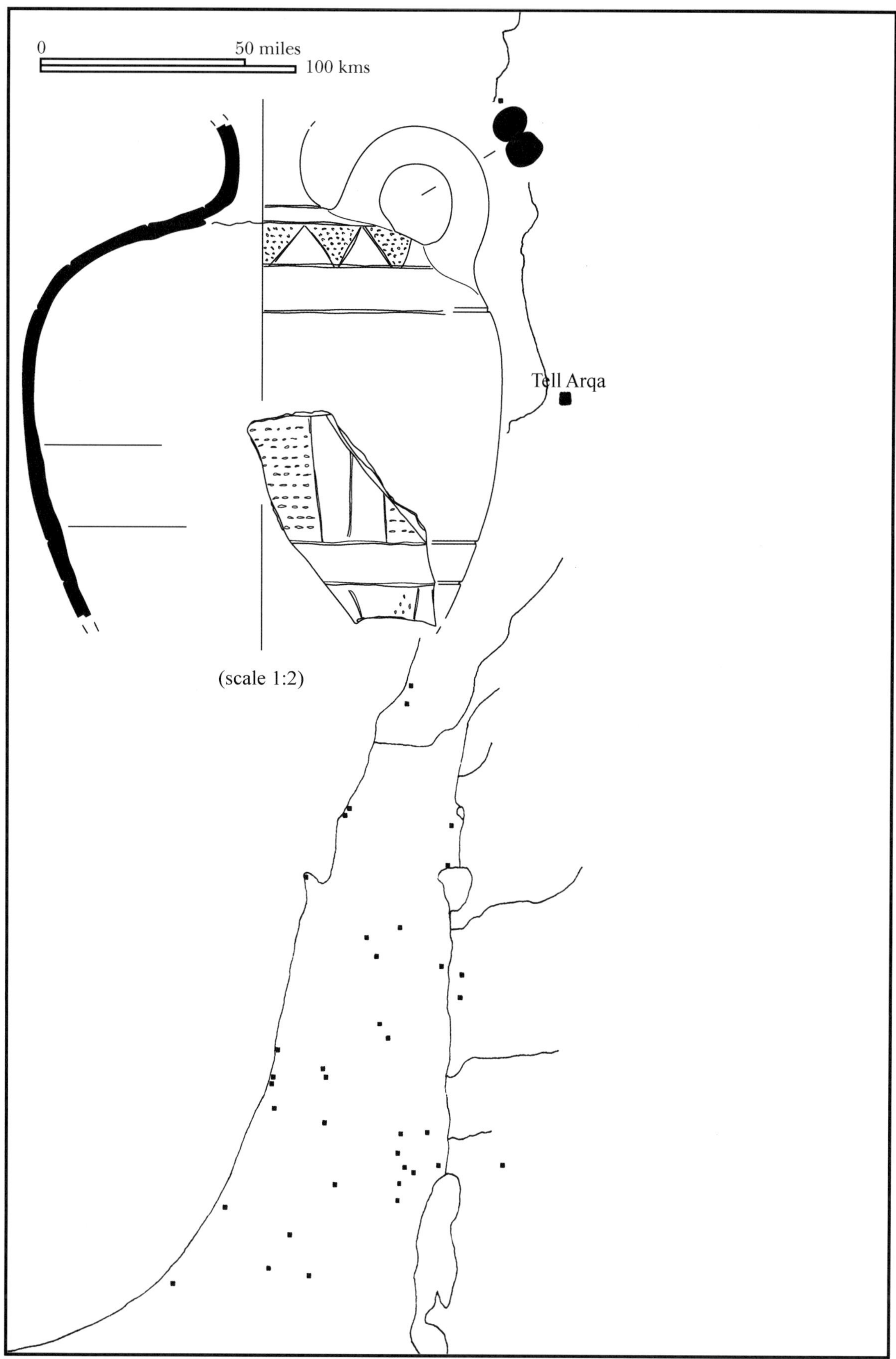

Fig. 81 Distribution and Shape Class of Type Group I.1.1

Type Group I.1.2 (Figs. 82, 86)

Type group I.1.2 is represented by an incomplete vessel from Level 13 at Tell Arqa.[347] The clay from which this jug was made is a marl with *Terra Rossa* additions, possibly deriving from Arqa or at the site of Ardé some 20 km to the south-east. Like the earlier vessel from Arqa, above type group I.1.1, this vessel has a loop handle placed on the slanting shoulder which imitates locally produced MB IIB jugs. However, the thick handle is a single one punctured with holes filled with white chalk. One can assume that the little preserved decoration on the shoulder shows a triangle or a rhomboid. Faint traces of burnishing indicate that the vessel was burnished.

Type Group I.1.3 (Figs. 83, 86)

Vessels of group I.1.3 have kettle rims, tripartite handles, ring bases and four decorative zones consisting of joined pendant and standing triangles. They were subsumed into Kaplan's Ovoid 4, but are perhaps better seen as the earliest members of the Piriform 1 jugs of the Levanto-Egyptian group. Their style of decoration anticipates the decorative scheme which becomes very popular in this particular family. At present vessels of group I.1.3 are only known from Megiddo[348] and ᶜAfula,[349]

Type Group I.1.4 (Figs. 84, 86)

Type group I.1.4 is represented by two vessels from Megiddo, tombs 3123 and 4099, which are piriform in shape, have kettle rims, bipartite handles, ring bases and four horizontal zones of decoration.[350] The uppermost consists of comb imprints whilst the lower three comprise comb imprints with reserved zigzags.

Type Group I.1.5 (Figs. 85, 86)

Jugs of this group have a kettle rim, a double handle joining at the neck below the rim, incisions at the neck, ring bases and four zones of decoration. At present examples of such vessels are known only from Byblos,[351] Memphis,[352] the Fayoum[353] and Tell el-Dabᶜa (TD 3283). A vessel of which the place of discovery is unknown and now in the Fitzwilliam museum, Cambridge is made of a Levantine clay,[354] as is the Tell el-Dabᶜa vessel. As befits their early date the decorative schemes tend to be peculiar to each vessel.

I.2. Levanto-Egyptian II (Bietak's Piriform 1b)

Again, as with the Piriform 1a group, vessels of the Piriform 1b group can also be subdivided into those with a ring base and a tripartite (or more) handles, those with a ring base and bipartite handles, and, less common, those with disc and button bases. Jugs belonging to this type and the remaining I groups are now found in both Levantine and, as imitations, Egyptian clays.

Type Group I.2.1a (Figs. 87, 99)

Type group I.2.1a comprise those jugs with a kettle rim, a tripartite handle joining at the neck below the rim, incisions at the neck, ring bases and three zones of decoration. At present, however, this group is only known through one complete vessel found at Buhen,[355] made of a Nile Clay,[356] and other incomplete examples found at Edfu[357] and in tomb 303b at Tell el-Ajjul.[358] The decoration on all three vessels consists of an upper zone of standing triangles, a central zone of infilled rectangles and a lower zone of hanging triangles, a decorative scheme which is very popular at this time.

Type Group I.2.1b (Figs. 88, 99)

Jugs of this group are similar to I.2.1a in having a kettle rim, a tripartite handle joining at the neck below the rim, incisions at the neck, ring bases and three zones of decoration. At present examples of such vessels are known only through two vessels, an incom-

[347] H. Charaf, Arqa and its regional connections Redux, *Bulletin d'Architecture et d'Archéologie Libanaises* Hors-Série VI, (2009), 296, fig. 1.4; and cf. below 599.

[348] Jerusalem, Rockefeller Museum I.3121. Kaplan, *Tell el-Yahudiyeh Ware*, fig. 116b.

[349] Jerusalem, Rockefeller Museum 41.400. Sukenik, *JPOS* 41, 1948, 60, pl. 14.18, Kaplan, *Tell el-Yahudiyeh Ware*, fig. 116c.

[350] Loud, 1948, pl. 24.31; Kaplan, *Tell el-Yahudiyeh Ware*, fig. 116a.

[351] Beirut 8521. Kaplan, *Tell el-Yahudiyeh Ware*, fig. 29b.

[352] B. Bader, *TD XIX*, 2009, 496 no [6094].

[353] Weigall, Upper Egyptian Notes 11. A Pottery vase from Kahun, [105–112] *ASAE* 9, 1908, 110, fig. 5, Kaplan, *Tell el-Yahudiyeh Ware*, fig. 24a.

[354] Cambridge Fitzwilliam E.6.1972. Kaplan, *Tell el-Yahudiyeh Ware*, fig. 29a. The clay was checked by Manfred Bietak, personal observation.

[355] Philadelphia, UM E.10765. Randall-Maciver and Woolley, *Buhen*, 201–202, pl. 49.

[356] Kaplan, *Tell el-Yahudiyeh Ware*, 229 sample BH1.

[357] Cairo JE 46743. Merrillees, *Trade and Transcendance*, 67; Kaplan, *Tell el-Yahudiyeh Ware*, fig 25b.

[358] Jerusalem, Rockefeller Museum, Petrie 1933, 7, pl. 38.60M5; Kaplan, *Tell el-Yahudiyeh Ware*, fig 77b.

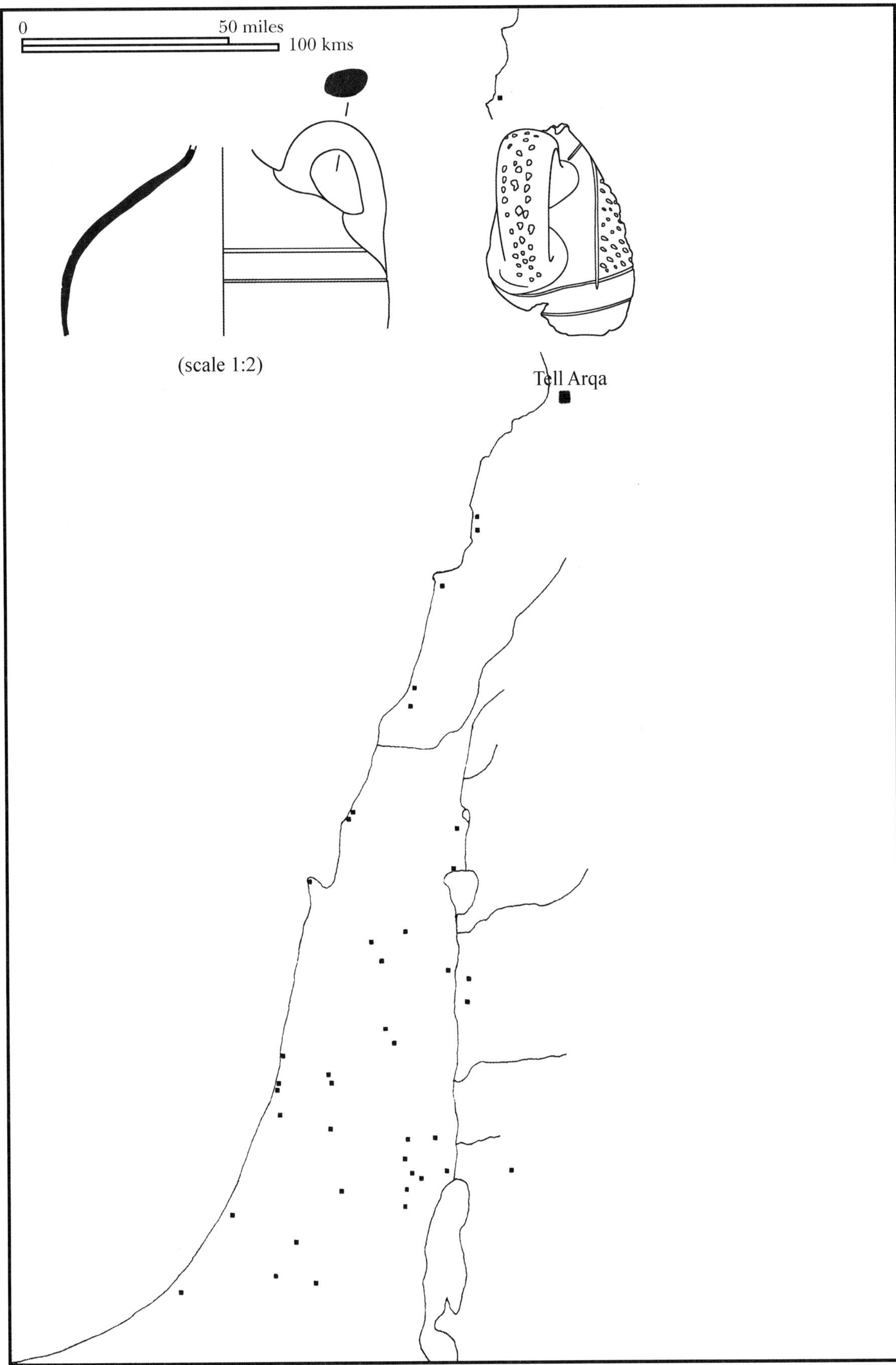

Fig. 82 Distribution and Shape Class of Type Group I.1.2

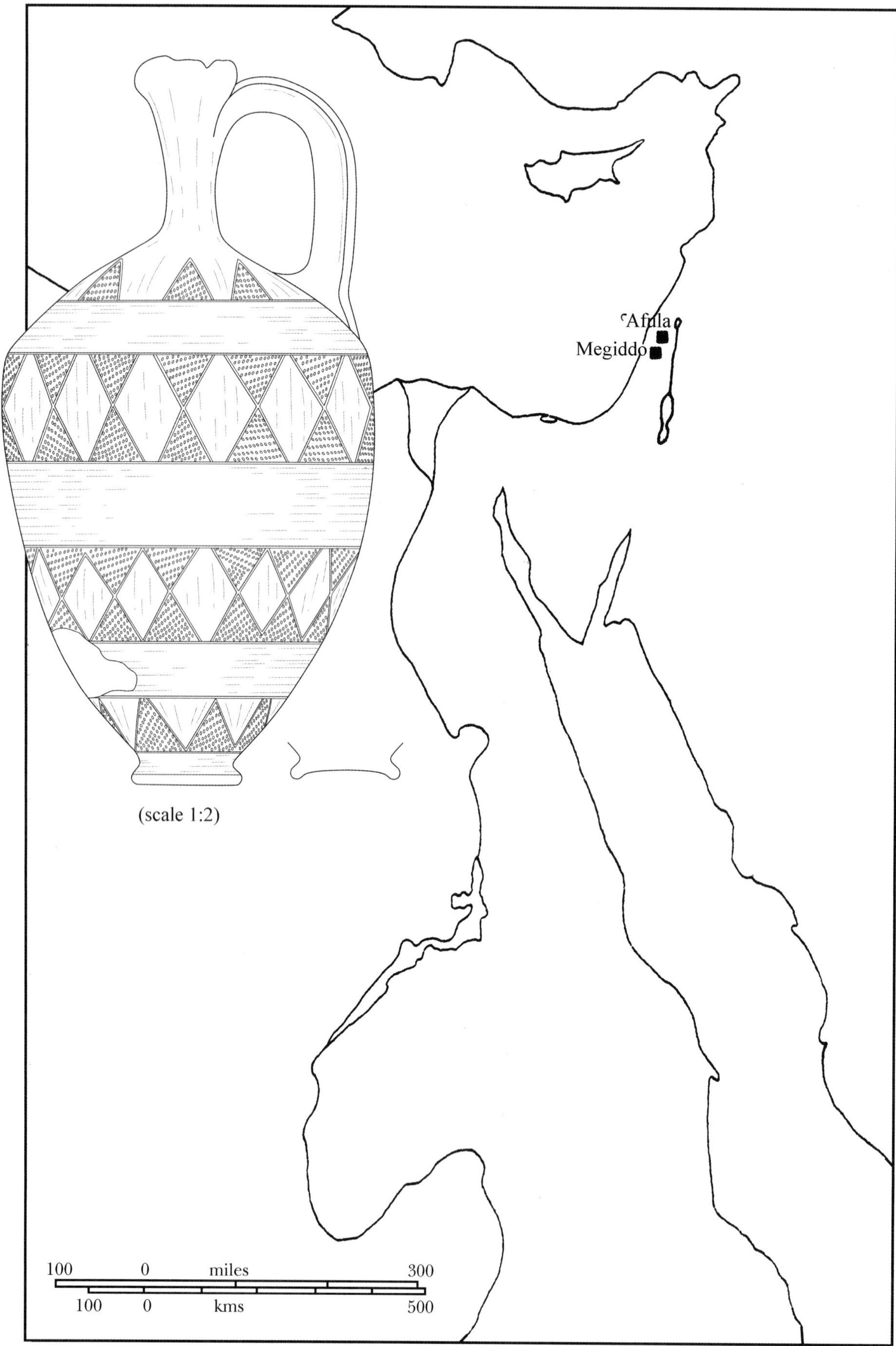

Fig. 83 Distribution and Shape Class of Type Group I.1.3

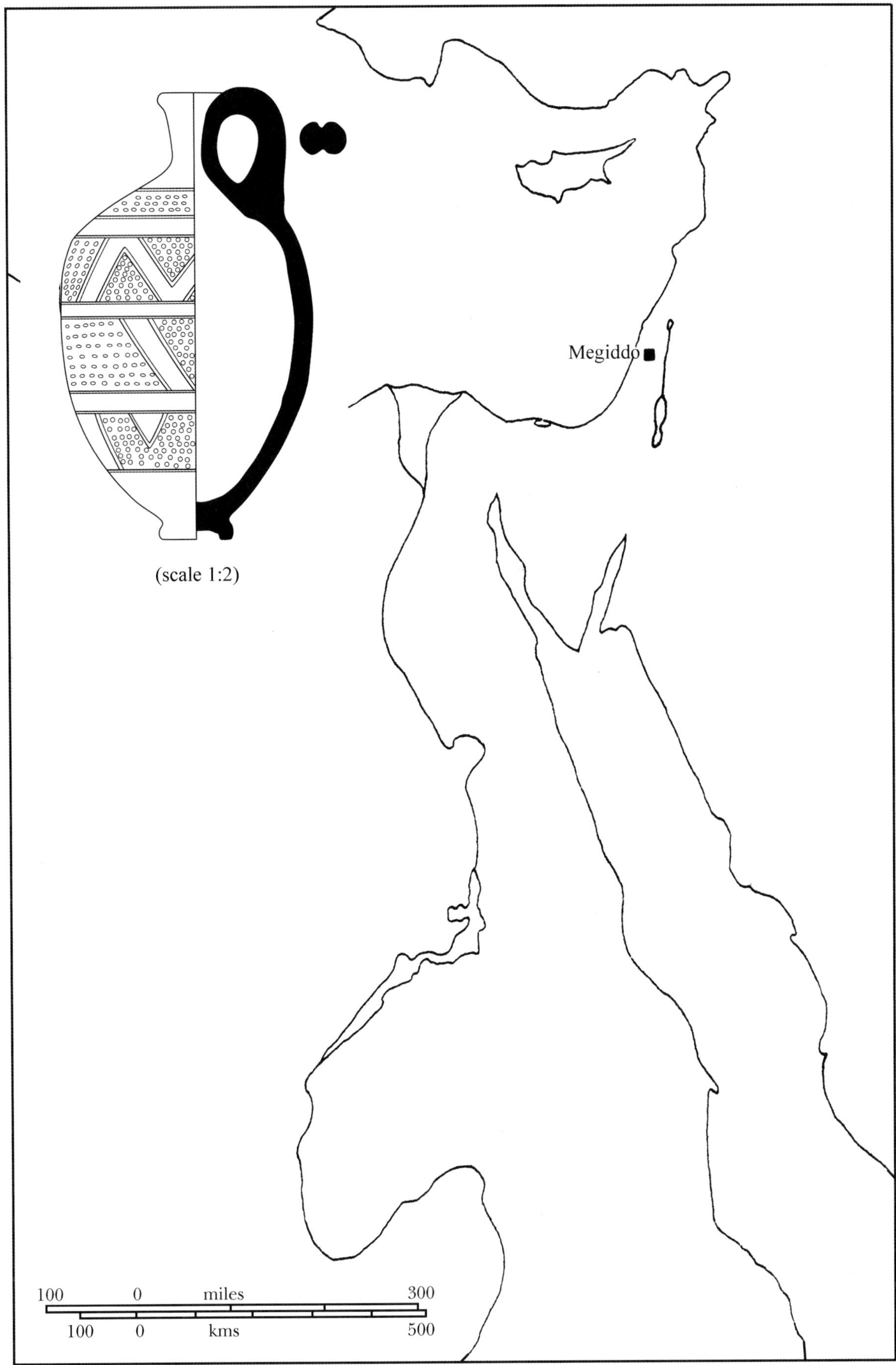

Fig. 84 Distribution and Shape Class of type Group I.1.4

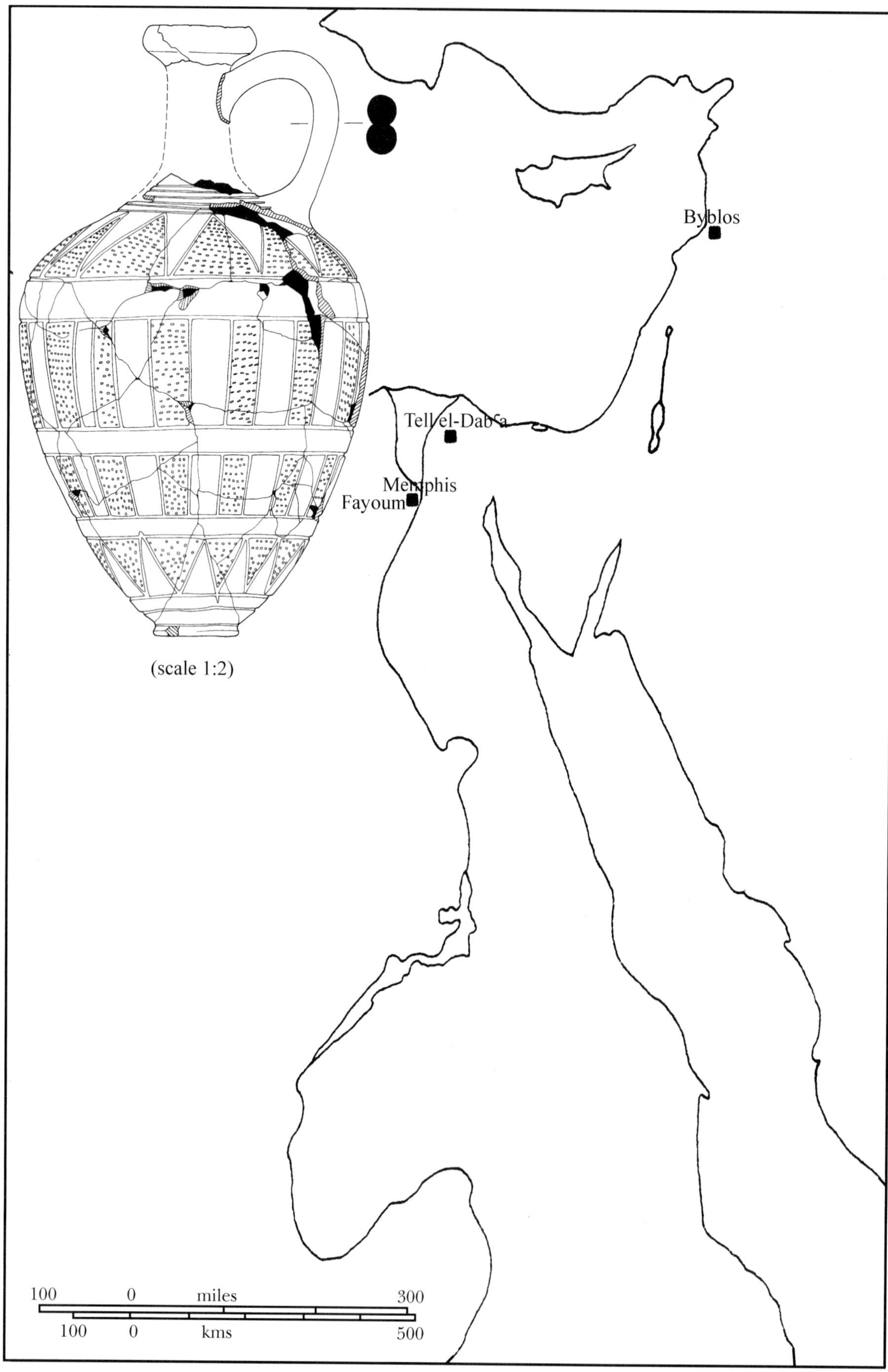

Fig. 85 Distribution and Shape Class of Type Group I.1.5

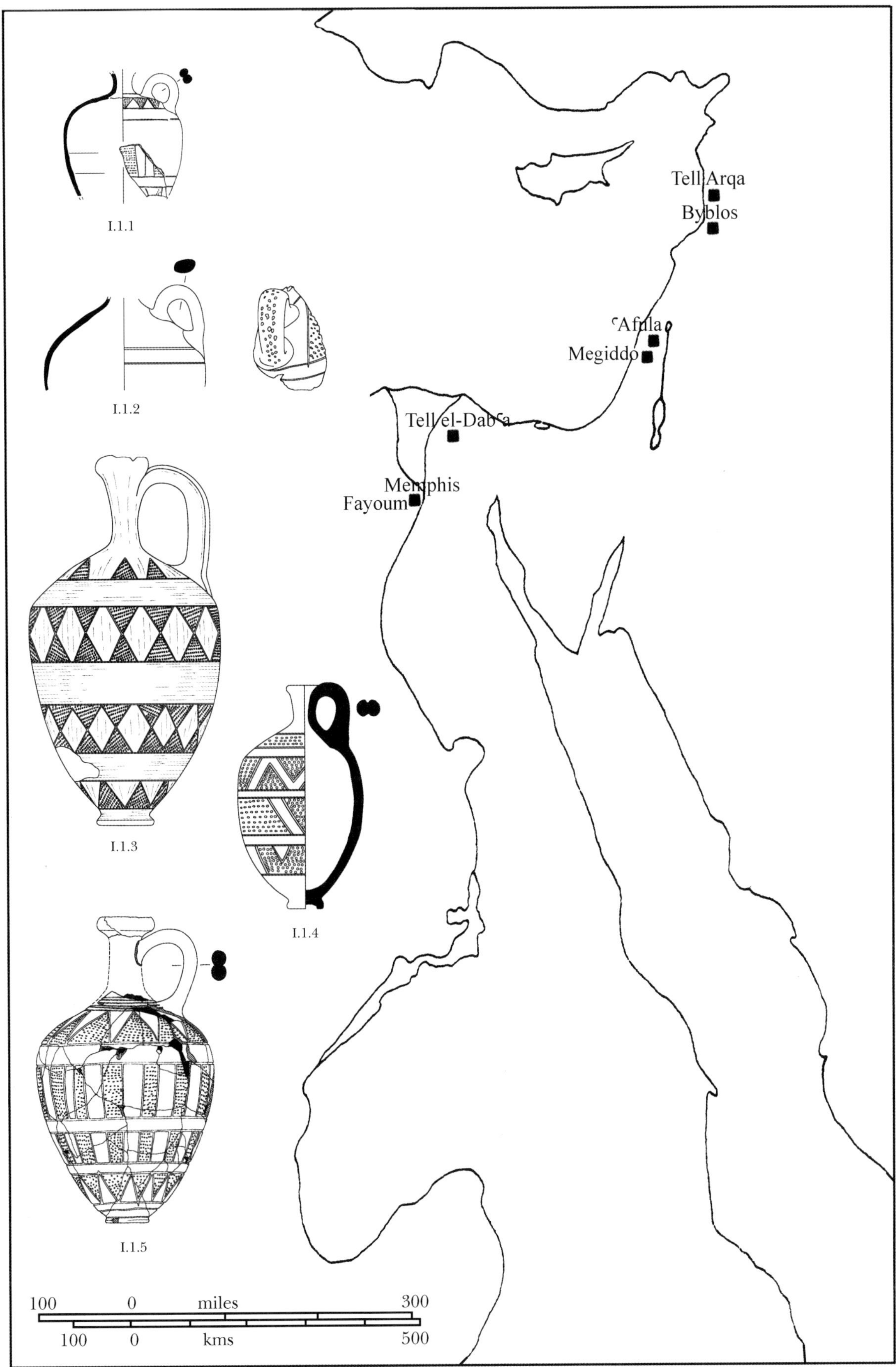

Fig. 86 Combined Distribution of Type Group I.1 (Piriform 1a)

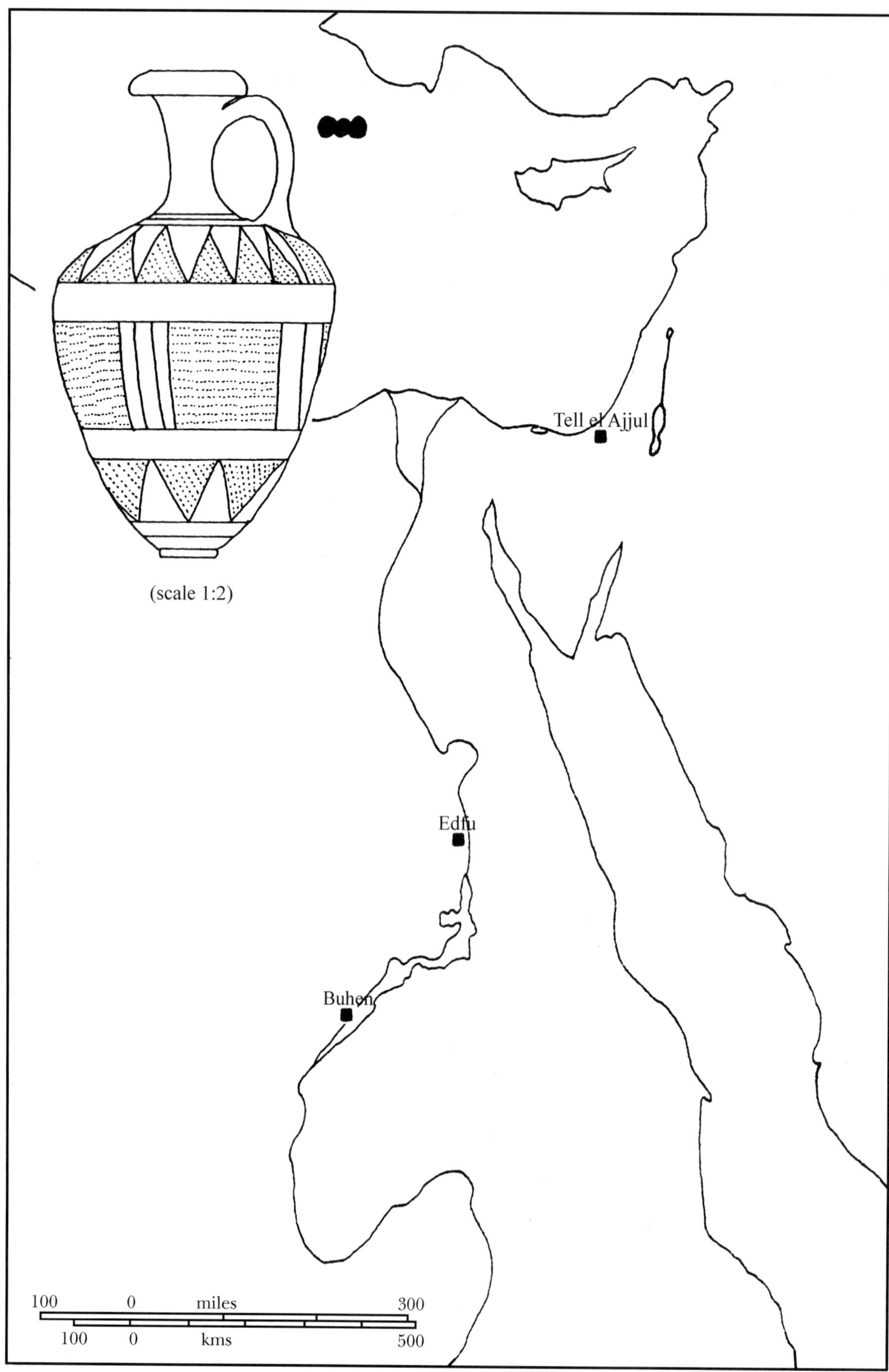

Fig. 87 Distribution and Shape Class of Type Group I.2.1a

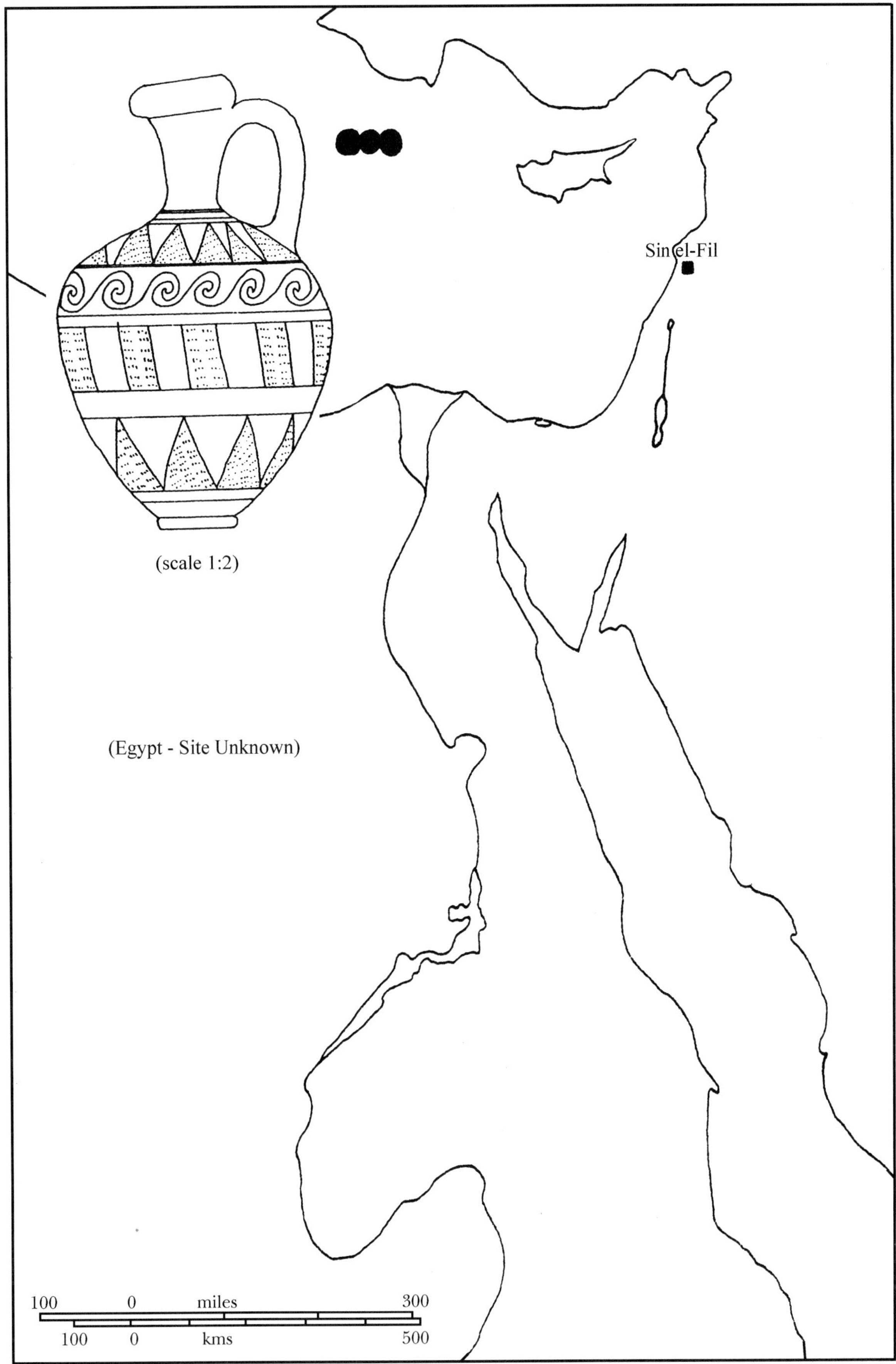

Fig. 88 Distribution and Shape Class of Type Group I.2.1b

plete one from Sin el-Fil,[359] and another from Egypt, site unknown, the latter made of a Nile clay.[360] The Sin el-Fil vessel is decorated with four zones of spirals, a motif which reappears in the second zone of the Egyptian vessel, though the other zones in comprising standing triangles - top and bottom zone, with the third zone consisting of squares.

Type Group I.2.2 (Figs. 89–96, 99)

Type group I.2.2 is in all respects similar to I.1.2, in that they have kettle rims, double handles joining at the neck below the rim, incisions at the neck, and ring bases, but by contrast there are now only three zones of decoration, and, at this stage, one begins to see more standardization in the styles of ornamentation. Of these the most common is I.2.2a, an uppermost zone consisting of standing triangles, a central zone of rectangles and a lower zone of pendant triangles found on vessels from Sin el-Fil,[361] Tell el-Dabᶜa vessels TD 3956 and TD 5436, Qasr el-Sagha,[362] Buhen,[363] and Arpera in Cyprus.[364] Variations on this scheme comprise I.2.2b in which the lowermost zone is replaced by one of standing triangles, a decorative scheme known from Byblos,[365] or I.2.2c in which the lowermost zone is replaced with a lowermost zone of rectangles, as in the example found in the tomb of Senwosretankh at Lisht.[366] Decorative style I.2.2d, comprising rectangles – standing triangles – rectangles comes from Byblos.[367] I.2.2e consisting of standing triangles – joined pendant and standing triangles – standing triangles was found at Elephantine.[368] I.2.2f standing triangles – pendant triangles – pendant triangles was found at Kumber, Sudan.[369] I.2.2.g, three zones of standing triangles is represented by an incomplete vessel which was reputedly found in Upper Egypt.[370] To this group should probably also be added another jug from Sin el-Fil, with a decoration comprising standing triangles – joined pendant and standing triangles – pendant triangles, but the published drawing of this vessel shows no incisions at the neck.[371]

Type Group I.2.3 (Figs. 97–99)

This group exists solely on the evidence of incomplete examples from Tell el-Dabᶜa. The best preserved, TD 5795, has a candlestick rim, double handle, incisions at the base of the neck, but in place of a ring base, a button, and three zones of decoration. TD 4518 is a fragmentary example missing the rim and neck. TD 5795 is decorated with three zones of standing triangles (I.2.3a), whilst TD 4518 has an uppermost zone of pendant triangles, a central one of rectangles and a lower one of pendant triangles (I.2.3b).

I.3. Levanto-Egyptian III (Bietak's Piriform 1c)

Type Group I.3.1 (Figs. 100–104, 110)

Tell el-Yahudiya jugs of group I.3.1 are piriform in shape, have kettle rims, double handles incisions at the base of the neck, ring bases, and only two decorative zones, one on the upper body and one on the lower body. Such vessels are very popular, and are known with various decorative styles: I.3.1a with an upper zone of standing triangles and a lower one of stylized lotus petals known only through a vessel presumably found in Cyprus;[372] I.3.1b, an upper zone of standing triangles and a lower one of pendant triangles, each of which are delineated by two incised lines, known on a vessel from Gezer, having presumably been imported from further north;[373] whilst the

[359] Chehab *Mélanges syriens*, 806, fig. 6a, Kaplan, *Tell el-Yahudiyeh Ware*, fig. 40b.

[360] Oxford Ashmolean 1896–1908.C.96. Petrie, *Kahun, Gurob and Hawara*, 199–200, Merrillees, *Trade and Transcendance*, 67, fig. 59, Kaplan, *Tell el-Yahudiyeh Ware*, fig. 40b. NAA analysis, Kaplan, *Tell el-Yahudiyeh Ware*, 230, UU21.

[361] Chehab, *Mélanges syriens*, 806 fig. 5c, Kaplan, *Tell el-Yahudiyeh Ware*, fig. 24b.

[362] Sliwa, Die Siedlung des Mittleren Reiches bei Qasr el-Sagha, *MDAIK* 48, 1992, 188, Abb 8.2.

[363] Philadelphia UM E.10765. Randall-MacIver and Woolley, *Buhen*, 201–202, pl. 49.

[364] Nicosia, Cyprus Museum. Merrillees *Trade and Transcendance*, 49, figs. 31.14, 38, Kaplan, *Tell el-Yahudiyeh Ware*, fig. 26b.

[365] Paris Louvre AO 9120. Dussaud, *Syria* 9, 1928, 149 fig. 16; Montet, *Byblos et l'Egypte*, 244, pl. 148, Kaplan, *Tell el-Yahudiyeh Ware*, fig. 23a

[366] Cairo JE 60263. Merrillees, *Trade and Transcendance*, 59, fig. 48, Kaplan, *Tell el-Yahudiyeh Ware*, fig. 25a.

[367] Beirut 12396. Dunand, *Fouilles à Byblos II*, 519, fig. 583, Kaplan, *Tell el-Yahudiyeh Ware*, fig. 24c.

[368] Cairo CG 4621. Kaplan *Tell el-Yahudiyeh Ware*, fig. 25c.

[369] Khartoum NM 23137. Kaplan *Tell el-Yahudiyeh Ware*, fig. 26a.

[370] London BM EA 50757, Myres *JHS* 17, 1897, 145; Kaplan *Tell el-Yahudiyeh Ware*, fig. 27b.

[371] Chehab, *Mélanges syriens*, 806, fig. 5b, Kaplan, *Tell el-Yahudiyeh Ware*, fig. 24d.

[372] Geneva P130. Merrillees *Trade and Transcendance*, 73, fig. 60, Kaplan, *Tell el-Yahudiyeh Ware*, fig. 35c.

[373] Macalister, *Gezer*, vol. 2, 156, 160, vol. 3, pl. 153.10, Kaplan, *Tell el-Yahudiyeh Ware*, fig. 34e.

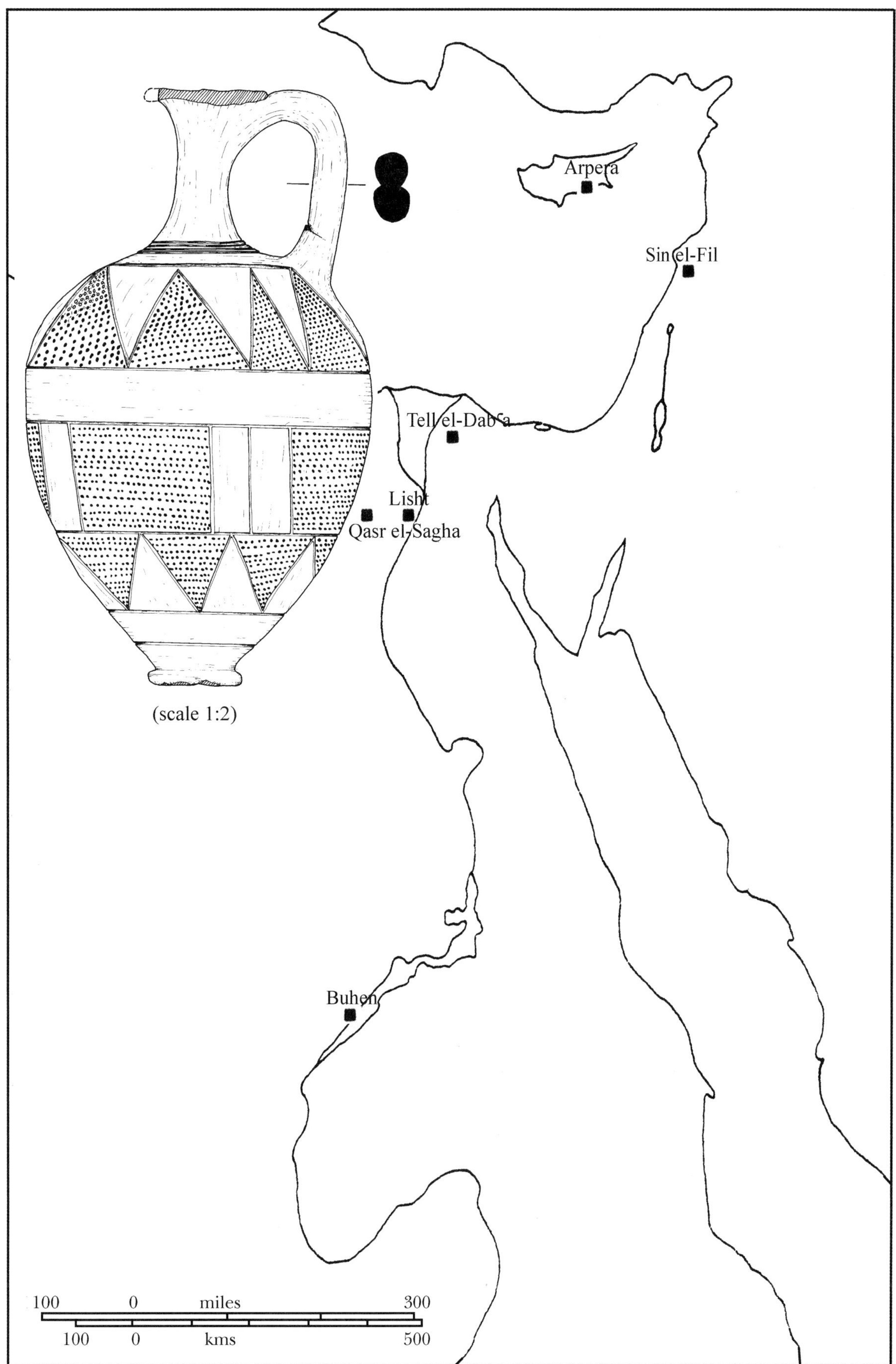

Fig. 89 Distribution and Shape Class of Type Group I.2.2a

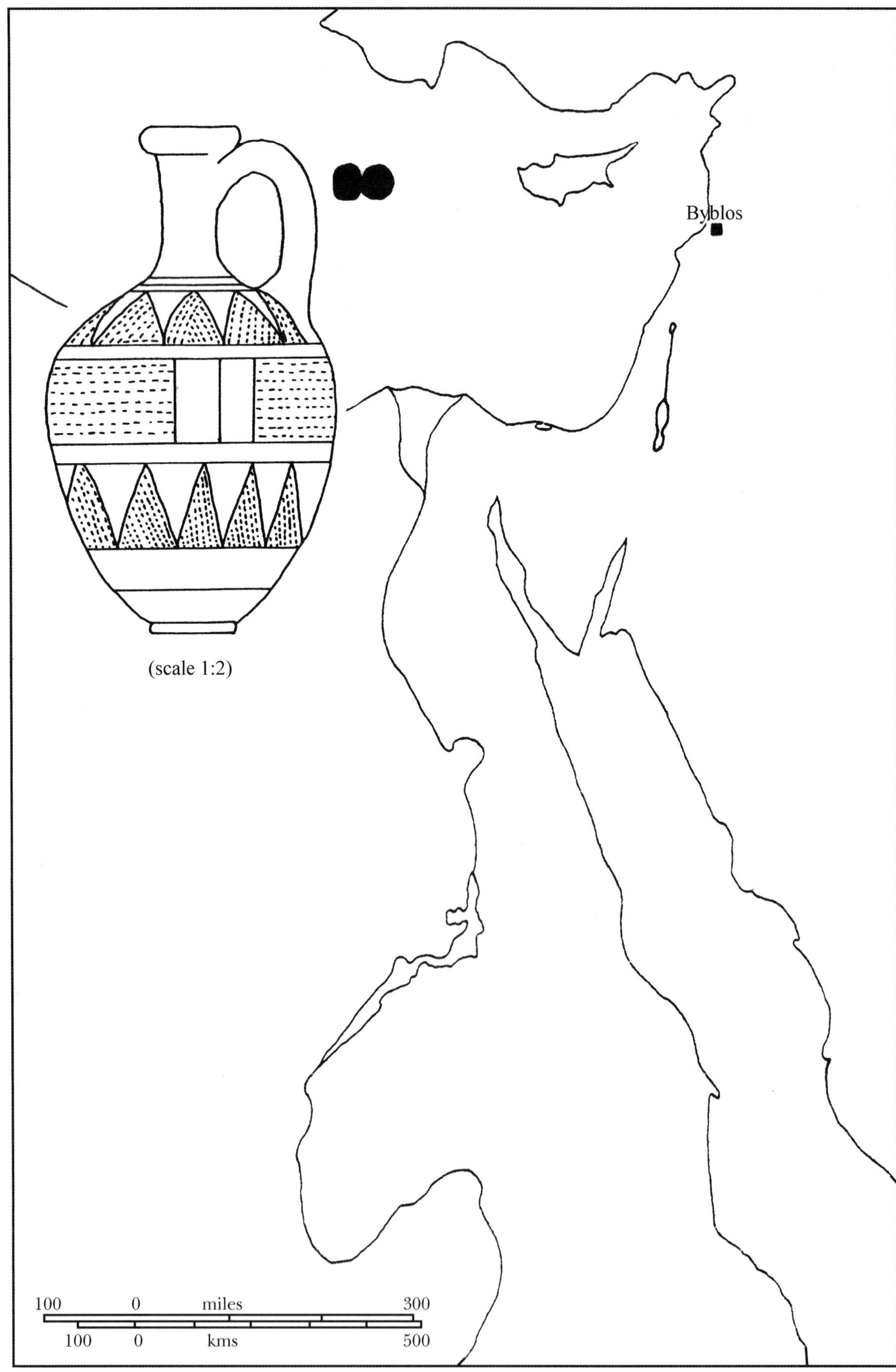

Fig. 90 Distribution and Shape Class of Type Group I.2.2b

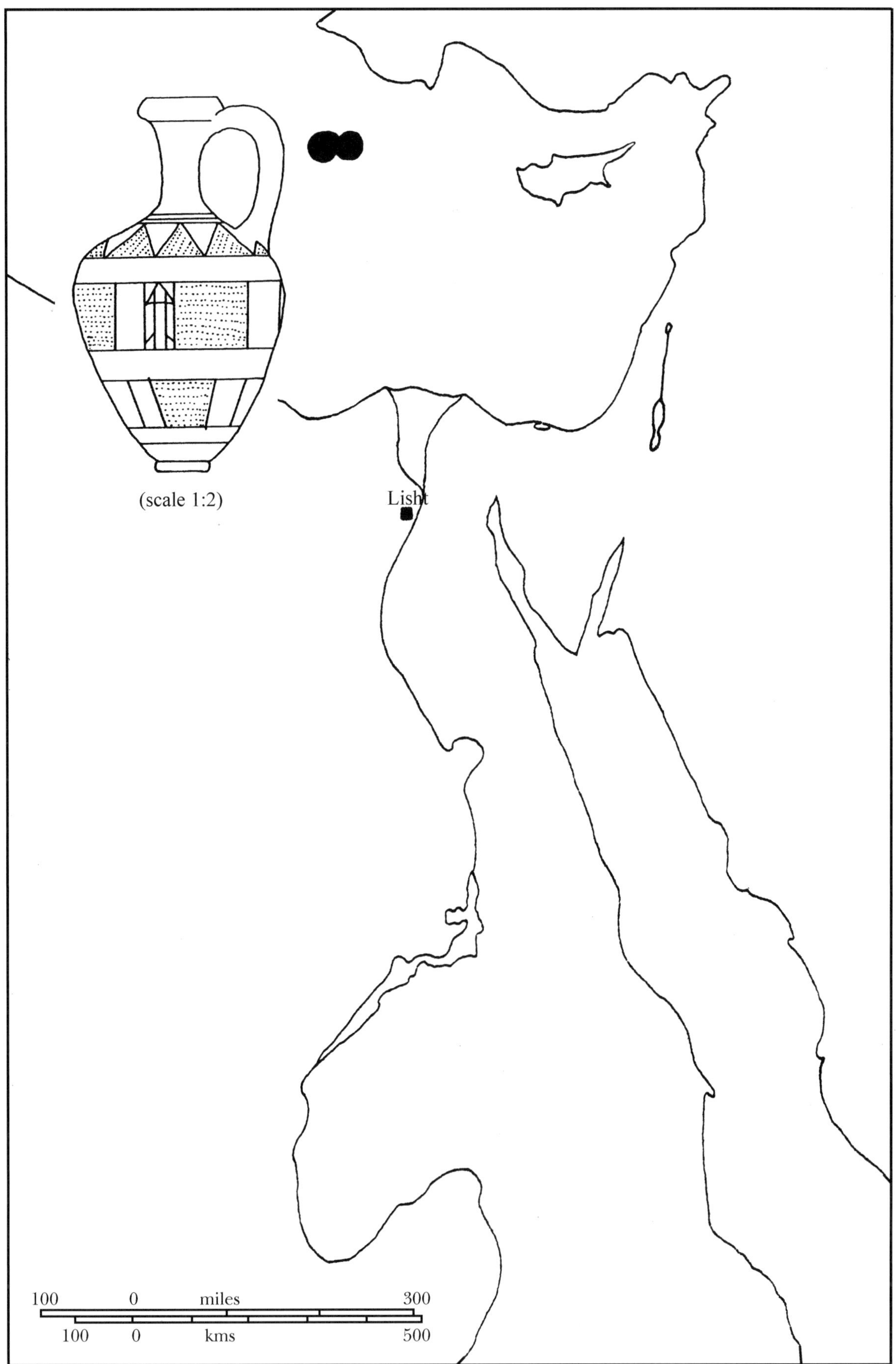

Fig. 91 Distribution and Shape Class of Type Group I.2.2c

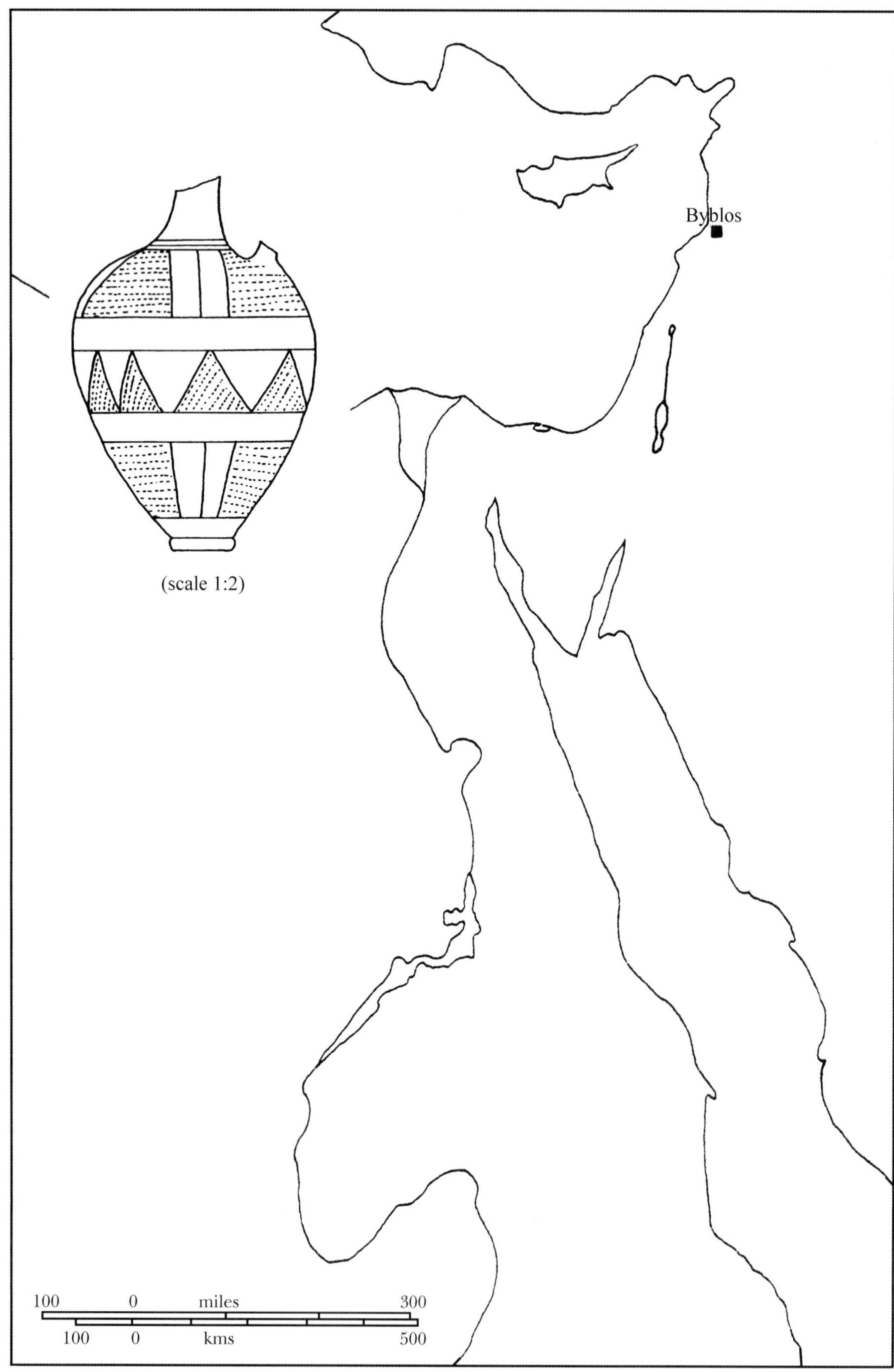

Fig. 92 Distribution and Shape Class of Type Group I.2.2d

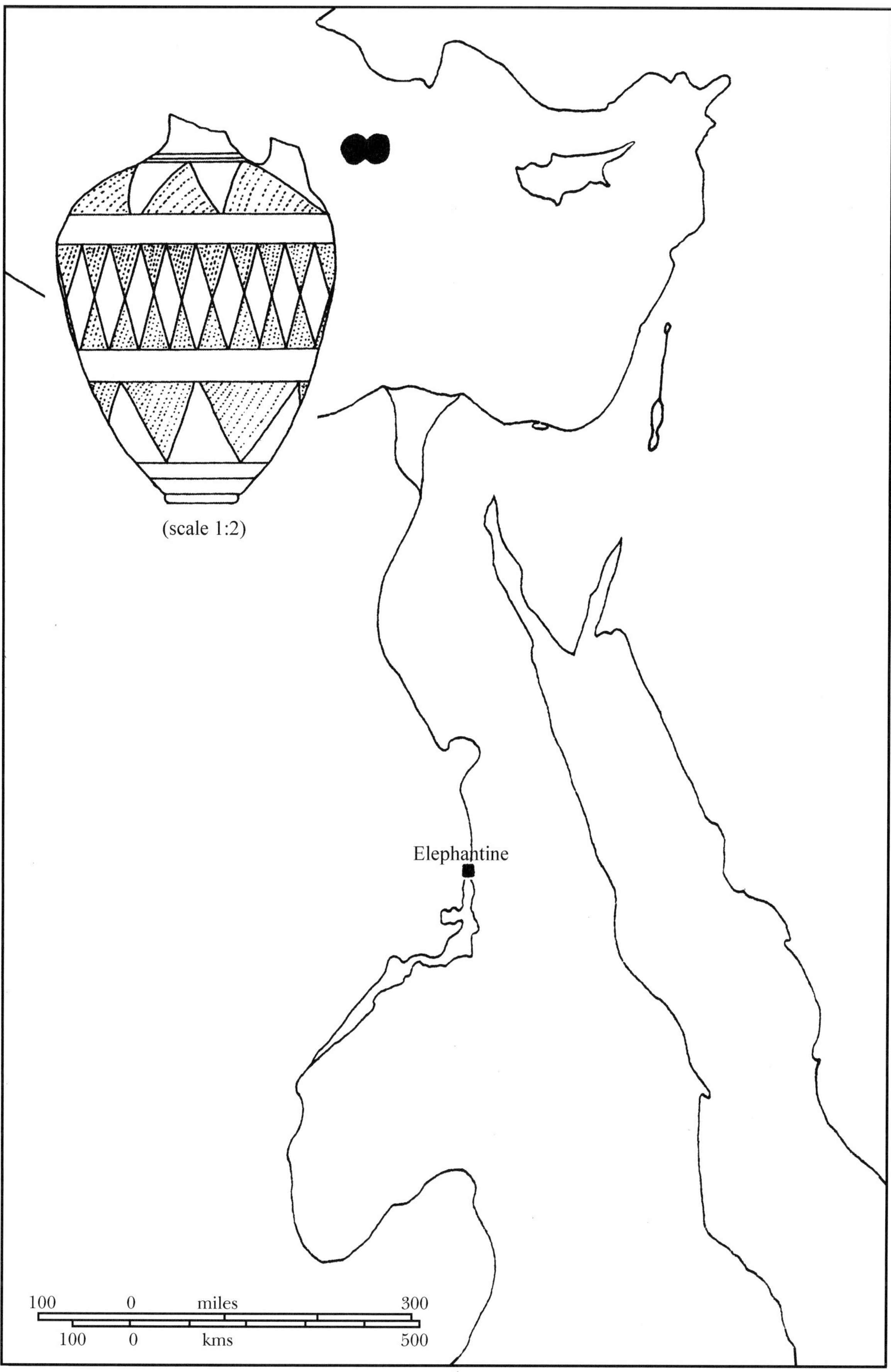

Fig. 93 Distribution and Shape Class of Type Group I.2.2e

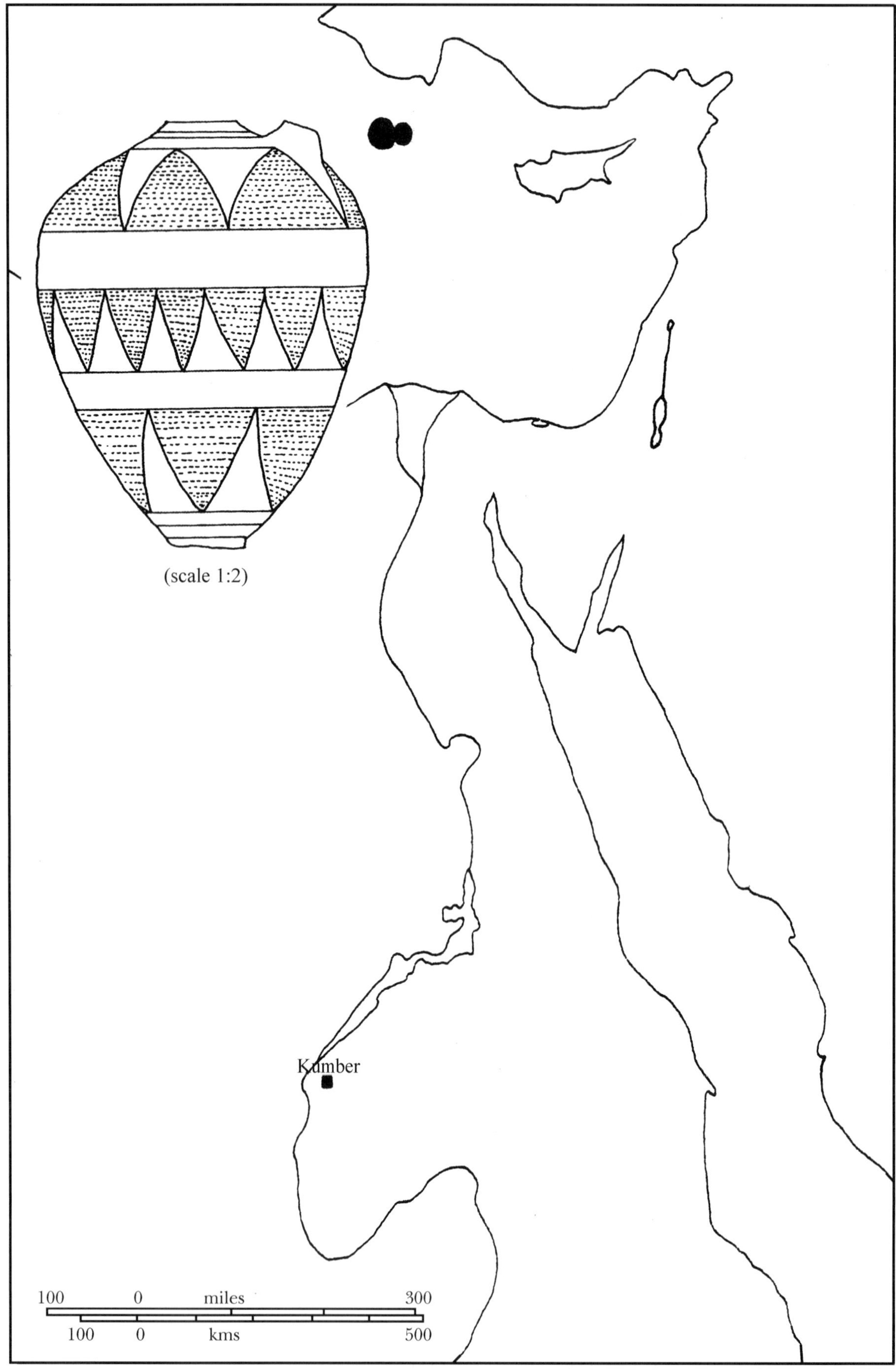

Fig. 94 Distribution and Shape Class of Type Group I.2.2f

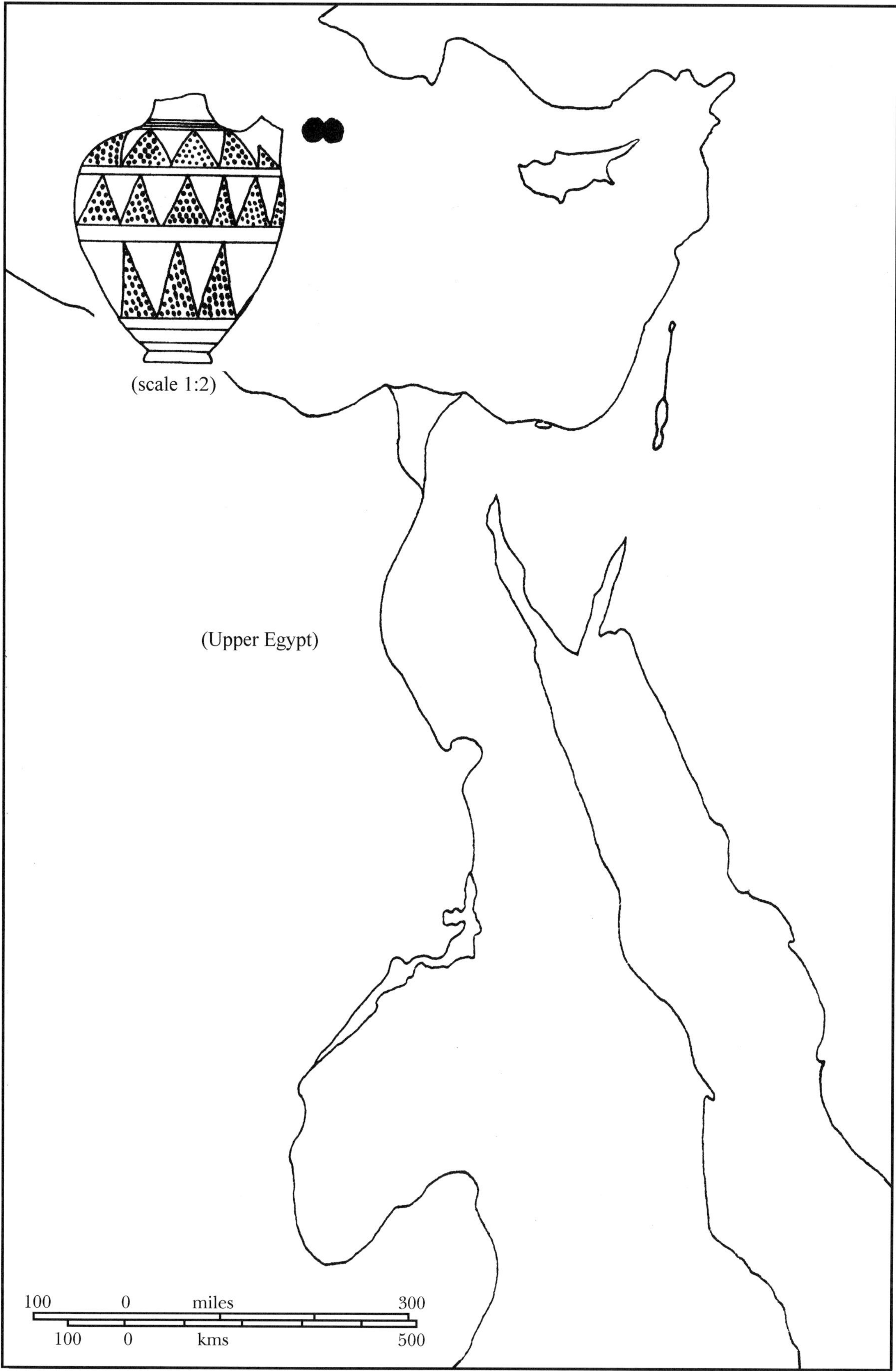

Fig. 95 Distribution and Shape Class of Type Group I.2.2g

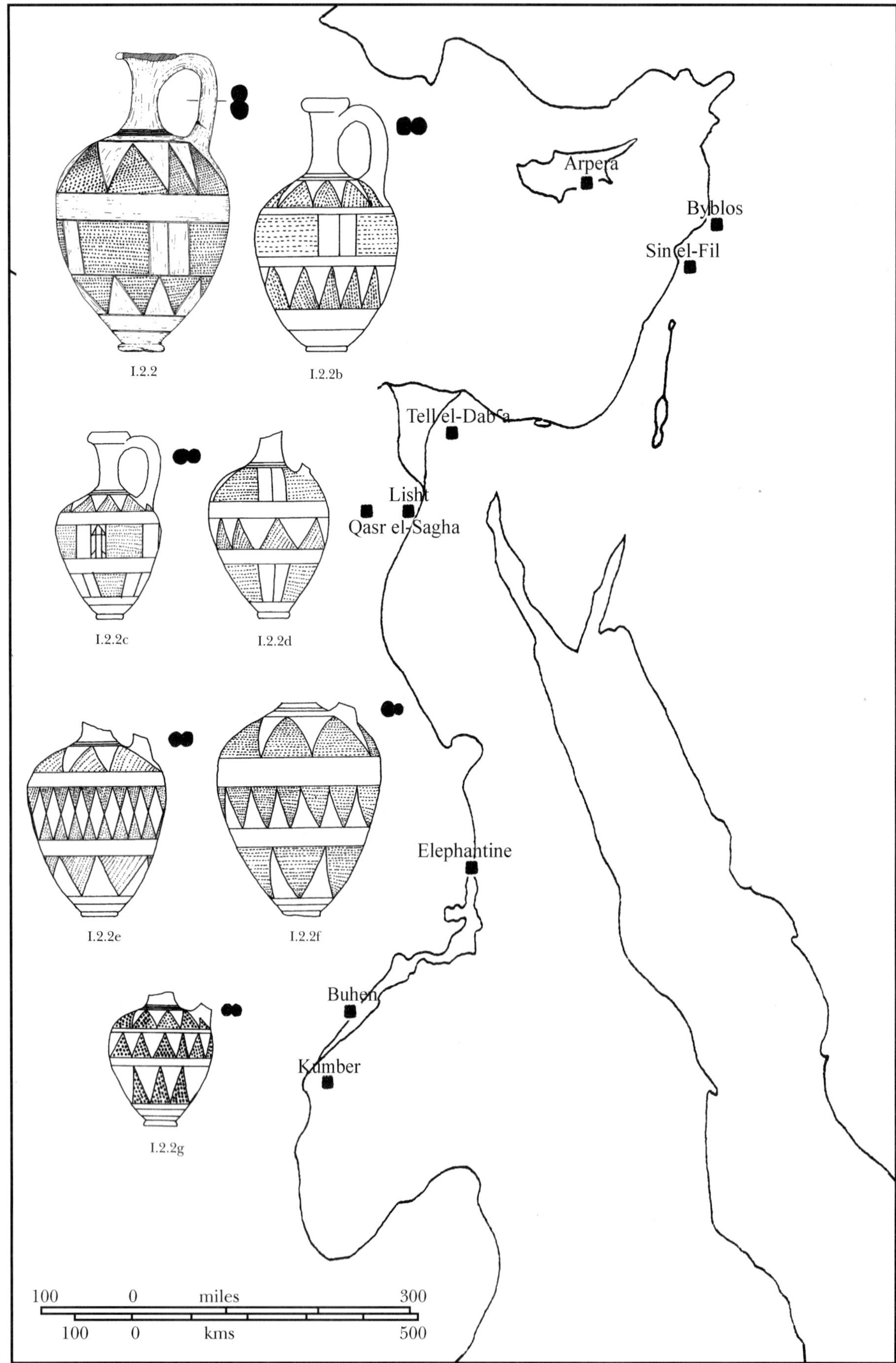

Fig. 96 Combined Distribution of Type Group I.2.2

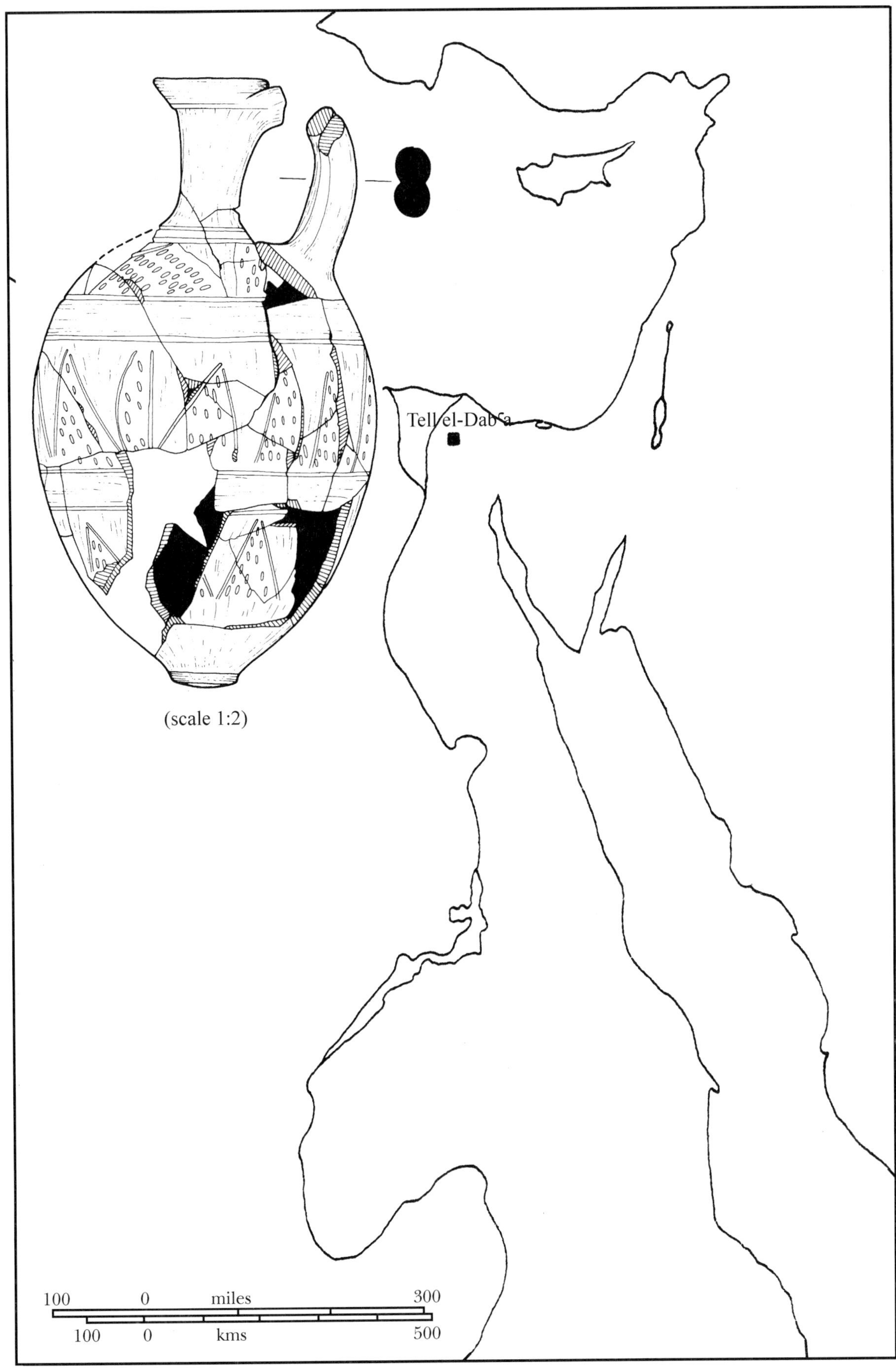

Fig. 97 Distribution and Shape Class of Type Group I.2.3a

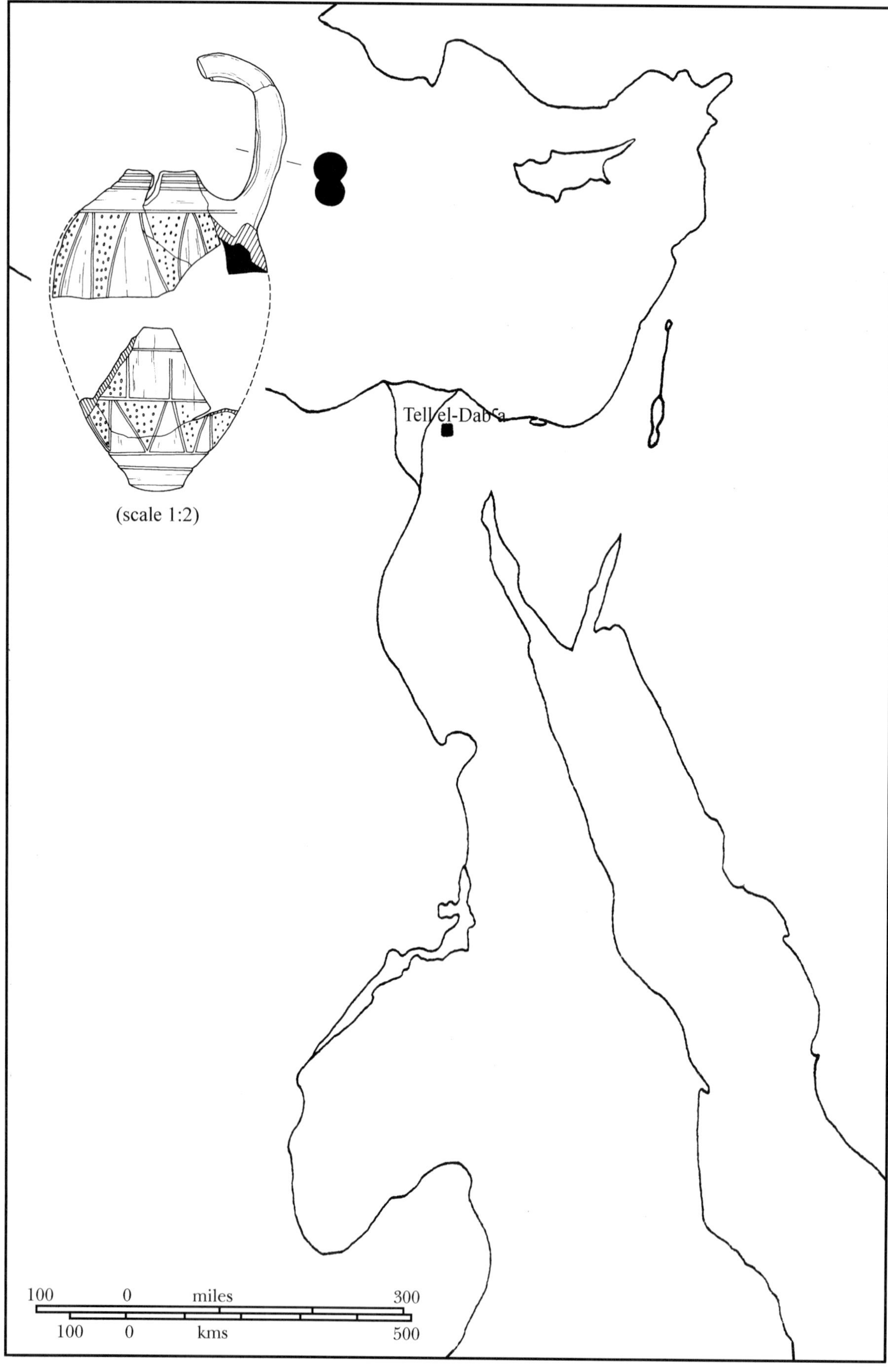

Fig. 98 Distribution and Shape Class of Type Group I.2.3b

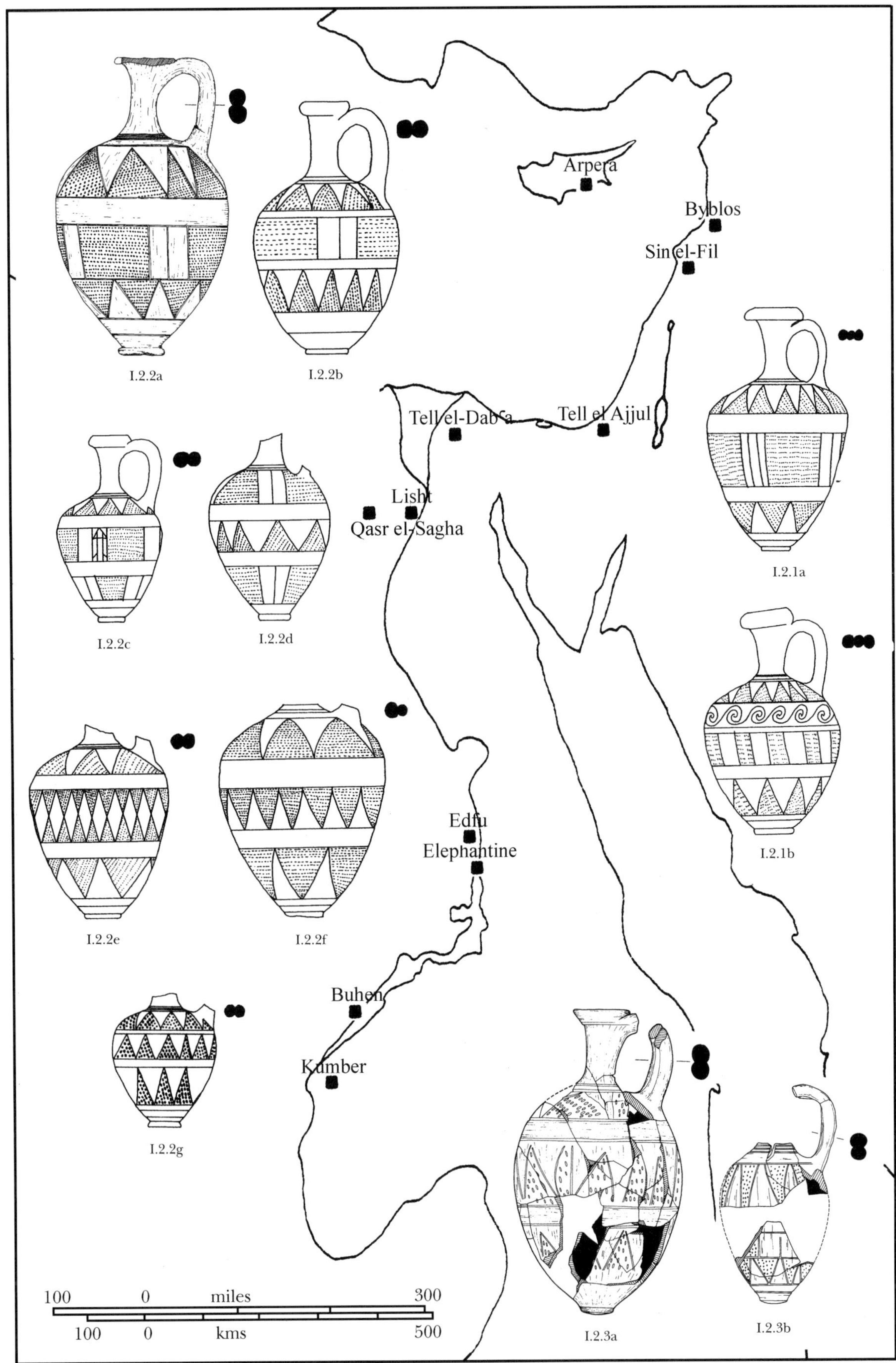

Fig. 99 Combined Distribution of Type Group I.2 (Piriform 1b)

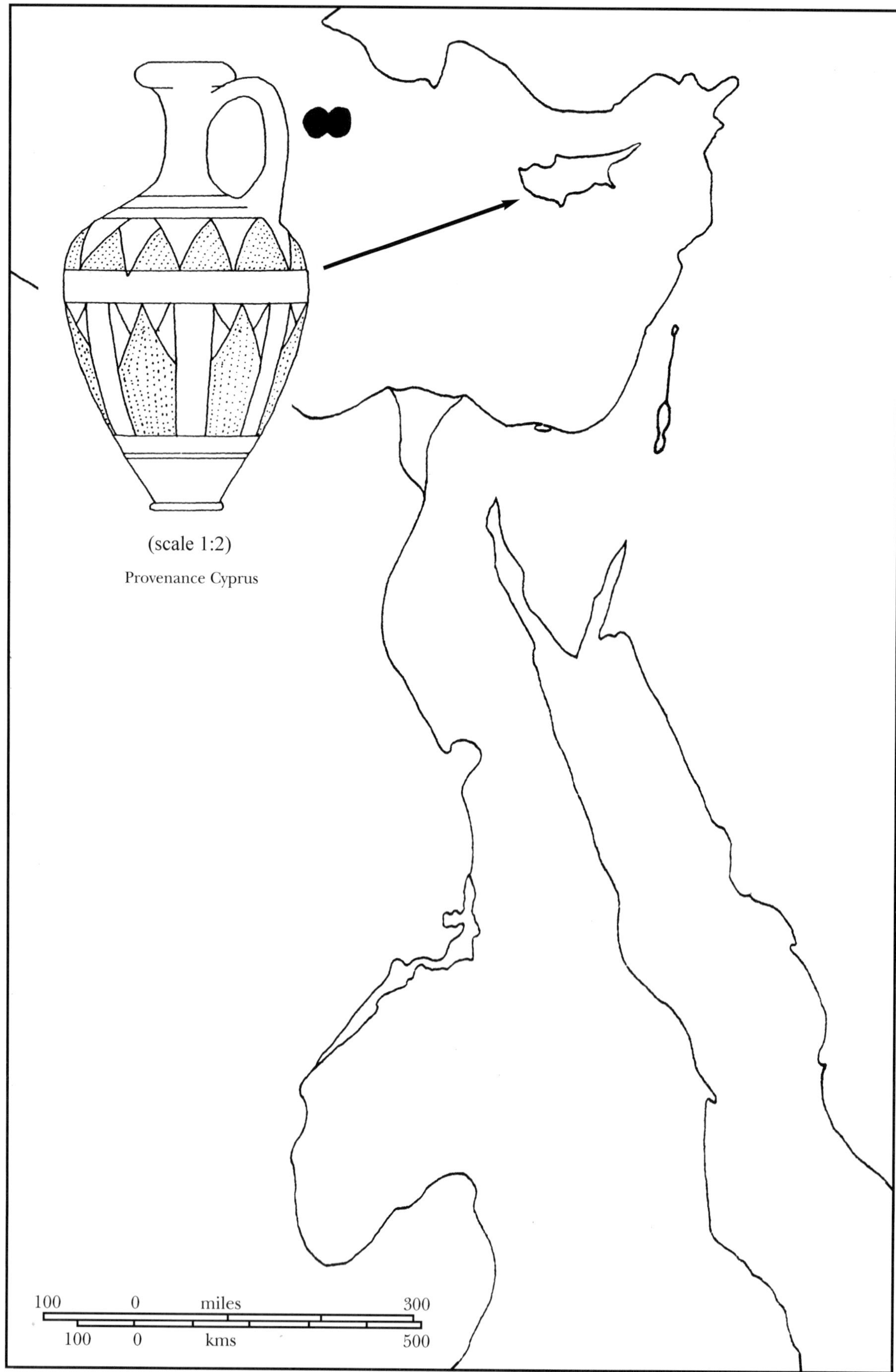

Fig. 100 Distribution and Shape Class of Type Group I.3.1a

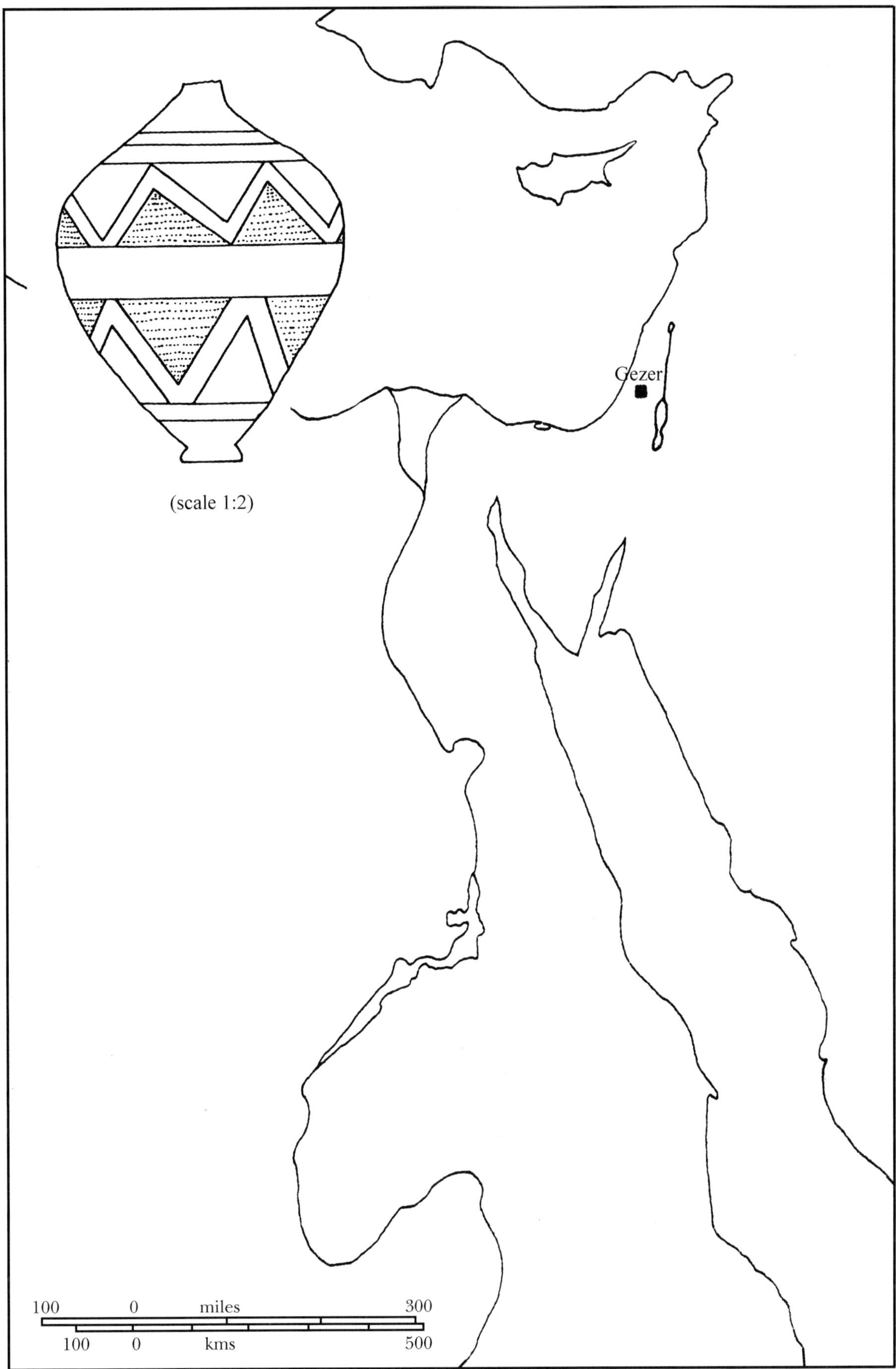

Fig. 101 Distribution and Shape Class of Type Group I.3.1b

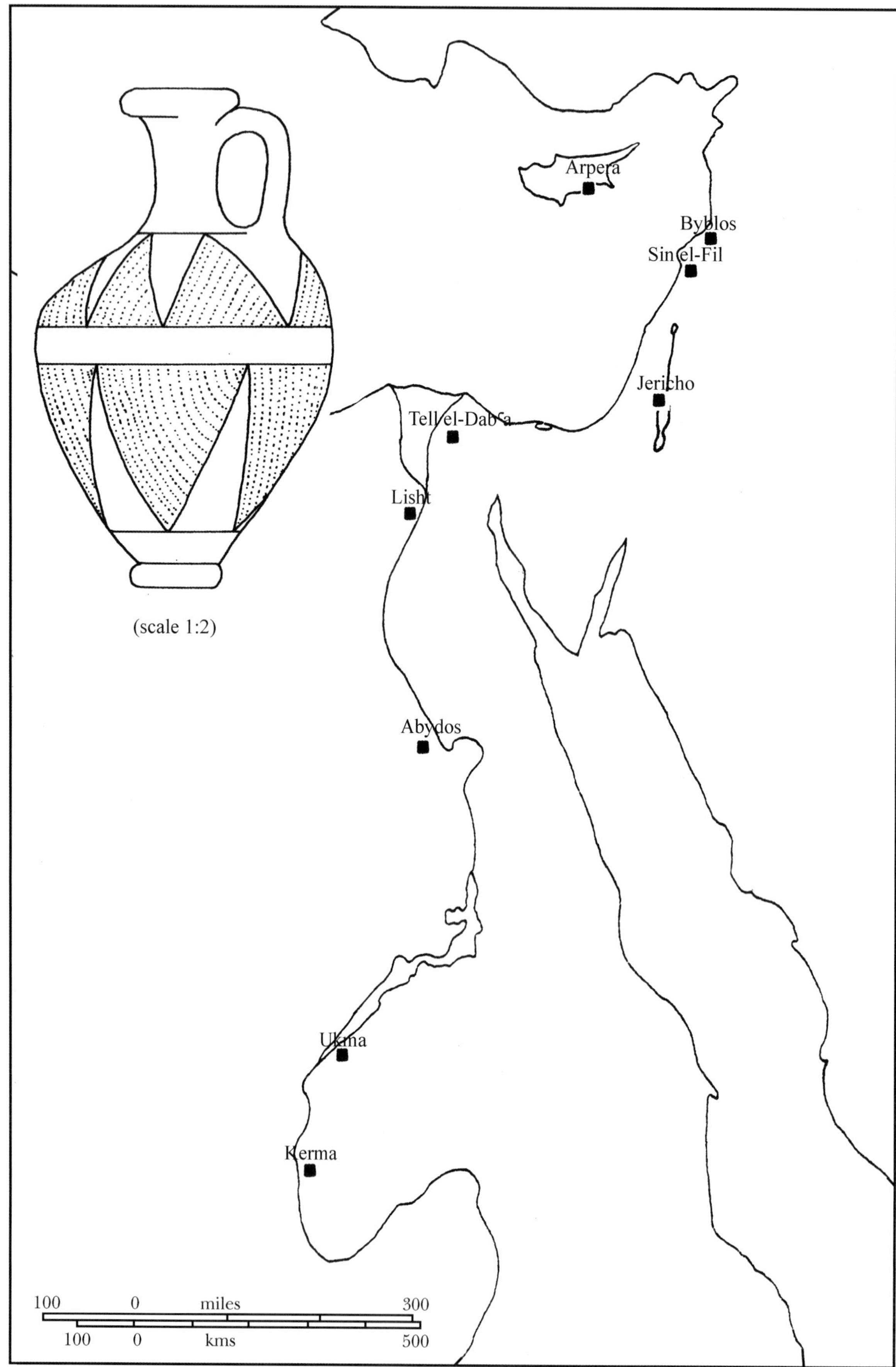

Fig. 102 Distribution and Shape Class of Type Group I.3.1c

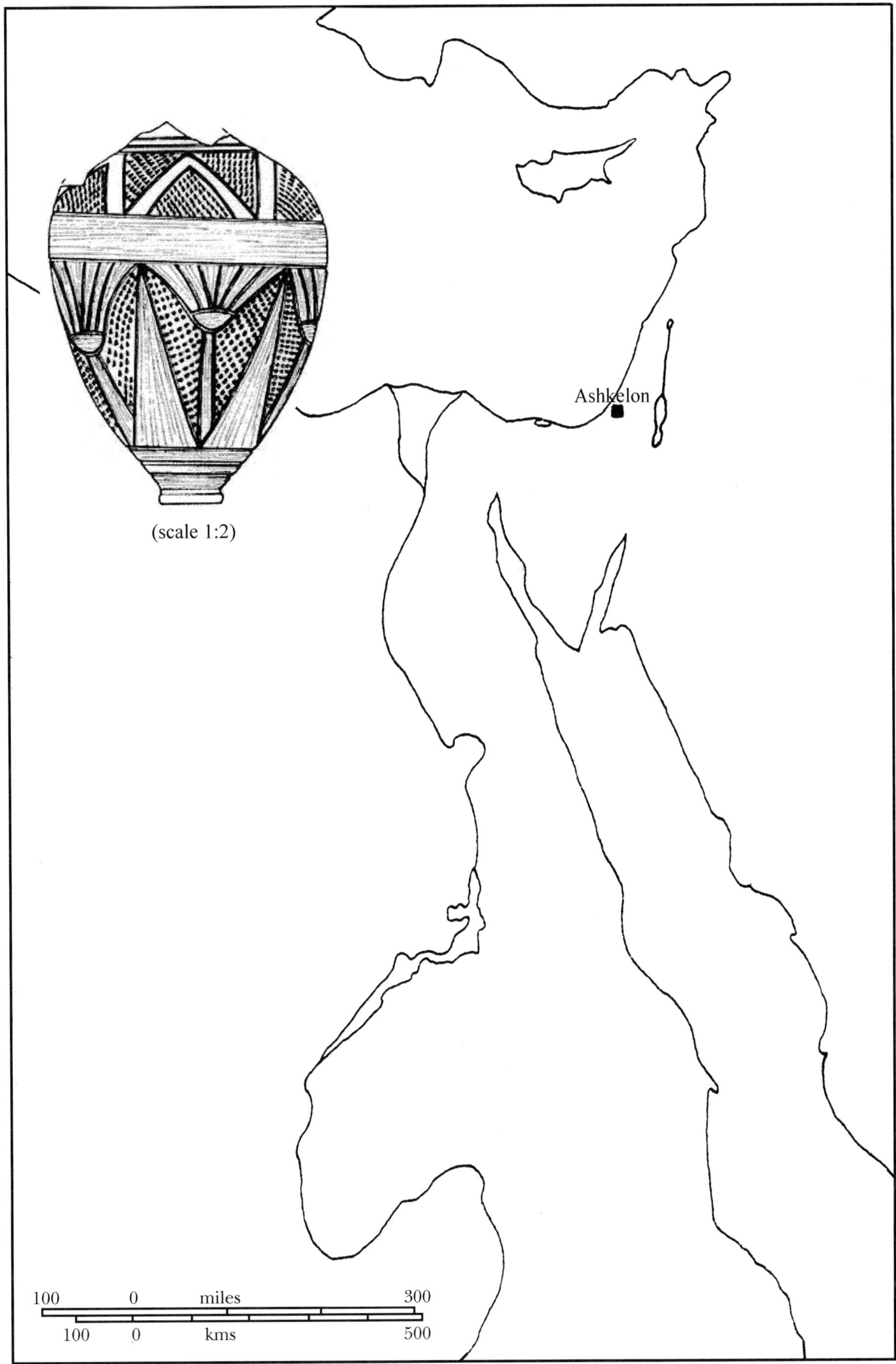

Fig. 103 Distribution and Shape Class of Type Group I.3.1d

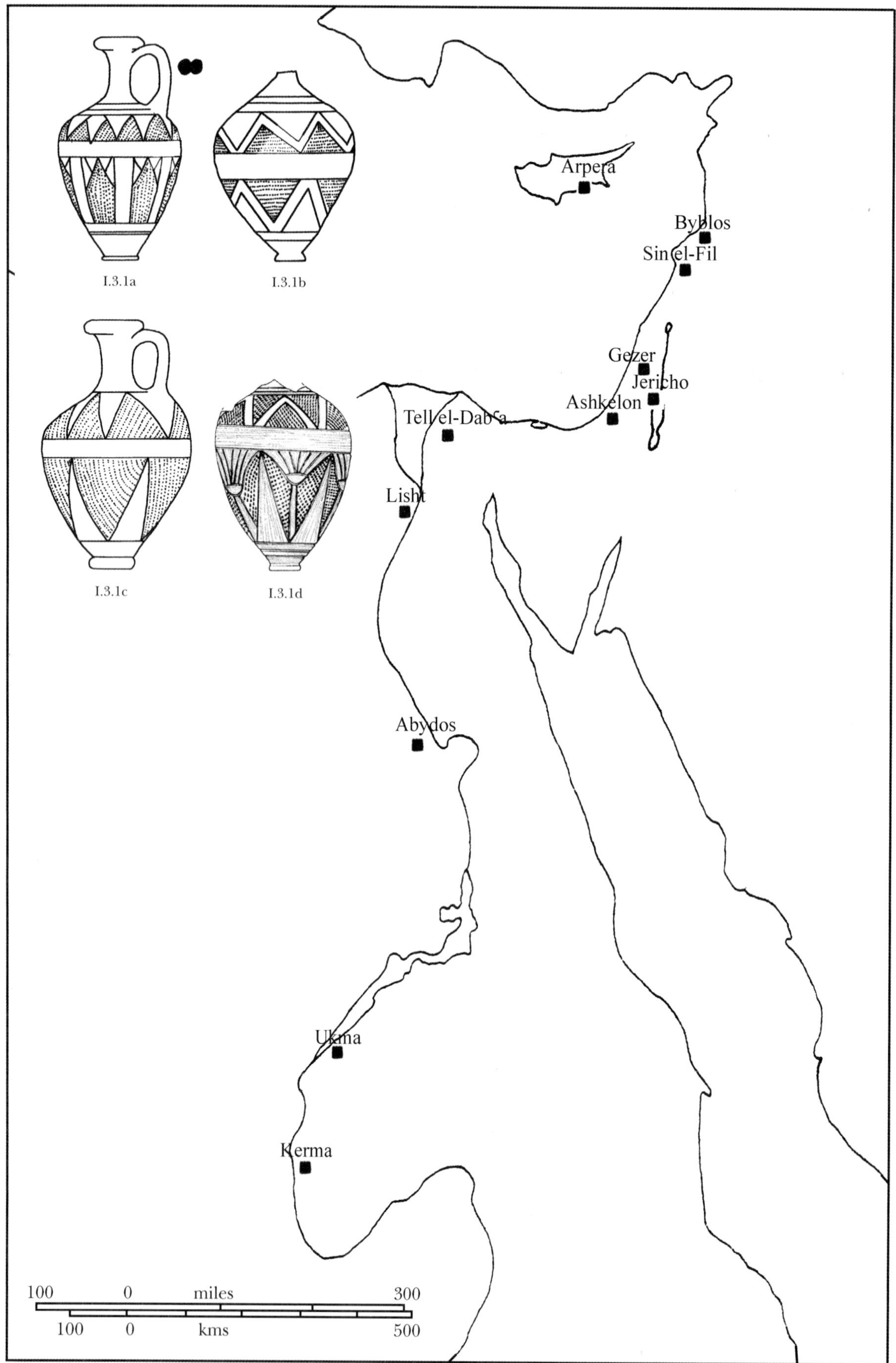

Fig. 104 Combined Distribution of Type Group I.3.1

most characteristic decorative motif, type I.3.1c comprises an upper band of standing triangles and a lower one of pendant triangles, with examples known from Byblos, tomb 917,[374] Sin el-Fil,[375] Jericho,[376] Tell el-Dabᶜa strata E/3 to E/2, Lisht tomb 879,[377] Abydos grave B.13,[378] Kerma Tumulus X, grave 1084,[379] Ukma,[380] and Arpera.[381] Decorative motif I.3.1d is known through a vessel from Ashkelon, and comprises an upper zone of alternating standing and pendant triangles with a lower zone of stylised lotus flowers and leaves.

Type Group I.3.2 (Figs. 105–108, 110)

Tell el-Yahudiya jugs of group I.3.2 are similar to those of group I.3.1, with kettle rims, double handles incisions at the base of the neck, but instead of a ring base have a disc or button base instead. Once again the most common decorative motif, type I.3.2a comprises an upper band of standing triangles and a lower one of pendant triangles, with most examples known from Tell el-Dabᶜa, with at least two other vessels known from Harageh tomb B297,[382] two more in Ukma,[383] and one in Ashkelon.[384] A variant of this style is found on a large jug from Mirgissa[385] where the upper zone comprises alternating standing and pendant triangles (I.3.2b). A third decorative style also known from Tell el-Dabᶜa, I.3.2c, consists of an upper band of standing triangles and a lower zone of intersecting pendant and standing triangles separated by a zigzag reserved zone. This type group, which is invariably made of Nile clay, is so standardised that we may assume they all derive from the same workshop.

Type Group I.3.3 (Figs. 109, 110)

Type group I.3.3 is known through a single vessel found at Mirgissa,[386] and possibly two other incomplete vessels from Kerma.[387] In shape the Mirgissa jug with its plump piriform shape, thickened rim, bipartite handle and slightly offset disc base, recalls the shape of the Middle Palestinian groups. On the other hand, the incisions at the base of the neck and its scheme of decoration place it firmly in the Levanto-Egyptian group. The vessel bears an upper zone of standing triangles and a lower one of pendant triangles in the style of Piriform 1c. The upper bodies of the two Kerma vessels are not preserved, but they are both plump and bear the same decorative scheme.

I4. Levanto-Egyptian IV (Piriform Id)

Type Group I.4 (Figs. 111–114)

Tell el-Yahudiya jugs of type group I.4 differ from the previous Levanto-Egyptian Piriform I types in having a candlestick, rather than a kettle rim. Vessels attributed to type group I.4 have candlestick rims, double handles, ring bases, and in some cases, incisions at the base of the neck, and are not common. A vessel, made of Nile clay, but found at Arpera in Cyprus has vertical bands of incised decoration;[388] a pot from Ras Shamra bears a single zigzag design which covers the entire body,[389] and a jug from Byblos[390] has three or four lozenges, a forerunner of the typical lozenge decoration found on the later Piriform 2a and 2b jugs. An incomplete vessel from Jaffa, which is missing the rim and neck, but has similar body decoration

---

374 Montet, *Byblos et l'Égypte*, 245, pl. 146, Kaplan, *Tell el-Yahudiyeh Ware,* fig. 34b.

375 Chehab, *Mélanges syriens*, 806, fig. 5a, Kaplan, *Tell el-Yahudiyeh Ware,* fig. 35b.

376 Kenyon, *Jericho I*, 1960, fig. 122.15, Kaplan, *Tell el-Yahudiyeh Ware,* fig. 35a

377 Bourriau, *FS. Simpson*, 1996, 113, fig. 8.

378 London BM EA 49344. Peet and Loat, *Cemeteries of Abydos III*, 54, pl. 13.8 centre, Kaplan, *Tell el-Yahudiyeh Ware,* fig. 33b.

379 Boston MFA 1920.1700. Reisner *Excavations at Kerma IV–V*, 381–388, fig. 264.25, pl. 70.3, Kaplan, *Tell el-Yahudiyeh Ware,* fig. 30c.

380 Khartoum 19122. Kaplan, *Tell el-Yahudiyeh Ware,* fig. 30b.

381 Nicosia, Cyprus Museum. Merrillees, *Trade and Transcendance*, 52, figs. 31, 40, Kaplan, *Tell el-Yahudiyeh Ware,* fig. 33a.

382 Cambridge, Fitzwilliam E.68.1914. Oxford Ashmolean 1914.687. Engelbach, *Harageh*, pl. 91.49f, j, Kaplan, *Tell el-Yahudiyeh Ware,* fig. 37 a–b.

383 Khartoum National Museum 19117 and 19122. Kaplan, *Tell el-Yahudiyeh Ware,* fig. 31 a–b.

384 See below page 000

385 Lille University Museum L.1036, Vercoutter, *Kush* 13, 1965, 69–72, pl. 7.1; Idem, 1975, 44–49, fig. 11.4; Kaplan, *Tell el-Yahudiyeh Ware,* fig. 32b.

386 Khartoum 14017. Vercoutter, *Kush* 13, 1965, 69–71, pl. 7.1, Kaplan, *Tell el-Yahudiyeh Ware,* fig. 38b.

387 From Tumulus X, graves 1042 and 1045. Reisner, *Excavations at Kerma IV–V*, 381–388, fig 264.23, Kaplan, *Tell el-Yahudiyeh Ware,* figs. 42e, 43a.

388 Nicosia, Cyprus Museum. Merrillees, *Trade and Transcendance*, 49, figs. 31, 39. Kaplan, *Tell el-Yahudiyeh Ware,* fig. 41c. NAA analysis. Kaplan, *Tell el-Yahudiyeh Ware,* 229 no. CM15.

389 Paris Louvre AO 15735. Schaeffer, *Syria* 14, 1933, 110, fig. 10.7, Kaplan, *Tell el-Yahudiyeh Ware,* fig. 42a

390 Montet, *Byblos et l'Egypte*, 119, 244, pl. 146, Kaplan, *Tell el-Yahudiyeh Ware,* fig. 62b.

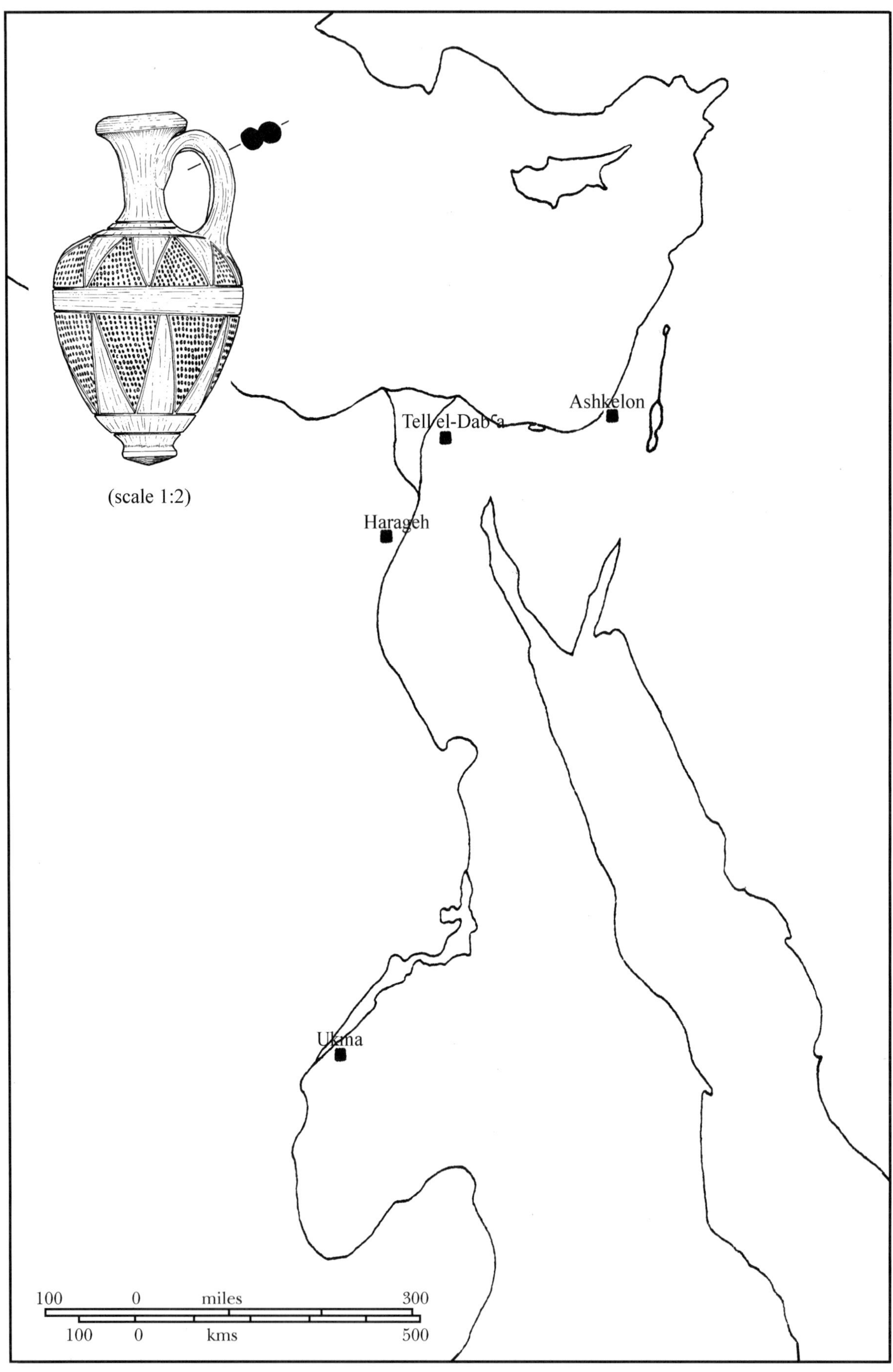

Fig. 105 Distribution and Shape Class of Type Group I.3.2a

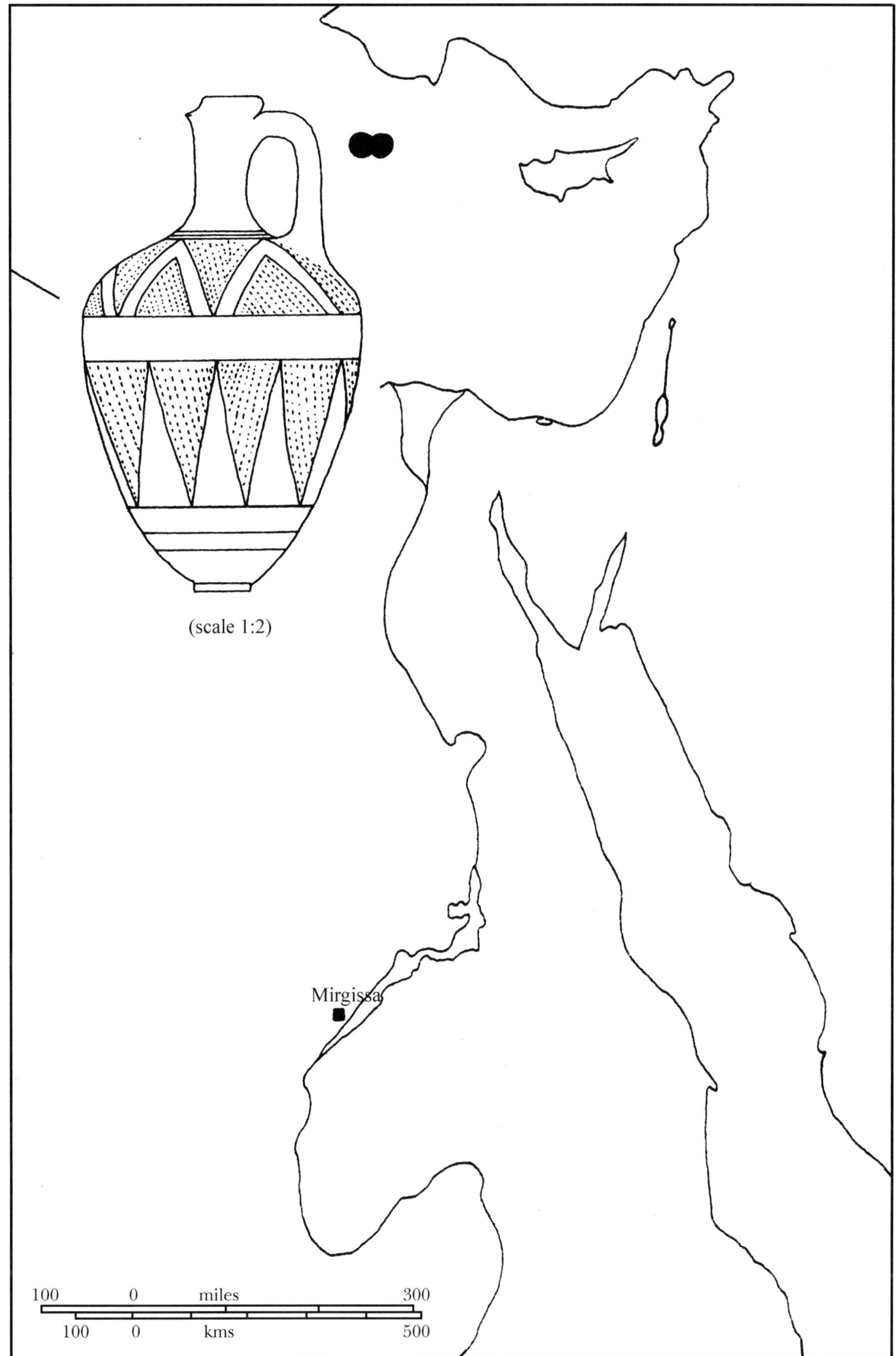

Fig. 106 Distribution and Shape Class of Type Group I.3.2b

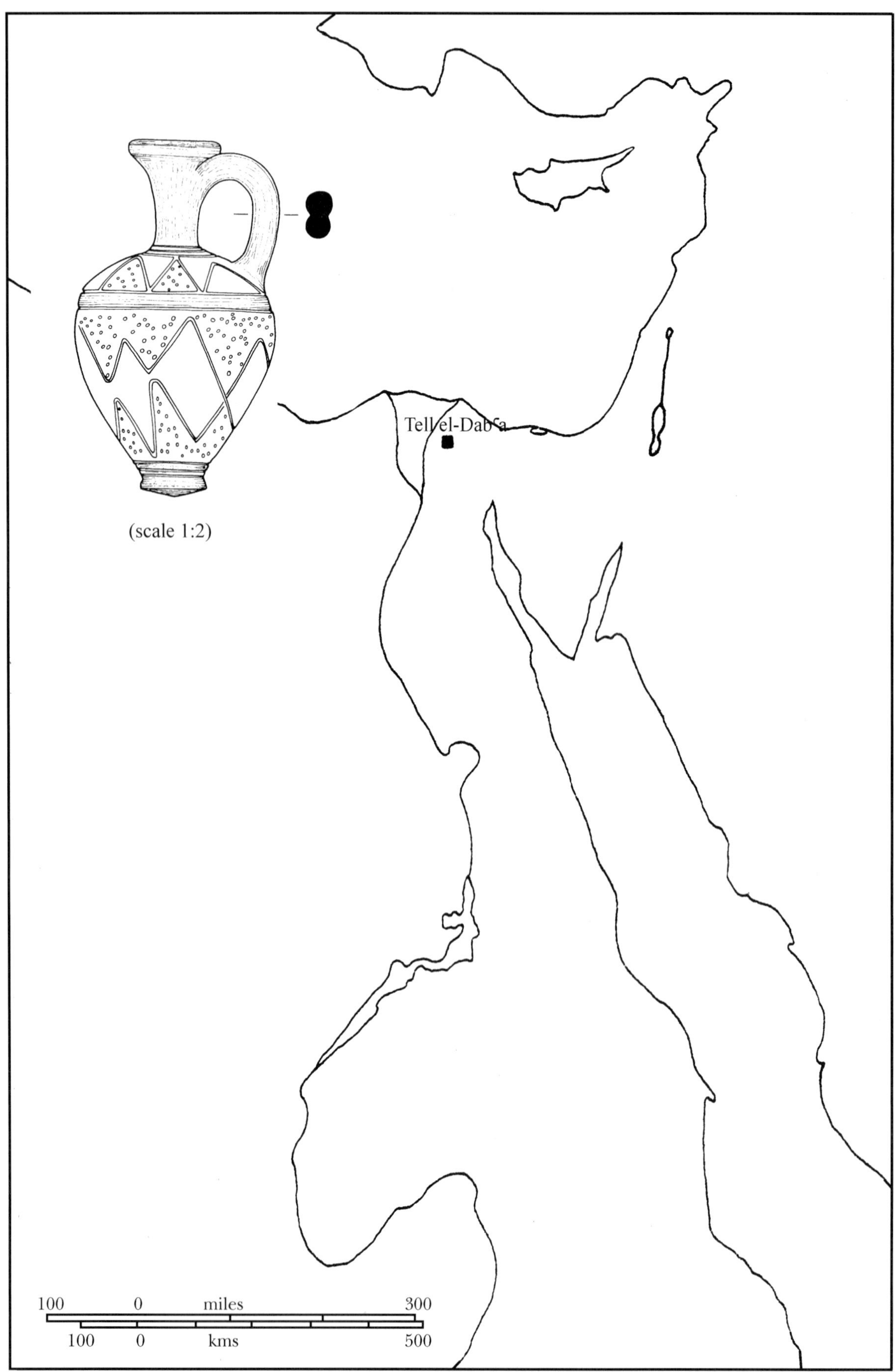

Fig. 107 Distribution and Shape Class of Type Group I.3.2c

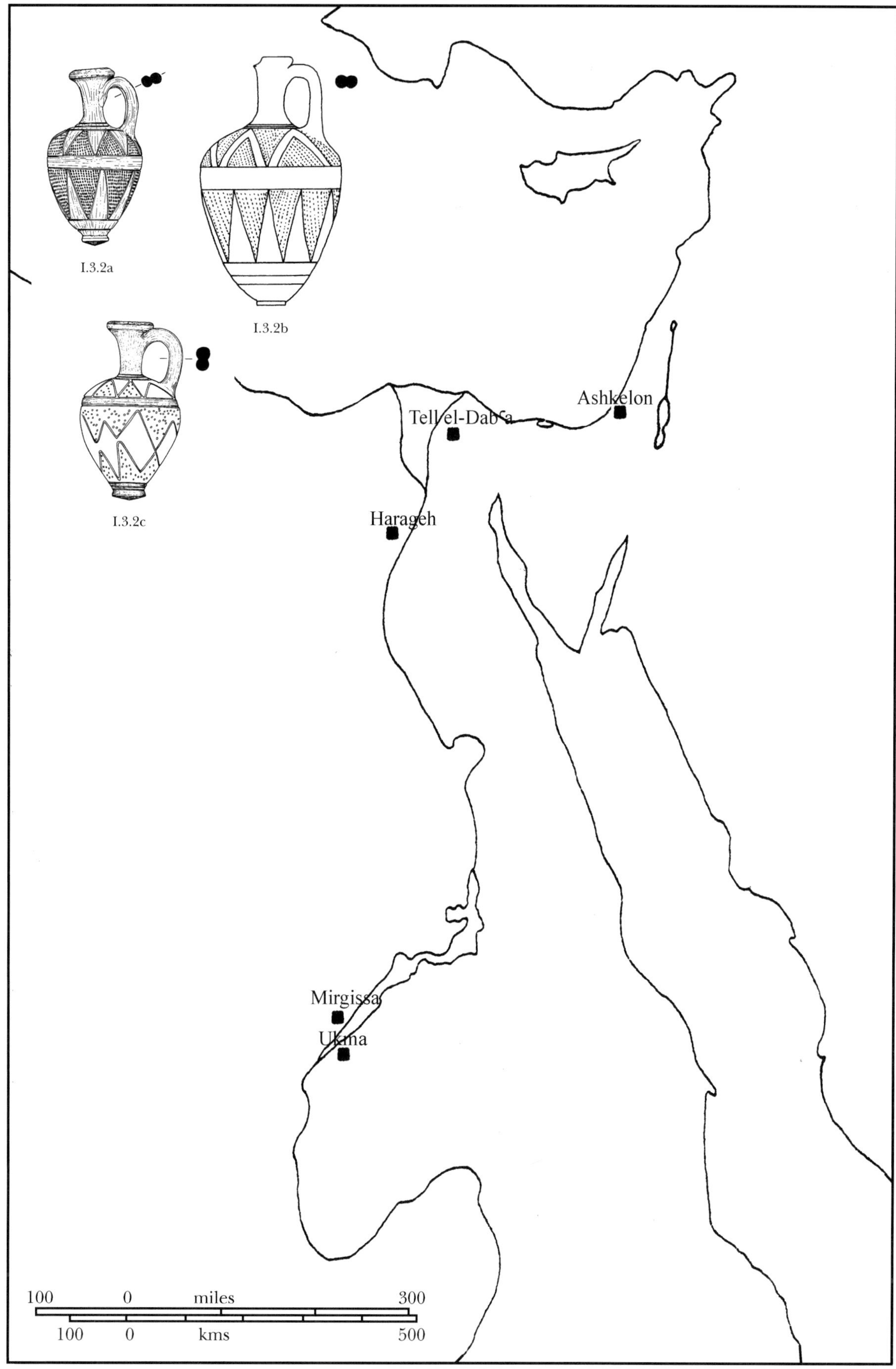

Fig. 108 Combined Distribution of Type Group I.3.2

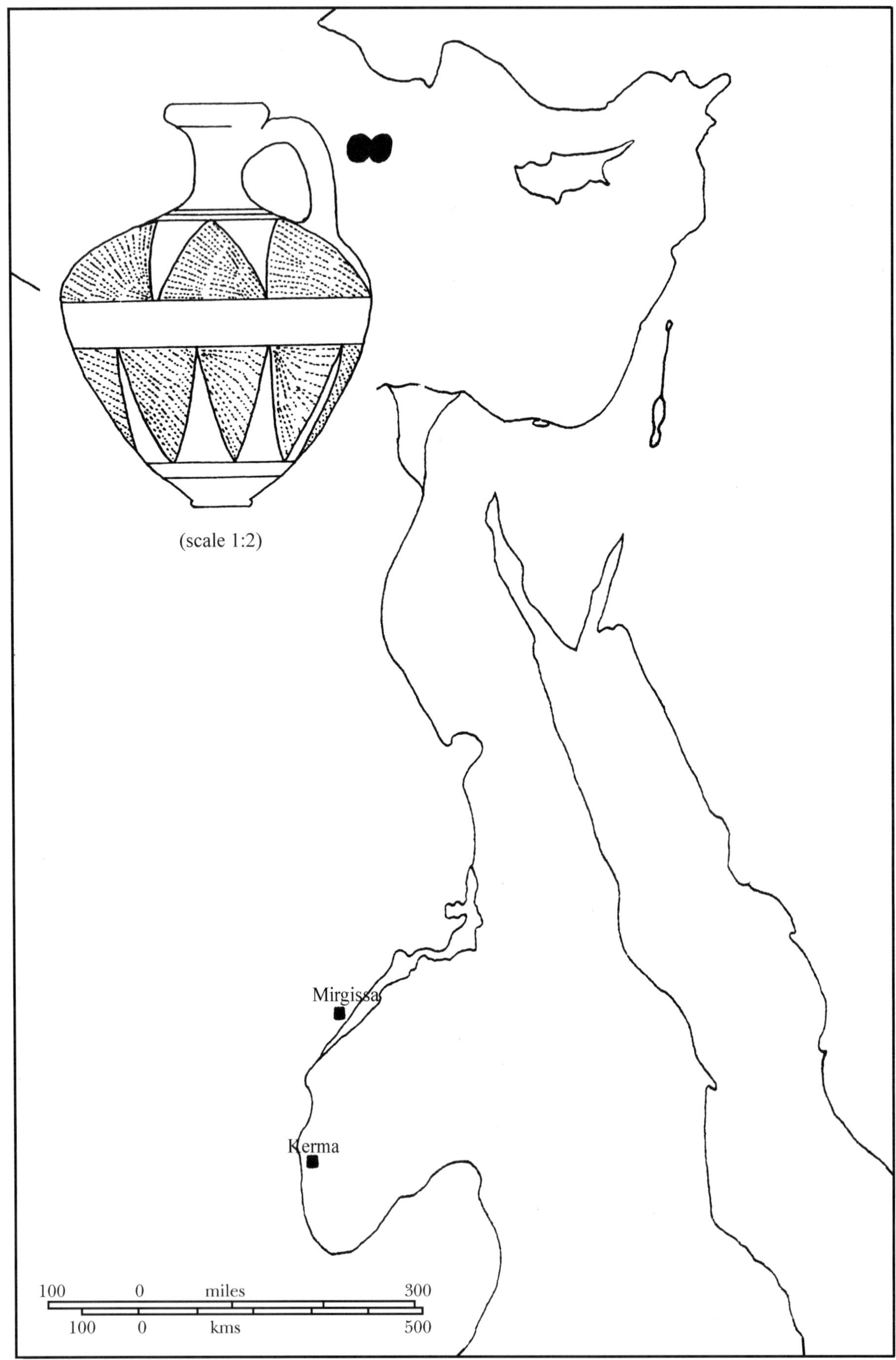

Fig. 109 Distribution and Shape Class of Type Group I.3.3

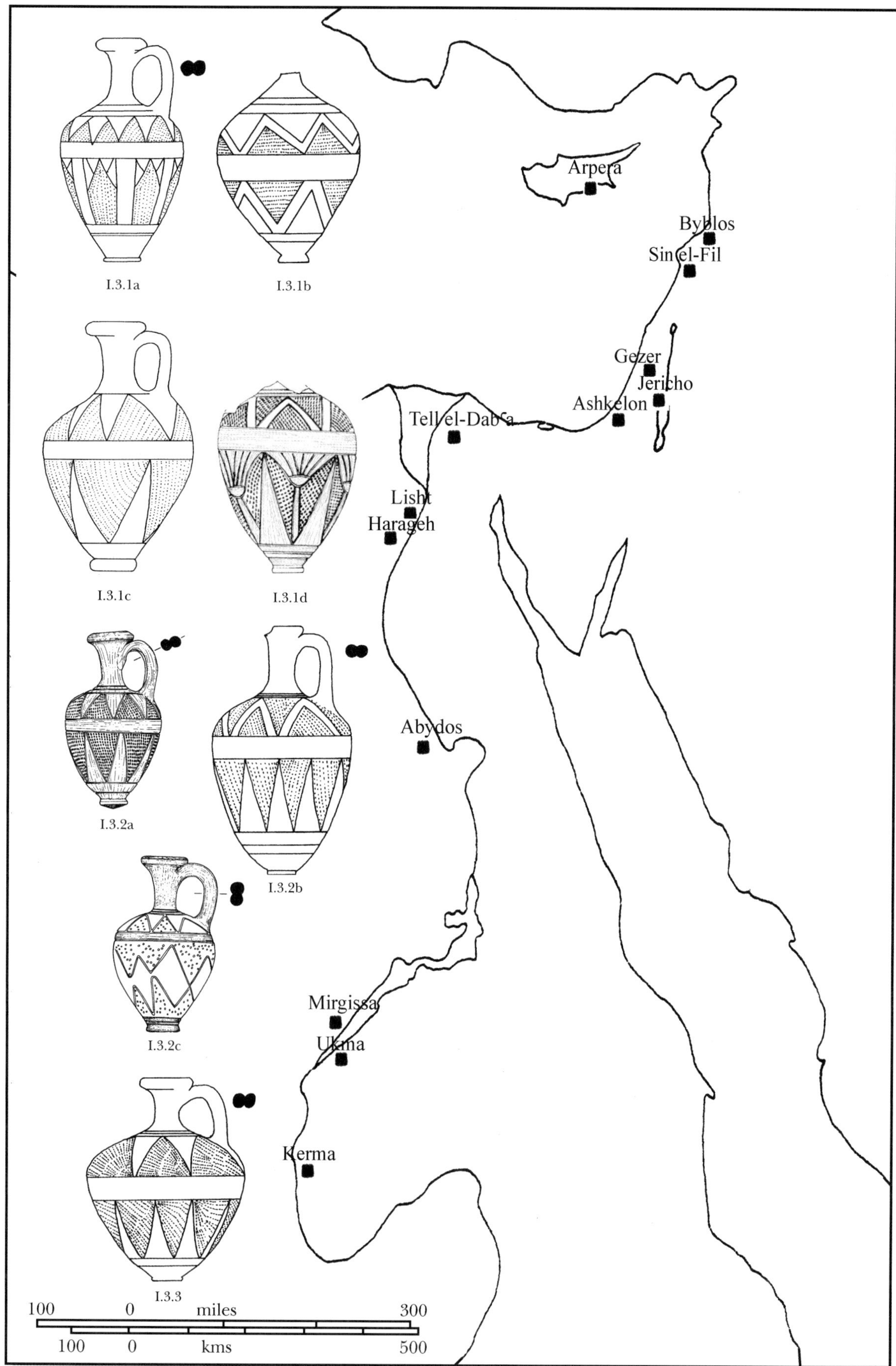

Fig. 110 Combined Distribution of Type Group I.3 (Piriform 1c)

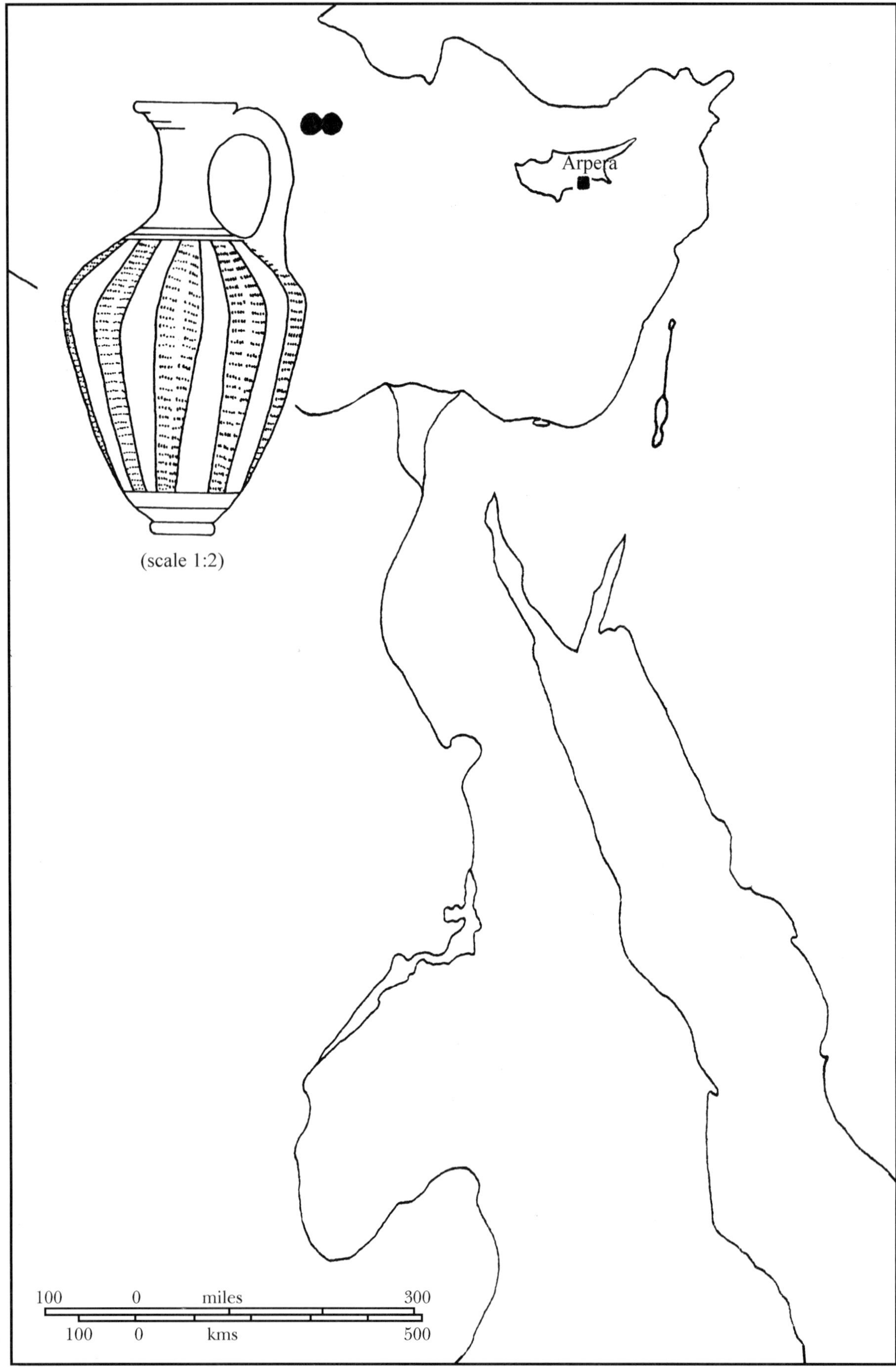

Fig. 111 Distribution and Shape Class of Type Group I.4.1a

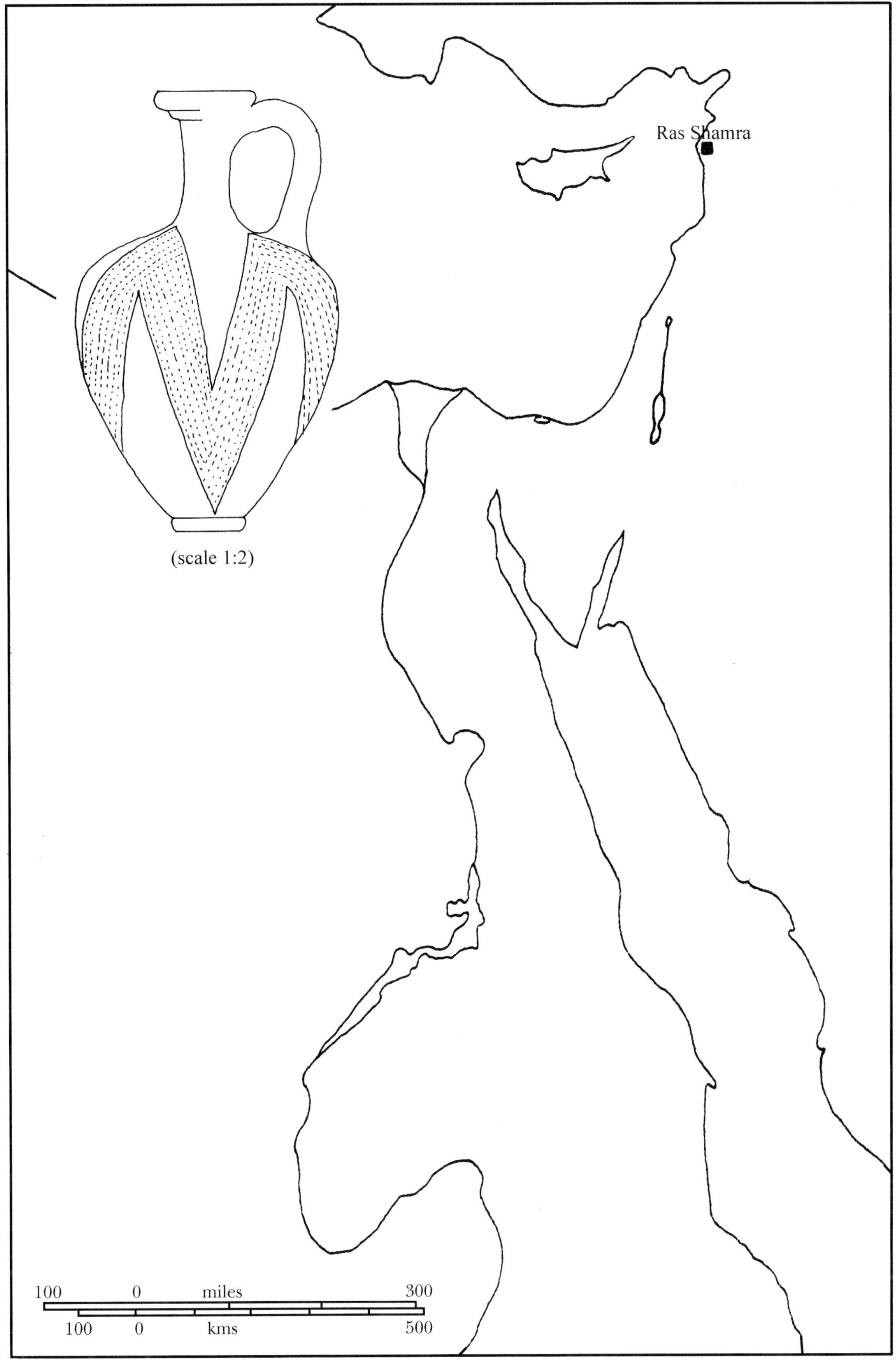

Fig. 112 Distribution and Shape Class of Type Group I.4.1b

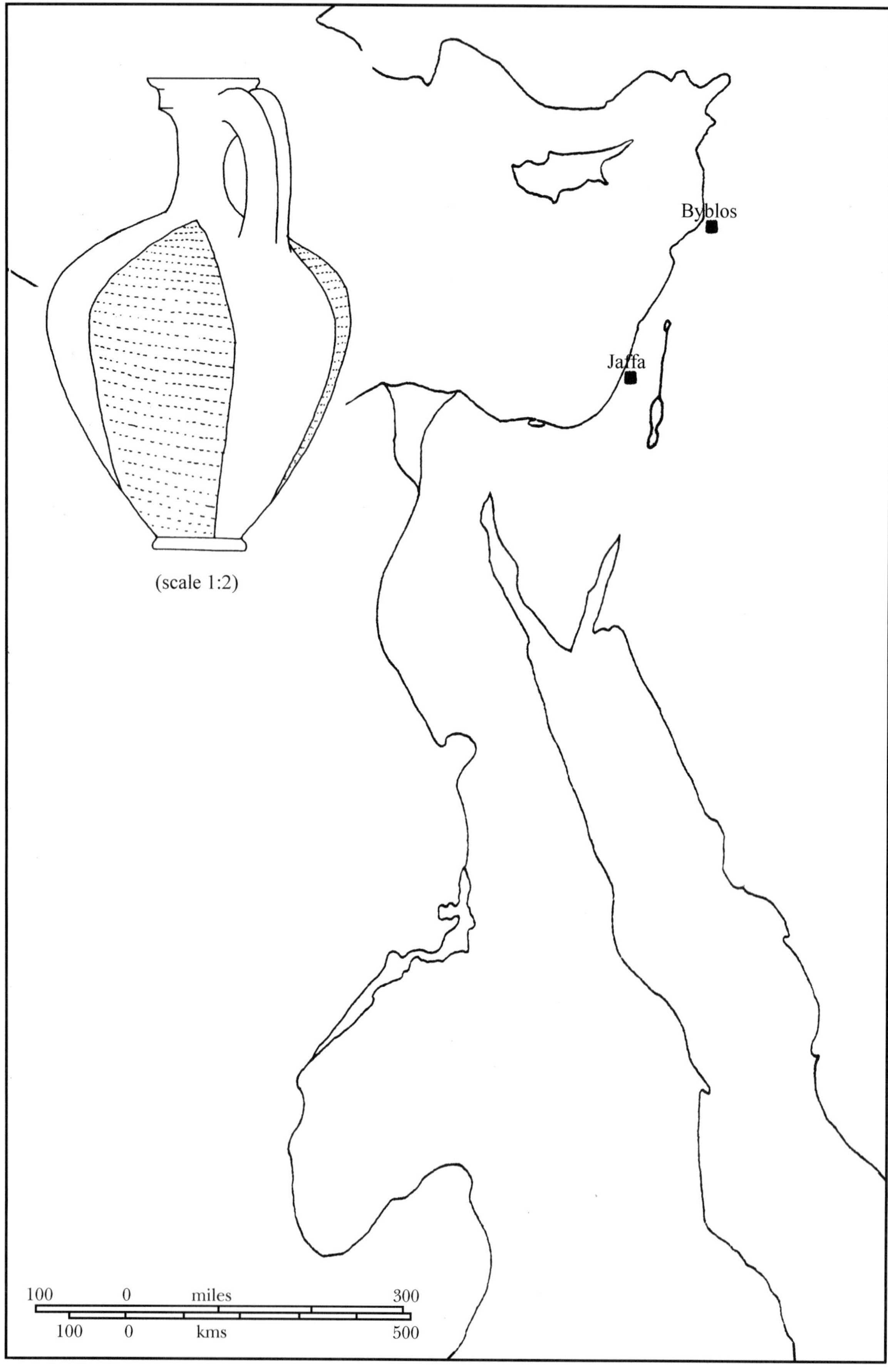

Fig. 113 Distribution and Shape Class of Type Group I.4.1c

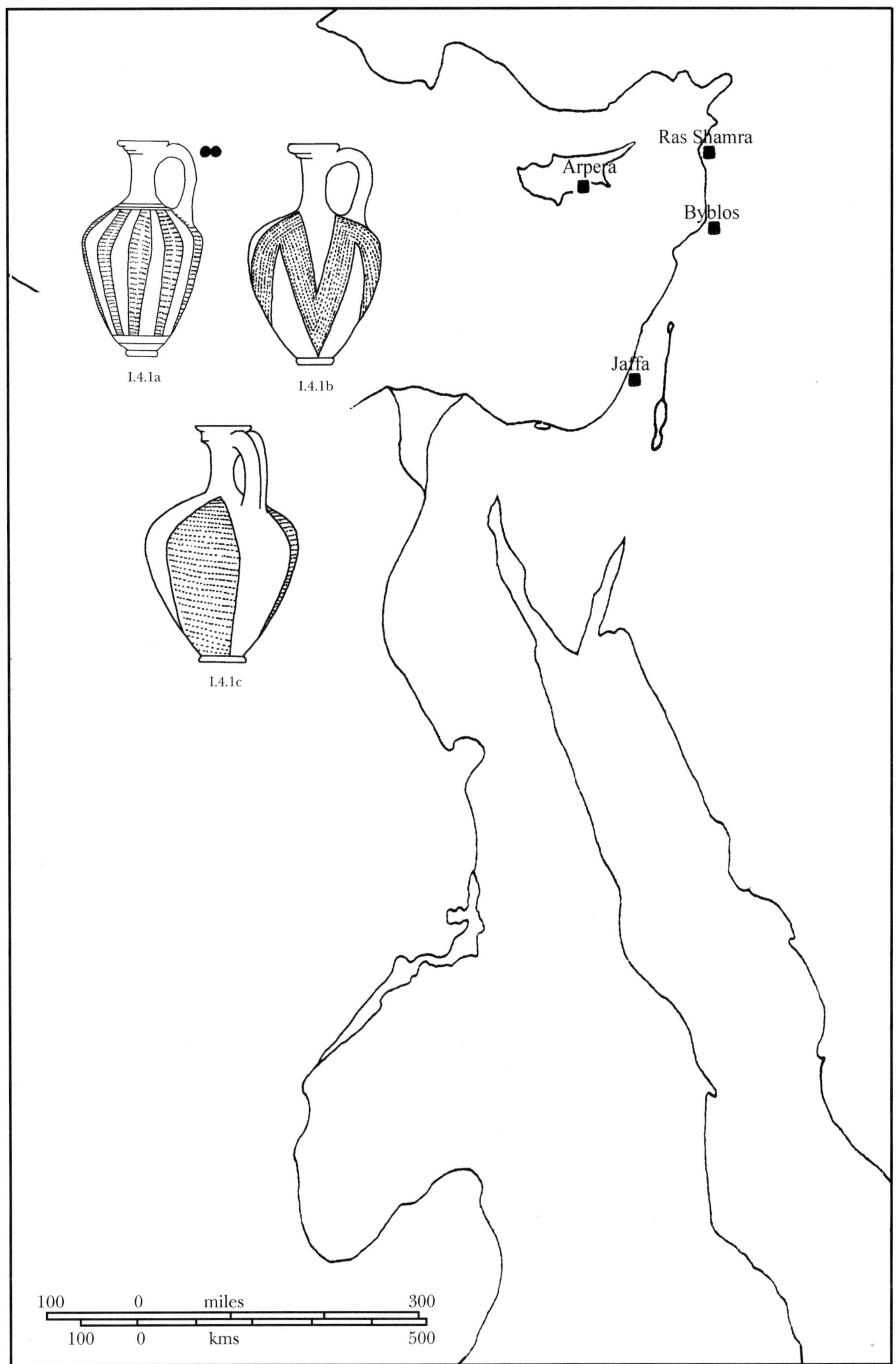

Fig. 114 Combined Distribution of Type Group I.4 (Piriform 1d)

to the Byblos vessel, either belongs to this group, or the hybrid type M.1.[391]

I.5. Levanto-Egyptian V

Levanto-Egyptian Group V is a somewhat heterogeneous grouping consisting of a number of model piriform jugs with designs often found on the contemporary, but larger, Piriform 1b and Piriform 1c.

Type Group I.5.1 (Figs. 115, 121)

Vessels of group I.5.1 are smaller than those of groups I.1–4 and are characterised as having candlestick rims, double handles, and ring bases, but this time no incisions at the base of the neck. Two such vessels are known from Tell el-Dabᶜa, each having three zones of decoration, in the style of Piriform 1b jugs, an upper and lower band of intersecting pendant and standing triangles separated by a zigzag reserved zone, and a central one of rectangles.

Type Group I.5.2 (Figs. 116, 121)

Type group I.5.2 comprises small piriform, almost ovoid jugs, between 8 and 9 cm. tall, known from Tell el-Dabᶜa. They have a rolled rim, double handle button base and are decorated with an upper zone of standing triangles, a wide central band of pendant triangles and a lower zone of pendant triangles.

Type Group I.5.3 (Figs. 117, 118, 121)

Vessels of group I.5.3 comprise piriform vessels with rolled rims, double handles, button bases, and, usually, no incisions at the base of the neck. Several such, somewhat carelesly made, vessels are known from Tell el-Dabᶜa, and all have three zones of decoration. They can be divided into two sub-groups. I.5.3a sports an upper and lower band of aternating pendant and standing triangles separated by a zigzag reserved zone, and a central one of rectangles, whilst I.5.3b are decorated with an upper and middle band of intersecting pendant and standing triangles separated by a zigzag reserved zone, and a lower one of pendant triangles.

Type Group I.5.4 (Figs. 119, 121)

Type Group I.5.4 consists of small piriform vessels with double handles and button bases. The decoration, in the style of Piriform 1b, consists of an upper zone of alternating pendant and standing triangles, a central zone of rectangles and a lower zone of pendant triangles.

Type Group I.5.5 (Figs. 120, 121)

Vessels of group I.5.5 comprise model piriform vessels with double handles, button bases, and once again no incisions at the base of the neck. Examples from Tell el-Dabᶜa, such as TD 1841, have an upper zone of standing triangles and a lower zone of pendant triangles.

I.6. Levanto-Egyptian VI

Type Group I.6.1 (Figs. 122, 126)

Vessels of type group I.6.1 consist of Biconical jugs with a rolled rim, bipartite handle and ring base, and three decorative zones. Such vessels are known from Tell el-Dabᶜa, where TD 4238, found in Phase b/2 (= E/3), has three decorative zones comprising an upper band of standing triangles, a central zone of six infilled rectangles and a lower band of pendant triangles.

Type Group I.6.2 (Figs. 123, 126)

Vessels of type group I.6.2 consist of Biconical jugs with a rolled rim, bipartite handle and ring base. Such vessels are known from Tell el-Dabᶜa where they are decorated with an upper zone of standing triangles and a lower one of pendant triangles with the addition of a horizontal infilled band just above the base (TD 1839). To this group should perhaps also be added TD 1833 which is more piriform but bears the same decorative scheme as TD 1839.

Type Group I.6.3 (Figs. 124, 126)

Jugs belonging to Type Group I.6.3 are so far known only at Tell el-Dabᶜa. They are around 12 cms. tall, and consist of jugs with rolled rims, strap handles, biconical to piriform bodies, and ring bases. The decoration shows an upper zone of touching standing triangles and a lower one of touching pendant triangles with the addition of a horizontal band of incisions below the lower zone of pendant triangles (TD 5935).

Type Group I.6.4 (Figs. 125, 126)

Type group I.6.4 consists of a single jug reputedly found in Egypt,[392] but from the published drawing the details of the shape of the rim and base are not

[391] Tel Aviv, Jaffa Archaeological Museum. Kaplan, *'Atiqot* 1, 1955, 10, fig. 3.4, Kaplan, *Tell el-Yahudiyeh Ware,* fig. 62a.

[392] Toronto, ROM 900.2.134. Kaplan, *Tell el-Yahudiyeh Ware,* fig. 42b.

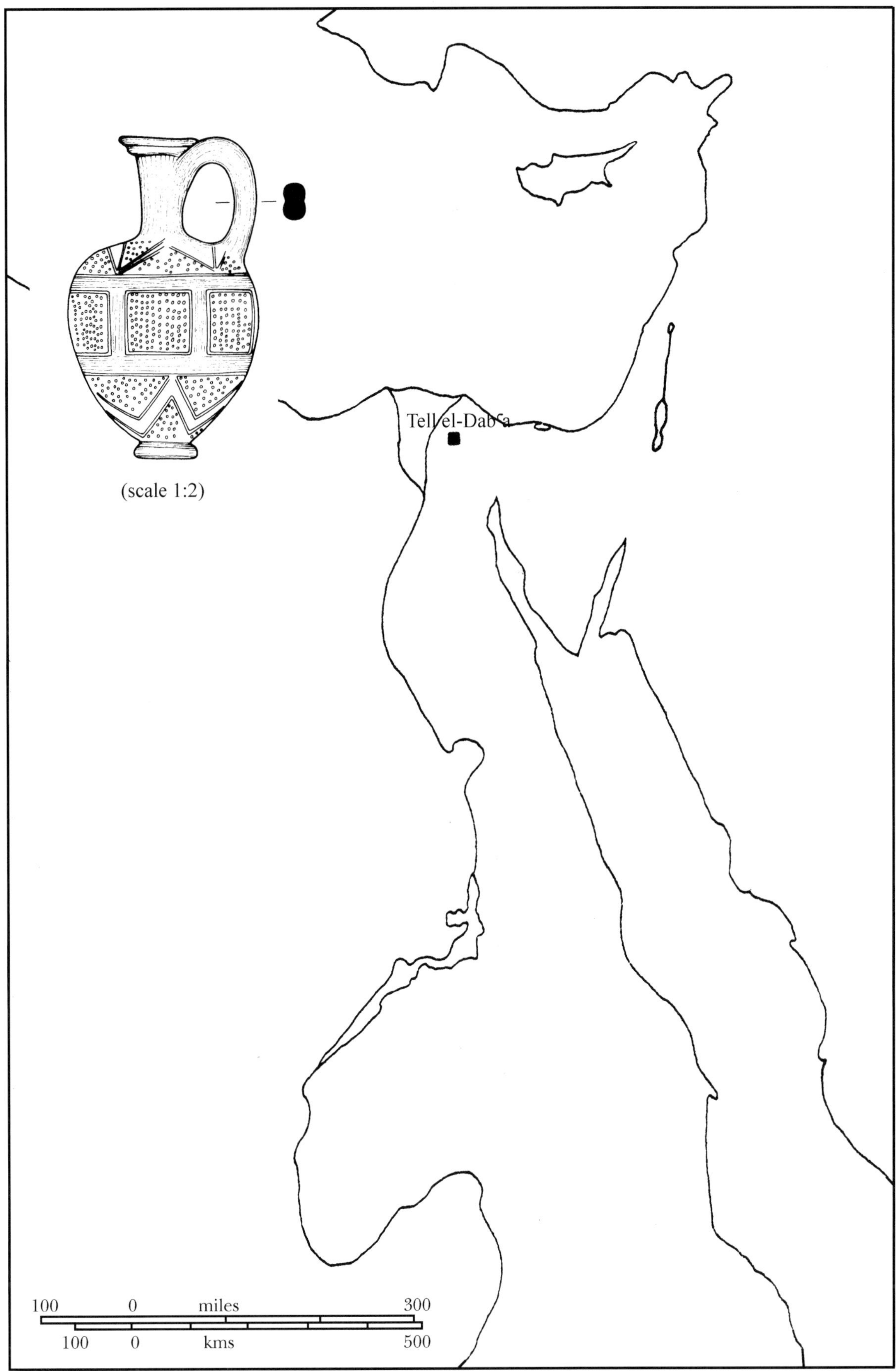

Fig. 115 Distribution and Shape Class of Type Group I.5.1

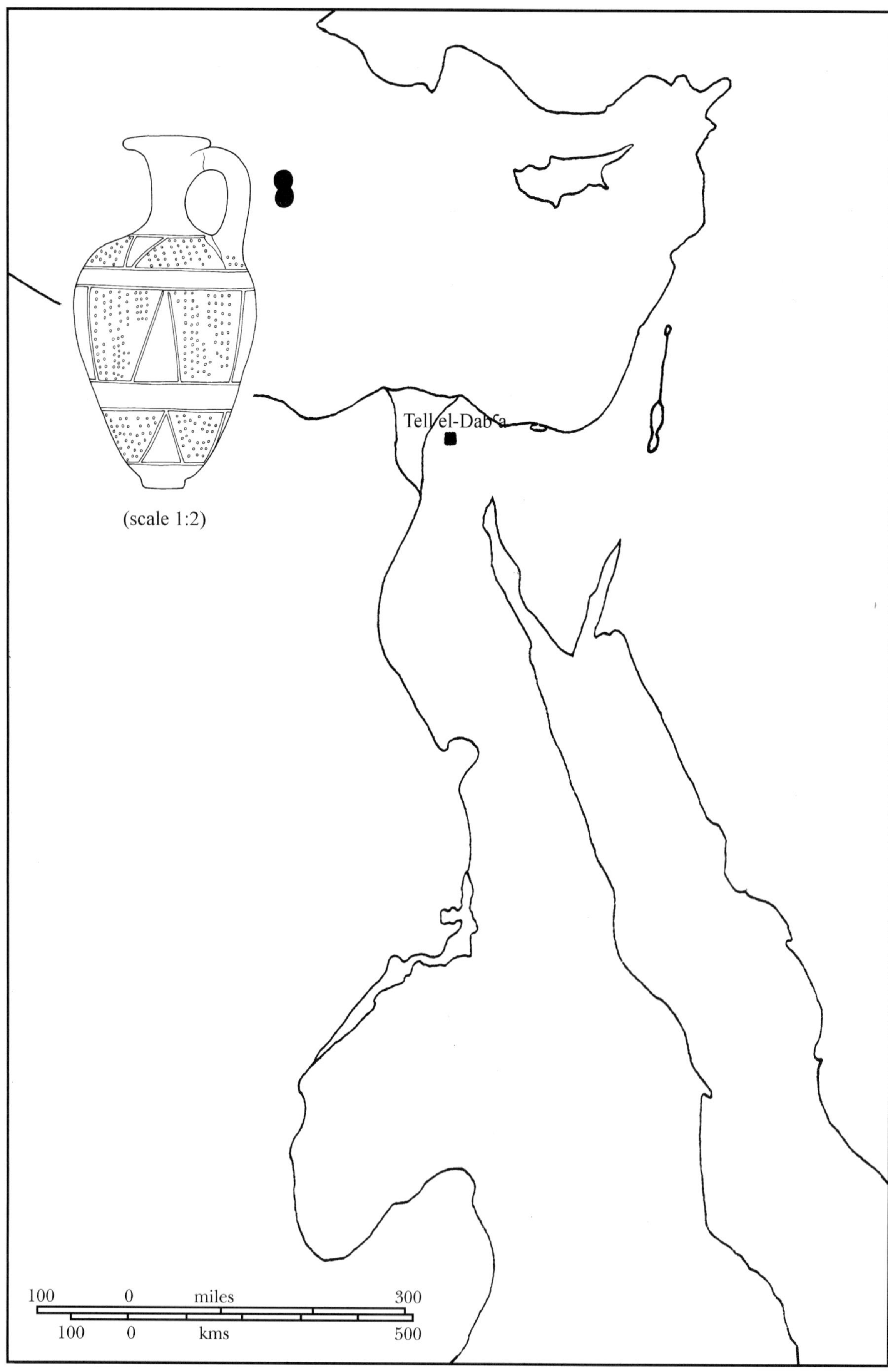

Fig. 116 Distribution and Shape Class of Type Group I.5.2

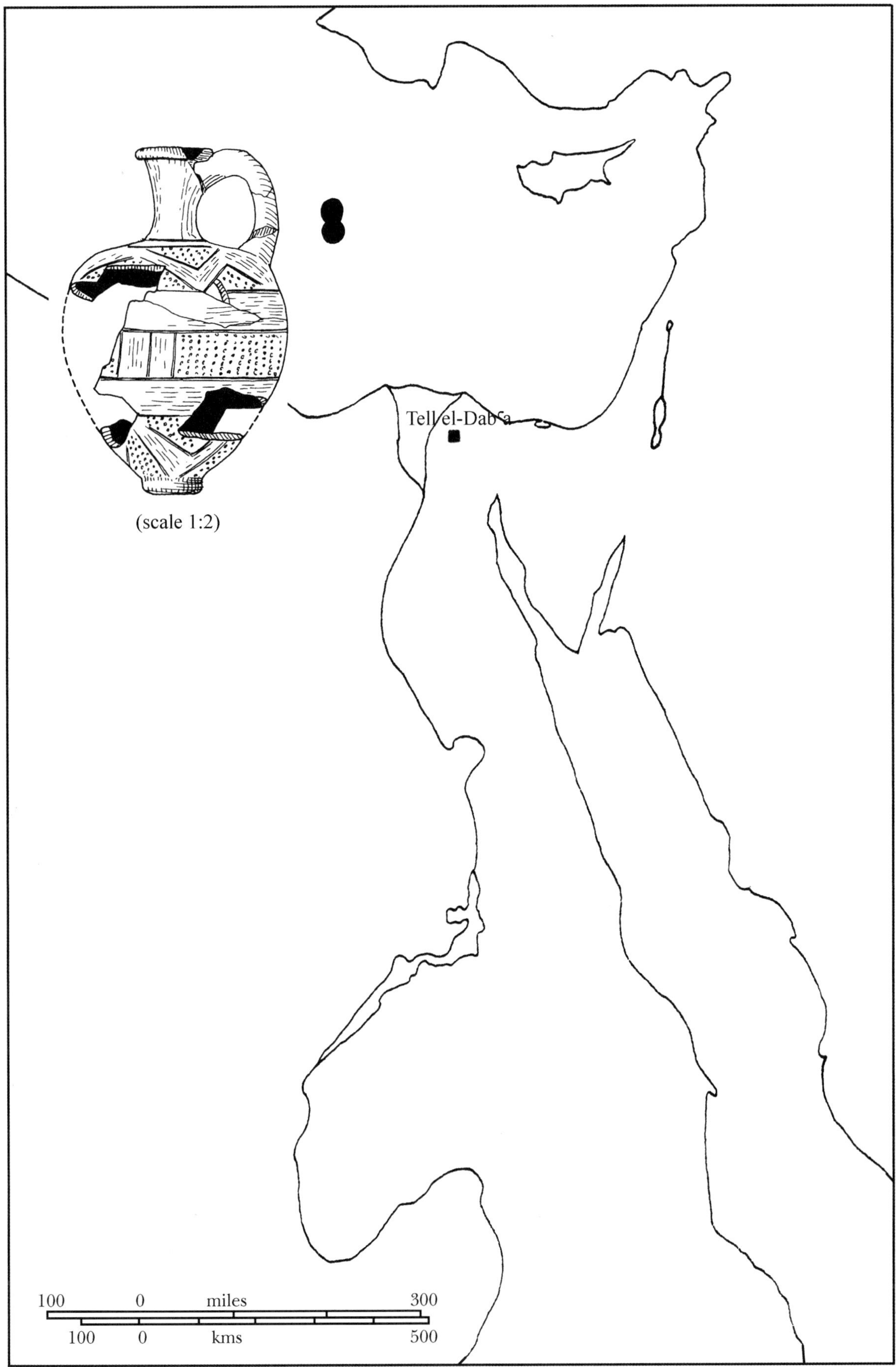

Fig. 117 Distribution and Shape Class of Type Group I.5.3a

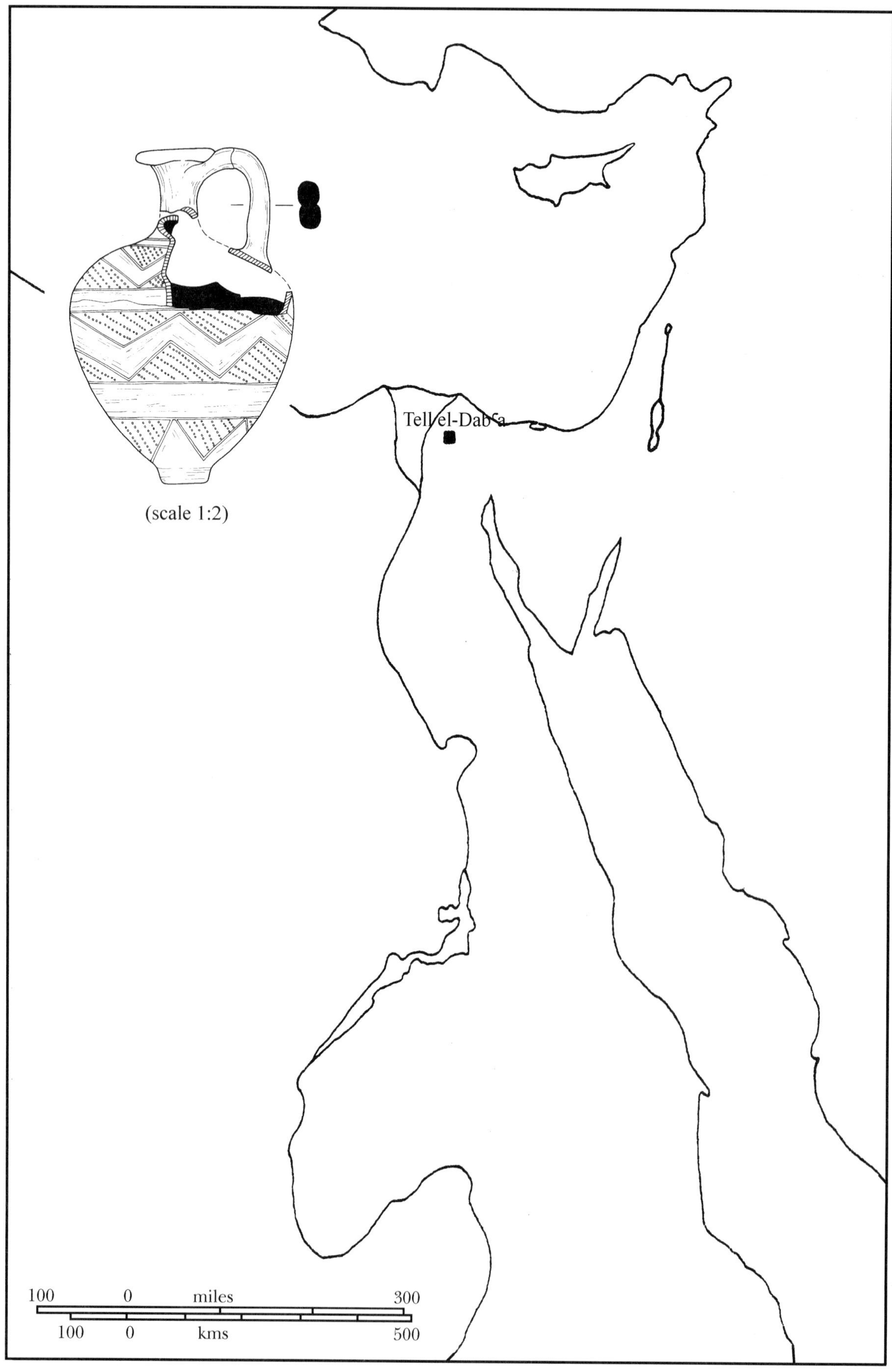

Fig. 118 Distribution and Shape Class of Type Group I.5.3b

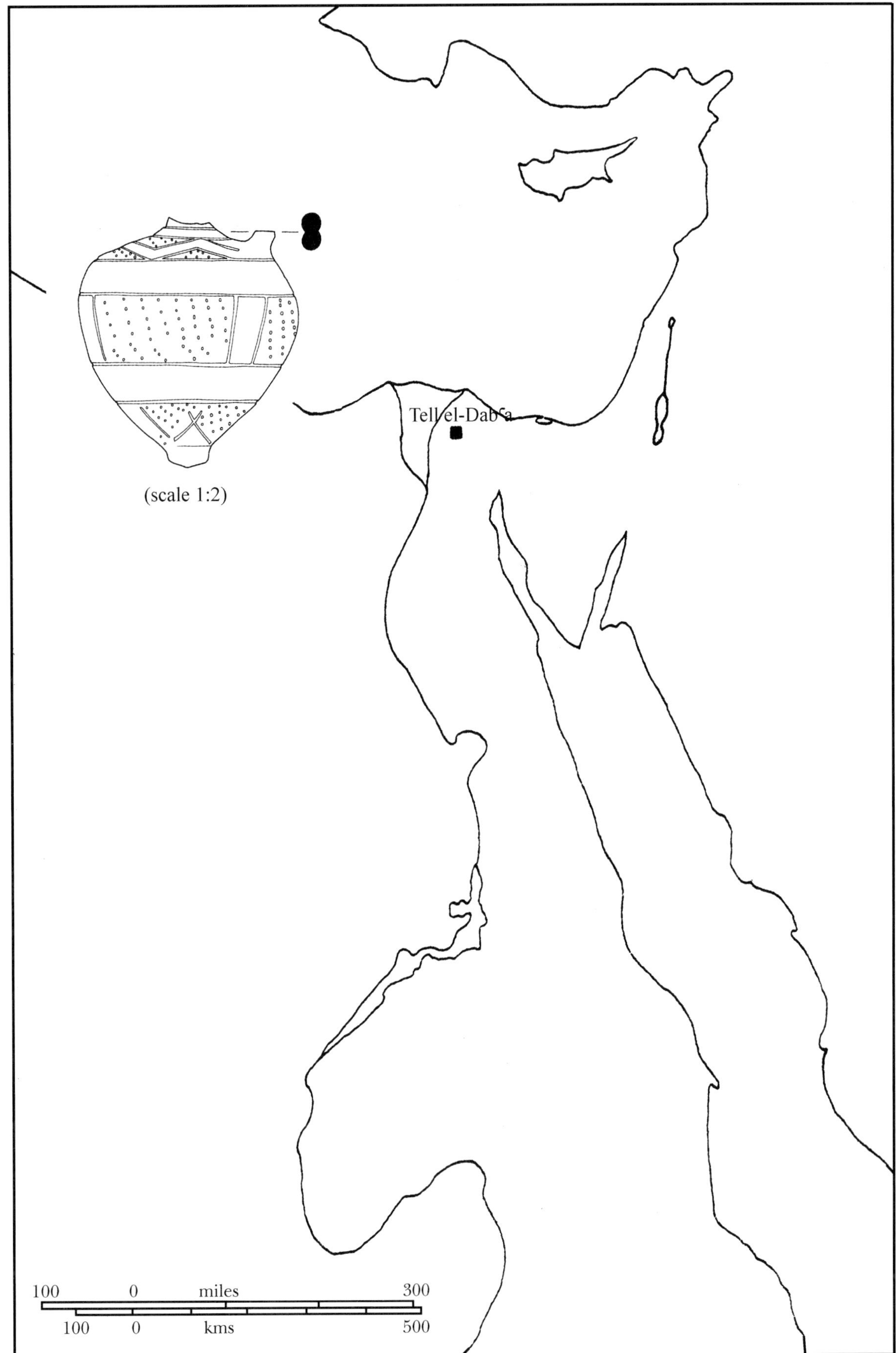

Fig. 119 Distribution and Shape Class of Type Group I.5.4

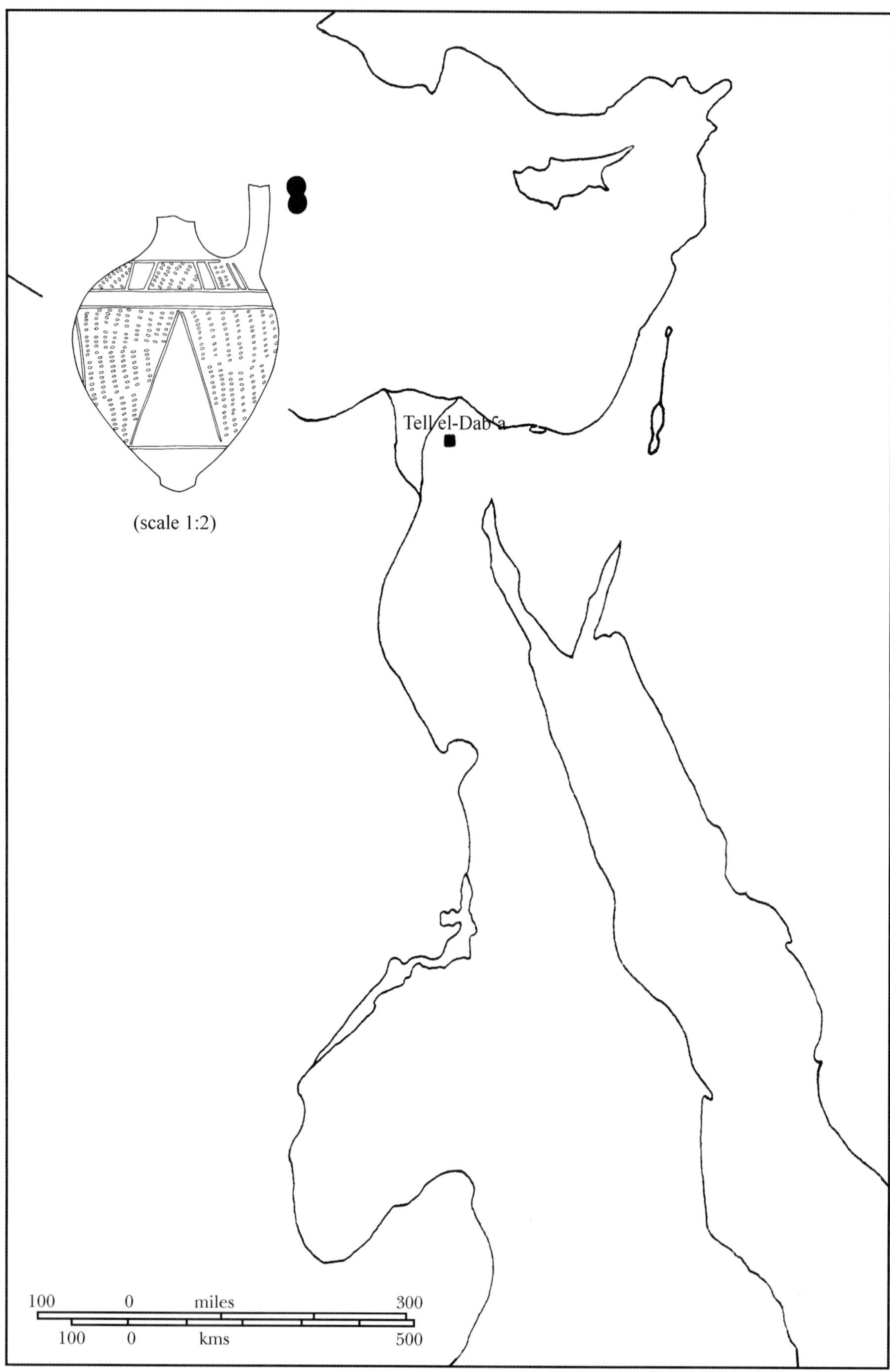

Fig. 120 Distribution and Shape Class of Type Group I.5.5

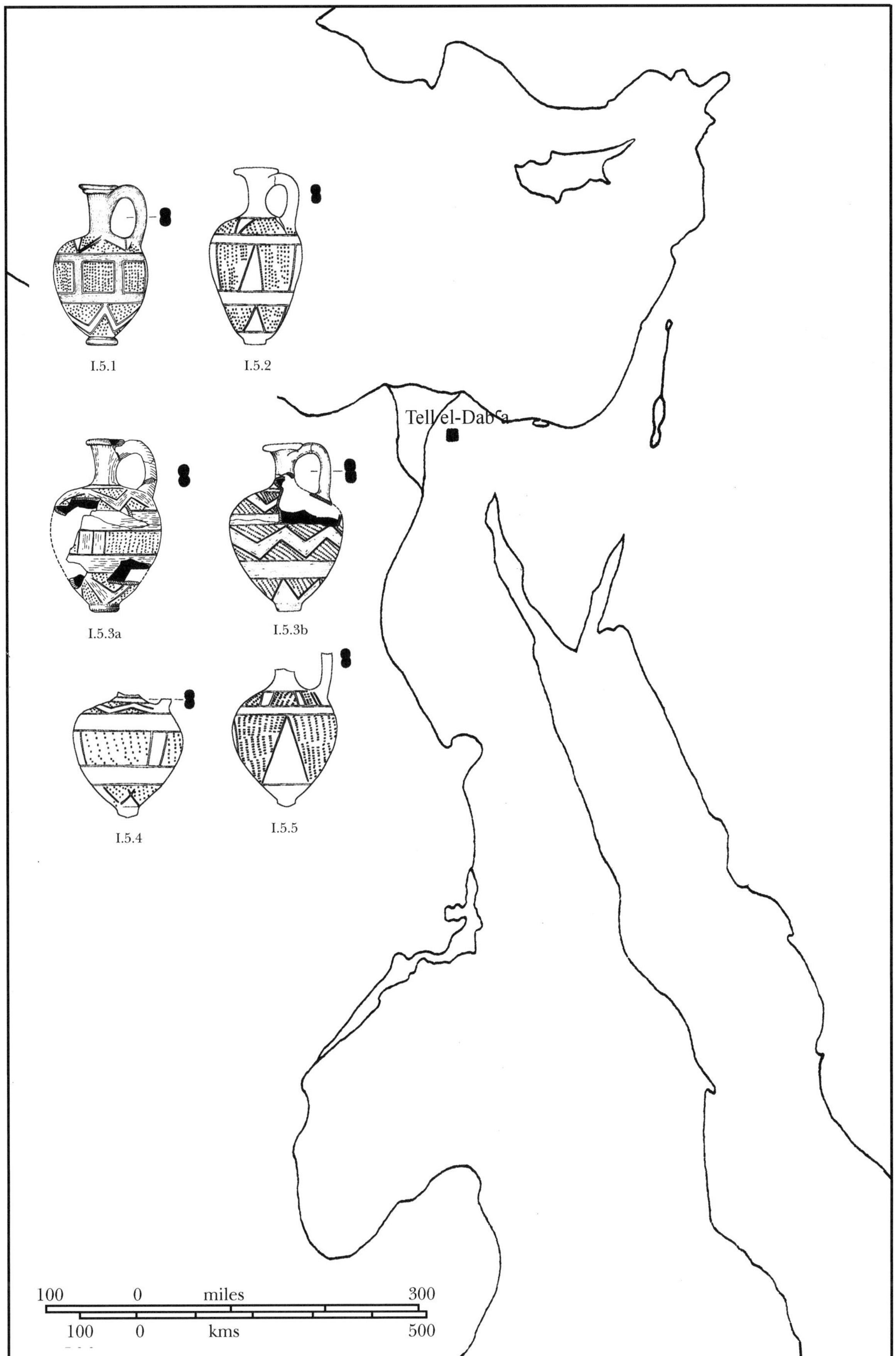

Fig. 121 Combined Distribution of Type Group I.5

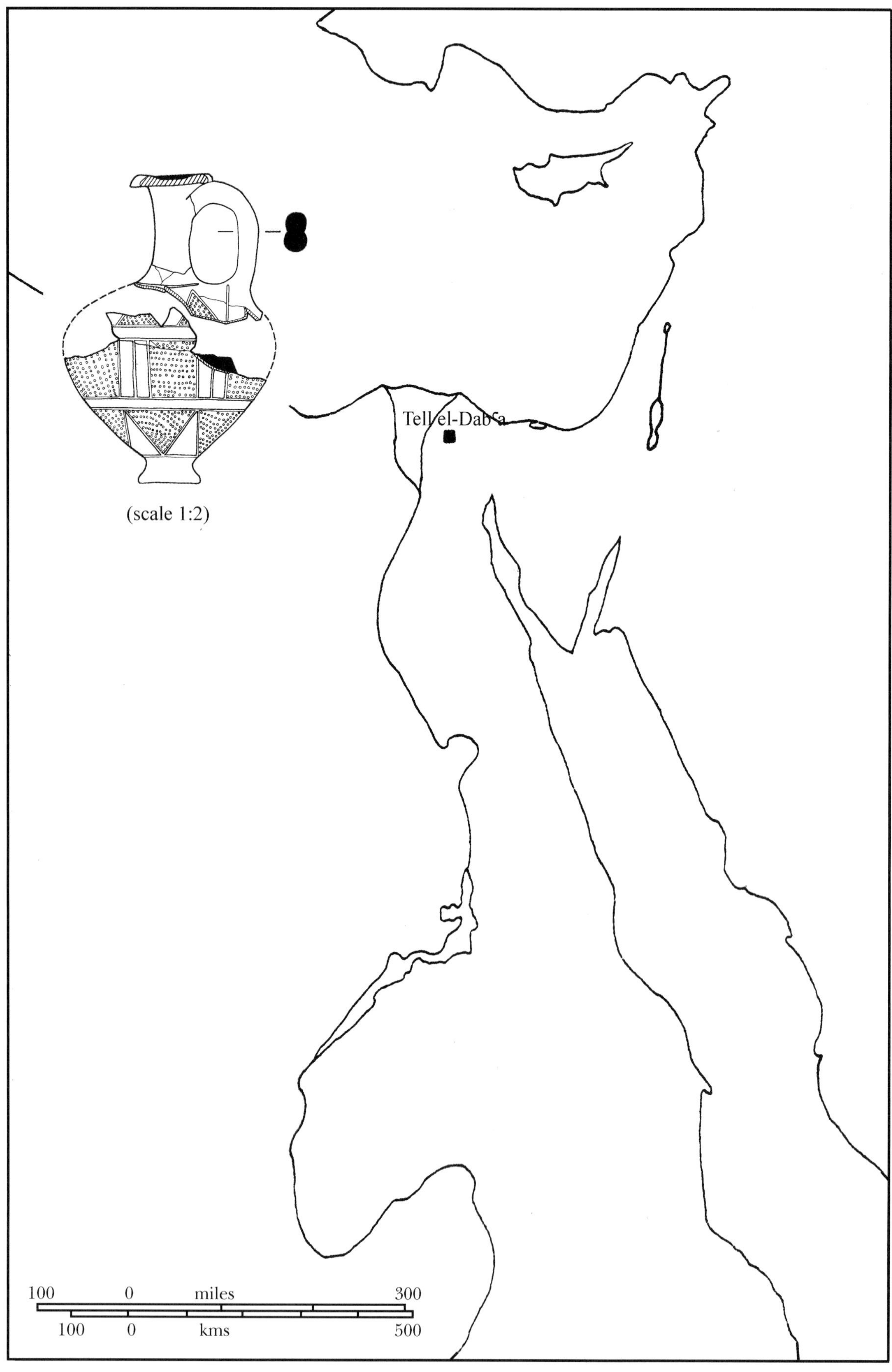

Fig. 122 Distribution and Shape Class of Type Group I.6.1

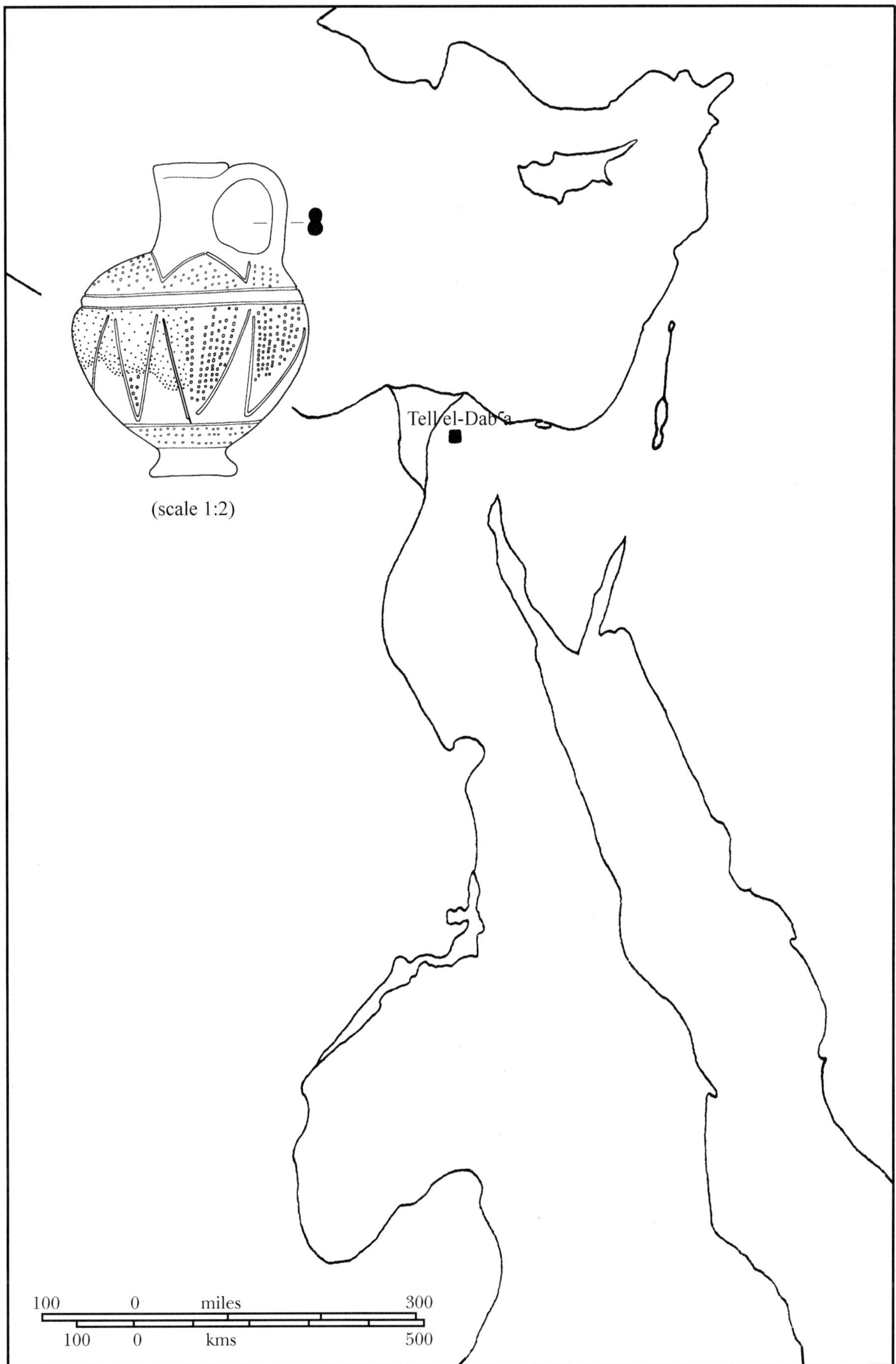

Fig. 123 Distribution and Shape Class of Type Group I.6.2

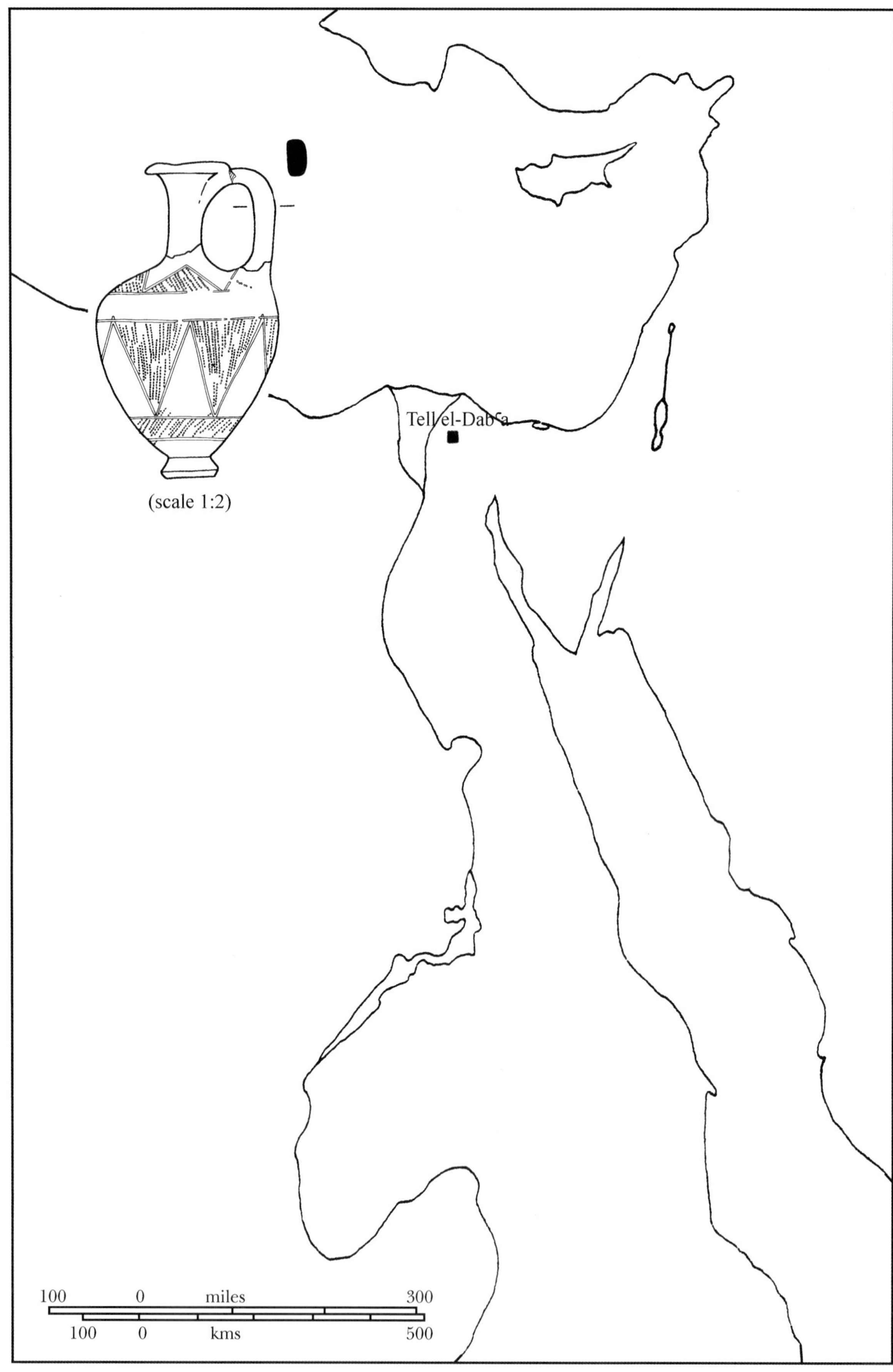

Fig. 124 Distribution and Shape Class of Type Group I.6.3

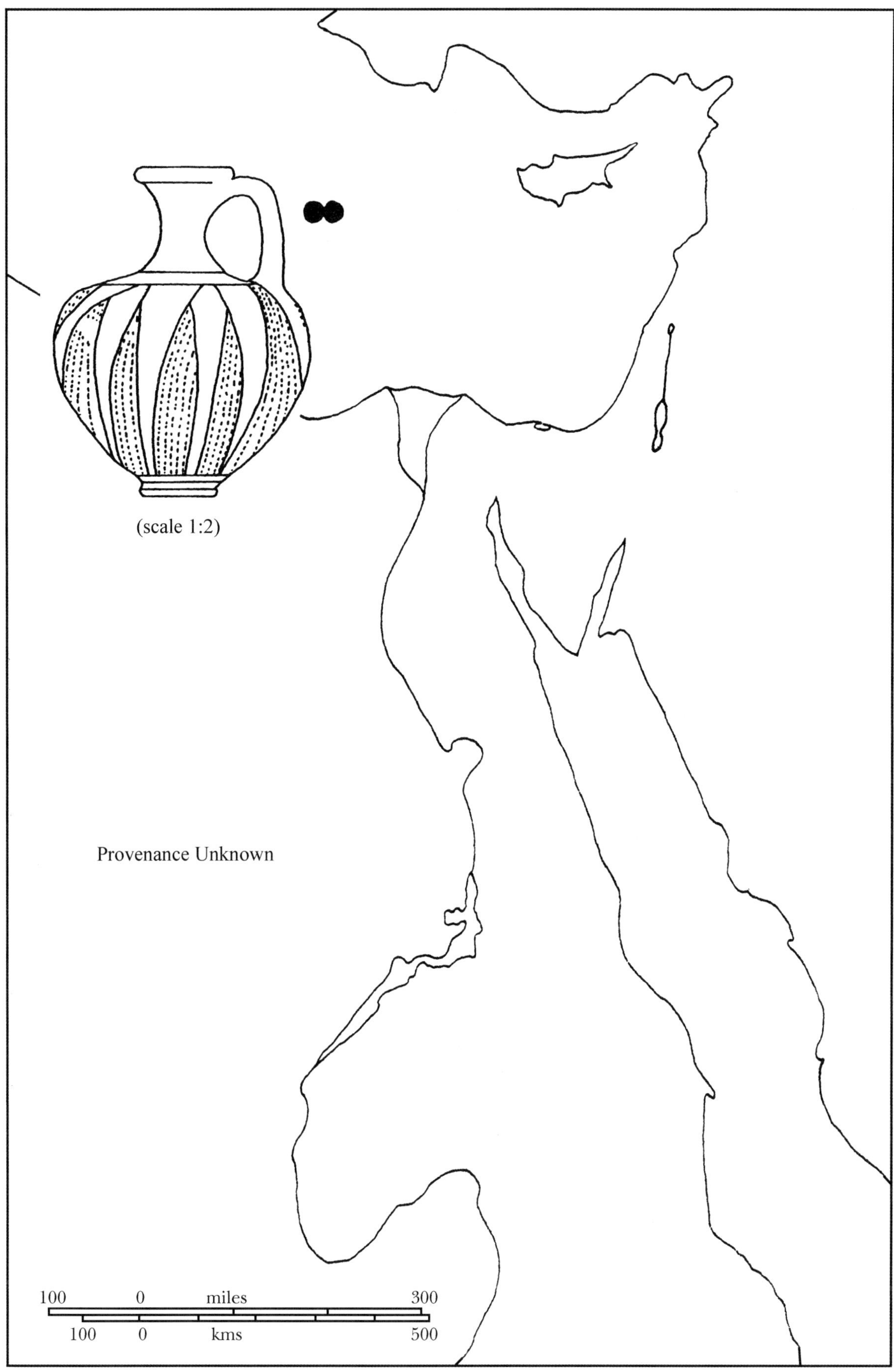

Fig. 125 Distribution and Shape Class of Type Group I.6.4

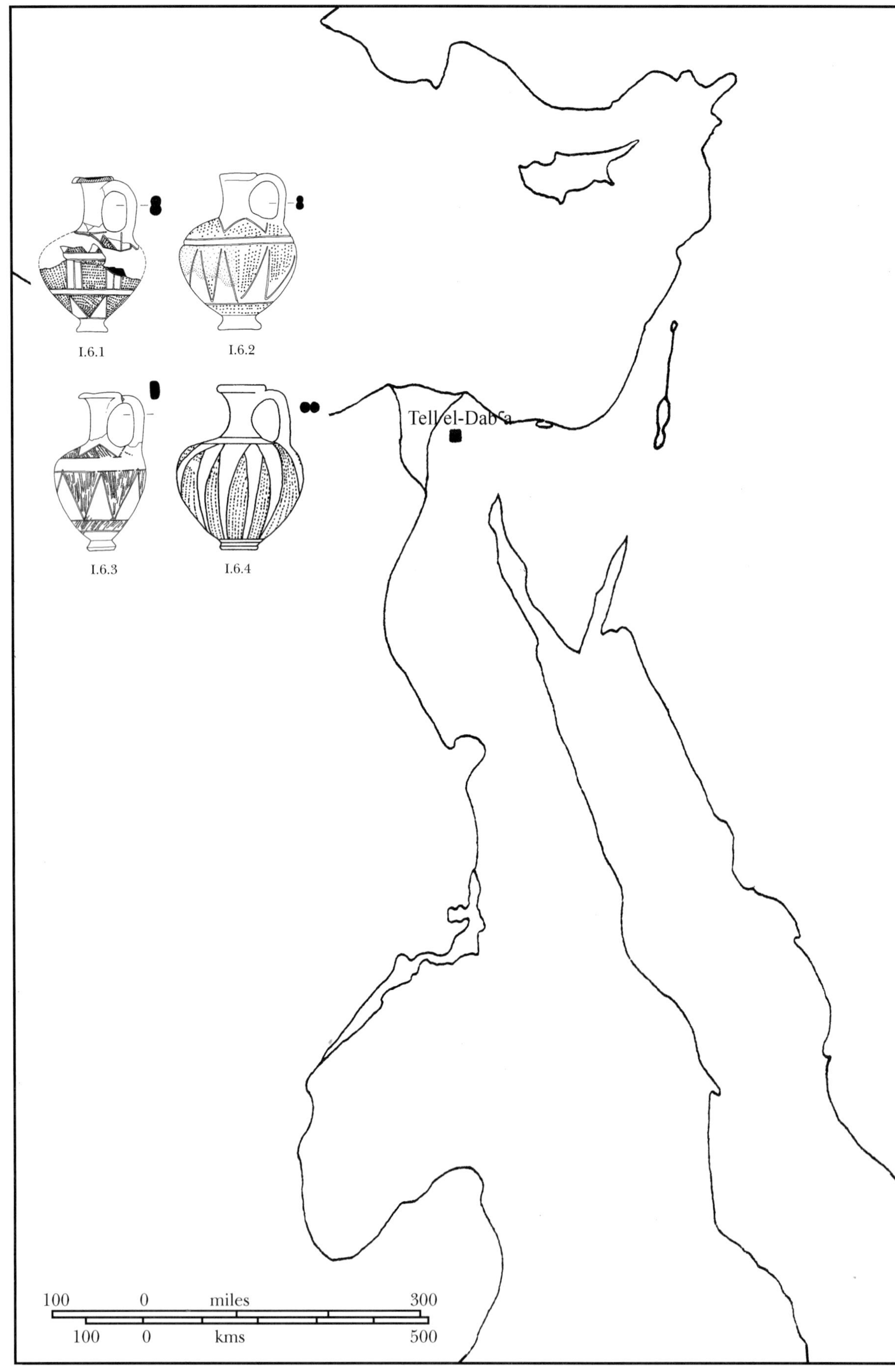

Fig. 126 Combined Distribution of Type Group I.6

clear. The decoration – perhaps lozenges similar to those found on the I.4 group – is probably early.

Branch J: Levanto-Egyptian Vessels with Naturalistic Designs

To the Levanto-Egyptian group also belong those jugs in which the entire surface is covered with naturalistic designs. Essentially all such jugs are piriform in shape and usually contain marsh scenes with representations of lotus flowers, lotus petals and birds. In addition two fragments probably from the same vessel found at Kahun (London BM 50789), and one sherd from Ashkelon (Jerusalem Rockefeller Museum P 2094) show herbivores nibbling on a tree, whilst a sherd from Lisht bears a representation of a human arm and hand.[393] Wherever NAA analysis has been done on these vessels, it is clear that most were made in Egypt,[394] although the one example found at Toumba tou Skouru was apparently made in the Byblos area.[395] In order to be consistent these jugs are divided according to their physical attributes, though this is perhaps over-fussy since so few vessels are known, and body sherds cannot be attributed to a given type:

Type Group J.1.1 (Figs. 127, 135)

A distinctly unusual vessel, which belongs in this group, is known from Bernasht and bears an upper zone of standing triangles, a central zone of stylised lotus flowers, and a lower zone of pendant triangles.[396]

Type Group J.1.2 (Figs. 128, 135)

Vessels of Type Group J.1.2 comprise piriform jugs with candlestick rims, double handles and slightly offset button bases. The complete example from Tell el-Dab^ca (TD 7461) shows one opened tall lotus blossom and three buds(?), each separated by single lotus leaves. The unincised areas are burnished. Another complete example from Tell el-Ghassil, stratum X, shows an upper row of five birds, and below two more pairs, slightly larger with palm trees between each pair.[397]

Type Group J.1.3 (Figs. 129, 135)

Vessels of Type Group J.1.3 comprise piriform jugs with rolled rims, double handles and ring or disc bases of which the only complete example comes from Toumba tou Skourou.[398] It bears a hanging garland of united lotus petals at the shoulder, and an upright garland of lotus flowers at the base. The lower band also has a series of incised birds between the blossoms. Negbi has suggested that the vessel found at Toumba tou Skourou was made in Cyprus, and should be dated to the Middle Cypriote III or Late Cypriote IA. However this is unlikely on both counts. The vessel clearly belongs in the same traditions as the remaining vessels of the J.1 family, which strongly suggests both a Levanto-Egyptian origin for the vessel and a Late Thirteenth Dynasty/Second Intermediate Period date. Its presence therefore in a Late Cypriote IA context can only be explained as an heirloom.

Type Group J.1.4 (Figs. 130, 135)

Vessels of Type Group J.1.4 comprise piriform jugs with rolled rims, strap handles and button bases, of which at least four examples have been found at Tell el-Dab^ca (TD 7483, 7484, 7485). All four have a pattern of lotus petals on the shoulder which radiate out from the base of the neck, a reserved band, and a lower zone of three lotus blossoms and alternating birds. The other has no distinct reserved zone, but one which is created by the fact that the decoration on the body comes up from the base and thus there is a gap between that, which consists of a rishi pattern, and the tips of the lotus petals.

Type Group J.1.5 (Figs. 131, 135)

Vessels of Type Group J.1.5 comprise squat piriform jugs with rolled rims (?), incisions at the base of the neck, bipartite handles and ring bases, again known from a single incomplete example from Tell el-Dab^ca (TD 7518). It has a pattern of lotus petals on the shoulder which radiate out from the base of the neck, a reserved band, and a lower zone of three lotus blossoms, though this time without any intervening birds.

Type Group J.1.6 (Figs. 132, 135)

Type group J.1.6 is known through an incomplete vessel from Tell el Dab^ca, TD 7463. It consists of a squat piriform to biconical vessel with a bipartite handle and a button base. It has a pattern of lotus petals on the shoulder which radiate out from the base of the

---

[393] Smith, *Interconnections*, fig. 48d; Merrillees, *Trade and Transcendance*, fig. 42, Amiran *IMN* 10, 1975, pl. c.1.

[394] Kaplan, *Tell el-Yahudiyeh Ware*, 235.

[395] M. Artzy, personal communication.

[396] London UC 13478, Merrillees, *Trade and Transcendance*, 64, fig. 51, Kaplan, *Tell el-Yahudiyeh Ware*, fig. 41a.

[397] Doumit-Serhal, *Berytus* 42, 54, pl. I.2; Eadem, *Les fouilles de Tell el-Ghassil de 1972 à 1974*, 1996, 33, 197, pl. 15.2.

[398] Vermeule, *Toumba tou Skourou*, 1974, 8, fig. 17a; Yon, *Manuel de céramique chypriote* I, 1976, 67, fig. 17d; O. Negbi, Cypriote Imitations of Tell el-Yahudiyeh Ware, *AJA* 82, 1978, 143–147, Kaplan, *Tell el-Yahudiyeh Ware*, fig. 127g.

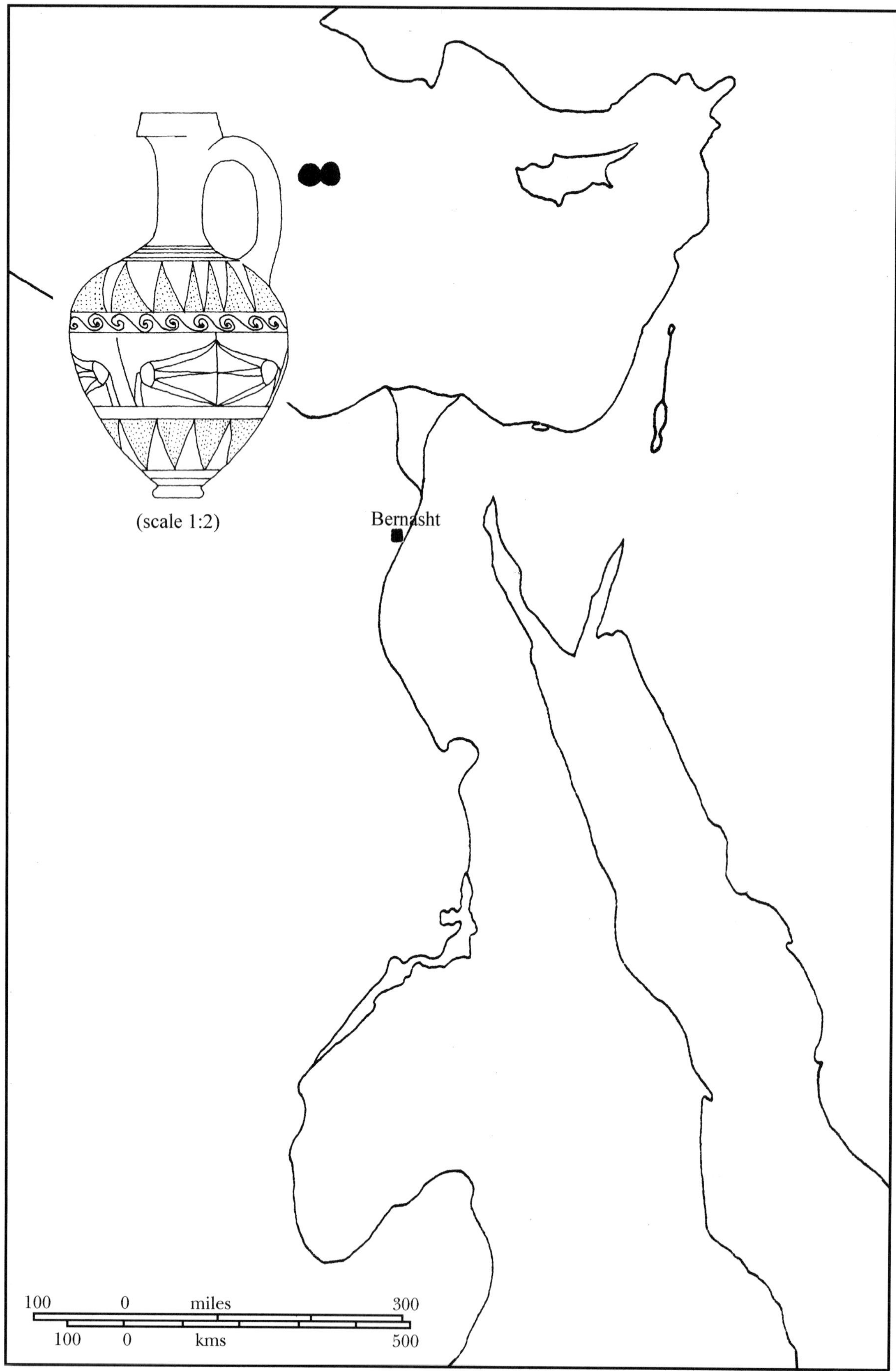

Fig. 127 Distribution and Shape Class of Type Group J.1.1

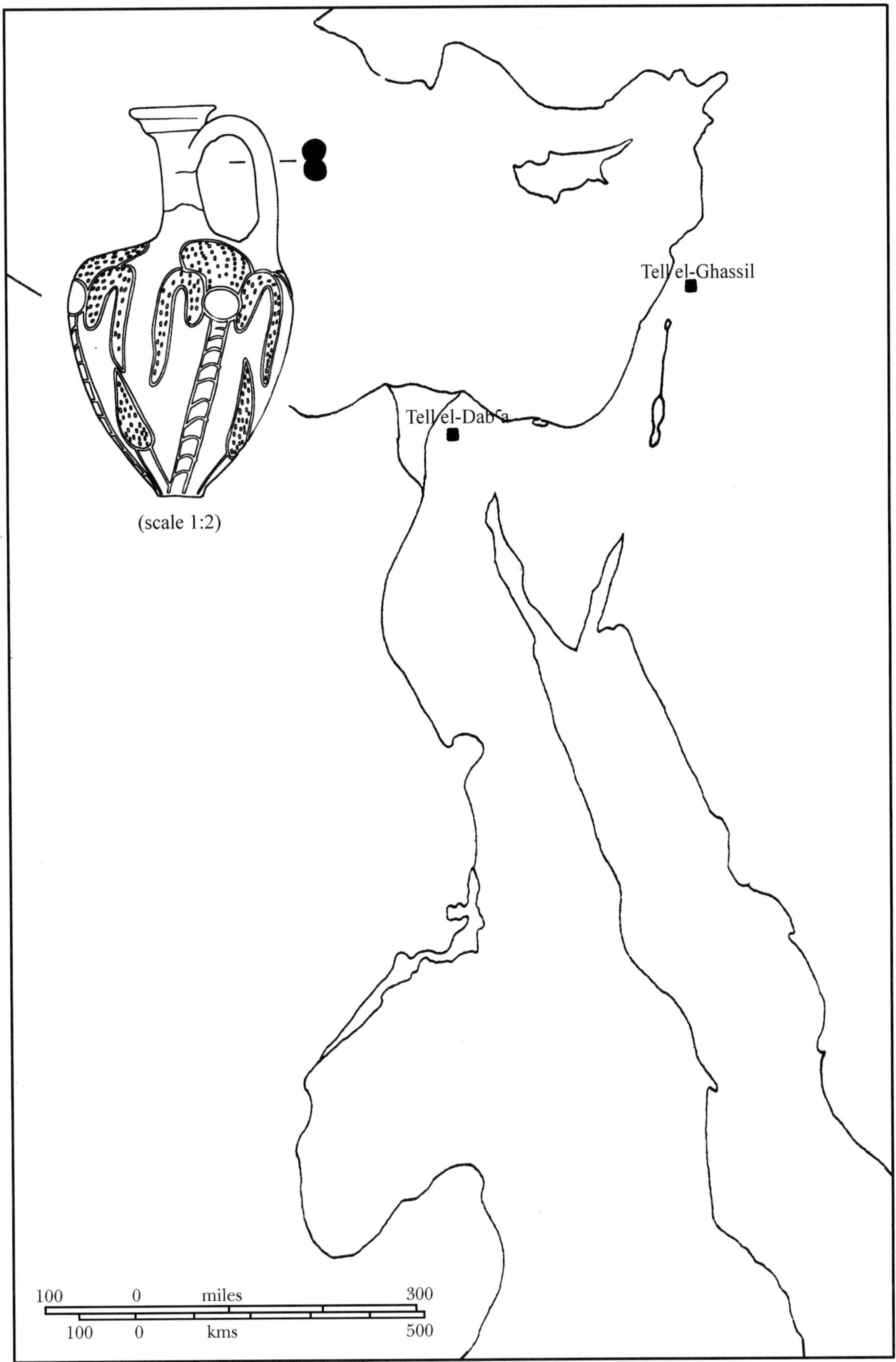

Fig. 128 Distribution and Shape Class of Type Group J.1.2

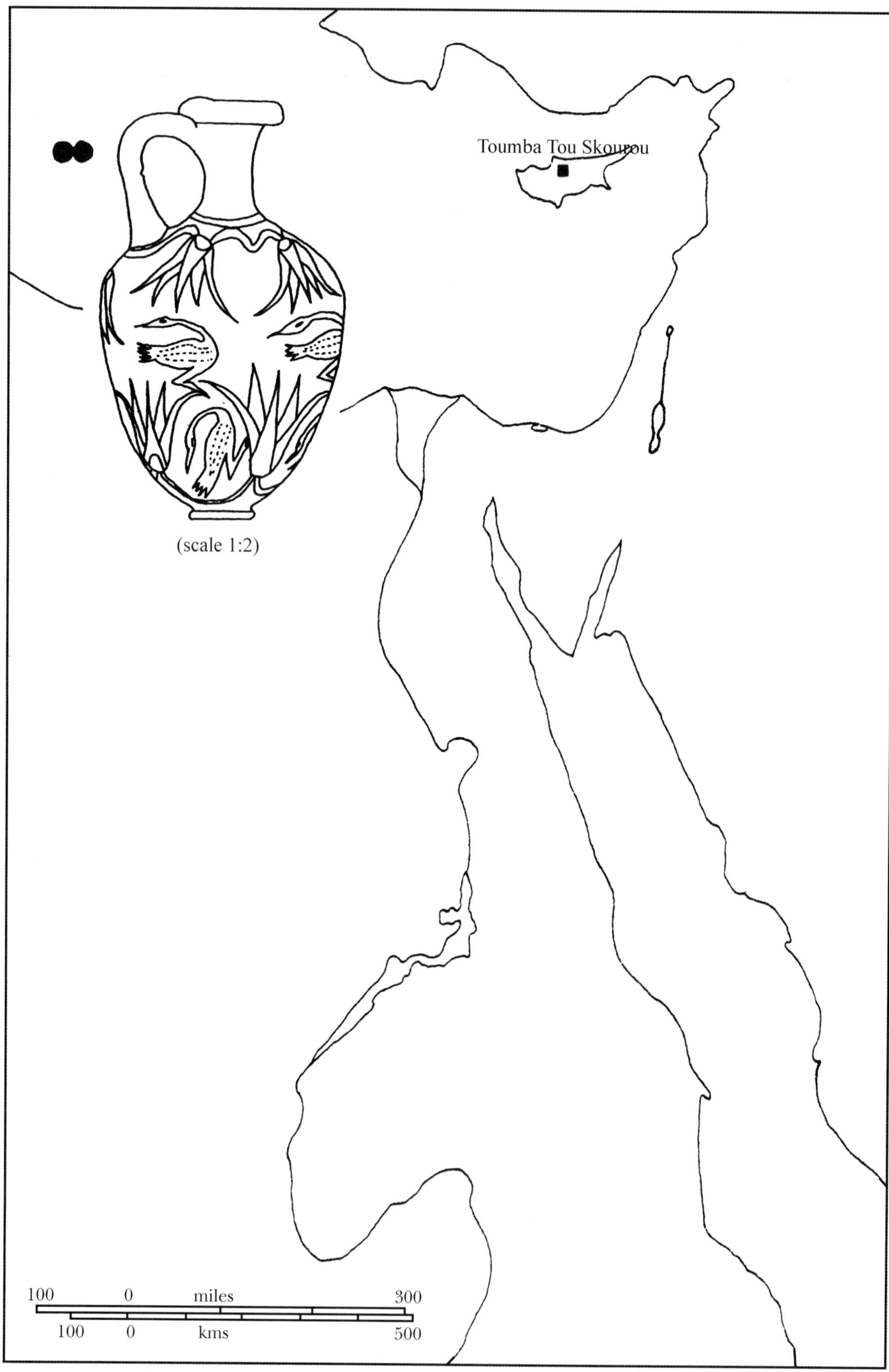

Fig. 129 Distribution and Shape Class of Type Group J.1.3

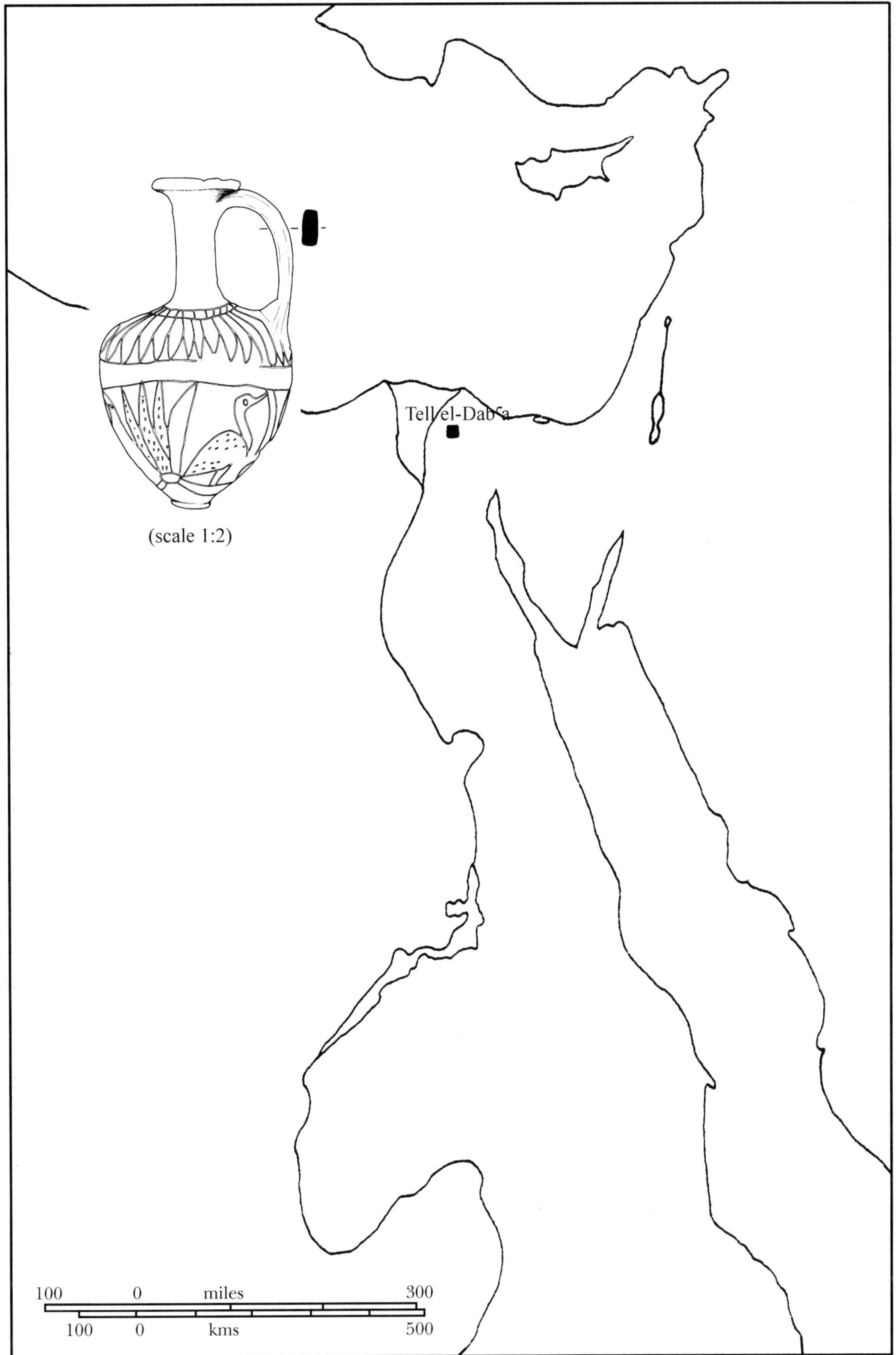

Fig. 130 Distribution and Shape Class of Type Group J.1.4

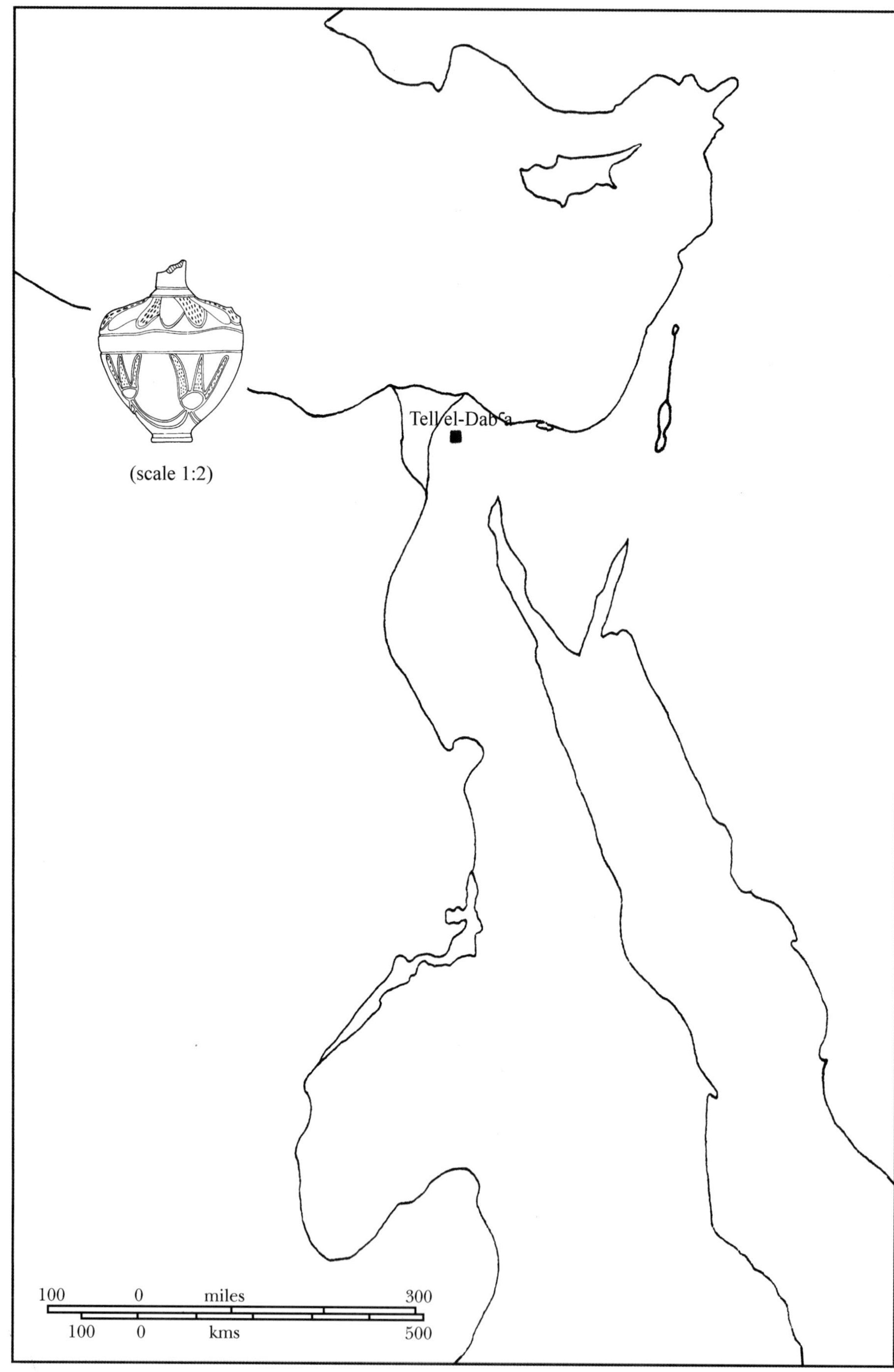

Fig. 131 Distribution and Shape Class of Type Group J.1.5

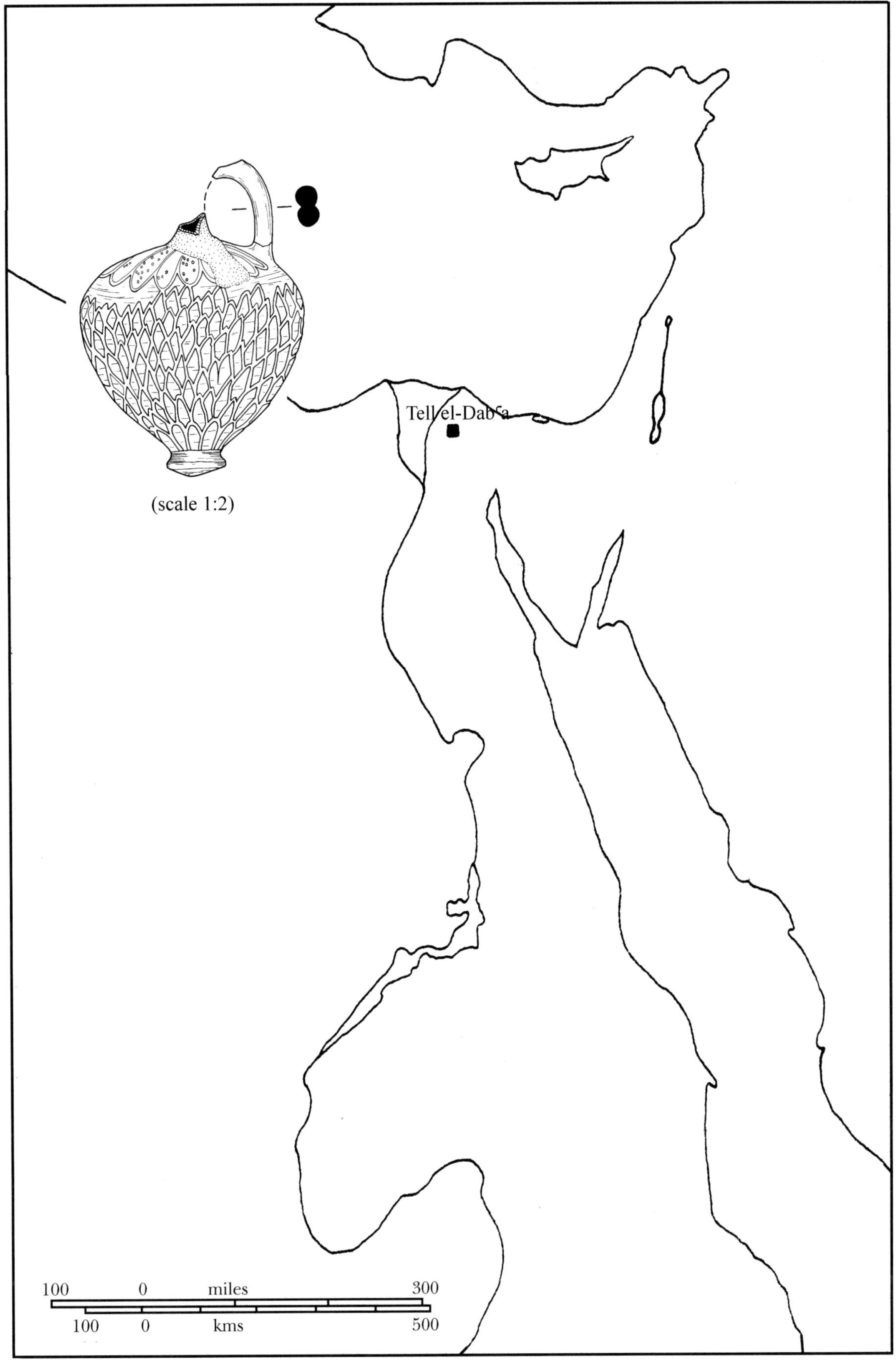

Fig. 132 Distribution and Shape Class of Type Group J.1.6

neck, but this time the body of the vessel is decorated with a rishi feather pattern.

Type Group J.1.7 (Figs. 133, 135)

Vessels of Type Group J.1.7 comprise piriform jugs with everted rims, double handles and button bases, of which three examples are now known from Tell el-Dabᶜa (TD 1122, 1630, 3545). They are all decorated with three upright lotus flowers on a long stem alternating with three stylised waterfowl which have long legs and long curved necks.

Type Group J.1.8 (Figs. 134, 135)

Vessels of Type Group J.1.8 comprise piriform jugs with rolled rims, double bodies, strap handles and disc bases known from a single example found at Thebes.[399] This unique vessel has a running spiral around the shoulder of each vessel, and around the bodies three tall lotus flowers, interspersed with three smaller examples.

*

Several other fragments of decorated vessels are also known, and where enough is preserved to give some indication of shape it is clear that they are all piriform. Such pieces include the lower body and ring base from Harageh,[400] which shows lotus blossoms waving in the breeze; a body sherd also from Harageh with fragments of lotus flowers and a running spiral;[401] body sherds from Lisht showing birds;[402] a large part of the body from Tuna el-Gebel, which has two bands of lotus blossoms, separated by a cross-hatched band which runs around the pot at the maximum diameter;[403] a shoulder from Abydos tomb D.11 showing lotus petals;[404] and a sherd from Kerma with part of a lotus flower.[405]

*

To this branch should perhaps belong the following two vessels which differ slightly from the previous examples of Group J.1, but are clearly related to them:

Type Group J.2 (Fig. 136)

Tell el-Yahudiya jugs of type group J.2 are represented by an incomplete vessel, missing its rim and neck, from Ashkelon (below 567) which is decorated with a rishi, or scale pattern.

Type Group J.3 (Fig. 137)

Vessels of Type Group J3 comprise piriform jugs with rolled (?) rims, double handles and ring bases of which the most complete example was found in Cyprus, site unknown.[406] This vessel has a series of sitting ducks around the shoulder and others shown in flight below. Similar fragments with poorly drawn bird motifs were found at Shechem[407] and Ardé.[408] It is not clear whether these vessels should be placed here or in the early Palestinian group. On the one hand, the style of decoration is very reminiscent to that found on the group B.6.1 vessel, which would suggest a placing in the early Palestinian grouping, but the overall form is very close to a number of vessels of groups J.1.4–6, which rather suggests that the J.3 vessels are Palestinian copies of Levanto-Egyptian vessels. Other fragmentary pieces which probably belong in this group include a ring base with a garland of lotus flowers from Byblos,[409] one of only two analysed examples to be made of a Levantine clay, rather then Egyptian Nile silt,[410] though the decoration is clearly inspired by examples from Egypt; and another base from Byblos showing lotus petals and reserved diamonds.[411]

Branch K: Late Syrian

As explained earlier, the late Syrian development of the Levanto-Egyptian branch of Tell el-Yahudiya ware is very poorly known owing to the lack of published material from Syrian sites dating to the MB IIB period. However the letter K is reserved for subsequent discoveries which may, one day, be attributed to this branch of the ware.

---

399 New York MMA 23.3.39. Winlock, *BMMA* 18, 1923, 31, fig. 25, Kaplan, *Tell el-Yahudiyeh Ware*, fig. 127c.

400 Oxford. Ashmolean 1914.671. Kaplan, *Tell el-Yahudiyeh Ware*, fig. 126e.

401 London UC 18646. Merrillees, *Trade and Transcendance*, 64, fig. 51b.

402 Merrillees, *Trade and Transcendance*, 59 fig. 42 left.

403 Paris Louvre E.11314. Kaplan, *Tell el-Yahudiyeh Ware*, fig. 126h.

404 Oxford Ashmolean E.2776. Kaplan, *Tell el-Yahudiyeh Ware*, fig. 126i.

405 Smith, *Interconnections*, 43, fig. 18c.

406 Nicosia, Cyprus Museum 1953/II-6/12. Åström, *Alasia I*, 13, figs. 8–9, Kaplan, *Tell el-Yahudiyeh Ware*, fig. 128b.

407 Jerusalem. Rockefeller Museum I.859. Kaplan, *Tell el-Yahudiyeh Ware*, fig. 127e.

408 Kaplan, *Tell el-Yahudiyeh Ware*, fig. 127f.

409 Dussaud, 1928, 149, fig. 18.

410 Kaplan, *Tell el-Yahudiyeh Ware*, 235, sample BYB3, and cf. below, 595.

411 Beirut 13199. Dunand, *Fouilles de Byblos II*, 581, fig. 675 no. 13199, pl. 209. As far as we know this vessel has not been subject to an NAA analysis.

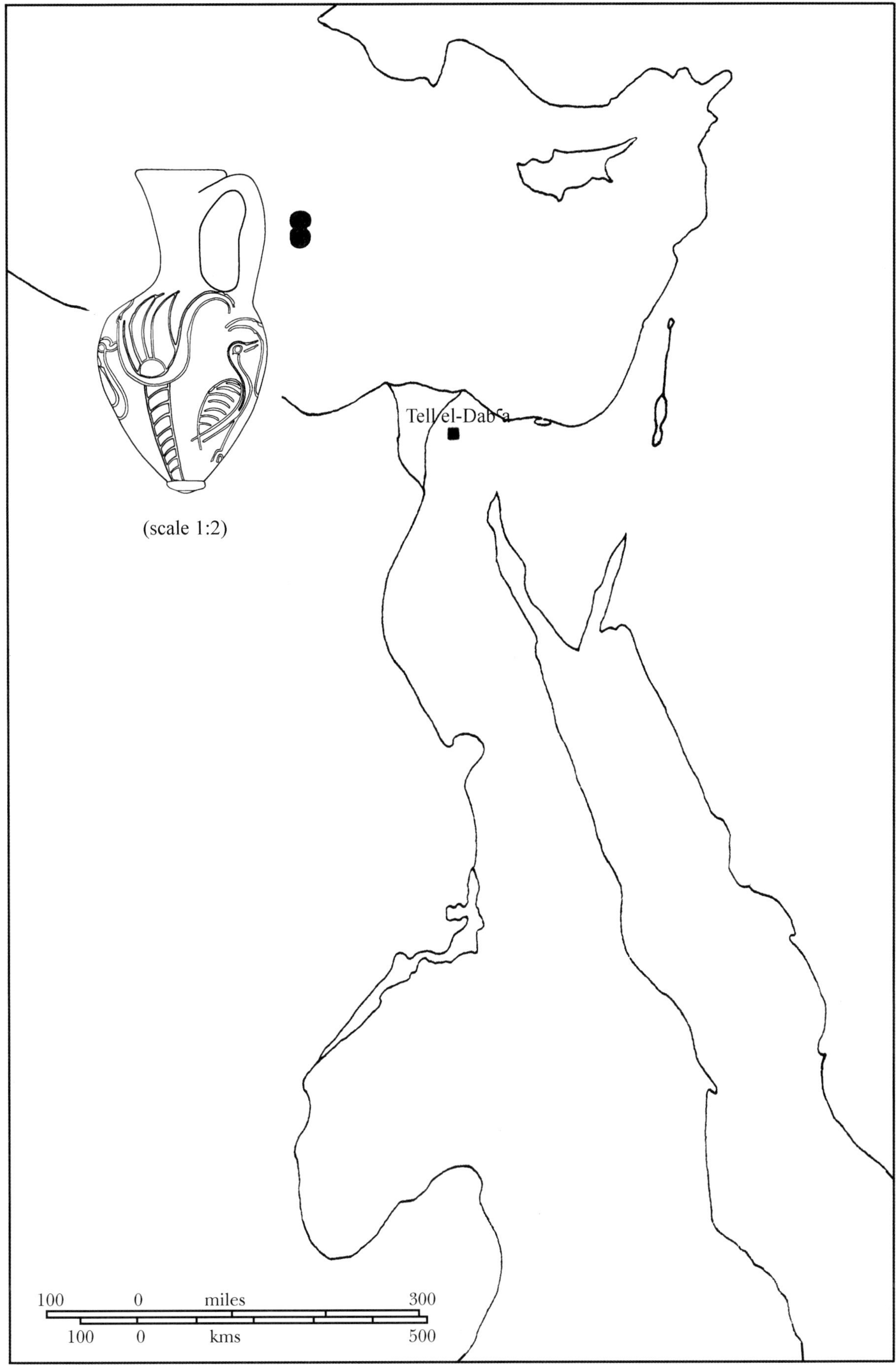

Fig. 133 Distribution and Shape Class of Type Group J.1.7

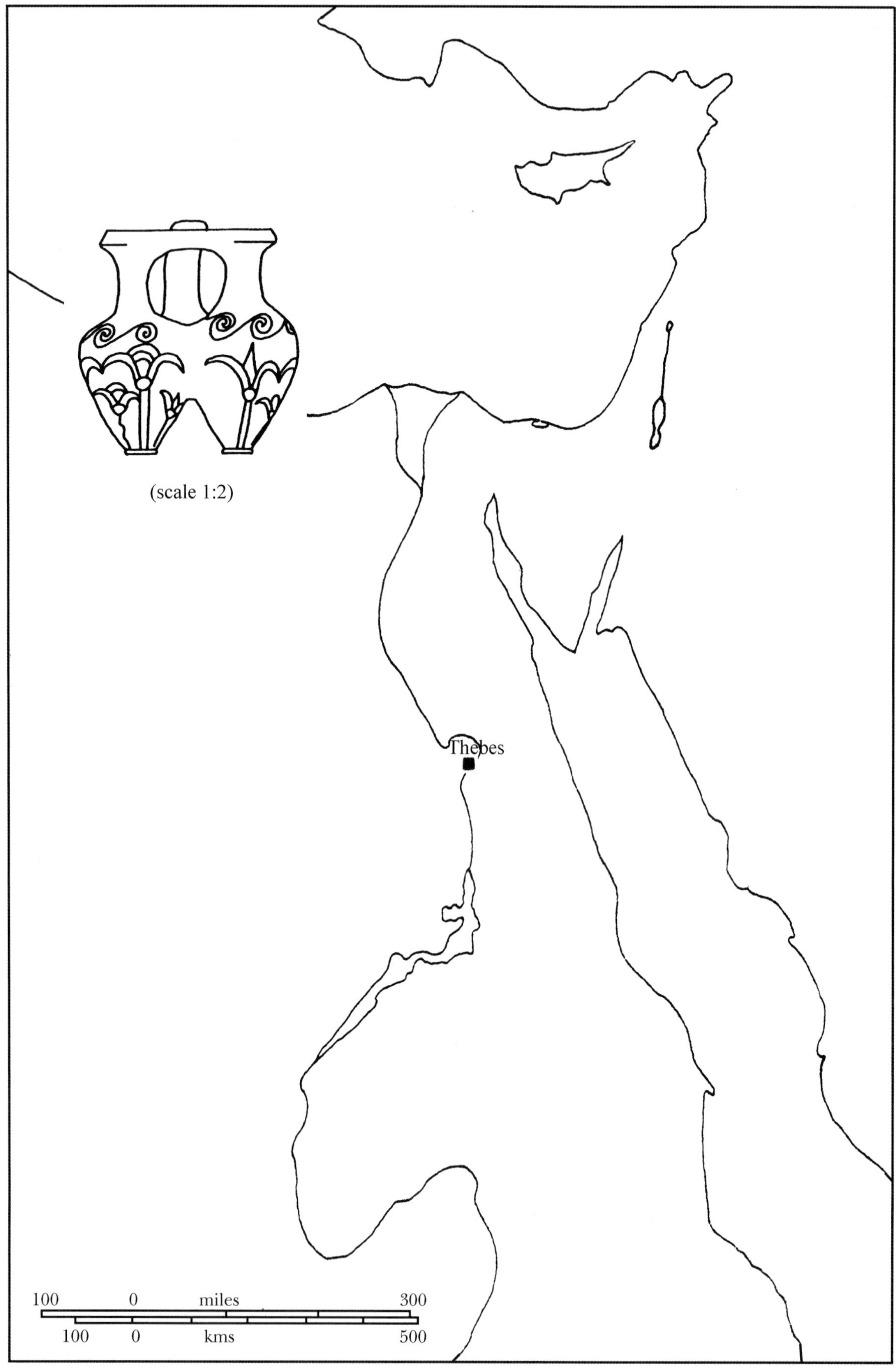

Fig. 134 Distribution and Shape Class of Type Group J.1.8

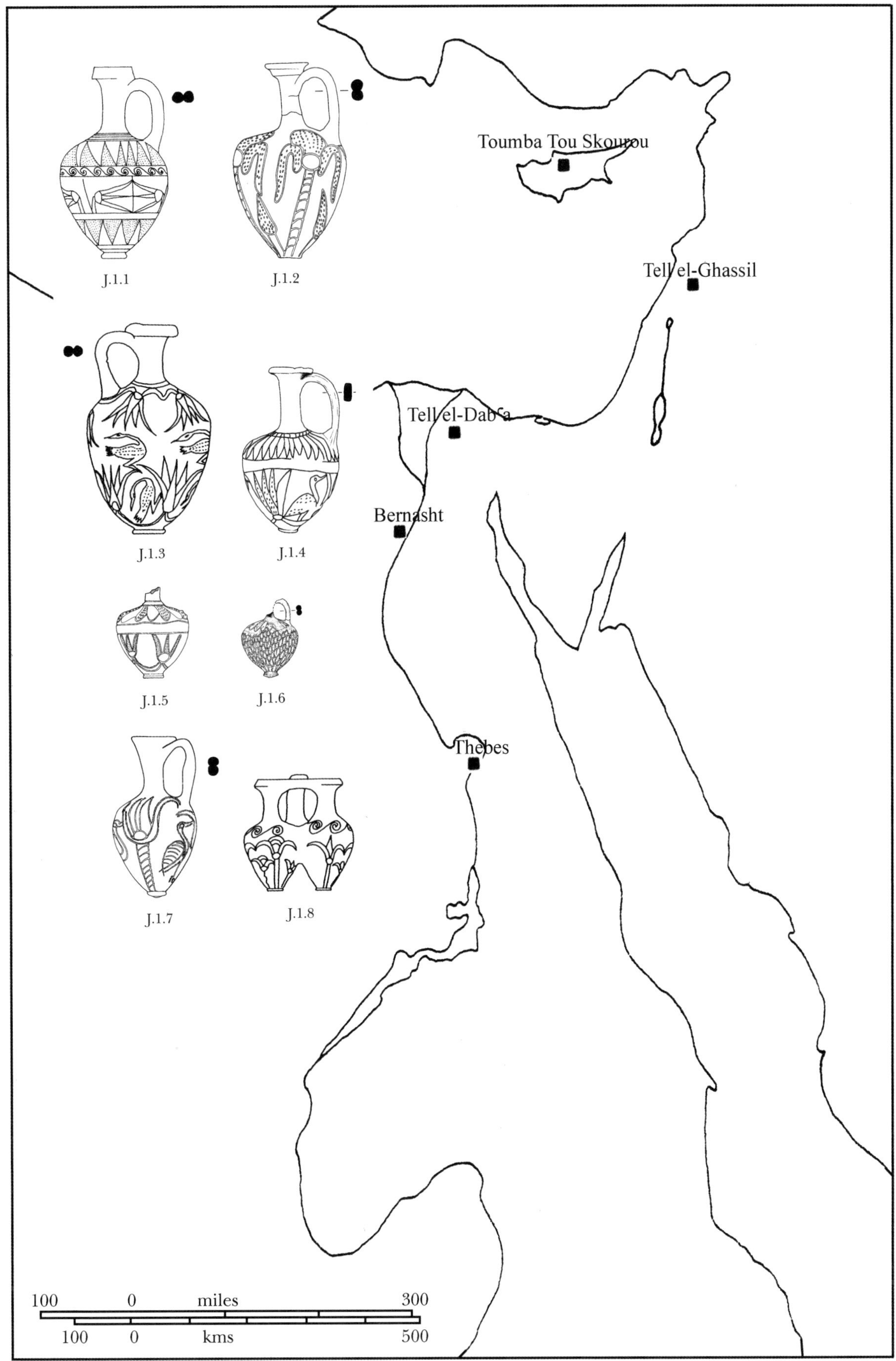

Fig. 135 Combined Distribution of Type Group J.1

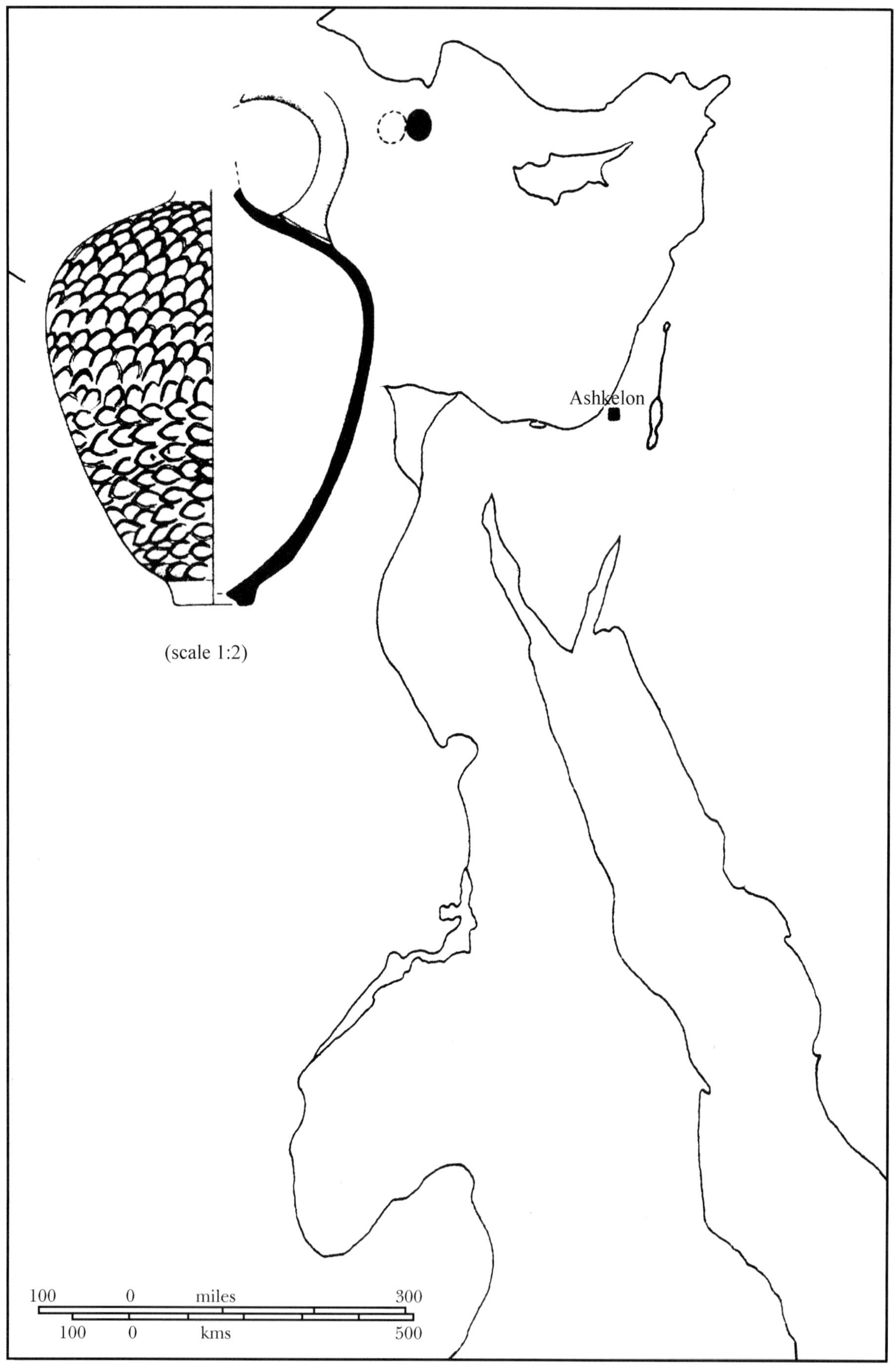

Fig. 136 Distribution and Shape Class of Type Group J.2

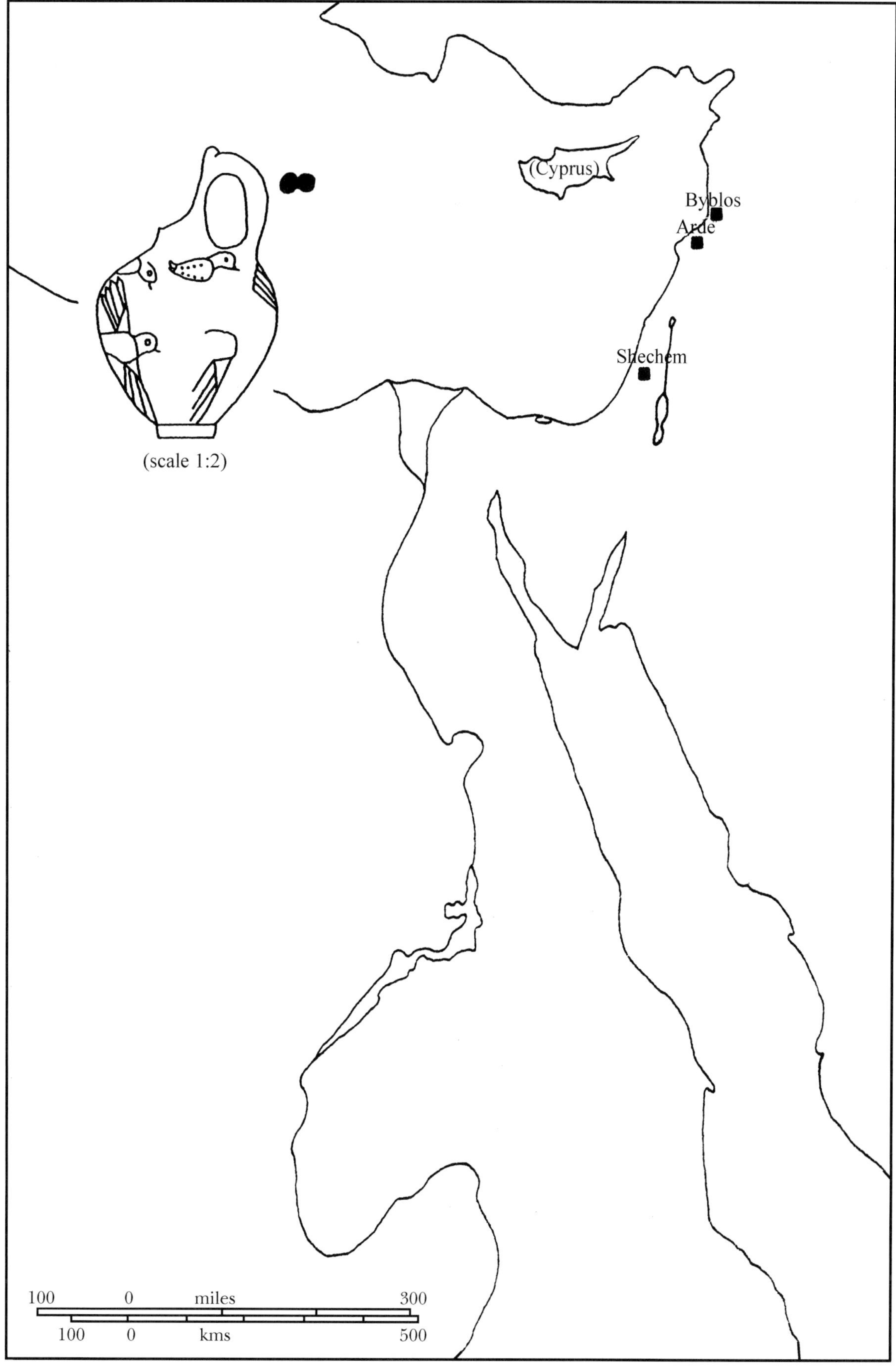

Fig. 137 Distribution and Shape Class of Type Group J.3

Branch L. Late Egyptian

As mentioned above it is only shortly before the onset of the Hyksos Period that this kind of pottery shows signs of mass production and standardization, a trend which can be observed both in Palestine and in Egypt. Within Egypt proper there are five main groups, Kaplan's Biconical 1, Piriform 2a, Globular, Cylindrical and Quadrilobal, all of which vary little in their style of decoration.

L.1. Late Egyptian I (Piriform 2a)

Late Egyptian I comprise those vessels of Kaplan's Piriform 2a with lozenge decoration, each lozenge being clearly defined by incised borders (L.1.1–L.1.5), or in the case of groups L.1.6–8 undelinated lozenge decoration.

Type Group L.1.1 (Figs. 138, 147)

One complete vessel, TD 1674, along with another, incomplete example, TD 3269A, have been attributed to this type. The complete example forms a link between the Levanto-Egyptian group I4, in that it has a candlestick rim and a ring base, but by contrast, it has a single strap, rather than a bipartite, handle which links it with the Late Egyptian Piriform 2a group. Both vessels are decorated with a number of lozenges, again reminiscent of the true Piriform 2a group, each infilled with rows of dots made with a comb. However the findspots of both vessels clearly indicate their earlier dating.

Type Group L.1.2 (Large Piriform 2a) (Figs. 139, 140, 147)

Large Piriform 2a jugs, type group L.1.2, with a height of between 14 and 18 cms, which contrasts with more 'normal' jugs which generally vary in height between 7 and 13 cms., with the average being around 10 cms, come from settlement sites and are somewhat rare. Of the five complete (or at least published) examples so far known, two have ring bases, type L.1.2a, (Tell el-Dabᶜa TD 3346 and London UC13468, from Egypt, site unknown[412]), and the others, Oxford Ashmolean E.4243 from Hu,[413] and London UC 8865 from Tell el-Yahudiya,[414] a disc base, type L.1.2b.

Type Group L.1.3 (Piriform 2a) (Figs. 141, 147)

Type groups L.1.3–L.1.4 are equivalent to Kaplan's classic Piriform 2a Tell el Yahudiya jugs,[415] in that they comprise vessels with a rolled rim, strap handle, flattened to rounded shoulders, a piriform to rounded body and a ring, disc or button base. In terms of size they generally vary in height between 7 and 13 cms., with the average being around 10 cms. Such Piriform 2a jugs are here divided into groups L.1.3 with a ring base, L.1.4 with a disc base, and L.1.5 with a button base. The decoration invariably consists only of lozenges (gores), usually three or four, though sometimes five or only two, filled with a herringbone pattern of incised dots. The comb used for this generally had eight or more teeth, and the area of incision is usually delineated. Burnishing occurs on the unincised areas. Although in previous publications the number of lozenges is not always indicated, they may be divided into decorative styles based on the number of lozenges present, namely L.1.3a with five lozenges, L.1.3b with four, L.1.3c with three and L.1.3d with two. Vessels of group L.1.3 with ring bases are known from Tell el-Dabᶜa,[416] Tell el-Yahudiya[417] Giza,[418] Koptos,[419] Buhen,[420] Kerma,[421] and have also been found in Cyprus,[422] whilst an Egyptian example was found at Beth Shan.[423]

A variant ring base is known on at least seven vessels from Tell el-Dabᶜa, (TD 231, 367, 2138, 2142, 3050, 4902 and 9180), and in one example from Ashkelon (below 570), where the centre of the base

---

[412] Kaplan, *Tell el-Yahudiyeh Ware,* fig. 46b.

[413] Kaplan, *Tell el-Yahudiyeh Ware,* fig. 46a.

[414] Griffith, The Antiquities of Tell el-Yahudiyah, 1890, pl. 9.1, Kaplan, *Tell el-Yahudiyeh Ware,* fig. 47a.

[415] Kaplan, *Tell el-Yahudiyeh Ware,* 21–22, figs. 48–60.

[416] See below and add London BM 27472. Hall, *The Oldest Civilization Of Greece,* 68, fig. 29.2; Adam, *ASAE* 56, 1959, 207, pl. 15.

[417] Oxford Ashmolean 1888.268. Griffith, *The Antiquities of Tell el-Yahudiyeh,* 40, pl. 9.1, Oxford Ashmolean E.3502. Petrie, *Hyksos and Israelite Cities,* 11, 15, pl. viiia.81; Boston MFA 1888.989. Griffith, *The Antiquities of Tell el-Yahudiyeh,* 40, pl. 9.1; Manchester 3490, Petrie, *Hyksos and Israelite Cities,* 11, 15, pl. viiia.86; London UC 13471. Griffith, *The Antiquities of Tell el-Yahudiyeh,* 40, pl. 9.2; Adam, *ASAE* 55, 1958, 309 pl. 17b.

[418] Cairo JE 72328. Hassan, *Excavations at Giza II,* 108, pl. 35.1.

[419] Boston MFA 1947.1665. Kaplan, *Tell el-Yahudiyeh Ware,* fig. 53d.

[420] Philadelphia UM E.10876. Randall-MacIver and Woolley, *Buhen,* 215–216, pl. 92.

[421] Khartoum 1296. Kaplan, *Tell el-Yahudiyeh Ware,* fig. 55b.

[422] Nicosia Cyprus Museum. Kaplan, *Tell el-Yahudiyeh Ware,* fig. 54d.

[423] Cf. A. Maeir and R. Mullins, below page 585.

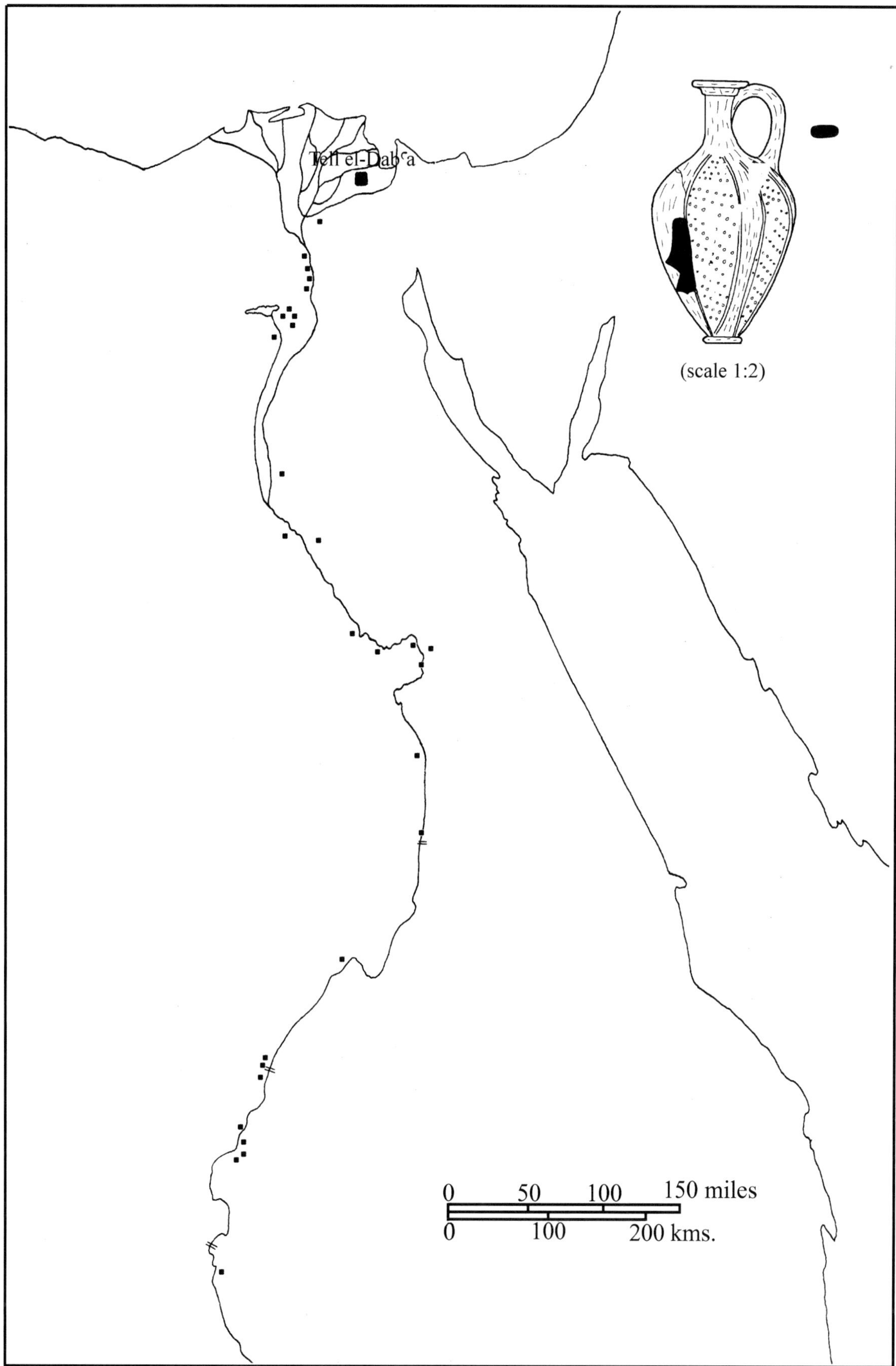

Fig. 138 Distribution and Shape Class of Type Group L.1.1

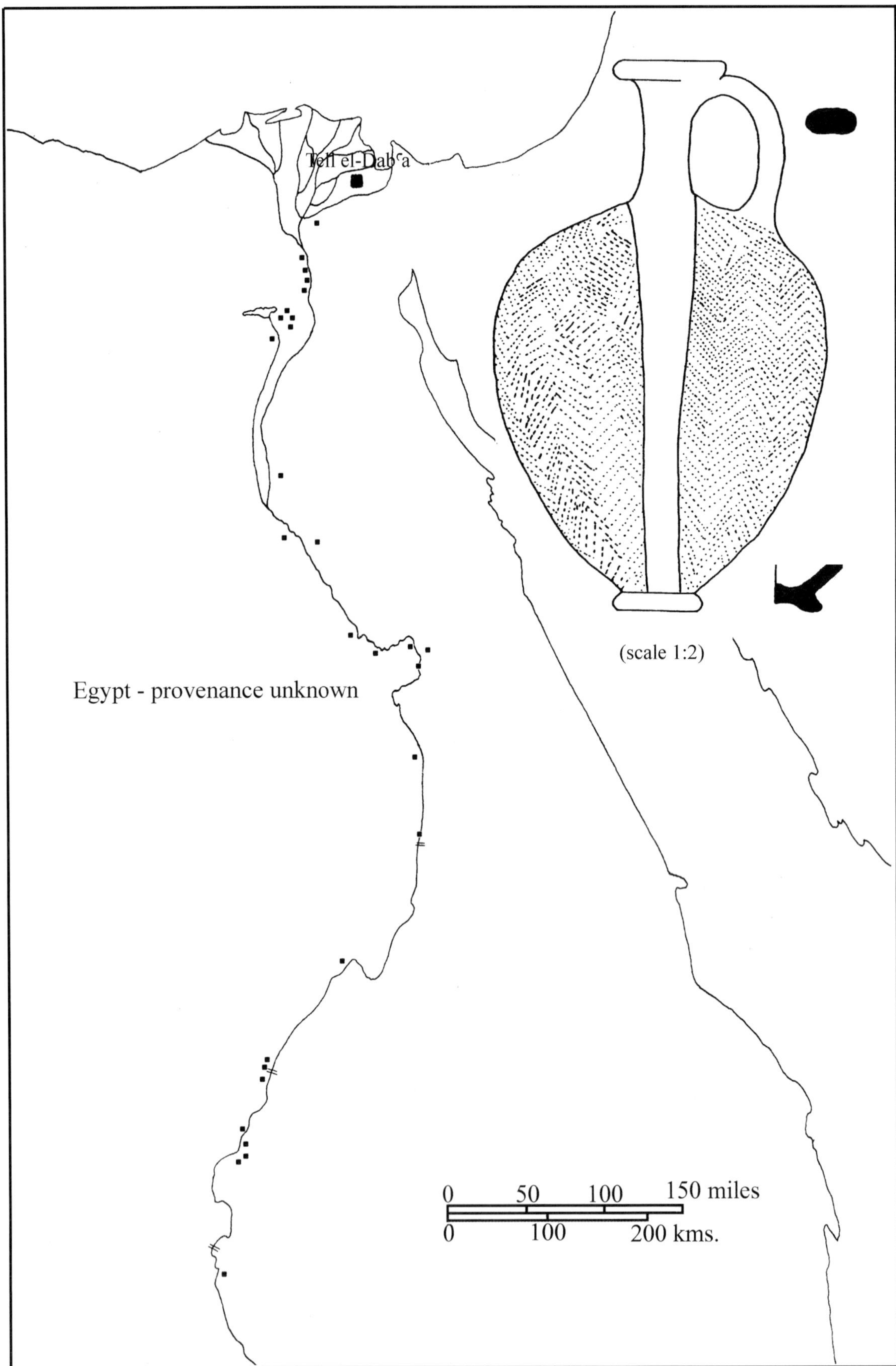

Fig. 139 Distribution and Shape Class of Type Group L.1.2a

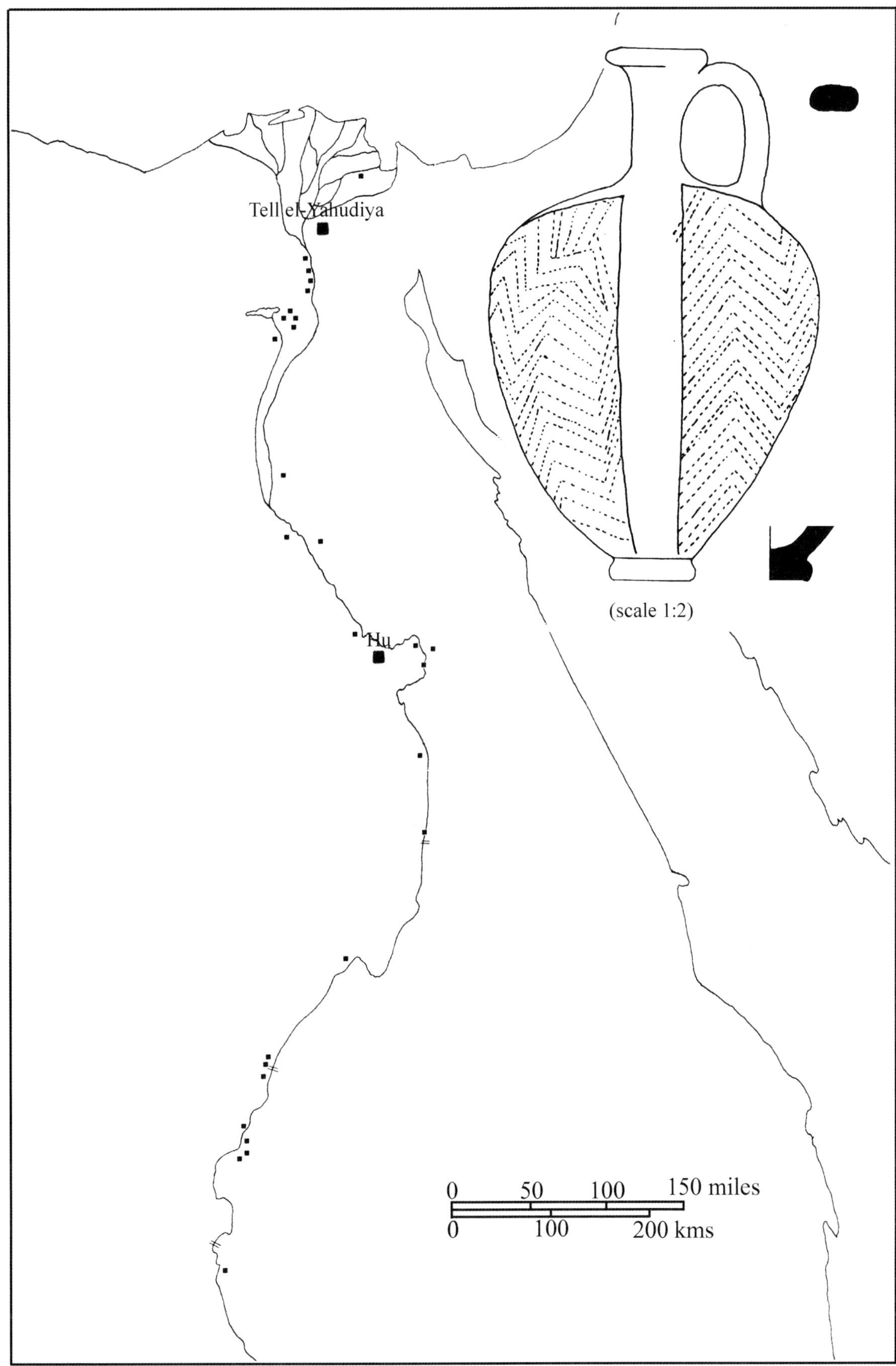

Fig. 140 Distribution and Shape Class of Type Group L.1.2b

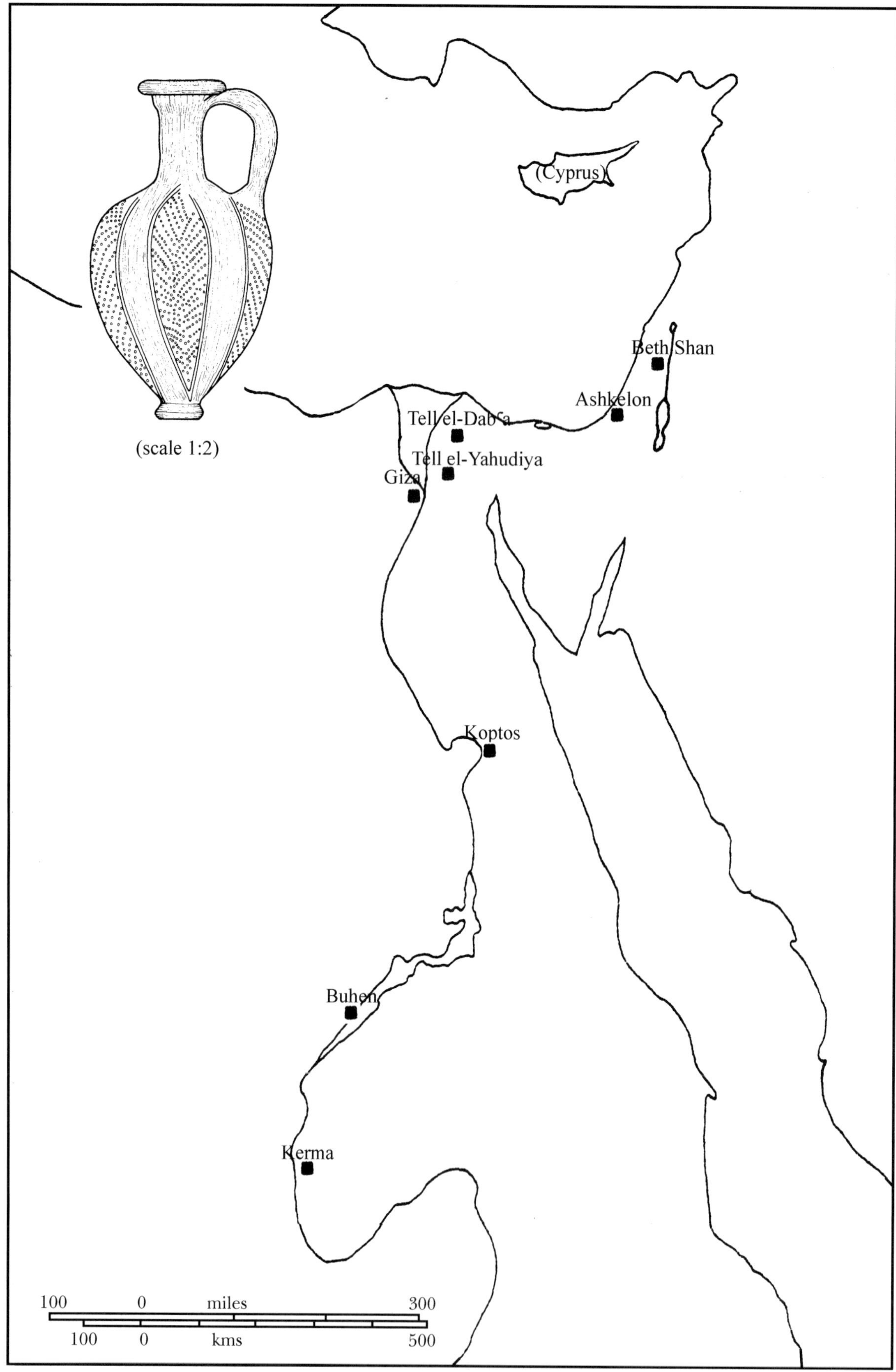

Fig. 141 Distribution and Shape Class of Type Group L.1.3

Type Group L.1.4 (Piriform 2a) (Figs. 142, 147)

Type group L.1.4 is similar to the previous group but in place of a ring base, the bases were left as a flat disc. Vessels of this group were also decorated with delineated lozenges, decorative styles L.1.4a, with four lozenges, Ll.4b with three and Ll.4c with two. Vessels with delineated lozenges are known from Tell el-Dabᶜa [424] Buhen,[425] Tell Nagila,[426] ᶜAin Karem,[427] Gibeon,[428] and Enkomi[429] and Milia[430] in Cyprus.

Type Group L.1.5 (Figs. 143, 147)

Type group L.1.5 is another branch of the 'normal' size Piriform 2a family, which, however, was not mentioned by Kaplan. In this group the vessels have a rolled rim, a strap handle a piriform body, but in contrast to groups L.1.3 and L.1.4, a distinct button base, and such vessels seem confined to Tell el-Dabᶜa. These jugs again have four (L.1.5a) or three (L.1.5b) delineated decorative lozenges. One variant vessel (TD 888) also has a bulging neck.

An incomplete vessel, of either groups L.1.3–L.1.5 was also found at Tel Nagila.[431]

Type group L.1.6 (Large Piriform 2a) (Figs. 144, 147)

Vessels of group L.1.6 are similar in all respects to type group L.1.3, but the lozenge decoration is not bordered by incised lines. At present only two complete vessels are known to us, New York MMA 74.51.1230, found on Cyprus[432] and TD 6117 from Tell el-Dabᶜa.

Type group L.1.7 (Piriform 2a) (Figs. 145, 147)

Vessels of type group L.1.7 are the undelineated equivalent of group L.1.3. Thus they comprise vessels with a rolled rim, strap handle, flattened to rounded shoulders, a piriform to rounded body and a ring base. Examples of such vessels have been found at both, Tell el-Yahudiya and Tell el-Dabᶜa.[433]

Type Group L.1.8 (Figs. 148, 147)

Vessels of type group L.1.8 are the undelineated equivalent of group L.1.4. Thus they comprise vessels with a rolled rim, strap handle, flattened to rounded shoulders, a piriform to rounded body and a disc or button base. Vessels of type group L.1.8 with undelineated lozenges come from unknown locations in Egypt.[434]

L.2 Late Egyptian II (Biconical I)

The term Biconical I is here used to refer to those vessels of the Late Egyptian group which are clearly ovoid to biconical in shape, although different to the traditional Biconical 1 of Kaplan and Bietak, yet bear styles of decoration usually associated with the Late Egyptian biconical group.

Type Group L.2.1 Large Biconical I (Figs. 148, 153)

To type group L.2.1 belongs a large slender piriform to biconical jug known from Tell el-Dabᶜa (TD 900) which has a rolled, slightly undercut rim, strap handle and ring base. It is decorated with an upper zone of non-touching rounded rectangles, each containing a herringbone pattern made with a multi-toothed comb.

Type Group L.2.2 (Figs. 149, 153)

Type group L.2.2 consists of two ovoid vessels with ring bases, one known from Ashkelon (below 570) and the other from Tell el-Dabᶜa (TD 1925) which should perhaps be related to the Biconical 1 jugs by their style of decoration. Whilst typologically they are not quite the same, the Ashkelon vessel having an undercut rolled rim and a strap handle, whilst the Tell el Dabᶜa vessel has a ledged rim and a round handle, – both of which features are early within the Late phase – they seem sufficiently similar to be considered a single group. The decoration on both vessels consists of an upper zone of delineated standing triangles, a reserved band at the mid point and a lower zone of pendant triangles.

Type Group L.2.3 (Figs. 150, 153)

Type Group L.2.3 comprises biconical vessels with a rolled rim, strap handle and a ring or disc base. They are decorated with an upper zone of standing triangles and a lower one of pendant triangles.

---

424 London, BM 27473. Kaplan, *Tell el-Yahudiyeh Ware,* fig. 48c.

425 Philadelphia UM E.10527, 10617, 10887b. Randall-MacIver and Woolley, *Buhen,* 161–162, pl. 49, Philadelphia UM E.10887b. Kaplan, *Tell el-Yahudiyeh Ware,* fig. 53f.

426 Jerusalem, Israel Museum 66.911. Kaplan, *Tell el-Yahudiyeh Ware,* fig. 51c.

427 Jerusalem, Museum of the Flagellation. Kaplan, *Tell el-Yahudiyeh Ware,* fig. 55c.

428 Pritchard, *Gibeon,* 49, pl. 46.3.

429 London BM Greek and Roman Antiquities, 97/4–1/1305. Kaplan, *Tell el-Yahudiyeh Ware,* fig. 56b.

430 Nicosia Cyprus Museum. Westholm, *QDAP* 8, 1939, 4, pl. 1.

431 Cf. Kaplan, *Tell el-Yahudiyeh Ware,* fig. 51c.

432 Myres, *Cessnola Collection,* 42–43, fig. 383, Kaplan, *Tell el-Yahudiyeh Ware,* fig. 47b.

433 Petrie, *Hyksos and Israelite Cities,* 11, 15 pl. viiia.78, 87.

434 Berlin 81/71, London UC 13472. Kaplan, *Tell el-Yahudiyeh Ware,* fig. 55d–e.

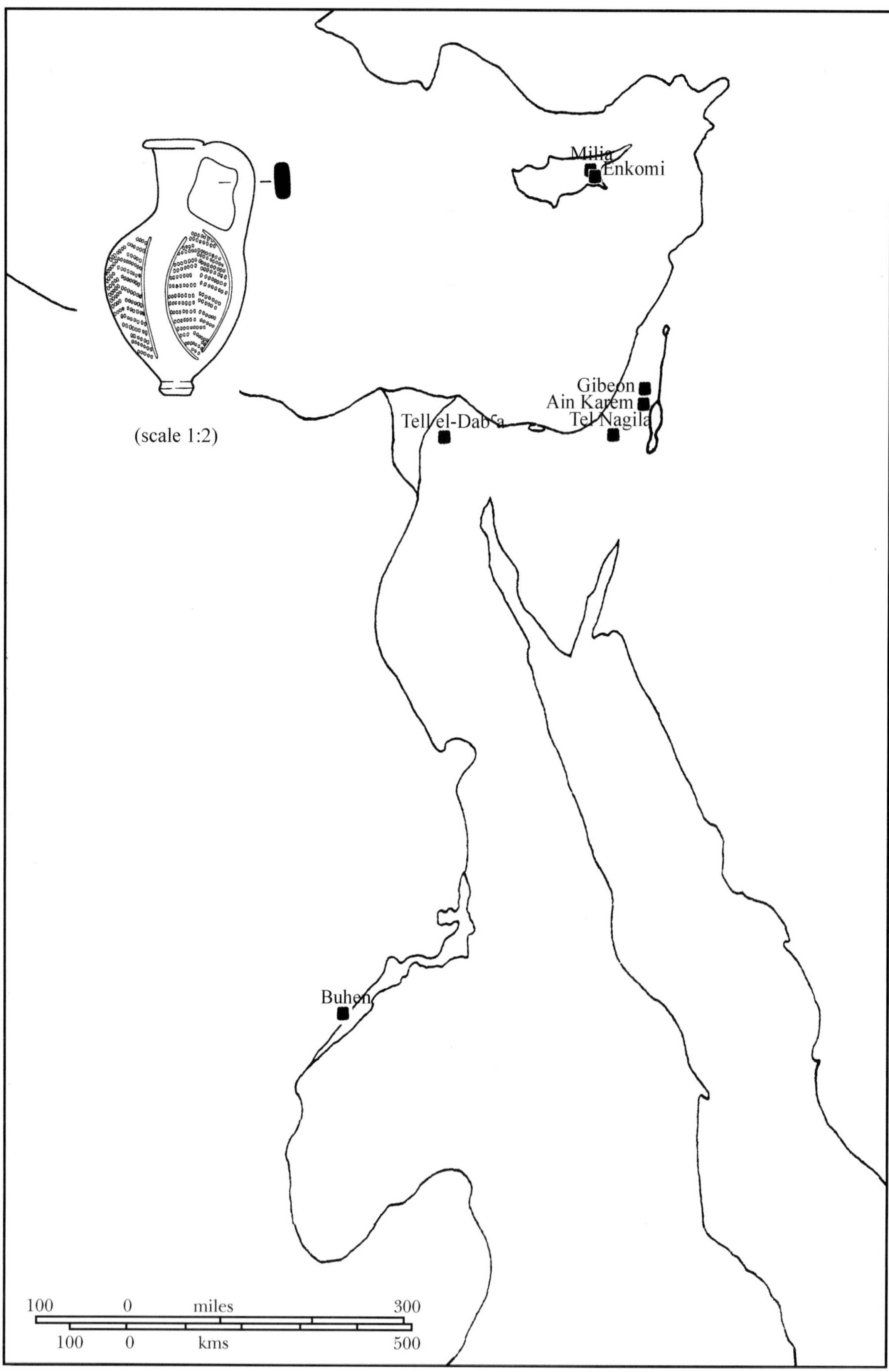

Fig. 142 Distribution and Shape Class of Type Group L.1.4

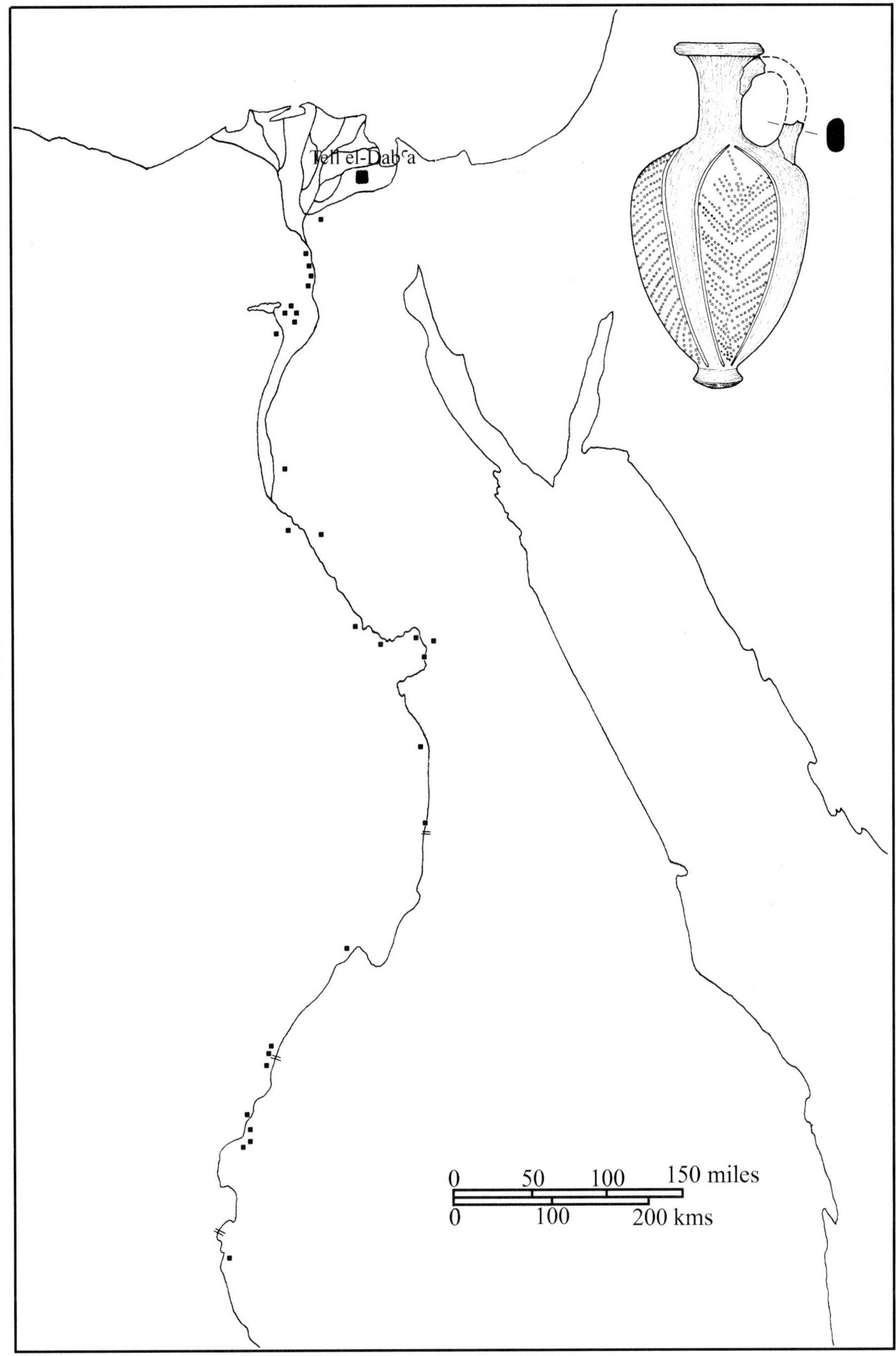

Fig. 143 Distribution and Shape Class of Type Group L.1.5

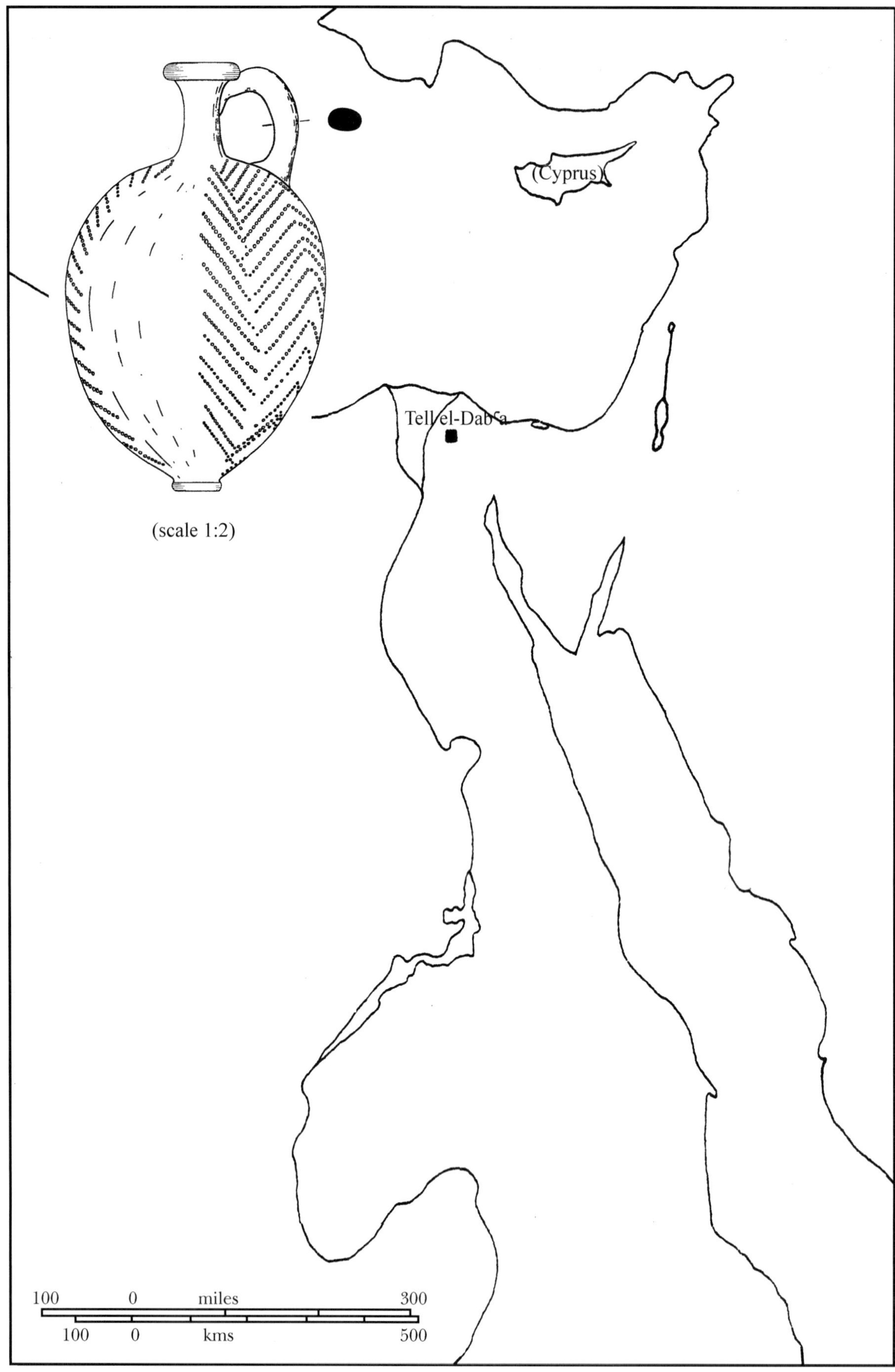

Fig. 144 Distribution and Shape Class of Type Group L.1.6

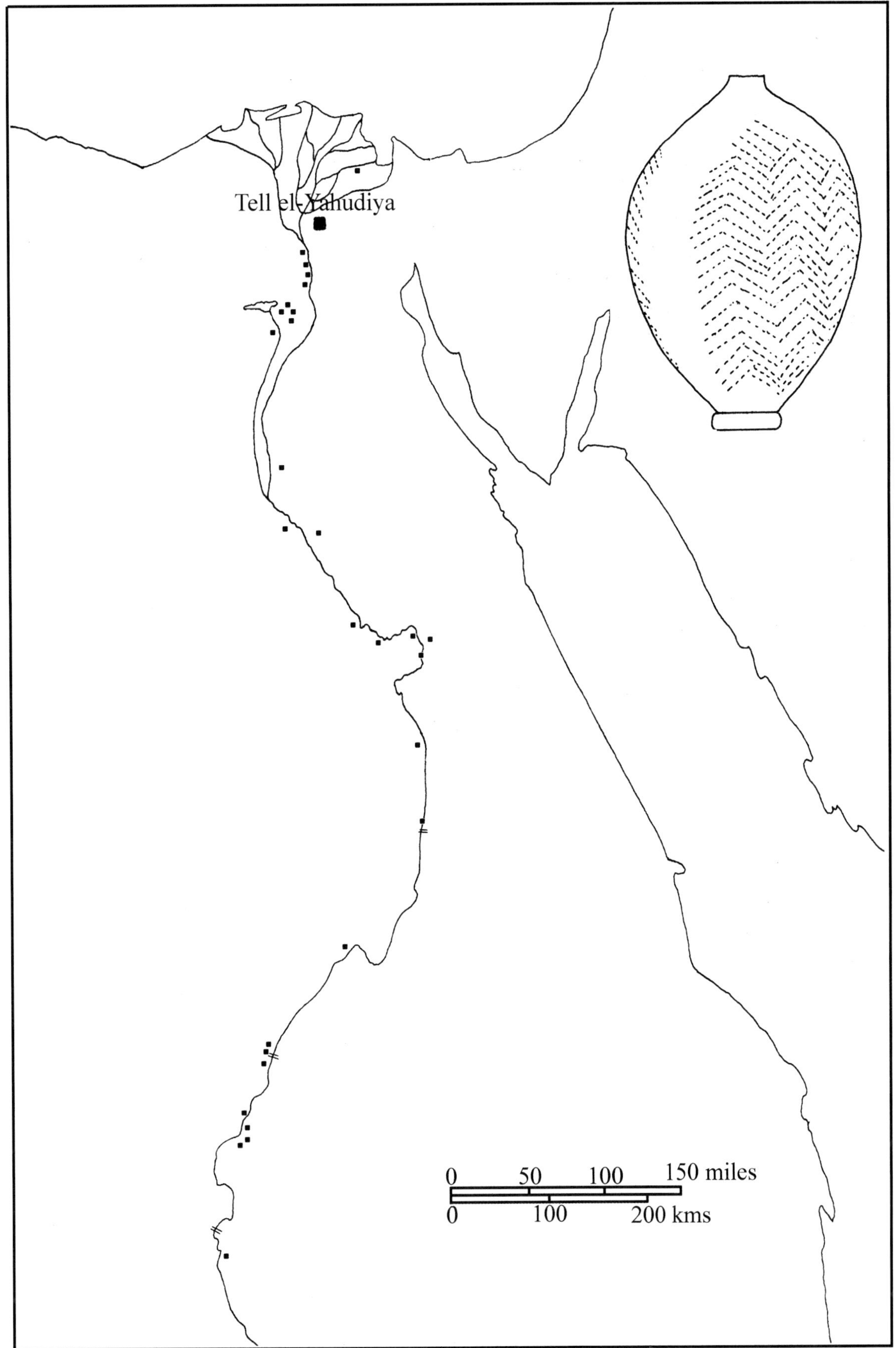

Fig. 145 Distribution and Shape Class of Type Group L.1.7

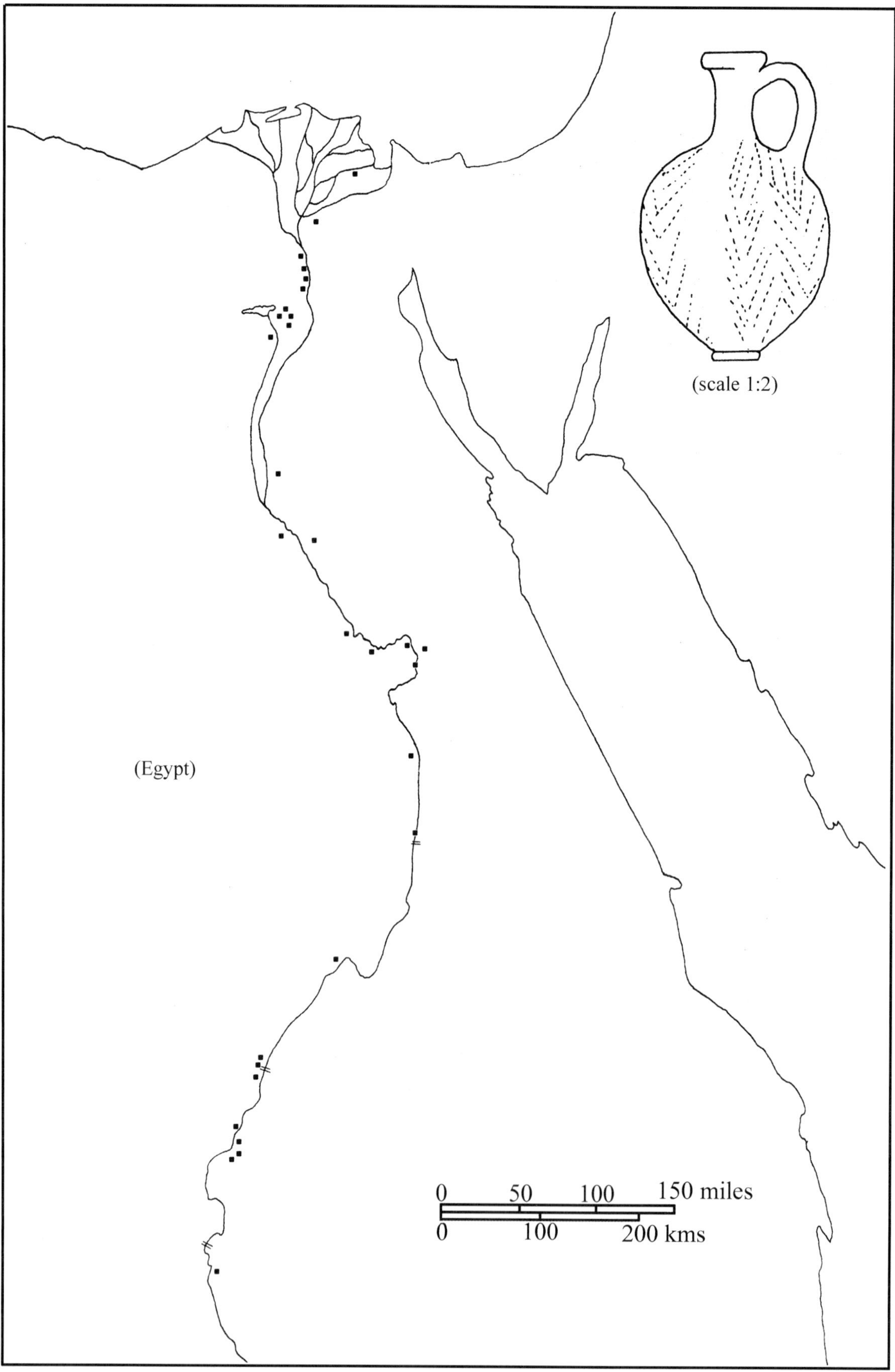

Fig. 146 Distribution and Shape Class of Type Group L.1.8

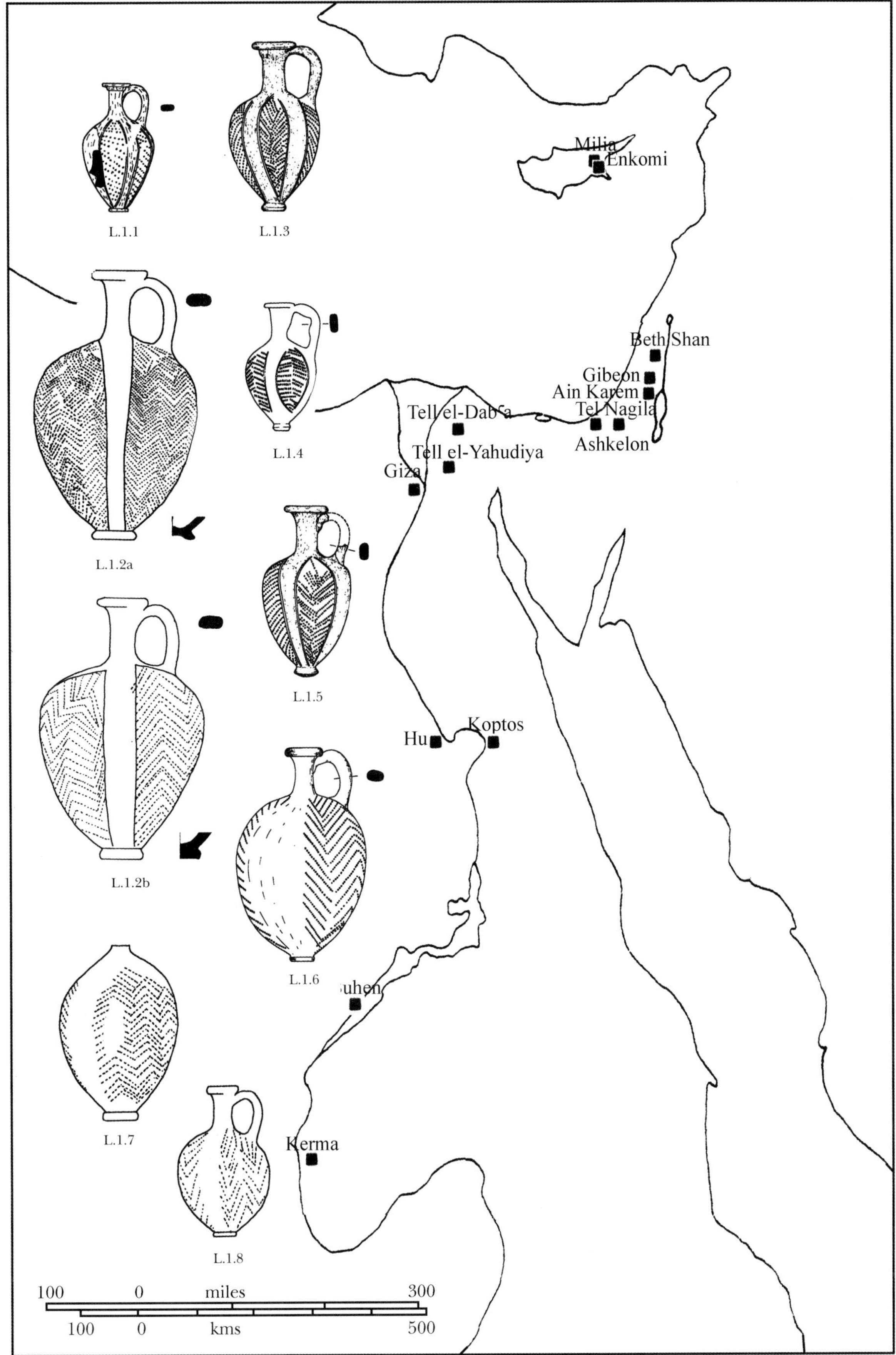

Fig. 147 Combined Distribution of Type Group L.1 (Piriform 2a)

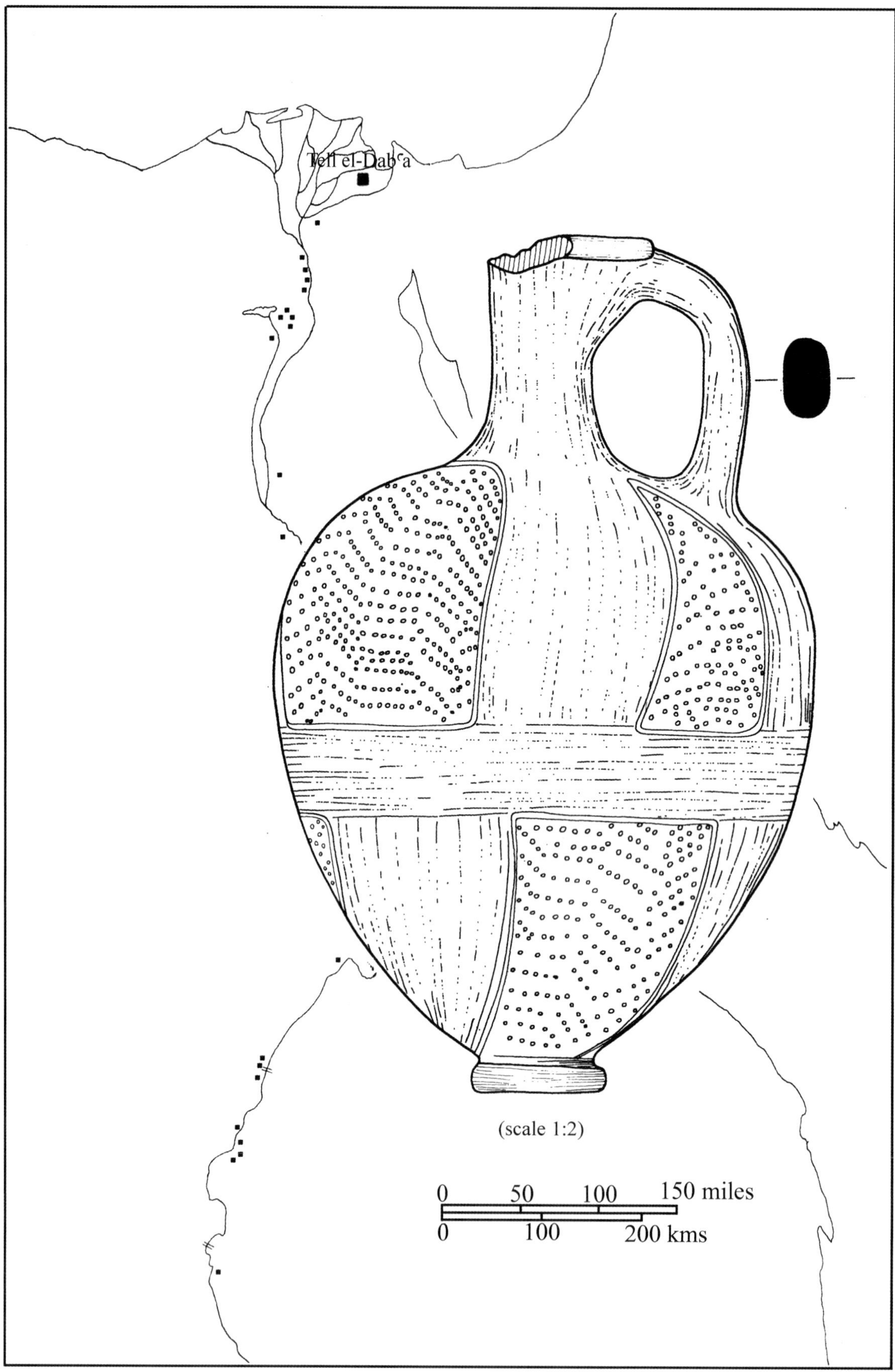

Fig. 148 Distribution and Shape Class of Type Group L.2.1

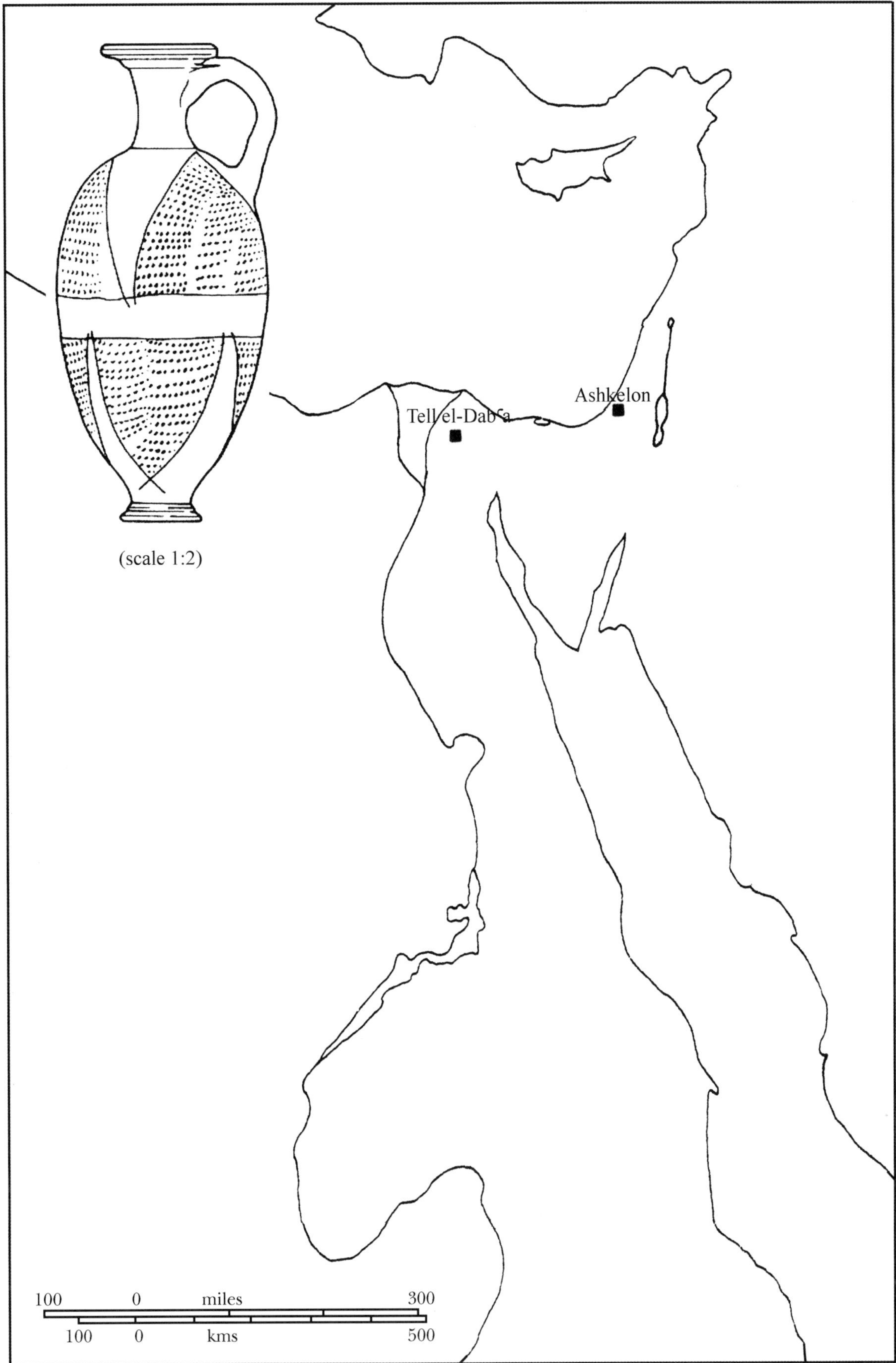

Fig. 149 Distribution and Shape Class of Type Group L.2.2

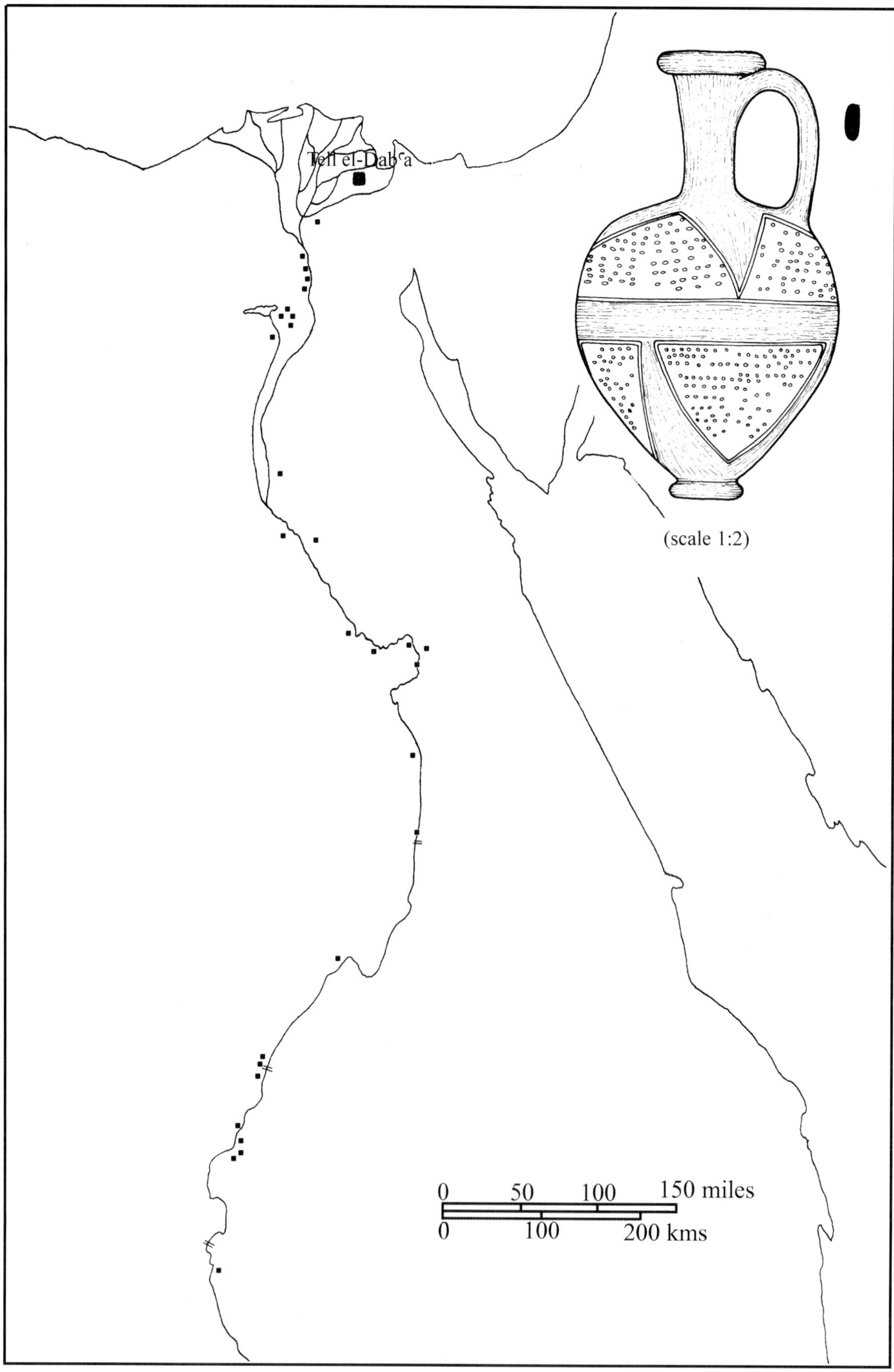

Fig. 150 Distribution and Shape Class of Type Group L.2.3

Type Group L.2.4 (Figs. 151, 153)

Related to group L.2.3 are five vessels from Tell el-Dabᶜa, TD 1520, 2055, 8670, 8674 and 8684, which are similar to group L.2.3 but have button bases rather than an offset disc. Once again their decoration comprises an upper zone of standing triangles and a lower one of pendant ones, which usually touch one another (L.2.4b), but in TD 1520, the triangles are non-touching (L.2.4a). At least one other example of unknown provenience can be added to this group.[435]

Type Group L.2.5 (Figs. 152, 153)

Jugs belonging to Type Group L.2.5 are so far known only at Tell el-Dabᶜa. They are around 12 cms. tall, and consist of jugs with rolled rims, strap handles, biconical to piriform bodies, and ring bases. They have two styles of decoration which closely relate them to vessels of the rounded biconical L.5 group. The decorative patterns comprise L.2.5a which consists of an upper zone of non-touching standing triangles and a lower one of non-touching pendant triangles (TD 4468C, 7651); and L.2.5b which is similar but the triangles are touching (TD 3401, 8671).

Type Group L.3 Late Egyptian III (Carinated Biconical)

Type Group L.3 consists of a small number of vessels whose typological position is somewhat hard to ascertain. They have clear links to both the classic Piriform 2a and to Biconical I vessels.

Type Group L.3.1 (Figs. 154, 156)

Type group L.3.1 is known through a single example from Tell el-Dabᶜa (TD 3963) which has a strap handle, sharply carinated, almost biconical, body and a disc base. The rim is not preserved but was presumably rolled. Clearly related to the Biconical 1 vessels in shape, this jug is decorated with the typical lozenge style associated with the very common Piriform 2a jugs of Kaplan. Around the body are three infilled lozenges.

Type Group L.3.2 (Figs. 155, 156)

Type group L.3.2 consists of a single vessel, Tell el-Dabᶜa TD 2702 which has a rolled rim, strap handle, sharply biconical body and a ring base. The decoration scheme is unusual in that the upper body has three infilled triangles, delineated only on their upper two sides, whilst the lower body remains undecorated.

L.4. Late Egyptian IV (Biconical II)

Late Egyptian IV vessels are generally omitted from the work of Kaplan, since they come exclusively from Tell el-Dabᶜa, and were not published at the time she was writing. In terms of their general shape, and the fact that the decoration is always in two zones, separated by a narrow burnished band around the maximum body diameter, this class is evidently related to Kaplan's Biconical 1 group (here considered as Late Egyptian V). In contrast to the latter, in which the upper and lower decorative zones are usually filled with horizontal chevrons, a herringbone pattern or oblique lines, the decoration found on the somewhat earlier Late Egyptian IV jugs is confined to standing triangles in the upper zone, and pendant triangles in the lower zone.

Type Group L.4.1 (Figs. 157, 159)

Type group L.4.1 is made up of Biconical II jugs with rolled rims, swollen necks, strap handles and ring bases. They are confined to Phase E/1 at Tell el-Dabᶜa, and are again decorated with an upper zone of standing triangles and a lower one of pendant triangles.

Type Group L.4.2 (Figs. 158, 159)

Type group L.4.2 is currently known from a single example, TD 781, with direct everted rim, strap handle and a button base. It is decorated with an upper zone of standing triangles and a lower one of pendant triangles.

L.5. Late Egyptian V (Biconical III)

Vessels of the Biconical III (Kaplan's Biconical 1) group tend to vary in height from 7.8 to 16 cms., with an average of around 10.4 cm., though there are larger exceptions. As defined by Kaplan, vessels of this group always have rolled rims, single handles and ring or disc bases, to which can be added those with a distinct button. The decoration invariably covers most of the body leaving only a narrow burnished band around the mid point. The upper and lower decorative zones are usually filled with horizontal chevrons, a herringbone pattern or oblique lines, and at times these lines radiate straight out from the base or neck.

[435] Würzburg, Martin von Wagner Museum A.34, cf. S. Petschel in: *Pharao siegt immer – Krieg und Frieden im Alten Ägypten*, Hamm, 2004, 199 no. 184b.

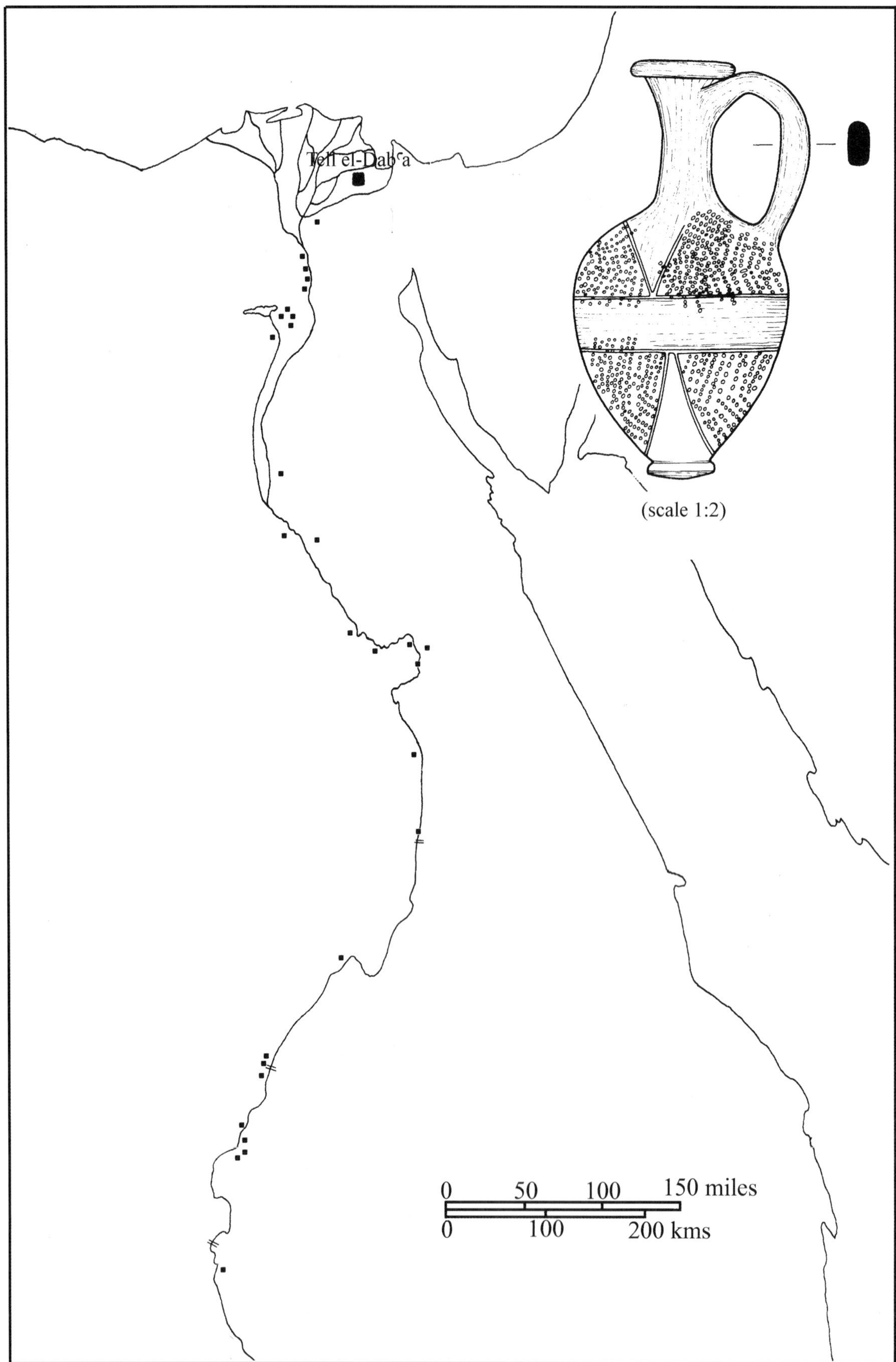

Fig. 151 Distribution and Shape Class of Type Group L.2.4

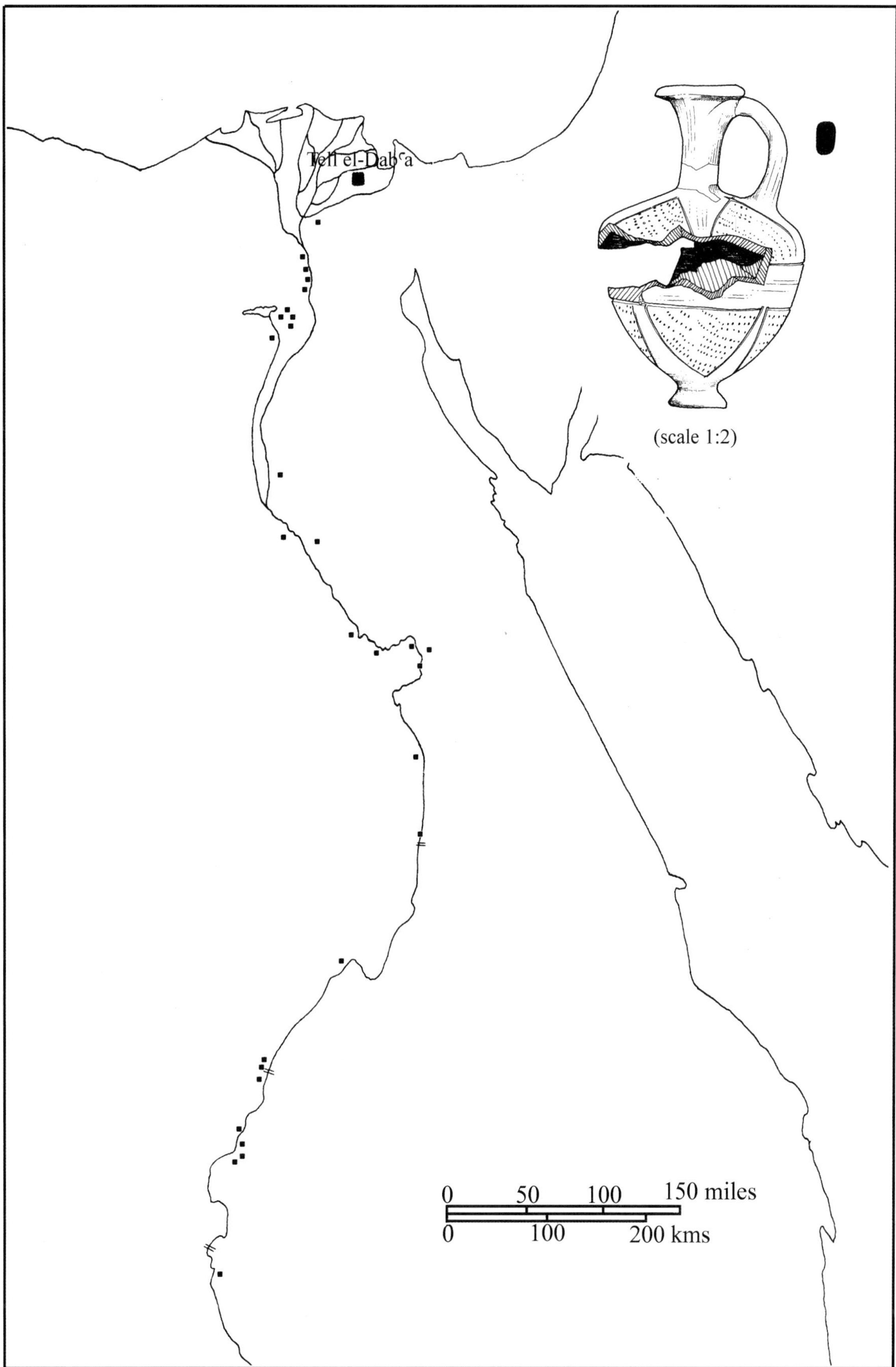

Fig. 152 Distribution and Shape Class of Type Group L.2.5

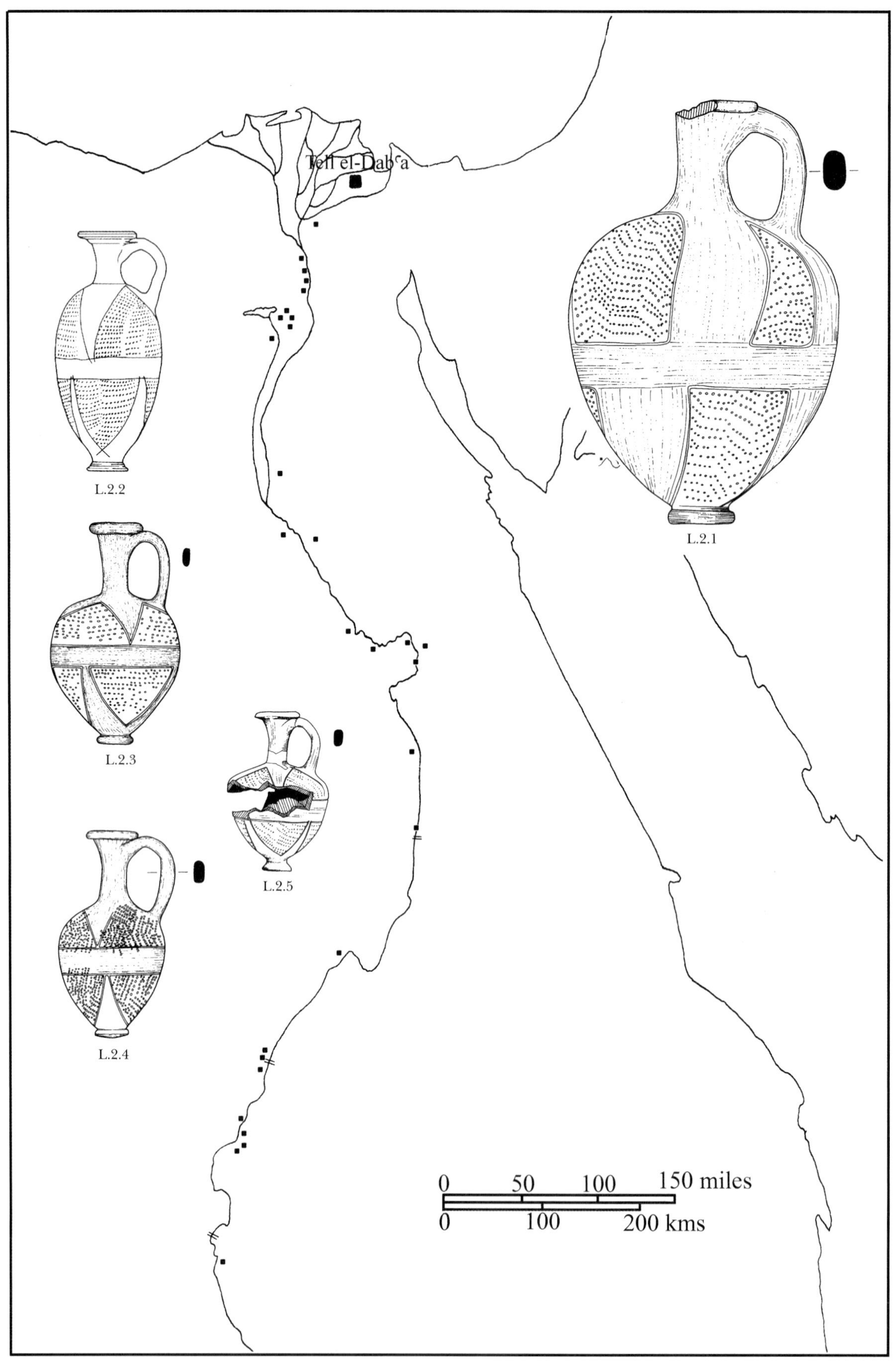

Fig. 153 Combined Distribution of Type Group L.2

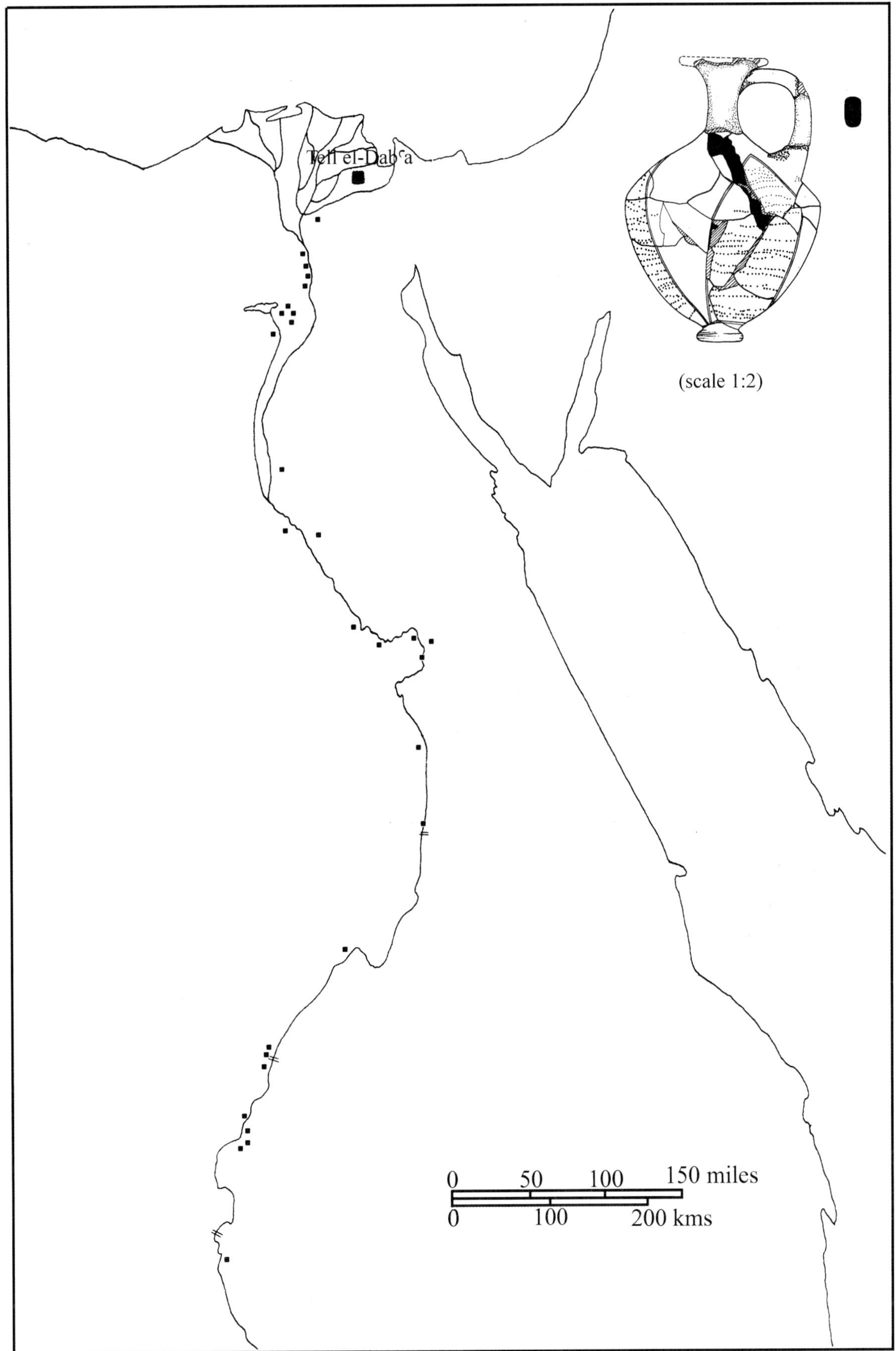

Fig. 154 Distribution and Shape Class of Type Group L.3.1

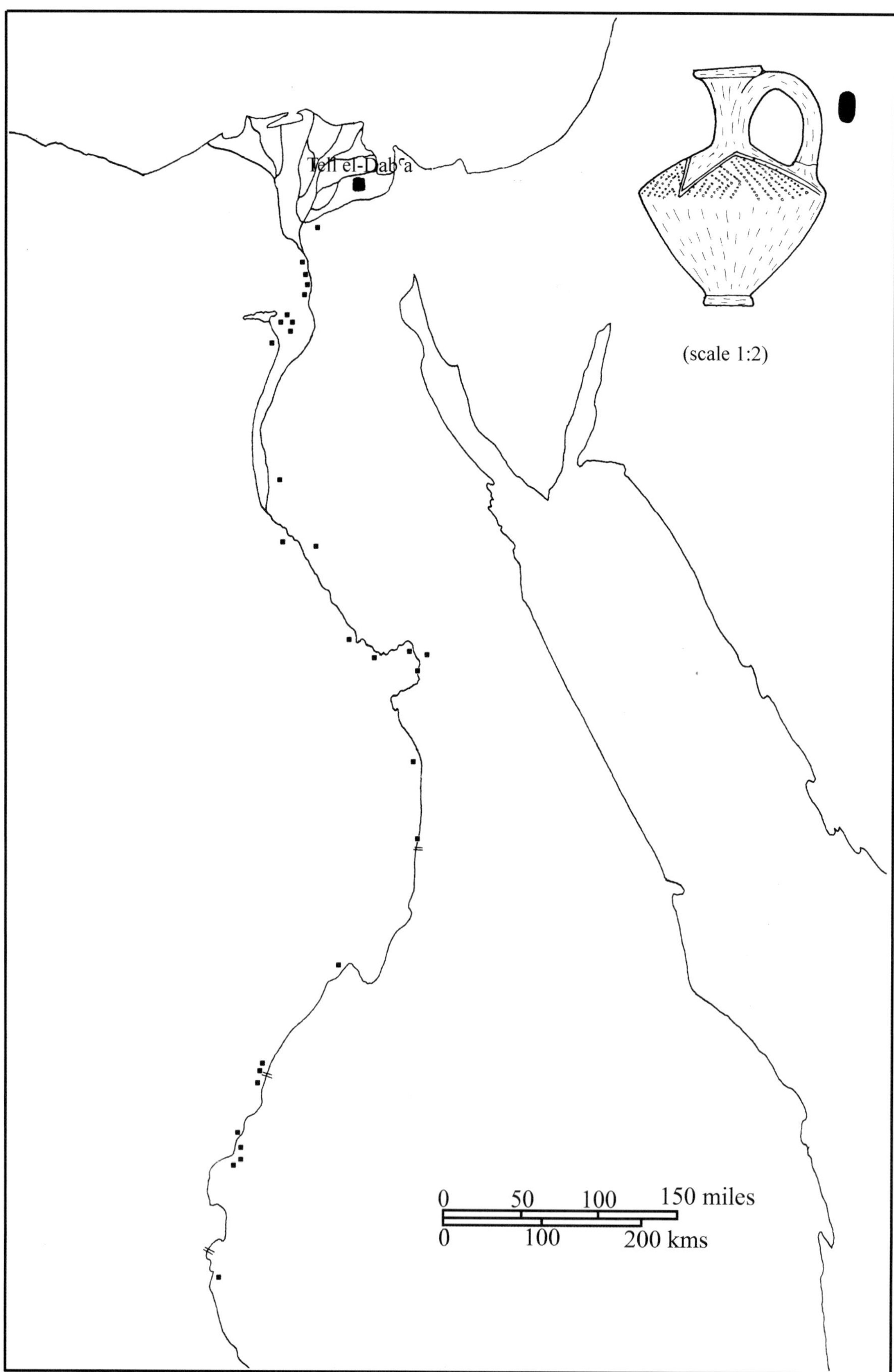

Fig. 155 Distribution and Shape Class of Type Group L.3.2

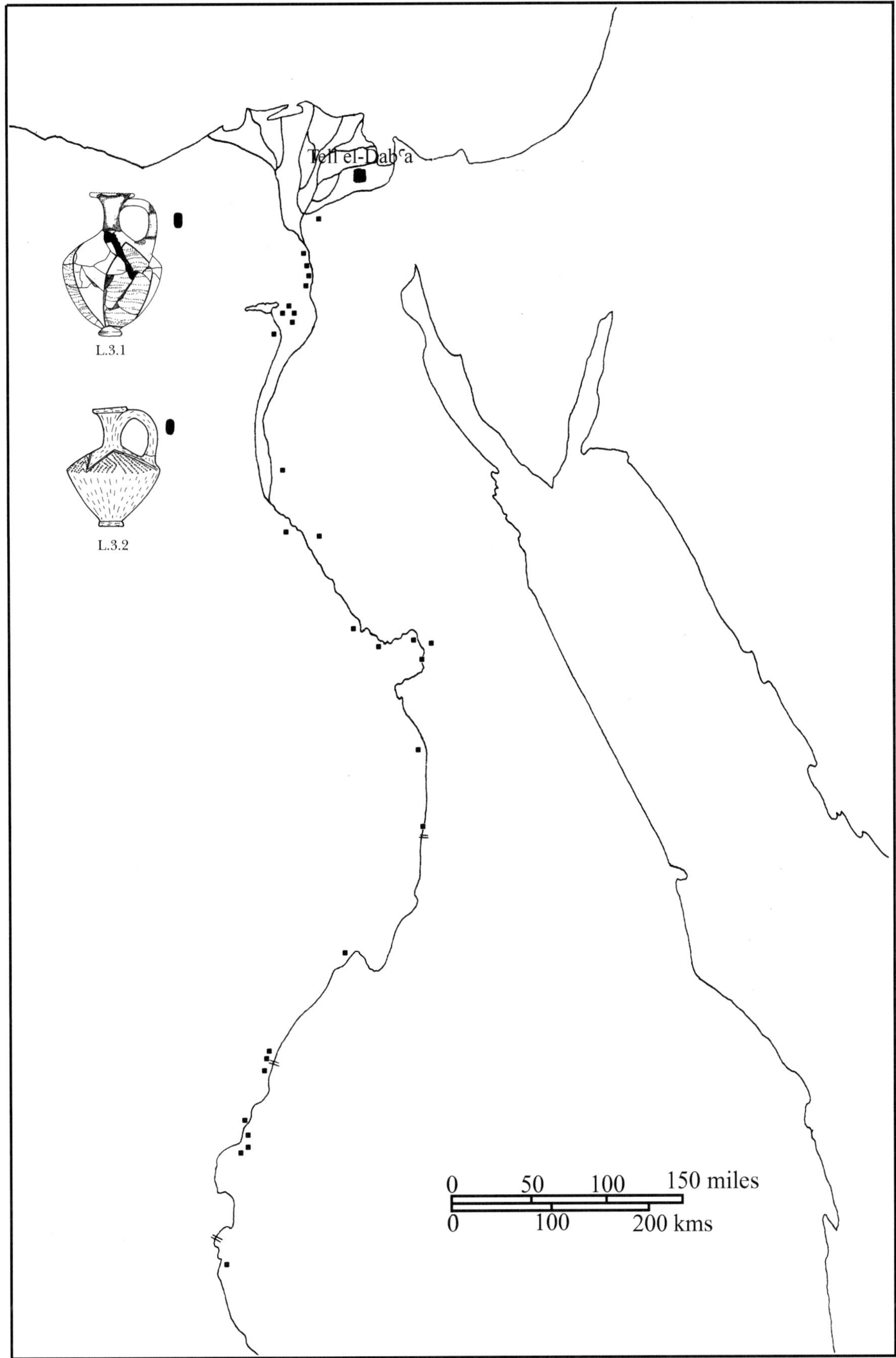

Fig. 156 Combined Distribution of Type Group L.3

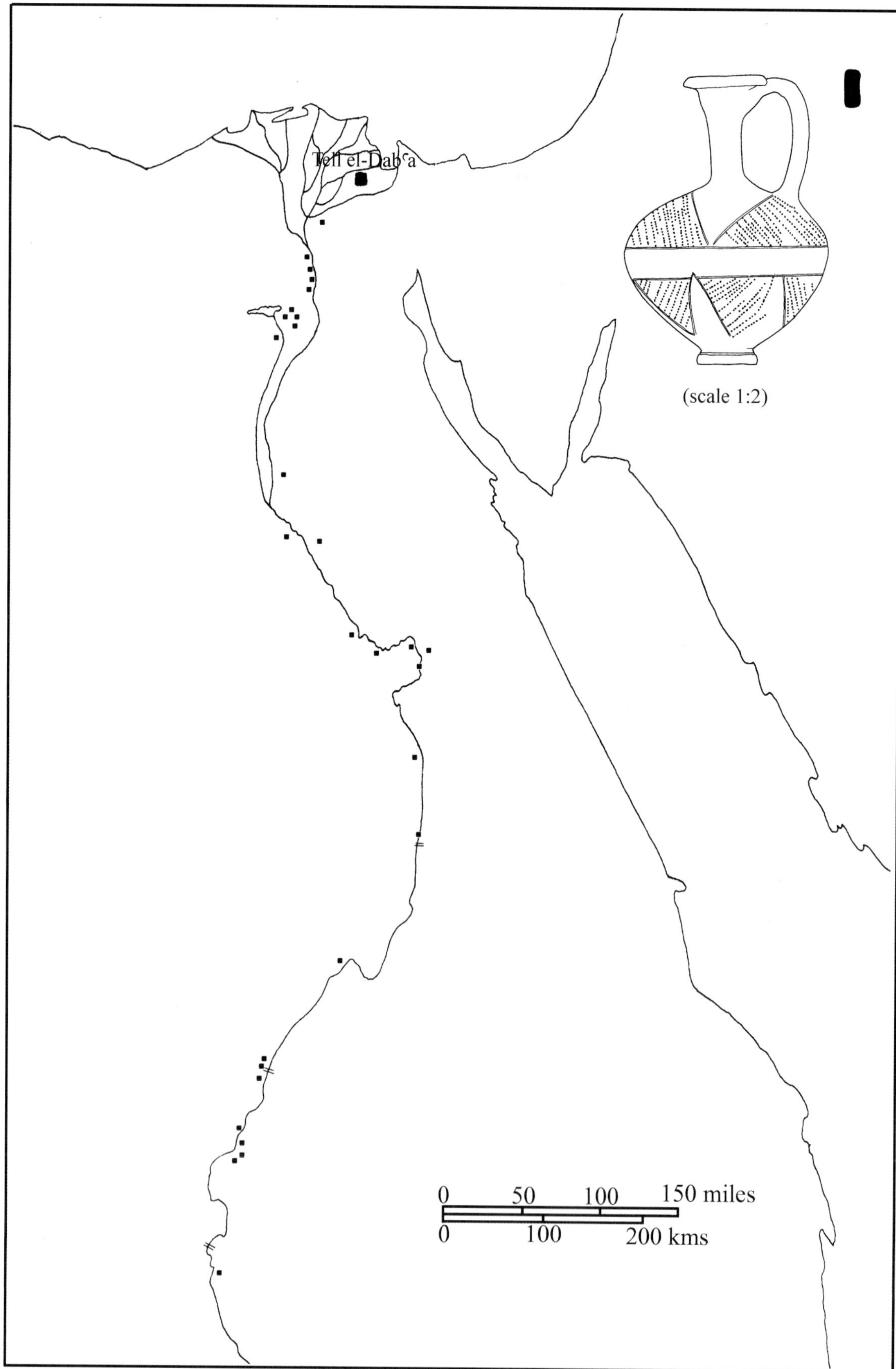

Fig. 157 Distribution and Shape Class of Type Group L.4.1

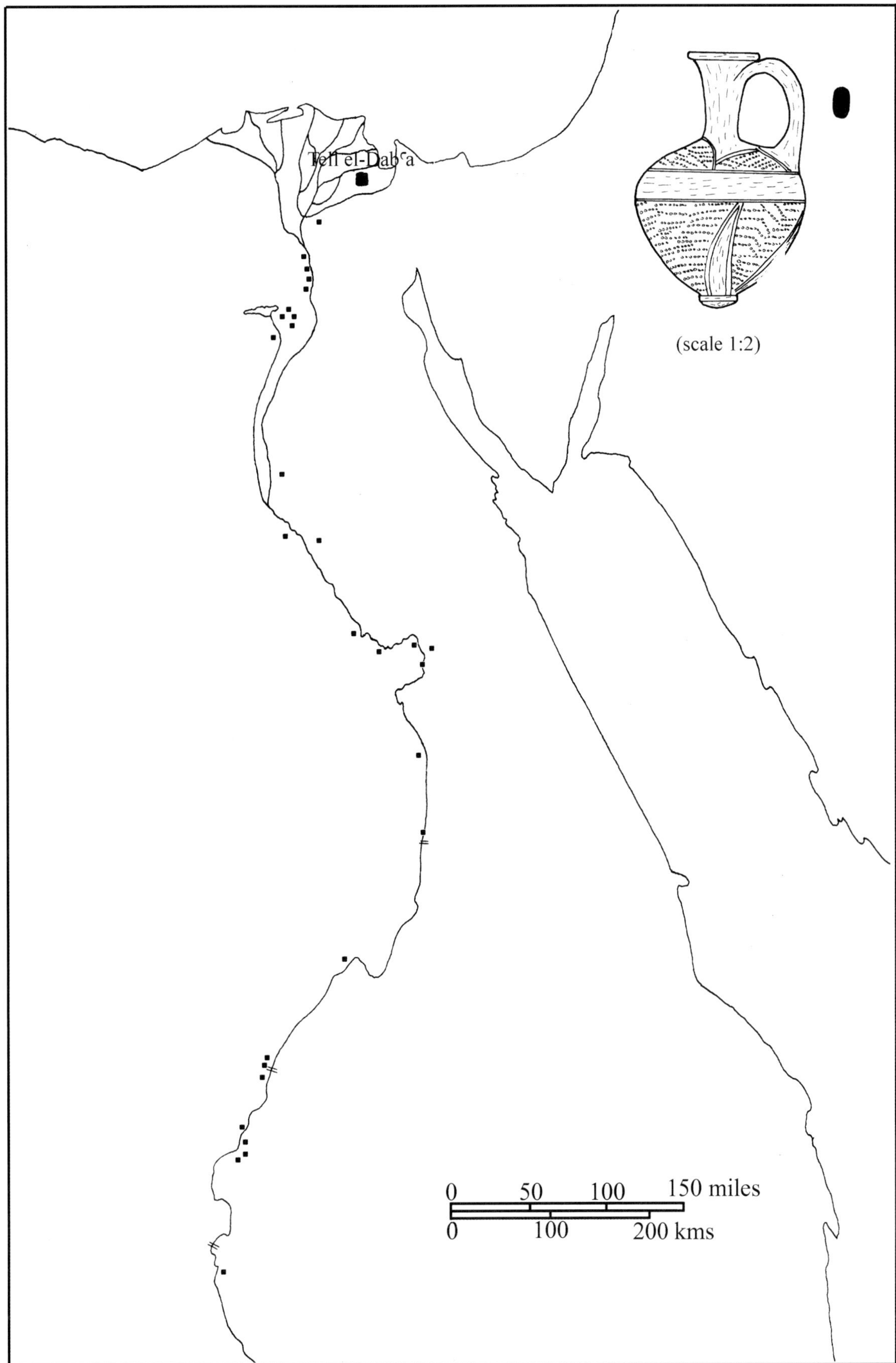

Fig. 158 Distribution and Shape Class of Type Group L.4.2

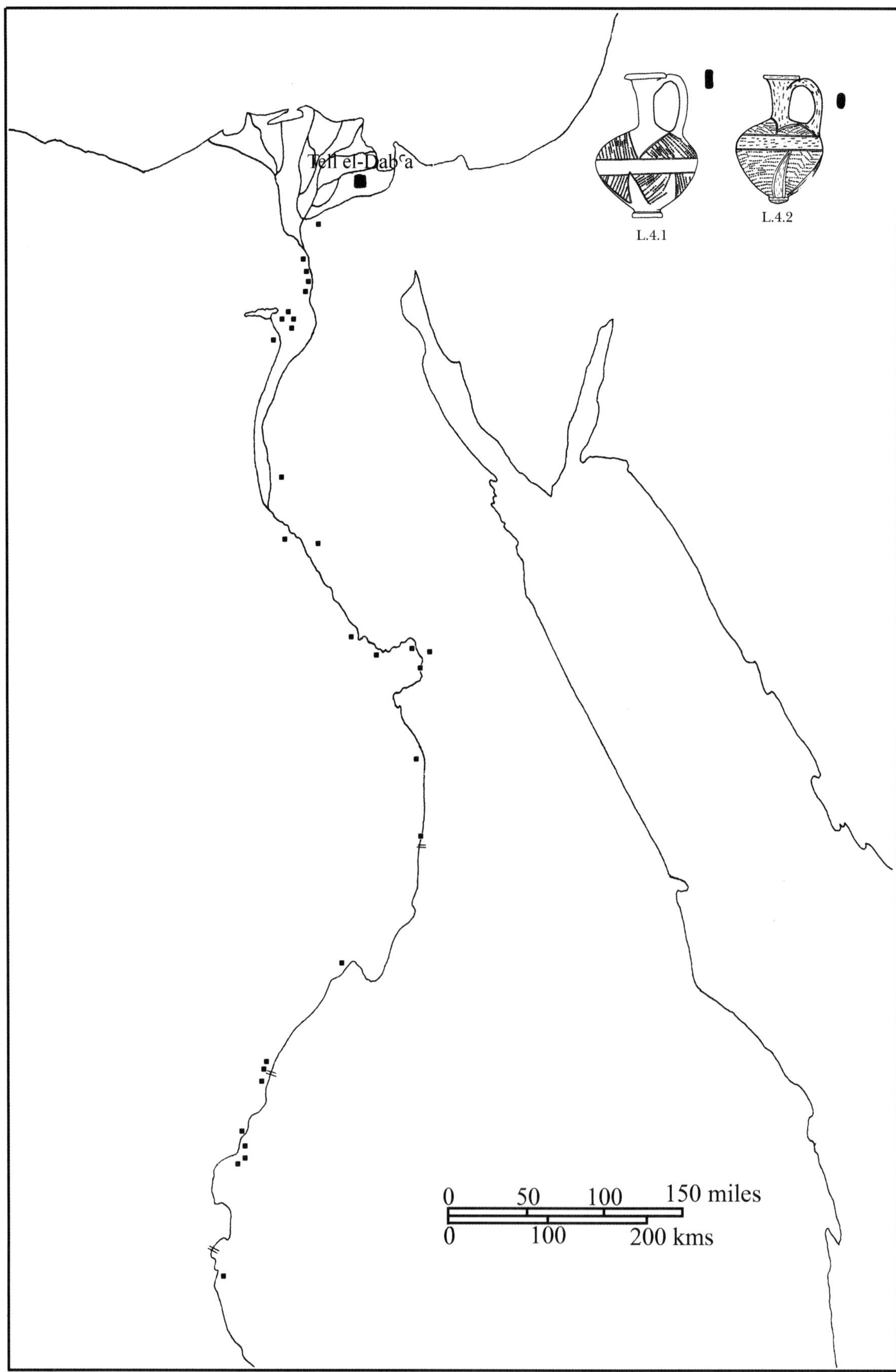

Fig. 159 Combined Distribution of Type Group L.4

In vessels assigned to this group, the areas of decoration are consistently set off from the rest of the vessel by incised lines which act as frames for the decorative zones. This is in contrast to the L.7 vessels on which no frame lines are present. The motifs themselves are made with a comb having eight or more points.

Type Group L.5.1 (Figs. 160, 167)

Type group L.5.1 consists of a single Biconical 1 jug with rolled rim, swollen neck, strap handle and a ring base, TD 174. It is decorated with two zones of chevrons delineated at the lower edge of the upper zone, and the upper edge of the lower zone.

Type Group L.5.2 (Figs. 161, 167)

Type group L.5.2 known through a single Biconical 1 jug, (TD 183), with rolled rim, swollen neck, strap handle and button base, is similar to the previous group, but with a different base form. It is decorated with two zones of chevrons delineated at the lower edge of the upper zone, and the upper edge of the lower zone.

Type Group L.5.3 (Figs. 162–164, 167)

This is the classic Biconical 1 of Kaplan, namely jugs with rolled rims, strap handles and ring or disc bases. The upper and lower decorative zones are usually filled with horizontal chevrons, (L.5.3a), or oblique lines (L.5.3b), and at times these lines radiate straight out from the base or neck. Combinations such as chevrons in the upper zone and oblique lines in the lower one, or vice versa may also occur (L.5.3c). This type group is extremely common with examples of type L.5.3a – two zones of chevrons each delineated by incised lines at top and bottom, – found at Ras Shamra,[436] Thera,[437] and Milia, Cyprus.[438] L.5.3a vessels in which the zones are only bordered at the belly of the pot, i.e. the lower edge of the uppermost zone, and the uppermost edge of the bottom zone, are known from Tell el-Yahudiya,[439] Abydos,[440] Buhen,[441] Arpera,[442] Kalopsidha[443] and Enkomi.[444] Conversely a vessel from Hu[445] is delineated in the opposite fashion - the upper edge of the uppermost zone, and the lowermost edge of the bottom zone. Type L.5.3b is known from Tell el-Yahudiya[446] and Tell el-Dabᶜa. Vessels with decorative scheme L.5.3c come from Tell el-Yahudiya,[447] and Tell el-Dabᶜa. Sherds from vessels of L.5, exact decorative scheme unknown since no complete shapes are preserved, are known from Ashkelon (below 572–574). The recent attribution of an L.5.3 sherd from Ashkelon to a vessel of type group L.6.1b is incorrect;[448] since the sherd in question comes from a much smaller vessel and has a much flatter shoulder. However, since jugs of type group L.5.3 are known at Tell el-Dabᶜa, from strata E2/1, certainly as late as D/2 and, as sherds, even into the early New Kingdom, this does not affect a correlation of Ashkelon Stratum 10 with Tell el-Dabᶜa Phases D/3–D/1.

Type Group L.5.4 (Figs. 165, 167)

Vessels attributed to type group L.5.4 comprises vessels which are similar to the common L.5.3 group, but have distinct button, rather than ring or disc bases. All the examples so far known have two zones of chevrons.

Type Group L.5.5 (Figs. 166, 167)

Type group L.5.5 is represented by a single incomplete vessel from Tell el-Dabᶜa, TD 299, which is biconical in shape and has a button base. This vessel has a single reserved band running around the midpoint, and is burnished above and below it. In the middle of this reserved band is a single incised wavy line.

---

436 Paris Louvre RS 7427. SCHAEFFER, 1936a 131, 144, fig, 18d.

437 ASTRÖM, *Thera Ist Acts*, 1971, 415–418, fig. 1.

438 Nicosia, Cyprus Museum. WESTHOLM, *QDAP* 8, 1939, 4, pl. 1.

439 London UC 8867. GRIFFITH, *The Antiquities of Tell el-Yahudiyeh*, 40, pl. 9.3.

440 Cambridge Fitzwilliam E.21.1913. London UC 13467. RANDALL-MACIVER and MACE, *El Amrah and Abydos*, 92, 98, pl. liv.13.

441 Philadelphia UM E.10595. RANDALL-MACIVER and WOOLLEY, *Buhen*, 171, pl. 49.

442 Jerusalem, Rockefeller Museum V.1512. KAPLAN, *Tell el-Yahudiyeh Ware*, 1980, fig. 100a.

443 Oxford Ashmolean E.3456. MYRES, *JHS* 17, 1897, 140, fig. 4.24; Nicosia Cyprus Museum A.1445 (?). MYRES *JHS* 17, 1897, 141, fig. 5.6.

444 London BM Greek and Roman Antiquities, 97/4–1/1306. MURRAY *et al*, *Excavations in Cyprus*, 1900, 6, fig. 9 second from left; Stockholm MM. SCE 4.1 569–570, pl. 87.3.

445 Oxford Ashmolean E.2026. PETRIE, *Diospolis Parva*, 50–52, pl. xxxvi.187, KAPLAN, *Tell el-Yahudiyeh Ware*, fig. 85d.

446 Manchester 3443, 3444, 3447. PETRIE, *Hyksos and Israelite Cities*, 11, pl. vii.23, vii.3; Cairo. ADAM, *ASAE* 55, 1958, 309, pl. 17a, KAPLAN, *Tell el-Yahudiyeh Ware*, fig. 86b, 90a, 90c.

447 Manchester 3446. PETRIE, *Hyksos and Israelite Cities*, 11, pl. vii.25, KAPLAN, *Tell el-Yahudiyeh Ware*, fig. 95e.

448 M. BIETAK, K. KOPETZKY and L. STAGER, Synchronization of stratigraphies, Ashkelon and Tell el-Dabᶜa, *Ä&L* 18, 2008, 55, fig. 7 nos. 2 and 6.

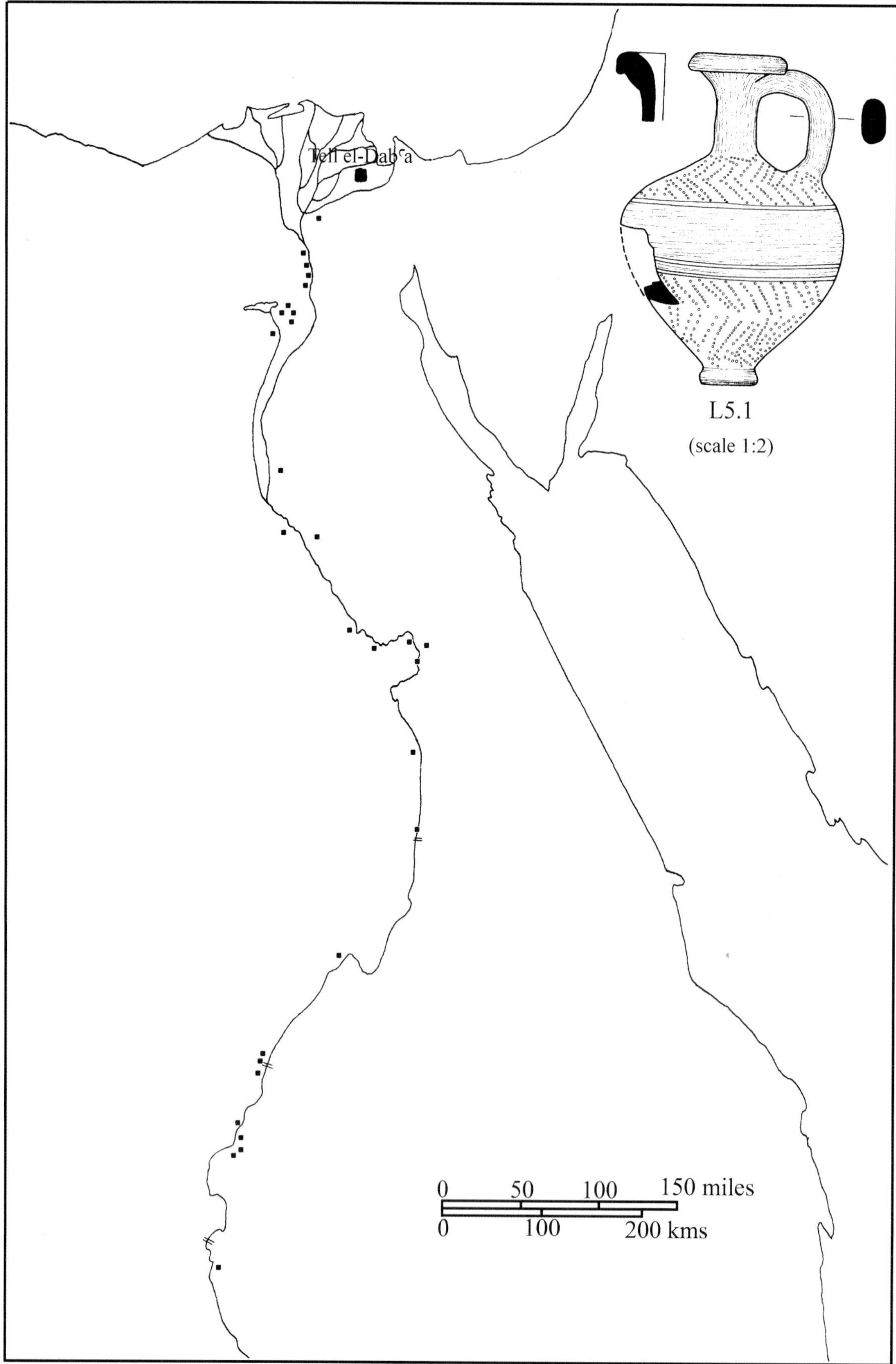

Fig. 160 Distribution and Shape Class of Type Group L.5.1

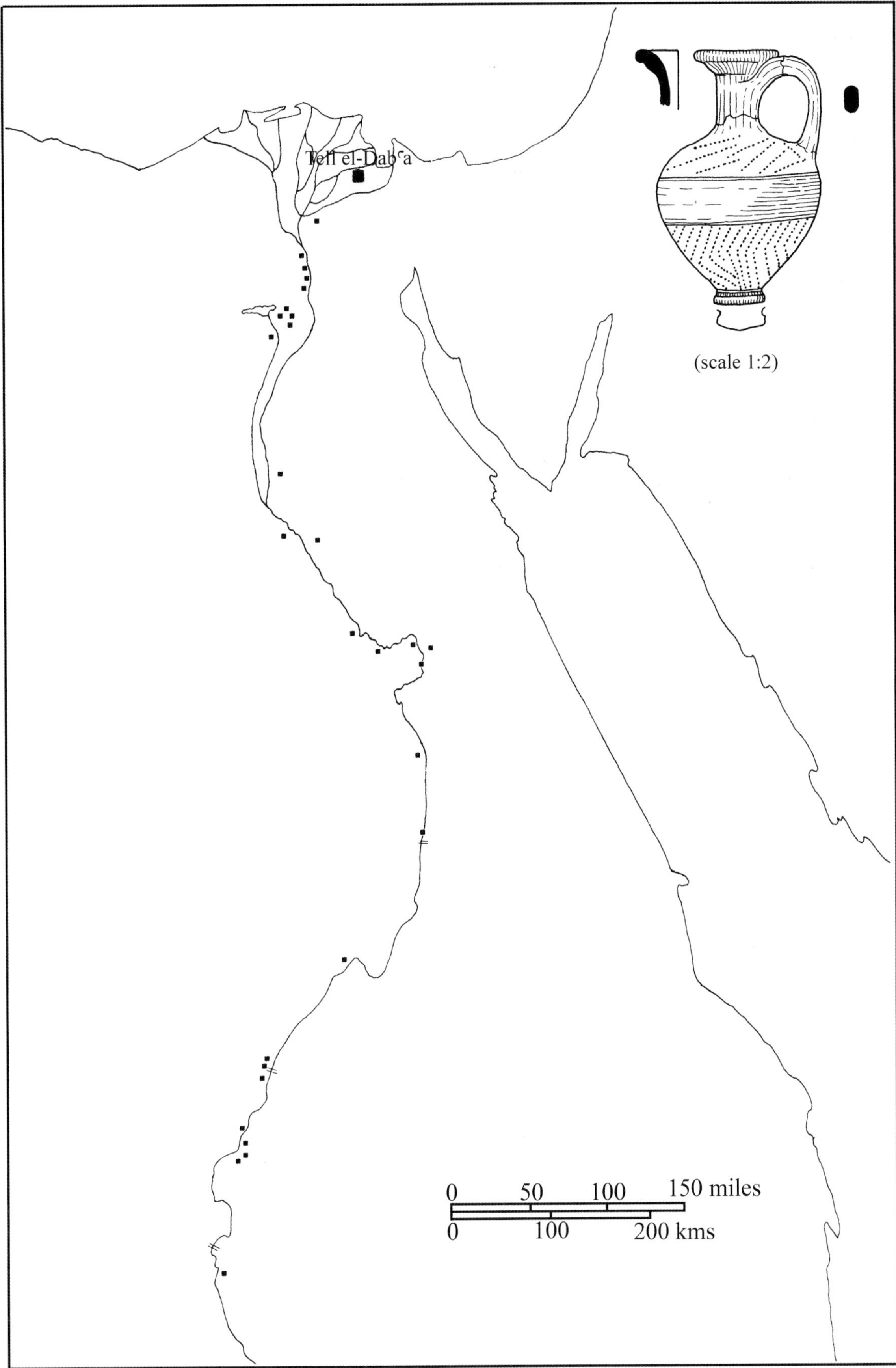

Fig. 161 Distribution and Shape Class of Type Group L.5.2

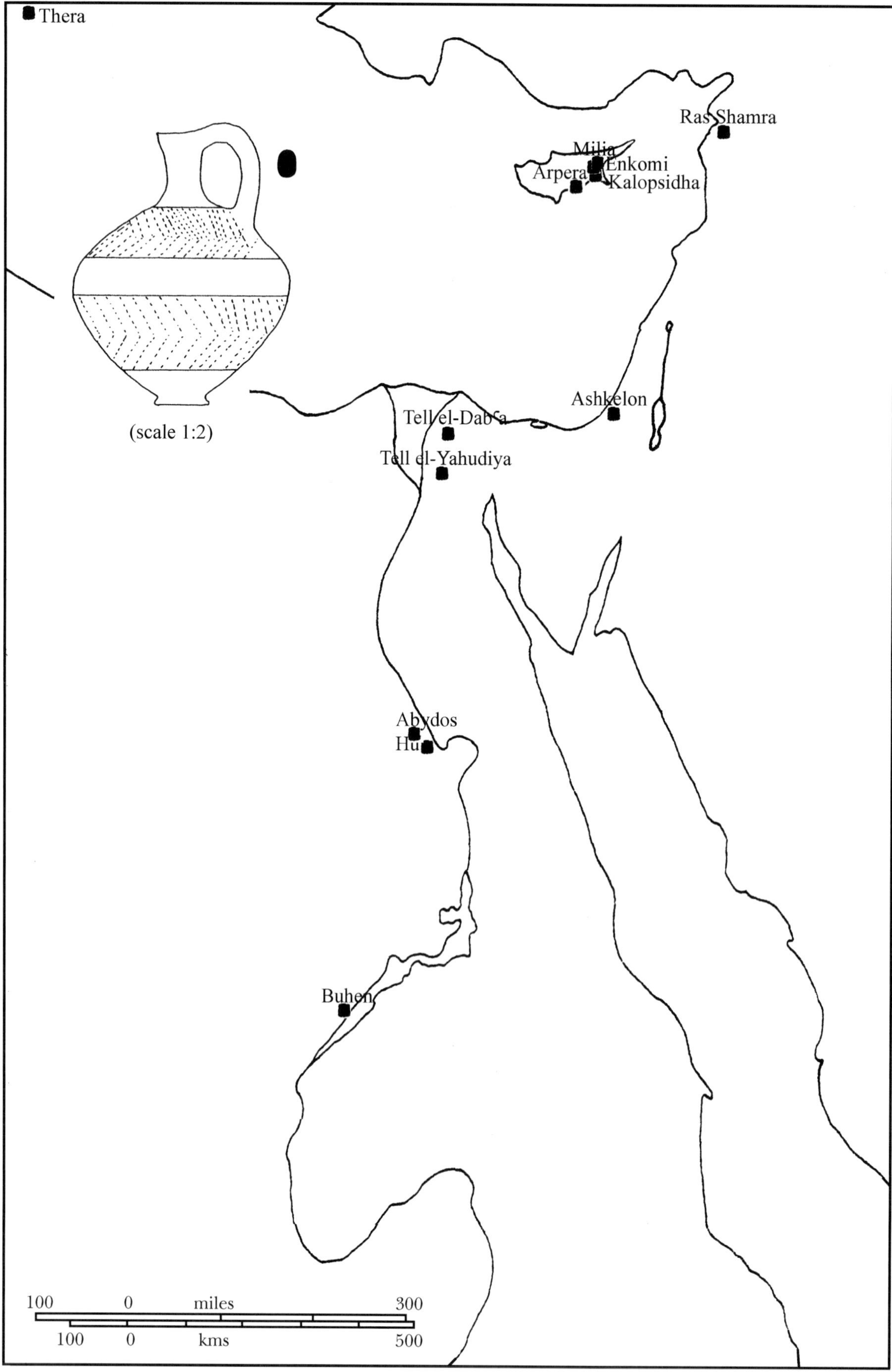

Fig. 162 Distribution and Shape Class of Type Group L.5.3a

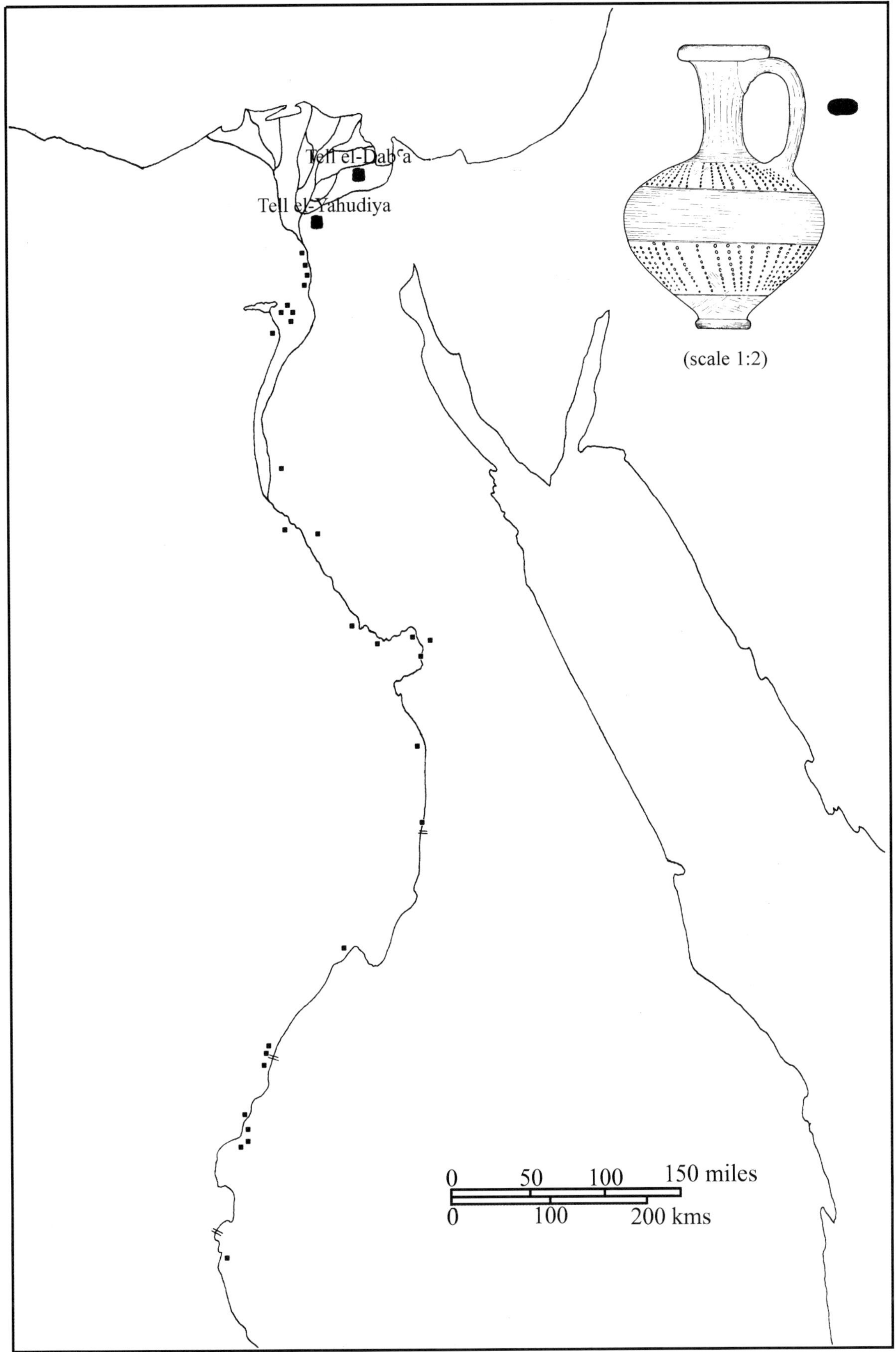

Fig. 163 Distribution and Shape Class of Type Group L.5.3b

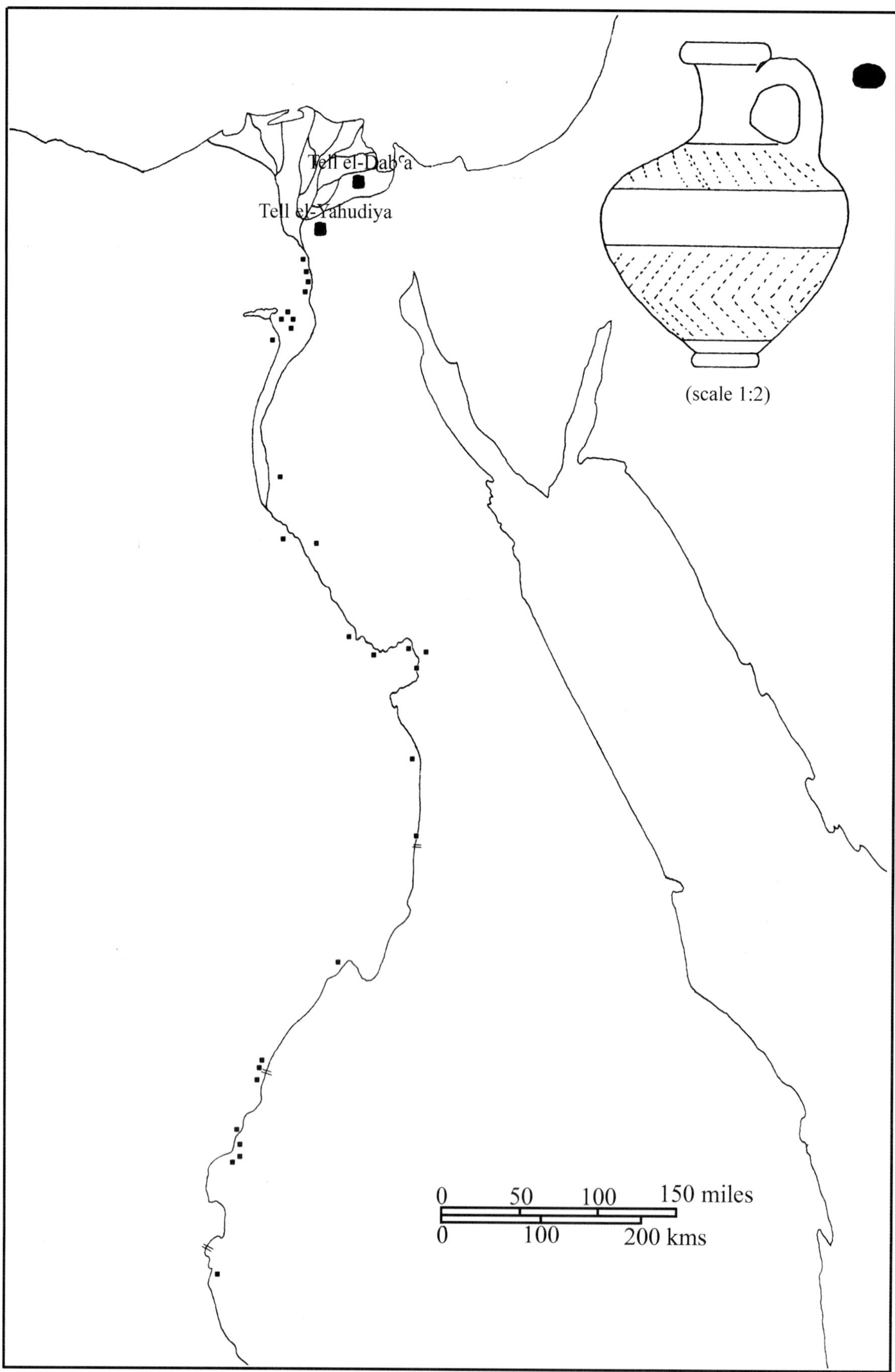

Fig. 164 Distribution and Shape Class of Type Group L.5.3c

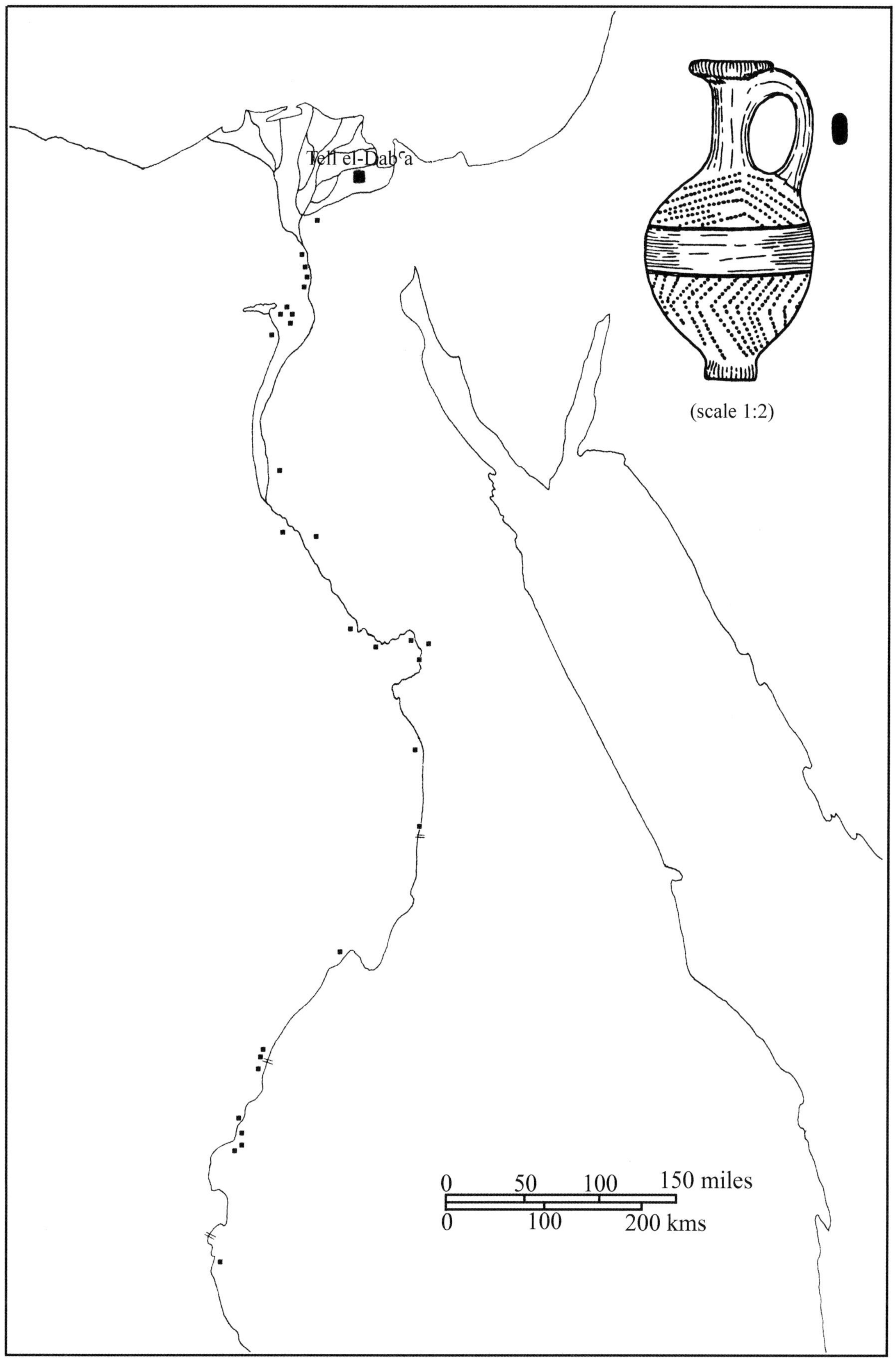

Fig. 165 Distribution and Shape Class of Type Group L.5.4

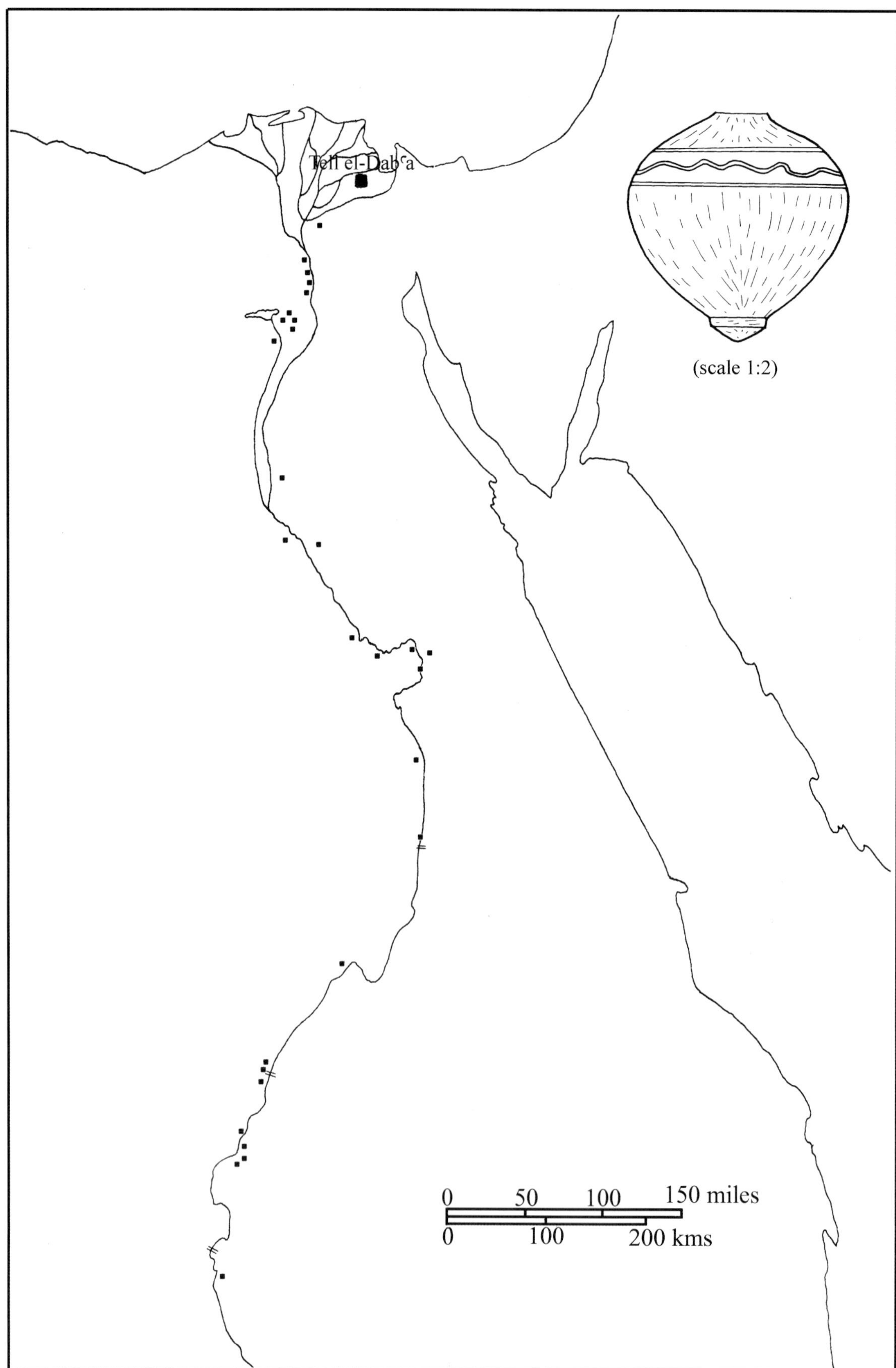

Fig. 166 Distribution and Shape Class of Type Group L.5.5

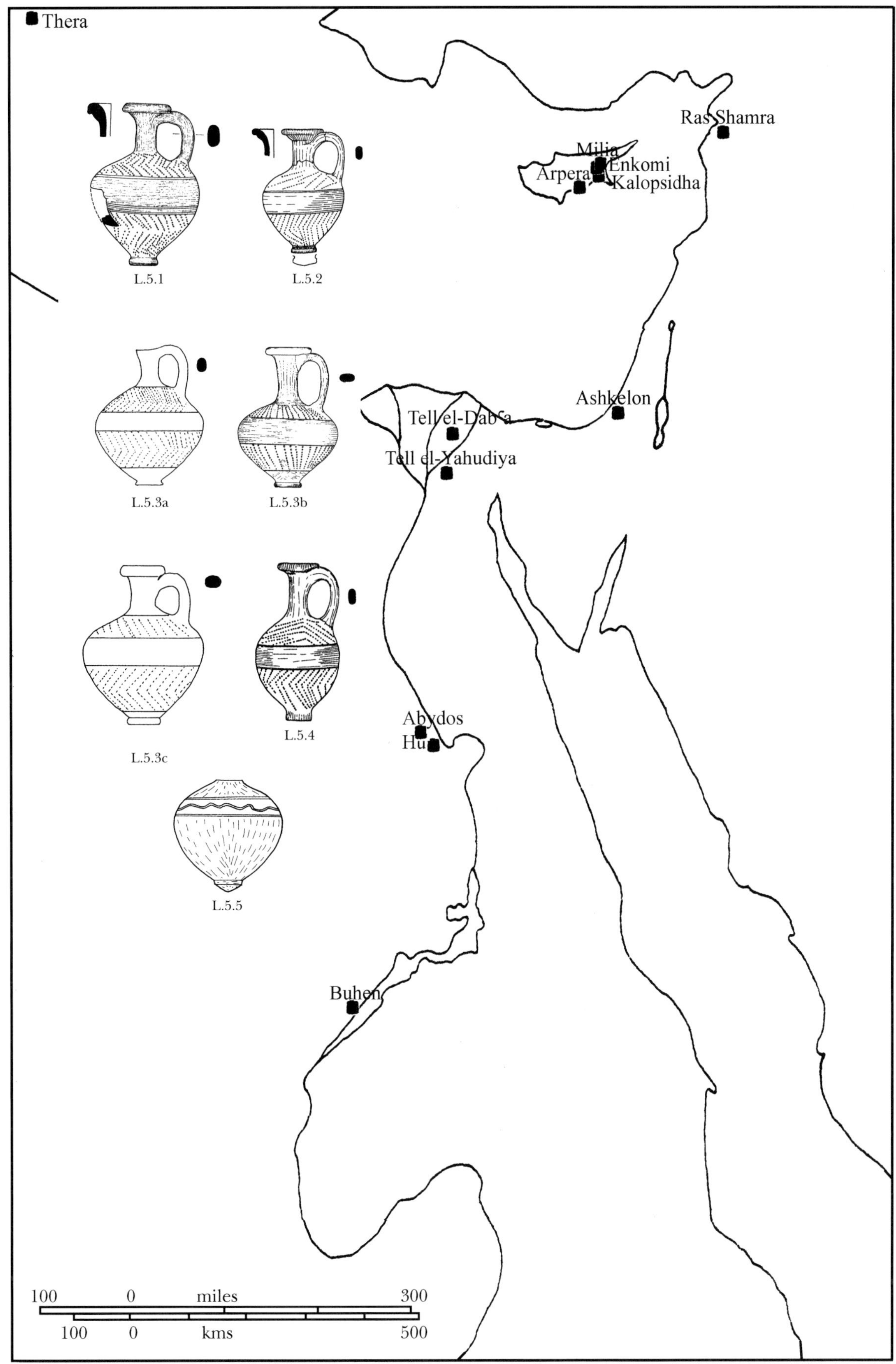

Fig. 167 Combined Distribution of Type Group L.5

L.6. Late Egyptian VI (Large Biconical I)

Type Group L.6.1 (Figs. 168–172)

This type of large biconical jug is known from an example now in Cairo which is 17.2 cm. high and 16 cm. wide at its maximum point,[449] and several others from Tell el-Dabᶜa. The Cairo jug consists of a biconical jug with rolled rim, rounded biconical body, strap handle and ring base with two decorative zones, the upper one consisting of standing triangles and below three or four large pendant traingles filled with a vertical herringbone pattern (L.6.1a). At Tell el-Dabᶜa it is distinctly noticeable that these larger examples always come from settlement areas, and the smaller ones from tomb contexts. Consequently it is likely that the Cairo jug also originally derived from a habitation context. The Tell el-Dabᶜa examples have four different decorative styles: L.6.1b which consists of two bands of chevrons which are only framed at the belly of the pot, ie. the lower edge of the uppermost zone, and the uppermost edge of the bottom zone, (TD 469, 5927B, 3051, 6807, 6466B, 8436U, 6807D, 6135, 3007, 8446L, 6500X, 8446N, 6489R, 8875B): L.6.1c which comprises an upper band of diagonal lines, and a lower zone decorated in a herringbone pattern (TD 6806B), and L.6.1d which consists of two zones of horizontal dots bordered at the belly of the pot, (TD 261, 6466C). Again a recent attribution of a sherd from Ashkelon to a vessel of type group L.6.1a is probably incorrect;[450] the sherd in question is more likely to be of type L.6.1b, which at Tell el-Dabᶜa is current from Phases E/1 to D/2.

L.7. Late Egyptian VII (Large Biconical II)

Vessels of the Late Egyptian VII, group are similar to those of the Late Egyptian VI differing only by the fact that the two zones of decoration are not bordered by incised frame lines. They may be divided into the following groups:

Type Group L.7.1 (Figs. 173, 175)

The one vessel, attributed to type Group L.7.1 is a somewhat unique pot reputedly found on Cyprus,[451] which may be a local Cypriote copy. Although distinctly piriform in shape, resembling a typical Piriform 2a type jug, it is here added to the biconical group since its style of decoration, – two undelineated bands of horizontal chevrons with a reserved zone around the belly, – is otherwise only found on Late Egyptian biconical vessels.

Type Group L.7.2 (Figs. 174, 175)

Type group L.7.2 is known through an example from Aniba which is 16 cm. tall.[452] It is clearly a Large Biconical II jug with a rolled rim, strap handle and round base and is perhaps related to the large wheel-made globular group (L.9.6), although its style of decoration is clearly related to the biconical group. It has a large upper zone of undelineated vertical chevrons, and a lower one of straight lines radiating out from the base. The two zones are separated by a reserved band situated in the lower third of the vessel. Several more possible, incomplete examples, however, are also known from Tell el-Dabᶜa.

Type Group L.8. (Biconical IV)

Vessels of the Biconical IV group are similar to those of the Biconical III group, but the decorative zones are not defined by incised borders. Indeed these are probably the forerunners of the combed group of Tell el-Yahudiya ware (below group L.13), especially where the decoration consists solely of undelineated rows of dots.

Type Group L.8.1 (Figs. 176–180, 182)

Type group L.8.1 is the Biconical IV equivalent of type group L.5.3 in the Biconical III group, and is also subsumed within the classic Biconical 1 of Kaplan, namely jugs with rolled rims, strap handles and ring or disc bases. The upper and lower decorative zones are usually formed by horizontal chevrons, L.8.1a, a herringbone pattern in the lower zone L.8.1b, an upper zone of horizontal dots and a lower zone of chevrons, L.8.1c, and rarely, rows of horizontal dots (L.8.1d), or oblique lines (L.8.1e), and at times these lines radiate straight out from the base or neck. Combinations of any of the above, such as chevrons in the upper zone and oblique lines in the lower, or vice versa may also occur

---

449 Cairo JE 49072. Kaplan *Tell el-Yahudiyeh Ware,* fig. 39b.

450 M. Bietak, K. Kopetzky and L. Stager, Synchronization of stratigraphies, Ashkelon and Tell el-Dabᶜa, *Ä&L* 18, 2008, 55, fig. 5 nos. 3 and 9. a better parallel is the L.6.1b vessel illustrated there on p. 57 fig. 7.2.

451 Kaplan, *Tell el-Yahudiyeh Ware,* fig. 85a.

452 Steindorff, *Aniba* II, 38–40, 125–127, 170, pl. 86.4b2, Kaplan, *Tell el-Yahudiyeh Ware,* fig. 92e.

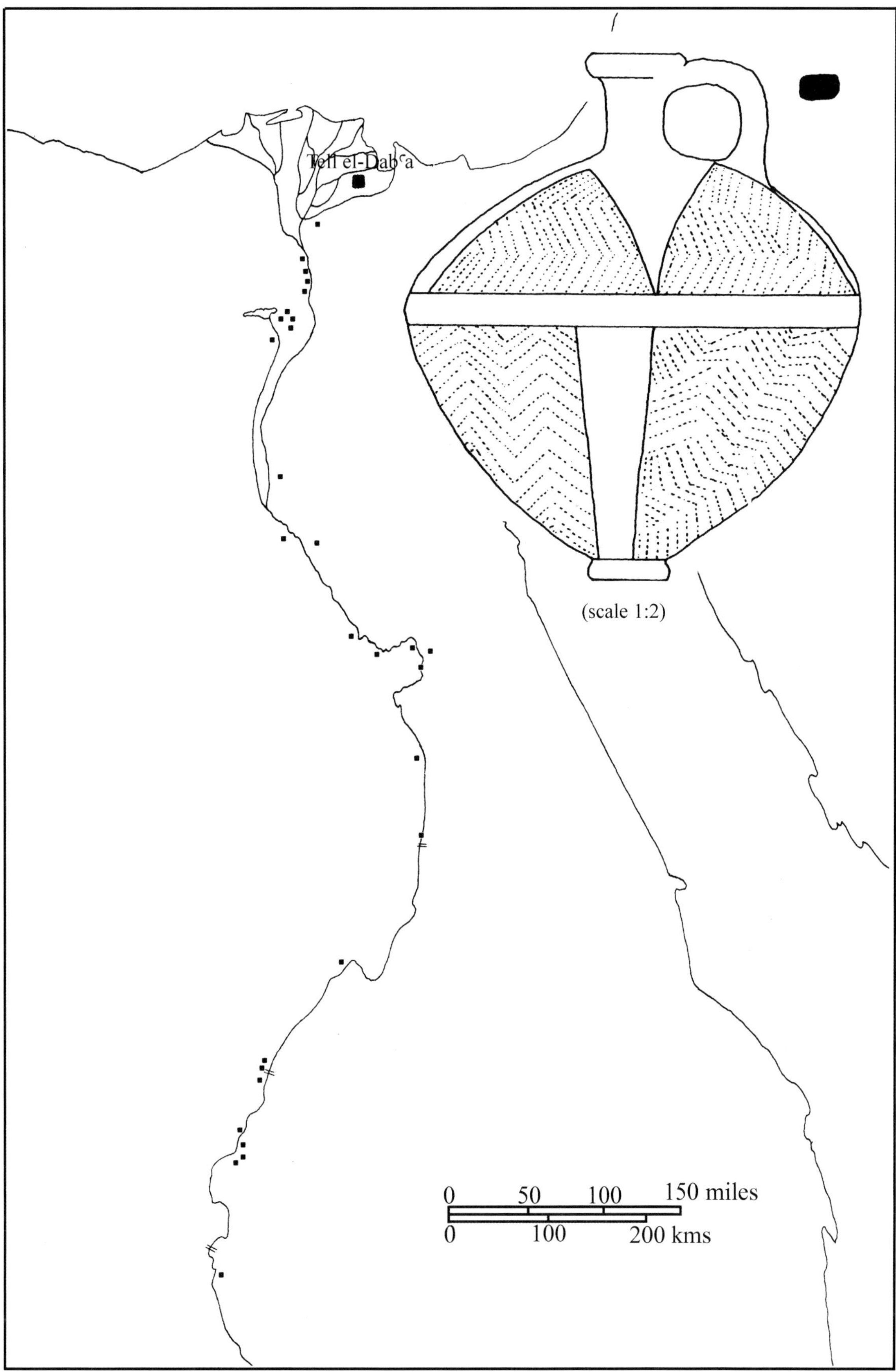

Fig. 168 Distribution and Shape Class of Type Group L.6.1a

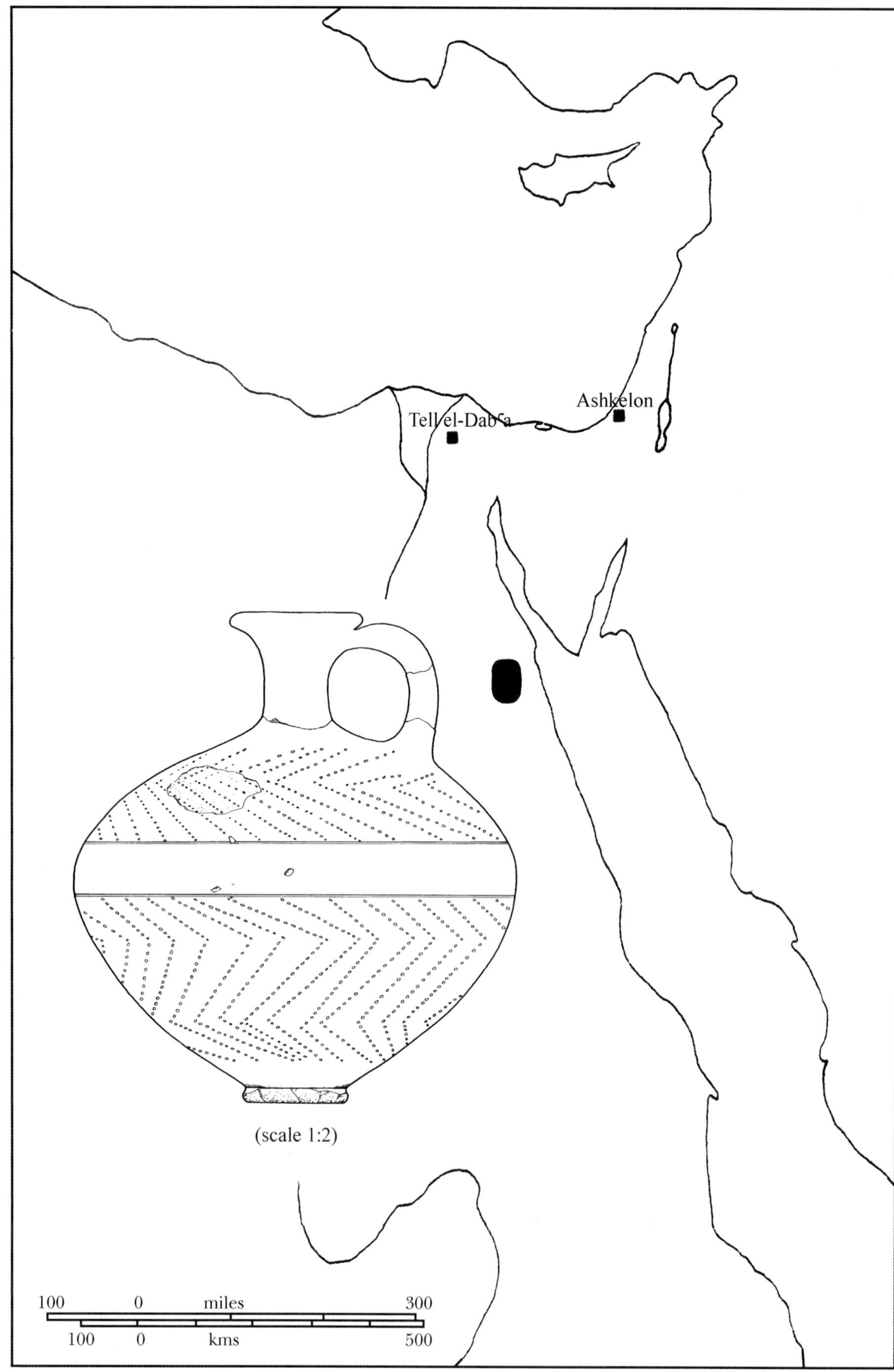

Fig. 169 Distribution and Shape Class of Type Group L.6.1b

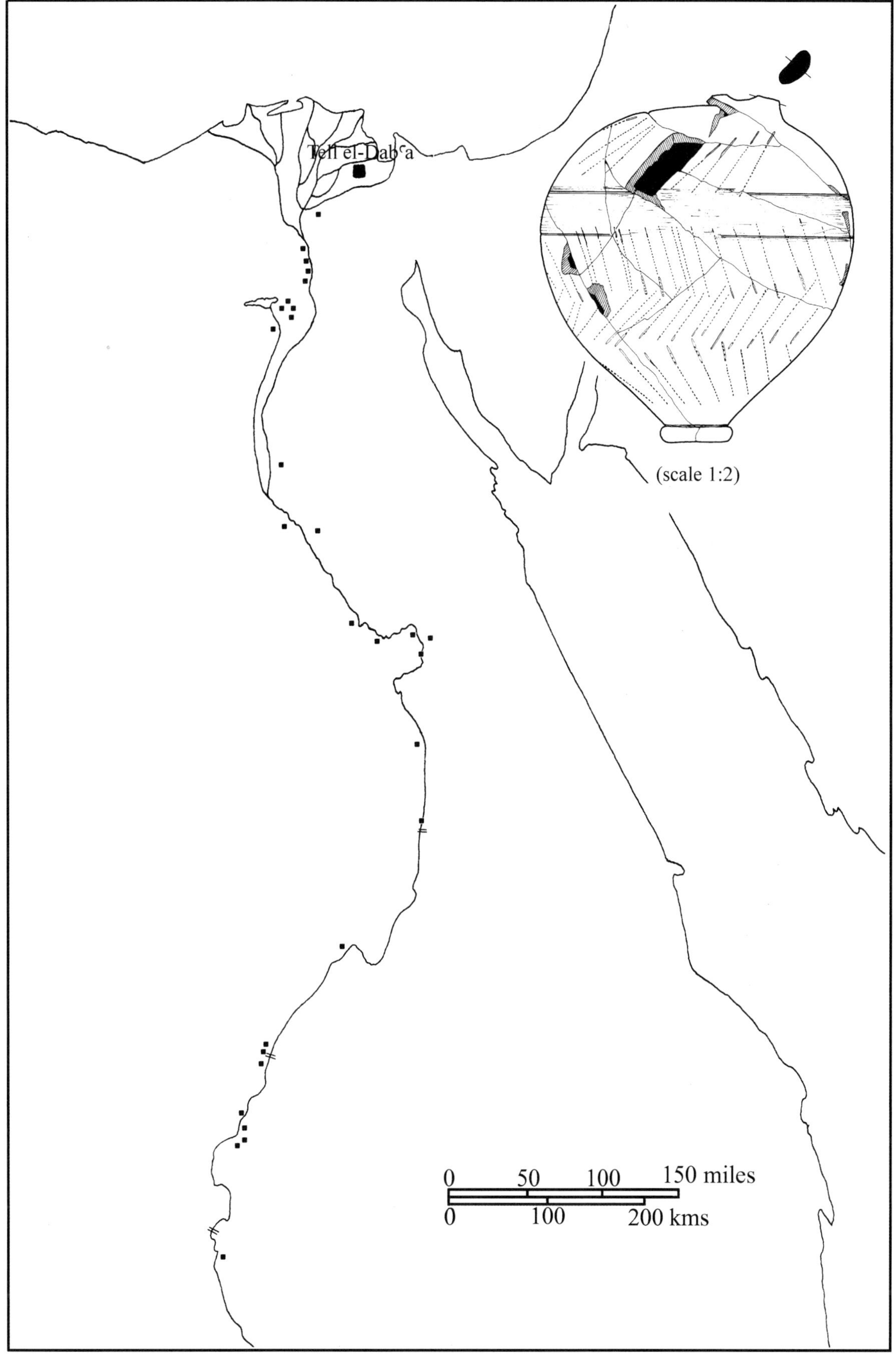

Fig. 170 Distribution and Shape Class of Type Group L.6.1c

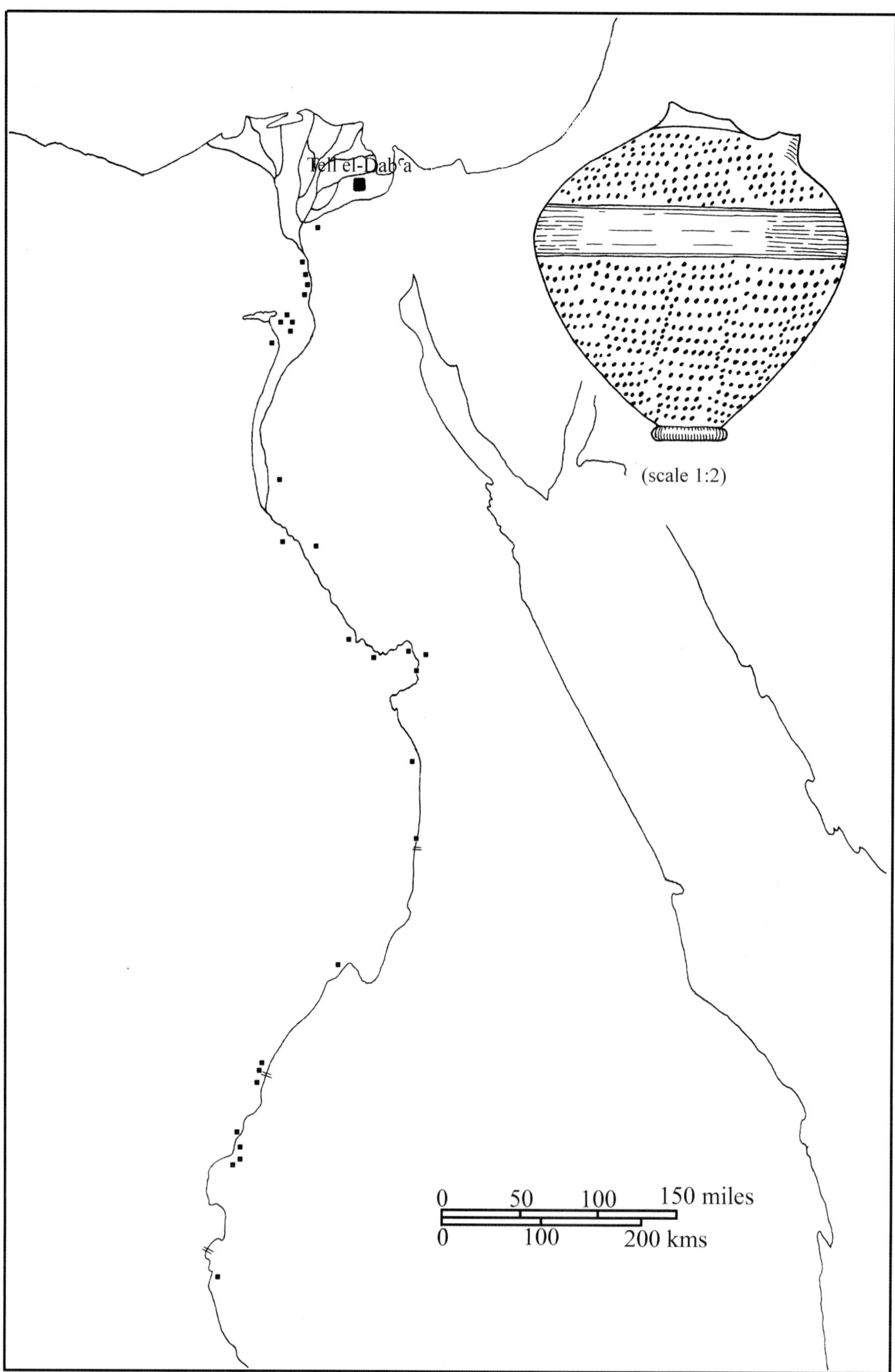

Fig. 171 Distribution and Shape Class of Type Group L.6.1d

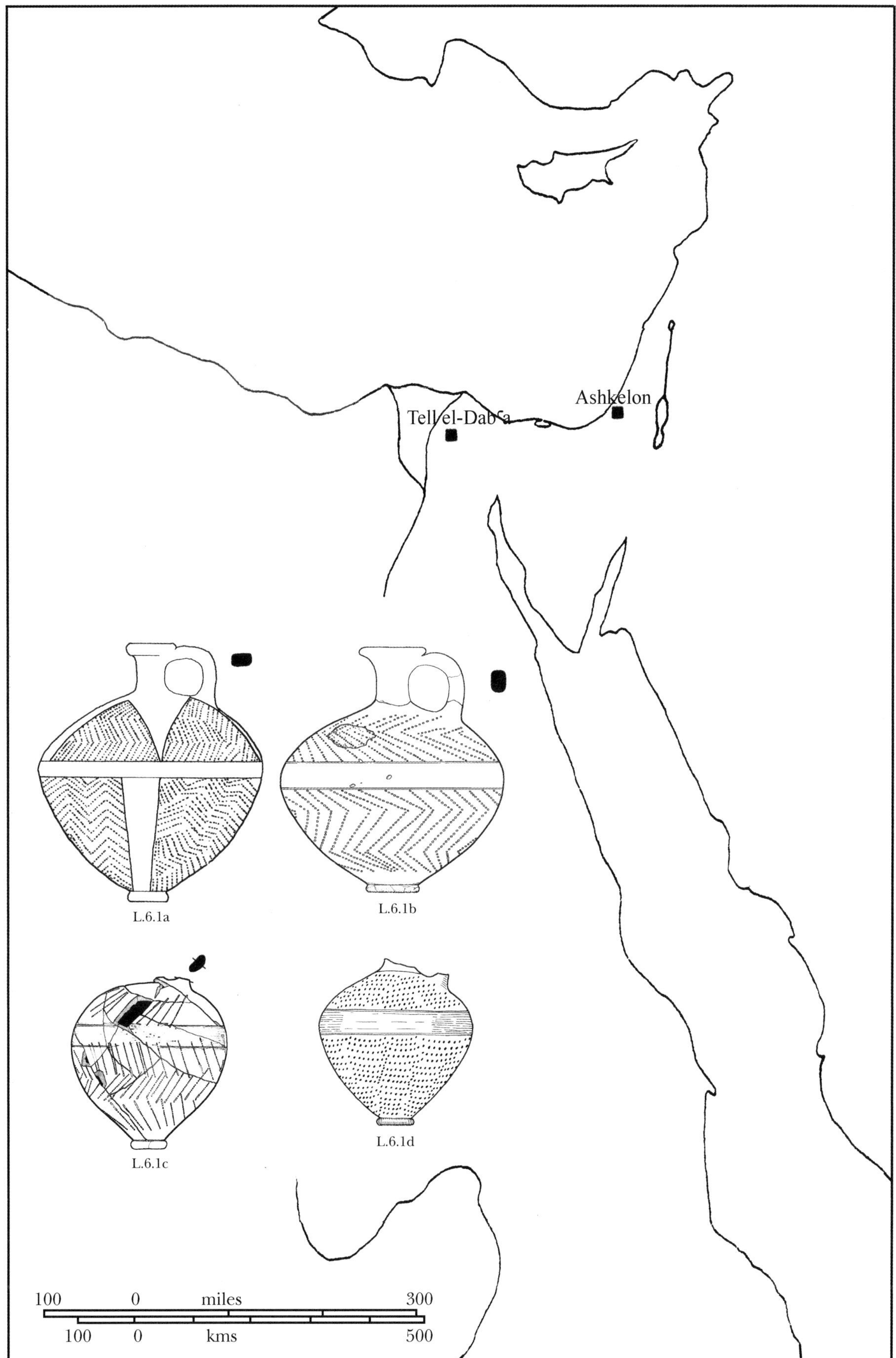

Fig. 172 Combined Distribution of Type Group L.6.1

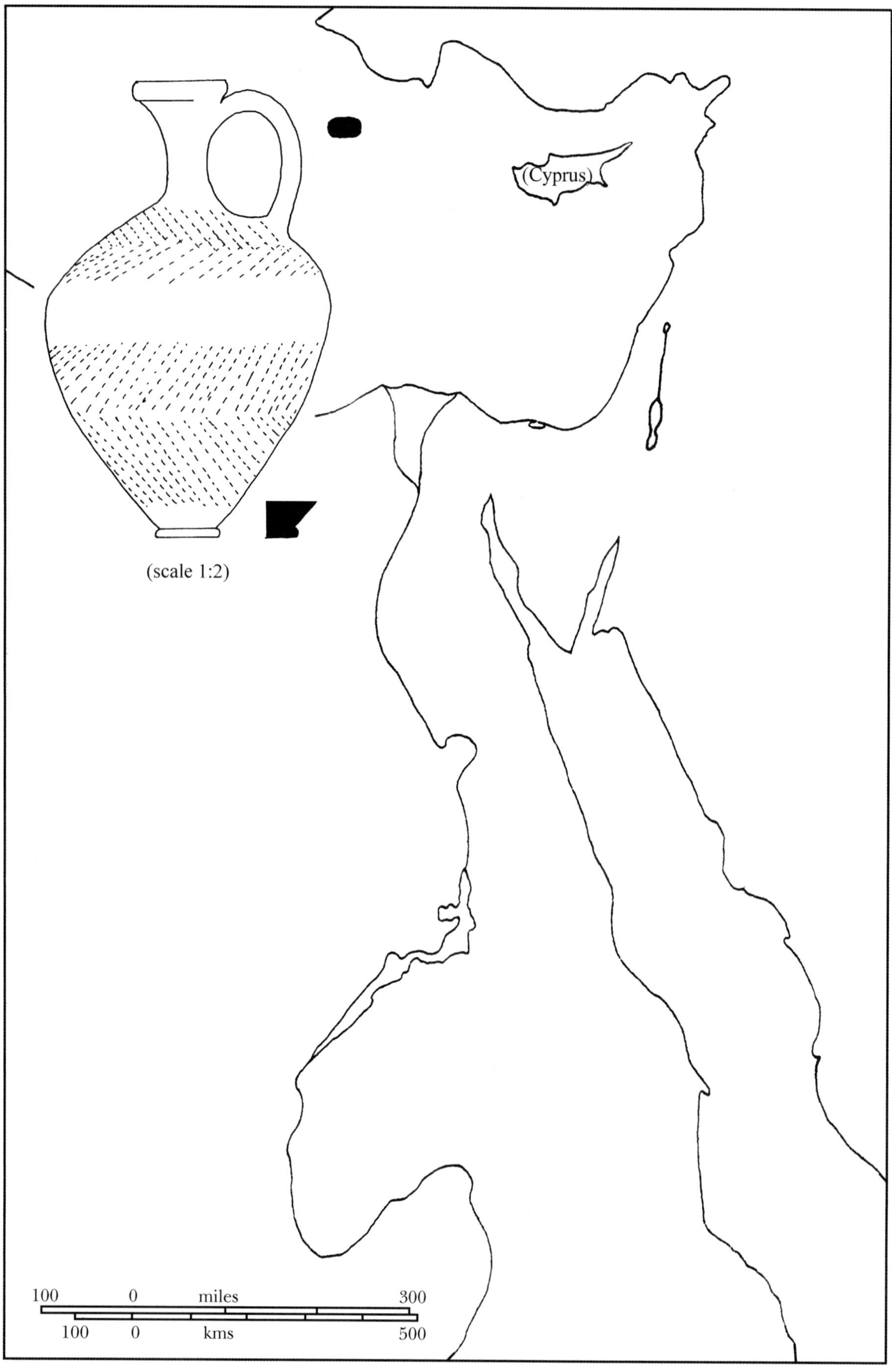

Fig. 173 Distribution and Shape Class of Type Group L.7.1

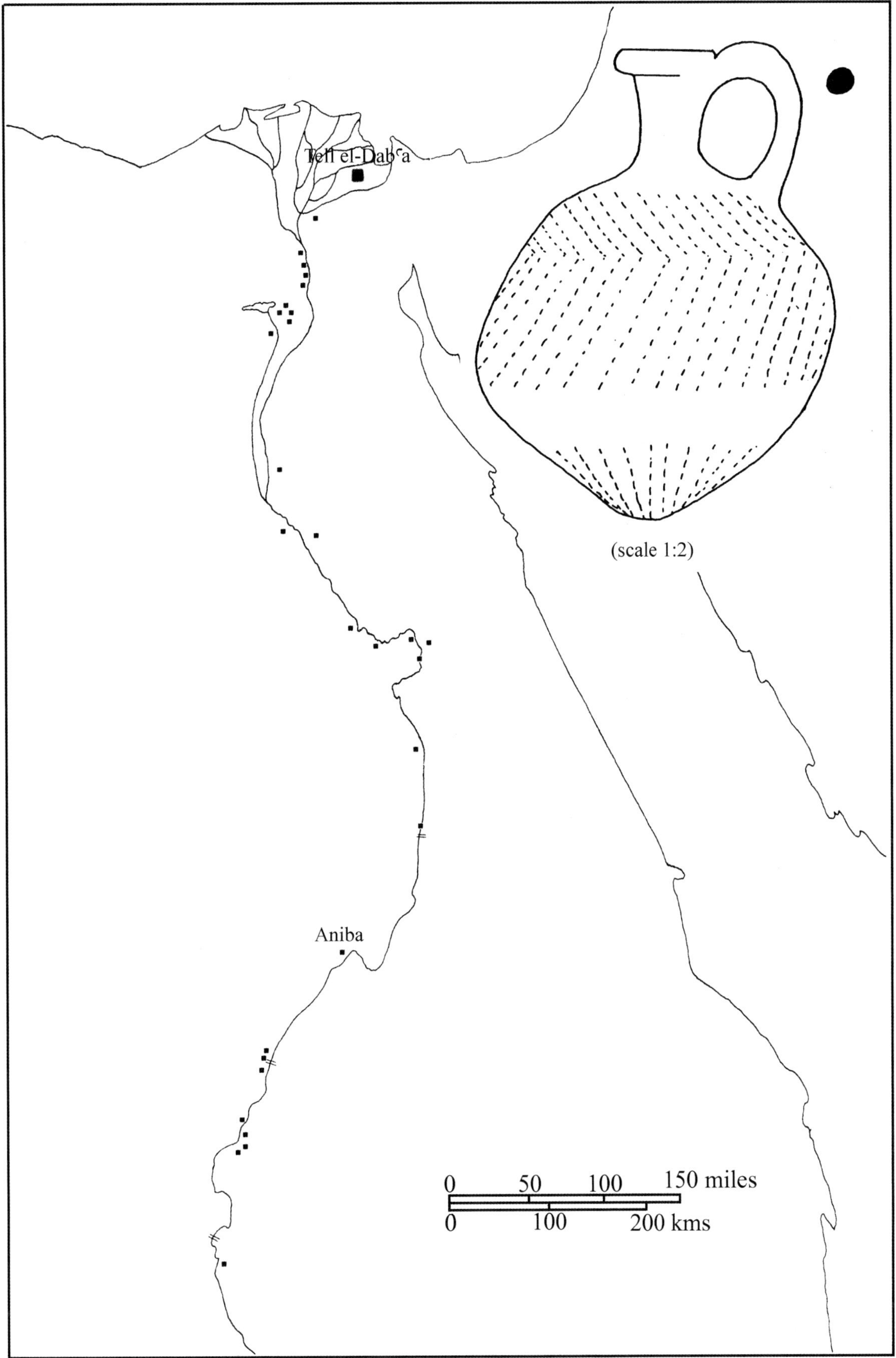

Fig. 174 Distribution and Shape Class of Type Group L.7.2

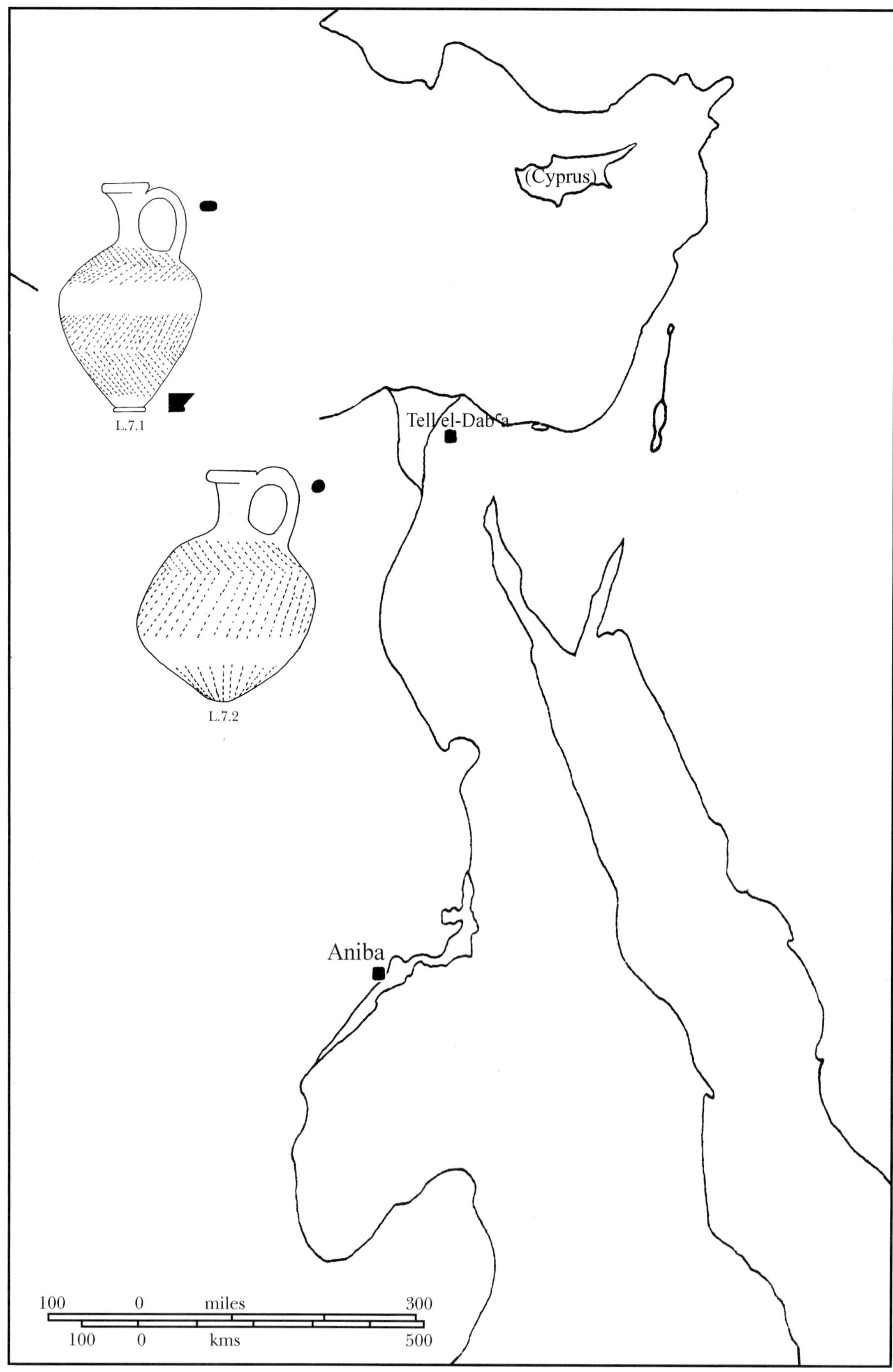

Fig. 175 Combined Distribution of Type Group L.7

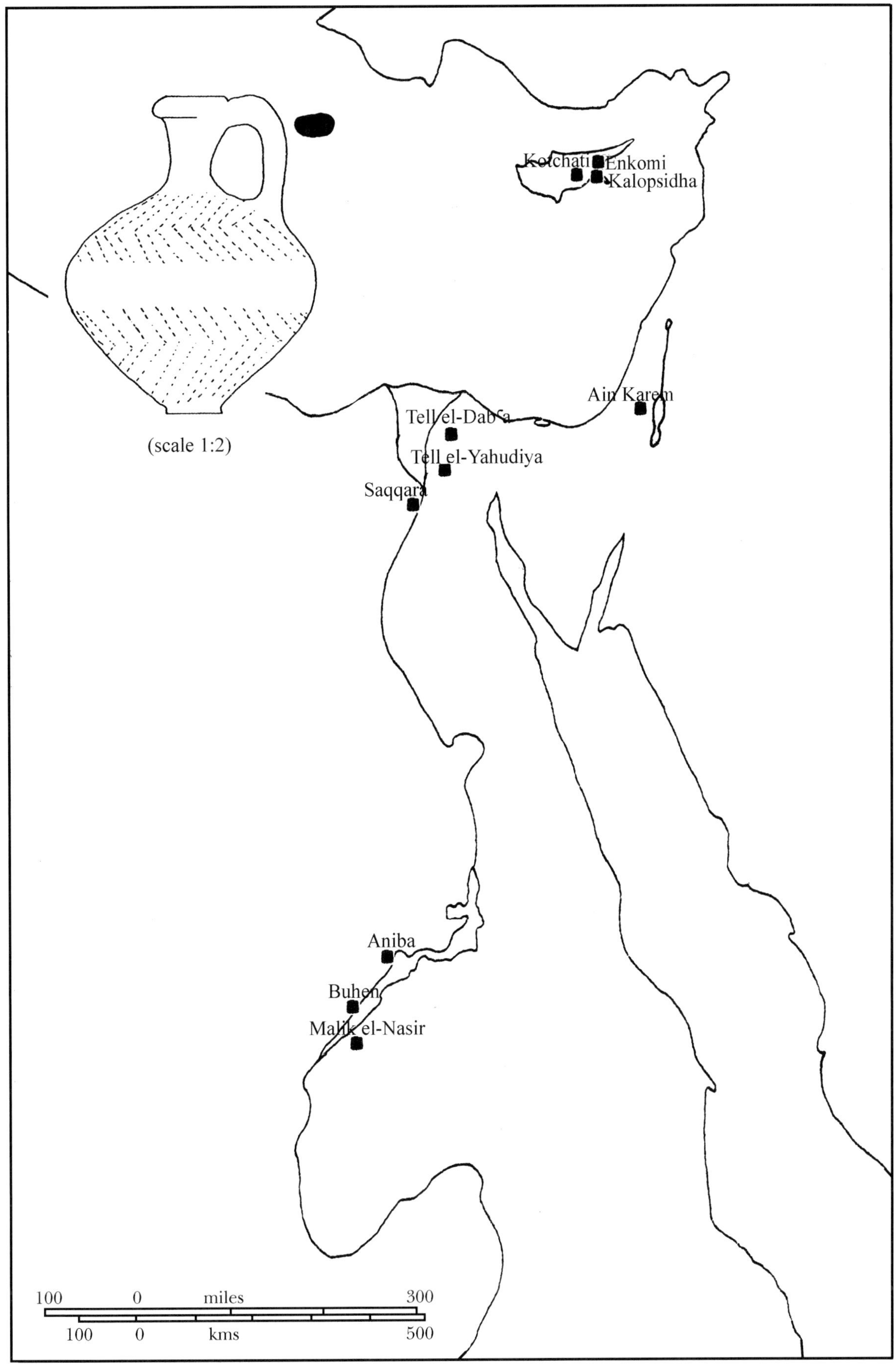

Fig. 176 Distribution and Shape Class of Type Group L.8.1a

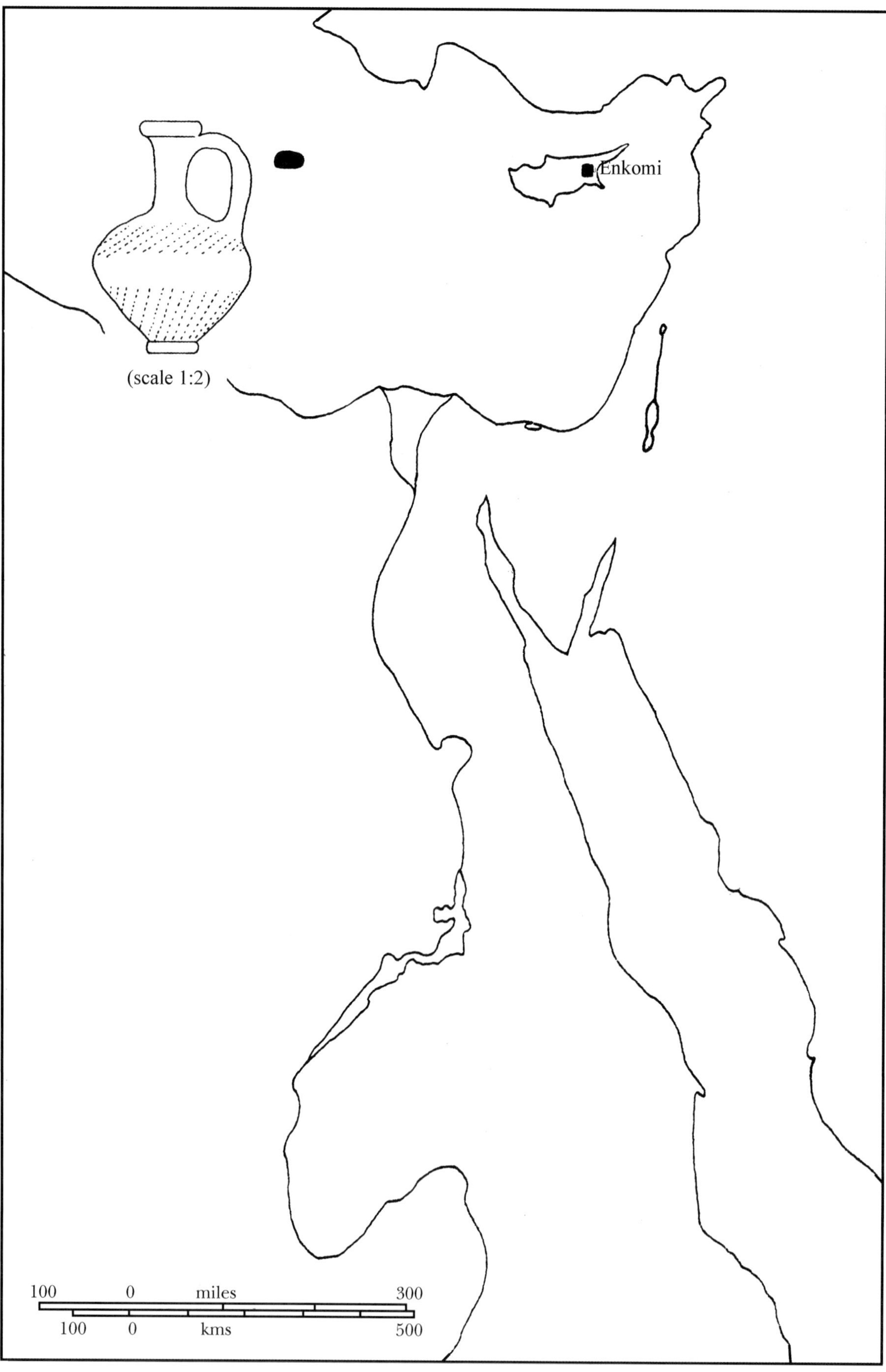

Fig. 177 Distribution and Shape Class of Type Group L.8.1b

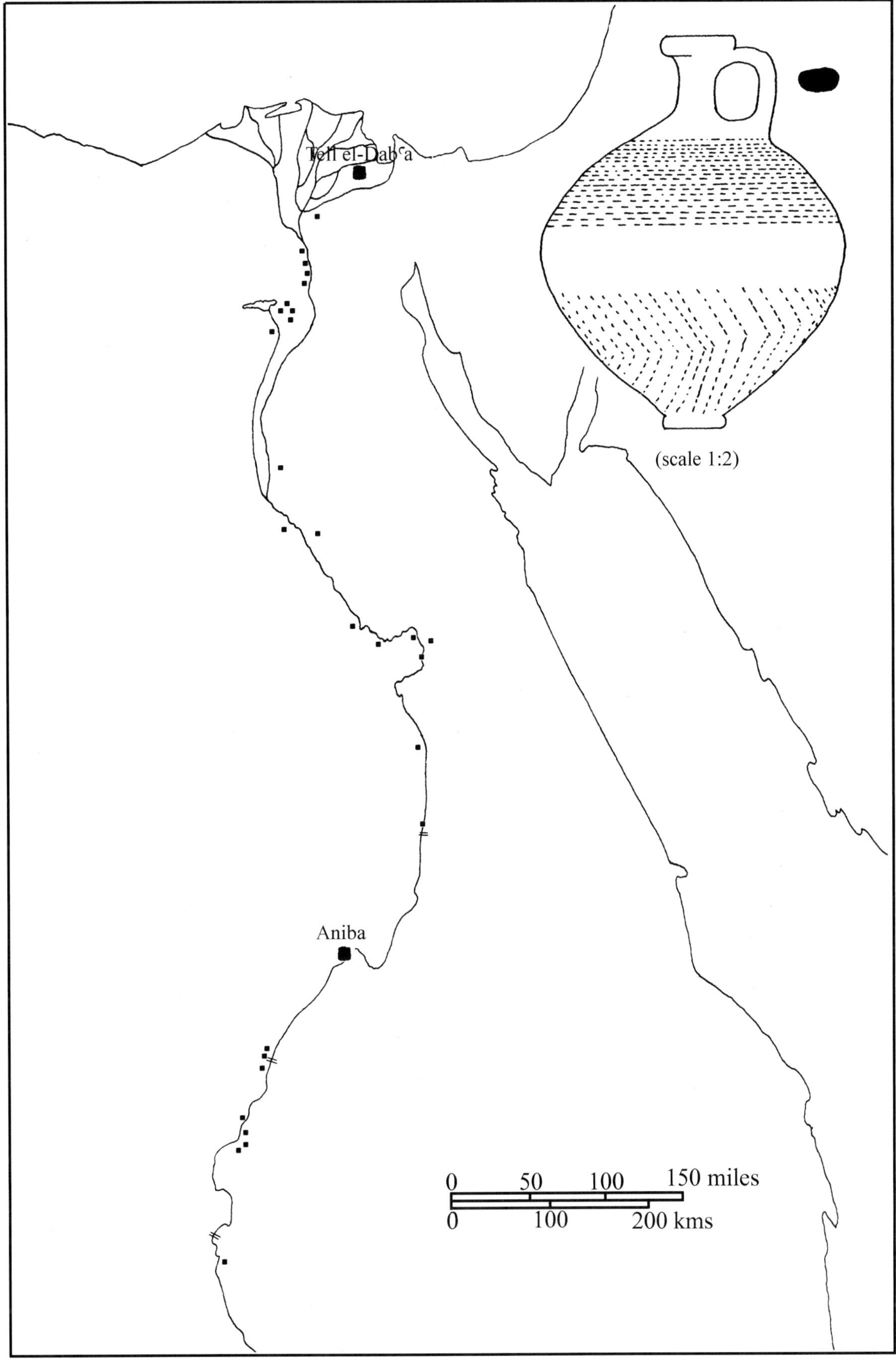

Fig. 178 Distribution and Shape Class of Type Group L.8.1c

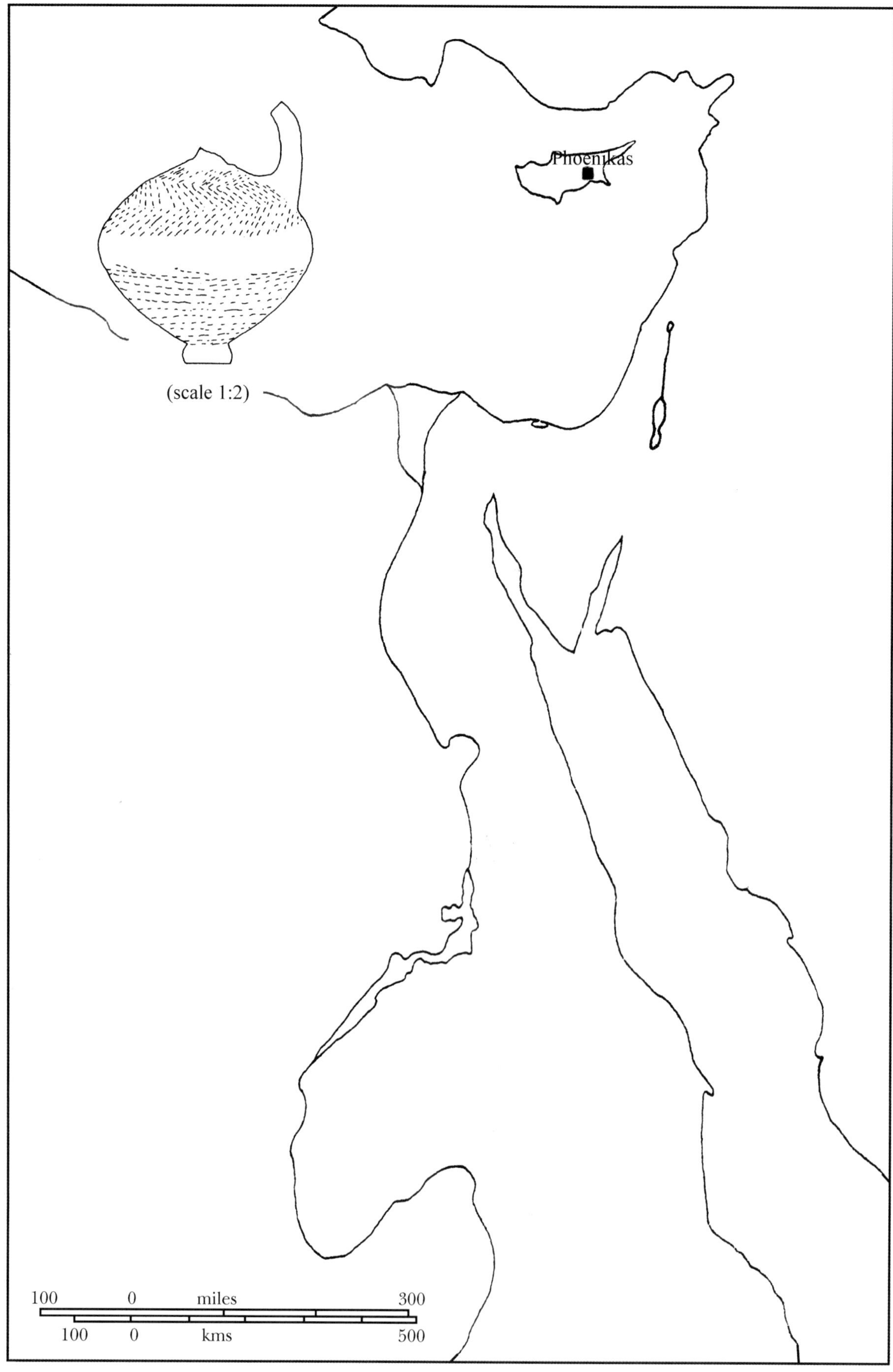

Fig. 179 Distribution and Shape Class of Type Group L.8.1d

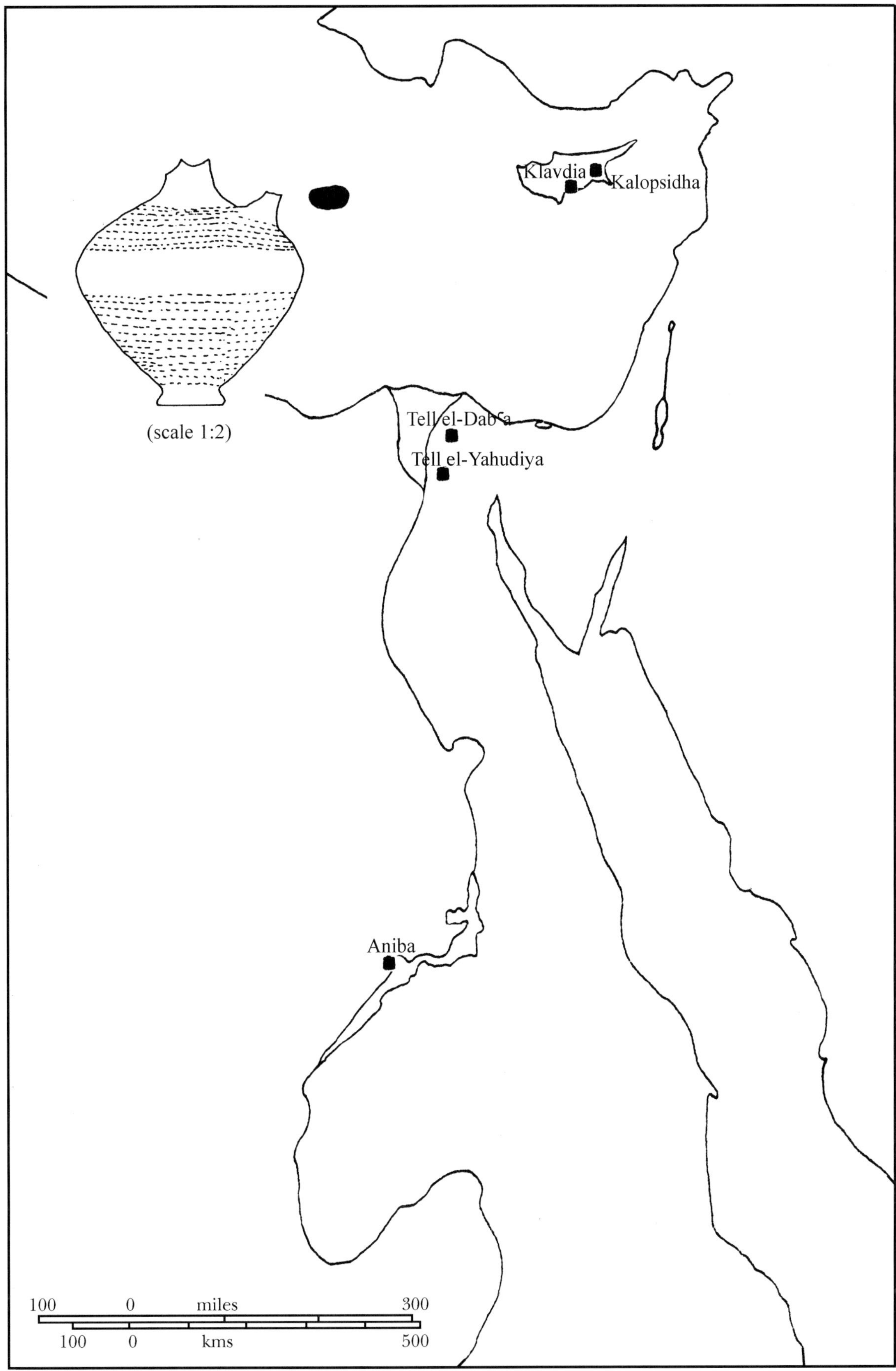

Fig. 180 Distribution and Shape class of Type Group L.8.1e

(L.8.1f). This group is also common with examples of decorative style L.8.1a known from Tell el-Dabᶜa (TD 3417), Tell el-Yahudiya,[453] Saqqara,[454] Buhen,[455] Aniba,[456] Malik el Nasir,[457] ᶜAin Karem,[458] Enkomi,[459] Kotchati,[460] and Kalopsidha.[461] The herringbone pattern L.8.1b is found on a vessel from Enkomi.[462] an upper zone of horizontal dots and a lower zone of chevrons, L.8.1c is known from Aniba;[463] L.8.1d, two zones of undelineated horizontal dots, is known from Phoenikas, Cyprus;[464] and finally two horizontal zones of undelineated oblique lines, L.8.1e are known from Tell el-Yahudiya,[465] Aniba,[466] Kalopsidha[467] and Klavdia.[468] Combinations (L.8.1f) are known on vessels from Tell el-Yahudiya[469] Buhen,[470] and Enkomi;[471] (uppermost zone of oblique lines and a lower zone of chevrons), Aniba[472] (an uppermost zone of undelineated horizontal dots, and a lower one of undelineated chevrons), and Giza[473] and Aniba,[474] (an uppermost zone of chevrons and a lower zone of oblique lines).

Type Group L.8.2 (Figs. 181, 182)

Type group L.8.2, which is clearly a smaller version of type group L.7.3, is known through a complete vessel, 10 cm. high with a maximum body diameter of 9.2 cms, from Cyprus, site unknown.[475] It is clearly a Biconical IV jug with a rolled rim, round handle and round base again perhaps related to the wheel-made globular group (L.9), although its style of decoration – undelineated upper and lower zones of horizontal dots, with a reserved zone at the maximum body diameter – is clearly related to the biconical group. Several more incomplete examples, however, are also known from Tell el-Dabᶜa.

L.9. Late Egyptian IX ('Wheel-made Globular')

Kaplan has defined her (wheel-made) globular vessels as being very homogeneous, in that the rim is primarily rolled, the handle is a single strap and that there is a general progression from globular to squat globular. The most common decoration is three or four vertical lozenges (gores) filled with a herringbone pattern, reminiscent of the piriform 2a vessels, with which they are contemporary. Other minor variations include two broad bands of triangles, two broad bands of chevrons or random lines of pricking. The vessels are usually burnished outside of the decorated areas.

---

[453] Philadelphia UM E.2834. Petrie, *Hyksos and Israelite Cities*, 11, pl. viii.38, Kaplan, *Tell el-Yahudiyeh Ware*, fig. 94d; Ashmolean Museum 1896–1908 E.3511, Petrie, *Hyksos and Israelite Cities*, 1906, pl. 8a.71, Kaplan, *Tell el-Yahudiyeh Ware*, fig. 100f.

[454] Cairo JE 56469. Kaplan, *Tell el-Yahudiyeh Ware*, fig. 85e.

[455] Philadelphia UM E.10621. Randall-MacIver and Woolley, *Buhen*, 177, pl. 49, Kaplan, *Tell el-Yahudiyeh Ware*, fig. 97a.

[456] Steindorff, pl. 86, 45b1, Kaplan, *Tell el-Yahudiyeh Ware*, fig. 93f.

[457] Khartoum 20342. Kaplan, *Tell el-Yahudiyeh Ware*, fig. 89a.

[458] Jerusalem, Museum of the Flagellation. Kaplan, *Tell el-Yahudiyeh Ware*, fig. 99b.

[459] Paris, Louvre, AM 2583. Kaplan, *Tell el-Yahudiyeh Ware*, fig. 88a; Nicosia Cyprus Museum 1939/VII-18/1 (F), Kaplan, *Tell el-Yahudiyeh Ware*, fig. 100c, 1939/VII-18/1 (G). Kaplan, *Tell el-Yahudiyeh Ware*, fig. 88b, 1939/VII-18/1 (H). Kaplan, *Tell el-Yahudiyeh Ware*, fig. 98c.

[460] Nicosia Cyprus Museum 1950/VI-16/1. Kaplan, *Tell el-Yahudiyeh Ware*, fig. 91c.

[461] Oxford, Ashmolean C.31. Myres, *JHS* 17, 1897, 145, fig. 4.23, Kaplan, *Tell el-Yahudiyeh Ware*, fig. 87c.

[462] London BN Greek and Roman Dept. 97/4–1/1303, Murray *et al.*, 1900 6 fig. 9, Kaplan, *Tell el-Yahudiyeh Ware*, fig. 98a.

[463] Steindorff, *Aniba*, pl. 86.45b3; Kaplan, *Tell el-Yahudiyeh Ware*, fig. 94b.

[464] London BM Greek and Roman Antiquities, 84/12–10/85. Murray, *Handbook of Greek Archaeology*, 1892, 6, fig. 1. Kaplan, *Tell el-Yahudiyeh Ware*, fig. 90b. Kaplan, *Tell el-YahudiyehWare*, 300, suggests that this vessel is of Cypriote manufacture, but since no NAA analysis has been made on it, an Egyptian origin, as suggested by Murray could well be correct.

[465] Cairo JE 51916. Kaplan, *Tell el-Yahudiyeh Ware*, fig. 95c; Oxford Ashmolean E.3500, E.3553. Petrie, *Hyksos and Israelite Cities*, 11, pls. viii.49, vii.22; Jerusalem, Biblical Institute. Amiran, *Ancient Pottery of the Holy Land*, 1969, 121, photo 123; London UC 13473, Petrie, *Hyksos and Israelite Cities*, 11, 15, pl. viiia.72; Brussels E2569. Petrie, *Hyksos and Israelite Cities*, 11, pl. vii.11; Cairo. Adam, *ASAE* 55, 1958, 309, pls. 17 a–b, 20.1; Kaplan, *Tell el-Yahudiyeh Ware*, figs. 85f, 86e, 86h, 92d, 92f, 93c, 95c, 103c.

[466] Steindorff, *Aniba* II, 38–40, 125–137, 197, pl. 86.45a1, Kaplan, *Tell el-Yahudiyeh Ware*, fig. 103a.

[467] Nicosia Cyprus Museum A.1443. Myres, *JHS* 17, 1897, 141, fig. 5.7, Kaplan, *Tell el-Yahudiyeh Ware*, fig. 103b.

[468] London BM Greek and Roman Antiquities, 99/12–29/100. Kaplan, *Tell el-Yahudiyeh Ware*, fig. 101c.

[469] London UC 8866. Griffith, *The Antiquities of Tell el-Yahudiyeh*, 40, pl. 9.3; Brussels E2570. Petrie, *Hyksos and Israelite Cities*, 11, pl. vii.12, Kaplan, *Tell el-Yahudiyeh Ware*, figs. 92c, 94c.

[470] Philadelphia UM E.10869. Randall MacIver and Woolley, 1911, 214–215, pl. 92, Kaplan, *Tell el-Yahudiyeh Ware*, fig. 85b.

[471] Nicosia Cyprus Museum 1939/VII-18/1 (E). Kaplan, *Tell el-Yahudiyeh Ware*, fig. 100b.

[472] Steindorff, *Aniba* II, 38–40, 125–137, 227–229, pl. 86.45b3.

[473] Cairo T.43/16/5/1. Hassan, *Excavations at Giza II*, 108, pl. 35.2; Kaplan, *Tell el-Yahudiyeh Ware*, fig. 93b.

[474] Steindorff, *Aniba II*, 38–40, 125–137, 167, pl. 86.45b1; Kaplan, *Tell el-Yahudiyeh Ware*, fig. 94b.

[475] Nicosia, Cyprus Museum A.1446. Kaplan, *Tell el-Yahudiyeh Ware*, fig. 91b.

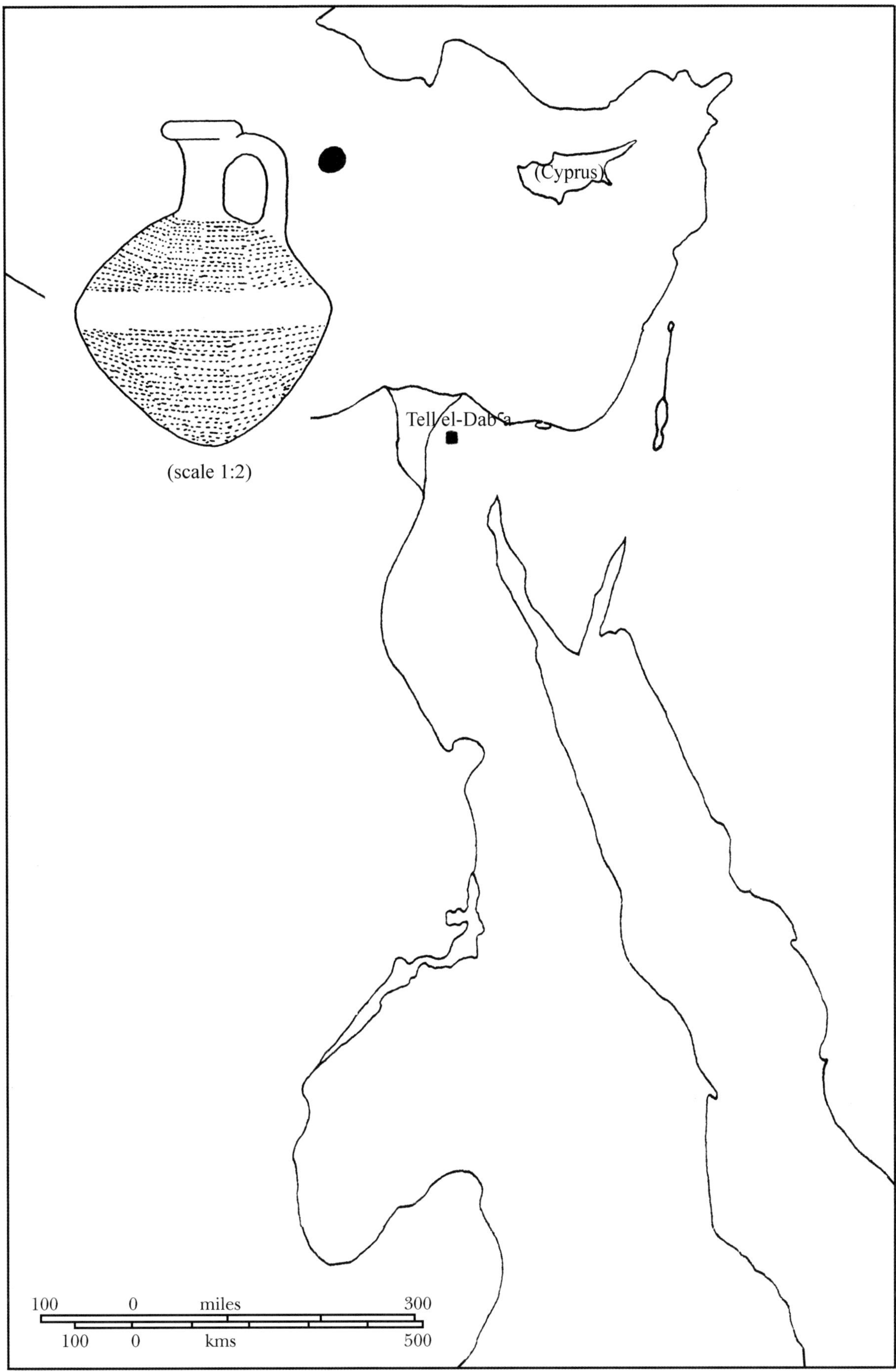

Fig. 181 Distribution and Shape Class of Type Group L.8.2

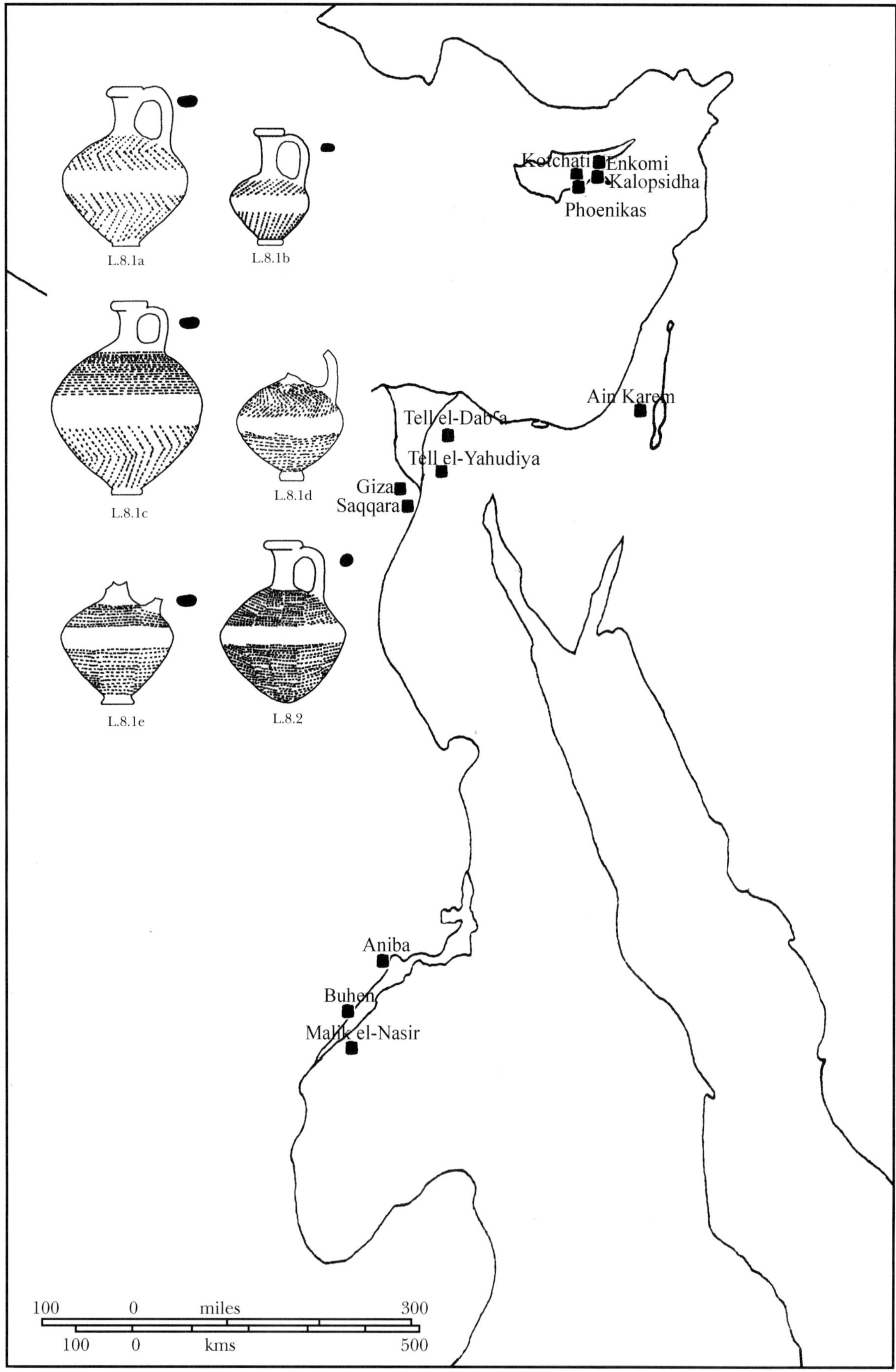

Fig. 182 Combined Distribution of Type Group L.8

Type Group L.9.1 (Figs. 183, 189)

Type group L.9.1 comprises a series of spherical jugs with a rolled rim and strap handle. Like the Biconical 1 vessels these jugs always have a broad reserved burnished zone around the maximum point, and the decoration consists of an upper zone of delineated standing triangles, and a lower one of delineated pendant triangles. Both zones usually contain between four and six such triangles. Such vessels are known from Tell el-Dab^ca and Harageh.[476]

Type Group L.9.2 (Figs. 184, 189)

Type Group L.9.2 is somewhat similar to the previous type but the body is distinctly carinated rather than spherical. Like the previous group the decoration consists of an upper zone of delineated standing triangles, and a lower one of delineated pendant triangles.

Type Group L.9.3 (Figs. 185, 189)

Type group L.9.3 is defined from a single incomplete example found at Tell el-Dabᶜa (TD 2093) which has a small plump body with three delineated circles, infilled with chevrons (?) on the body.

Type Group L.9.4 (Figs. 186, 189)

Type group L.9.4 consists of drop-shaped globular jugs with a rolled rim and strap handle, and are very common. They vary in height between around 9 and 16 cms., with most in the 10–12 cm. range. They are decorated with three or four infilled delineated lozenges with examples known from Tell el-Dabᶜa, Tell el-Yahudiya,[477] Illahun,[478] Harageh,[479] Deir Rifeh,[480] Abydos,[481] Buhen,[482] and Salamis.[483]

Type Group L.9.5 (Figs. 187, 189)

Type group L.9.5, which consists of drop-shaped globular jugs with a rolled rim and strap handle, is similar to L.9.4, but the decorative zones are not defined by an incised border. Again they vary in height between around 9 and 16 cms., with most in the 10–12 cm. range, and have two distinctive styles of decoration: L.9.5a undelineated infilled lozenges known from Tell el-Yahudiya[484] and Edfu;[485] and L.9.5b, an upper and lower zone of horizontal chevrons, known from Tell el-Yahudiya;[486] Enkomi,[487] and perhaps Tell el-Dabᶜa (TD 5925A), though the latter is incomplete and the attribution to this type is only tentative.

Type Group L.9.6 Large Globular Jugs (Figs. 188, 189)

Large globular jugs with a rolled rim, strap handle, drop shaped body and a total height of around 28–30 cms. are not common, but since such vessels were not deposited in tombs, their chances of preservation are much less. Nevertheless examples are known from Tell el-Dabᶜa,[488] Tell el-Ajjul,[489] Ashkelon (?),[490] and from an unknown location in Cyprus.[491] They are all similarly decorated with two zones separated by a wide band at the middle. The uppermost zone consists of delineated triangles and the lower one, delineated pendant triangles.

L.10. Late Egyptian X (Quadrilobal Jugs)

---

476 Oxford Ashmolean 1914.644. ENGELBACH, *Harageh*, 2, 10–11, 13, pl. xli.99d, KAPLAN, *Tell el-Yahudiyeh Ware*, fig. 19c.

477 Ex London Victoria. and Albert Museum. 530.1906. KAPLAN, *Tell el-Yahudiyeh Ware*, fig. 13f; Oxford Ashmolean E3506, PETRIE, *Hyksos and Israelite Cities*, 11, 15, pl. viiia.76; Boston MFA 1888.988. GRIFFITH, *The Antiquities of Tell el-Yahudiyeh*, 40, pl. 9.5.

478 London BM 53948. KAPLAN, *Tell el-Yahudiyeh Ware*, fig. 18b.

479 Cambridge Fitzwilliam E.69.1914. ENGELBACH, *Harageh*, pl. lv.99m.

480 PETRIE, *Gizeh and Rifeh*, 20–21, pls. xxiii.38, xxviim.

481 Oxford Ashmolean E.2330. GARSTANG, *El Arabeh*, 12, 28–29, pl. 17 tomb E10.

482 Philadelphia UM E.10831, RANDALL-MACIVER and WOOLLEY, *Buhen*, 310–311, pl. 49; 10887b, KAPLAN, *Tell el-Yahudiyeh Ware*, fig. 13d.

483 Nicosia Cyprus Museum A.1447. KAPLAN, *Tell el-Yahudiyeh Ware*, fig. 17b.

484 Paris Louvre, no number, KAPLAN, *Tell el-Yahudiyeh Ware*, fig. 14b; Oxford Ashmolean E.3501, PETRIE, *Hyksos and Israelite Cities*, 11, 15, pl. viii.48; Philadelphia UM E.2833, E2835, PETRIE, *Hyksos and Israelite Cities*, 11, 15, pls. viii.40, viiia.84; Boston MFA 1888.898. KAPLAN, *Tell el-Yahudiyeh Ware*, fig. 15a; Brussels E573, PETRIE, *Hyksos and Israelite Cities*, 11, 15, pl. viii.39; London BM 30444. HALL, *The Oldest Civilization of Greece*, fig. 29 left: Cairo JE 51917. KAPLAN, *Tell el-Yahudiyeh Ware*, fig. 17d; Manchester 3489, PETRIE, *Hyksos and Israelite Cities*, 11, 15, pl. viiia.77.

485 Stockholm MM 979. KAPLAN, *Tell el-Yahudiyeh Ware*, fig. 17e.

486 Munich Äg. Seminar 4427. PETRIE, *Hyksos and Israelite Cities*, 11, 15, pl. viii.41.

487 London BM Greek and Roman Antiquities, 97/4–1/1304. MURRAY *et al*, *Excavations in Cyprus*, 6, fig. 9.

488 See below, and add ADAM, *ASAE* 56, 1959, 207, pl. 16.2, KAPLAN, *Tell el-Yahudiyeh Ware*, fig. 20a.

489 Jerusalem, Rockefeller Museum 35.4412. PETRIE, *Ancient Gaza IV*, 13, pl. lv.68j, KAPLAN, *Tell el-Yahudiyeh Ware*, fig. 20b.

490 Cf. below page 572.

491 Nicosia, Cyprus Museum A.1440. BUCHHOLZ and KARAGEORGHIS, *Prehistoric Greece and Cyprus*, 1973, 148, pl. 417, KAPLAN, *Tell el-Yahudiyeh Ware*, fig. 20c. Another vessel of unknown provenance is in the Haaretz Museum, Tel Aviv, KAPLAN, *Tell el-Yahudiyeh Ware*, fig. 36b.

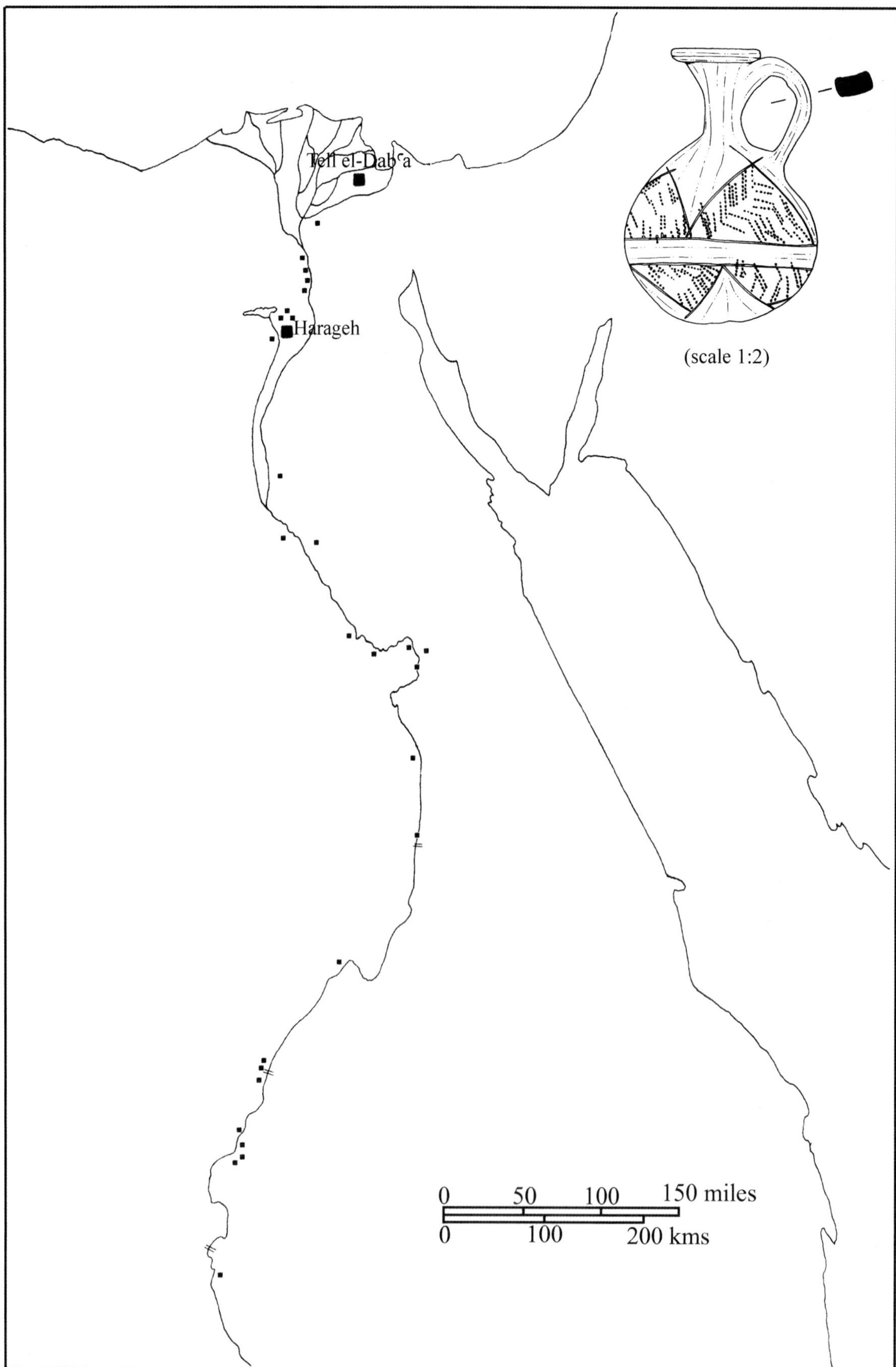

Fig. 183 Distribution and Shape Class of Type Group L.9.1

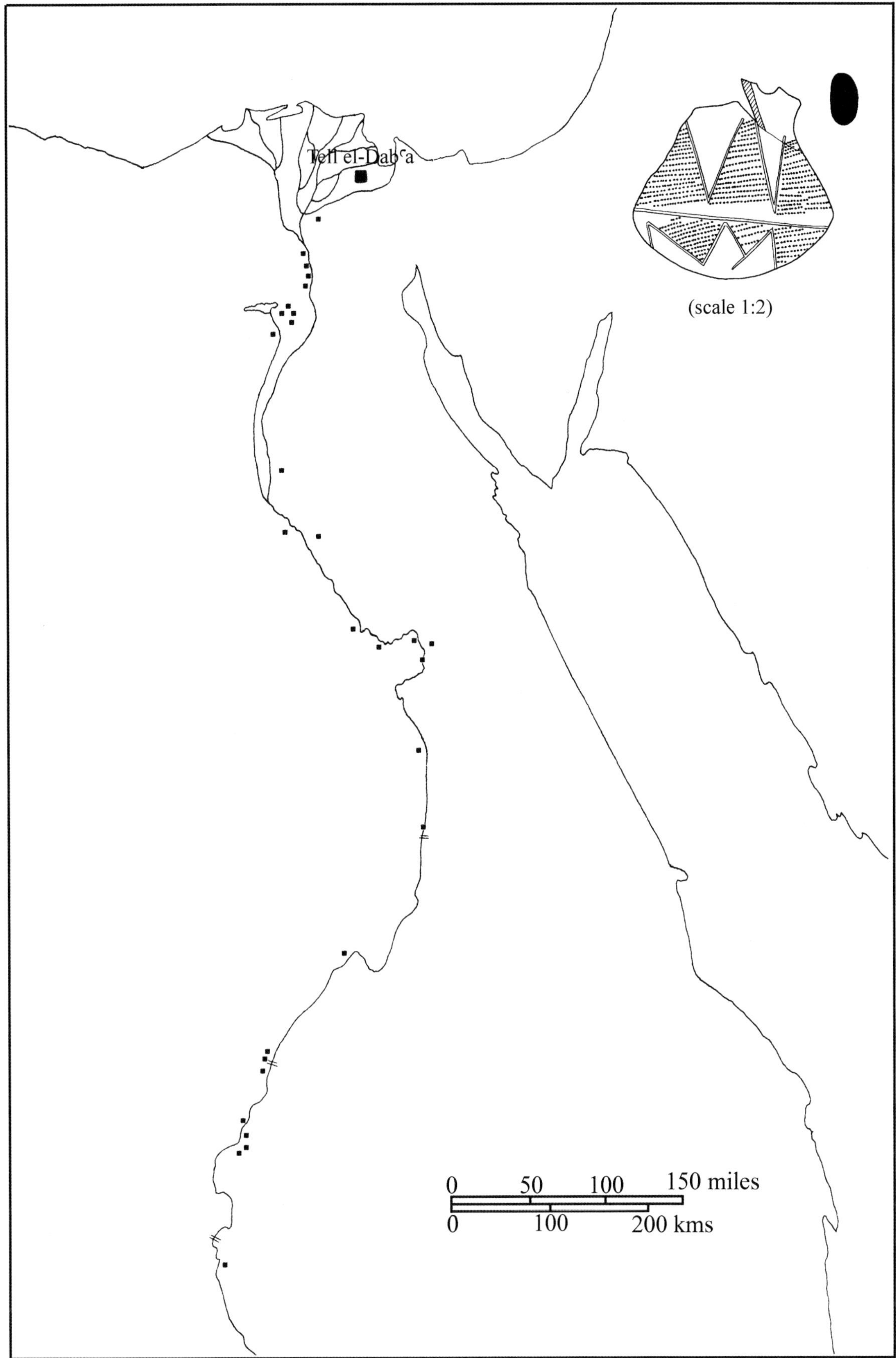

Fig. 184 Distribution and Shape Class of Type Group L.9.2

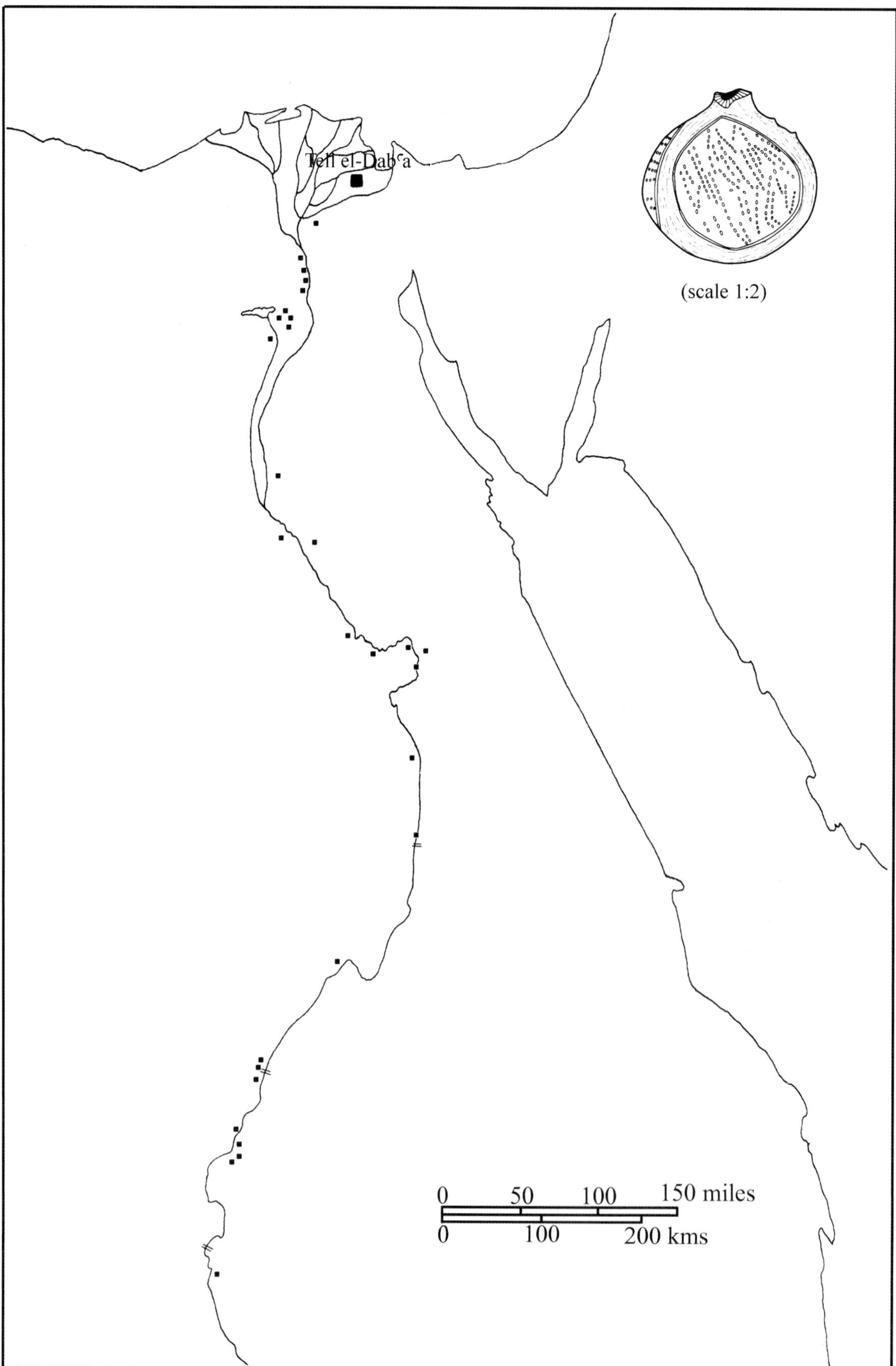

Fig. 185 Distribution and Shape Class of Type Group L.9.3

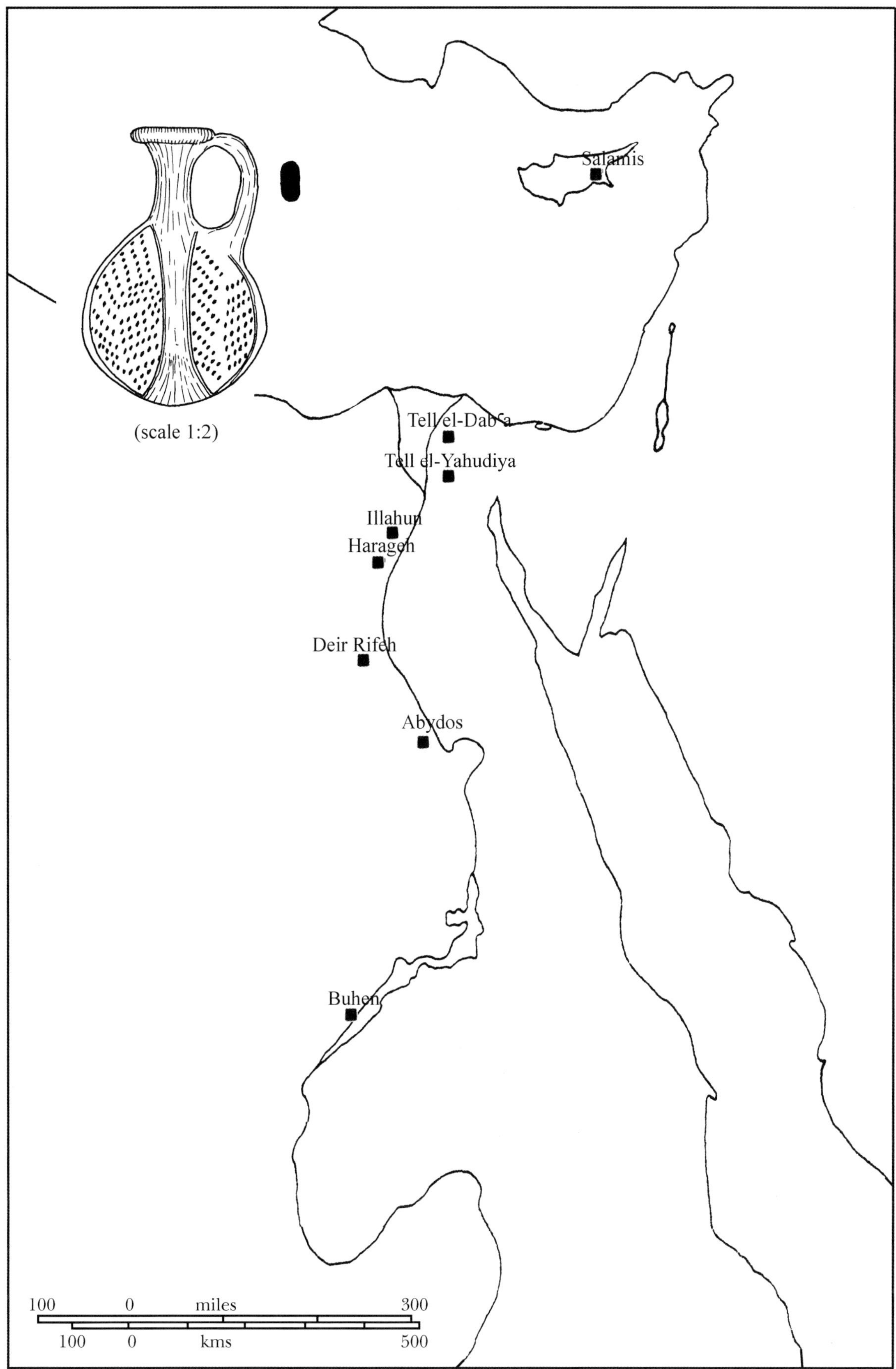

Fig. 186 Distribution and Shape Class of Type Group L.9.4

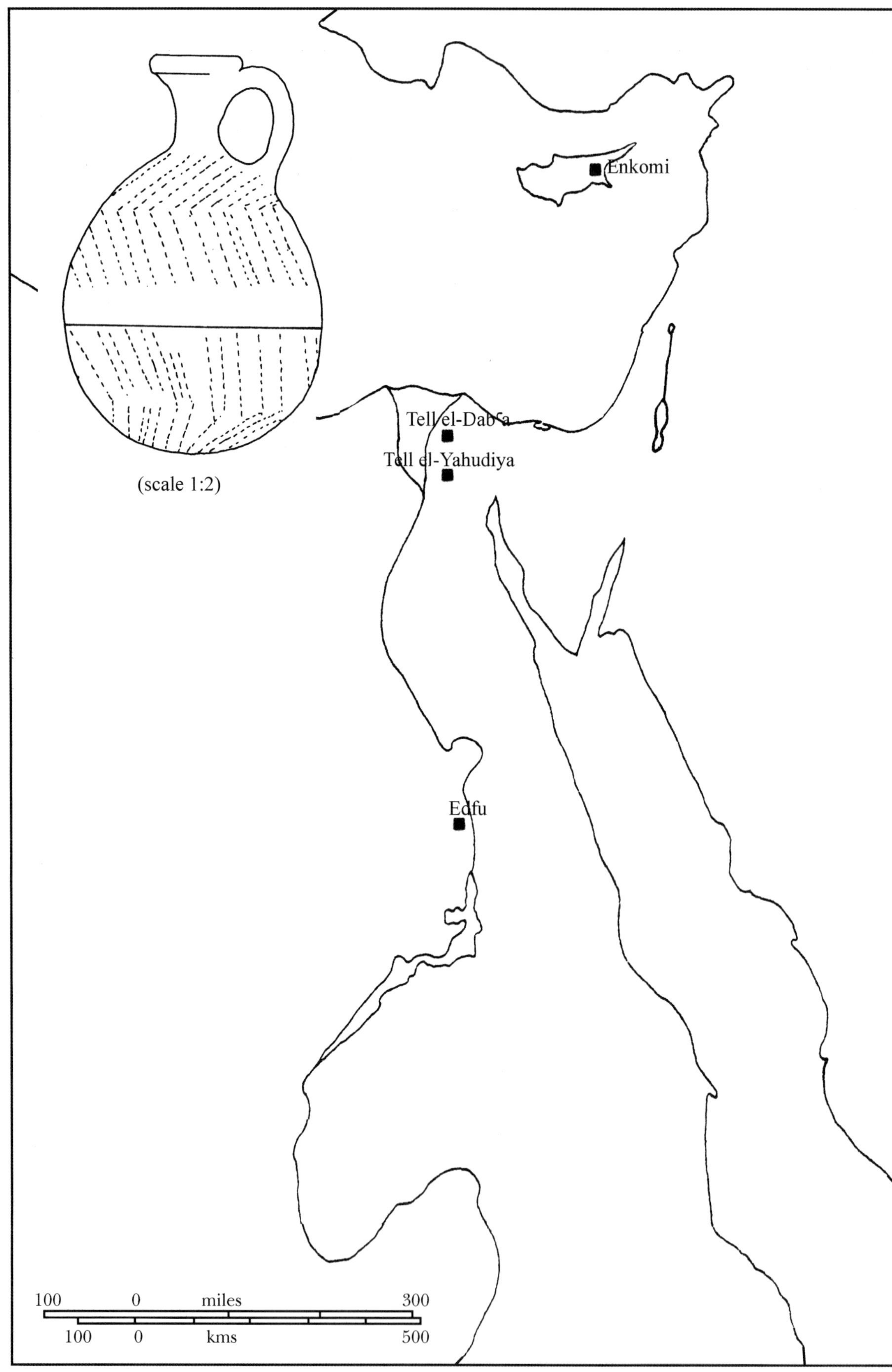

Fig. 187 Distribution and Shape Class of Type Group L.9.5

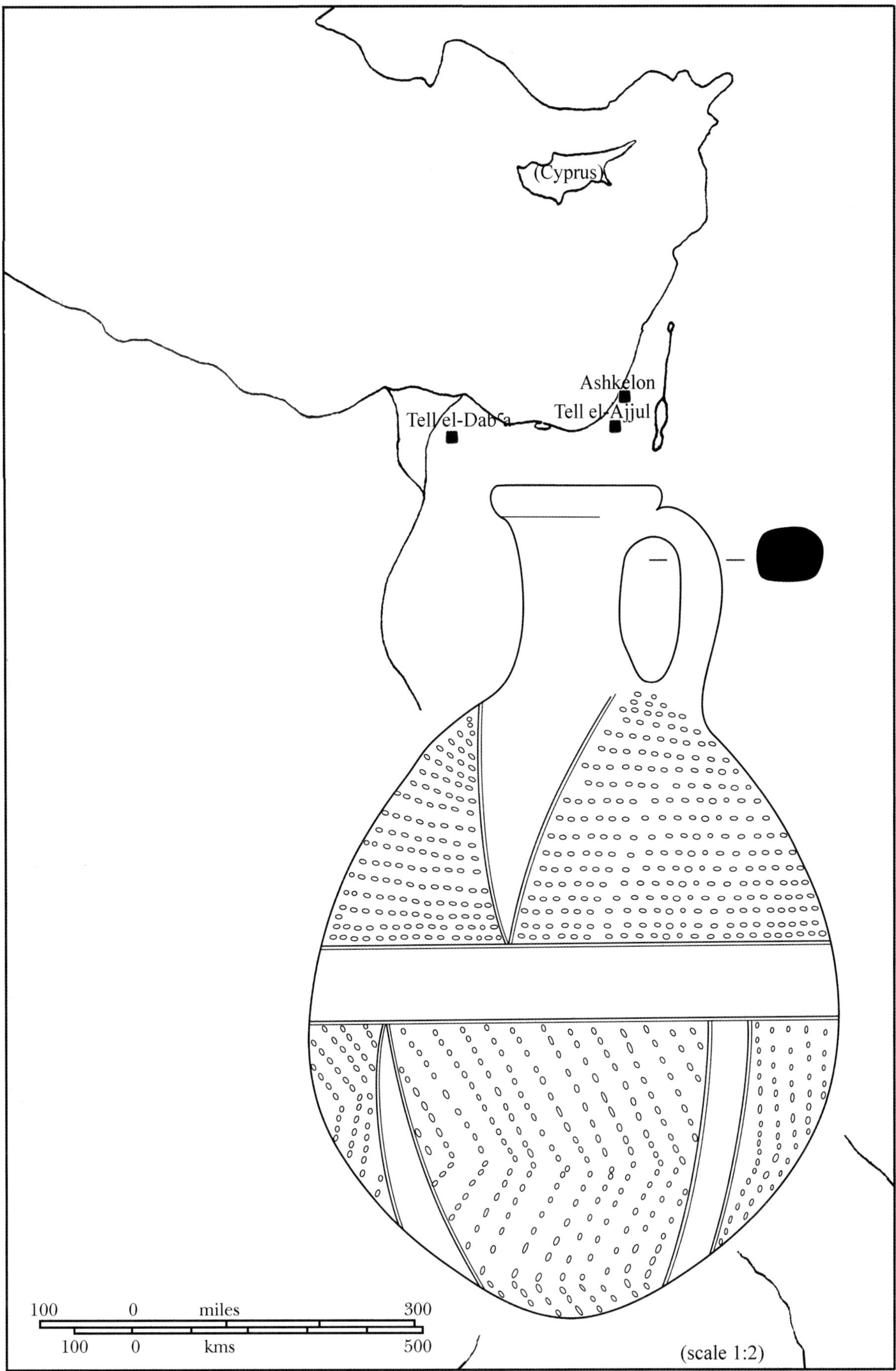

Fig. 188 Distribution and Shape Class of Type Group L.9.6

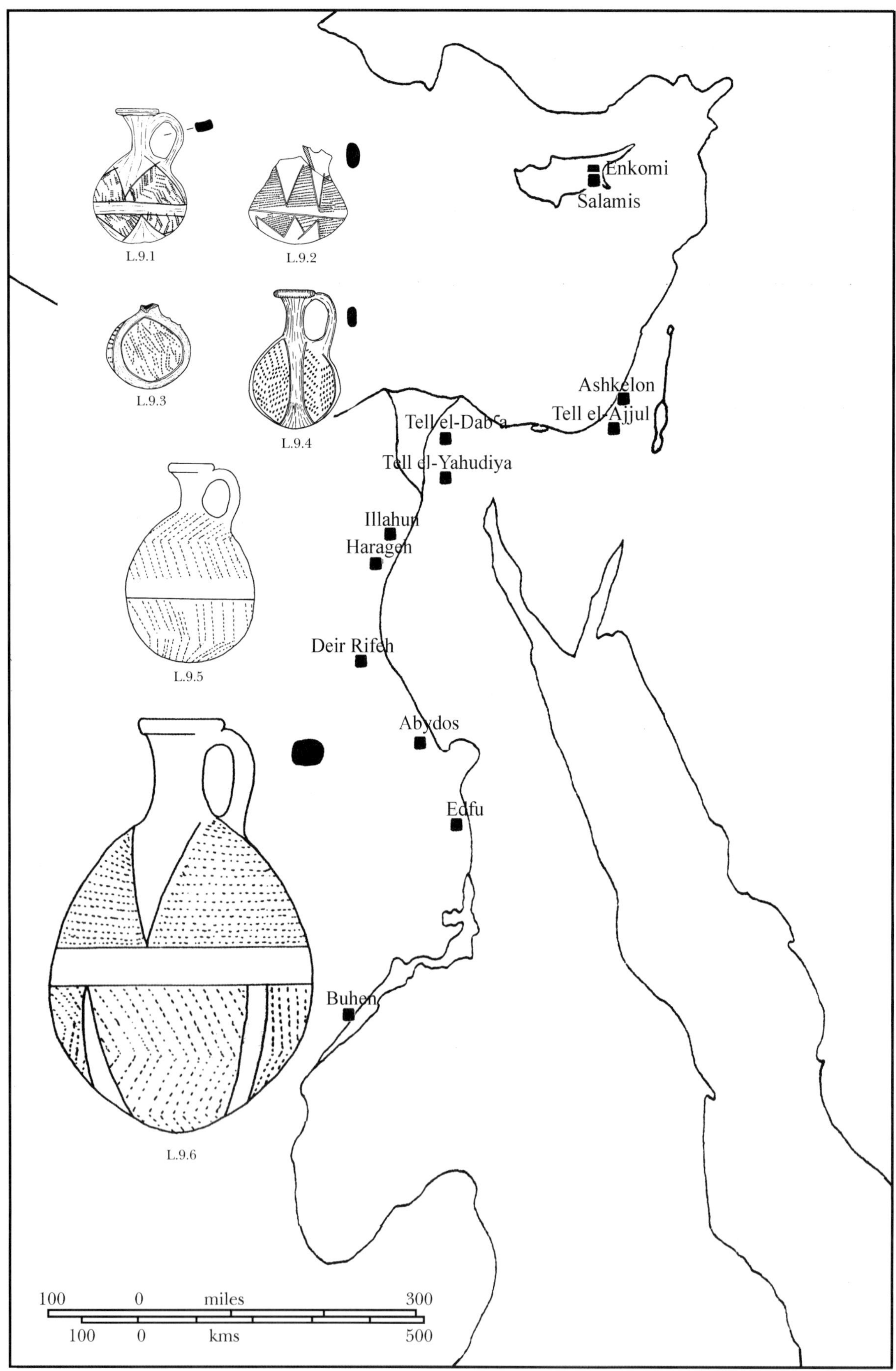

Fig. 189 Combined Distribution of Type Group L.9

Type Group L.10 (Figs. 190–192)

Quadrilobal jugs are not common, having only been found at Tell el-Dabᶜa and at Tell el-Yahudiya.[492] In their body proportions they are similar to the globular jugs of type group L.9, and like them, have rolled rims and strap handles. What sets them apart, however, is that the body is indented in such a manner as to form four lobes. The incised decoration outlines each of these lobes, and in style L.10.1a, this decoration has an incised border, and in L.10.1b it does not.

L.11. Late Egyptian XI (Cylindrical I) (Figs. 193, 194)

Three examples of this type are known, all of which are broken off at the base of the neck. They consist of Cylindrical 1 jugs with ring bases, and in the case of the two examples from Tell el-Dabᶜa (TD 2583D, 3438) are decorated with vertical chevrons (L.11.1a). Another example, of which the find location is unknown, London UC 13459,[493] is decorated with a horizontal herringbone pattern (L.11.1b).

L.12. Late Egyptian XII (Cylindrical II)

Late Egyptian Cylindrical II (Kaplan's Cylindrical 1) jugs are small, with a size range of 7.6 to 12.6 cms., and are generally around 9 cms. The bases tend to be rounded often showing no sign of carination as the vertical plane of the body is reached. The transition from the shoulder to the body is less angular than in the contemporary Palestinian types (Kaplan's Cylindrical 2, above group D.6.3). Cylindrical II jugs have rolled (which are sometimes undercut), or everted rims, single strap handles and decoration restricted to the vertical plane of the body.

Type Group L.12.1 (Figs. 195, 201)

This group is defined through the presence of a single example from Tell el-Dabᶜa (TD 212) and a fragment from Kahun.[494] They are somewhat narrower than the other Cylindrical 1 jugs, have a sharper shoulder and are unusually decorated with a series of standing triangles (TD 212) or alternating standing and pendant triangles (Kahun). Another incomplete vessel from Tell el-Yahudiya, with undelineated standing triangles (?) may also belong with this group.[495]

Type Group L.12.2 (Figs. 196–201)

This group comprises the classic Cylindrical 1 jug as defined by Kaplan and is relatively common.[496] The various decorative schemes associated with this type comprise L.12.2a horizontal chevrons, found at Tell el-Dabᶜa,[497] Tell el-Yahudiya;[498] Galinoporni[499] and elsewhere on Cyprus;[500] L.12.2b vertical chevrons known from Tell el-Yahudiya,[501] and Gibeon;[502] L.12.2c oblique striations, known from Tell el-Yahudiya;[503] L.12.2d horizontal striations found at Tell el-Dabᶜa, Tell el-Yahudiya,[504] Mostagedda,[505] Deir el-Ballas,[506] Aniba,[507] and Enkomi;[508] and L.12.2e with an upper zone of oblique lines and a lower one of chevrons, so far only known from an unknown site in Egypt.[509]

Two vessels, one from Tell el-Dabᶜa (TD 227), the other from Egypt, site unknown,[510] have distinctly flat bases, but whether this will turn out to be a distinct type or simply an accident of production must await further excavations.

L.13. Late Egyptian XIII (Combed Tell el-Yahudiya Ware)

During the latest phase of the Hyksos Period, Tell el-Yahudiya ware developed into its final decorative phase, a series of incised grooves, in which no pig-

---

[492] Oxford Ashmolean E.3496. Petrie, *Hyksos and Israelite Cities,* 11, 15, pl. viiia.65; London UC 13474. Petrie, *Hyksos and Israelite Cities,* 11, 15, pl. viiia.64, Kaplan, *Tell el-Yahudiyeh Ware,* fig. 22a–d.

[493] Kaplan, *Tell el-Yahudiyeh Ware,* fig. 6b.

[494] Manchester 461c. Kaplan, *Tell el-Yahudiyeh Ware,* fig. 8b.

[495] Oxford Ashmolean 1872.993. Kaplan, *Tell el-Yahudiyeh Ware,* fig. 8a.

[496] Kaplan, *Tell el-Yahudiyeh Ware,* figs. 4a–6a, 6c–d, 6f, 7a–f.

[497] See below and add Petrie, *Hyksos and Israelite Cities,* 35–47, pls. xxxixb.3.

[498] Oxford Ashmolean E.3509, 3510, Petrie, *Hyksos and Israelite Cities,* 11, pls. viiia.66, vii.5.

[499] Kaplan, *Tell el-Yahudiyeh Ware,* fig. 7d.

[500] London BM 1967/11-3/9. Kaplan, *Tell el-Yahudiyeh Ware,* fig. 6d.Nicosia, Cyprus Museum A.1448. Buchholz and Karageorghis, *Prehistoric Greece and Cyprus,* pl. 417 no. 1537.

[501] Manchester 3445. Petrie, *Hyksos and Israelite Cities,* 11, pl. vii.26.

[502] Jerusalem, Rockefeller Museum 45.122. Kaplan, *Tell el-Yahudiyeh Ware,* fig. 7b.

[503] Brussels E.2571. Petrie, *Hyksos and Israelite Cities,* 11, pl. vii.13; Kaplan, *Tell el-Yahudiyeh Ware,* fig. 7c.

[504] Oxford Ashmolean 1888.269. Griffith, *The Antiquities of Tell el-Yahudiyeh,* 40, pl. 9.6.

[505] Oxford Ashmolean 1930.486. Brunton, *Mostagedda,* 117, pl. lxxi, lxxii.60.

[506] Philadelphia UM E.1042. Kaplan, *Tell el-Yahudiyeh Ware,* fig. 4c.

[507] Steindorff, *Aniba II,* 38–40, 125–137, 194, pl. 86.45b5.

[508] Paris, Louvre AM 2582. Schaeffer, *Missions en Chypre,* 68–72, fig. 30.4, pl. 31c.

[509] London UC 13457. Kaplan, *Tell el-Yahudiyeh Ware,* fig. 4f.

[510] London UC 13455. Kaplan, *Tell el-Yahudiyeh Ware,* fig. 4a.

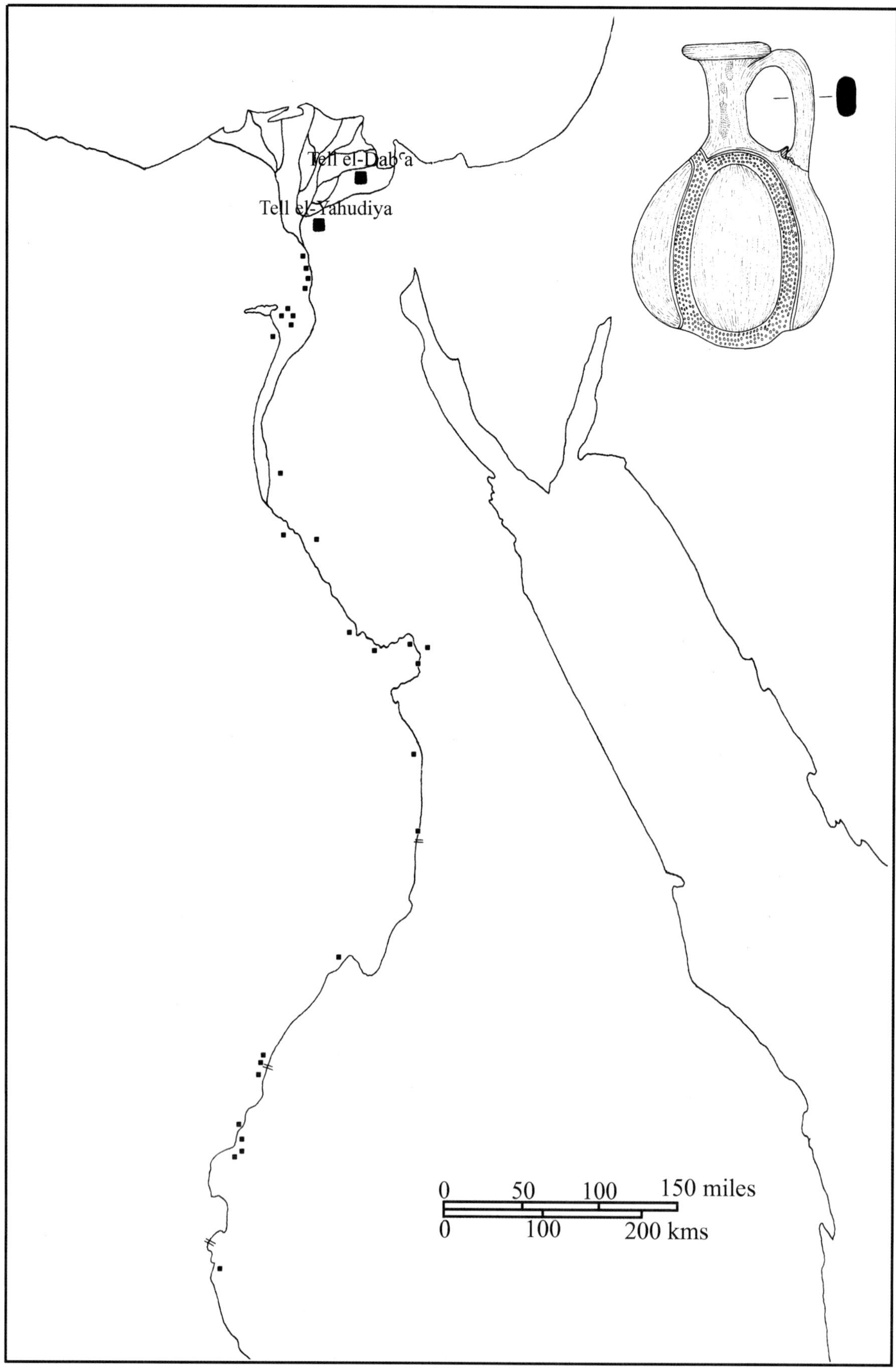

Fig. 190 Distribution and Shape Class of Type Group L.10.1a

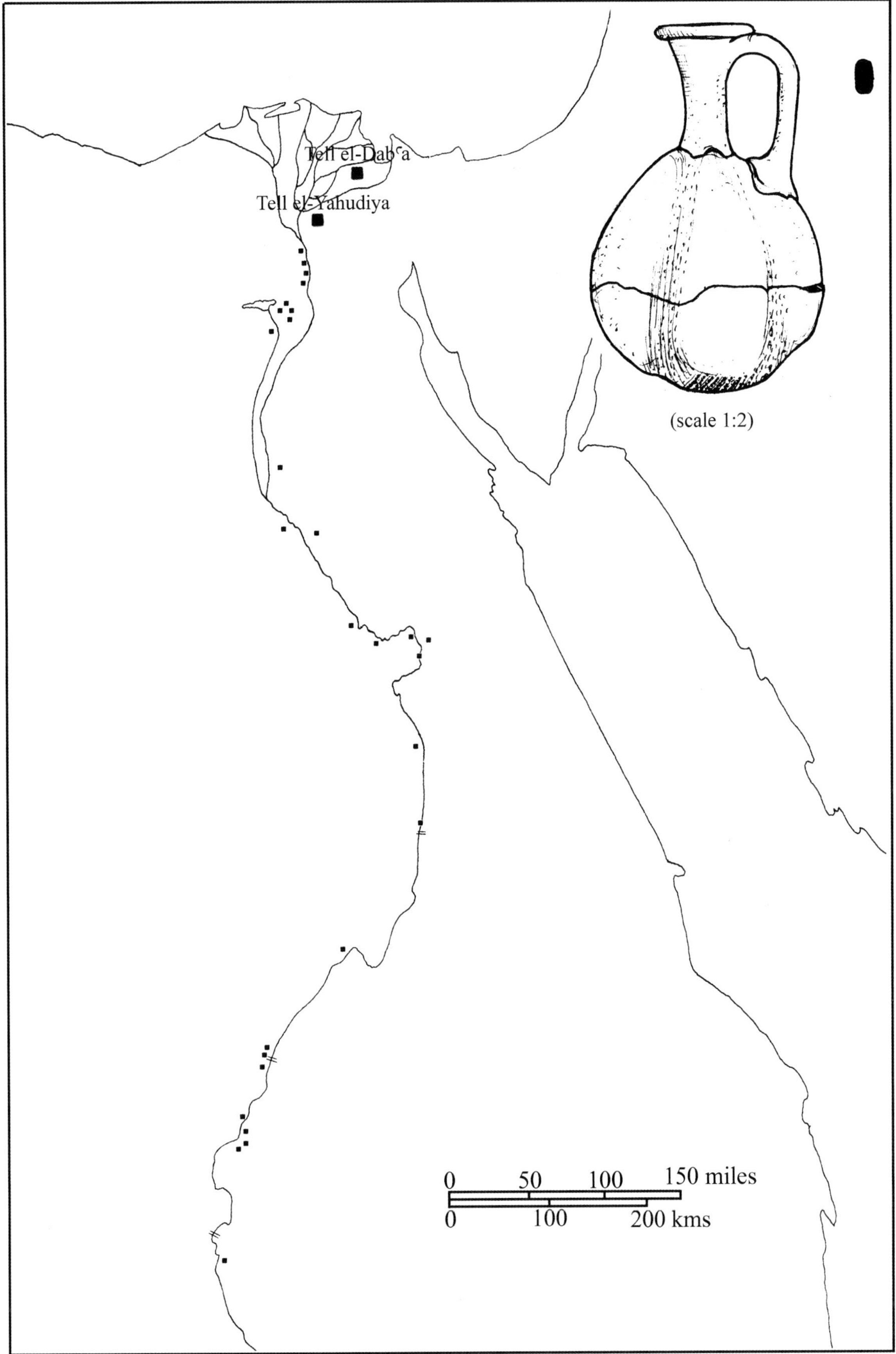

Fig. 191 Distribution and Shape Class of Type Group L.10.1b

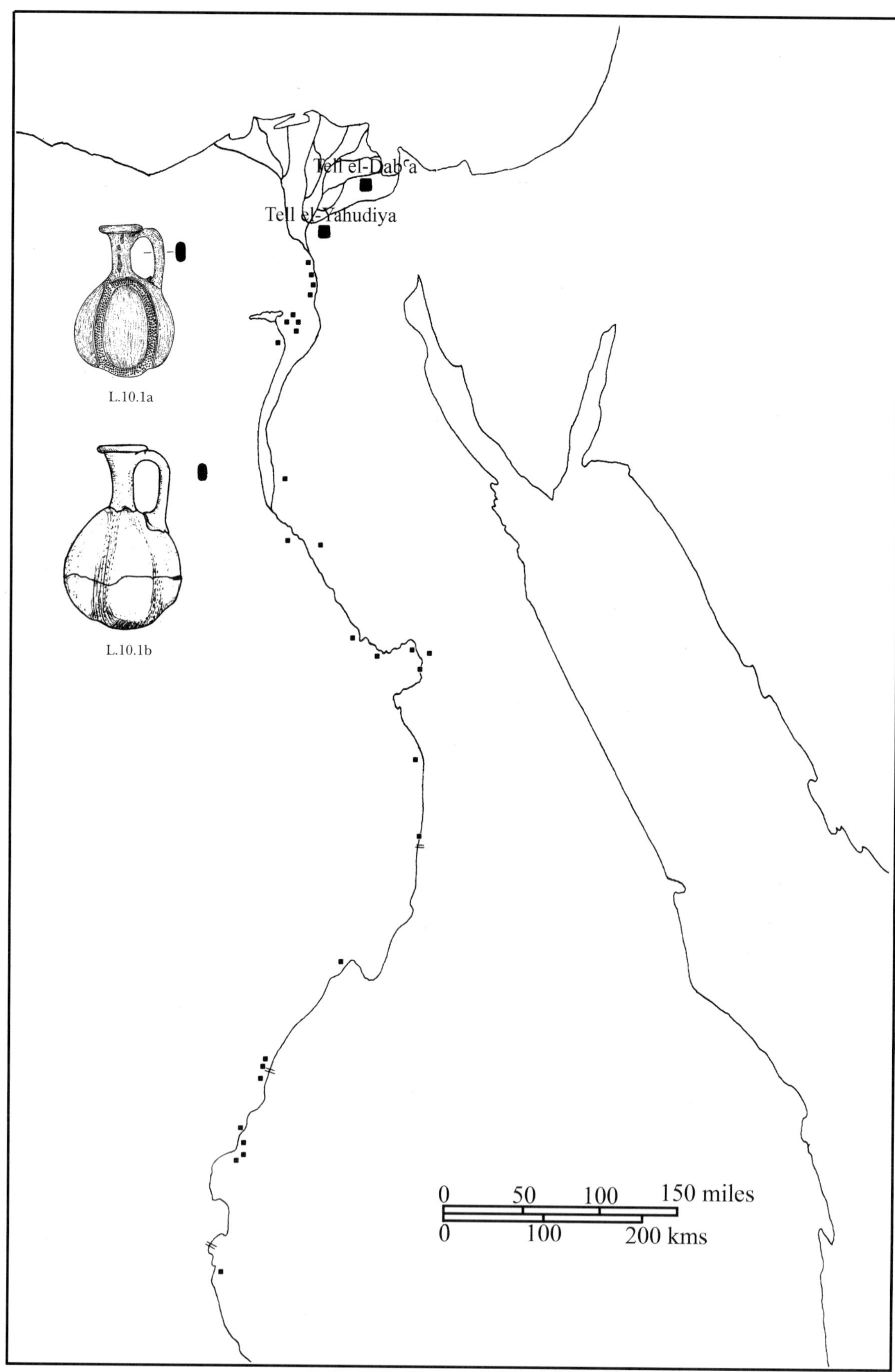

Fig. 192 Combined Distribution of Type Group L.10

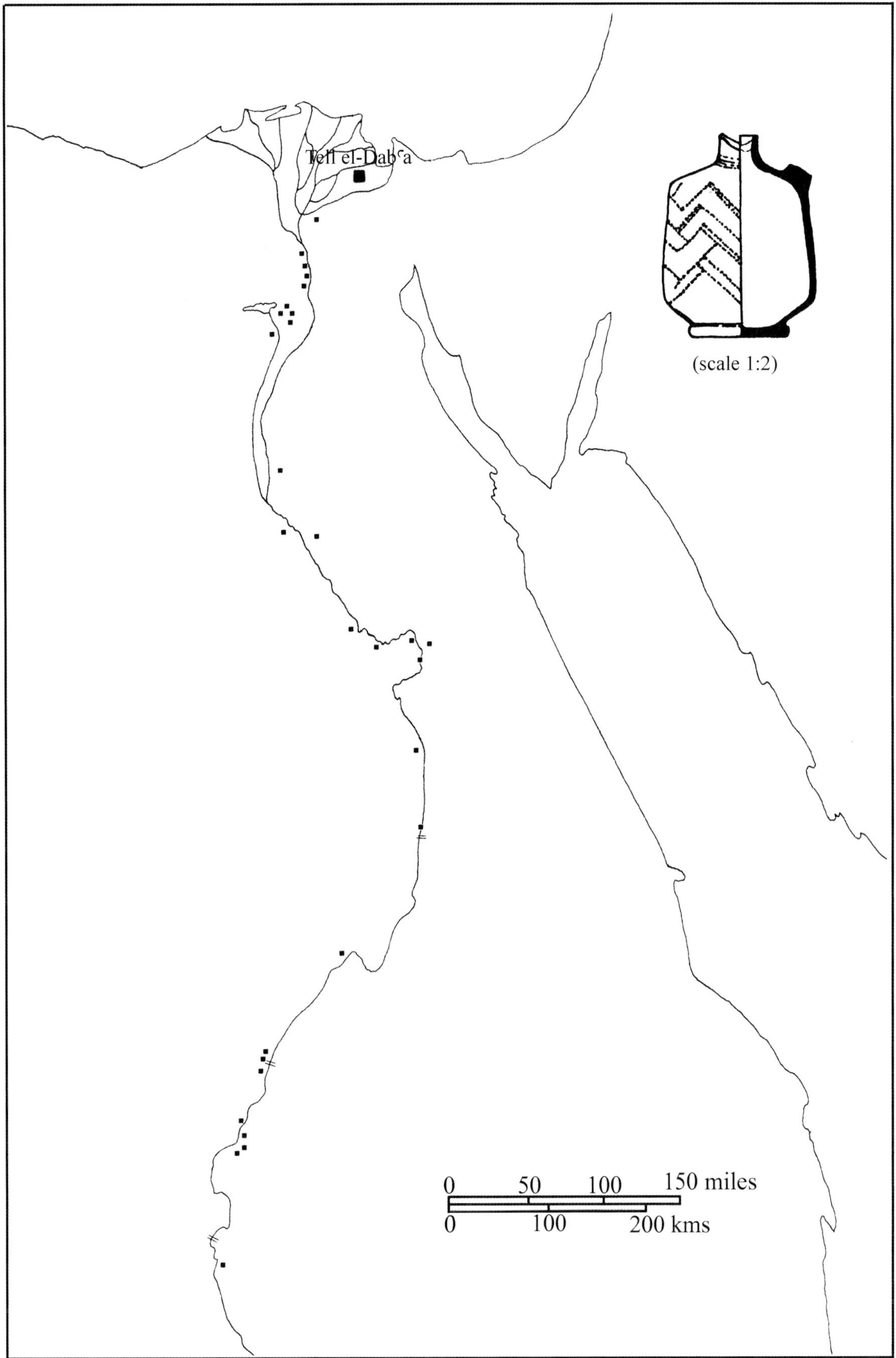

Fig. 193 Distribution and Shape Class of Type Group L.11.1a

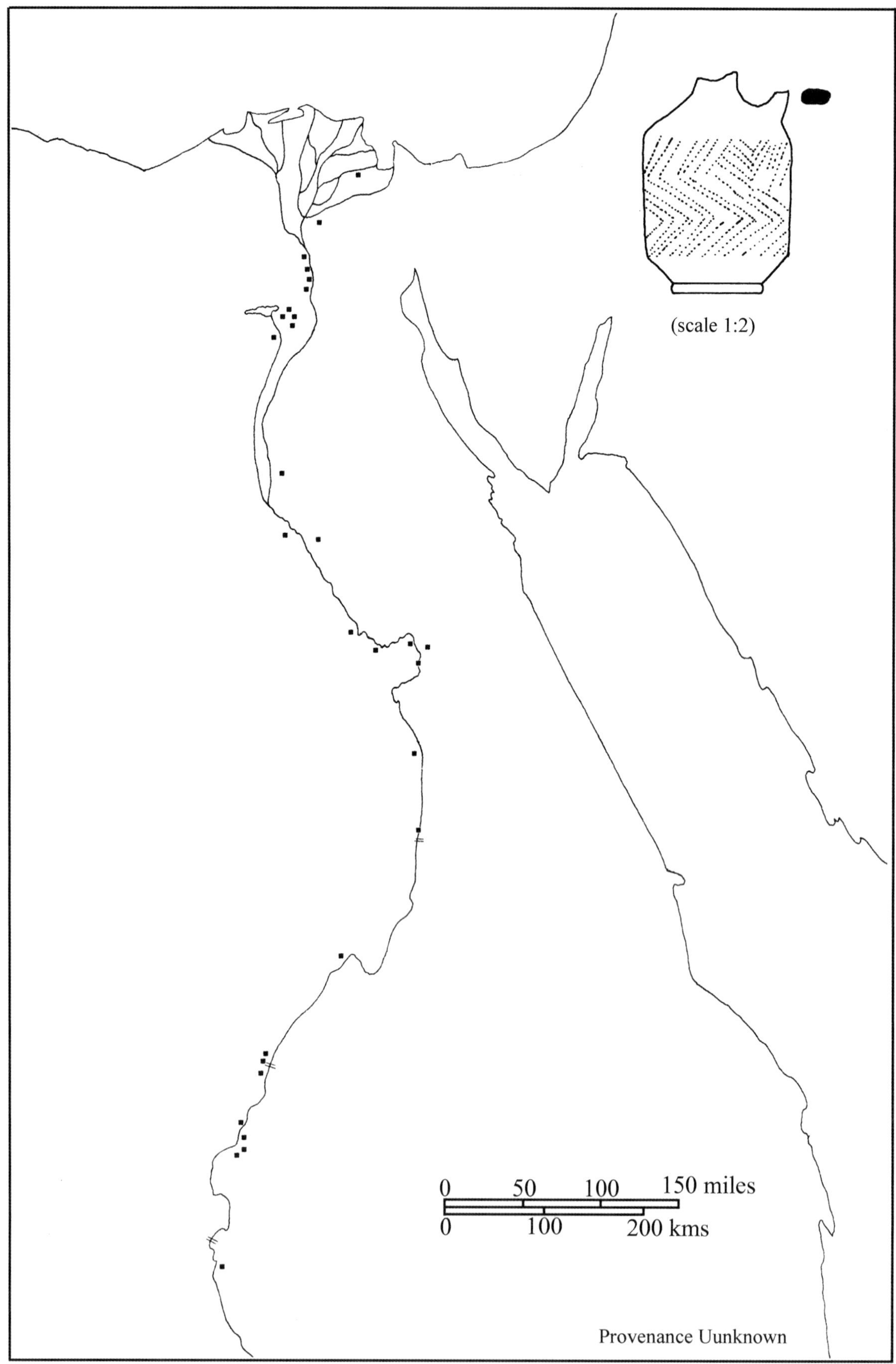

Fig. 194 Distribution and Shape Class of Type Group L.11.1b

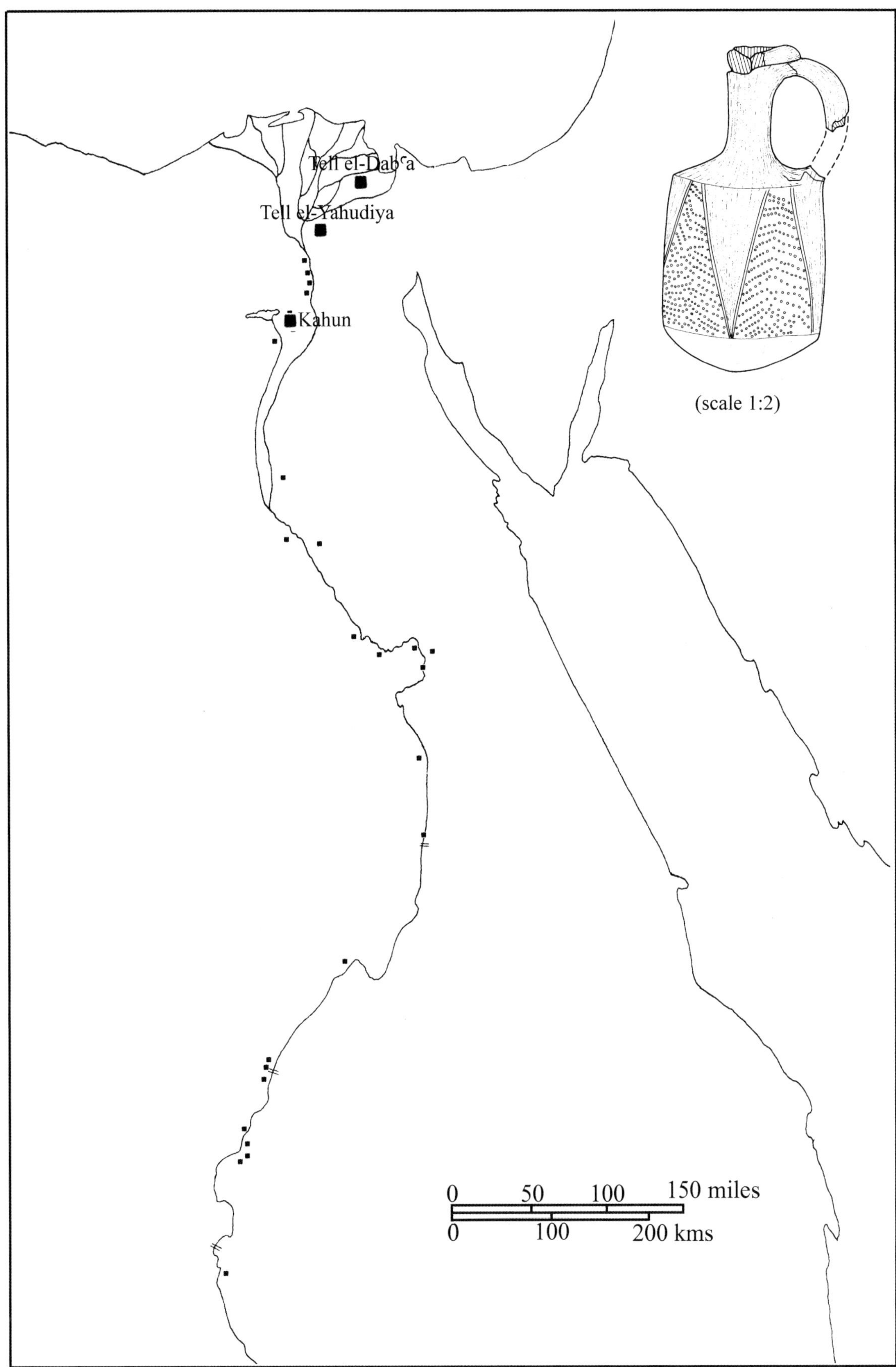

Fig. 195 Distribution and Shape Class of Type Group L.12.1

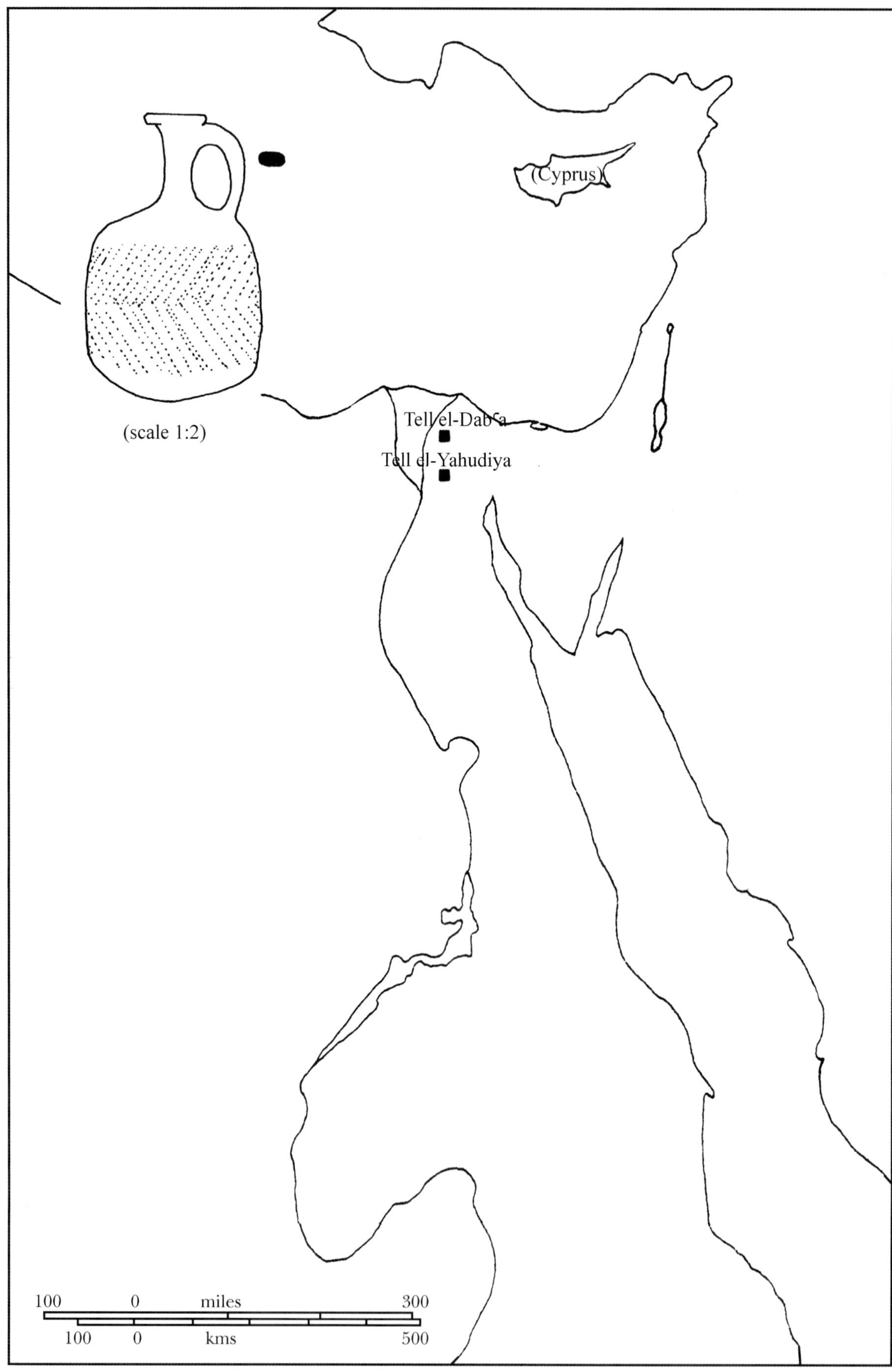

Fig. 196 Distribution and Shape Class of Type Group L.12.2a

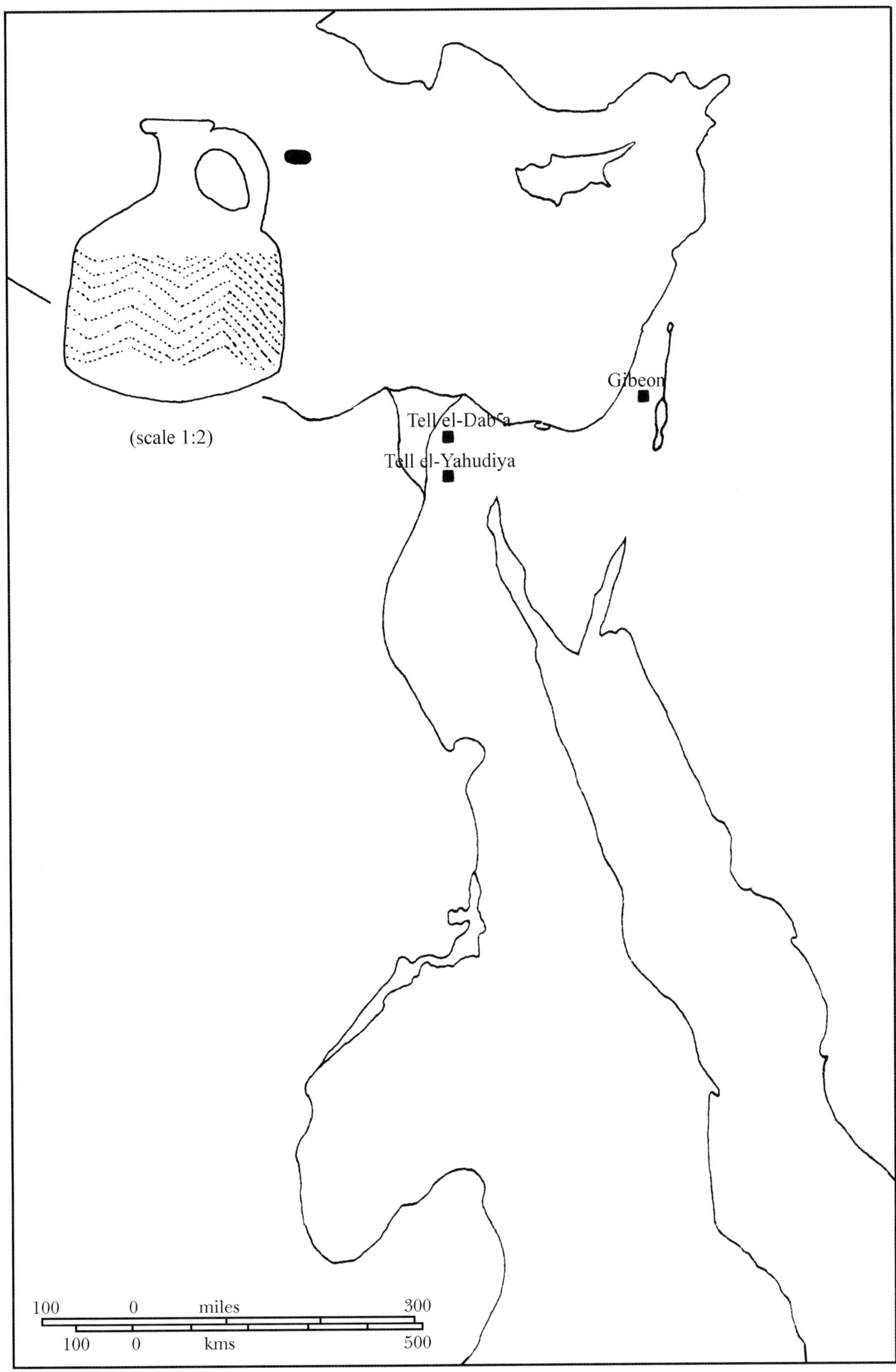

Fig. 197 Distribution and Shape Class of Type Group L.12.2b

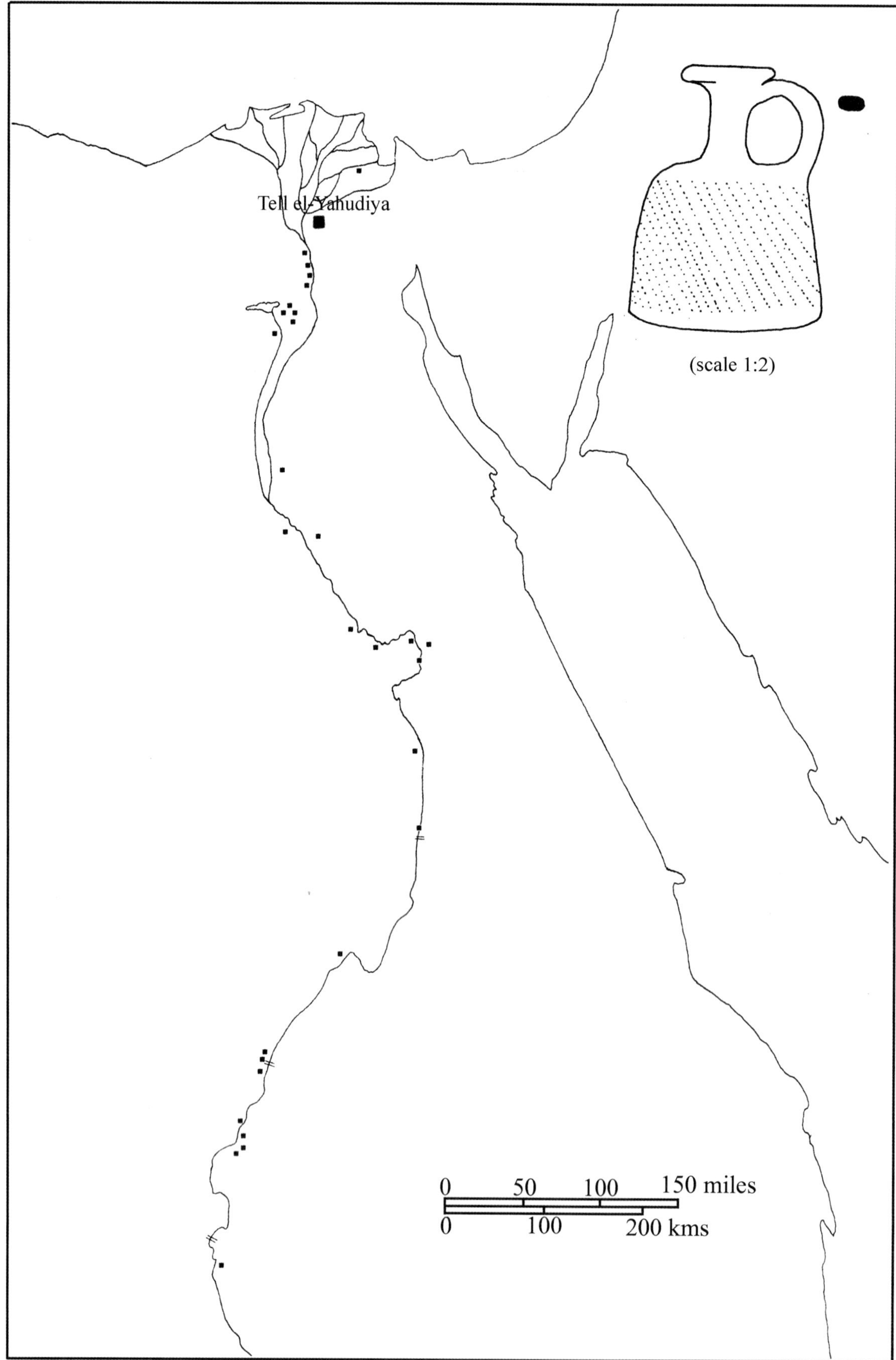

Fig. 198 Distribution and Shape Class of Type Group L.12.2c

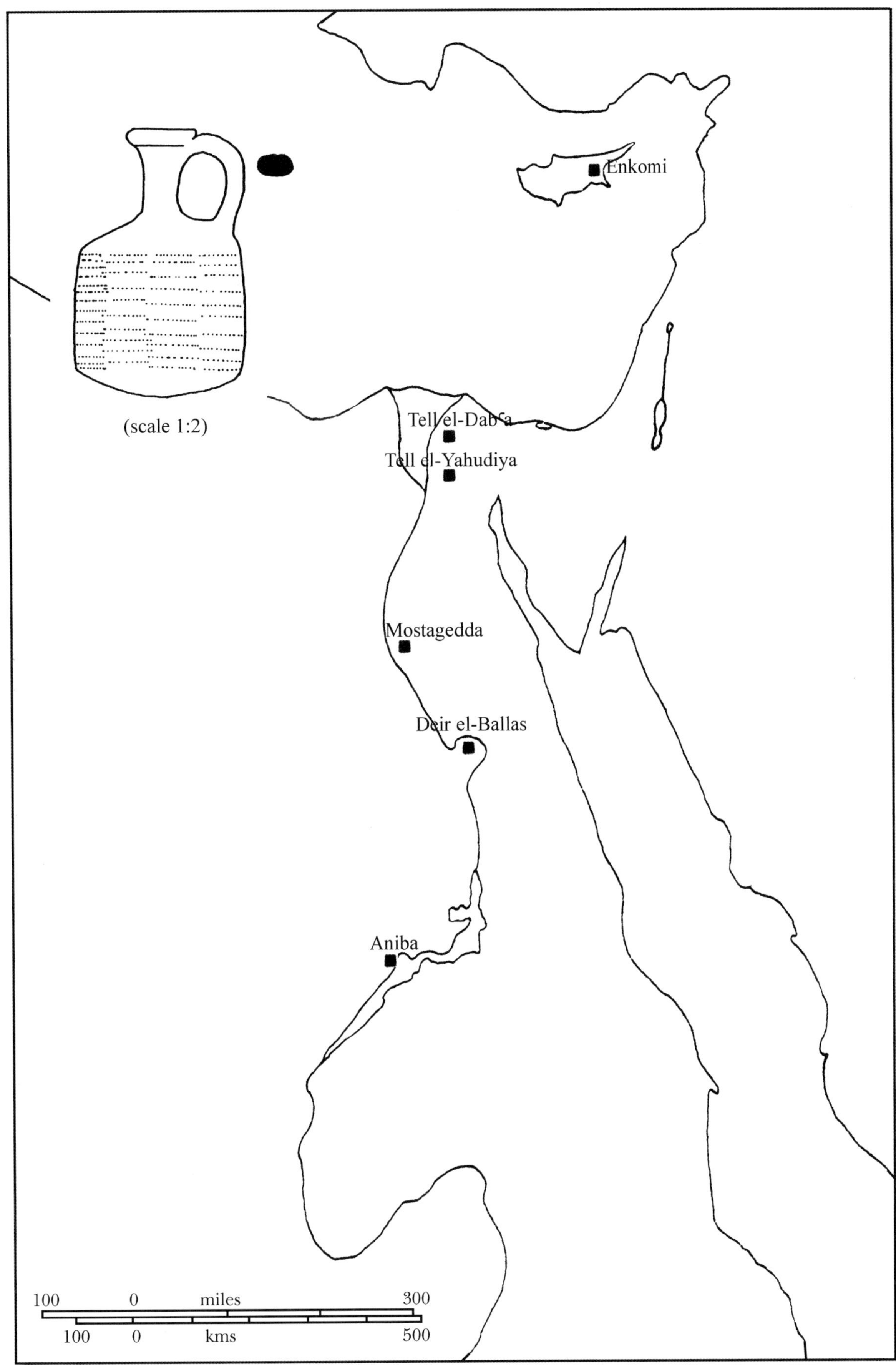

Fig. 199 Distribution and Shape Class of Type Group L.12.2d

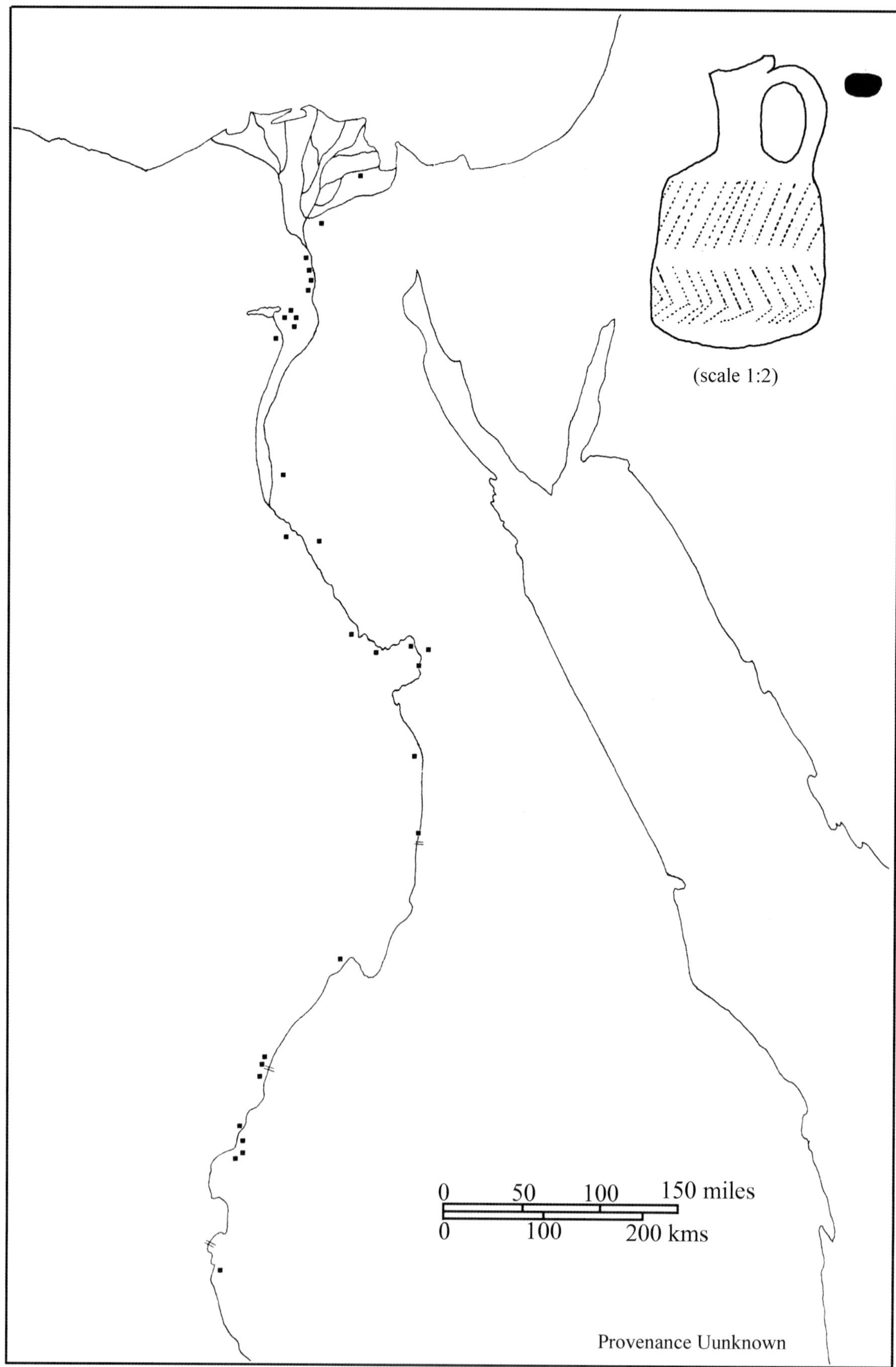

Fig. 200 Distribution and Shape Class of Type Group L.12.2e

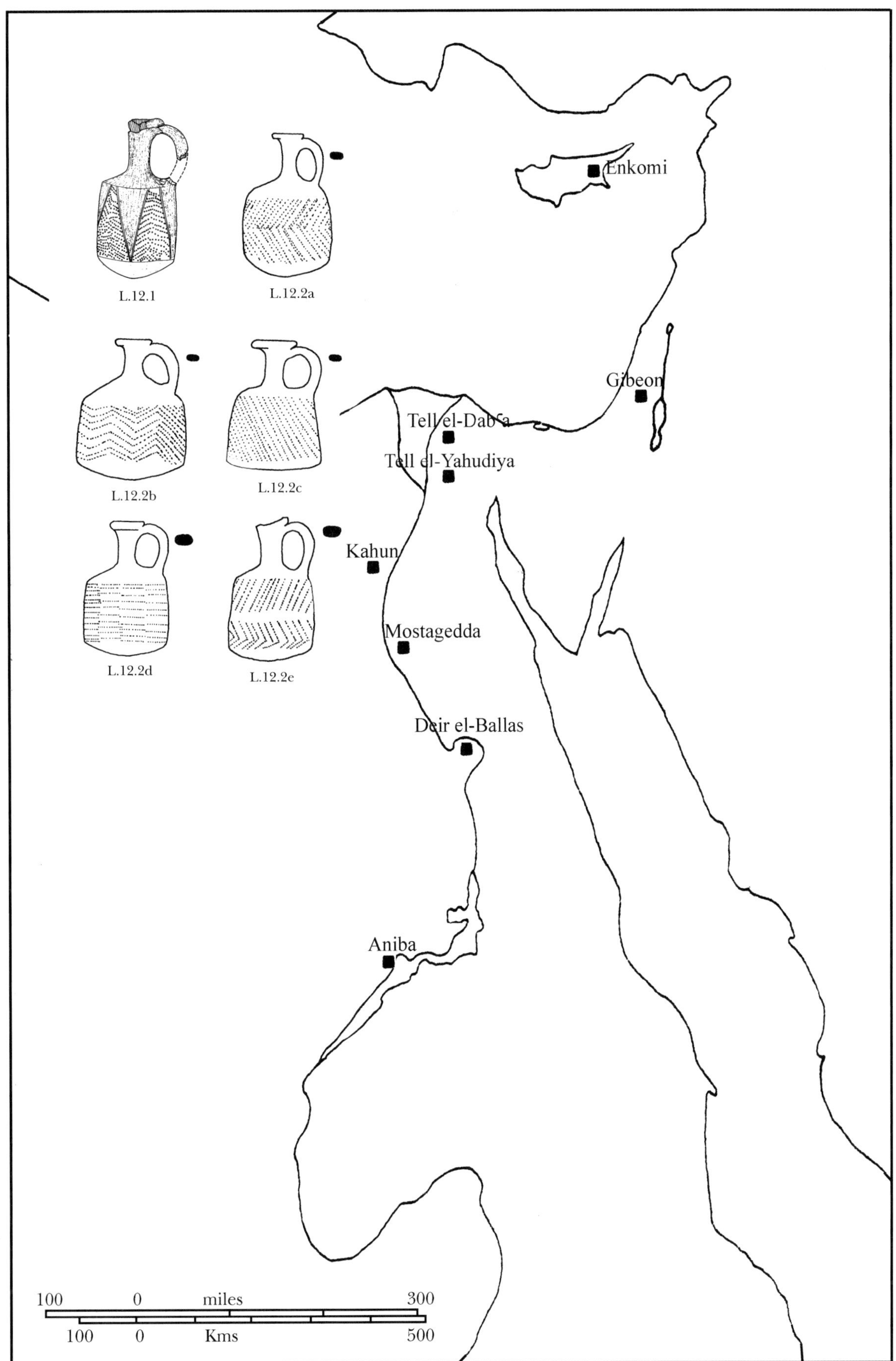

Fig. 201 Combined Distribution of Type Group L.12

ment was added, running horizontally around the body of the vessel, the grooving almost certainly being made with a comb whilst the vessel was still on the wheel. Whilst they were undoubtedly made in Egypt, the vagaries of archaeological excavation are such that most of the extant complete examples were found in Cyprus. Where such vessels can be closely dated it is apparent that the vessels with bands of incised grooves are earlier than those in which the entire surface is combed. The following shape groups exist:

Type Group L.13.1 Piriform (Figs. 202, 206)

Piriform vessels with combed decoration are so far only known from Cyprus,[511] and if the vessels TD 6128G, 6489T, 6783G, have been correctly assigned to this type, Tell el-Dabᶜa. They have a rolled rim, strap handles and disc bases.

Type Group L.13.2 Biconical (Figs. 203, 206)

This is the most common form of combed Tell el-Yahudiya. Such vessels have a rolled rim, strap handle, a rounded biconial to piriform body and a ring or disc base. The horizontal grooves are separated by a reserved band at the mid-point of the vessel. Whilst it is possible to sub-divide these vessels into a distinctly biconical and a distinctly piriform shape, the decoration into an upper and a lower zone owes its antecedents to the biconical rather than the piriform 2a shapes. Examples of group L.13.2 are known from Tell el-Dabᶜa, Tell el-Yahudiya,[512] Enkomi,[513] and many others from Cyprus.[514]

Type Group L.13.3 Globular (Figs. 204, 206)

Globular vessels with combed decoration, which also have a reserved zone around the mid point of the vessel are known from Enkomi,[515] and elsewhere in Cyprus.[516]

Type Group L.13.4 Cylindrical (Figs. 205, 206)

Cylindrical vessels with grooved decoration are rare. At present they are only known from Sedment,[517] and possibly Tell el-Dabᶜa (TD 6857G).

L.14. Late Egyptian XIV Miniature Jugs

In addition to the above categories, there are a number of Tell el-Yahudiya jugs known which are somewhat small in scale and can probably be seen as miniature jugs.

Type Group L.14.1 (Fig. 207)

Closely related to the piriform 2a jugs of group I3 are a series of squat vessels, which are smaller in size being approximately 6–8 cms. high with piriform to spherical bodies, which are known from Tell el-Dabᶜa, Tell el-Yahudiya[518] and Kerma.[519] They may be divided into two groups, one having a ring base, L.14.1, and the other a button, L.14.2. Like the slender, taller Piriform 2a vessels the decoration invariably consists only of lozenges (gores), usually three or four, filled with a herringbone pattern of incised dots. The comb used for this generally had eight or more points, and the area of incision is usually delineated. Burnishing occurs on the unincised areas.

Type group L.14.1 comprise those squat piriform vessels with rolled rims, strap handles, piriform to spherical bodies and ring bases. Two decorative schemes are associated with this type comprising four (L.14.1a) or three (L.14.1b) delinated infilled lozenges.

Type group L.14.2 (Fig. 208)

Type group L.14.2 is similar to group L.14.1, but the jugs of this group have distinct button bases. At present the only decorative scheme associated with these vessels are four (L.14.2a) or three (L.14.2b) infilled lozenges.

Type Group L.14.3 (Fig. 209)

Group L.14.3 is represented by a single model vessel of unknown provenance. It has a kettle rim, strap handle and distinctly pointed base. Decoration consists of three undelineated bands of incisions made with a four-toothed comb.[520]

Type Group LI4.4 (Fig. 210)

Type group L.14.4 consists of two incomplete pots from Tell el-Dabᶜa, TD 7247A and TD 296, which although piriform in shape are also decorated in

[511] Kaplan, *Tell el-Yahudiyeh Ware*, figs. 118b, 120b.

[512] Oxford Ashmolean E.3498, Petrie, *Hyksos and Israelite Cities*, 11, pl. viii.52, Kaplan, *Tell el-Yahudiyeh Ware*, fig. 121a.

[513] London BM Greek and Roman Dept 97/4-1/1307, Murray *et al. Excavations in Cyprus*, 6, fig. 9; 97/4-1/1308. Kaplan, *Tell el-Yahudiyeh Ware*, fig. 119b.

[514] Kaplan, *Tell el-Yahudiyeh Ware*, figs. 119c, 120a.

[515] London BM Greek and Roman Dept 1921/6-17/1. Kaplan *Tell el-Yahudiyeh Ware*, fig. 117e.

[516] Nicosia Cyprus Museum A.1444. Kaplan, *Tell el-Yahudiyeh Ware*, fig. 118a.

[517] Oxford Ashmolean 1921.1390. Petrie and Brunton, *Sedment II*, pl. xlv.64, xlvi, Kaplan, *Tell el-Yahudiyeh Ware*, fig. 117d.

[518] Kaplan, *Tell el-Yahudiyeh Ware*, fig. 57d.

[519] Kaplan, *Tell el-Yahudiyeh Ware*, fig. 57e.

[520] Stockholm MM E.1064. Kaplan, *Tell el-Yahudiyeh Ware*, fig. 117a.

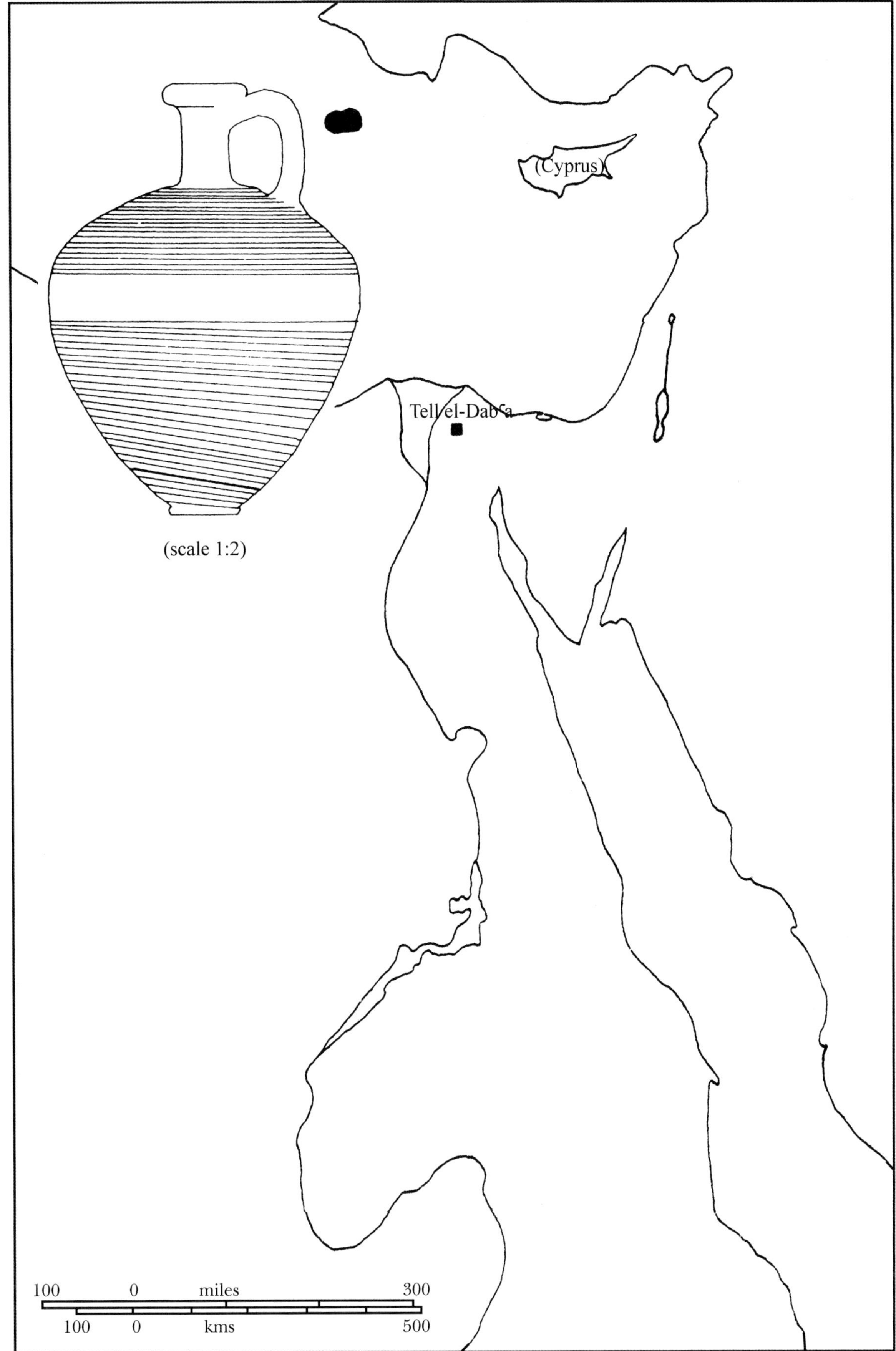

Fig. 202 Distribution and Shape Class of Type Group L.13.1

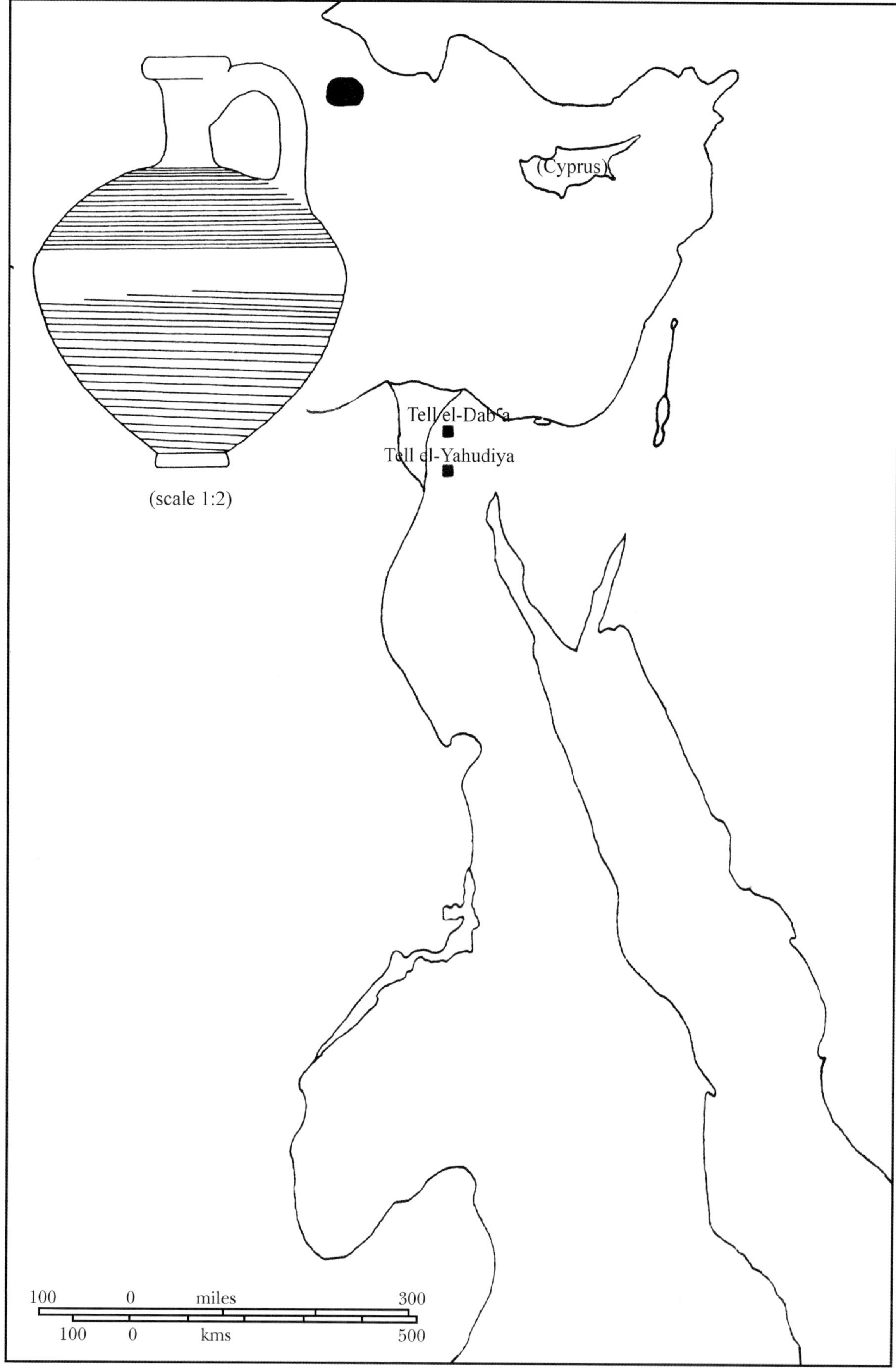

Fig. 203 Distribution and Shape Class of Type Group L.13.2

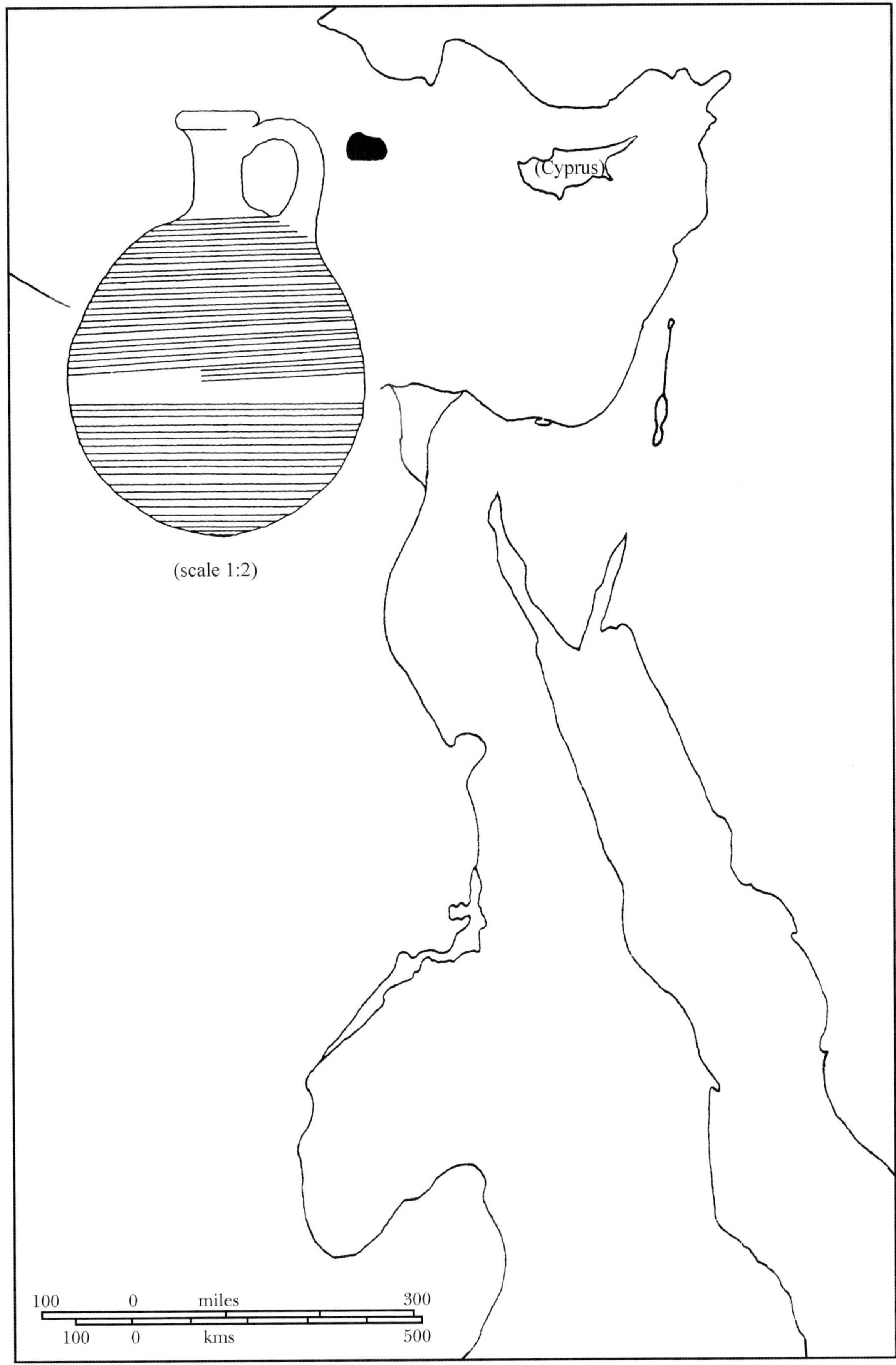

Fig. 204 Distribution and Shape Class of Type Group L.13.3

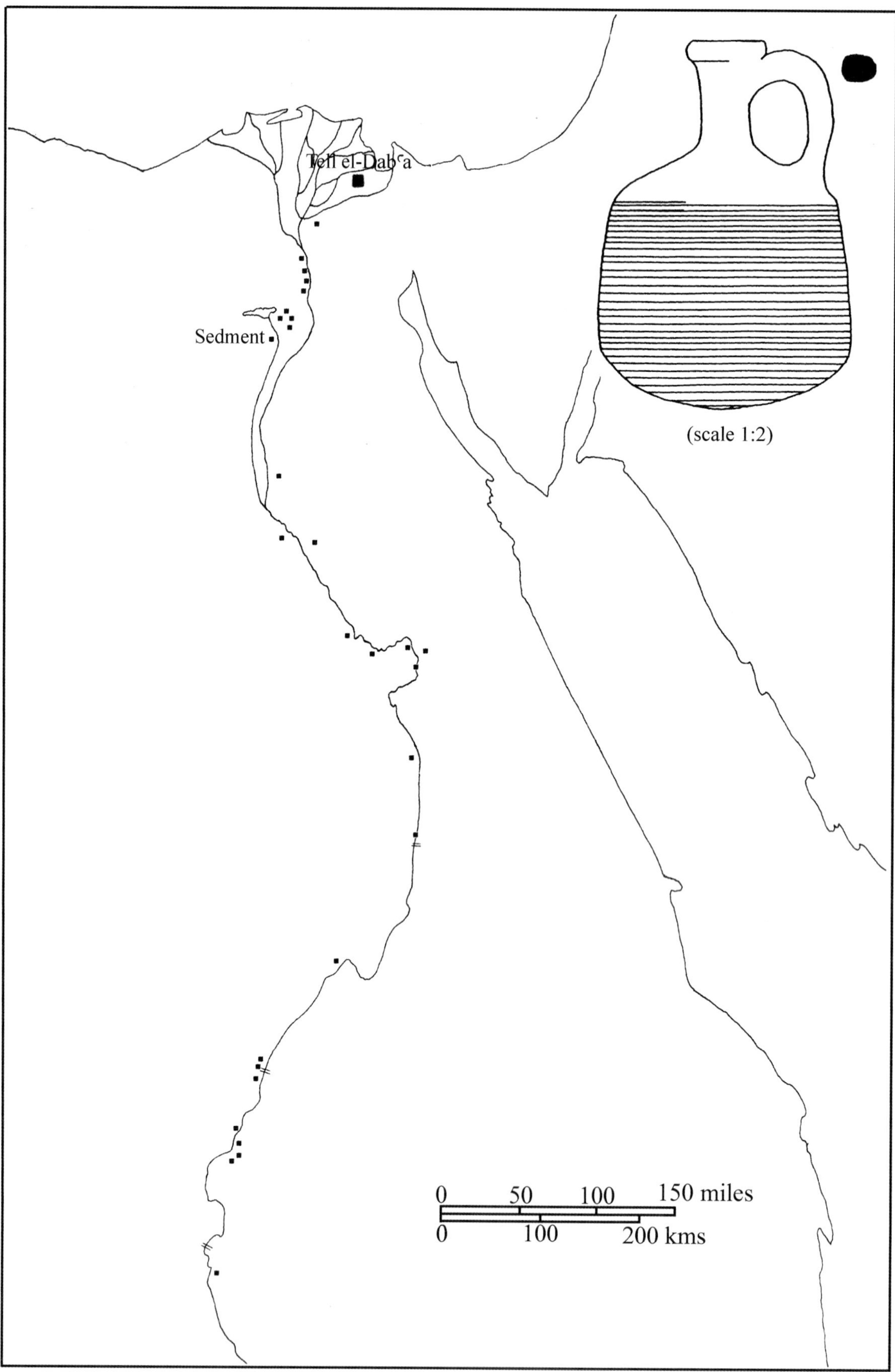

Fig. 205 Distribution and Shape Class of Type Group L.13.4

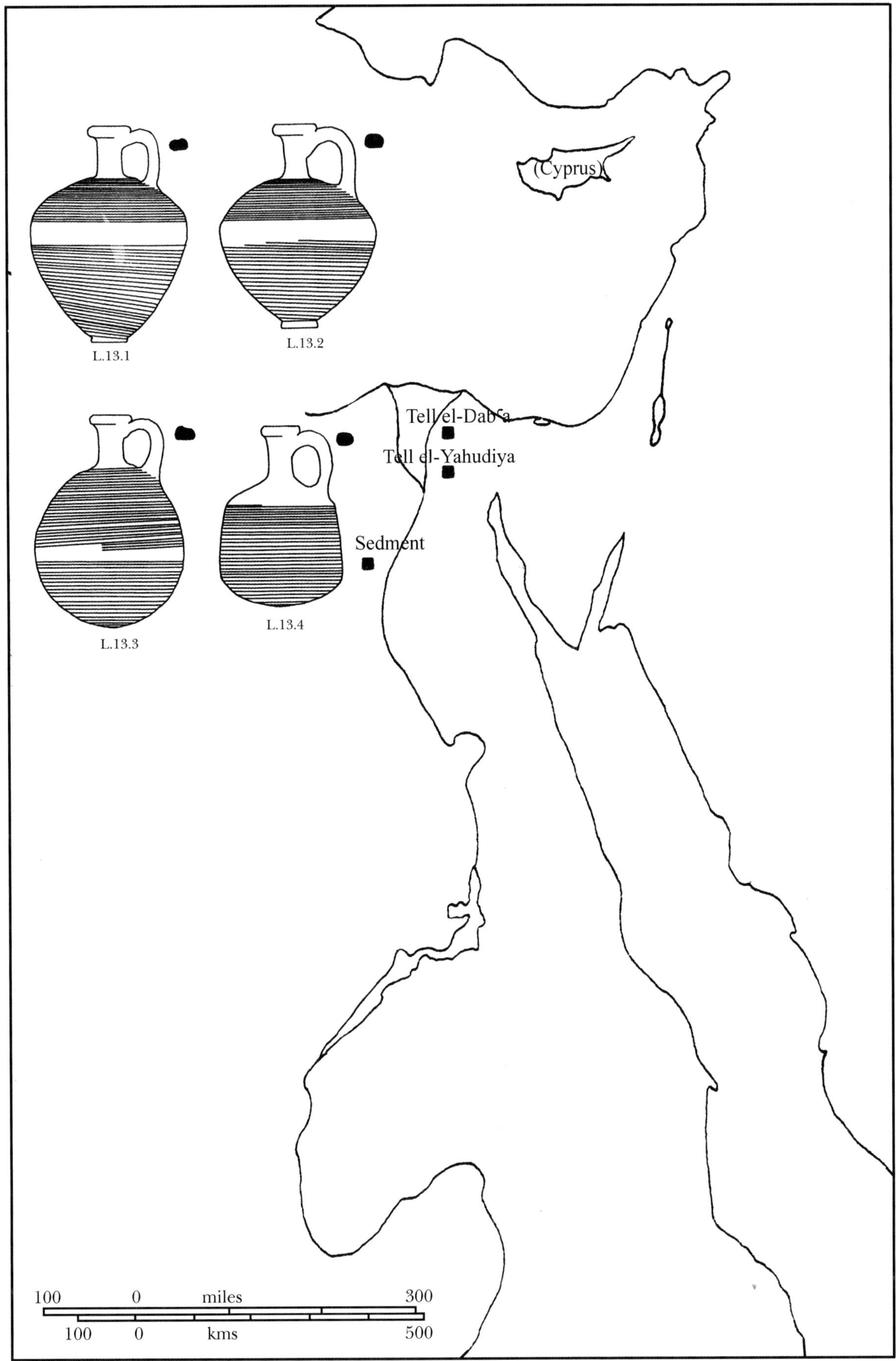

Fig. 206 Combined Distribution of Type Group L.13

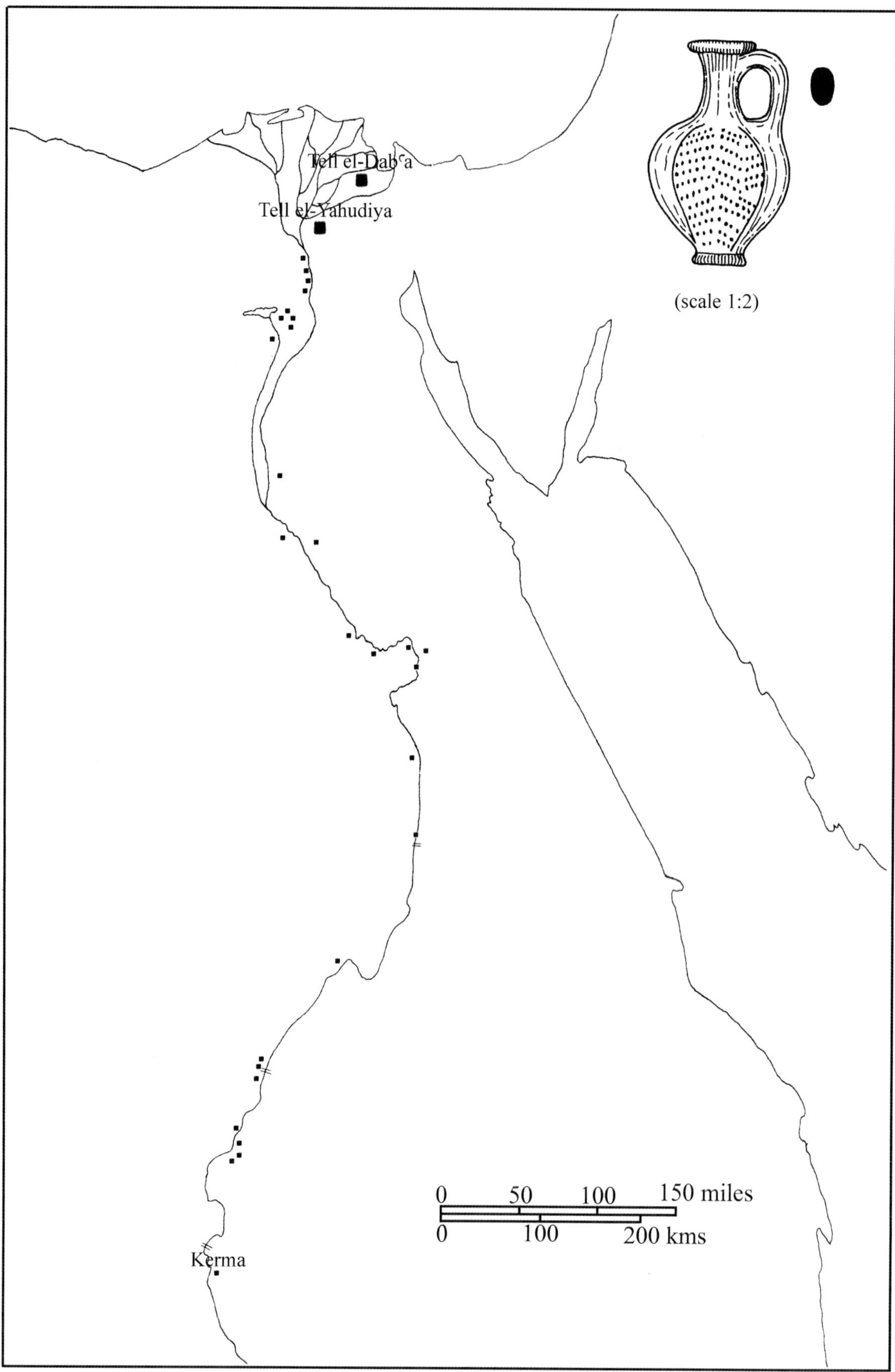

Fig. 207 Distribution and Shape Class of Type Group L.14.1

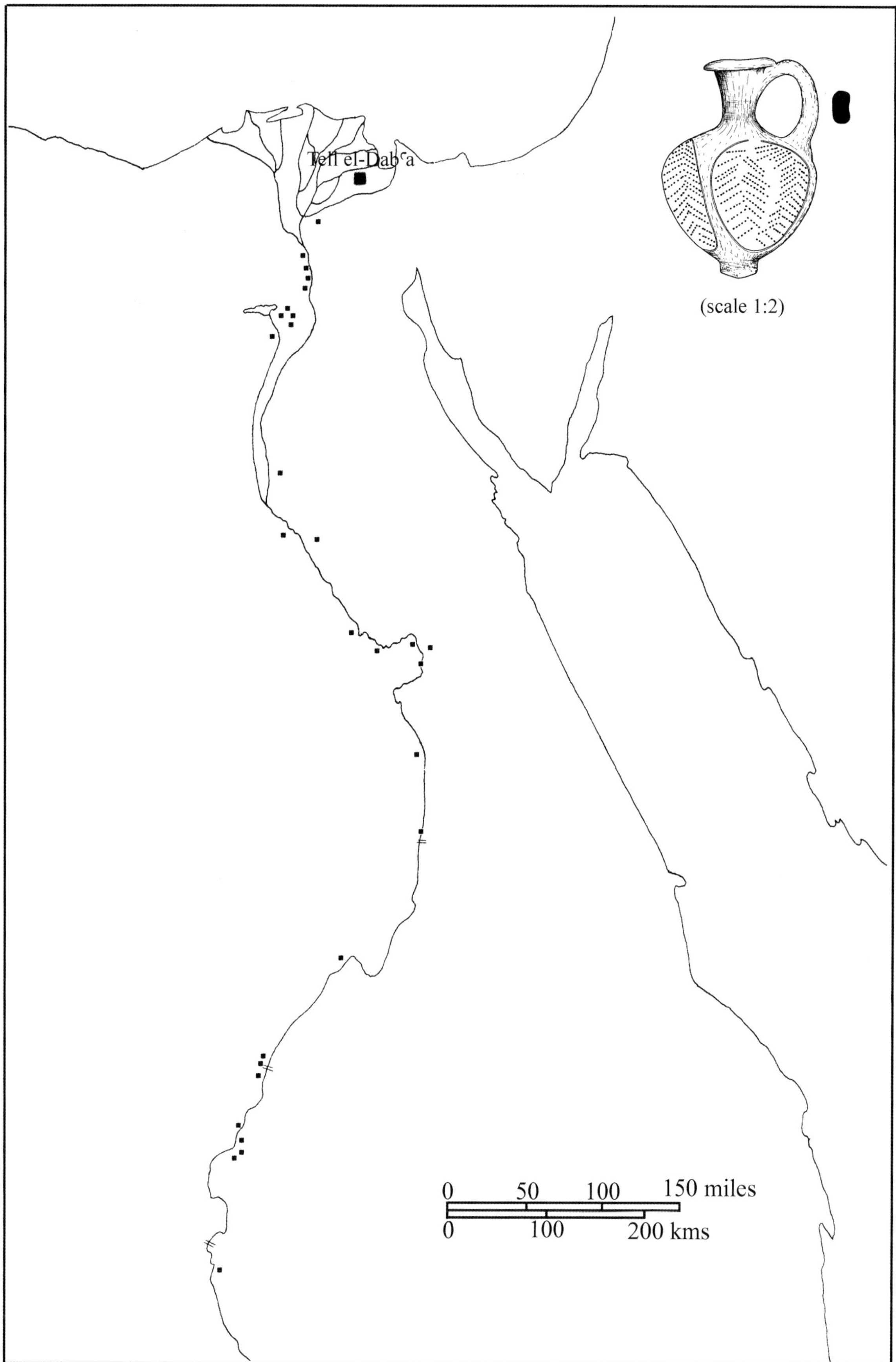

Fig. 208 Distribution and Shape Class of Type Group L.14.2

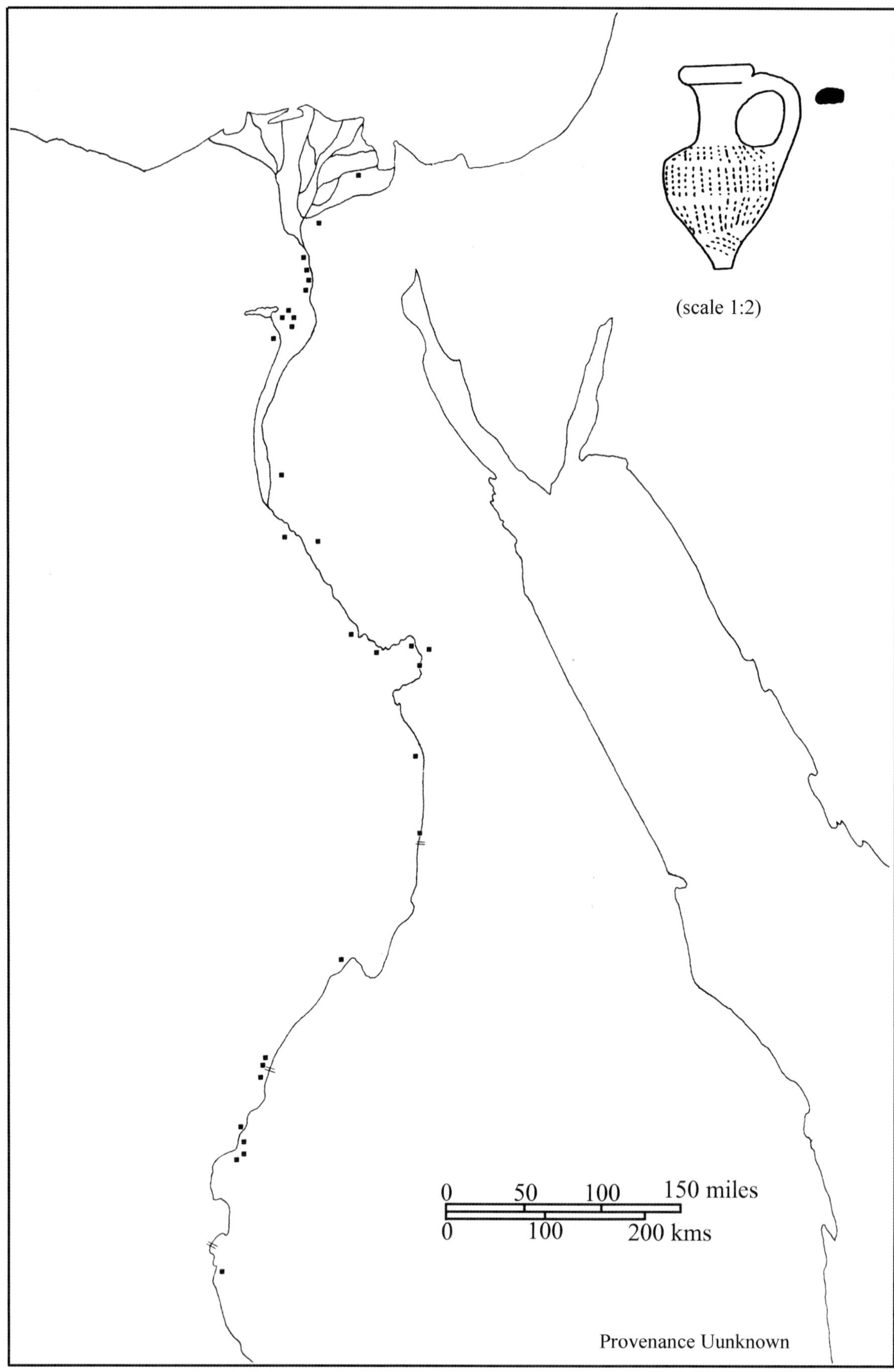

Fig. 209 Distribution and Shape Class of Type Group L.14.3

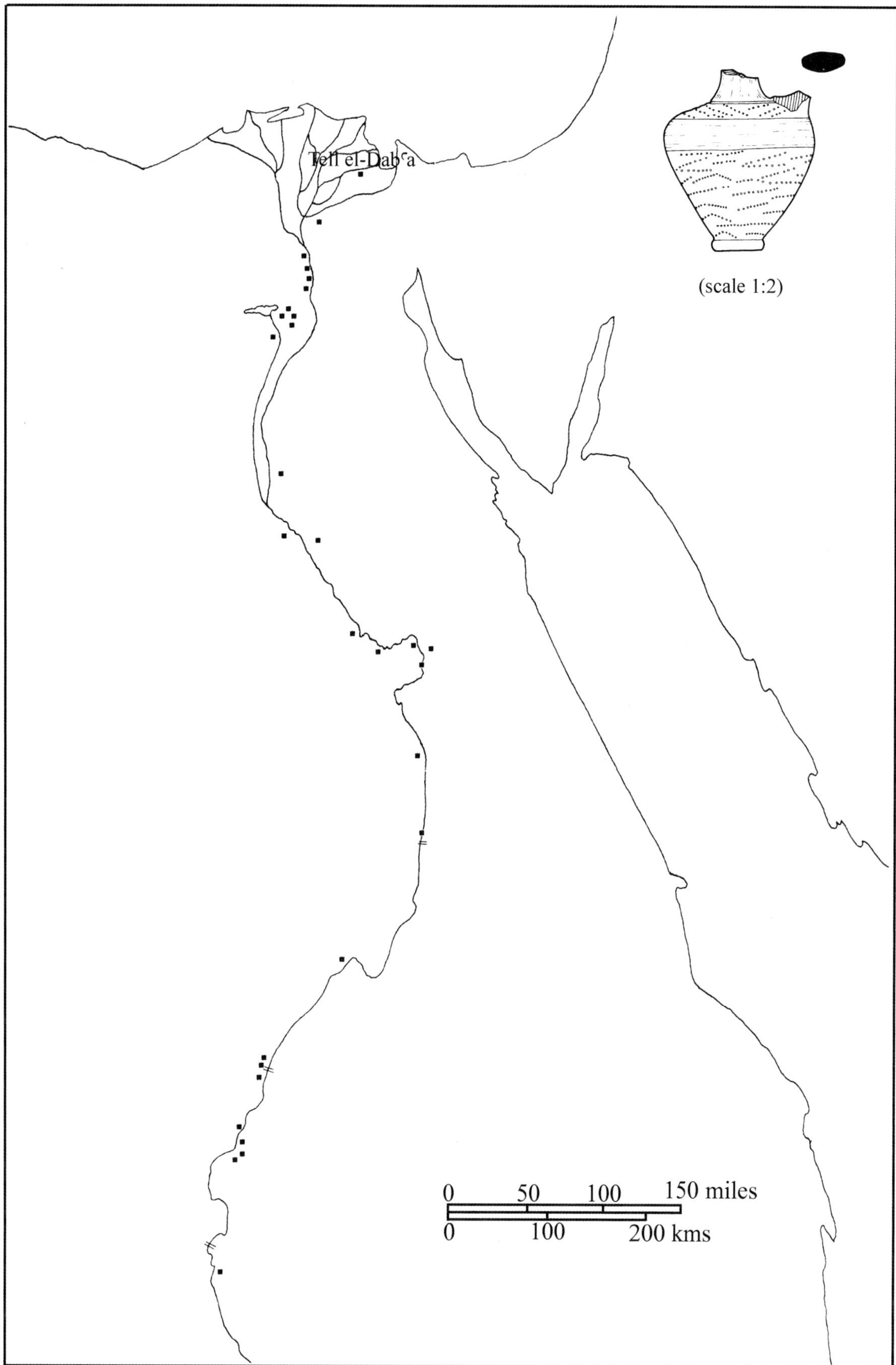

Fig. 210 Distribution and Shape Class of Type Group L.14.4

styles usually associated with Late Egyptian biconical vessels in which a reserved zone runs around the midpoint. Above and below this reserved band are standing and pendant triangles (TD 296, L.14.4a), or rows of dots made with an eight-toothed comb (TD 7297A, L.14.4b). Burnishing occurs only on the neck and reserved zone.

Although no examples are known to us, probable model globular, Type group L.14.5, and model cylindrical, Type Group L.14.6, are to be expected.

L.15. Late Egyptian XV (Late Egyptian Figural Jugs)

Late Egyptian figural jugs which date to the early Hyksos Period, are not common, but do show some similarity to one another, and in contrast to the figural vessels of the Late Palestinian group are all functional. So far the only clearly recognisable types are ducks, hawks, fish and a fly. Other miscellaneous fragments are known at Tell el-Dabᶜa, (Cf. below, catalogue nos. 647–650), but the creatures represented cannot be ascertained with any certainty.

Type Group L.15.1 Ducks (Figs. 211–213)

Only four complete duck vessels are known, and of these only one was scientifically excavated, being found at Thebes. This, London UC 13479,[521] is the largest and most realistic vessel of this type, with the modelling of the head and neck well made. The handle is double and is situated entirely on the back of the bird, the spout being situated at the back of the head. The entire vessel beneath the neck is decorated with a rishi feather design. The remaining complete duck vessels differ, but are somewhat similar to each other. Two vessels now in London (UC 13475)[522] and Oxford (Ashmolean 1971.946)[523] are double bodied which join to a single neck and have a single (UC 13475) or a double handle. Both are covered with a series of small comb incisions. Finally the fourth, Cairo JE 46741, said to come from Upper Egypt,[524] is similar to the previous two, but has only a single body. Among the incomplete examples is a vessel found in the tomb of Yuy at Thebes, (New York MMA 23.3.40),[525] and TD 3389F from Tell el-Dabᶜa.

Type Group L.15.2 Hawks (Fig. 214)

A complete hawk-shaped bird from the Fayoum area, now in the British Museum (BM EA 17046), is typical of jugs of this type.[526] The neck and single strap handle rise from the top of the head, whilst the bird stands on its legs and tail. The wings, back and chest are decorated with incised striations. Fragments of similar vessels are known from Tell el-Dabᶜa, (Cf. below, catalogue nos. 639–640), Lisht[527] and Gebel Zeit.[528]

Type Group L.15.3 Fishes (Fig. 215)

Of the figural group of late Egyptian Tell el-Yahudiya ware, the fish vessels have, by chance, survived better with practically complete examples known from Tell el-Yahudiya,[529] Tell el-Dabᶜa, Tell el-Kuᶜa,[530] Tell Hebwa I,[531] and Cyprus, site unknown.[532] As noted by Merrillees in his discussion of such vessels,[533] the dorsal fin is a long continuous ridge, whilst the ventral fins are small projections. The eyes and gills are usually drawn into clay. The handle is, in some cases, bipartite, whilst in others a single strap running from the mouth of the fish to the juglet rim. Bipartite handles occur on the earlier examples. The body is usually covered with a herringbone pattern. Whilst most fish are single, as in nature, one example, Manchester II.c.36, has a double body.[534] All such vessels are clearly wheel made; Kaplan suggests that the potters may have thrown a piriform jug and then compressed it until a fish shape was attained.[535]

Type Group L.15.4 Flies (Fig. 216)

This group is known only from a complete example, Hildesheim 6350.[536] The jug has a rolled rim, strap handle and a body modelled in the form of a fly. The Tell el-Yahudiya style, with its white incrustations on a

521 Petrie, *Qurneh*, 1909, 2–3, pl. ix B23, xii. B23, Kaplan, *Tell el-Yahudiyeh Ware*, fig. 122a.

522 Kaplan, *Tell el-Yahudiyeh Ware*, fig. 122b.

523 Payne, *Burlington Magazine* June 1972, 399, fig. 59, Kaplan, *Tell el-Yahudiyeh Ware*, fig. 122c.

524 Kaplan, *Tell el-Yahudiyeh Ware*, fig. 122d.

525 Kaplan, *Tell el-Yahudiyeh Ware*, fig. 123c.

526 Hall, *The Oldest Civilization of Greece*, 69, fig. 30.

527 Merrillees *Trade and Transcendance*, 59, figs. 43, 47, Kaplan, *Tell el-Yahudiyeh Ware*, fig. 123a.

528 Exhibition catalogue, *25 ans de découvertes archéologiques sur les chantiers de l'IFAO, 1981–2006*, (Cairo, 2007), 56 no. 37.

529 Adam, *ASAE* 55, 1958, 309, pl. 19a, Kaplan, *Tell el-Yahudiyeh Ware*, fig. 125c., cf. also figs.125e–f, 126a–d.

530 Unpublished. A. Eshmawy, personal communication.

531 Unpublished. M. Abd el-Maksoud, personal communication.

532 New York MMA 74.51.831. Myres, *Cessnola Collection*, 42, fig. 384, Kaplan, *Tell el-Yahudiyeh Ware*, fig. 124c.

533 Merrillees, *Levant* 10, 1978, 81.

534 Prag, *Levant* 5, 1973, 128–131.

535 Kaplan, *Tell el-Yahudiyeh Ware*, 33.

536 Seidel, in: Eggebrecht (ed.), *Pelizaeus Museum, Hildesheim*, 1993, 49 no. 40.

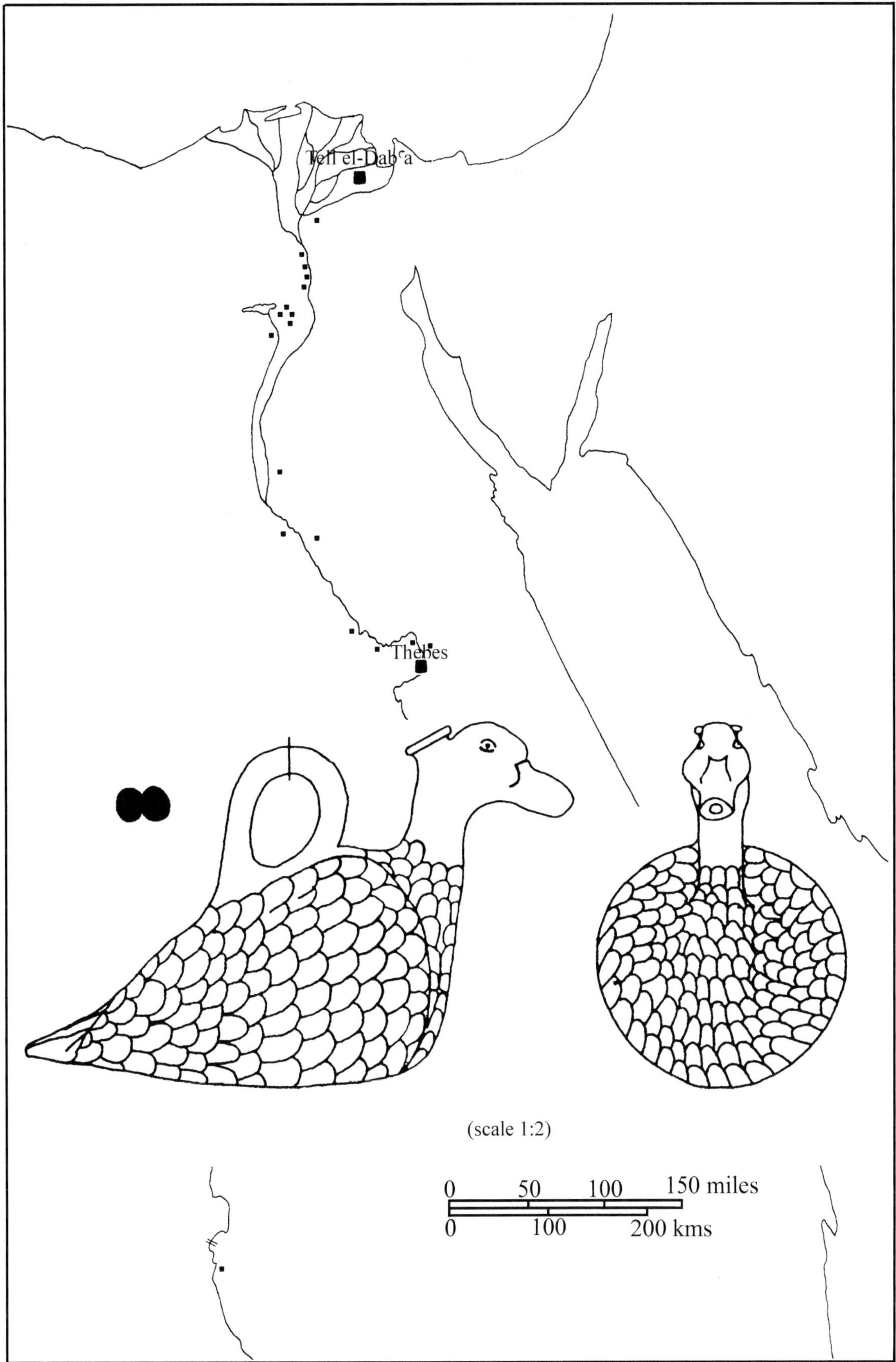

Fig. 211 Distribution and Shape Class of Type Group L.15.1-1

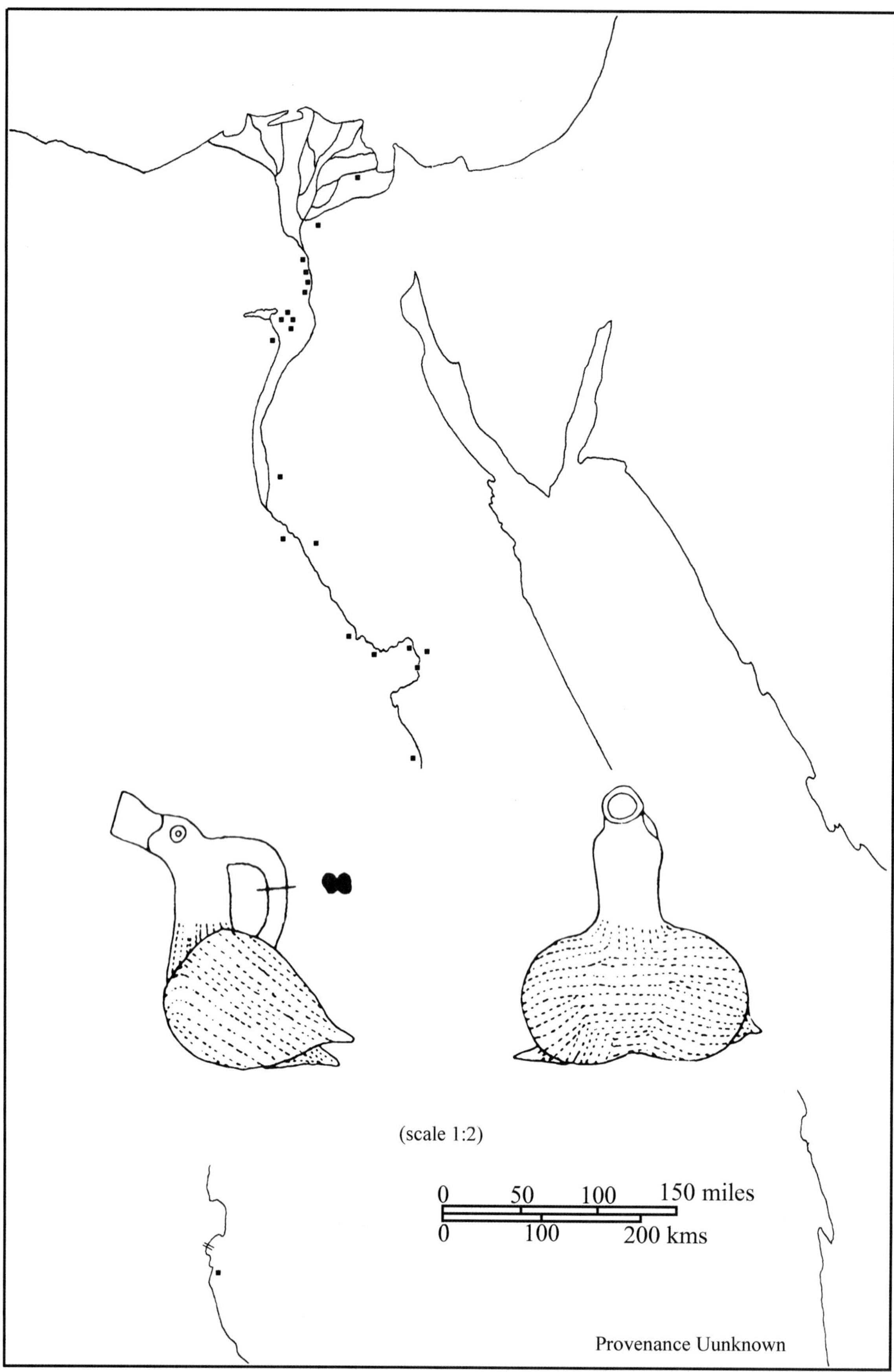

Fig. 212 Distribution and Shape Class of Type Group L.15.1–2

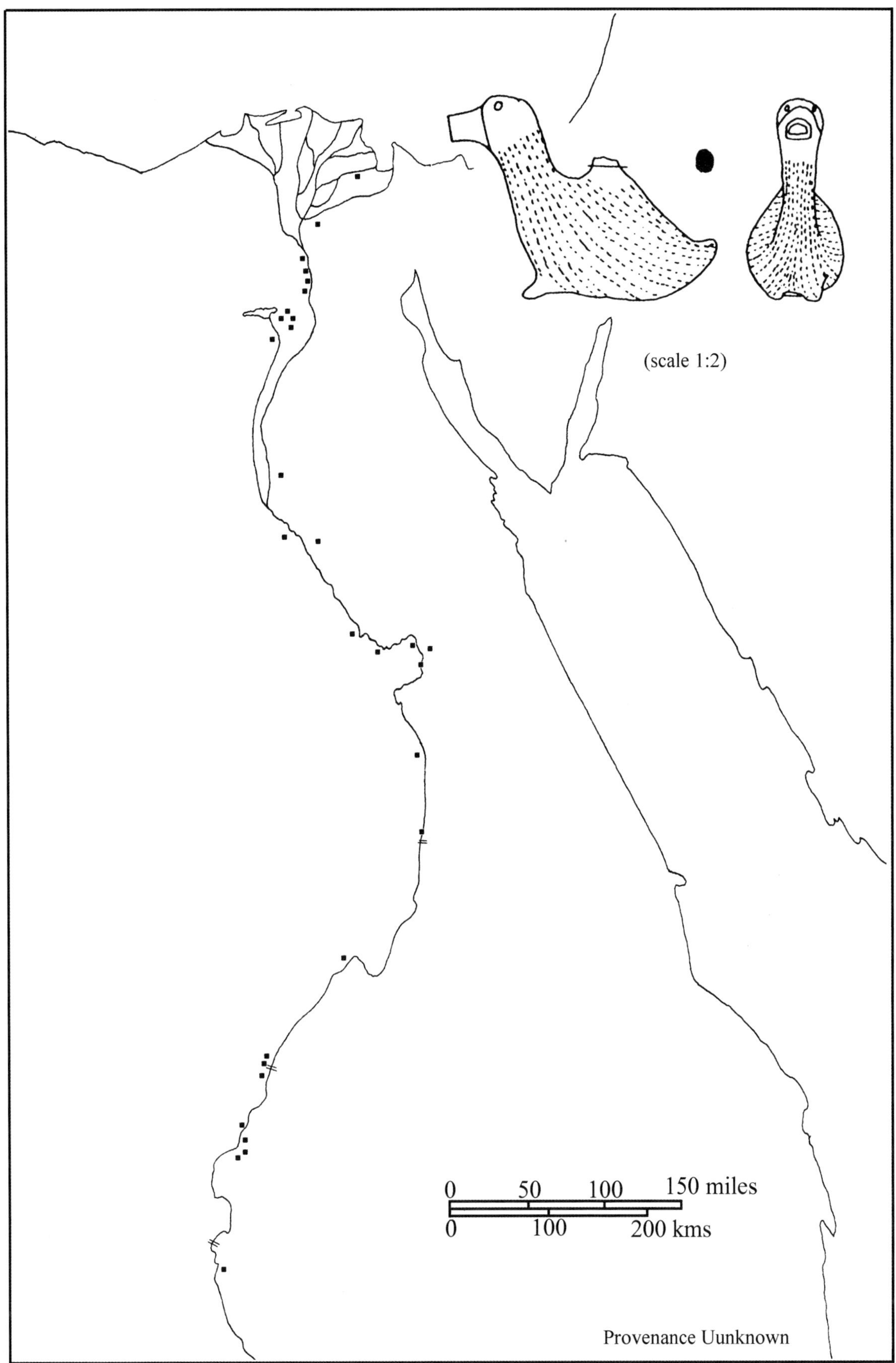

Fig. 213 Distribution and Shape Class of Type Group L.15.1–3

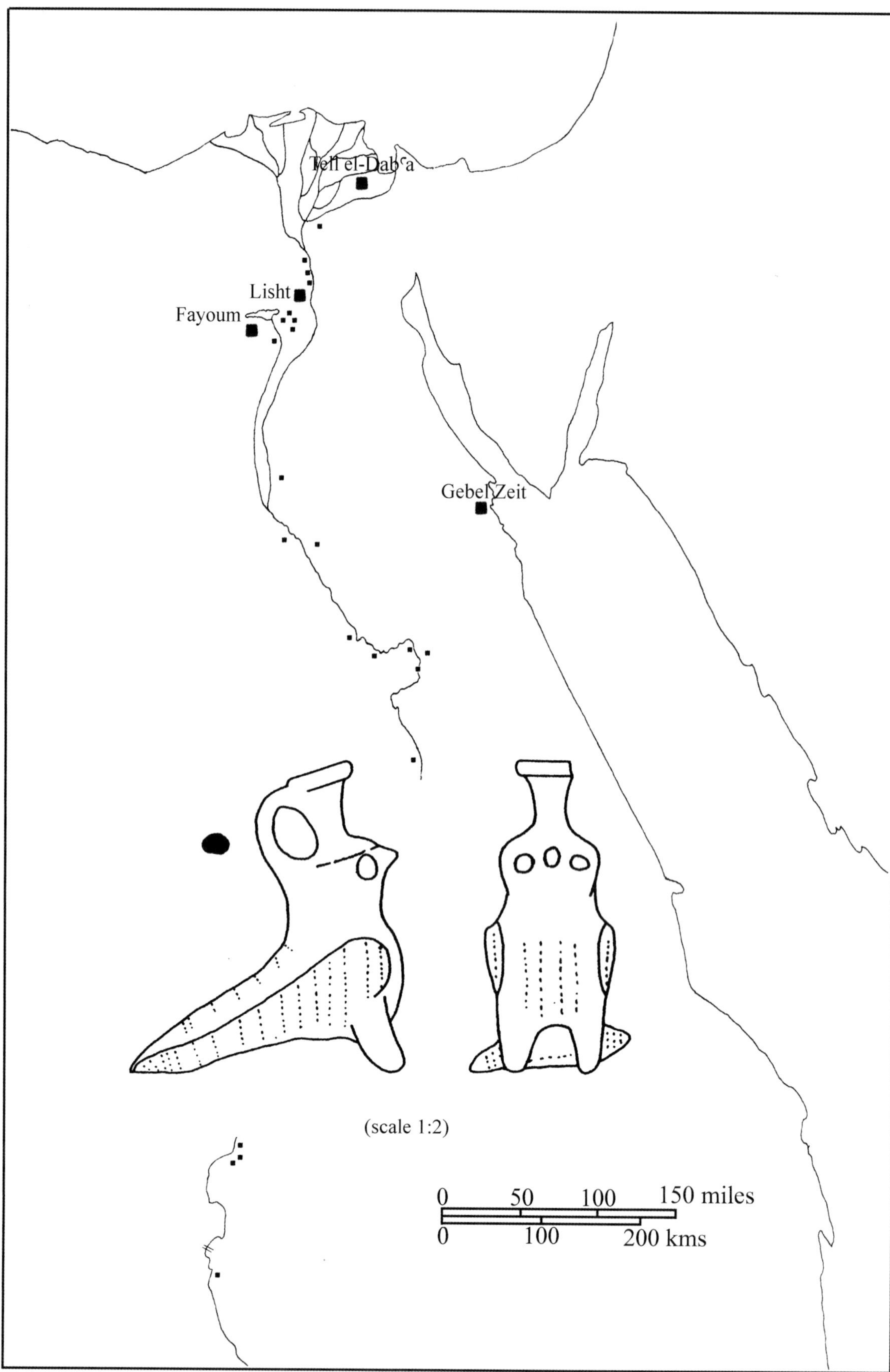

Fig. 214 Distribution and Shape Class of Type Group L.15.2

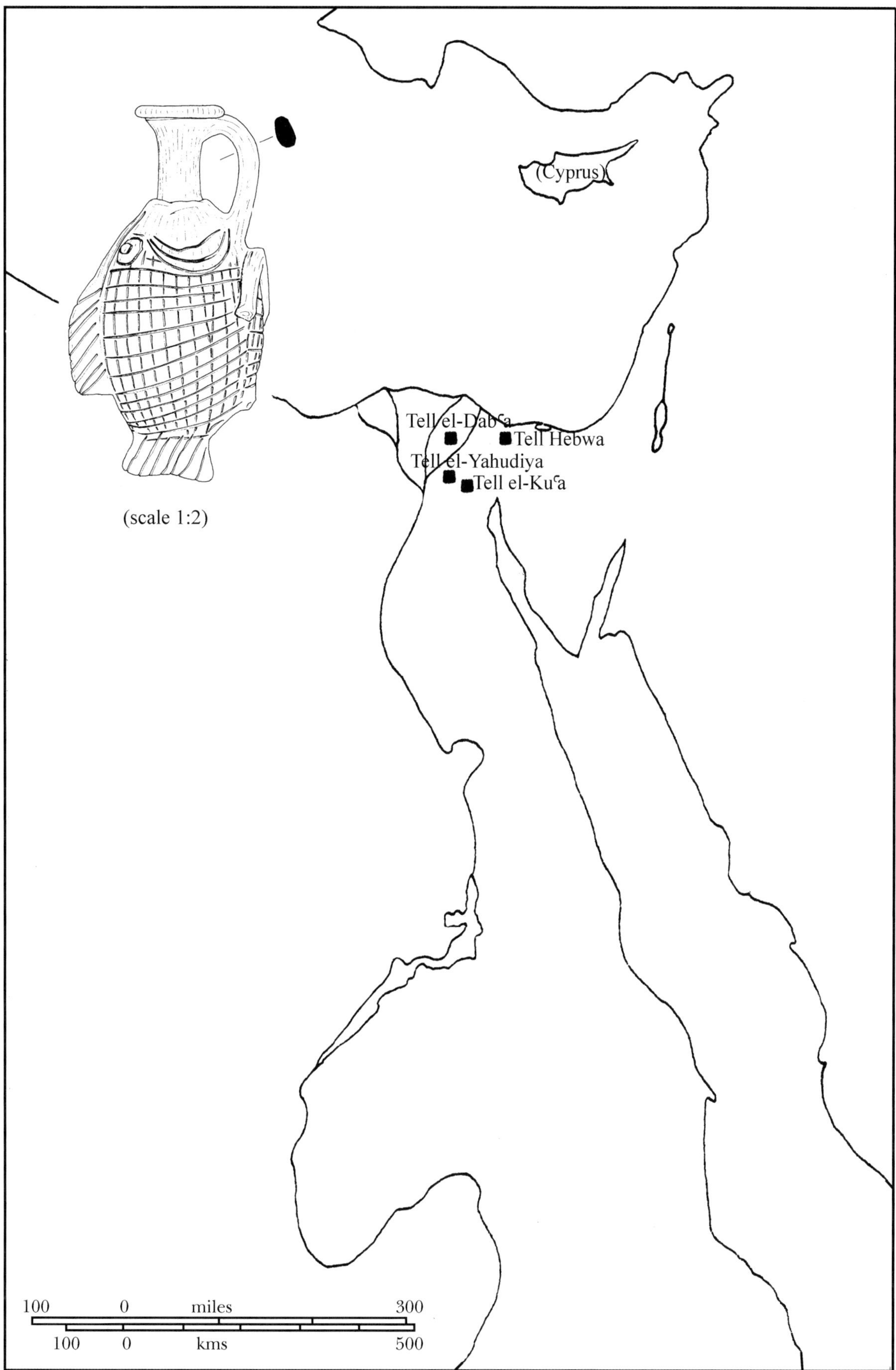

Fig. 215 Distribution and Shape Class of Type Group L.15.3

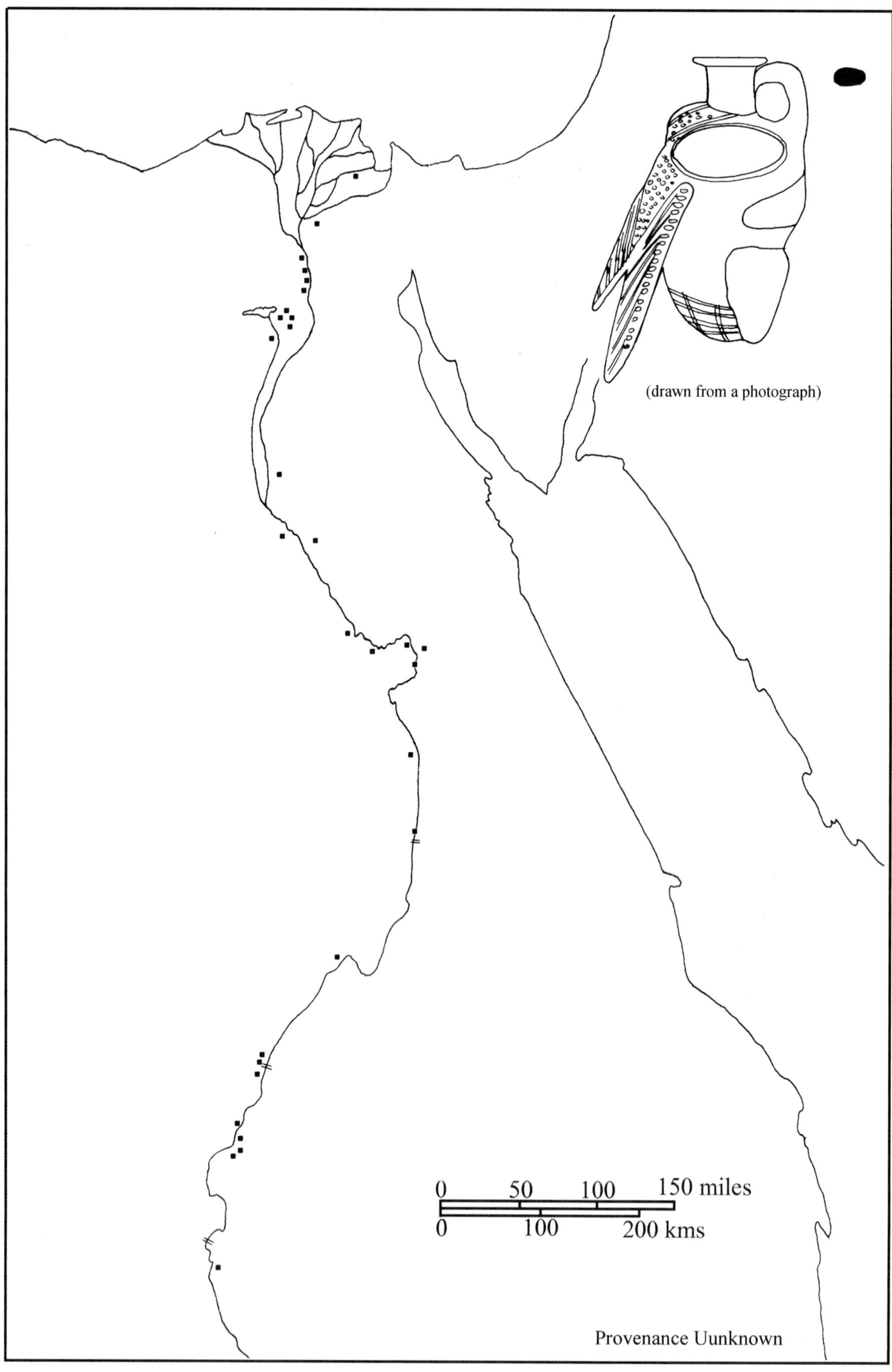

Fig. 216 Distribution and Shape Class of Type Group L.15.4

black ground lends itself well to such an insect. Unfortunately its place of origin and stratigraphic date remain unknown, but the underlying shape clearly belongs with the late Egyptian group, and moreover may be associated with the traditional Egyptian motif of the flies of honour.

Type Group L.15.5 Cattle (?) (Fig. 217)

An unusual, but unfortunately incomplete vessel from Khatana, pit complex L81, TD 9018X, appears to represent the neck and foreparts of a quadruped, most probably a cow.

Branch M: Hybrids

Contact in Southern Palestine between the Hyksos kingdoms centred on Tell el-Dab^c^a and Sharuhen, brought about a hybrid blend of both Late Palestinian and Egyptian designs. Most probably these piriform, and to a lesser extent, cylindrical hybrids were produced locally in Southern Palestine. They may be divided into the following groups:

Type Group M.1 (Kaplan's Piriform 2b) (Fig. 218)

Type group M.1 clearly owes its origins to the Piriform 2a vessels of the Late Egyptian Group L.1. However neutron activation analysis of such vessels shows them to have been made of Palestinian clays.[537] Such vessels, which are known from Ashkelon,[538] Jericho[539] and Tell Ajjul,[540] have rolled rims; piriform bodies, and like the Egyptian vessels which inspired them, infilled lozenge decoration. In contrast to the Egyptian vessels, however, this type always has a double handle, and usually a button or offset disc base.

Type Group M.2 (Piriform 2b hybrids) (Fig. 219)

By contrast two vessels found at Tell el-Dab^c^a (TD 67 and TD 3434) comprise Piriform 2b vessels with rolled rims, double handles and ring bases. Both are decorated with undelineated infilled lozenges. Both, however are made of Nile clay and are evident copies of Late Palestinian forms.

Type Group M.3 (Piriform 3) (Fig. 220)

Type group M.3 comprises a number of Kaplan's Piriform 3 vessels which are very similar to the contemporary Late Egyptian Piriform 2a (type group LI), but can be distinguished not only by their findspots – all examples currently known come from Megiddo, and Tell el-^c^Ajjul[541] – but by their style of decoration. In contrast to the Egyptian examples, which were invariably decorated with lozenge patterns, jugs of type group M.3 bear horizontal herringbone patterns which run around the entire vessel. They are perhaps to be seen as hybrids.[542] Kaplan also points out that the jugs of this type also tend to have proportionally shorter necks than her Piriform 2a and 2b vessels, but whether this is a consistent observation must await further discoveries.

Type Group M.4 (Piriform 3) (Fig. 221)

Vessels of this group, which again belong in Kaplan's Piriform 3 group, have been found at Lachish[543] and Jericho,[544] and are characterised by an ornamental pattern which consists of one horizontal band around the belly of the pot, with, evidently borrowed from Egypt, segments or pendant triangles on either the shoulder or lower body, which may, or may not be delineated by incised frame lines. An incomplete vessel, with an apparent mix of Palestinian and Egyptian style decoration found at Tell el-Ajjul may also belong in this group.[545]

Type Group M.5 (Cylindrical 2 hybrids) (Fig. 222)

Cylindrical 2 hybrids consist of Palestinian style Cylindrical 2 jugs with double handles but having Egyptian style decoration. Thus a jug from Megiddo,[546] produced from Palestinian Red Field clay,[547] has the flat base of the Cylindrical 2 jugs, but shows a combination of the standing triangles common on jugs of the Late Egyptian Group, as well as the more typical Palestinian band decoration on the body (M.5a). Another cylindrical 2 jug from Jericho with the typical Cylindrical 2 features of Palestinian jugs is deco-

---

[537] Kaplan, *Tell el-Yahudiyeh Ware*, 231, Piriform 2b.

[538] Cf. below page 570.

[539] Birmingham City Museum 1032.52. Kenyon, *PEQ* 1952, pl. 22, fig. 1; Oxford Ashmolean 1954.576. Kenyon, *Jericho I*, 315–330, fig. 122.14; Jerusalem, Rockefeller Museum V.588. Kaplan, *Tell el-Yahudiyeh Ware*, fig. 61c–e.

[540] Jerusalem, Rockefeller Museum, 32.2088. Petrie, *Ancient Gaza II*, pl. xxxiv 60M6, Kaplan, *Tell el-Yahudiyeh Ware*, fig. 61a.

[541] Kaplan, Tell el-Yahudiyeh Ware, fig. 77c–f.

[542] Perhaps the incomplete vessel Jerusalem Rockefeller Museum 32.1694 also belongs in this group – Kaplan, *Tell el-Yahudiyeh Ware*, fig. 76.

[543] Tufnell, *Lachish IV*, 1958, 272, pls. 50.17, 77.729; Kaplan, *Tell el-Yahudiyeh Ware*, fig. 77a.

[544] Garstang, *LAAA* 19, 1932, 51–54, pl. 41.1; Kaplan, *Tell el-Yahudiyeh Ware*, fig. 76a.

[545] Petrie, *Ancient Gaza III*, 1933, pl. 38.60M5; Kaplan, *Tell el-Yahudiyeh Ware*, fig. 77b.

[546] Jerusalem, Rockefeller Museum 34.1725. Guy, *Megiddo Tombs*, 64–68, pl. 28.40.

[547] Kaplan, *Tell el-Yahudiyeh Ware*, 229 sample M1.

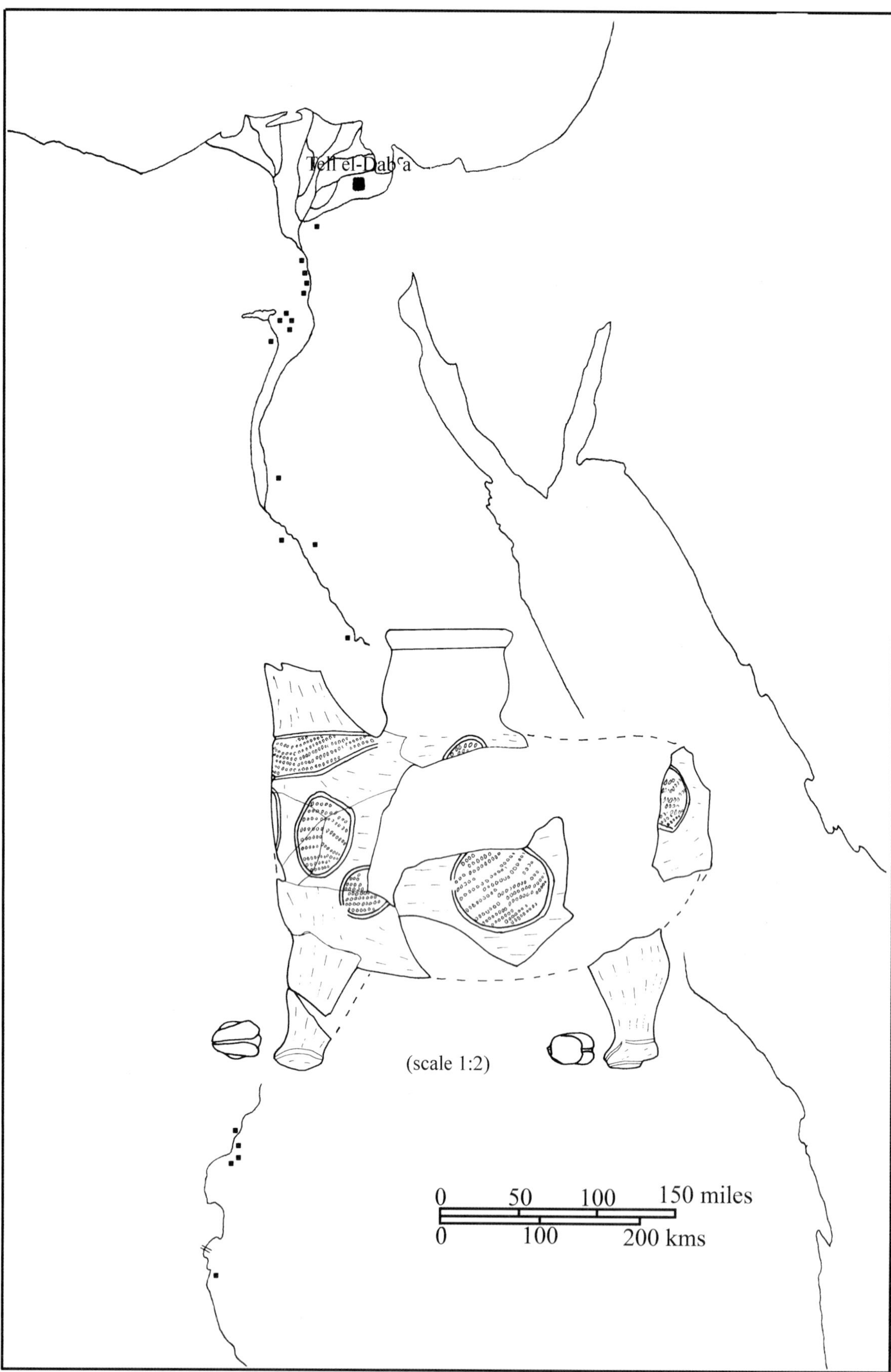

Fig. 217 Distribution and Shape Class of Type Group L.15.5

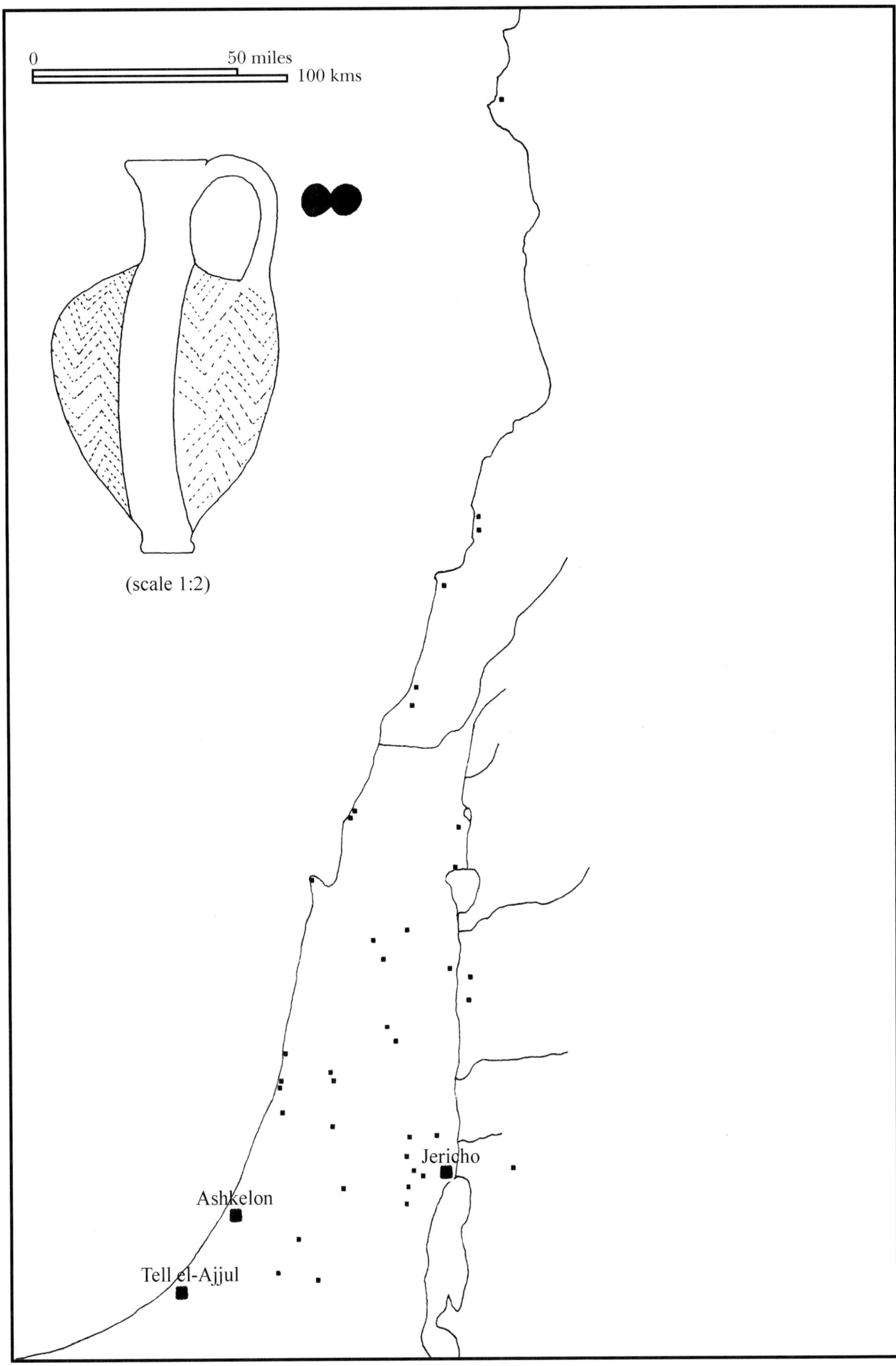

Fig. 218 Distribution and Shape Class of Type Group M.1

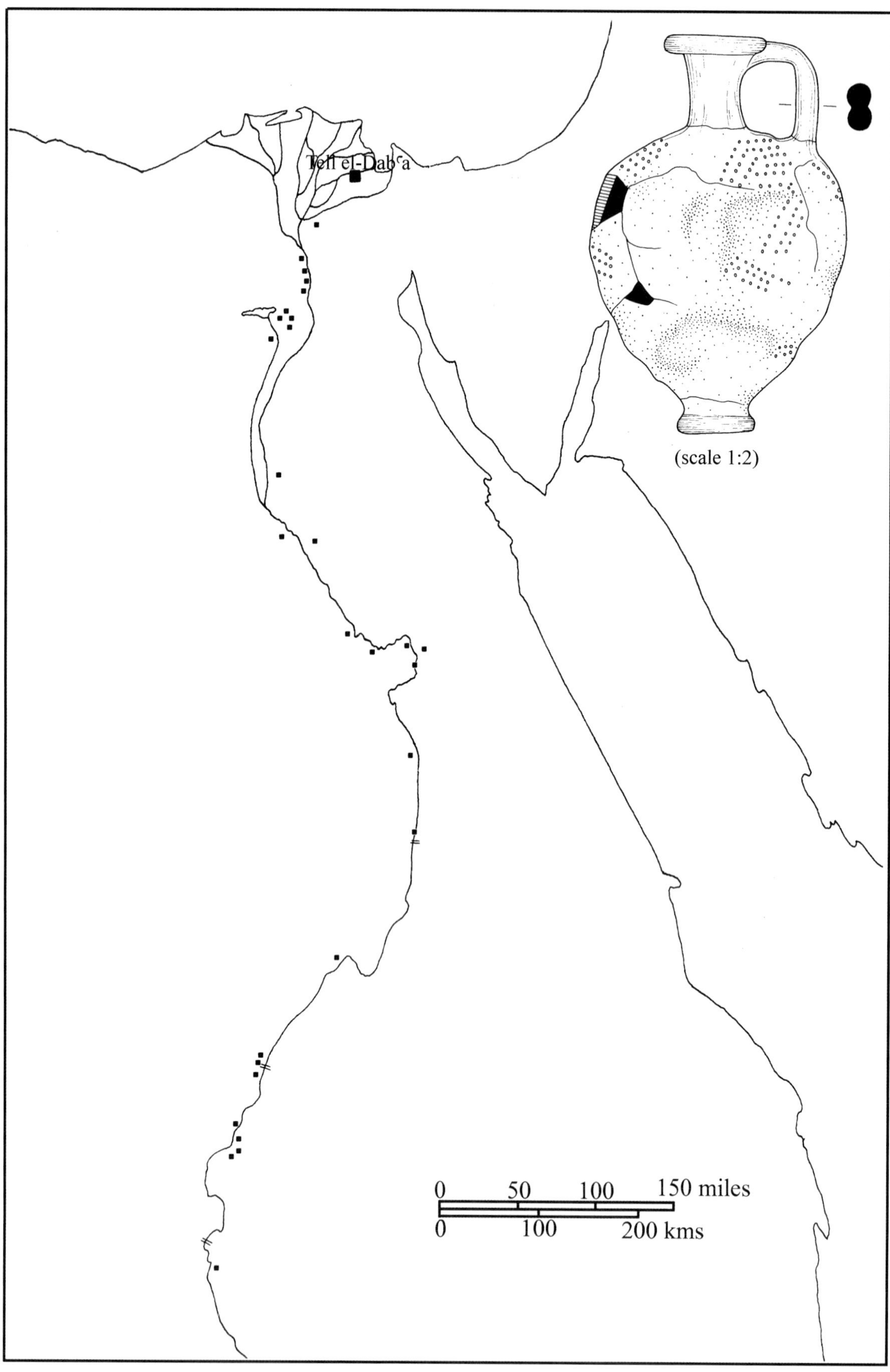

Fig. 219 Distribution and Shape Class of Type Group M.2

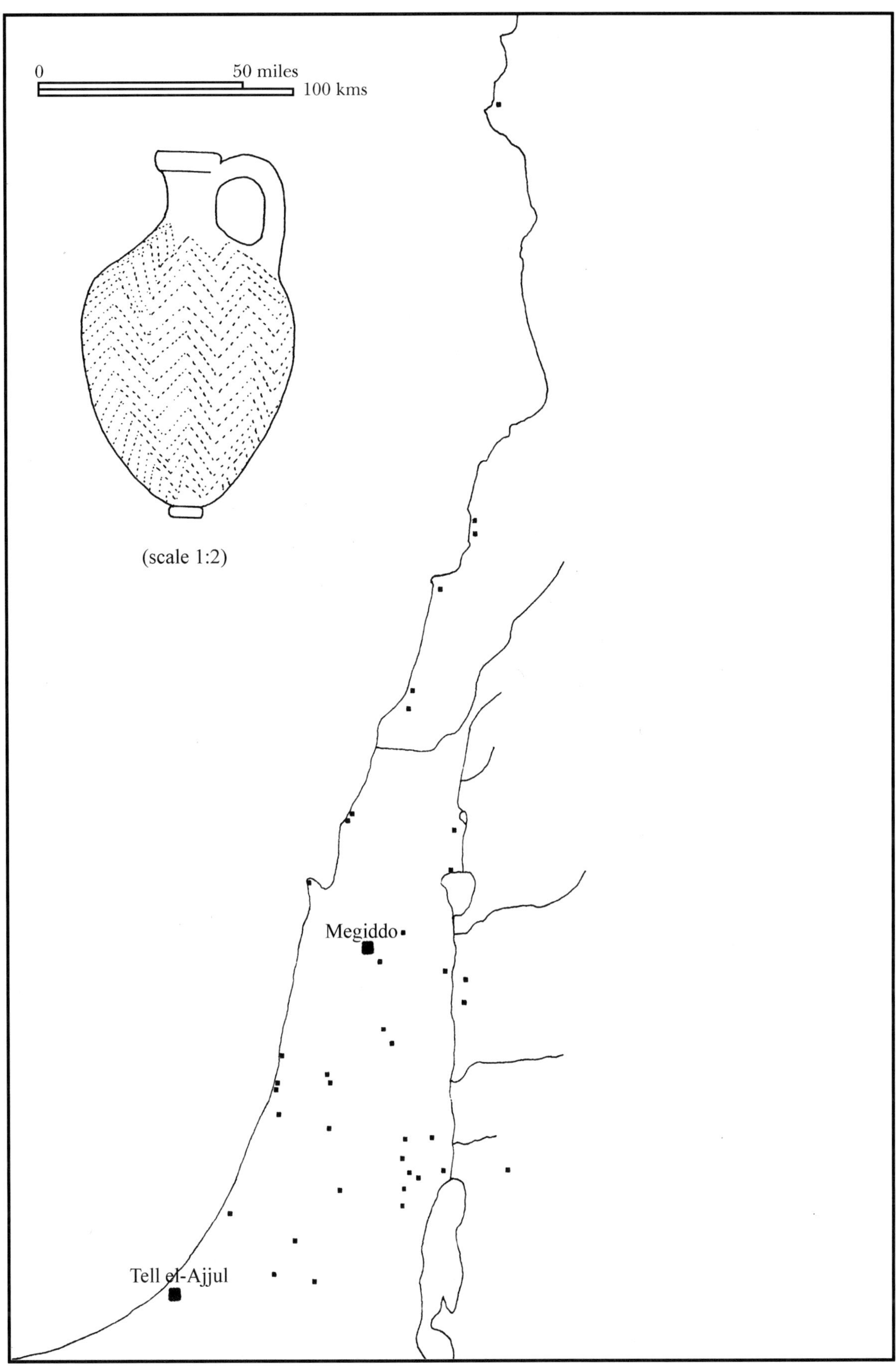

Fig. 220 Distribution and Shape Class of Type Group M.3

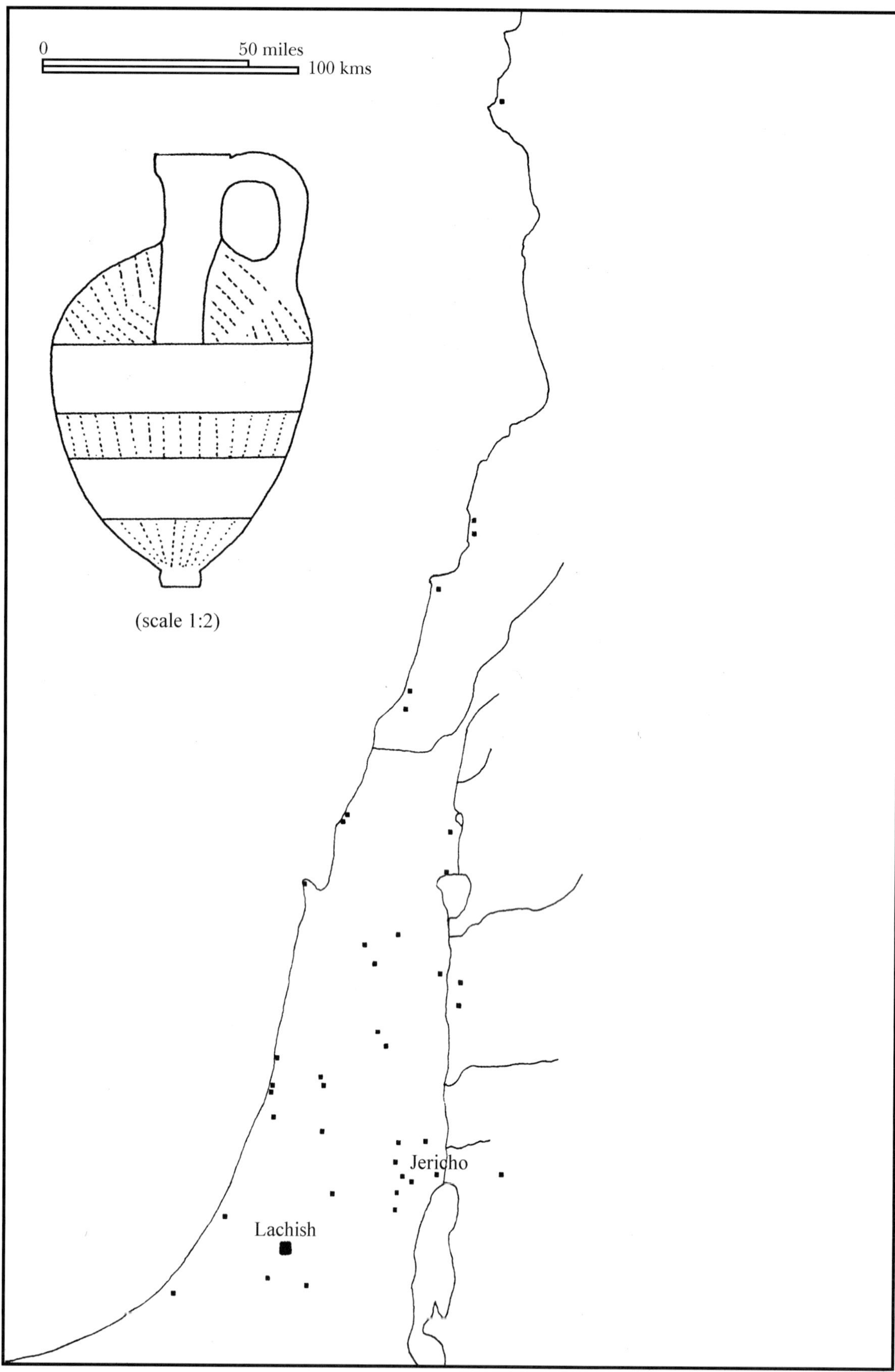

Fig. 221 Distribution and Shape Class of Type Group M.4

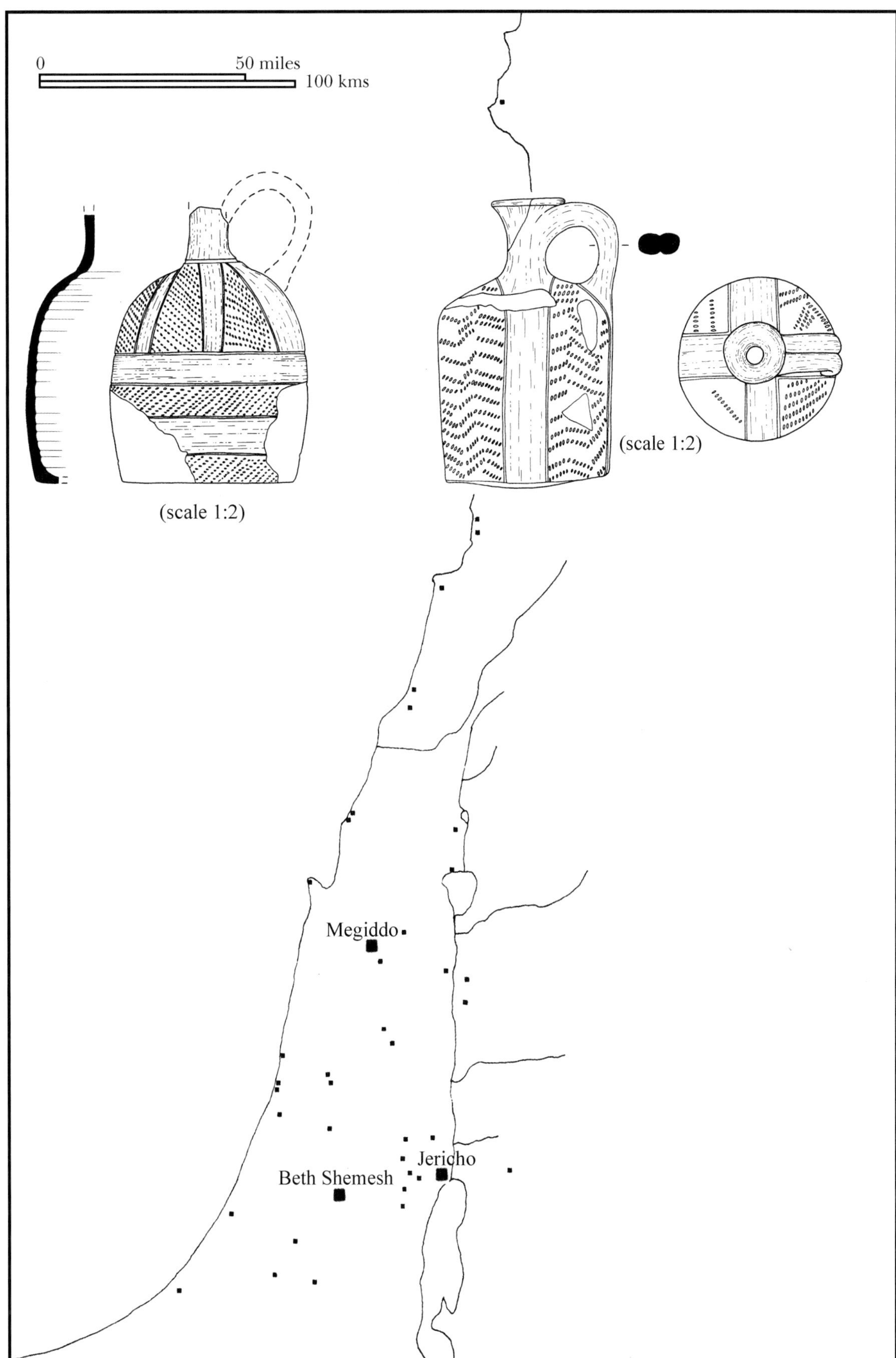

Fig. 222 Distribution and Shape Class of Type Group M.5

rated with the typical lozenge decoration of the Late Egyptian Globular and Piriform 2a vessels (M.5b).[548]

Branch N: Handmade Globular

As a group the handmade globular type of Tell el-Yahudiya ware is, in the main, absent from the work of Kaplan, but occurs fairly frequently in Tell el-Dabᶜa. Being handmade these vessels differ from all other types of Tell el-Yahudiya ware, and whilst they may have developed out of the original Primeval group, it is also possible that they developed out of a Cypriot tradition where pottery was traditionally handmade throughout the Middle Bronze Age. Moreover all these handmade globular vessels have their handles pushed through the vessel wall, a particularly Cypriot technique. Åström seems to have been the first to point out the close connection between Cypriot Black Slip III ware and Tell el-Yahudiya ware, both in terms of decoration and shape,[549] and this was subsequently followed by Negbi.[550] Black Slip III exists with a number of incised elements comprising groups of parallel, straight or zigzag lines, hatched triangles; hatched diamonds, hatched bands; hatched chevrons, plain diamonds with framed hatched borders; vertical or horizontal punctured straight bands or zigzags; triangles with horizontal rows of short vertical strokes; herring bone patterns; networks and vertical or horizontal bands filled with parallel zigzag lines. Close parallels in shape can be distinguished in a number of jugs with button or pedestal bases and ovoid bodies, whilst Late Black Slip Ware jugs with fin-like projections down the sides may be related to the fish-shaped juglets of group L.15.3. Since Black Slip III is contemporary with the Late Egyptian group I, Black Slip III is somewhat later than the handmade globular jugs listed here. However, it is possible that both Black Slip III and the Handmade Globular Tell el-Yahudiya Ware have a common ancestor in Cypriot Black Slip II Ware.[551] The jugs of the latter ware usually have horizontal decoration on the neck and body, – straight or zigzag lines or alternating straight and wavy or zigzag relief bands or incised lines. Sometimes only the neck is incised with parallel zigzag, encircling lines. Both a vertical and a horizontal arrangement also occur; sometimes straight and wavy lines are placed horizontally on the neck and body, and vertically in front from neck to base and below the handle. Of particular interest is the fact that the jugs of Åström's Type VIIIB6e[552] have panels with punctured dots on the shoulder or vertical stripes with punctured triangles alternating with zigzag bands bordered by punctured dots on the shoulder. At least one of these jugs was reputedly found in Egypt,[553] which may indicate that such jugs were exported to Egypt during the MC II period, and may well have provided the inspiration for the form of the Handmade Globular jugs in Tell el-Yahudiya Ware, which were decorated in typical Egyptian style.

These Tell el-Yahudiya Ware Handmade Globular jugs, which are generally brown polished and burnished, indicative of their early date, strata F–E/3, may be divided into the following groups dependant on their attributes and style of decoration:

Type Group N.1 (Figs. 223, 227)

At present only one vessel can be attributed to this group, Tell el-Dabᶜa TD 8698, from a grave dated to Phase E/3. With a cut-away spout, incisions at the base of the neck and double handle, it is clearly an early vessel, and although no NAA analysis has yet been carried out on this vessel, visual observation indicates that it is made of a Nile clay. Three horizontal zones of decoration are found on the vessel extending from immediately below the neck to the lower body. The first zone is decorated with standing triangles which are themselves delineated by incised lines; the second band comprises a zigzag again delineated by incised lines, and finally the lower band consists solely of groups of three incised lines arranged in a zigzag pattern.

Type Group N.2 (Figs. 224–227)

Type Group N.2 consists of hand made globular jugs with slightly everted or kettle rims and double handles, which may be sub-divided into three subgroups N.2.1 a–c by the decorative styles. In N.2.1a the vessel has an incised line at the height of the base of the handle, thence vertical incised lines running down towards the base; N.2.1b, in which the decoration consists of two bands of upright triangles; and N.2.1c with

---

548 Jerusalem, Rockefeller Museum I.10089. Garstang, *LAAA* 21, 1934, 119, pl. 17.19, Kaplan, *Tell el-Yahudiyeh Ware*, fig. 8c.

549 Åström, *The Middle Cypriote Bronze Age*, 108, 226.

550 O. Negbi, Cypriot Imitations of Tell el-Yahudiyeh Ware, *AJA* 78, 1982, 137–149.

551 Åström, *The Middle Cypriote Bronze Age*, 103–104, pls. xxv–xxx.

552 Åström, *The Middle Cypriote Bronze Age*, 95, 104.

553 Stockholm, MM 389. Åström, *The Middle Cypriote Bronze Age*, 95, pl. xxvi.12.

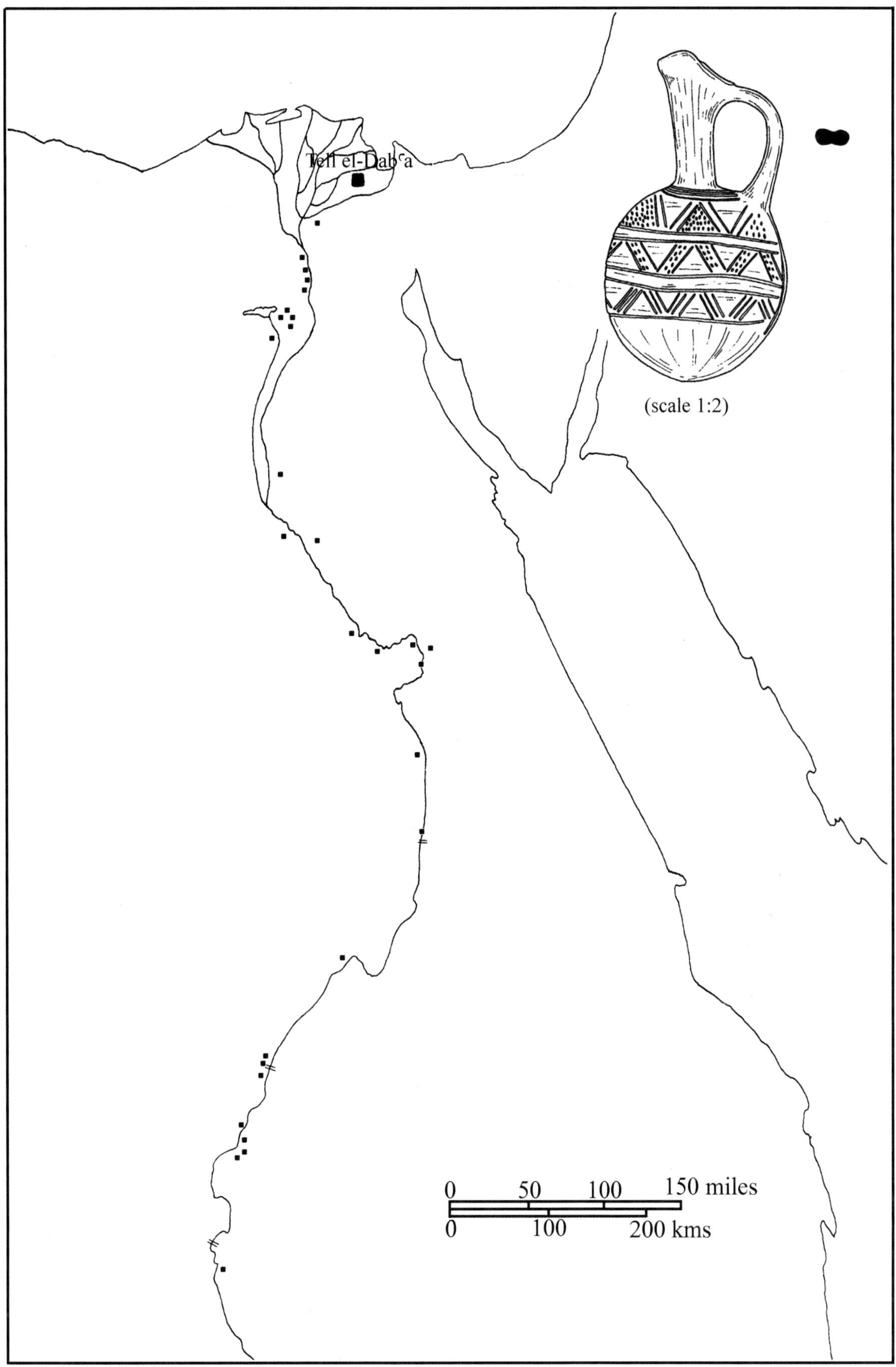

Fig. 223 Distribution and Shape Class of Type Group N.1

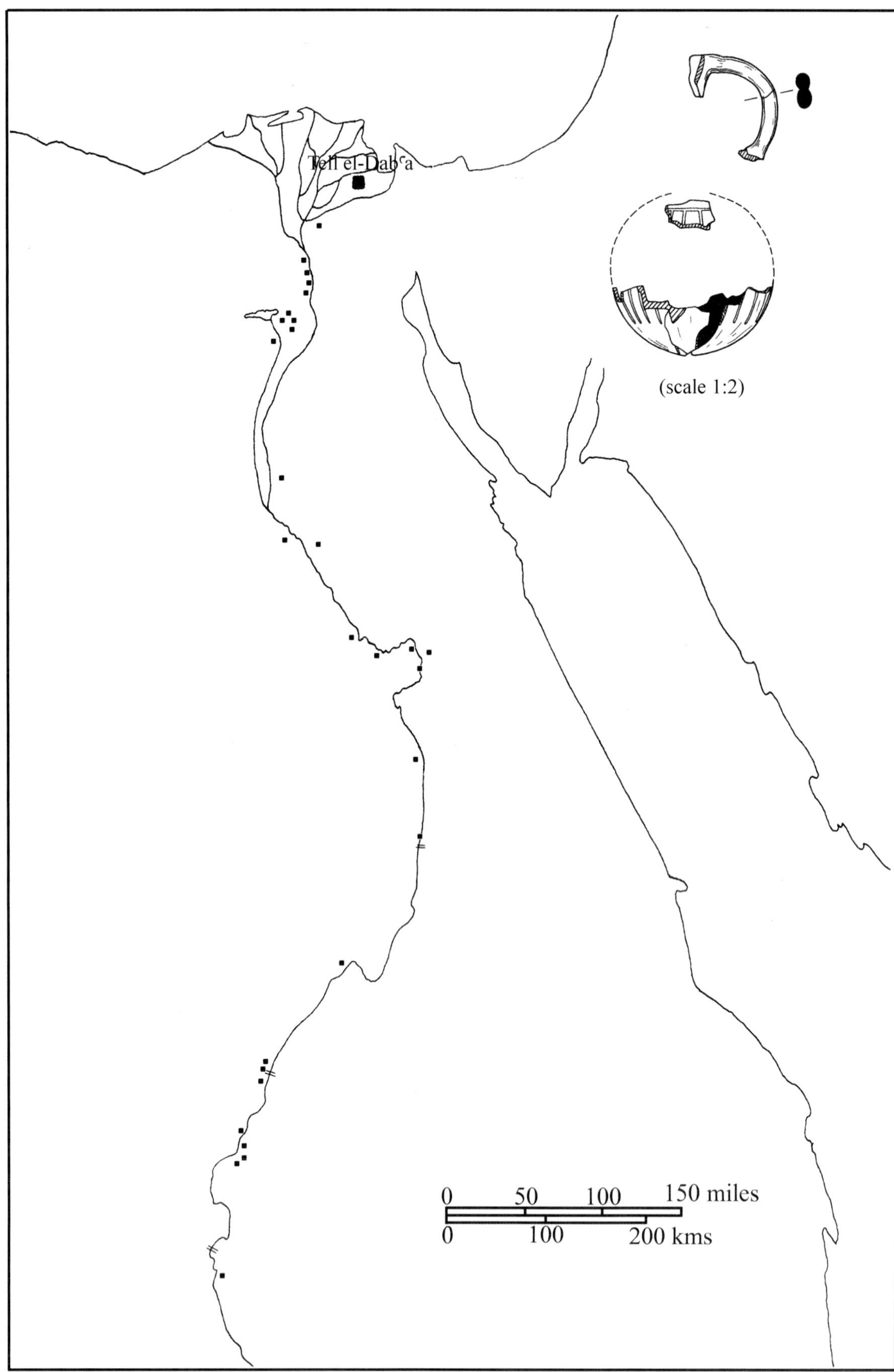

Fig. 224 Distribution and Shape Class of Type Group N.2.1a

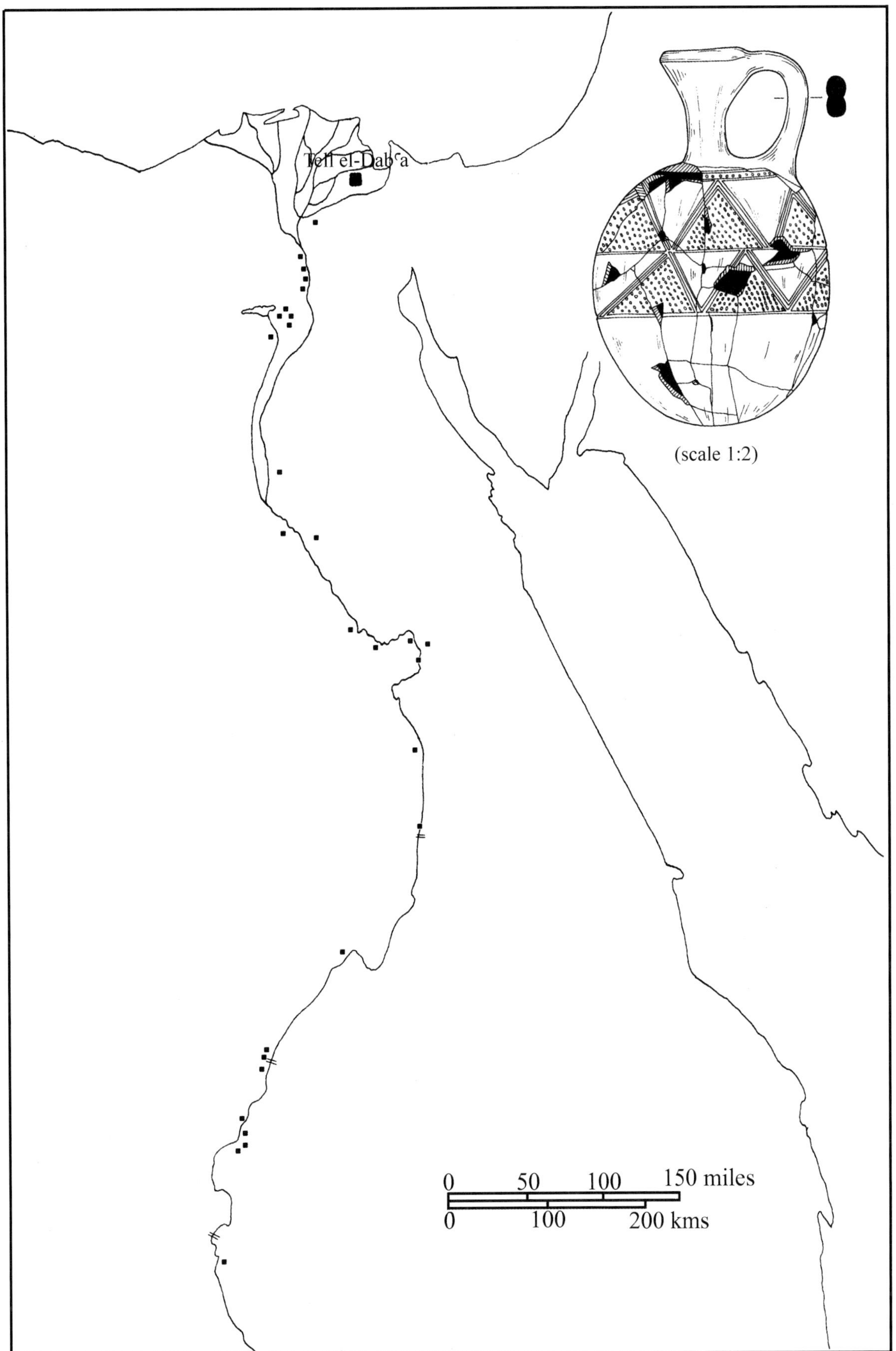

Fig. 225 Distribution and Shape Class of Type Group N.2.1b

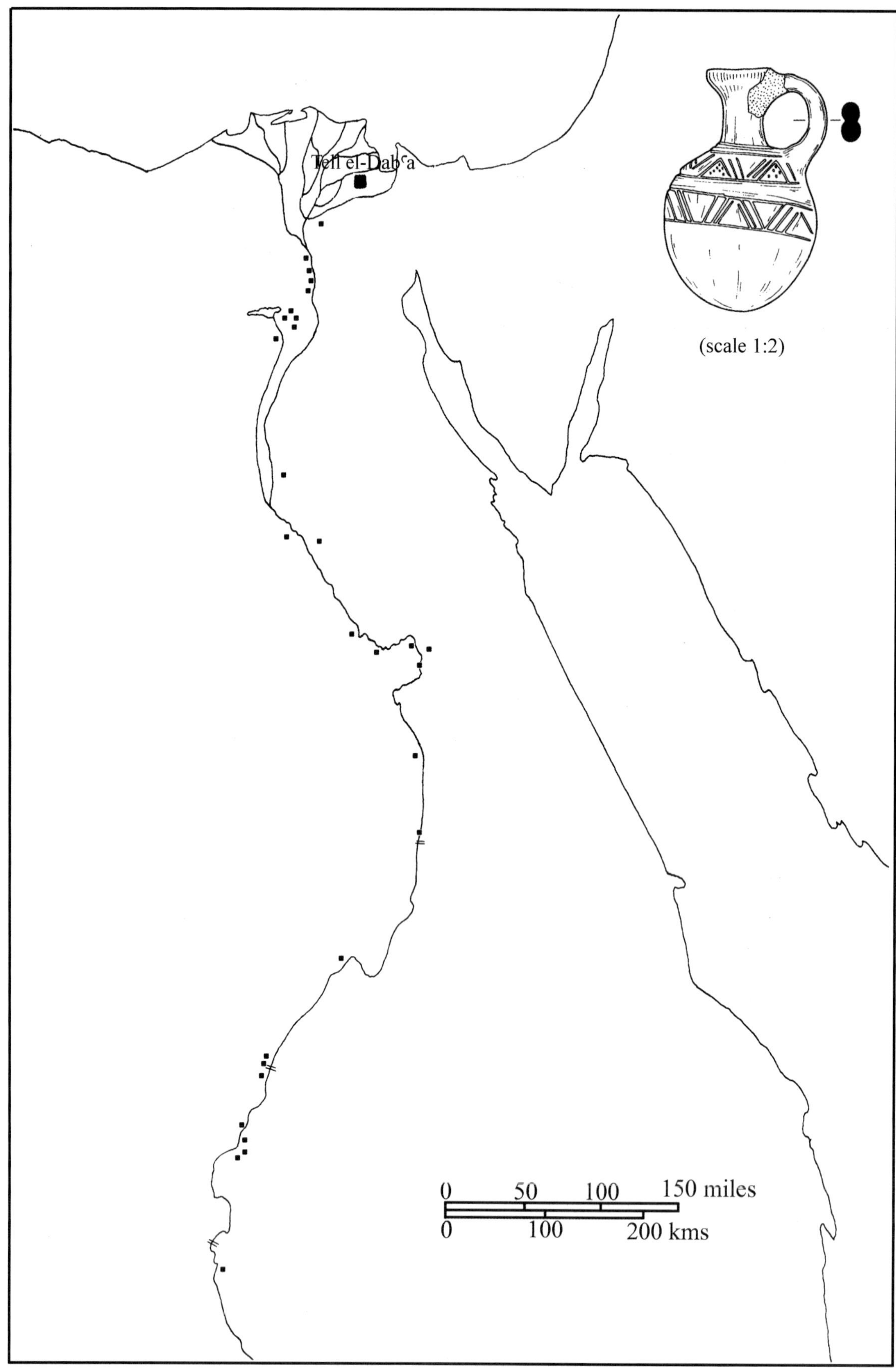

Fig. 226 Distribution and Shape Class of Type Group N.2.1c

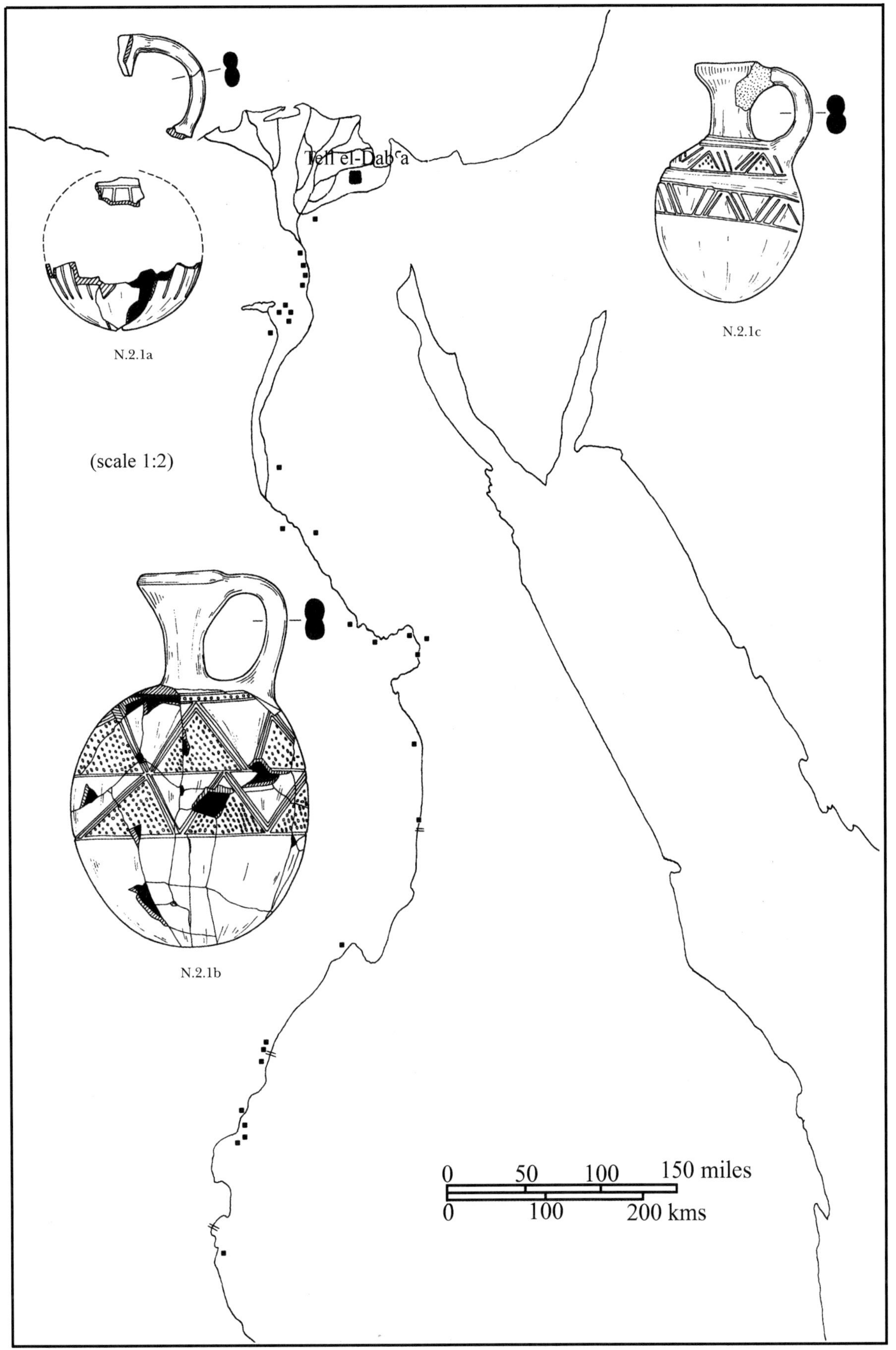

Fig. 227 Combined Distribution of Type Group N.2

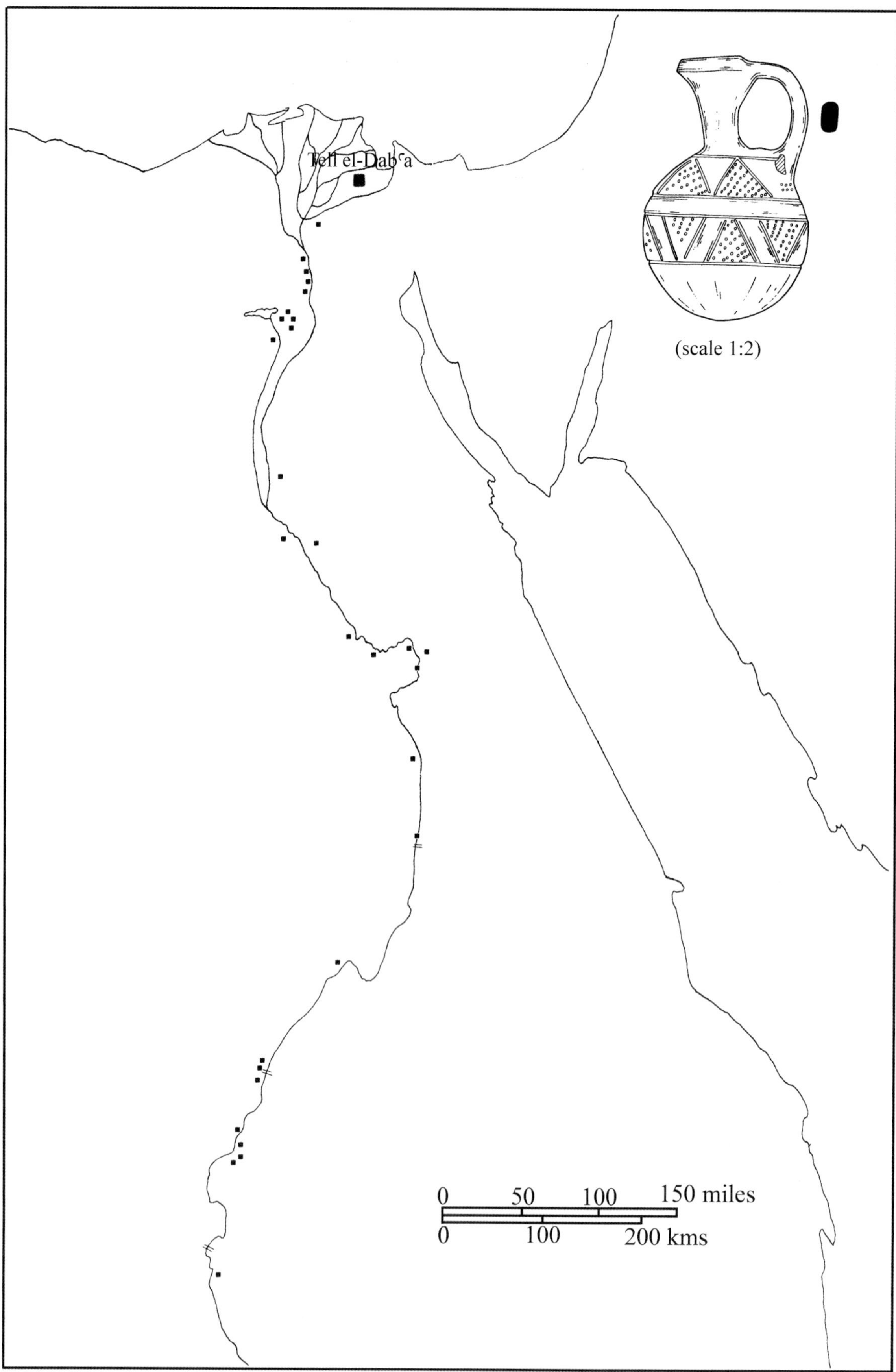

Fig. 228 Distribution and Shape Class of Type Group N.3.1a

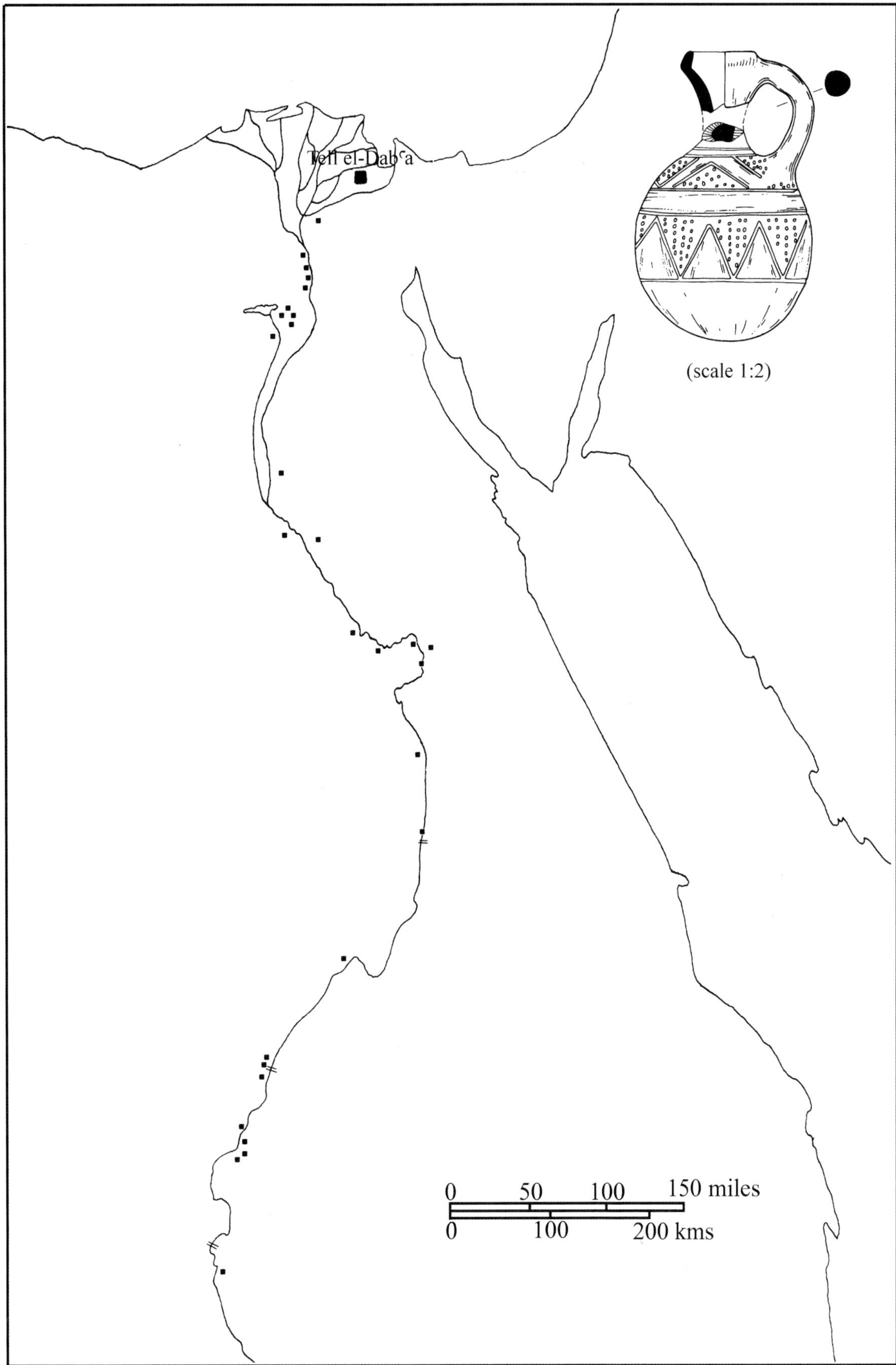

Fig. 229 Distribution and Shape Class of Type Group N.3.1b

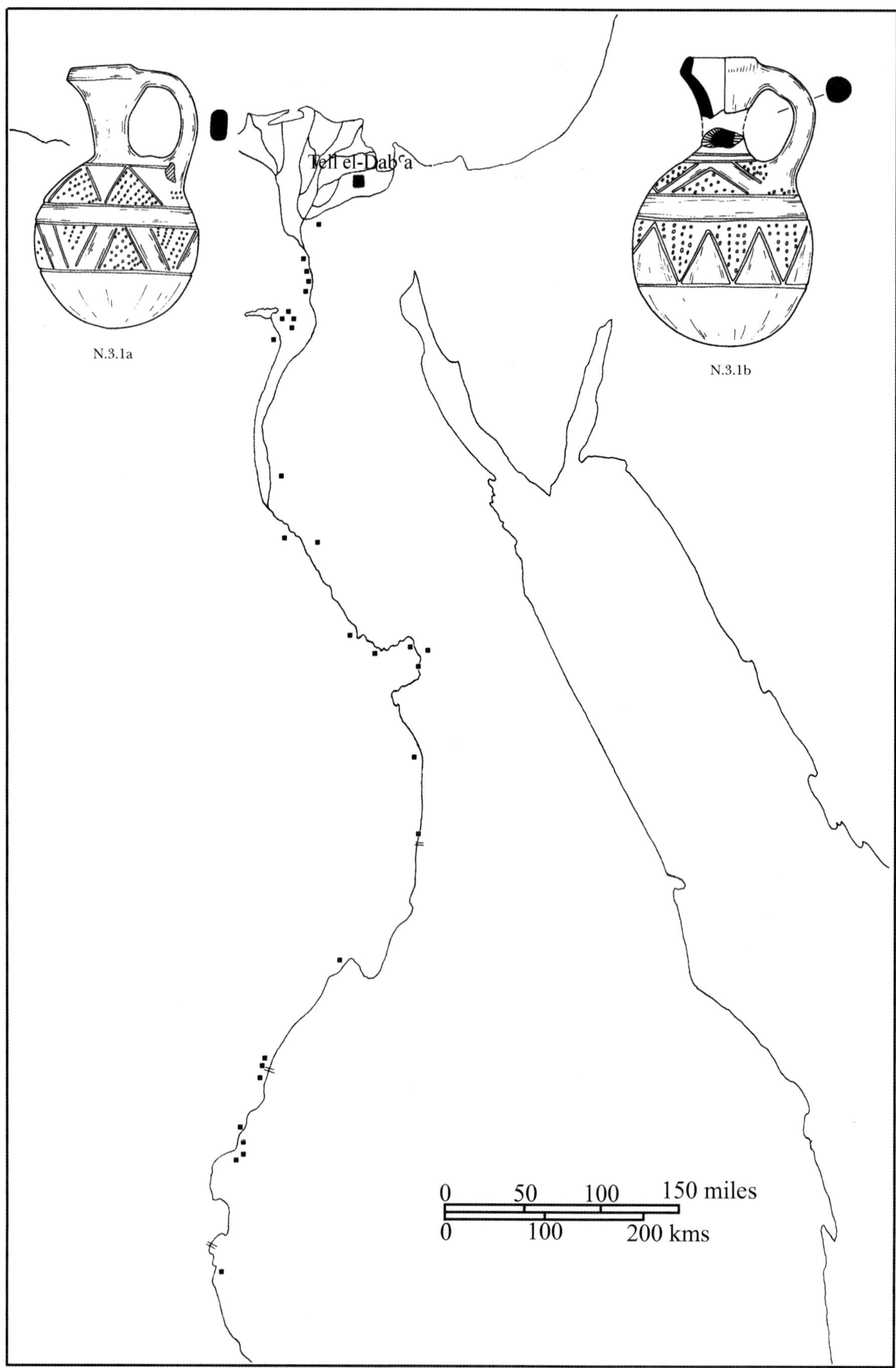

Fig. 230 Combined Distribution of Type Group N.3

an upper band of upright triangles and a lower band consisting of groups of three incised lines arranged in a zigzag pattern.

Type Group N.3 (Figs. 228–230)

Type Group N.3 comprises similar vessels to type group N.2, but in place of a double handle, have a single strap handle. Vessels attributed to group N.3 have two decorative schemes N.3.1a, in which the decoration consists of two zones of alternating standing and pendant triangles; and N.3.1b which has a row of alternating standing and pendant triangles and a row of pendant triangles below.

Type Group N.4 (Figs. 231–235)

Type group N.4 consists of globular jugs, which in contrast to jugs of type group N.2 have much smaller bodies in comparison to their total height. They have an upright rim and double handle which comes from the rim to a point low down on the shoulder. Four decorative styles are associated with this type: N.4.1a in which a band of decoration is wrapped around the vessel; N.4.1b which consists of one zone of intersecting standing and pendant triangles separated by a reserved zigzag; N.4.1c which has a horizontal band filled with vertical dots above and a row of standing triangles below; and N.4.1d which has two rows of standing triangles.

Type Group N.5 (Globular 1 hybrids) (Fig. 236)

Type Group N.5 is formed by at least three globular jugs, known from Tell el-Dabᶜa which are evidently Egyptian in shape (cf. above group N.3), but bear one band of impressed decoration which certainly owes its inspiration to the Palestinian group. Whether this group originated in the Levant is not clear since a preliminary visual analysis would attribute TD 3642 to a Palestinian clay, whilst the others are seemingly made of a Nile clay. A slightly similar jug, TD 6042, has a horizontal band around the upper belly with a zigzag pattern above.

Type Group N.6 (Fig. 237)

Type Group N.6 is known through a single example found at Tell el-Dabᶜa, TD 8856, which is a handmade globular jug with everted rim, strap handle and a simple decoration consisting of horizontal and oblique lines.

Type Group N.7 Three-Footed Jug (Fig. 238)

Type Group N.7 is also known through only one vessel, Tell el-Dabᶜa, TD 8665, which has a thickened rolled rim, double handle and a trilobal body, decorated with incised lines.

*

Perhaps related to the handmade globular jugs are the vessels here defined as belonging to groups N.8–N.11.

Type Group N.8 (Fig. 239)

Type group N.8 is represented by a strange vessel found at Gezer.[554] It has an everted rim, round handle and pointed base. The decoration consists of the typical Palestinian three bands, filled with individual dots.

Type Group N.9 (Fig. 240)

Vessels of Type Group N.9 comprise squat piriform jugs with rolled rims, double handles and ring bases, known from a single, poorly preserved example from Tell el-Dabᶜa (TD 5934). The preserved decoration comprises a rishi pattern around the neck.

Type Group N.10 (Fig. 241)

Type group N.10 consists of a piriform jug with kettle rim, tripartite handle joining at the neck below the rim, incisions at the neck, ring bases and two zones of decoration. In terms of their decoration these vessels fit ornamentally after the vessels of group I.5.4, but are placed here because of their tripartite handles. At present only one vessel with an upper zone of standing triangles and a lower one which is completely incised except for reserved 'spade' motifs is known.[555]

Type Group N.11 (Fig. 242)

Vessels of type N.11 are recognised through a model vessel, of unknown provenance, with kettle rim, bipartite handle and offset disc base.[556] The body is decorated with an incised scale pattern.

[554] Tel Aviv, Haaretz Museum 55060. Kaplan, *Tell el-Yahudiyeh Ware,* fig. 115a

[555] Boston MFA 1965.1740. Kaplan, *Tell el-Yahudiyeh Ware,* fig. 41b.

[556] London BM EA 21976; Hall, 1901, 68, fig. 29 right; Kaplan, *Tell el-Yahudiyeh Ware,* fig. 117b.

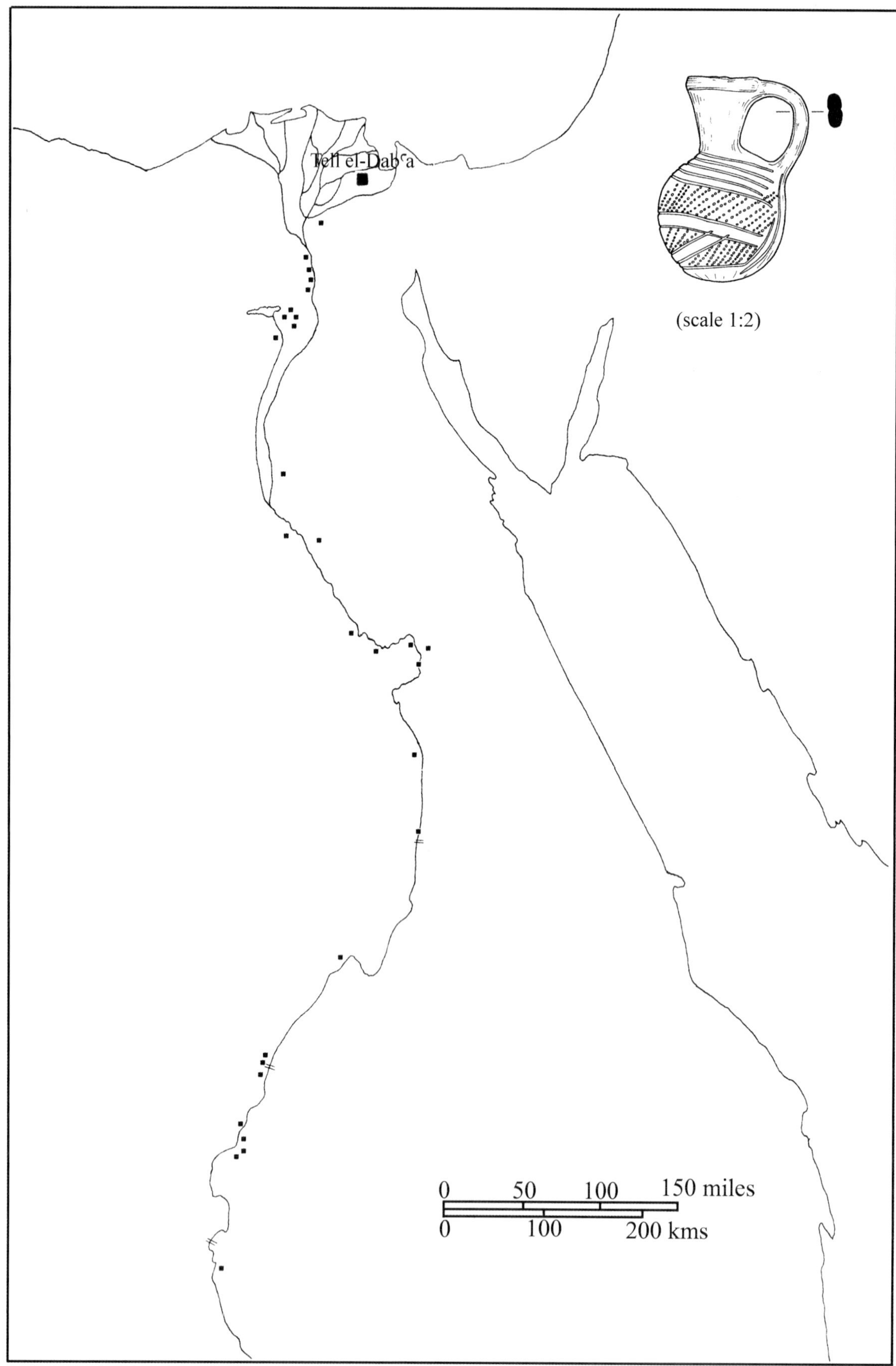

Fig. 231 Distribution and Shape Class of Type Group N.4.1a

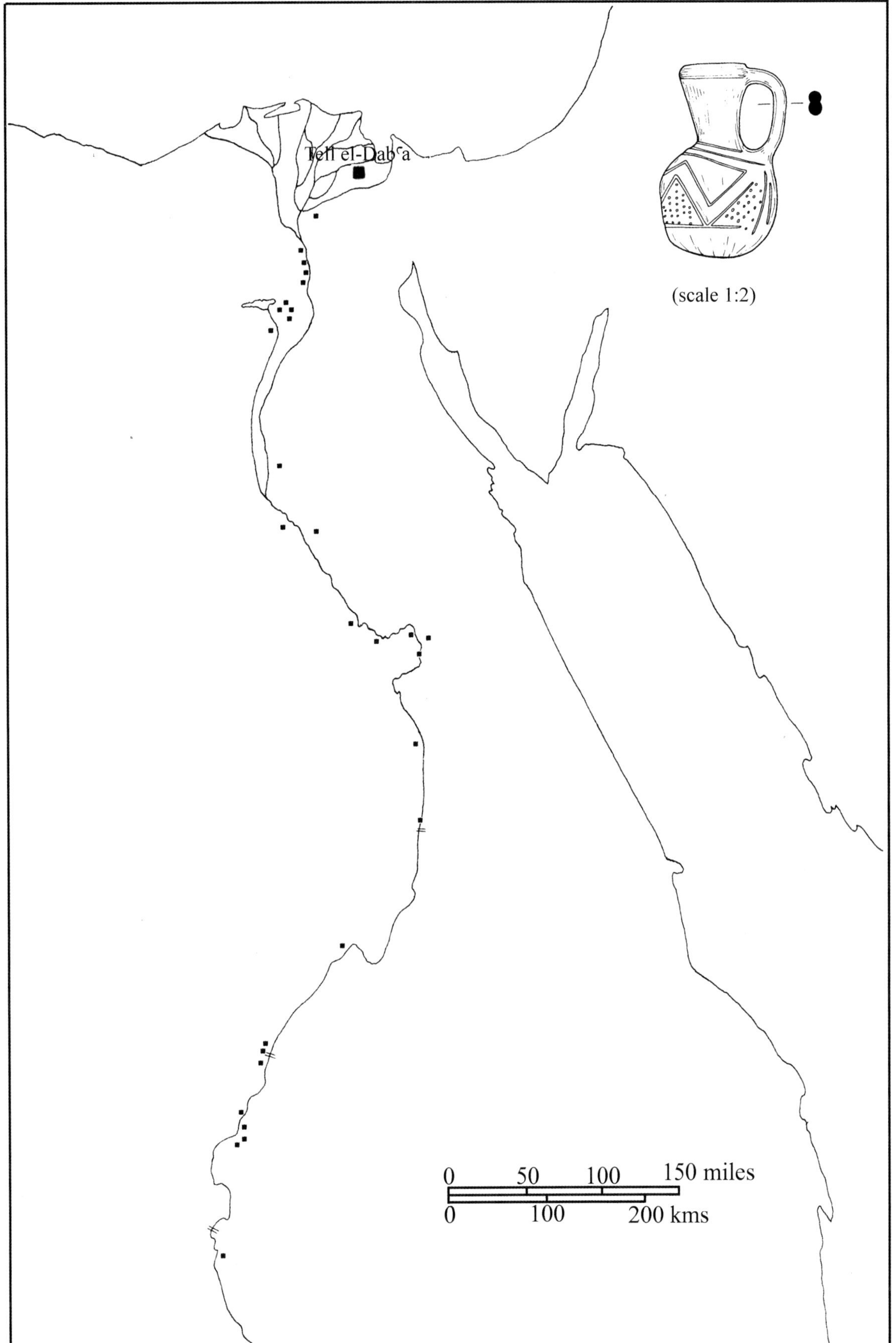

Fig. 232 Distribution and Shape Class of Type Group N.4.1b

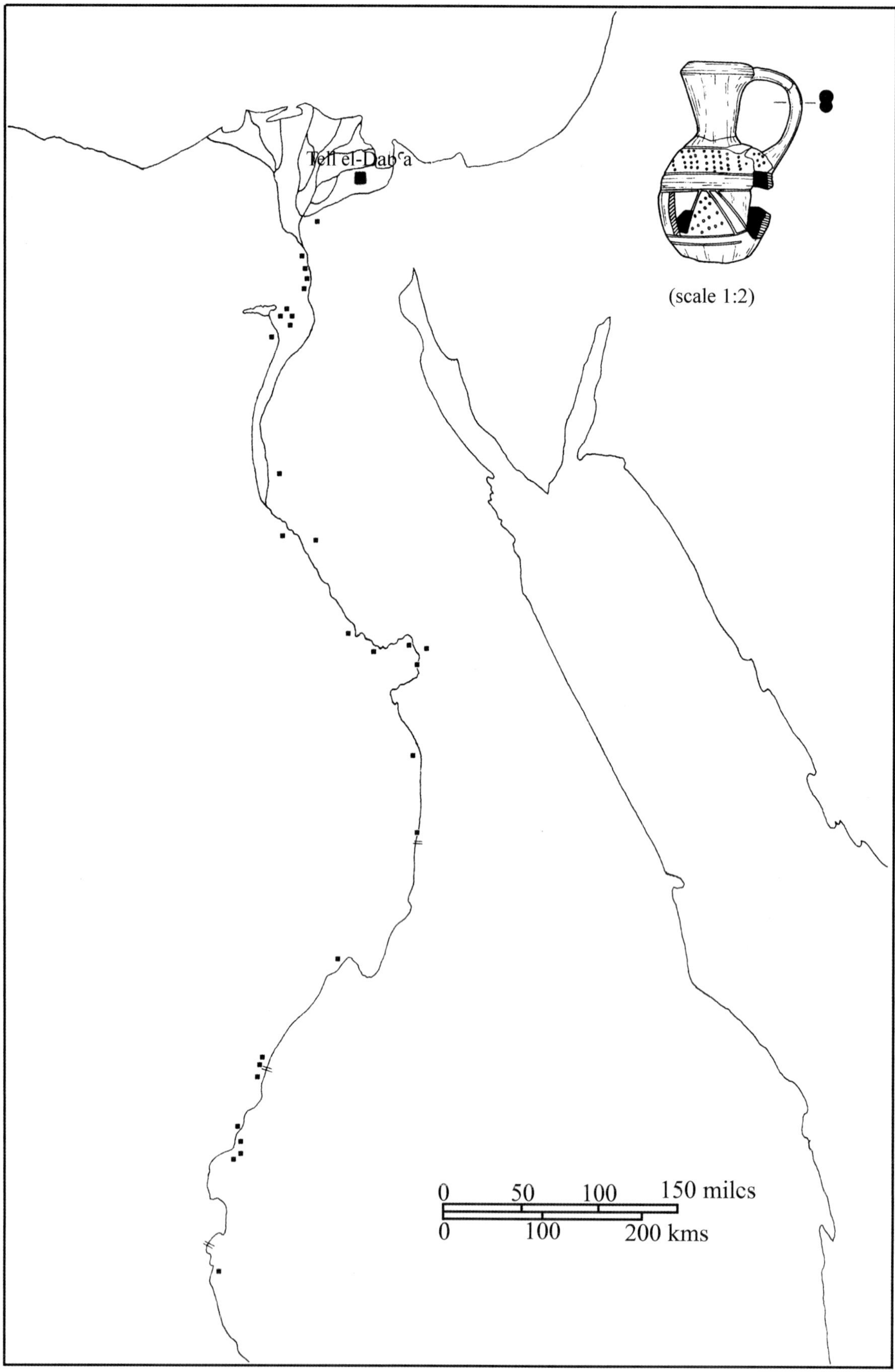

Fig. 233 Distribution and Shape Class of Type Group N.4.1c

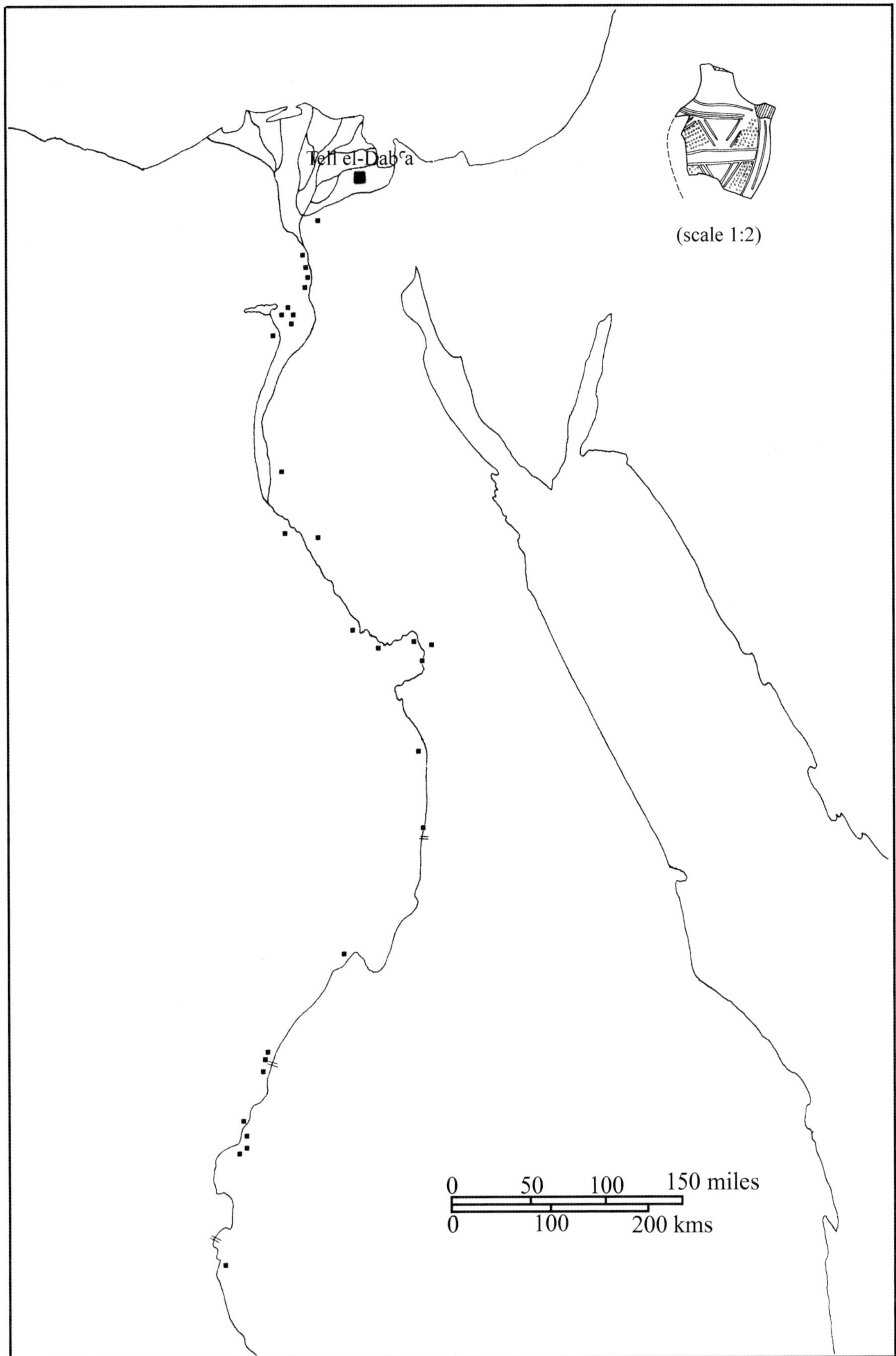

Fig. 234 Distribution and Shape Class of Type Group N.4.1d

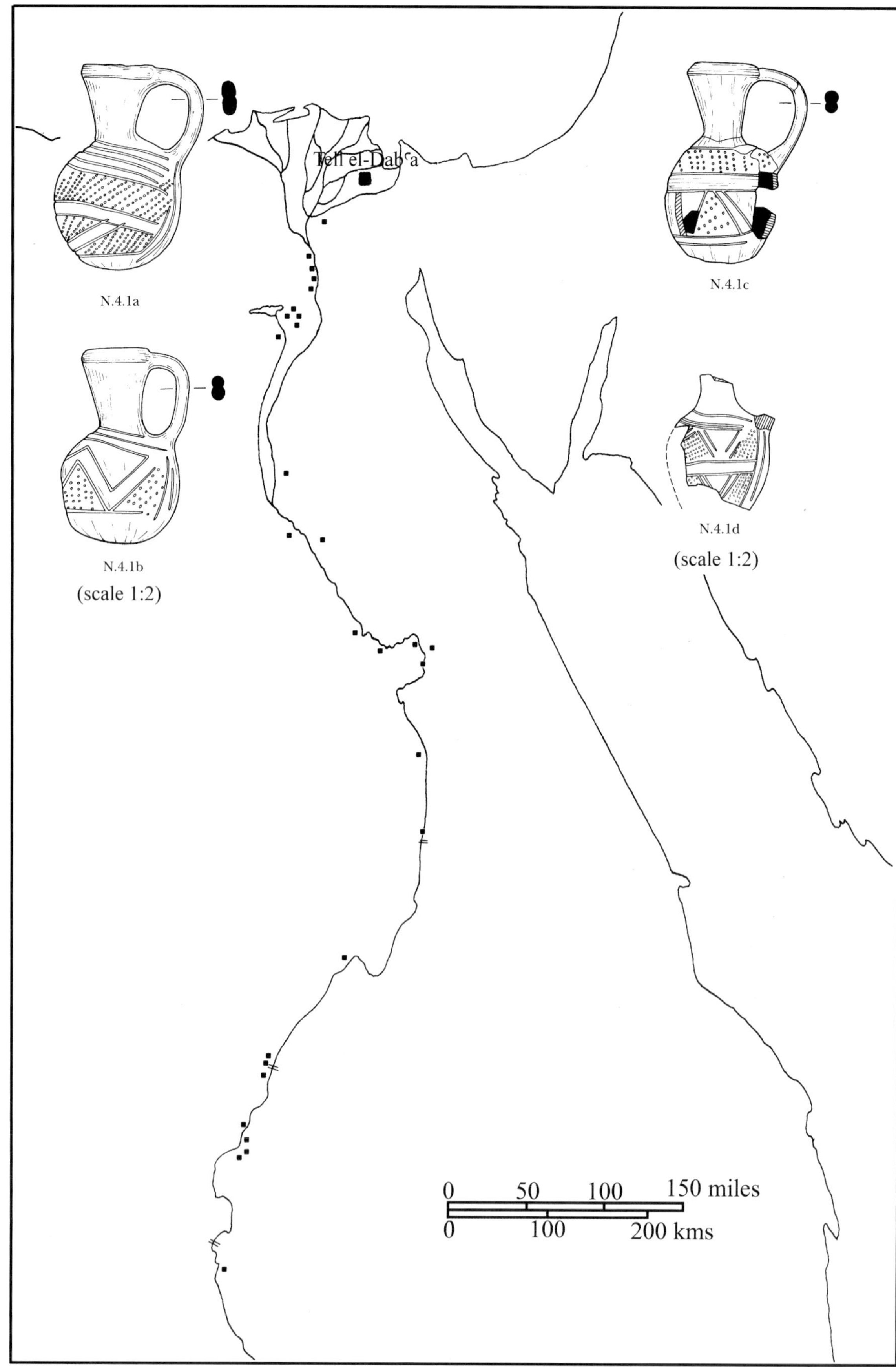

Fig. 235 Combined Distribution of Type Group N.4

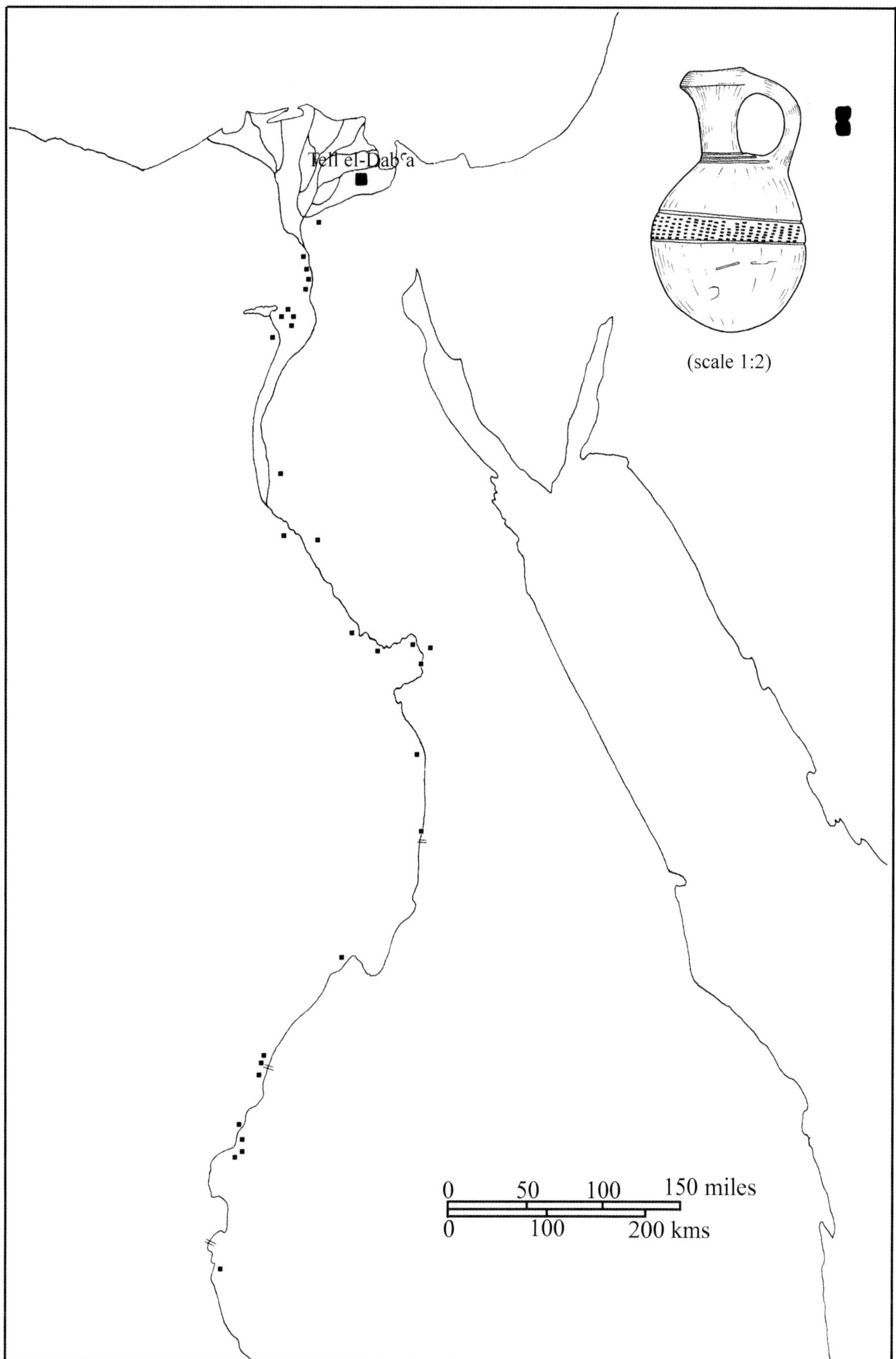

Fig. 236 Distribution and Shape Class of Type Group N.5

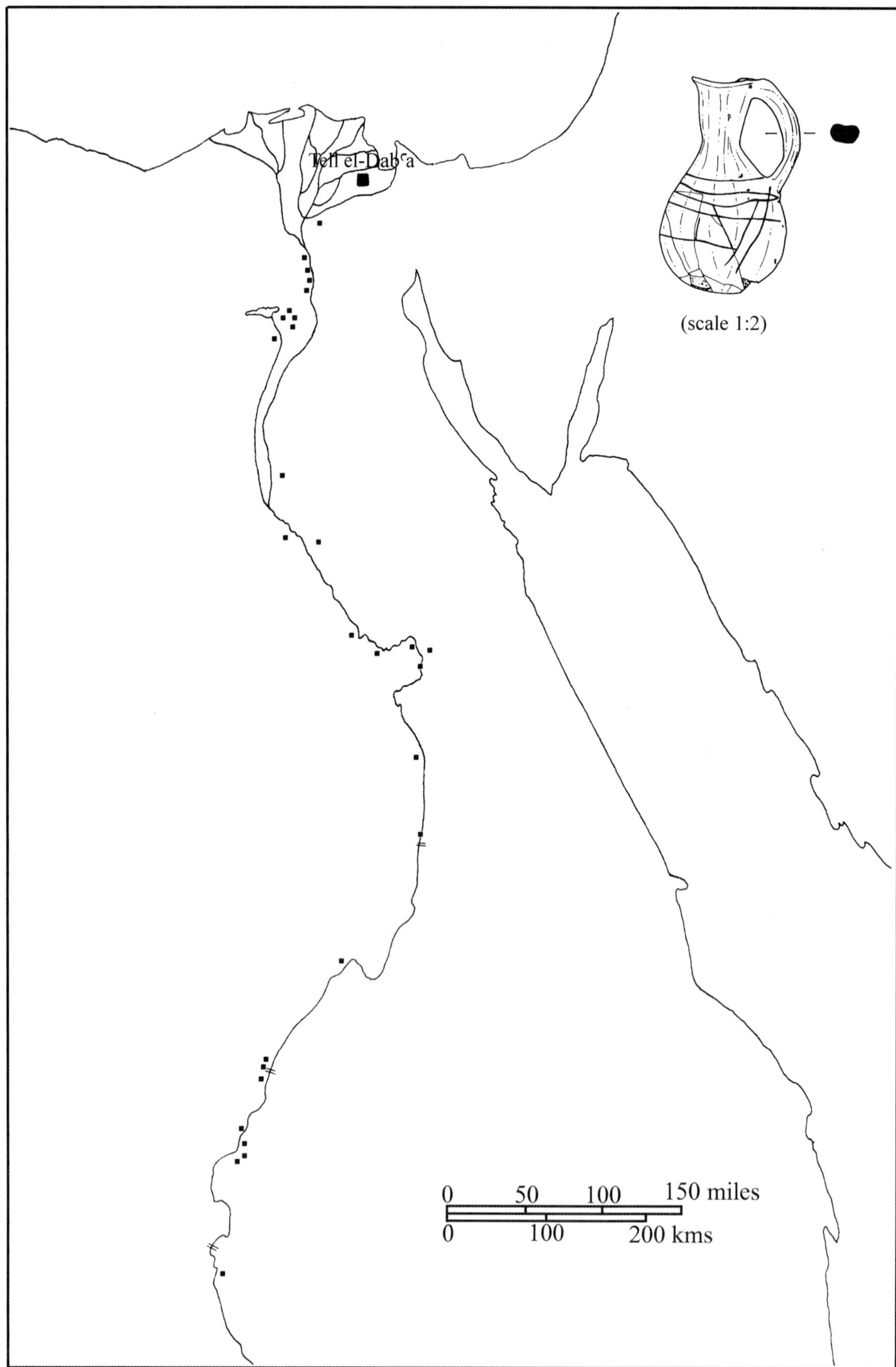

Fig. 237 Distribution and Shape Class of Type Group N.6

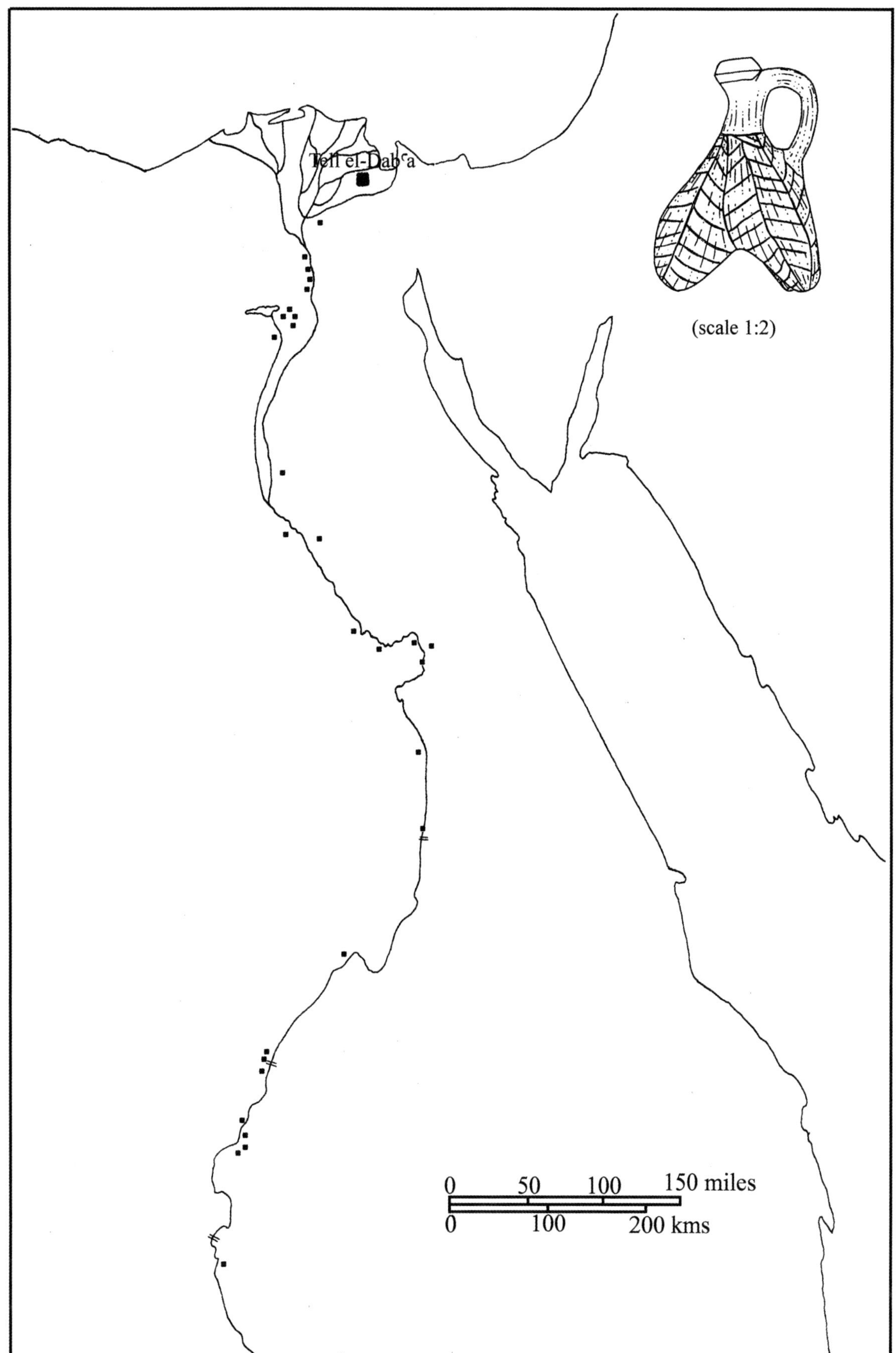

Fig. 238 Distribution and Shape Class of Type Group N.7

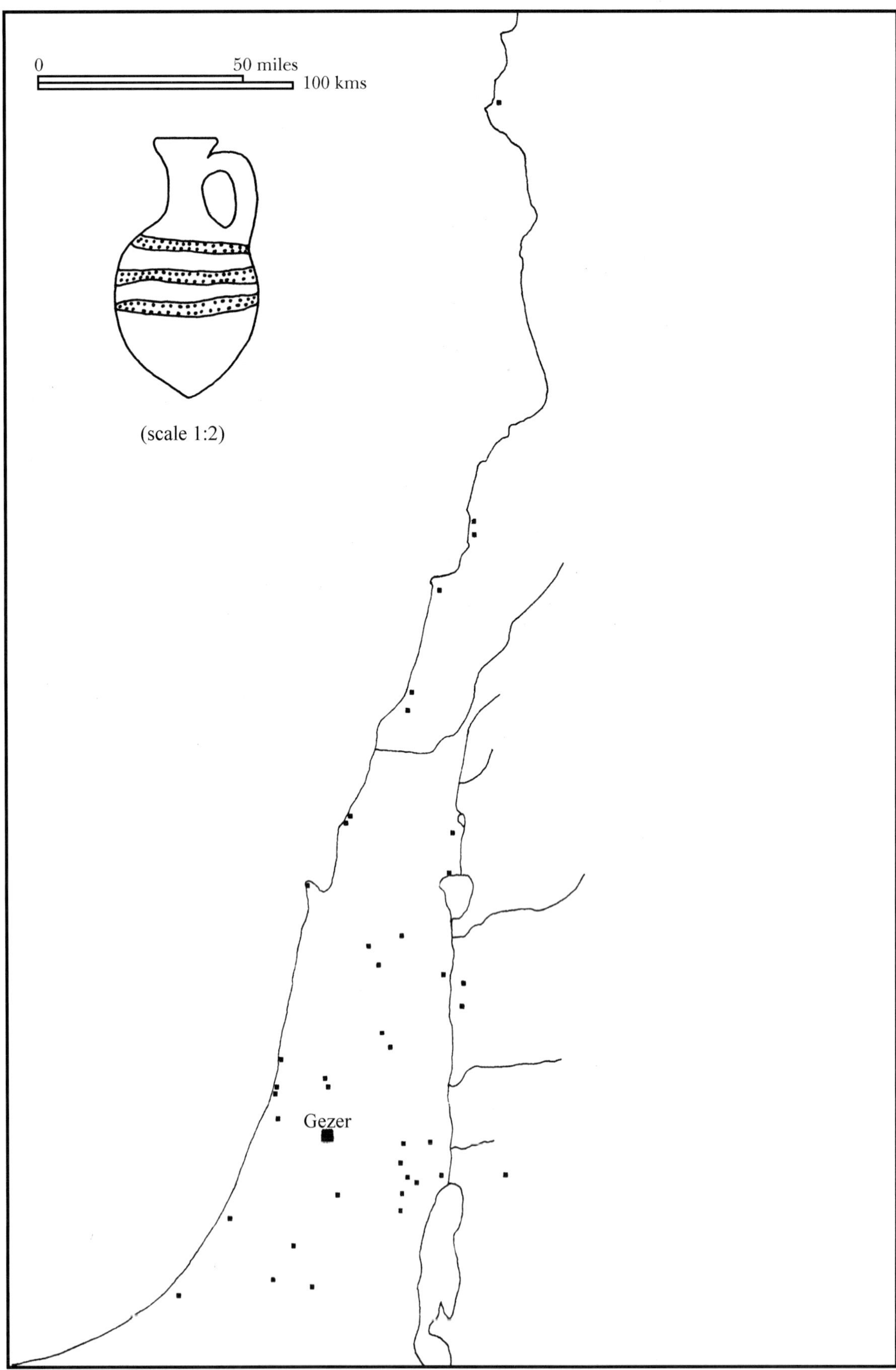

Fig. 239 Distribution and Shape Class of Type Group N.8

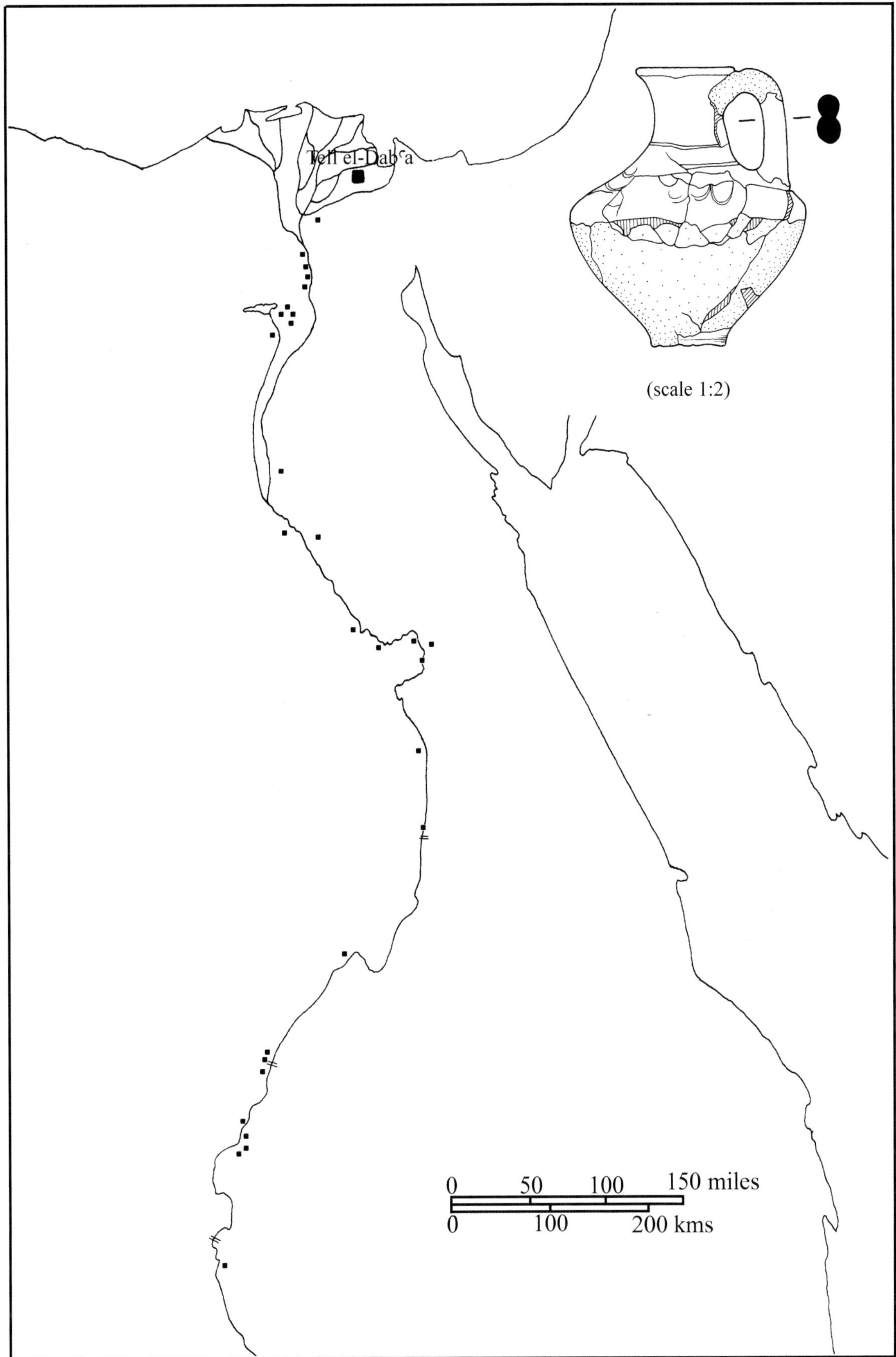

Fig. 240 Distribution and Shape Class of Type Group N.9

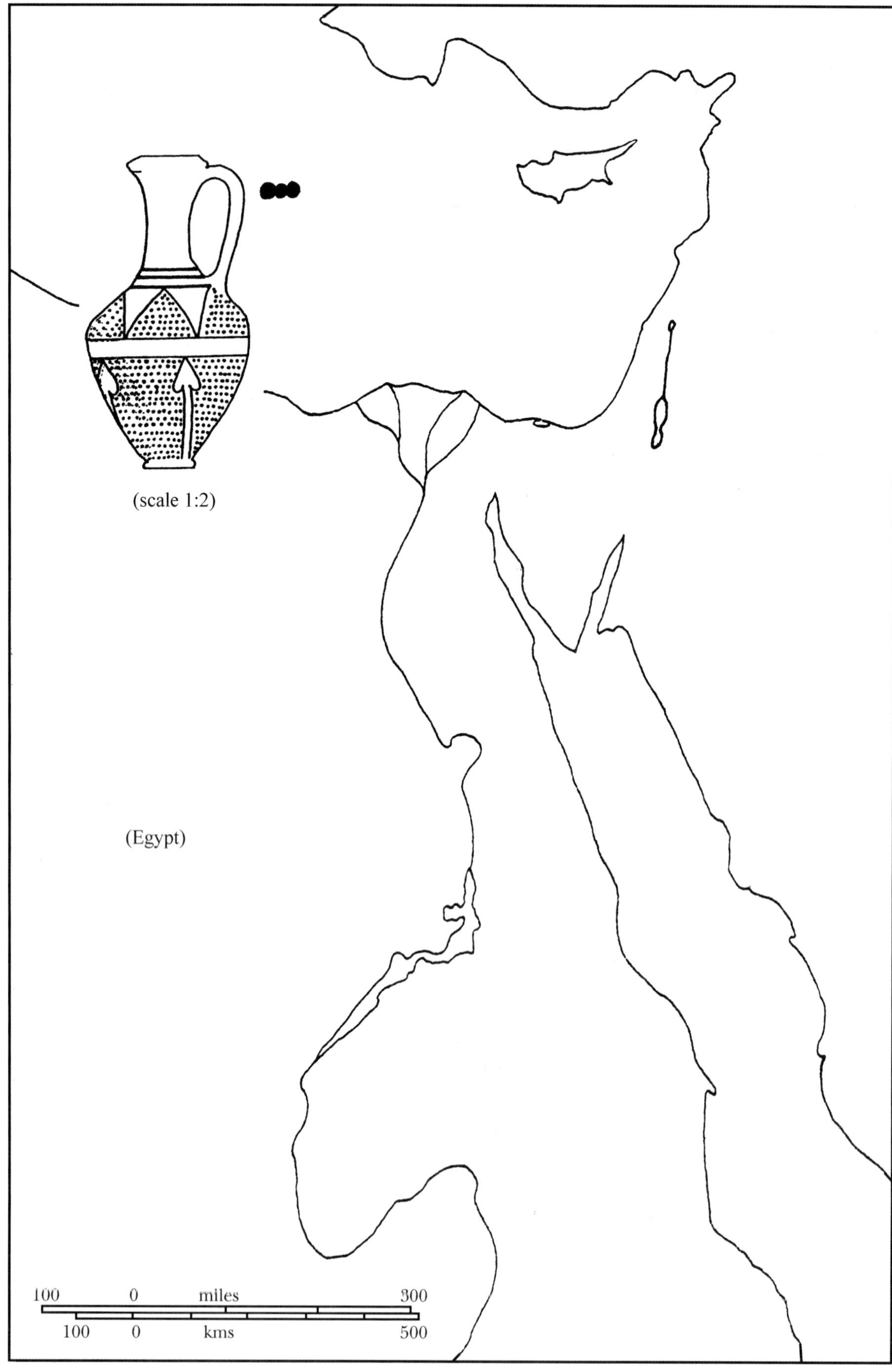

Fig. 241 Distribution and Shape Class of Type Group N.10

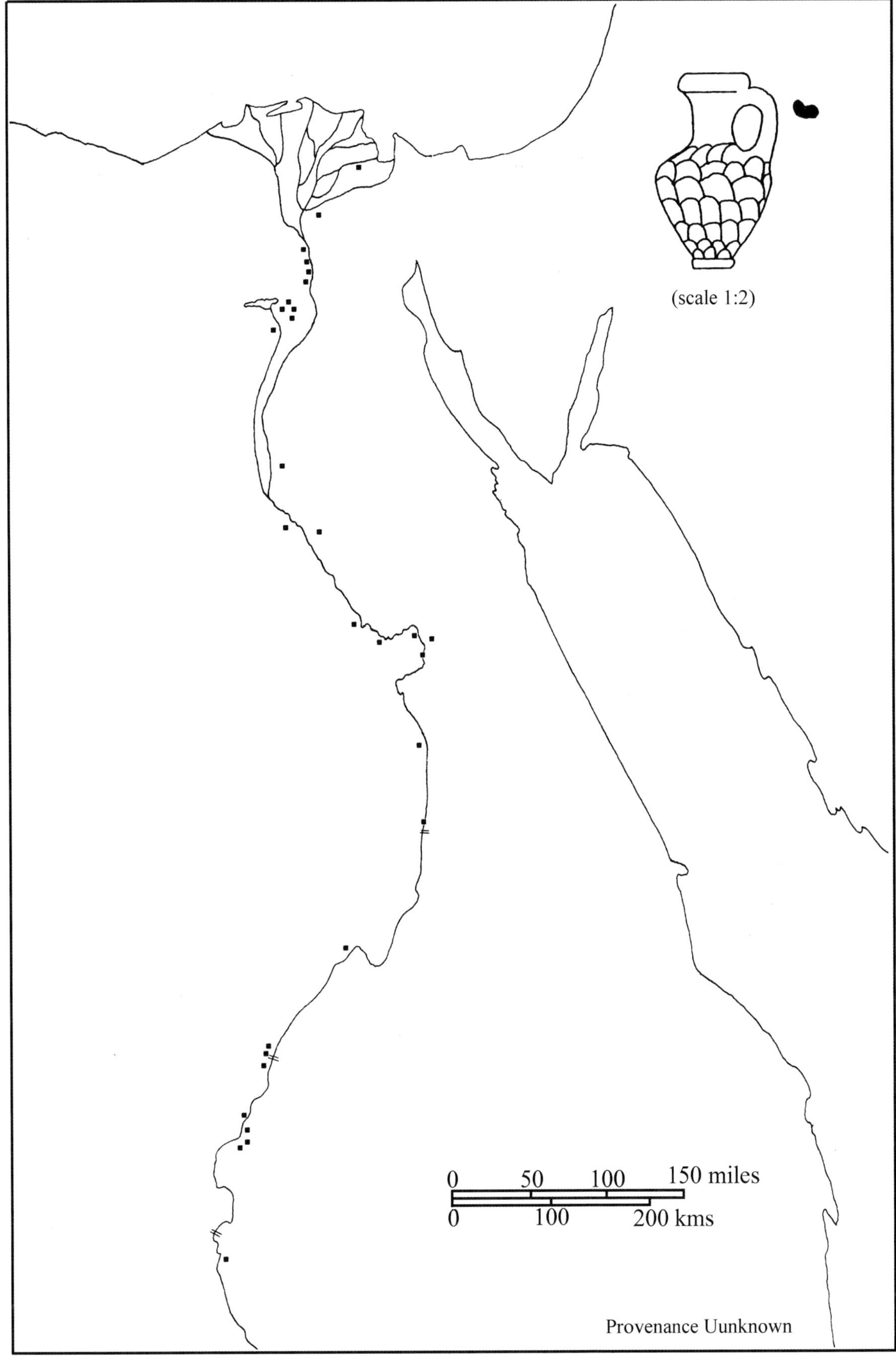

Fig. 242 Distribution and Shape Class of Type Group N.11

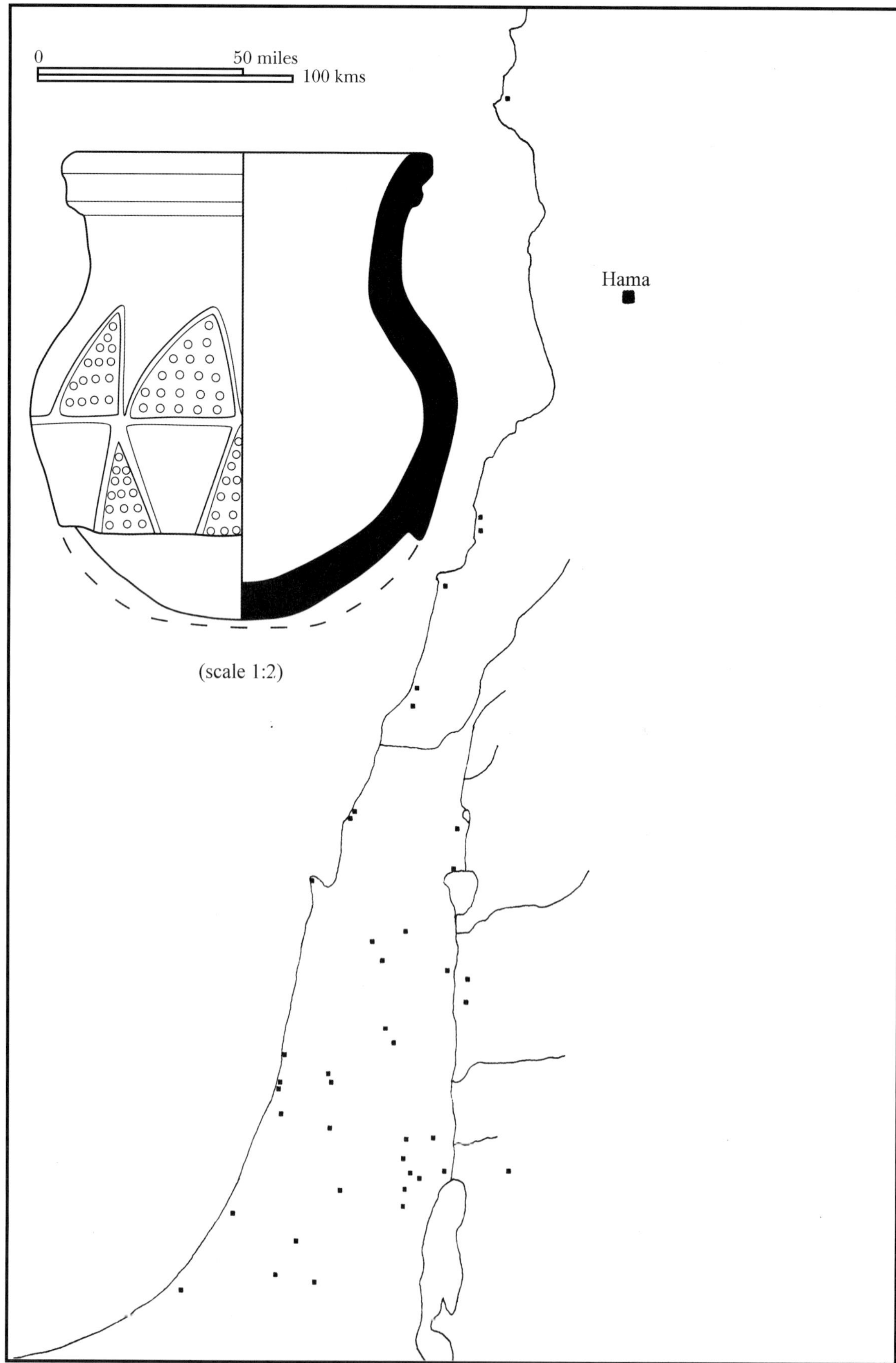

Fig. 243 Distribution and Shape Class of Type Group O.1

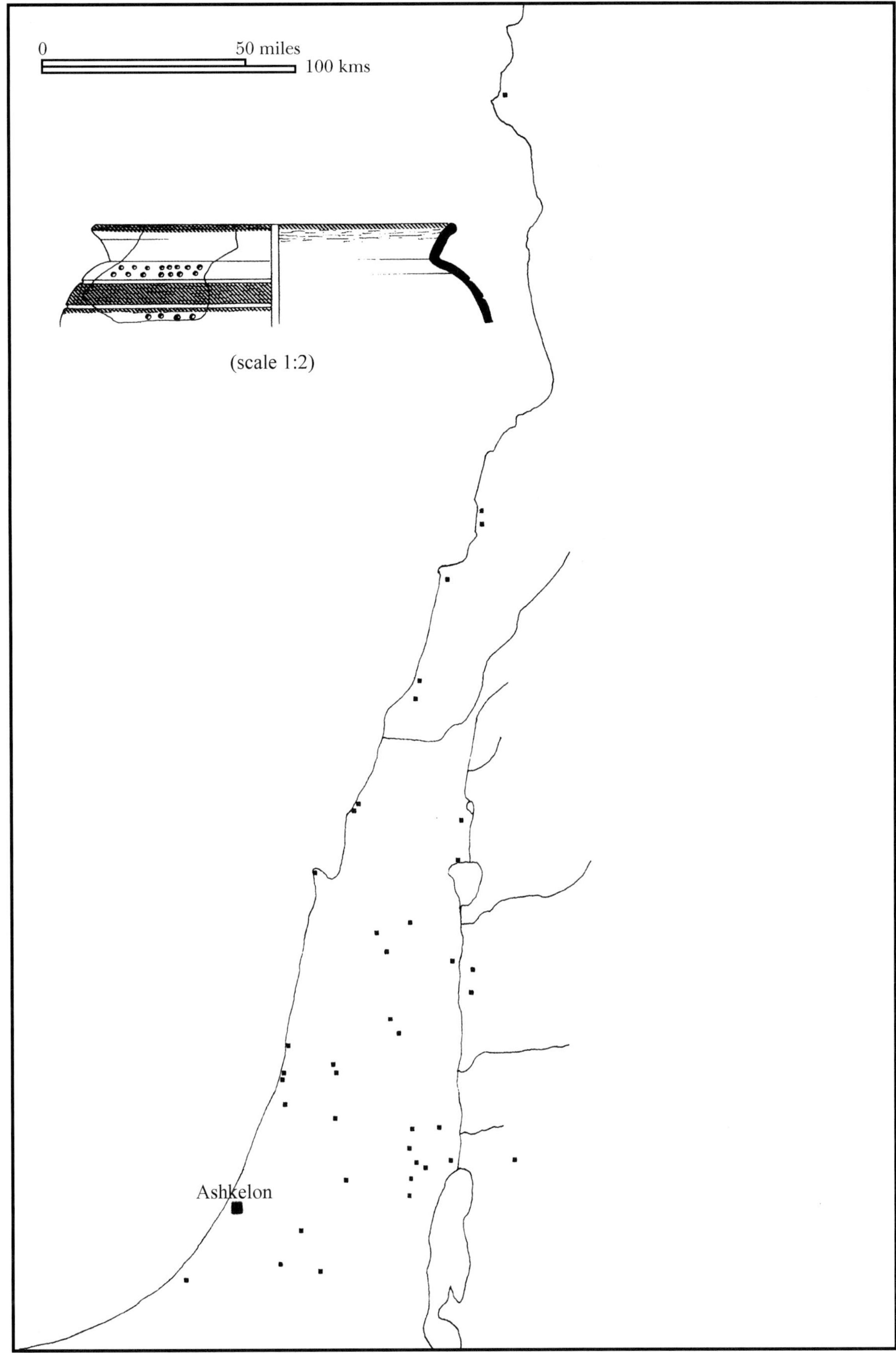

Fig. 244 Distribution and Shape Class of Type Group O.2

Branch O: Jars (Figs. 243, 244)

Whilst most known Tell el-Yahudiya style vessels are jugs, a small number of jars are also known, of which the most complete is a vessel from Hama stratum H.[557] This jar has two bands of standing triangles containing a number of dots infilled with white pigment. As befits the early date of this vessel, the MB IIA, the infilled dots were made with an awl, rather than a comb. From the 'Moat Deposit' at Ashkelon comes a restricted vessel with, as preserved, two horizontal bands of dots, infilled with a white pigment, separated from each other by a red burnished band.[558] The Moat Deposit belongs in Ashkelon Phase 13 which again dates to the MB IIA. Other incomplete, and later, vessels are known from Tell el-Daba (TD 4138E and TD 3415B). Whether the so-called "Kerma vase"[559] should be considered as an example of Tell el-Yahudiya ware as Kopetzky has suggested,[560] is open to question but it is probably unlikely. The vessel is handmade and bears incised decoration infilled with both red and white pigments. At present the only handmade vessels in true Tell el-Yahudiya style are the handmade globular jugs of group N, which may owe their origins to Cypriote inspiration, whilst no (other) Tell el-Yahudiya vessel is known with red filling. Moreover as Lacovara points out the decoration on the shoulder of the vessel has affinities with Kerman pottery, whilst the spiral and lotus motifs which adorn the body of the vase are known in the Kerman culture. It thus seems more probable, that although unique, the Kerma vase should probably be seen as the product of a potter entrenched in the Kerman culture.

A fragment of a spouted vessel, TD 9026K, found in pit L81 at Tell el-Daba, decorated with at least one infilled lotus flower, also appears to come from a closed vessel since there are signs of deep wheel ridging on the interior. As such this unusual piece is here considered to belong with the jars of Branch O.

Branch P: Open Vessels

Open vessels decorated in typical Tell el-Yahudiya technique are rare, but most of the known examples have recently been collated by Kopetzky.[561] The only complete shapes known to us are a dish from Pella, and two cups of a typical Middle Bronze shape from Megiddo tombs 5202 and 5171, which are decorated with oblique lines of incision just under the rim.[562] Since these clearly copy local vessels it is probable that they were locally made. Several fragments of other types of open vessels, however, have since come to light at Tell el-Dabᶜa. These, below catalogue entries 689–698, are most often decorated with running spirals, incised triangles, and in two, or three, cases lotus flowers. A spiral on a sherd from Lisht[563] looks, from the published drawing, somewhat similar to those found on the open shapes at Tell el-Dabᶜa, and thus may also be from a similar vessel. They may be preliminarily classified into the following groups:

Type Group P.1 Dishes

Only two Tell el-Yahudiya style dishes are known to us, and both are clearly Middle Bronze Levantine rather than Egyptian in style, although the example from type group P.1.2 is made of a Nile Clay.

Type Group P.1.1 (Fig. 245)

Type group P.1.1 is known from a single, complete, example from Burial Feature 106 at Pella. It consists of a burnished dish with slightly inturned rim and a spiral tripod foot.[564] Impressed into the interior are three rows of singular dots, each infilled with a white pigment.

Type Group P.1.2 (Fig. 246)

Type group P.1.2 is known from the rim sherd Tell el-Dabᶜa, TD 9026H, which evidently derives form a dish with modeled rim, two, or four, handles and pre-

[557] E. Fugmann, *Hama II. Fouilles et recherches 1931–38*, fig. 139b/5 B 265; Kopetzky, Gefässe im Tell el-Yahudiya Stil, in: E. Cerny, I. Hein, H. Hunger, D. Melmann, A. Schwab (eds.), *Timelines. Studies in Honour of Manfred Bietak II*, OLA 149.2, Leuven, 2006, 178.

[558] K. Kopetzky, Gefässe in Tell el-Yahudiya Stil, 177, 2006; cf also below page 561 no. 17.

[559] P. Lacovara, An Incised Vase from Kerma, *JNES* 44, 1985, 211–226.

[560] K. Kopetzky, Gefässe in Tell el-Yahudiya Stil, 2006, 179–181.

[561] K. Kopetzky, Gefässe in Tell el-Yahudiya Stil, 2006, 177–186.

[562] Loud, *Megiddo II*, 186, 187, pls. 9.10, 14.35, Kaplan, *Tell el-Yahudiyeh Ware*, fig. 129d.

[563] Smith W.S., *The Art and Architecture of Ancient Egypt*, 1965, 118, fig. 48d. Merrillees, *Trade and Transcendance*, fig. 49, top row, second from right.

[564] S. Bourke, R. Sparks and M. Schroeder, Pella in the Middle Bronze Age, in: P.M. Fischer (ed.), *The Chronology of the Jordan Valley during the Middle and Late Bronze Ages: Pella, Tell Abu al-Kharaz, and Tell Deir 'Alla*, Vienna, 2006, 48–49, figs. 41–42.

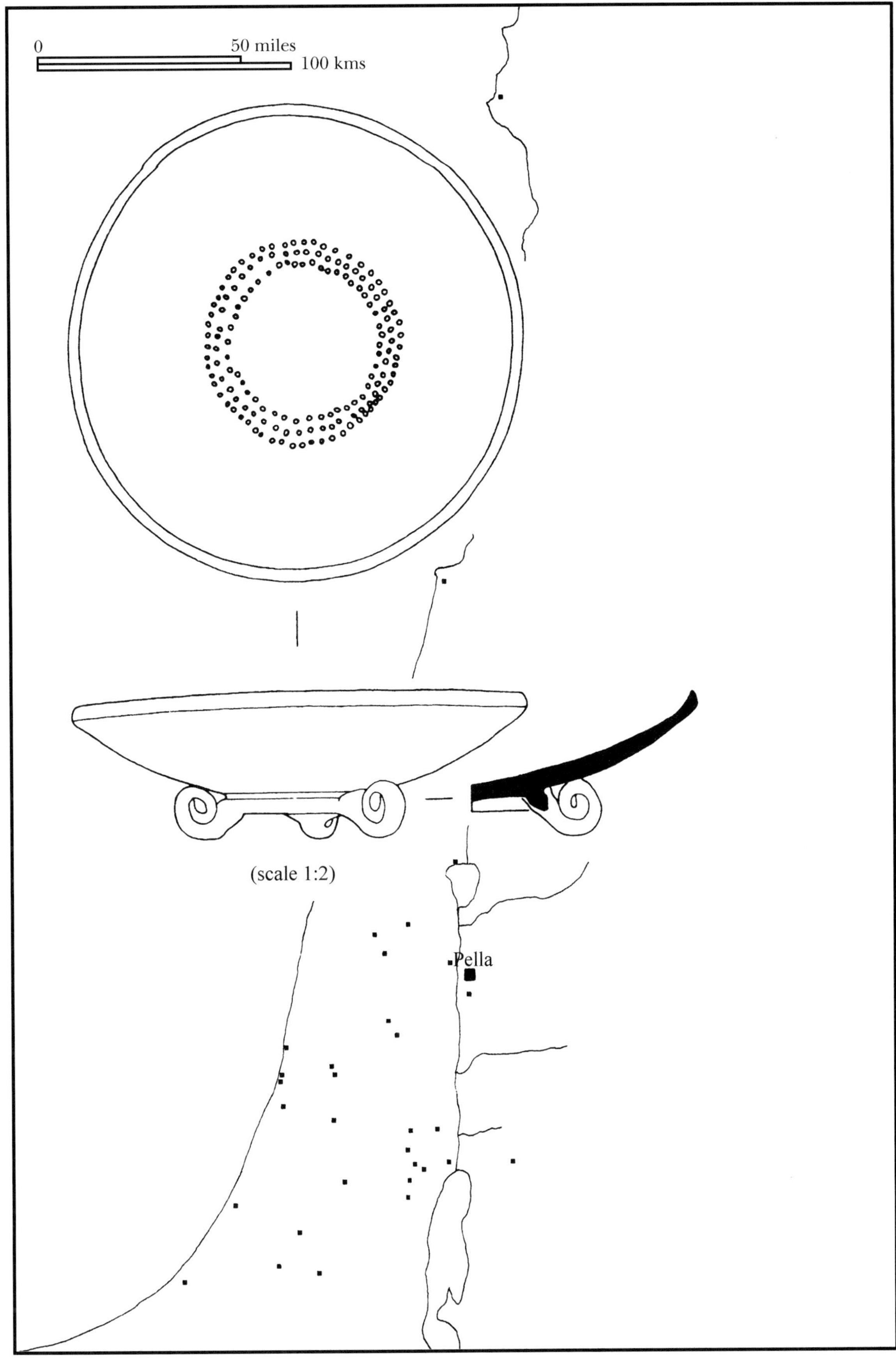

Fig. 245 Distribution and Shape Class of Type Group P.1.1

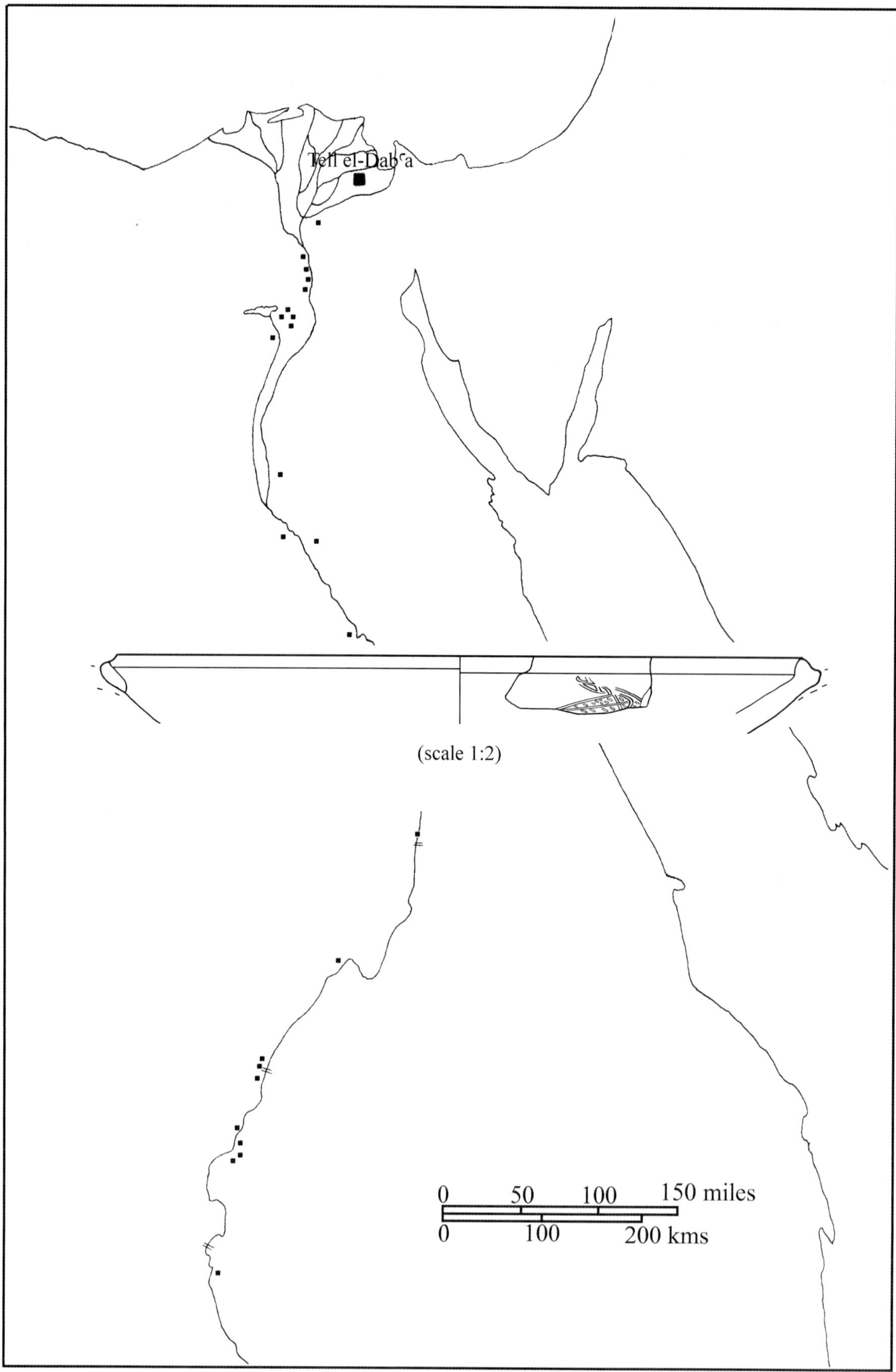

Fig. 246 Distribution and Shape Class of Type Group P.1.2

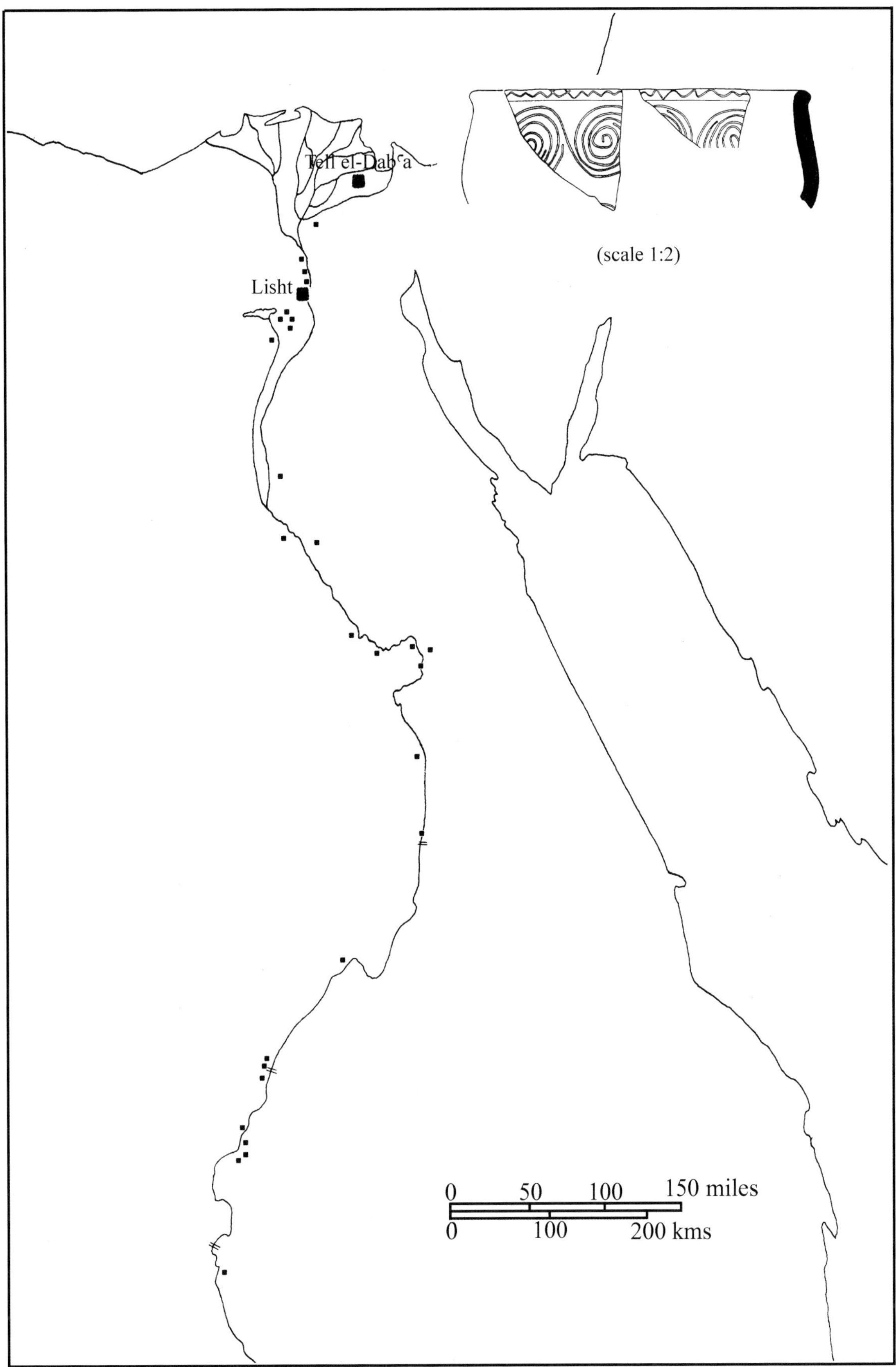

Fig. 247 Distribution and Shape Class of Type Group P.2

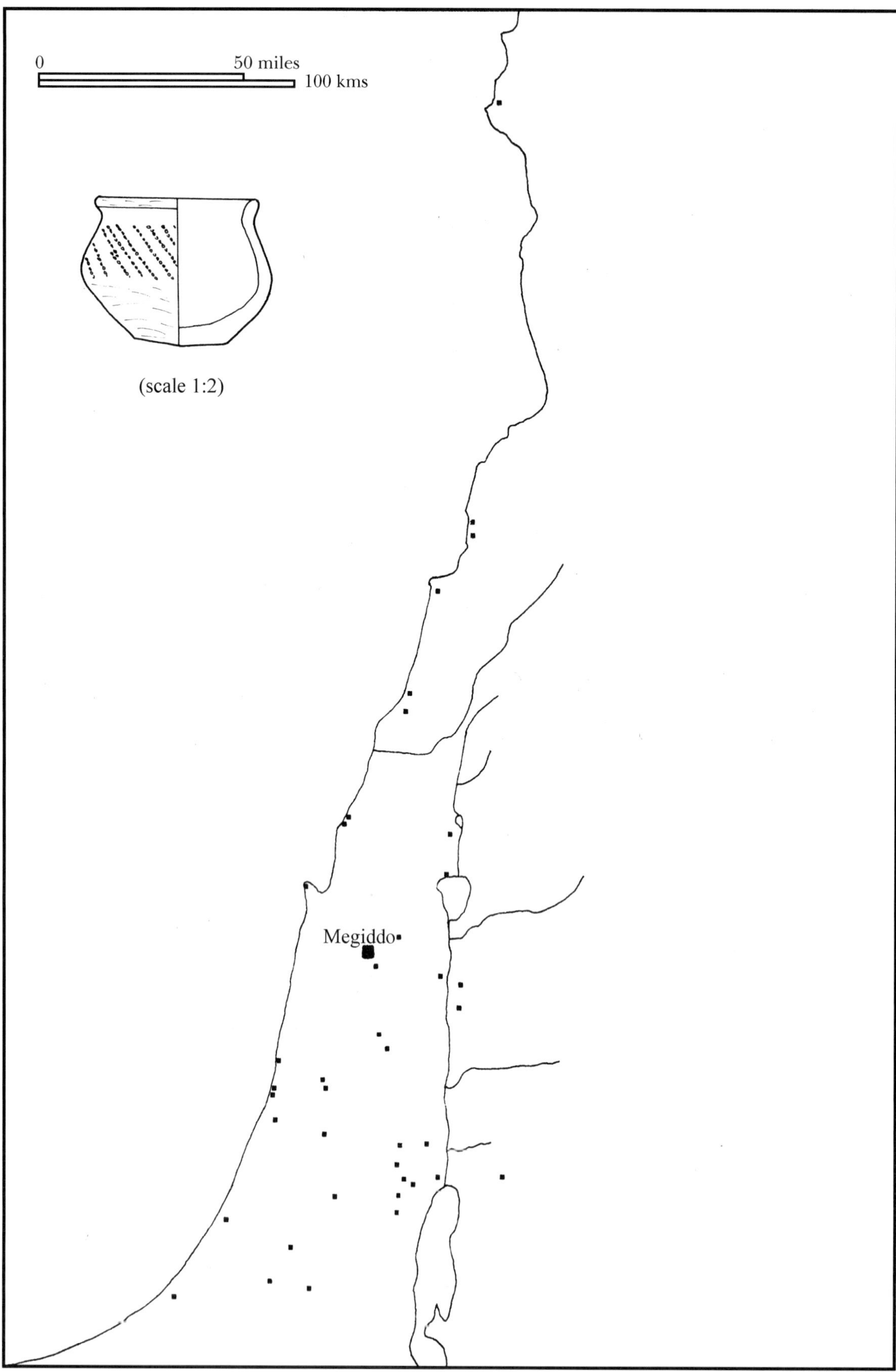

Fig. 248 Distribution and Shape Class of Type Group P.3

sumably a ring base, although only a rim sherd which bears a handle scar is preserved.

Type Group P.2 Ring (?)-based Cups (Fig. 247)

As yet type group P.2 which consists of open vessels, possibly ring-based cups, are the most common. They are usually decorated with spirals and examples have been found at both Tell el-Dabᶜa and Lisht (?).[565]

Type Group P.3 Flat-based Cups (Fig. 248)

Type group P.3 comprises the small cups found at Megiddo described above.

Type Group P.4 Round-based Cups (Fig. 249)

Type group P.4 is recognised through an incomplete cup from Tell el-Dabᶜa, TD 4242. It resembles contemporary Egyptian cups and is decorated with stylised lotus flowers.

Type Group P.5 Beakers (Fig. 250)

Type group P.5 is known from an incomplete beaker from Tell el-Dabᶜa, TD 9012H. It resembles contemporary Egyptian beakers and is decorated with stylised lotus flowers, decorated in typical Tell el-Yahudiya technique.

Branch Q: Ringstands (Fig. 251)

It is not certain that ringstands in Tell el-Yahudiya ware actually exist. However a fragment from Khatana, pit complex L81, TD 9018W, is possibly part of a ringstand. It is burnished on the interior, and on the inner rim are a series of incised vertical lines made with a ten-toothed comb. Since however it is incomplete, the possibility that this piece is actually the neck of an unknown jug type cannot be discounted.

---

565 Smith W.S., *The Art and Architecture of Ancient Egypt*, 1965, 118, fig. 48d. Merrillees, *Trade and Transcendance*, fig. 49, top row, second from right.

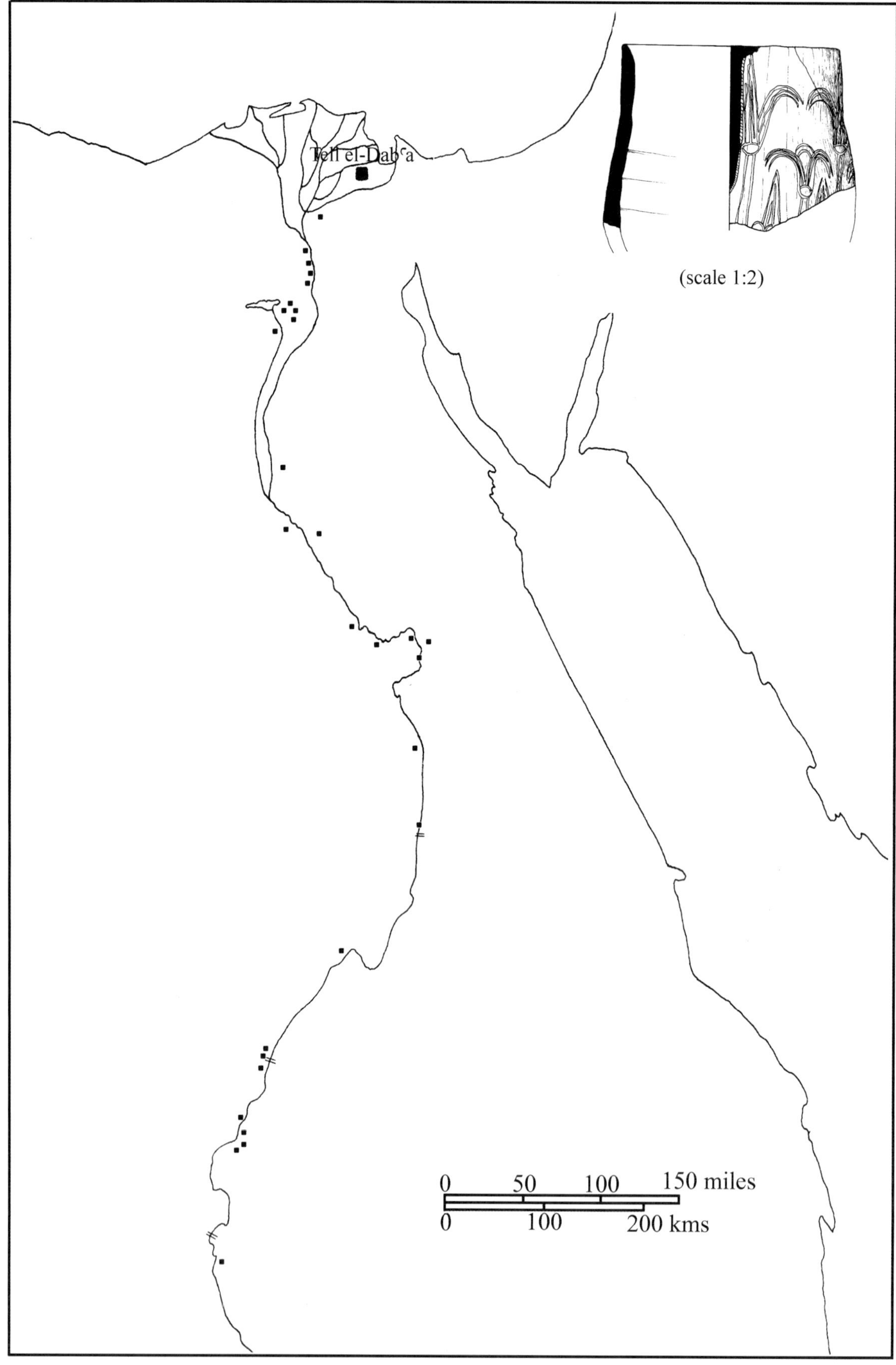

Fig. 249 Distribution and Shape Class of Type Group P.4

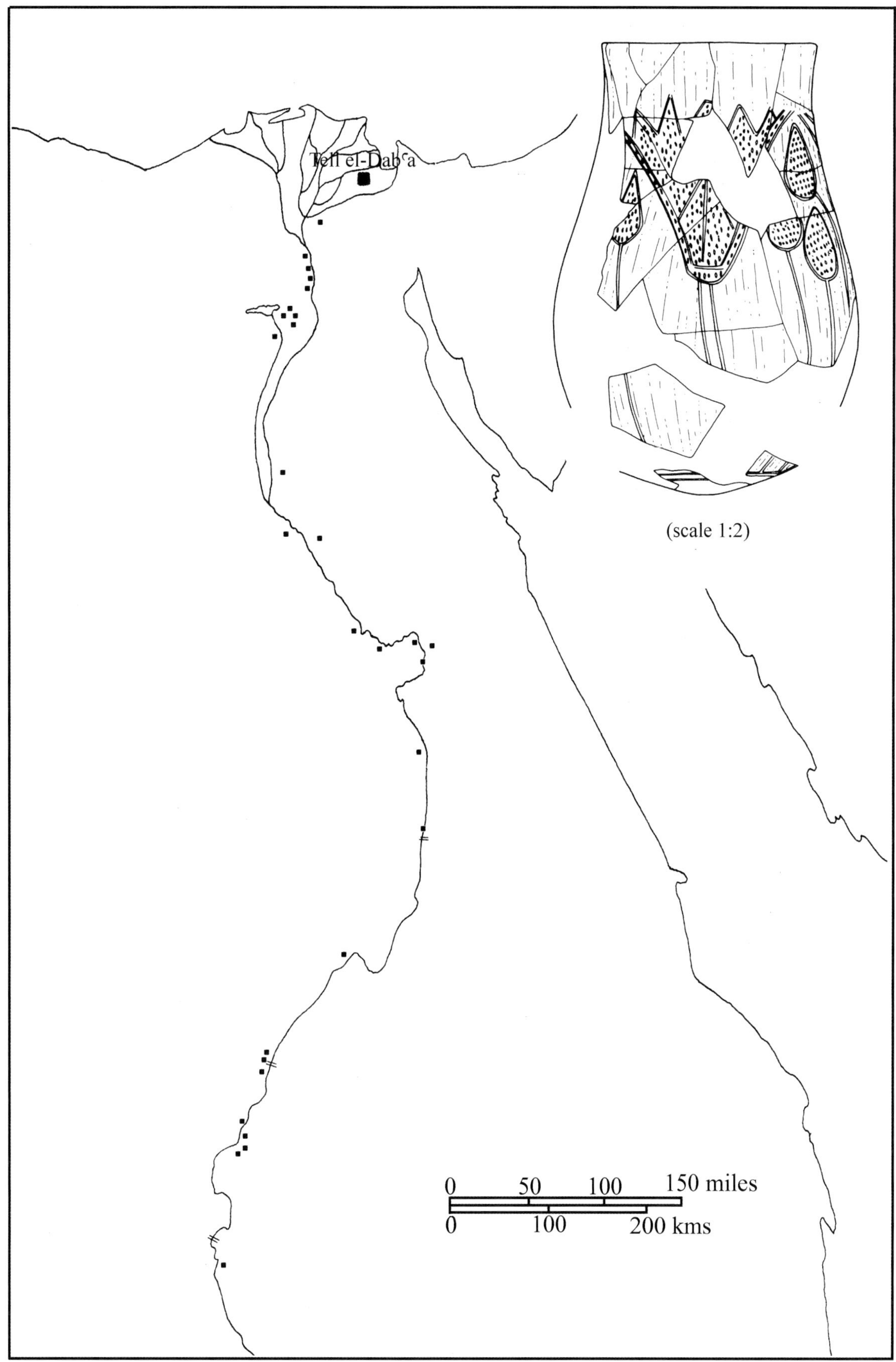

Fig. 250 Distribution and Shape Class of Type Group P.5

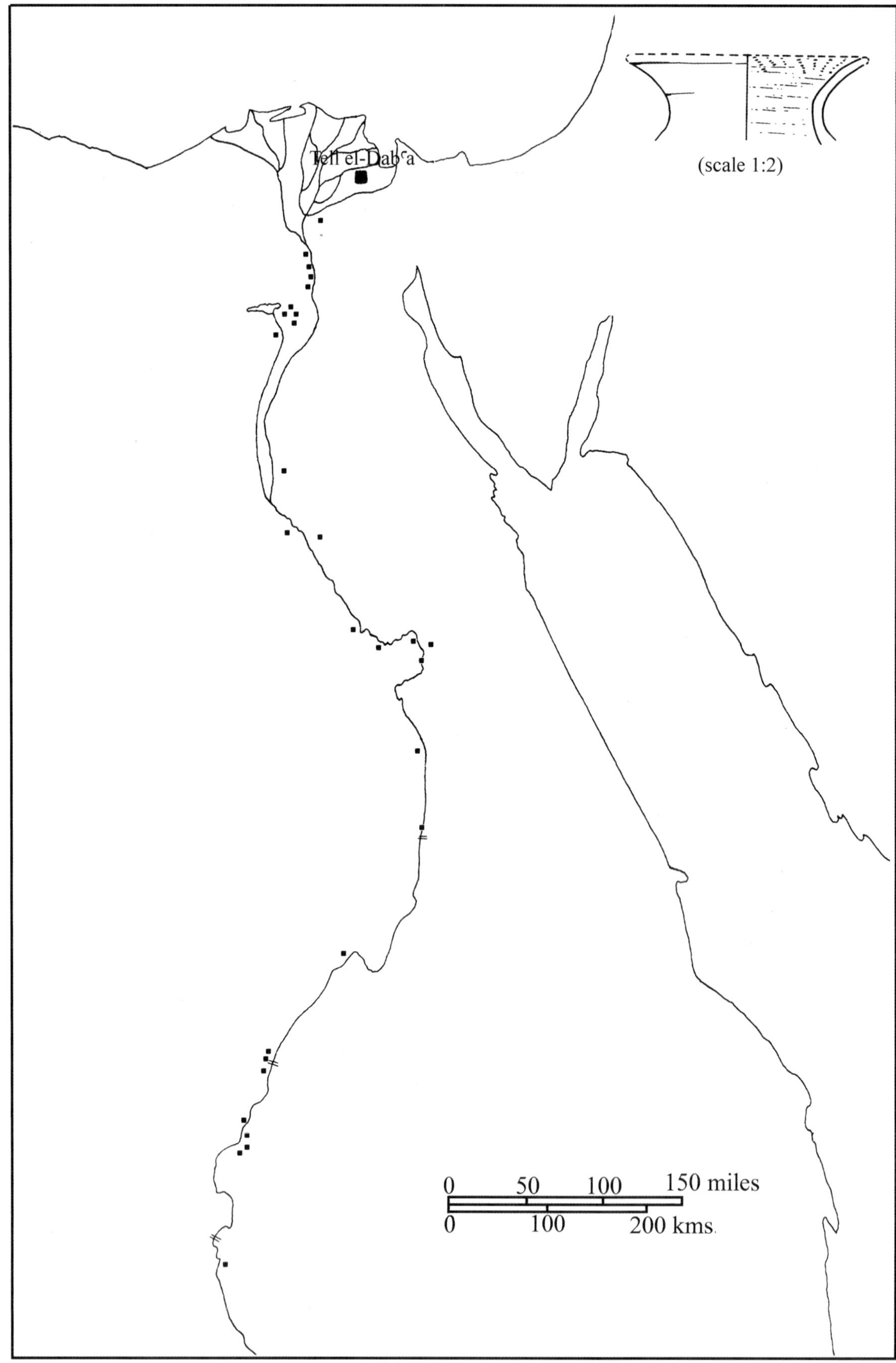

Fig. 251 Distribution and Shape Class of Type Group Q

III. Catalogue of Tell el-Yahudiya Vessels found at Tell el-Dab^ca

Introduction

In this section. all Tell el-Yahudiya vessels, or parts thereof, discovered at Tell el-Dab^{c}a, are listed according to the typology established in Part Two. In common with the other types of pottery published in *Tell el-Dab^{c}a X–XIX*, all vessel descriptions in this corpus include a small table such as

BPI	I-d	f–vf	W2	Bd. gef	mi	3	2R

In these tables the first box refers to the ware, the second to the fabric, the third to the quality, the fourth to the method of manufacture, the fifth to the way the base was made, the sixth to the firing method, the seventh to the hardness and the eighth, when necessary, to the type of handle. These can be interpreted as follows:

Ware Terminology

The ware terms met in the first box are as follows:

BPI ("braunpoliert, weiß inkrustiert") Brown slipped burnished with white incrusted decoration. This is an early form of "Tell el-Yahudiya" ware in which the firing conditions have resulted in the vessel being fired brown rather than the usual black.

GPI ("weiß-bis gelbpoliert") Uncoated, burnished ware with white incrusted decoration.

RPI ("rotpoliert, weiß inkrustiert") Red slipped burnished with white incrusted decoration. This is a form of "Tell el-Yahudiya" ware in which the firing conditions have resulted in the vessel firing red rather than the usual black.

SPI ("schwarzpoliert, weiß inkrustiert") Black slipped burnished with white incrusted decoration. (Typical "Tell el-Yahudiya" ware).

TG ("tongrundig") Uncoated.

Fabric Terminology

Fabrics used for the production of Tell el-Yahudiya Ware found at Tell el-Dab^{c}a comprise:

Fabric I-b-2

In the "Vienna System", this is a typical Nile silt B2 fabric,[566] differing from I-b-1 by the fact that mineral and organic inclusions occur in larger quantities and in greater sizes. The section is usually zoned with a range of colour lying between strong brown 7.5 YR 5/6 to yellowish red 5 YR 4/6 at the surface with, in thin walled and better fired pieces, a red 10 R 5/8 core. Most examples, however, are not completely oxidised and have a black core. The added temper consists of chaff, which is conspicuous and in the region of 2–3 mm. in length, with mineral inclusions such as mica and quartz up to 1 mm. in size. In a few cases fragments of shell and small limestone particles are found but this seems accidental,[567] deriving from Delta geziras. This clay fabric is used for a wide variety of shapes and is associated with a large number of different wares: uncoated, uncoated with red or white slipped rims, decorated, red slipped, white slipped, red slipped burnished and black slipped burnished.

Fabric I-d

The diagnostic property of Nile D clays, to which group in the Vienna System, fabric I-d belongs, is the inclusion of, in addition to particles of chaff and silica formations, conspicuous amounts of limestone. The latter tends to dominate the clay and is easily visible to the naked eye. At Tell el-Dab^{c}a the porosity of fabric I-d varies but is characteristically hard and fine. The groundmass is generally similar to fabrics I-a or I-b-1, and only rarely, I-b-2, with the addition of limestone particles which vary in size from 0.3 to 1.0 mm. The fracture usually shows zones of yellowish red and red with, in closed vessels an ash grey core, though sometimes it is completely red in colour. It occurs with a large number of basic surface treatments, uncoated, uncoated with a red slipped rim, red slipped, red slipped burnished, black slipped, black slipped burnished, brown slipped burnished, and yellow slipped burnished.

References to imported clays found in this book refer to the classification nomenclature published by

[566] H.-Å. Nordström and J. Bourriau, *Ceramic technology: clays and fabrics*, 171–172.

[567] For added lime temper see below fabric group I-d.

BIETAK in *TD V*, 328–330, thus the following fabric terms are found in this book:

Fabric IV-1

Fabric IV-1 is a limestone tempered clay characterised by the distinct 10R4/6–2.5YR 4/6 red break of the fired pottery.

Fabric IV-2

In this common type of imported clay, the surface fires from 5YR7/6–8/7 reddish yellow to 2.5YR6/6 light red. In thin walled vessels the break fires the same colour as the surface whilst in thicker-walled vessels there is often a thin grey core.

Fabric IV-3

Fabric IV-3 is a marl type clay which usually fires to a very pale brown to pink colour.

*

All the above imported clays are further subdivided into a, b and c variants, IV-1-a, IV-2-b, IV-3-c etc. depending on the size of the limestone particles thus a) no visible, limestone particles, at 10× magnification, b) fine limestone particles no larger than 8 mm. and c) large limestone particles, in the region of 0.5–2.0 mm.

FINENESS

The fineness depends on the porosity and sand particles present in the clay:

vf very fine, indicates that the clay is very compact and fine grained whilst the sand particles are few and smaller than 0.5 mm. in size.

f fine, indicates that the clay is fine grained and slightly porous with few sand particles. Those present, however, are no larger than 0.8 mm. in size.

m medium, a porous clay with numerous sand particles in the range 0.5–0.8 mm., sometimes extending upto 1.0 mm.

r rough, a very porous clay, poorly levigated with sand particles larger than 1.0 mm.

METHOD OF MANUFACTURE

H, handmade. This is sometimes divided into H1 where the vessel is clearly made by a "non-radial"[568] method such as hollowing and pinching or by paddle and anvil techniques; and H2 where the pot is made by a "free-radial" method, such as coiling. In the latter case the rim may be finished on the wheel.

W1 refers to wheel made vessels produced on a "simple low wheel" and W2 to vessels made on a "tall stemmed simple wheel".[569] Where the wheel head is placed on top of a tall stem it has the ability to spin with more force than when the stem is low. Consequently vessels made by method W2 tend to be finer and better made than those made on the low wheel. It would appear that the tall stemmed simple wheel was first introduced during the Late Thirteenth Dynasty. During the Late Second Intermediate Period, the low wheel was improved slightly and vessels could be thrown with more force; this being particularly noticeable in New Kingdom pottery.[570] This is indicated at Tell el-Dabᶜa by the code W1–2.

Base Production

The bases of Tell el-Yahudiya vessels found at Tell el-Dabᶜa were finished in a number of ways:

Bd. abg. ("abgeschnitten") Cut from the wheel with a knife or string, to form a flat base, with no further finishing. Assymmetrical circles are often noticeable on the underside of the base when this technique is used.

Bd. gef. ("geformt") Opened at the base and finally closed on the wheel.

Bd. gesp. ("gespatelt") Cut from the wheel and scraped smooth.

Bd. H ("handgemacht") Handmade. It does not necessarily follow that all hand made vessels had hand made bases since some were clearly made in a mould. Conversely some wheel made bases are finished by hand.

FIRING METHOD

Pots are either fired in an oxidising or a reducing atmosphere. Whilst it is often assumed that pots fired in an oxidising atmosphere, fire red, and those in a reducing atmosphere, grey to black, this is an oversimplification.[571] An oxidising atmosphere is one in which free oxygen is present whilst a reducing atmos-

568 For these terms, see DO. ARNOLD, Techniques and traditions of Manufacture in the Pottery of Ancient Egypt, in: DO. ARNOLD and J. BOURRIAU, (eds.), *An Introduction to Ancient Egyptian Pottery*, 1993, 15–40.

569 For these terms, see DO. ARNOLD, Techniques and traditions of Manufacture in the Pottery of Ancient Egypt, 41–78.

570 DO. ARNOLD, Techniques and traditions of Manufacture in the Pottery of Ancient Egypt, 62–63.

571 Cf. P. NICHOLSON, The firing of Pottery, in: DO. ARNOLD and J. BOURRIAU, (eds.), *An Introduction to Ancient Egyptian Pottery*, 1993, 104.

phere takes free oxygen away from the clay. As a rough approximation, pots fired in an oxidising atmosphere tend to have bright, clear colours whilst those fired in a reducing atmosphere tend to have dulled or smudged colours which often results in an entirely grey ware. In the tables ox ("oxydierend") indicates that the pot was fired in an oxidising atmosphere and re ("reduzierend") in a reducing atmosphere. The term mi ("mittel") is used to indicate a 'half-way' stage which tends to produce a deep brown surface, and was probably produced accidentally.

Hardness

Whilst it is known that Nile silt clays register between 2 and 3 and marl clays between 3 and 4 on the Mohs scale, at Tell el-Dabᶜa, a system to describe the hardness of a given vessel has been defined as follows:

1 ("weich") soft. The pot can be easily scratched with a finger nail. Such pieces tend to be underfired.

2 ("mittelhart") medium hard. Mohs scale 2–3. This is the usual hardness of most silt clays.

3 ("hart") hard. The vessel is scarcely scratchable with a finger nail. This tends to be the standard of highly fired silt clays and Marl C.

4 ("sehr hart") very hard. In these cases the vessel can be scarcely scratched with an iron nail.

Handle Types

1B ("1 Bandhenkel") Single strap handle which is flat in section.

1R ("1 Rundhenkel") Single handle which is round in section

2R ("2 Rundhenkel") Double Handle formed by two parallel loops, round in section

3R ("3 Rundhenkel") Triple handle formed either by three parallel loops, round in section, or in a triangle with two rows on the inner side and one on the outer side.

*

Since the above information is thus provided in this small table for every pot, this information is generally not repeated in the individual descriptions of the vessel types. The descriptions of the different types, found at Tell el-Dabᶜa are also reproduced here to avioid having to continuously refer back to the typological analysis in Part Two.

Tell el-Yahudiya Vessels belonging to the Primeval Group of Tell el-Yahudiya Ware

Type Group A.1

As mentioned above the earliest Tell el-Yahudiya jug so far found at Tell el-Dabᶜa belongs in this primeval Ovoid 1 group. This jug fragment, TD 4211, was retrieved from a palace of Phase d/1 = Phase G/4, which, according to pottery seriation, is dated approximately to the beginning of the Thirteenth Dynasty, before the middle of the 18th century BC. It is very similar to a fragment found at Byblos.[572] where the position of the handle attachment on the shoulder close to the neck is in close agreement with the piece from Tell el-Dabᶜa. This Byblos vessel also relates to TD 5250A, another shoulder fragment from Tell el-Dabᶜa, with a handle attached near to the base of the neck. It was found in a Phase G/1–3 dump which thus provides a *terminus ad quem*, and could thus derive from Phase H (end of the Twelfth Dynasty). NAA analysis indicates that it is not of Egyptian manufacture, though its exact origin could not be determined.[573] The same is true for another fragment of a brown burnished vessel, TD 5971E,[574] which also seems to derive from an Ovoid 1 vessel of the Primeval Group, with a specially fine fabric and an extremely thin wall, incised with a vertical grooved decoration outlining segments. 3116A and 7067F were also found in early contexts and are probably to be associated with this early group. The sherd 6138C found in a Phase E/1 context is obviously an earlier piece and must be considered residual, and it too probably belongs either with this primeval group, or perhaps the Early Palestinian Group.

It is surely no coincidence that all five Tell el Dabᶜa pieces mentioned above have been found in very early strata at Tell el-Dabᶜa. They are all foreign imports and all share an ovoid shape.

1. 5971E (TD) F/I-m/19 planum 0–1 Phase d/2 (87/152)
Plates 1, 127

BPI	IV-2-d	f	W2	–	re	3–4

[572] Beirut, American University 4906, 4908, Merrillees, *Levant* 10, 1978, figs. 1, 2.

[573] P. McGovern, *The Foreign Relations of the Hyksos*, Oxford, 2000, 152 no. JH911

[574] P. McGovern, *The Foreign Relations of the Hyksos*, Oxford, 2000, 154 no. MB024.

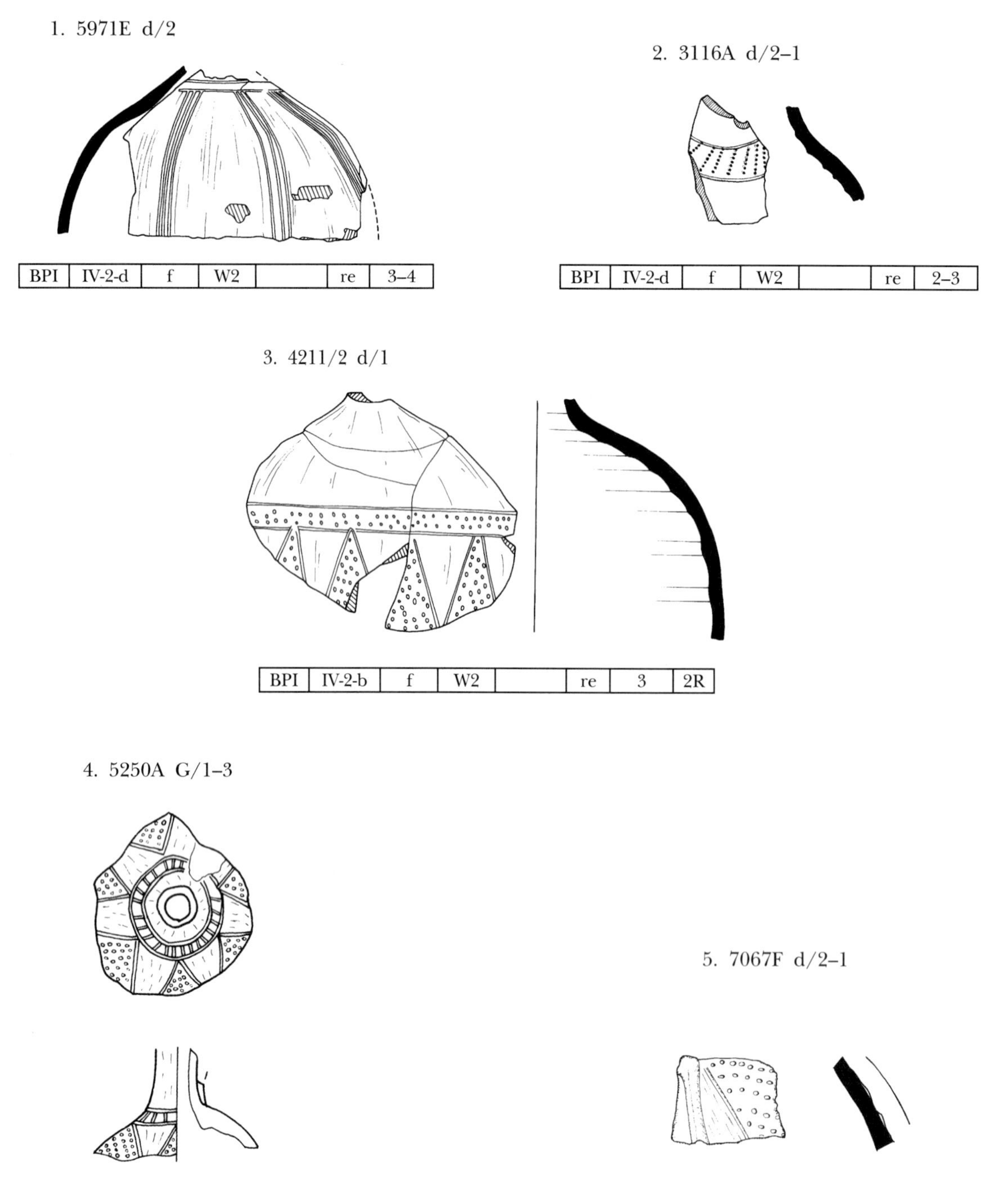

1:2

Type Group A.1

Plate 1

Wd. 0.45 cm.
Body sherd
Restored from sherds, incomplete
Surface colour: 5YR4/2 dark reddish grey; burnished slip 10YR3/4 dark yellowish brown
Break: uniform greyish brown
Decoration: Incised lines at base of neck and three extant groups of three vertical lines incised in body. Incised lines filled with white pigment.
BNL MB024 no parallels[575]

2. 3116A (TD) F/I-i/21 planum 3–4 Phase d/2–1 (80/084) Plate 1

BPI	IV-2-d	f	W2	–	re	2–3

Wd. 0.45 cm.
Body sherd
Restored from sherds, incomplete
Surface colour: 5YR4/2 dark reddish grey; burnished slip 10YR3/4 dark yellowish brown
Decoration: Band of vertical lines on shoulder, dots made with a single-pointed tool.
Break: reddish brown core, grey reduction zones

3. 4211 (TD) F/I-i/22 planum 5 Phase d/1 (82/334) Plate 1

BPI	IV-2-b	f	W2	–	re	3	2R

pht. 6.4 cm. Md. 11.5 cm. Wd. 0.4 cm.
Incomplete
Surface colour: burnished slip 10YR6/2 light brownish grey;
Decoration: Band at base of shoulder and the remains of four standing triangles, all infilled with dots made with a single-pointed tool.
Break: grey core, light red oxidation zones
BNL JH690 red field clay, southern Palestine

4. 5250A (TD) A/II-m/15 planum 5 Phase G (75/017) Plates 1, 127

BPI	IV-2-b	f	W2	–	re	3

Nd. 1.4 cm. pht. 3.2 cm. Wd. 0.53 cm.
Incomplete
Surface colour: 10YR6/2 light brownish grey; burnished slip 10YR5/3 brown
Break: grey core, light reddish brown oxidation zones
Decoration: Band of 25 incised rectangles at base of neck. Six standing triangles on shoulder, filled with dots made with a single-pointed tool.
BNL JH911 unknown provenience[576]

5. 7067F TD F/I-l/23 planum 4–5 Phase d/2–1 (87/096) Plate 1

SPI	IV-2-b	m	H1	–	re	2	2R

Nd. 1.7 cm. pht. upper part 2.2 cm. lower part 2.6 cm. Wd. 0.5 cm.
Incomplete
Surface colour: 2.5Y5/1 grey; burnished slip: 10YR6/1 grey
Break: grey in, brown out
Decoration: made with a single-pointed tool.

Tell el-Yahudiya Vessels belonging to the Early Palestinian Group of Tell el-Yahudiya Ware

As the Early Palestinian Group is mainly found in what is today northern Israel, with others coming from southern Lebanon and Transjordan, and, as is to be expected, all are made of Levantine clays, it was thus something of a surprise to find four examples belonging to this group at Tell el-Dabca where they were excavated in Phase G-F contexts.

Type Group B.3.1. Early Palestinian III

To the sub-group B.3.1 belongs TD 7505A with three horizontal ornament bands, produced of Levantine clay (IV-2-b), found in a transitional MBIIA-B context. This jug has a straight direct rim without lip, a bipartite handle and sloping outwards at the upper attachment of the handle whereas the lower joint of the handle is near the base of the neck, similar to the typical pieces of the Primeval Group. The small base is slightly set off and convex. The burnishing in between the decoration zones is brown. A very similar piece, made of Red Field clay comes from Chamber II of tomb JR 59 in El-Jisr, not far from Tel Aviv.[577] It perfectly matches the cited Tell el-Dabca jug, except that it has a pointed base, and was classified by Kaplan as an Ovoid 2. Looking at both examples the shoulder seems flat enough to classify them as plump piriform.

6. 7505A (TD) A/IV-h/6 grave 13 Phase G/1–3 or F (91/174) Plates 2, 127

BPI	IV-2-b	f	W2	Bd. gef	re	3	2R

D. 1.6 cm. Nd. 1.3 cm. Bd. 1.5 cm. est H. 16.0 cm. Md. 9.5 cm. Wd. 0.3 cm.
Incomplete
Surface colour: 10YR4/1 dark gray brown; burnished slip 7.5YR6/2–4 pink
Break: reddish brown at the inner surface, grey towards the outside
Decoration: Three bands infilled with oblique lines made with a five-toothed comb.

Type Group B.4. Early Palestinian IV

Two jugs from Tell el-Dabca can be attributed to group B.4. Both of them TD 2518 and TD 2519, were

[575] P. McGovern, *The Foreign Relations of the Hyksos*, Oxford, 2000, 154 no. MB024.

[576] P. McGovern, *The Foreign Relations of the Hyksos*, Oxford, 2000, 152 no. JH911.

[577] Jerusalem 42.271, Ory, A Middle Bronze Age Tomb at El-Jisr, *QDAP* 12, 1946, 38–39, pl. 12.50: Kaplan, *Tell el-Yahudiyeh Ware*, fig. 113d, 232, JS1.

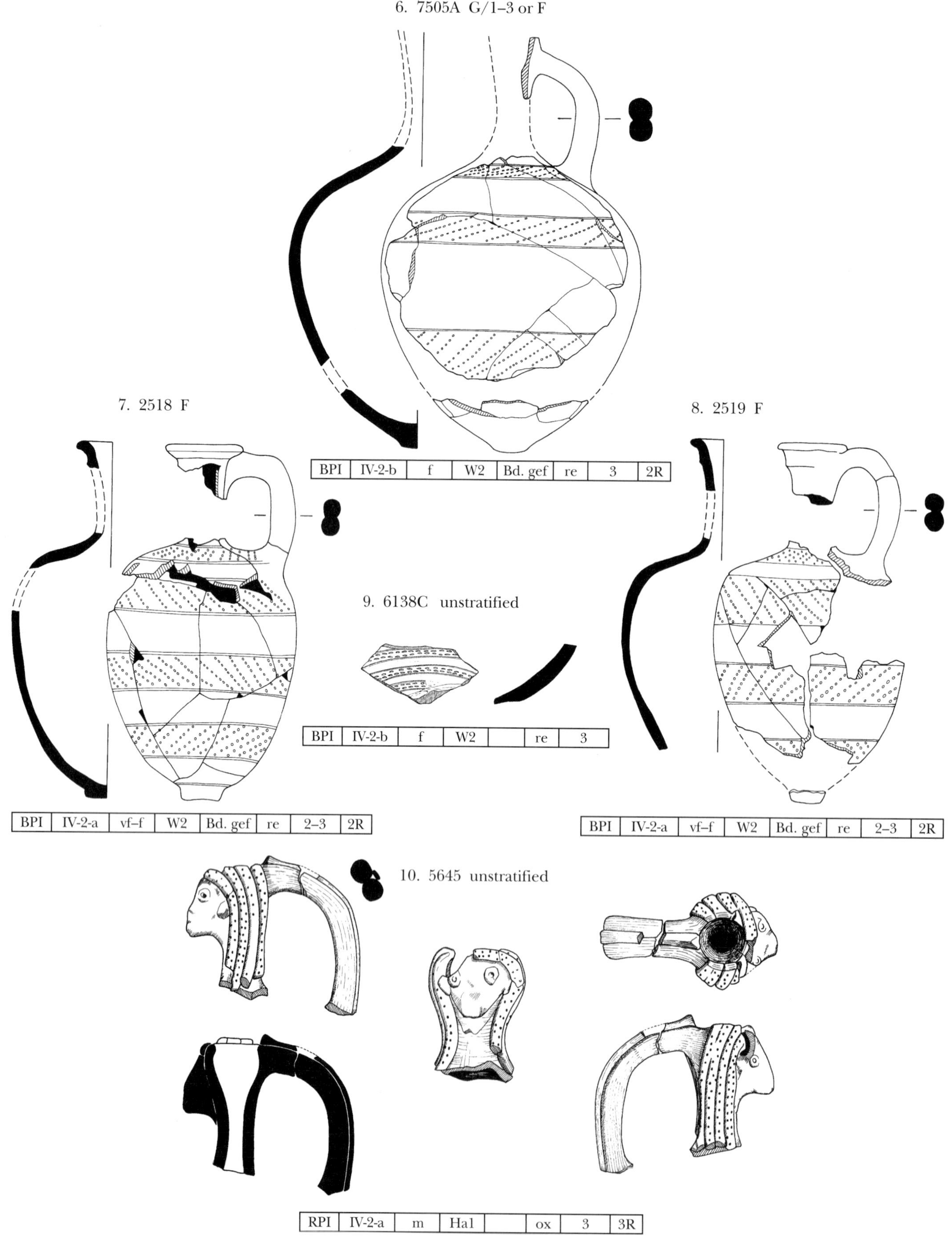

Early Palestinian Type Groups B.3.1, B.4, B.6 1:2

Plate 2

found in an early Phase F, (transitional MB IIA/B), tomb, but, as mentioned above, these may be old vessels originating from Phase G/1–3. Both of them bear horizontal ornament bands, a style of decoration which, as seen in the typological chapter is characteristic of Palestine. As such these vessels must surely be imports, as indeed indicated by an NAA analysis carried out by Maureen Kaplan.[578] The more recent analysis by McGovern, suggesting a production area in the Nile Valley is thus somewhat strange, and one can only assume that McGovern accidentally misplaced his records.[579]

7. 2518 Cairo ? A/II-m/15 planum 5 grave 8 Phase F (75/025) Plates 2, 127

BPI	IV-2-a	vf–f	W2	Bd. gef	re	2–3	2R

D. 3.0 cm. Bd. 1.5 cm. H. 13.1 cm. Md. 7.4 cm. Wd. 0.6 cm.
Incomplete
Surface colour: 10YR4/1 dark grey brown; burnished slip 10YR5/1 dark grey
Break: light brown core, dark brown reduction zones
Decoration: Four bands impressed with an eight tooth comb, from lower left to upper right in the uppermost and lowermost bands, and from upper left to lower right in the middle two bands.
BNL JH 322 most similar to Nile clay[580]
Previously published: AP 246; *TD XVI,* 154, fig. 91, no. 5.

8. 2519 Cairo ? A/II-m/15 planum 5 grave 8 Phase F (75/027)

BPI	IV-2-a	vf–f	W2	Bd. gef	re	2–3	2R

Plate 2
D. 2.85 cm. Bd. 1.4 cm. H. 13.5 cm. Md. 7.4 cm. Wd. 0.6 cm.
Incomplete
Surface colour: 10YR4/1 dark grey brown; burnished slip 10YR5/1 dark grey
Break: light brown core, dark brown reduction zones
Decoration: Four bands impressed with an eight tooth comb, from lower left to upper right in the uppermost and third bands, and from upper left to lower right in the second and lowest band.
Previously published: AP 246; *TD XVI,* 154, fig. 91, no. 6.

9. 6138C (TD) A/II-k/17 planum 3 unstratified (87/282) Plate 2

BPI	IV-2-b	f	W2	–	re	3

pht. 1.8 cm. Wd. 0.5 cm.
Incomplete
Surface colour: 10R5/1 reddish grey; burnished slip 7.5YR4/2 brown
Break: dark grey core, brown zones
Decoration: Three irregular delineated bands filled with irregular dots made with a single-pointed tool. Incised lines and dots filled with white pigment.
Previously published: Kopetzky, *The MB IIB-Corpus of the Hyksos Period at Tell el-Dabᶜa*, 2007, 199, fig. 4.6.

Type Group B.6. Early Palestinian VI ("Palestinian Figural Vases")

The fragmentary jug, TD 5645, clearly belongs in group B.6.1, female-headed Palestinian figural vases. Unfortunately it was found in a disturbed context – a tomb pit with ceramic material of both Phase c and at least one later Hyksos vessel. The swollen neck of TD 5645, however, is reminiscent of the Ovoid 1 jugs of the Primeval Group, and it is probably correct to assign this piece to the earliest use of the tomb. TD 5645 is wheel made, bears a reddish brown burnished slip, and from a visual examination would appear to be made of a Levantine clay. Only the neck and tripartite handle are preserved, the latter joining with the back of the head. Around the neck a female head was modelled with thick braids falling down on both sides of the head. The facial features are more crudely modelled than on the Jericho jug[581] (see above page 86), with which it may be compared.

10. 5645 (TD) F/I-k/19 silo unstratified (85/399) Plates 2, 128

RPI	IV-2-a	m	Ha1	–	ox	3	3R

D. 1.6 cm. Nd. 1.3 cm. Bd. 1.5 cm. est H. 16.0 cm. Md. 9.5 cm. Wd. 0.3 cm.
Incomplete
Surface colour: 7.5YR6/4 light brown; burnished slip 2.5YR4/4 reddish brown
Break: uniform brown
The strands of the wig, four to each side of the head are decorated with dots made with a single-pointed tool. The eyes are represented by small perforated nodules of clay.

Branches C and D: Middle and Late Palestinian Vessels

At present no vessels which can be attributed to the Middle or Late Palestinian groups have been found at Tell el-Dabᶜa.

[578] Kaplan, *Tell el-Yahudiyeh Ware,* 232 TD3.
[579] P. McGovern, *The Foreign Relations of the Hyksos,* Oxford, 2000, 129 no. JH322.
[580] P. McGovern, *The Foreign Relations of the Hyksos,* Oxford, 2000, 129 no. JH322.
[581] Amman, National Museum J.5173. Åström, *Alasia I,* 1971, 13, Merrillees, *Levant* 10, 1978, 83, Kaplan, *Tell el-Yahudiyeh Ware,* fig. 131c.

11. 5588 c

RPI	IV-2-a	m	Ha1		ox	3	3R

13. 3139 F

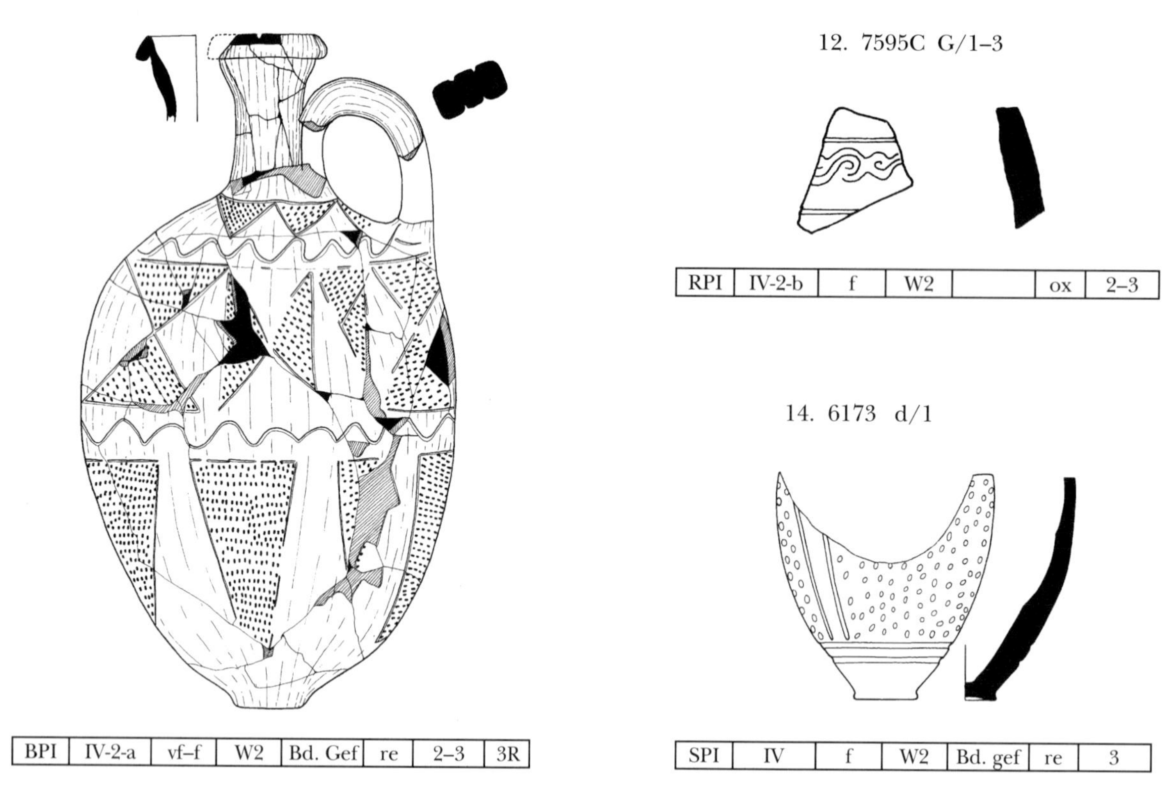

BPI	IV-2-a	vf–f	W2	Bd. Gef	re	2–3	3R

12. 7595C G/1–3

RPI	IV-2-b	f	W2		ox	2–3

14. 6173 d/1

SPI	IV	f	W2	Bd. gef	re	3

1:2

Early Levantine Type Groups E.1, E.2, F.1

Plate 3

Vessels belonging to the Early Levantine Group

Type Group E.1 Early Levantine I

TD 5588 is only one of two definite known examples which can be assigned to Type group E.1. It is an incomplete large biconical jug with a maximum body diameter of 25 cm. and is an import, being a red slipped vessel, made of Levantine clay, decorated with five or more horizontal zones comprising three zones of wavy bands filled with six-toothed comb imprints alternating with two zones of running spirals. TD 7595C may also belong in this group.

11. 5588 (TD) F/I-l/19 grave 1 Phase c (85/397) Plates 3, 129

RPI	IV-2-b	f	W2	–	ox	2–3

pht. 15.0 cm. Md. 25.0 cm. Wd. 0.6 cm.
Incomplete
Surface colour: 5YR7/4–6 pink; burnished slip 10R5/6 red
Break: grey core, pink oxidation zones
Decoration: consists of incised lines, and as far as it is preserved two rows of broad wavy lines separated by rows of running spirals. The delineated wavy bands are infilled with oblique lines made with a six-toothed comb. Below are the remains of an unidentifiable motif. The running spirals may be Minoan influenced.
Previously published: TD XVIII, 354, fig. 310.

12. 7595C (TD) A/IV-l/19 grave 1 Phase c (91/216) Plate 3

RPI	IV-2-b	f	W2	–	ox	2–3

pht. 3.1 cm. Wd. 0.6 cm.
Incomplete
Surface colour: 5YR7/4–6 pink; burnished slip 10R5/6 red
Break: grey core, pink oxidation zones
Decoration: Running spirals between twon incised lines.

Type Group E.2 Early Levantine II

As explained above, this vessel is at present, the only one of its type. It has a rolled rim, a distinct swelling of the neck, a triple loop handle, which comes from the base of the handle to the base of the shoulder, and a button base. The decoration consists of four zones of pendant or standing triangles with an incised wavy line in the reserved zones between the first and second, and between the third and fourth decorative zones.

13. 3139 Cairo A/II-m/16 grave 3 Phase F (80/094) Plates 3, 129

BPI	IV-2-a	vf–f	W2	Bd. Gef	re	2–3	3R

D. 3.3 cm. Nd. 1.8 cm. Bd. 2.1 cm. H. 18.2 cm. Md. 10.4 cm. Wd. 0.6 cm.
Incomplete
Surface colour: 5YR4/4 reddish brown; burnished slip 10R5/6 red
Break: light brown core, dark brown reduction zones
Decoration: At the base of the neck a zone of pendant triangles, a middle zone of pendant and standing triangles in an 'egg-timer fashion' with a lower zone of large pendant triangles. The decorative zones are separated from each other by an incised wavy line.
Previously published: Apht. 121, 345, *PuF* 230 nr 278; *TD XVI,* 172, fig. 97b, no. 11.

Type Group F.1 Early Levantine IV

Type group F.1 comprises small piriform, almost ovoid jugs, between 8 and 9 cm. tall, known from Byblos, with one incomplete example being found at Tell el-Dab^ca . They have a rolled rim, double handle, button base and have one zone of large rectangles around the major part of the body.

14. 6173 TD F/I-k/19 planum ? Phase d/1, water system of the palace (86/276) Plates 3, 130

SPI	IV	f	W2	Bd. gef	re	3

Bd. 1.7 cm. pht. 5.4 cm. Md. 5.9 cm. Wd. 0.5 cm.
Incomplete
Surface colour: 5YR7/6–8 reddish yellow; burnished slip 5YR5.5/6 reddish yellow
Break: uniform reddish yellow
Decoration: two large rectangles infilled with dots made by a single-pointed tool.

Type Group F.3 Early Levantine V

15. 4465F TD F/I-k/20 planum 2–3 Phase d/1–c (83/096) Plate 4

BPI	IV	f–m	W2	Bd. gef	re	3

Bd. 2.2 cm. pht. 4.9 cm. Wd. 0.5 cm.
Incomplete
Surface colour: 7.5YR5.5/3 brown; burnished slip 7.5YR5/4 brown
Break: uniform greyish brown
Decoration: zone of rectangles infilled with dots made by a single-pointed tool.
BNL JH830 Southern Palestine[582]

16. 8470B TD F/I-j/23n planum 3–4 Phase c (96/004) Plate 4

SPI	IV-1	m	W2	–	re	2–3

pht. 6.9 cm. Wd. 0.4 cm.
Incomplete
Surface colour: 7.5YR5.5/3 brown; burnished slip 10YR4/1 dark grey
Break: dark grey in, reddish brown out
Decoration: Three rows of rectangles preserved, each infilled with dots made by a single-pointed tool.

Type Group F.4

Tell el-Yahudiya jugs of group F.4 are piriform in shape, have double handles, incisions at the base of the neck, ring bases, and only two decorative zones,

[582] P. McGovern, *The Foreign Relations of the Hyksos,* Oxford, 2000, 147 no. JH835.

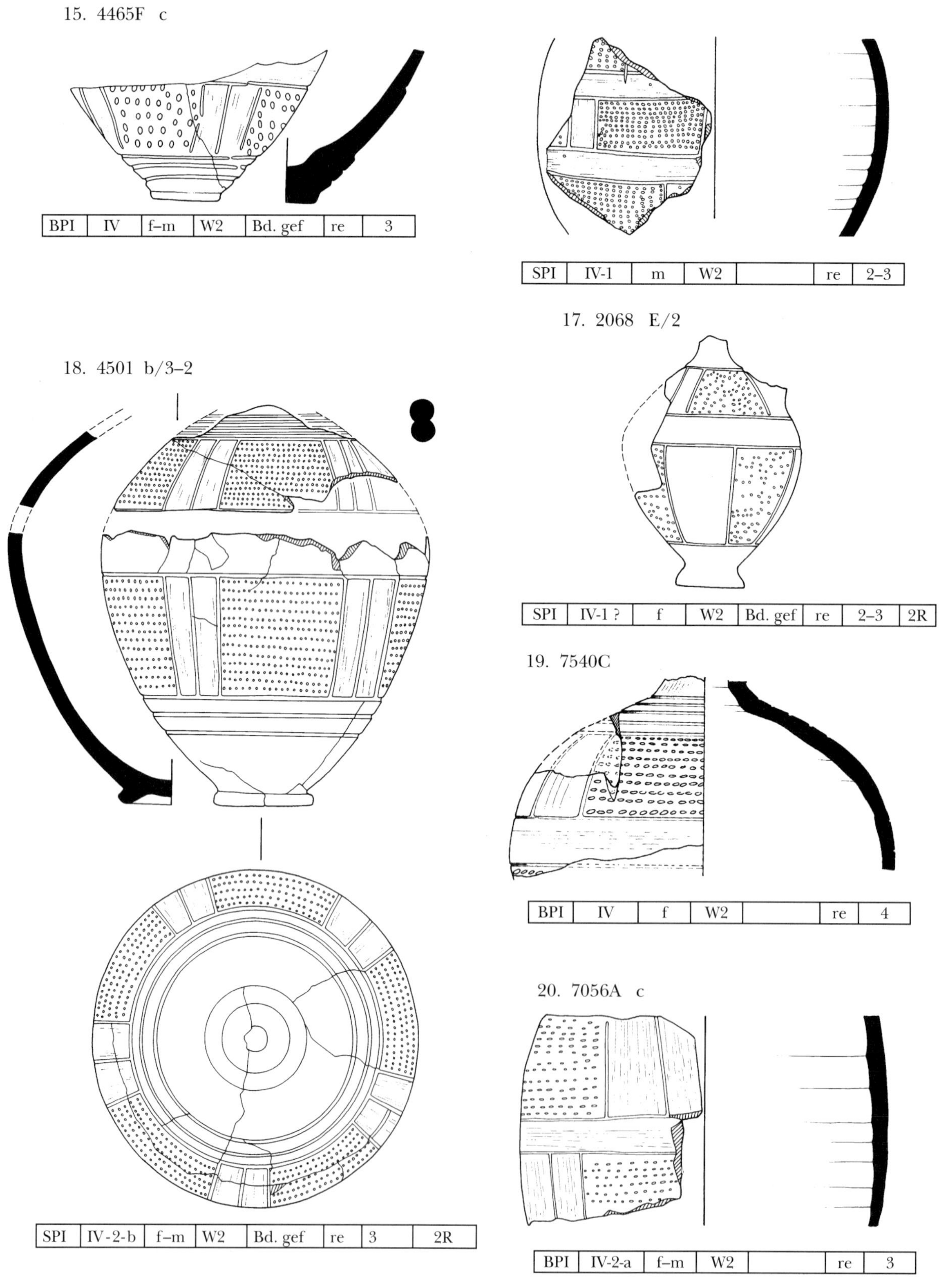

1:2

Early Levantine Type Groups F.3, F.4, F.5

Plate 4

one on the upper body and one on the lower body, and presumably kettle rims. The type group is known from an example found at Tell el-Dabᶜa, TD 2068, which bears two zones of rectangles separated by reserved zones.

17. 2068 Vienna A3391 A/II-o/12 grave 8 Phase E/2 (69/030) Plate 4, 130

SPI	IV-1 ?	f	W2	Bd. gef	re	2–3	2R

Nd 1.2 cm. Bd. 2.4 cm. pht. 8.3 cm. Md. 6.3 cm. Wd. 0.35 cm.
Incomplete
Surface colour: 10YR6/1 grey; burnished slip: 2.5YR2/0 black
Break: dark grey core, dark grey brown reduction zones
Decoration: On the shoulder four standing trapezoids, followed by a reserved band running aound the maximum body diameter, then below five hanging trapezoids. The trapezoids are decorated with a seven-toothed comb, impressed vertically on the shoulder and horizontally on the lower body.
Previously published: TD V, 152

Type Group F.5 Early Levantine VII

Tell el-Yahudiya jugs of group F.5 are piriform in shape, have kettle rims, double handles incisions at the base of the neck, ring bases, and only two decorative zones, one on the upper body and one on the lower body. The best example of such a vessel known to us is an incomplete example from Tell el-Dabᶜa (TD 4501).

18. 4501 TD F/I-k/21 grave 15 Phase b/3–2 (83/132) Plates 4, 130

SPI	IV-2-b	f–m	W2	Bd. gef	re	3	2R

Bd. 3.0 cm. pht. 13.0 cm. Md. 11.2 cm. Wd. 0.45 cm.
Restored from sherds, incomplete
Surface colour: 2.5YR5/4 reddish brown; burnished slip 10YR4/1 dark grey
Break: uniform orange brown
Decoration: consists of two zones of four rectangles infilled with a five-toothed comb. Traces of white pigment still survive in both the comb impressions and in the incised lines dividing the rectangles from one another.
BNL JH824 Southern Palestine[583]

19. 7540C TD A/IV-h/6 pit 14 Phase b/3 (91/185) Plates 4, 130

BPI	IV	f	W2	–	re	4

Md 12.0 cm. Wd. 0.4 cm.
Restored from sherds, incomplete
Surface colour: 5YR5/3 reddish brown; burnished slip 5YR4/1 dark grey
Break: dark grey core, reddish brown reduction zones
Decoration: Irregularly impresed white infilled dots in a trapezoidal frame. Lines at base of neck and around maximum diameter also infilled with white pigment.

20. 7056A TD F/I-p/20 granary 11 Phase c (89/143) Plate 4

BPI	IV-2-a	f–m	W2	–	re	3

pht. 6.2 cm. Wd. 0.4 cm.
Incomplete
Surface colour: 5YR5/1 grey; burnished slip 5YR5/3 reddish brown
Break: uniform reddish brown
Decoration: Parts of three rectangles (?) from two different registers infilled with dots made by a single-pointed tool.

Type Group H.1.2 Early Levantine VIII

Type Group H.1.2 is known through the fragmentary jug Tell el-Dabᶜa TD 1734 which would also appear to have four zones of decoration, an upper large one of rectangles, followed by a band of pendant triangles, a band of swimming fish and a lower zone of connected standing and pendant triangles. TD 883 is probably a further fragment of the same vessel.

21. 1609+1610+1611+1734 Vienna A1691 A/II-m/11 planum 6 Phase G (68/112) Plates 5, 131

BPI	IV-2-c	f–m	W2	Bd. gef	re	3	3R

Bd. 9.45 cm. pht. 29.0 cm. Md. 29.0 cm. Wd. 0.9 cm.
Incomplete
Surface colour: 10YR4/1–5/2 dark grey; burnished slip 7.5YR3–4/2 dark brown
Break: grey core, light red to pink oxidation zones
Decoration: consists of large rectangles on the upper part of the pot, infilled with dots made made with a single-pointed tool. This is separated from a frieze of pendant triangles by a reserved band. The triangles are again infilled with dots made with a single-pointed tool. A reserved zone separates this from a frieze of swimming fish, whose bodies are made up of dots made with a single-pointed tool. Immediately below them is a frieze of interlocking standing and pendant triangles each infilled with dots made with a single-pointed tool.
BNL JH338 Southern Palestine ?[584]
Previously published: Bietak, *MDAIK* 26, Taf 19c; *FA*, 78 Abb 61 H5, Kaplan, *Tell el-Yahudiyeh Ware*, fig. 128d, *TD V*, 28, *PuF* 235 nr. 290; *Pharao Siegt Immer*, 150 nr. 149.
A sherd with very similar decoration was also found at Dahshur.[585]

22. 0883 Cairo JE91172 A/II-m/11 grave 6 burial 2 Phase G (67/029) Plate 5

BPI	IV-2-b	f	W2	–	re	3

Wd. 0.9 cm.
Incomplete

---

[583] P. McGovern, *The Foreign Relations of the Hyksos*, Oxford, 2000, 146 no. JH824.

[584] P. McGovern, *The Foreign Relations of the Hyksos*, Oxford, 2000, 131 no. JH338.

[585] Do. Arnold, *MDAIK* 33, 1977, Taf. 4.

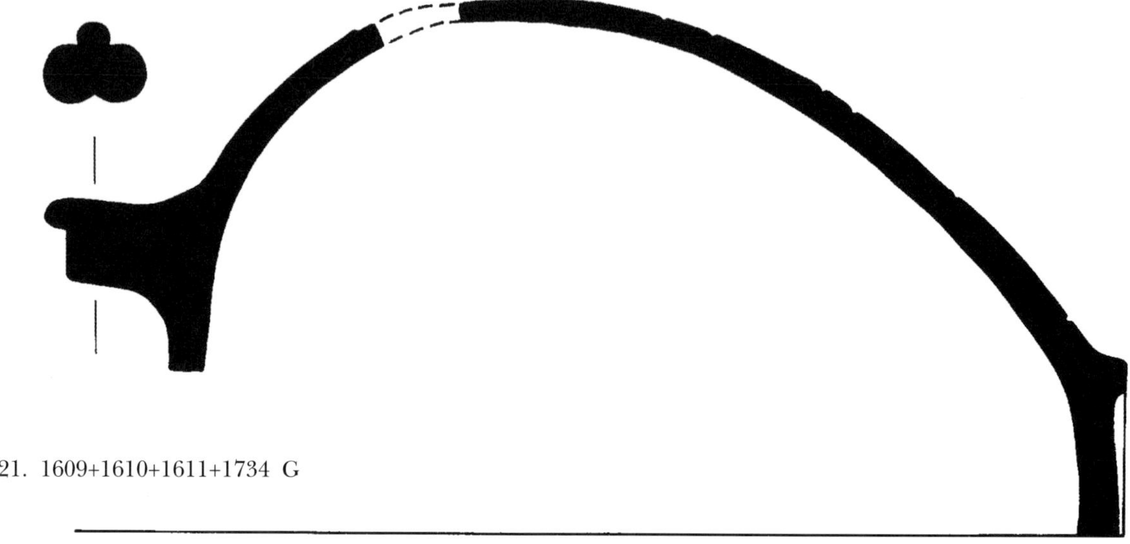

21. 1609+1610+1611+1734 G

BPI	IV-2-c	f–m	W2	Bd. gef	re	3	3R

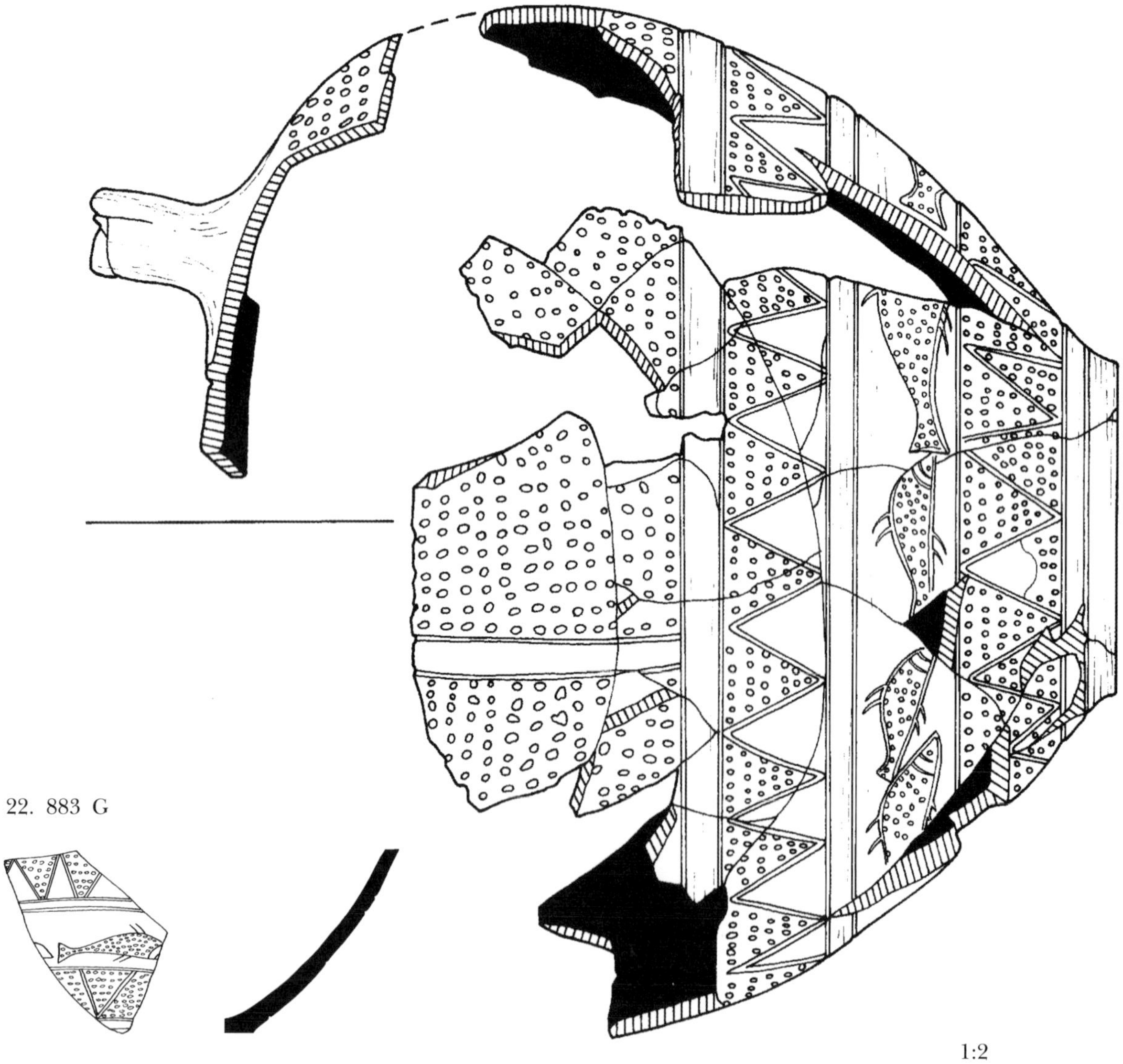

22. 883 G

1:2

BPI	IV-2-b	f	W2		re	3

Early Levantine Group H.1.2

Plate 5

Surface colour: 10YR4/1–5/2 dark grey; burnished slip 7.5YR3–4/2 dark brown
Break: grey core, light red to pink oxidation zones
Probably belongs with the previous vessel
Previously published: Bietak, *MDAIK* 23, pl. 32a.

Vessels belonging to the Levanto-Egyptian Group

Type Group I.1.5 Piriform 1a

As befits the Levanto-Egyptian nature of this group, most of these vessels are evident imports from the Levant whilst TD 3283 is made of an Egyptian Nile clay. Piriform 1a jugs of group I.1.5 have a kettle rim, a double handle joining at the neck below the rim, incisions at the neck, ring bases and four zones of decoration.

23. 3283 F/I-i/21 planum 3 grave 34 Phase c (80/140) Plates 6, 131

BPI	I-d	f–m	W2	Bd. gef	re	2	2R

D. 4.2 cm. Nd 2.2 cm. Bd. 3.0 cm. pht. 19.0 cm. Md. 12.0 cm. Wd. 0.9 cm.
Incomplete
Surface colour: 7.5YR5.5/3 brown; burnished slip 7.5YR5/4 brown
Break: uniform greyish brown
Decoration: consists of four zones. On the shoulder eleven standing triangles, around the body of the pot two bands of fourteen rectangles and a lower frieze of pendant triangles, each infilled with dots made with a single-pointed tool.

24. 4436A TD F/I-k/20 grave 4 Phase b/3 ? (94/118) Plate 6

BPI	IV-1a	f–m	W2	Bd. gef	re	2–3

Bd. 2.7 cm. pht. 4.3 cm. Wd. 0.5 cm.
Incomplete
Surface colour: 7.5YR5.5/3 brown; burnished slip 7.5YR5/4 brown
Break: uniform greyish brown
Decoration: Only parts of the lower frieze of pendant triangles, infilled with dots made with a single-pointed tool is preserved.

25. 8442R TD F/I-k/20 grave 4 Phase b/3 ? (94/151) Plate 6

BPI	IV-1-b	f	H1	–	re	3

pht. 6.2 cm. Md 5.5 cm. Wd. 0.35 cm.
Restored from sherds, incomplete
Surface colour: 10YR7/2 light grey; burnished slip 7.5YR5/4 brown
Break: uniform light grey
Decoration: Parts of three standing triangles on shoulder infilled with oblique lines made with a ten (?)-toothed comb.

26. 7046G TD F/I-p/19 grave 12 Phase d/1 or c (90/017) Plate 6

BPI	IV-2-b	f	W2		re	3

pht. 5.8 cm. Md. 12.0 cm. Wd. 0.55 cm.
Incomplete
Surface colour: 7.5YR5/4 brown burnished slip 10YR5/4 yellowish brown
Break: dark brown in, yellowish red oxidation zones
Decoration: Only parts of two standing triangles and two rectangles, each filled with dots made with a single-pointed tool are preserved.

Type Group I.2.2

Type Group I.2.2a Piriform 1b

Type group I.2.2 comprise jugs with kettle rims, double handles joining at the neck below the rim, incisions at the neck, and ring bases, and three zones of decoration. Of these the most common is I.2.2a, an uppermost zone consisting of standing triangles, a central zone of rectangles and a lower zone of pendant triangles

27. 7498 A/IV-h/6 grave 13 Phase F–E/3 (90/278) Plates 6, 131

BPI	IV-2-b	f	W2	Bd. gef	re	3	2R

D. 4.9 cm. Nd. 1.8 cm. Bd. 3.0 cm. H. 21.4 cm. Md. 12.5 cm. Wd. 0.45 cm.
Restored from sherds, complete
Surface colour: 7.5YR8/2 pinkish white; burnished slip 7.5YR6/2 brown
Break: grey core, orange oxidation zones
Decoration: On shoulder eight standing triangles, on body five rectangles and on lower body eight pendant triangles, each infilled with dots made with an eight-toothed comb.
Previously published: PuF 230 nr 277

28. 3956 Cairo F/I-i/22 grave 33 Phase c (82/077) Plate 7

BPI	IV-2-a	m	W2	Bd. gef	re	2	2R

D. 4.4 cm. Nd. 1.8 cm. Bd. 3.4 cm. H. 20.5 cm. Md. 12.5 cm. Wd. 0.4 cm.
Restored from sherds, complete
Surface colour: 10YR6/1 grey; burnished slip grey to dark brown
Break: grey core, brown re zones
Decoration: consists of eight standing triangles on the shoulder, divided from a frieze of four rectangles, by a reserved zone. Beneath the rectangles is a band of nine pendant triangles. All the decorated elements are infilled with dots made with a single-pointed tool.
Previously published: PuF 229 nr 275

29. 5436 TD A/II-k/17 grave 30 burial 2 Phase F (85/272) Plate 7

BPI	IV-1	m	W2	Bd. gef	re	2	2R

D. 4.1 cm. Nd. 1.9 cm. Bd. 3.2 cm. H. 19.6 cm. Md. 11.0 cm. Wd. 0.4 cm.
Restored from sherds, incomplete
Surface colour: 10YR6/1 grey; burnished slip 10YR7/6 reddish yellow
Break: reddish brown core, light greyish brown oxidation zones
Decoration: Upper zone of seven unequal standing triangles, a central zone of rectangles (only part of one preserved) and a lower zone of eight pendant triangles, all infilled with lines made with an three (?)-toothed comb.
Previously published: TD XVI, 146, fig. 84b, no. 11.

30. 3145 Cairo F/I-j/21 planum 0–1 grave 4? Phase b/3 (80/033) Plate 7

BPI	I-d	f–m	W2	–	re	2

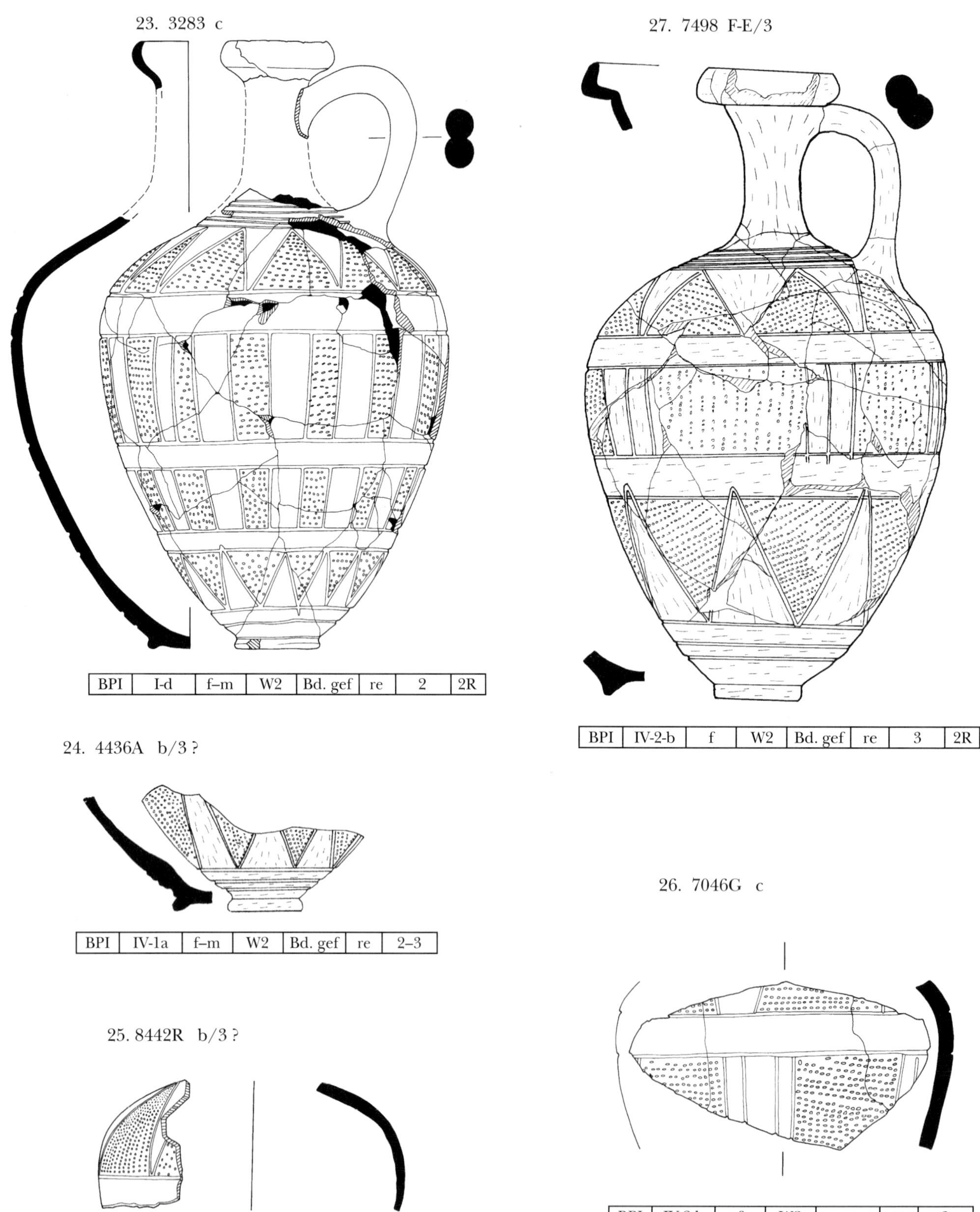

23. 3283 c

BPI	I-d	f–m	W2	Bd. gef	re	2	2R

27. 7498 F-E/3

BPI	IV-2-b	f	W2	Bd. gef	re	3	2R

24. 4436A b/3 ?

BPI	IV-1a	f–m	W2	Bd. gef	re	2–3

26. 7046G c

BPI	IV-2-b	f	W2		re	3

25. 8442R b/3 ?

BPI	IV-1-b	f	H1		re	3

1:2

Levanto-Egyptian Type Group I.1.5, I.2.2a

Plate 6

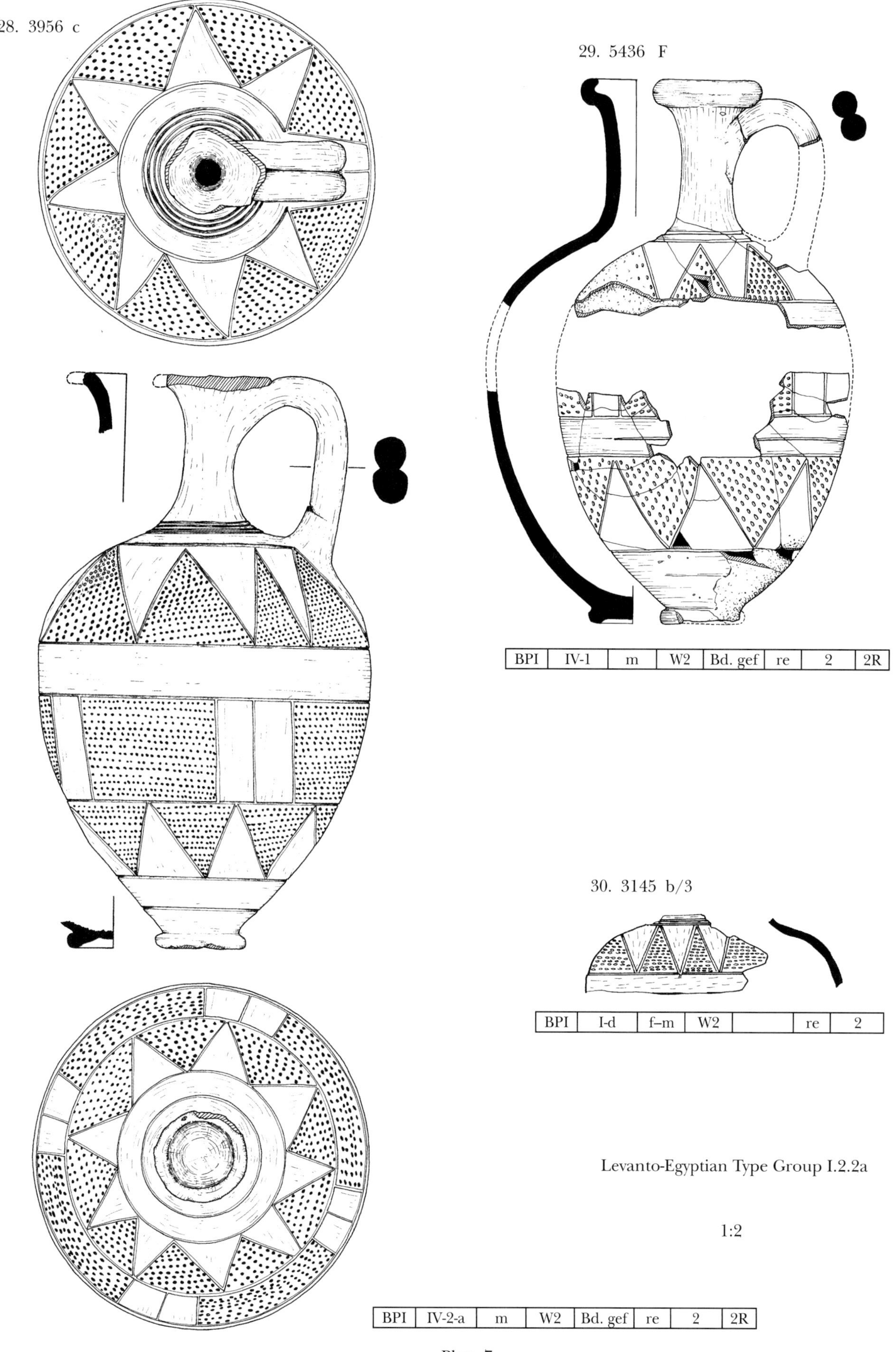

29.

BPI	IV-1	m	W2	Bd. gef	re	2	2R

30.

BPI	I-d	f–m	W2		re	2

Levanto-Egyptian Type Group I.2.2a

1:2

28.

BPI	IV-2-a	m	W2	Bd. gef	re	2	2R

Plate 7

D. 2.4 cm. Nd. 1.6 cm. pht. 2.8 cm. Md. 7.3 cm. Wd. 0.4 cm.
Incomplete
10YR6/1 grey; burnished slip 10YR7/6 reddish yellow
Break: reddish brown core, light greyish brown oxidation zones.
Decoration: Remains of four standing triangles filled with dots made with a five-toothed comb.

31. 1886 Vienna A3276 A/II-m/13 planum 6/7 grave 13 Phase E/3 (68/200) Plate 8

BPI	I-d	f	W2	Bd. Gef	mi	3	2R

D. 2.45 cm Nd. 1.1 cm. Bd. 1.63 cm. H. 8.6+ cm. Md. 5.4 cm. Wd. 0.35 cm.
Restored from sherds, incomplete
Surface colour: 10YR6/3 pale brown; burnished slip 5YR4/3 lt red brown
Break: grey core, with light brown outer zones
Rim trimmed and fashioned into a kettle rim
Decoration: Three decorative zones with matt reserved zones: in the centre are matt rectangles divided by two vertical incisions, and above and below, standing and pendant triangles separated from each other by a reserved zigzag. Decorated areas were made by means of a multi-toothed comb applied in an irregular pattern.
Previously published: TD V, 86.

32. 4266A (TD) F/I-i/23 planum 5 Phase c (82/199) Plate 8

BPI	IV-2-b	f–m	W2	Bd. gef	re	3

pht. 4.4 cm. Wd. 0.45 cm.
Restored from sherds, incomplete
Surface colour: 7.5YR8/2 pinkish white; burnished slip 7.5YR6/2 brown
Break: brown core, reddish brown oxidation zones
Decoration: Pendant triangles filled with dots made with a single pointed tool.
BNL JH 872 Southern Palestine[586]

Type Group I.2.3

This group exists solely on the evidence of incomplete examples from Tell el-Dabᶜa. The best preserved, TD 5795, has a candlestick rim, double handle, incisions at the base of the neck, but in place of a ring base, a button, and three zones of decoration. TD 4518 is a fragmentary example missing the rim and neck. TD 5795 is decorated with three zones of standing triangles (I.2.3a), whilst TD 4518 has an uppermost zone of pendant triangles, a central one of rectangles and a lower one of pendant triangles (I.2.3b). To this group should also probably be attributed TD 4539 with a decoration of standing triangles – diamonds – standing triangles.

Type Group I.2.3a Piriform 1b

33. 5795 TD F/I-m/19 grave 11 Phase c (86/028) Plates 8, 132

BPI	I-d	f	W2	Bd. gef	re	3	2R

D. 3.2 cm Nd. 1.75 cm. Bd. 1.8 cm. H. 16.6 cm. Md. 9.6 cm. Wd. 0.48 cm.
VI 57.83
Restored from sherds, incomplete
Surface colour: 7.5YR4/4 dark brown; burnished slip 7.5YR3/0 very dark grey
Break: red core, light grey reduction zones
Decoration: consists of three bands of pendant triangles, five on the shoulder, eleven at the maximum diameter and eight on the lower body, each infilled with dots made with a single pointed tool.

34. 4539 F/I-k/22 grave 7 Phase c (84/122) Plate 8

BPI	I-d	vf	W2	Bd. gef	re	3–4

Bd. 2.3 cm. pht. 13.0 cm. Md. 11.9 cm. Wd. 0.4 cm.
Restored from sherds, incomplete
Surface colour: 10YR7/2 light grey; burnished slip: worn off
Break: grey core, orange oxidation zones
Decoration: consists of three bands, a topmost one of pendant triangles, of which only three are preserved, a middle row of diamonds, of which four are preserved and a lower zone of standing triangles each infilled with dots made with a single pointed tool.
BNL JH152 Egyptian Nile Clay[587]

Type Group I.2.3b Piriform 1b

35. 4287B/4518 TD F/I-j/22 planum 6–7 Phase c ? (82/255) Plate 9

BPI	IV-2-c	vf	W2	Bd. gef	re	3	2R

Nd. 2.0 cm. Bd. 1.8 cm. pht. 14.0 cm. Md. 7.6 cm. Wd. 0.7 cm.
Restored from sherds, complete
Surface colour: 7.5YR6/4 light brown; burnished slip 7.5YR5/4 brown
Break: grey core, reddish brown oxidation zones
Decoration: consists, probably of an upper zone of pendant triangles, separated by a reserved band from a frieze of rectangles and a lower band of eight pendant triangles.
BNL JH870 Southern Palestine[588]

36. 4964B TD F/I-m/22 Schnitt 17 Phase c–b/3 (85/040) Plate 9
Bd 2.2 cm. pht. 4.9 cm. Wd. 0.43 cm.
Incomplete

BPI	IV-2-b	f	W2	Bd. gef	re	1–2

Surface colour: 5YR5/4 reddish brown; burnished slip 5.R6/6 reddish yellow
Break: uniform grey
Decoration: Parts of two standing triangles infilled with individually made dots.
BNL JH857 Southern Palestine[589]

[586] P. McGovern, *The Foreign Relations of the Hyksos*, Oxford, 2000, 150 no. JH872.

[587] P. McGovern, *The Foreign Relations of the Hyksos*, Oxford, 2000, 124 no. JH152.

[588] P. McGovern, *The Foreign Relations of the Hyksos*, Oxford, 2000, 149 no. JH870.

[589] P. McGovern, *The Foreign Relations of the Hyksos*, Oxford, 2000, 149 no. JH857.

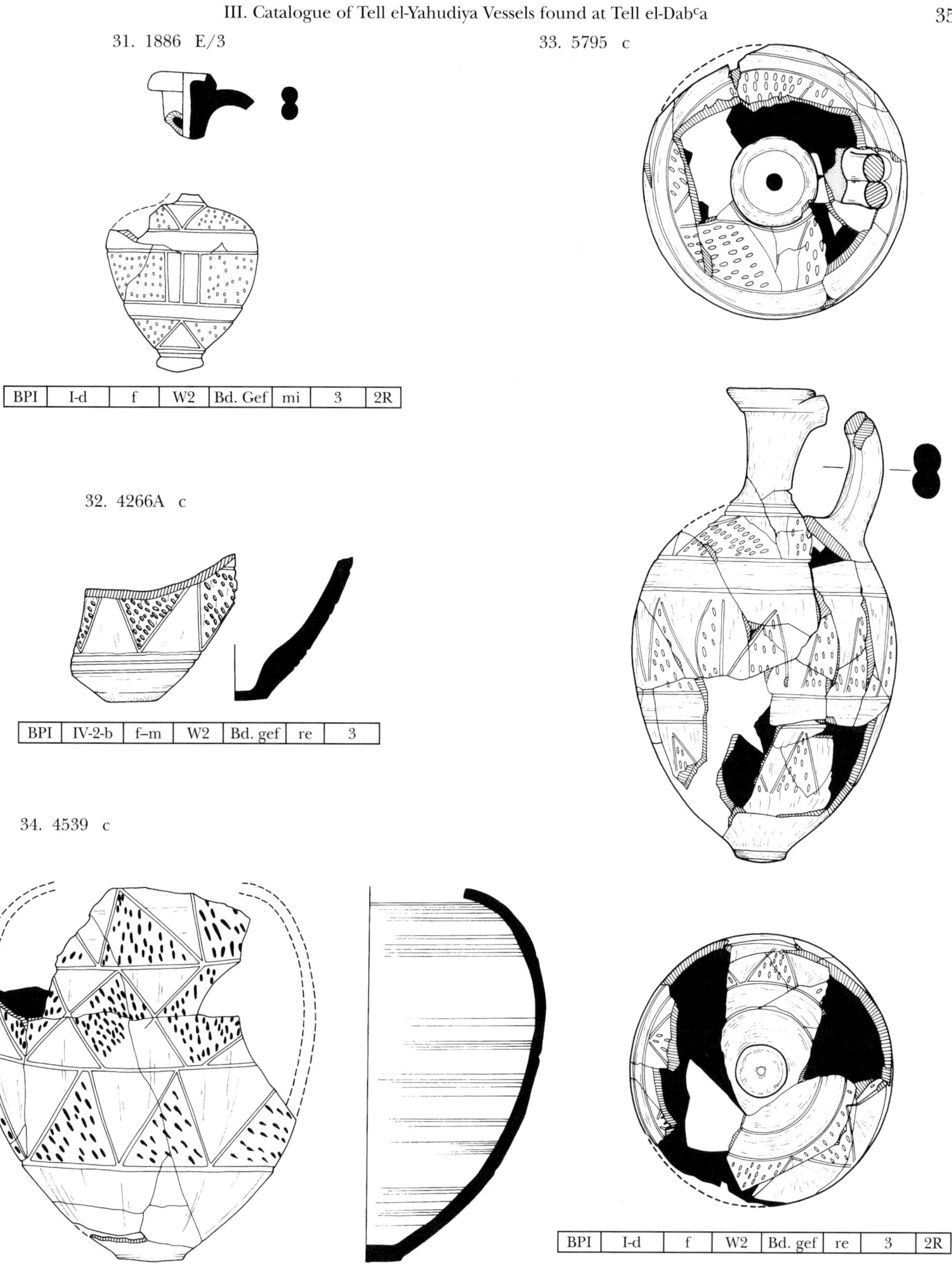

BPI	I-d	f	W2	Bd. Gef	mi	3	2R

BPI	IV-2-b	f–m	W2	Bd. gef	re	3

BPI	I-d	f	W2	Bd. gef	re	3	2R

BPI	I-d	vf	W2	Bd. gef	re	3–4

1:2

Levanto-Egyptian Type Groups I.2.2a, I.2.3a

Plate 8

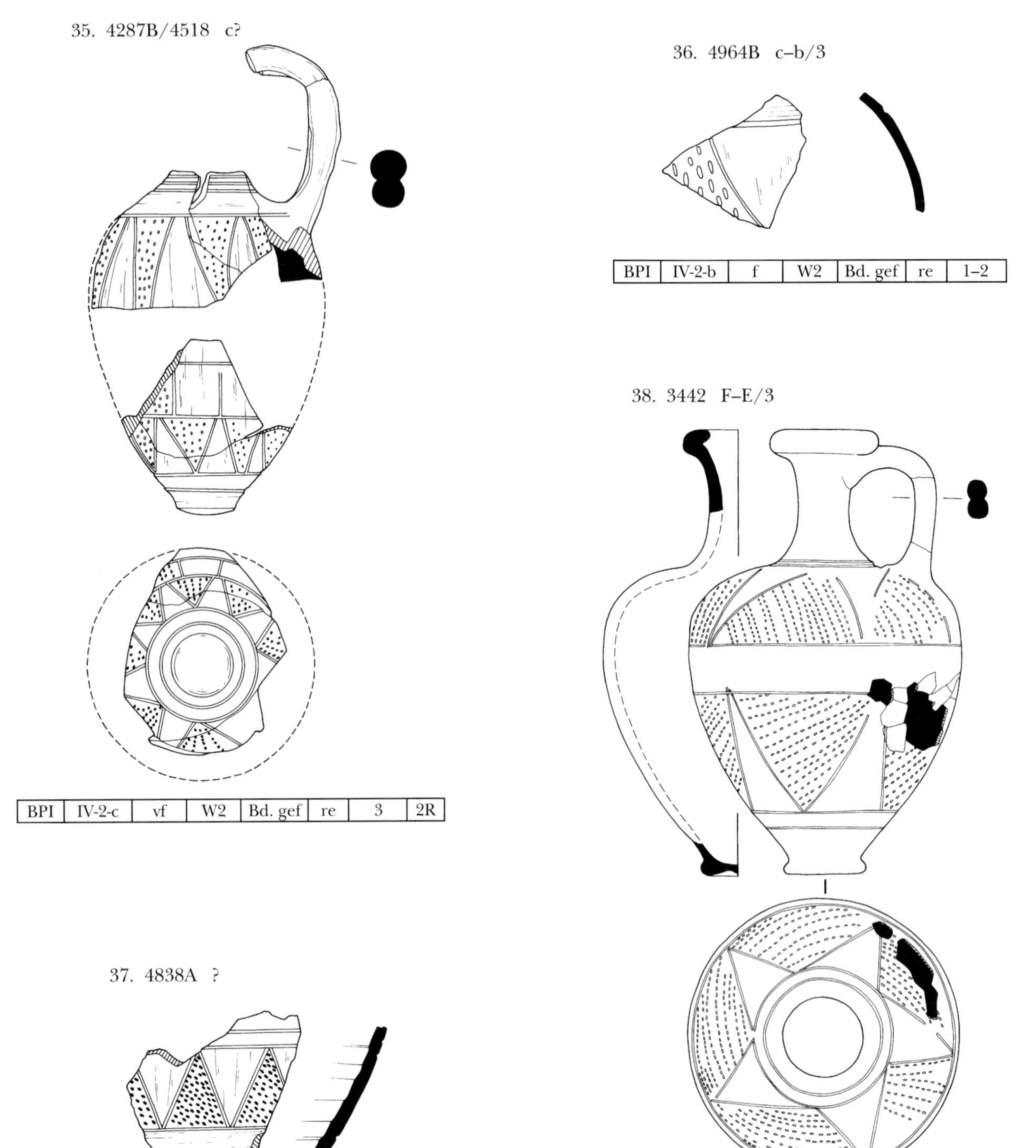

BPI	IV-2-c	vf	W2	Bd. gef	re	3	2R

BPI	IV-2-b	f	W2	Bd. gef	re	1–2

BPI	IV-1-c	f	W2		re	3

SPI	IV-2-b	f	W2	Bd. gef	re	2–3	2R

1:2

Levanto-Egyptian Type Groups I.2.3b, I.3.1c

Plate 9

37. 4838A TD F/I-l/21 grave 12 Phase ? (85/084) Plate 9

BPI	IV-1-c	f	W2		re	3

pht. 4.7 cm. Wd. 0.4 cm.
Incomplete
Surface colour: 10R6/1 reddish grey; burnished slip 5YR4/1 dark grey
Break: yellowish red core, thin grey reduction zones
Decoration: Standing triangles infilled with dots made by a single-pointed tool.
BNL JH825 Southern Palestine[590]

Type Group I.3.1

Type Group I.3.1c Piriform 1c

Tell el-Yahudiya jugs of group I.3.1 are piriform in shape, have kettle rims, double handles incisions at the base of the neck, ring bases, and only two decorative zones, one on the upper body and one on the lower body. Such vessels are very popular, and are known with various decorative styles, but the most characteristic decorative motif, type I.3.1c comprises an upper band of standing triangles and a lower one of pendant triangles.

38. 3442 Cairo F/I-j/22 planum 1 grave 2 Phase b/3–b/2

SPI	IV-2-b	f	W2	Bd. gef	re	2–3	2R

(81/088) Plate 9
D. 3.5 cm. Nd. 1.6 cm. Bd. 2.4 cm. H. 14.2 cm. Md. 8.8 cm. Wd. 0.45 cm.
Restored from sherds, complete
Surface colour: 2.5YR5/4 reddish brown; burnished slip 10YR4/1 dark grey
Break: uniform orange brown
Decoration: Upper zone of five standing triangles and a lower one of five pendant triangles made with an eight-toothed comb.

Type Group I.3.2

Tell el-Yahudiya jugs of group I.3.2 are similar to those of group I.3.1, with kettle rims, double handles incisions at the base of the neck, but instead of a ring base have a disc or button base instead. Once again the most common decorative motif, type I.3.2a comprises an upper band of standing triangles and a lower one of pendant triangles. A variant of this style is found on a large jug from Mirgissa[591] where the upper zone comprises alternating standing and pendant triangles. A third decorative style also known from Tell el-Dab^ca, I.3.2c, consists of an upper band of standing triangles and a lower zone of intersecting pendant and standing triangles separated by a zigzag reserved zone. This type group, which is invariably made of Nile clay, is so standardised that we may assume they all derive from the same workshop.

Type Group I.3.2a

39. 7476 TD A/IV-h/4 grave 11 Phase F ? (91/387) Plate 10

SPI	I-d	f	W2	Bd. gef	re	3	2R

D. 3.0 cm Nd. 1.8 cm. Bd. 1.7 cm. H. 9.7 cm. Md. 5.8 cm. Wd. 0.4 cm.
VI 59.79
Restored from sherds, incomplete
Surface colour: 7.5YR6/4 light brown; burnished slip 5Y4/1 olive
Break: dark grey in, greyish brown reduction zones
Decoration: Three incised lines at base of neck. Nine (? – only seven preserved –) standing triangles on shoulder, and nine pendant triangles below, all of which are infilled by a nine-toothed comb.

40. 4241 TD F/I-i/23 grave 32 Phase b/2 (82/191)
Plates 10, 132

SPI	I-d	f–vf	W2	Bd. gef	re	2	2R

D. 3.4 cm Nd. 1.3 cm. Bd. 2.0 cm. H. 13.2 cm. Md. 7.6 cm. Wd. 0.5 cm.
VI 57.57
Restored from sherds, incomplete
Surface colour: 5YR6/3 light red brown; burnished slip 2.5YR3/0 dark grey
Break: grey black core, light brown ox zones
Decoration: Three incised lines at base of neck. Eight standing triangles on shoulder, and nine pendant triangles below, all of which are infilled by a twelve-toothed comb. Three incised lines under the handle.
BNL JH869 Egyptian Nile Clay[592]

41. 4240 TD F/I-i/23 grave 32 Phase b/2 (82/189) Plate 10

SPI	I-d	f–vf	W2	Bd. gef	re	2	2R

D. 3.35 cm Nd. 1.5 cm. Bd. 2.0 cm. H. 12.3 cm. Md. 7.0 cm. Wd. 0.5 cm.
VI 56.91
Restored from sherds, incomplete
Surface colour: dark grey; burnished slip 2.5YR3/0 dark grey
Break: uniform dark grey
Decoration: Three incised lines at base of neck. Eight standing triangles on shoulder, and nine pendant triangles below, all of which are infilled by a twelve-toothed comb. Three incised lines under the handle.
BNL JH871 Egyptian Nile Clay[593]

42. 7513 TD A/IV-h/7 grave 4 Phase E/3 ? (91/177)
Plates11, 132

SPI	I-d	f	W2	Bd. gef	re	3–4	2R

[590] P. McGovern, *The Foreign Relations of the Hyksos*, Oxford, 2000, 146 no. JH825.
[591] Lille University Museum L.1036, Vercoutter, Excavations at Mirgissa II, *Kush* 13, 1965, 69–72, pl. 7.1; Idem, 1975, 44–49, fig. 11.4; Kaplan, *Tell el-Yahudiyeh Ware*, fig. 32b.
[592] P. McGovern, *The Foreign Relations of the Hyksos*, Oxford, 2000, 149 no. JH869.
[593] P. McGovern, *The Foreign Relations of the Hyksos*, Oxford, 2000, 150 no. JH871.

39. 7476 F

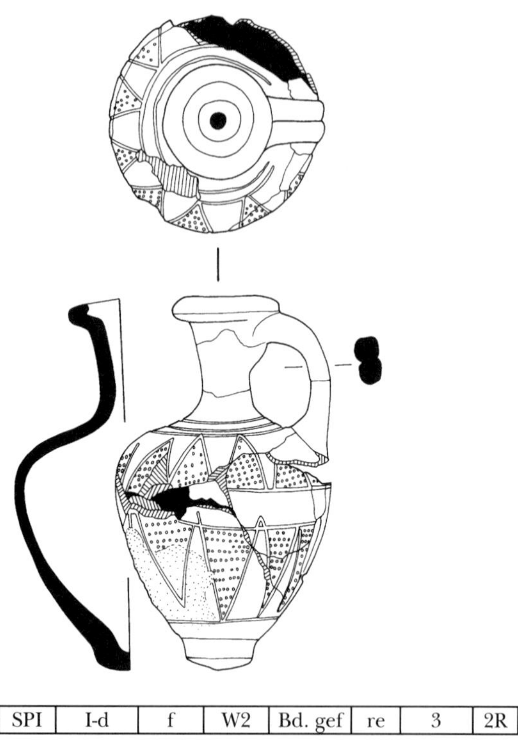

SPI	I-d	f	W2	Bd. gef	re	3	2R

40. 4241 b/2

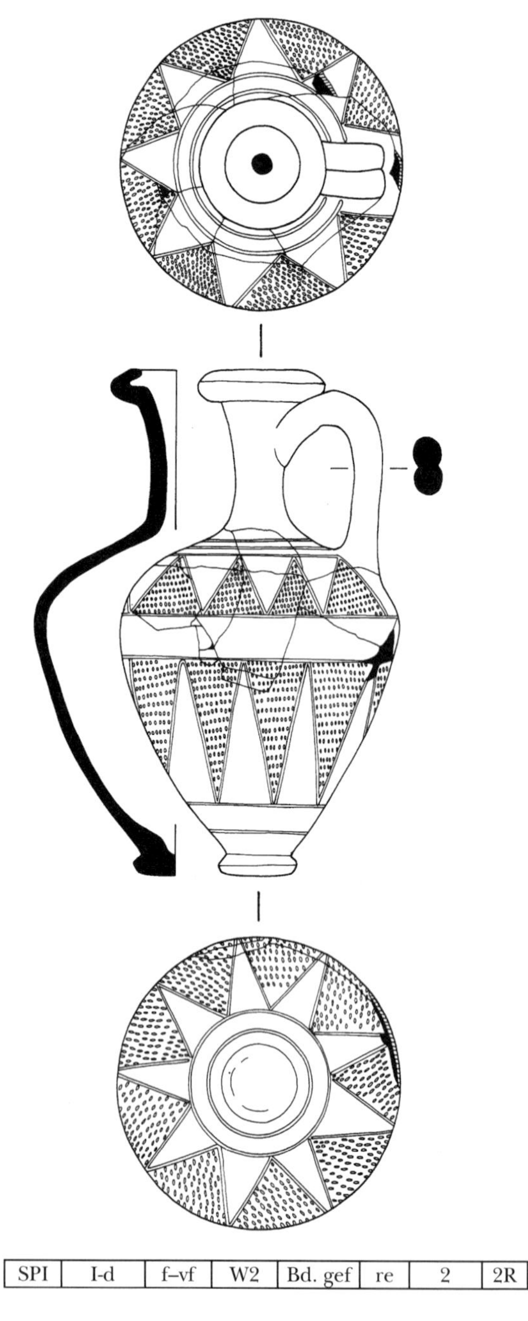

SPI	I-d	f–vf	W2	Bd. gef	re	2	2R

41. 4240 b/2

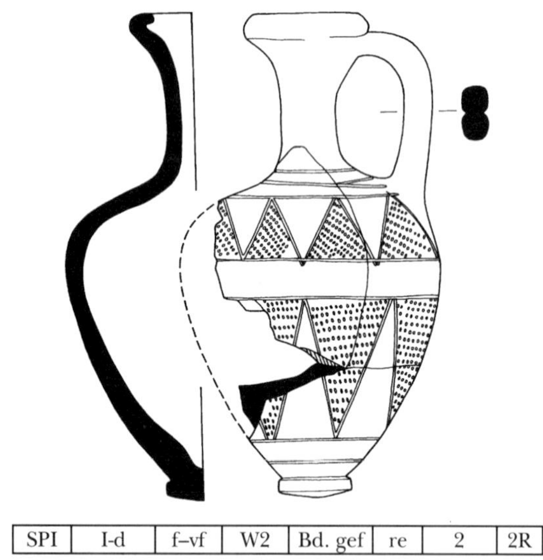

SPI	I-d	f–vf	W2	Bd. gef	re	2	2R

1:2

Levanto-Egyptian Type Group I.3.2a

Plate 10

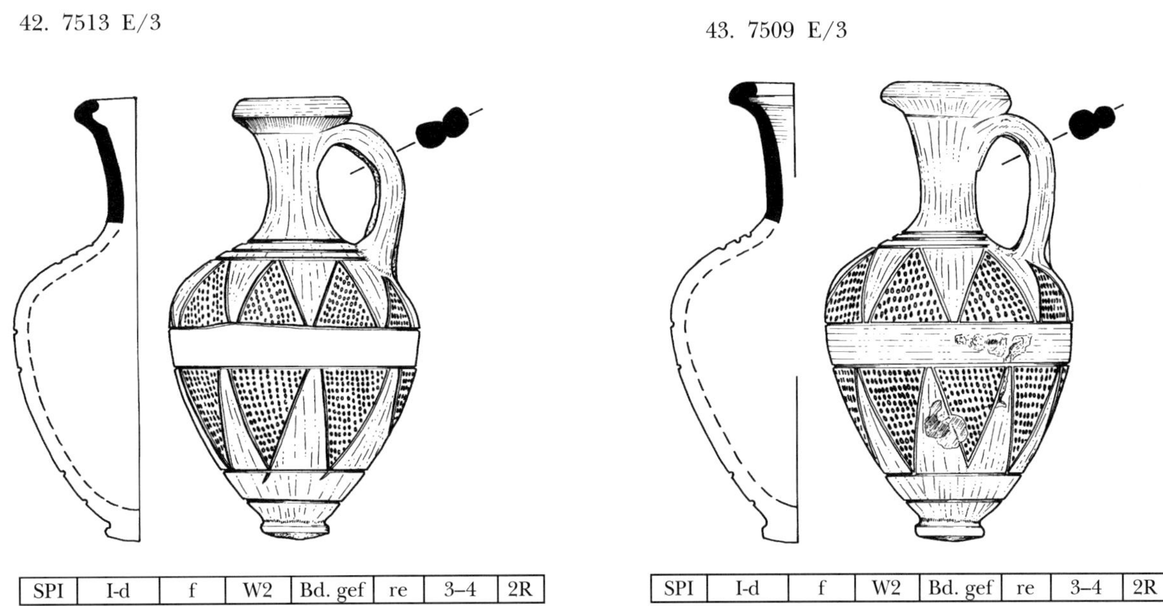

42. 7513 E/3

SPI	I-d	f	W2	Bd. gef	re	3–4	2R

43. 7509 E/3

SPI	I-d	f	W2	Bd. gef	re	3–4	2R

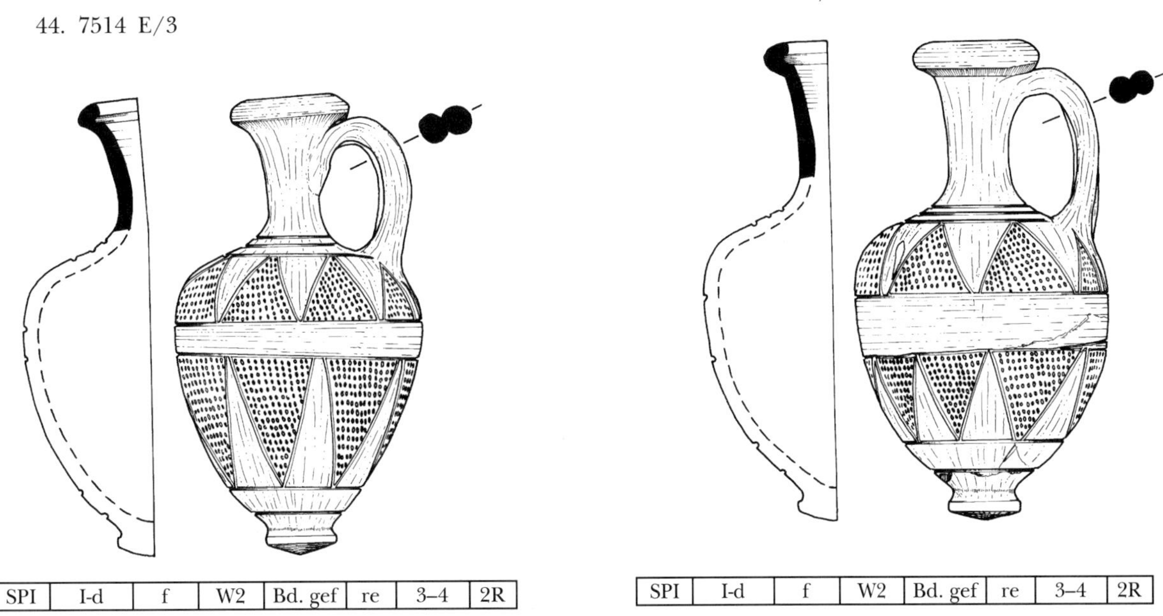

44. 7514 E/3

SPI	I-d	f	W2	Bd. gef	re	3–4	2R

45. 7508 E/3

SPI	I-d	f	W2	Bd. gef	re	3–4	2R

1:2

Levanto-Egyptian Type Group I.3.2a

Plate 11

D. 3.3 cm. Nd. 1.6 cm. Bd. 1.8 cm. H. 11.8 cm. Md. 6.7 cm. Wd. 0.45 cm.
VI 56.77
Intact
Surface colour: 10R5/2 weak red; burnished slip 10YR3/1 dark brown
Break: not visible
Decoration: Three incised lines at base of neck. Nine standing triangles on shoulder, and eight pendant triangles below, all of which are infilled by a seven-toothed comb. Three incised lines under the handle.
Previously published: PuF 177 nr 182

43. 7509 TD A/IV-h/7 grave 4 Phase E/3 ? (91/177) Plate 11

SPI	I-d	f	W2	Bd. gef	re	3–4	2R

D. 3.6 cm. Nd. 1.5 cm. Bd. 1.95 cm. H. 12.4 cm. Md. 6.8 cm. Wd. 0.45 cm.
VI 54.83
Intact
Surface colour: 5YR4/1 dark grey; burnished slip 5YR3/1 very dark grey
Break: not visible
Decoration: Three incised lines at base of neck. Eight standing triangles on shoulder, and nine pendant triangles below, all of which are infilled by a five-toothed comb. Three incised lines under the handle.
Previously published: PuF 177 nr 178

44. 7514 TD A/IV-h/7 grave 4 Phase E/3 ? (91/178) Plate 11

SPI	I-d	f	W2	Bd. gef	re	3–4	2R

D. 3.4 cm. Nd. 1.45 cm. Bd. 1.95 cm. H. 12.2 cm. Md. 6.7 cm. Wd. 0.45 cm.
VI 54.91
Intact
Surface colour: 10R5/2 weak red; burnished slip 5YR4/1 dark grey
Break: not visible
Decoration: Three incised lines at base of neck. Eight standing triangles on shoulder, and eight pendant triangles below, all of which are infilled by a six or seven-toothed comb. Three incised lines under the handle.
Previously published: PuF 177 nr 183

45. 7508 TD A/IV-h/7 grave 4 Phase E/3 ? (91/178) Plate 11

SPI	I-d	f	W2	Bd. gef	re	3–4	2R

D. 3.55 cm. Nd. 1.65 cm. Bd. 2.0 cm. H. 12.8 cm. Md. 6.95 cm. Wd. 0.45 cm.
VI 54.29
Intact
Surface colour: 5YR4/1 dark grey; burnished slip 5Y3/1 very dark grey
Break: not visible
Decoration: Three incised lines at base of neck. Seven standing triangles on shoulder, and nine pendant triangles below, all of which are infilled horizontally by a five-toothed comb. Three incised lines under the handle.
Previously published: PuF 177 nr 177

46. 7516A TD A/IV-h/7 grave 4 Phase E/3 ? (91/180) Plate 12

SPI	I-d	f	W2	Bd. gef	re	3–4	2R

D. 3.25 cm. Nd. 1.6 cm. Bd. 1.8 cm. H. 12.3 cm. Md. 6.7 cm. Wd. 0.45 cm.
VI 54.47
Restored from sherds, incomplete
Surface colour: 5YR4/1 dark grey; burnished slip 7.5YR3/2 dark brown
Break: dark greyish brown core, dark grey reduction zones
Decoration: Three incised lines at base of neck. Seven (?) standing triangles (four preserved) on shoulder, and eight pendant triangles below, all of which are infilled by an eight-toothed comb. Three incised lines under the handle.

47. 7512 TD A/IV-h/7 grave 4 Phase E/3 ? (91/100) Plate 12

SPI	I-d	f	W2	Bd. gef	re	3–4	2R

D. 3.4 cm. Nd. 1.5 cm. Bd. 2.05 cm. H. 12.2 cm. Md. 6.6 cm. Wd. 0.45 cm.
VI 54.09
Intact
Surface colour: 5YR4/1 dark grey; burnished slip 10YR3/1 dark brown
Break: not visible
Decoration: Three incised lines at base of neck. Nine standing triangles on shoulder, and eight pendant triangles below, all of which are infilled by a nine-toothed comb. Three incised lines under the handle.
Previously published: PuF 177 nr 181

48. 7511 TD A/IV-h/7 grave 4 Phase E/3 ? (91/099) Plate 12

SPI	I-d	f	W2	Bd. gef	re	3–4	2R

D. 3.3 cm. Nd. 1.4 cm. Bd. 1.9 cm. H. 11.8 cm. Md. 6.3 cm. Wd. 0.45 cm.
VI 53.38
Intact
Surface colour: 5YR4/1 dark grey; burnished slip 10YR4/2 very dark grey
Break: not visible
Decoration: Three incised lines at base of neck. Eight standing triangles on shoulder, and eight pendant triangles below, all of which are infilled with vertical lines made by a six-toothed comb. Three incised lines under the handle.
Previously published: PuF 177 nr 180

49. 7510 TD A/IV-h/7 grave 4 Phase E/3 ? (91/179) Plate 12

SPI	I-d	f	W2	Bd. gef	re	3–4	2R

D. 3.35 cm. Nd. 1.5 cm. Bd. 2.0 cm. H. 11.5 cm. Md. 6.2 cm. Wd. 0.45 cm.
VI 53.91
Intact
Surface colour: 5YR4/1 dark grey; burnished slip 10YR4/2 very dark grey
Break: not visible
Decoration: Three incised lines at base of neck. Eight standing triangles on shoulder, and nine pendant triangles below, all of which are infilled by an eleven-toothed comb. Three incised lines under the handle.
Previously published: PuF 177 nr 179

50. 7516B TD A/IV-h/7 grave 4 Phase E/3 ? (91/180) Plate 13

SPI	I-d	f	W2	Bd. gef	re	3–4	2R

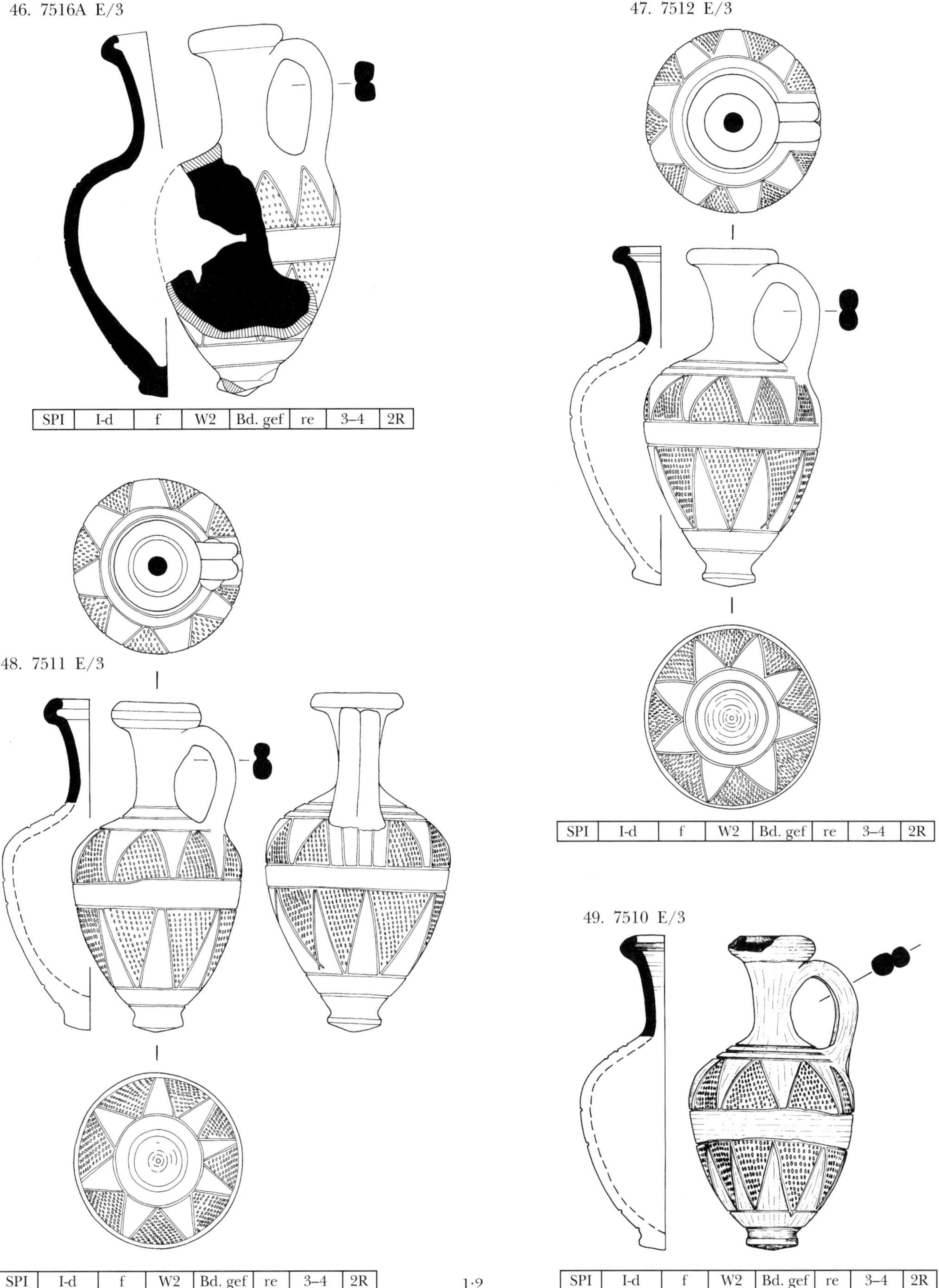

46. 7516A E/3

SPI	I-d	f	W2	Bd. gef	re	3–4	2R

48. 7511 E/3

SPI	I-d	f	W2	Bd. gef	re	3–4	2R

47. 7512 E/3

SPI	I-d	f	W2	Bd. gef	re	3–4	2R

49. 7510 E/3

SPI	I-d	f	W2	Bd. gef	re	3–4	2R

1:2

Levanto-Egyptian Type Group I.3.2a

Plate 12

D. 3.2 cm. Nd. 1.5 cm. Bd. 1.8 cm. H. 12.4 cm. Md. 6.6 cm. Wd. 0.4 cm.
VI 53.22
Restored from sherds, incomplete
Surface colour: 5YR4/1 dark grey; burnished slip 2.5YR3/0 dark grey
Break: dark greyish brown core, dark grey reduction zones
Decoration: Three incised lines at base of neck. Eight standing triangles on shoulder, and nine pendant triangles below, all of which are infilled by an eight-toothed comb. Three incised lines under the handle.

51. 7515 TD A/IV-h/7 grave 4 Phase E/3 ? (91/179) Plate 13

SPI	I-d	f	W2	Bd. gef	re	3–4	2R

D. 3.2 cm. Nd. 1.5 cm. Bd. 2.2 cm. H. 13.3 cm. Md. 6.8 cm. Wd. 0.45 cm.
VI 51.13
Part of handle missing
Surface colour: 5YR4/1 dark grey; burnished slip 5YR3/2 dark reddish brown
Break: uniform grey
Decoration: Three incised lines at base of neck. Seven standing triangles above mid-point and eight pendant triangles below, all filled with vertical lines made with an eight-toothed comb. Three incised lines under the handle.

52. 7516 TD A/IV-h/7 grave 4 Phase E/3 ? (91/180) Plate 13

SPI	I-d	f	W2	Bd. gef	re	3–4	2R

Nd. 1.5 cm. Bd. 2.0 cm. H. 11.5 cm. Md. 6.6 cm. Wd. 0.45 cm.
VI 57.39
Incomplete
Surface colour: 5YR4/1 dark grey; burnished slip 2.5YR3/0 dark grey
Break: dark greyish brown core, dark grey reduction zones
Decoration: Three incised lines at base of neck. Eight standing triangles on shoulder, and nine pendant triangles below, all of which are infilled by an eight-toothed comb. Three incised lines under the handle.

53. 8684 TD A/II-p/14 locus 173 grave 4 Phase E/2 (98/085) Plate 13

SPI	I-d	m	W2	Bd. gef	re	2–3	1B

D. 3.7 cm. Nd. 1.7 cm. Bd. 1.7 cm. H. 12.0 cm. Md 7.2 cm. Wd. 0.4 cm.
VI 60.00
Intact
Surface colour: 10YR4/1 dark grey; burnished slip: 10YR3/4 dark yellowish brown
Break: not visible
Decoration: Three incised lines at the base of the neck. On the shoulder ten standing triangles infilled with comb decoration from upper left to lower right. On the lower body seven pendant triangles infilled with comb decoration from upper left to lower right.
Previously published: TD XVI, 240, fig. 172, no. 3.

54. 1123 Vienna AS2276 A/II-m/12 grave 9 Phase E/2 (68/022) Plate 14

SPI	I-d	f–vf	W2	Bd. gef	re	3–4	2R

Nd. 1.3 cm. Bd. 2.0 cm. pht. 10.4 cm. Md 6.4 cm. Wd. 0.4 cm.
Restored from sherds, incomplete
Surface colour: 10YR5/2 greyish brown; burnished slip: 7.5YR6/4 light brown
Break: not visible
Decoration: Three incised lines at the base of the neck. On the shoulder nine standing triangles infilled with comb decoration from upper left to lower right. On the lower body eight pendant triangles infilled with comb decoration from upper left to lower right.
Previously published: BIETAK, *MDAIK* 26, pl 20d; KAPLAN *Tell el-Yahudiyeh Ware* fig. 34c; *TD V,* 123, 125.

Type Group I.3.2c

55. 1675 Vienna AS1430 A/II-l/14 grave 7 Phase E/3 (68/117) Plates 14, 132

SPI	I-d	f–vf	W2	Bd. gef	re	3	2R

D. 3.25 cm Nd. 1.3 cm. Bd. 2.35 cm. H. 12.3 cm. Md. 7.2 cm. Wd. 0.4 cm.
VI 58.53
Intact
Surface colour: 2.5Y5/1 gray: burnished slip 10YR2/1 black
Break: not visible
Decoration: Three incised lines at the base of the neck. On the shoulder six standing triangles with comb decoration. On the body a wide zone of opposing pendant and standing triangles infilled with comb decoration. The areas not decorated are burnished.
Previously published: BIETAK, *MDAIK* 26, pl. 20d; BIETAK, *Antike Welt* 6, 32, fig. 8; KAPLAN, *Tell el-Yahudiyeh Ware,* fig. 34d; *TD XVI,* 197, fig. 115, no. 5.

56. 3653A Vienna A3942 F/I-i/23 grave 26 Phase b/2 (81/523) Plate 14

SPI	I-d	f–vf	W2	Bd. gef	re	3	2R

D. 3.55 cm Nd. 1.4 cm. Bd. 2.15 cm. H. 14.0 cm. Md. 7.4 cm. Wd. 0.4 cm.
VI 52.85
Restored from sherds, incomplete
Surface colour: 7.5YR6/4 light brown; burnished slip 10YR5/2–3 grey brown
Break: uniform black
Decoration: Six standing triangles on shoulder, six (?) small hanging triangles and five tall standing triangles on body. Triangles infilled with a series of individually made dots.
BNL JH902 Egyptian Nile Clay[594]

Type Group I.5.1

Vessels of group I.5.1 are smaller than those of groups I.1–4 and are characterised as having candlestick rims, double handles, and ring bases, but this time no incisions at the base of the neck. Two such

[594] P. MCGOVERN, *The Foreign Relations of the Hyksos,* Oxford, 2000, 152 no. JH902.

50. 7516B E/3

SPI	I-d	f	W2	Bd. gef	re	3–4	2R

51. 7515 E/3

SPI	I-d	f	W2	Bd. gef	re	3–4	2R

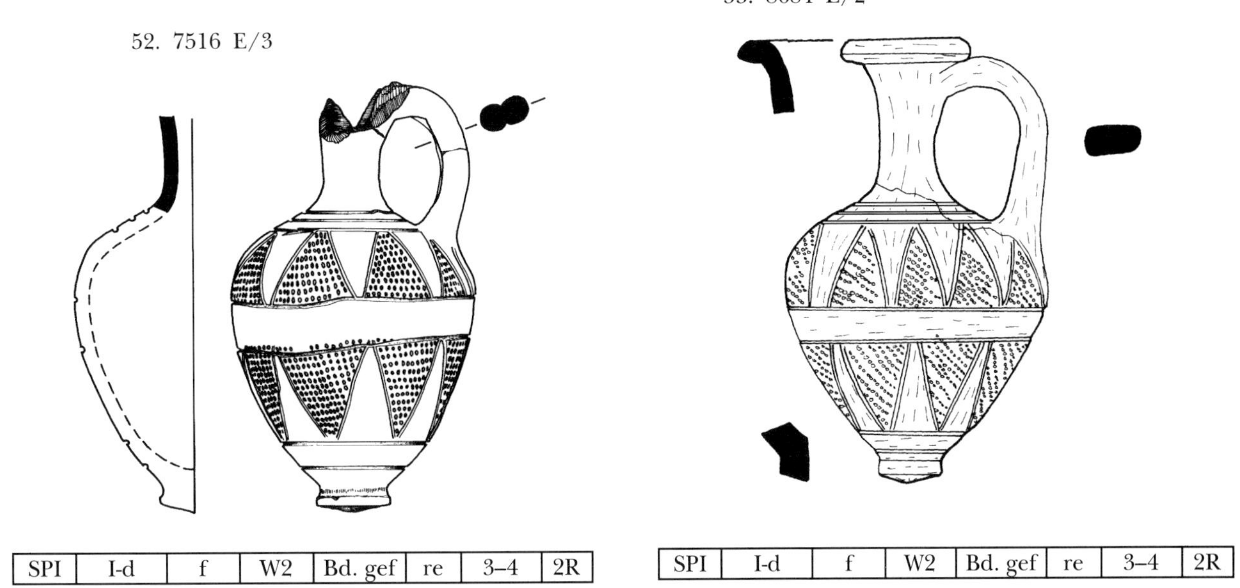

52. 7516 E/3

SPI	I-d	f	W2	Bd. gef	re	3–4	2R

53. 8684 E/2

SPI	I-d	f	W2	Bd. gef	re	3–4	2R

1:2

Levanto-Egyptian Type Group I.3.2a

Plate 13

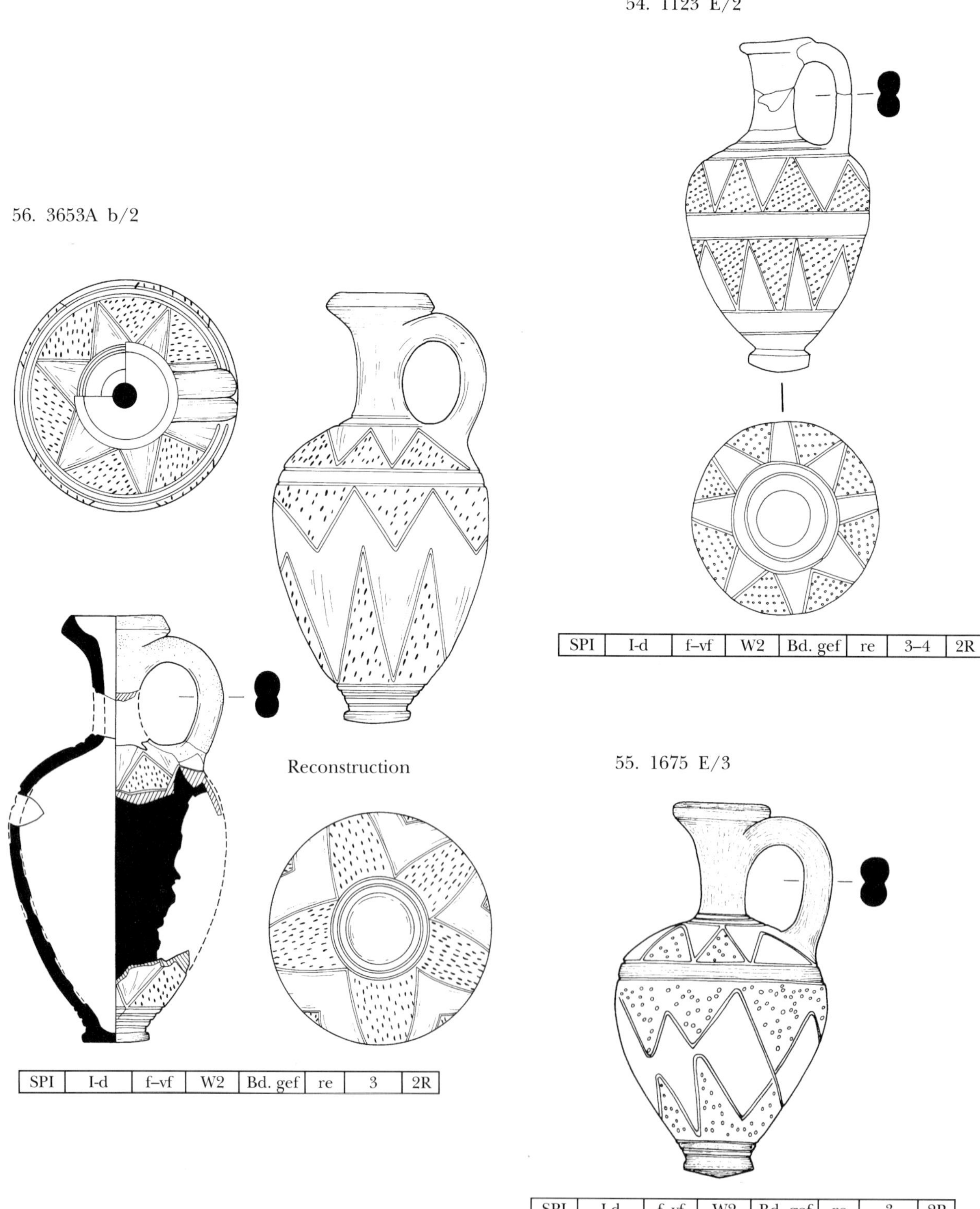

1:2

Levanto-Egyptian Type Groups I.3.2a, I.3.2c

Plate 14

vessels are known from Tell el-Dab[c]a, each having three zones of decoration, in the style of Piriform 1b jugs, an upper and lower band of intersecting pendant and standing triangles separated by a zigzag reserved zone, and a central one of rectangles.

57. 1676 Vienna A1683 A/II-l/14 grave 7 Phase E/3 (68/117) Plates 15, 133

BPI	I-d	f	W2	Bd. gef	re	3	2R

D. 2.75 cm Nd. 1.3 cm. Bd. 2.25 cm. H. 11.0 cm. Md. 5.8 cm. Wd. 0.4 cm.
Intact
Surface colour: 7.5YR4/2 dark brown; burnished slip 5YR4/3 red brown
Break: not visible
Decoration: Band of pendant and standing triangles on the shoulder and lower body. Around the maximum point of the jug a zone of rectangles, all infilled with comb decoration.
Previously published: BIETAK, *MDAIK* 26, pl. 21a; KAPLAN, *Tell el-Yahudiyeh Ware,* fig. 27c; *TD XVI,* 197, fig. 115, no. 2.

58. 1679 Vienna A3143 A/II-l/14 grave 7 Phase E/3 (68/118) Plate 15

SPI	I-d	f	W2	Bd. gef	re	3	2R

Bd. 2.4 cm. pht. 8.8 cm. Md. 7.2 cm. Wd. 0.4 cm.
Intact
Surface colour: 7.5YR4/2 dark brown; burnished slip 5YR4/3 red brown
Break: not visible
Decoration: Similar to 1676.
Previously published: TD XVI, 197, fig. 115, no. 3.

Type Group I.5.2

Type group I.5.2 comprises small piriform, almost ovoid jugs, between 8 and 9 cm. tall, known from Byblos and Tell el-Dab[c]a. They have a rolled rim, double handle button base and all have different decorative styles.

59. 1842 Cairo JE 91632 A/II-n/13 planum 6–7 grave 8 Phase E/3 (68/167) Plate 15

BPI	I-d	f	W2	Bd. gef	re	2	2R

D. 3.0 cm Nd. 1.4 cm. Bd. 1.5 cm. H. 11.8 cm. Md. 6.4 cm. Wd. 0.27 cm.
VI 54.23
Intact
Surface colour: 7.5YR5/2 brown; burnished slip 2.5YR4/4 reddish brown– 5YR4/2 dark reddish grey
Break: not visible
Decoration: consists of three zones with comb filled decoration. An upper zone of four standing triangles. a central one of five hanging triangles and a lower zone of three hanging trapezoids.
Previously published: TD V, 89, 91

Type Group I.5.3

Vessels of group I.5.3a comprise piriform vessels with rolled rims, double handles, button bases, and, usually, incisions at the base of the neck. Several such vessels are known from Tell el-Dab[c]a, and all have three zones of decoration. They can be divided into two sub-groups. I.5.3a sports an upper and lower band of aternating pendant and standing triangles separated by a zigzag reserved zone, and a central one of rectangles, whilst I.5.3b are decorated with an upper and middle band of intersecting pendant and standing triangles separated by a zigzag reserved zone, and a lower one of pendant triangles.

Type Group I.5.3a

60. 1769 Vienna A3191 A/II-m/10 planum 6 grave 8 Phase F (68/146) Plates 16, 133

BPI	I-d	f–vf	W2	Bd. gef	re	3	2R

Nd. 1.25 cm. Bd. 1.2 cm. pht. 9.0 cm. Md. 6.4 cm. Wd. 0.3 cm.
Restored from sherds, incomplete
Surface colour: 5YR4.5/1 dark grey; burnished slip 5YR3–4/2 dark reddish brown
Break: brown core, grey reduction zones
Decoration: Three decorative zones with matt reserved zones: in the centre are divided rectangles, and above and below, standing and pendant triangles separated from each other by a reserved zigzag. White incrusted decorated areas were made by means of a multi-toothed comb. Metallic burnish.
Previously published: TD V, 66, 67

61. 1786 Vienna A3205 A/II-m/10 planum 6 grave 8 Phase F (68/148) Plates 16, 133

BPI	I-d	f	W2	Bd. gef	re	3	2R

D. 2.9 cm Nd. 1.4 cm. Bd. 1.4 cm. H. 11.9 cm. Md. 7.9 cm. Wd. 0.3 cm.
Restored from sherds, incomplete
Surface colour: 10YR4/1 grey; burnished slip 10YR6/3 dark brown
Break: grey core, with light grey outer zone
Rim undercut and horizontally trimmed.
Decoration: Three decorative zones with matt reserved zones: in the centre are divided rectangles, and above and below, standing and pendant triangles separated from each other by a reserved zigzag. Decorated areas were made by means of an eight-toothed comb. Metallic burnish.
Previously published: TD V, 66, 67

62. 7441B (TD) A/IV-h/4 grave 11 Phase F ? (91/059) Plates 16, 133

SPI	I-d	f	W2	Bd. gef	re	3	2R

Nd. 1.4 cm. Bd. 1.2 cm. pht. 8.1 cm. Md. 7.6 cm. Wd. 0.3 cm.
Restored from sherds, incomplete
Surface colour: 10YR4/2 dark brownish grey; burnished slip 10YR6/3 dark brown
Break: dark grey core, grey reduction zones
Decoration: Three decorative zones with matt reserved zones: in the centre are divided rectangles, and above and below, standing and pendant triangles separated from each other by a reserved zigzag. Decorated areas were made by means of an eight-toothed comb. Metallic burnish.

63. 3301C TD F/I-j/21 planum 1 Phase b/1 (80/106) Plate 16

SPI	I-d	f	W2	–	re	3	2R

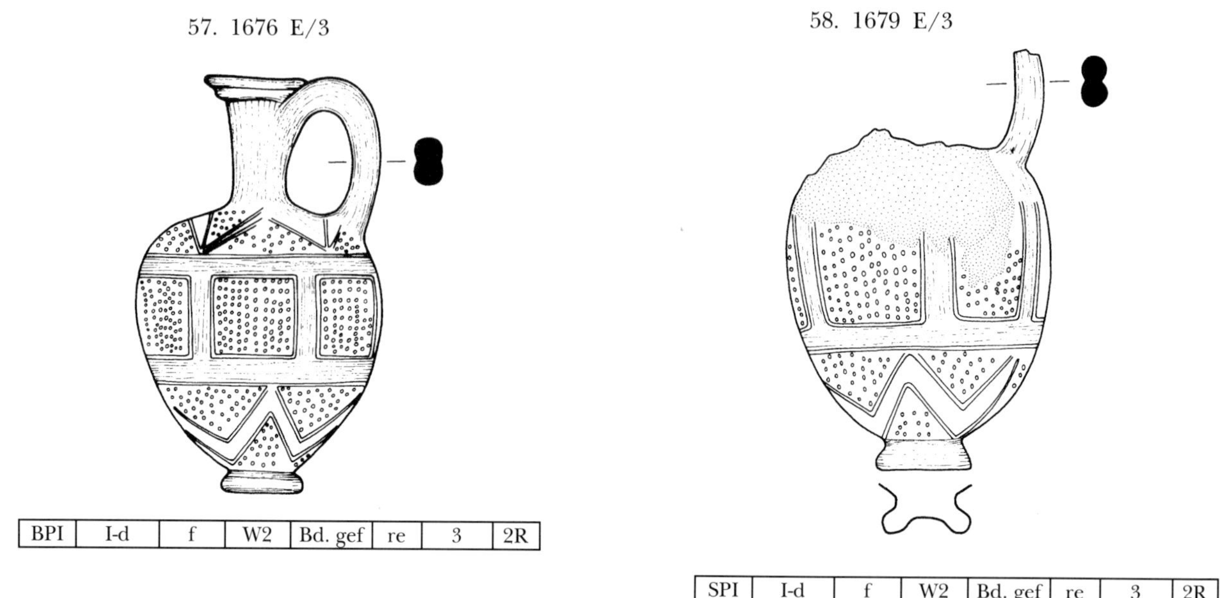

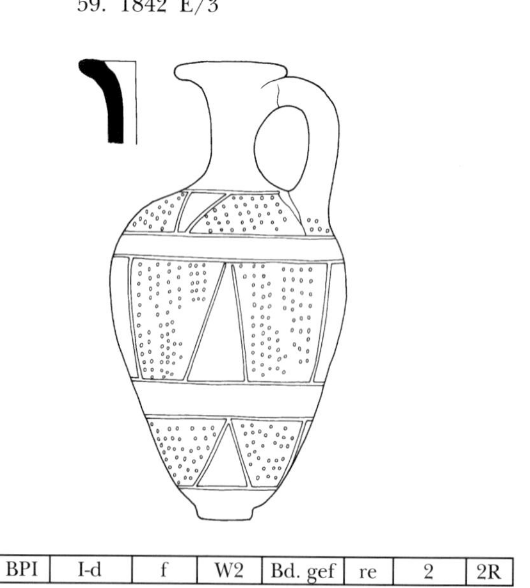

1:2

Levanto-Egyptian Type Groups I.5.1, I.5.2

Plate 15

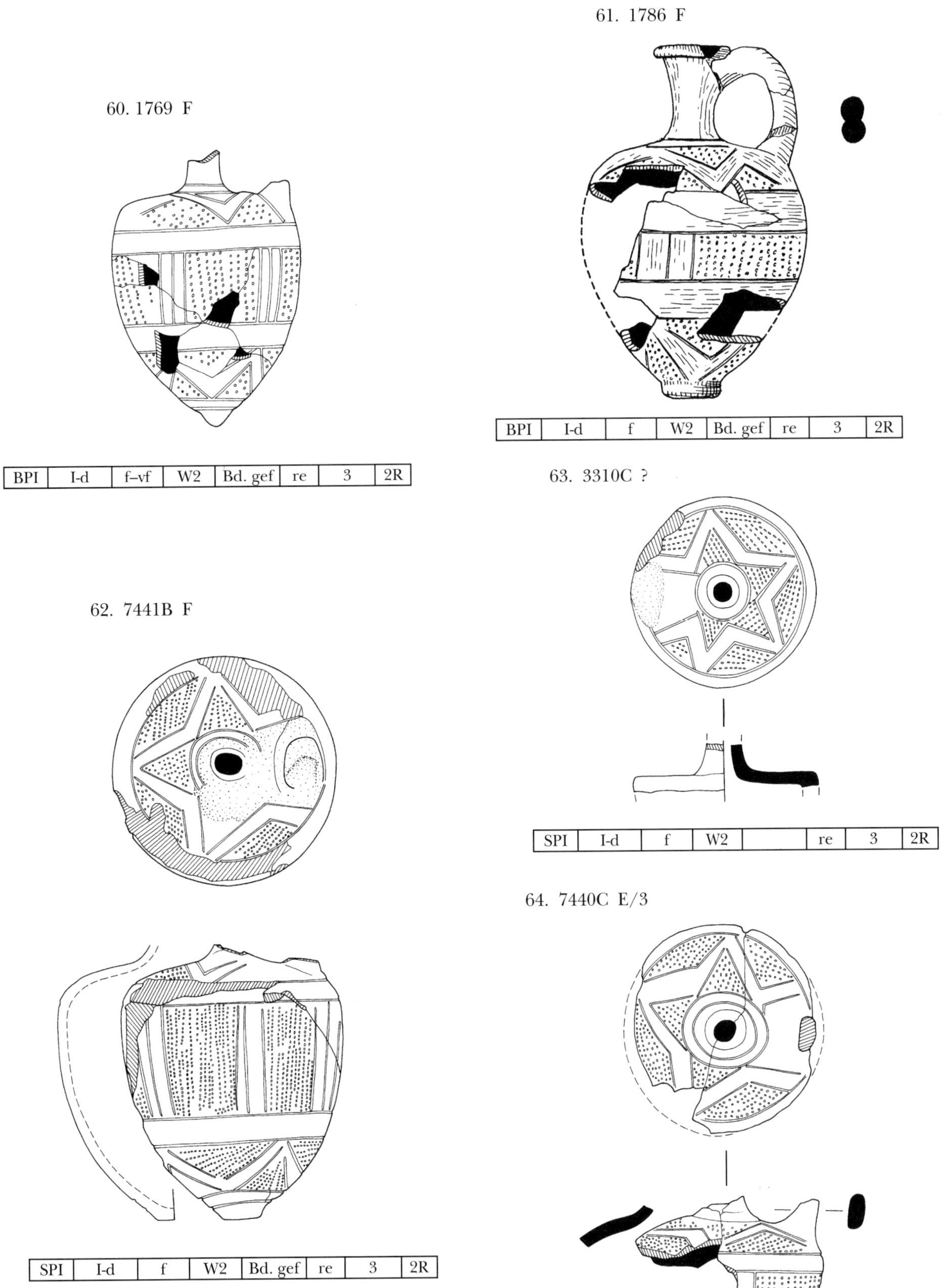

1:2

Levanto-Egyptian Type Group I.5.3a

Plate 16

Nd. 1.2 cm. pht. 1.4 cm. Md. 6.3 cm. Wd. 0.5 cm.
Incomplete
Surface colour: 10YR5/1–6/2 dark grey brown; burnished slip 10YR4/1 dark grey
Break: beige core, dark grey reduction zones
Decoration: consists of four alternating standing and pendant triangles, each infilled with a six-toothed comb.

64. 7440C TD A/IV-h/4 grave 11 Phase F ? (91/065) Plate 16

SPI	I-d	f	W2	–	re	3	2R

Nd. 1.8 cm. pht. 2.0 cm. Md. 6.8 cm. Wd. 0.3 cm.
Incomplete
Surface colour: 10YR5/1–6/2 dark grey brown; burnished slip worn off
Break: brown core, dark grey reduction zones
Decoration: Three pendant and four standing triangles on shoulder, infilled with a five-toothed comb.

65. 6044 TD F/I-o/21 grave 5 Phase b/3 (87/073) Plate 17

SPI	I-d	f–m	W2	Bd. gef	re	2	2R

D. 3.3 cm Nd. 1.3 cm. Bd. 1.6 cm. H. 10.2 cm. Md. 6.7 cm. Wd. 0.4 cm.
Restored from sherds, incomplete
Surface colour: 10YR5/1 grey; burnished slip 10YR6/3 dark brown
Break: dark grey core, light grey brown reduction zones
Rim undercut and horizontally trimmed.
Decoration: Three decorative zones with matt reserved zones: in the centre are divided rectangles, and above and below, standing and pendant triangles separated from each other by a reserved zigzag. Decorated areas were made by means of a multi-toothed comb. Metallic burnish.

Type Group I.5.3b

66. 1758 Vienna A3183 A/II-m/10 planum 6 grave 8 Phase F (68/144) Plates 17, 134

BPI	I-d	f	W2	Bd. gef	re	3	2R

D. 2.65 cm Nd. 1.5 cm. Bd. 1.7 cm. H. 11.2 cm. Md. 7.6 cm. Wd. 0.4 cm.
VI 67.85
Incomplete
Surface colour: 10YR3/2–5YR4/2 very dark grey; burnished slip 10YR6/3 dark brown
Break: uniform grey
Carefully burnished
Decoration: consists of mat standing and pendant triangles in three zones. The triangles are infilled by mean of a ten-toothed comb.
Previously published: TD V, 64, 65

67. 1759 Vienna A3184 A/II-m/10 planum 6 grave 8 Phase F (68/144) Plate 17

BPI	I-d	f	W2	Bd. gef	re	3	2R

D. 2.65 cm Nd. 1.3 cm. Bd. 1.7 cm. H. 11.4 cm. Md. 7.65 cm. Wd. 0.4 cm.
VI 62.65
Restored from sherds, Incomplete
Surface colour: 7.5YR5/3 brown; burnished slip 7.5YR5/3 brown
Break: uniform grey
Very carefully burnished
Decoration: consists of matt standing and pendant triangles in three zones. The triangles are infilled by mean of a multi-toothed comb.
Previously published: TD V, 64

68. 3028 Cairo F/I-i/20 grave 3 Phase b/2 (79/215) Plate 17

BPI	I-d	f	W2	Bd. gef	re	2	2R

D. 2.8 cm Nd. 1.3 cm. Bd. 1.67 cm. H. 11.5 cm. Md. 7.9 cm. Wd. 0.27 cm.
VI 68.69
Restored from sherds, incomplete
Surface colour: 7.5YR5/3 brown; burnished slip 7.5YR5/3 brown
Break: uniform grey
Very carefully burnished
Decoration: consists of mat standing and pendant triangles in three zones. The triangles are infilled by mean of a multi-toothed comb.

69. 1762 Vienna A3187 A/II-m/10 planum 6 grave 8 Phase F (68/144) Plate 18

BPI	I-d	f–vf	W2	Bd. gef	mi	3	2R

Bd. 1.8 cm. pht. 8.5 cm. Md. 7.7 cm. Wd. 0.4 cm.
Restored from sherds, incomplete
Surface colour: 5YR5/4 red brown; burnished slip 2.5YR4/2 weak red
Break: grey core, light brown and thin brown oxidation zones
Well burnished
Decoration: consists of matt standing and pendant triangles in three zones. The triangles are infilled by mean of a nine-toothed comb.
Previously published: TD V, 64

70. 5985C TD F/I-n/21 grave 3 Phase b/3 (87/174) Plate 18

BPI	I-d	f	W2	Bd. gef	re	2–3	2R

D. 2.75 cm Nd. 1.75 cm. pht. 3.35 + 1.95 cm. Wd. 0.4 cm.
Restored from sherds, incomplete
Surface colour: 7.5YR5/3 brown; burnished slip 7.5YR4/2 dark brown
Break: dark grey in, greenish grey out
Decoration: Three incised lines at base of neck. Only uppermost zone preserved which consists of standing and pendant triangles separated by a burnished zigzag. The triangles are infilled by mean of a six-toothed comb.

Type Group I.5.4

Type Group I.5.4 consists of small piriform vessels with double handles and button bases. The decoration consists of an upper zone of alternating pendant and standing triangles, a central zone of rectangles and a lower zone of pendant triangles.

71. 1760 Vienna A3185 A/II-m/10 planum 6 grave 8 Phase F (68/144) Plate 18

BPI	I-d	f	W2	Bd. gef	mi	3	2R

Bd. 1.5 cm. pht. 8.5 cm. Md. 6.4 cm. Wd. 0.4 cm.
Restored from sherds, incomplete
Surface colour: 5YR4.5/4 red brown; burnished slip 2.5YR4/2–4YR4.5/6 weak red to reddish yellow
Break: grey core, brown oxidation zones

65. 6044 b/3

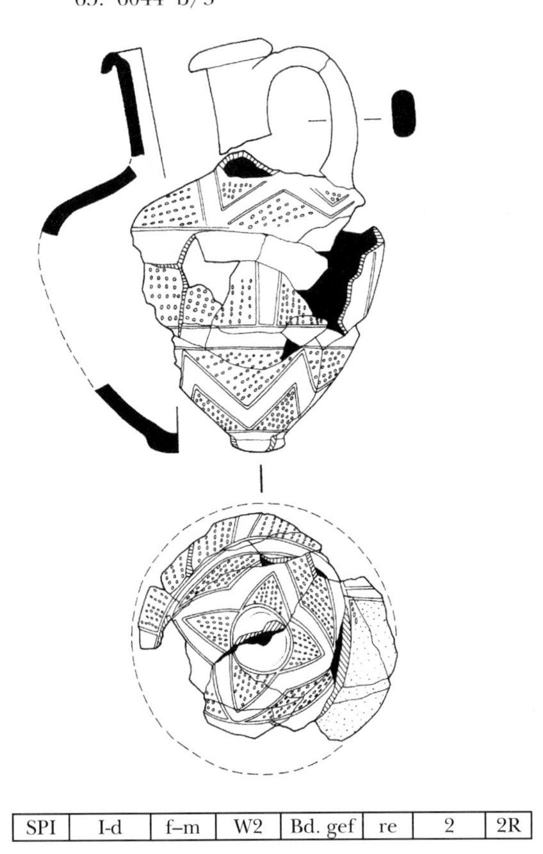

SPI	I-d	f–m	W2	Bd. gef	re	2	2R

66. 1758 F

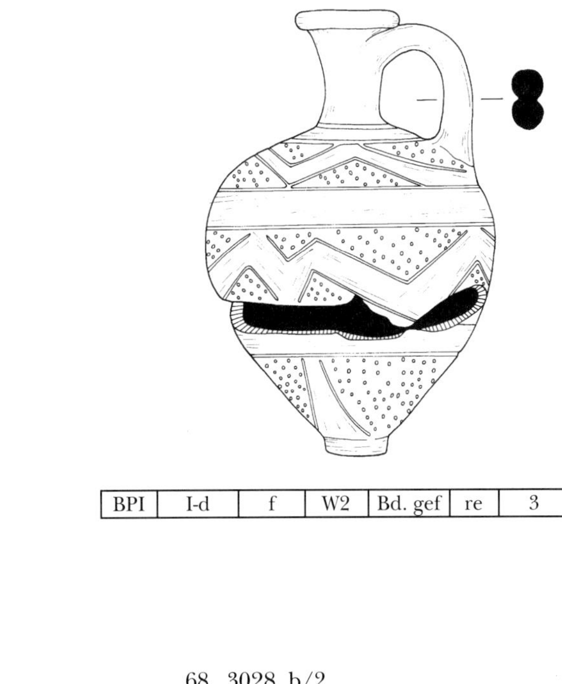

BPI	I-d	f	W2	Bd. gef	re	3	2R

67. 1759 F

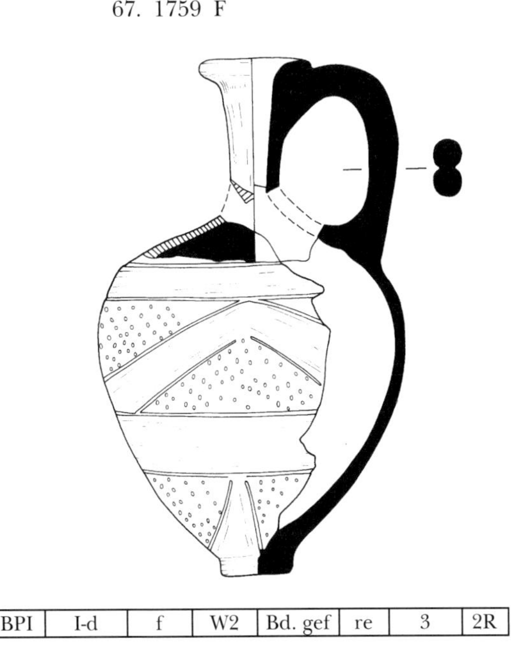

BPI	I-d	f	W2	Bd. gef	re	3	2R

68. 3028 b/2

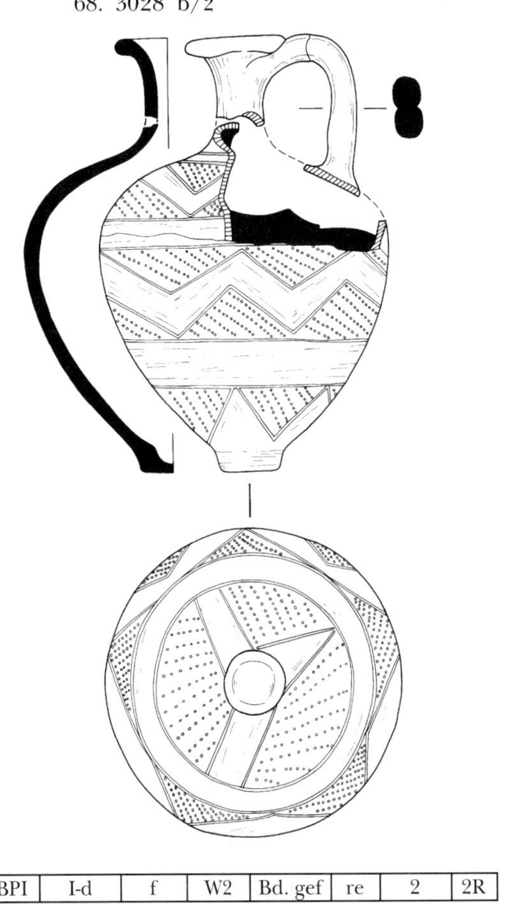

BPI	I-d	f	W2	Bd. gef	re	2	2R

1:2

Levanto-Egyptian Type Groups I.5.3a–b

Plate 17

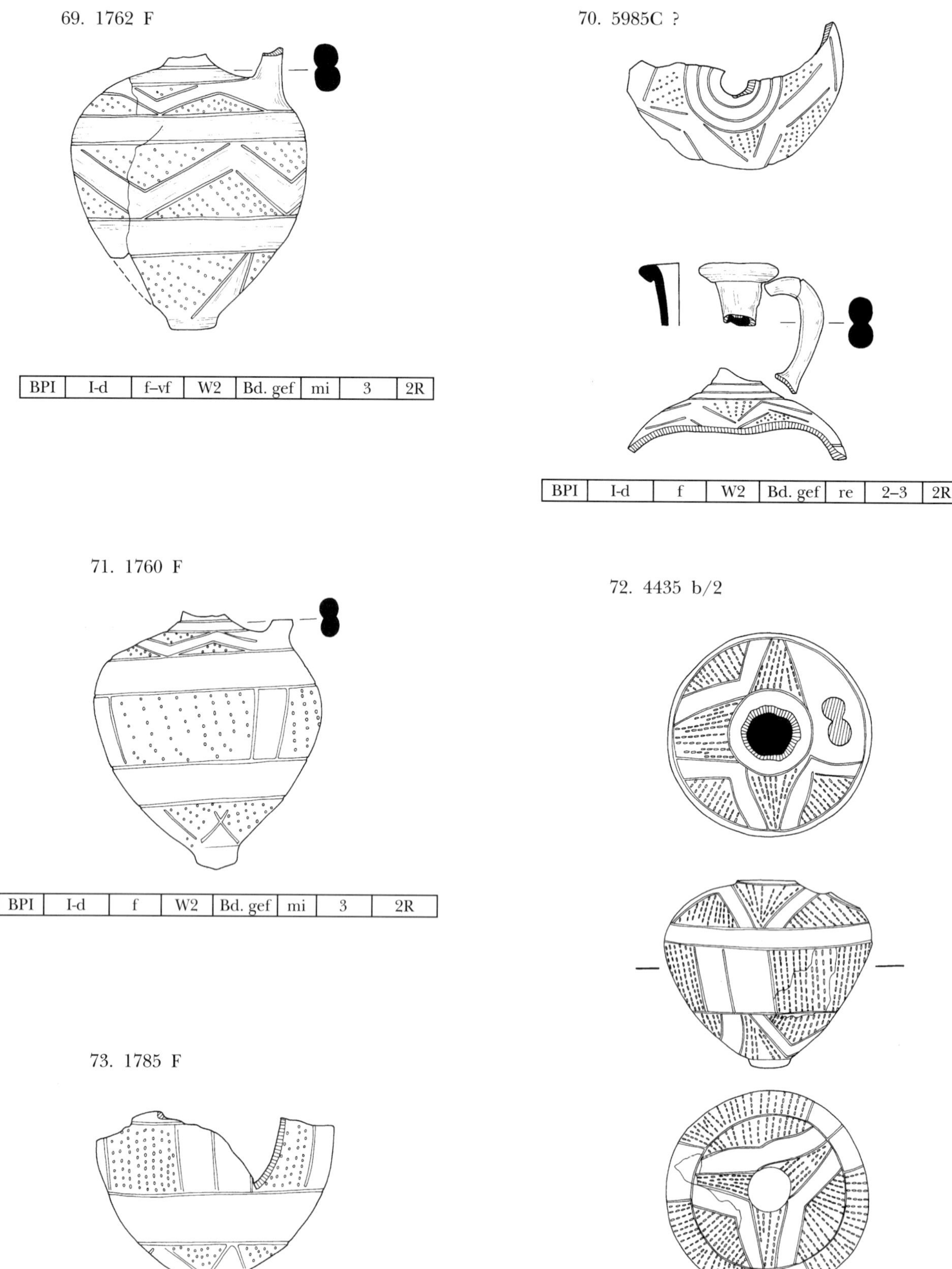

69. 1762 F

BPI	I-d	f–vf	W2	Bd. gef	mi	3	2R

70. 5985C ?

BPI	I-d	f	W2	Bd. gef	re	2–3	2R

71. 1760 F

BPI	I-d	f	W2	Bd. gef	mi	3	2R

73. 1785 F

BPI	I-d	f–vf	W2	Bd. gef	re	2–3	2R

72. 4435 b/2

SPI	I-d	f–m	W2	Bd. gef	re	2	2R

1:2

Levanto-Egyptian Type Groups I.5.3b, I.5.4

Plate 18

Button base has a slight bulb
Decoration: Three decorative zones with matt reserved zones: in the centre are divided rectangles, and above and below, standing and pendant triangles separated from each other by a reserved zigzag. White incrusted decorated areas were made by means of a ten-toothed comb. Metallic burnish.
Previously published: TD V, 64

To this group should probably also be attributed the following squatter vessels:

72. 4435 F/I-k/20 grave 1 Phase b/2 (83/055) Plates 18, 134

SPI	I-d	f–m	W2	Bd. gef	re	2	2R

Nd. 1.6 cm. Bd. 1.3 cm. pht. 6.2 cm. Md. 6.9 cm. Wd. 0.4 cm.
Incomplete
Surface colour: 10YR6/2 lt grey brown; burnished slip 5YR5/3 reddish brown
Break: uniform grey
Decoration: Three decorative zones with matt reserved zones: in the centre are divided rectangles, and above and below, standing and pendant triangles separated from each other by a reserved zigzag. White incrusted decorated areas were made by means of a multi-toothed comb. Metallic burnish.

73. 1785 Vienna A3204 A/II-m/10 planum 6 grave 8 Phase F (68/148) Plate 18

BPI	I-d	f–vf	W2	Bd. gef	re	2–3	2R

Bd. 1.4 cm. pht. 5.8 cm. Md. 6.4 cm. Wd. 0.3 cm.
Incomplete
Surface colour: 10YR6/2 lt grey brown; burnished slip 5YR4/2–5/4 dark reddish grey
Break: brown core, grey reduction zones
Decoration: Presumably originally three decorative zones with matt reserved zones, of which only the lower two are preserved: in the centre are divided rectangles, and below, standing and pendant triangles separated from each other by a reserved zigzag. White incrusted decorated areas were made by means of a six-toothed comb. Metallic burnish.
Previously published: TD V, 66, 67.

Type Group I.5.5

Vessels of group I.5.5 comprise model piriform vessels with double handles, button bases, and once again no incisions at the base of the neck. Examples from Tell el-Dab^ca, such as TD 1841, have an upper zone of standing triangles and a lower zone of pendant triangles.

74. 1841 Vienna A3247 A/II-n/13 planum 6–7 grave 8 Phase E/3 (68/200) Plates 19, 134

SPI	I-d	f	W2	Bd. gef	re	2	2R

Nd. 1.4 cm. Bd. 1.4 cm. pht. 8.8 cm. Md. 6.8 cm. Wd. 0.45 cm.
Incomplete
Surface colour: 5YR5/3 reddish brown; burnished slip 5YR4/2 dark reddish grey
Break: greyish brown core, dark grey reduction zones
Decoration: consists of two zones with irregular multi-toothed comb filled decoration. An upper zone of five matt trapezoids, and on the body four hanging trapezoids.
Previously published: TD V, 89, 91

Type Group I.6.1

Vessels of type group I.6.1 consist of Biconical jugs with a rolled rim, bipartite handle and ring base, and three decorative zones. Such vessels are known from Tell el-Dab^ca, where TD 4238, found in Phase b/2 (= Phase E/3), has three decorative zones comprising an upper band of standing triangles, a central zone of six infilled rectangles and a lower band of pendant triangles.

75. 4238 (TD) F/I-i/23 grave 32 Phase b/2 (82/188) Plate 19

SPI	I-d	f	W2	Bd. gef	re	2	2R

D. 2.9 cm Nd. 1.1 cm. Bd. 2.2 cm. H. 10.5 cm. Md. 7.5 cm. Wd. 0.3 cm.
VI 71.42
Restored from sherds, incomplete
Surface colour: 5YR5/2 reddish grey; burnished slip 10R5/3 dark red
Break: uniform grey
Decoration: An upper band of standing triangles, a central zone of six infilled rectangles and a lower band of five pendant triangles. Dots made with a six-toothed comb.

Type Group I.6.2

Vessels of type group I.6.2 consist of Biconical jugs with a rolled rim, bipartite handle and ring base. Such vessels are known from Tell el-Dab^ca where they are decorated with an upper zone of standing triangles and a lower one of pendant triangles with the addition of a horizontal infilled band just above the base (TD 1839). To this group should perhaps also be added TD 1833 which is more piriform but bears the same decorative scheme as TD 1839.

76. 1839 Vienna A3246 A/II-n/13 planum 6–7 grave 8 Phase E/3 (68/200) Plates 19, 134

BPI	I-d	f–vf	W2	Bd. gef	re	2–3	2R

D. 3.0 cm Nd. 1.5 cm. Bd. 2.9 cm. H. 10.2 cm. Md. 8.0 cm. Wd. 0.3 cm.
VI 78.43
Incomplete
Surface colour: 2.5YR6/2 pale red; burnished slip 7.5YR3.5/2 dark brown
Break: uniform greyish brown
Decoration: On the shoulder five standing triangles, and below the maximum diameter, eight hanging triangles separated by matt zones. The triangles are infilled with white dots made by a multi-toothed comb. Above the foot a horizontal band filled with oblique comb punctures.
Previously published: TD V, 90, 91

77. 1833 Vienna A3241 A/II-n/13 planum 6–7 grave 8 Phase E/3 (68/166) Plate 19

BPI	I-d	f	W2	Bd. gef	re	2–3	2R

D. 3.0 cm Nd. 1.45 cm. Bd. 3.2 cm. H. 13.1 cm. Md. 7.9 cm. Wd. 0.3 cm.

74. 1841 E/3

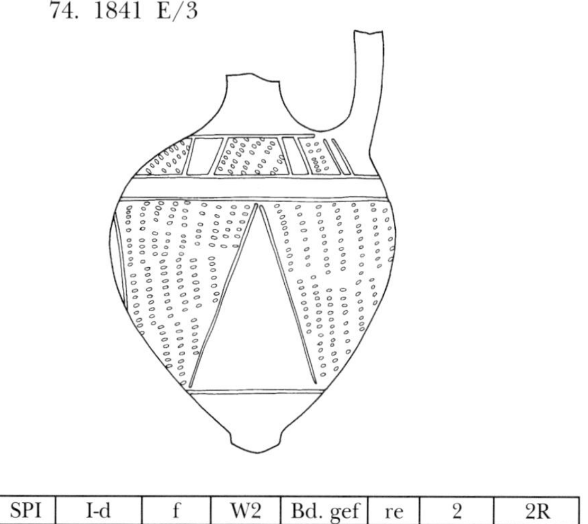

SPI	I-d	f	W2	Bd. gef	re	2	2R

75. 4238 b/2

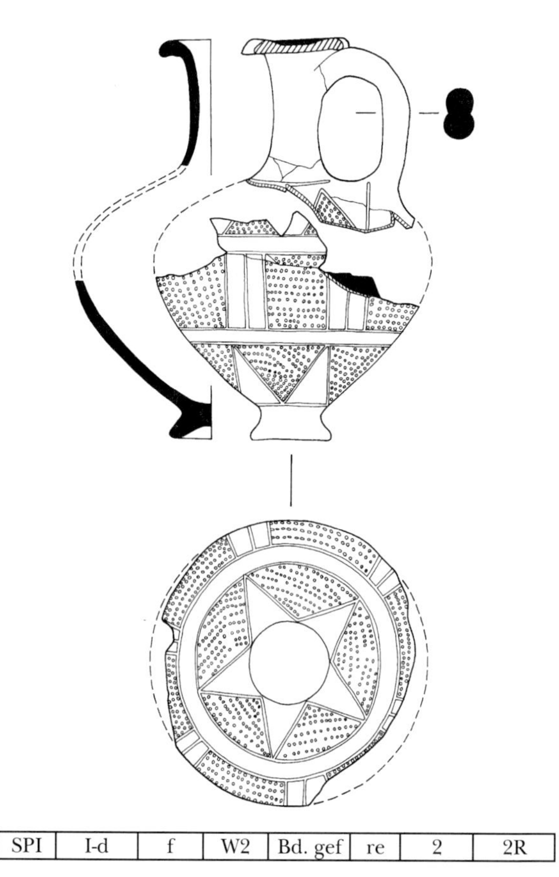

SPI	I-d	f	W2	Bd. gef	re	2	2R

76. 1839 E/3

BPI	I-d	f–vf	W2	Bd. gef	re	2–3	2R

77. 1833 E/3

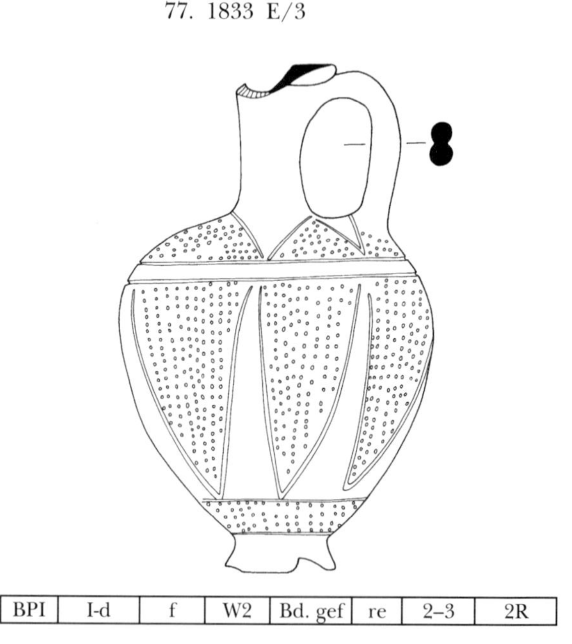

BPI	I-d	f	W2	Bd. gef	re	2–3	2R

1:2

Levanto-Egyptian Type Groups I.5.5, I.6.1, I.6.2

Plate 19

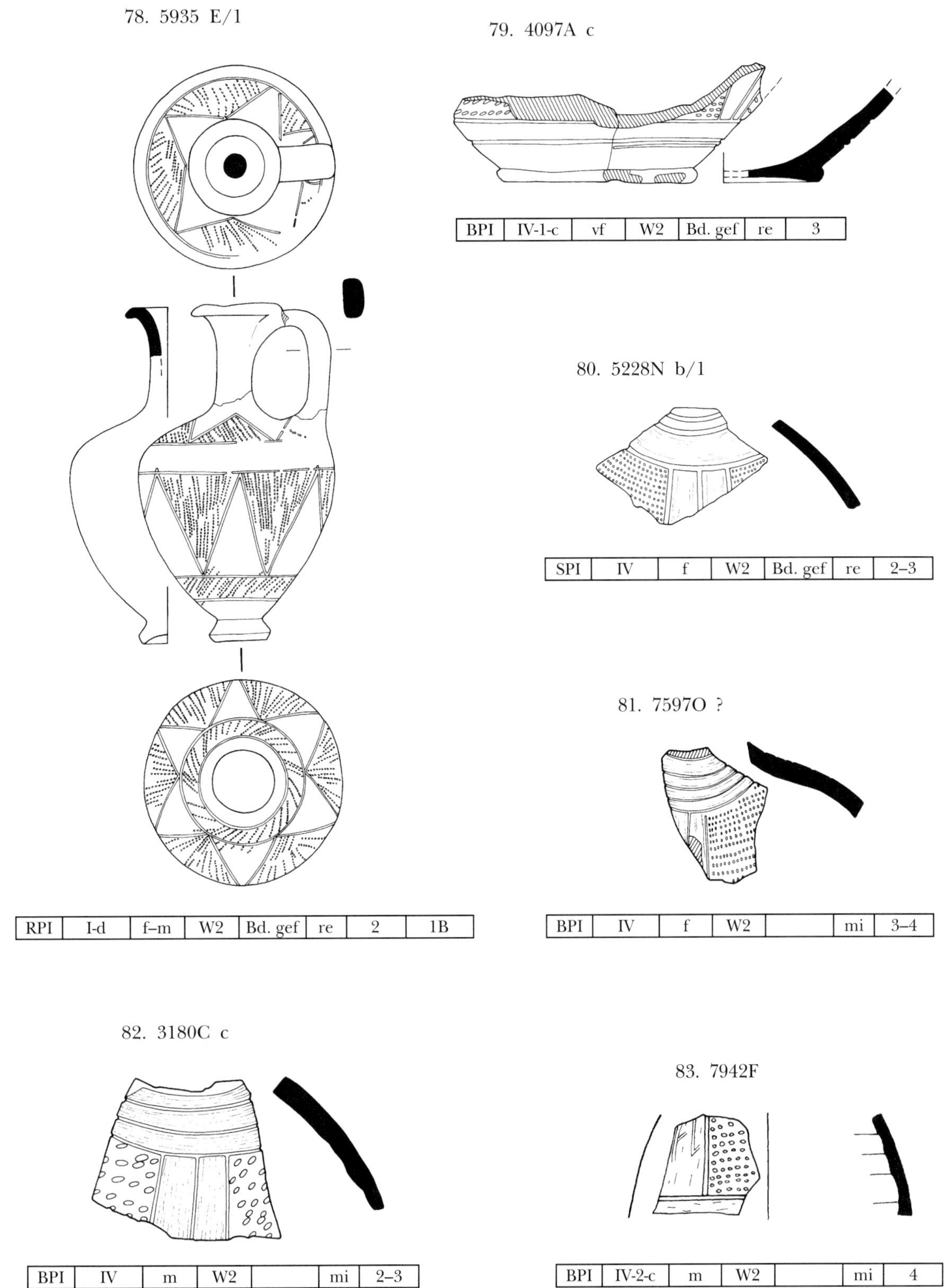

78. 5935 E/1

RPI	I-d	f–m	W2	Bd. gef	re	2	1B

79. 4097A c

BPI	IV-1-c	vf	W2	Bd. gef	re	3

80. 5228N b/1

SPI	IV	f	W2	Bd. gef	re	2–3

81. 7597O ?

BPI	IV	f	W2		mi	3–4

82. 3180C c

BPI	IV	m	W2		mi	2–3

83. 7942F

BPI	IV-2-c	m	W2		mi	4

1:2

Levanto-Egyptian Type Group I.6.3 and miscellaneous early imported sherds

Plate 20

VI 60.30
Incomplete
Surface colour: 10YR6/2 light brownish grey; burnished slip 5YR4/4 reddish brown
Break: uniform greyish brown
Decoration: On the shoulder five standing triangles, and below the maximum diameter, six hanging triangles separated by matt zones. The triangles are infilled with white dots made by a multi-toothed comb. Above the foot a horizontal band filled with oblique comb punctures.
Previously published: BIETAK, *MDAIK* 26 pl. 21b; KAPLAN, *Tell el-Yahudiyeh Ware,* fig. 34a, *TD V,* 90, 91

Type Group I.6.3

78. 5935 TD A/II-n/19 grave 4 Phase E/1 (84/163)
Plates 20, 135

RPI	I-d	f–m	W2	Bd. gef	re	2	1B

D. 3.0 cm. Nd. 1.2 cm. Bd. 2.0 cm. H. 10.6 cm. Md 6.4 cm. Wd. 0.3 cm.
VI 60.37
Restored from sherds, complete
Surface colour: 2.5YR 4–3 dark grey; burnished slip: 5YR4/2 dark reddish grey
Break: not visible
Decoration: Four standing triangles on shoulder infilled with striations from upper left to lower right made with a twelve-toothed comb. On body a frieze of six pendant triangles infilled with a twelve-toothed comb. Band at base infilled with vertical striations made with an eight-toothed comb.

Miscellaneous sherds from Groups I.1–I.6

a) Imports

a.1 Bases

79. 4097A TD F/I-j/22 planum 3 Phase c (82/004) Plate 20

BPI	IV-1-c	vf	W2	Bd. gef	re	3

Bd. 6.6 cm. pht. 2.4 cm. Wd. 1.2 cm.
Incomplete
Surface colour: 10YR6/2 light reddish grey; burnished slip 5YR5.5/6 reddish yellow
Break: wide yellowish red core, thin red oxidation zones
Decoration: Parts of three rectangles (?) preserved infilled with individually made dots. Incised lines also filled with pigment.
BNL JH908 Southern Palestine[595]

a.2. Body Sherds

80. 5228N TD F/I-k/23 pit 3 Phase b/1 (83/096) Plate 20

SPI	IV	f	W2	Bd. gef	re	2–3

Wd. 0.4 cm.
Incomplete
Surface colour: 7.5YR5.5/3 brown; burnished slip 7.5YR5/4 brown
Break: uniform 3.5Y5/8 reddish yellow
Decoration: Remains of two rectangles infilled with an eight-toothed comb.
BNL JH828 Southern Palestine[596]

81. 7597O TD A/IV-h/5 planum 3–4 pit 15 Phase ? (91/204)
Plate 20

BPI	IV	f	W2	–	mi	3–4

pht. 1.5 cm. Wd. 0.4 cm.
Incomplete
Surface colour: 10YR5/1 grey; burnished slip 5YR4/6 yellowish red
Break: uniform grey
Decoration: Remains of one rectangle infilled with an eight-toothed comb.

82. 3180C TD F/I-i/21 planum 1–2 Phase b/2 (80/038)
Plate 20

BPI	IV	m	W2	–	mi	2–3

pht. 4.5 cm. Wd. 0.6 cm.
Incomplete
Surface colour: 10YR6/2 light reddish grey; burnished slip 5YR5/3 reddish brown
Break: uniform yellowish red
Decoration: Remains of two rectangles infilled with dots made a single pointed tool.

83. 7942F TD A/IV-g/6 planum 1 surface (01/065) Plate 20

BPI	IV-2-c	m	W2	–	mi	4

pht. 3.0 cm. Wd. 0.45 cm.
Incomplete
Surface colour: 7.5YR6/4 light brown; burnished slip 7.5YR5/4 brown
Break: dark brown in, yellowish red oxidation zones
Decoration: Preserved decoration shows a horizontal line with a vertical line framing probably a rectangular panel filled wih irregular impressed dots. athe lines and dots are filled with white pigment.
Vertically burnished

84. 8441D A/IV-garage planum 6–7, Phase ? (94/136)
Plate 21

BPI	IV-2	f–m	W2	–	mi	2–3

pht. 2.2 cm. Wd. 0.45 cm.
Incomplete
Surface colour: 5YR4/1 dark grey; burnished slip 5YR5/2 reddish grey
Break: wide grey core, thin red and grey reduction zones
Decoration: Dots impressed with a multi-toothed comb, and both dots and incised lines are infilled with white pigment.

85. 7044L TD F/I-p/19 grave 1 disturbed context (89/187)
Plate 21

BPI	IV	f	W2	–	mi	3

[595] P. McGOVERN, *The Foreign Relations of the Hyksos,* Oxford, 2000, 152 no. JH908.

[596] P. McGOVERN, *The Foreign Relations of the Hyksos,* Oxford, 2000, 146–7 no. JH828.

84. 8441D ?

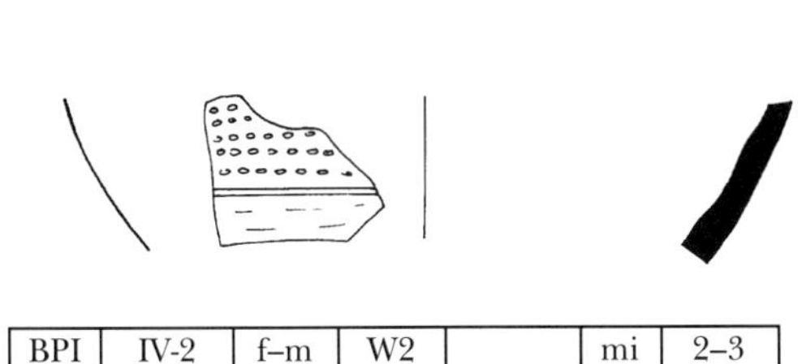

BPI	IV-2	f–m	W2		mi	2–3

85. 7044L ?

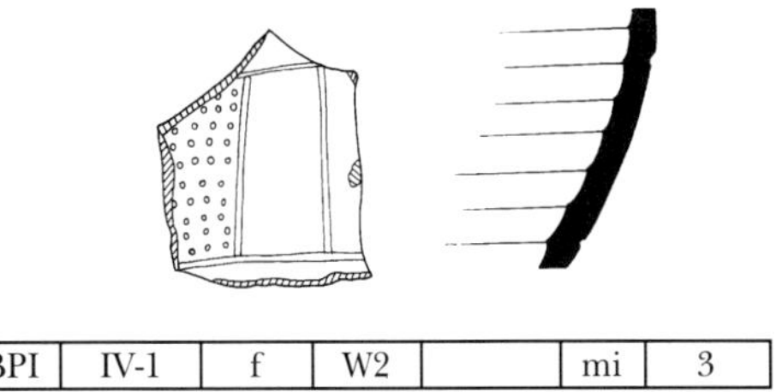

BPI	IV-1	f	W2		mi	3

86. 7597K F–E/3

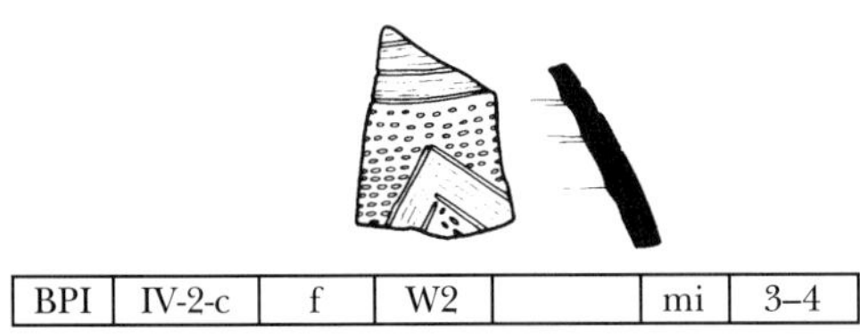

BPI	IV-2-c	f	W2		mi	3–4

87. 5823 c–b/3

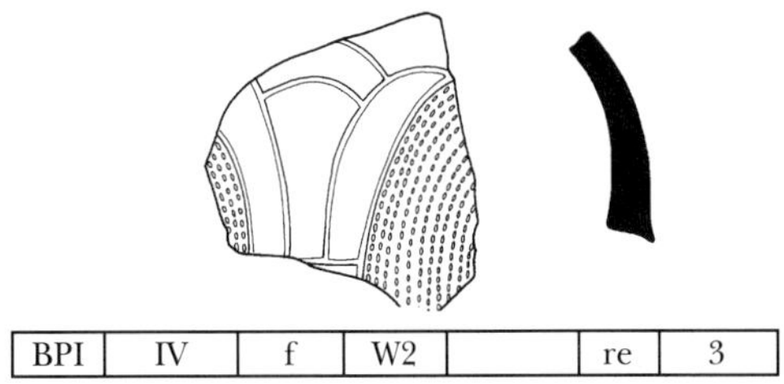

BPI	IV	f	W2		re	3

88. 7596W ?

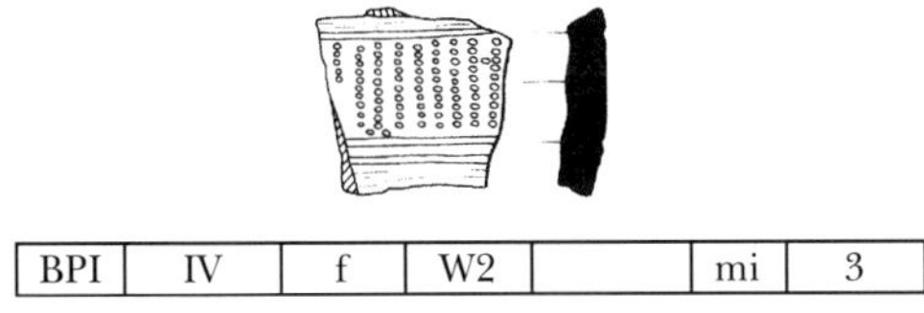

BPI	IV	f	W2		mi	3

89. 8441B G–F

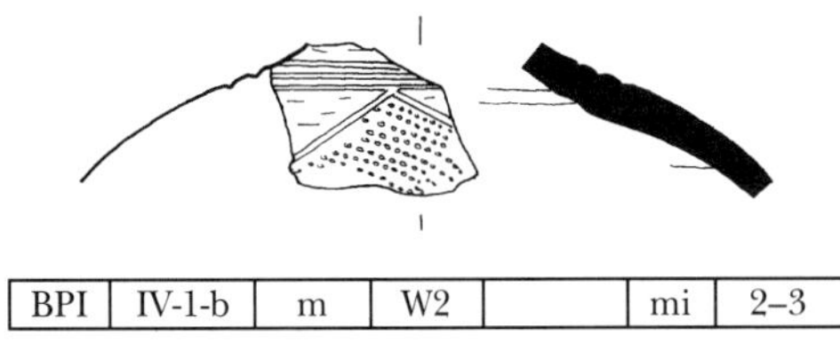

BPI	IV-1-b	m	W2		mi	2–3

90. 7351O E/3

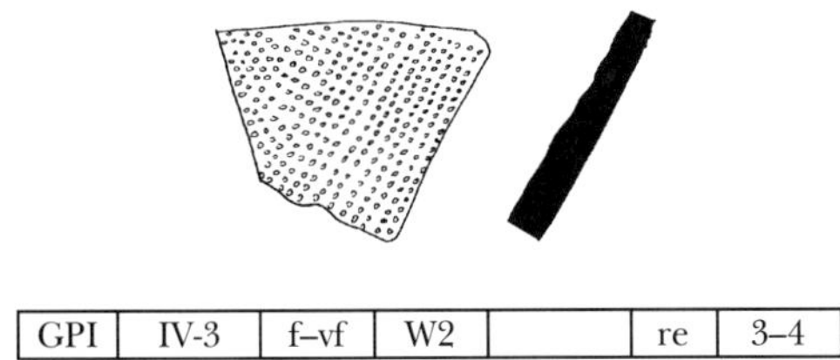

GPI	IV-3	f–vf	W2		re	3–4

1:2

Miscellaneous early imported sherds

Plate 21

pht. 2.0 cm. Wd. 0.55 cm.
Incomplete
Surface colour: 2.5YR6/4 light reddish brown; burnished slip 2.5YR6/4 light reddish brown
Break: grey core, light red oxidation zones
Decoration: Part of one rectangle preserved infilled with dots made by a single-pointed tool.
Previously published: TD XVIII, 290, fig. 230, no. 11.

86. 7597K TD A/IV-h/5 planum 2–3 Phase F–E/3 (91/203) Plate 21

BPI	IV-1	f	W2	–	mi	3

pht. 3.0 cm. Wd. 0.4 cm.
Incomplete
Surface colour: 10YR7/4 very pale brown; burnished slip 7.5 YR7/4 pink
Break: grey core, yellowish brown oxidation zones
Decoration: Probably parts of alternating standing and pendant triangles infilled with dots made by a single-pointed tool.

87. 5823 TD F/I-l/18 planum 0–1 Phase c–b/3 (85/398) Plate 21

BPI	IV-2-c	f	W2	–	mi	3–4

pht. 3.3 cm. Wd. 0.5 cm.
Incomplete
Surface colour: 10YR6/2 light reddish grey; burnished slip 5YR6/6 reddish yellow
Break: uniform reddish yellow
Decoration: stylised lotus flower (?) between areas infilled with a comb.

88. 7596W TD A/IV-h/4 planum 1–2 Phase ? (91/149) Plate 21

BPI	IV	f	W2	–	re	3

pht. 2.3 cm. Wd. 0.6 cm.
Incomplete
Surface colour: burnished slip 10YR6/2 light brownish grey
Break: uniform greyish brown
Decoration: part of a band of vertical striations made with a ten-toothed comb.

89. 8441B TD A/IV-garage locus 27 stratrum G–F (94/143) Plate 21

BPI	IV-1-b	m	W2	–	mi	2–3

pht. 2.8 cm. Wd. 0.5 cm.
Incomplete
Surface colour: 10YR6/1 light grey; burnished slip 5YR5/3 reddish brown
Break: uniform light grey
Decoration: Three incised lines at base of neck. One standing triangle preserved infilled with oblique lines made with a multi-toothed comb.

90. 7351O TD A/II-k/16 planum 5–6 Phase E/2 ? (90/096) Plate 21

GPI	IV-3	f–vf	W2	–	re	3–4

pht. 1.7 cm. Wd. 0.5 cm.
Incomplete
Surface colour: 10YR8–7/3 v pale brown
Break: light grey interior, white out
Decoration: made with a ten-toothed comb.

b) Locally produced

b.1 bases

91. 4297E TD F/I-j/23n planum 1–2 Phase b/3–2 (82/267) Plate 22

BPI	I-d	vf	W2	Bd. gef	re	2–3

Bd. 1.5 cm. pht. 3.0 cm. Wd. 0.5 cm.
Incomplete
Surface colour: 7.5YR5.5/3 brown; burnished slip 5YR4/3 reddish brown
Break: uniform grey
Decoration: Pendant triangles infilled with chevrons made with an eight-toothed comb.

92. 3445H TD A/II-o/19 planum 2–3 pit mixed date (01/065) Plates 22, 135

RPI	I-d	f	W2	Bd. gef	re	2–3

Bd. 1.9 cm. pht. 3.1 cm. Wd. 0.5 cm.
Incomplete
Surface colour: 5YR6/3 light reddish brown; burnished slip 10R5/6 red
Break: dark grey core, brown reduction zones
Decoration: At least three pendant triangles preserved filled with irregular white incrusted dots.

b.2. Body sherds

93. 3532C TD A/II-n/19 planum 2–3 Phase E/1 (01/065) Plate 22

BPI	I-d	vf	W2	–	re	2–3	2R

Nd. 1.5 cm. pht. 2.5 cm. Wd. 0.5 cm.
Incomplete
Surface colour: 7.5YR5.5/3 brown; burnished slip 5YR4/3 reddish brown
Break: uniform grey
Decoration: Only part of a standing triangle preserved infilled with a multi-toothed comb.

94. 8942D TD A/II-o/18 sebakh pit (01/032) Plate 22

BPI	I-d	f	W2	–	re	3

pht. 2.3 cm. Wd. 0.4 cm.
Incomplete
Surface colour: 10YR6/2 light brownish grey; burnished slip 10YR5/4 yellowish brown
Break: very dark grey in, light brown out
Decoration: Incised lines below the neck. Remains of two standing triangles filled with a V-shaped pattern made with a multi-toothed comb.

95. 7021D F/I-m/18 grave 2 disturbed context (89/008) Plate 22

BPI	I-d	m	W2	–	re	3

pht. 7.4 cm. Wd. 0.5 cm.
Incomplete
Surface colour: 10YR6/2 light reddish grey; burnished slip 10YR4/1–2 dark grey

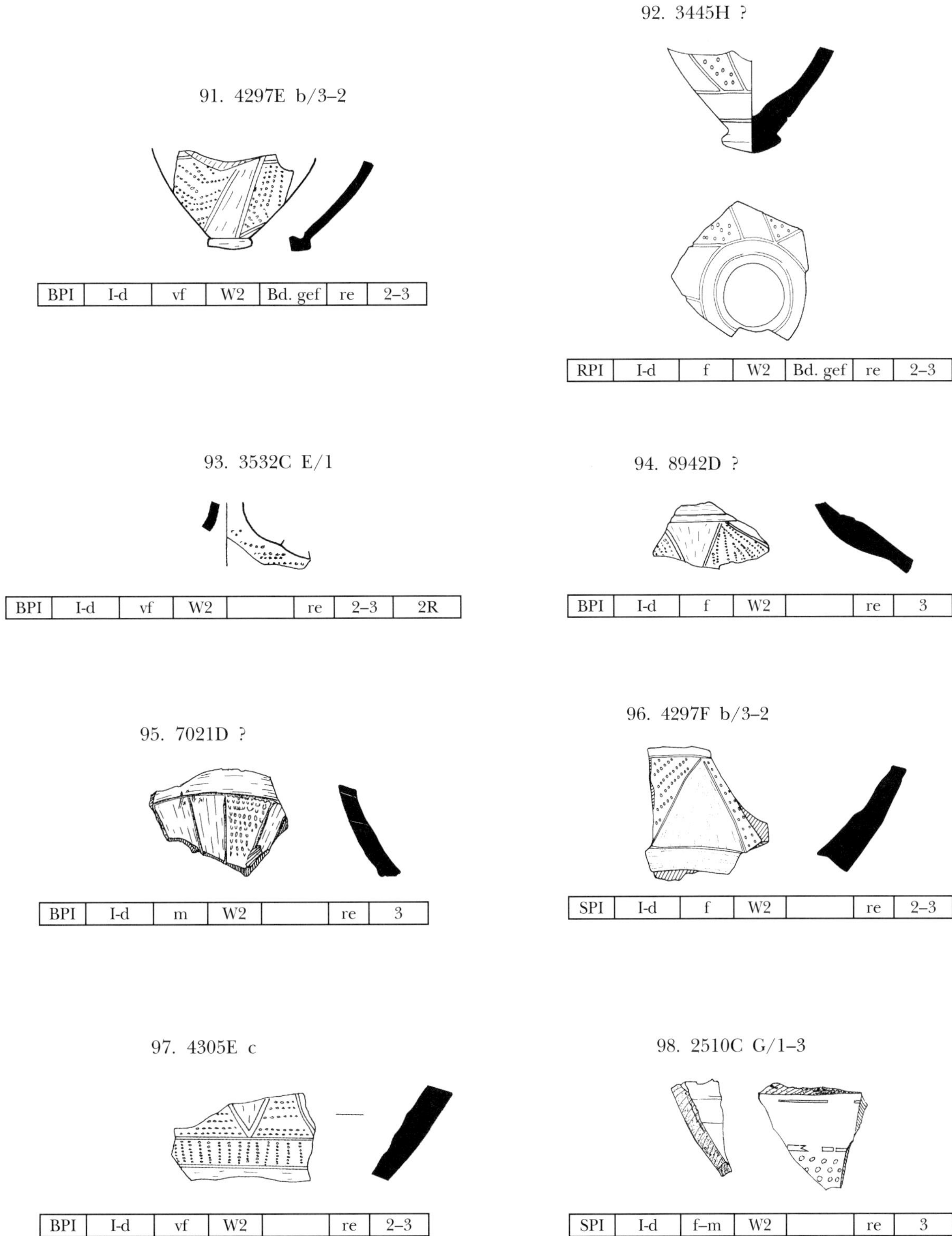

91. 4297E b/3–2

BPI	I-d	vf	W2	Bd. gef	re	2–3

92. 3445H ?

RPI	I-d	f	W2	Bd. gef	re	2–3

93. 3532C E/1

BPI	I-d	vf	W2		re	2–3	2R

94. 8942D ?

BPI	I-d	f	W2		re	3

95. 7021D ?

BPI	I-d	m	W2		re	3

96. 4297F b/3–2

SPI	I-d	f	W2		re	2–3

97. 4305E c

BPI	I-d	vf	W2		re	2–3

98. 2510C G/1–3

SPI	I-d	f–m	W2		re	3

1:2

Miscellaneous early sherds

Plate 22

Break: dark grey core, thin light grey eduction zone
Decoration: Part of one standing triangle preserved with reserved bipartite rectangle. Triangle filled with oblique lines made with an eight-toothed comb.

96. 4297F TD F/I-j/23n planum 1–2 Phase b/3–2 (83/065) Plate 22

SPI	I-d	f	W2	–	re	2–3

pht. 4.0 cm. Wd. 0.6 cm.
Incomplete
Surface colour: 10YR6/2 light reddish grey; burnished slip 5YR4/1 dark grey
Break: uniform yellowish red
Decoration: Pendant triangles infilled with a multi-toothed comb.

97. 4305E TD F/I-j/23n planum 3–4 Phase c (82/267) Plate 22

BPI	I-d	vf	W2	–	re	2–3

pht. 3.3 cm. Wd. 0.5 cm.
Incomplete
Surface colour: 7.5YR4/2 dark brown; burnished slip 5YR4/3 reddish brown
Break: grey core, light brown oxidation zones
Decoration: One band of vertical dots with pendant triangles above, all infilled with a six-toothed comb.

98. 2510C TD A/II-o/15 planum 3–4 Phase G/1–3 (75/022) Plate 22

SPI	I-d	f–m	W2	–	re	3

pht. 2.8 cm. Wd. 0.4 cm.
Incomplete
Surface colour: 10YR4/2 dark grey brown; burnished slip 10R4/4 weak red
Break: dark brown core, red brown reduction zones
Decoration: dots made a single-pointed tool.
BNL: Nile clay

99. 1328 Vienna A2907 A/II-n/11 planum 1 Phase D/3 (68/077) Plate 23

SPI	I-d	f	W2	–	re	3

pht. 5.3 cm. Wd. 0.7 cm.
Incomplete
Surface colour: 10YR4/3 brown; burnished slip 5YR3/1 very dark grey
Break: dark grey core, brown reduction zones
Decoration: parts of two pendant triangles infilled with dots made with a six-pointed comb.

100. 4964A TD F/I-m/22 Schnitt 17 Phase c–b/3 (85/040) Plate 23

BPI	I-d	f	W2	–	re	3

pht. 4.2 cm. Wd. 0.35 cm.
Incomplete
Surface colour: 10YR4/2 dark grey brown; burnished slip 5YR6/4–6 light reddish brown
Break: grey core, yellowish grey reduction zones
Decoration: Lower zone of standing triangles and a upper zone which is not discernible. Dots made with a single pointed tool.
BNL JH862 Southern Palestine[597]

101. 3254C TD A/II-m/17 planum 7 Phase G/1–3 (80/004) Plate 23

BPI	I-d	f	W2	–	re	3

pht. 3.9 cm. Wd. 0.4 cm.
Incomplete
Surface colour: 10YR4/2 dark grey brown; burnished slip 10R4/4 weak red
Break: dark brown core, red brown reduction zones
Decoration: Not discernible. Dots made with a single pointed tool.

102. 7598A TD A/IV-h/7 grave 4 Phase ? (91/217) Plate 23

SPI	I-d	f–m	W2	–	mi	3–4

pht. 1.3 cm. Wd. 0.4 cm.
Incomplete
Surface colour: 10YR5/1 grey; burnished slip 10YR3/1 very dark grey
Break: dark grey in, dark brown ox zones
Decoration: Shoulder zone of alternating standing and pendant triangles infilled with a ten-toothed comb.

103. 8470C TD F/I-j/23n planum 3–4 Phase c (96/003) Plate 23

SPI	I-d	r	W2	–	re	2–3

pht. 4.7 cm. Wd. 0.6 cm.
Incomplete
Surface colour: 10YR4/2 dark grey brown; burnished slip 10YR4/2 dark grey brown
Break: wide dark grey band in, thin red and dark grey bands out
Decoration: Vertical lines made with a multi-toothed comb.

104. 8470D TD F/I-j/23n planum 3–4 Phase c (96/003) Plate 23

RPI	I-d	r	W2	–	mi	3

pht. 3.0 cm. Wd. 0.5 cm.
Incomplete
Surface colour: 10YR4/2 dark grey brown; burnished slip 10R4/4 weak red
Break: wide dark grey band in, thin red and dark grey bands out
Decoration: Freeze of pendant triangles above a band filled with vertical lines. Dots made with a multi-toothed comb.

105. 7597N TD A/IV-h/5 planum 3–4 pit 15 Phase ? (91/204) Plates 23, 135

BPI	I-d	f–m	W2	–	mi	3

[597] P. McGovern, *The Foreign Relations of the Hyksos*, Oxford, 2000, 149 no. JH862.

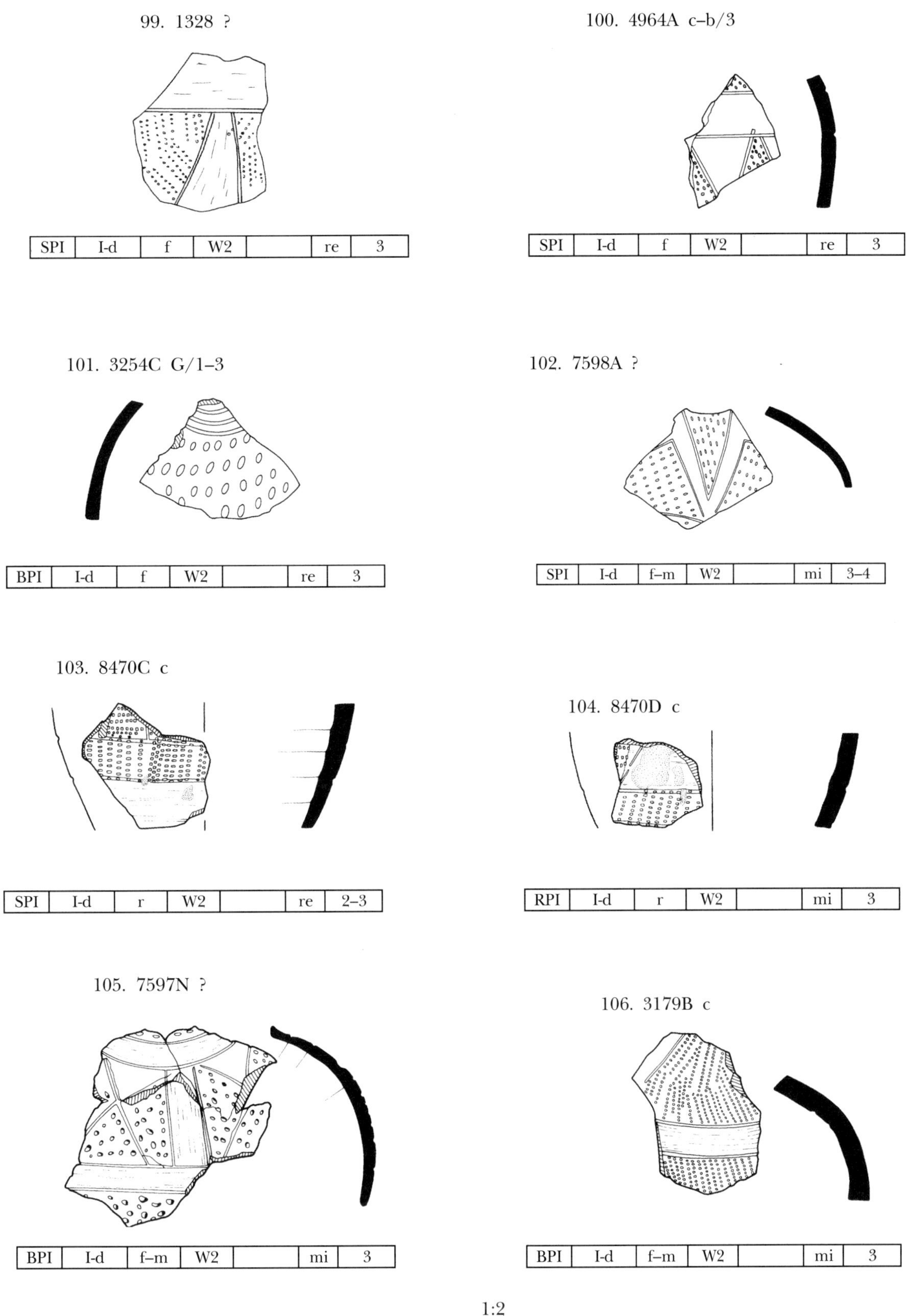

1:2

Miscellaneous early sherds

Plate 23

pht. 6.0 cm. Wd. 0.5 cm.
Incomplete
Surface colour: 7.5YR5.5/3 brown; burnished slip 7.5YR6/4 light brown
Break: uniform brown
Decoration: band of dots at neck, reserved zone, then shoulder decoration, reserved zone, and the beginning of the next frieze. The shoulder decoration comprises a series of rectangles divided into four by a "Saint Andrews" cross, the uppermost triangle thus formed being left undecorated. Infilled dots made with a single-pointed tool.

106. 3179B TD F/I-i/21 planum 1–2 Phase b/2 (80/038) Plate 23

BPI	I-d	f–m	W2	–	mi	3

pht. 4.2 cm.
Incomplete
Surface colour: 7.5YR5.7/2 pinkish grey; burnished slip 2.5YR4/4 reddish brown
Break: grey in, brown oxidation zone
Decoration: Upper zone of chevrons plus lower zone of chevrons or vertical lines impressed with a twelve-toothed comb.

107. 7942Y TD A/IV-j/4 planum 1–2 Phase ? (93/579) Plate 24

SPI	I-d	f–m	W2	–	re	3

pht. 2.0 cm. Wd. 0.45 cm.
Incomplete
Surface colour 10YR3/2 very dark brown; burnished slip 10R5/1 reddish grey
Break: uniform light grey
Decoration: not discernible.
Vertically burnished

108. 3241D1 TD F/I-i/21 planum 1–2 Phase c (80/084) Plate 24

SPI	I-d	f	W2	–	re	3

pht. 1.1 cm. Wd. 0.3 cm.
Incomplete
Surface colour: 10YR3/2 very dark brown; burnished slip 10R5/1 reddish grey
Break: uniform grey
Decoration: not discernible, made with a multi-toothed comb.

109. 1810 Vienna A3226 A/II-n/11 planum ? Phase ? (68/157) Plate 24

SPI	I-d	f–m	W2	–	re	3

pht. 2.2 cm. Wd. 0.3 cm.
Incomplete
Surface colour: 7.5YR5.5/3 brown; burnished slip 10R5/1 reddish grey
Break: uniform grey
Decoration: part of a rectangle infilled with dots made with a ten-toothed comb.

110. 7149F TD F/I-o/21 grave 5 Phase b/3 (90/030) Plate 24

SPI	I-d	vf	W2	–	re	2–3

pht. 2.9 + 1.8 cm. Wd. 0.3 cm.
Incomplete
Surface colour: 5YR5/1 grey; burnished slip 5YR4/2 grey
Break: uniform dark grey
Decoration: Fragments of rectangles infilled with a multi-toothed comb.

111. 3241E TD F/I-i/21 planum 1–2 Phase c (80/084) Plate 24

SPI	I-d	f	W2	–	re	3

pht. 2.2 cm. Wd. 0.3 cm.
Incomplete
Surface colour: 7.5YR5.5/3 brown; burnished slip 10R5/1 reddish grey
Break: uniform grey
Decoration: not discernible.

112. 3241D2 TD F/I-i/21 planum 1–2 Phase c (80/084) Plate 24

SPI	I-d	f	W2	–	re	3

pht. 1.1 cm. Wd. 0.3 cm.
Incomplete
Surface colour: 7.5YR5.5/3 brown; burnished slip 10R5/1 reddish grey
Break: uniform grey
Decoration: part of a rectangle infilled with dots made with a multi-toothed comb.

113. 3545A TD F/I-i/23 planum 1–2 grave 11 Phase b/2 (81/179) Plate 24

SPI	I-d	vf	W2	–	re	4

pht. 6.5 cm. Wd. 0.5 cm.
Incomplete
Surface colour: 7.5YR5.5/3 brown; burnished slip 10R5/1 reddish grey
Break: dark brown in, yellowish red oxidation zones
Decoration: Remains of a frieze of pendant triangles infilled with a ten-toothed comb.

114. 8346C TD A/IV-dep planum 5–6 Phase ? (94/314) Plate 24

SPI	I-d	f	W2	–	re	3

pht. 2.2 cm. Wd. 0.3 cm.
Incomplete
Surface colour: 7.5YR5.5/3 brown; burnished slip 10R5/1 reddish grey
Break: uniform grey
Decoration: not discernible.

Type Group J.1.2

Vessels of Type Group J.1.2 comprise piriform jugs with candlestick rims, double handles and slightly offset button bases. The complete example from Tell el-Dab^ca (TD 7461) shows one opened tall lotus blossom and three buds(?), each separated by single lotus leaves. The unincised areas are burnished.

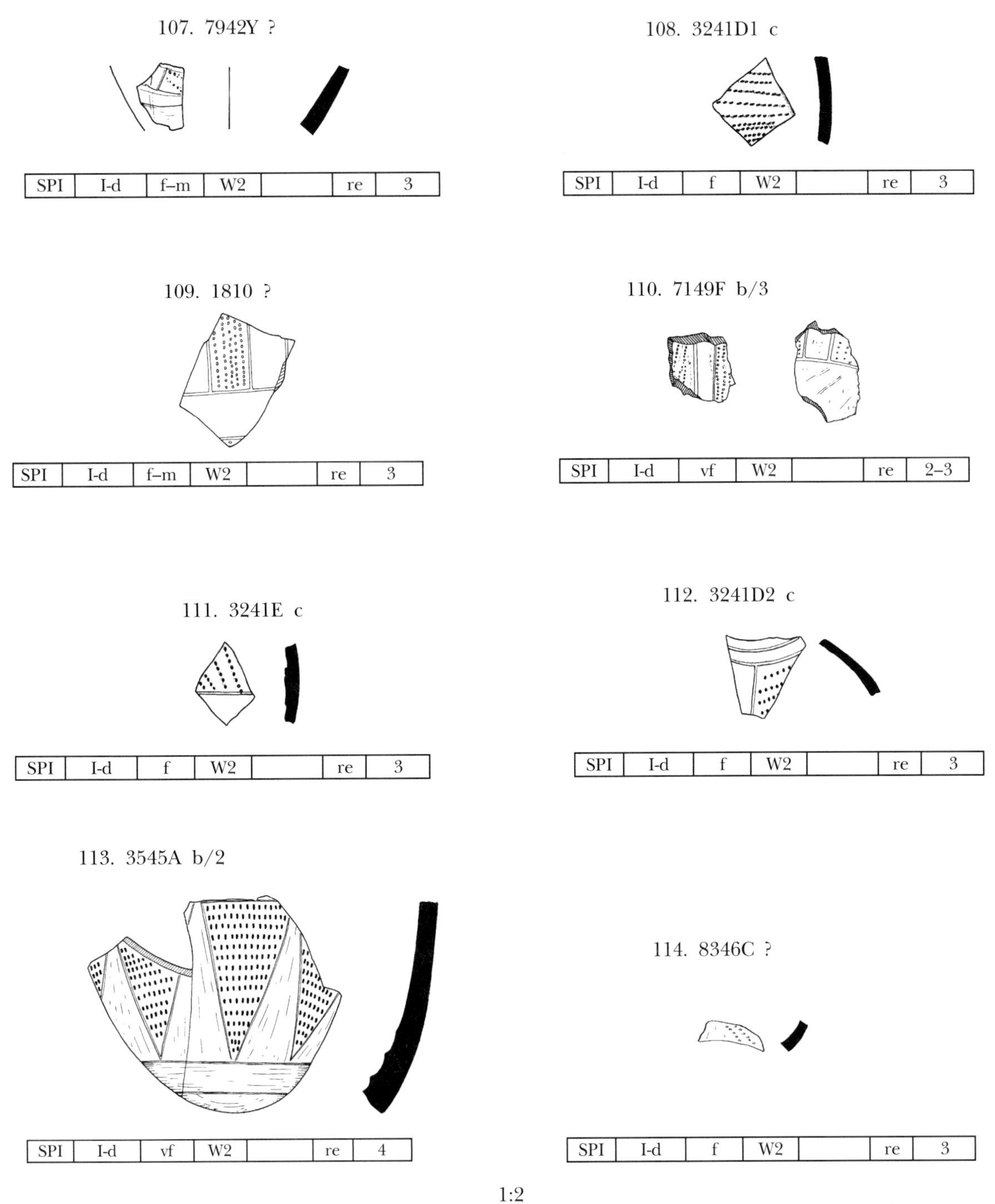

Miscellaneous early sherds

Plate 24

115. 7461 TD A/IV-h/7 grave 7 Phase F–E/3 (92/020)
Plats 26, 136

SPI	I-d	f	W2	Bd. gef	re	3	2R

D. 3.2 cm. Nd. 1.2 cm. Bd. 1.2 cm. H. 13.2 cm. Md 7.8 cm. Wd. 0.3 cm.
VI 59.09
Intact
Surface colour: 5YR6/3 light red brown; burnished slip 5YR4/1 dark grey
Break: not visible
Asymmetrical
Decoration: Marsh scene of a lotus flower and three lilies, infilled with dots made with a single pointed tool.
Previously published: PuF 232 nr. 283

Type Group J.1.4

Vessels of Type Group J.1.4 comprise piriform jugs with rolled rims, strap handles and button bases, of

115. 7461 F–E/3

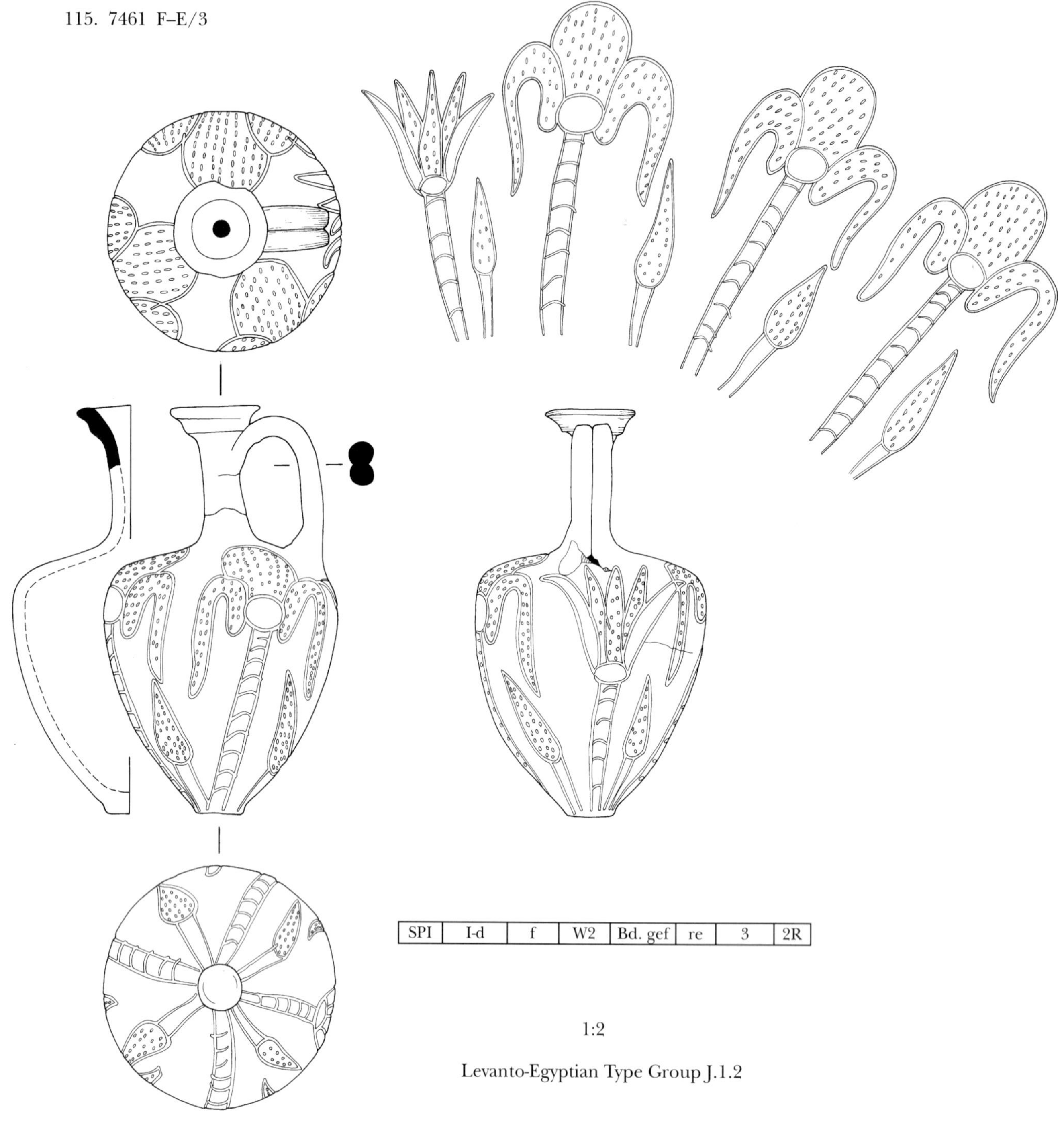

SPI	I-d	f	W2	Bd. gef	re	3	2R

1:2

Levanto-Egyptian Type Group J.1.2

Plate 25

which at least three examples have been found at Tell el-Dab^c^a (TD 7483, 7484, 7485). All four have a pattern of lotus petals on the shoulder which radiate out from the base of the neck, a reserved band, and in three cases a lower zone of three lotus blossoms and alternating birds. The other has no distinct reserved zone, but one which is created by the fact that the decoration on the body comes up from the base and thus there is a gap between that, which consists of a rishi pattern, and the tips of the lotus petals.

116. 7483 TD A/IV-h/4 grave 11 Phase F ? (90/267)
Plates 26, 136

SPI	I-d	f	W2	Bd. gef	re	3	1B

D. 2.85 cm. Nd. 1.3 cm. Bd. 1.7 cm. H. 10.5 cm. Md 6.7 cm. Wd. 0.3 cm.
VI 63.80
Restored from sherds, incomplete
Surface colour: 7.5–10YR4/2 dark greyish brown; burnished slip 2.5YR4/0 dark grey
Break: uniform dark brownish grey
Decoration: Decoration: 29 small rectangles at base of neck cre-

ated by the incising of 29 blue lotus petals on the shoulder which continued over the two incisions at the base of the neck. On lower body three five-petalled intertwined lotus flowers, with three wading birds in between the flowers. The innermost three petals and bird wings are infilled with gashes made with a single-pointed instrument.

117. 7485 TD A/IV-h/4 grave 11 Phase F ? (92/218)
Plates 26, 135

SPI	I-d	f	W2	Bd. gef	re	3	1B

D. 2.8 cm. Nd. 1.4 cm. Bd. 1.5 cm. H. 10.9 cm. Md 6.5 cm. Wd. 0.35 cm.
VI 59.63
Restored from sherds, incomplete
Surface colour: 7.5–10YR4/2 dark greyish brown; burnished slip 5Y4/1 dark grey
Break: dark grey core, reddish brown and olive grey reduction zones
Decoration: 24 small rectangles at base of neck. 27 blue lotus petals incised on shoulder. On lower body three five-petalled intertwined lotus flowers, with three wading birds in between the flowers. The innermost three petals and bird wings are infilled with gashes made with a single-pointed instrument.
Previously published: PuF 232 nr. 284

118. 7484 TD A/IV-h/4 grave 11 Phase F ? (92/039)
Plates 27, 137

SPI	I-d	f–vf	W2	Bd. gef	re	3–4	1B

D. 3.2cm. Nd. 1.4 cm. Bd. 1.5 cm. H. 11.5 cm. Md 7.0 cm. Wd. 0.35 cm.
VI 60.86
Restored from sherds, incomplete
Surface colour: 7.5–10YR4/2 dark greyish brown; burnished slip 10YR3/1 very dark grey
Break: uniform dark brown
Decoration: 22 small rectangles at base of neck. 27 blue lotus petals incised on shoulder. On lower body three five-petalled intertwined lotus flowers, with three wading birds in between the flowers. The innermost three petals and bird wings are infilled with gashes made with a single-pointed instrument.

Type Group J.1.5

Vessels of Type Group J.1.5 comprise squat piriform jugs with rolled rims (?), incisions at the base of the neck, bipartite handles and ring bases, again known from a single incomplete example from Tell el-Dab^ca (TD 7518). It has a pattern of lotus petals on the shoulder which radiate out from the base of the neck, a reserved band, and a lower zone of three lotus blossoms, though this time without any intervening birds.

119. 7518 TD A/IV-h/7 grave 4 Phase E/3 ? (91/181)
Plates 27, 137

SPI	I-d	f	W2	Bd. gef	re	3	1B

Nd. 1.0 cm. Bd. 1.4 cm. pht. 6.1 cm. Md 5.05 cm. Wd. 0.25 cm.
Incomplete
Surface colour: 10YR5/3 brown; burnished slip 5Y3–4/1 dark grey
Break: uniform dark grey
Decoration: Two incised lines at base of neck. Eleven petals on shoulder, six of which are left blank, and the alternating five are infilled with gashes made by a single-pointed instrument. Below are five interlinked lotus flowers, four of which have three petals, as shown in the drawing, whereas the fifth, on the other side of the vessel as drawn has five. The flowers with three petals and the innermost three of the five-petalled flower are decorated with a series of single gashes made with the same single-pointed instrument as used on the shoulder.
Previously published: PuF 178 nr. 185

Type Group J.1.6

Type group J.1.6 is known through an incomplete vessel from Tell el Dab^ca, TD 7463. It consists of a squat piriform to biconical vessel with a bipartite handle and a button base. It has a pattern of lotus petals on the shoulder which radiate out from the base of the neck, but this time the body of the vessel is decorated with a rishi feather pattern.

120. 7463 TD A/IV-h/7 grave 7 Phase E/3 ? (92/043)
Plates 27, 137

SPI	I-d	f–m	W2	Bd. gef	re	3	2R

Bd. 2.1 cm. pht. 10.5 cm. Md 7.9 cm. Wd. 0.35 cm.
Incomplete
Surface colour: 10YR6/2 light reddish grey; burnished slip 7.5YR3/0 very dark grey
Break: dark grey core, light grey reduction zones
Decoration: eighteen lotus petals on shoulder, each alternate one being infilled with dots made with a single pointed tool. Below the shoulder a number of petals arranged in a rishi fashion.

Type Group J.1.7

Vessels of Type Group J.1.7 comprise piriform jugs with everted rims, double handles and button bases, of which three examples are now known from Tell el-Dab^ca (TD 1122, 1630, 3545). They are all decorated with three upright lotus flowers on a long stem alternating with three stylised waterfowl which have long legs and long curved necks.

121. 1122 Vienna A2775 A/II-m/12 planum 5 grave 9 Phase E/2 (68/023) Plates 28, 137

SPI	I-d	f–vf	W2	Bd. gef	re	3–4	2R

D. 3.3 cm. Nd. 1.3 cm. Bd. 1.2 cm. H. 10.3 cm. Md 5.1 cm. Wd. 0.3 cm.
VI 49.51
Incomplete
Surface colour: 7.5–10YR4/2 dark greyish brown; burnished slip 10YR3/1 very. dark. grey
Break: not visible
Asymmetrical
Decoration: consists of three stylised lotus flowers with upturned blossoms between.
Previously published: BIETAK, *MDAIK* 26 Tf. 20b; KAPLAN, *Tell el-Yahudiyeh Ware,* fig. 127b; *FA* 79 Abb 65; *TD V,* 123, *PuF* 225 nr. 264.

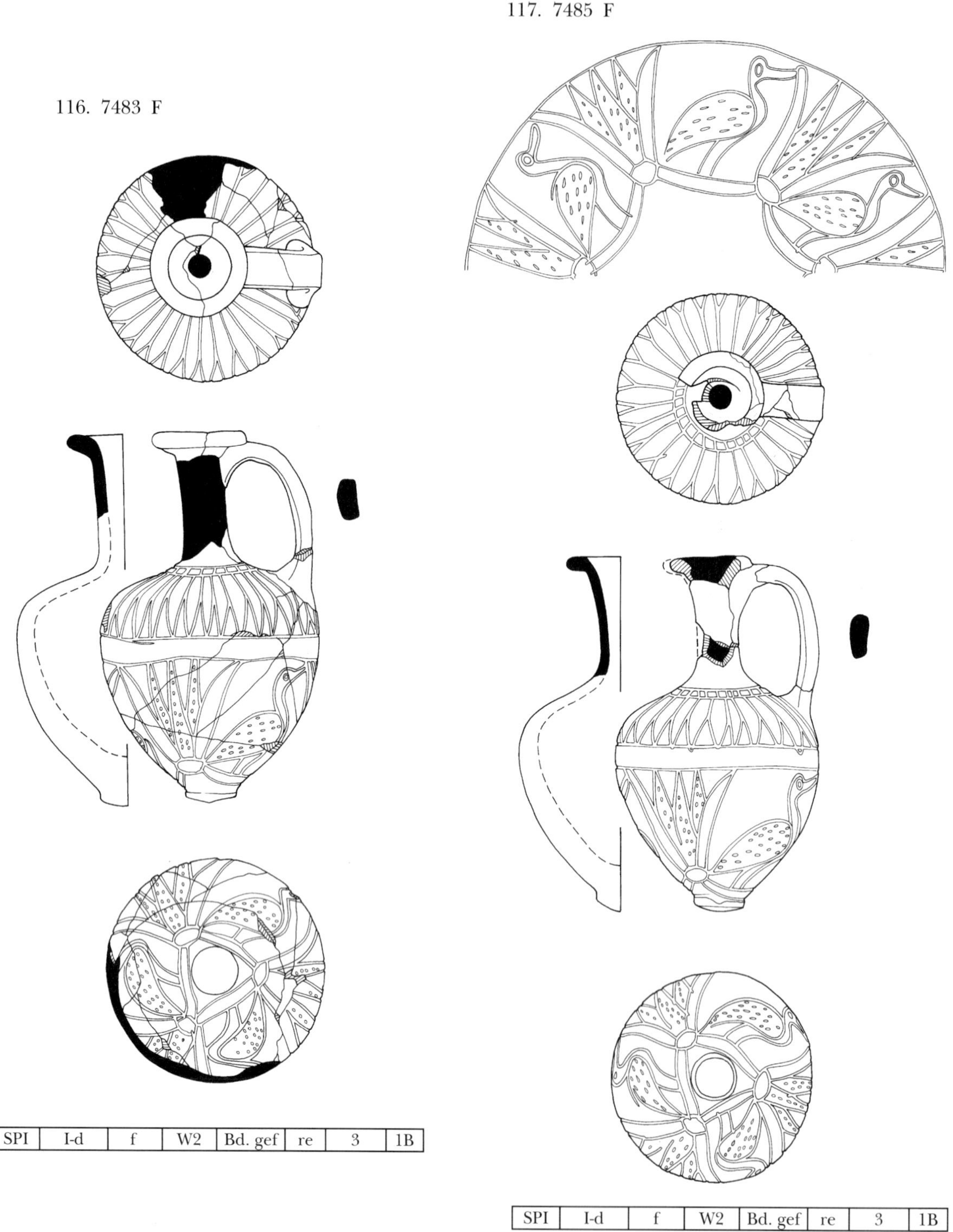

SPI	I-d	f	W2	Bd. gef	re	3	1B

SPI	I-d	f	W2	Bd. gef	re	3	1B

1:2

Levanto-Egyptian Type Group J.1.4

Plate 26

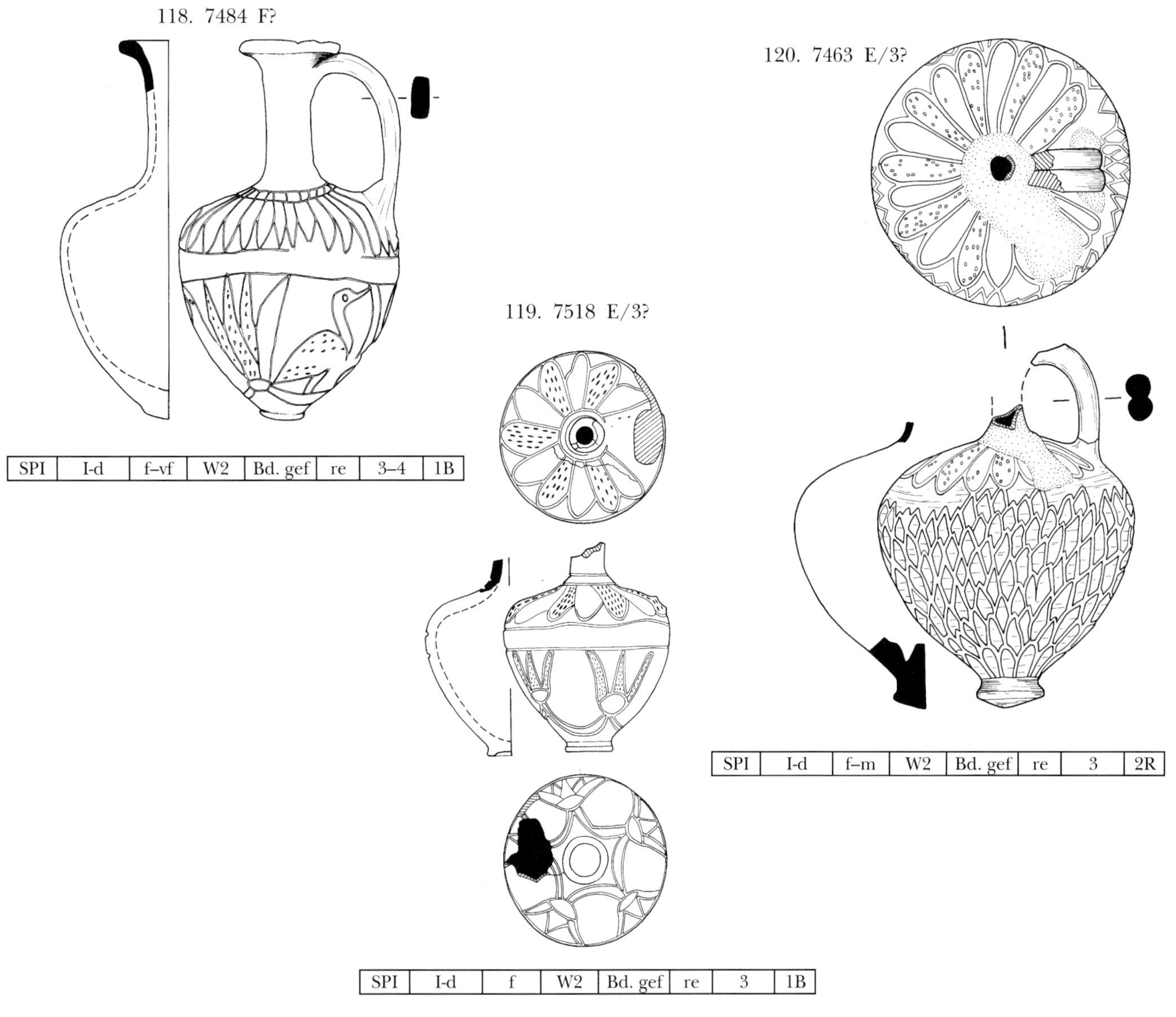

1:2

Type Groups J.1.4–6

Plate 27

122. 1630 Cairo JE 91179 A/II-m/12 planum 5 grave 9 Phase E/2 (68/097) Plates 28, 138

SPI	I-d	f–vf	W2	Bd. gef	re	3–4	2R

D. 3.3 cm. Nd. 1.4 cm. Bd. 1.4 cm. H. 11.2 cm. Md 5.7 cm. Wd. 0.3 cm.
VI 50.89
Intact
Surface colour: 7.5–10YR4/2 dark greyish brown; burnished slip 10YR3/1 very. dark. grey
Break: not visible
Asymmetrical
Decoration: consists of three stylised lotus flowers with birds between.
Previously published: Bietak, *MDAIK* 26, pl. 20a; Kaplan, *Tell el-Yahudiyeh Ware*, fig. 128a; *TD V*, 123, *PuF* 231 nr. 282

123. 3545 Cairo F/I-i/23 planum 1–2 grave 11 Phase a/2 (81/179) Plate 27

SPI	I-d	vf	W2	Bd. gef	re	4

Bd. 1.6 cm. pht. 4.2 cm. Md 5.7 cm. Wd. 0.4 cm.
Incomplete
Surface colour: 7.5–10YR4/2 dark greyish brown; burnished slip 10YR3/1 very. dark. grey
Break: not visible
Asymmetrical
Decoration: Presumably similar to TD 1630.

Miscellaneous Decorated Sherds

a) Imports

124. 3360C TD F/I-j/20 planum 3 Phase ? (92/030)
Plate 29

GPI	IV-3	f–m	W2	–	re	3

pht. 4.5 cm. Wd. 0. cm.
Incomplete
Surface colour: 2.5Y7/2 light grey; burnished slip 2.5Y8/4 pale yellow
Break: uniform greyish pink
Decoration: Incised herringbone pattern.

b) Local

125. 8942Q TD Stray find (01/078)
Plate 29

BPI	I-d	vf	W2	–	Re	3–4	3R

pht. 4.2 cm. Wd. 0.4 cm.
Incomplete
Surface colour: not visible; burnished slip 5YR4/4 reddish brown
Break: uniform black
Decoration: Incised lines, possibly the tops of lotus flowers.

126. 3339 Cairo Khatana E/I/C stray find (80/180)
Plate 29

BPI	I-d	vf	W2	–	Re	3	1B

pht. 1.5 cm. Md 9.2 cm. Wd. 0.5 cm.
Incomplete
Surface colour: 10YR6/2 light reddish grey; burnished slip 7.5YR3/0 very dark grey
Break: grey core, brown reduction zones
Decoration: Rectangles at the base of the neck. Remaining decoration presumably represents a marsh scene with lotus flowers.

127. 1587 Vienna A3082 A/II-l/14 planum 2–3 grave 5 ? Phase E/1 (68/120) Plate 29

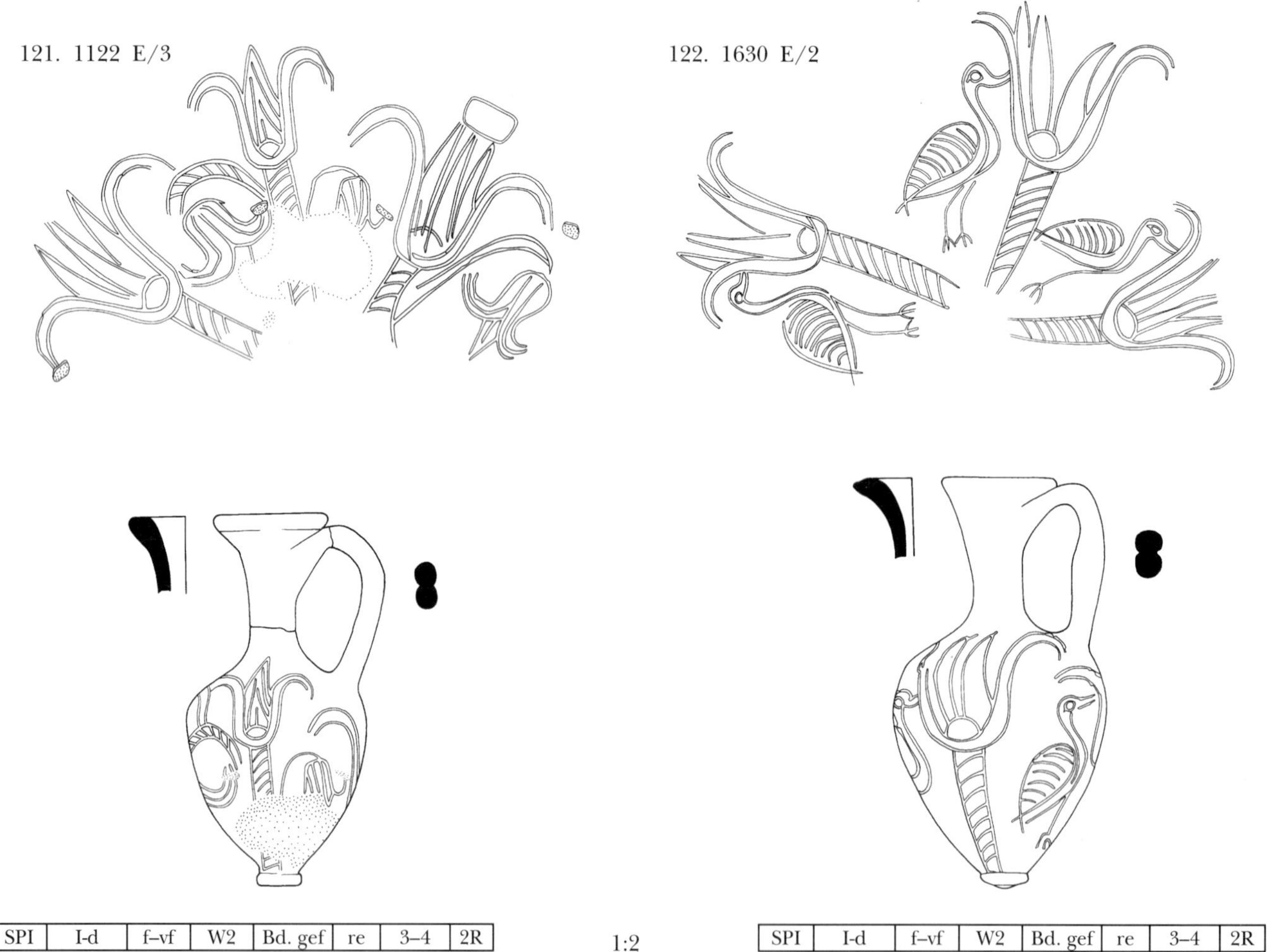

SPI	I-d	f–vf	W2	Bd. gef	re	3–4	2R

SPI	I-d	f–vf	W2	Bd. gef	re	3–4	2R

Levanto-Egyptian Type Group J.1.7

Plate 28

SPI	I-d	vf	W2	–	re	3

pht. 4.0 cm. Md 9.2 cm. Wd. 0.5 cm.
Incomplete
Surface colour: 10YR6/2 light reddish grey; burnished slip 7.5YR3/0 very dark grey
Break: grey core, brown reduction zones
Decoration: uncertain, Lilies ?
Previously published: Bietak, *MDAIK* 26, pl. 19d; Kaplan, *Tell el-Yahudiyeh Ware,* fig. 127d.

128. 7373E TD F/I-q/24 planum 1–2 Phase b/2–1 (91/007) Plate 30

BPI	I-d	m	W2	–	re	3

pht. 7.4 cm. Wd. 0.5 cm.
Incomplete
Surface colour: 10YR6/2 light reddish grey; burnished slip 5YR5/4 reddish brown
Break: uniform yellowish red
Decoration: Part of a bird standing on a lotus flower, decorated with a single-pointed tool.

129. 4127C TD A/II-l/17 planum 5 Phase E/3–2 (82/163) Plate 30

RPI	IV	f	W2	–	mi	2	2R

pht. 3.2 cm. Wd. 0.35–45 cm.
Incomplete
Surface colour: 5Y5/6 reddish yellow; burnished slip: 10YR6/1 grey
Break: grey core, thin light brown oxidation zones
Decoration: presumably part of a bird, infilled with dots made with a single-pointed tool

130. 6457A TD A/II-h/16 planum 5 Phase F–E/3 (88/106) Plate 30

BPI	IV	vf	W2	–	re	3

pht. 2.4 cm. Md 9.2 cm. Wd. 0.4 cm.
Incomplete
Surface colour: 7.5YR7/4 pink; burnished slip 7.5YR6/4 light brown
Break: uniform pink
Decoration: Lotus petal (?) filled with individual dashes.

131. 7347C TD F/I-m/17 pit 12 Phase ? (90/012) Plate 30

BPI	I-d	f–vf	W2	–	re	3

Nd. 1.2 cm. pht. 2.0 cm. Md 9.2 cm. Wd. 0.4 cm.
Incomplete
Surface colour: 10YR6/2 light reddish grey; burnished slip 10YR4/2 dark grey
Break: grey core, brown reduction zones
Decoration: Petals arranged in a rishi pattern.

132. 1558 Vienna A1743 A/II-m/14 planum 2–3 Phase E/1 (68/078) Plate 30

SPI	I-d	m	W2	–	re	3

pht. 2.5 cm. Wd. 0.5 cm.
Incomplete, shoulder
Surface colour: 7.5YR5/1 grey; burnished slip 7.5YR5/4 reddish brown
Break: wide grey core, brown and grey reduction zones
Decoration: Part of a schematic plant ?

133. 4151B=4759E TD A/II-o/20 planum 5 Phase F–E/3 (82/226) Plate 30

BPI	I-d	vf	W2	–	re	3

pht. 3.0 cm. Wd. 0.4 cm.
Incomplete
Surface colour: 7.5YR4/2 brown; burnished slip 10YR5/4 yellowish brown
Break: uniform grey
Decoration: Lower part of a horizontal band filled with oblique lines with figural decoration below.

The following thirty-three pieces derive from a number of different vessels found in pit complex L81. Unfortunately only a number of disjointed body sherds and one base were found so it is now impossible to know how many of these decorated vessels were originally deposited in this pit complex.

134. 9026G-10 TD F/II-r/22 L81 Phase a/2 (09/070) Plate 31

SPI	I-d	f	W2	–	re	3

pht. 8.2 cm.
Incomplete
Surface colour: burnished slip: 7.5Y4/1 dark grey
Break: wide grey core, thin brown reduction zones
Decoration: Upper parts of three flowers.

135. 9026G-1 TD F/II-r/22 L81 Phase a/2 (09/069) Plate 31

SPI	I-d	f	W2	–	re	3

pht. 4.6 cm.
Incomplete
Surface colour: burnished slip: 7.5Y5/1 gray
Break: wide grey core, brown reduction zones
Decoration: Upper part of a flower.

136. 9026G-5 TD F/II-r/22 L81 Phase a/2 (09/069) Plate 31

SPI	I-d	f	W2	–	re	3

pht. 4.0 cm.
Incomplete
Surface colour: burnished slip: 5YR5/1 gray
Break: wide grey core, brown reduction zones
Decoration: Upper part of a flower.

137. 9026G-2 TD F/II-r/22 L81 Phase a/2 (09/069) Plate 31

SPI	I-d	f	W2	–	re	3

pht. 3.2 cm.
Incomplete
Surface colour: burnished slip: 5YR3/1 dark gray

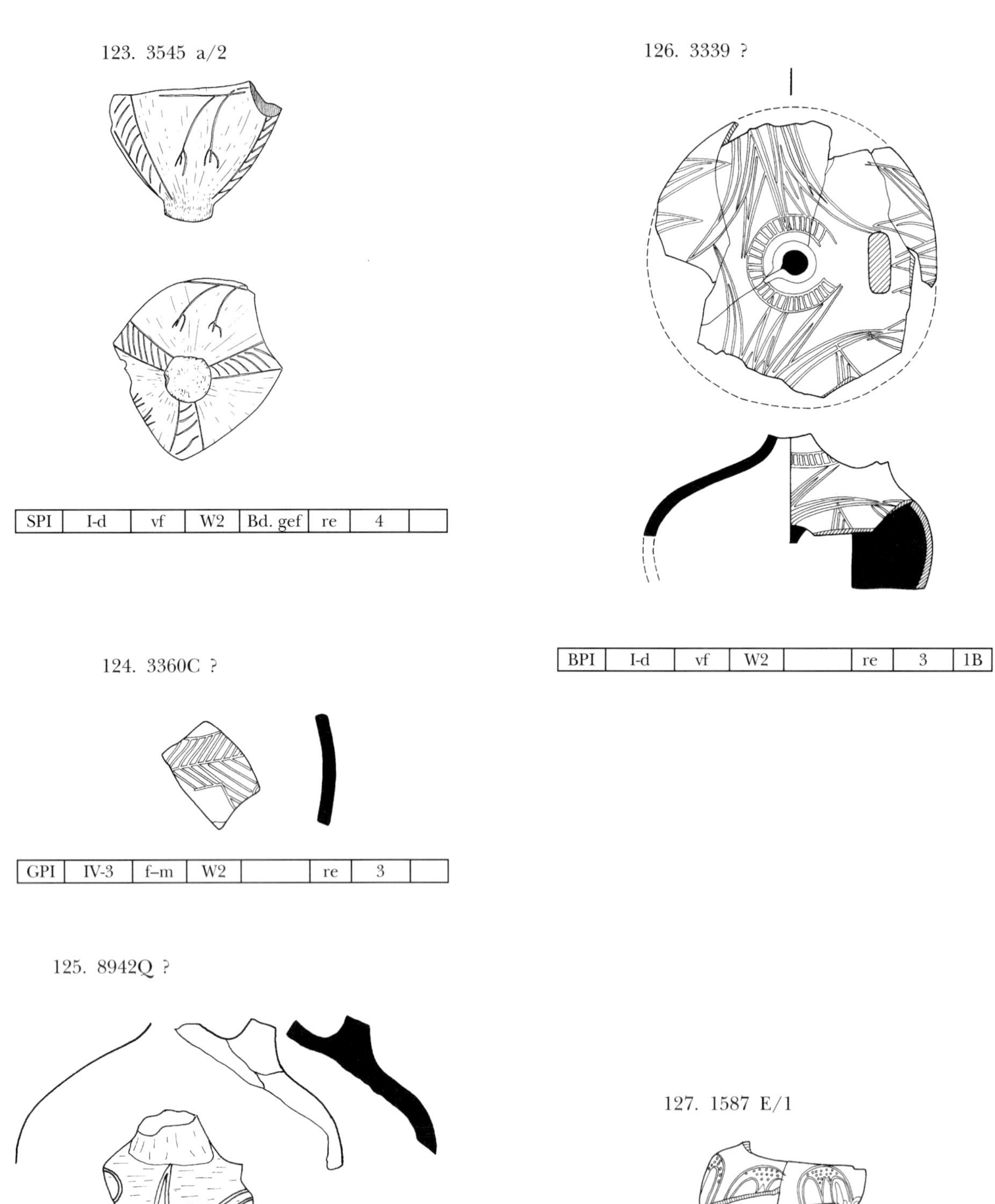

123. 3545 a/2

SPI	I-d	vf	W2	Bd. gef	re	4	

126. 3339 ?

BPI	I-d	vf	W2		re	3	1B

124. 3360C ?

GPI	IV-3	f–m	W2		re	3	

125. 8942Q ?

BPI	I-d	vf	W2		re	3–4	3R

127. 1587 E/1

BPI	I-d	vf	W2		re	3	1B

1:2

Levanto-Egyptian Type Group J.1.7 and miscellaneous decorated sherds

Plate 29

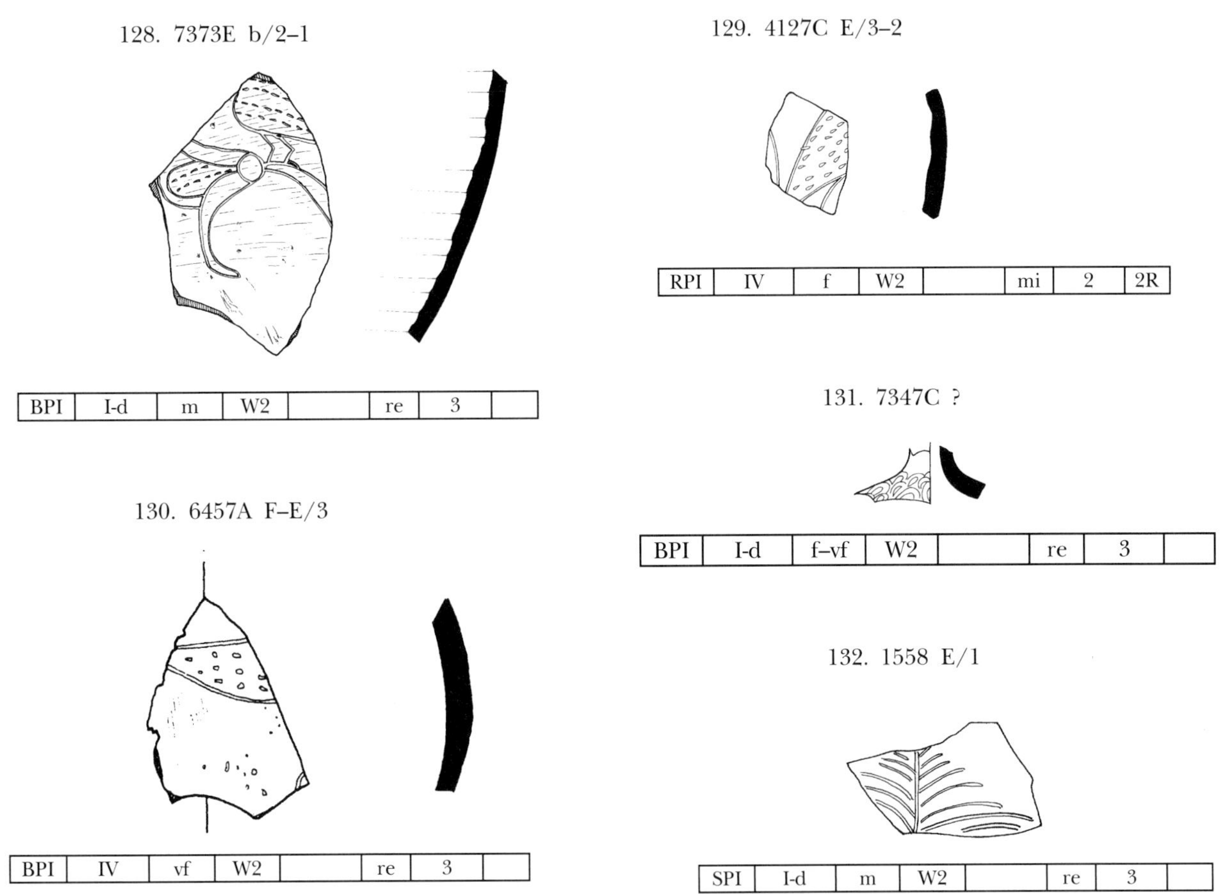

133. 4151B F–E/3

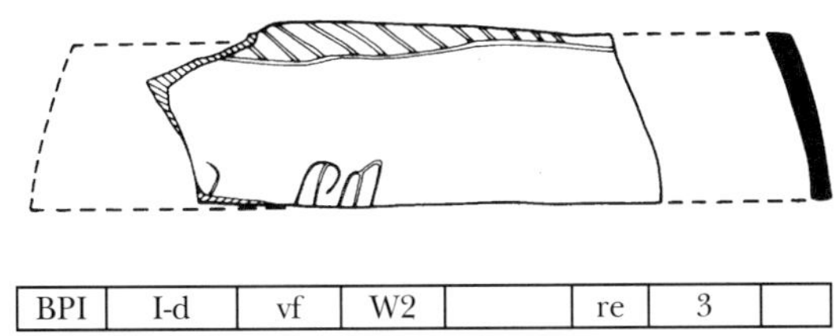

BPI	I-d	vf	W2		re	3	

1:2

Miscellaneous decorated sherds

Plate 30

Break: wide grey core, thin brown reduction zones
Decoration: Upper part of a flower.

138. 9026G-28 TD F/II-r/22 L81 Phase a/2 (09/072)
Plate 31

SPI	I-d	f	W2	–	re	3

pht. 5.3 cm.
Incomplete
Surface colour: burnished slip: 5YR4/1 dark gray
Break: wide grey core, brown reduction zones
Decoration: Upper parts of two different flowers and a floral bud.
Handle pushed through body wall

139. 9026G-9 TD F/II-r/22 L81 Phase a/2 (09/070)
Plate 31

SPI	I-d	f	W2	–	re	3

pht. 6.3 cm.
Incomplete
Surface colour: burnished slip: 7.5YR4/1 dark gray
Break: wide grey core, thin brown reduction zones
Decoration: Upper part of a flower plus floral stems and leaves (?).

140. 9026G-3 TD F/II-r/22 L81 Phase a/2 (09/069)
Plate 32

SPI	I-d	f	W2	–	re	3

pht. 3.5 cm.
Incomplete
Surface colour: burnished slip: 5YR4/1 dark gray
Break: wide grey core, thin brown reduction zones
Decoration: Upper part of two flowers.

141. 9026G-12 TD F/II-r/22 L81 Phase a/2 (09/070)
Plate 32

SPI	I-d	f	W2	–	re	3

pht. 2.8 cm.
Incomplete
Surface colour: burnished slip: 7.5YR4/1 dark gray
Break: wide grey core, thin brown reduction zones
Decoration: Upper part of a flower.

142. 9026G-7 TD F/II-r/22 L81 Phase a/2 (09/070)
Plate 32

SPI	I-d	f	W2	–	re	3

pht. 3.6 cm.
Incomplete
Surface colour: burnished slip: 5YR4/1 dark gray
Break: black core, red and grey reduction zones
Decoration: Upper part of two flowers.

143. 9026G-4 TD F/II-r/22 L81 Phase a/2 (09/069)
Plate 32

SPI	I-d	f	W2	–	re	3

pht. 5.8 cm.
Incomplete
Surface colour: burnished slip: 7.5YR4/1 dark gray
Break: wide grey core, brown reduction zones
Decoration: Parts of two flowers and a floral bud.

144. 9026G-6 TD F/II-r/22 L81 Phase a/2 (09/069)
Plate 32

SPI	I-d	f	W2	–	re	3

pht. 4.0 cm.
Incomplete
Surface colour: 5YR5/1 gray, burnish worn off
Break: black inner, brown outer
Decoration: Parts of two flowers.

145. 9026G-13 TD F/II-r/22 L81 Phase a/2 (09/071)
Plate 32

SPI	I-d	f	W2	–	re	3

pht. 5.8 cm.
Incomplete
Surface colour: burnished slip: 5YR4/1 dark gray
Break: grey core, brown reduction zones
Decoration: Part of a flower and floral stems.

146. 9026G-15 TD F/II-r/22 L81 Phase a/2 (09/071)
Plate 32

SPI	I-d	f	W2	–	re	3

pht. 3.4 cm.
Incomplete
Surface colour: burnished slip: 5YR4/1 dark gray
Break: grey core, brown reduction zones
Decoration: Parts of a flower and floral stems.

147. 9026G-14 TD F/II-r/22 L81 Phase a/2 (09/071)
Plate 32

SPI	I-d	f	W2	–	re	3

pht. 3.8 cm.
Incomplete
Surface colour: burnished slip: 5YR4/1 dark gray
Break: grey core, brown zones
Decoration: Parts of a flower.

148. 9026G-16 TD F/II-r/22 L81 Phase a/2 (09/071)
Plate 33

SPI	I-d	f	W2	–	re	3

pht. 3.1 cm.
Incomplete
Surface colour: burnished slip: 5YR4/1 dark gray
Break: grey core, brown reduction zones
Decoration: Parts of a flower.

149. 9026G-18 TD F/II-r/22 L81 Phase a/2 (09/071)
Plate 33

SPI	I-d	f	W2	–	re	3

pht. 2.2 cm.
Incomplete
Surface colour: burnished slip: 5YR4/1 dark gray
Break: grey core, brown reduction zones
Decoration: Parts of a flower.

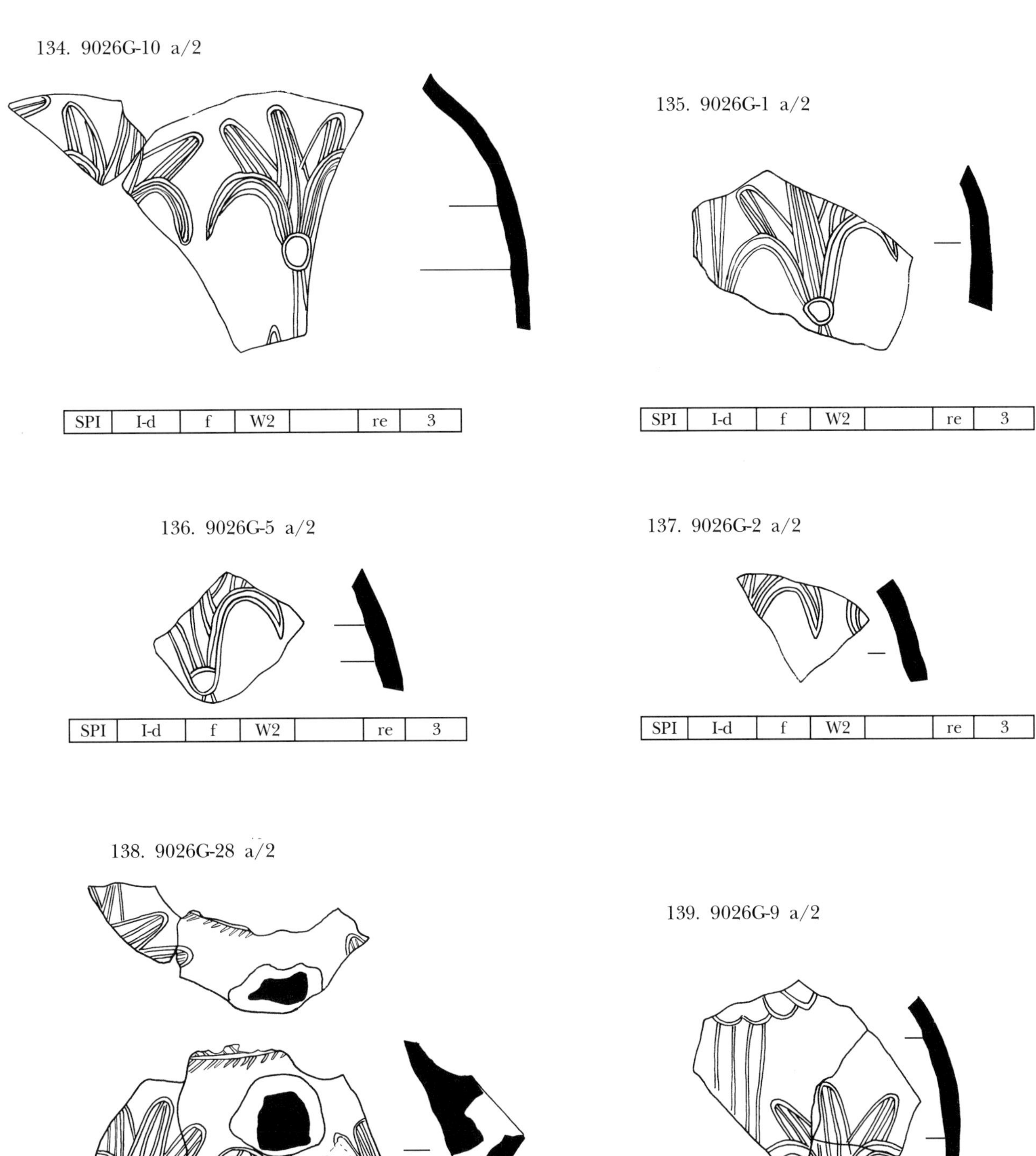

SPI	I-d	f	W2		re	3

SPI	I-d	f	W2		re	3

SPI	I-d	f	W2		re	3

SPI	I-d	f	W2		re	3

SPI	I-d	f	W2		re	3

SPI	I-d	f	W2		re	3

1:2

Miscellaneous decorated sherds

Plate 31

140. 9026G-3 a/2

SPI	I-d	f	W2		re	3

141. 9026G-12 a/2

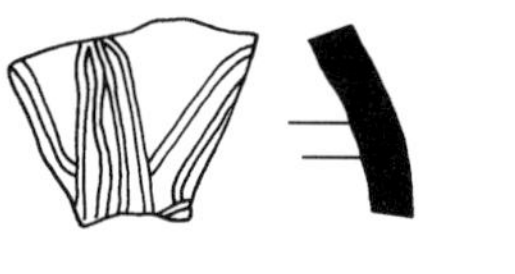

SPI	I-d	f	W2		re	3

142. 9026G-7 a/2

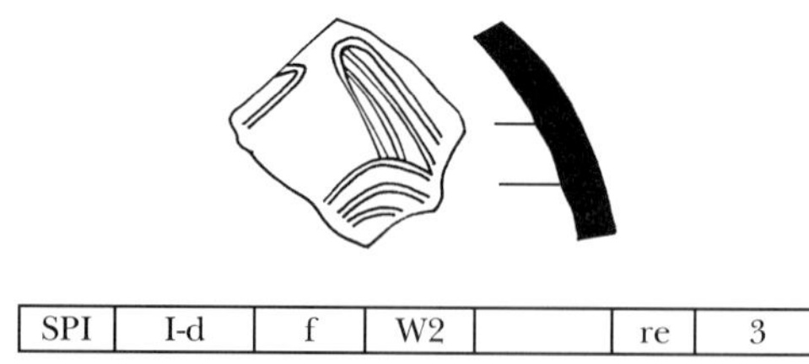

SPI	I-d	f	W2		re	3

143. 9026G-4 a/2

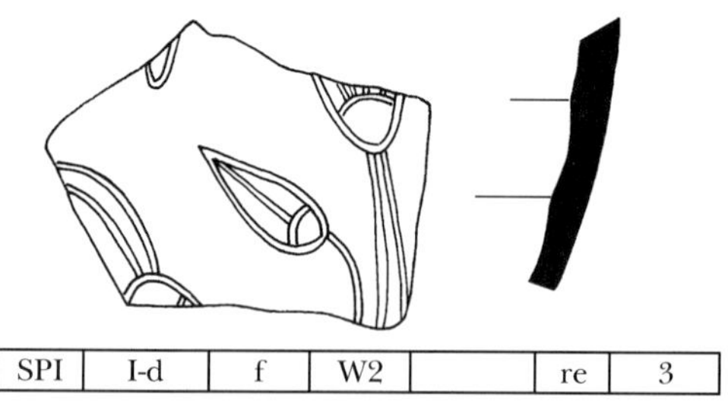

SPI	I-d	f	W2		re	3

144. 9026G-6 a/2

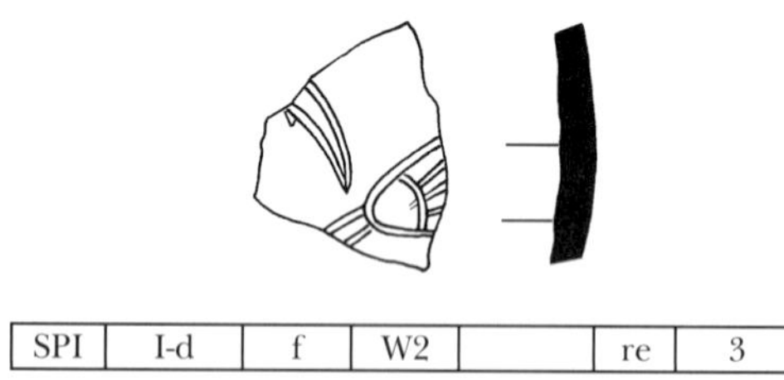

SPI	I-d	f	W2		re	3

145. 9026G-13 a/2

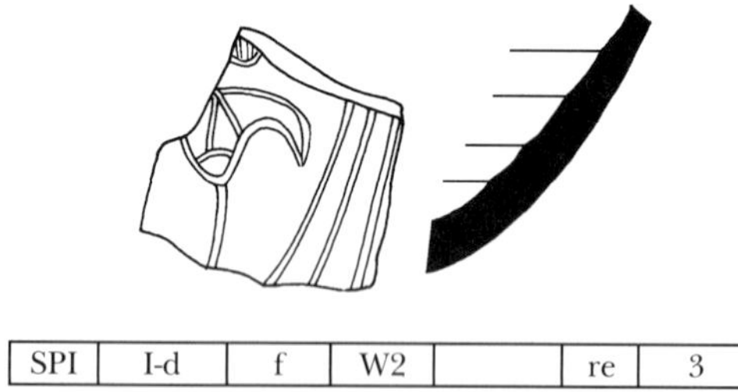

SPI	I-d	f	W2		re	3

146. 9026G-15 a/2

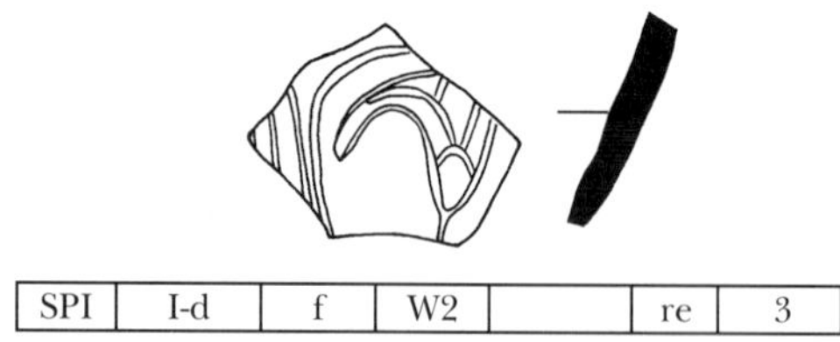

SPI	I-d	f	W2		re	3

147. 9026G-14

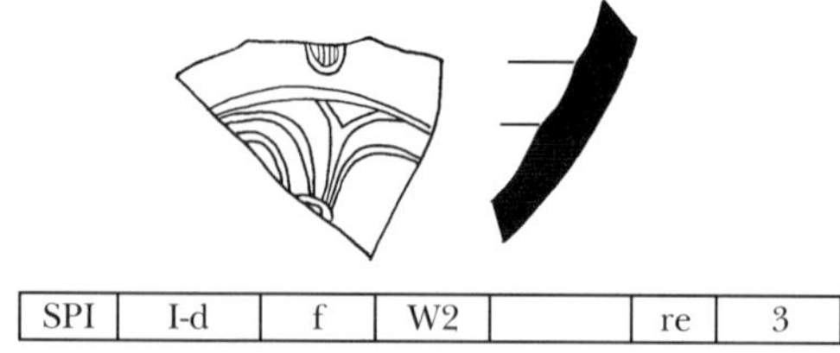

SPI	I-d	f	W2		re	3

1:2

Miscellaneous decorated sherds

Plate 32

150. 9026G-8 TD F/II-r/22 L81 Phase a/2 (09/070)
Plate 33

SPI	I-d	f	W2	–	re	3

pht. 5.5 cm.
Incomplete
Surface colour: burnished slip: 5YR4/1 dark gray
Break: grey core, brown reduction zones
Decoration: Floral stems.

151. 9026G-29 TD F/II-r/22 L81 Phase a/2 (09/072)
Plate 33

SPI	I-d	f	W2	–	re	3

pht. 5.5 cm.
Incomplete
Surface colour: burnished slip: 7.5YR3/1 very dark gray
Break: grey inner, brown outer
Decoration: Floral stems.

152. 9026G-17 TD F/II-r/22 L81 Phase a/2 (09/071)
Plate 33

SPI	I-d	f	W2	–	re	3

pht. 2.9 cm.
Incomplete
Surface colour: burnished slip: 5YR4/1 dark gray
Break: grey core, brown reduction zones
Decoration: Floral stems.

153. 9026G-21 TD F/II-r/22 L81 Phase a/2 (09/071)
Plate 33

SPI	I-d	f	W2	–	re	3

pht. 3.1 cm.
Incomplete
Surface colour: burnished slip: 5YR3/1 very dark gray
Break: grey core, brown reduction zones
Decoration: Floral stems.

154. 9026G-20 TD F/II-r/22 L81 Phase a/2 (09/071)
Plate 33

SPI	I-d	f	W2	–	re	3

pht. 2.5 cm.
Incomplete
Surface colour: burnished slip: 5YR4/1 dark gray
Break: grey core, brown reduction zones
Decoration: Floral stems.

155. 9026G-19 TD F/II-r/22 L81 Phase a/2 (09/071)
Plate 33

SPI	I-d	f	W2	–	re	3

pht. 1.7 cm.
Incomplete
Surface colour: burnished slip: 5YR4/1 dark gray
Break: grey core, brown reduction zones
Decoration: Floral stems.

156. 9026G-22 TD F/II-r/22 L81 Phase a/2 (09/072)
Plate 33

SPI	I-d	f	W2	–	re	3

pht. 2.7 cm.
Incomplete
Surface colour: burnished slip: 5YR4/1 dark gray
Break: grey core, brown reduction zones
Decoration: Floral stems.

157. 9026G-23 TD F/II-r/22 L81 Phase a/2 (09/072)
Plate 33

SPI	I-d	f	W2	–	re	3

pht. 1.8 cm.
Incomplete
Surface colour: burnished slip: 5YR4/1 dark gray
Break: grey inner, brown outer
Decoration: Floral stems.

158. 9026G-24 TD F/II-r/22 L81 Phase a/2 (09/072)
Plate 34

SPI	I-d	f	W2	–	re	3

pht. 2.3 cm.
Incomplete
Surface colour: burnished slip: 5YR4/1 dark gray
Break: uniform grey
Decoration: Floral stems.

159. 9026G-25 TD F/II-r/22 L81 Phase a/2 (09/072)
Plate 34

SPI	I-d	f	W2	–	re	3

pht. 2.3 cm.
Incomplete
Surface colour: burnished slip: 5YR4/1 dark gray
Break: uniform grey
Decoration: Floral stems.

160. 9026G-26 TD F/II-r/22 L81 Phase a/2 (09/072)
Plate 34

SPI	I-d	f	W2	–	re	3

pht. 2.2 cm.
Incomplete
Surface colour: burnished slip: 5YR4/1 dark gray
Break: uniform grey
Decoration: Floral stems.

161. 9026G-27 TD F/II-r/22 L81 Phase a/2 (09/072)
Plate 34

SPI	I-d	f	W2	–	re	3

pht. 3.0 cm.
Incomplete
Surface colour: burnished slip: 5YR4/1 dark gray
Break: uniform grey
Decoration: Floral stems.

162. 9026G-33 TD F/II-r/22 L81 Phase a/2 (09/073)
Plate 34

SPI	I-d	f	W2	–	re	3

pht. 2.4 cm.

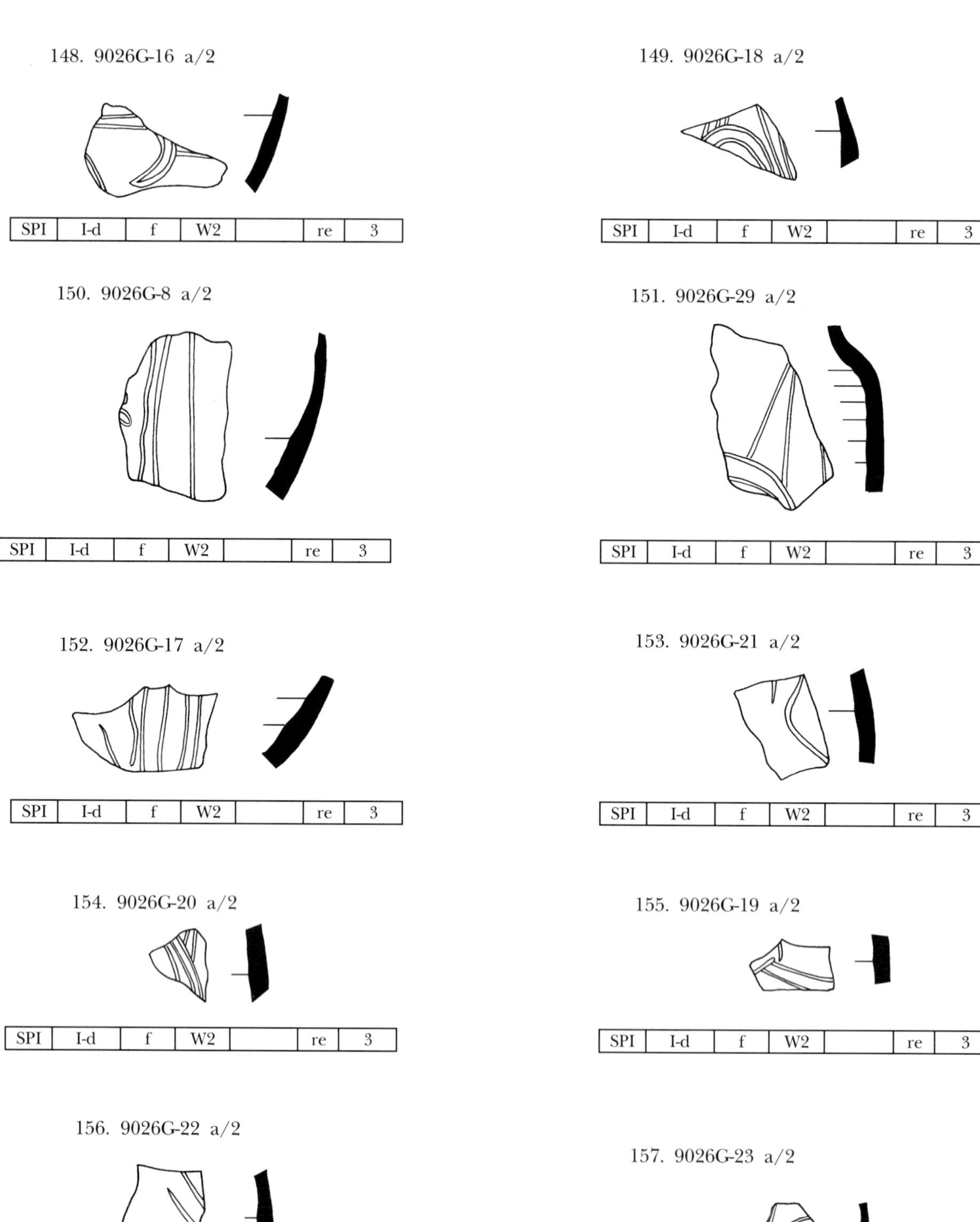

1:2

Miscellaneous decorated sherds

Plate 33

158. 9026G-24 a/2

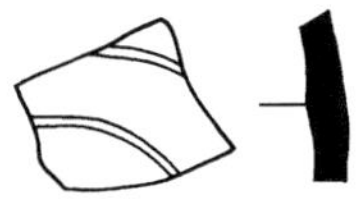

SPI	I-d	f	W2		re	3

159. 9026G-25 a/2

SPI	I-d	f	W2		re	3

160. 9026G-26 a/2

SPI	I-d	f	W2		re	3

161. 9026G-27 a/2

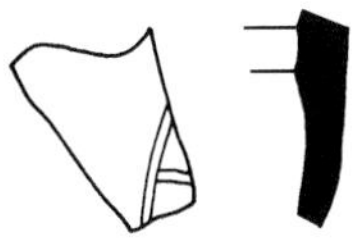

SPI	I-d	f	W2		re	3

162. 9026G-33 a/2

SPI	I-d	f	W2		re	3

163. 9026G-11 a/2

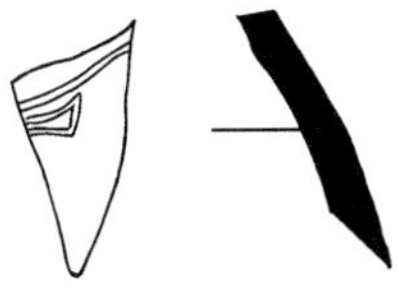

SPI	I-d	f	W2		re	3

164. 9026G-31 a/2

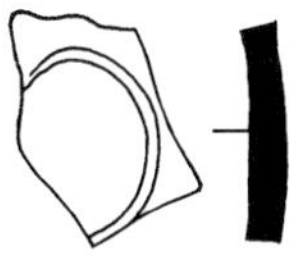

SPI	I-d	f	W2		re	3

165. 9026G-32 a/2

SPI	I-d	f	W2		re	3

166. 9026G-30 a/2

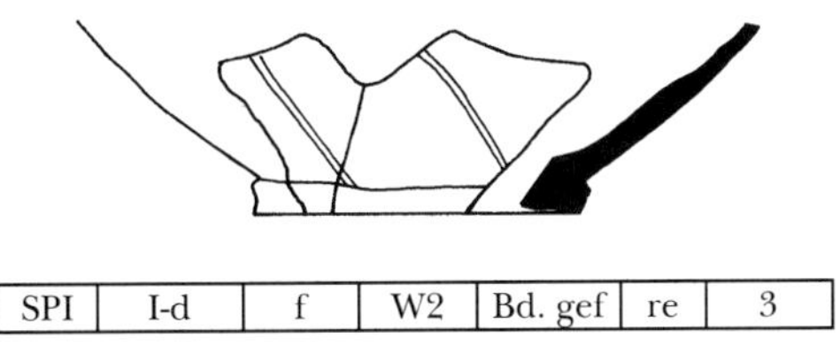

SPI	I-d	f	W2	Bd. gef	re	3

1:2

Miscellaneous decorated sherds

Plate 34

Incomplete
Surface colour: burnished slip: 5YR4/1 dark gray
Break: grey core, brown reduction zones
Decoration: Floral stems (?).

163. 9026G-11 TD F/II-r/22 L81 Phase a/2 (09/073)
Plate 34

SPI	I-d	f	W2	–	re	3

pht. 2.4 cm.
Incomplete
Surface colour: 7.5YR6/1 gray, burnish worn off
Break: grey core, brown reduction zones
Decoration: Floral stems (?).

164. 9026G-31 TD F/II-r/22 L81 Phase a/2 (09/073)
Plate 34

SPI	I-d	f	W2	–	re	3

pht. 2.4 cm.
Incomplete
Surface colour: 7.5YR5/1 gray, burnish worn off
Break: grey core, brown reduction zones
Decoration: Floral stems (?).

165. 9026G-32 TD F/II-r/22 L81 Phase a/2 (09/073)
Plate 34

SPI	I-d	f	W2	Bd. gef	re	3

pht. 2.4 cm.
Incomplete
Surface colour: burnished slip: 5YR4/1 dark gray
Break: uniform grey
Decoration: Floral stems (?).

166. 9026G-30 TD F/II-r/22 L81 Phase a/2 (09/073)
Plate 34

SPI	I-d	f	W2	Bd. gef	re	3

Base diam. 5.0 cms. pht. 2.9 cms.
Incomplete
Surface colour: burnished slip: 5YR4/1 dark gray
Break: uniform grey
Decoration: Floral stems.

Late Egyptian Tell El-Yahudiya Vessels

Type Group L.1.1

One complete vessel, TD 1674, along with another, incomplete example, TD 3269A, have been attributed to this type. The complete example forms a link between the Levanto-Egyptian group I4, in that it has a candlestick rim and a ring base, but by contrast, it has a single strap, rather than a bipartite, handle which links it with the Late Egyptian Piriform 2a group. Both vessels are decorated with a number of lozenges, again reminiscent of the true Piriform 2a group, each infilled with rows of dots made with a comb. However the findspots of both vessels clearly indicate their earlier dating.

167. 1674 Vienna A3141 A/II-l/14 grave 7 Phase E/3 (68/117) Plates 35, 138

SPI	I-d	f	W2	Bd. gef	re	2	1B

D. 2.85 cm. Nd. 1.2 cm. Bd. 2.1 cm. H. 12.3 cm. Md 7.35 cm. Wd. 0.35 cm.
VI 59.75
Restored from sherds, incomplete
Surface colour: 2.5Y5/1 grey; burnished slip: 2.5Y3/1 light olive brown
Break: uniform grey
Decoration: Five lozenges infilled with lines from upper left to lower right made with an eight-toothed comb.
Previously published: TD XVI, 197, fig. 115, no. 4.

168. 3269A TD F/I-j/20 grave 10 Phase b/3 (68/117)
Plates 35, 138

SPI	I-d	f	W2	Bd. gef	re	2–3	1B

Nd. 1.4 cm. Bd. 1.75 cm. pH: 8.1 cm. Md 5.8 cm. Wd. 0.35 cm.
Incomplete
Surface colour: 2.5Y5/2 greyish brown, burnished slip: 2.5Y3/2 very dark greyish brown
Break: uniform grey
Decoration: Eight vertical bands from the neck to the base filled with oblique lines made with a five-toothed comb.
BNL JH895 Egyptian Nile Clay[598]

Type Group L.1.2 (Large Piriform 2a)

Large Piriform 2a jugs of type group L.1, with delineated lozenges, and a height of between 14 and 18 cms. come from settlement sites, and are somewhat rare. Of the examples found at Tell el-Dabca one has a ring base (TD 3346) and the others a disc base.

Type Group L.1.2a

169. 3346 Cairo Khatana E/I/J planum ? Phase ? (80/185)
Plates 35, 139

SPI	I-d	f	W2	Bd. gef	re	2–3	1B

D. 3.1 cm. Nd 1.4 cm. Bd. 2.5 cm. H. 15.2 cm. Md. 9.1 cm. Wd. 0.3 cm.
VI 59.86
Restored from sherds, complete

[598] P. McGovern, *The Foreign Relations of the Hyksos*, Oxford, 2000, 151 no. JH895.

167. 1674 E/3

SPI	I-d	f	W2	Bd. gef	re	2	1B

168. 3269A b/3

SPI	I-d	f	W2	Bd. gef	re	2–3	1B

169. 3346 ?

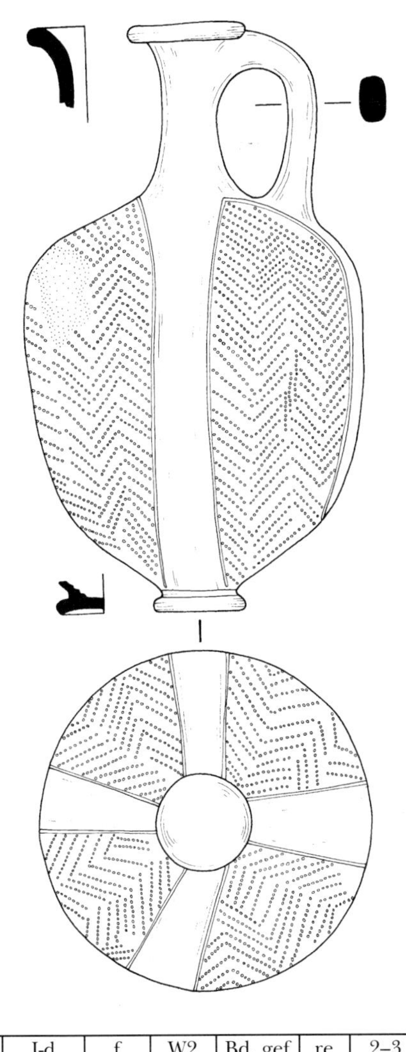

SPI	I-d	f	W2	Bd. gef	re	2–3	1B

170. 2045 ?

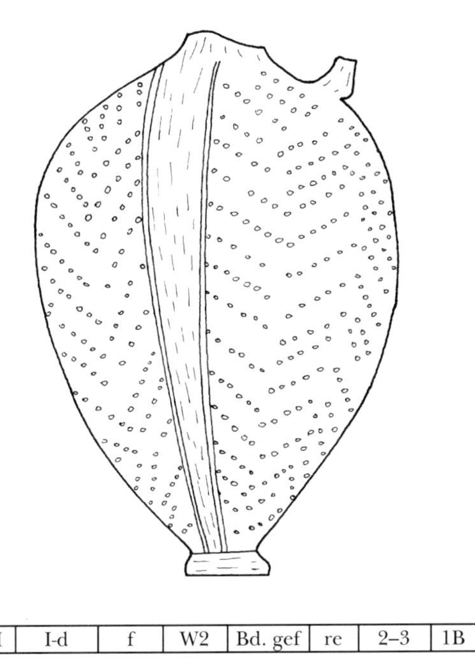

SPI	I-d	f	W2	Bd. gef	re	2–3	1B

1:2

Late Egyptian Type Groups L.1.1– 2

Plate 35

Surface colour 2.5Y5/1 grey; burnished slip: 10YR3/1 very dark grey
Break: not visible
Decoration: four lozenges infilled with horizontal zigzags made with a twelve-toothed comb.

Type Group L.1.2b

170. 2045 Vienna A3378 A/II-o/13 planum 3 Phase ? (69/046) Plate 35

SPI	I-d	f	W2	Bd. gef	re	2–3	1B

Nd. 1.9 cm. Bd. 2.3 cm. pht. 14.0 cm. Md. 10.0 cm. Wd. 0.45 cm.
Incomplete
Surface colour 2.5Y5/1 grey; burnished slip: 2.5Y3/1 very dark grey
Break: dark grey core, light grey reduction zones
Decoration: four lozenges infilled with horizontal zigzags made with an eight-toothed comb.

171. 8971R TD H/VI-x/20 planum 6 rel Phase f (Phase D/3) (02/255) Plates 36, 139

SPI	I-d	f	W2	Bd. gef	re	2–3	1B

Nd 1.8 cm. Bd. 2.35 cm. pht. 11.5 cm. Md. 8.7 cm. Wd. 0.55 cm.
Incomplete
Surface colour 2.5Y5/1 grey; burnished slip: 2.5Y3/1 very dark grey, burnish almost worn off
Break: dark grey core, light grey reduction zones
Decoration: Three lozenges with infilled zigzags made with a twenty-toothed comb.

172. 6023D TD F/I-o/21 planum 1 Phase ? (87/203) Plate 36

SPI	I-d	f	W2	Bd. gef	re	3	1B

Bd. 2.15 cm. pht. 9.2 cm. Md. 8.6 cm. Wd. 0.5 cm.
Incomplete
Surface colour: 5YR4/1 dark grey; burnished slip: 7.5YRN3 very dark grey
Break: greyish brown core, very dark grey reduction zones
Decoration: Three lozenges infilled with carelessly drawn chevrons made with a ten-toothed comb. Intervening areas vertically burnished.

Type Group L.I.3

Type groups L.1.3–L.1.5 are equivalent to Kaplan's classic Piriform 2a Tell el Yahudiya jugs, in that they comprise vessels with a rolled rim, strap handle, flattened to rounded shoulders, a piriform to rounded body and a ring, disc or button base. Such Piriform 2a jugs are here divided into groups L.1.3 with a ring base, L.1.4 with a disc base, and L.1.5 with a button base. The first two types are very common, and generally vary in height between 7 and 13 cms., with the average being around 10 cms. The decoration invariably consists only of lozenges (gores), usually three or four, though sometimes five or only two, filled with a herringbone pattern of incised dots. The comb used for this generally had eight or more teeth, and the area of incision is usually delineated. Burnishing occurs on the unincised areas. Although in previous publications the number of lozenges is not always indicated, they may be divided into decorative styles based on the number of lozenges present, namely L.I.3a with five lozenges, L.1.3b with four, L.1.3c with three and L.1.3d with two.

A variant ring base is known on at least seven vessels from Tell el-Dab^c^a, (TD 231, 367, 2138, 2142, 3050, 4904 and 9180, catalogue numbers 364–370), where the centre of the base forms a distinct bulb.

Type Group L.1.3a

173. 0170 Cairo A/II-l/12 grave 2 Phase E/1 (66/038) Plate 36

SPI	I-d	f	W2	Bd. gef	re	3	1B

D. 3.15 cm. Nd. 1.5 cm. Bd. 1.8 cm. H. 11.7 cm. Md 6.6 cm. Wd. 0.4 cm.
VI 56.41
Intact
Surface colour: 10YR5/2 grey brown; burnished slip: 10YR2/1 black
Break: grey core, brown reduction zones
Decoration: Five lozenges infilled with horizontal chevrons from upper left to lower right made with an eight-toothed comb.
Previously published; Bietak, *MDAIK* 23, fig. 8; Kaplan, *Tell el-Yahudiyeh Ware,* fig. 50f; *TD V,* 187, 188

Type Group L.1.3b

174. 1410 Vienna A2960 A/II-l/14 grave 5 Phase E/1 (68/094) Plate 36

SPI	I-d	f	W2	Bd. gef	re	3	1B

D. 2.0 cm. Nd 1.6 cm. Bd. 1.8 cm. H. 8.45 cm. Md. 6.3 cm. Wd. 0.3 cm.
VI 74.55
Incomplete
Surface colour: 10YR6/2 grey brown; burnished slip: 10YR5/1 dark grey
Break: not visible
Decoration: Four unequal lozenges infilled with horizontal chevrons with an eight-toothed comb.
Previously published: TD XVI, 254, fig. 189b, no. 18.

175. 2323 Vienna A1730 A/II-m/15 grave 3 Phase D/3 (69/111) Plate 37

SPI	I-d	f	W2	Bd. gef	re	2	1B

D. 3.0 cm. Nd. 1.5 cm. Bd. 1.7 cm. H. 9.9 cm. Md 6.6 cm. Wd. 0.3 cm.
VI 66.66
Intact
Surface colour: 10YR4/1 dark grey; burnished slip: 10YR3/1 very dark grey
Break: not visible

172. 6023D ?

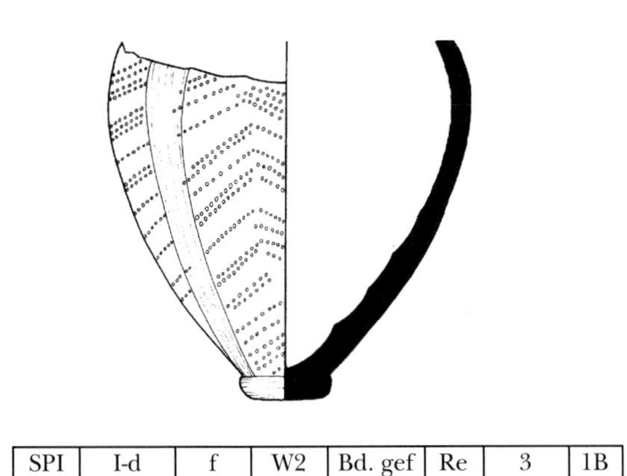

SPI	I-d	f	W2	Bd. gef	Re	3	1B

171. 8971R D/3

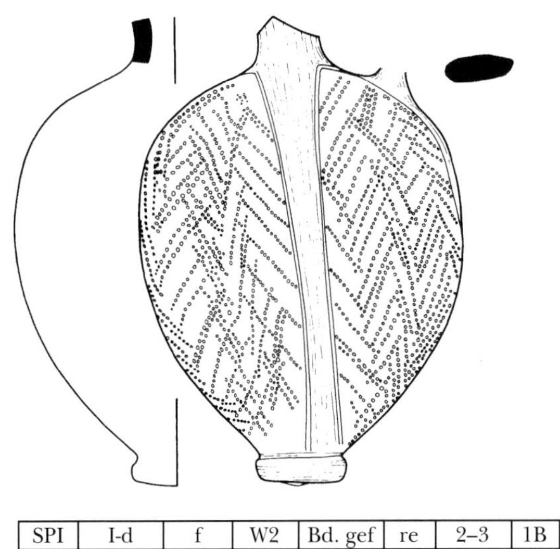

SPI	I-d	f	W2	Bd. gef	re	2–3	1B

173. 170 E/1

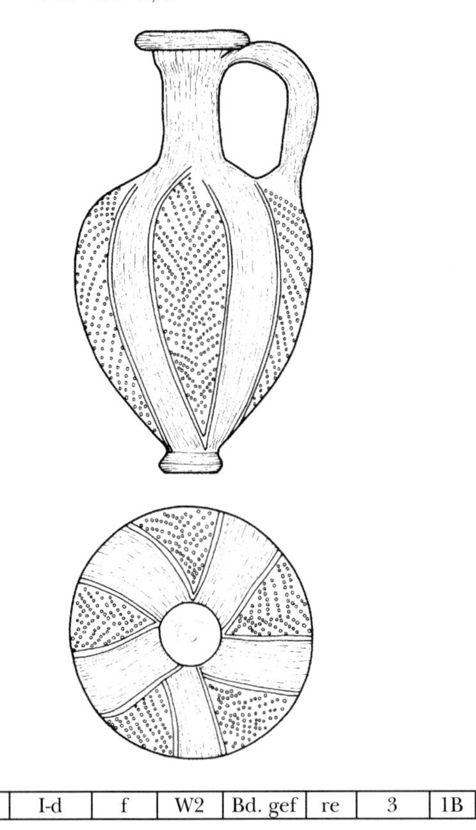

SPI	I-d	f	W2	Bd. gef	re	3	1B

174. 1410 E/1

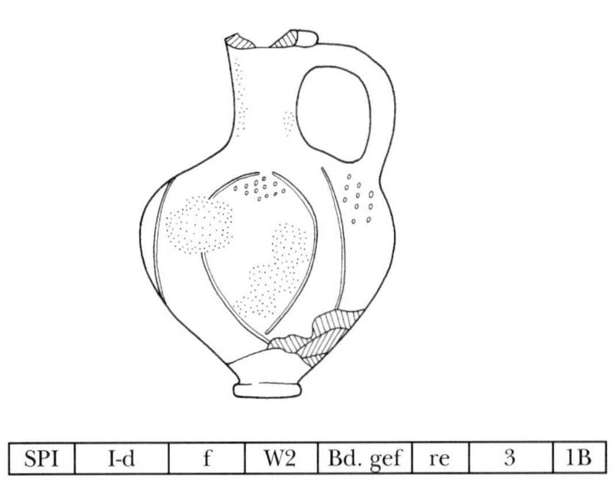

SPI	I-d	f	W2	Bd. gef	re	3	1B

1:2

Late Egyptian Type Groups L.1.2b–3b

Plate 36

175. 2323 D/3

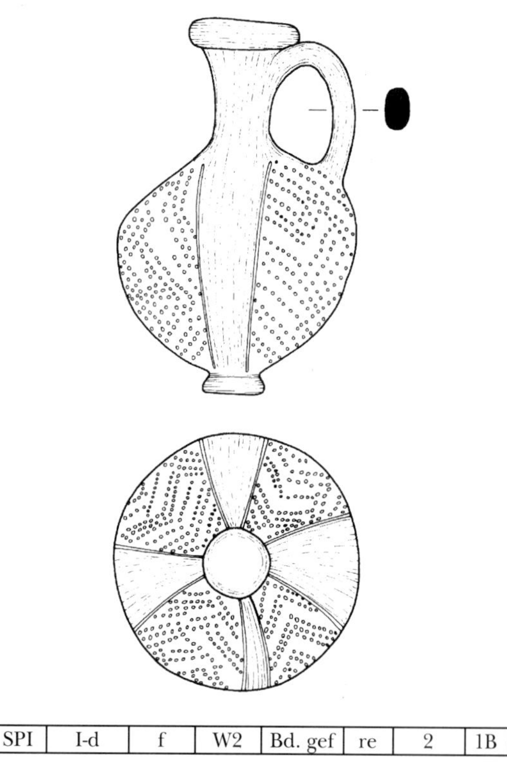

SPI	I-d	f	W2	Bd. gef	re	2	1B

176. 1385 E/1

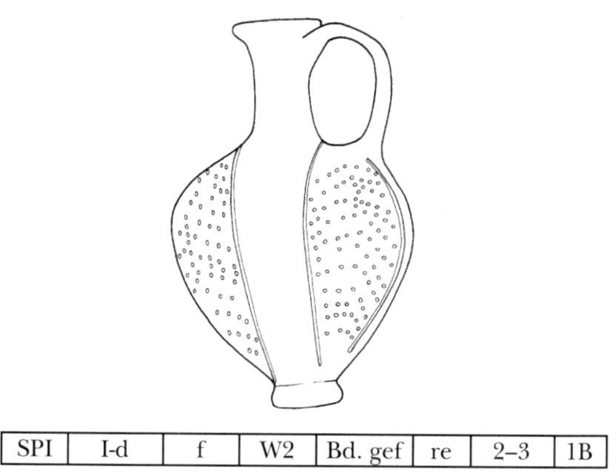

SPI	I-d	f	W2	Bd. gef	re	2–3	1B

177. 5764 a/2

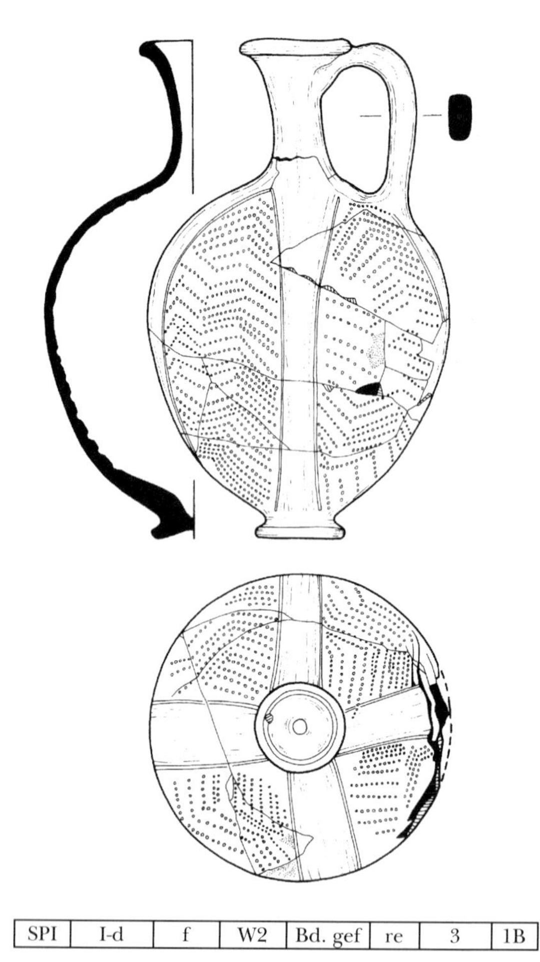

SPI	I-d	f	W2	Bd. gef	re	3	1B

178. 885 E/1

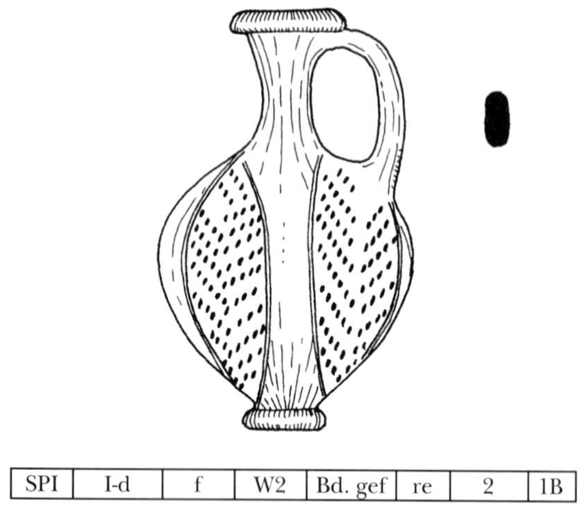

SPI	I-d	f	W2	Bd. gef	re	2	1B

1:2

Late Egyptian Type Group L.1.3b

Plate 37

Decoration: Four unequal lozenges infilled with horizontal chevrons with an eight-toothed comb.
Previously published: TD XVI, 315, fig. 235, no. 27.

176. 1385 Vienna A1665 A/II-l/14 planum 3 grave 5 Phase E/1 (68/090) Plate 37

SPI	I-d	f	W2	Bd. gef	re	2–3	1B

D. 2.0 cm. Nd. 1.2 cm. Bd. 1.5 cm. H. 8.5 cm. Md 5.5 cm. Wd. 0.3 cm.
VI 64.70
Intact
Surface colour: 2.5Y6/1 grey: burnished slip: 2.5Y3/1 light olive brown
Break: not visible
Decoration: Four unequal lozenges infilled with horizontal chevrons with an eight-toothed comb.
Previously published: TD XVI, 254, fig. 189b, no. 17.

177. 5764 TD F/I-m/19 grave 7 Phase a/2 (86/003) Plate 37

SPI	I-d	f	W2	Bd. gef	re	3	1B

D. 3.0 cm. Nd. 1.3 cm. Bd. 2.4 cm. H. 13.3 cm. Md 8.5 cm. Wd. 0.4 cm.
VI 63.90
Restored from sherds, incomplete
Surface colour: 5YR5/1 dark grey; burnished slip: 5YR2/1 black
Break: uniform dark grey
Decoration: Four unequal lozenges infilled with horizontal chevrons with a ten-toothed comb.

178. 0885 Vienna A1411 A/II-m/11 grave 7 Phase E/1 (67/026) Plate 37

SPI	I-d	f	W2	Bd. gef	re	2	1B

D. 2.9 cm. Nd 1.25 cm. Bd. 2.0 cm. H. 10.0 cm. Md. 6.3 cm. Wd. 0.3 cm.
VI 63.00
Intact
Surface colour: 5YR5/1 grey; burnished slip: 10YR3/1 very dark grey
Break: uniform grey
Decoration: Four unequal lozenges infilled with horizontal chevrons with an eight-toothed comb.
Previously published: TD V, 190, 191; *PuF* 226, nr 267; *Pharao siegt immer,* 151 no. 150.

179. 0836 Cairo JE 91580 A/III planum 2–3 Phase D/3–2 (67/031) Plate 38

SPI	I-d	f	W2	Bd. gef	re	2	1B

D. 3.1 cm. Nd 1.2 cm. Bd. 1.9 cm. H. 9.6 cm. Md. 5.95 cm. Wd. 0.3 cm.
VI 61.97
Intact
Surface colour: 10YR6/2 grey; burnished slip: 10YR6/1 dark grey
Break: not visible
Decoration: Four unequal lozenges infilled with horizontal chevrons with a ten-toothed comb.

180. 2315 Vienna A3542 A/II-m/15 grave 3 Phase D/3 (69/109) Plate 38

SPI	I-d	f	W2	Bd. gef	re	2	1B

D. 2.8 cm. Nd. 1.25 cm. Bd. 1.8 cm. H. 9.4 cm. Md 5.8 cm. Wd. 0.35 cm.
VI 61.70
Intact
Surface colour: eroded; burnished slip: eroded
Break: not visible
Decoration: Four unequal lozenges, infilled with poorly made chevrons, made with a six-toothed comb.
BNL JH389 Egyptian Nile Clay[599]
Previously published: TD XVI, 315, fig. 235, no. 18.

181. 2314 Vienna A3541 A/II-m/15 grave 3 Phase D/3 (69/109) Plate 38

SPI	I-d	F	W2	Bd. gef	re	2–3	1B

D. 2.8 cm. Nd. 1.5 cm. Bd. 1.8 cm. H. 9.4 cm. Md 5.8 cm. Wd. 0.3 cm.
VI 61.70
Restored from sherds, complete
Surface eroded
Break: not visible
Decoration: Four unequal lozenges infilled with horizontal chevrons with an eight-toothed comb.
Previously published: TD XVI, 315, fig. 235, no. 17.

182. 7931 TD A/IV-g/6 grave 11 Phase ? (92/201) Plate 38

SPI	I-d	f–m	W2	Bd. gef	re	3	1B

D. 2.6 cm. Nd. 1.2 cm. Bd. 2.0 cm. H. 9.8 cm. Md 6.0 cm. Wd. 0.4 cm.
VI 61.22
Incomplete
Surface colour: 10YR3/1 dark grey; burnished slip: 10YR2/1 black
Break: not visible
Decoration: Four unequal lozenges filled on three instances with horizontal chevrons, and in the fourth, narrower lozenge, oblique lines made with an eight-toothed comb.

183. 0876 Vienna A2638 A/II-m/11 planum 3–4 grave 6 Phase E/2–1 (67/024) Plate 39

SPI	I-d	f	W2	Bd. gef	re	2–3	1B

D. 2.2 cm. Nd. 1.3 cm. Bd. 1.7 cm. H. 9.6 cm. Md 5.8 cm. Wd. 0.35 cm.

599 P. McGovern, *The Foreign Relations of the Hyksos,* Oxford, 2000, 134 no. JH389.

179. 836 D/3–2

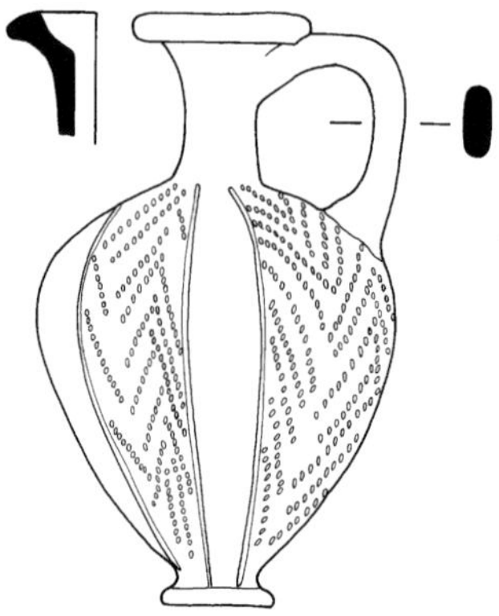

SPI	I-d	f	W2	Bd. gef	re	2	1B

180. 2315 D/3

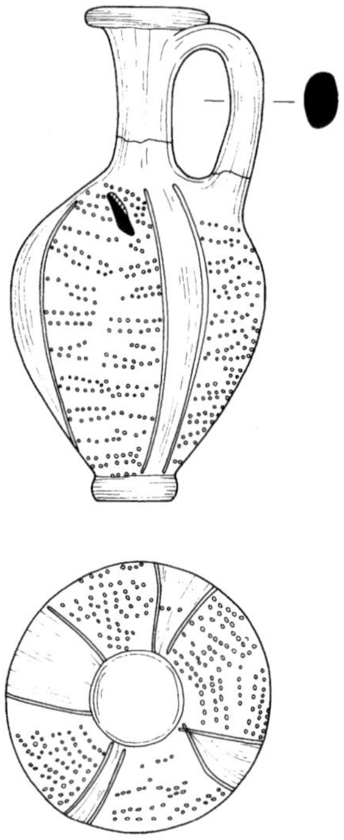

SPI	I-d	f	W2	Bd. gef	re	2	1B

181. 2314 D/3

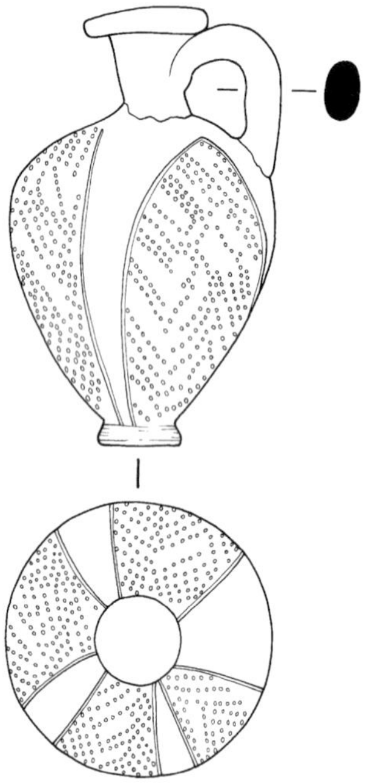

SPI	I-d	f	W2	Bd. gef	re	2–3	1B

182. 7931 ?

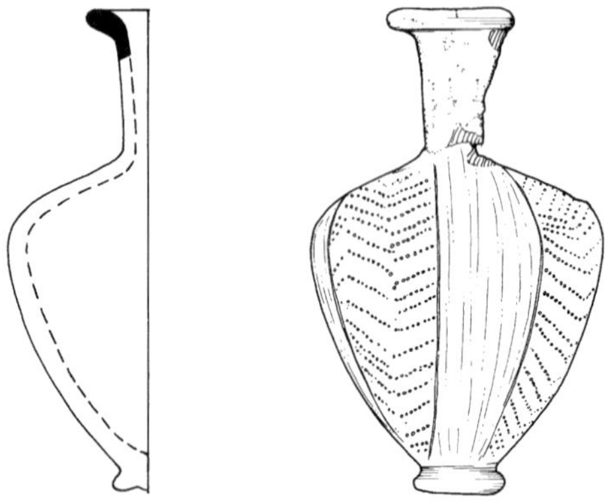

SPI	I-d	f–m	W2	Bd. gef	re	3	1B

1:2

Late Egyptian Type Group L.1.3b

Plate 38

183. 876 E/2–1

SPI	I-d	f	W2	Bd. gef	re	2–3	1B

184. 2154 E/1

SPI	I-d	f	W2	Bd. gef	re	2	1B

185. 2276 E/1 or D/3

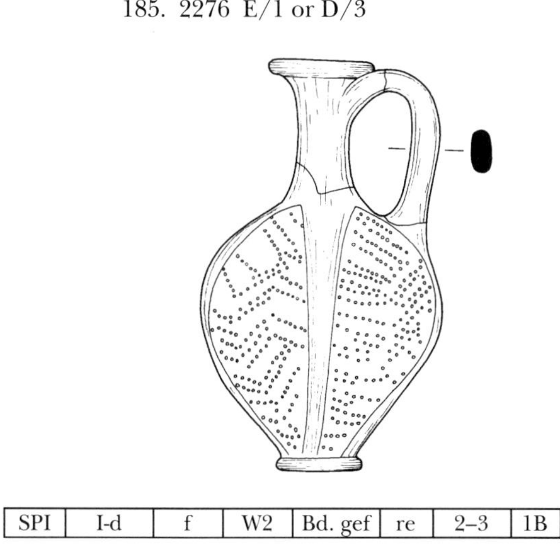

SPI	I-d	f	W2	Bd. gef	re	2–3	1B

186. 8781B E/1

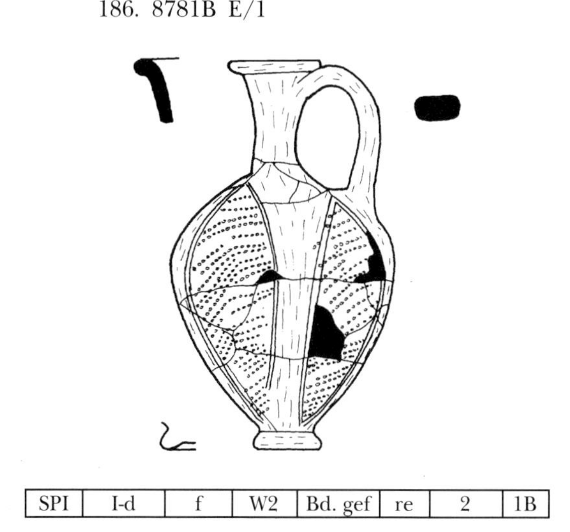

SPI	I-d	f	W2	Bd. gef	re	2	1B

1:2

Late Egyptian Type Group L.1.3b

Plate 39

VI 60.41
Incomplete
Surface colour: 10YR3/3 dark brown: burnished slip: 10YR4/1 dark grey
Break: grey core, brown reduction zones
Decoration: Four unequal lozenges infilled with horizontal chevrons with a six-toothed comb.
Previously published: TD V, 157, 158.

184. 2154 Vienna A1722 A/II-l/16 grave 2 Phase E/1 (69/064) Plates 39, 139

SPI	I-d	f	W2	Bd. gef	re	2	1B

D. 2.8 cm. Nd. 1.2 cm. Bd. 2.0 cm. H. 9.6 cm. Md 5.8 cm. Wd. 0.3 cm.
VI 60.41
Intact
Surface colour: 2.5Y4/1 grey: burnished slip: 2.5Y3/1 very dark grey
Break: not visible
Decoration: Four lozenges infilled with well made chevrons, made with an eight-toothed comb.
Previously published: TD XVI, 269, fig. 194a, no. 5.

185. 2276 Vienna A1725 A/II-k/14 grave 1 Phase E/1 or D/3 (69/087) Plate 39

SPI	I-d	f	W2	Bd. gef	re	2–3	1B

D. 2.7 cm. Nd. 1.2 cm. Bd. 2.2 cm. H. 10.4 cm. Md 6.2 cm. Wd. 0.3 cm.
VI 59.61
Restored from sherds, complete
Surface colour: 2.5Y5/1 grey: burnished slip: 2.5Y3/1 very dark grey
Break: not visible
Decoration: Four lozenges with poorly made chevrons, made with an eight-toothed comb.
BNL JH396 Egyptian Nile Clay[600]
Previously published: TD XVI, 297, fig. 216b, no. 9.

186. 8781B TD A/II-o/14 grave 43 Phase E/1 (98/072) Plates 39, 139

SPI	I-d	f	W2	Bd. gef	re	2	1B

D. 2.5 cm. Nd. 1.1 cm. H. 10.4 cm. Md. 6.2 cm. Wd. 0.3 cm.
VI 59.61
Restored from sherds, Incomplete
Surface colour: 10YR4/3 brown; burnished slip: 10YR3/1 very dark grey
Break: uniform 10YR4/3 light grey brown
Decoration: Four lozenges filled with oblique lines made with a ten-toothed comb.
Previously published: TD XVI, 286, fig. 208a, no. 2.

187. 4903 TD F/I-k/24 pit 2 Phase b/1–a/2 (84/044) Plate 40

SPI	I-d	vf	W2	Bd. gef	re	3	1B

D. 3.2 cm. Nd. 1.3 cm. Bd. 1.85 cm. H. 10.6 cm. Md 6.3 cm. Wd. 0.4 cm.
VI 59.43
Rim chipped
Surface colour: 10YR4/1 dark grey; burnished slip: 10YR2/1 black
Break: uniform grey
Decoration: Four lozenges infilled with horizontal chevrons made with a sixteen-toothed comb. Undecorated parts vertically burnished. rim horizontally burnished.

188. 3516 Cairo A/II-s/18 grave 1 Phase E/1 (81/400) Plate 40

SPI	I-d	vf	W2	Bd. gef	re	3	1B

D. 2.5 cm. Nd. 1.2 cm. Bd. 1.75 cm. H. 9.1 cm. Md 5.4 cm. Wd. 0.4 cm.
VI 59.34
Intact
Surface colour: 10YR1/1 dark grey; burnished slip: 10YR2/1 black
Break: uniform greyish brown
Decoration: Four lozenges with well made chevrons, in two cases zigzags, made with an eight-toothed comb.
Previously published: TD XVI, 293, fig. 214, no. 1.

189. 2278 Vienna A3522 A/II-k/14 grave 1 Phase E/1 or D/3 (69/087) Plate 40

SPI	I-d	f	W2	Bd. gef	re	2–3	1B

D. 2.6 cm. Nd. 1.2 cm. Bd. 2.0 cm. H. 10.3 cm. Md 6.1 cm. Wd. 0.3 cm.
VI 59.22
Restored from sherds, complete
Surface colour: 2.5Y5/1 grey: burnished slip: 2.5Y3/1 very dark grey
Break: not visible
Decoration: Four unequal lozenges infilled with horizontal chevrons made with an eight-toothed comb.
Previously published: TD XVI, 297, fig. 216b, no. 11.

190. 4902 TD F/I-k/24 planum ? grave ? Phase a/2 (84/043) Plate 40

SPI	I-d	f	W2	Bd. gef	re	2–3	1B

D. 2.95 cm. Nd. 1.28 cm. Bd. 1.8 cm. H. 10.5 cm. Md 6.2 cm. Wd. 0.3 cm.
VI 59.04
Intact
Surface colour: 10YR6–5/3 brown: burnished slip: 10YR2/1 black
Break: not visible
Decoration: Four lozenges infilled with horizontal chevrons made with a sixteen-toothed comb. Undecorated parts vertically burnished. rim horizontally burnished.

191. 0214 Cairo JE 91560 A/II-l/12 grave 1 Phase E/1 (66/036) Plate 40

SPI	I-d	f	W2	Bd. gef	re	2	1B

D. 2.6 cm. Nd. 1.2 cm. Bd. 1.8 cm. H. 8.7 cm. Md 5.1 cm. Wd. 0.4 cm.
VI 58.62

[600] P. McGovern, *The Foreign Relations of the Hyksos,* Oxford, 2000, 134 no. JH396.

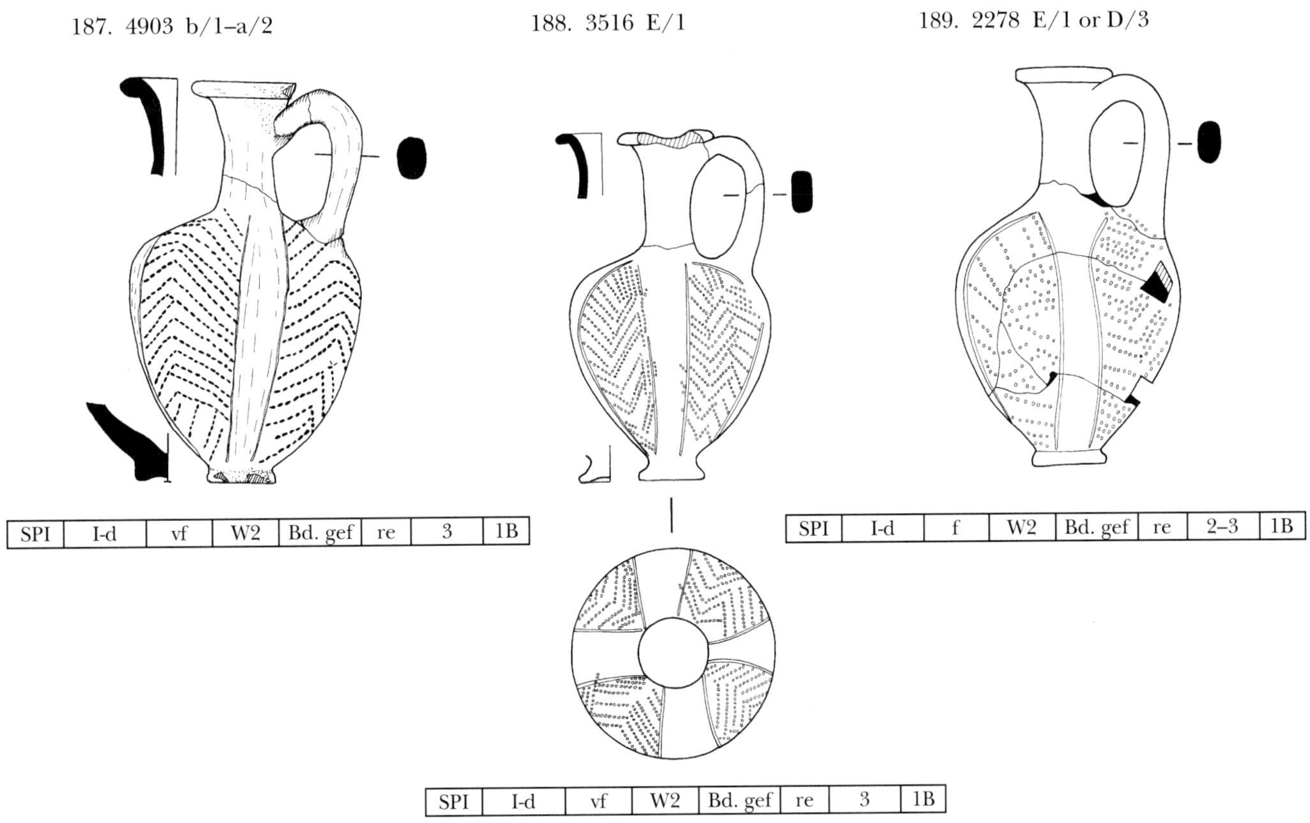

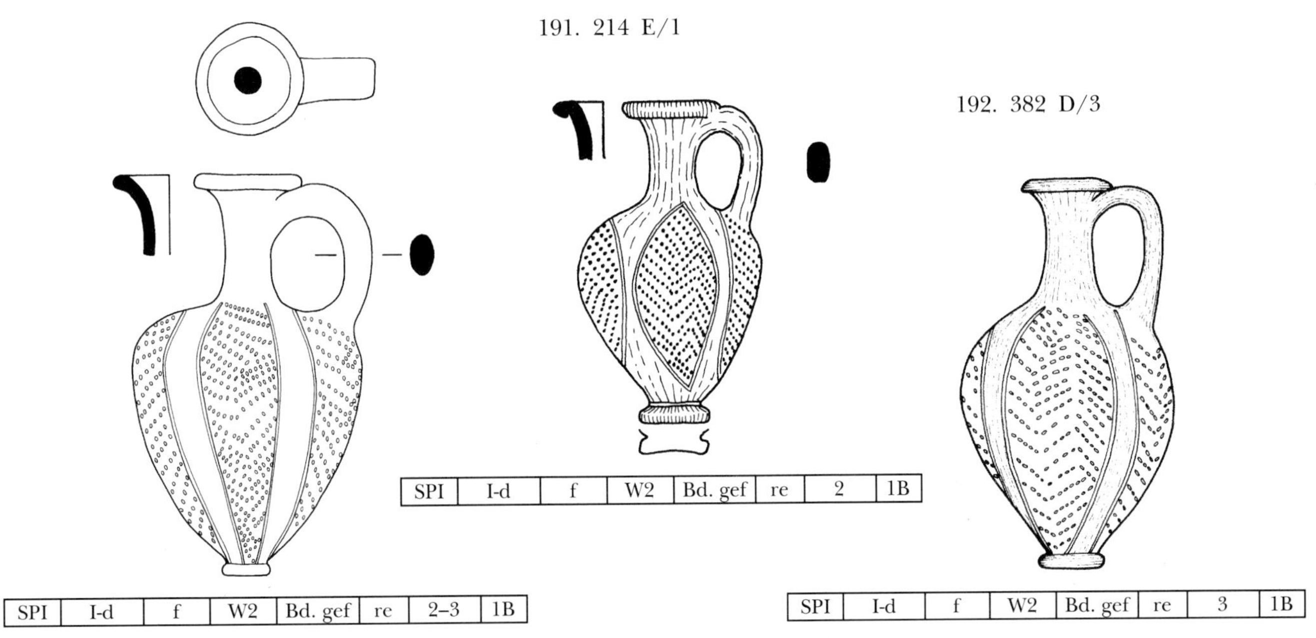

1:2

Late Egyptian Type Group L.1.3b

Plate 40

Restored from sherds, incomplete
Surface colour: 10YR5/3 brown; burnished slip: 10YR3/1 very dark grey
Break: black core, grey brown reduction zones
Decoration: Four unequal lozenges infilled with horizontal chevrons or zigzags made with a ten-toothed comb.
Previously published: TD V, 177, 179.

192. 0382 Vienna A1604 A/I-g/3 grave 1 Phase D/3 (66/056) Plate 40

SPI	I-d	f	W2	Bd. gef	re	3	1B

D. 2.5 cm. Nd. 1.15 cm. Bd. 1.8 cm. H. 10.4 cm. Md 6.0 cm. Wd. 0.4 cm.
VI 57.69
Intact
Surface colour: 10YR4/2 dark grey; burnished slip: 10YR3/1 very dark grey
Break: not visible
Decoration: Four unequal lozenges infilled with horizontal chevrons or zigzags made with an eight-toothed comb.

193. 5415 Cairo A/II-k/17 grave 30 burial 1 Phase E/1 (85/262) Plate 41

SPI	I-d	f	W2	Bd. gef	re	2–3	1B

D. 2.3 cm. Nd. 1.2 cm. Bd. 1.65 cm. H. 10.8 cm. Md 6.0 cm. Wd. 0.4 cm.
VI 55.55
Intact
Surface colour: 10YR5/3 brown; burnished slip: 10YR3/1 very dark grey
Break: not visible
Decoration: Four unequal lozenges, one infilled with bipartite horizontal chevrons one with a tripartite horizontal chevron, and two with oblique lines all made with an eight-toothed comb. Undecorated parts vertically burnished. rim horizontally burnished
Previously published: TD XVI, 248 fig. 184, no. 4.

194. 2317 Cairo JE 91711C A/II-m/15 grave 3 Phase D/3 (69/110) Plate 41

SPI	I-d	f	W2	Bd. gef	re	2–3	1B

D. 2.7 cm. Nd. 1.3 cm. Bd. 2.05 cm. H. 10.5 cm. Md 5.8 cm. Wd. 0.4 cm.
VI 55.23
Intact
Surface colour: 10YR5/1 dark grey; burnished slip: 10YR2/1 black
Break: not visible
Decoration: Four unequal lozenges with poorly made chevron decoration, made with an eight-toothed comb.
Previously published: TD XVI, 315, fig. 235, no. 21.

195. 1389 Cairo ? A/II-l/14 planum 3 grave 5 Phase E/1 (68/090) Plate 41
D. 2.8 cm. Nd. 1.2 cm. Bd. 1.5 cm. H. 10.5 cm. Md 5.8 cm.

SPI	I-d	f	W2	Bd. gef	re	2–3	1B

Wd. 0.3 cm.
VI 55.23
Intact
Surface colour: 2.5Y6/1 grey: burnished slip: 2.5Y3/1 light olive brown
Break: not visible
Decoration: Four lozenges with well made chevrons or zigzags made with an eight-toothed comb.
Previously published: TD XVI, 254, fig. 189b, no. 13.

196. 0192 Vienna A2215 A/II-l/12 grave 2 Phase E/1 (66/014) Plate 41

SPI	I-d	f	W2	Bd. gef	re	3	1B

D. 3.15 cm. Nd. 1.2 cm. Bd. 1.65 cm. H. 9.2 cm. Md 5.0 cm. Wd. 0.4 cm.
VI 54.34
Intact
Surface colour: 10YR1/1 dark grey; burnished slip: 10YR2/1 black
Break: not visible
Decoration: Four unequal lozenges infilled with horizontal chevrons made with an eight-toothed comb.
Previously published: TD V, 187, 188.

197. 0837 Vienna A1655 A/III planum 2–3 Phase ? (67/015) Plate 41

SPI	I-d	f	W2	Bd. gef	re	2	1B

D. 3.1 cm. Nd 1.2 cm. Bd. 2.0 cm. H. 10.7 cm. Md. 5.7 cm. Wd. 0.3 cm.
VI 53.27
Intact
Surface colour: 10YR6/2 grey; burnished slip: 10YR6/1 dark grey
Break: not visible
Decoration: Four unequal lozenges infilled with horizontal chevrons made with an eight-toothed comb.

198. 4121 TD A/II-l/17 planum 1–2 Phase D/3 (82/158) Plate 41

SPI	I-d	vf	W2	Bd. gef	re	3	1B

D. 2.9 cm. Nd. 1.3 cm. Bd. 1.8 cm. H. 10.1 cm. Md 5.25 cm. Wd. 0.4 cm.
VI 51.98
Intact
Surface colour: 10YR5/1 dark grey; burnished slip: 10YR2/1 black
Break: not visible
Decoration: Four unequal lozenges, three infilled with horizontal chevrons made with a six-toothed comb, the fourth filled with oblique striations made with an eight-toothed comb. Undecorated parts vertically burnished. Rim horizontally burnished.

199. 1396 Vienna A2950 A/II-l/14 planum 3 grave 5 Phase E/1 (68/092) Plate 42

SPI	I-d	f	W2	Bd. gef	re	2–3	1B

D. 2.9 cm. Nd. 1.2 cm. Bd. 1.9 cm. H. 11.4 cm. Md 5.72 cm. Wd. 0.3 cm.
VI 50.17
Intact
Surface colour: 10YR6/1 grey: burnished slip: 10YR4/1 dark grey
Break: dark brown core, black reduction zones
Decoration: Four unequal lozenges infilled with zigzags made with an eight-toothed comb.
Previously published: TD XVI, 254, fig. 189b, no. 14.

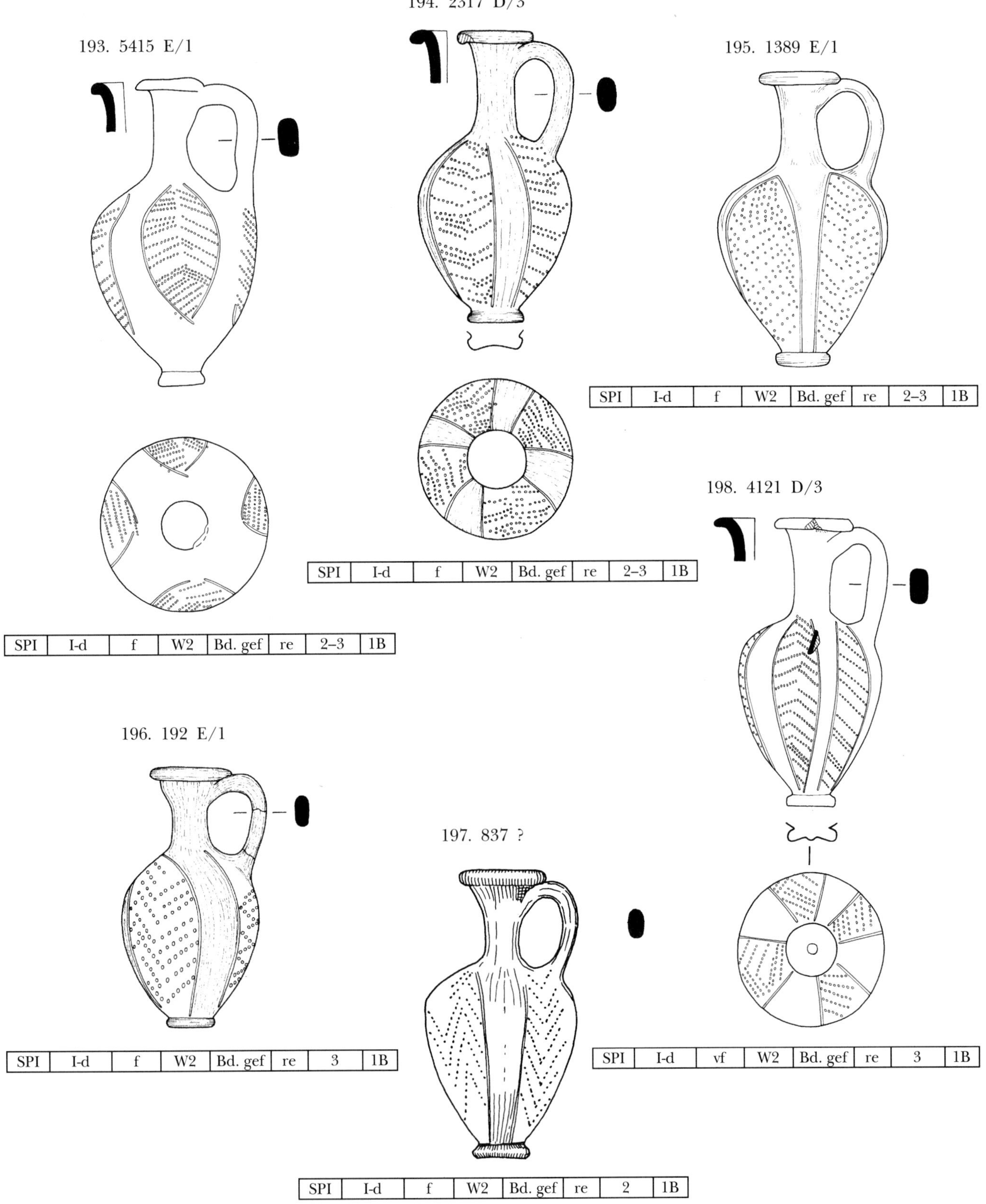

SPI	I-d	f	W2	Bd. gef	re	2–3	1B

SPI	I-d	f	W2	Bd. gef	re	2–3	1B

SPI	I-d	f	W2	Bd. gef	re	2–3	1B

SPI	I-d	f	W2	Bd. gef	re	3	1B

SPI	I-d	vf	W2	Bd. gef	re	3	1B

SPI	I-d	f	W2	Bd. gef	re	2	1B

1:2

Late Egyptian Type Group L.1.3b

Plate 41

200. 0877 Vienna A2639 A/II-m/11 planum 3–4 grave 6 Phase E/2–1 (67/025) Plate 42

SPI	I-d	f	W2	Bd. gef	re	3	1B

D. 2.7 cm. Nd. 1.2 cm. pht. 9.4 cm. Md 5.6 cm. Wd. 0.4 cm.
Incomplete
Surface colour: 7.5YR5–6/6 brown red: burnished slip: 10YR4/1 dark grey
Break: grey core, brown reduction zones
Decoration: Four unequal lozenges infilled with horizontal chevrons made with an eight-toothed comb.
Previously published: TD V, 157, 158.

201. 2954 Vienna TDS 2954 A/II-m/17 grave 3 Phase D/2 (79/128) Plate 42

SPI	I-d	f	W2	Bd. gef	mi	2	1B

Nd. 1.2 cm. Bd. 1.85 cm. pht. 7.6 cm. Md. 5.55 cm. Wd. 0.3 cm.
Intact
Surface colour: 5YR5/1 grey; burnished slip: 10YR3/1 very dark grey
Break: dark grey core, thin red oxidation zones
Decoration: Four unequal lozenges infilled with horizontal chevrons made with an eight-toothed comb.
Previously published: TD XVI, 372, fig. 297, no. 11.; KOPETZKY, *The MB IIB-Corpus of the Hyksos Period at Tell el-Dab^ca,* 2007, 198 fig. 3.12.

202. 1378 Vienna A2938 A/II-l/14 planum 3 grave 5 Phase E/1 (68/089) Plate 42

SPI	I-d	f	W2	Bd. gef	re	2–3	1B

Nd. 1.35 cm. Bd. 1.8 cm. pht. 8.8 cm. Md 6.1 cm. Wd. 0.3 cm.
Intact
Surface colour: 2.5Y5/1 grey: burnished slip: 2.5Y5/3 light olive brown
Break: uniform grey
Decoration: Four unequal lozenges infilled with horizontal chevrons made with an eight-toothed comb.
Previously published: TD XVI, 254, fig. 189b, no. 16.

203. 3519 Cairo A/II-s/18 grave 1 Phase E/1 (81/401) Plate 42

SPI	I-d	vf	W2	Bd. gef	re	3	1B

Nd. 1.2 cm. Bd. 1.6 cm. pht. 7.1 cm. Md 5.1 cm. Wd. 0.4 cm.
Incomplete
Surface colour: 10YR1/1 dark grey; burnished slip: 10YR2/1 black
Break: uniform greyish brown
Decoration: Four unequal lozenges infilled with carelessly executed horizontal chevrons made with an eight-toothed comb.
Previously published: TD XVI, 293, fig. 214, no. 4.

204. 1359 Vienna A2928 A/II-n/11 grave 5 Phase E/1 (68/085) Plate 42

SPI	I-d	f	W2	Bd. gef	re	2	1B

Nd. 1.2 cm. Bd. 1.7 cm. pht. 7.2 cm. Md 6.0 cm. Wd. 0.3 cm.
Incomplete
Surface colour: 10YR5/1–2 grey; burnished slip: 7.5YR2/0 black
Break: grey brown core, grey reduction zones
Decoration: Four unequal lozenges infilled with horizontal chevrons made with an eight-toothed comb.
Previously published: TD V, 199, 200.

205. 2143 Vienna A3440 A/II-l/16 grave 2 Phase E/1 (69/075) Plate 42

SPI	I-d	f	W2	Bd. gef	re	2–3	1B

Bd. 1.9 cm. pht. 6.9 cm. Md 6.9 cm. Wd. 0.25 cm.
Incomplete
Surface colour: 2.5Y5/1 grey: burnished slip: 2.5Y3/1 very dark grey
Break: uniform grey
Decoration: Four unequal lozenges infilled with poorly fashioned horizontal chevrons made with an eight-toothed comb.
BNL JH393 Egyptian Nile Clay[601]
Previously published: TD XVI, 263, fig. 192a, no. 14.

206. 8396B TD A/IV-dep planum 5–6 pit 112 Phase ? (94/314) Plate 42

SPI	I-d	f	W2	Bd. gef	re	2	1B

Bd. 2.05 cm. pht. 8.2 cm. Md 6.0 cm. Wd. 0.4 cm.
Incomplete
Surface colour: 10YR6/8 brownish yellow; burnished slip: 2.5YR5/2 mat red
Break: brown in, thin black reduction zones
Decoration: Four unequal lozenges infilled with horizontal chevrons made with an eight-toothed comb.

207. 2162 Vienna A3453 A/II-l/16 grave 2 Phase E/1 (69/065) Plate 43

SPI	I-d	f	W2	Bd. Gef	re	3	1B

Nd. 1.3 cm. Bd. 1.9 cm. pht. 7.1 cm. Md. 5.4 cm. Wd. 0.3 cm.
Restored from sherds, incomplete
Surface colour: 2.5Y6/1 grey; burnished slip: 2.5Y4/1 dark grey
Break: red core, red and grey reduction zones
Decoration: Four unequal lozenges infilled with horizontal zigzags made with a twelve-toothed comb.
Previously published: TD XVI, 269, fig. 194a, no. 8.

208. 7062L TD F/I-p/21 pit 3 Phase a/2 (89/060) Plate 43

SPI	I-b-2	f	W2	Bd. gef	re	2–3	1B

Bd. 1.7 cm. pht. 6.0 cm. Md 5.3 cm. Wd. 0.4 cm.
Incomplete
Surface colour: 5Y2/1–2 black: burnished slip: 10YR3/1 very dark grey
Break: brown in, thin black reduction zones
Decoration: Remains of three (out of four ?) unequal lozenges preserved filled with carelessly made horizontal chevrons impressed with a six-toothed comb.

209. 0879A Vienna A2641 A/II-m/11 grave 6 Phase E/2–1 (67/025) Plate 43

SPI	I-d	f	W2	Bd. gef	re	2–3	1B

Bd. 2.1 cm. pht. 2.0 cm. Md 5.6 cm. Wd. 0.5 cm.
Incomplete

[601] P. McGOVERN, *The Foreign Relations of the Hyksos,* Oxford, 2000, 134 no. JH393.

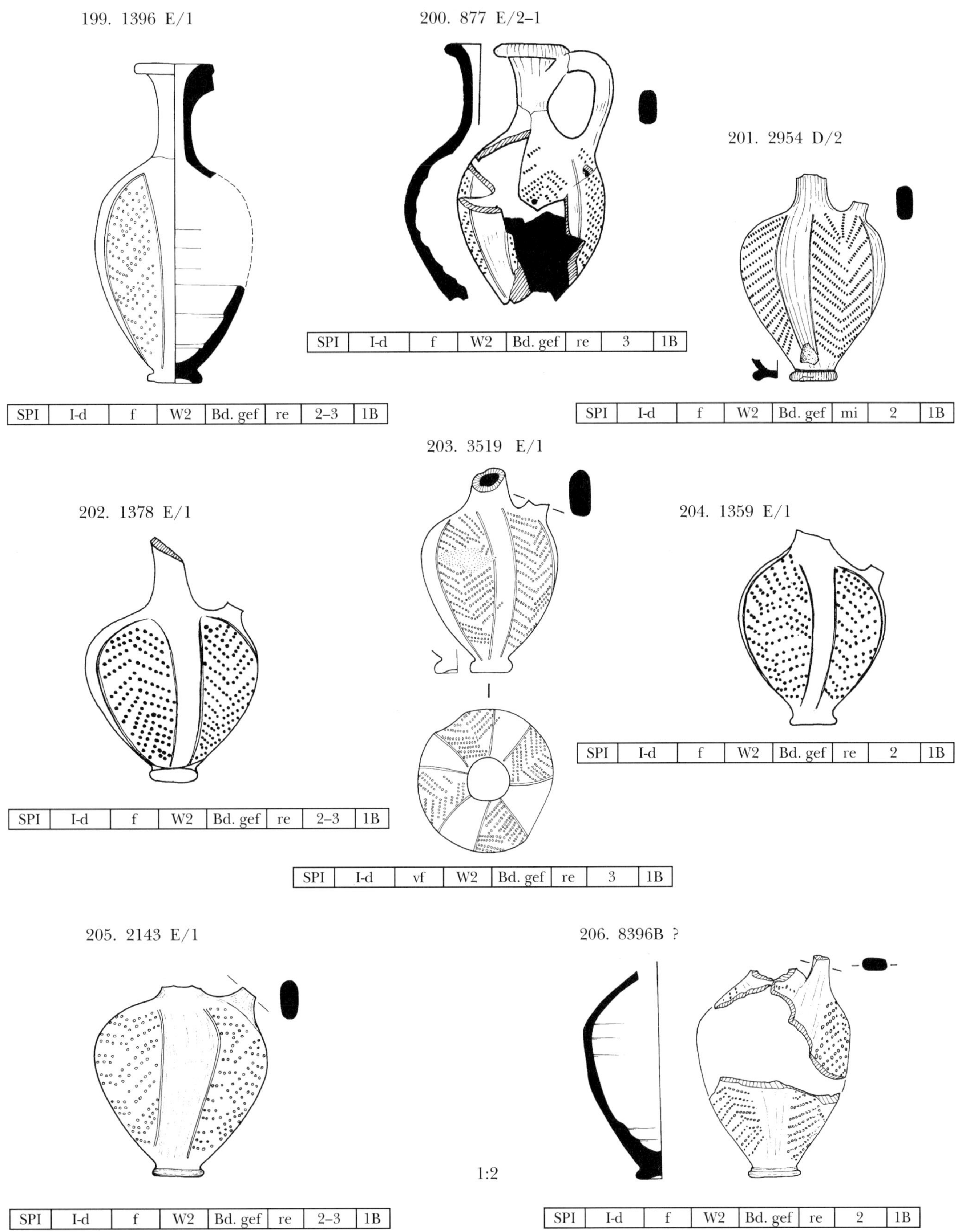

Late Egyptian Type Group L.1.3b

Plate 42

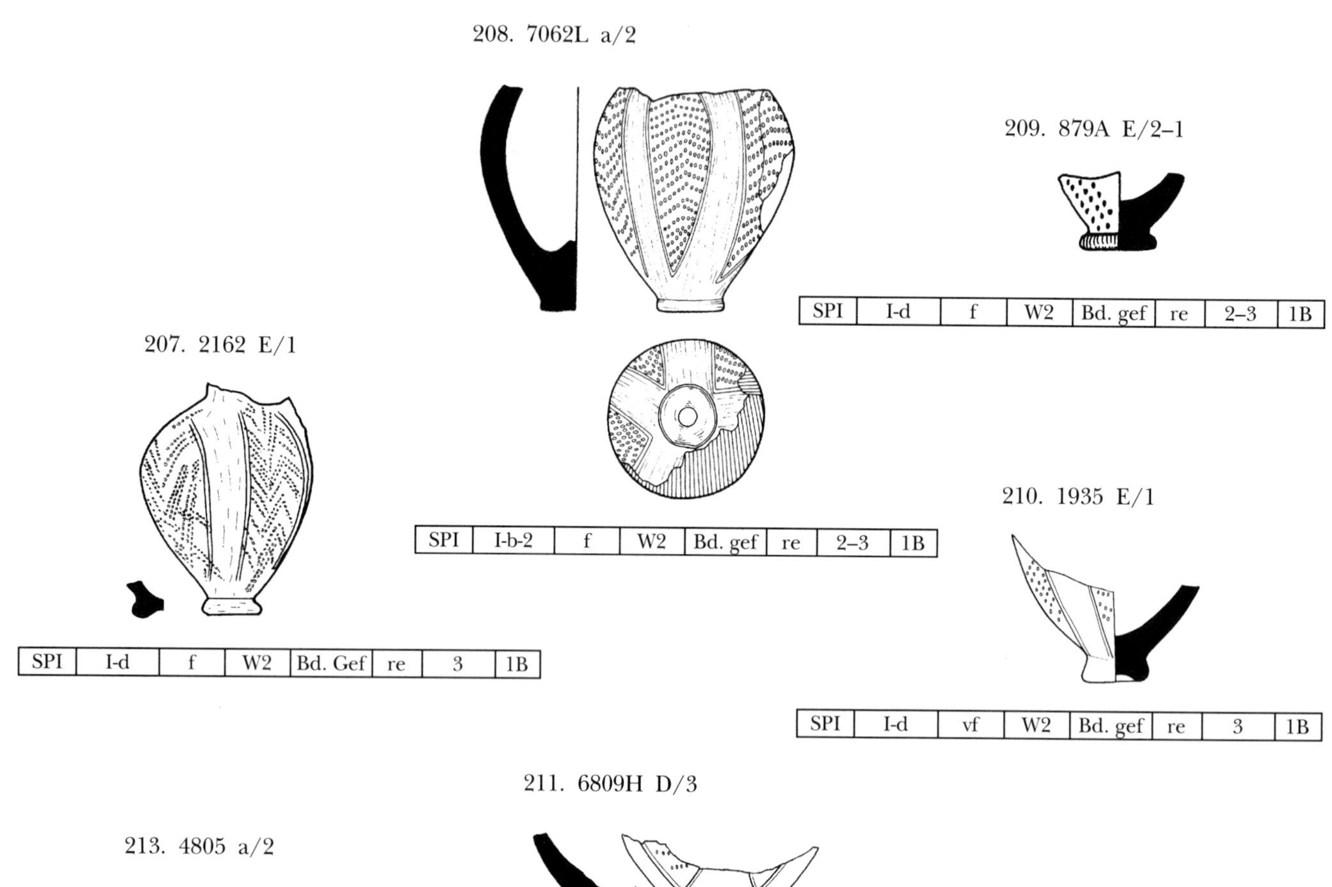

208. 7062L a/2

SPI	I-b-2	f	W2	Bd. gef	re	2–3	1B

209. 879A E/2–1

SPI	I-d	f	W2	Bd. gef	re	2–3	1B

207. 2162 E/1

SPI	I-d	f	W2	Bd. Gef	re	3	1B

210. 1935 E/1

SPI	I-d	vf	W2	Bd. gef	re	3	1B

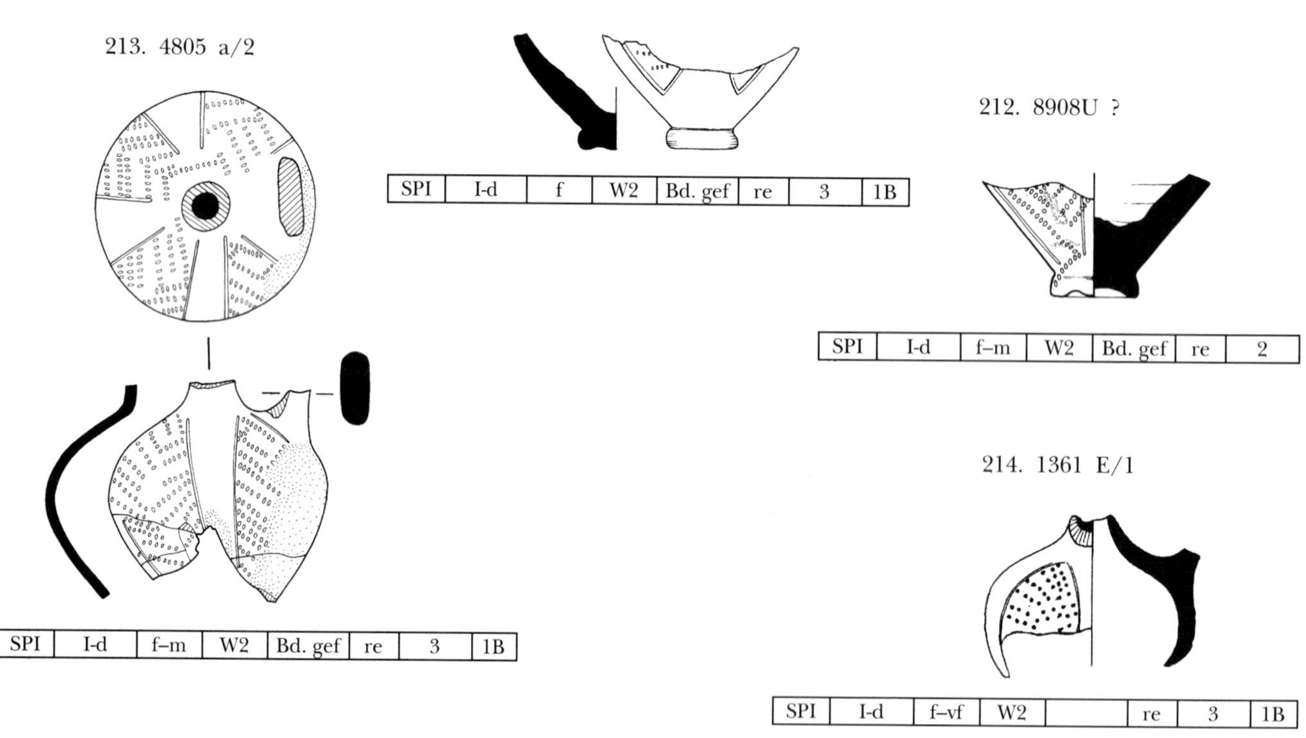

211. 6809H D/3

SPI	I-d	f	W2	Bd. gef	re	3	1B

213. 4805 a/2

SPI	I-d	f–m	W2	Bd. gef	re	3	1B

212. 8908U ?

SPI	I-d	f–m	W2	Bd. gef	re	2

214. 1361 E/1

SPI	I-d	f–vf	W2		re	3	1B

1:2

Late Egyptian Type Group L.1.3b

Plate 43

Surface colour: 7.5YR5–6/6 brown red: burnished slip: 10YR4/1 dark grey
Break: grey core, brown reduction zones
Decoration: Four unequal lozenges infilled with horizontal chevrons made with an eight-toothed comb.
Previously published: TD V, 157, 158.
Possibly base to 0877

210. 1935 Vienna A3310 A/II-n/11 grave 5 Phase E/1 (69/006) Plate 43

SPI	I-d	vf	W2	Bd. gef	re	3	1B

Bd. 1.8 cm. pht. 3.9 cm. Wd. 0.35 cm.
Incomplete
Surface colour: 10YR6/3 light brown; burnished slip: 10YR4/1–5/4 dark grey – yellow brown
Break: black core, brown reduction zones
Decoration: Four unequal lozenges infilled with horizontal chevrons made with an eight-toothed comb.
Previously published: TD V, 199–200.
Possibly base to 1361

211. 6809H TD A/V-p/19 planum 4–5 Phase D/3 (88/056) Plate 43

SPI	I-d	f	W2	Bd. gef	re	3	1B

Bd. 2.0 cm. pht. 2.5 cm. Wd. 0.5 cm.
Incomplete
Surface colour: 10YR4/1 dark grey; burnished slip: 5YR2/1 black
Break: uniform dark grey
Decoration: Four unequal lozenges infilled with horizontal chevrons made with an eight-toothed comb. Remainder vertically burnished.
Previously published: TD XI, 41–42 no. 11.

212. 8908U TD H/III-t/14 planum 1–2 Phase ? (99/145) Plate 43

SPI	I-d	f–m	W2	Bd. gef	re	2

Bd. 2.1 cm. pht. 3.4 cm. Wd. 0.8 cm.
Restored from sherds, incomplete
Surface colour: 10YR5/2 grey brown; burnished slip: 5YR4/1 dark grey
Break: dark grey interior, brown exterior
Decoration: Four unequal lozenges infilled with horizontal chevrons made with an eight-toothed comb.

213. 4805 TD F/I-l/20 intrusive within grave 23 (84/174) Plate 43

SPI	I-d	f–m	W2	Bd. gef	re	3	1B

Nd. 1.3 cm. pht. 6.0 cm. Md. 6.0 cm. Wd. 0.3 cm.
Intact
Surface colour: 10YR6/5 brownish grey; burnished slip: 7.5YR4/2 dark brown
Break: brown core, dark grey reduction zones
Decoration: Four unequal lozenges infilled with horizontal chevrons made with an eight-toothed comb.

214. 1361 Vienna A2930 A/II-n/11 grave 5 Phase E/1 (68/085) Plate 43

SPI	I-d	f–vf	W2	–	re	3	1B

Nd. 1.3 cm. pht. 4.6 cm. Md. 5.8 cm. Wd. 0.35 cm.
Incomplete
Surface colour: 10YR4/1–5/2 dk grey; burnished slip: 10YR3/1–4/2 very dark grey
Break: grey brown core, dark grey reduction zones
Decoration: Four unequal lozenges infilled with horizontal chevrons made with an eight-toothed comb.
Previously published: TD V, 199.

Type Group L.1.3c

215. 2335 Vienna A3557 A/II-m/15 grave 3 Phase D/3 (69/104) Plate 44

SPI	I-d	f	W2	Bd. gef	re	2–3	1B

D. 3.1 cm. Nd 1.3 cm. Bd. 1.8 cm. H. 10.2 cm. Md. 7.0 cm. Wd. 0.3 cm.
VI 68.62
Intact
Surface colour: 2.5Y5/1 grey; burnished slip: 2.5Y5/1 grey
Break: dark grey core, brownish grey reduction zones
Decoration: Three unequal lozenges infilled with poorly executed horizontal zigzags made with an eight-toothed comb.
Previously published: TD XVI, 310, fig. 231, no. 10.

216. 0537 Vienna A2380 A/II-m/13 grave 3 Phase D/3 (67/084) Plate 44

SPI	I-d	f	W2	Bd. gef	re	3	1B

D. 2.4 cm. Nd 1.5 cm. Bd. 2.0 cm. H. 10.4 cm. Md. 7.1 cm. Wd. 0.4 cm.
VI 68.26
Incomplete
Surface colour: 10YR5/1.5–3 grey brown; burnished slip: 10YR3.5/1 very dark grey
Break: grey core, light grey reduction zones
Decoration: Three unequal lozenges infilled with horizontal zigzags made with a ten-toothed comb.
Previously published: TD V, 266.

217. 8677 TD A/II-o/14 grave 43 Phase E/1 (98/085) Plate 44

SPI	I-d	f	W2	Bd. gef	re	2–3	1B

D. 3.0 cm. Nd 1.3 cm. Bd. 2.0 cm. H. 9.8 cm. Md. 6.6 cm. Wd. 0.4 cm.
VI 67.34
Intact
Surface colour: 10YR5/3 brown; burnished slip: 10YR4/1 dark grey
Break: dark grey in, greenish brownish grey out
Decoration: Three lozenges infilled with horizontal lines made with an eight-toothed comb.
Previously published: TD XVI, 289, fig. 209, no. 28.

218. 0184 Cairo JE 91557H A/II-l/12 grave 2 Phase E/1 (66/039) Plate 44

SPI	I-d	f	W2	Bd. gef	re	3	1B

D. 2.75 cm. Nd 1.2 cm. Bd. 1.9 cm. H. 9.3 cm. Md. 6.1 cm. Wd. 0.3 cm.
VI 65.59
Intact
Surface colour: 5YR5/2 reddish grey; burnished slip: 5YR2/2 dark red brown

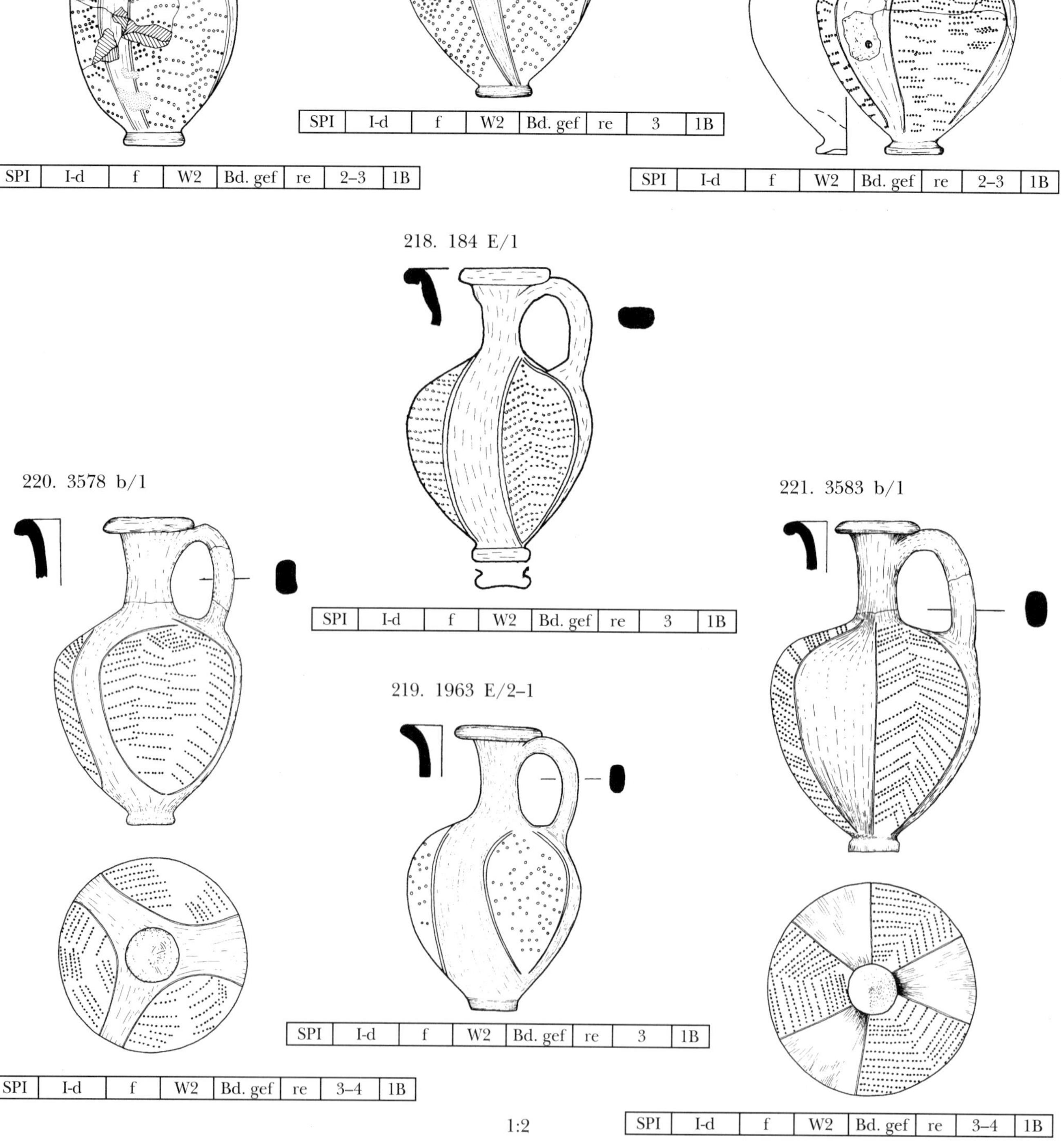

Late Egyptian Type Group L.1.3c

Plate 44

Break: not visible
Decoration: Three unequal lozenges infilled with horizontal zigzags made with an eight-toothed comb.
Previously published: *TD V*, 188.

219. 1963 Vienna A1707 A/II-m/12 grave 10 Phase E/2–1 (69/003) Plate 44

SPI	I-d	f	W2	Bd. gef	re	3	1B

D. 2.9 cm. Nd 1.3 cm. Bd. 1.7 cm. H. 9.2 cm. Md. 6.0 cm. Wd. 0.3 cm.
VI 65.21
Intact
Surface colour: 10YR5/1–2 grey; burnished slip: 10YR3/1 very dark grey
Break: not visible
Decoration: Three unequal lozenges infilled with horizontal zigzags made with an eight-toothed comb.
Previously published: *TD V*, 161, 164.

220. 3578 Cairo F/I-i/22 grave 7 Phase b/1 (81/167) Plate 44

SPI	I-d	f	W2	Bd. gef	re	3–4	1B

D. 3.0 cm. Nd 1.4 cm. Bd. 1.6 cm. H. 10.0 cm. Md. 6.5 cm. Wd. 0.4 cm.
VI 65.00
Intact
Surface colour: 10YR4/1 dark grey; burnished slip: 10YR2/1 black
Break: not visible
Decoration: Three unequal lozenges infilled with horizontal zigzags made with an eight-toothed comb.

221. 3583 Cairo F/I-i/22 grave 7 Phase b/1 (81/169) Plate 44

SPI	I-d	f	W2	Bd. gef	re	3–4	1B

D. 2.9 cm. Nd 1.3 cm. Bd. 1.7 cm. H. 10.8 cm. Md. 7.0 cm. Wd. 0.4 cm.
VI 64.81
Intact
Surface colour: 10YR4/1 dark grey; burnished slip: 10YR3/1 very dark grey
Break: not visible
Decoration: Three unequal lozenges infilled with horizontal zigzags made with an eight-toothed comb.
Previously illustrated: KOPETZKY, *The MB IIB-Corpus of the Hyksos Period at Tell el-Dab^ca*, 2007, 198 fig. 3.2.

222. 2144 Vienna A3441 A/II-l/16 grave 2 Phase E/1 (69/075) Plate 45

SPI	I-d	f	W2	Bd. gef	re	3	1B

D. 3.0 cm. Nd 1.2 cm. Bd. 1.6 cm. H. 9.2 cm. Md. 5.8 cm. Wd. 0.3 cm.
VI 63.04
Intact
Surface colour: 2.5Y5/1 grey; burnished slip: 2.5Y3/1 very dark grey
Break: not visible
Decoration: Three unequal lozenges infilled with horizontal chevrons made with an eight-toothed comb.
Previously published: *TD XVI*, 263, fig. 192a, no. 13.

223. 2277 Cairo JE 91706 A/II-k/14 grave 1 Phase E/1 or D/3 (69/087) Plate 45

SPI	I-d	f	W2	Bd. gef	re	2–3	1B

D. 3.1 cm. Nd 1.2 cm. Bd. 1.9 cm. H. 9.4 cm. Md. 5.9 cm. Wd. 0.3 cm.
VI 62.75
Intact
Surface colour: 10YR6/2 grey; burnished slip: 10YR3/1 very dark grey
Break: not visible
Decoration: Three lozenges infilled with poorly made chevrons made with an eight-toothed comb.
Previously published: *TD XVI*, 297, fig. 216b, no. 10.

224. 1289 Vienna A2875 A/II-n/11 grave 3 Phase E/1 (68/033) Plate 45

SPI	I-d	f–m	W2	Bd. gef	re	2	1B

D. 3.2 cm. Nd 1.3 cm. Bd. 2.0 cm. H. 10.7 cm. Md. 6.7 cm. Wd. 0.4 cm.
VI 62.61
Incomplete
Surface colour: 10YR4/2 dark grey brown; burnished slip: 2.5Y/1 black
Break: brown core, dark grey reduction zones
Decoration: Three unequal lozenges infilled with horizontal zigzags made with an eight-toothed comb.
Previously published: *TD V*, 234, 235.

225. 1924 Vienna A1704 A/II-n/12 grave 7 Phase E/1 (69/002) Plate 45

SPI	I-d	f	W2	Bd. gef	re	3	1B

D. 2.75 cm. Nd 1.4 cm. Bd. 1.7 cm. H. 9.6 cm. Md. 6.0 cm. Wd. 0.3 cm.
VI 62.50
Intact
Surface colour: 10YR5/1–6/3 grey; burnished slip: 10YR3/1 very dark grey
Break: brown core, grey reduction zones
Decoration: Three unequal lozenges infilled with horizontal zigzags made with an eight-toothed comb.
Previously published: BIETAK, *EI* 21, 14*; *TD V*, 208, 209; *PuF* 224 nr 261.

226. 2938 Cairo A/II-p/20 grave 4 Phase E/1 (79/119) Plate 45

SPI	I-d	f	W2	Bd. gef	re	3	1B

D. 3.1 cm. Nd 1.36 cm. Bd. 1.7 cm. H. 10.9 cm. Md. 6.8 cm. Wd. 0.4 cm.
VI 62.38
Restored from sherds, incomplete
Surface colour: 10YR4/1 dark grey; burnished slip: 10YR3/1 very dark grey
Break: not visible
Decoration: Three unequal lozenges infilled with poorly executed horizontal zigzags made with a fourteen-toothed comb.

227. 1926 Vienna A3348 A/II-n/12 grave 7 Phase E/1 (69/003) Plate 45

SPI	I-d	f	W2	Bd. gef	re	3	1B

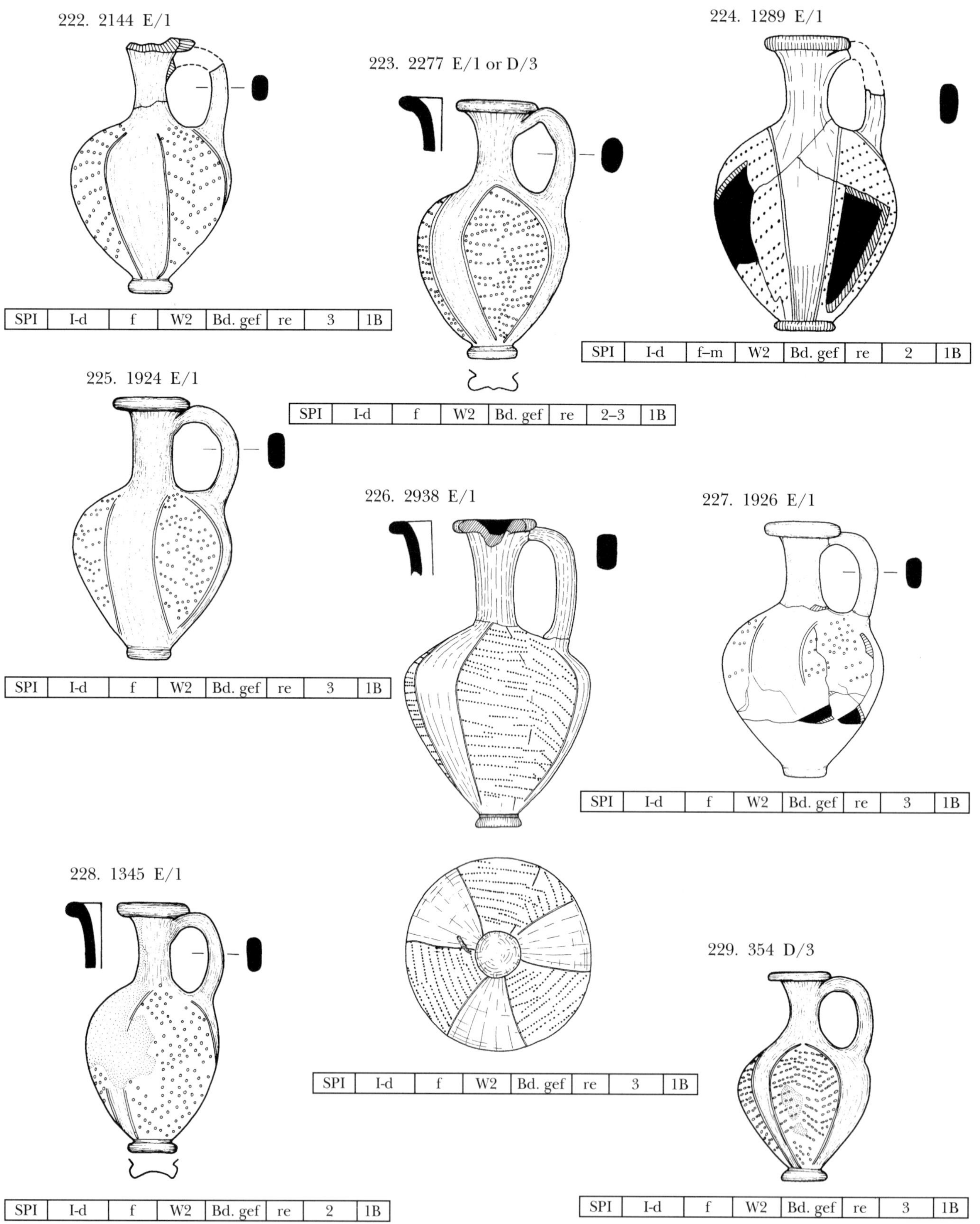

1:2

Late Egyptian Type Group L.1.3c

Plate 45

D. 2.7 cm. Nd 1.15 cm. Bd. 1.6 cm. H. 9.3 cm. Md. 5.8 cm. Wd. 0.3 cm.
VI 62.36
Incomplete
Surface colour: 10YR6/2–3 light grey brown; burnished slip: 10YR3/1 very dark grey
Break: black core, thin dark grey brown reduction zones
Decoration: Three unequal lozenges infilled with horizontal zigzags made with an eight-toothed comb.
Previously published: BIETAK, *EI* 21, 14*; *TD V,* 208, 209.

228. 1345 Cairo JE 91610 A/II-l/14 grave 5 Phase E/1 (68/080) Plate 45

SPI	I-d	f	W2	Bd. gef	re	2	1B

D. 2.6 cm. Nd 1.2 cm. Bd. 1.7 cm. H. 8.3 cm. Md. 5.1 cm. Wd. 0.3 cm.
VI 61.44
Intact
Surface colour: 10YR6/2 grey; burnished slip: 10YR3/1 very dark grey
Break: not visible
Decoration: Three unequal lozenges infilled with poorly executed horizontal zigzags made with an eight-toothed comb.
Previously published: TD XVI, 254, fig. 189b, no. 21.

229. 0354 Vienna A1640 A/I-g/3 grave 1 Phase D/3 (66/052) Plate 45

SPI	I-d	f	W2	Bd. gef	re	3	1B

D. 2.7 cm. Nd 1.2 cm. Bd. 1.75 cm. H. 10.0 cm. Md. 6.15 cm. Wd. 0.3 cm.
VI 61.50
Intact, rim chipped
Surface colour: 2.5Y5/1 grey; burnished slip: 2.5Y5/1 grey
Break: black core, grey and dark grey reduction zones
Decoration: Three unequal lozenges infilled with horizontal zigzags made with an eight-toothed comb.

230. 2117 Vienna A1713 A/II-l/16 grave 1 Phase E/1 (69/051) Plate 46

SPI	I-d	f	W2	Bd. gef	re	3	1B

D. 2.4 cm. Nd 1.2 cm. Bd. 1.7 cm. H. 8.9 cm. Md. 5.4 cm. Wd. 0.3 cm.
VI 60.67
Intact
Surface colour: 10YR6/1 grey; burnished slip: 10YR3/1 very dark grey
Break: not visible
Decoration: Three unequal lozenges infilled with horizontal zigzags made with an eight-toothed comb.
Previously published: TD XVI, 263, fig. 192a, no. 2.

231. 2132 Vienna A3433 A/II-l/16 grave 1 Phase E/1 (69/061) Plate 46

SPI	I-d	f	W2	Bd. gef	re	3	1B

D. 2.4 cm. Nd 1.1 cm. Bd. 2.0 cm. H. 9.4 cm. Md. 5.7 cm. Wd. 0.3 cm.
VI 60.63
Restored from sherds, complete
Surface colour: 10YR5/1 grey; burnished slip: 10YR3/1 very dark grey
Break: dark grey core, light grey reduction zones
Decoration: Three unequal lozenges infilled with horizontal zigzags made with an eight-toothed comb.
Previously published: TD XVI, 263, fig. 192a, no. 7.

232. 5794 TD F/I-m/19 grave 11 Phase b/1 (86/037) Plates 46, 140

SPI	I-d	f	W2	Bd. gef	re	3–4	1B

D. 2.35 cm. Nd 1.25 cm. Bd. 1.95 cm. H. 8.25 cm. Md. 5.0 cm. Wd. 0.4 cm.
VI 60.60
Intact
Surface colour: 10YR4/1 dark grey; burnished slip: 7.5YR3/0 black
Break: not visible
Decoration: Three unequal lozenges infilled with horizontal zigzags made with a twelve-toothed comb.

233. 2124 Vienna A3427 A/II-l/16 grave 1 Phase E/1 (69/052) Plate 46

SPI	I-d	f	W2	Bd. gef	re	3	1B

D. 2.4 cm. Nd 1.2 cm. Bd. 1.9 cm. H. 9.1 cm. Md. 5.5 cm. Wd. 0.3 cm.
VI 60.43
Incomplete
Surface colour: 2.5Y6/1 grey; burnished slip: 2.5Y4/1 very dark grey
Break: dark grey core, light grey reduction zones
Decoration: Three unequal lozenges infilled with poorly executed horizontal zigzags made with an eight-toothed comb.
Previously published: TD XVI, 263, fig. 192a, no. 4.

234. 2153 Vienna A3448 A/II-l/16 grave 2 Phase E/1 (69/064) Plate 46

SPI	I-d	f	W2	Bd. gef	re	3	1B

D. 2.8 cm. Nd 1.2 cm. Bd. 2.0 cm. H. 9.6 cm. Md. 5.8 cm. Wd. 0.3 cm.
VI 60.41
Intact
Surface colour: 2.5Y5/1 grey; burnished slip: 2.5Y3/1 very dark grey
Break: not visible
Decoration: Three unequal lozenges infilled with horizontal zigzags made with a twelve-toothed comb.
Previously published: TD XVI, 269, fig. 194a, no. 7.

235. 0369 Vienna A2303 A/I-g/3 grave 1 Phase D/3 (66/052) Plate 46

SPI	I-d	f	W2	Bd. gef	re	3	1B

D. 2.55 cm. Nd 1.1 cm. Bd. 1.8 cm. H. 8.8 cm. Md. 5.3 cm. Wd. 0.3 cm.
VI 60.22
Intact, rim chipped
Surface colour: 2.5Y5/1 grey; burnished slip: 2.5Y4/1 dark grey
Break: black core, grey and dark grey reduction zones
Decoration: Three unequal lozenges infilled with horizontal zigzags made with an eight-toothed comb.

236. 1500 Cairo JE 91617 A/II-n/13 grave 5 Phase E/1 (69/003) Plate 46

SPI	I-d	f–vf	W2	Bd. gef	re	3	1B

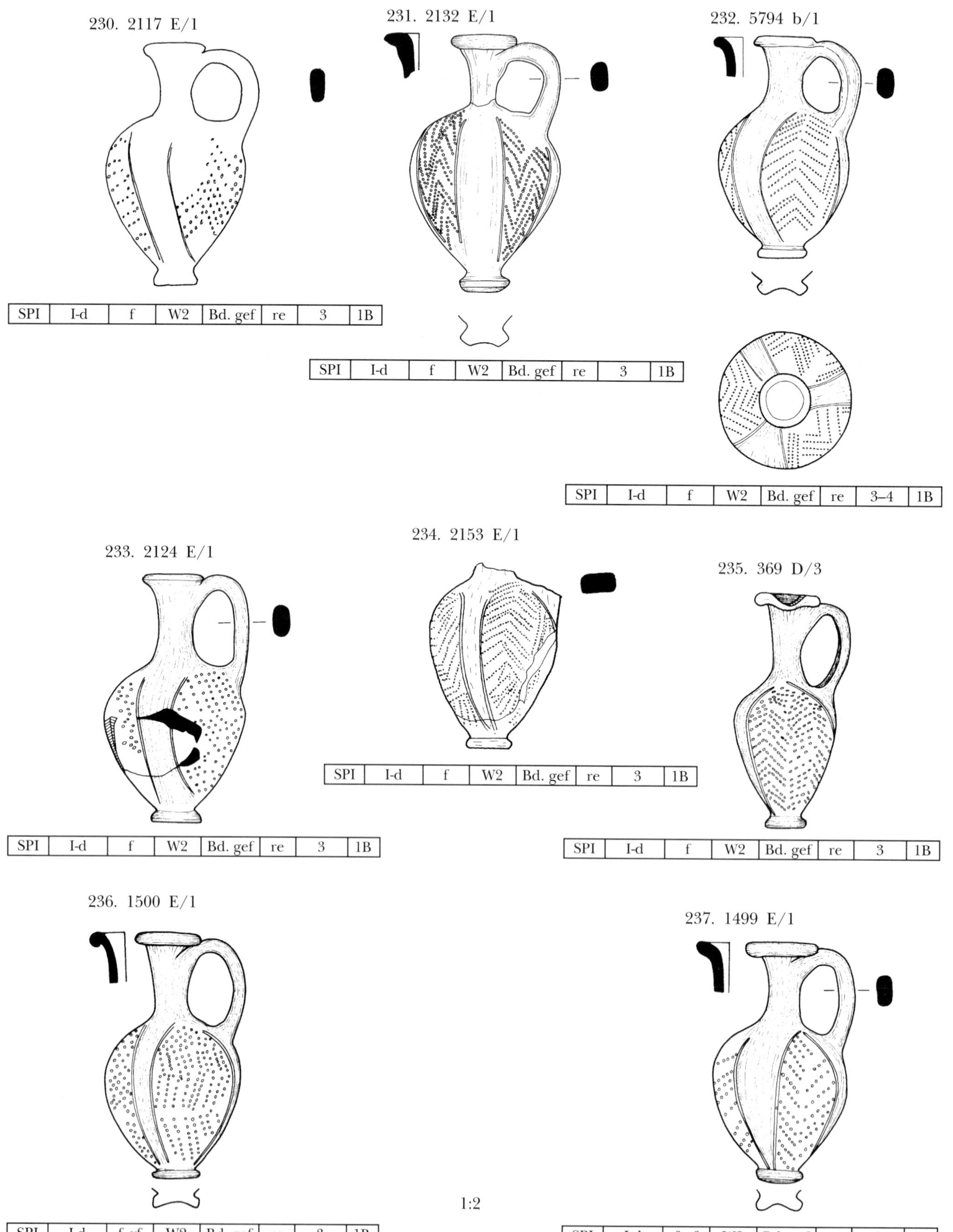

230. 2117 E/1	SPI	I-d	f	W2	Bd. gef	re	3	1B
231. 2132 E/1	SPI	I-d	f	W2	Bd. gef	re	3	1B
232. 5794 b/1	SPI	I-d	f	W2	Bd. gef	re	3–4	1B
233. 2124 E/1	SPI	I-d	f	W2	Bd. gef	re	3	1B
234. 2153 E/1	SPI	I-d	f	W2	Bd. gef	re	3	1B
235. 369 D/3	SPI	I-d	f	W2	Bd. gef	re	3	1B
236. 1500 E/1	SPI	I-d	f–vf	W2	Bd. gef	re	3	1B
237. 1499 E/1	SPI	I-d	f–vf	W2	Bd. gef	re	3	1B

Late Egyptian Type Group L.1.3c

Plate 46

D. 2.6 cm. Nd 1.3 cm. Bd. 1.7 cm. H. 8.8 cm. Md. 5.3 cm. Wd. 0.3 cm.
VI 60.22
Intact
Surface colour: 5YR5/3 red brown; burnished slip: 5YR3/1 very dark grey
Break: not visible
Decoration: Three unequal lozenges infilled with vertical zigzags made with an eight-toothed comb.
Previously published; Bietak, *MDAIK* 26, pl. 19d; Kaplan, *Tell el-Yahudiyeh Ware,* fig. 50a; *TD V,* 211.

237. 1499 Cairo JE 91616 A/II-n/13 grave 5 Phase E/1 (69/003) Plate 46

SPI	I-d	f–vf	W2	Bd. gef	re	3	1B

D. 2.6 cm. Nd 1.3 cm. Bd. 1.7 cm. H. 8.8 cm. Md. 5.3 cm. Wd. 0.3 cm.
VI 60.22
Intact
Surface colour: 5YR5/3 red brown; burnished slip: 5YR3/1 very dark grey
Break: not visible
Decoration: Three unequal lozenges infilled with horizontal zigzags made with an eight-toothed comb.
Previously published: TD V, 211.

238. 2316 Vienna A3543 A/II-m/15 grave 3 Phase D/3 (69/110) Plate 47

SPI	I-d	F	W2	Bd. gef	re	2–3	1B

D. 3.0 cm. Nd. 1.4 cm. Bd. 1.7 cm. H. 9.5 cm. Md 5.7 cm. Wd. 0.4 cm.
VI 60.00
Restored from sherds, complete
Surface colour: 2.5Y5/1 grey; burnished slip: 2.5Y3/1 light olive brown
Break: not visible
Decoration: Three unequal lozenges infilled with horizontal zigzags made with a twelve-toothed comb.
Previously published: TD XVI, 315, fig. 235, no. 19.

239. 3571 Cairo F/I-i/22 grave 4 Phase b/1 (81/253) Plate 47

SPI	I-d	f–m	W2	Bd. gef	re	3	1B

D. 2.8 cm. Nd 1.3 cm. Bd. 2.05 cm. H. 11.6 cm. Md. 6.6 cm. Wd. 0.3 cm.
VI 60.00
Incomplete
Surface colour: 10YR6/2 grey; burnished slip: 10YR3/1 very dark grey
Break: uniform dark grey
Decoration: Three unequal lozenges infilled with horizontal zigzags made with a ten-toothed comb.

240. 3517 Cairo A/II-s/18 grave 1 Phase E/1 (81/400) Plate 47

SPI	I-d	vf	W2	Bd. gef	re	3	1B

D. 2.8 cm. Nd 1.7 cm. Bd. 2.25 cm. H. 9.0 cm. Md. 5.4 cm. Wd. 0.4 cm.
VI 60.00
Intact
Surface colour: 10YR4/1 dark grey; burnished slip: 10YR3/1 very dark grey
Break: not visible
Decoration: Three unequal lozenges infilled with horizontal zigzags or chevrons made with an eight-toothed comb.
Previously published: TD XVI, 293, fig. 214, no. 2.

241. 0050 Vienna A2264 A/II-l/12 grave ?? Phase ? (66/006) Plate 47

SPI	I-d	f	W2	Bd. gef	re	2–3	1B

D. 3.2 cm. Nd 1.2 cm. Bd. 1.78 cm. H. 9.5 cm. Md. 5.7 cm. Wd. 0.4 cm.
VI 60.00
Intact
Surface colour: 10YR5/1–2 brown; burnished slip: 10YR2/1 black
Break: dark brown core, dark grey reduction zones
Decoration: Three unequal lozenges infilled with horizontal zigzags or chevrons made with an eight-toothed comb.

242. 1923 Vienna A1703 A/II-n/12 grave 7 Phase E/1 (69/002) Plate 47

SPI	I-d	f	W2	Bd. gef	re	3	1B

D. 2.9 cm. Nd 1.2 cm. Bd. 1.5 cm. H. 10.1 cm. Md. 6.0 cm. Wd. 0.3 cm.
VI 59.40
Intact
Surface colour: 10YR5–6/2–3 light greyish brown; burnished slip: 10YR3/1 very dark grey
Break: brown core, grey reduction zones
Decoration: Three unequal lozenges infilled with horizontal zigzags made with an eight-toothed comb.
Previously published: Bietak, *EI* 21, 14*; *TD V,* 208, 209.

243. 2330 Cairo JE 91714C A/II-m/15 grave 3 Phase D/3 (69/103) Plate 47

SPI	I-d	f	W2	Bd. gef	re	2–3	1B

D. 2.9 cm. Nd 1.3 cm. Bd. 1.9 cm. H. 9.3 cm. Md. 5.5 cm. Wd. 0.3 cm.
VI 59.13
Intact
Surface colour 10YR5/1 grey; burnished slip: 10YR3/1 very dark grey
Break: light brown core, grey reduction zones
Decoration: Three unequal lozenges infilled with poorly executed horizontal zigzags made with an eight-toothed comb.
Previously published: TD XVI, 310, fig. 231, no. 3.

244. 0230 Cairo JE 91563A A/II-l/12 grave 1 Phase E/1 (66/032) Plate 54

SPI	I-d	f	W2	Bd. gef	re	3	1B

D. 3.1 cm. Nd 1.4 cm. Bd. 2.3 cm. H. 11.4 cm. Md. 6.7 cm. Wd. 0.3 cm.
VI 58.77
Intact
Surface colour: 10YR4/2 dark grey brown; burnished slip: 10YR2/1 black
Break: dark grey core, greyish brown reduction zones
Decoration: Three unequal lozenges infilled with horizontal zigzags made with a ten-toothed comb.
Previously published: TD V, 176 179.

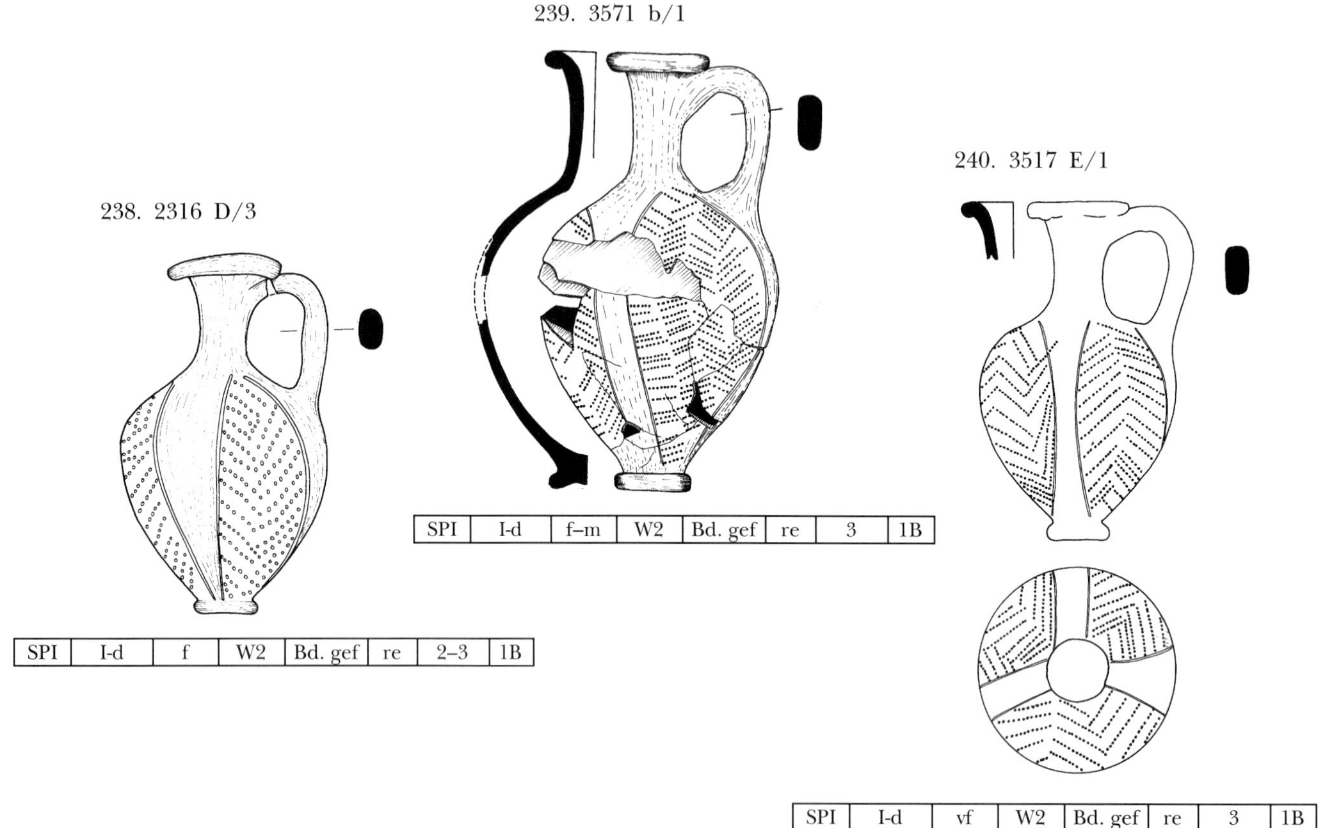

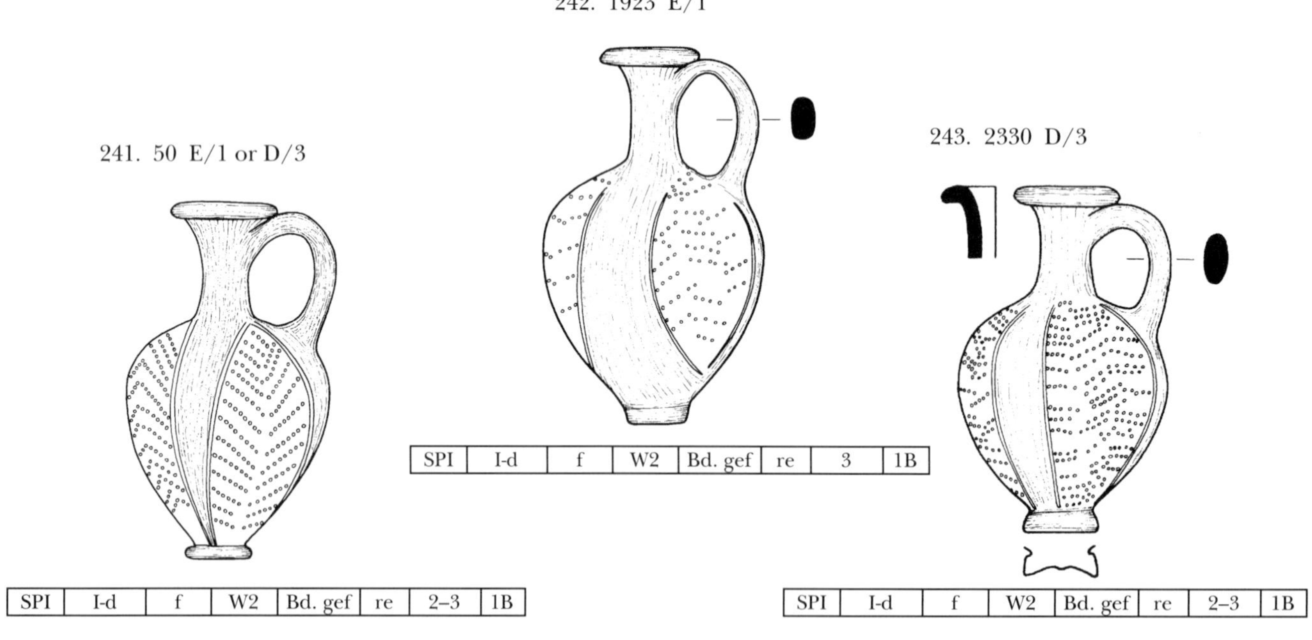

1:2

Late Egyptian Type Group L.1.3c

Plate 47

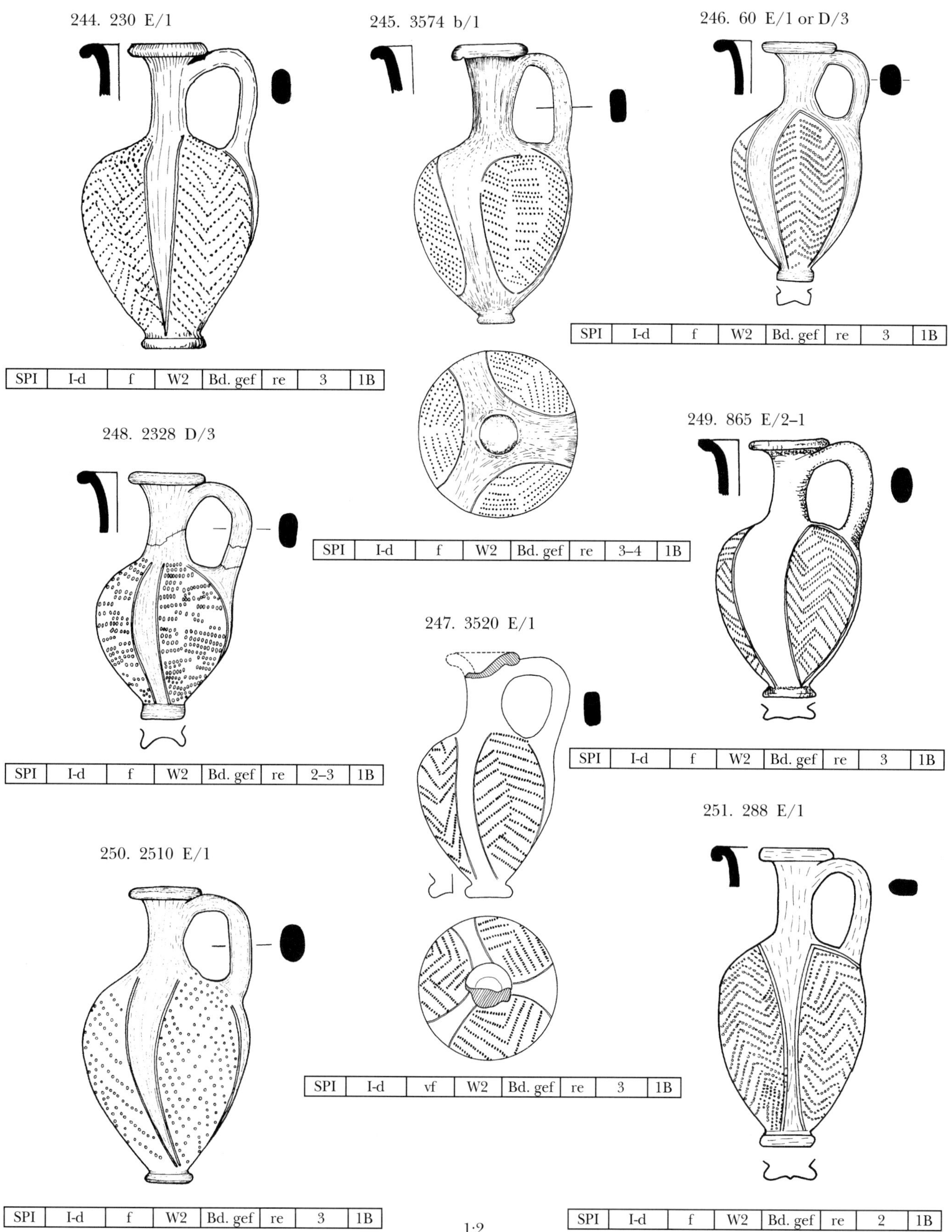

SPI	I-d	f	W2	Bd. gef	re	3	1B

SPI	I-d	f	W2	Bd. gef	re	3–4	1B

SPI	I-d	f	W2	Bd. gef	re	3	1B

SPI	I-d	f	W2	Bd. gef	re	2–3	1B

SPI	I-d	f	W2	Bd. gef	re	3	1B

SPI	I-d	vf	W2	Bd. gef	re	3	1B

SPI	I-d	f	W2	Bd. gef	re	3	1B

SPI	I-d	f	W2	Bd. gef	re	2	1B

1:2

Late Egyptian Type Group L.1.3c

Plate 48

245. 3574 Cairo F/I-i/22 grave 7 Phase b/1 (81/122) Plate 48

SPI	I-d	f	W2	Bd. gef	re	3–4	1B

D. 3.0 cm. Nd 1.4 cm. Bd. 1.4 cm. H. 10.4 cm. Md. 6.1 cm. Wd. 0.4 cm.
VI 58.65
Intact
Surface colour: 10YR4/1 dark grey; burnished slip: 10YR2/1 black
Break: not visible
Decoration: Three unequal lozenges infilled with horizontal zigzags made with an eight-toothed comb.

246. 0060 Cairo JE 91553 A/II-l/12 grave ?? Phase E/1 or D/3 (66/003) Plate 48

SPI	I-d	f	W2	Bd. gef	re	3	1B

D. 2.8 cm. Nd 1.3 cm. Bd. 1.4 cm. H. 8.7 cm. Md. 5.1 cm. Wd. 0.3 cm.
VI 58.62
Intact
Surface colour: 10YR3/1 very dark grey; burnished slip: 10YR5/2 brown
Break: not visible
Decoration: Three unequal lozenges infilled with horizontal zigzags made with an eight-toothed comb.

247. 3520 Cairo A/II-s/18 grave 1 Phase E/1 (81/402) Plate 48

SPI	I-d	vf	W2	Bd. gef	re	3	1B

D. 2.8 cm. Nd 1.3 cm. Bd. 1.8 cm. H. 9.0 cm. Md. 5.25 cm. Wd. 0.4 cm.
VI 58.33
Intact
Surface colour: 10YR4/1 dark grey; burnished slip: 10YR3/1 very dark grey
Break: not visible
Decoration: Three unequal lozenges infilled with horizontal chevrons or zigzags made with an eight-toothed comb.
Previously published: TD XVI, 293, fig. 214, no. 5.

248. 2328 Cairo JE 91714B A/II-m/15 grave 3 Phase D/3 (69/103) Plate 48

SPI	I-d	f	W2	Bd. gef	re	2–3	1B

D. 2.9 cm. Nd 1.3 cm. Bd. 1.7 cm. H. 9.2 cm. Md. 5.35 cm. Wd. 0.3 cm.
VI 58.15
Intact
Surface colour10YR5/1 grey; burnished slip: 10YR3/1 very dark grey
Break: uniform greyish brown
Decoration: Three unequal lozenges infilled with poorly executed horizontal zigzags made with an eight-toothed comb.
Previously published: TD XVI, 310, fig. 231, no. 1.

249. 0865 Cairo JE 91583 A/II-m/11 grave 6 Phase E/2–1 (67/030) Plate 48

SPI	I-d	f	W2	Bd. gef	re	3	1B

D. 3.0 cm. Nd 1.3 cm. Bd. 2.1 cm. H. 9.65 cm. Md. 5.6 cm. Wd. 0.35 cm.
VI 58.03
Restored from sherds, complete
Surface colour: 5YR5/1–2 grey-reddish grey; burnished slip: 5YR3/1 very dark grey
Break: uniform grey brown
Decoration: Three unequal lozenges infilled with horizontal zigzags made with a twelve-toothed comb.
Previously published: TD V, 157, 158.

250. 2120 Vienna A1714 A/II-l/16 grave 1 Phase E/1 (69/052) Plate 48

SPI	I-d	f	W2	Bd. gef	re	3	1B

D. 2.8 cm. Nd 1.3 cm. Bd. 1.8 cm. H. 10.9 cm. Md. 6.3 cm. Wd. 0.3 cm.
VI 57.79
Intact
Surface colour: 10YR6/1 grey; burnished slip: 10YR3/1 very dark grey
Break: not visible
Decoration: Three unequal lozenges infilled with horizontal zigzags made with an eight-toothed comb.
Previously published: TD XVI, 263, fig. 192a, no. 3.

251. 0288 Cairo JE 91176 A/II-l/12 planum 2–3 Phase E/1 (66/038) Plate 48

SPI	I-d	f	W2	Bd. gef	re	2	1B

D. 2.6 cm. Nd 1.3 cm. Bd. 1.9 cm. H. 10.2 cm. Md. 5.9 cm. Wd. 0.3 cm.
VI 57.84
Restored from sherds, complete
Surface colour: 10YR5/3 brown; burnished slip: 10YR3/1 very dark grey
Break: uniform grey
Decoration: Three unequal lozenges infilled with horizontal zigzags made with a twelve-toothed comb.
Previously published: TD V, 175, 177

252. 0131 Cairo JE 91555 A/II-l/12 grave 1 Phase E/1 (68/027) Plate 49

SPI	I-d	f–m	W2	Bd. gef	re	3	1B

D. 2.6 cm. Nd 1.15 cm. Bd. 1.7 cm. H. 8.1 cm. Md. 4.65 cm. Wd. 0.3 cm.
VI 57.40
Intact
Surface colour: 5YR4/1 dark grey; burnished slip: 5YR4/1 very dark grey
Break: not visible
Decoration: Three unequal lozenges infilled with horizontal zigzags made with a twelve-toothed comb.
Previously published: TD V, 174.

253. 5759 TD F/I-m/19 planum 1 pit 5 Phase b/1–a/2 (86/014) Plate 49

SPI	I-d	vf	W2	Bd. gef	re	3	1B

D. 2.7 cm. Nd 1.4 cm. Bd. 2.25 cm. H. 10.7 cm. Md. 6.2 cm. Wd. 0.4 cm.
VI 57.24
Intact
Surface colour: 10YR4/1 dark grey; burnished slip: 10YR3/1 very dark grey
Break: not visible

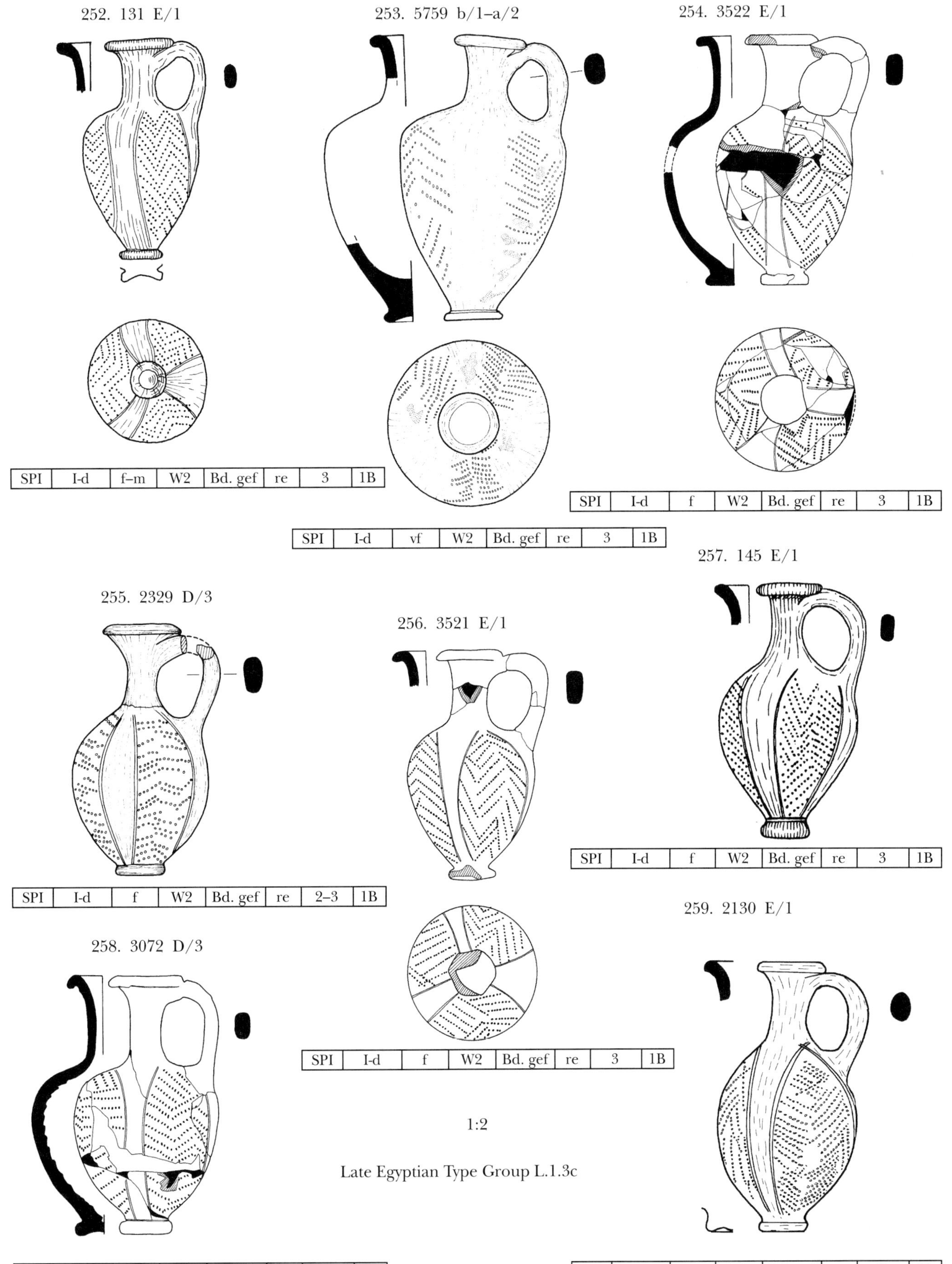
252. 131 E/1
SPI I-d f–m W2 Bd. gef re 3 1B
253. 5759 b/1–a/2
SPI I-d vf W2 Bd. gef re 3 1B
254. 3522 E/1
SPI I-d f W2 Bd. gef re 3 1B
255. 2329 D/3
SPI I-d f W2 Bd. gef re 2–3 1B
256. 3521 E/1
SPI I-d f W2 Bd. gef re 3 1B
257. 145 E/1
SPI I-d f W2 Bd. gef re 3 1B
258. 3072 D/3
SPI I-d f W2 Bd. gef re 3 1B
259. 2130 E/1
SPI I-d f W2 Bd. gef re 3 1B
1:2
Late Egyptian Type Group L.1.3c

Decoration: Three lozenges infilled with horizontal chevrons made with a fourteen-toothed comb. Undecorated parts vertically burnished. Rim horizontally burnished. Surface poorly preserved.

254. 3522 Cairo A/II-s/18 grave 1 Phase E/1 (81/406) Plate 49

SPI	I-d	f	W2	Bd. gef	re	3	1B

D. 2.8 cm. Nd 1.35 cm. Bd. 1.8 cm. H. 9.3 cm. Md. 5.3 cm. Wd. 0.4 cm.
VI 56.98
Restored from sherds, incomplete
Surface colour: 10YR4/1 dark grey; burnished slip: 10YR3/1 very dark grey
Break: not visible
Decoration: Three unequal lozenges infilled with horizontal zigzags made with an eight-toothed comb.
Previously published: TD XVI, 293, fig. 214, no. 7.

255. 2329 Vienna A3648 A/II-m/15 grave 3 Phase D/3 (69/103) Plate 49

SPI	I-d	f	W2	Bd. gef	re	2–3	1B

D. 3.0 cm. Nd 1.3 cm. Bd. 1.8 cm. H. 9.3 cm. Md. 5.3 cm. Wd. 0.3 cm.
VI 56.98
Intact
Surface colour: 2.5Y5/1 grey; burnished slip: 2.5Y5/1 grey
Break: light brown core, grey reduction zones
Decoration: Three unequal lozenges infilled with poorly executed horizontal zigzags made with an eight-toothed comb.
Previously published: TD XVI, 310, fig. 231, no. 2.

256. 3521 Cairo A/II-s/18 grave 1 Phase E/1 (81/402) Plate 49

SPI	I-d	f	W2	Bd. gef	re	3	1B

D. 2.6 cm. Nd 1.3 cm. Bd. 1.8 cm. H. 8.6 cm. Md. 4.9 cm. Wd. 0.4 cm.
VI 56.97
Restored from sherds, incomplete
Surface colour: 10YR4/1 dark grey; burnished slip: 10YR3/1 very dark grey
Break: not visible
Decoration: Three unequal lozenges infilled with horizontal zigzags made with a ten-toothed comb.
Previously published: TD XVI, 293, fig. 214, no. 6.

257. 0145 Vienna A1591 A/II-l/12 grave 2 Phase E/1 (66/036) Plate 49

SPI	I-d	f	W2	Bd. gef	re	3	1B

D. 2.47 cm. Nd 1.26 cm. Bd. 1.8 cm. H. 9.5 cm. Md. 5.4 cm. Wd. 0.27 cm.
VI 56.84
Incomplete
Surface colour: 10YR5–6/1 grey; burnished slip: 10YR 3/1 very dark grey
Break: uniform grey
Decoration: Three unequal lozenges infilled with horizontal zigzags made with a ten-toothed comb.
Previously published: TD V, 182, 183.

258. 3072 Cairo A/II-p/21 grave 3 Phase D/3 (79/121) Plate 49

SPI	I-d	f	W2	Bd. gef	re	3	1B

D. 2.9 cm. Nd. 1.2 cm. Bd. 2.1 cm. H. 9.6 cm. Md 5.6 cm. Wd. 0.2 cm.
VI 58.33
Restored from sherds, incomplete
Surface colour: 2.5Y5/1 grey; burnished slip: 2.5Y3/1 light olive brown
Break: not visible
Decoration: Three unequal lozenges infilled with horizontal zigzags made with a ten-toothed comb.

259. 2130 Vienna A3431 A/II-l/16 grave 1 Phase E/1 (69/061) Plate 49

SPI	I-d	f	W2	Bd. gef	re	3	1B

D. 2.7 cm. Nd 1.2 cm. Bd. 1.7 cm. H. 9.2 cm. Md. 5.2 cm. Wd. 0.3 cm.
VI 56.52
Restored from sherds, complete
Surface colour: 2.5Y5/1 grey; burnished slip: 2.5Y3/1 very dark grey
Break: dark grey core, light grey reduction zones
Decoration: Three unequal lozenges infilled with horizontal zigzags made with a twelve-toothed comb.

260. 2327 Vienna A3547 A/II-m/15 grave 3 Phase D/3 (69/103) Plate 50

SPI	I-d	f	W2	Bd. gef	re	2–3	1B

D. 2.8 cm. Nd 1.4 cm. Bd. 1.9 cm. H. 9.4 cm. Md. 5.3 cm. Wd. 0.3 cm.
VI 56.38
Intact
Surface colour: 2.5Y5/1 grey; burnished slip: 2.5Y3/1 very dark grey
Break: uniform grey
Decoration: Three unequal lozenges infilled with horizontal zigzags made with an eight-toothed comb.
Previously published: TD XVI, 310, fig. 231, no. 6.

261. 0869 Vienna A2632 A/II-m/11 grave 6 Phase E/2–1 (67/023) Plate 50

SPI	I-d	f	W2	Bd. gef	re	2–3	1B

D. 3.1 cm. Nd 1.5 cm. Bd. 1.85 cm. H. 12.1 cm. Md. 6.8 cm. Wd. 0.3 cm.
VI 56.19
Incomplete
Surface colour: 10YR5/2–3 grey brown; burnished slip: 10YR3/1 very dark grey
Break: uniform grey brown
Decoration: Three unequal lozenges infilled with horizontal zigzags made with a twelve-toothed comb.
Previously published: TD V, 157, 158.

262. 2432 Cairo JE 94651 A/II-l/15 grave 1 Phase D/3 or D/2 (69/123) Plate 50

SPI	I-d	f	W2	Bd. gef	re	2–3	1B

D. 2.7 cm. Nd 1.2 cm. Bd. 1.7 cm. H. 9.8 cm. Md. 5.5 cm. Wd. 0.3 cm.

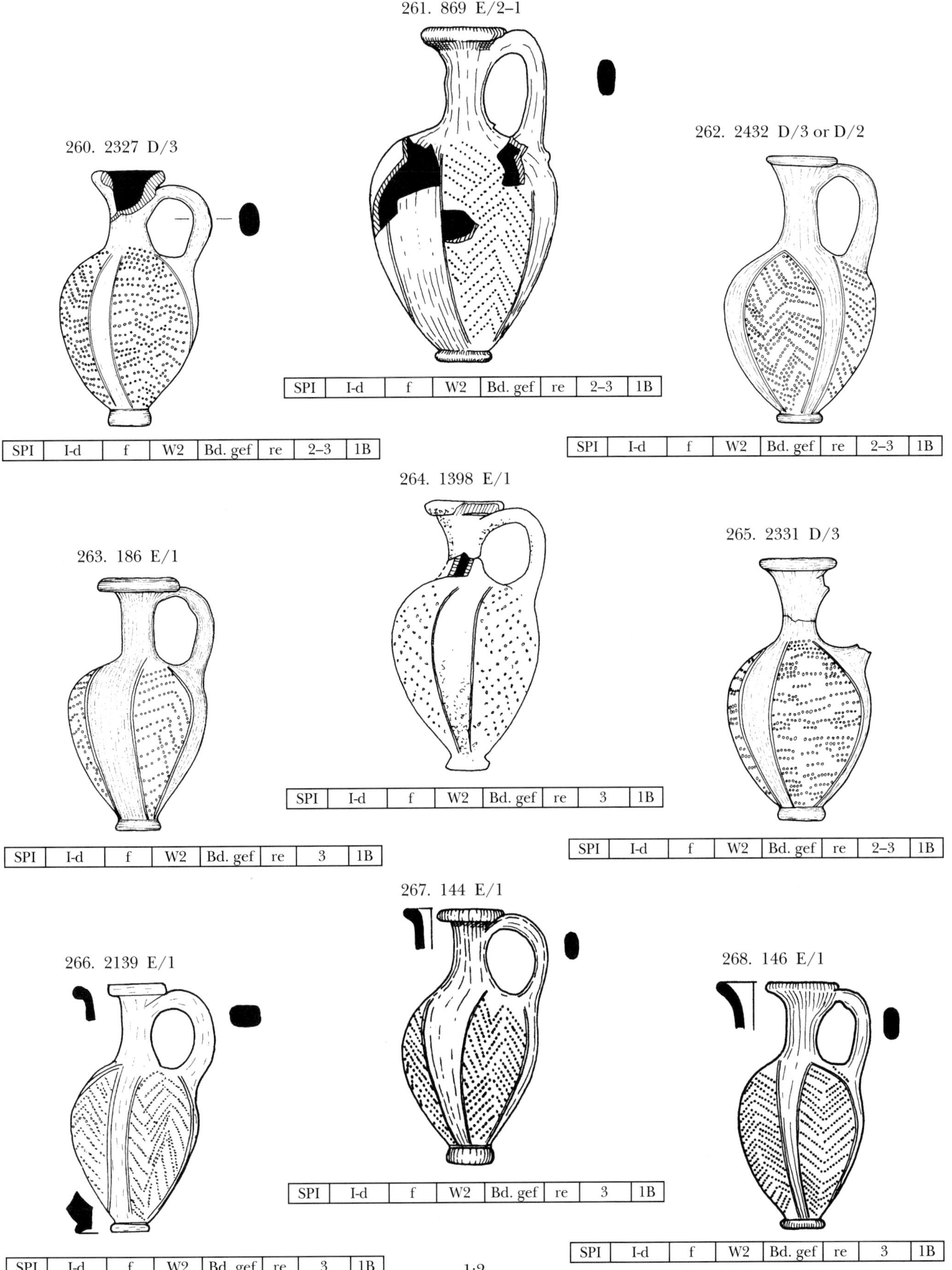

Late Egyptian Type Group L.1.3c

Plate 50

VI 56.12
Intact
Surface colour: 10YR4/1 grey; burnished slip: 10YR2/1 black
Break: not visible
Decoration: Three unequal lozenges infilled with horizontal zigzags made with an eight-toothed comb.
Previously published: TD XVI, 337, fig. 261, no. 1.

263. 0186 Vienna A1631 A/II-l/12 grave 2 Phase E/1 (66/039) Plate 50

SPI	I-d	f	W2	Bd. gef	re	3	1B

D. 3.0 cm. Nd 1.13 cm. Bd. 1.8 cm. H. 9.3 cm. Md. 5.2 cm. Wd. 0.34 cm.
VI 55.91
Intact
Surface colour: 10YR5–6/1–2 light brownish grey; burnished slip: 10YR3/1 black
Break: not visible
Decoration: Three unequal lozenges infilled with horizontal zigzags made with an eight-toothed comb.
Previously published: TD V, 187, 188

264. 1398 Vienna A2951 A/II-l/14 grave 5 Phase E/1 (68/092) Plate 50

SPI	I-d	f	W2	Bd. gef	re	3	1B

D. 2.7 cm. Nd 1.2 cm. Bd. 1.5 cm. H. 9.85 cm. Md. 5.5 cm. Wd. 0.3 cm.
VI 55.83
Intact
Surface colour: 10YR6/2 light brownish grey; burnished slip: 10YR5/2 greyish brown
Break: brown core, grey reduction zones
Decoration: Three unequal lozenges infilled with horizontal zigzags made with an eight-toothed comb.
Previously published: TD XVI, 254, fig. 189b, no. 22.

265. 2331 Vienna A3549 A/II-m/15 grave 3 Phase D/3 (69/103) Plate 50

SPI	I-d	f	W2	Bd. gef	re	2–3	1B

D. 2.9 cm. Nd 1.3 cm. Bd. 1.8 cm. H. 9.7 cm. Md. 5.4 cm. Wd. 0.3 cm.
VI 55.67
Intact
Surface colour: 2.5Y5/1 grey; burnished slip: 2.5Y5/1 grey
Break: dark grey core, brownish grey reduction zones
Decoration: Three lozenges infilled with horizontal lines made with a five toothed comb.
Previously published: TD XVI, 310, fig. 231, no. 5.

266. 2139 Vienna A1412 A/II-l/16 grave 1 Phase E/1 (69/062) Plate 50

SPI	I-d	f	W2	Bd. gef	re	3	1B

D. 2.7 cm. Nd 1.3 cm. Bd. 1.6 cm. H. 9.25 cm. Md. 5.1 cm. Wd. 0.3 cm.
VI 55.13
Intact
Surface colour: 10YR5/1 grey; burnished slip: 10YR3/1 very dark grey
Break: not visible
Decoration: Three unequal lozenges infilled with horizontal zigzags made with a twelve-toothed comb.
Previously published: TD XVI, 263, fig. 192a, no. 11.

267. 0144 Cairo JE 91556C A/II-l/12 grave 2 Phase E/1 (66/036) Plate 50

SPI	I-d	f	W2	Bd. gef	re	3	1B

D. 2.4 cm. Nd 1.2 cm. Bd. 1.7 cm. H. 9.1 cm. Md. 5.0 cm. Wd. 0.3 cm.
VI 54.94
Intact
Surface colour: 10YR5/2 grey brown; burnished slip: 10YR 3/1 very dark grey
Break: not visible
Decoration: Three unequal lozenges infilled with horizontal zigzags made with a ten-toothed comb.
Previously published: TD V, 182, 183.

268. 0146 Vienna A1592 A/II-l/12 grave 2 Phase E/1 (66/036) Plate 50

SPI	I-d	f	W2	Bd. gef	re	3	1B

D. 2.75 cm. Nd 1.2 cm. Bd. 1.6 cm. H. 9.1 cm. Md. 5.0 cm. Wd. 0.2 cm.
VI 54.94
Incomplete
Surface colour: 10YR5–6/1 grey; burnished slip: 10YR 3/1 very dark grey
Break: light grey core, dark grey reduction zones
Decoration: Three unequal lozenges infilled with horizontal zigzags made with a twelve-toothed comb.
Previously published: TD V, 182, 183.

269. 0143 Cairo JE 91556B A/II-l/12 grave 2 Phase E/1 (69/003) Plate 51

SPI	I-d	f–m	W2	Bd. gef	re	3	1B

D. 2.4 cm. Nd 1.2 cm. Bd. 1.8 cm. H. 10.2 cm. Md. 5.6 cm. Wd. 0.3 cm.
VI 54.90
Intact
Surface colour: 10YR5/3 brown; burnished slip: 10YR 3/1 very dark grey
Break: not visible
Decoration: Three unequal lozenges infilled with horizontal zigzags made with a fourteen-toothed comb.
Previously published: TD V, 182, 183.

270. 0371 Cairo JE 91568 A/I-g/3 grave 1 Phase D/3 (66/055) Plates 51, 140

SPI	I-d	f	W2	Bd. gef	re	3	1B

D. 2.9 cm. Nd 1.2 cm. Bd. 2.2 cm. H. 10.6 cm. Md. 5.8 cm. Wd. 0.3 cm.
VI 54.71
Intact
Surface colour: 10YR6/3 dark brown: burnished slip: 10YR3/1 dark grey
Break: not visible
Decoration: Three unequal lozenges infilled with horizontal zigzags made with an eight-toothed comb.

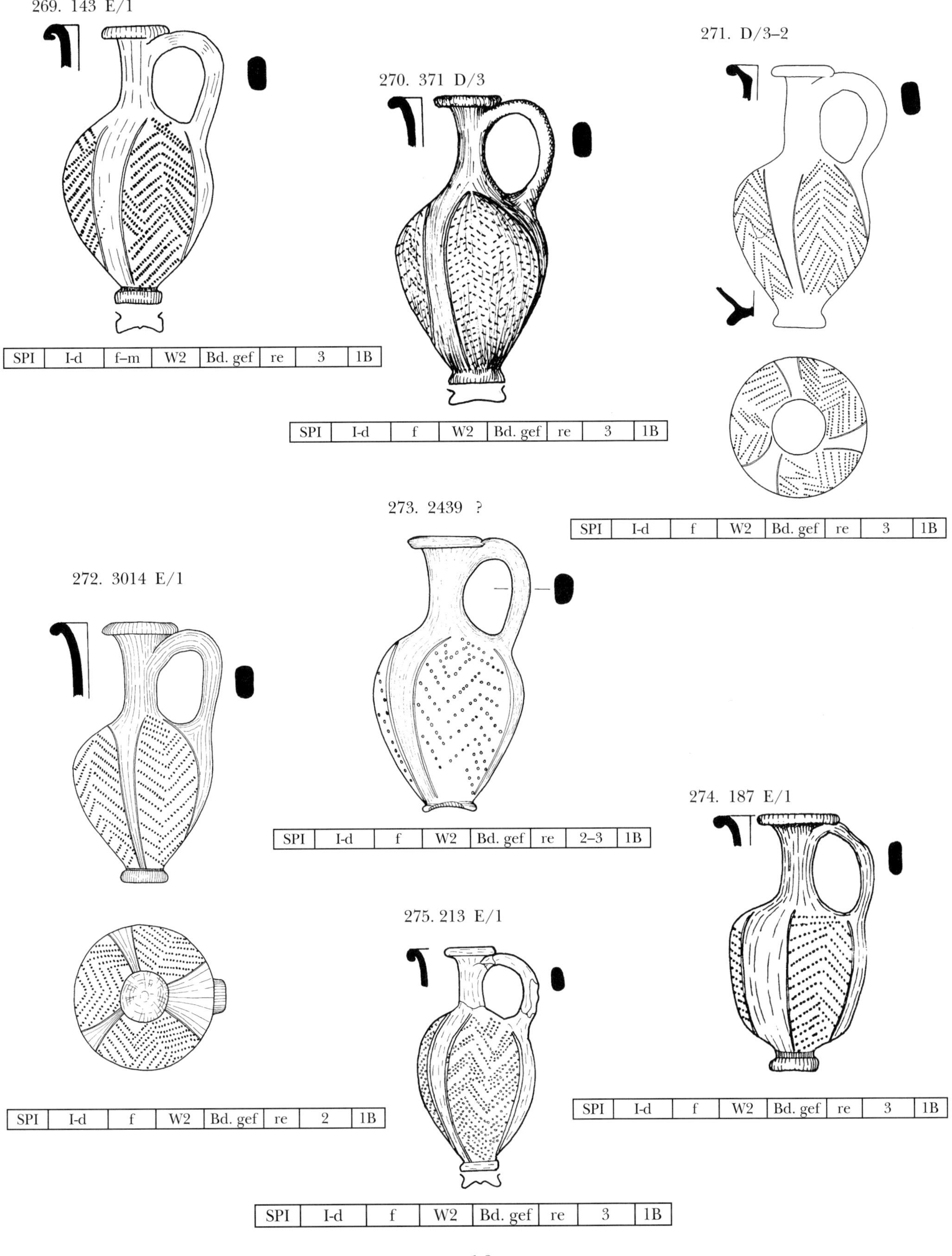

1:2

Late Egyptian Type Group L.1.3c

Plate 51

271. 3454 Cairo A/II-l/17 grave 2 Phase D/3–2 (81/270) Plate 51

SPI	I-d	f	W2	Bd. gef	re	3	1B

D. 2.45 cm. Nd 1.45 cm. Bd. 2.0 cm. H. 9.6 cm. Md. 5.25 cm. Wd. 0.4 cm.
VI 54.68
Restored from sherds, complete
Surface colour: 10YR4/1 dark grey; burnished slip: 10YR3/1 very dark grey
Break: dark grey in, light grey out
Decoration: Three unequal lozenges infilled with horizontal zigzags made with a fourteen-toothed comb.
Previously published: TD XVI, 360, fig. 287, no. 1.

272. 3014 Cairo A/II-p/20 grave 3 Phase E/1 (79/199) Plate 51

SPI	I-d	f	W2	Bd. gef	re	2	1B

D. 2.87 cm. Nd 1.33 cm. Bd. 1.75 cm. H. 9.6 cm. Md. 5.24 cm. Wd. 0.4 cm.
VI 54.58
Restored from sherds, complete
Surface colour: 10YR4/1 dark grey; burnished slip: 10YR3/1 very dark grey
Break: dark grey in, light grey out
Decoration: Three unequal lozenges infilled with horizontal zigzags made with a twelve-toothed comb.

273. 2439 Vienna TDS 2439 A/II-l/15 grave ? Phase ? (69/136) Plate 51

SPI	I-d	f	W2	Bd. gef	re	2–3	1B

D. 2.8 cm. Nd 1.2 cm. Bd. 1.7 cm. H. 10.1 cm. Md. 5.5 cm. Wd. 0.3 cm.
VI 54.45
Intact
Surface colour: 2.5Y7/1 light grey; burnished slip: 2.5Y4/1 dark grey
Break: not visible
Decoration: Three unequal lozenges infilled with horizontal zigzags made with an eight-toothed comb.

274. 0187 Vienna A1632 A/II-l/12 grave 2 Phase E/1 (66/039) Plate 51

SPI	I-d	f	W2	Bd. gef	re	3	1B

D. 2.3 cm. Nd 1.15 cm. Bd. 1.7 cm. H. 9.37 cm. Md. 5.1 cm. Wd. 0.3 cm.
VI 54.42
Incomplete
Surface colour: 10YR6/2 grey brown; burnished slip: 10YR3/1 very dark grey
Break: dark grey core, greyish brown reduction zones
Decoration: Three unequal lozenges infilled with horizontal chevrons made with a twelve-toothed comb.
Previously published: TD V, 187 188.

275. 0213 Cairo JE 91559 A/II-l/12 grave 1 Phase E/1 (66/031) Plate 51

SPI	I-d	f	W2	Bd. gef	re	3	1B

D. 2.7 cm. Nd 1.2 cm. Bd. 1.9 cm. H. 11.4 cm. Md. 6.2 cm. Wd. 0.3 cm.
VI 54.38
Incomplete
Surface colour: 10YR5/2 grey brown; burnished slip: 2.5YR4/4 red brown
Break: dark grey core, greyish brown reduction zones
Decoration: Three unequal lozenges infilled with horizontal zigzags made with a twelve-toothed comb.
Previously published: TD V, 177 179.

276. 0360 Cairo JE 91567 A/I-g/3 grave 1 Phase D/3 (66/051) Plate 52

SPI	I-d	f	W2	Bd. gef	re	2–3	1B

D. 2.8 cm. Nd 1.2 cm. Bd. 2.1 cm. H. 10.6 cm. Md. 5.7 cm. Wd. 0.3 cm.
VI 53.77
Intact
Surface colour: 5YR3/1 grey: burnished slip: 5YR5/1 dark grey
Break: not visible
Decoration: Three unequal lozenges infilled with horizontal zigzags made with an eight-toothed comb.

277. 2129 Vienna A3430 A/II-l/16 grave 1 Phase E/1 (69/053) Plate 52

SPI	I-d	F	W2	Bd. gef	re	3	1B

D. 2.6 cm. Nd 1.1 cm. Bd. 1.5 cm. H. 11.2 cm. Md. 6.0 cm. Wd. 0.3 cm.
VI 53.57
Restored from sherds, complete
Surface colour: 2.5Y6/1 grey; burnished slip: 2.5Y4/1 very dark grey
Break: dark grey core, light grey reduction zones
Decoration: Three unequal lozenges infilled with horizontal zigzags made with an eight-toothed comb.
Previously published: TD XVI, 263, fig. 192a, no. 6.

278. 5763 TD F/I-m/19 grave 7 Phase a/2 (86/002) Plates 52, 140

SPI	I-d	f	W2	Bd. gef	re	3–4	1B

D. 2.6 cm. Nd 1.27 cm. Bd. 1.73 cm. H. 9.9 cm. Md. 5.3 cm. Wd. 0.4 cm.
VI 53.53
Intact
Surface colour: 10YR4/1 dark grey; burnished slip: 10YR2/1 black
Break: not visible
Decoration: Three lozenges infilled with horizontal chevrons made with a twelve-toothed comb. Undecorated parts vertically burnished. Rim horizontally burnished.

279. 0402 Vienna A1413 A/I-g/3 grave 1 Phase D/3 (66/029) Plate 52

SPI	I-d	f	W2	Bd. gef	re	3	1B

D. 2.6 cm. Nd 1.1 cm. Bd. 1.8 cm. H. 9.0 cm. Md. 4.8 cm. Wd. 0.4 cm.
VI 53.33
Intact
Surface colour: 10YR4–5/1 dark grey; burnished slip: 10YR3/1 very dark grey
Decoration: Three unequal lozenges infilled with horizontal zigzags made with a ten-toothed comb.

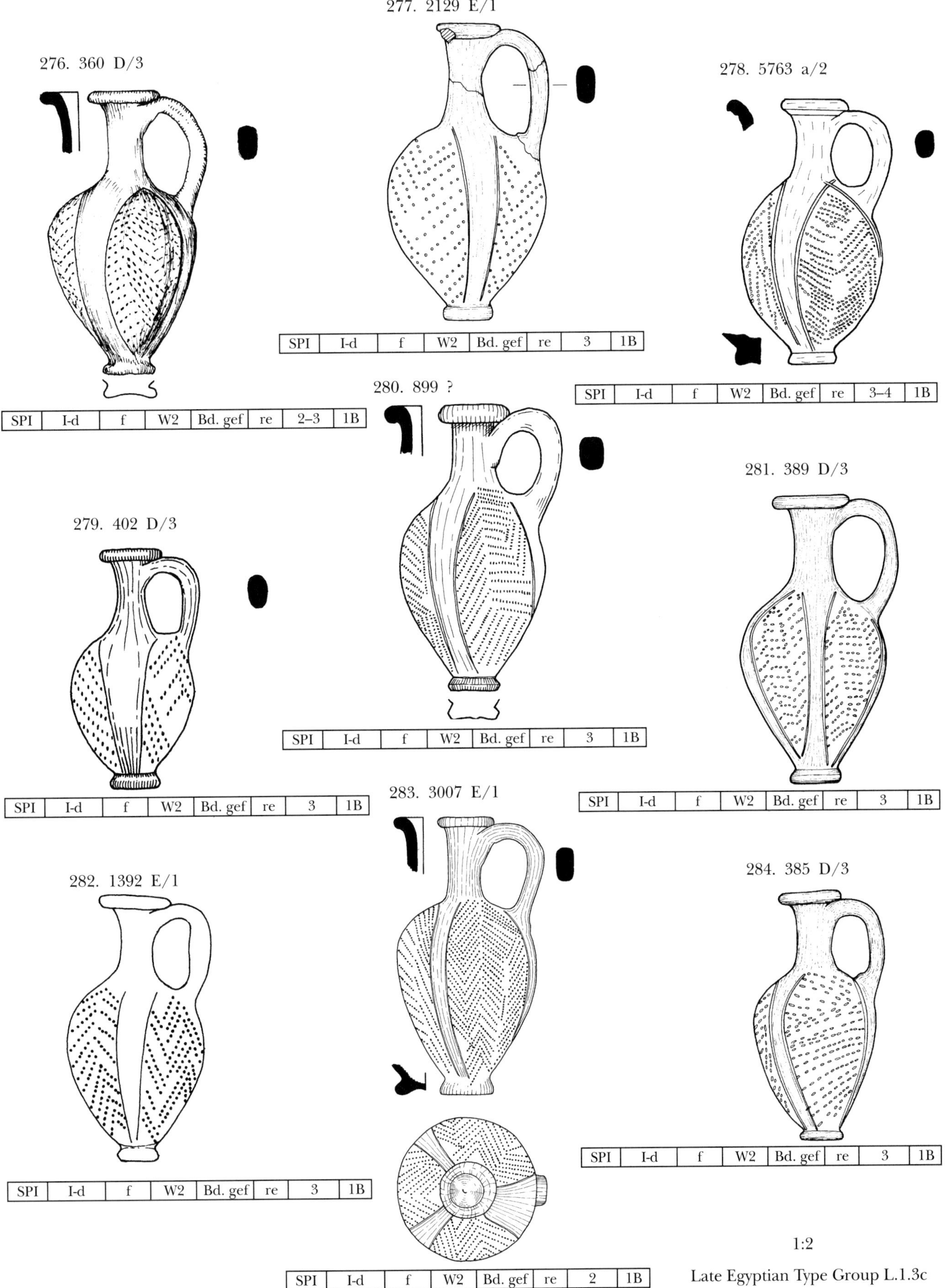

Late Egyptian Type Group L.1.3c

Plate 52

280. 0899 Cairo JE 91586 A/III Suchgraben Phase ? (69/001) Plate 52

SPI	I-d	f	W2	Bd. gef	re	3	1B

D. 2.7 cm. Nd 1.4 cm. Bd. 2.0 cm. H. 10.5 cm. Md. 5.6 cm. Wd. 0.3 cm.
VI 53.33
Intact
Surface colour: 5YR4/1 grey; burnished slip: 10YR3/1 very dark grey
Break: not visible
Decoration: Three unequal lozenges infilled with horizontal zigzags made with a fourteen-toothed comb.

281. 0389 Vienna A1645 A/I-g/3 grave 1 Phase D/3 (66/056) Plate 52

SPI	I-d	f	W2	Bd. gef	re	3	1B

D. 3.0 cm. Nd 1.3 cm. Bd. 1.9 cm. H. 10.7 cm. Md. 5.7 cm. Wd. 0.34 cm.
VI 53.27
Intact
Surface colour: 10YR4/1 dark grey; burnished slip: 10YR2/1 black
Decoration: Three unequal lozenges infilled with horizontal zigzags made with an eight-toothed comb.

282. 1392 Vienna A1666 A/II-l/14 grave 5 Phase E/1 (68/091) Plate 52

SPI	I-d	f	W2	Bd. gef	re	3	1B

D. 2.7 cm. Nd 1.25 cm. Bd. 1.7 cm. H. 9.95 cm. Md. 5.3 cm. Wd. 0.3 cm.
VI 53.26
Intact
Surface colour: 2.5Y5/1 grey; burnished slip: 2.5Y/1 black
Break: dark grey core, light grey reduction zones
Decoration: Three unequal lozenges infilled with horizontal zigzags made with a ten-toothed comb.
Previously published: TD XVI, 254, fig. 189b, no. 11.

283. 3007 Cairo A/II-p/20 grave 3 Phase E/1 (79/200) Plate 52

SPI	I-d	f	W2	Bd. gef	re	2	1B

D. 2.16 cm. Nd 1.31 cm. Bd. 2.0 cm. H. 10.3 cm. Md. 5.46 cm. Wd. 0.4 cm.
VI 53.00
Restored from sherds, complete
Surface colour: 10YR4/1 dark grey; burnished slip: 10YR3/1 very dark grey
Break: dark grey in, light grey out
Decoration: Three unequal lozenges infilled with horizontal zigzags made with a twelve-toothed comb.

284. 0385 Vienna A1607 A/I-g/3 grave 1 Phase D/3 (66/056) Plate 52

SPI	I-d	f	W2	Bd. gef	re	3	1B

D. 2.35 cm. Nd 1.1 cm. Bd. 1.6 cm. H. 9.1 cm. Md. 4.8 cm. Wd. 0.34 cm.
VI 52.74
Intact
Surface colour: 10YR5/2 dark greyish brown; burnished slip: 10YR3/1 very dark grey
Break: not visible
Decoration: Three unequal lozenges infilled with poorly executed horizontal zigzags made with an eight-toothed comb.

285. 0154 Vienna A2213 A/II-l/12 grave 3 Phase E/1 (66/036) Plate 53

SPI	I-d	f–m	W2	Bd. gef	re	3	1B

D. 2.6 cm. Nd 1.34 cm. Bd. 1.95 cm. H. 11.0 cm. Md. 5.75 cm. Wd. 0.3 cm.
VI 52.27
Incomplete
Surface colour: 10YR4/2 dark grey; burnished slip: 10YR2/1 black
Break: dark grey core, greyish brown reduction zones
Decoration: Three unequal lozenges infilled with poorly executed horizontal zigzags made with a twelve-toothed comb.
Previously published: TD V, 182, 183.

286. 0522 Vienna A2369 A/II-m/11 grave ? Phase D/2 (67/080) Plate 53

SPI	I-d	f	W2	Bd. gef	re	3	1B

D. 2.5 cm. Nd 1.35 cm. Bd. 1.7 cm. H. 10.2 cm. Md. 5.3 cm. Wd. 0.4 cm.
VI 51.96
Intact
Surface colour: 10YR4.5/1–3 grey brown; burnished slip: 10YR3/1 very dark grey
Break: grey core, brown reduction zones
Decoration: Three unequal lozenges infilled with horizontal chevrons made with a fourteen-toothed comb.
Previously published: TD V, 292.

287. 3012 Cairo A/II-p/20 grave 3 Phase E/1 (79/199) Plate 53

SPI	I-d	f	W2	Bd. gef	re	2	1B

D. 2.78 cm. Nd 1.33 cm. Bd. 1.67 cm. H. 9.8 cm. Md. 5.07 cm. Wd. 0.4 cm.
VI 51.73
Restored from sherds, complete
Surface colour: 10YR4/1 dark grey; burnished slip: 10YR3/1 very dark grey
Break: dark greyin, light grey out
Decoration: Three unequal lozenges infilled with horizontal zigzags made with a twelve-toothed comb.

288. 2318 Vienna A3544 A/II-m/15 grave 3 Phase D/3 (69/110) Plate 53

SPI	I-d	f	W2	Bd. gef	re	2–3	1B

D. 3.2 cm. Nd. 1.2 cm. Bd. 1.9 cm. H. 10.1 cm. Md 5.2 cm. Wd. 0.4 cm.
VI 51.48
Restored from sherds, complete
Surface colour: 10YR5/1 grey; burnished slip: 10YR3/2 very dark greyish brown
Break: not visible
Decoration: Three unequal lozenges infilled with horizontal chevrons made with a twelve-toothed comb.
Previously published: TD XVI, 315, fig. 235, no. 20.

289. 2126 Vienna A1715 A/II-l/16 grave 1 Phase E/1 (69/053) Plate 53

SPI	I-d	f	W2	Bd. gef	re	3	1B

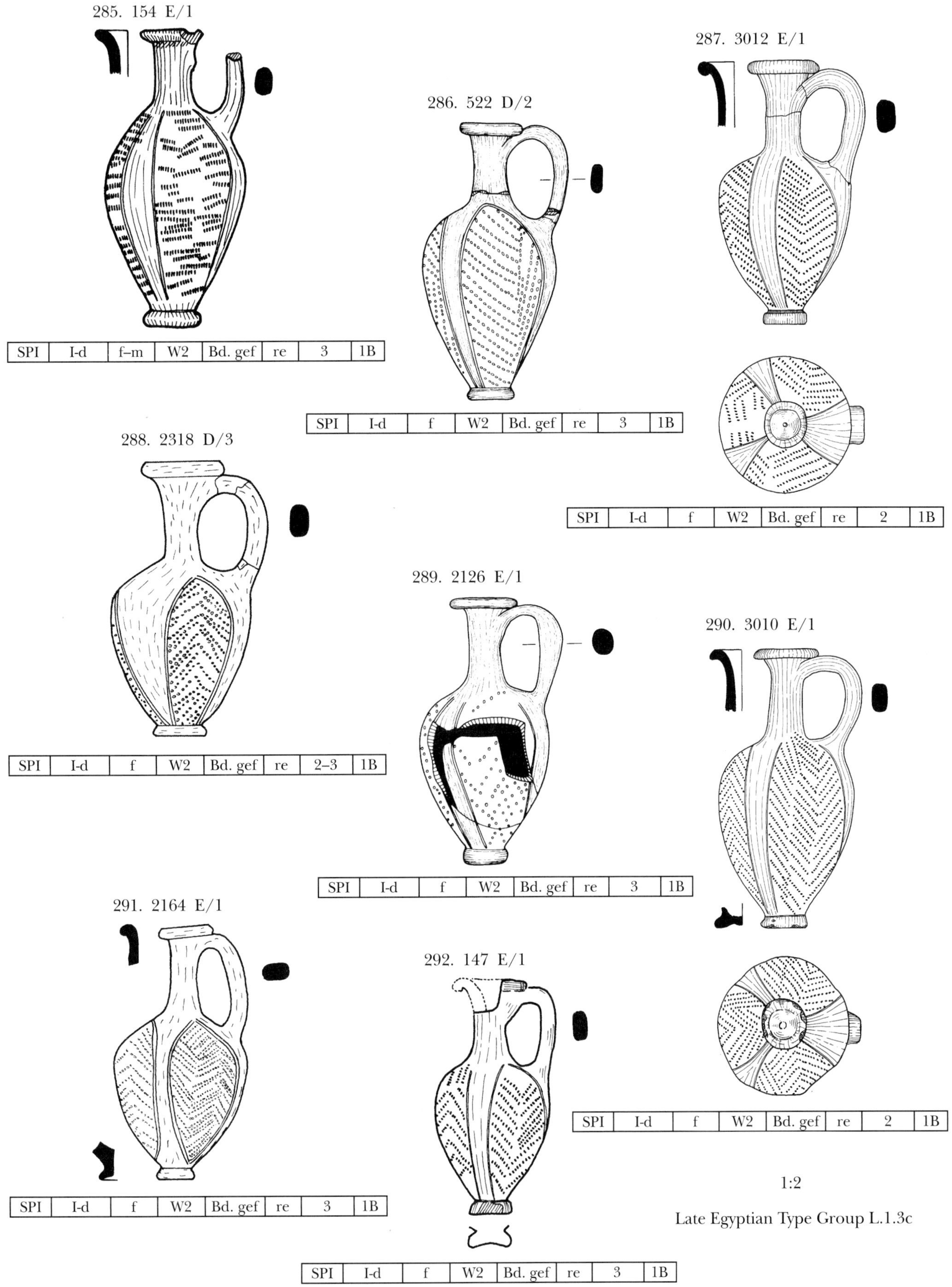

285. 154 E/1

SPI	I-d	f–m	W2	Bd. gef	re	3	1B

286. 522 D/2

SPI	I-d	f	W2	Bd. gef	re	3	1B

287. 3012 E/1

SPI	I-d	f	W2	Bd. gef	re	2	1B

288. 2318 D/3

SPI	I-d	f	W2	Bd. gef	re	2–3	1B

289. 2126 E/1

SPI	I-d	f	W2	Bd. gef	re	3	1B

290. 3010 E/1

SPI	I-d	f	W2	Bd. gef	re	2	1B

291. 2164 E/1

SPI	I-d	f	W2	Bd. gef	re	3	1B

292. 147 E/1

SPI	I-d	f	W2	Bd. gef	re	3	1B

1:2

Late Egyptian Type Group L.1.3c

Plate 53

D. 2.6 cm. Nd 1.1 cm. Bd. 1.5 cm. H. 9.8 cm. Md. 5.0 cm. Wd. 0.3 cm.
VI 51.02
Incomplete
Surface colour: 2.5Y6/1 grey; burnished slip: 2.5Y4/1 very dark grey
Break: dark grey core, light grey reduction zones
Decoration: Three unequal lozenges infilled with horizontal zigzags made with an eight-toothed comb.
Previously published: TD XVI, 263, fig. 192a, no. 5.

290. 3010 Cairo A/II-p/20 grave 3 Phase E/1 (79/200) Plate 53

SPI	I-d	f	W2	Bd. gef	re	2	1B

D. 2.53 cm. Nd 1.2 cm. Bd. 1.8 cm. H. 10.3 cm. Md. 5.25 cm. Wd. 0.4 cm.
VI 50.97
Restored from sherds, complete
Surface colour: 10YR4/1 dark grey; burnished slip: 10YR3/1 very dark grey
Break: dark grey in, light grey out
Decoration: Three unequal lozenges infilled with horizontal zigzags made with a twelve-toothed comb.

291. 2164 Vienna A1723 A/II-l/16 grave 2 Phase E/1 (69/067) Plates 53, 140

SPI	I-d	f	W2	Bd. gef	re	3	1B

D. 2.8 cm. Nd 1.15 cm. Bd. 1.8 cm. H. 10.6 cm. Md. 5.4 cm. Wd. 0.3 cm.
VI 50.94
Intact
Surface colour: 2.5Y6/1 grey; burnished slip: 2.5Y4/1 very dark grey
Break: not visible
Decoration: Three unequal lozenges infilled with horizontal zigzags made with a twelve-toothed comb.
Previously published: TD XVI, 269, fig. 194a, no. 9.

292. 0147 Vienna A1593 A/II-l/12 grave 2 Phase E/1 (69/014) Plate 53

SPI	I-d	f	W2	Bd. gef	re	3	1B

D. 2.4 cm. Nd 1.1 cm. Bd. 1.7 cm. H. 8.7 cm. Md. 4.4 cm. Wd. 0.3 cm.
VI 50.57
Incomplete
Surface colour: 10YR4–5/2 grey brown; burnished slip: 10YR 3/1 very dark grey
Break: light grey core, dark grey reduction zones
Decoration: Three unequal lozenges infilled with horizontal zigzags or chevrons made with a twelve-toothed comb.
Previously published: TD V, 182, 183.

293. 0792 Cairo JE 91557 A/II-m/13 grave 4 Phase E/1 (69/002) Plate 54

SPI	I-d	f–m	W2	Bd. gef	re	3	1B

D. 2.6 cm. Nd 1.25 cm. Bd. 1.7 cm. H. 10.3 cm. Md. 5.2 cm. Wd. 0.4 cm.
VI 50.48
Intact
Surface colour: 10YR5–6/2 grey; burnished slip: 10YR3/1 very dark grey
Break: grey core, light grey reduction zones
Decoration: Three unequal lozenges infilled with horizontal zigzags made with a twelve-toothed comb.
Previously published: TD V, 201.

294. 0142 Cairo JE 91556A A/II-l/12 grave 2 Phase E/1 (66/036) Plate 54

SPI	I-d	f–m	W2	Bd. gef	re	2–3	1B

D. 2.6 cm. Nd 1.2 cm. Bd. 2.0 cm. H. 11.0 cm. Md. 5.5 cm. Wd. 0.3 cm.
VI 50.00
Intact
Surface colour: 10YR5/1–2 grey; burnished slip: 10YR 3/1 very dark grey
Break: not visible
Decoration: Three unequal lozenges infilled with horizontal zigzags made with a twelve-toothed comb.
Previously published: TD V, 182, 183.

295. 2106 Cairo JE 91664 A/II-l/16 grave 2 Phase E/1 (69/041) Plate 54

SPI	I-d	f	W2	Bd. gef	re	2–3	1B

D. 2.5 cm. Nd 1.2 cm. Bd. 1.6 cm. H. 10.0 cm. Md. 5.0 cm. Wd. 0.3 cm.
VI 50.00
Intact
Surface colour: 10YR5/2 grey; burnished slip: 10YR 2/1 black
Break: not visible
Decoration: Three unequal lozenges infilled with poorly executed horizontal zigzags made with an eight-toothed comb.
Previously published: TD XVI, 268, fig. 193, no. 44.

296. 0368 Vienna A1644 A/I-g/3 grave 1 Phase D/3 (66/052) Plate 54

SPI	I-d	f	W2	–	re	3	1B

D. 2.9 cm. Nd 1.35 cm. Bd. eroded H. 9.6 cm. Md. 4.9 cm. Wd. 0.3 cm.
Incomplete
Surface colour: 10YR2/1 black; burnished slip: 10YR5/2 grey brown
Break: not visible
Decoration: Three unequal lozenges infilled with horizontal zigzags made with a twelve-toothed comb.

297. 0370 Vienna A2304 A/I-g/3 grave 1 Phase D/3 (66/055) Plate 54

SPI	I-d	f	W2	–	re	3	1B

D. 3.2 cm. Nd 1.35 cm. Bd. eroded H. 8.5 cm. Md. 5.3 cm. Wd. 0.3 cm.
Incomplete
Surface colour: 2.5Y6/1 grey; burnished slip: 2.5Y4/1 grey
Break: uniform greyish brown
Decoration: Three unequal lozenges infilled with horizontal zigzags made with an eight-toothed comb.

298. 0864 Vienna A2629 A/II-m/11 grave 6 Phase E/2–1 (67/023) Plate 54

SPI	I-d	f–m	W2	Bd. gef	re	3	1B

D. 3.0 cm. Nd 1.3 cm. Bd. 1.75 cm. H. 10.0 cm. Md. 5.8 cm. Wd. 0.35 cm.

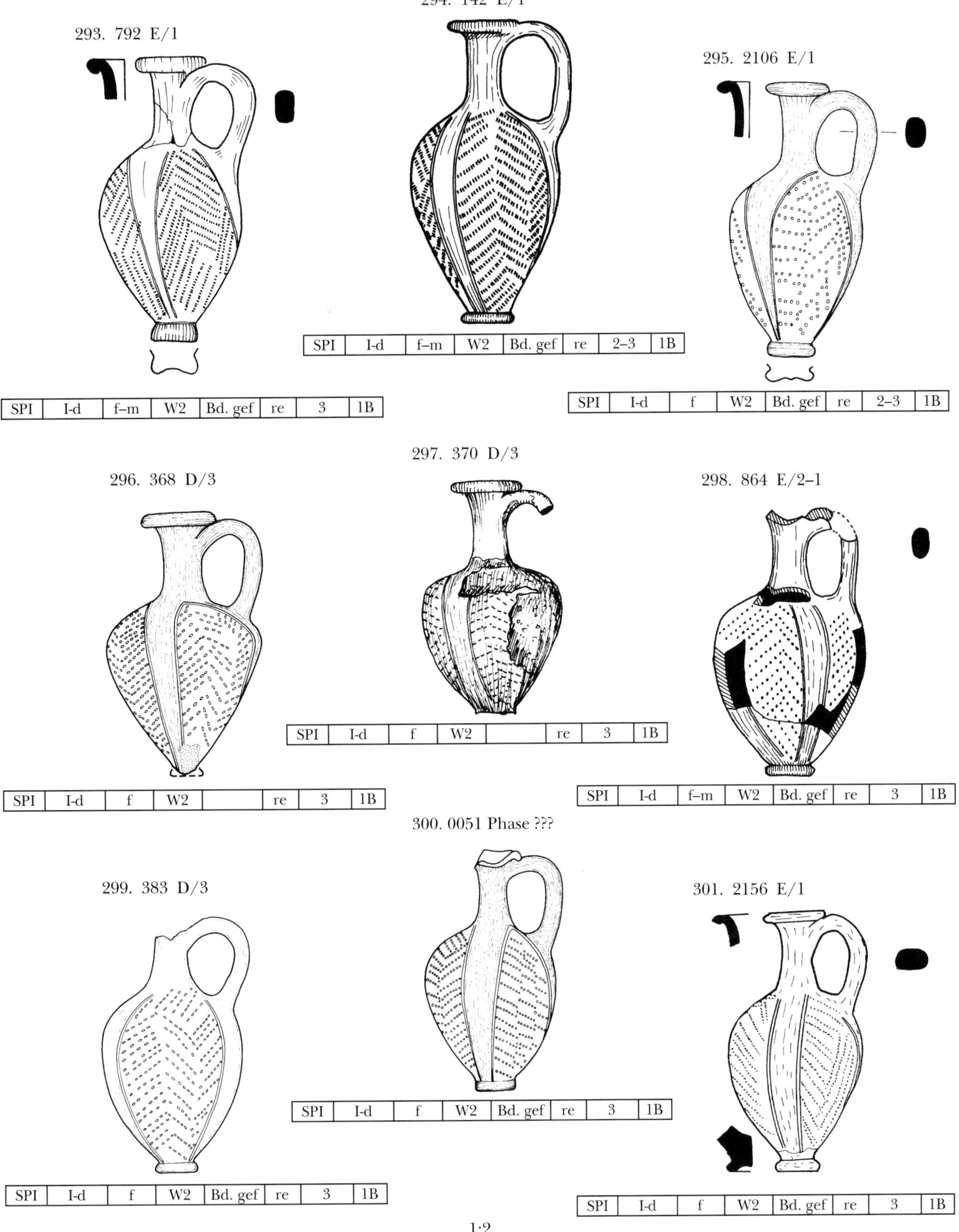

Late Egyptian Type Group L.1.3c

Plate 54

VI 58.00
Incomplete
Surface colour: 10YR4/3–5/1 brown to grey; burnished slip: 10YR3/1–2 dark grey
Break: uniform grey brown
Decoration: Three unequal lozenges infilled with horizontal zigzags made with a twelve-toothed comb.
Previously published: TD V, 157, 158.

299. 0383 Vienna A1605 A/I-g/3 grave 1 Phase D/3 (66/056) Plate 54

SPI	I-d	f	W2	Bd. gef	re	3	1B

D. 2.4 cm. Nd 1.15 cm. Bd. 1.6 cm. H. 9.4 cm. Md. 5.2 cm. Wd. 0.34 cm.
VI 55.31
Intact, rim chipped
Surface colour: 10YR5/2 dark greyish brown; burnished slip: 10YR3/1 very dark grey
Break: dark grey core, light grey reduction zones
Decoration: Three unequal lozenges infilled with horizontal zigzags made with an eight-toothed comb.

300. 0051 Vienna A2161 A/II-l/12 grave ?? Phase ? (66/006) Plate 54

SPI	I-d	f	W2	Bd. gef	re	3	1B

D. 3.0 cm. Nd 1.1 cm. Bd. 1.4 cm. H. 8.9 cm. Md. 4.9 cm. Wd. 0.3 cm.
VI 55.05
Intact
Surface colour: 10YR5/2–3 brown; burnished slip: 10YR2/1 black
Break: dark grey core, greyish brown reduction zones
Decoration: Three unequal lozenges infilled with poorly executed horizontal zigzags made with a twelve-toothed comb.

301. 2156 Vienna A3449 A/II-l/16 grave 2 Phase E/1 (69/064) Plate 54

SPI	I-d	f	W2	Bd. gef	re	3	1B

D. 2.7 cm. Nd 1.2 cm. Bd. 1.9 cm. H. 10.5 cm. Md. 5.7 cm. Wd. 0.3 cm.
VI 54.28
Restored from sherds, incomplete
Surface colour: 2.5Y6/1 grey; burnished slip: 2.5Y4/1 dark grey
Break: red core, red and grey reduction zones
Decoration: Three unequal lozenges infilled with horizontal zigzags made with a twelve-toothed comb.
Previously published: TD XVI, 269, fig. 194a, no. 6.

302. 0390 Vienna A2310 A/I-g/3 grave 1 Phase D/3 (66/056) Plate 55

SPI	I-d	f	W2	Bd. gef	re	3	1B

D. 3.0 cm. Nd 1.2 cm. Bd. 2.1 cm. H. 10.5 cm. Md. 5.6 cm. Wd. 0.34 cm.
VI 53.33
Intact
Surface colour: 2.5Y5/1 grey; burnished slip: 2.5Y3/1 very dark grey
Break: uniform grey
Decoration: Three unequal lozenges infilled with horizontal zigzags made with a twelve-toothed comb.

303. 2341 Cairo JE 94628 A/II-m/15 grave 3 Phase D/3 (69/104) Plate 55

SPI	I-d	f	W2	Bd. gef	re	3	1B

Nd. 1.4 cm. Bd. 1.8 cm. pht. 8.7 cm. Md. 5.1 cm. Wd. 0.3 cm.
Intact
Surface colour: 10YR6/2 grey; burnished slip: 10YR3/1 very dark grey
Break: dark grey core, brownish grey reduction zones
Decoration: Three unequal lozenges infilled with horizontal zigzags made with an eight-toothed comb.
Previously published: TD XVI, 310, fig. 231, no. 7.

304. 0149 Vienna A1595 A/II-l/12 grave 2 Phase E/1 (66/014) Plate 55

SPI	I-d	f	W2	Bd. gef	re	3	1B

Nd. 1.1 cm. Bd. 1.7 cm. H. 8.42 cm. Md. 5.14 cm. Wd. 0.3 cm.
Incomplete
Surface colour: 10YR5/2 grey brown; burnished slip: 10YR6/1 dark grey
Break: uniform grey
Decoration: Three unequal lozenges infilled with horizontal zigzags made with a twelve-toothed comb.
Previously published: TD V, 182, 183.

305. 6084 TD F/I-o/21 grave 6 Phase b/1–a/2 (87/217) Plate 55

SPI	I-d	f	W2	Bd. gef	re	3	1B

D. 2.65 cm. Nd 1.15 cm. Bd. 1.8 cm. H. 9.8 cm. Md. 6.6 cm. Wd. 0.4 cm.
VI 67.34
Restored from sherds, incomplete
Surface colour: 10YR5/3 brown; burnished slip: 10YR4/1 dark grey
Break: dark grey in, greenish brownish grey out
Decoration: Three unequal lozenges infilled with poorly executed horizontal zigzags made with a twelve-toothed comb.
Previously published: TD XVIII, 311, fig. 261, no. 3.

306. 3509A TD A/II-o/21 offering pit 8 Phase E/1–D/3 (81/347) Plate 55

SPI	I-d	vf	W2	Bd. gef	re	3	1B

D. 2.2 cm. Nd 1.2 cm. Bd. 1.5 cm. H. 8.0 cm. Md. 5.8 cm. Wd. 0.4 cm.
VI 72.50
Restored from sherds, incomplete
Surface colour: 10YR4/1 dark grey; burnished slip: 10YR3/1 very dark grey
Break: dark grey in, light grey out
Decoration: Three delineated lozenges infilled with tripartite chevrons made with an eight-toothed comb.
Previously published: TD XVII, I, 294, fig. 168, no. 12.

307. 0861 Vienna A2626 A/II-m/11 grave 6 Phase E/2–1 (67/022) Plate 55

SPI	I-d	f	W2	Bd. gef	re	3	1B

D. 3.2 cm. Nd 1.3 cm. Bd. 1.8 cm. H. 11.0 cm. Md. 6.7 cm. Wd. 0.25 cm.
VI 60.90
Incomplete

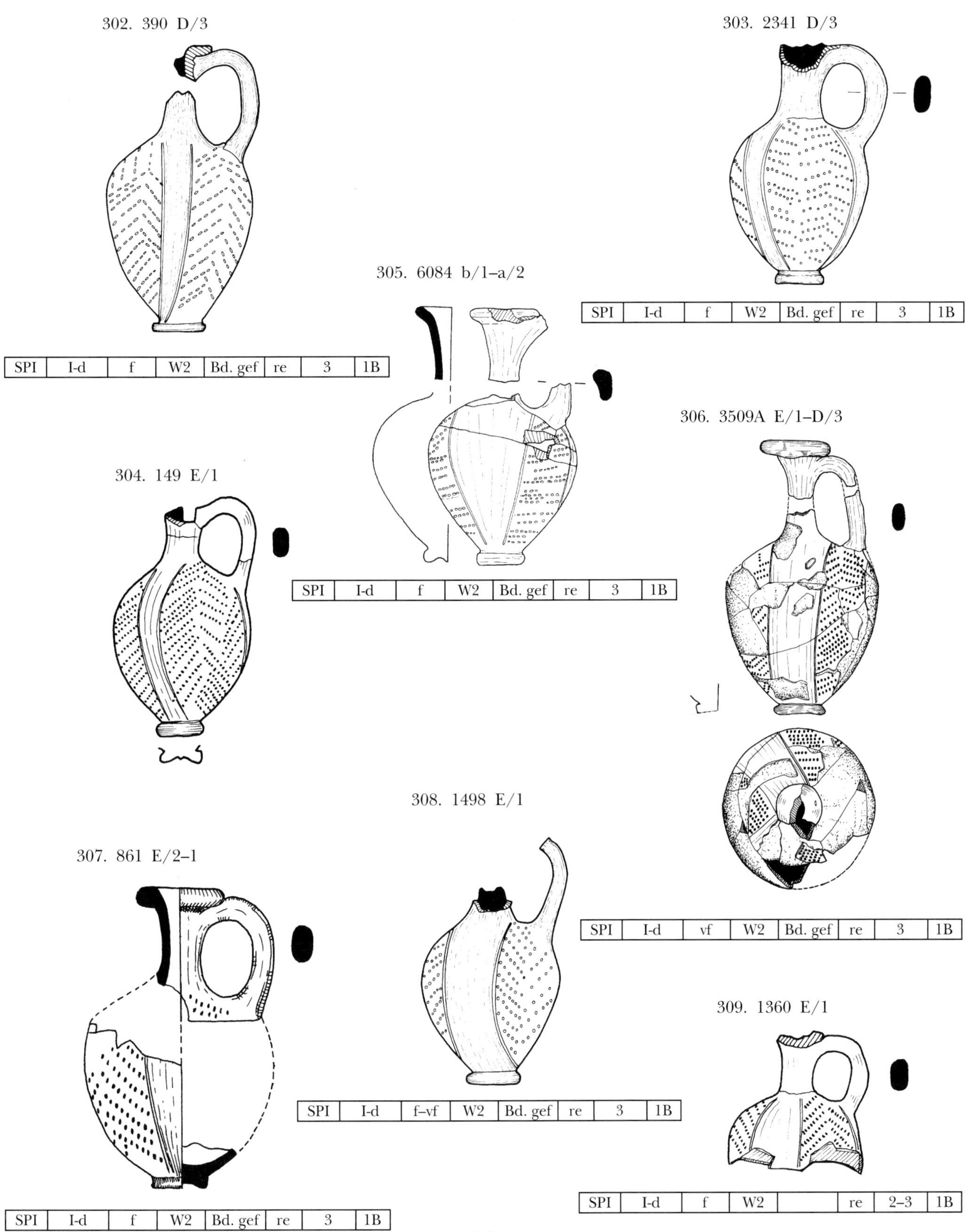

1:2

Late Egyptian Type Group L.1.3c

Plate 55

Surface colour: 10YR4/1 dark grey brown; burnished slip: 10YR3/1 very dark grey
Break: grey core, light grey reduction zones
Decoration: Three unequal lozenges infilled with horizontal zigzags made with a twelve-toothed comb.
Previously published: *TD V*, 157, 158.

308. 1498 Vienna A3028 A/II-n/13 grave 5 Phase E/1 (68/105) Plate 55

SPI	I-d	f–vf	W2	Bd. gef	re	3	1B

Nd. 1.2 cm. Bd. 1.9 cm. pht. 9.0 cm. Md. 5.2 cm. Wd. 0.4 cm.
Incomplete
Surface colour: 10YR4/8 v dark greyish brown: burnished slip: 5YR2/1 black
Break: dusty red core, dark grey reduction zones
Decoration: Three unequal lozenges infilled with horizontal chevrons made with a twelve-toothed comb.
Previously published: *TD V*, 211.

309. 1360 Vienna A2929 A/II-n/11 grave 5 Phase E/1 (69/011) Plate 55

SPI	I-d	f	W2	–	re	2–3	1B

Nd. 1.1 cm. pht. 7.0 cm. Md. 5.0 cm. Wd. 0.4 cm.
Incomplete
Surface colour: 10YR5/2 grey; burnished slip: 10YR3/1 very dark grey
Break: grey core, brown re zones
Decoration: Three unequal lozenges infilled with horizontal chevrons made with a twelve-toothed comb.
Previously published: *TD V*, 199, 200.

310. 3280C TD F/I-i/23 planum 0–1 Phase b/1–a/2 (80/101) Plate 56

SPI	I-d	f	W2	Bd. gef	re	3	1B

Nd. 1.2 cm. Bd. 1.7 cm. pht. 8.9 cm. Md. 5.8 cm. Wd. 0.4 cm.
Incomplete
Surface colour: 10YR4/1 dark grey; burnished slip: 10YR2/1 black
Break: not visible
Decoration: Three delineated lozenges filled with zigzags made with a nine-toothed comb.

311. 0451 Vienna A2331 A/I-g/3 grave 1 Phase D/3 (66/070) Plate 56

SPI	I-d	f	W2	Bd. gef	re	3	1B

Bd. 2.05 cm. pht. 9.0 cm. Md. 5.3 cm. Wd. 0.3 cm.
Incomplete
Surface colour: 2.5Y6/1 grey; burnished slip: 10YR3/2 very dark greyish brown
Break: uniform grey
Decoration: Three unequal lozenges infilled with horizontal zigzags made with a twelve-toothed comb.

312. 2115 Vienna A3420 A/II-l/16 grave 1 Phase E/1 (69/051) Plate 56

SPI	I-d	f	W2	Bd. gef	re	3	1B

Nd. 1.2 cm. Bd.1.6 cm. pht. 8.8 cm. Md. 4.8 cm. Wd. 0.3 cm.
Incomplete
Surface colour: 2.5Y5/1 grey; burnished slip: 2.5Y3/1 very dark grey
Break: uniform grey
Decoration: Three unequal lozenges infilled with horizontal zigzags made with a twelve-toothed comb.
Previously published: *TD XVI*, 263, fig. 192a, no. 1.

313. 0391 Vienna A2311 A/I-g/3 grave 1 Phase D/3 (66/063) Plate 56

SPI	I-d	f	W2	Bd. gef	re	3	1B

Nd. 1.2 cm. Bd.1.5 cm. pht. 7.5 cm. Md. 4.8 cm. Wd. 0.34 cm.
Incomplete
Surface colour: 2.5Y5/1 grey; burnished slip: 2.5Y3/1 very dark grey
Break: uniform grey
Decoration: Three unequal lozenges infilled with horizontal zigzags made with a twelve-toothed comb.

314. 6030 TD F/I-o/21 intrusive within grave 4 unstratified (87/209) Plate 56

SPI	I-d	f	W2	Bd. gef	re	3	1B

Nd. 1.3 cm. Bd. 1.9 cm. pht. 6.9 cm. Md. 5.35 cm. Wd. 0.4 cm.
Incomplete
Surface colour: 5YR4/1 dark grey; burnished slip: 2.5YN2 black
Break: not visible
Decoration: Three unequal lozenges infilled with horizontal zigzags made with a twelve-toothed comb.

315. 1856 Vienna A3259 A/II-m/13 grave 14 Phase E/1 (68/159) Plate 56

SPI	I-d	f	W2	Bd. gef	re	3	1B

Nd. 1.5 cm. Bd. 1.8 cm. pht. 8.1 cm. Md. 5.7 cm. Wd. 0.3 cm.
Incomplete
Surface colour: 10YR4/1 grey; burnished slip: 10YR3/1 very dark grey
Break: grey core, brownish grey reduction zones
Decoration: Three unequal lozenges infilled with horizontal zigzags made with an eight-toothed comb.
Previously published: *TD V*, 203.

316. 0185 Vienna A1630 A/II-l/12 grave 2 Phase E/1 (66/036) Plate 56

SPI	I-d	f	W2	Bd. gef	re	3	1B

Nd. 1.35 cm. Bd. 1.8 cm. pht. 6.7 cm. Md. 5.4 cm. Wd. 0.3 cm.
Incomplete
Surface colour: 10YR5–6/2 grey brown; burnished slip: 10YR3/1 very dark grey
Break: dark grey core, brown reduction zones
Decoration: Three unequal lozenges infilled with horizontal zigzags made with a twelve-toothed comb.
Previously published: *TD V*, 187, 188.

317. 1251 Vienna A2837 A/II-l/14 grave 5 Phase E/1 (66/068) Plate 56

SPI	I-d	f	W2	Bd. gef	re	2	1B

Bd. 2.5 cm. pht. 9.5 cm. Md. 7.3 cm. Wd. 0.3 cm.
Incomplete
Surface colour: 10YR6/2 grey; burnished slip: 10YR6/1 dark grey
Break: dark grey core, brown reduction zones
Decoration: Three unequal lozenges infilled with horizontal zigzags made with a twelve-toothed comb.
Previously published: *TD XVI*, 254, fig. 189b, no. 23.

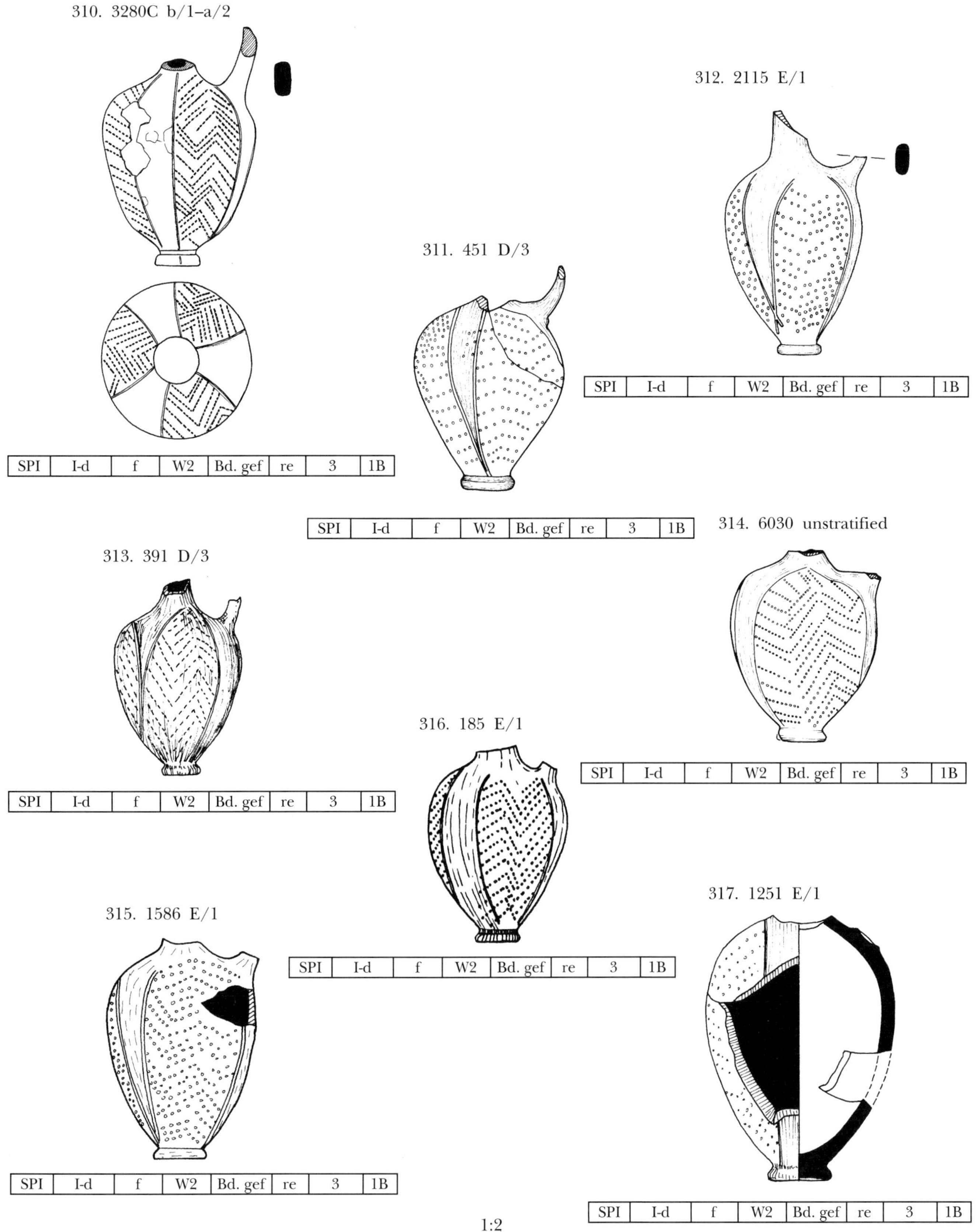

Late Egyptian Type Group L.1.3c

Plate 56

318. 1276 Vienna A2862 A/II-n/11 grave 3 Phase E/1 (68/030) Plate 57

SPI	I-d	f	W2	Bd. gef	re	3	1B

Nd. 1.15 cm. Bd. 1.5 cm. pht. 8.0 cm. Md. 5.3 cm. Wd. 0.4 cm.
Incomplete
Surface colour: 10YR5–6/3 brown; burnished slip: 2.5Y/1 black
Break: dark grey core, brown reduction zones
Decoration: Three unequal lozenges infilled with horizontal zigzags made with a twelve-toothed comb.
Previously published: TD V, 234, 235.

319. 0193 Vienna A2216 A/II-l/12 grave 2 Phase E/1 (66/014) Plate 57

SPI	I-d	f	W2	Bd. gef	re	3	1B

Bd. 1.85 cm. pht. 8.0 cm. Md. 5.8 cm. Wd. 0.5 cm.
Incomplete
Surface colour: 10YR5/2–3 dark greyish brown; burnished slip: 10YR2/1 black
Break: uniform light grey
Decoration: Three unequal lozenges infilled with horizontal zigzags made with a twelve-toothed comb.
Previously published: TD V, 187 189.

320. 3518 Cairo A/II-s/18 grave 1 Phase E/1 (80/401) Plate 57

SPI	I-d	f	W2	Bd. gef	re	3	1B

Nd. 1.3 cm. Bd. 1.6 cm. pht. 7.8 cm. Md. 5.0 cm. Wd. 0.4 cm.
Incomplete
Surface colour: 10YR4/1 dark grey; burnished slip: 10YR2/1 black
Break: not visible
Decoration: Three unequal lozenges infilled with horizontal zigzags made with a ten-toothed comb.
Previously published: TD XVI, 293, fig. 214, no. 3.

321. 0352 Vienna A2299 A/I-g/3 profile Phase ? (66/050) Plate 57

SPI	I-d	f	W2	Bd. gef	re	3	1B

Nd. 1.3 cm. Bd. 1.6 cm. pht. 7.4 cm. Md 5.0 cm. Wd. 0.3 cm.
Incomplete
Surface colour: 2.5Y5/1 grey; burnished slip: 2.5Y3/2 black
Break: uniform dark grey
Decoration: Three unequal lozenges infilled with horizontal zigzags made with an eight-toothed comb.

322. 4121B TD A/II-l/17 planum 4 Phase E/2 (82/160) Plate 57

SPI	I-d	f	W2	Bd. gef	re	3	1B

Bd. 1.7 cm. pht. 8.0 cm. Md. 5.8 cm. Wd. 0.3 cm.
Restored from sherds, incomplete
Surface colour: 10YR2/1 black; burnished slip: 7.5YR4/4 dark brown
Break: uniform grey brown
Decoration: Three unequal lozenges infilled with horizontal zigzags made with a twelve-toothed comb.

323. 2135 Vienna A3436 A/II-l/16 grave 1 Phase E/1 (69/061) Plate 57

SPI	I-d	f	W2	Bd. gef	re	3	1B

Bd. 1.7 cm. pht. 7.8 cm. Md. 5.7 cm. Wd. 0.3 cm.
Incomplete
Surface colour: eroded
Break: uniform grey
Decoration: Three unequal lozenges infilled with horizontal zigzags made with a twelve-toothed comb.
Previously published: TD XVI, 263, fig. 192a, no. 8.

324. 0054 Vienna A2163 A/II-l/12 grave ?? Phase ? (66/006) Plate 57

SPI	I-d	f	W2	Bd. gef	re	3	1B

Bd. 1.8 cm. pht. 8.0 cm. Md. 6.3 cm. Wd. 0.3 cm.
Incomplete
Surface colour: 10YR6/1 grey; burnished slip: 10YR3/2 very dark greyish brown
Break: dark grey core, greyish brown reduction zones
Decoration: Three unequal lozenges infilled with horizontal zigzags made with a twelve-toothed comb.

325. 4164C TD A/II-o/21 planum 2–3 Phase ? (01/065) Plate 57

SPI	I-d	vf	W2	Bd. gef	re	3	1B

Bd. 2.0 cm. pht. 4.9 cm. Wd. 0.4 cm.
Incomplete
Surface colour: 10YR4/1 dark grey; burnished slip: 10YR2/1 black
Break: uniform grey brown
Unusually thick at base
Decoration: Three unequal lozenges infilled with horizontal zigzags made with a twelve-toothed comb.

326. 3453B TD A/II-m/18 planum 1–2 Phase D/3–2 (81/125) Plate 57

SPI	I-d	f	W2	Bd. gef	re	3	1B

Bd. 1.4 cm. pht. 4.8. Wd. 0.4 cm.
Incomplete
Surface colour: 5YR4/1 dark grey; burnished slip: 2.5YN2 black
Break: uniform light grey
Decoration: Three lozenges infilled with horizontal zigzags made with a twelve-toothed comb.

327. 6089A TD F/I-o/21 offering pit 9 unstratified (87/089) Plate 58

SPI	I-d	F	W2	Bd. gef	re	3	1B

Nd. 1.4 cm. Bd. 1.9 cm. pht. 4.85. Wd. 0.4 cm.
Incomplete
Surface colour: 5YR4/1 dark grey; burnished slip: 2.5YN2 black
Break: uniform light grey
Decoration: three lozenges infilled with zigzags made with a six toothed comb.
Same pot as next ?
Previously published: TD XVII, I, 364, fig. 212, no. 10.

328. 6089B TD F/I-o/21 offering pit 9 unstratified (87/089) Plate 58

SPI	I-d	f	W2	Bd. gef	re	3	1B

Nd. 1.4 cm. Bd. 1.9 cm. pht. 4.85. Wd. 0.4 cm.
Incomplete
Surface colour: 5YR4/1 dark grey; burnished slip: 2.5YN2 black

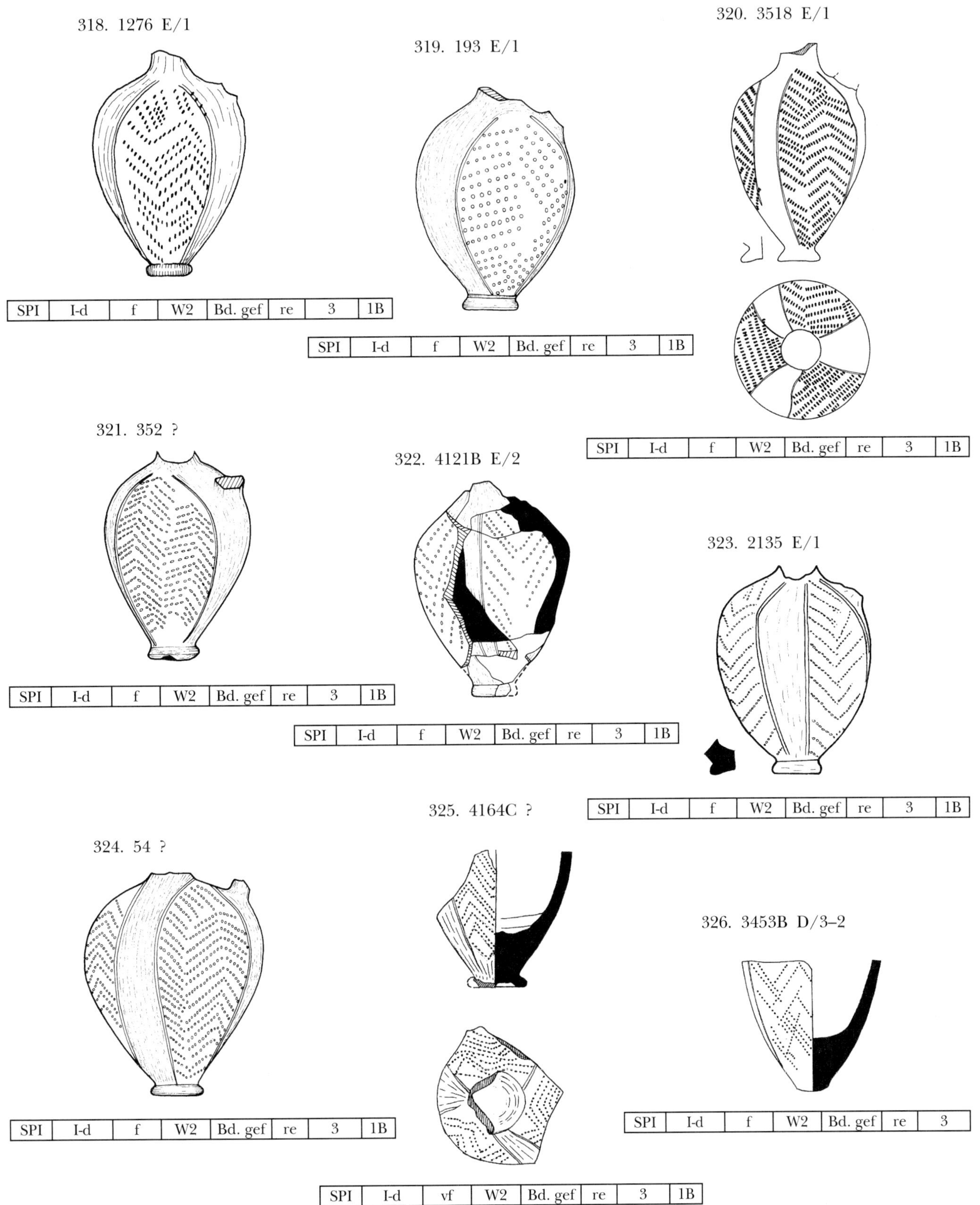

1:2

Late Egyptian Type Group L.1.3c

Plate 57

328. 6089B unstratified

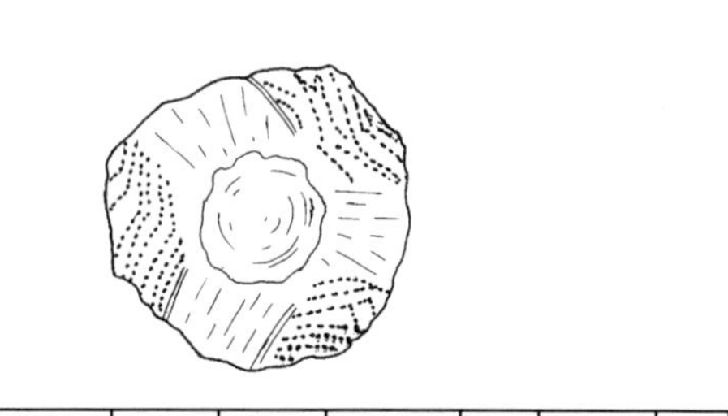

SPI	I-d	f	W2	Bd. gef	re	3	1B

330. 21A unstratified

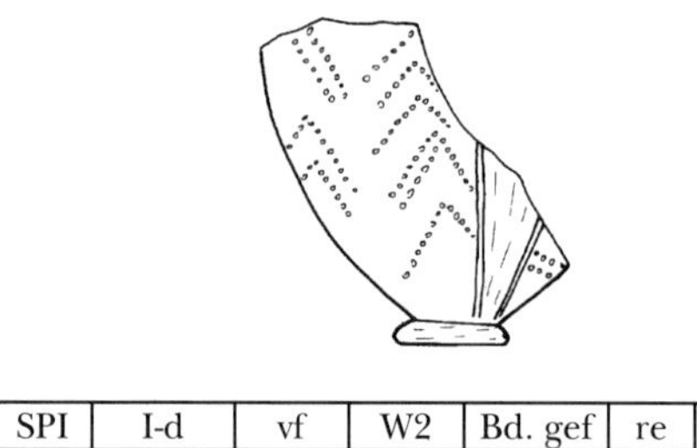

SPI	I-d	vf	W2	Bd. gef	re	3	1B

331. 2141 E/3

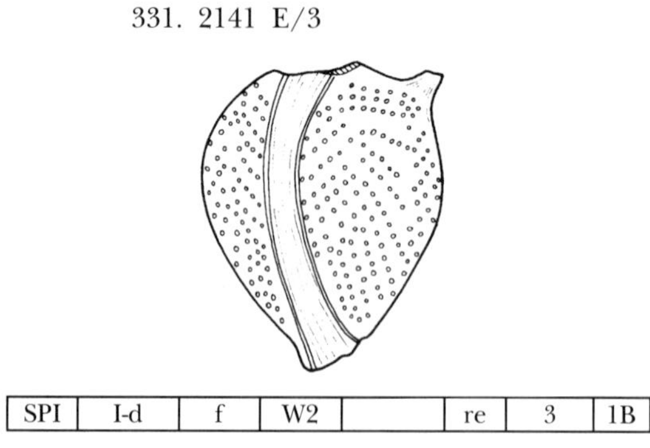

SPI	I-d	f	W2		re	3	1B

327. 6089A unstratified

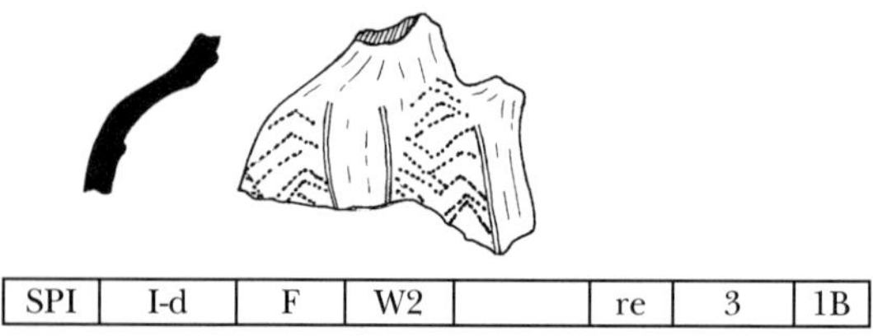

SPI	I-d	F	W2		re	3	1B

329. 4164D ?

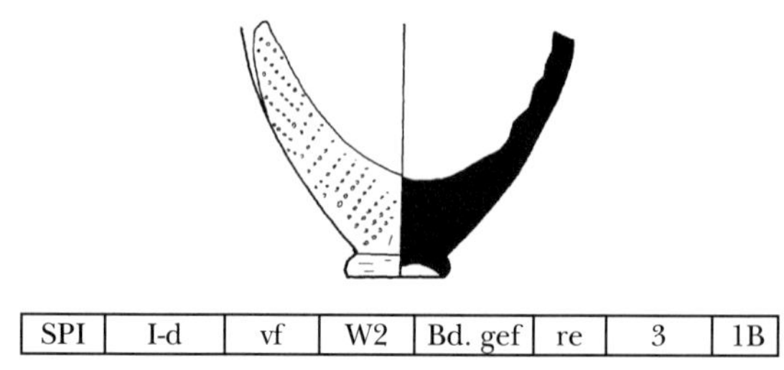

SPI	I-d	vf	W2	Bd. gef	re	3	1B

332. 9180 a/2

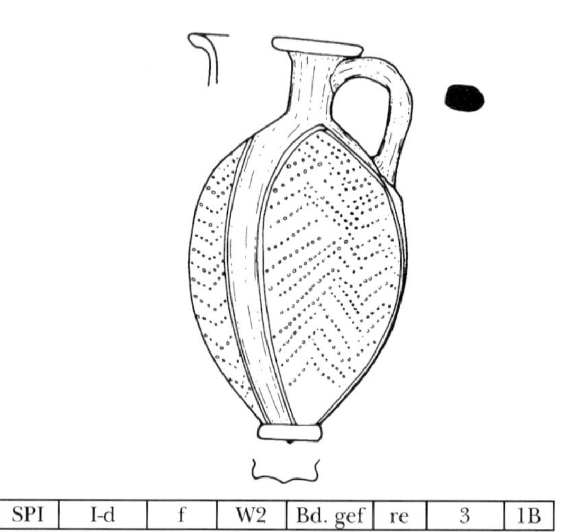

SPI	I-d	f	W2	Bd. gef	re	3	1B

1:2

Late Egyptian Type Group L.1.3c

Plate 58

Break: uniform light grey
Decoration: three lozenges infilled with zigzags made with a six toothed comb.
Same pot as previous ?
Previously published: TD XVII, I, 364, fig. 212, no. 11.

329. 4164D TD A/II-o/21 planum 2–3 Phase ? (82/027) Plate 58

SPI	I-d	vf	W2	Bd. gef	re	3	1B

Bd. 1.7 cm. pht. 4.7 cm. Wd. 0.3 cm.
Incomplete
Surface colour: 5YR6/1 grey; burnished slip 5YR2/2 dark reddish brown
Break: wide black core, brown reduction zones
Decoration: Three delineated lozenges with horizontal zigzags infilled with a twelve-toothed comb. Intervening areas vertically burnished.

330. 0021A Vienna A2141a A/I-g/6 planum 0–1 surface find (66/006) Plate 58

SPI	I-d	vf	W2	Bd. gef	re	3	1B

Bd. 1.2 cm. pht. 4.7 cm. Wd. 0.3 cm.
Incomplete
Surface colour: 10YR4/1 dark grey; burnished slip: 10YR2/1 black
Break: uniform grey brown
Decoration: Three unequal lozenges infilled with horizontal zigzags made with a twelve-toothed comb.

331. 2141 Vienna A3439 A/II-l/16 grave 1 Phase E/1 (69/075) Plate 58

SPI	I-d	f	W2	Bd. gef	re	3	1B

pht. 6.4 cm. Md. 5.3 cm. Wd. 0.3 cm.
Incomplete
Surface colour: 2.5Y5/1 grey; burnished slip: 2.5Y3/1 very dark grey
Break: not visible
Decoration: Three unequal lozenges infilled with horizontal zigzags made with a twelve-toothed comb.
Previously published: TD XVI, 263, fig. 192a, no. 15.

Type Group L.1.3c with Variant Base

332. 9180 F/II-r/22 L81 Phase a/2 (06/154) Plates 58, 141

SPI	I-d	f	W2	Bd. gef	re	3	1B

D. 2.8 cm. Nd 1.2 cm. Bd. 2.1 cm. H. 10.2 cm. Md. 5.4 cm. Wd. 0.3 cm.
VI 52.94
Intact
Surface colour: 2.5Y5/1 grey; burnished slip: 2.5Y4/1 very dark grey
Break: not visible
Decoration: three lozenges with zig-zag decoration. No burnish on rim.

333. 0367 Vienna A1643 A/I-g/3 grave 1 Phase D/3 (66/052) Plate 59

SPI	I-d	f	W2	Bd. gef	re	3	1B

D. 3.05 cm. Nd 1.45 cm. Bd. 2.2 cm. H. 9.9 cm. Md. 6.4 cm. Wd. 0.3 cm.
VI 64.64
Intact
Surface colour: 10YR4/1 grey; burnished slip: 10YR2–3/1 black – very dark grey
Break: not visible
Decoration: Three unequal lozenges infilled with horizontal zigzags made with a twelve-toothed comb.

334. 2138 Vienna A1718 A/II-l/16 grave 1 Phase E/1 (69/062) Plate 59

SPI	I-d	f	W2	Bd. gef	re	3	1B

D. 2.7 cm. Nd 1.2 cm. Bd. 2.0 cm. H. 9.1 cm. Md. 5.5 cm. Wd. 0.3 cm.
VI 60.43
Intact
Surface colour: 2.5Y6/1 grey; burnished slip: 2.5Y4/1 dark grey
Break: red core, red and grey reduction zones
Decoration: Three unequal lozenges infilled with horizontal zigzags made with a twelve-toothed comb.
Previously published: TD XVI, 263, fig. 192a, no. 10.

335. 3050 Vienna A3338 A/II-p/21 grave 1 Phase E/1 (79/124) Plate 59

SPI	I-d	f	W2	Bd. gef	re	3	1B

D. 2.6 cm. Nd 1.4 cm. Bd. 2.2 cm. H. 9.5 cm. Md. 5.6 cm. Wd. 0.3 cm.
VI 58.94
Incomplete
Surface colour: 2.5Y5/1 grey; burnished slip: 2.5Y4/1 very dark grey
Break: uniform grey
Decoration: Three unequal lozenges infilled with horizontal zigzags made with a twelve-toothed comb.

336. 0231 Cairo JE 91563B A/II-l/12 grave 1 Phase E/1 (66/032) Plate 59

SPI	I-d	m	W2	Bd. gef	re	2–3	1B

D. 2.55 cm. Nd 1.3 cm. Bd. 1.9 cm. H. 9.2 cm. Md. 5.4 cm. Wd. 0.3 cm.
VI 58.69
Intact
Surface colour: 10YR4/1 dark grey; burnished slip: 10YR3/1 very dark grey
Break: dark grey core, greyish brown reduction zones
Decoration: Three unequal lozenges infilled with horizontal zigzags made with a twelve-toothed comb.
Previously published: TD V, 176 179.

337. 4904 TD F/I-k/24 planum 0–1 Phase b/1–a/2 (84/060) Plate 59
D. 2.6 cm. Nd 1.25 cm. Bd. 1.9 cm. H. 10.2 cm. Md. 5.6 cm.

SPI	I-d	f	W2	Bd. gef	re	3	1B

Wd. 0.3 cm.
VI 54.90
Intact
Surface colour: 10YR6–7/3–4 pale brown; burnished slip: 10YR3/2 very dark greyish brown
Break: not visible
Decoration: Three unequal lozenges infilled with horizontal chevrons made with a fourteen-toothed comb. Undecorated parts vertically burnished. Rim horizontally burnished.

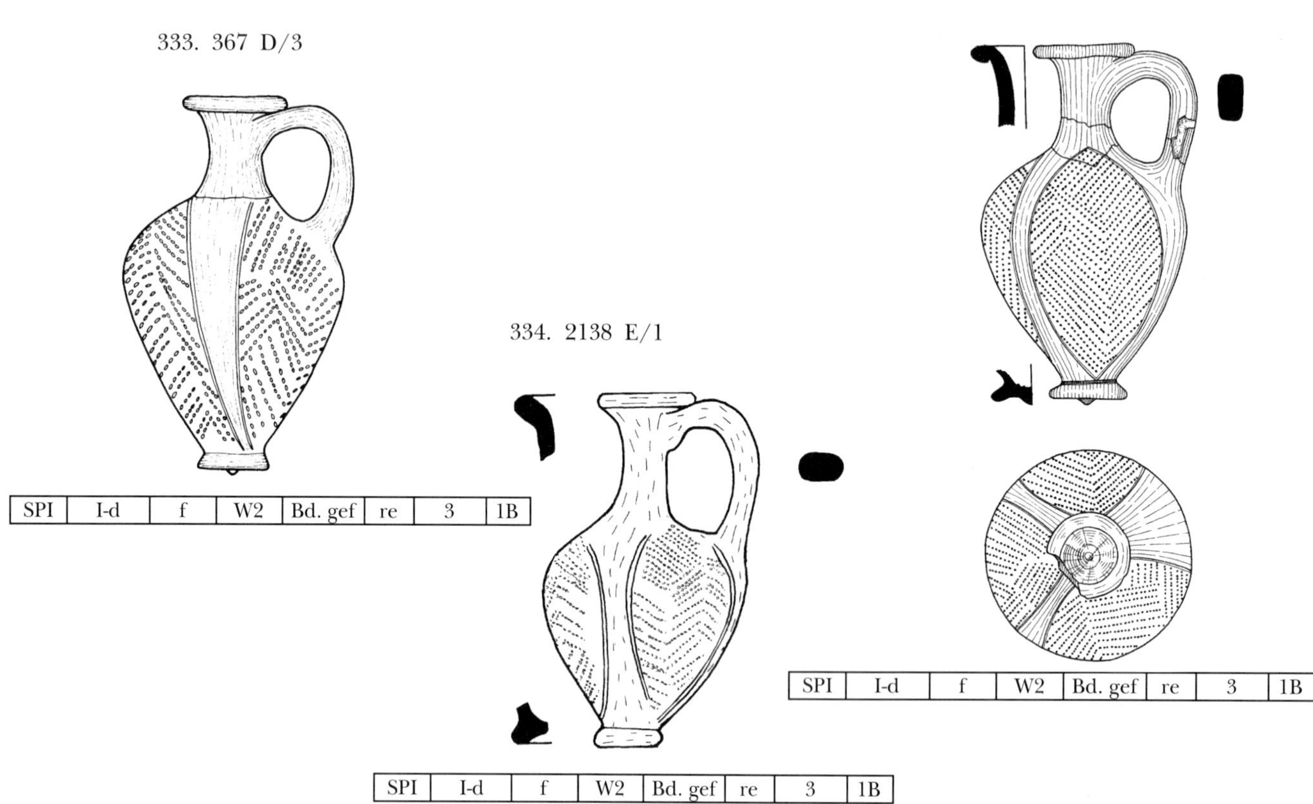

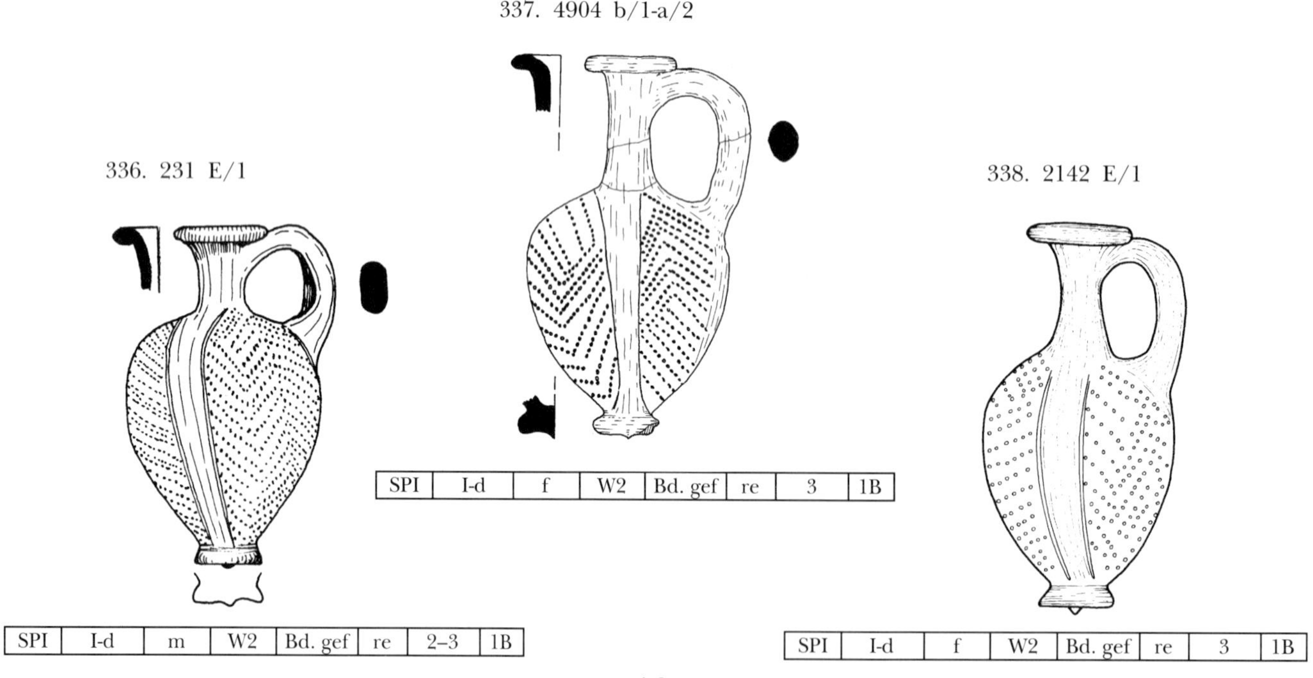

1:2

Late Egyptian Type Group L.1.3c variant

Plate 59

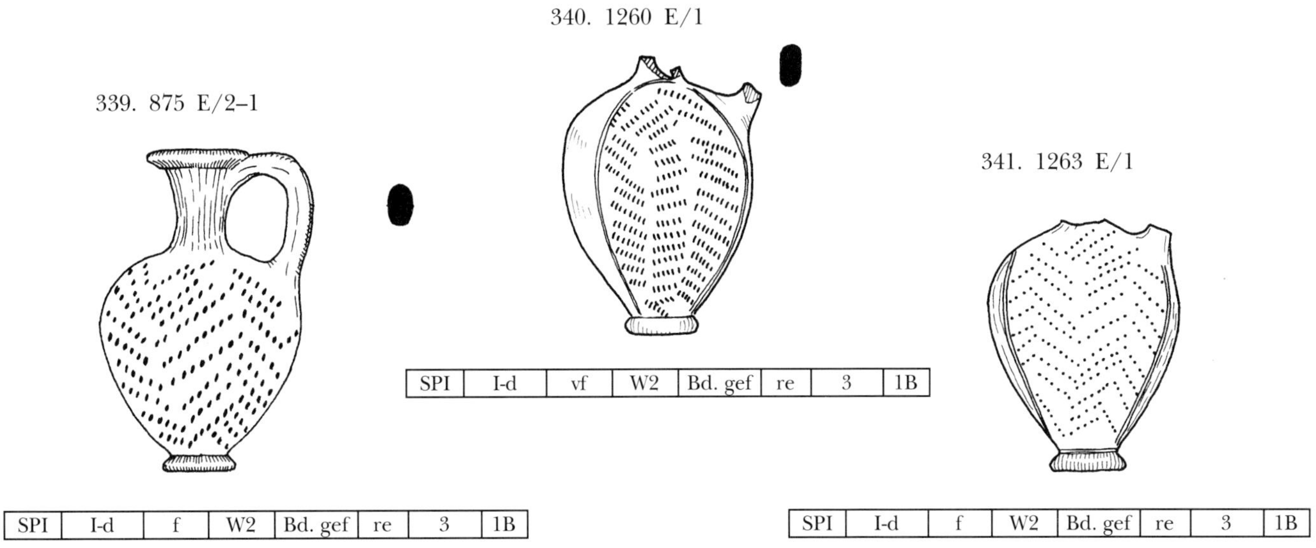

339. 875 E/2–1

SPI	I-d	f	W2	Bd. gef	re	3	1B

340. 1260 E/1

SPI	I-d	vf	W2	Bd. gef	re	3	1B

341. 1263 E/1

SPI	I-d	f	W2	Bd. gef	re	3	1B

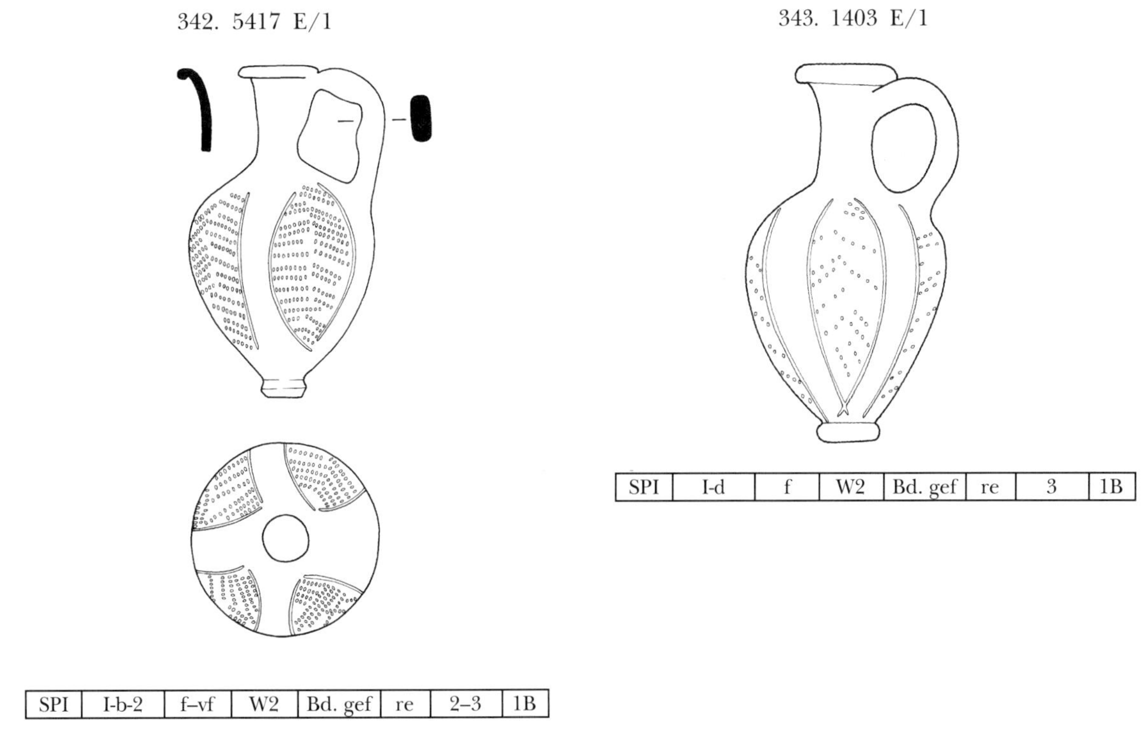

342. 5417 E/1

SPI	I-b-2	f–vf	W2	Bd. gef	re	2–3	1B

343. 1403 E/1

SPI	I-d	f	W2	Bd. gef	re	3	1B

1:2

Late Egyptian Type Groups L.1.3d and L.1.4a

Plate 60

338. 2142 Vienna A1719 A/II-l/16 grave 1 Phase E/1 (69/075) Plate 59

SPI	I-d	f	W2	Bd. gef	re	3	1B

D. 2.8 cm. Nd 1.2 cm. Bd. 2.1 cm. H. 10.2 cm. Md. 5.4 cm. Wd. 0.3 cm.
VI 52.94
Intact
Surface colour: 2.5Y5/1 grey; burnished slip: 2.5Y4/1 very dark grey
Break: not visible
Decoration: Three unequal lozenges infilled with horizontal zigzags made with a twelve-toothed comb.
Previously published: TD XVI, 263, fig. 192a, no. 12.

Type Group L.1.3d

339. 0875 Vienna A1656 A/II-m/11 grave 6 Phase E/2–1 (67/024) Plates 60, 141

SPI	I-d	f	W2	Bd. gef	re	3	1B

D. 2.7 cm. Nd 1.35 cm. Bd. 1.9 cm. H. 8.7 cm. Md. 5.5 cm. Wd. 0.3 cm.
VI 63.21
Intact
Surface colour: 10YR4/2 dark grey brown; burnished slip: 10YR3/1 very dark grey
Break: not visible
Decoration: Two unequal lozenges with horizontal zigzags made with a twelve-toothed comb.
Previously published: TD V, 157, 159.

340. 1260 Vienna A2848 A/II-n/11 grave 3 Phase E/1 (69/012) Plate 60

SPI	I-d	vf	W2	Bd. gef	re	3	1B

Bd. 1.9 cm. pht. 6.9 cm. Md. 5.0 cm. Wd. 0.3 cm.
Incomplete
Surface colour: 10YR5/2–3 grey brown; burnished slip: 10YR3/1 very dark grey
Break: uniform grey
Decoration: Two unequal lozenges infilled with horizontal zigzags made with a twelve-toothed comb.
Previously published: TD V, 234, 235.

341. 1263 Vienna A2850 A/II-n/11 grave 3 Phase E/1 (69/028) Plate 60

SPI	I-d	f	W2	Bd. gef	re	3	1B

Bd. 1.8 cm. pht. 6.5 cm. Md. 5.1 cm. Wd. 0.35 cm.
Incomplete
Surface colour: 10YR5/2 grey brown; burnished slip: 10YR3/1 very dark grey
Break: uniform dark grey
Decoration: Two unequal lozenges infilled with horizontal zigzags made with a twelve-toothed comb.
Previously published: TD V, 234, 235.

Type Group L.1.4 (Piriform 2a)

Type group L.1.4 is similar to the previous group but in place of a ring base, the bases were left as a flat disc. Vessels of this group were also decorated with delineated lozenges, decorative styles L.1.4a, with four lozenges, L.1.4b with three and L.1.4c with two. Vessels of all three sub-types are found at Tell el-Dab^ca.

Type Group L.1.4a

342. 5417 TD A/II-k/17 grave 30 burial 1 Phase E/1 (85/263) Plates 60, 141

SPI	I-b-2	f–vf	W2	Bd. gef	re	2–3	1B

D. 2.2 cm. Nd 1.0 cm. Bd. 2.2 cm. H. 8.6 cm. Md. 5.0 cm. Wd. 0.3 cm.
VI 58.13
Intact
Surface colour: 2.5Y4/0 dark grey; burnished slip: 2.5YR3–4/0 very dark grey
Break: not visible
Decoration: Four unequal lozenges infilled with horizontal chevons made with a seven-toothed comb, somewhat carelessly done.
Previously published: TD XVI, 248, fig. 184, no. 6.

343. 1403 Vienna A1668 A/II-l/14 grave 5 Phase E/1 (68/093) Plate 60

SPI	I-d	f	W2	Bd. gef	re	3	1B

D. 2.78 cm. Nd. 1.3 cm. Bd. 1.7 cm. H. 9.8 cm. Md 5.4 cm. Wd. 0.4 cm.
VI 55.10
Intact
Surface colour: 2.5Y5/1 grey; burnished slip: 2.5Y3/2 black
Break: uniform dark grey
Decoration: Four unequal lozenges infilled with horizontal chevons made with a six-toothed comb.
Previously published: TD XVI, 254, fig. 189b, no. 12.

Type Group L.1.4b

344. 2275 Vienna A1724 A/II-k/14 grave 1 Phase E/1 or D/3 (69/087) Plates 61, 141

SPI	I-d	f	W2	Bd. gef	re	3	1B

D. 3.0 cm. Nd 1.2 cm. Bd. 1.8 cm. H. 9.9 cm. Md. 5.4 cm. Wd. 0.3 cm.
VI 54.54
Intact
Surface colour: 2.5Y7/1 light grey; burnished slip: 2.5Y2.5/1 black
Break: not visible
Decoration: Three unequal lozenges with chevrons or zigzag decoration, made with a twelve-toothed comb.
Previously published: TD XVI, 297, fig. 216b, no. 8.

345. 0384 Vienna A1606 A/I-g/3 grave 1 Phase D/3 (66/056) Plate 61

SPI	I-d	f	W2	Bd. gef	re	3	1B

D. 2.6 cm. Nd 1.2 cm. Bd. 2.1 cm. H. 9.3 cm. Md. 6.02 cm. Wd. 0.35 cm.
VI 64.73
Intact
Surface colour: 10YR5/2 dark grey brown; burnished slip: 10YR3–4/1 dark grey
Break: not visible

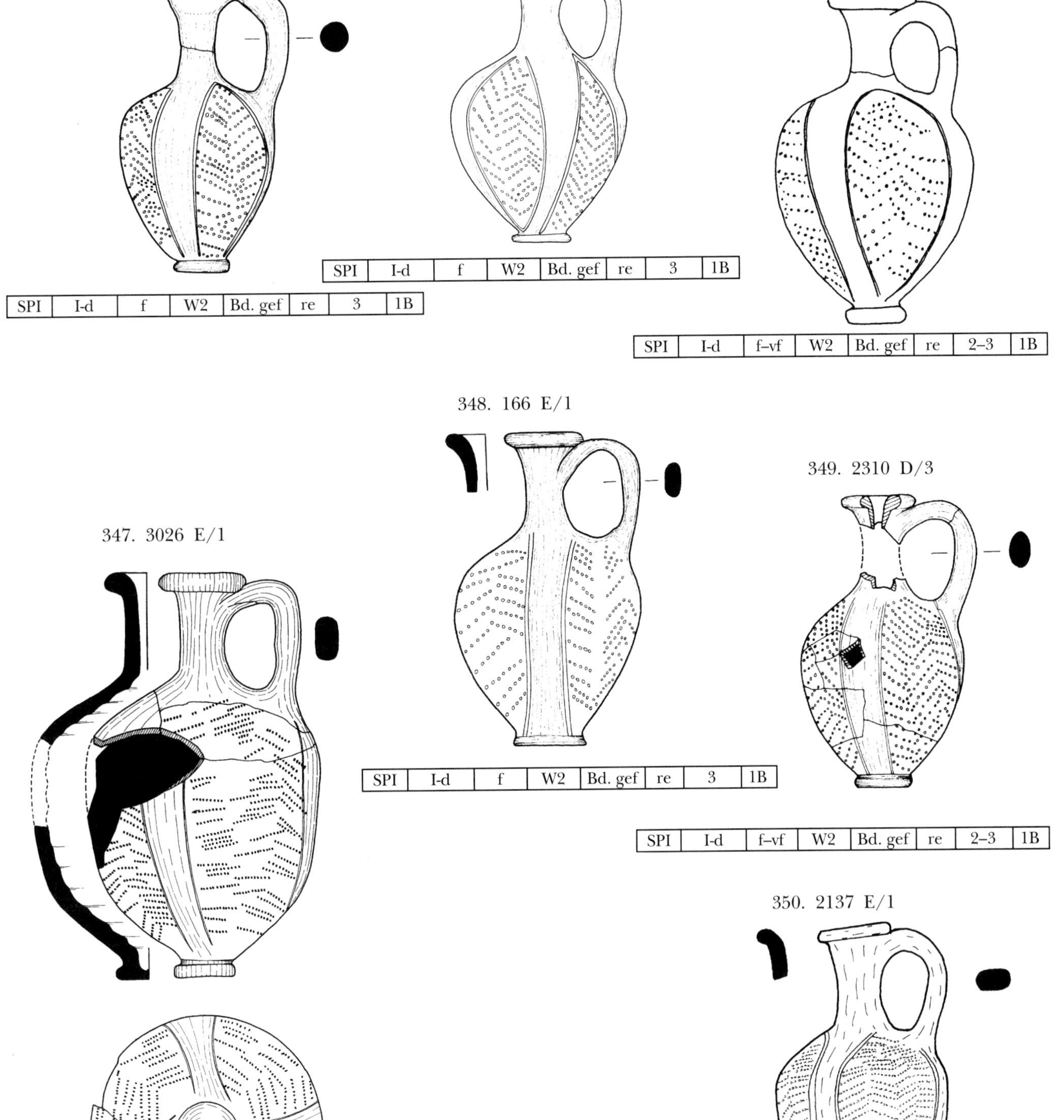

344.

SPI	I-d	f	W2	Bd. gef	re	3	1B

345.

SPI	I-d	f	W2	Bd. gef	re	3	1B

346.

SPI	I-d	f–vf	W2	Bd. gef	re	2–3	1B

348.

SPI	I-d	f	W2	Bd. gef	re	3	1B

349.

SPI	I-d	f–vf	W2	Bd. gef	re	2–3	1B

347.

SPI	I-d	f	W2	Bd. gef	re	2–3	1B

350.

SPI	I-d	f	W2	Bd. gef	re	3	1B

1:2

Late Egyptian Type Group L.1.4b

Plate 61

Decoration: Three unequal lozenges with chevrons or zigzag decoration, made with a twelve-toothed comb.
Previously published: TD V, 157, 158.

346. 1386 Vienna A2943 A/II-l/14 grave 5 Phase E/1 (68/090) Plate 61

SPI	I-d	f–vf	W2	Bd. gef	re	2–3	1B

D. 2.5 cm. Nd 1.25 cm. Bd. 2.1 cm. H. 11.1 cm. Md. 6.7 cm. Wd. 0.4 cm.
VI 60.36
Restored from sherds, complete
Surface colour: 2.5Y5/1 grey; burnished slip: 2.5Y2.5/1 black
Break: uniform grey
Decoration: Three unequal lozenges with zigzag decoration, made with an eight-toothed comb.
Previously published: TD XVI, 254, fig. 189b, no. 15.

347. 3026 Cairo A/II-p/20 grave 3 Phase E/1 (79/202) Plate 61

SPI	I-d	f	W2	Bd. gef	re	2–3	1B

D. 3.01 cm. Nd. 1.52 cm. Bd. 2.1 cm. H. 13.6 cm. Md 8.2 cm. Wd. 0.4 cm.
VI 60.29
Restored from sherds, incomplete
Surface colour: 2.5Y5/1 grey; burnished slip: 2.5Y3/1 light olive brown
Break: not visible
Decoration: Three unequal lozenges with poorly executed zigzag decoration, made with a twelve-toothed comb.

348. 0166 Vienna A1600 A/II-l/12 grave 2 Phase E/1 (66/037) Plate 61

SPI	I-d	f	W2	Bd. gef	re	3	1B

D. 2.65 cm. Nd 1.2 cm. Bd. 2.3 cm. H. 10.6 cm. Md. 6.2 cm. Wd. 0.3 cm.
VI 58.49
Intact
Surface colour: 10YR6/1 grey; burnished slip: 10YR3/1 very dark grey
Break: not visible
Decoration: Three unequal lozenges with zigzag decoration, made with an eight-toothed comb.
Previously published: TD V, 185.

349. 2310 Vienna A3539 A/II-m/15 grave 3 Phase D/3 (69/108) Plate 61

SPI	I-d	f–vf	W2	Bd. gef	re	2–3	1B

D. 2.6 cm. Nd 1.2 cm. Bd. 2.0 cm. H. 9.8 cm. Md. 5.6 cm. Wd. 0.2 cm.
VI 57.14
Incomplete
Surface colour: 2.5Y5/1 grey; burnished slip: 2.5Y2.5/1 black
Break: uniform grey
Decoration: Three unequal lozenges with zigzag decoration, made with a twelve-toothed comb.
Previously illustrated: *TD XVI,* 313, fig. 234, no. 9.

350. 2137 Vienna A1717 A/II-l/16 grave 1 Phase E/1 (66/062) Plate 61

SPI	I-d	f	W2	Bd. gef	re	3	1B

D. 2.7 cm. Nd 1.6 cm. Bd. 1.9 cm. H. 10.2 cm. Md. 5.6 cm. Wd. 0.3 cm.
VI 54.90
Intact
Surface colour: 2.5Y6/1 grey; burnished slip: 2.5Y3/1 very dark grey
Break: not visible
Decoration: Three unequal lozenges with zigzag decoration, made with a twelve-toothed comb.
Previously published: TD XVI, 263, fig. 192a, no. 9.

351. 3013 Vienna TDS 3013 A/II-p/20 grave 3 Phase E/1 (79/201) Plate 62

SPI	I-d	f	W2	Bd. gef	re	2–3	1B

Bd. 1.5 cm. pht. 11.2 cm. Wd. 0.3 cm.
Incomplete
Surface colour: 2.5Y3/1 dark grey; burnished slip: 2.5Y3/1 dark grey
Break: uniform brownish grey
Decoration: Three unequal lozenges with zigzag decoration, made with a twelve-toothed comb.

352. 0866 Vienna A2630 A/II-m/11 grave 6 Phase E/2 (68/023) Plate 62

SPI	I-d	f	W2	Bd. gef	re	3	1B

D. 2.6 cm. Nd 1.45 cm. Bd. 1.85 cm. H. 11.3 cm. Md. 6.1 cm. Wd. 0.35 cm.
VI 53.98
Incomplete
Surface colour: 10YR5–6/2 light brown grey; burnished slip: 10YR3–4/1 dark grey
Break: brown core, grey reduction zones
Decoration: Three unequal lozenges with zigzag decoration, made with an eight-toothed comb.
Previously published: TD V, 157, 158.

Type Group L.1.4c

353. 1358 Vienna A2927 A/II-n/11 grave 5 Phase E/1 (68/085) Plate 62

SPI	I-d	f–vf	W2	Bd. gef	re	2–3	1B

D. 2.5 cm. Nd 1.2 cm. Bd. 1.8 cm. H. 9.3 cm. Md. 5.4 cm. Wd. 0.4 cm.
VI 58.06
Restored from sherds, complete
Surface colour: 10YR5/2–4/1 grey brown; burnished slip: 10YR3/1 very dark grey
Break: dark grey core, brown and light grey reduction zones
Decoration: Two unequal lozenges with zigzag decoration, made with an eight-toothed comb.
Previously published: TD V, 199, 200.

354. 0525 Vienna A2370 A/II-m/13 oven Phase D/3 (67/084) Plate 62

SPI	I-d	f–m	W2	Bd. gef	re	3	1B

Nd. 1.5 cm. Bd. 1.5 cm. pht. 7.0 cm. Md. 6.4 cm. Wd. 0.3 cm.
Incomplete
Surface colour: 10YR5.5/2 grey brown; burnished slip: 10YR4/1 dark grey
Break: light grey core, grey reduction zones

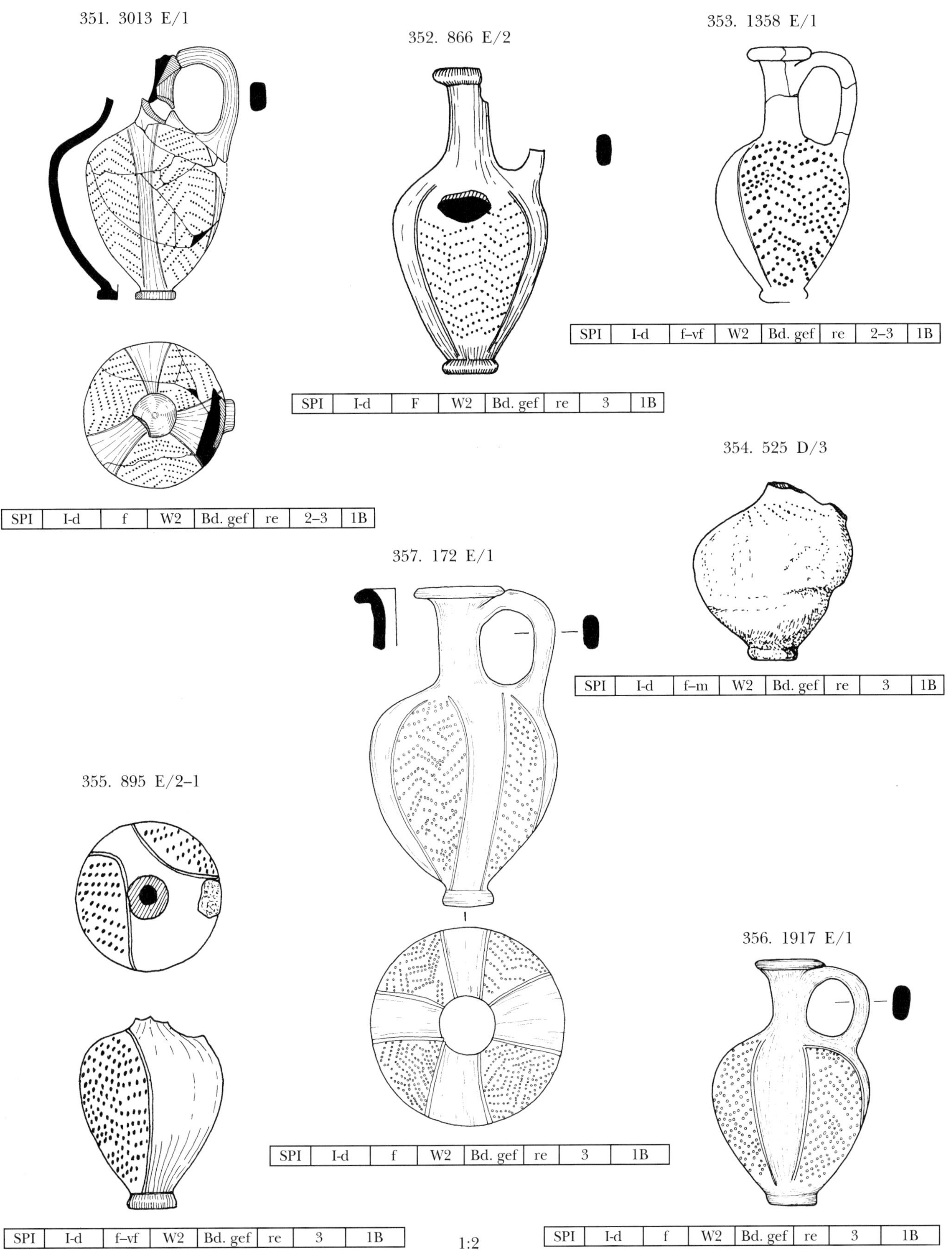

Late Egyptian Type Groups L.1.4b–c, L.1.5a

Plate 61

Decoration: eroded.
Previously published: *TD V*, 259.

355. 0895 Vienna A2648 A/II-m/11 planum 4 Phase E/2–1 (67/028) Plate 62

SPI	I-d	f–vf	W2	Bd. gef	re	3	1B

Nd. 1.4 cm. Bd. 1.65 cm. pht. 7.0 cm. Md 5.6 cm. Wd. 0.4 cm.
Incomplete
Surface colour: 10YR4/1–5/2 dark grey; burnished slip: 10YR2/1 black
Break: grey core, brown reduction zones
Decoration: two decorative lozenges filled with regular, deeply incised chevrons made with an eight-toothed comb.
Previously published: *TD V*, 160.

Variant with kettle rim

356. 1917 Vienna A1701 A/II-n/12 grave 7 Phase E/1 (69/001) Plate 62

SPI	I-d	f	W2	Bd. gef	re	3	1B

D. 2.9 cm. Nd 1.2 cm. Bd. 2.0 cm. H. 8.9 cm. Md. 6.1 cm. Wd. 0.4 cm.
Intact
Surface colour: 10YR4/2–6/3 dark grey brown; burnished slip: 10YR3/1 very dark grey
Break: uniform grey
Decoration: Three unequal lozenges with zigzag decoration, made with an eight-toothed comb.
Previously published: *TD V*, 207–208.

Type Group L.1.5

Type group L.1.5 is another branch of the Piriform 2a family, which, however, was not mentioned by Kaplan. In this group the vessels have a rolled rim, a strap handle a piriform body, but in contrast to groups L.1.3 and L.1.4, a distinct button base, and such vessels seem confined to Tell el-Dab^ca. These jugs again have four (L.1.5a) or three (L.1.5b) delineated decorative lozenges. One variant vessel (TD 888) also has a bulging neck.

Type Group L.1.5a

357. 0172 Cairo JE 91777 A/II-l/12 grave 2 Phase E/1 (66/038) Plate 62

SPI	I-d	f	W2	Bd. gef	re	3	1B

D. 3.2 cm. Nd. 1.4 cm. Bd. 1.8 cm. H. 11.7 cm. Md 7.0 cm. Wd. 0.4 cm.
VI 63.63
Intact
Surface colour: 10YR5/2 grey brown; burnished slip: 10YR2/1 black
Break: not visible
Decoration: Four unequal lozenges with zigzag or chevron decoration, made with an eight-toothed comb.
Previously published: Bietak, *MDAIK* 23, fig. 8; Kaplan, *Tell el-Yahudiyeh Ware*, fig. 50d; *TD V*, 187, 188.

358. 0888 Cairo JE 91585 A/II-m/11 grave 7 Phase E/1 (67/030) Plate 63

SPI	I-d	f	W2	Bd. gef	re	3	1B

D. 2.6 cm. Nd. 1.2 cm. Bd. 1.3 cm. H. 8.2 cm. Md 5.1 cm. Wd. 0.4 cm.
VI 62.19
Almost complete
Surface colour: 7.5YR5–6/0 grey; burnished slip: 5YR3/1 very dark grey
Break: brown core, grey reduction zones
Decoration: Four unequal lozenges with chevron decoration, made with a twelve-toothed comb.
Previously published: *TD V*, 190, 191.

359. 0459 Vienna A2338 A/I-g/3 grave 1 Phase D/3 (67/069) Plates 63, 142

SPI	I-d	f	W2	Bd. gef	re	2–3	1B

D. 2.6 cm. Nd. 1.2 cm. Bd. 1.7 cm. H. 9.7 cm. Md 6.0 cm. Wd. 0.4 cm.
VI 61.85
Intact
Surface colour: 2.5Y6/1 grey; burnished slip: 2.5Y4/1 grey
Break: brown core, grey reduction zones
Decoration: Four unequal lozenges with chevron decoration, made with an eight-toothed comb.
Previously published: *TD V*, 187, 188.

360. 0173 Vienna A1603 A/II-l/12 grave 2 Phase E/1 (66/006) Plate 63

SPI	I-d	f	W2	Bd. gef	re	3	1B

D. 2.15 cm. Nd. 1.5 cm. Bd. 1.8 cm. H. 11.2 cm. Md 6.6 cm. Wd. 0.4 cm.
VI 58.92
Intact
Surface colour: 10YR6–7/2 light grey brown; burnished slip: 10YR4/2 dark grey brown
Break: uniform grey
Decoration: Four unequal lozenges with chevron decoration, made with an eight-toothed comb.
Previously published: Bietak, *MDAIK* 23, fig. 8; Kaplan, *Tell el-Yahudiyeh Ware*, fig. 50e; *TD V*, 187, 188.

361. 5420 TD A/II-k/17 grave 30 burial 1 Phase E/1 (85/264) Plate 63

SPI	I-d	f–vf	W2	Bd. gef	re	2–3	1B

D. 2.3 cm. Nd 1.15 cm. Bd. 1.4 cm. H. 10.0 cm. Md. 5.5 cm. Wd. 0.3 cm.
VI 55.00
Intact
Surface colour: 10YR6/2 grey; burnished slip: 10YR3/1 very dark grey
Break: not visible
Decoration: Four unequal lozenges, two filled with zigzags and two filled with bipartite chevrons made with an eight-toothed comb.
Previously published: *TD XVI*, 248, fig.184, no. 8.

362. 1394 Vienna A2948 A/II-l/14 grave 5 Phase E/1 (68/091) Plate 63

SPI	I-d	vf	W2	Bd. gef	rc	3	1B

Bd. 1.2 cm. pht. 7.0 cm. Md 5.0 cm. Wd. 0.3 cm.

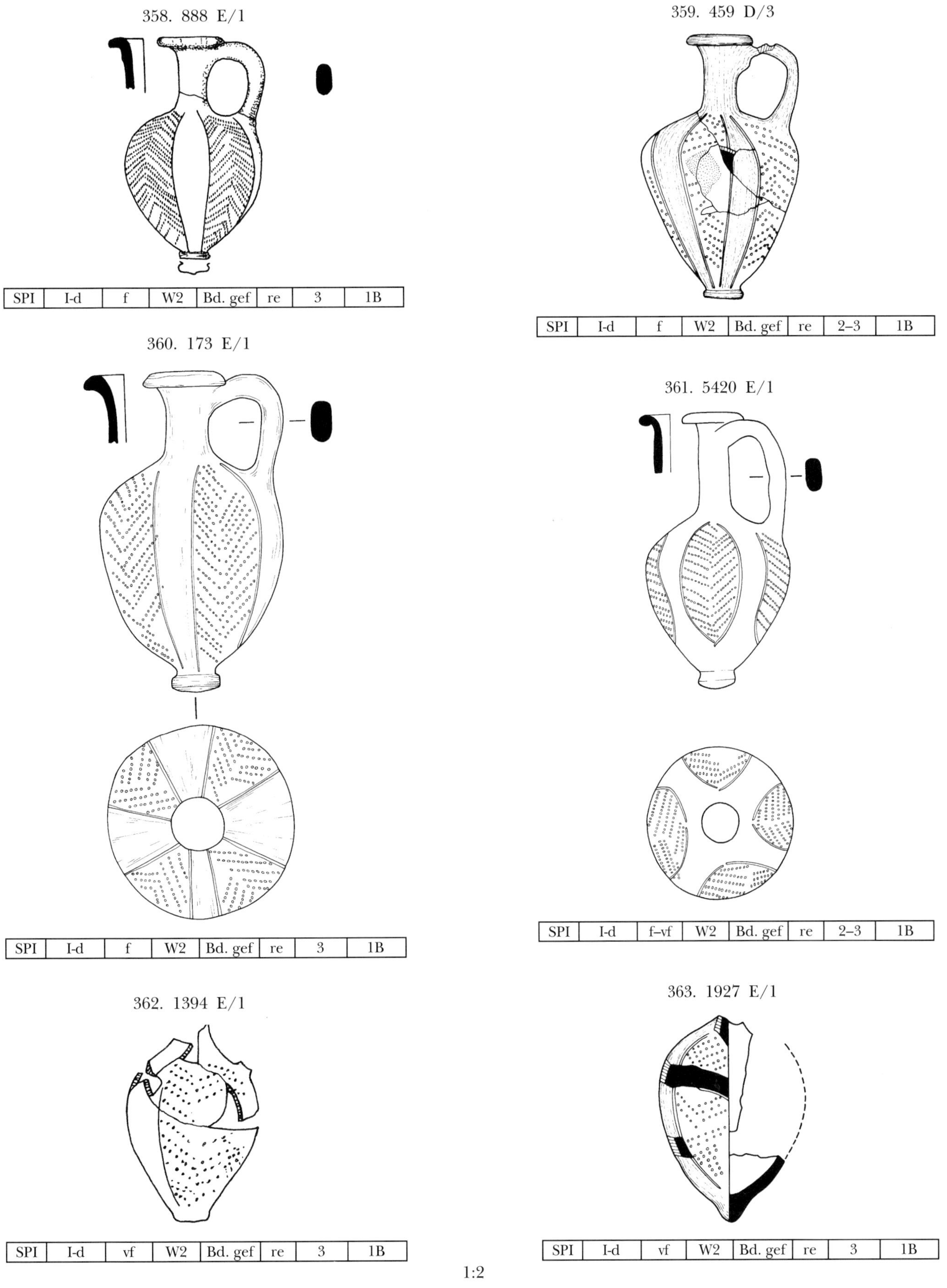

1:2

Late Egyptian Type Group L.1.5a

Plate 61

Incomplete
Surface colour: 10YR5/3 brown; burnished slip: 10YR3/1 very dark grey
Break: thin dark grey core, brown reduction zones
Decoration: Four unequal lozenges with chevron decoration, made with an eight-toothed comb.
Previously published: Bietak, *EI* 21, 14*; *TD V*, 208, 209; *TD XVI*, 254, fig. 189b. no. 19.

363. 1927 Vienna A3305 A/II-n/12 grave 7 Phase E/1 (69/003) Plate 63

SPI	I-d	vf	W2	Bd. gef	re	3	1B

Bd. 0.9 cm. pht. 7.8 cm. Md 5.8 cm. Wd. 0.35 cm.
Incomplete
Surface colour: 10YR5/3 brown; burnished slip: 10YR3/1 very dark grey
Break: thin dark grey core, brown reduction zones
Decoration: Four unequal lozenges with chevron decoration, made with an eight-toothed comb.
Previously published: Bietak, *EI* 21, 14*; *TD V*, 208, 209.

Type Group L.1.5b

364. 7932A TD A/IV-g/6 grave 11 Phase ? (93/047) Plate 70

SPI	I-d	f	W2	Bd. gef	re	2	1B

Nd. 1.3 cm. Bd. 1.7 cm. pht. 6.5 cm. Md. 5.0 cm. Wd. 0.3 cm.
Incomplete
Surface colour: 10YR6/2 grey; burnished slip: 2.5YR4/0 dark grey
Break: uniform dark grey brown
Decoration: Three lozenges filled with horizontal chevrons made with an eight-toothed comb.

365. 2274 Vienna A521 A/II-k/14 grave 1 Phase E/1 or D/3 (69/136) Plate 64

SPI	I-d	f	W2	Bd. gef	re	2–3	1B

D. 3.0 cm. Nd 1.25 cm. Bd. 2.0 cm. H. 9.0 cm. Md. 6.0 cm. Wd. 0.3 cm.
VI 66.66
Restored from sherds, complete
Surface colour: 2.5Y5/1 grey; burnished slip: 2.5Y2.5/1 black
Break: not visible
Decoration: Three lozenges filled with poorly executed horizontal chevrons made with an eight-toothed comb.
BNL JH381 Egyptian Nile Clay[602]
Previously published: *TD XVI*, 297, fig. 216b, no. 7.

366. 3577 Cairo F/I-i/22 grave 7 Phase b/1 (81/166) Plate 64

SPI	I-d	f	W2	Bd. gef	re	3	1B

D. 2.7 cm. Nd 1.6 cm. Bd. 1.5 cm. H. 10.0 cm. Md. 6.0 cm. Wd. 0.3 cm.
VI 60.00
Intact
Surface colour: 2.5Y5/1 grey; burnished slip: 2.5Y4/1 very dark grey
Break: not visible
Decoration: Three lozenges filled with poorly executed horizontal chevrons made with a ten-toothed comb.

367. 0874 Vienna A2637 A/II-m/11 grave 6 Phase E/2–1 (67/024) Plate 64

SPI	I-d	f	W2	Bd. gef	re	3	1B

D. 2.8 cm. Nd. 1.3 cm. Bd. 1.8 cm. H. 10.3 cm. Md 6.0 cm. Wd. 0.4 cm.
VI 58.25
Intact
Surface colour: 10YR5/1–2 grey brown; burnished slip: 10YR2–3/1 dark grey - black
Break: grey core, greyish brown reduction zones
Decoration: Three lozenges filled with poorly executed horizontal chevrons made with an eight-toothed comb.
Previously published: *TD V*, 157, 158.

368. 0171 Vienna A1627 A/II-l/12 grave 2 Phase E/1 (66/038) Plate 64

SPI	I-d	f	W2	Bd. gef	re	3	1B

D. 3.2 cm. Nd. 1.44cm. Bd. 1.6 cm. H. 11.8 cm. Md 6.4 cm. Wd. 0.4 cm.
VI 57.62
Incomplete
Surface colour: 10YR6/2 grey brown; burnished slip: 7.5YR4–5/1 dark grey
Break: uniform dark grey
Decoration: Three lozenges filled with poorly executed horizontal chevrons made with a twelve-toothed comb.
Previously published: Bietak, *MDAIK* 23, fig. 8; Kaplan, *Tell el-Yahudiyeh Ware,* fig. 50g; *TD V*, 187, 188.

369. 7490 TD A/IV-h/5 grave 21 Phase ? (91/182) Plate 64

SPI	I-d	f	W2	Bd. gef	re	3–4	1B

D. 2.75 cm. Nd 1.25 cm. Bd. 1.9 cm. H. 9.95 cm. Md. 5.6 cm. Wd. 0.35 cm.
VI 56.28
Restored from sherds, incomplete
Surface colour: 5YR5/1 grey; burnished slip: 5YR2/1 black
Break: not visible
Decoration: Three delineated lozenges filled with horizontal zigzags made with a ten-toothed comb.

370. 8692 TD A/II-o/14 grave 3 Phase D/3 (98/085) Plate 64

SPI	I-d	m	W2	Bd. gef	re	2–3	1B

D. 2.6 cm. Nd 1.4 cm. Bd. 1.5 cm. H. 8.9 cm. Md. 4.8 cm. Wd. 0.4 cm.
VI 53.93
Intact
Surface colour: 10YR5/4 yellowish brown; burnished slip: 10YR4/1 dark grey
Break: not visible
Decoration: Three lozenges filled with poorly executed horizontal chevrons made with a twelve-toothed comb.
Previously published: *TD XVI*, 326, fig. 245b, no. 21.

602 P. McGovern, *The Foreign Relations of the Hyksos*, Oxford, 2000, 133 no. JH381.

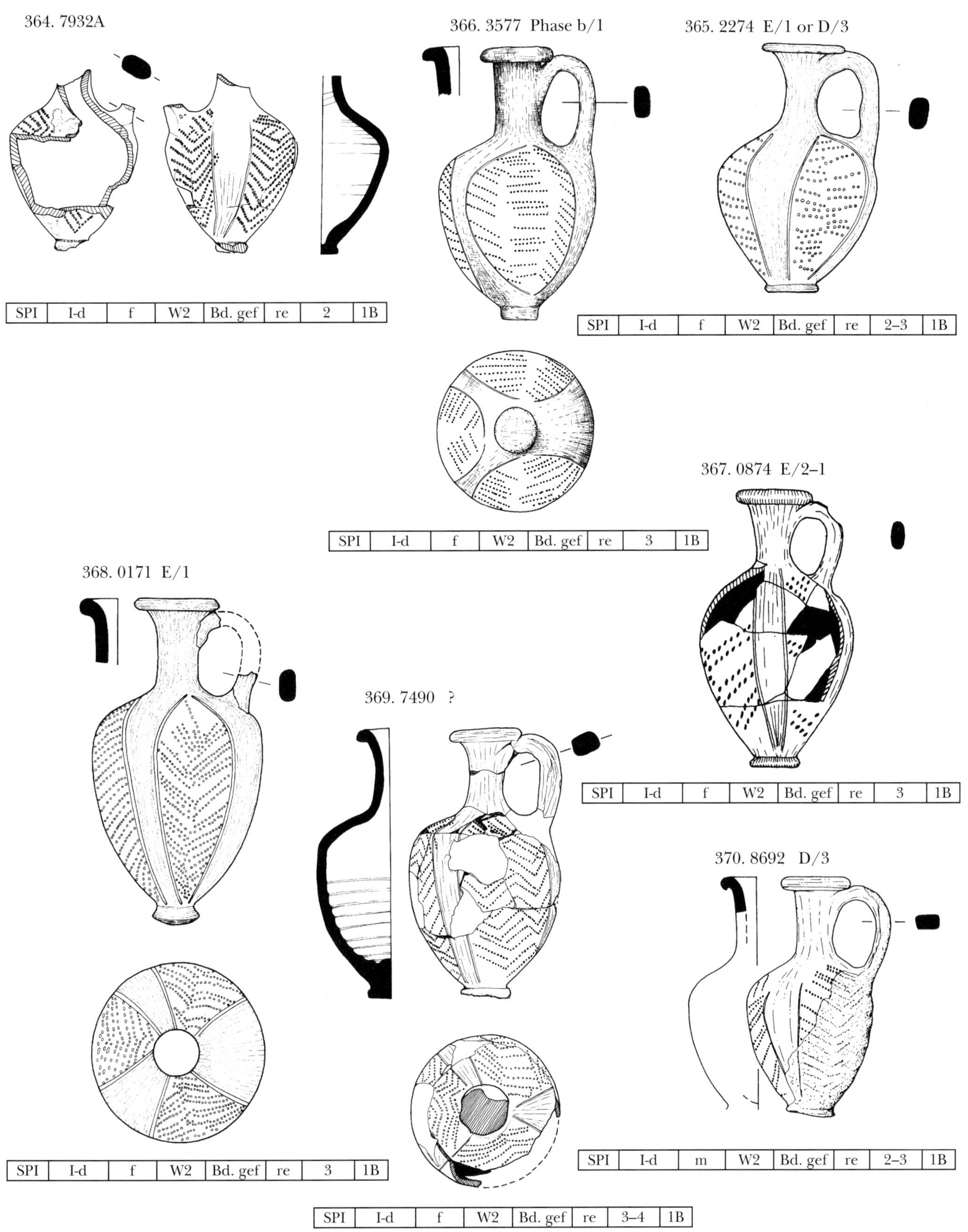

1:2

Late Egyptian Type Group L.1.5b

Plate 61

371. 8802 TD A/II-o/14 grave 3 Phase D/3 (98/073) Plate 65

SPI	I-d	f	W2	Bd. gef	re	3	1B

D. 2.6 cm. Nd 1.2 cm. Bd. 1.5 cm. H. 9.0 cm. Md. 4.8 cm. Wd. 0.3 cm.
VI 53.33
Intact
Surface colour: 10YR5/2 grey brown; burnished slip: 10YR4/1 dark grey
Break: uniform 10YR5/2 light grey brown
Decoration: Three lozenges filled with poorly executed horizontal chevrons made with a twelve-toothed comb.
Previously published: TD XVI, 326, fig. 245b, no. 22.

372. 2668 Vienna TDS 2668 A/II-m/17 grave 2 Phase D/3–2 (77/058) Plate 65

SPI	I-d	f	W2	Bd. gef	re	3	1B

D. 2.66 cm. Nd 1.68 cm. Bd. 1.7 cm. H. 9.73 cm. Md. 6.0 cm. Wd. 0.3 cm.
Incomplete
Surface colour: 2.5Y5/1 grey; burnished slip: 2.5Y4/1 very dark grey
Break: not visible
Decoration: Three lozenges filled with poorly executed horizontal chevrons made with a twelve-toothed comb.

373. 7150 TD stray find (89/044) Plate 65

SPI	I-d	m	W2	Bd. gef	re	3	1B

Nd. 1.75 cm. Bd. 2.0 cm. pht. 7.3 cm. Md. 5.15 cm. Wd. 0.3 cm.
Incomplete
Surface colour: 2.5Y5/1 grey; burnished slip: 10YR4/1 very dark grey
Break: uniform dark grey
Decoration: Three lozenges filled with poorly executed horizontal chevrons made with a twelve-toothed comb.

374. 0777 Vienna A2579 A/II-m/11 grave 13 Phase E/2–1 (69/030) Plate 65

SPI	I-d	f	W2	Bd. gef	re	2	1B

Bd. 1.5 cm. pht. 6.8 cm. Md 5.8 cm. Wd. 0.4 cm.
Incomplete
Surface colour: 10YR6/3 light brown; burnished slip: 10R3/1 very dark grey
Break: dark grey core, brown reduction zones
Decoration: Three asymmetrical decorative fields filled with chevrons and zigzags made with a multi-toothed comb, very well impressed.
Previously published: TD V, 160.

375. 7932B TD A/IV-g/6 grave 11 Phase ? (93/047) Plate 65

SPI	I-d	f–m	W2	Bd. gef	re	3	1B

Bd. 1.95 cm. pht. 6.5 cm. Md. 5.6 cm. Wd. 0.3 cm.
Incomplete
Surface colour: 10YR6/2 grey; burnished slip: 10YR3/1 dark grey
Break: brown core, grey reduction zones
Decoration: Three lozenges infilled with horizontal chevrons, made with a twelve-toothed comb.

376. 3423A Cairo A/II-l/17 grave 3 Phase D/2 (81/132) Plate 65

SPI	I-d	f	W2	Bd. gef	re	3	1B

Bd. 1.1 cm. pht. 2.2 cm. Wd. 0.3 cm.
Incomplete
Surface colour: 10YR6/3 light brown; burnished slip: 10R3/1 very dark grey
Break: dark grey core, brown reduction zones
Decoration: Three unequal lozenges. The parts preserved show one lozenge with horizontal tripartite chevrons, one with bipartite chevrons, and one with oblique lines made with a multi-toothed (nine ?) comb. Intervening areas are vertically burnished.

Type Group L.1.6

Vessels of group L.1.6 are similar in all respects to type group L.2.1, but the lozenge decoration is not bordered by incised lines. At present only two complete vessels are known to us, New York MMA 74.51.1230, found on Cyprus[603] and TD 6117 from Tell el-Dab^c^a.

377. 6117 TD A/V-m/18 grave 12 Phase D/2 (87/280) Plates 66, 142

SPI	I-d	f–vf	W2	Bd. gef	mi	3–4	1B

D. 3.0 cm. Nd 1.3 cm. Bd. 1.85 cm. H. 14.0 cm. Md. 8.9 cm. Wd. 0.5 cm.
Intact
Surface colour: 10YR5/1 grey; burnished slip: 10YR6/1 dark grey
Break: not visible
Decoration: Three lozenges decorated with horizontal zigzags made with a sixteen-toothed comb.
Previously published: TD XI, 74 no. 1.

378. 6846B TD A/V-p/19 planum 6 Phase D/3 (88/151) Plate 66

SPI	I-d	f	W2	Bd. gef	re	3	1B

Nd. 1.5 cm. pht. 4.3 cm. Md 8.15 cm. Wd. 0.4 cm.
Restored from sherds, incomplete
Surface colour: 10YR4/1 dark grey; burnished slip: 10YR3–2/1 very dark grey
Break: greyish brown core, dark grey reduction zones
Decoration: Three lozenges filled with vertical chevrons made with a sixteen-toothed comb.
Previously published: TD XI, 39–40 no. 13.

379. 0021B Vienna A2141b A/I-g/6 planum 0–1 surface find (66/006) Plate 66

SPI	I-d	vf	W2	Bd. gef	re	3	1B

Bd. 2.8 cm. pht. 3.5 cm. Wd. 0.4 cm.
Incomplete
Surface colour: 10YR4/1 dark grey; burnished slip: 10YR3.5/1 very dark grey
Break: uniform grey brown
Decoration: Three lozenges filled with vertical chevrons made with an eight-toothed comb.

[603] Myres, *Cessnola Collection,* 42–43, fig. 383, Kaplan, *Tell el-Yahudiyeh Ware,* fig. 47b.

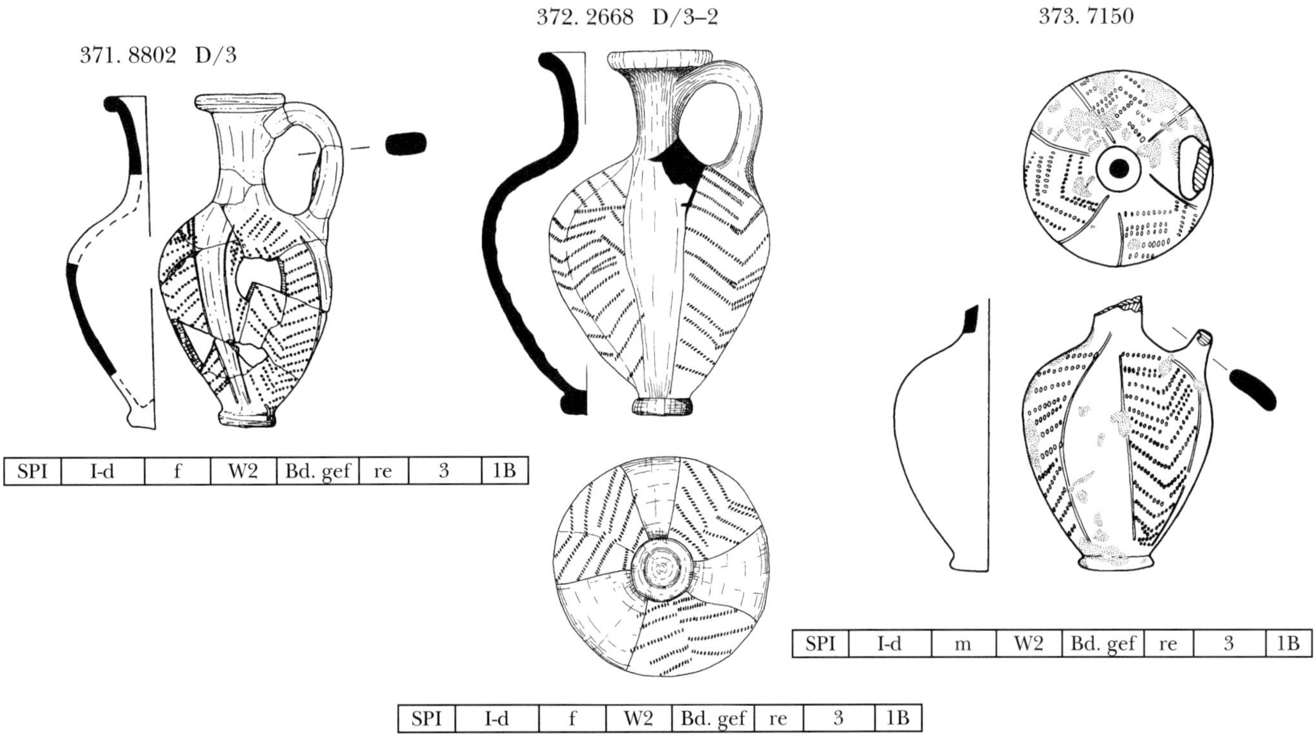

371. 8802 D/3

SPI	I-d	f	W2	Bd. gef	re	3	1B

372. 2668 D/3–2

SPI	I-d	f	W2	Bd. gef	re	3	1B

373. 7150

SPI	I-d	m	W2	Bd. gef	re	3	1B

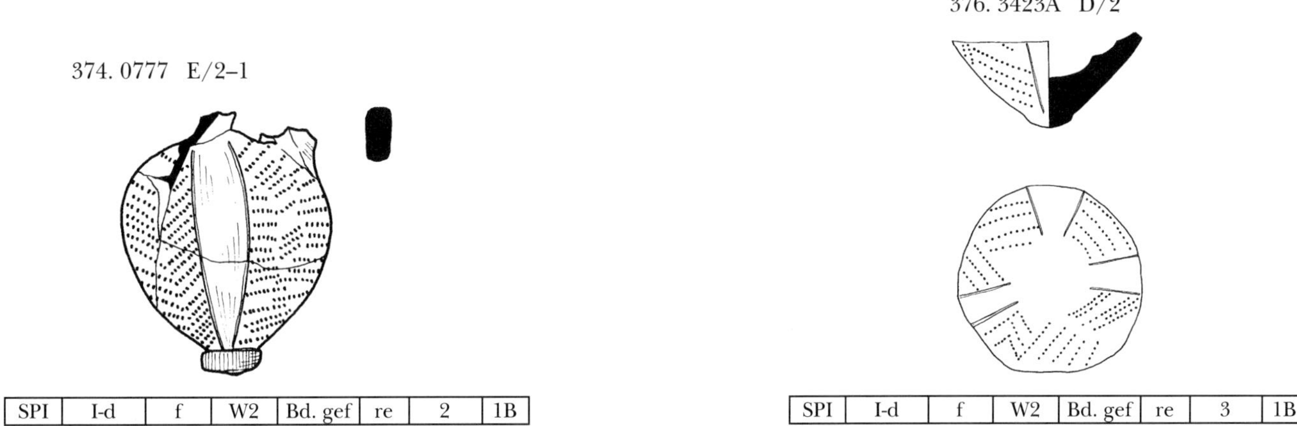

374. 0777 E/2–1

SPI	I-d	f	W2	Bd. gef	re	2	1B

376. 3423A D/2

SPI	I-d	f	W2	Bd. gef	re	3	1B

375. 7932B

SPI	I-d	f–m	W2	Bd. gef	re	3	1B

1:2

Late Egyptian Type Group L.1.5b

Plate 65

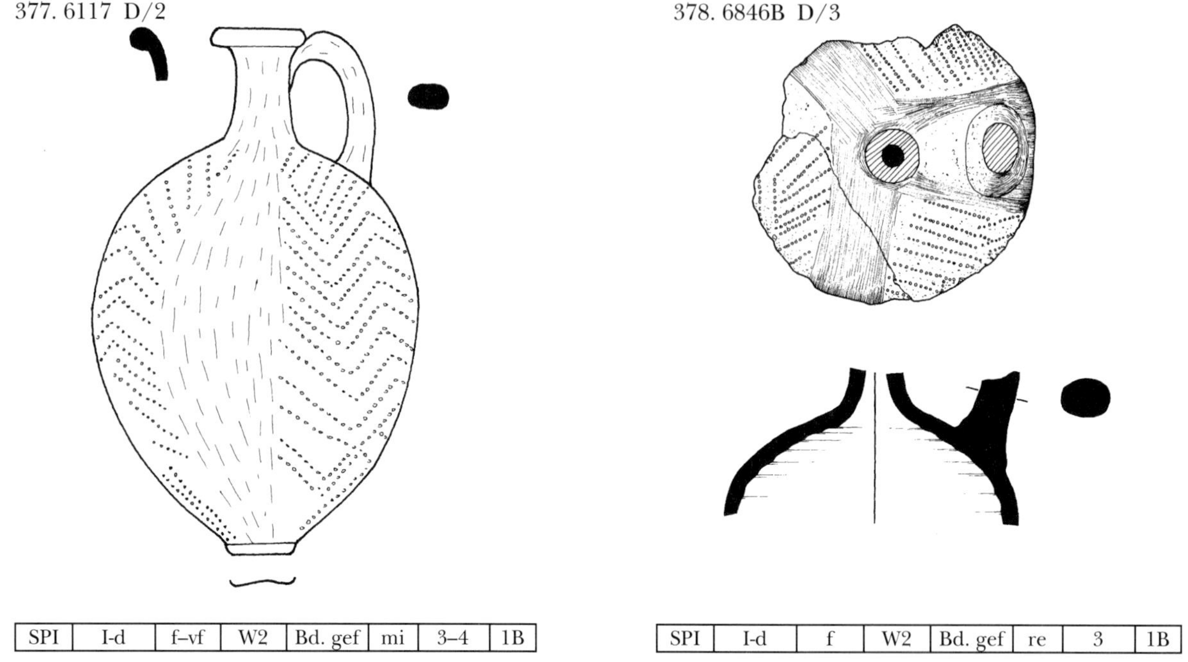

379. 0021B

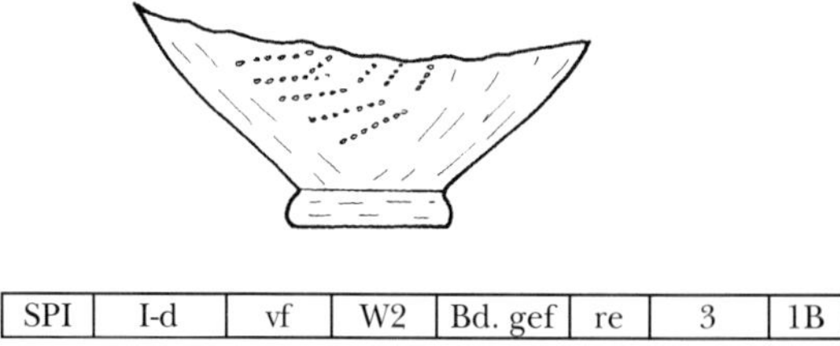

1:2

Late Egyptian Type Group L.1.6

Plate 66

Type Group L.1.7

Vessels of type group L.1.7 are the undelineated equivalent of group L.2.2. Thus they comprise vessels with a rolled rim, strap handle, flattened to rounded shoulders, a piriform to rounded body and a ring base. Examples of such vessels have also been found at Tell el-Yahudiya.[604]

380. 0148 Vienna A1594 A/II-l/12 grave 2 Phase E/1 (66/036) Plate 67

SPI	I-d	f	W2	Bd. gef	mi	3	1B

D. 2.5 cm. Nd 1.22 cm. Bd. 1.6 cm. H. 8.7 cm. Md. 5.25 cm. Wd. 0.3 cm.

VI 60.34
Intact
Surface colour: 10YR5/2 grey brown; burnished slip: 10YR6/1 dark grey
Break: not visible
Decoration: Three unequal areas infilled with horizontal zigzags made with a twelve-toothed comb.
Previously published: TD V, 182, 183.

381. 0039B Vienna A2155b A/I-f/6 planum 0–1 surface find (66/018) Plate 67

SPI	I-d	f	W2	Bd. gef	re	3	1B

Bd. 2.0 cm. pht. 3.7 cm. Wd. 04 cm.
Incomplete

604 Petrie, *Hyksos and Israelite Cities,* 11, 15 pl. viiia.78, 87.

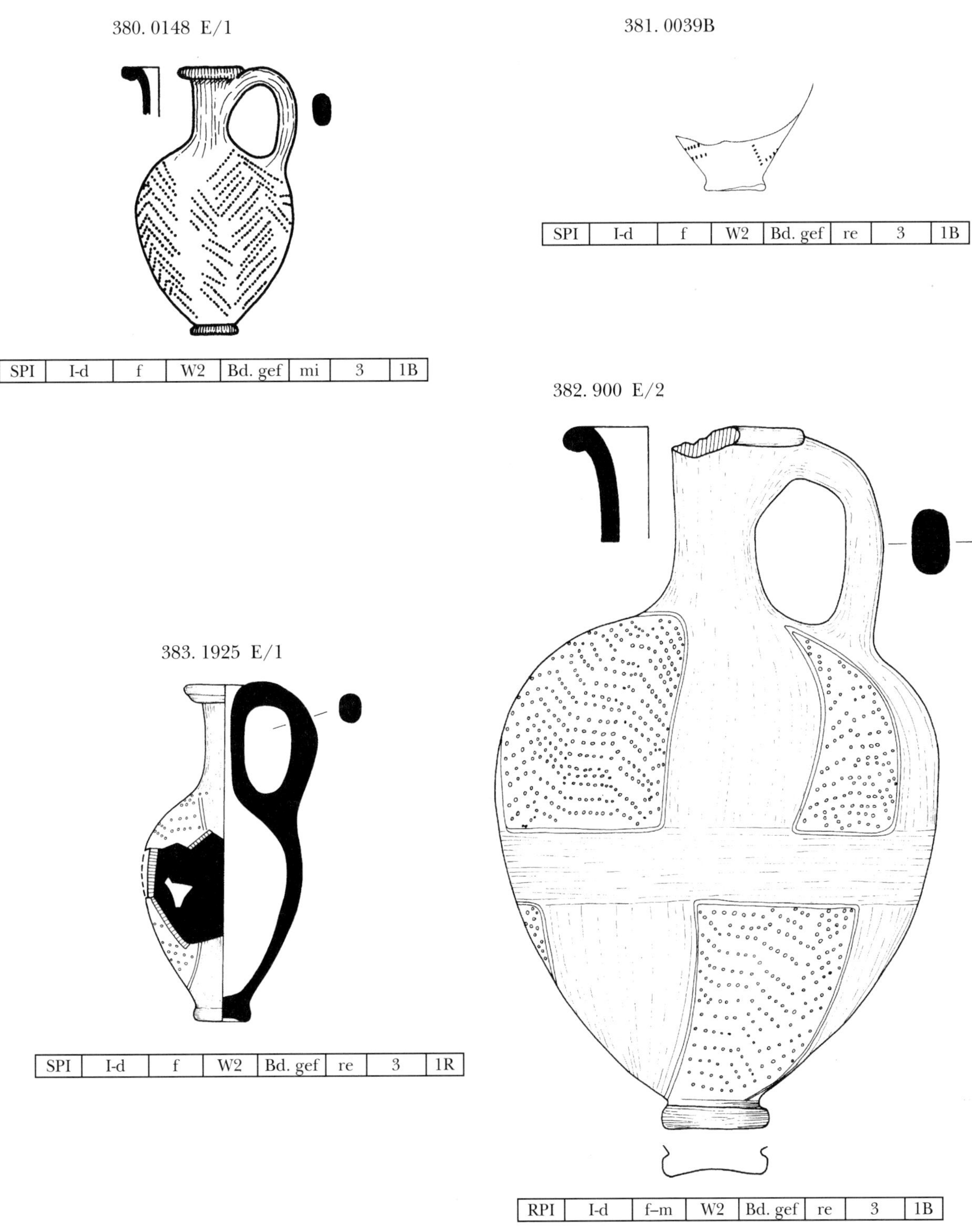

1:2

Late Egyptian Type Groups L.1.7, L.2.1, L.2.2

Plate 67

Surface colour: 10YR4/1 dark grey; burnished slip: 10YR2/1 black
Break: uniform grey brown
Decoration: Three unequal areas infilled with horizontal zigzags made with a twelve-toothed comb.

Type Group L.2.1

To type group L.2.1 belongs the large slender piriform to biconical jug TD 900 which has a rolled, slightly undercut rim, strap handle and ring base. It is decorated with an upper zone of non-touching rounded rectangles, each containing a herringbone pattern made with a multi-toothed comb.

382. 0900 Cairo JE 91587 A/II-k/11 planum 3 temple 1 Phase E/2 (67/092) Plates 67, 142

RPI	I-d	f–m	W2	Bd. gef	re	3	1B

D. 5.6 cm. Nd. 2.6 cm. Bd. 3.5 cm. H. 23.3 cm. Md 14.8 cm. Wd. 0.5 cm.
VI 63.51
Rim chipped
Surface colour: 5YR5–6/3 light reddish brown; burnished slip: 2.5YR3/6 dark red
Break: reddish grey core, grey oxidation zones
Decoration: Three trapezoidal lozenges on shoulder and three on lower body, each infilled with vertical zigzags made with a six-toothed comb. Burnish applied firstly in a horizontal pattern and thence vertically.
Previously published: TD V, 112, 114.

Type Group L.2.2

Type group L.2.2 consists of a single vessel (Tell el-Dabᶜa TD 1925) which should perhaps be related to the Biconical 1 jugs by its style of decoration. It is, however, distinctly ovoid, has a stepped rim, round handle and a ring base, all of which features are early within the Late phase. The decoration consists of an upper zone of delineated standing triangles, a reserved band at the mid point and a lower zone of pendant triangles.

383. 1925 Vienna A3304 A/II-n/12 planum 4 grave 7 Phase E/1 (69/003) Plates 67, 142

SPI	I-d	f	W2	Bd. gef	re	3	1R

D. 2.2 cm. Nd. 1.25 cm. Bd. 1.8 cm. H. 11.2 cm. Md 5.3 cm. Wd. 0.4 cm.
VI 48.18
Incomplete
Surface colour: 10YR5/2–3 grey brown; burnished slip: 10YR3/1 very dark grey
Break: dark grey core, light grey reduction zones
Decoration: Upper zone of delineated standing triangles, a reserved band at the mid point and a lower zone of pendant triangles, infilled with horizontal zigzags made with a five-toothed comb. White incrustation partly preserved.
Previously published: Bietak, *EI* 21, 14*, *TD V,* 208, 209.

Type Group L.2.3

Type Group L.2.3 comprises biconical vessels with a rolled rim, strap handle and a ring or disc base. They are decorated with an upper zone of standing triangles and a lower one of pendant triangles.

384. 1409 Vienna A2959 A/II-l/14 grave 5 Phase E/1 (68/094) Plate 68

SPI	I-d	f–vf	W2	Bd. gef	re	3	1B

D. 3.3 cm. Nd. 1.45 cm. Bd. 1.9 cm. H. 12.5 cm. Md 7.6 cm. Wd. 0.3 cm.
Restored from sherds, incomplete.
Surface colour: 10YR4/2 dark greyish brown; burnished slip: 10YR4/4 dark yellowish brown
Break: grey core, brown reduction zones
Decoration: Upper zone of standing triangles and a lower zone of pendant triangles, each infilled with dots made with a six-toothed comb.
BNL JH359 Egyptian Nile Clay[605]
Previously published: Bietak, MDAIK 23, fig. 8; Kaplan, *Tell el-Yahudiyeh Ware,* fig. 93a; *TD XVI,* 254, fig. 189b, no. 10.

385. 1405 Vienna A1670 A/II-l/14 grave 5 Phase E/1 (68/093) Plate 68

SPI	I-d	f	W2	Bd. gef	re	3	1B

D. 3.14 cm. Nd. 1.4 cm. Bd. 1.9 cm. H. 11.0 cm. Md 7.5 cm. Wd. 0.3 cm.
VI 68.18
Restored from sherds, complete
Surface colour: 10YR5–6/3 brown–pale brown; burnished slip: 10YR3–4/1 dark grey
Break: not visible
Decoration: On shoulder three standing triangles and a lower zone of five pendant triangles each infilled with dots made with a six-toothed comb.
BNL JH350 Egyptian Nile Clay[606]
Previously published: TD XVI, 254, fig. 189b, no. 9.

386. 1382 Vienna A2941 A/II-l/14 grave 5 Phase E/1 (68/089) Plates 68, 143

SPI	I-d	f	W2	Bd. gef	re	3	1B

D. 3.14 cm. Nd. 1.4 cm. Bd. 1.9 cm. H. 11.0 cm. Md 7.0 cm. Wd. 0.3 cm.
VI 63.63
Restored from sherds, complete
Surface colour: 10YR6/1 grey; burnished slip: 10YR4/1 dark grey
Break: not visible
Decoration: On shoulder three standing triangles and a lower zone of four pendant triangles infilled with striations made with a twelve-toothed comb.
Previously published: TD XVI, 254, fig. 189b, no. 8.

---

[605] P. McGovern, *The Foreign Relations of the Hyksos,* Oxford, 2000, 132 no. JH359.

[606] P. McGovern, *The Foreign Relations of the Hyksos,* Oxford, 2000, 131 no. JH350.

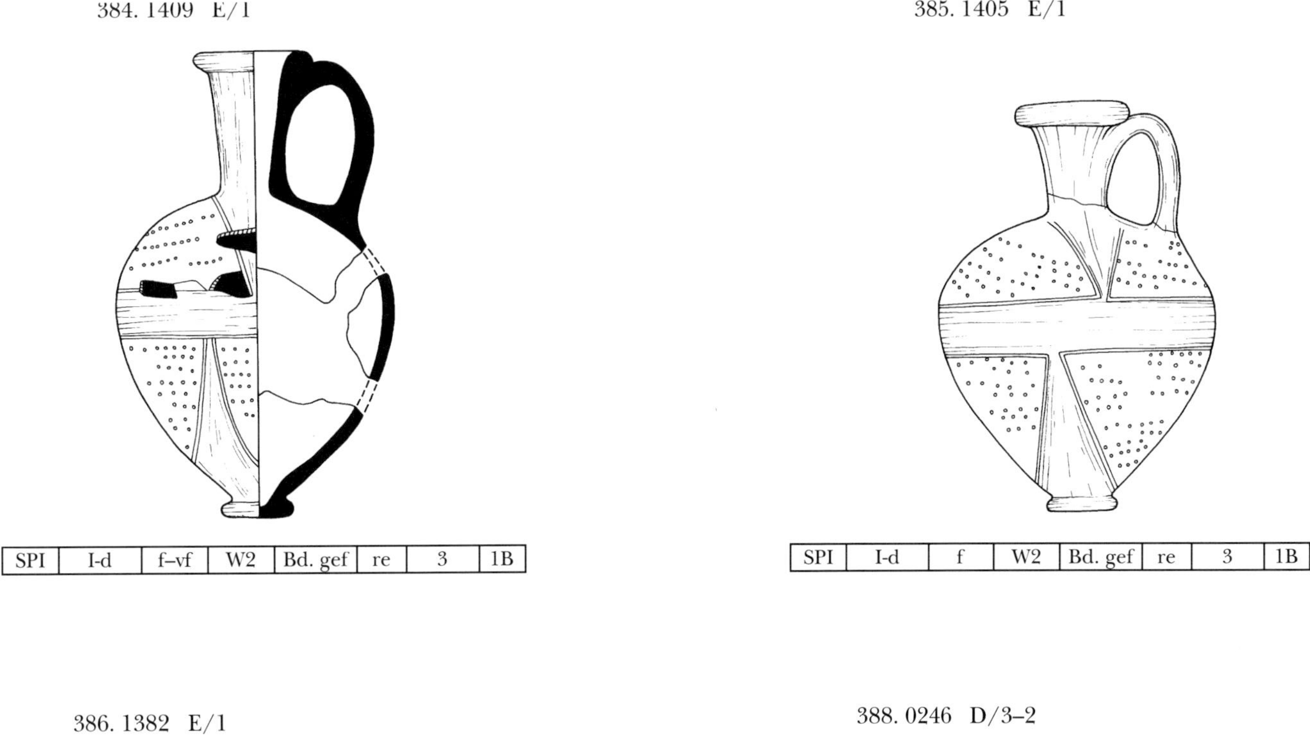

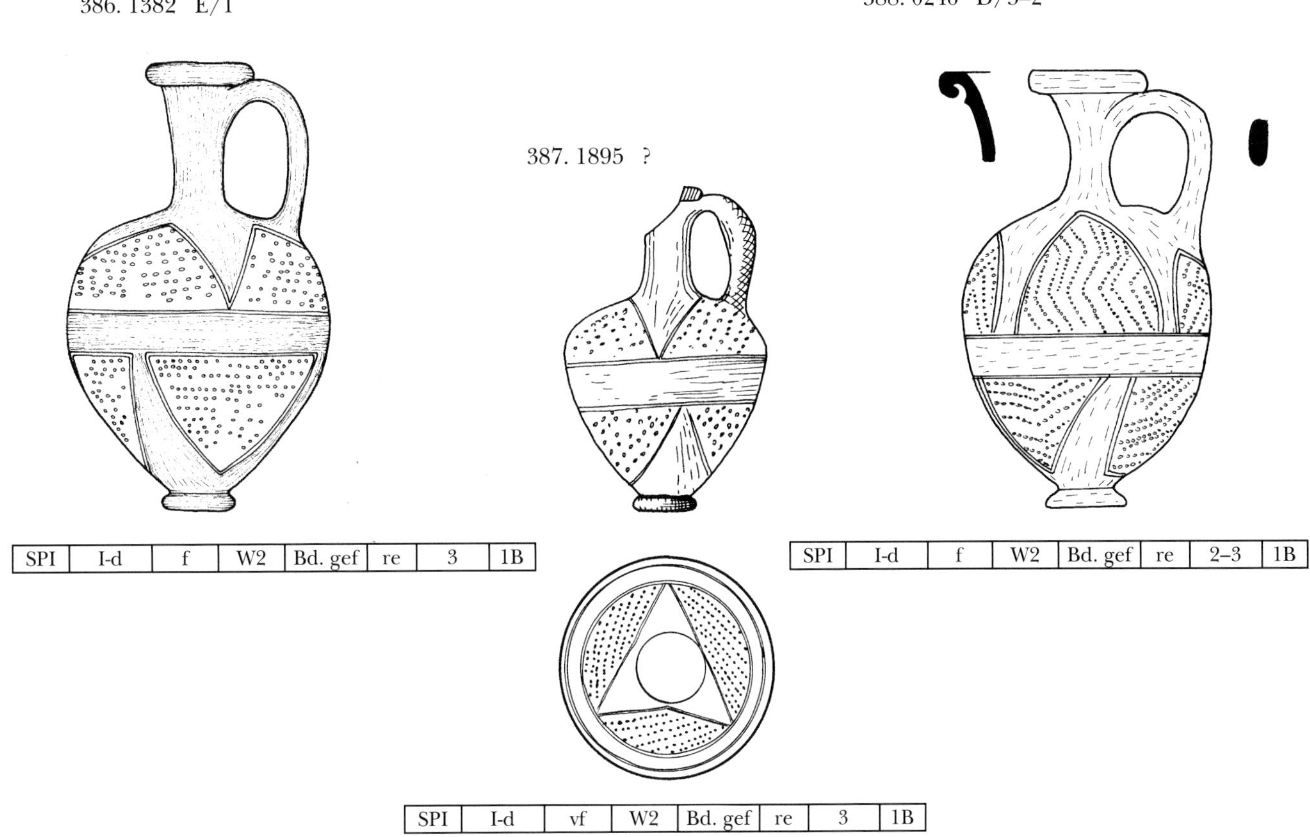

1:2

Late Egyptian Type Group L.2.3

Plate 68

387. 1895 Vienna A3281 A/II-l/12 grave 5 intrusive within a grave from Phase F (68/180) Plate 68

SPI	I-d	vf	W2	Bd. gef	re	3	1B

D. 2.2 cm. Nd. 1.1 cm. Bd. 1.55 cm. H. 8.7 cm. Md 5.55 cm. Wd. 0.25 cm.
VI 63.79
Restored from sherds, complete
Surface colour: 10YR6/1 light grey; burnished slip: 2.5YR2/0 dark grey
Break: uniform grey
Decoration: On shoulder three standing triangles and a lower zone of four pendant triangles infilled with striations made with a twelve-toothed comb.
Previously published: TD V, 54, 57.

388. 0246 Cairo JE 91564 A/II-l/13 grave 2 Phase D/3–2 (66/038) Plates 68, 143

SPI	I-d	f	W2	Bd. gef	re	2–3	1B

D. 3.3 cm. Nd. 1.25 cm. Bd. 2.2 cm. H. 11.4 cm. Md 6.5 cm. Wd. 0.3 cm.
VI 57.01
Incomplete
Surface colour: 10YR4/2 brown; burnished slip: 10YR2/1 black
Break: uniform grey
Decoration: On shoulder five standing triangles and a lower zone of four pendant triangles infilled with vertical zigzags and horizontal chevrons made with a twelve-toothed comb.
Undercut rim

Type Group L.2.4

Related to group L.2.3 are five vessels from Tell el-Dab^ca, TD 1520, 2055, 8670, 8674 and 8684, which are similar to group L.2.3 but have button bases rather than an offset disc. Once again their decoration comprises an upper zone of standing triangles and a lower one of pendant ones, which usually touch one another (L.2.4b), but in TD 1520, the triangles are non-touching (L.2.4a). At least one other example of unknown provenience can be added to this group.[607]

Type Group L.2.4a

389. 1520 Vienna A3042 A/II-n/14 grave 1 Phase E/1 (69/033) Plate 69

SPI	I-d	f	W2	Bd. gef	re	3	1B

D. 3.0 cm. Nd 1.5 cm. Bd. 1.4 cm. H. 11.0 cm. Md. 6.0 cm. Wd. 0.4 cm.
VI 54.54
Restored from sherds, incomplete.
Surface colour: 7.5YR4/0 dark grey; burnished slip: 5YR3/1 very dark grey
Break: brown core, dark grey reduction zones
Decoration: Upper zone of non-touching standing triangles, and a lower zone of non-touching pendant triangles, filled with horizontal chevrons made with a twelve-toothed comb.
Previously published: TD V, 207.

Type Group L.2.4b

390. 8670 TD A/II-o/14 locus 393 grave 43 Phase E/1 (98/011) Plate 69

SPI	I-d	f	W2	Bd. gef	re	2–3	1B

D. 2.75 cm. Nd. 1.3 cm. Bd. 1.7 cm. H. 8.5 cm. Md 5.4 cm. Wd. 0.4 cm.
VI 63.52
Intact
Surface colour: 10YR5/4 yellowish brown; burnished slip: 10YR6/2 light brownish grey
Break: not visible
Decoration: Four standing triangles on the shoulder, and four pendant triangles on the lower body, each filled with poorly made chevrons.
Previously published: TD XVI, 286, fig. 208a, no. 3.

391. 8674 TD A/II-o/14 locus 393 grave 43 Phase E/1 (98/012) Plates 69, 143

SPI	I-d	m	W2	Bd. gef	re	2	1B

D. 3.0 cm. Nd. 1.1 cm. Bd. 1.8 cm. H. 11.0 cm. Md 6.3 cm. Wd. 0.4 cm.
VI 57.27
Restored from sherds, incomplete
Surface colour: 10YR5/2 greyish brown; burnished slip: 10YR4/1dark grey
Break: uniform grey
Decoration: Upper zone of three standing triangles and a lower one of three pendant triangles, each filled with poorly made chevrons.
Previously published: TD XVI, 286, fig. 208a, no. 5.

392. 2055 Cairo JE 91679 A/II-o/12 grave 3 Phase D/3 (69/044) Plates 69, 143

SPI	I-d	f	W2	Bd. gef	re	3	1B

D. 2.8 cm. Nd 1.2 cm. Bd. 1.8 cm. H. 11.2 cm. Md. 5.9 cm. Wd. 0.4 cm.
VI 52.67
Intact
Surface colour: 5YR5/1 grey; burnished slip: 10YR3/1 very dark grey
Break: uniform grey
Decoration: Upper zone of three standing triangles and a lower one of three pendant triangles, each filled with poorly made chevrons made with a ten-toothed comb.
Previously published: TD V, 286.

393. 3052 Vienna A3340 A/II-q/21 grave 1 Phase E/1 (79/125) Plate 70

SPI	I-d	f	W2	Bd. gef	re	2–3

[607] Würzburg, Martin von Wagner Museum A.34. cf. Suzanne Petschel in: *Pharao siegt immer – Krieg und Frieden im Alten Ägypten,* Hamm, 2004, 199 no. 184b.

389. 1520 E/1

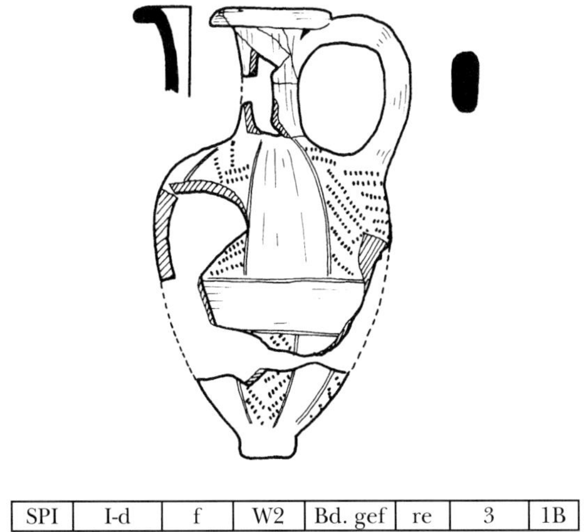

SPI	I-d	f	W2	Bd. gef	re	3	1B

390. 8670 E/1

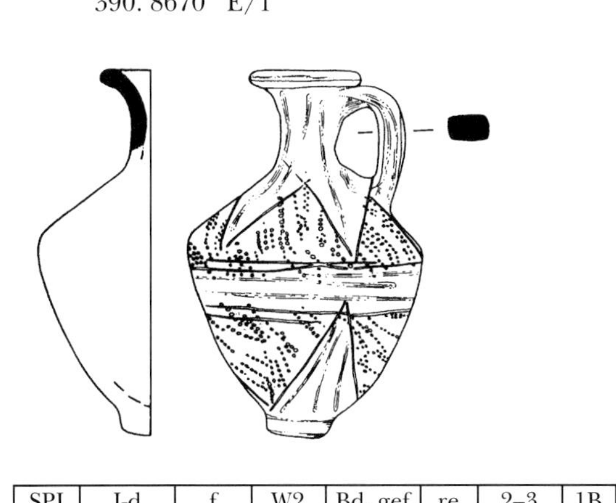

SPI	I-d	f	W2	Bd. gef	re	2–3	1B

391. 8674 E/1

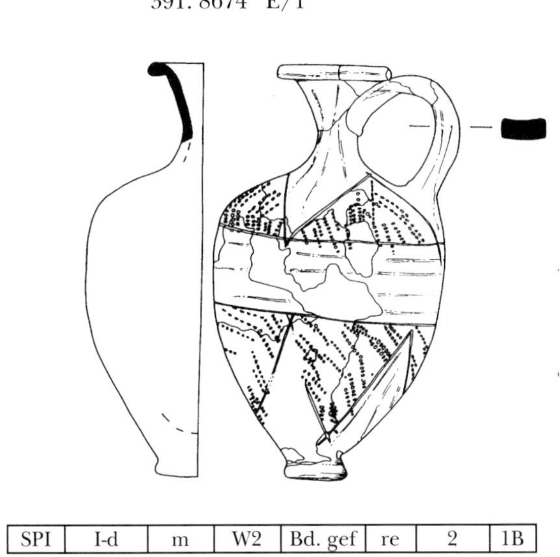

SPI	I-d	m	W2	Bd. gef	re	2	1B

392. 2055 D/3

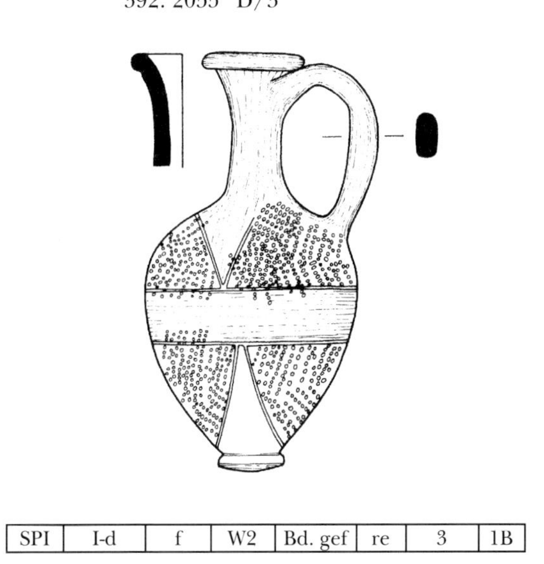

SPI	I-d	f	W2	Bd. gef	re	3	1B

1:2

Late Egyptian Type Group L.2.4a–4b

Plate 69

393. 3052 E/1

SPI	I-d	f	W2	Bd. gef	re	2–3

394. 5210 b/3–2

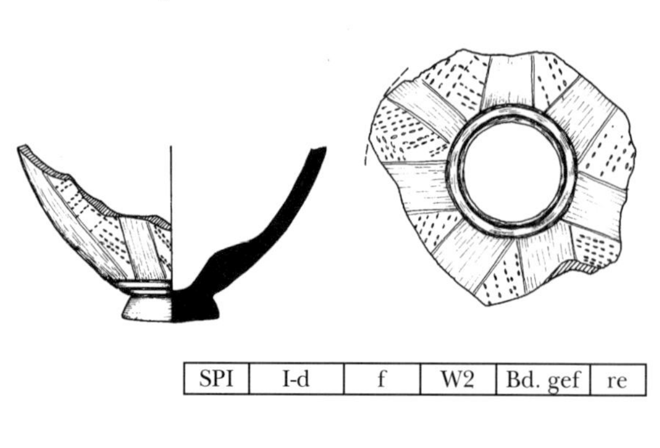

SPI	I-d	f	W2	Bd. gef	re

395. 7651 E/2

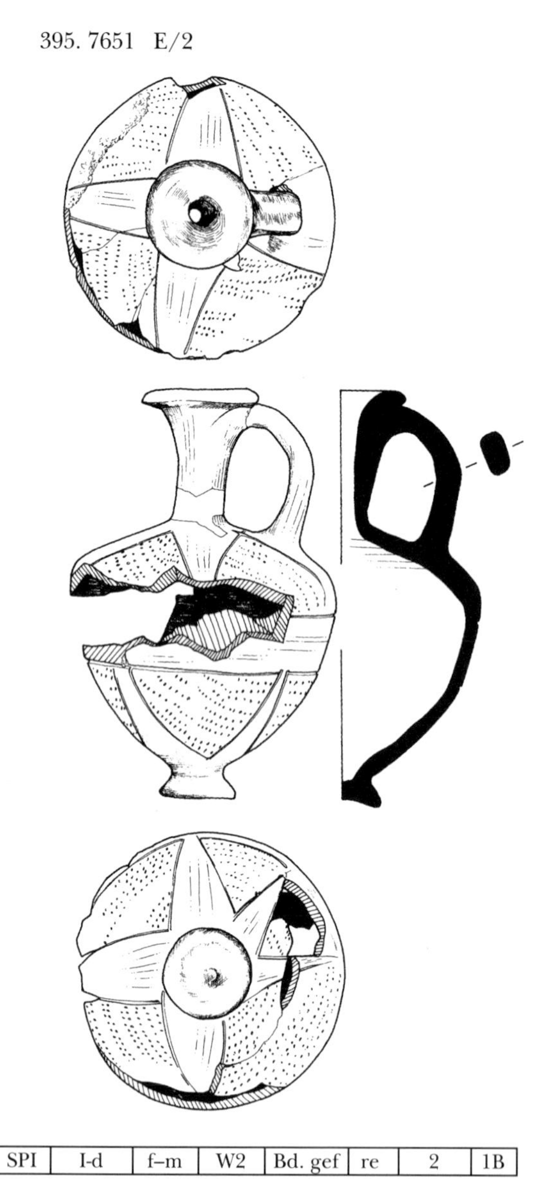

SPI	I-d	f–m	W2	Bd. gef	re	2	1B

396. 4468C b/1–a/2

SPI	I-d	f–m	W2	Bd. gef	re	3	1B

1:2

Late Egyptian Type Group L.2.4b, L.2.5a

Plate 70

Bd. 2.3 cm. pht. 6.3 cm. Wd. 0.6 cm.
Restored from sherds, incomplete.
Surface colour: light grey to reddish brown; burnished slip: 10YR3/1 very dark grey
Break: dark grey core, red reductuion zones
Decoration: lower frieze of eight pendant triangles, each filled with striations from upper left to lower right made with a multi-toothed comb.

394. 5210 TD F/I-k/24 grave 42 Phase b/3–2 (85/082) Plate 70

SPI	I-d	f	W2	Bd. gef	re

Bd. 2.3 cm. pht. 3.9 cm. Wd. 0.35 cm.
Restored from sherds, incomplete.
Surface colour: 10YR5/1 grey; burnished slip: 10YR3/1 very dark grey
Break: dark grey core, light grey reduction zones
Decoration: Lower frieze of six pendant triangles, each filled with horizontal chevrons made with a multi-toothed comb.

Type Group L.2.5

Jugs belonging to Type Group L.2.5 are so far known only at Tell el-Dab^ca. They are around 12 cms. tall, and consist of jugs with rolled rims, strap handles, biconical to piriform bodies, and ring bases. They have two styles of decoration which closely relate them to vessels of the rounded biconical L.5 group. The decorative patterns comprise L.2.5a which consists of an upper zone of non-touching standing triangles and a lower one of non-touching pendant triangles (TD 4468C, 7651); and L.2.5b which is similar but the triangles are touching (TD 3401, 8671).

Type Group L.2.5a

395. 7651 TD A/II-k/14 grave 8 Phase E/2 (91/278) Plates 70, 144
D. 3.05 cm. Nd. 1.35 cm. Bd. 2.35 cm. H. 10.7 cm. Md 7.1 cm.

SPI	I-d	f–m	W2	Bd. gef	re	2	1B

Wd. 0.3 cm.
VI 66.35
Restored from sherds, incomplete
Surface colour: 2.5YR 4–3 dark grey; burnished slip: dark grey
Break: uniform dark grey
Decoration: Four standing triangles on shoulder, and five unequal pendant triangles below. decoration impressed with a six-toothed comb.
Previously published: TD XVI, 223, fig. 146, no. 8.

396. 4468C TD F/I-k/21 planum 0–1 Phase b/1–a/2 (83/059) Plate 70

SPI	I-d	f–m	W2	Bd. gef	re	3	1B

Nd. 1.3 cm. Bd. 1.65 cm. pht. 6.6 cm. Md 6.15 cm. Wd. 0.3 cm.
Incomplete
Surface colour: 2.5YR 4–3 dark grey; burnished slip: 5Y2/1 black
Break: uniform grey
Decoration: Four standing triangles on shoulder and four pendant triangles below reserved burnished band. All triangles are infilled with oblique lines made with an eight-toothed comb.

Type Group L.2.5b

397. 3401 Vienna TDS 3401 F/I-j/23 planum ? Phase b/2–1 (80/102) Plate 71

SPI	I-d	vf	W2	Bd. gef	re	3	1B

D. 3.0 cm. Nd. 1.3 cm. Bd. 4.3 cm. H. 11.7 cm. Md 7.3 cm. Wd. 0.5 cm.
VI 62.39
Restored from sherds, incomplete
Surface colour: 2.5YR 4–3 dark grey; burnished slip: 2.5Y3/1 very dark grey
Break: dark grey core, grey brown reduction zones
Decoration: Six standing triangles in the upper zone, and seven pendant triangles in the lower zone, infilled with dots made with a ten-toothed comb.

398. 8671 TD A/II-o/14 locus 393 grave 43 Phase E/1 (98/012) Plates 71, 144

SPI	I-d	m	W2	Bd. gef	re	2	1B

D. 2.8 cm. Nd. 1.25 cm. Bd. 1.7 cm. H. 10.2 cm. Md 6.7 cm. Wd. 0.5 cm.
VI 65.68
Intact
Surface colour: 10YR5/2 grey brown; burnished slip: 10YR4/1dark grey
Break: not visible
Decoration: Upper zone of four standing triangles and a lower one of four pendant triangles, each infilled with comb decoration from upper left to lower right, made with an eight-toothed comb
Previously published: TD XVI, 286, fig. 208a, no. 4.

399. 3401A TD F/I-j/23 planum ? presumably from a disturbed grave (80/103) Plate 71

SPI	I-d	f	W2	Bd. gef	re	3	1B

D. 3.2 cm. Nd. 1.3 cm. Bd. 2.1 cm. H. 11.5 cm. Md 8.0 cm. Wd. 0.38 cm.
VI 69.56
Restored from sherds, incomplete
Surface colour: 2.5YR 4–3 dark grey; burnished slip: 2.5Y3/1 very dark grey
Break: dark grey core, grey brown reduction zones
Decoration: Six standing triangles in the upper zone, and seven pendant triangles in the lower zone.

400. 8682 TD A/II-o/14 locus 393 grave 43 Phase E/1 (98/214) Plate 71

SPI	I-d	m	W2	Bd. gef	re	2–3	1B

D. 2.75 cm. Nd. 1.3 cm. Bd. 1.75 cm. H. 10.2 cm. Md 6.3 cm. Wd. 0.4 cm.
VI 61.76
Incomplete
Surface colour: 10YR6/8 brownish yellow: burnished slip: 10YR4/1 dark grey
Break: uniform grey

397. 3401 b/2–1

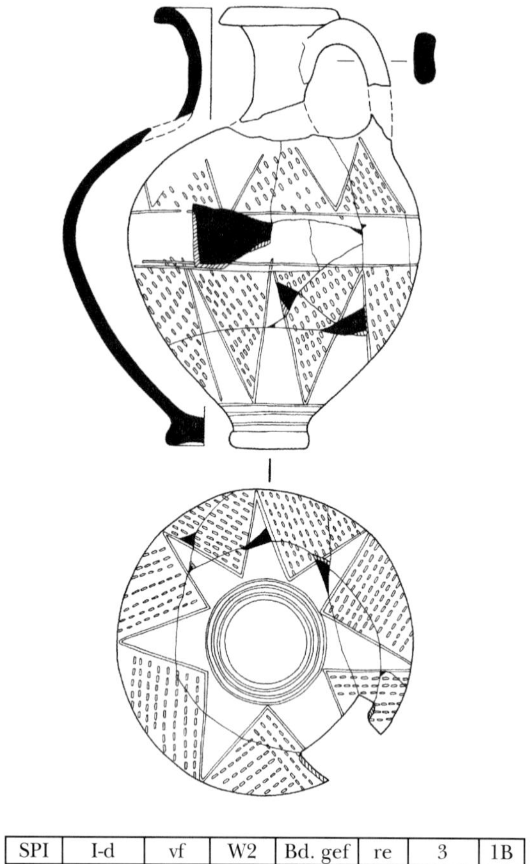

SPI	I-d	vf	W2	Bd. gef	re	3	1B

398. 8671 E/1

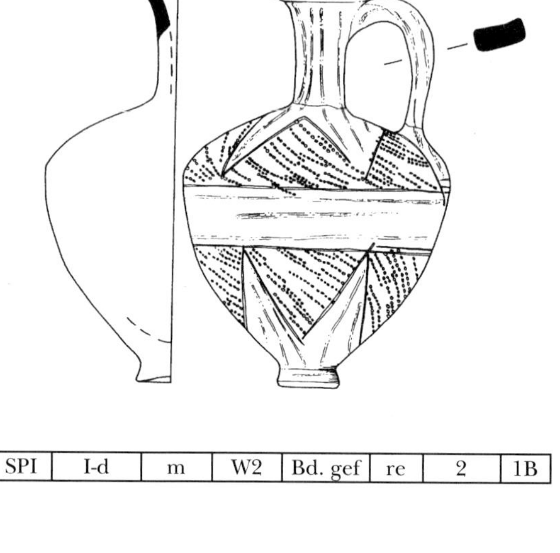

SPI	I-d	m	W2	Bd. gef	re	2	1B

399. 3401A ?

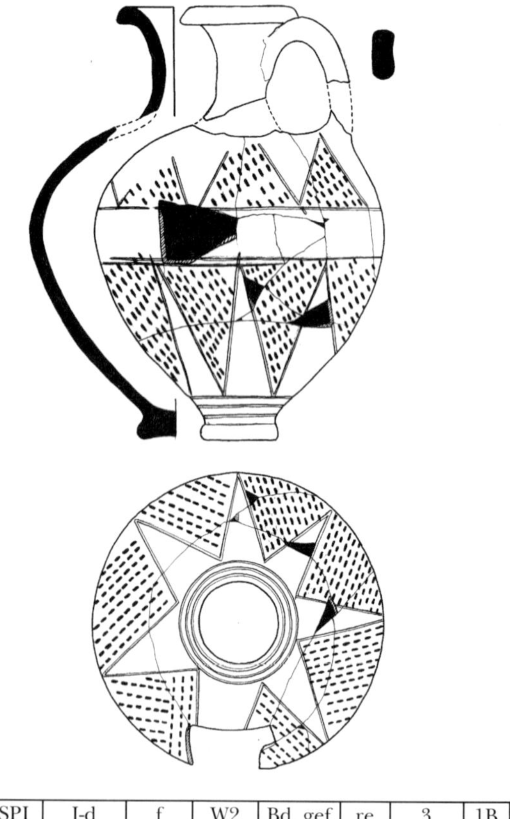

SPI	I-d	f	W2	Bd. gef	re	3	1B

400. 8682 E/1

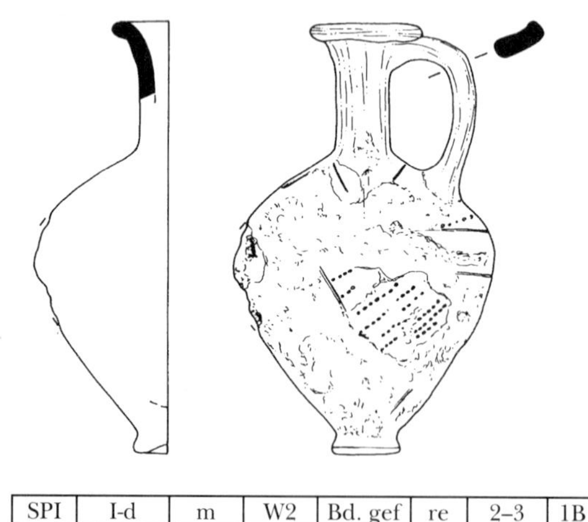

SPI	I-d	m	W2	Bd. gef	re	2–3	1B

1:2

Late Egyptian Type Group L.2.5b

Plate 71

Decoration: Badly preserved.
Previously published: TD XVI, 289, fig. 209, no. 30.

401. 6449D TD A/II-i/11 planum 6 Phase D/2 or later, probably residual (88/109) Plate 72

SPI	I-d	f	W2	Bd. gef	re	3	1B

Bd. 2.6 cm. pH.2.6 cm. Wd. 0.6 cm.
Restored from sherds, complete
Surface colour: 10YR6/1 light grey; burnished slip: 2.5YR2/0 dark grey
Break: uniform grey
Decoration: Three pendant triangles preserved, carelessly infilled with a muilti-toothed comb.

Type Group L.3.1

Type group L.3.1 is known through a single example from Tell el-Dab[c]a (TD 3963) which has a strap handle, sharply carinated, almost biconical, body and a disc base. The rim is not preserved but was presumably rolled. Clearly related to the Biconical 1 vessels in shape, this jug is decorated with the typical lozenge style associated with the very common Piriform 2a jugs of Kaplan. Around the body are three infilled lozenges.

402. 3963 Cairo A/II-n/19 grave 5 Phase E/1 (82/091) Plate 72

SPI	I-d	f	W2	Bd. gef	re	2–3	1B

D. 2.8 cm. Nd 1.2 cm. Bd. 1.7 cm. H. 9.65 cm. Md. 6.8 cm. Wd. 0.3 cm.
VI 70.46
Intact
Surface colour: 10YR4/1 grey; burnished slip: 10YR2/1 black
Break: uniform grey
Decoration: Three lozenges filled with horizontal chevrons made with a ten-toothed comb.

Type Group L.3.2

Type group L.3.2 consists of a single vessel, Tell el-Dab[c]a TD 2702 which has a rolled rim, strap handle, sharply biconical body and a ring base. The decoration scheme is unusual in that the upper body has three infilled triangles, delineated only on their upper two sides, whilst the lower body remains undecorated.

403. 2702 Vienna TDS 2702 AII-m/17 grave 6 Phase E/1 or D/3 (78/013) Plates 72, 144

SPI	I-d	f	W2	Bd. gef	re	2	1B

D. 2.7 cm. Nd. 1.35 cm. Bd. 1.75 cm. H. 7.8 cm. Md 6.4 cm. Wd. 0.3 cm.
VI 82.05
Restored from sherds, complete
Surface colour: 10YR5/3 brown; burnished slip: black
Break: uniform dark grey
Decoration: Three standing triangles on the shoulder, infilled with vertical chevrons and vertical lines running from top left to bottom right.
Previously published: AP pl. xxxA; *TD XVI,* 274, fig. 198, no. 1.

Type Group L.4.1

Type group L.4.1 is made up of Biconical II jugs with rolled rims, swollen necks, strap handles and ring bases. They are confined to Strata E/2–E/1 at Tell el-Dab[c]a, and are again decorated with an upper zone of standing triangles and a lower one of pendant triangles.

404. 2940 ?? A/II-p/20 grave 4 Phase E/2 (79/120) Plate 73

SPI	I-d	f	W2	Bd. gef	re	2	1B

D. 2.5 cm. Nd 1.2 cm. Bd. 1.82 cm. H. 7.95 cm. Md. 5.86 cm. Wd. 0.4 cm.
VI 73.71
Restored from sherds, incomplete
Surface colour: 10YR4/3 brown; burnished slip: 10YR3/1 very dark grey
Break: uniform dark grey
Decoration: On shoulder four standing triangles and a lower zone of four pendant triangles infilled with striations made with a twelve-toothed comb.
Previously published: TD V, 286.

405. 2941 ?? A/II-p/20 grave 4 Phase E/2 (79/120) Plate 73

SPI	I-d	f	W2	Bd. gef	re	2	1B

D. 2.8 cm. Nd 1.14 cm. Bd. 2.1 cm. H. 9.84 cm. Md. 7.12 cm. Wd. 0.4 cm.
VI 72.35
Intact
Surface colour: 10YR4/3 brown; burnished slip: 10YR3/1 very dark grey
Break: uniform dark grey
Decoration: On shoulder four standing triangles and a lower zone of five pendant triangles infilled with striations made with a twelve-toothed comb.
Previously published: PuF 225 nr 265.

406. 2942 ?? A/II-p/20 grave 4 Phase E/2 (79/128) Plate 73

SPI	I-d	f	W2	–	re	2	1B

D. 2.66 cm. Nd 1.2 cm. pht. 2.8 cm. Wd. 0.4 cm.
Restored from sherds, incomplete
Surface colour: 10YR4/3 brown; burnished slip: 10YR3/1 very dark grey
Break: uniform dark grey
Decoration: On shoulder five standing triangles infilled with striations made with a twelve-toothed comb.

407. 3077 TD A/II-p/20 grave 4 Phase E/2 (94/212) Plate 73

SPI	I-d	f	W2	–	re	3	1B

D. 3.0 cm. Nd 1.1 cm. pht. 5.8 cm. Md. 5.8 cm. Wd. 0.25 cm.
Incomplete
Surface colour: 10YR4/3 brown; burnished slip: 10YR3/1 very dark grey
Break: uniform grey
Decoration: Four standing triangles infilled with oblique lines made with a nine-toothed comb.
Top to 2945 ?

401. D/2 or later

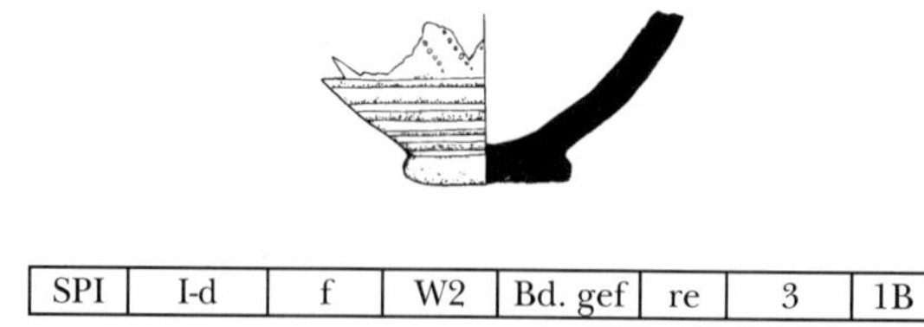

SPI	I-d	f	W2	Bd. gef	re	3	1B

402. 3963 E/1

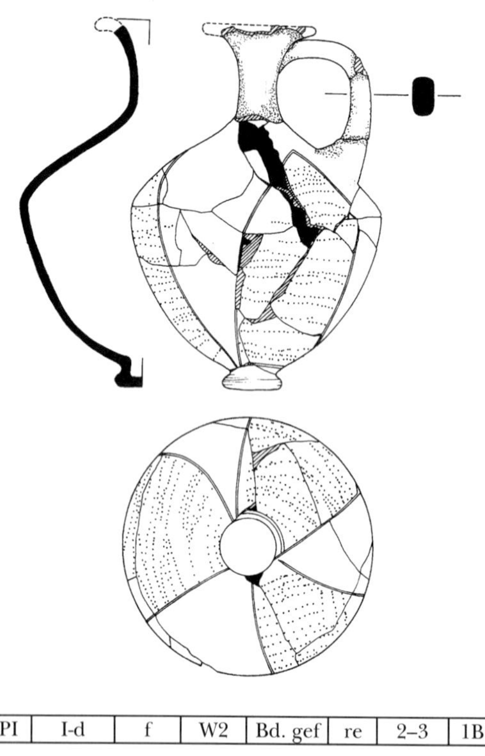

SPI	I-d	f	W2	Bd. gef	re	2–3	1B

403. 2702 E/1 or D/3

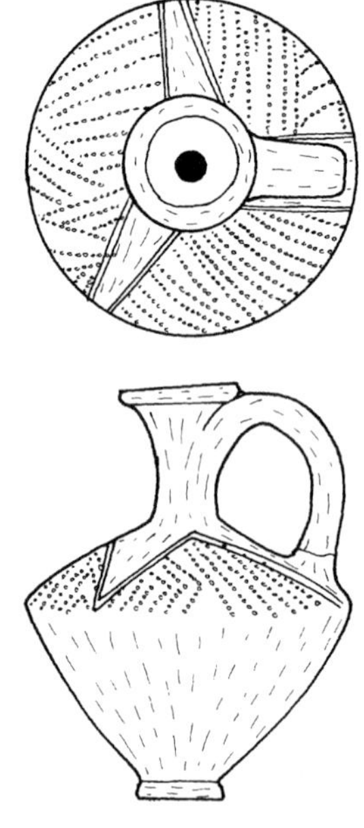

SPI	I-d	f	W2	Bd. gef	re	2	1B

1:2

Late Egyptian Type Group L.2.5b, L.3.1, L.3.2

Plate 72

408. 3077A TD A/II-p/20 grave 4 Phase E/2 (94/212) Plate 73

SPI	I-d	f	W2	–	re	3	1B

D. 2.5 cm. Nd 1.2 cm. pht. 4.2 Wd. 0.3 cm.
Incomplete
Surface colour: 10YR4/3 brown; burnished slip: 10YR3/1 very dark grey
Break: uniform grey
Decoration: Part of one standing triangle preserved infilled with a nine (?) toothed comb.

409. 1423 Vienna A2971 A/II-l/11 Temple wall Phase E/2 (69/077) Plate 73

SPI	I-d	m	W2	Bd. gef	re	1–2	1B

Bd. 3.4 cm. pht. 3.0 cm. Wd. 0.4 cm.
Incomplete
Surface colour: 10YR2–5/1 black to grey; burnished slip: 10YR3/1 very dark grey
Break: uniform grey
Decoration: Remains of four pendant triangles infilled with striations made with a multi-toothed comb.
Previously published: TD V, 116.

410. 2945 ?? A/II-p/20 grave 4 Phase E/2 (88/423) Plate 73

SPI	I-d	F	W2	Bd. gef	re	2	1B

Bd. 1.63 cm. pht. 2.8 cm. Wd. 0.3 cm.
Incomplete
Surface colour: 2.5Y5/1 grey; burnished slip: 2.5Y3/2 black

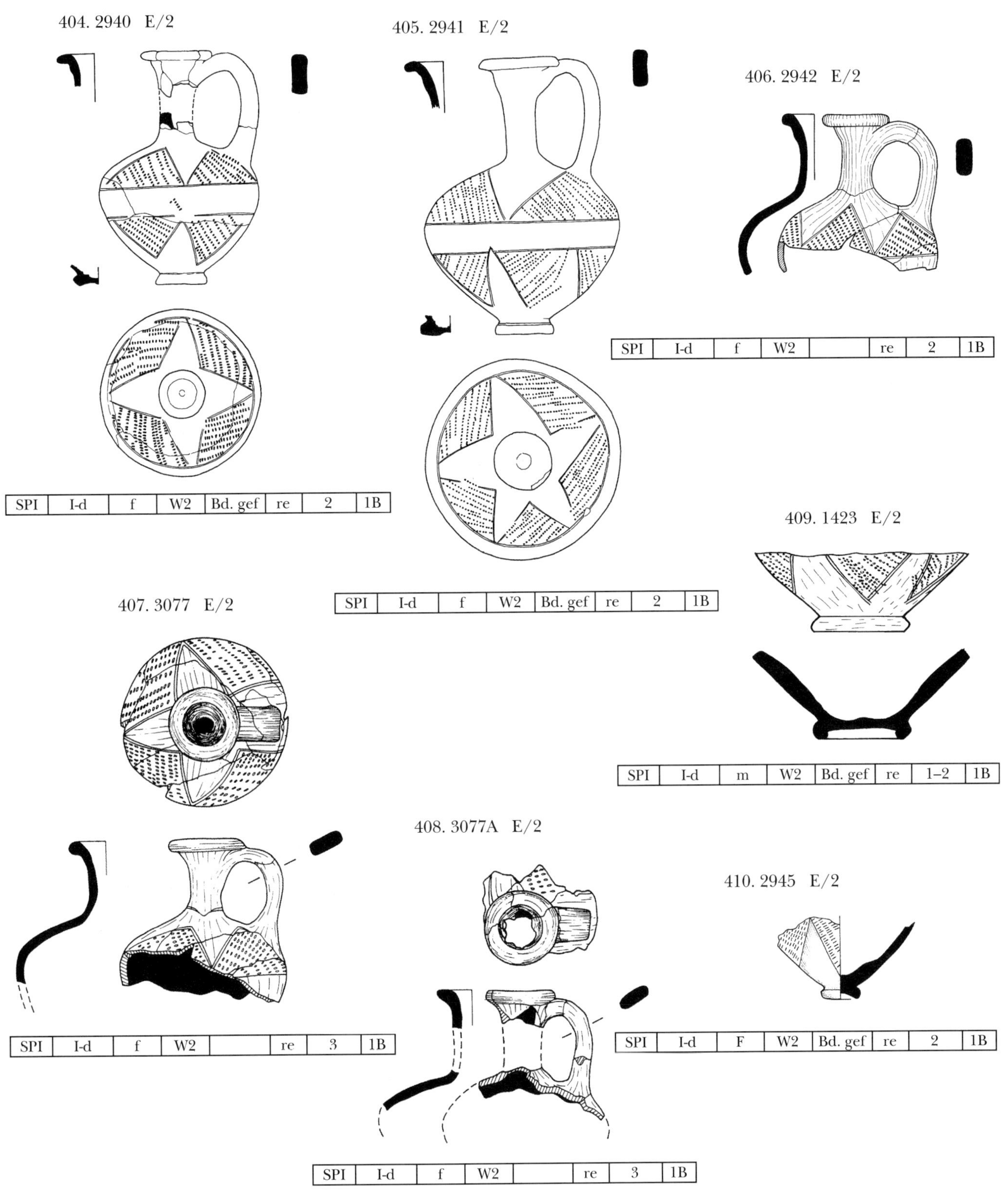

404. 2940 E/2

SPI	I-d	f	W2	Bd. gef	re	2	1B

405. 2941 E/2

SPI	I-d	f	W2	Bd. gef	re	2	1B

406. 2942 E/2

SPI	I-d	f	W2		re	2	1B

407. 3077 E/2

SPI	I-d	f	W2		re	3	1B

408. 3077A E/2

SPI	I-d	f	W2		re	3	1B

409. 1423 E/2

SPI	I-d	m	W2	Bd. gef	re	1–2	1B

410. 2945 E/2

SPI	I-d	F	W2	Bd. gef	re	2	1B

1:2

Late Egyptian Type Group L.4.1

Plate 73

Break: uniform dark grey
Decoration: Remains of four pendant triangles infilled with striations made with a multi-toothed comb.
Base to 3077?

411. 2939 Vienna TDS 2939 A/II-p/20 grave 4 Phase E/2–1 (79/119) Plates 74, 144

SPI	I-d	f	W2	Bd. gef	re	2	1B

D. 2.5 cm. Nd. 1.1 cm. Bd. 1.75 cm. H. 7.62 cm. Md 5.5 cm. Wd. 0.4 cm.
VI 72.17
Intact
Surface colour: 10YR5/4 yellowish brown; burnished slip: 10YR3/1 very dark grey
Break: not visible
Decoration: Upper zone of five standing triangles, and a lower zone of five pendant triangles, filled with striations running from upper left to lower right made made with a twelve-toothed comb.

412. 8675 TD A/II-o/14 locus 393 grave 43 Phase E/1 (98/011) Plate 74

SPI	I-d	f–m	W2	Bd. gef	re	2	1B

D. 3.05 cm. Nd. 1.3 cm. Bd. 1.8 cm. H. 9.4 cm. Md 6.5 cm. Wd. 0.4 cm.
VI 69.14
Intact
Surface colour: 10YR5/3 brown; burnished slip: 10YR4/1 dark grey
Break: not visible
Decoration: Upper zone of four standing triangles, and a lower one of four pendant triangles, with comb decoration from upper left to lower right, made with an eight-toothed comb.
Previously published: TD XVI, 289, fig. 209, no. 32.

413. 8702 TD A/II-o/14 locus 393 grave 43 Phase E/1 (98/062) Plate 74

SPI	I-d	m	W2	Bd. gef	re	2–3	1B

D. 2.8 cm. Nd. 1.2 cm. Bd. 1.7 cm. H. 9.5 cm. Md 6.5 cm. Wd. 0.4 cm.
VI 68.42
Intact
Surface colour: 10YR5/4 yellowish brown; burnished slip: 10YR3/1 very dark grey
Break: not visible
Decoration: Upper zone of four standing triangles and a lower one of four pendant triangles, each infilled with comb decoration from upper left to lower right, made with an eight-toothed comb.
Previously published: TD XVI, 286, fig. 208a, no. 6.

414. 8672 TD A/II-o/14 locus 393 grave 43 Phase E/1 (98/013) Plate 74

SPI	I-d	m	W2	Bd. gef	re	2–3	1B

D. 3.15 cm. Nd. 1.3 cm. Bd. 1.8 cm. H. 10.1 cm. Md 6.8 cm. Wd. 0.4 cm.
VI 67.32
Restored from sherds, incomplete
Surface colour: 10YR5/2 greyish brown; burnished slip: 10YR4/1 dark grey
Break: uniform dark grey
Decoration: Upper zone of five standing triangles and a lower one of five pendant triangles, each infilled with comb decoration from upper left to lower right, made with an eight-toothed comb.
Previously published: TD XVI, 289, fig. 209, no. 31.

415. 8782 TD A/II-o/14 locus 393 grave 43 Phase E/1 (98/003) Plate 74

SPI	I-d	f–m	W2	Bd. gef	re	2	1B

D. 3.0 cm. Nd. 1.3 cm. Bd. 2.1 cm. H. 12.1 cm. Md 7.7 cm. Wd. 0.3 cm.
VI 63.63
Restored from sherds, incomplete
Surface colour: 10YR4/3 brown; burnished slip: 10YR3/1 very dark grey
Break: uniform dark grey
Decoration: Upper zone of three standing triangles and a lower one of three pendant triangles, each infilled with comb decoration from upper left to lower right, made with a ten-toothed comb.
Previously published: TD XVI, 289, fig. 209, no. 29; Kopetzky, *The MB IIB-Corpus of the Hyksos Period at Tell el-Dab^ca,* 2007, 198, fig. 3.1.

416. 6034A TD F/I-o/21 intrusive within grave 4 unstratified (87/216) Plate 75

SPI	I-d	f	W2	Bd. gef	re	3	1B

D. 2.5 cm. Nd. 1.2 cm. pht. 7.5 cm. Md 5.6 cm. Wd. 0.4 cm.
Intact
Surface colour: 5YR5/1 grey; burnished slip: 5Y2/1 black
Break: black in, dark grey out
Decoration: Four (?) standing triangles on shoulder (three preserved) and four below reserved central band (two preserved), filled with oblique lines made with a five-toothed comb.
Previously published: TD XVIII, 462, fig. 417, no. 5.

417. 1608 Vienna A3100 A/II-k/11 planum 4–5 Phase E/3–2 (68/203) Plate 75

SPI	I-d	f	W2	Bd. gef	re	3	1B

D. 3.0 cm. pht. 10.0 cm. Md 7.4 cm. Wd. 0.3 cm.
Restored from sherds, incomplete
Surface colour: 10YR6/1 light grey; burnished slip: 2.5YR2/0 dark grey
Break: uniform grey
Decoration: Four (?) standing triangles on shoulder (three preserved) and four below reserved central band (two preserved), filled with oblique lines made with an eight-toothed comb.
BNL JH376 Egyptian Nile Clay[608]

[608] P. McGovern, *The Foreign Relations of the Hyksos,* Oxford, 2000, 133 no. JH376.

411. 2939 E/2–1

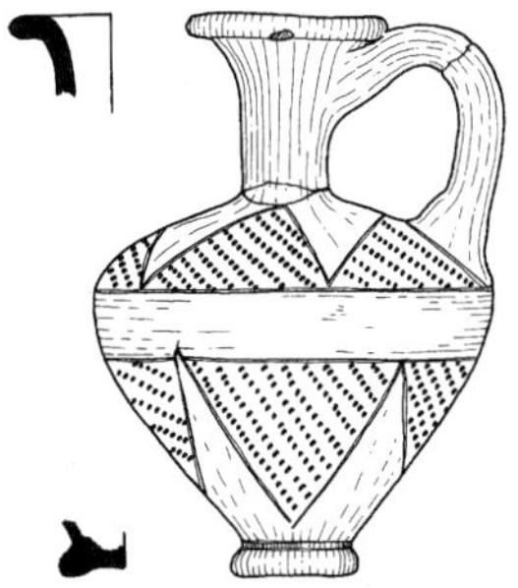

SPI	I-d	f	W2	Bd. gef	re	2	1B

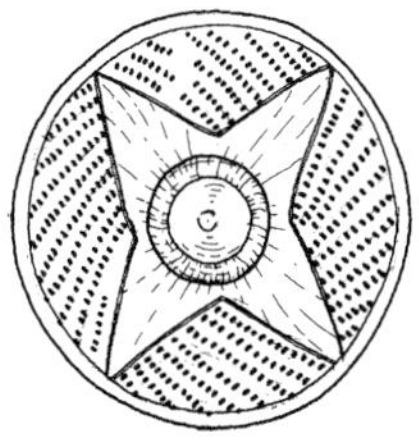

412. 8675 E/1

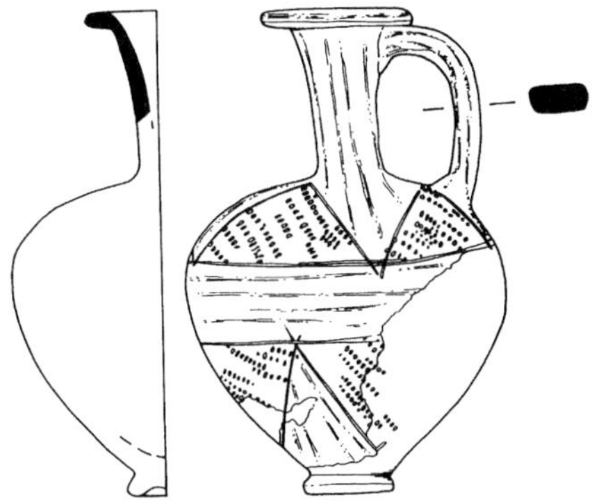

SPI	I-d	f–m	W2	Bd. gef	re	2	1B

413. 8702 E/1

SPI	I-d	m	W2	Bd. gef	re	2–3	1B

414. 8672 E/1

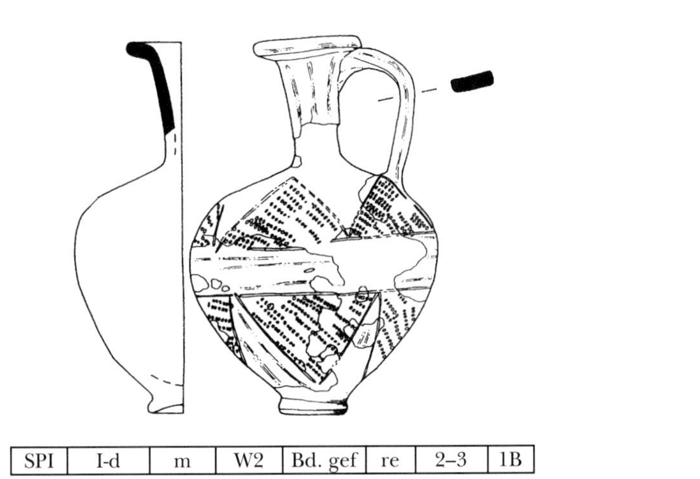

SPI	I-d	m	W2	Bd. gef	re	2–3	1B

415. 8782 E/1

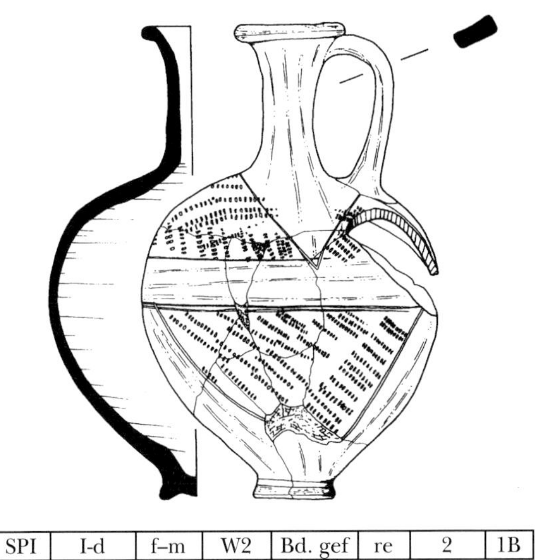

SPI	I-d	f–m	W2	Bd. gef	re	2	1B

1:2

Late Egyptian Type Group L.4.1

Plate 74

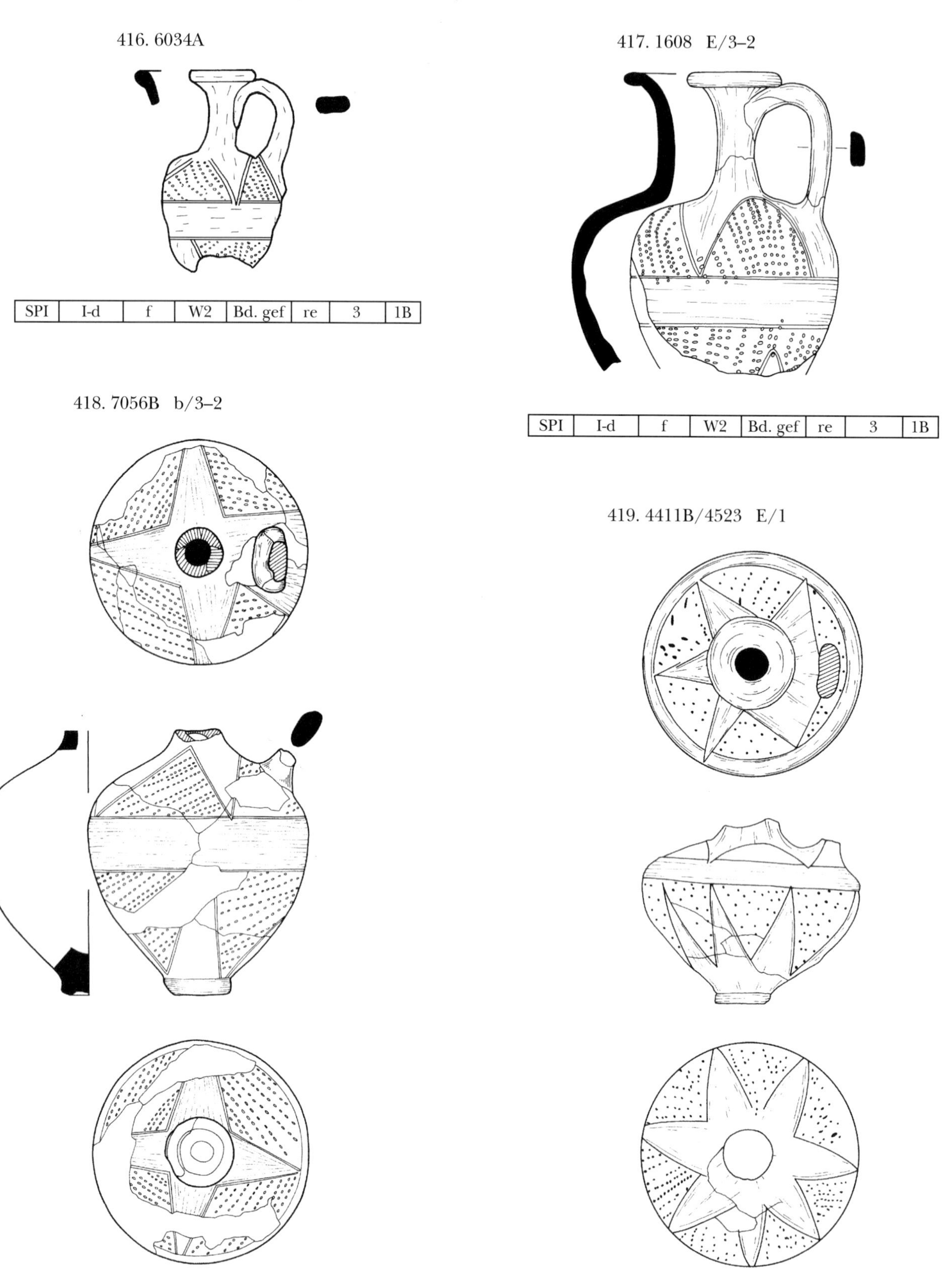

SPI	I-d	f	W2	Bd. gef	re	3	1B

SPI	I-d	f	W2	Bd. gef	re	3	1B

SPI	I-d	f	W2	Bd. gef	re	3	1B

SPI	I-d	m	W2	Bd. gef	re	1–2	1B

1:2

Late Egyptian Type Group L.4.1

Plate 75

418. 7056B TD F/I-p/20 grave 13 Phase b/3–2 (89/142) Plate 75

SPI	I-d	f	W2	Bd. gef	re	3	1B

Nd. 1.6 cm. Bd. 2.3 cm. pht. 8.5 cm. Md 7.7 cm. Wd. 0.45 cm.
Restored from sherds, incomplete
Surface colour: 5Y4/4 reddish brown; burnished slip: 10YR4/1 dark grey
Break: not visible
Decoration: Upper zone of four standing triangles and a lower one of four pendant triangles, each infilled with comb decoration from upper left to lower right, made with an eight-toothed comb.

Perhaps to this group should also be assigned the more squat vessel TD 4411B/4523

419. 4411B/4523 TD F/I-i/22 offering pit 12 Phase E/1 (83/019) Plate 75

SPI	I-d	m	W2	Bd. gef	re	1–2	1B

Nd. 1.8 cm. Bd. 1.94 cm. pht. 6.2 cm. Md 7.64 cm. Wd. 0.4 cm.
Incomplete
Surface colour: 2.5Y3/3 very dark greyish brown; burnished slip: 2.5Y3/0 very dark greyish brown
Break: uniform grey
Decoration: Four standing triangles on shoulder, seven pendant triangles on lower body, all infilled with a twelve-toothed comb.
Previously published: TD XVII, I, 32, fig. 8, no. 29.
BNL JH868 Egyptian Nile Clay[609]

Type Group L.4.2

Type group L.4.2 is currently known from a single example, TD 781, with direct everted rim, strap handle and a button base. It is decorated with an upper zone of standing triangles and a lower one of pendant triangles.

420. 0781 Cairo JE 91178 A/II-m/11 planum 4/5 grave 5 Phase E/2–1 (66/039) Plates 76, 145

SPI	I-d	f	W2	Bd. gef	re	3	1B

D. 2.6 cm. Nd 1.2 cm. Bd. 1.3 cm. H. 8.7 cm. Md. 5.9 cm. Wd. 0.4 cm.
Intact
Surface colour: 10YR5/2 grey brown; burnished slip: 5YR3/1 very dark grey
Break: not visible
Decoration: On shoulder three standing triangles and a lower zone of four pendant triangles infilled with poorly executed zigzags made with a twelve-toothed comb.
Previously published: KOPETZKY, *The MB IIB-Corpus of the Hyksos Period at Tell el-Dab^ca*, 2007, 198 fig. 3.3.

Type Group L.5.1

Type group L.5.1 consists of a single Biconical III jug with rolled rim, swollen neck, strap handle and a ring base, TD 174. It is decorated with two zones of chevrons delineated at the lower edge of the upper zone, and the upper edge of the lower zone.

421. 0174 Vienna A1628 A/II-l/12 grave 2 Phase E/1 (66/038) Plates 76, 145

SPI	I-d	f	W2	Bd. gef	re	3	1B

D. 3.5 cm. Nd 1.4 cm. Bd. 2.1 cm. H. 11.2 cm. Md. 8.0 cm. Wd. 0.4 cm.
VI 72.72
Restored from sherds, incomplete.
Surface colour: 10YR4/1 dark grey; burnished slip: 10YR3/1 very dark grey
Break: uniform dark grey
Decoration: Upper zone of vertical chevrons pointing left, and lower zone of vertical zigzags, made with a twelve-toothed comb.
Previously published: TD V, 187, 188.

Type Group L.5.2

Type group L.5.2 known through a single Biconical III jug, TD 183, with rolled rim, swollen neck, strap handle and button base, is similar to the previous group, but with a different base form. It is decorated with two zones of chevrons delineated at the lower edge of the upper zone, and the upper edge of the lower zone.

422. 0183 Cairo JE 91557G A/II-l/12 grave 2 Phase E/1 (66/034) Plates 76, 145

SPI	I-d	vf	W2	Bd. gef	re	3	1B

D. 2.7 cm. Nd 1.4 cm. Bd. 1.7 cm. H. 8.5 cm. Md. 5.5 cm. Wd. 0.4 cm.
Intact
Surface colour: 5YR5/1 grey; burnished slip: 5YR2/1 black
Break: not visible
Decoration: Upper zone of vertical striations from upper right to lower left, and lower zone of vertical chevrons pointing left, made with a twelve-toothed comb.
Previously published: TD V, 187, 188.

Type Group L.5.3

This is the classic Biconical 1 of Kaplan, namely jugs with rolled rims, strap handles and ring or disc bases. The upper and lower decorative zones are usually filled with horizontal chevrons, (L.5.3a), or oblique

[609] P. MCGOVERN, *The Foreign Relations of the Hyksos*, Oxford, 2000, 149 no. JH868.

420. 781 E/2–1

SPI	I-d	f	W2	Bd. gef	re	3	1B

421. 0174 E/1

SPI	I-d	f	W2	Bd. gef	re	3	1B

422. 0183 E/1

SPI	I-d	vf	W2	Bd. gef	re	3	1B

1:2

Late Egyptian Type Group L.4.2, L.5.1, L.5.2

Plate 76

lines (L.5.3b), and at times these lines radiate straight out from the base or neck. Combinations such as chevrons in the upper zone and oblique lines in the lower, or vice versa may also occur (L.5.3c). This type group is extremely common.

Type Group L.5.3a

423. 0867 Vienna A2631 A/II-m/11 planum 3/4 grave 6 Phase E/2–E/1 (67/023) Plate 77

SPI	I-d	f	W2	Bd. gef	re	3	1B

D. 2.75 cm. Nd. 1.3 cm. Bd. 1.85 cm. H. 8.2 cm. Md 6.3 cm. Wd. 0.35 cm.
VI 76.82
Incomplete
Surface colour: 10YR4/1 dark grey; burnished slip: 10YR3/1 very dark grey
Break: uniform grey
Decoration: Upper zone of vertical chevrons pointing right, and lower zone of vertical chevrons pointing left made with a twelve-toothed comb.
Previously published: TD V, 157, 158.

424. 0182 Cairo JE 91557F A/II-l/12 grave 2 Phase E/1 (66/034) Plate 77

SPI	I-d	f	W2	Bd. gef	re	3	1B

D. 2.8 cm. Nd. 1.3 cm. Bd. 1.6 cm. H. 8.3 cm. Md 5.7 cm. Wd. 0.4 cm.
VI 68.67
Intact
Surface colour: 7.5YR6/2 pinkish grey; burnished slip: 5YR3/1 very dark grey
Break: not visible
Decoration: Upper zone of vertical chevrons pointing right, and

423. 0867 E/2–E/1

424. 0182 E/1

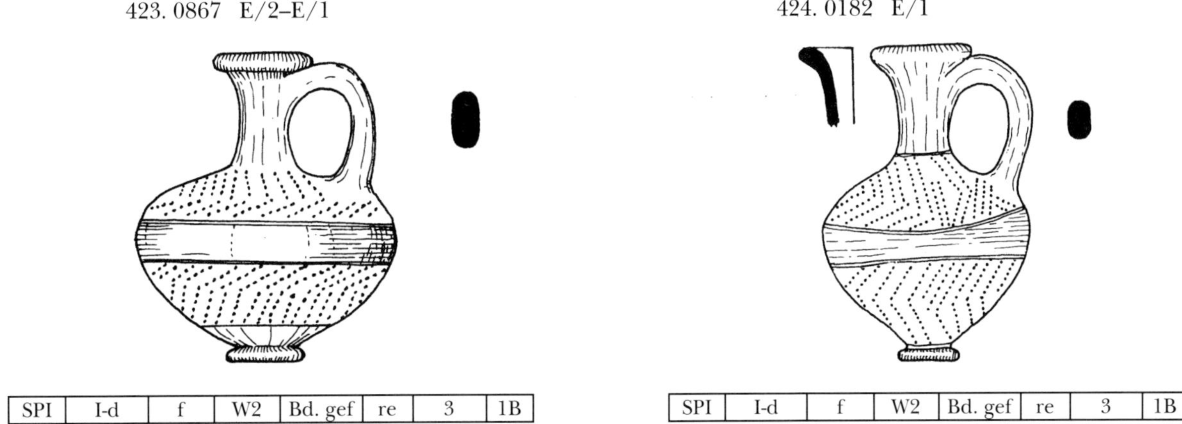

SPI	I-d	f	W2	Bd. gef	re	3	1B

SPI	I-d	f	W2	Bd. gef	re	3	1B

425. 178 E/1

426. 858 E/2–E/1

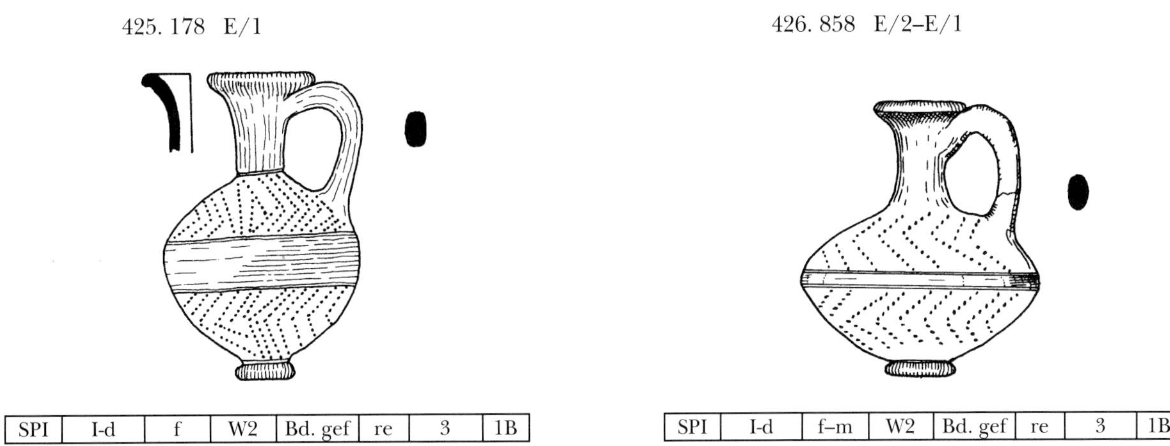

SPI	I-d	f	W2	Bd. gef	re	3	1B

SPI	I-d	f–m	W2	Bd. gef	re	3	1B

427. 388 D/3

428. 2319 D/3

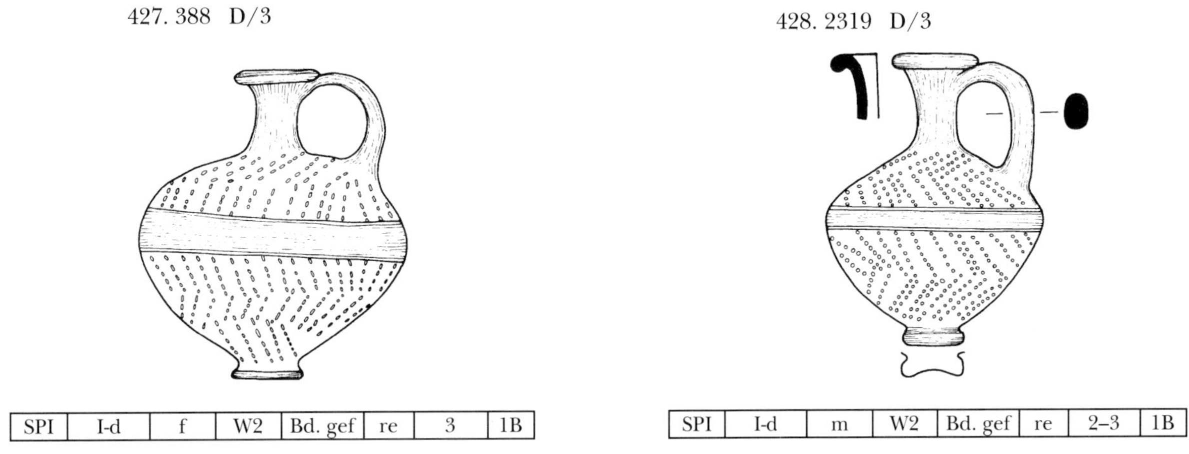

SPI	I-d	f	W2	Bd. gef	re	3	1B

SPI	I-d	m	W2	Bd. gef	re	2–3	1B

1:2

Late Egyptian Type Group L.5.3a

Plate 77

lower zone of vertical chevrons pointing left made with a twelve-toothed comb.
Previously published: TD V, 186–188.

425. 0178 Cairo JE 91557C A/II-l/12 grave 2 Phase E/1 (66/034) Plate 77

SPI	I-d	f	W2	Bd. gef	re	3	1B

D. 2.8 cm. Nd. 1.2 cm. Bd. 1.7 cm. H. 8.2 cm. Md 5.6 cm. Wd. 0.4 cm.
VI 62.92
Intact
Surface colour: 7.5YR6/2 pinkish grey; burnished slip: 5YR3/1 black
Break: uniform grey
Decoration: Upper zone of vertical chevrons pointing right, and lower zone of vertical chevrons pointing left made with a twelve-toothed comb.
Previously published: TD V, 187, 188.

426. 0858 Vienna A2624 A/II-m/11 planum 3–4 grave 6 Phase E/2–E/1 (67/021) Plate 77

SPI	I-d	f–m	W2	Bd. gef	re	3	1B

D. 2.55 cm. Nd. 1.25 cm. Bd. 1.6 cm. H. 7.3 cm. Md 6.5 cm. Wd. 0.3 cm.
VI 89.04
Incomplete.
Surface colour: 10YR-2.5Y5/2 greyish brown; burnished slip: 5YR3/1 very dark grey
Break: brown core, grey reduction zones
Decoration: Upper zone of vertical chevrons pointing left, and lower zone of vertical chevrons pointing left made with an eight-toothed comb.
Previously published: TD V, 157, 158, *PuF* 225 nr. 263.

427. 0388 Vienna A1409 A/I-g/3 grave 1 Phase D/3 (66/056) Plate 77

SPI	I-d	f	W2	Bd. gef	re	3	1B

D. 2.5 cm. Nd. 1.24 cm. Bd. 2.1 cm. H. 8.4 cm. Md 7.3 cm. Wd. 0.3 cm.
VI 86.90
Intact
Surface colour: 10YR5/1 grey; burnished slip: 10YR3/1 very dark grey
Break: not visible
Decoration: Upper zone of vertical chevrons pointing left, and lower zone of vertical zigzags made with an eight-toothed comb.

428. 2319 Vienna A3545 A/II-m/15 grave 3 Phase D/3 (69/110) Plate 77

SPI	I-d	m	W2	Bd. gef	re	2–3	1B

D. 2.4 cm. Nd. 1.1 cm. Bd. 1.8 cm. H. 7.8 cm. Md 6.05 cm. Wd. 0.3 cm.
VI 77.56
Intact
Surface colour: 10YR6/4 light yellow brown; burnished slip: 10YR3/1 very dark grey
Break: not visible
Decoration: Upper zone of vertical chevrons pointing left, and lower zone of vertical chevrons pointing right, made with a twelve-toothed comb.
Previously published: TD V, 226, 228; *TD XVI*, 315, fig. 235, no. 24.

429. 0860 Cairo JE 91582 A/II-m/11 planum 3/4 grave 6 Phase E/2–E/1 (67/030) Plate 78

SPI	I-d	vf	W2	Bd. gef	re	3	1B

D. 2.7 cm. Nd. 1.4 cm. Bd. 2.05 cm. H. 8.2 cm. Md 6.25 cm. Wd. 0.3 cm.
VI 76.21
Intact
Surface colour: 7.5YR6/1–2 pinkish grey; burnished slip: 5YR4/1,5/2 dark grey, reddish grey
Break: not visible
Decoration: Upper zone of vertical chevrons pointing right, and lower zone of vertical chevrons pointing left made with a twelve-toothed comb.
Previously published: TD V, 157, 158.

430. 2111 Vienna A3416 A/II-l/16 grave 1 Phase E/1 (69/050) Plate 78

SPI	I-d	f	W2	Bd. gef	re	3	1B

D. 2.5 cm. Nd 1.2 cm. Bd. 1.5 cm. H. 7.0 cm. Md. 5.0 cm. Wd. 0.3 cm.
VI 71.42
Incomplete
Surface colour: eroded
Break: uniform grey
Decoration: Upper zone of vertical chevrons pointing left, and lower zone of vertical chevrons pointing right made with a twelve-toothed comb.
BNL JH384 Egyptian Nile Clay[610]

431. 0180 Cairo JE 91557D A/II-l/12 grave 2 Phase E/1 (66/034) Plate 78

SPI	I-d	vf	W2	Bd. gef	re	3	1B

D. 2.7 cm. Nd. 1.3 cm. Bd. 1.5 cm. H. 8.1 cm. Md 5.4 cm. Wd. 0.3 cm.
VI 66.66
Intact
Surface colour: 5YR5/1 grey; burnished slip: 5YR3/1 very dark grey
Break: uniform grey
Decoration: Upper zone of vertical chevrons pointing right, and lower zone of vertical chevrons pointing left made with a eight-toothed comb.
Previously published: TD V, 187, 188.

432. 5774 TD F/I-m/19 grave 7 Phase a/2 (86/011) Plates 78, 145

SPI	I-d	f–m	W2	Bd. gef	re	3	1B

[610] P. McGovern, *The Foreign Relations of the Hyksos*, Oxford, 2000, 134 no. JH384.

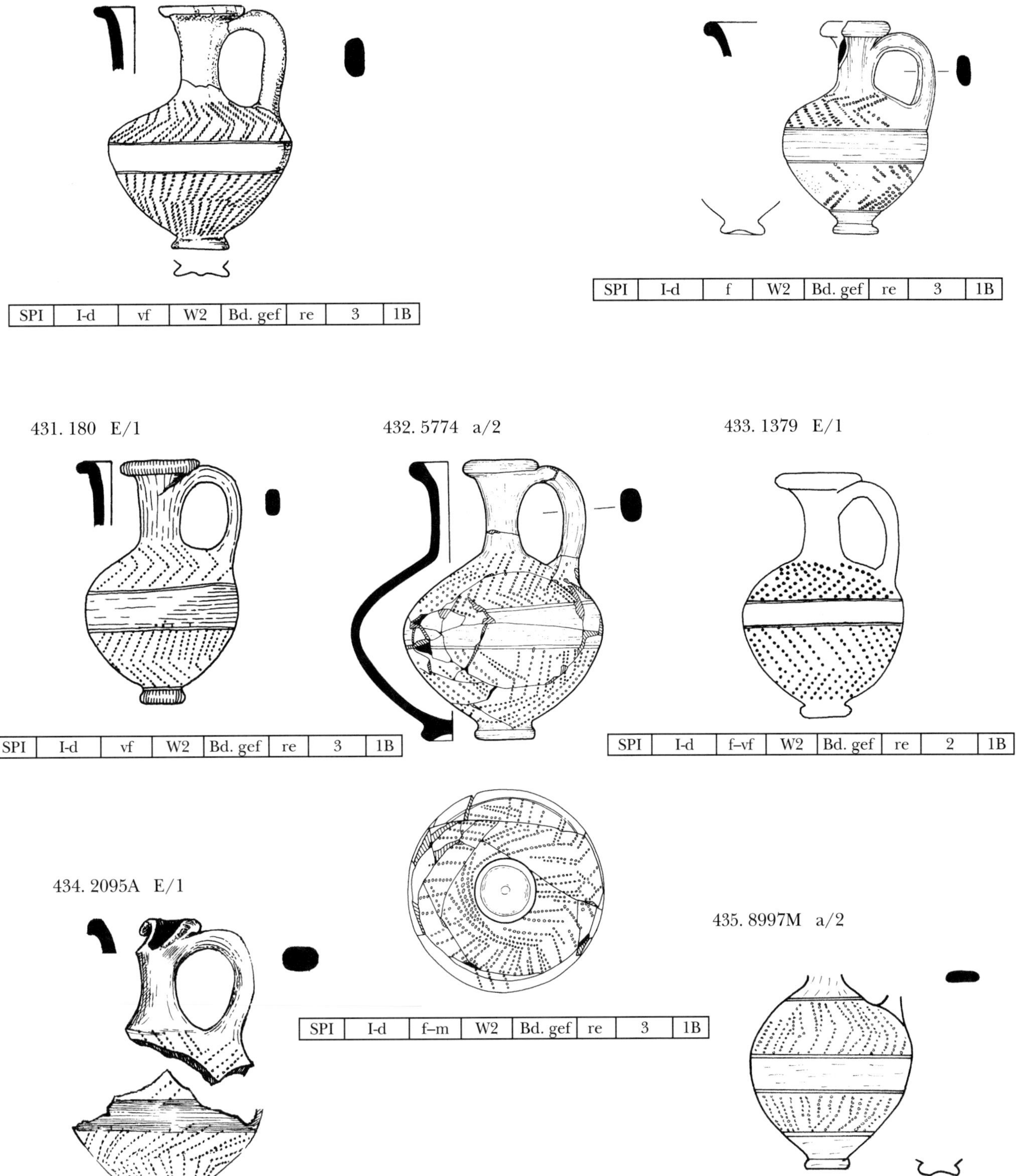

429. 860 E/2–E/1

SPI	I-d	vf	W2	Bd. gef	re	3	1B

430. 2111 E/1

SPI	I-d	f	W2	Bd. gef	re	3	1B

431. 180 E/1

SPI	I-d	vf	W2	Bd. gef	re	3	1B

432. 5774 a/2

SPI	I-d	f–m	W2	Bd. gef	re	3	1B

433. 1379 E/1

SPI	I-d	f–vf	W2	Bd. gef	re	2	1B

434. 2095A E/1

SPI	I-d	f	W2	Bd. gef	re	2–3	1B

435. 8997M a/2

SPI	I-b-2	f	W2	Bd. gef	re	3–4	1B

1:2

Late Egyptian Type Group L.5.3a

Plate 78

D. 2.64 cm. Nd. 1.14 cm. Bd. 2.13 cm. H. 9.5 cm. Md 6.9 cm. Wd. 0.3 cm.
VI 72.63
Restored from sherds, incomplete.
Surface colour: 10YR5/2 grey brown; burnished slip: 10YR5/2 grey brown
Break: uniform grey
Decoration: Upper zone of vertical chevrons pointing left, and lower zone of vertical chevrons pointing right made with a fourteen-toothed comb.

433. 1379 Vienna A1663 A/II-l/14 grave 5 Phase E/1 (68/089) Plate 78

SPI	I-d	f–vf	W2	Bd. gef	re	2	1B

D. 2.65 cm. Nd. 1.2 cm. Bd. 2.15 cm. H. 8.1 cm. Md 5.7 cm. Wd. 0.3 cm.
VI 70.37
Intact
Surface colour: 2.5Y6/1 grey; burnished slip: 2.5Y4/1 dark grey
Break: not visible
Decoration: Upper zone of vertical chevrons pointing right, and lower zone of vertical chevrons also pointing right, made with a twelve-toothed comb.
Previously published: TD XVI, 254, fig. 189b, no. 7.

434. 2095A Vienna TDS 2095A A/II-n/10 planum 3 grave 5 Phase E/1 (75/005) Plate 78

SPI	I-d	f	W2	Bd. gef	re	2–3	1B

D. 3.0 cm. Nd. 1.1 cm. Bd. 1.6 cm. H. 9.8 cm. Md 7.0 cm. Wd. 0.3 cm.
VI 71.42
Incomplete.
Surface colour: 10YR-2.5Y5/2 greyish brown; burnished slip: 5YR3/1 very dark grey
Break: uniform dark grey
Decoration: Upper zone of vertical chevrons pointing left, and lower zone of vertical chevrons pointing right made with a twelve-toothed comb.
Previously published: TD V, 226, 228.

435. 8997M TD F/II-r/22 planum 1 L81 Phase a/2 (06/284) Plate 78

SPI	I-b-2	f	W2	Bd. gef	re	3–4	1B

Nd. 1.3 cm. Bd. 1.5 cm. pht. 6.6 cm. Md 5.6 cm. Wd. 0.35 cm.
Incomplete.
Surface colour: 10R5/1 reddish gray; burnished slip: 5YR2.5/1 black
Break: uniform grey
Decoration: Upper zone of vertical chevrons pointing right, and lower zone of vertical chevrons pointing left made with an eight-toothed comb.

436. 5351 TD A/II-k/17 planum 2–3 pit 1 unstratified (85/230) Plate 79

SPI	I-d	f–m	W2	Bd. gef	re	3	1B

Bd. 1.8 cm. pht. 6.9 cm. Md 6.6 cm. Wd. 0.35 cm.
Incomplete.
Surface colour: 10YR6/1–3 grey to grey brown; burnished slip: 10YR3/1–4/2
Break: uniform grey
Decoration: Upper zone of vertical chevrons pointing right, and lower zone of vertical chevrons pointing right made with a twelve-toothed comb.

437. 0373 Vienna A2306 A/I-g/3 planum 0–1 grave 1 burial 1 Phase D/3 (66/052) Plate 79

SPI	I-d	f	W2	Bd. gef	re	3	1B

Nd. 1.2 cm. Bd. 1.95 cm. pht. 5.0 cm. Md 5.3 cm. Wd. 0.3 cm.
Incomplete
Surface colour: 2.5Y5/1 grey; burnished slip: 2.5YR2.5/1 black
Break: uniform grey
Decoration: Upper zone of vertical chevrons pointing left, and lower zone of vertical chevrons pointing left made with a twelve-toothed comb.

438. 1430 Vienna A2978 A/II-n/12 planum 2 Phase D/3 (68/074) Plate 79

SPI	I-d	f	W2	Bd. gef	re	3	1B

Nd. 1.4 cm. Bd. 1.8 cm. pht. 6.5 cm. Md 6.5 cm. Wd. 0.3 cm.
Incomplete
Surface colour: 10YR4/1–5/2 dark grey; burnished slip: 10R3/2 dusty red
Break: uniform dark grey
Decoration: Upper zone of vertical chevrons pointing right, and lower zone of vertical chevrons pointing left made with a twelve-toothed comb.
Previously published: TD V, 260; *TD XVII,* II, 200, fig. 173.

439. 2136 Vienna A3437 A/II-l/16 grave 1 Phase E/1 (69/062) Plate 79

SPI	I-d	f	W2	Bd. gef	re	2–3	1B

Nd. 1.2 cm. Bd. 2.3 cm. pht. 4.7 cm. Md 5.0 cm. Wd. 0.4 cm.
Incomplete
Surface colour: 10YR6/2 light brownish grey; burnished slip: 10YR4/3 dark brown
Break: uniform dark grey
Decoration: Upper zone of vertical chevrons pointing left, made with a twelve-toothed comb: lower zone eroded.
BNL JH392 Egyptian Nile Clay[611]
Previously published: TD XVI, 263, fig. 192a, no. 18.

440. 2322 Cairo JE 91711B A/II-m/15 grave 3 Phase D/3 (69/111) Plates 79, 146

SPI	I-d	vf	W2	Bd. gef	re	3	1B

D. 2.8 cm. Nd. 1.2 cm. Bd. 1.8 cm. H. 8.85 cm. Md 6.7 cm. Wd. 0.3 cm.
VI 75.70
Intact
Surface colour: 10YR6/2 light brownish gray; burnished slip: 10YR3/1 very dark grey

[611] P. McGovern, *The Foreign Relations of the Hyksos,* Oxford, 2000, 134 no. JH392.

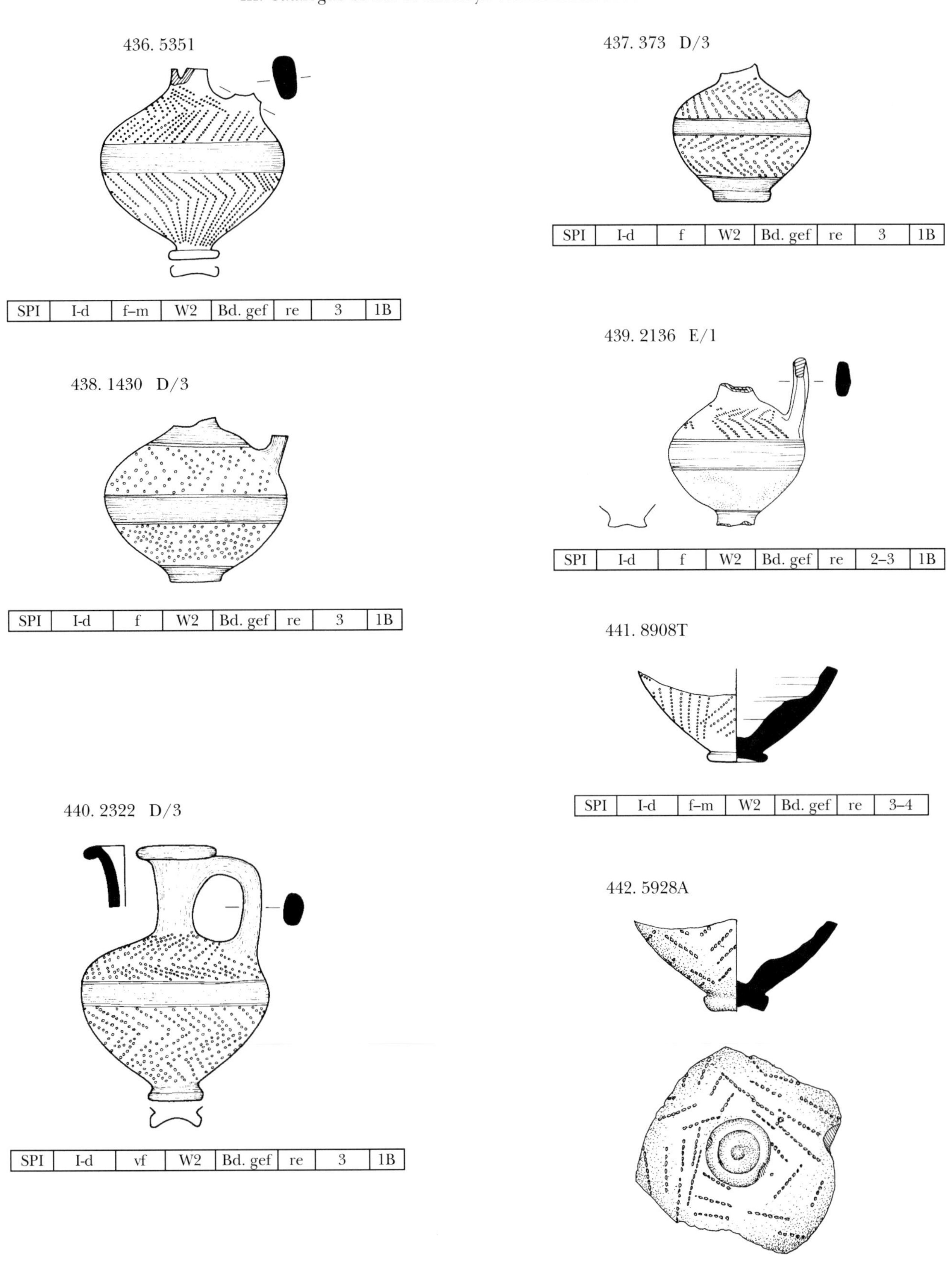

436. 5351

SPI	I-d	f–m	W2	Bd. gef	re	3	1B

437. 373 D/3

SPI	I-d	f	W2	Bd. gef	re	3	1B

438. 1430 D/3

SPI	I-d	f	W2	Bd. gef	re	3	1B

439. 2136 E/1

SPI	I-d	f	W2	Bd. gef	re	2–3	1B

440. 2322 D/3

SPI	I-d	vf	W2	Bd. gef	re	3	1B

441. 8908T

SPI	I-d	f–m	W2	Bd. gef	re	3–4

442. 5928A

1:2

SPI	I-d	f	W2	Bd. gef	re	3	1B

Late Egyptian Type Group L.5.3a

Plate 79

Break: not visible
Decoration: Upper zone of vertical chevrons pointing right, and lower zone of vertical zigzags pointing left made with a twelve-toothed comb.
Previously published: TD XVI, 315, fig. 235, no. 23.

441. 8908T TD H/VI-j/17 planum 0–1 unstratified (99/143) Plate 79

SPI	I-d	f–m	W2	Bd. gef	re	3–4

Bd. 2.1 cm. pht. 3.3 cm. Wd. 0.45 cm.
Incomplete
Surface colour: 10YR4/2 dark grey brown; burnished slip 5YR4/1 dark grey
Break: dark brown core, red brown reduction zones
Decoration: Lower zone of vertical chevrons pointing left made with a twelve-toothed comb.

442. 5928A TD A/II-l/19 unstratified (86/275) Plate 79

SPI	I-d	f	W2	Bd. gef	re	3	1B

Bd. 2.2 cm. pht. 3.2 cm. Wd. 0.4–8 cm.
Incomplete
Surface colour: 5YR5/1 grey
Break: dark grey core, thin red oxidation zones
Decoration: Lower zone of horizontal chevrons pointing left made with a six-toothed comb.

Type Group L.5.3b

443. 0028 Vienna A2147 A/I-g/4 planum 1 Phase D/3 (66/006) Plates 80, 146

SPI	I-d	f	W2	Bd. gef	re	3	1B

D. 2.8 cm. Nd. 1.2 cm. Bd. 2.0 cm. H. 8.7 cm. Md 7.0 cm. Wd. 0.3 cm.
VI 80.45
Restored from sherds, incomplete
Surface colour: 2.5Y5/1 grey; burnished slip: 7.5YR4/1 dark grey
Break: reddish grey core, grey reduction zones
Decoration: Upper zone of vertical chevrons pointing right, and lower zone of vertical lines, made with a twelve-toothed comb.

444. 6813 TD A/V-p/19 planum 5 grave 33 Phase D/3 (88/377) Plate 80

SPI	I-d	f	W2	Bd. gef	re	3	1B

D. 3.2 cm. Nd. 1.4 cm. Bd. 2.0 cm. H. 9.7 cm. Md 7.1 cm. Wd. 0.3 cm.
VI 73.19
Intact
Surface colour: 10YR5/1 gray; burnished slip: 5Y2/1 black
Break: not visible
Decoration: Two horizontal zones of delineated oblique lines made with an eight-toothed comb in the upper zone, and with an eleven-toothed comb in the lower zone.
Previously published: TD XI, 59 no. 1, pl. xxxA.

445. 9009Z TD F/II-r/22 planum 1 L81 Phase a/2 (06/519) Plate 80

SPI	I-b-2	f	W2	Bd. gef	re	3	1B

Nd. 1.2 cm. Bd. 1.8 cm. pht. 5.4 cm. Md 6.2 cm. Wd. 0.3 cm.
Incomplete
Surface colour: 7.5YR5/1 grey; burnished slip: 7.5Y3/1 dark grey
Break: uniform black
Decoration: Two horizontal zones of delineated oblique lines made with a sixteen-toothed comb.

446. 8943G TD H/VI-u/13 planum 12 Phase D/3 (01/118) Plate 80

SPI	I-d	f–m	W2	Bd. gef	re	3	1B

Nd. 1.5 cm. Bd. 1.9 cm. pht. 7.7 cm. Wd. 0.3 cm.
Restored from sherds, incomplete.
Surface colour: 5YR6/1 grey; burnished slip: 5YR6/1 grey
Break: thin black core, red and brown reduction zones
Decoration: Two zones of oblique lines made with a sixteen-toothed comb.

447. 0361 Vienna A2302 A/I-g/3 grave 1 Phase D/3 (66/052) Plate 80

SPI	I-d	f	W2	Bd. gef	re	3	1B

Nd. 1.1 cm. Bd. 1.5 cm. pht. 4.4 cm. Md 5.35 cm. Wd. 0.3 cm.
Incomplete
Surface colour: 2.5Y6/1 grey; burnished slip: 2.5Y4/1 dark grey
Break: light grey core, reddish grey and grey reduction zones
Decoration: Two zones of oblique lines made with a sixteen-toothed comb.

448. 1986A TD A/II-n/10 grave 1 Phase D/2 (69/052) Plate 80

SPI	I-d	f	W2	Bd. gef	re	2–3	1B

Bd. 2.9 cm. pht. 2.3 cm. Wd. 0.4 cm.
Incomplete.
Surface colour: 10YR4/1–2 grey; burnished slip: 10YR3/1 very dark grey
Break: uniform dark grey
Decoration: Lower zone of oblique lines made with a sixteen-toothed comb.
Previously published: TD V, 312, 313.

Type Group L.5.3c

449. 2308 Cairo JE 91711E A/II-m/15 grave 3 Phase D/3 (69/108) Plate 81

SPI	I-d	f	W2	Bd. gef	re	3	1B

D. 3.1 cm. Nd. 1.3 cm. Bd. 1.8 cm. H. 10.0 cm. Md 7.2 cm. Wd. 0.3 cm.
VI 72.00
Intact
Surface colour: 10YR5/1 grey; burnished slip: 10YR2/1 very dark grey brown
Break: uniform dark grey
Decoration: Upper zone of vertical lines, and lower zone of poorly made vertical chevrons pointing right made with a ten-toothed comb.
Previously published: TD XVI, 313, fig. 234, no. 11.

450. 2332 Cairo JE 91714A A/II-m/15 grave 3 Phase D/3 (69/104) Plates 81, 146

SPI	I-d	f	W2	Bd. gef	re	2–3	1B

443. 28 D/3

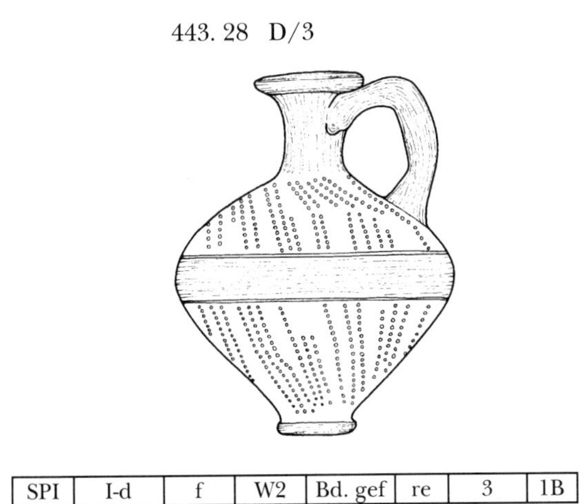

SPI	I-d	f	W2	Bd. gef	re	3	1B

444. 6813 D/3

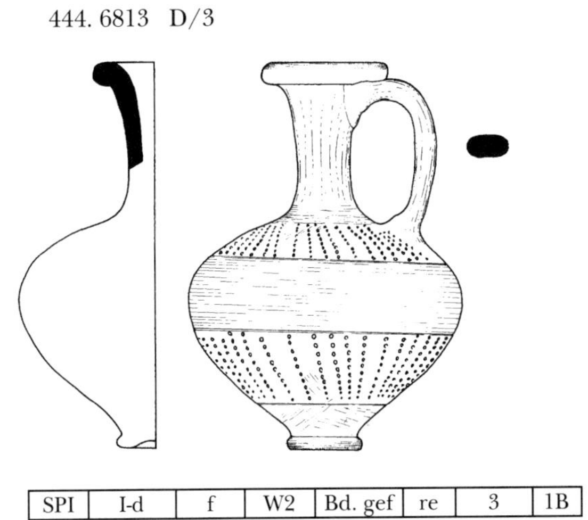

SPI	I-d	f	W2	Bd. gef	re	3	1B

445. 9009Z a/2

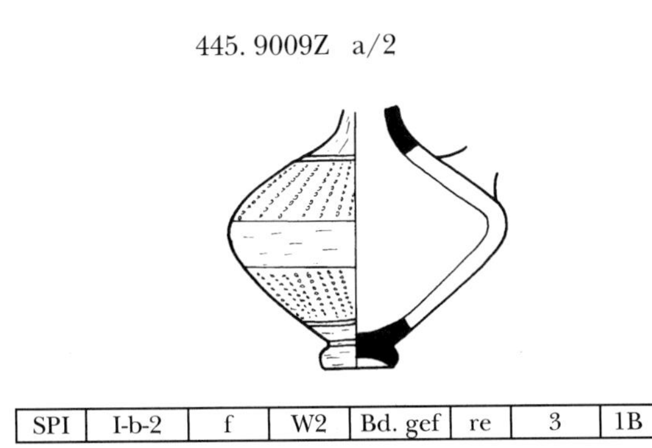

SPI	I-b-2	f	W2	Bd. gef	re	3	1B

446. 8943G D/3

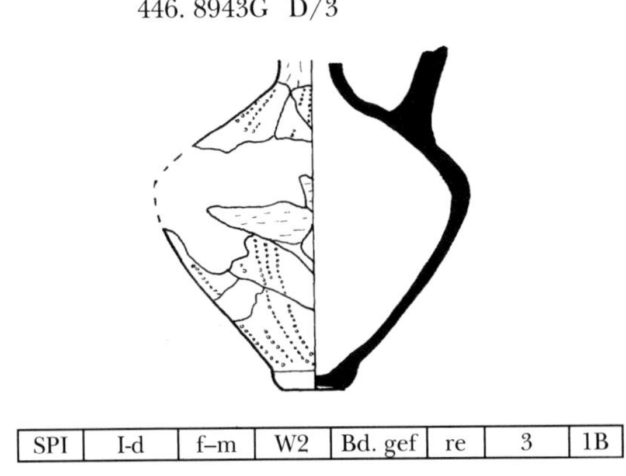

SPI	I-d	f–m	W2	Bd. gef	re	3	1B

447. 0361 D/3

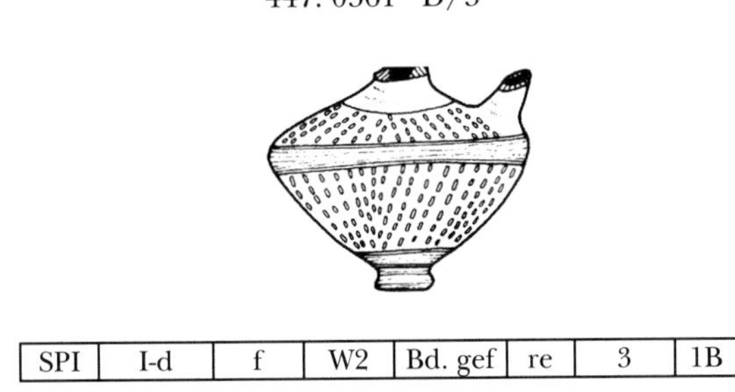

SPI	I-d	f	W2	Bd. gef	re	3	1B

448. 1986A D/2

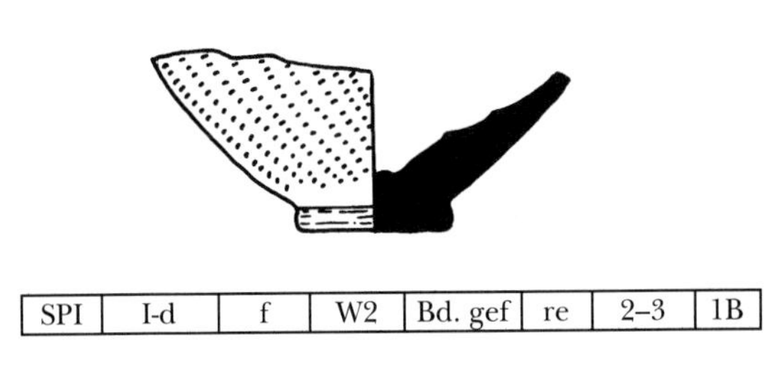

SPI	I-d	f	W2	Bd. gef	re	2–3	1B

1:2

Late Egyptian Type Group L.5.3b

Plate 80

D. 3.05 cm. Nd. 1.25 cm. Bd. 2.3 cm. H. 8.45 cm. Md 8.0 cm. Wd. 0.4 cm.
VI 94.67
Intact
Surface colour: 10YR6/2 light brownish grey; burnished slip: 10YR4/3 dark brown
Break: uniform dark grey
Decoration: Upper zone of lines running from bottom left to top right, and lower zone of vertical chevrons pointing left made with a twelve-toothed comb.
Previously published: TD XVI, 310, fig. 231, no. 8; Kopetzky, *The MB IIB-Corpus of the Hyksos Period at Tell el-Dab^ca*, 2007, 198 fig. 3.6.

451. 2333 Vienna A3550 A/II-m/15 grave 3 Phase D/3 (69/104) Plates 81, 146

SPI	I-d	F	W2	Bd. gef	re	2–3	1B

D. 2.9 cm. Nd. 1.0 cm. Bd. 1.9 cm. H. 9.1 cm. Md 7.2 cm. Wd. 0.4 cm.
VI 79.12
Intact
Surface colour: 10YR6/2 light brownish grey; burnished slip: 10YR4/3 dark brown
Break: uniform dark grey
Decoration: Upper zone of lines running from top left to bottom right, and lower zone of vertical chevrons pointing right made with a twelve-toothed comb.
Previously published: TD XVI, 310, fig. 231, no. 9.

452. 2309B TD A/II-m/15 grave 3 Phase D/3 (69/108) Plate 81

SPI	I-d	f–vf	W2	Bd. gef	re	2	1B

D. 3.2 cm. Nd. 1.1 cm. Bd. 2.0 cm. H. 10.2 cm. Md 7.1 cm. Wd. 0.3 cm.
VI 69.60
Incomplete
Surface colour: 10YR2/1 very dark grey brown; burnished slip: 10YR2/1 black
Break: uniform grey
Decoration: Upper zone of vertical striations, and lower zone of vertical chevrons pointing left made with a twelve-toothed comb.
Previously published: TD XVI, 313, fig. 234, no. 13.

453. 8826 TD A/II-p/13 locus 3 grave 4 Phase D/2 (98/073) Plates 81, 147

SPI	I-d	F	W2	Bd. gef	re	2–3	1B

D. 2.9 cm. Nd. 1.2 cm. Bd. 2.1 cm. H. 9.4 cm. Md 7.9 cm. Wd. 0.35 cm.
VI 84.04
Intact
Surface colour: 10YR6/4 light yellow brown; burnished slip: 10YR4/1 dark grey
Break: uniform grey
Decoraton: Upper zone of vertical lines, and lower zone of vertical chevrons pointing right made with a twelve-toothed comb.
Previously published: TD XVI, 381, fig. 307, no. 3.; Kopetzky, *The MB IIB-Corpus of the Hyksos Period at Tell el-Dab^ca*, 2007, 198 fig. 3.1.

454. 0868 Cairo JE 91584 A/II-m/11 planum 3/4 grave 6 Phase E/2–E/1 (67/030) Plate 81

SPI	I-d	f–m	W2	Bd. gef	re	3	1B

D. 2.9 cm. Nd. 1.3 cm. Bd. 1.8 cm. H. 9.0 cm. Md 7.0 cm. Wd. 0.3 cm.
VI 77.77
Intact
Surface colour: 7.5YR6/2 pinkish grey; burnished slip: 10YR3/1 very dark grey
Break: not visible
Decoration: Upper zone of vertical chevrons pointing right, and lower zone of vertical striations made with a twelve-toothed comb.
Previously published: TD V, 156, 157.

455. 1431 Vienna A1671 A/II-n/12 planum 2 Phase D/3 (68/074) Plates 82, 147

SPI	I-d	f	W2	Bd. gef	re	3	1B

D. 3.0 cm. Nd. 1.35 cm. Bd. 2.15 cm. H. 8.7 cm. Md 6.6 cm. Wd. 0.3 cm.
VI 75.86
Intact
Surface colour: 10YR5/1–2 grey brown; burnished slip: 10YR3/1 very dark grey
Break: not visible
Decoration: Upper zone of vertical chevrons pointing right, and lower zone of vertical lines, made with a twelve-toothed comb.
Previously published: TD V, 260, *PuF* 226 nr 268; *TD XVII,* II, 200, fig. 173.

456. 0456 Vienna A2336 A/I-g/3 planum 3/4 grave 1 Phase D/3 (67/069) Plate 82

SPI	I-d	f	W2	Bd. gef	re	3	1B

Nd. 1.2 cm. Bd. 1.95 cm. H. 8.4 cm. Md 6.34 cm. Wd. 0.4 cm.
VI 75.47
Incomplete
Surface colour: 2.5Y6/1 grey; burnished slip: 2.5Y3/1 very dark grey
Break: uniform grey
Decoration: Upper zone of vertical chevrons pointing right, and lower zone of vertical lines, made with a twelve-toothed comb.

457. 0454 Vienna A2334 A/I-g/3 planum 3–4 grave 1 Phase D/3 (67/070) Plate 82

SPI	I-d	f	W2	Bd. gef	re	3	1B

D. 3.0 cm. Nd. 1.3 cm. Bd. 2.1 cm. H. 7.9 cm. Md 5.86 cm. Wd. 0.35 cm.
VI 74.17
Incomplete
Surface colour: 10YR6/1 grey; burnished slip: 10YR3/1 very dark grey
Break: uniform grey
Decoration: Upper zone of vertical chevrons pointing right, and lower zone of vertical lines, made with a twelve-toothed comb.

458. 1717 Vienna A1688 A/II-l/14 grave 4 Phase E/1 (68/123) Plate 82

SPI	I-d	f–vf	W2	Bd. gef	re	2	1B

449. 2308 D/3

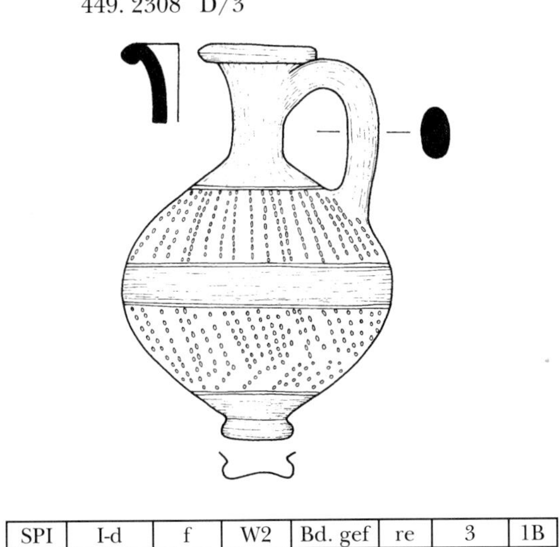

SPI	I-d	f	W2	Bd. gef	re	3	1B

450. 2332 D/3

SPI	I-d	f	W2	Bd. gef	re	2–3	1B

451. 2333 D/3

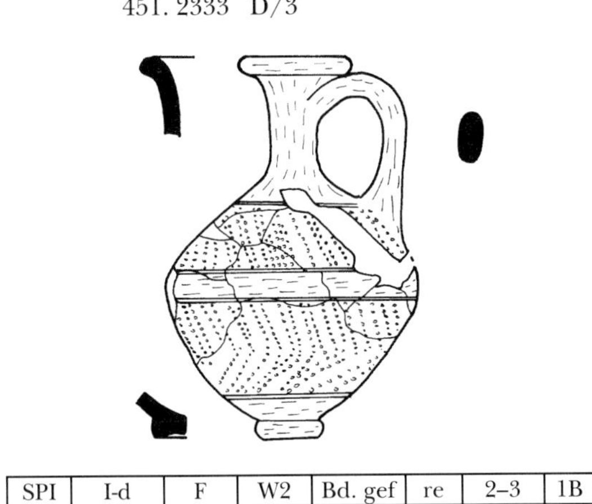

SPI	I-d	F	W2	Bd. gef	re	2–3	1B

452. 2309B D/3

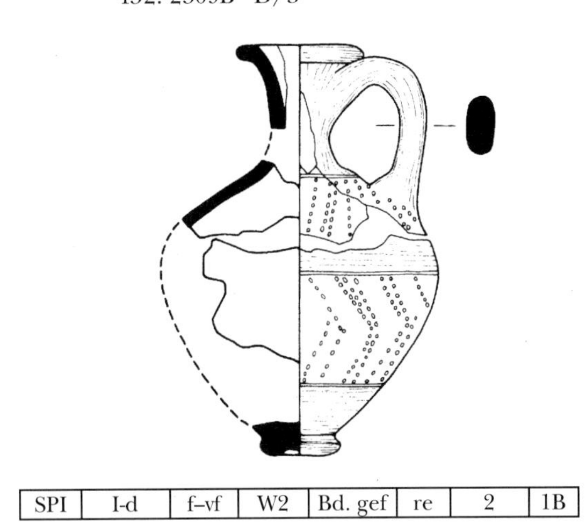

SPI	I-d	f–vf	W2	Bd. gef	re	2	1B

453. 8826 D/2

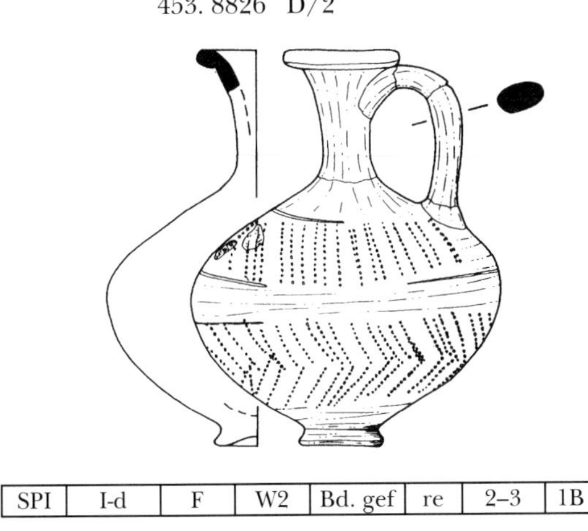

SPI	I-d	F	W2	Bd. gef	re	2–3	1B

454. 0868 E/2–E/1

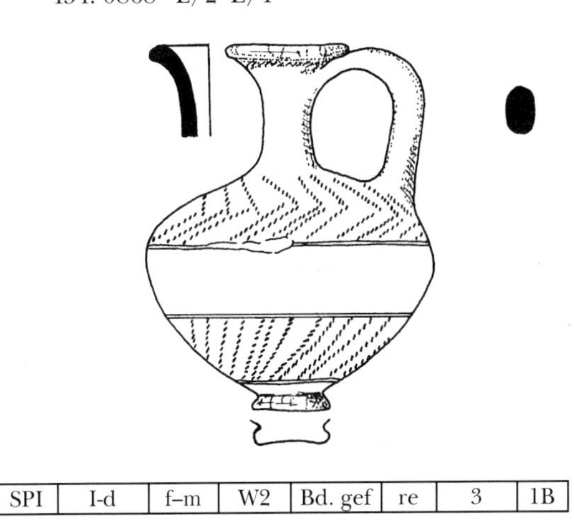

SPI	I-d	f–m	W2	Bd. gef	re	3	1B

1:2

Late Egyptian Type Group L.5.3c

Plate 81

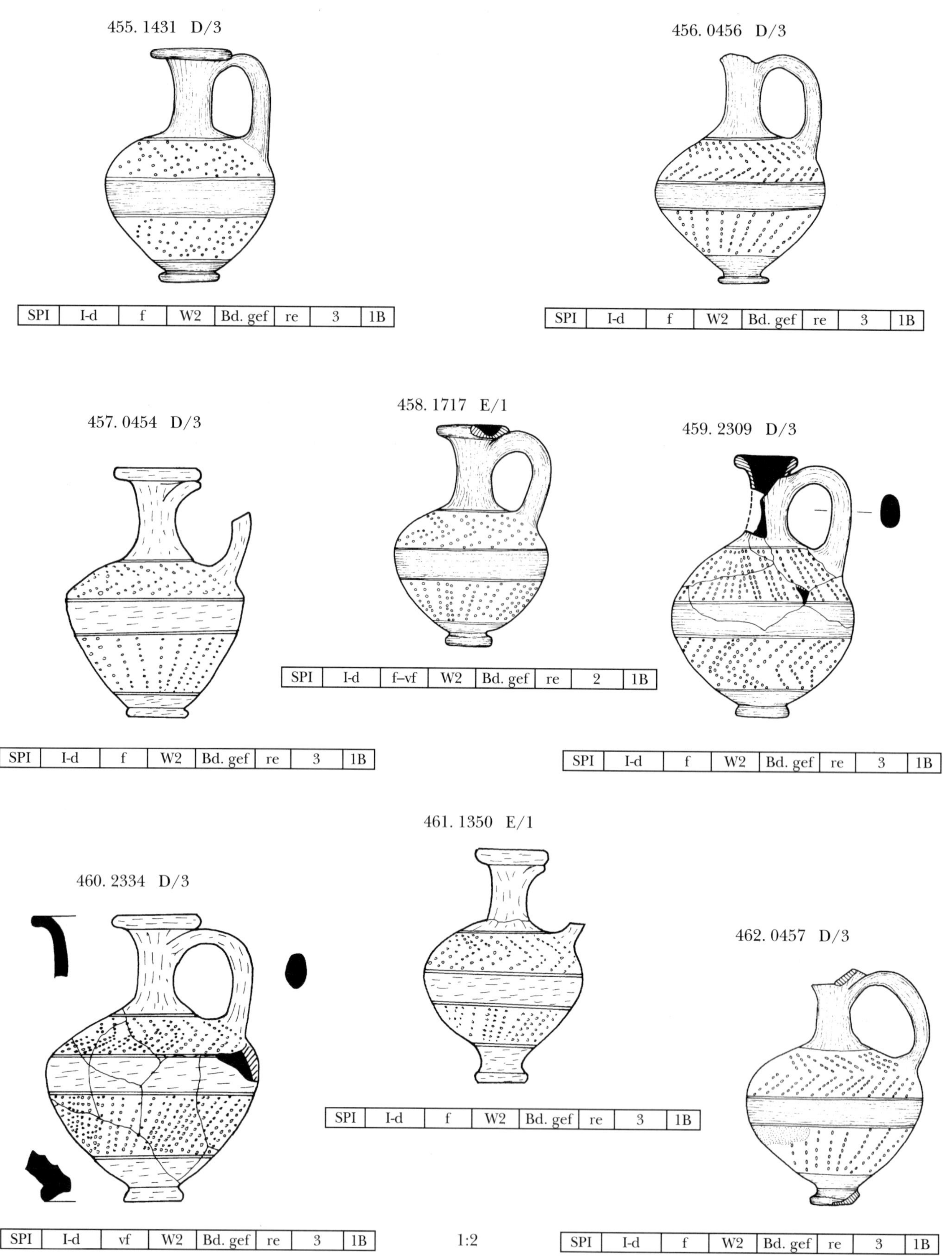

455. 1431 D/3

SPI	I-d	f	W2	Bd. gef	re	3	1B

456. 0456 D/3

SPI	I-d	f	W2	Bd. gef	re	3	1B

457. 0454 D/3

SPI	I-d	f	W2	Bd. gef	re	3	1B

458. 1717 E/1

SPI	I-d	f–vf	W2	Bd. gef	re	2	1B

459. 2309 D/3

SPI	I-d	f	W2	Bd. gef	re	3	1B

460. 2334 D/3

SPI	I-d	vf	W2	Bd. gef	re	3	1B

461. 1350 E/1

SPI	I-d	f	W2	Bd. gef	re	3	1B

462. 0457 D/3

SPI	I-d	f	W2	Bd. gef	re	3	1B

1:2

Late Egyptian Type Group L.5.3c

Plate 82

D. 2.7 cm. Nd. 1.2 cm. Bd. 1.65 cm. H. 8.2 cm. Md 5.8 cm. Wd. 0.3 cm.
VI 70.73
Incomplete
Surface colour: 10YR3/1 very dark grey; burnished slip: 10YR2/1 black
Break: uniform grey
Decoration: Upper zone of vertical chevrons pointing right, and lower zone of vertical lines, made with a twelve-toothed comb.
Previously published: TD XVI, 251, fig. 187, no. 11.

459. 2309 Vienna A3528 A/II-m/15 grave 3 Phase D/3 (69/108) Plate 82

SPI	I-d	f	W2	Bd. gef	re	3	1B

Nd. 1.6 cm. Bd. 2.0 cm. H. 9.7 cm. Md 6.7 cm. Wd. 0.3 cm.
VI 69.07
Incomplete
Surface colour: 2.5Y5/2 greyish brown; burnished slip: 2.5Y3/2 very dark greyish brown
Break: uniform grey
Decoration: Upper zone of lines running from top left to bottom right, and lower zone of vertical chevrons pointing right made with a twelve-toothed comb.
Previously published: TD XVI, 313, fig. 234, no. 12.

460. 2334 Vienna A1731 A/II-m/15 grave 3 Phase D/3 (69/104) Plate 82

SPI	I-d	vf	W2	Bd. gef	re	3	1B

D. 3.0 cm. Nd. 1.3 cm. Bd. 1.9 cm. H. 10.5 cm. Md 5.6 cm. Wd. 0.3 cm.
VI 53.33
Intact
Surface colour: 2.5Y4/1 grey; burnished slip: 2.5Y4/1 dark grey
Break: not visible
Decoration: Upper zone of vertical chevrons pointing right, and lower zone of vertical lines, made with a twelve-toothed comb.
Previously published: TD XVI, 310, fig. 231, no. 4.

461. 1350 Vienna A2921 A/II-l/14 planum 3 grave 5 Phase E/1 (68/080) Plate 82

SPI	I-d	f	W2	Bd. gef	re	3	1B

D. 2.7 cm. Nd. 1.2 cm. Bd. 1.75 cm. H. 8.5 cm. Md 5.8 cm. Wd. 0.4 cm.
VI 68.23
Incomplete
Surface colour: 10YR4/4 dark yellowish brown; burnished slip: 10YR3/1 very dark grey
Break: dark grey core, greyish brown reduction zones
Decoration: Upper zone of chevrons pointing right, lower zone of vertical lines.
Previously published: TD XVI, 254, fig. 189b, no. 6.

462. 0457 Vienna A2337 A/I-g/3 planum 3/4 grave 1 Phase D/3 (67/069) Plate 82

SPI	I-d	f	W2	Bd. gef	re	3	1B

Nd. 1.2 cm. Bd. 2.0 cm. H. 8.5 cm. Md 5.7 cm. Wd. 0.4 cm.
VI 67.05
Incomplete
Surface colour: 7.5YR6/1 grey; burnished slip: 7.5YR3/1–2 very dark gray – dark brown
Break: dark grey core, greyish brown reduction zones
Decoration: Upper zone of vertical chevrons pointing right, and lower zone of striations running from top right to bottom left made with an eight-toothed comb.

463. 0458 Vienna A1651 A/I-g/3 planum 3/4 grave 1 Phase D/3 (67/069) Plate 83

SPI	I-d	f	W2	Bd. gef	re	3	1B

D. 2.8 cm. Nd. 1.2 cm. Bd. 1.7 cm. H. 8.3 cm. Md 5.7 cm. Wd. 0.4 cm.
VI 68.67
Incomplete
Surface colour: 10YR5/2 grayish brown; burnished slip: 10YR3/2 very dark grayish brown
Break: uniform grey
Decoration: Upper zone of vertical chevrons pointing right, and lower zone of striations running from top right to bottom left made with an eight-toothed comb.

464. 0886 Vienna A2645 A/II-m/11 grave 7 Phase E/1 (67/026) Plate 83

SPI	I-d	f–vf	W2	Bd. gef	re	2	1B

D. 2.75 cm. Nd. 1.2 cm. Bd. 1.9 cm. H. 8.5 cm. Md 6.1 cm. Wd. 0.3 cm.
VI 71.76
Restored from sherds complete
Surface colour: 10YR2/1 very dark grey brown; burnished slip: 10YR2/1 black
Break: uniform grey
Decoration: Upper zone of striations from upper right to lower left, and lower zone of chevrons pointing left made with a twelve-toothed comb.
Previously published: TD V, 190, 191.

465. 0047 Vienna A2158 A/II-l/12 planum ? Phase ? (66/006) Plate 83

SPI	I-d	f	W2	Bd. gef	re	3	1B

Nd. 1.3 cm. Bd. 2.05 cm. pht. 8.0 cm. Md 6.0 cm. Wd. 0.3 cm.
Incomplete
Surface colour: 10YR4/1 dark grey; burnished slip: 10YR5/1 grey
Break: uniform grey
Decoration: Upper zone of striations from upper right to lower left, and lower zone of chevrons pointing left made with a twelve-toothed comb.

466. 2116 Vienna A3421 A/II-l/16 grave 1 Phase E/1 (69/051) Plate 83

SPI	I-d	f	W2	Bd. gef	re	3	1B

Nd. 1.2 cm. Bd. 2.1 cm. pht. 5.8 cm. Md 6.5 cm. Wd. 0.3 cm.
Incomplete
Surface colour: 10YR5/2 reddish gray; burnished slip: 10YR3/2 very dark greyish brown
Break: uniform dark grey
Decoration: Upper zone of poorly made vertical chevrons pointing left, made with a ten tooth comb, and lower zone of lines from top left to bottom right made with a sixteen-tooth comb.
Previously published: TD XVI, 263, fig. 192a, no. 17.

463. 0458 D/3

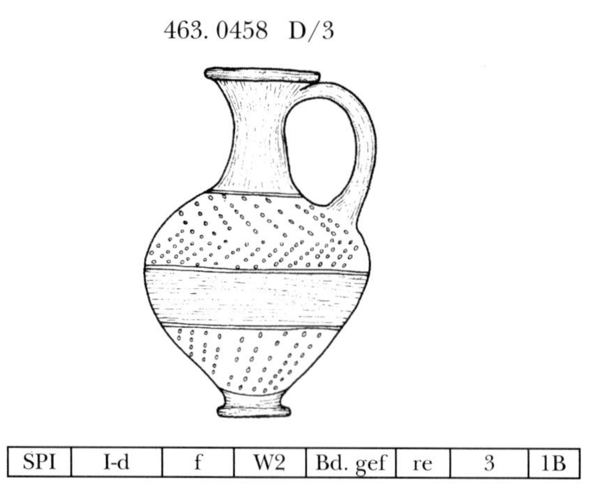

SPI	I-d	f	W2	Bd. gef	re	3	1B

464. 0886 E/1

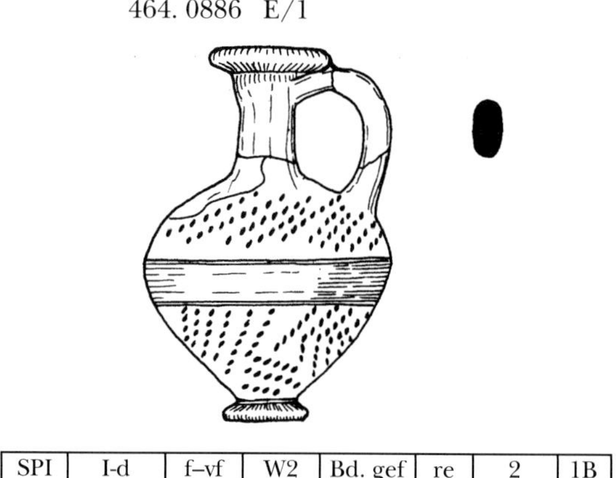

SPI	I-d	f–vf	W2	Bd. gef	re	2	1B

465. 0047 ?

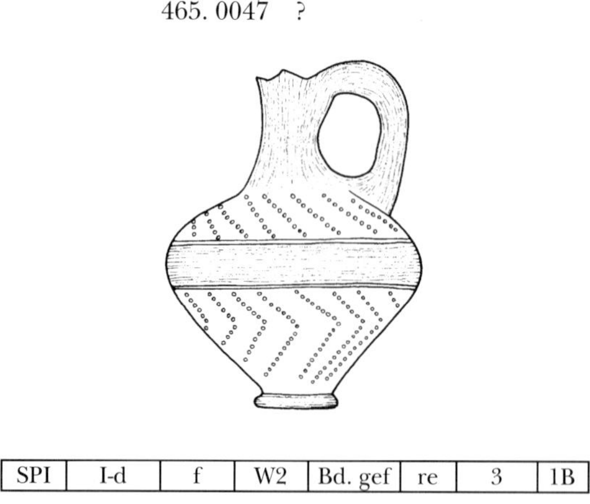

SPI	I-d	f	W2	Bd. gef	re	3	1B

466. 2116 E/1

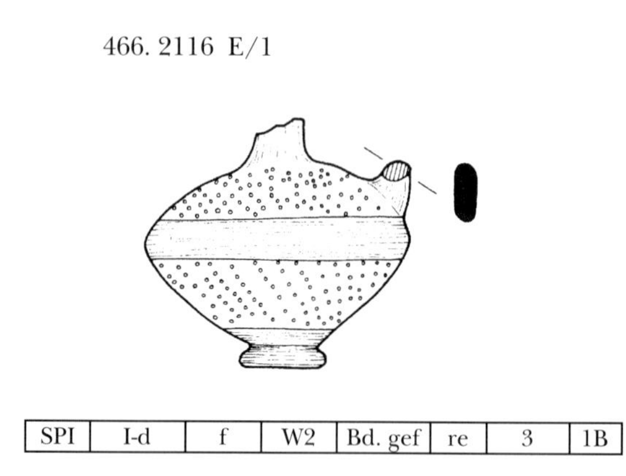

SPI	I-d	f	W2	Bd. gef	re	3	1B

467. 8992R a/2

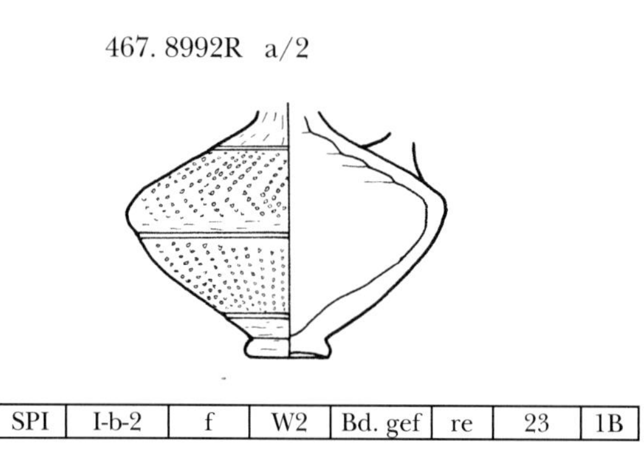

SPI	I-b-2	f	W2	Bd. gef	re	23	1B

468. 0536 D/3

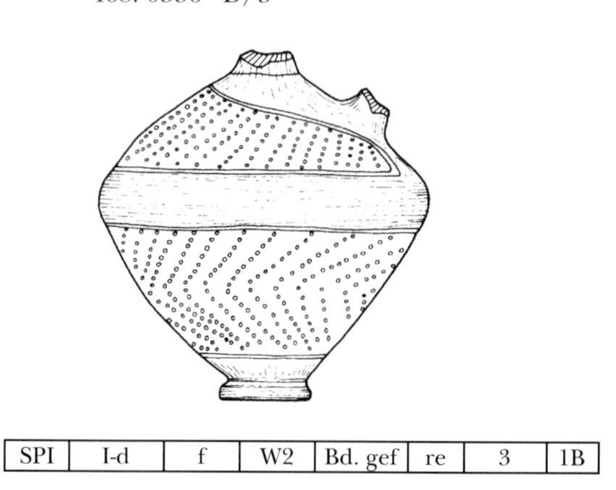

SPI	I-d	f	W2	Bd. gef	re	3	1B

1:2

Late Egyptian Type Group L.5.3c

Plate 83

469. 0177 E/1

SPI	I-d	f	W2	Bd. gef	re	3	1B

471. 0175 E/1

SPI	I-d	vf	W2	Bd. gef	re	3	1B

473. 0181 E/1

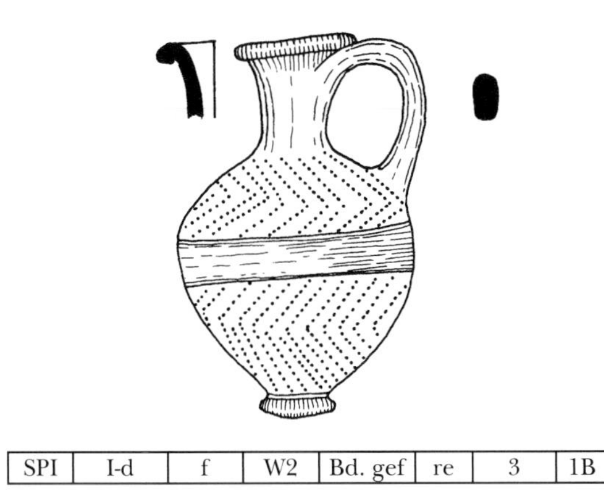

SPI	I-d	f	W2	Bd. gef	re	3	1B

470. 0176 E/1

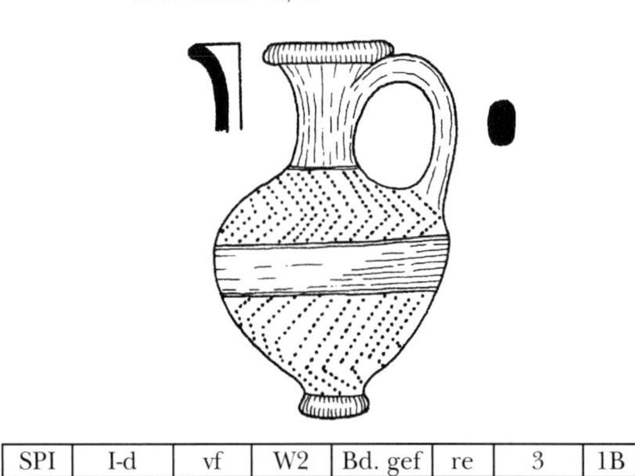

SPI	I-d	vf	W2	Bd. gef	re	3	1B

472. 0179 E/1

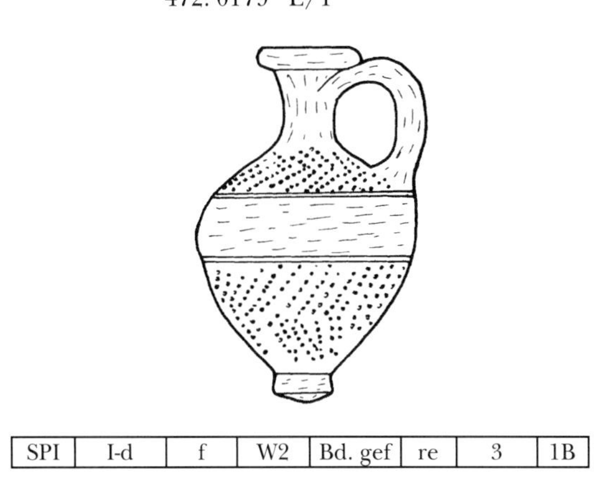

SPI	I-d	f	W2	Bd. gef	re	3	1B

474. 6128F2

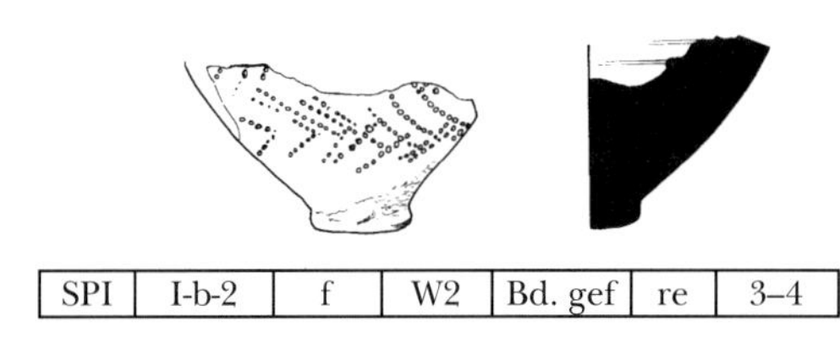

SPI	I-b-2	f	W2	Bd. gef	re	3–4

475. 6500L D/2

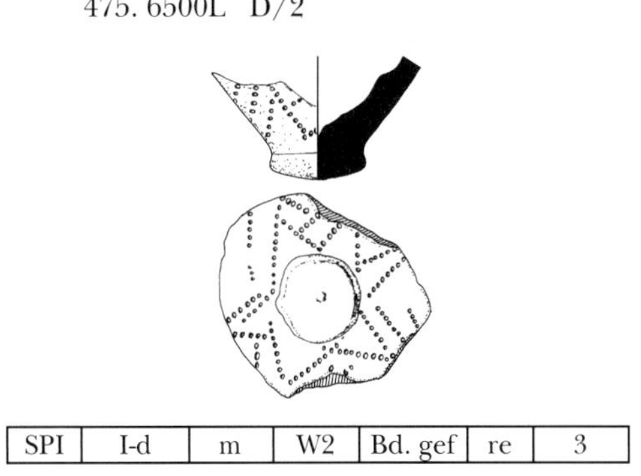

SPI	I-d	m	W2	Bd. gef	re	3

1:2

Late Egyptian Type Group L.5.4

Plate 84

467. 8992R TD F/II-r/22 planum 1 L81 Phase a/2 (08/026) Plate 83

SPI	I-b-2	f	W2	Bd. gef	re	23	1B

Bd. 1.9 cm. pht. 5.2 cm. Md 7.1 cm. Wd. 0.3 cm.
Incomplete
Surface colour: 5YR4/1 dark gray; burnish worn off
Break: not visible
Decoration: Upper band of chevrons made with a twelve-toothed comb, and a lower band of vertical lines made with a fourteen-toothed comb in the lower zone.

468. 0536 Vienna A2379 A/II-m/13 planum 3–4 Phase D/3 (67/084) Plate 83

SPI	I-d	f	W2	Bd. gef	re	3	1B

Nd. 1.3 cm. Bd. 2.3 cm. pht. 8.2 cm. Md 7.9 cm. Wd. 0.4 cm.
Incomplete
Surface colour: 7.5YR5/2 brown and 10YR5–6/1–2 grey; burnished slip: 10YR3/1 very dark grey
Break: dark brown core, dark grey reduction zones
Decoration: Upper zone of vertical striations, and lower zone of vertical chevrons pointing left made with a twelve-toothed comb.
Previously published: TD V, 264, 265.

Type Group L.5.4

Vessels attributed to type Group L.5.4 comprises vessels which are similar to the common L.5.3 group, but have distinct button, rather than ring or disc bases. All the examples so far known have two zones of chevrons.

469. 0177 Cairo JE 91557B A/II-l/12 grave 2 Phase E/1 (66/034) Plate 84

SPI	I-d	f	W2	Bd. gef	re	3	1B

D. 2.8 cm. Nd 1.3 cm. Bd. 1.4 cm. H. 7.8 cm. Md. 5.5 cm. Wd. 0.4 cm.
VI 70.51
Intact
Surface colour: 7.5YR4/0 dark grey; burnished slip: 5YR3/1 black
Break: not visible
Decoration: Upper zone of vertical chevrons pointing right, and lower zone of vertical chevrons pointing left made with a twelve-toothed comb.
Previously published: TD V, 187, 188.

470. 0176 Cairo JE 91557A A/II-l/12 grave 2 Phase E/1 (66/034) Plates 84, 147

SPI	I-d	vf	W2	Bd. gef	re	3	1B

D. 2.8 cm. Nd 1.2 cm. Bd. 1.5 cm. H. 8.1 cm. Md. 5.4 cm. Wd. 0.4 cm.
VI 66.66
Intact
Surface colour: 2.5YR4/0 dark grey; burnished slip: 5YR3/1 black
Break: not visible
Decoration: Upper zone of vertical chevrons pointing right, and lower zone of vertical chevrons pointing left made with a twelve-toothed comb.
Previously published: TD V, 187, 188.

471. 0175 Cairo JE 91557H A/II-l/12 grave 2 Phase E/1 (66/034) Plate 84

SPI	I-d	vf	W2	Bd. gef	re	3	1B

D. 2.8 cm. Nd 1.2 cm. Bd. 1.7 cm. H. 8.5 cm. Md. 5.6 cm. Wd. 0.4 cm.
VI 65.88
Intact
Surface colour: 2.5YR4/0 dark grey; burnished slip: 5YR3/1 black
Break: not visible
Decoration: Upper zone of horizontal chevrons pointing right, and lower zone of vertical chevrons pointing left made with a twelve-toothed comb.
Previously published: Bietak, *MDAIK* 23, fig. 8; Kaplan, *Tell el-Yahudiyeh Ware,* fig. 92b; *TD V,* 187, 188.

472. 0179 Vienna A1629 A/II-l/12 grave 2 Phase E/1 (66/036) Plate 84

SPI	I-d	f	W2	Bd. gef	re	3	1B

D. 2.7 cm. Nd 1.2 cm. Bd. 1.7 cm. H. 8.5 cm. Md. 5.6 cm. Wd. 0.4 cm.
VI 65.88
Intact
Surface colour: 10YR4/1–5/2 grey brown; burnished slip: 10YR3/1 very dark grey
Break: not visible
Decoration: Upper zone of vertical chevrons pointing right, and lower zone of vertical chevrons pointing left made with a twelve-toothed comb.
Previously published: TD V, 187, 188.

473. 0181 Cairo JE 91557E A/II-l/12 grave 2 Phase E/1 (66/034) Plate 84

SPI	I-d	f	W2	Bd. gef	re	3	1B

D. 2.8 cm. Nd 1.3 cm. Bd. 1.7 cm. H. 8.8 cm. Md. 5.6 cm. Wd. 0.4 cm.
VI 63.63
Intact
Surface colour: 7.5YR6/2 pinkish grey; burnished slip: 5YR3/1 very dark grey
Break: not visible
Decoration: Upper zone of vertical chevrons pointing right, and lower zone of vertical chevrons pointing left made with a twelve-toothed comb.
Previously published: TD V, 187, 188.

474. 6128F2 TD A/V-q/17 planum 1 surface (94/078) Plate 84

SPI	I-b-2	f	W2	Bd. gef	re	3–4

Bd. 1.7 cm. pht. 3.0 cm. Wd. 0.4 cm.
Incomplete
Surface colour: 10R5/1 grey; burnished slip not preserved
Break: uniform blackish grey
Decoration: lower zone of vertical chevrons pointing right made with a ten-toothed comb.
Previously published: TD XI, 216–217 no. 5.

475. 6500L TD A/V-n/17 planum 1–2 Phase D/2 (88/166) Plate 84

SPI	I-d	m	W2	Bd. gef	re	3

Bd. 2.1 cm. pht. 2.0 cm. Wd. 0.4 cm.
Incomplete
Surface colour: 10YR5/2 greyish brown; burnished slip 7.5YR5/4 brown
Break: brown core, grey reduction zones
Decoration: Horizontal chevrons made with an eight-toothed comb.
Previously published: TD XI, 67–68 no. 22.

Type Group L.5.5

Type group L.5.5 is represented by a single incomplete vessel from Tell el-Dabᶜa, TD 299, which is biconical in shape and has a button base. This vessel has a single reserved band running around the mid-point, and is burnished above and below it. In the middle of this reserved band is a single incised wavy line.

476. 0299 Vienna AS2262 A/I-g/4 planum 3 Phase E/1–D/3 (66/027) Plates 85, 147

SPI	I-d	f–m	W2	Bd. gef	re	3	1B

Bd. 1.7 cm. pht. 7.6 cm. Md. 7.6 cm. Wd. 0.6 cm.
Incomplete
Surface colour: 10YR6/2 light reddish grey; burnished slip 5YR5/3 reddish brown
Break: uniform yellowish red
Decoration: reserved zone on shoulder with an incised wavy line.
BNL JH353 Nile Clay

L.6. Late Egyptian VI (Large Biconical I)

Type Group L.6.1

This type of large biconical jug is well-known, and, at Tell el-Dabᶜa it is distinctly noticeable that these larger examples always come from settlement areas, and the smaller ones from tomb contexts. The Tell el-Dabᶜa examples have four different decorative styles: L.6.1a an upper zone consisting of standing triangles and below three or four large pendant traingles filled with a vertical herringbone pattern: L.6.1b which consists of two bands of chevrons which are only framed at the belly of the pot, ie. the lower edge of the uppermost zone, and the uppermost edge of the bottom zone, (TD 469, 5927B, 3051, 6807, 6466B, 8436U, 6807D, 6135, 3007, 8446L, 6500X, 8446N, 6489R, 8875B): L.6.1c which comprises an upper band of diagonal lines, and a lower zone decorated in a herringbone pattern (TD 6806B), and L.6.1d which consists of two zones of horizontal dots bordered at the belly of the pot, (TD 261, 6466C).

Type Group L.6.1a

477. 8875B TD A/II-p/13 locus 33 grave 3 Phase D/2 (98/098) Plate 85

SPI	I-d	f	W2	Bd. gef	re	2	1B

D. 3.3 cm. Nd 1.5 cm. Bd. 2.3 cm. H. 10.4 cm. Md. 7.4 cm. Wd. 0.4 cm.
VI 71.15
Restored from sherds, incomplete
Surface colour: 10YR4/1 dark grey; burnished slip: 10YR3/1 very dark grey
Break: dark grey in, light grey out
Decoration: Three standing triangles on shoulder and four pendant triangles below maximum point. Shoulder triangles filled with horizontal lines and lower triangles with vertical zigzags and or horizontal chevrons made with a twelve-toothed comb.
Previously published: TD XVI, 376, fig. 305, no. 1.

478. 6839A TD A/V-p/19 grave 28 Phase D/3–2 (88/168) Plates 85, 148

SPI	I-d	m	W2	Bd. gef	re	2	1B

Bd. 3.1 cm. pht. 12.0 cm. Md. 11.9 cm. Wd. 0.35 cm.
Intact
Surface colour: 5YR4/1 dark grey
Break: grey core, dark grey reduction zones
Decoration: Upper zone of four standing triangles filled with straight and oblique lines made with a twelve-toothed comb. Below a reserved zone are three pendant triangles similarly filled. There are no traces of burnishing on the vessel, either because the vessel was never burnised, or because the burnish has worn off.
Previously published: TD XI, 53–54 no. 5, pl. xxxD.

479. 8942G TD A/V-p/19 planum 3–4 Phase ? (01/066) Plate 85

SPI	I-d	f	W2	–	re	3

pht. 5.5 cm. Md 10.0 cm. Wd. 0.5 cm.
Incomplete.
Surface colour: 5Y5/1 grey; burnished slip: 5Y4/1 dark grey
Break: dark grey core, brown reduction zones
Decoration: Part of chevrons preserved above and below a reserved band, made with a fourteen(or more)-toothed comb.

Type Group L.6.1b

480. 0469 Vienna A1653 A/II-m/13 planum ? Phase ? (67/085) Plate 86

SPI	I-d	m	W2	Bd. gef	re	2	1B

D. 3.05 cm. Nd 1.6 cm. Bd. 2.7 cm. H. 12.4 cm. Md. 9.1 cm. Wd. 0.4 cm.
VI 73.38
Intact
Surface colour: 10YR4/1 dark grey; burnished slip: 10YR3/1 very dark grey
Break: not visible
Decoration: Upper zone of vertical chevrons pointing right, and lower zone of vertical chevrons pointing left made with a twelve-toothed comb.

481. 3051 Vienna A3339 A/II-o/21 grave 1 Phase E/1 (79/164) Plate 86

SPI	I-d	f	W2	Bd. gef	re	2–3	1B

D. 3.15 cm. Nd 1.5 cm. Bd. 2.3 cm. H. 11.5 cm. Md. 8.9 cm. Wd. 0.4 cm.
VI 77.39

476. 0299 E/1–D/3

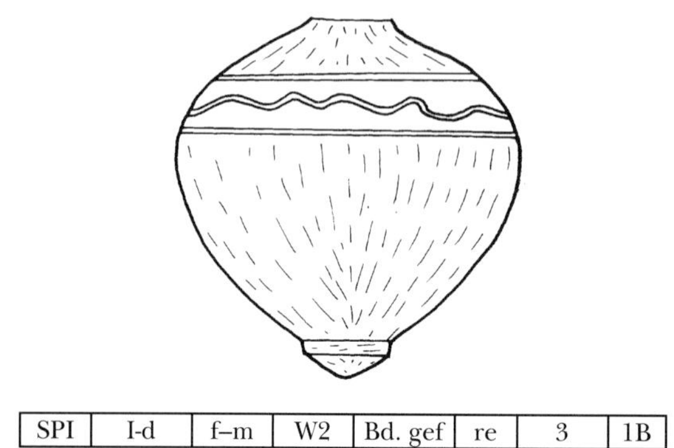

SPI	I-d	f–m	W2	Bd. gef	re	3	1B

477. 8875B D/2

SPI	I-d	f	W2	Bd. gef	re	2	1B

478. 6839A D/3–2

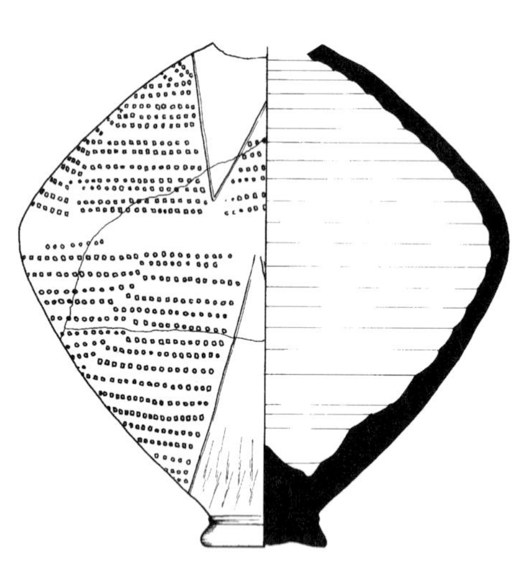

SPI	I-d	m	W2	Bd. gef	re	2	1B

479. 8942G ?

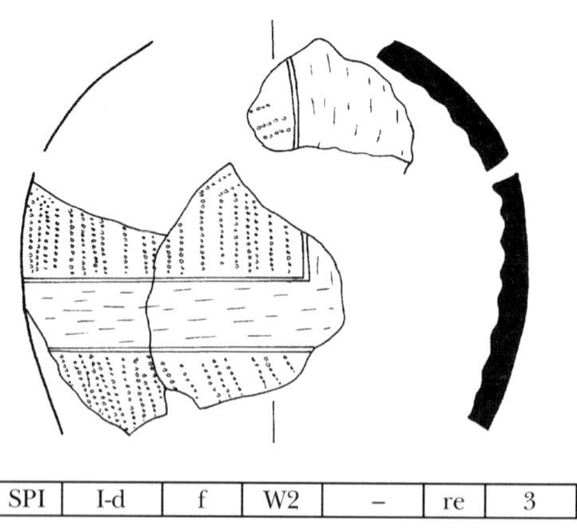

SPI	I-d	f	W2	–	re	3

1:2

Late Egyptian Type Group L.5.5, L.6.1a

Plate 85

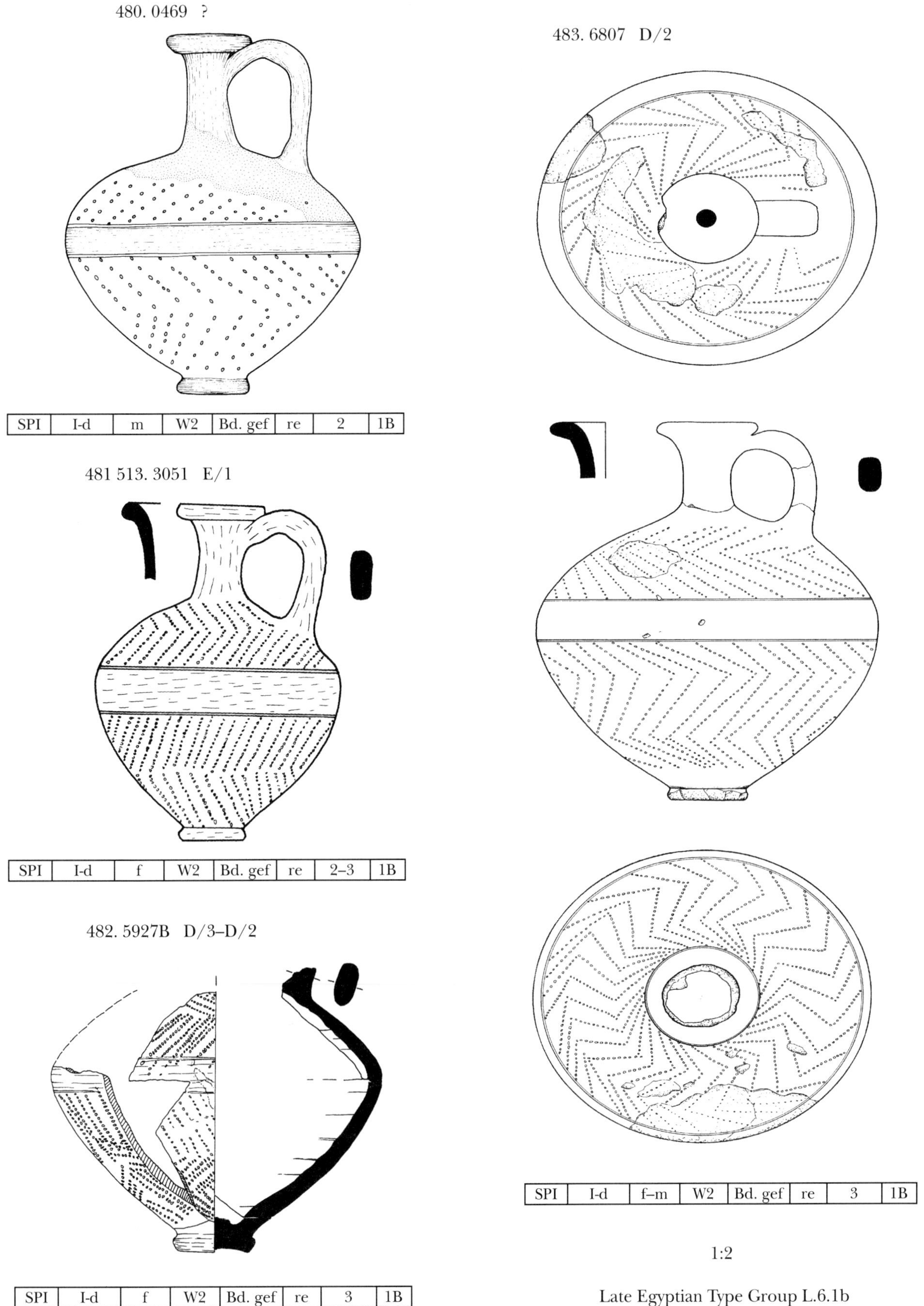

1:2

Late Egyptian Type Group L.6.1b

Intact
Surface colour: 10YR4/1 dark grey; burnished slip: 10YR3/1 very dark grey
Break: uniform grey
Decoration: Upper zone of vertical chevrons pointing right, and lower zone of vertical chevrons pointing left made with a twelve-toothed comb.

482. 5927B TD A/II-i/11 planum 6–7 Phase D/3–D/2 (86/273) Plate 86

SPI	I-d	f	W2	Bd. gef	re	3	1B

Bd. 2.9 cm. H. 9.3 cm. Md. 12.0 cm. Wd. 0.5 cm.
Intact
Surface colour: 10YR4/1 dark grey; burnished slip: 2.5YR5/4 reddish brown
Break: black inner zone, yellowish brown outer zones
Decoration: Vertical chevrons pointing right on shoulder and vertical zigzags on body made with a 22-toothed comb.

483. 6807 TD A/V-p/19 planum 2 Phase D/2 (88/017) Plates 86, 148

SPI	I-d	f–m	W2	Bd. gef	re	3	1B

D. 3.8 cm. Nd 1.8 cm. Bd. 2.9 cm. H. 16.0 cm. Md. 12.5 cm. Wd. 0.5 cm.
VI 78.13
Restored from sherds, complete
Surface colour: 2.5YR4/1 dark grey; burnished slip: 10YR3/1 very dark grey
Break: dark grey in, greyish brown reduction zones out
Decoration: Delineated vertical chevrons above and below mid-point, made with an eighteen-toothed comb.
Previously published: TD XI, 155–156 no. 1, pl. xxxE.

484. 6466B+6466J4 TD A/V-m/18 planum 1–2 Phase D/2 (88/428) Plate 87

SPI	I-b-2	f	W2	–	re	3	1B

pht. 7.6 cm. Md. 15.0 cm. Wd. 0.4 cm.
Incomplete
Surface colour: 5YR4–5/4 reddish brown; burnished slip: 10YR3/1 very dark grey
Break: light brown core, dark grey reduction zones
Decoration: Chevrons made with a multi-toothed comb.
Previously published: TD XI, 67–68 no. 4.

485. 6807D TD A/V-p/19 planum 2 Phase D/2 (88/014) Plate 87

SPI	I-b-2	f	W2	–	re	3

pht. 6.6 cm. Wd. 0.5 cm.
Incomplete
Surface colour: 10YR3/1–2 very dark grey; burnished slip: 2.5YR5/4 reddish brown
Break: thin matt red core, grey and grey brown reduction zones
Decoration: Part of vertical chevrons preserved made with a twenty-toothed comb.
Previously published: TD XI, 156–157 no. 2.

486. 6135 TD A/V-q/19 planum 2 Phase D/2 (94/074) Plate 87

SPI	I-d	f	W2	Bd. gef	re	3	1B

Nd. 1.5 cm. Bd. 2.1 cm. pht. 7.0 cm. Md 7.5 cm. Wd. 0.3 cm.
Incomplete
Surface colour: 10YR5/1–2 grey brown; burnished slip: 5YR5/1 grey
Break: grey core, red and brown reduction zones
Decoration: Two zones of vertical chevrons made with a sixteen-toothed comb.
Previously published: TD XI, 171–172 no. 3, pl. xxxC.

487. 8446L TD H/III-q/19 planum 3–4 Phase D/2 (95/148) Plate 87

SPI	I-d	vf	W2	–	re	3	1B

pht. 6.0 cm. Md. 14.0 cm. Wd. 0.6 cm.
Incomplete
Surface colour: 5YR4/1 dark grey; burnished slip: 10YR3/1 very dark grey
Break: beige grey core, black reduction zones
Decoration: One zone of vertical chevrons on shoulder made with a fourteen-toothed comb.

488. 6500X TD A/V-o/16 planum 1 surface (88/137) Plate 87

SPI	I-b-2	f–vf	W2	Bd. gef	re	3

pht. 6.0 cm. Md. 11.0 cm. Wd. 0.5 cm.
Incomplete
Surface colour: 5YR5/4 red brown; burnished slip: 2.5YR5/4 reddish brown
Break: dark grey core, dark brown reduction zones
Decoration: Horizontal chevrons made with an eighteen-toothed comb.
Previously published: TD XI, 216–217 no. 1.

489. 8446N TD H/III-q/19 planum 4–5 Phase rel e/2 (95/114) Plate 87

SPI	I-d	f–m	W2	–	re	3	1B

Bd 1.6 cm pht. 8.5 cm. Md. 10.0 cm. Wd. 0.8 cm.
Incomplete
Surface colour: 10YR5/1 dark greyish brown; burnished slip: 10YR6/3 pale brownish grey
Break: dark grey in, brown out
Decoration: Vertical chevrons pointing right on shoulder and lower body, made with a sixteen-toothed comb. Horizontally burnished on the reserved band.

490. 6489R TD A/V-m/17 planum 1–2 Phase D/2 (88/379) Plates 88, 148

SPI	I-b-2	f–m	W2	Bd. gef	re	3	1B

Nd. 2.2 cm. Bd. 2.8 cm. pht. 12.6 cm. Md. 11.5 cm. Wd. 0.5 cm.
Incomplete
Surface colour: 10YR5/1 grey; burnished slip: 10YR3/1 very dark grey
Break: dark brown core, dark grey reduction zones
Decoration: vertical chevrons on shoulder pointing left, vertical zigzags on body below reserved bands, all made with a twenty-toothed comb.
Previously published: TD XI, 82–83 no. 16.

Type Group L.6.1c

491. 6806B TD A/V-p/18 planum 2 Ansammlung 16 Phase D/2 (88/024) Plates 88, 148

SPI	I-b-2	f	W2	Bd. gef	re	3	1B

Bd. 2.6 cm. pht. 11.8 cm. Md 11.1 cm. Wd. 0.3 cm.
Incomplete

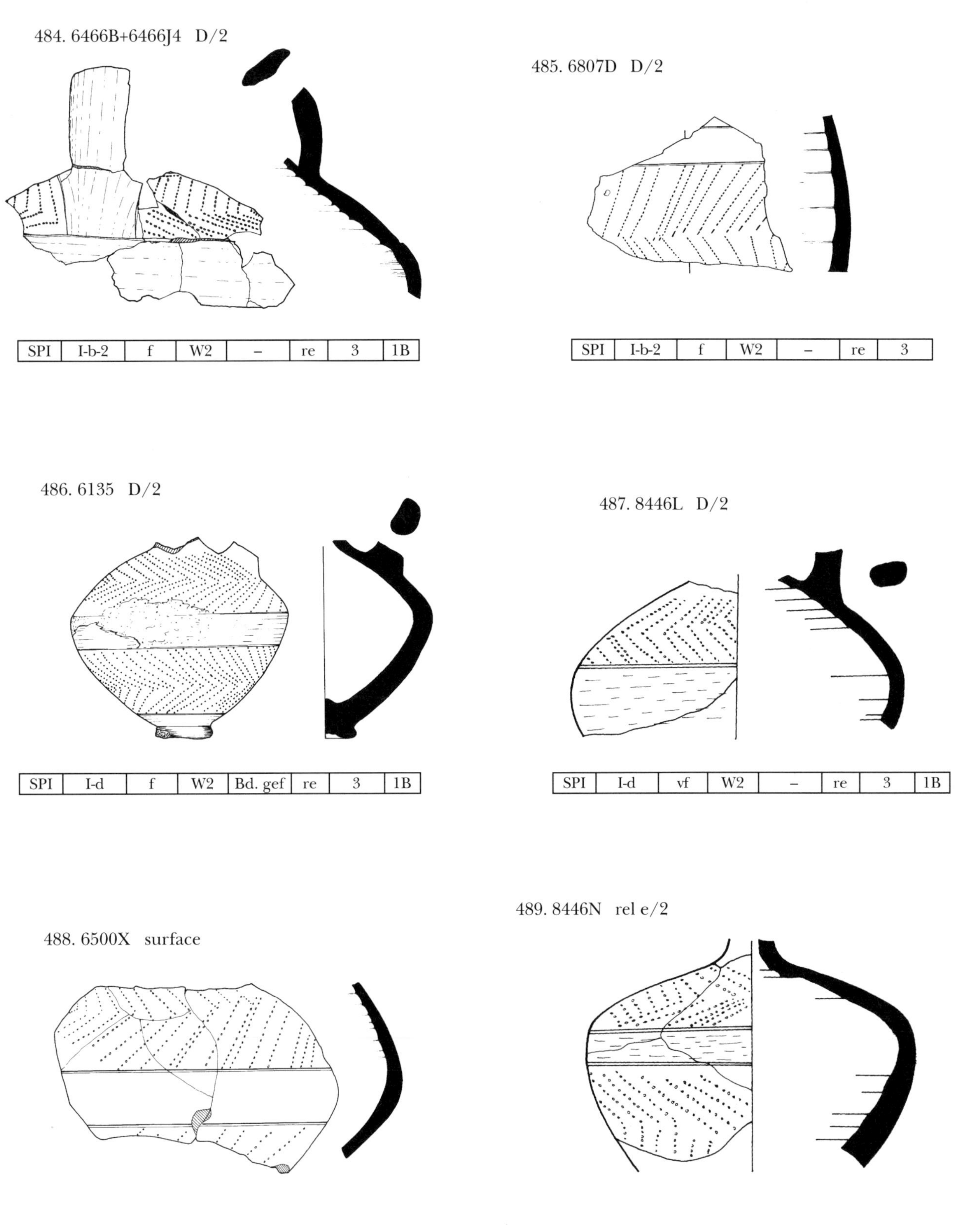

1:2

Late Egyptian Type Group L.6.1b

Plate 87

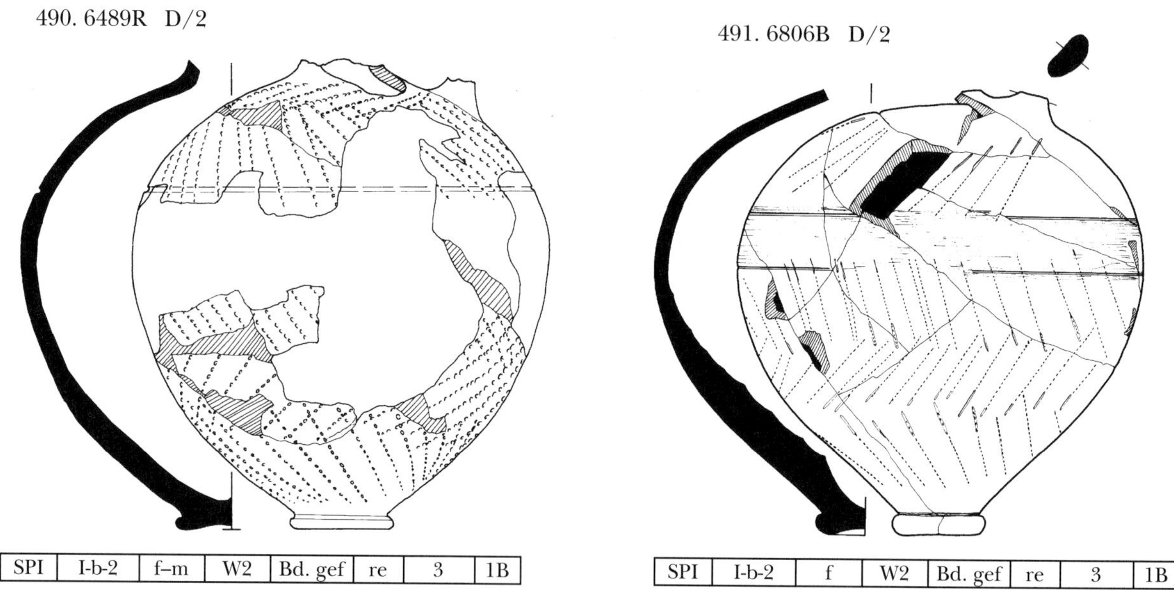

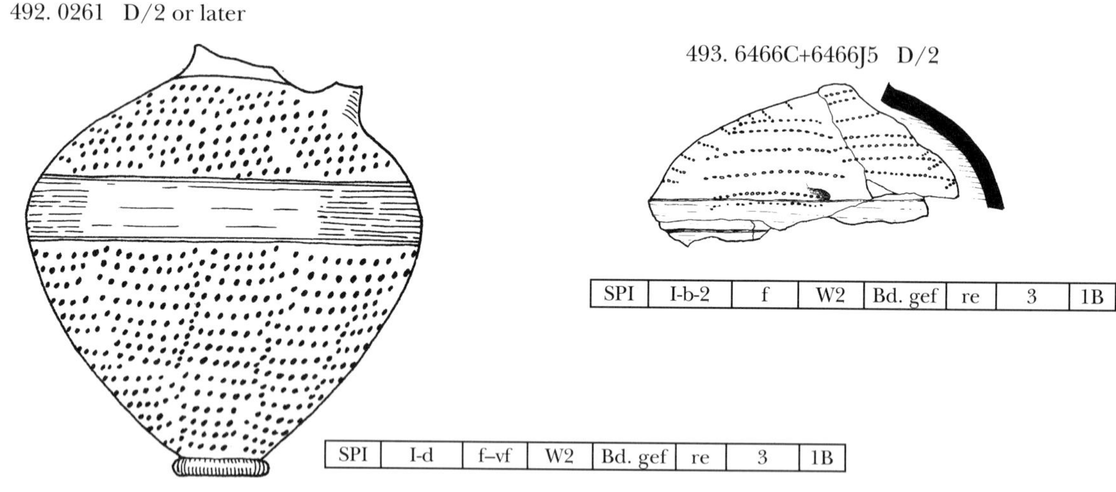

1:2

Late Egyptian Type Group L.6.1b, L.6.1c, L.6.1d

Plate 88

Surface colour: 10YR5/1 grey; burnished slip: 10YR3/1 very dark grey
Break: dark grey core, brown zones
Decoration: Oblique lines on shoulder and vertical zigzags on lower body, carelessly made with a sixteen-toothed comb. Vertically burnished below handle and horizontally burnished around mid-point.
Previously published: TD XI, 143 no. 1, pl. xxxB; *TD XVII,* II, 200, fig. 173.

Type Group L.6.1d

492. 0261 Vienna A2239 A/I-g/3 planum 3 Phase D/2 or later (66/024) Plates 88, 149

SPI	I-d	f–vf	W2	Bd. gef	re	3	1B

Bd. 2.5 cm. pht. 11.0 cm. Md 11.0 cm. Wd. 0.5 cm.
Incomplete.
Surface colour: 10YR5/1 grey; burnished slip: 10YR3/1 very dark grey
Break: grey core, brown reduction zones
Decoration: upper and lower zones of vertical lines made with an eight-toothed comb.

493. 6466C+6466J5 TD A/V-m/18 planum 1–2 Phase D/2 (88/428) Plate 88

SPI	I-b-2	f	W2	Bd. gef	re	3	1B

pht. 5.7 cm. Md. 11.3 cm. Wd. 0.4 cm.
Incomplete.
Surface colour: 10YR5/1–2 greenish grey brown; burnished slip: 10YR3/1 very dark grey

Break: brown core, dark grey reduction zones
Decoration: Horizontal lines on shoulder made with a twenty-toothed comb. Reserved band horizontally burnished.
Previously published: TD XI, 67–68 no. 5.

Type Group L.7.1

Vessels of type group L.7.1 are, in all respects similar to the vessels of type group L.6 except for the fact that the decorative zones are not delineated by incised frame lines. Only one decorative style is known at Tell el-Dab[c]a, L.7.1a which consists of two bands of undelineated chevrons.

494. 3417 Cairo A/II-o/21 planum 7 Phase E/1–D/3 (81/074) Plates 89, 149

SPI	I-d	f	W2	Bd. gef	re	2–3	1B

D. 3.0 cm. Nd. 1.6 cm. Bd. 3.2 cm. H. 14.2 cm. Md 10.8 cm. Wd. 0.5 cm.
VI 76.05
Incomplete.
Surface colour: 10YR5/1 grey; burnished slip: 10YR3/1 very dark grey
Break: uniform grey
Decoration: Upper zone of vertical chevrons pointing left, and lower zone of vertical chevrons pointing right made with a sixteen-toothed comb.

495. 6135H TD A/V-q/19 planum 2 Phase D/2 (94/074) Plate 89
pht. 5.7 cm. Md. 12.4 cm Wd. 0.5 cm

SPI	I-d	f	W2	–	re	3

Incomplete
Surface colour: 10YR4/1 dark gray; burnished slip 5YR5/1 grey
Break: uniform dark grey brown
Decoration: Upper zone of vertical chevrons pointing left, and lower zone of vertical chevrons (?) pointing left made with a sixteen-toothed comb.
Previously published: TD XI, 172–173 no. 5.

496. 5230N TD A/II-e/24 planum 0–1 Phase D/3–2 ? (01/066) Plate 89

SPI	I-b-2	f	W2	Bd. gef	re	3	1B

Bd. 2.5 cm. pht. 6.6 cm. Md. 8.7 cm. Wd. 0.5 cm.
Incomplete
Surface colour: 10YR4/1 dark grey; burnished slip: 10YR3.5/1 very dark grey
Break: wide grey core, red and brown reduction zones
Decoration: Lower zone of vertical chevrons made with a fourteen-toothed comb.

497. 8436U TD A/V-o/17 pit 1 Surface (94/041) Plate 95

SPI	I-d	m	W2	Bd. gef	re	3

pht. 4.6 cm. Md. 13.2 cm. Wd. 0.5 cm.
Incomplete.
Surface colour: 7.5YR4/0 dark grey; burnished slip: 5YR5–4/1 grey – dark reddish grey
Break: uniform grey
Decoration: Upper zone of vertical chevrons pointing left made with a fourteen-toothed comb.
Previously published: TD XI, 216–217 no. 3.

Miscellaneous sherds from large biconical vessesls

498. 6120A TD A/V-m/18 planum 2 Phase D/2 (94/075) Plate 89

SPI	I-d	f–vf	W2	–	re	4	1B

D. 3.3 cm. Nd. 1.7 cm. pht. 6.7 cm. Md 10.0 cm. Wd. 0.3 cm.
Incomplete
Surface colour: 10YR5/1–2 grey brown; burnished slip: 5YR5/1 grey
Break: uniform dark grey
Decoration: not discernible.
Previously published: TD XI, 161–162 no. 2.

499. 8166G TD Khatana E/I/G planum 3–4 grave 1 Phase ? (93/503) Plate 90

SPI	I-d	f–m	W2	–	re	2	1B

D. 3.2 cm. Nd. 1.6 cm. pht. 5.7 cm. Wd. 0.5 cm.
Incomplete
Surface colour: 10YR5/1 grey; burnished slip: 10YR4/2 dark grey brown
Break: uniform grey
Decoration: Part of oblique lines or vertical chevrons on shoulder made with a multi-toothed comb.

500. 1192 Vienna A2801 A/II-n/12 grave 12 Phase D/3 (68/058) Plate 90

RPI	I-d	f	W2	–	re	3

pht. 8.3 cm. Md. 19–20 cm. Wd. 0.4–55 cm.
Incomplete
Surface colour: 5YR5.5/3 light red brown; burnished slip 2.5YR4/4 red brown
Break: dark grey core, thin red oxidation zones
Decoration: Two horizontal mat decorative fields with impressed decoration made with a multi-toothed comb. The upper zone is bordered at the bottom by an irregular wavy line.
Previously published: TD V, 262–263.

501. 8205P TD H/III-r/18 planum 2–3 Phase ? (94/106) Plate 90

SPI	I-d	f–m	W2	–	re	2–3

Md. 13.0 cm. Wd. 0.55 cm.
Incomplete
Surface colour: 7.5YR5/0 grey; burnished slip: 7.5YR4/0 dark grey
Break: uniform dark grey
Decoration: Parts of upper and lower zones preserved. Decoration of upper zone not clear, lower zone appears to be vertical zigzags made with an eighteen toothed comb.

502. 1575 Vienna A3072 A/II-m-n/13 planum 5 Phase E/1 (69/028) Plate 90

SPI	I-d	f–vf	W2	Bd. gef	re	3

Bd. 2.65 cm. pht. 5.2 cm. Wd. 0.5 cm.
Incomplete
Surface colour: 10YR4–5/2 grey brown; burnished slip: 10YR3/1 very dark grey
Break: uniform dark grey

494. 3417 E/1–D/3

SPI	I-d	f	W2	Bd. gef	re	2–3	1B

495. 6135H D/2

SPI	I-d	f	W2	–	re	3

496. 5230N D/3–2 ?

SPI	I-b-2	f	W2	Bd. gef	re	3	1B

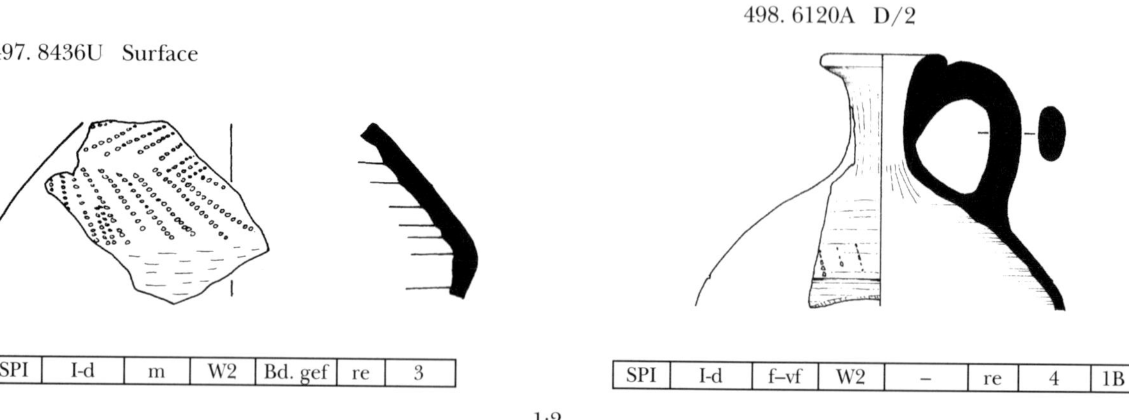

497. 8436U Surface

SPI	I-d	m	W2	Bd. gef	re	3

498. 6120A D/2

SPI	I-d	f–vf	W2	–	re	4	1B

1:2

Late Egyptian Type Group L.7.1a and miscellaneous large biconical vessesls

Plate 89

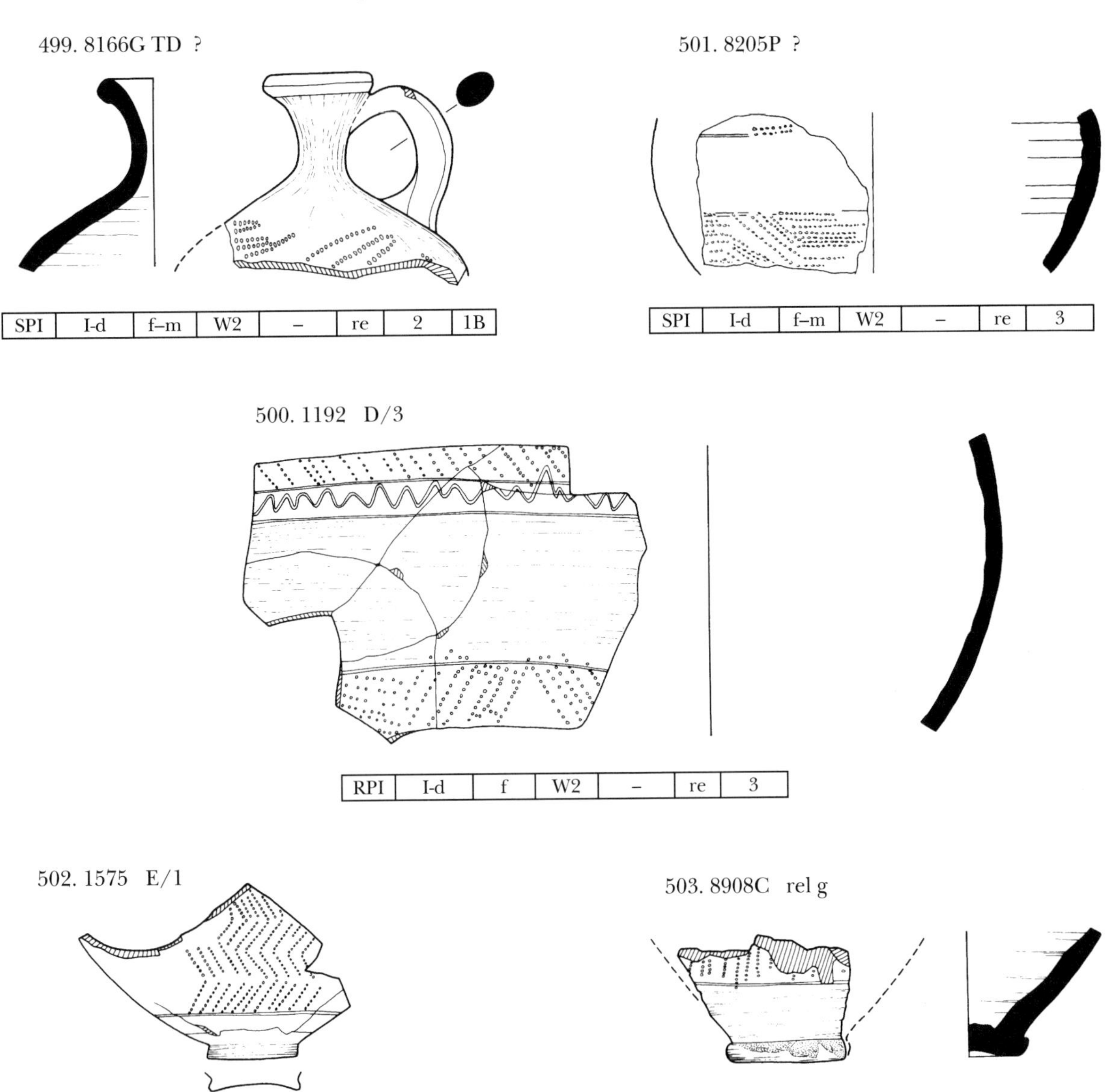

Late Egyptian large biconical vessels

Plate 90

Decoration: Lower zone of vertical zigzags made with a twelve-toothed comb.
Previously published: TD V, 205–206.

503. 8908C TD H/III-u/16 planum 8 Phase rel g (99/153) Plate 90

SPI	I-d	f–m	W2	Bd. gef	re	2–3

Bd. 3.5 cm. pht. 3.4 cm. Wd. 0.45 cm.
Incomplete
Surface colour: 5YR3/1 very dark grey; burnished slip: 2.5Y2.5/1 black
Break: uniform dark grey
Decoration: not discernible.

504. 4506A TD F/I-k/23 surface (83/138) Plate 91

SPI	I-b-2	m	W2	Bd. gef	re	3

Bd. 2.75 cm. pht. 3.1 cm. Wd. 0.65 cm.
Incomplete
Surface colour: 10YR5/2 grey brown; burnished slip: not preserved
Break: wide dark grey core, yellowish brown outer zone
Decoration: Chevrons made with a sixteen (?)-toothed comb.

505. 5987B TD F/I-o/19 intrusive within grave 1 (87/090) Plate 91

SPI	I-d	f	W2	Bd. gef	re	3

Bd. 2.0 cm. pht. 3.0 cm. Wd. 0.3 cm.
Incomplete
Surface colour: 2.5Y5/2 greenish grey; burnished slip 10YR4/1 very dark grey
Break: dark grey in, red and dark grey reduction zones
Decoration: Vertical chevrons made with a ten-toothed comb.

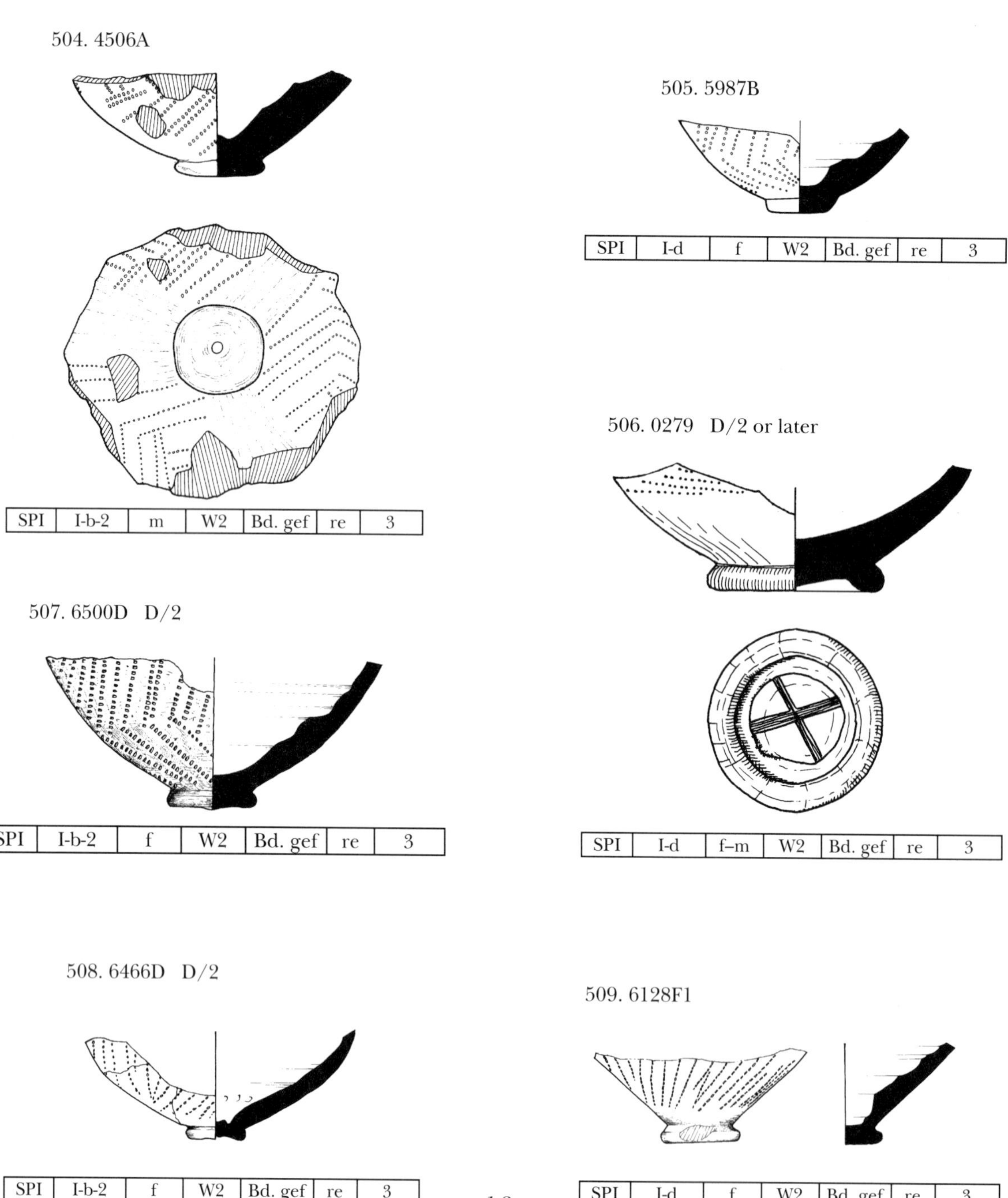

Late Egyptian large biconical vessesls

Plate 91

506. 0279 Vienna A2251 A/I-g/3 planum 3 Phase D/2 or later (66/030) Plate 91

SPI	I-d	f–m	W2	Bd. gef	re	3

Bd. 2.0 cm. pht. 2.8 cm. Wd. 0.45 cm.
Incomplete
Surface colour: 7.5YR5.5/3 brown; burnished slip 10YR5/6 light red
Break: uniform grey
Decoration: not discernible.

507. 6500D TD A/V-n/17 planum 2 Phase D/2 (88/150) Plate 91

SPI	I-b-2	f	W2	Bd. gef	re	3

Bd. 2.8 cm. pht. 4.7 cm. Wd. 0.45 cm.
Restored from sherds, incomplete.
Surface colour: 10R6/1 grey; burnished slip 7.5YR5/0 grey
Break: grey core, brown and grey reduction zones
Decoration: Vertical chevrons made with a 20-toothed comb.
Previously published: TD XI, 79–80 no. 10.

508. 6466D TD A/V-m/18 planum 1–2 Phase D/2 (88/428) Plate 91

SPI	I-b-2	f	W2	Bd. gef	re	3

pht. 3.3 cm. Bd. 2.0 cm. Wd. 0.35 cm.
Incomplete
Surface colour: 5YR4–5/4 reddish brown; burnished slip: 5YR5/1 grey
Break: dark grey core, red and grey reduction zones
Decoration: vertical lines made with a multi-toothed comb
Base to 6466B ?
Previously published: TD XI, 67–68 no. 11.

509. 6128F1 TD A/V-q/17 planum 1 surface (94/078) Plate 91

SPI	I-d	f	W2	Bd. gef	re	3

Bd. 2.5 cm. pht. 2.9 cm. Wd. 0.4 cm.
Incomplete
Surface colour: 10R5/1 grey; burnished slip 10YR4/1 dark grey
Break: uniform blackish grey
Decoration: Oblique lines made with a twelve-toothed comb.
Previously published: TD XI, 216–217 no. 6.

Type Group L.8

Vessels of the Type Group L.8 are similar to those of the L.5 group, but the decorative zones are not defined by incised borders.

Type Group L.8.1

Type group L.8.1 is also subsumed within the classic Biconical 1 of Kaplan, namely jugs with rolled rims, strap handles and ring or disc bases. The upper and lower decorative zones are usually formed by horizontal chevrons, L.8.1a, a herringbone pattern in the lower zone L.8.1b, or oblique lines (L.8.1c), and at times these lines radiate straight out from the

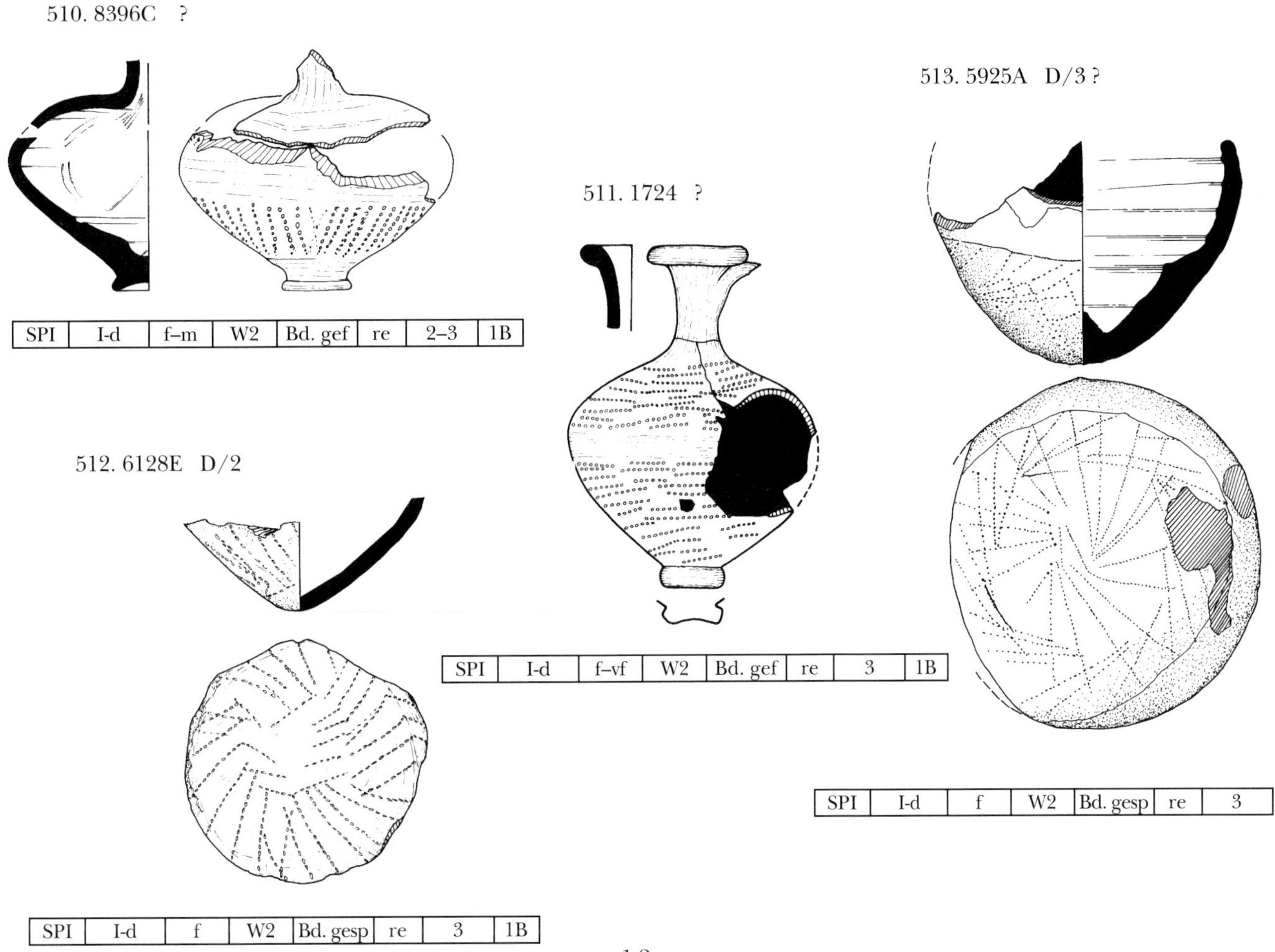

Late Egyptian Type Group L.8.1b, L.8.1c, L.8.2

Plate 92

base or neck, and rarely, rows of horizontal dots (L.8.1d). Combinations of any of the above, such as chevrons in the upper zone and oblique lines in the lower, or vice versa may also occur (L.8.1e). This group is also common.

Type Group L.8.1b

510. 8396C TD A/IV-dep planum 3–4 pit 112 Phase ? (94/314) Plate 92

SPI	I-d	f–m	W2	Bd. gef	re	2–3	1B

Bd. 2.0 cm. pht. 4.3 cm. Md. 7.8 cm Wd. 0.45 cm
Incomplete
Surface colour: 10YR4/1 gray; burnished slip 2.5YR3–4/4 reddish brown
Break: dark grey in, brown and dark grey reduction zones
Decoration: Lower zone of vertical striations made with a twelve-toothed comb.

Type Group L.8.1c

511. 1724 Vienna A3168 A/II-l/10 Phase ? (69/028) Plate 92

SPI	I-d	f–vf	W2	Bd. gef	re	3	1B

D. 2.8 cm. Nd. 1.2 cm. Bd. 1.9 cm. H. 9.2 cm. Md 7.2 cm. Wd. 0.3 cm.
Restored from sherds, incomplete.
Surface colour: 10YR4/1–2 grey; burnished slip: 10YR3/1 very dark grey
Break: grey core, brown reduction zones
Decoration: Two undelineated zones of horizontal striations made with an eight-toothed comb.

Type Group L.8.2 ?

Type group L.8.2, refers to Biconical IV jugs with rolled rims, round handles and round bases again perhaps related to the wheel-made globular group (L.9). The following sherds are assigned to this group but it is not clear if they really derive from jugs of this type or from the L.9 globular vessels.

512. 6128E TD A/V-q/16 planum 0–1 Phase D/2 (88/430) Plate 92

SPI	I-d	f	W2	Bd. gesp	re	3	1B

pht. 3.0 cm. Wd. 0.45 cm.
Incomplete
Surface colour: 10YR5/1 grey; burnished slip: not preserved
Break: red brown core, grey reduction zones
Decoration: Oblique lines of dots made with a twelve-toothed comb.
Previously published: TD XI, 175 no. 2.

513. 5925A TD A/II-k/15 planum 2 pit 5A Phase D/3 ? (86/283) Plate 92

SPI	I-d	f	W2	Bd. gesp	re	3

pht. 6.2 cm. Md. 6.2 cm. Wd. 0.5 cm.
Incomplete
Surface colour: 10YR4/2 dark grey brown; burnished slip: 5YR4/1 dark grey
Break: black core, light brown reduction zones
Decoration: Poorly drawn chevrons made with a twenty-toothed comb.

Miscellaneous Late Egyptian Biconical Sherds

514. 8908B TD H/III-u/16 planum 7 Phase ? (99/152) Plate 93

SPI	I-d	f–m	W2	–	re	3

pht. 1.1 cm. Wd. 0.35 cm.
Incomplete
Surface colour: 7.5YR5/1 dark grey; burnished slip not preserved
Break: grey in, brown out
Decoration: Incised chevron pattern.

515. 3274L1 TD A/II-n/19 disturbance (01/065) Plate 93

SPI	I-d	f	W2	–	re	2–3

pht. 2.3 cm. Wd. 0.5 cm.
Incomplete
Surface colour: 5YR6/1 grey; burnished slip not preserved
Break: wide black core, brown reduction zones
Decoration: Part of a chevron made with a multi-toothed comb. Biconical Chevron decoration with a twelve (?) toothed comb.

516. 1468A Vienna A3007 A/II-n/13 planum 3 Phase D/2 (68/045) Plate 93

SPI	I-d	f	W2	–	re	3

pht. 4.0 cm. Md. 13.0 cm. Wd. 0.6 cm.
Incomplete
Surface colour: 10YR5.5/1 grey; burnished slip 10YR4/1 dark grey
Break: uniform grey
Decoration: not discerible.
Previously published: TD V, 300, 302.

517. 6386C TD F/I-m/18 grave 13 Phase ? (87/097) Plate 93

SPI	I-d	vf	W2	–	re	3	1B

pht. 1.5 cm. Wd. 0.4 cm.
Incomplete
Surface colour: 5YR6/1 grey; burnished slip 2.5YR2/0 black
Break: dark grey in, light brown and grey out
Decoration: Chevrons made with a multi-toothed comb.

518. 8904B TD H/III-t/15 planum 1 Phase ? (99/110) Plate 93

SPI	I-d	vf	W2	–	re	3

pht. 2.7 cm. Wd. 0.4 cm.
Incomplete
Surface colour: 10YR6/1–2 light brownish grey; burnished slip 7.5YR4/3 brown
Break: uniform 7.5YR4/3 brown
Decoration: Incised chevron pattern.

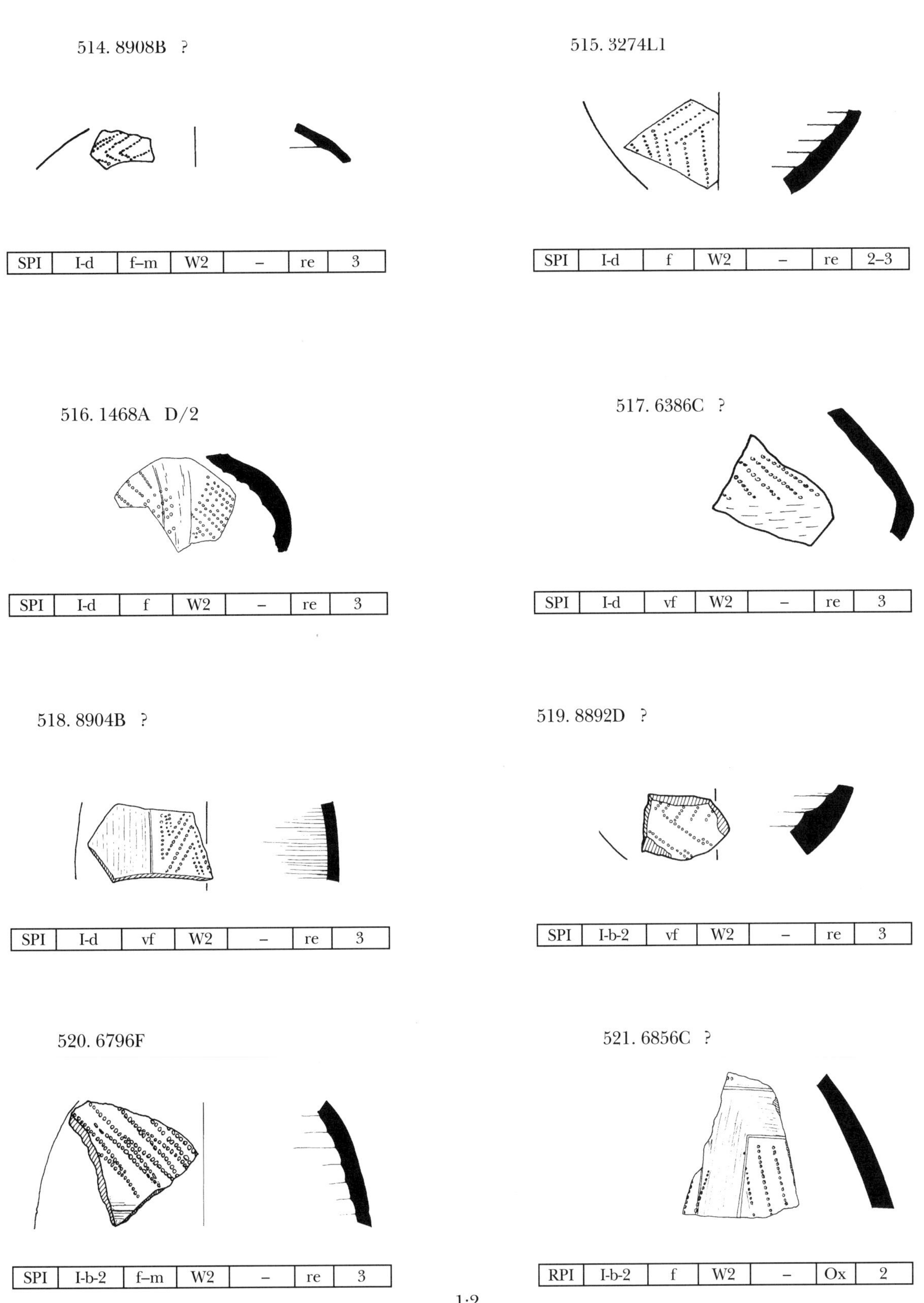

514. 8908B ?

SPI	I-d	f–m	W2	–	re	3

515. 3274L1

SPI	I-d	f	W2	–	re	2–3

516. 1468A D/2

SPI	I-d	f	W2	–	re	3

517. 6386C ?

SPI	I-d	vf	W2	–	re	3

518. 8904B ?

SPI	I-d	vf	W2	–	re	3

519. 8892D ?

SPI	I-b-2	vf	W2	–	re	3

520. 6796F

SPI	I-b-2	f–m	W2	–	re	3

521. 6856C ?

RPI	I-b-2	f	W2	–	Ox	2

1:2

Late Egyptian miscellaneous biconical vessels

Plate 93

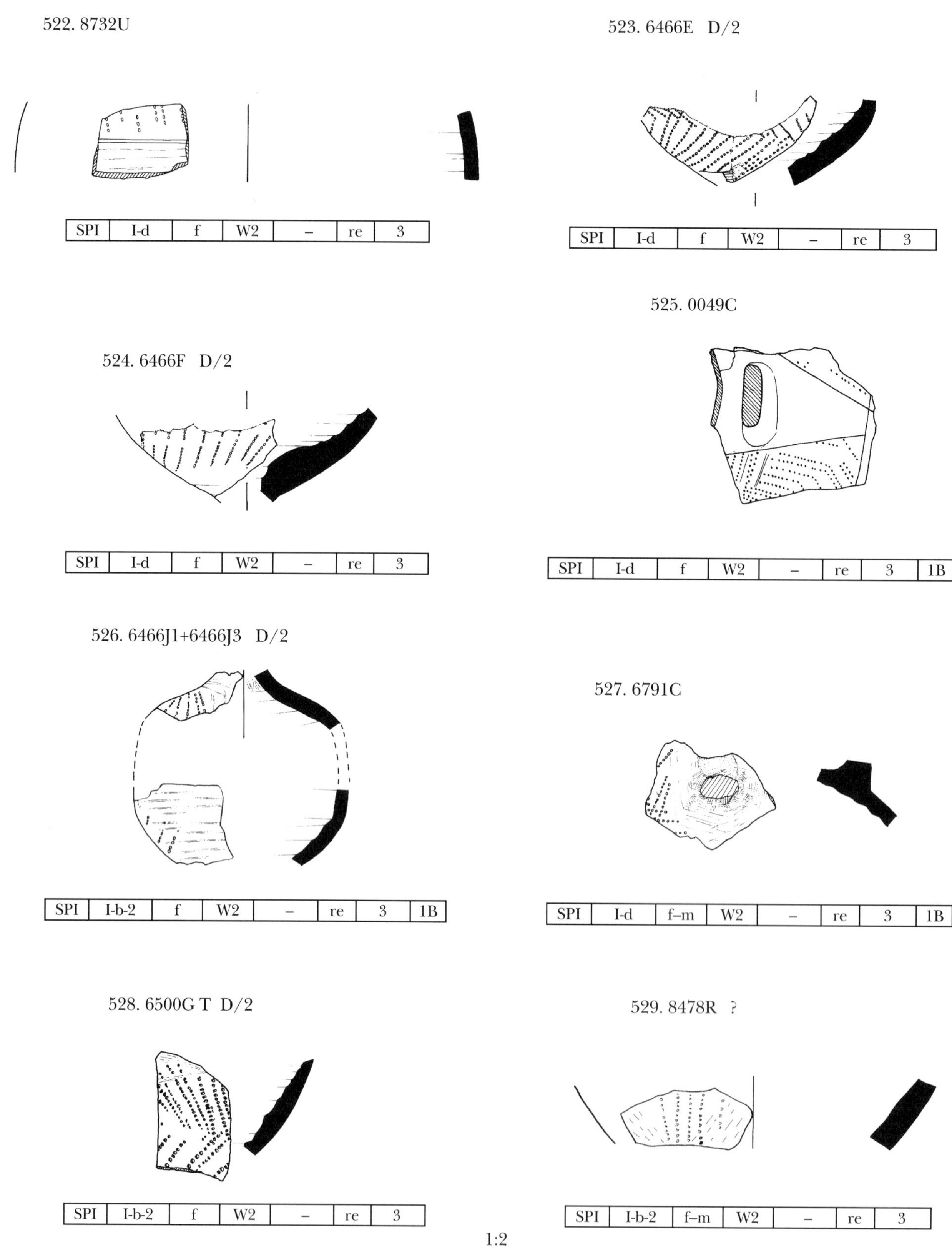

Late Egyptian miscellaneous biconical vessels

Plate 94

519. 8892D TD H/III-s/18 planum 0–1 Phase ? (99/132) Plate 93

SPI	I-b-2	vf	W2	–	re	3

pht. 2.1 cm. Wd. 0.5–0.8 cm.
Incomplete
Surface colour: 10YR4/1 dark grey; burnished slip 10YR3/1 very dark grey
Break: uniform grey
Decoration: Incised chevron pattern.

520. 6796F TD A/V-p/18 planum 1–2 surface (88/062) Plate 93

SPI	I-b-2	f–m	W2	–	re	3

pht. 4.3 cm. Wd. 0.5 cm.
Incomplete
Surface colour: 2.5YR6/6 light red; burnished slip: 5Y4/1 dark grey
Break: dark grey brown core, reddish brown reduction zones
Decoration: Vertical zigzag made with a multi-toothed comb
Probably same vessel as 6856C.
Previously published: TD XI, 216–217 no. 4.

521. 6856C TD A/V-o/18 planum 1–2 surface (88/262) Plate 93

RPI	I-b-2	f	W2	–	ox	2

pht. 3.4 cm.
Surface colour: 2.5YR5/8 red; burnished slip: 2.5YR3/6 dark red
Break: grey core, reddish brown oxidation zones
Decoration: Parts of two standing triangles filled with oblique lines or chevrons made with a multi-toothed comb.

522. 8732U TD H/III-t/17 profile (99/129) Plate 94

SPI	I-d	f	W2	–	re	3

pht. 2.5 cm. Md. 15.0 cm. 0.45 cm.
Incomplete
Surface colour: 2.5Y7/1 light grey; burnished slip 2.5Y6/1 grey
Break: thick black interior, reddish brown and grey reduction zones
Decoration: Incised chevron pattern.

523. 6466E TD A/V-m/18 planum 1–2 Phase D/2 (94/035) Plate 94

SPI	I-d	f	W2	–	re	3

pht. 3.0 cm. Wd. 0.5 cm.
Incomplete
Surface colour: 7.5YR4/0 reddish brown; burnished slip: 10YR3/1 very dark grey
Break: uniform dark grey
Decoration: Horizontal chevrons made with multi-toothed comb.
Previously published: TD XI, 67–68 no. 10.

524. 6466F TD A/V-m/18 planum 1–2 Phase D/2 (94/035) Plate 94

SPI	I-d	f	W2	–	re	3

pht. 3.0 cm. Wd. 0.6 cm.
Incomplete
Surface colour: 10YR5–6/1–2 grey; burnished slip: 10YR3/1 very dark grey
Break: black core, red and grey brown reduction zones
Decoration: Oblique lines made with a nine-toothed comb.
Previously published: TD XI, 67–68 no. 12.

525. 0049C ? A/II-l/12 planum 0–1 Surface (66/020) Plate 94

SPI	I-d	f	W2	–	re	3	1B

Wd. 0.4 cm.
Incomplete
Surface colour: 5YR5/4 reddish brown; burnished slip 10YR4/1 very dark grey
Break: light grey core, dark brown reduction zones
Decoration: Upper zone of vertical chevrons pointing right made with a fourteen-toothed comb.

526. 6466J1+6466J3 TD A/V-m/18 planum 1–2 Phase D/2 (94/034) Plate 94

SPI	I-b-2	f	W2	–	re	3	1B

pht. 6.7 cm. Wd. 0.4 cm.
Incomplete
Surface colour: 5YR5/4 reddish brown; burnished slip 10YR4/1 very dark grey
Break: dark grey in, red and dark grey reduction zones
Decoration: Parts of both the upper and lower zones preserved, but decoration not discernible.
Previously published: TD XI, 67–68 no. 6.

527. 6791C TD A/V-n/17 planum 0–1 surface (88/391) Plate 94

SPI	I-d	f–m	W2	–	re	3	1B

pht. 2.5 cm. Wd. 0.4 cm.
Incomplete
Surface colour: 5YR5/4 reddish brown; burnished slip 10YR4/1 very dark grey
Break: light grey core, dark brown reduction zones
Decoration: Only part of two rows of impressed dots preserved made with a comb.
Previously published: TD XI, 216–217 no. 2.

528. 6500G TD A/V-n/17 planum 1–2 Phase D/2 (88/167) Plate 94

SPI	I-b-2	f	W2	–	re	3

pht. 3.4 cm. Wd. 0.6 cm.
Incomplete
Surface colour: 7.5YR4/4 dark brown
Break: uniform reddish brown
Decoration: Vertical chevrons made with a multi-toothed comb.
Previously published: TD XI, 82–83 no. 21.

529. 8478R TD H/III-r/16 planum 3–4 rel g/h Phase ? (96/017) Plate 94

SPI	I-b-2	f–m	W2	–	re	3

pht. 2.4 cm. Wd. 0.8 cm.
Incomplete
Surface colour: 10YR5/1–6/2 dark grey brown; burnished slip 7.5YR5/0 grey
Break: wide dark grey core, red and dark grey reduction zones
Decoration: Part of a triangle or lozenge filled with vertical lines made with a multi-toothed comb.

530. 8477W TD H/V-m/10 planum 1 surface (96/016) Plate 95

SPI	I-b-2	f–m	W2	–	re	3

pht. 2.4 cm. Wd. 0.8 cm.
Incomplete
Surface colour: 10YR5/1–6/2 dark grey brown
Break: wide dark grey core, red and dark grey reduction zones
Decoration: Careless oblique lines made with a multi-toothed comb.

531. 6451E TD A/II-k/17 planum 3 Phase E/1–D/3 (88/112) Plate 95

SPI	I-d	f	W2	–	re	3

pht. 1.5 cm. Wd. 0.3 cm.
Incomplete
Surface colour: 5YR5/1 grey; burnished slip 5YR4/1 dark grey
Break: uniform dark grey
Decoration: Vertical lines made with a multi-toothed comb.

532. 1468B Vienna A3008 A/II-n/13 planum 3 Phase D/2 (68/045) Plate 95

SPI	I-d	f	W2	–	re	3	1B

pht. 3.5 cm. Md. 5.0 cm. Wd. 0.7 cm.
Incomplete
Surface colour: 10YR5.5/1 grey; burnished slip 10YR4/1 dark grey
Break: uniform grey
Decoration: Parts of both the upper and lower zones preserved, but decoration not discernible.
Previously published: TD V, 300, 302.

533. 3058K TD A/II-p/21 planum 2 offering pit 2 Phase E/1–D/3 (97/178) Plate 95

SPI	I-d	f	W2	–	re	2–3

pht. 1.8 cm. Wd. 0.5 cm.
Incomplete
Surface colour: 5YR6/1 grey; burnished slip not preserved
Break: wide black core, brown reduction zones
Decoration: Oblique line decoration with a twelve (?) toothed comb.
Previously published: TD XVII, I, 368, fig. 214, no. 10.

534. 8478E TD H/V-l/17 planum 3 Phase ? (96/007) Plate 95

SPI	I-d	f	W2	–	re	2–3

pht. 1.5 cm. Wd. 0.5 cm.
Incomplete
Surface colour: 5YR4/1 dark grey; burnished slip 7.5YR5/0 grey
Break: wide dark brown core, grey reduction zones
Decoration: Chevron decoration with a twelve toothed comb.

535. 8450S TD H/IV-k/3 planum 6–7 Phase D/2 (95/041) Plate 95

SPI	I-b-2	f	W2	–	re	2–3

pht. 1.7 cm. Wd. 0.7 cm.
Incomplete
Surface colour: 10YR6/1 grey; burnished slip not preserved
Break: light red core,dark, grey reduction zones
Decoration: Chevrons made with a twelve-toothed comb.

536. 8168C TD Khatana E/I/L planum ? Phase ? (93/435) Plate 95

SPI	I-d	f	W2	–	re	2	1B

pht. 2.4
Incomplete
Surface colour: 10YR4/3 brown; burnished slip: 5YR3/2 dark red brown
Break: greenish grey in, brownish grey out
Decoration: Four (?) lozenges or standing triangles – parts of only three preserved – filled with chevrons made with a multi-toothed (sixteen ?) comb.

537. 2095C TD A/II-m/10 planum 3 grave 5 Phase D/2 ? (75/005) Plate 95

SPI	I-d	f–m	W2	–	re	3

pht. 4.5 cm. Wd. 0.6 cm.
Incomplete
Surface colour: 10YR6/2 light reddish grey; burnished slip 5YR5/3 reddish brown
Break: uniform yellowish red
Decoration: not dicernible.

538. 6500H TD A/V-n/17 planum 1–2 Phase D/2 (88/167) Plate 96

SPI	I-b-2	f–m	W2	–	re	3

pht. 2.1 cm. Wd. 0.4 cm.
Incomplete
Surface colour: 10YR6/2 light reddish grey; burnished slip 5YR5/3 reddish brown
Break: thin red core, grey reduction zones
Decoration: Vertical chevrons made with a ten-toothed comb.
Previously published: TD XI, 82–83 no. 20.

539. 6466J2 TD A/V-m/18 planum 1–2 Phase D/2 (94/034) (possibly same vessel as 6466J6) Plate 96

SPI	I-b-2	f–m	W2	–	re	3

pht. 3.1 cm. Wd. 0.6 cm.
Incomplete
Surface colour: 5YR5/1 grey
Break: uniform grey
Decoration: Vertical chevrons made with a multi-toothed comb.
Previously published: TD XI, 67–68 no. 8.

540. 6466J6 TD A/V-m/18 planum 1–2 Phase D/2 (94/034) (possibly same vessel as 6466J2) Plate 96

SPI	I-b-2	f–m	W2	–	re	3

pht. 2.7 cm. Wd. 0.6 cm.
Incomplete
Surface colour: 5YR5/1 grey
Break: uniform grey
Decoration: Vertical lines made with a multi-toothed comb.
Previously published: TD XI, 67–68 no. 9.

541. 6095B2 TD F/I-o/21 modern pit by grave 11 (87/248) Plate 96

SPI	I-d	f–m	W2	–	re	3

pht. 4.5 cm. Wd. 0.6 cm.
Incomplete

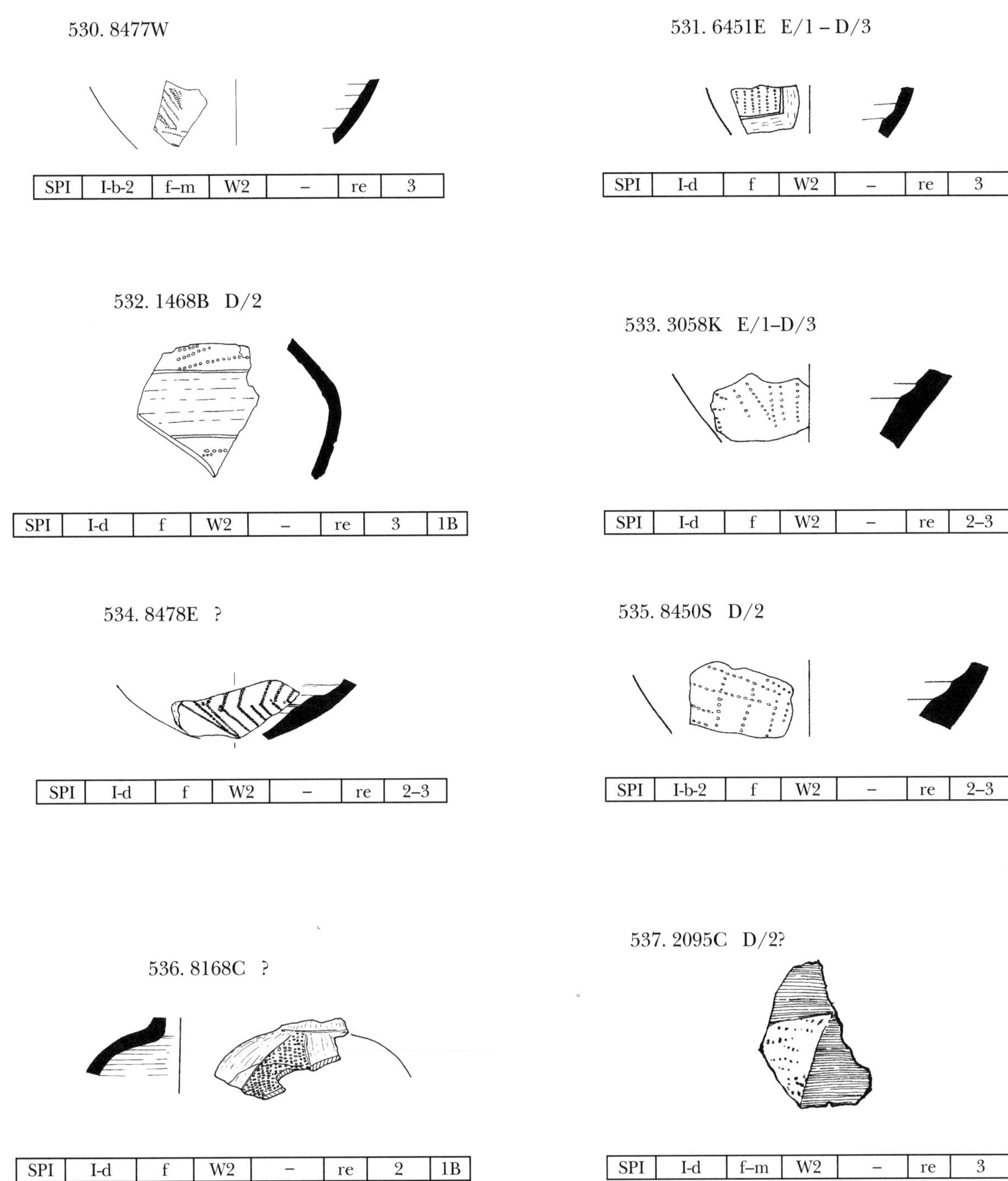

1:2

Late Egyptian miscellaneous biconical vessels

Plate 95

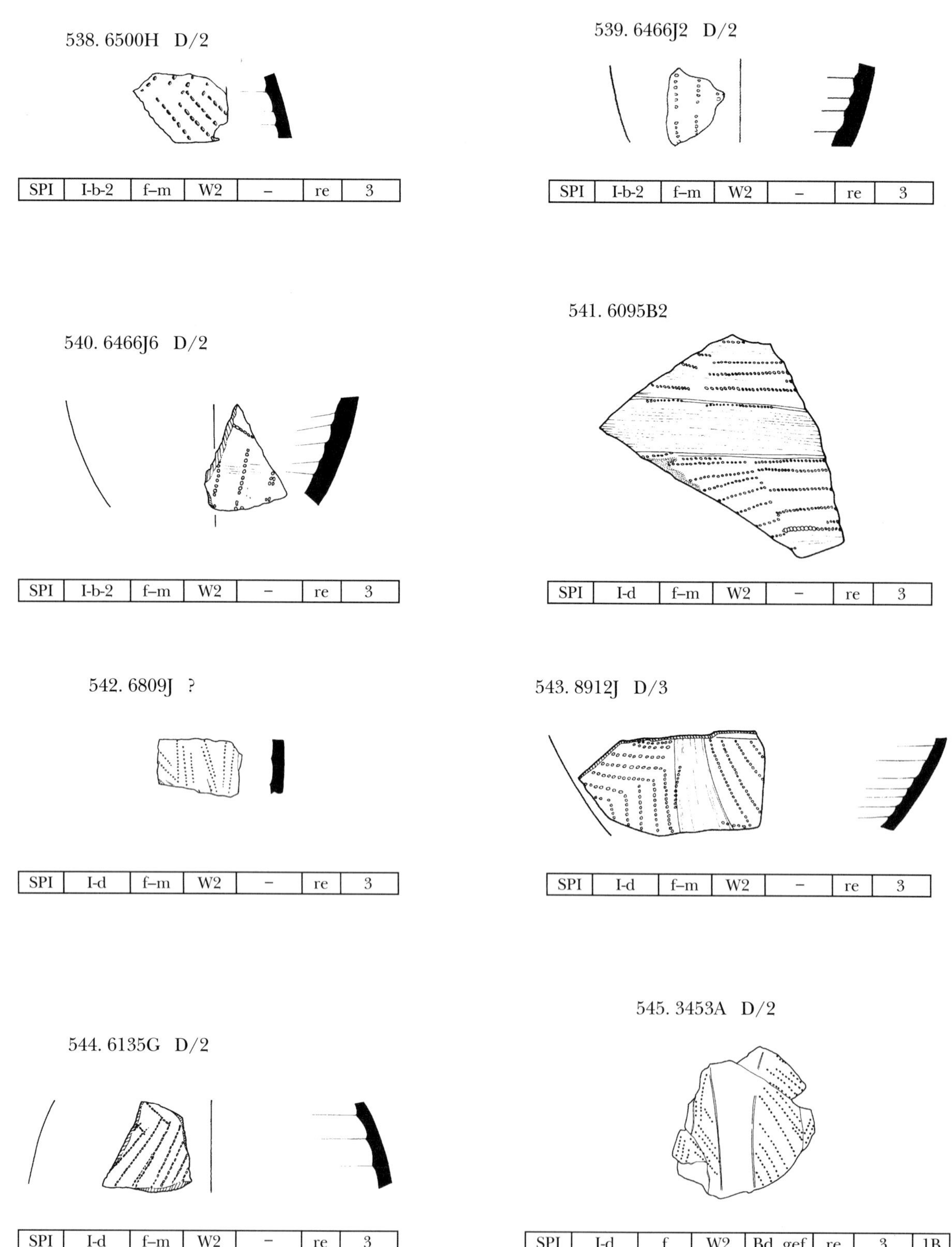

1:2

Late Egyptian miscellaneous biconical vessels

Plate 96

Surface colour: 5YR6/1 grey; burnished slip 7.5YR3/1 very dark grey
Break: uniform dark grey
Decoration: Horizontal and oblique lines made with a sixteen (?)-toothed comb.

542. 6809J TD A/V-n/19 planum 4–5 Phase ? (88/056)
Plate 96

SPI	I-d	f	W2	–	re	3

pht. 1.2 cm. Wd. 0.4 cm.
Incomplete
Surface colour: 5YR5/1 grey; burnished slip not preserved
Break: wide dark grey core, red and dark grey reduction zones
Decoration: Part of horizontal chevrons preserved made with a multi-toothed comb.

543. 8912J H/III-t/15 planum 1 Phase D/3 (00/107)
Plate 96

SPI	I-d	f	W2	–	re	3

pht. 2.3 cm. Wd. 0.35 cm.
Incomplete
Surface colour: 7.5YR5/2 dark grey brown; burnished slip 7.5YR4/2 grey
Break: wide dark grey core, grey reduction zones
Decoration: Chevrons carelessly made with a multi-toothed comb.

544. 6135G TD A/V-q/19 planum 2 Phase D/2 (94/074)
Plate 96

SPI	I-d	f	W2	–	re	3

pht. 3.0 cm. Md. 12.6 cm Wd. 0.5 cm
Incomplete
Surface colour: 7.5YR5/2 dark grey brown; burnished slip 5YR5/1 grey
Break: uniform dark grey brown
Decoration: Upper zone of vertical chevrons pointing right, and lower zone of vertical chevrons pointing right made with a sixteen-toothed comb.
Previously published: TD XI, 172–173 no.6.

545. 3453A TD A/II-m/18 grave 1 Phase D/2 (81/125)
Plate 96

SPI	I-d	f	W2	Bd. gef	re	3	1B

pht. 4.3 cm. Wd. 04 cm.
Incomplete
Surface colour: 10YR4/1 dark grey; burnished slip: 10YR2/1 black
Break: uniform grey brown
Decoration: Parts of two lozenges preserved, with tripartite chevrons made with a fourteen-toothed comb.

Type Group L.9.1

Type group L.9.1 comprises a series of spherical jugs with a rolled rim and strap handle. Like the Biconical 1 vessels these jugs always have a broad reserved burnished zone around the maximum point, and the decoration consists of an upper zone of delineated standing triangles, and a lower one of delineated pendant triangles. Both zones usually contain between four and six such triangles.

546. 8704 TD A/II-o/14 grave 43 Phase E/1 (98/062)
Plates 97, 149

SPI	I-d	m	W2	Bd. gesp	re	2–3	1B

D. 3.0 cm. Nd 1.2 cm. H. 9.3 cm. Md. 6.7 cm. Wd. 0.3 cm.
VI 72.04
Intact
Surface colour: 10YR6/3 pale brown; burnished slip: 10YR3/1 very dark grey
Break: not visible
Decoration: Three standing triangles, filled with vertical zigzags on upper body and four pendant triangles, filled with chevrons on lower body made with a ten-toothed comb.
Previously published: TD XVI, 286, fig. 208a, no. 7.

547. 8781D TD A/II-o/14 grave 43 Phase E/1 (98/072)
Plate 97

SPI	I-d	m	W2	Bd. gesp	re	2	1B

D. 3.3 cm. Nd 1.4 cm. H. 9.1 cm. Md. 6.5 cm. Wd. 0.4 cm.
VI 71.42
Restored from sherds, incomplete
Surface colour: 10YR4/3 brown; burnished slip: 10YR3/2 very dark grey
Break: uniform grey brown
Decoration: Three standing triangles on shoulder and three pendant triangles below reserved burnished band. Triangles infilled with oblique lines made with an eight-toothed comb.
Previously published: TD XVI, 286, fig. 208a, no. 8.

548. 8668 TD A/II-o/14 grave 43 Phase E/1 (97/371)
Plate 97

BPI	I-d	f	W2	Bd. gesp	re	2	1B

D. 3.2 cm. Nd 1.2 cm. H. 9.0 cm. Md. 6.4 cm. Wd. 0.3 cm.
VI 71.11
Intact
Surface colour: 10YR5/2 grey brown; burnished slip: 5YR5/6 reddish yellow
Break: not visible
Decoration: Three standing triangles, filled with zigzags on upper body and three pendant triangles, filled with chevrons on lower body. Dots made with an eight-toothed comb.
Previously published: TD XVI, 286, fig. 208a, no. 9.

549. 3400 Cairo F/I-j/23 grave 7 Phase b/1 (80/102)
Plate 97

SPI	I-d	f	W2	Bd. gesp	re	3	1B

D. 2.8 cm. Nd 1.2 cm. H. 10.2 cm. Md. 6.5 cm. Wd. 0.3 cm.
VI 63.72
Intact
Surface colour: 10YR5/1–6/4 grey; burnished slip: 7.5YR4/2 dark brown
Break: not visible
Decoration: Six triangles in upper zone, five triangles in the lower zone infilled with striations from upper right to lower left made with a ten-toothed comb.

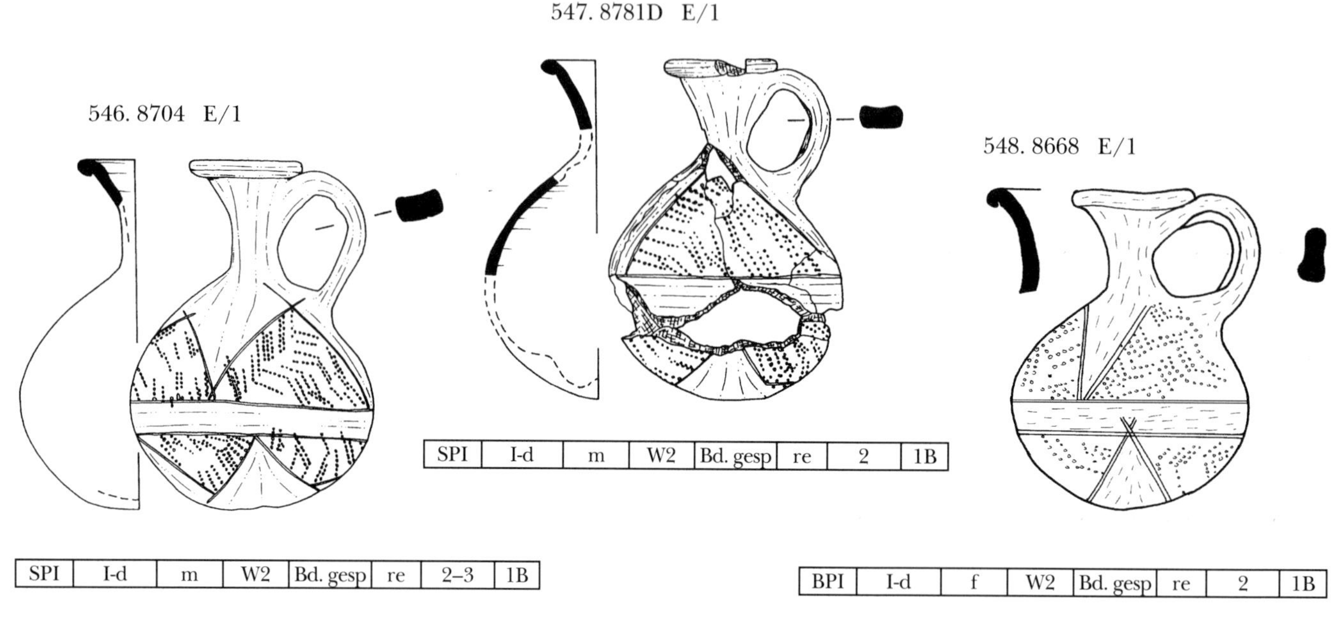

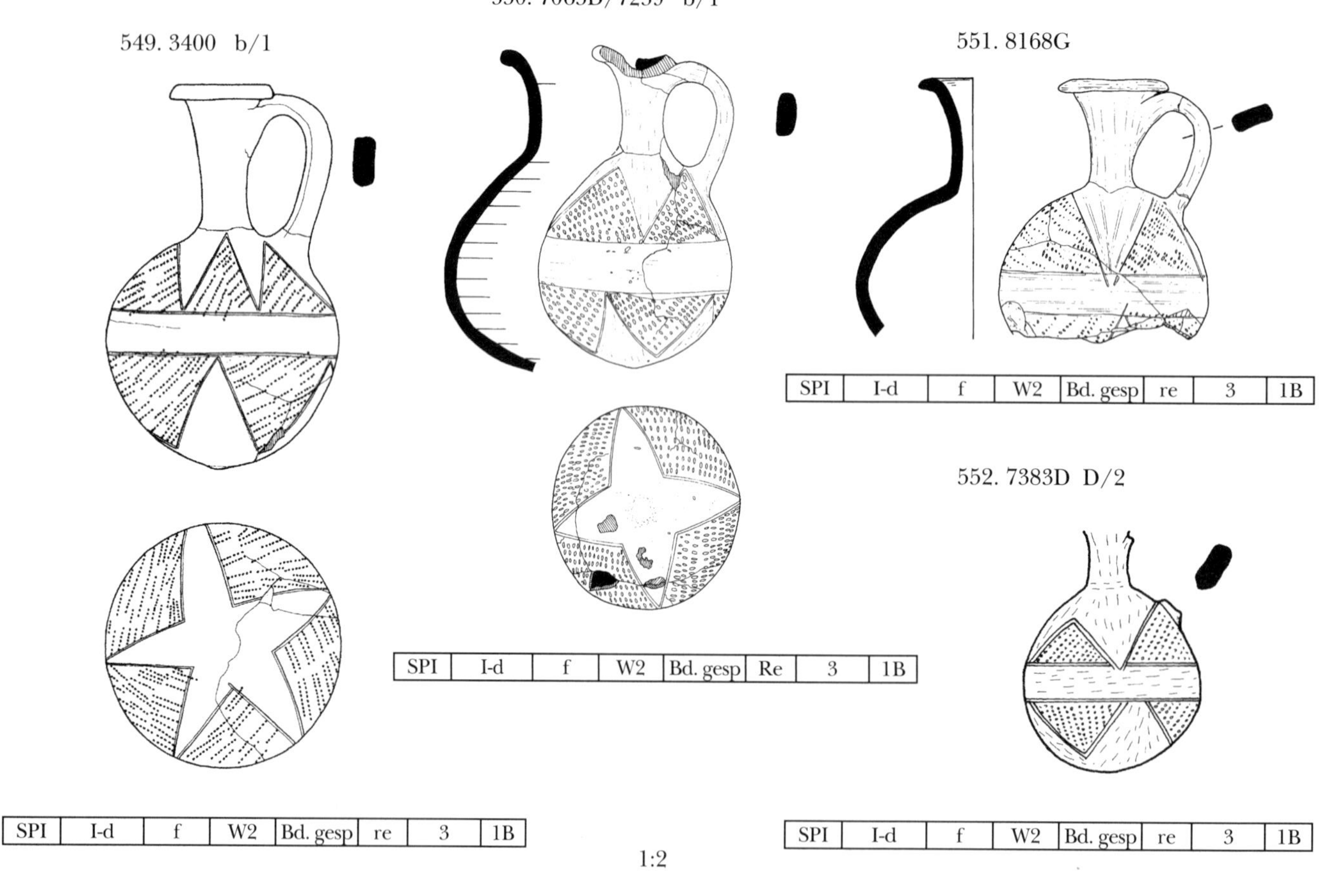

1:2

Late Egyptian Type Group L.9.1

Plate 97

550. 7065D/7239 TD F/I-l/23 planum 1 Phase b/1 (88/228) Plate 97

SPI	I-d	f	W2	Bd. gesp	re	3	1B

D. 2.6 cm. Nd 1.1 cm. H. 8.5 cm. Md. 5.4 cm. Wd. 0.3 cm.
VI 45.90
Restored from sherds, incomplete
Surface colour: 2.5YR5/4 reddish brown; burnished slip: 7.5YR4/2 dark brown
Break: not visible
Decoration: Four triangles in upper zone, four triangles in the lower zone infilled with striations from upper right to lower left made with an eight-toothed comb.

551. 8168G TD Khatana E/I/L planum ? Phase ? (93/411) Plate 97

SPI	I-d	f	W2	Bd. gesp	re	3	1B

D. 3.0 cm. Nd 1.0 cm. pht. 7.1 cm. Md. 5.8 cm. Wd. 0.3 cm.
Incomplete
Surface colour: 10YR4/3 brown; burnished slip: 10YR3/1 very dark grey
Break: greenish grey in, brownish grey out
Decoration: Four standing triangles on shoulder, and parts of two hanging triangles on lower body, infilled with oblique lines made with an eight-toothed comb.

552. 7383D TD A/IV-h/4 planum 1 Phase ? (90/011) Plates 97, 149

SPI	I-d	f	W2	Bd. gesp	re	3	1B

D. 3.0 cm. Nd 1.1 cm. pht. 6.8 cm. Md. 4.8 cm. Wd. 0.3 cm.
Incomplete
Surface colour: 10YR4/3 brown; burnished slip: 10YR2/1 black
Break: uniform dark greyish brown
Decoration: Four standing triangles on shoulder and four pendant triangles below mid point, each infilled with oblique lines made with an eight-toothed comb.

553. 8990R TD F/II-r/22 L81 Phase a/2 (08/053) Plate 98

SPI	I-b-2	f	W1	Bd. gesp	re	3	1B

Nd. 1.4 cm. pht. 5.8 cm. Md. 5.4 cm. Wd. 0.3 cm.
Incomplete
Surface colour: 10YR6/4 gray; burnished slip: 10YR4/3 brown
Break: black core, brown reduction zones
Decoration: Three standing triangles on shoulder, and three hanging triangles on lower body, infilled with chevrons made with a ten-toothed comb.

Type Group L.9.2

Type Group L.9.2 is somewhat similar to the previous type but the body is distinctly carinated rather than spherical. Like the previous group the decoration consists of an upper zone of delineated standing triangles, and a lower one of delineated pendant triangles.

554. 3368 Cairo Khatana E/I/G profile Phase ? (80/204) Plates 98, 150

SPI	I-d	f	W2	Bd. gesp	re	3	1B

pht. 5.3 cm. Md. 5.5 cm. Wd. 0.3 cm.
Incomplete
Surface colour: 10YR6/5 brownish grey; burnished slip: 7.5YR4/2 dark brown
Break: uniform dark grey
Decoration: Five triangles in upper zone, six triangles in the lower zone infilled with striations from upper right to lower left made with a ten-toothed comb.
Previously published: Kopetzky, *The MB IIB-Corpus of the Hyksos Period at Tell el-Dab^ca*, 2007, 198 fig. 3.7.

555. 7025B TD F/I-u/18 grave 7 Phase ? (89/210) Plate 98

SPI	I-d	f	W2	Bd. gesp	re	3	1B

Nd. 1.2 cm. pht. 4.5 cm. Md. 4.6 cm. Wd. 0.4 cm.
Incomplete
Surface colour: 5Y3/1–2 very dark grey; burnished slip: 7.5YR4/2 dark brown
Break: uniform dark grey
Decoration: Four triangles in upper zone, three triangles in the lower zone infilled with vertical chevrons or striations from upper right to lower left made with a twelve-toothed comb.

Type Group L.9.3

The only vessel which can be attributed to type group L.9.3 is the incomplete example, TD 2093, which has a small plump body with three delineated circles, infilled with chevrons (?) on the body.

556. 2093 Vienna A3105 A/II-n/10, grave 5 Phase E/1 (69/094) Plates 98, 150

SPI	I-d	f–m	W2	Bd. gesp	re	3

Nd. 1.3 cm. pht. 5.8 cm. Md. 5.9 cm. Wd. 0.4 cm.
Incomplete
Surface colour: 2.5YR4/0 dark grey; burnished slip: 10YR6/2 pale brown
Break: uniform grey
Decoration: Three circular areas infilled with vertical striations made with a ten toothed comb.
Previously published: TD V, 227, 228.

Type Group L.9.4

Type group L.9.4 consists of drop-shaped globular jugs with a rolled rim and strap handle, and are very common. They vary in height between around 9 and 16 cms., with most in the 10–12 cm. range. Several decorative styles are associated with this type though the most usual is L.9.4a, three or four infilled lozenges, and only L.9.4a has so far been unequivocally recorded at Tell el-Dab^ca.

Type Group L.9.4a

557. 3966 Cairo A/II-n/19 grave 5 Phase E/1 (82/091) Plate 99

RPI	I-d	f	W2	Bd. gesp	ox	2–3	1B

D. 2.3 cm. Nd 1.15 cm. H. 9.0 cm. Md. 6.3 cm. Wd. 0.3 cm.
VI 70.00
Intact

553. 8990R a/2

SPI	I-b-2	f	W1	Bd. gesp	re	3	1B

554. 3368 ?

SPI	I-d	f	W2	Bd. gesp	re	3	1B

555. 7025B ?

SPI	I-d	f	W2	Bd. gesp	re	3	1B

556. 2093 E/1

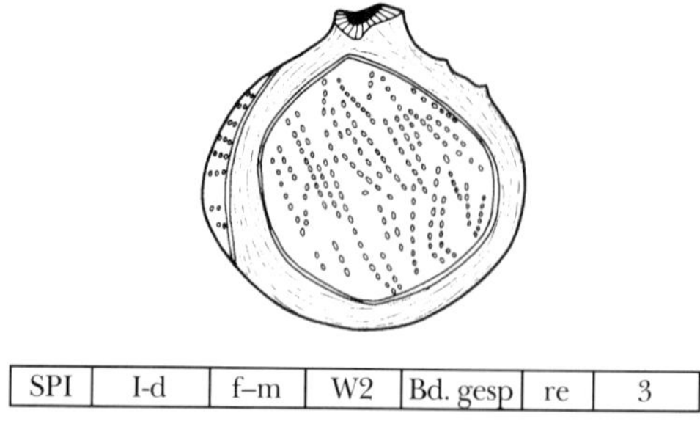

SPI	I-d	f–m	W2	Bd. gesp	re	3

1:2

Late Egyptian Type Groups L.9.1, L.9.2, L.9.3

Plate 98

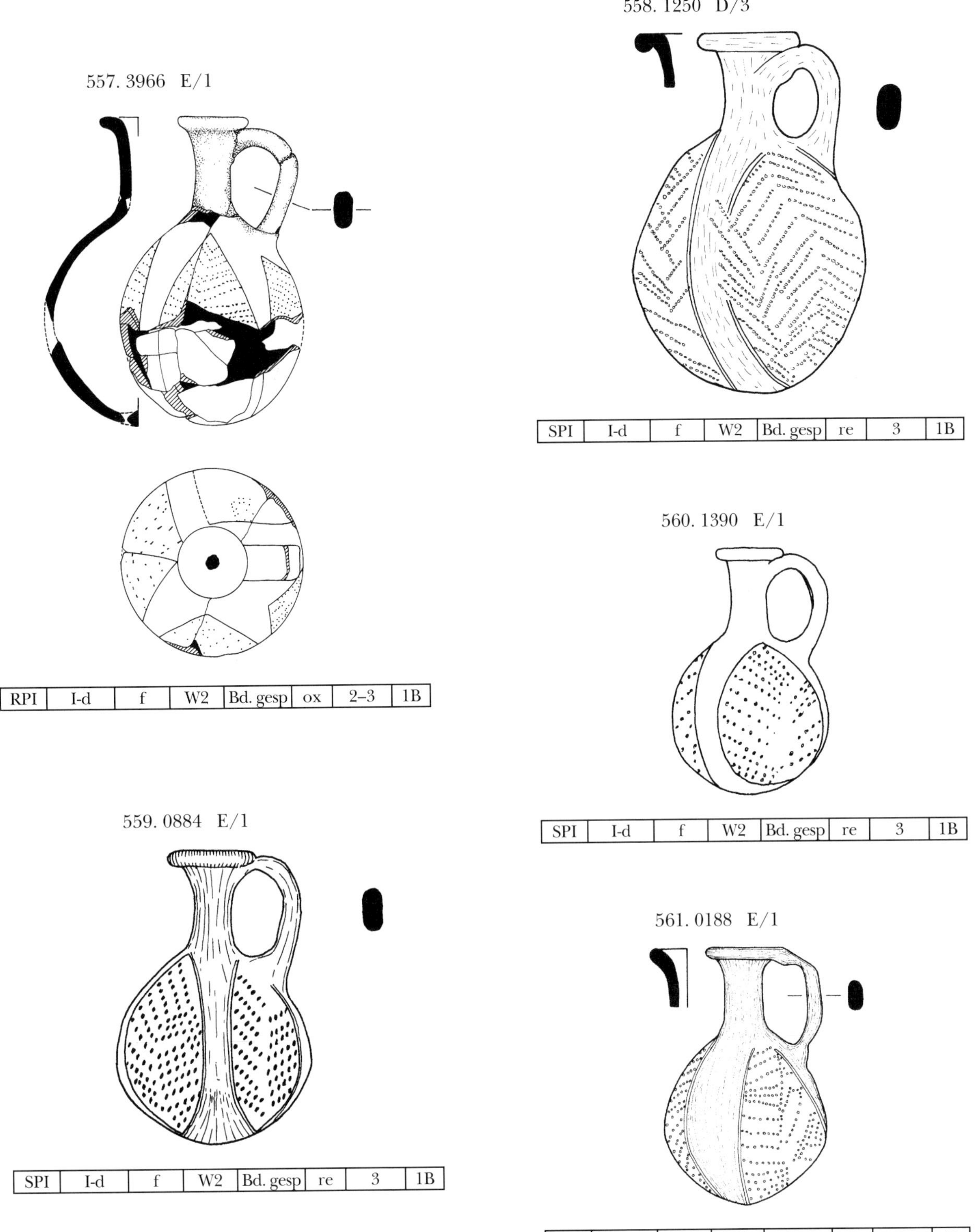

1:2

Late Egyptian Type Group L.9.4a

Plate 99

Surface colour: 7.5YR6/5 light brown; burnished slip: 10YR3/1 very dark grey
Break: brick red core, light reddish brown oxidation zones
Decoration: Four lozenges with vertical chevrons made with a twelve-toothed comb.
Previously published: TD V, 230.

558. 1250 Vienna A1660 A/II-n/13 grave 4 Phase D/3 (69/024) Plate 99

SPI	I-d	f	W2	Bd. gesp	re	3	1B

D. 3.3 cm. Nd 1.5 cm. H. 11.6 cm. Md. 7.8 cm. Wd. 0.2 cm.
VI 67.24
Intact
Surface colour: 10YR4/1–5/3 dark grey; burnished slip: 10YR3/1 very dark grey
Break: dark grey core, dark brown and dark grey reduction zones
Decoration: Three lozenges with infilled zigzags made with a twelve-toothed comb.
Previously published: TD V, 266.

559. 0884 Vienna A1657 A/II-m/11 grave 7 Phase E/1 (67/026) Plate 99

SPI	I-d	f	W2	Bd. gesp	re	3	1B

D. 3.0 cm. Nd 1.25 cm. H. 9.7 cm. Md. 6.5 cm. Wd. 0.3 cm.
VI 67.01
Intact
Surface colour: 7.5YR4/2 dark brown; burnished slip: 7.5YR3/1 dark grey brown
Break: not visible
Decoration: Four lozenges with infilled chevrons or zigzags made with an eight-toothed comb.
Previously published: FA, 79 abb 67 H13; *TD V,* 190, 191; *PuF,* 227 nr 271.

560. 1390 Vienna A2946 A/II-l/14 grave 5 Phase E/1 (68/091) Plate 99

SPI	I-d	f	W2	Bd. gesp	re	3	1B

D. 2.6 cm. Nd 1.2 cm. Bd. 2.0 cm. H. 7.95 cm. Md. 5.3 cm. Wd. 0.3 cm.
VI 66.66
Intact, chip in rim
Surface colour: 2.5Y5/1 grey; burnished slip: 2.5Y/1 black
Break: dark grey core, light grey reduction zones
Decoration: Three lozenges infilled with chevrons made with an eight-toothed comb.
Previously published: TD XVI, 254, fig. 189b, no. 24.

561. 0188 Vienna A1633 A/II-l/12 grave 2 Phase E/1 (66/039) Plate 99

SPI	I-d	f–m	W2	Bd. gesp	re	3	1B

D. 2.9 cm. Nd 1.14 cm. H. 8.4 cm. Md. 5.4 cm. Wd. 0.3 cm.
VI 64.28
Intact
Surface colour: 10YR5/4 yellow brown; burnished slip: 10YR5/1 grey
Break: not visible
Decoration: Three lozenges with infilled zigzags made with an eight-toothed comb.
Previously published: TD V, 187, 189.

562. 5416 TD A/II-k/17 grave 30 burial 1 Phase E/1 (85/262) Plate 100

SPI	I-b-2	f–vf	W2	Bd. gesp	re	3	1B

D. 2.25 cm. Nd 1.1 cm. H. 8.2 cm. Md. 5.4 cm. Wd. 0.3 cm.
VI 65.85
Intact
Surface colour: 10YR4/1 dark grey; burnished slip: 10YR3/1 very dark grey
Break: uniform light reddish brown
Decoration: Three lozenges filled with horizontal zigzags made with a nine-toothed comb.
Previously published: TD XVI, 248 fig 184, no. 5.

563. 5419 TD A/II-k/17 grave 30 burial 1 Phase E/1 (85/264) Plate 100

SPI	I-d	f	W2	Bd. gesp	re	2–3	1B

D. 2.3 cm. Nd 1.0 cm. H. 8.8 cm. Md. 5.5 cm. Wd. 0.3 cm.
VI 62.50
Intact
Surface colour: 10YR5/1 grey; burnished slip: 10YR3/1 very dark grey
Break: not visible
Decoration: Four lozenges filled with horizontal zigzags made with a six-toothed comb.
Previously published: TD XVI, 248, fig. 184, no. 7.

564. 2016 Vienna A1410 A/II-m-n/11 grave 11 Phase E/1 (69/028) Plate 100

SPI	I-d	f	W2	Bd. gesp	re	2–3	1B

D. 2.8 cm. Nd 1.22 cm. H. 9.27 cm. Md. 5.8 cm. Wd. 0.3 cm.
VI 62.56
Intact
Surface colour: 5YR4/1 dark grey; burnished slip: 5YR3/1 very dark grey
Break: not visible
Decoration: Three lozenges with infilled zigzags made with an eight-toothed comb.
Previously published: TD V, 230.

565. 0167 Vienna A1601 A/II-l/12 grave 2 Phase E/1 (66/037) Plate 100

SPI	I-d	f	W2	Bd. gesp	re	3	1B

D. 3.28 cm. Nd 1.5 cm. H. 12.2 cm. Md. 7.6 cm. Wd. 0.3 cm.
VI 62.29
Intact
Surface colour: 10YR5/2 grey brown; burnished slip: 10YR4/1 dark grey
Break: not visible
Decoration: Four lozenges with infilled zigzags made with a twelve-toothed comb.
Previously published: Bietak, *MDAIK* 23 fg. 8, pl. 30b, Kaplan, *Tell el-Yahudiyeh Ware,* fig. 16c; *TD V,* 185; Kopetzky, *The MB IIB-Corpus of the Hyksos Period at Tell el-Dabᶜa,* 2007, 198 fig. 3.8.

566. 0150 Vienna A1596 A/II-l/12 grave 2 Phase E/1 (66/036) Plates 100, 150

SPI	I-d	f–m	W2	Bd. gesp	re	3	1B

D. 2.5 cm. Nd 1.2 cm. H. 9.4 cm. Md. 5.7 cm. Wd. 0.3 cm.
VI 60.63

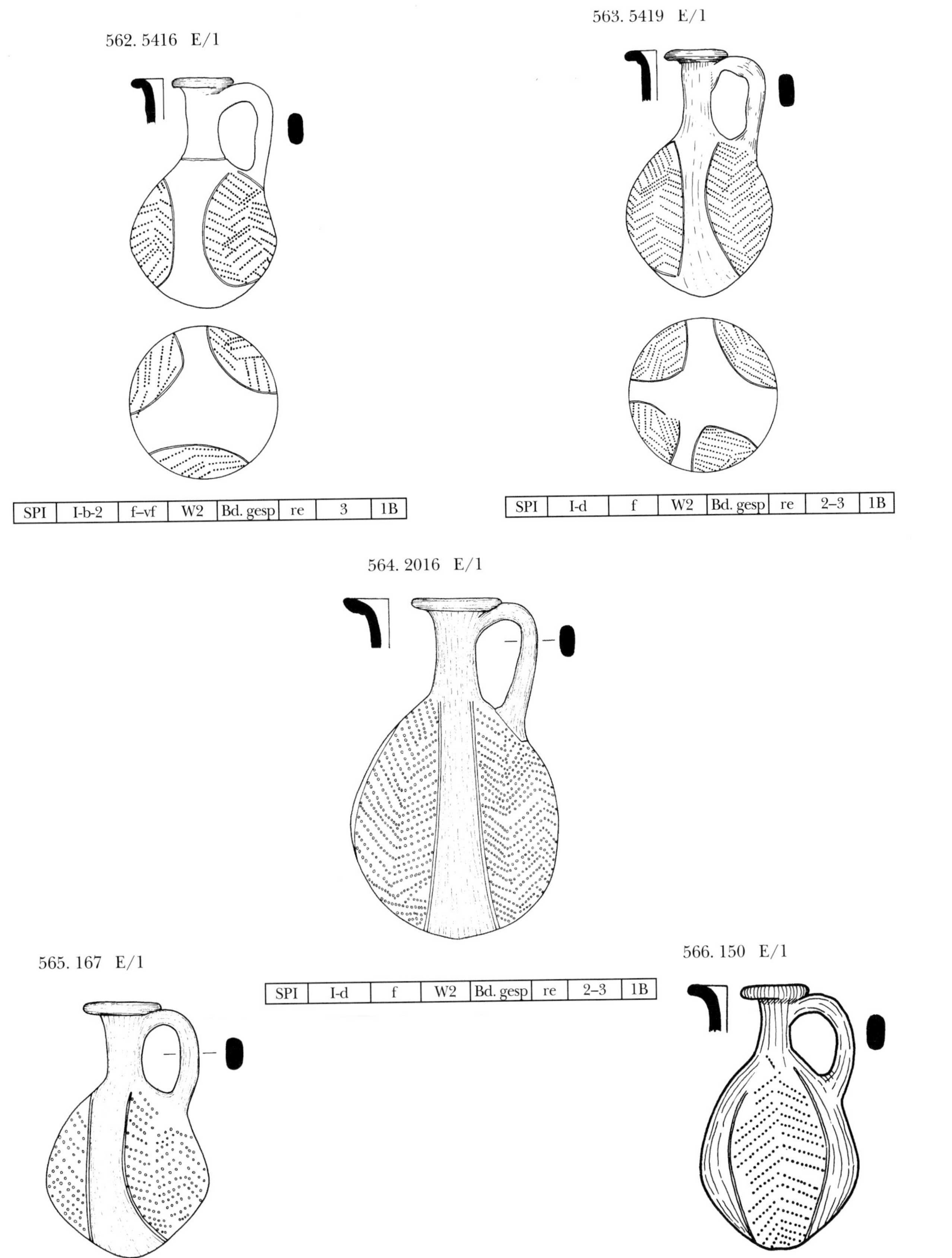

Late Egyptian Type Group L.9.4a

Plate 100

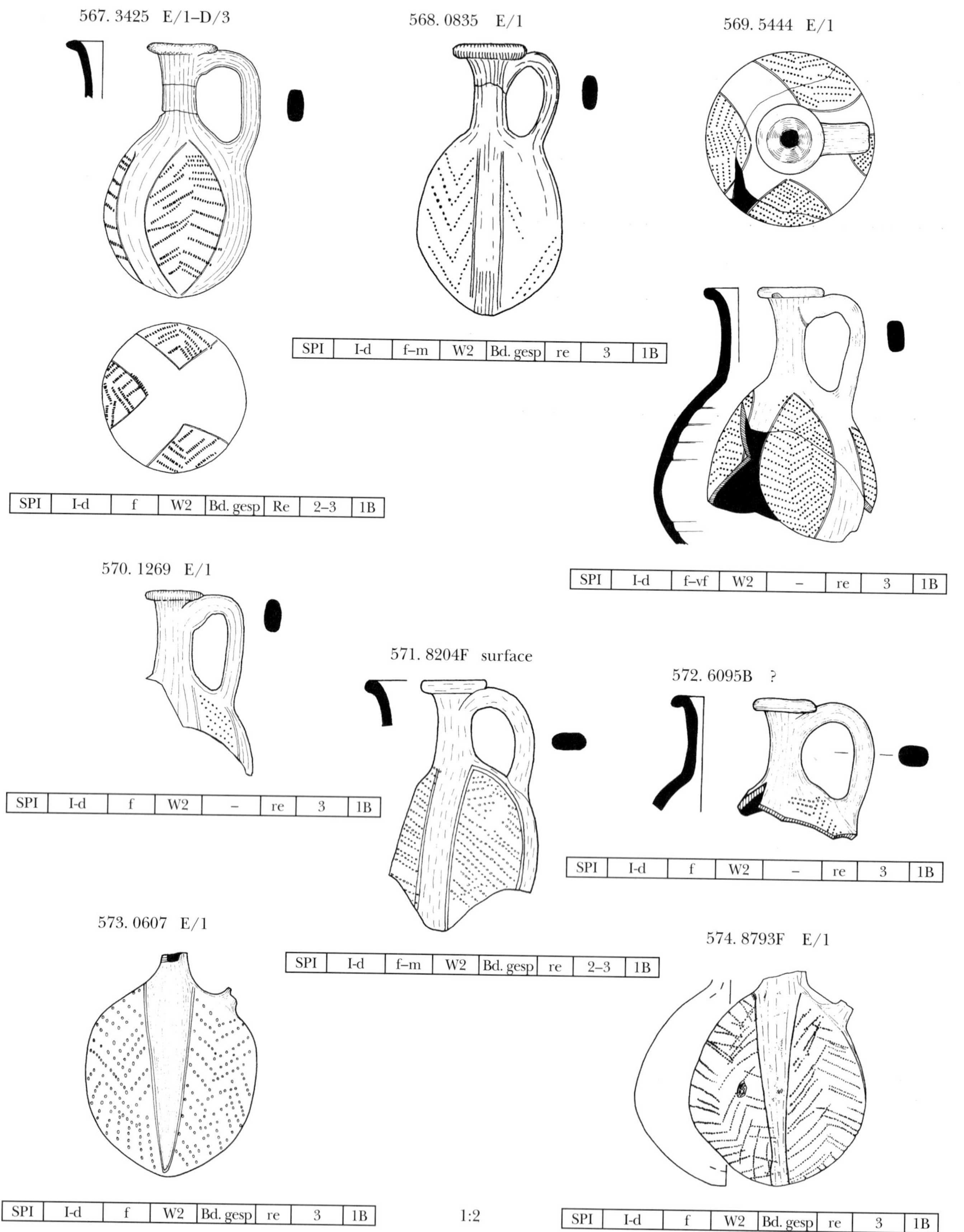

Late Egyptian Type Group L.9.4a

Plate 101

Intact
Surface colour: 10YR5/2 grey brown; burnished slip: 5YR3/2 dark red brown
Break: not visible
Decoration: Three lozenges with infilled chevrons made with a twelve-toothed comb.
Previously published: *TD V*, 182, 183.

567. 3425 Cairo A/II-p/21 grave 15 Phase E/1–D/3 (81/068) Plate 101

SPI	I-d	f	W2	Bd. gesp	Re	2–3	1B

D. 2.7 cm. Nd 1.3 cm. H. 9.5 cm. Md. 5.6 cm. Wd. 0.3 cm.
VI 58.94
Intact
Surface colour: 5YR4/1 dark grey; burnished slip: 5YR3/1 very dark grey
Break: not visible
Decoration: Three lozenges with infilled chevrons made with a twelve-toothed comb.
Previously published: *TD V*, 230.

568. 0835 Vienna A2607 A/III planum 2–3 Phase E/1 (67/015) Plates 101, 150

SPI	I-d	f–m	W2	Bd. gesp	re	3	1B

D. 2.3 cm. Nd 1.0 cm. H. 10.1 cm. Md. 5.5 cm. Wd. 0.3 cm.
VI 54.45
Intact
Surface colour: 2.5Y7/1 light grey; burnished slip: 2.5Y5/1 grey
Break: not visible
Decoration: Three lozenges with infilled zigzags made with a twelve-toothed comb.

569. 5444 TD A/II-k/17 grave 30 burial 1 Phase E/1 (82/275) Plate 101

SPI	I-d	f–vf	W2	–	re	3	1B

D. 2.6 cm. Nd. 1.1 cm. pht. 9.5 cm. Md. 6.5 cm. Wd. 0.35 cm.
Incomplete
Surface colour: 10YR4/1 grey; burnished slip: 2.5YR3/0 very dark grey
Break: grey core, dark grey reduction zones
Decoration: Four lozenges infilled with horizontal chevrons made with a twelve-toothed comb. Undecorated parts vertically burnished. Rim horizontally burnished.
Previously published: *TD XVI*, 248, fig. 184, no. 12.

570. 1269 Vienna A2855 A/II-n/11 grave 3 Phase E/1 (68/029) Plate 101

SPI	I-d	f	W2	–	re	3	1B

D. 2.2 cm. Nd. 1.12 cm. pht. 7.8 cm. Md. 6.0 cm. Wd. 0.35 cm.
Incomplete
Surface colour: 10YR5/2 grey brown; burnished slip: 10YR3/1 very dark grey
Break: dark grey core, grey brown reduction zones
Decoration: not discernible.
Previously published: *TD V*, 234, 235.

571. 8204F TD A/IV-dep planum 0–1 surface (93/684) Plate 101

SPI	I-d	f–m	W2	Bd. gesp	re	2–3	1B

D. 2.7 cm. Nd. 1.3 cm. pht. 9.7 cm. Md. 6.5 cm. Wd. 0.3 cm.
Incomplete
Surface colour: 7.5YRN5.5 dark grey; burnished slip: 5YR6/4–6 light reddish brown
Break: grey in, brown reduction zones out
Decoration: Three lozenges infilled with chrevrons made with an eight-toothed comb.

572. 6095B TD F/I-o/21 near grave 11 Phase ? (87/248) Plate 101

SPI	I-d	f	W2	–	re	3	1B

D. 2.5 cm. Nd. 1.1 cm. pht. 5.0 cm. Wd. 0.4 cm.
Incomplete
Surface colour: 10YR4/1 very dark grey; burnished slip: 10YR4/1 very dark grey
Break: black in, dark grey out
Decoration: Three (?) lozenges (two preserved) infilled with chevrons made with an eight-toothed comb.

573. 0607 Vienna A2430 A/II-m/10 planum 3 Phase E/1 (67/096) Plate 101

SPI	I-d	f	W2	Bd. gesp	re	3	1B

Nd. 1.0 cm. pht. 7.9 cm. Md. 6.5 cm. Wd. 0.3 cm.
Incomplete
Surface colour: 10YR5/4 yellow brown; burnished slip: 10YR5/1 grey
Break: not visible
Decoration: Three lozenges with infilled zigzags made with an eight-toothed comb.
Previously published: *TD V*, 187, 189.

574. 8793F TD A/II-p/13 planum 3 Phase E/1 (98/098) Plate 101

SPI	I-d	f	W2	Bd. gesp	re	3	1B

Nd. 1.6 cm. pht. 8.2 cm. Md. 6.95 cm. Wd. 0.3 cm.
Incomplete
Surface colour: 10YR5/2–3 grey brown; burnished slip: 10YR3/1 very dark grey
Break: wide grey core, thin light brown reduction zones
Decoration: Three delineated lozenges, two filled with tripartite lozenges and one with horizontal V-chevrons made with a twelve-toothed comb somewhat carelessly.

575. 7249 TD stray find (89/097) Plate 102

SPI	I-d	f–vf	W2	Bd. gesp	re	3	1B

Nd. 1.1 cm. pht. 6.6 cm. Md. 5.7 cm. Wd. 0.3 cm.
Incomplete
Surface colour: 10YR5/2 grey brown; burnished slip: 10YR3/1 very dark grey
Break: dark grey core, grey brown reduction zones
Decoration: Three lozenges with infilled zigzags made with a twelve-toothed comb.

576. 2065 Vienna A3390 A/II-o/12 planum 2–3 Phase E/1 (69/030) Plate 102

SPI	I-d	f–m	W2	Bd. gesp	re	3	1B

Nd. 1.2 cm. pht. 7.0 cm. Md. 6.4 cm. Wd. 0.35 cm.
Incomplete
Surface colour: 10YR5/2 grey brown; burnished slip: 10YR3/1 very dark grey

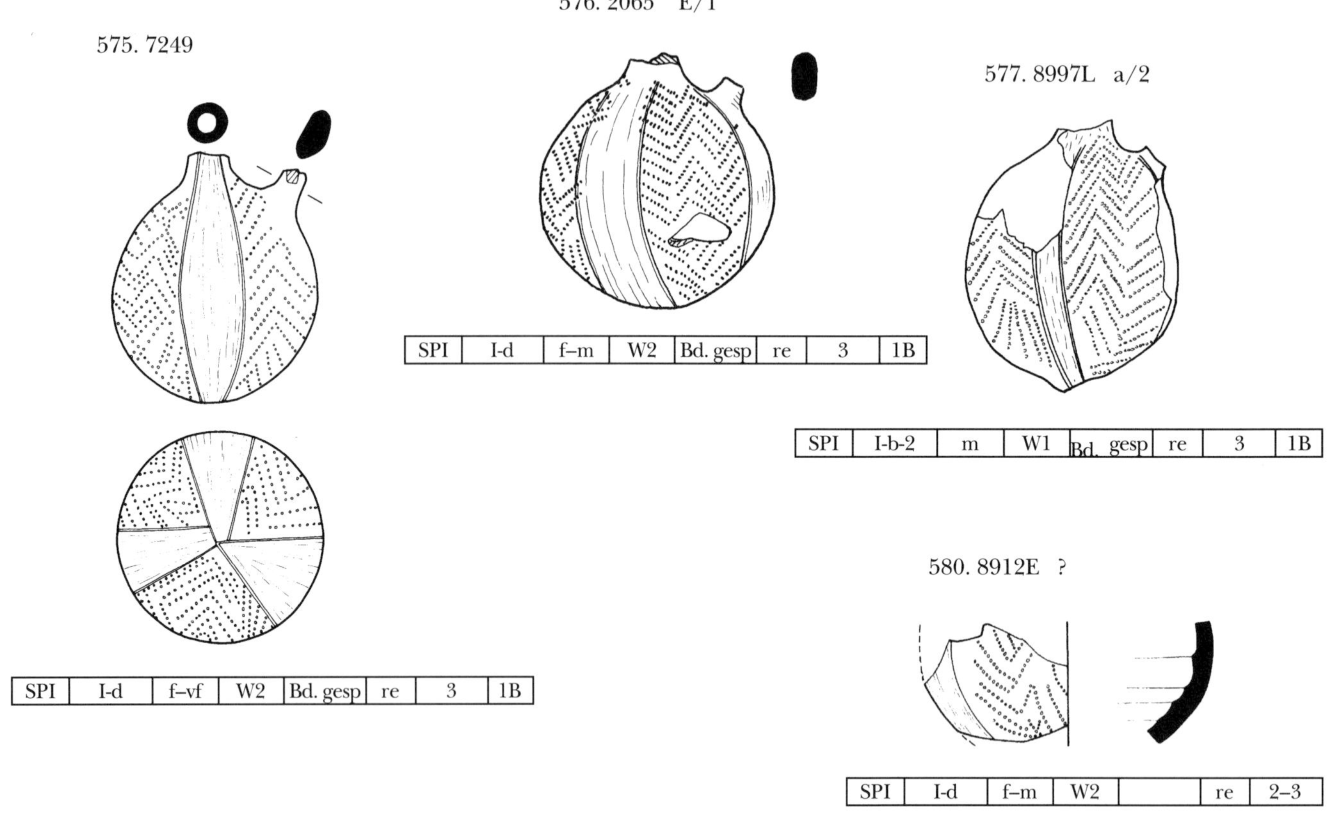

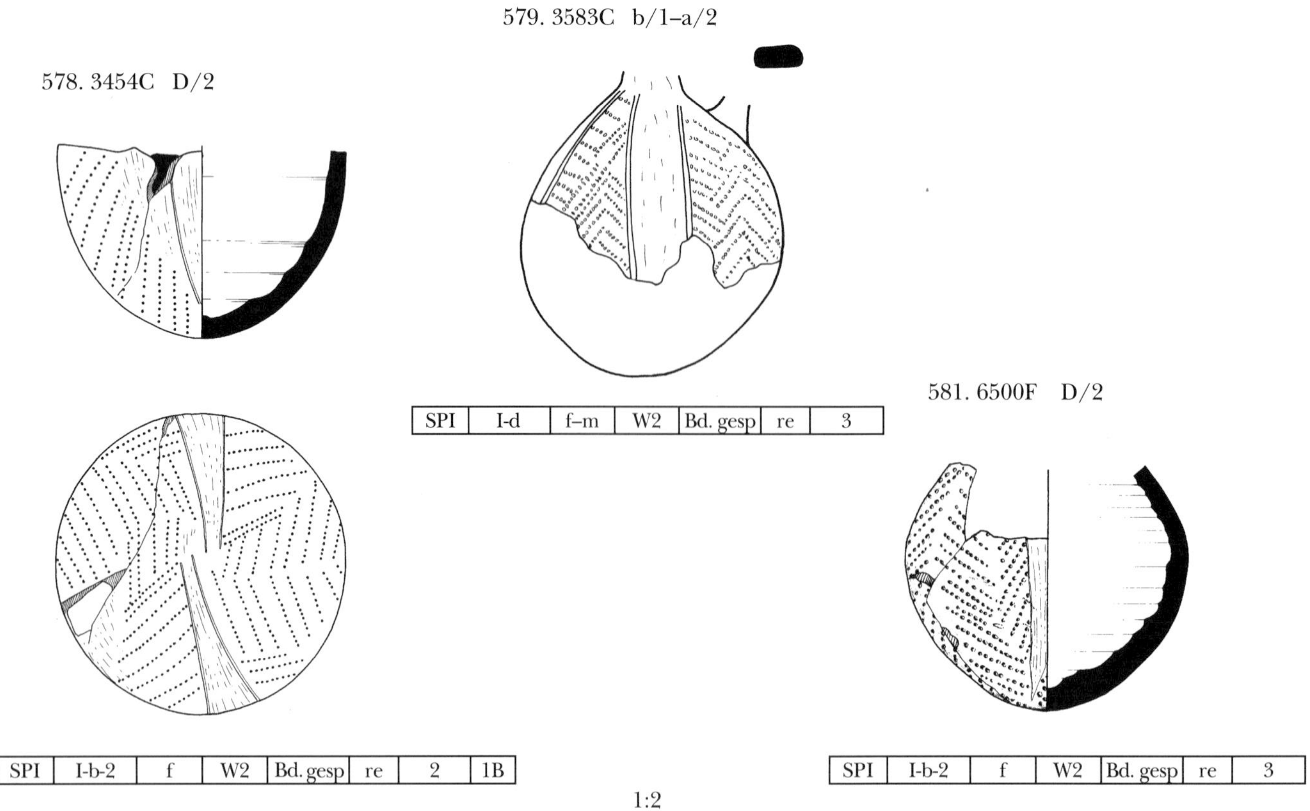

1:2

Late Egyptian Type Group L.9.4a

Plate 102

Break: dark grey core, grey brown reduction zones
Decoration: three lozenges with infilled zigzags made with a twelve-toothed comb.

577. 8997L TD F/II-r/22 L81 Phase a/2 (06/284)
Plate 102

SPI	I-b-2	m	W1	Bd. gesp	re	3	1B

Nd. 1.6 cm. pht. 8.2 cm. Md. 7.4 cm. Wd. 0.3 cm.
Incomplete
Surface colour: 5YR5/1 gray; burnished slip: 5YR4/1 dark gray
Break: uniform brownish black
Decoration: Four lozenges infilled with zigzags made with a ten-toothed comb.

578. 3454C TD A/II-l/17 grave 2 Phase D/2 (81/270)
Plate 102

SPI	I-b-2	f	W2	Bd. gesp	re	2	1B

Nd. 1.2 cm. pht. 7.4 cm. Md. 5.85 cm. Wd. 0.4 cm.
Incomplete
Surface colour: 10YR5/2 grey brown; burnished slip: 10YR3/1 very dark grey
Break: dark grey core, grey brown reduction zones
Decoration: Three delineated lozenges filled with tripartite chevrons made with a twelve-toothed comb. Intervening areas vertically burnished.
Surface poorly preserved.

579. 3583C TD F/I-i/22 grave 1 Phase b/1–a/2 (81/167)
Plate 102

SPI	I-d	f–m	W2	Bd. gesp	re	3

pht. 5.5 cm. Md. 8.0 cm. Wd. 0.55 cm.
Incomplete
Surface colour: 7.5YR5.5 dark grey; burnished slip: 10YR6/2–3 light brownish grey
Break: uniform dark grey
Decoration: Two lozenges filled with horizontal zigzags made with a sixteen-toothed comb

580. 8912E TD H/VIN-j/17 planum 0–1 Phase ? (00/118)
Plate 102

SPI	I-d	f–m	W2	–	re	2–3

pht. 2.0 cm. Wd. 0.5 cm.
Incomplete
Surface colour: 5Y5/1 grey; burnished slip: 7.5YR4/1 dark grey
Break: uniform dark grey
Decoration: One lozenge preserved filled with chevrons made with a multi-toothed comb

581. 6500F TD A/V-n/17, planum 1–2 Phase D/2 (88/167)
Plate 102

SPI	I-b-2	f	W2	Bd. gesp	re	3

pht. 6.8 cm. Md. 7.7 cm. Wd. 0.4 cm.
Incomplete
Surface colour: 7.5YR5.5 dark grey; burnished slip: 10YR6/2–3 light brownish grey
Break: uniform dark grey
Decoration: Three lozenges with infilled zigzags made with a twelve-toothed comb.
Previously published: TD XI, 82–83 no. 15.

Type Group L.9.5

Type Group L.9.5a

582. 8446M TD H/III-q/19, planum 3–5 disturbed area (95/108) Plate 103

SPI	I-b-2	f	W2	Bd. gesp	re	3

pht. 4.0 cm. Wd. 0.8 cm.
Incomplete
Surface colour: 7.5YRN5.5 dark grey; burnished slip: 7.5YRN/3 very dark grey
Break: uniform dark grey
Decoration: Three lozenges infilled with chrevrons made with an eight-toothed comb.

583. 5228R TD F/I-k/22s planum 0–1 Phase a/2 (85/150)
Plate 103

SPI	I-d	f	W2	Bd. gesp	re	3	1B

pht. 4.0 cm. Md. 6.2 cm. Wd. 0.9 cm.
Incomplete
Surface colour: 10YR4/2 dark grey brown; burnished slip: not preserved
Break: uniform black
Decoration: Zigzags made with an eighteen-toothed comb.

Type Group L.9.6 Large Globular Jugs

Large globular jugs with a rolled rim, strap handle, drop shaped body and a total height of around 28–30 cms. are not common, but since such vessels were not deposited in tombs, their chances of preservation are much less. Nevertheless examples are known from Tell el-Dab^c^a, where, with one exception, they are all similarly decorated with two zones separated by a wide band at the middle, L.9.6a. The uppermost zone consists of delineated triangles and the lower one, delineated pendant triangles. A single example, L.9.6b, is decorated with bands infilled with verical chevrons.

Type Group L.9.6a

584. 8887B TD A/II-p/13 profile Phase D/2 (98/257)
Plates 103, 151

SPI	I-d	f–m	W2	Bd. gesp	re	2–3	1B

Nd. 2.8 cm. pht. 20.0 cm. Md. 14.1 cm. Wd. 0.6 cm.
Incomplete
Surface colour: 10YR4/2 dark grey
Break: uniform grey brown
Decoration: Upper zone of four standing triangles and lower zone of four pendant triangles infilled with horizontal zigzags made with a twelve-toothed comb. No traces of burnishing.
Previously published: Kopetzky, *The MB IIB-Corpus of the Hyksos Period at Tell el-Dab^c^a*, 2007, 199 fig. 4.1.

585. 9019Z TD F/II-r/23 L81/6 Phase a/2 (08/096) Plate 104

SPI	I-b-2	f–m	W2	Bd. gesp	re	3	1B

Nd. 2.4 cm. pht. 15.5 cm. Md. 12.8 cm. Wd. 0.55 cm.
Incomplete
Surface colour: 5YR4/1 dark gray; burnish 10R2.5/1 very dark grey

583. 5228R a/2

582. 8446M

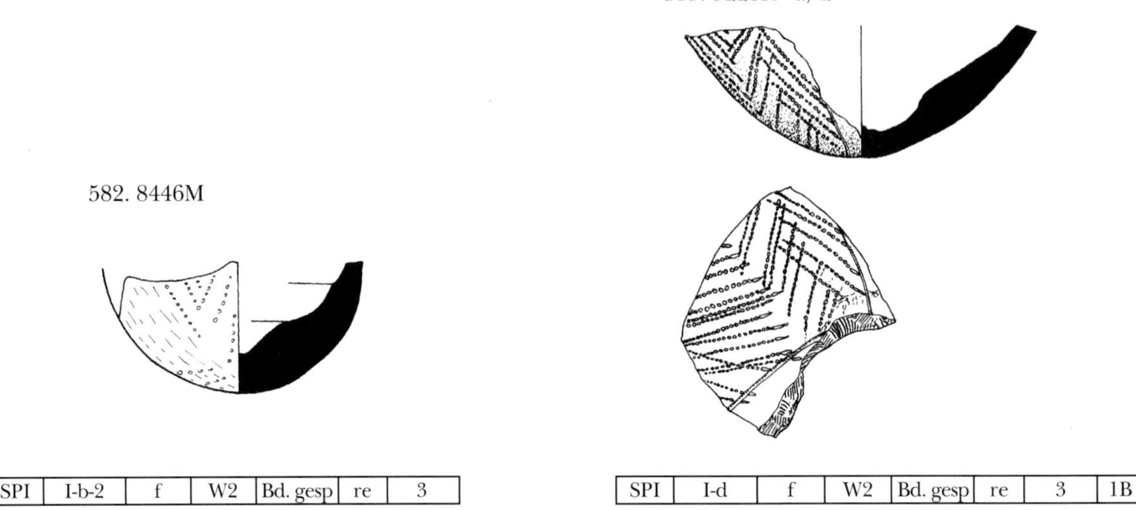

SPI	I-b-2	f	W2	Bd. gesp	re	3

SPI	I-d	f	W2	Bd. gesp	re	3	1B

584. 8887B D/2

SPI	I-d	f–m	W2	Bd. gesp	re	2–3	1B

1:2

Late Egyptian Type Groups L.9.5a, L.9.6a

Plate 103

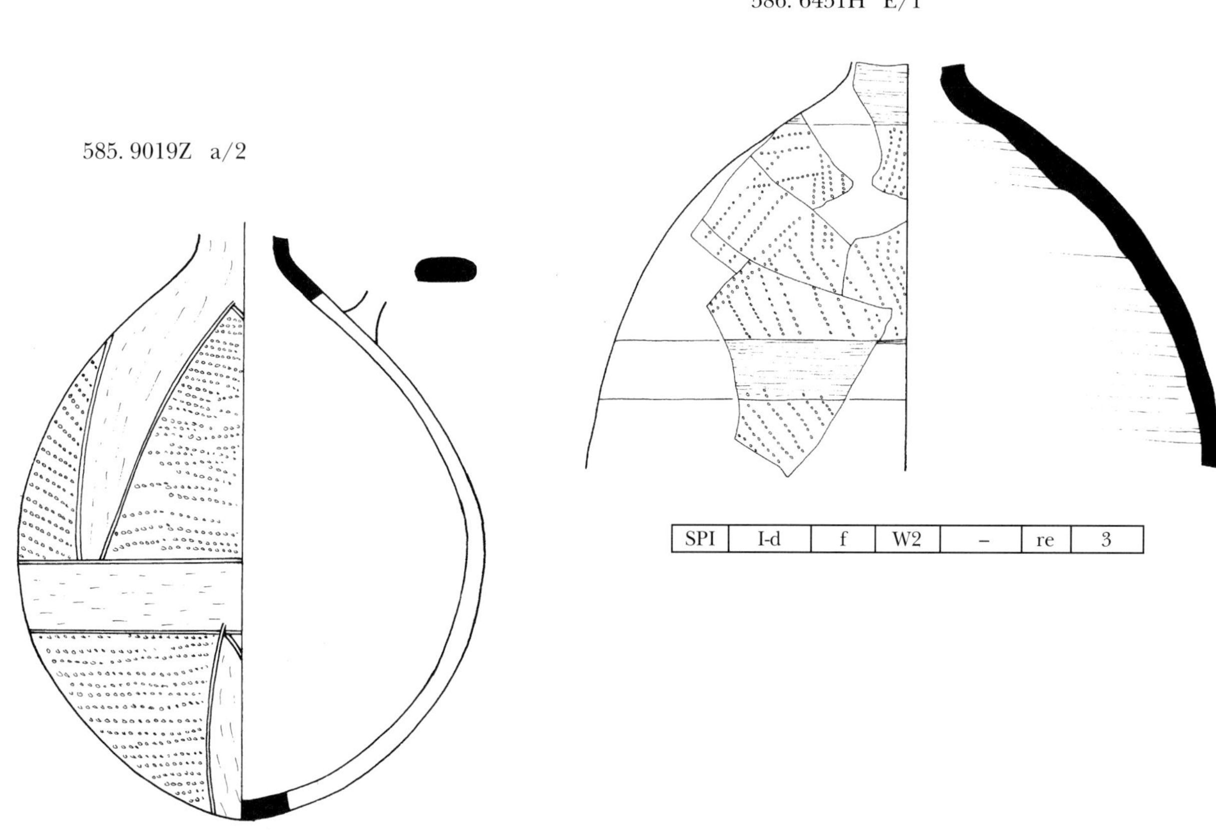

586. 6451H E/1

SPI	I-d	f	W2	–	re	3

585. 9019Z a/2

SPI	I-b-2	f–m	W2	Bd. gesp	re	3	1B

587. 6136E D/2

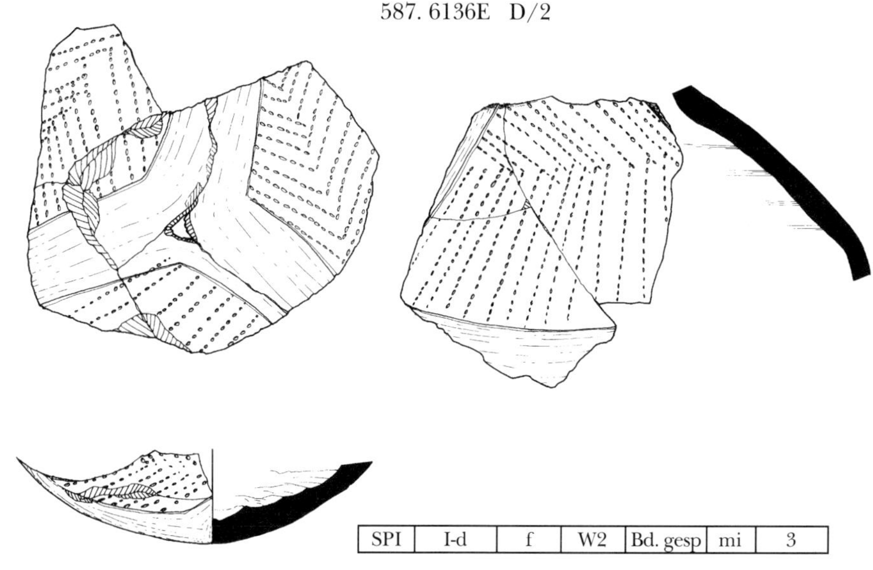

SPI	I-d	f	W2	Bd. gesp	mi	3

1:2

Late Egyptian Type Groups L.9.6a

Plate 104

Break: dark grey core, light grey reduction zones
Decoration: Upper zone of five standing triangles and lower zone of zone of four pendant triangles infilled with carelessly made horizontal zigzags punctured with a fourteen-toothed comb. No traces of burnishing.

586. 6451H TD A/II-k/16 planum 4 Phase E/1 (88/122)
Plate 104

SPI	I-d	f	W2	–	re	3

pht. 9.4 cm. Md. 17.6 cm. Wd. 0.6 cm.
Incomplete
Surface colour: 10YR4/2 dark grey; burnished slip: 10YR4/1 very dark grey
Break: dark reddish grey core, light grey and dark grey reduction zones
Decoration: Presumably similar to TD 8887B, vertical zigzags made with a sixteen toothed-comb.

587. 6136E TD A/V-p/17 planum 2 Phase D/2 (88/429)
Plate 104

SPI	I-d	f	W2	Bd. gesp	mi	3

pht. 2.5 cm. base 2.2 cm., shoulder 4.7 cm. Md. 11.4 cm. Wd. 0.6 cm.
Incomplete
Surface colour: 10YR5/1 grey; burnished slip: 10YR4/2 dark greyish brown
Break: red brown core, blackish reduction zones
Decoration: comprises (four ?) standing triangles above the maximum point and three pendant triangles below, each filled with horizontal chevrons made with a sixteen-toothed comb.
Previously published: TD XI, 112–113 nos. 5–6.

588. 6783F TD A/V-o/18 planum 1–2 Phase D/2 (88/405)
Plate 105

SPI	I-d	f	W2	Bd. gef	re	3	1B

pht. 7.5 cm. Wd. 0.5 cm.
Incomplete
Surface colour: 2.5YR3/0 very dark grey; burnished slip: 10YR3.5/1 very dark grey
Break: light grey core, dark brown reduction zones
Decoration: Remains of two standing triangles haphazardly infilled by means of a twelve-toothed comb.
Previously published: TD XI, 112 no. 1.

Type Group L.9.6b

589. 9012M TD F/II-r/22 L81 Phase a/2 (06/569)
Plates 105, 151

SPI	I-d	f	W2	Bd. gesp	re	3	1B

Nd. 3.0 cm. pht. 17.3 cm. Md. 14.0 cm. Wd. 0.5 cm.
Incomplete
Surface colour: 7.5YR5/1 gray; burnished slip: 5YR4/1 dark gray
Break: uniform brownish black
Decoration: Three horizontal bands infilled with vertical zigzags or chevrons made with a sixteen-toothed comb.

Type Group L.10. Late Egyptian X. Quadrilobal Jugs

Only two quadrilobal jugs have been found at Tell el-Dabᶜa, and in their body proportions they are similar to the globular jugs of type group L.9, and like them, have rolled rims and strap handles. What sets them apart, however, is that the body is indented in such a manner as to form four lobes. The incised decoration outlines each of these lobes.

Type Group L.10.1a

590. 0226 Cairo JE 91183 A/II-l/12 grave 1 Phase E/1 (66/031) Plate 106

SPI	I-d	f	W+M	Bd. m	re	2–3	1B

D. 3.0 cm. Nd. 1.2 cm. H. 10.2 cm. Md. 7.0 cm. Wd. 0.3 cm.
Intact
Surface colour: 10YR3/1 very dark grey; burnished slip: 7.5YR4/2 dark reddish grey
Break: dark grey core, grey brown reduction zones
Decoration: Underside of base lobes surrounded by a band of decoration made with a four-toothed comb.
Previously published: Bietak, *MDAIK* 23 fig 8 tf xxix; Kaplan, *Tell el-Yahudiyeh Ware,* fig. 22d; *TD V,* 176, 178; *PuF* 230 nr 279.

Type Group L.10.1b

591. 0244 Vienna 1407 A/II-l/13 grave 2 Phase E/1 (66/014)
Plates 106, 151

SPI	I-d	f	W+M	Bd. m	re	2–3	1B

D. 3.4 cm. Nd. 1.5 cm. H. 12.4 cm. Md. 7.6 cm. Wd. 0.3 cm.
Intact
Surface colour: 10YR4/2 dark greyish brown; burnished slip: 10YR2/2 black
Break: uniform grey
Decoration: Lines impressed with an eight-toothed comb outlining the lobes and over base.
Previously published: TD XVI, 249, fig 185, no. 1.

L.11. Late Egyptian XI (Kaplan's Cylindrical 1)

Two examples of this type are known at Tell el-Dabᶜa, both of which are broken off at the base of the neck. They consist of Cylindrical 1 jugs with ring bases, and in the case of the two examples from Tell el-Dabᶜa (TD 2583D, 3438) are decorated with vertical chevrons (L.11.1a).

Type Group L.11.1a

592. 2583D TD A/II-m/15 planum 8 Phase ? (76/015)
Plate 106

SPI	I-d	f–m	W2	Bd. gef	re	2–3	1B

Nd. 1.3 cm. Bd. 3.7 cm. pht. 7.0 cm. Md. 5.2 cm. Wd. 0.3 cm.
Incomplete
Surface colour: 10YR4/2 dark greyish brown; burnished slip: 5Y2/1 black
Break: uniform grey
Decoration: Horizontal zigzags made with a sixteen-toothed comb.

593. 3438 Cairo A/II-o/21 grave 4 Phase D/3 (81/115)
Plates 106, 152

SPI	I-d	f	W2	Bd. gef	re	3	1B

588. 6783F D/2

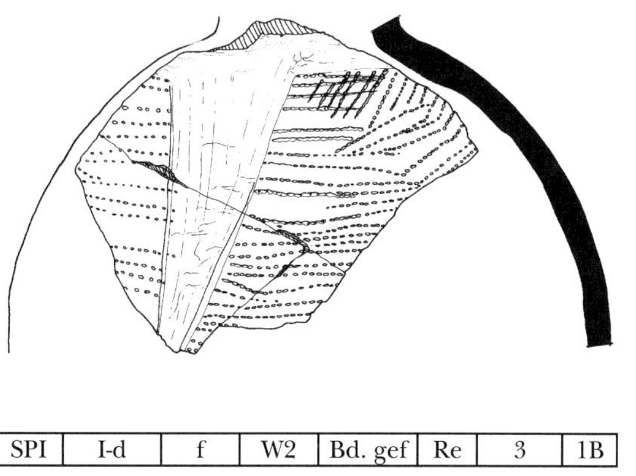

SPI	I-d	f	W2	Bd. gef	Re	3	1B

589. 9012M a/2

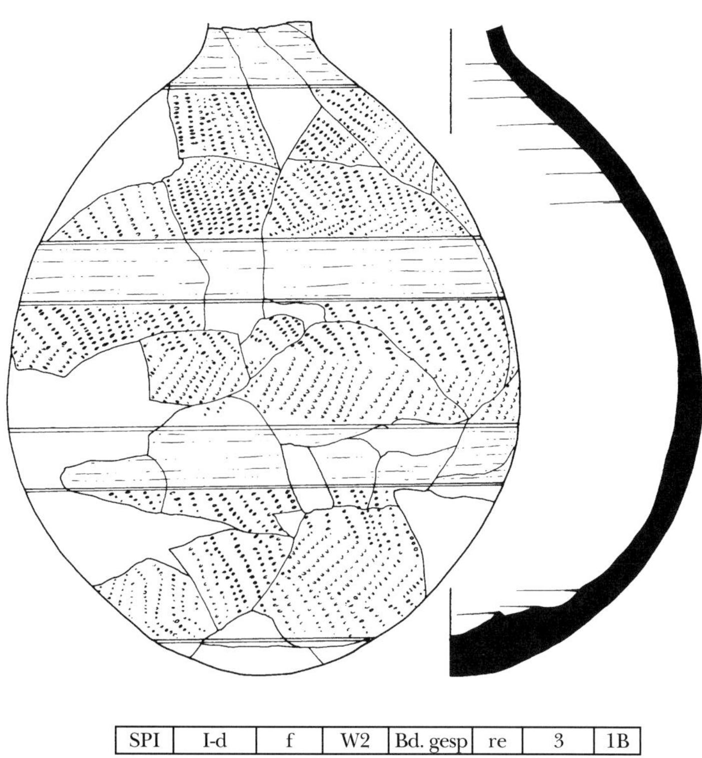

SPI	I-d	f	W2	Bd. gesp	re	3	1B

1:2

Late Egyptian Type Groups L.9.6a–b

Plate 105

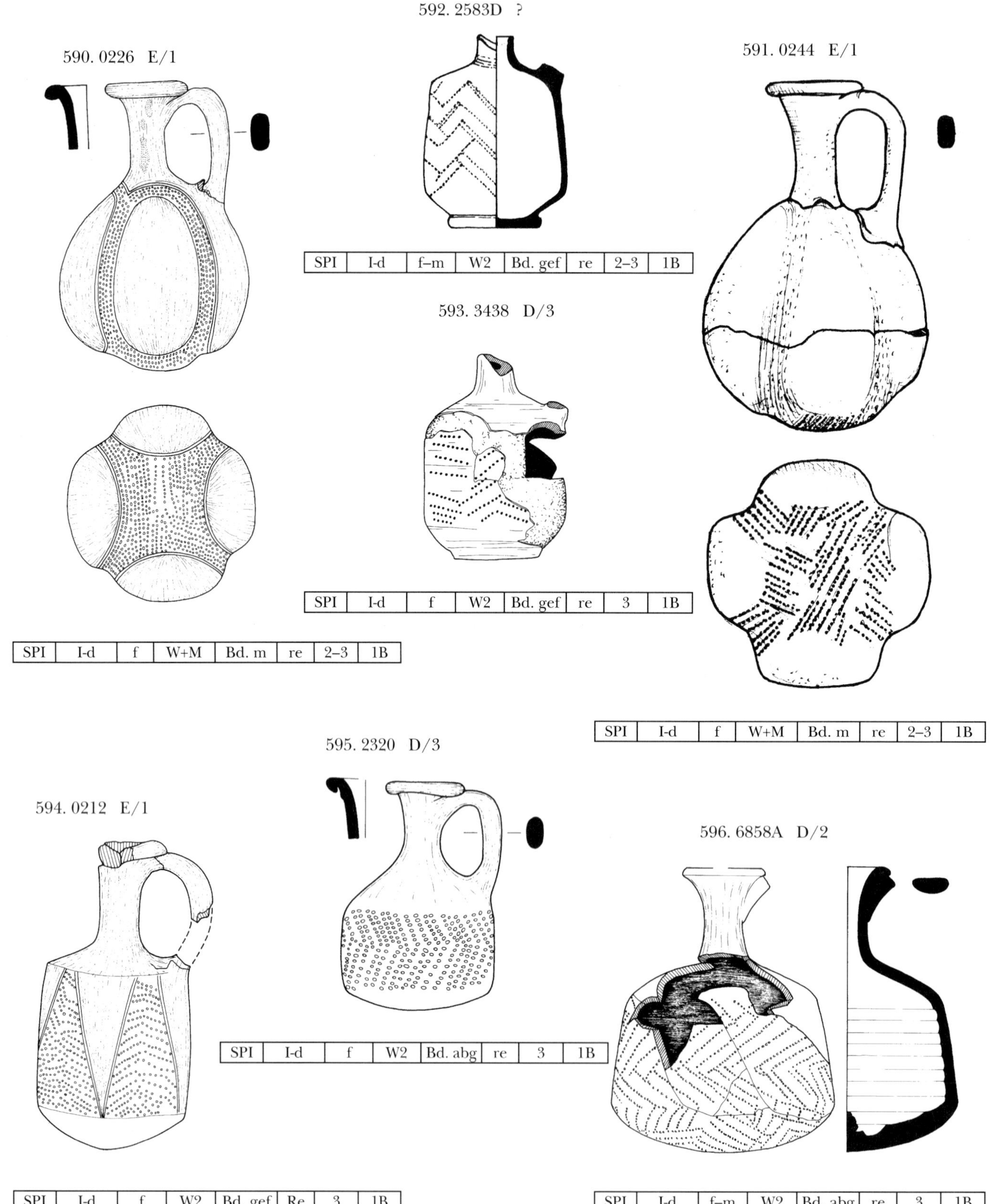

1:2

Late Egyptian Type Groups L.10.1a, L.11.1a, L.12.2a

Plate 106

Nd. 1.3 cm. Bd. 3.5 cm. pht. 7.4 cm. Md. 5.5 cm. Wd. 0.3 cm.
VI 74.32
Incomplete
Surface colour: 10YR4/2 dark greyish brown; burnished slip: 5Y2/1 black
Break: uniform greyish brown
Decoration: Horizontal zigzags made with an eight-toothed comb.

Type Group L.12.1

The single example of this type, TD 212 is decorated with a series of standing triangles.

594. 0212 Vienna A2222 A/II-l/12 grave 1 Phase E/1 (66/031) Plates 106, 151

SPI	I-d	f	W2	Bd. gef	Re	3	1B

D. 3.2 cm. Nd. 1.5 cm. Bd. 5.4 cm. H. 11.0 cm. Md. 5.9 cm. Wd. 0.4 cm.
VI 53.63
Incomplete
Surface colour: 10YR5/2 grey brown; burnished slip: 10YR3/1–2 very dark grey
Break: uniform grey
Decoration: Five standing triangles with poorly executed horizontal chevrons made with an eight-toothed comb.
Previously published: Bietak, *Bustan* 9.1, pl. 13 second from right, Idem, *MDAIK* 23, pl. 28a; Kaplan, *Tell el-Yahudiyeh Ware,* fig. 6e; *TD V,* 177, 179; Kopetzky., *The MB IIB-Corpus of the Hyksos Period at Tell el-Dab^{c}a,* 2007, 198 fig. 3.9.

Type Group L.12.2

This group comprises the classic Cylindrical 1 jug as defined by Kaplan and are relatively common at Tell el-Dab^{c}a, though the only decorative styles found are L.12.2a horizontal chevrons, and L.12.2d horizontal striations.

Type Group L.12.2a

595. 2320 Cairo JE 91712 A/II-m/15 grave 3 Phase D/3 (69/110) Plate 106

SPI	I-d	f	W2	Bd. abg	re	3	1B

D. 2.95. Nd. 1.2 cm. Bd. 5.3 cm. H. 8.3 cm. Md. 5.75 cm. Wd. 0.4 cm.
VI 69.27
Intact
Surface colour: 10YR6/2–4 light brownish grey–pale brown; burnished slip: 10YR3/1 very dark grey
Break: not visible
Decoration: Broad band of vertical chevrons pointing right mase with an eight-toothed comb.
Previously published: *TD V,* 177, 179; *TD XVI,* 315, fig. 235, no. 25.

596. 6858A TD A/V-o/18 planum 1–2 Phase D/2 (88/414) Plate 106

SPI	I-d	f	W2	Bd. abg	re	3	1B

D. 2.9. Nd. 1.4 cm. Bd. 8.2 cm. H. 10.5 cm. Md. 8.2 cm. Wd. 0.35 cm.
VI 78.09
Incomplete
Surface colour: 5YR4/1 dark grey–pale brown; burnished slip: 10YR3/1 very dark grey
Break: reddish grey core, grey reduction zones
Decoration: One band of undelineated vertical zigzags on body which continues on underside of base, made with an eighteen-toothed comb.
Previously published: *TD XI,* 139–140 no. 3, pl. xxxF; Kopetzky, *The MB IIB-Corpus of the Hyksos Period at Tell el-Dab^{c}a,* 2007, 198, fig. 3.11.

597. 0498 Vienna A2354 A/II-l/10 planum 1–2 Phase E/2 (67/032) Plate 107

SPI	I-d	f–m	W2	Bd. abg	re	3	1B

Nd. 1.3 cm. Bd. 4.8 cm. pht. 6.5 cm. Md. 5.1 cm. Wd. 0.3 cm.
Incomplete
Surface colour: 10YR4/1 dark grey–pale brown; burnished slip: 10YR3/1 very dark grey
Break: uniform grey
Decoration: One band of undelineated vertical chevrons pointing left on body which continues on underside of base, made with an eighteen-toothed comb. Burnished only on the shoulder.

598. 7940M TD A/IV-j/7 planum 0–1 Phase ? (93/052) Plate 107

SPI	I-d	f–m	W2	Bd. abg	re	3–4	1B

Nd. 2.7 cm. Bd. 9.3 cm. pht. 9.2 cm. Md. 10.4 cm. Wd. 0.5 cm.
Incomplete
Surface colour: 10YR7/2 light grey–pale brown; burnished slip: 10YR5/2 grey brown
Break: dark grey in, reddish grey out
Decoration: Vertical chevrons on body pointing right made with a 22-toothed comb. Base undecorated. Burnished only on the shoulder.

599. 6128I TD A/V-q/16 planum 0–1 Phase D/3–2 (88/430) Plate 107

SPI	I-d	f–m	W2	Bd. abg	re	3	1B

Bd. 8.5 cm. pht. 4.6 cm. Wd. 0.6 cm.
Incomplete
Surface colour: 10R5/1 reddish grey; burnished slip: not preserved
Break: reddish grey core, grey reduction zones
Decoration: Oblique lines of dots made with a twelve-toothed comb.
Previously published: *TD XI,* 175 no. 3.

Type group L.12.2d

600. 0228 Vienna A1408 A/II-l/12 grave 1 Phase E/1 (69/006) Plates 107

SPI	I-d	f	W2	Bd. gef	re	3	1B

D. 3.3 cm. Nd. 1.3 cm. Bd. 6.25 cm. H. 10.1 cm. Md. 6.5 cm. Wd. 0.5 cm.
VI 64.35
Intact
Surface colour: 10YR4/1 grey brown; burnished slip: 10YR2–3/1 very dark grey

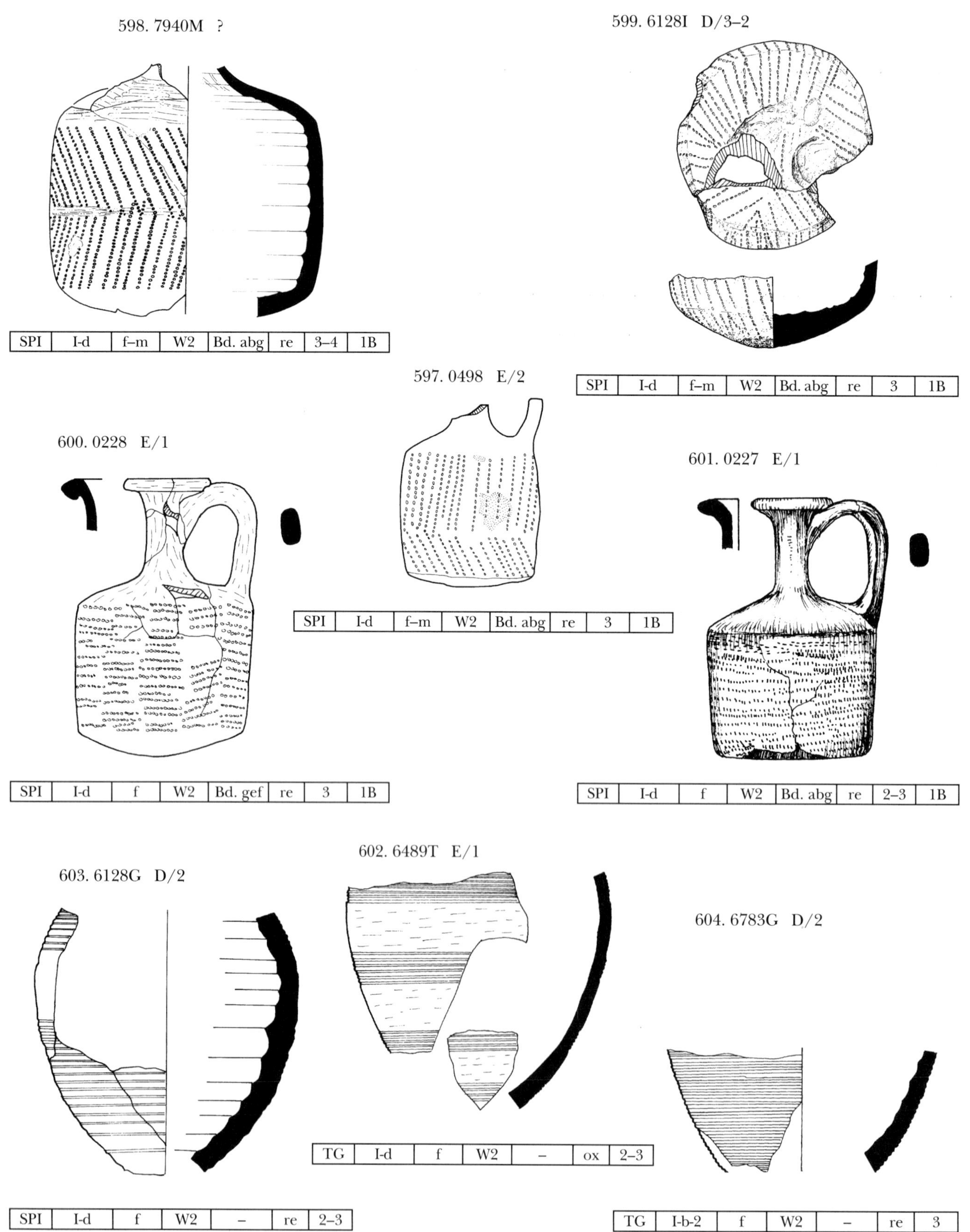

1:2

Late Egyptian Type Groups L.12.2a, L.12.2d, L.13.1

Plate 107

Break: uniform grey
Decoration: series of short horizontal lines running around the body of the vessel made with a twelve-toothed comb.
Previously published: BIETAK, *MDAIK* 23, pl. 29a; FA 83 H18; AP pl xxxd; KAPLAN, *Tell el-Yahudiyeh Ware,* fig. 6c; *TD V,* 177, 179; *PuF,* 226 nr. 26.

601. 0227 Cairo JE 91182 A/II-l/12 grave 1 Phase E/1 (66/032) Plate 107, 152

SPI	I-d	f	W2	Bd. abg	re	2–3	1B

D. 3.0 cm. Nd. 1.25 cm. Bd. 5.8 cm. H. 10.0 cm. Md. 6.45 cm. Wd. 0.4 cm.
VI 64.50
Intact
Surface colour: 10YR5/2 grey brown; burnished slip: 10YR3/1 very dark grey
Break: uniform grey
Decoration: series of short horizontal lines running around the body of the vessel made with a twelve-toothed comb.
Previously published: BIETAK, *Bustan,* 9.1 pl. 13, third from left; Idem, *MDAIK* 23, pl. 29 a–b; KAPLAN, *Tell el-Yahudiyeh Ware,* fig. 6a; *TD V,* 178; KOPETZKY K., *The MB IIB-Corpus of the Hyksos Period at Tell el-Dabᶜa,* 2007, 198 fig. 3.10.

Type Group L.13

During the latest phase of the Hyksos Period, Tell el-Yahudiya ware developed into its final decorative phase, a series of incised grooves, in which no pigment was added, running horizontally around the body of the vessel, the grooving almost certainly being made on the wheel. The examples found at Tell el-Dabᶜa can be assigned mostly to the biconical type, L.13.2, but the incomplete pieces, TD 6128G, 6489T, 6783G are probably to be seen as piriform vessels, group L.13.1.

Type Group L.13.1 Piriform

602. 6489T TD A/V-p/19 planum 7 Phase E/1 (88/184) Plate 107
pht. 6.4 cm. Wd. 0.5 cm.

TG	I-d	f	W2	–	ox	2–3

Incomplete
Surface colour: 5YR4/8 dark reddish brown
Break: wide grey in, thin red and brown oxidation zones out
Decoration: Parallel series of incised lines made with an eight-toothed comb at regular intervals around the shoulder and body of the vessel.
Previously published: TD XI, 30–31 no. 15.

603. 6128G TD A/V-q/17 planum 1 Phase D/2 (94/019) Plate 107
pht. 9.5 cm. Md. 9.7 cm. Wd. 0.6 cm.

SPI	I-d	f	W2	–	re	2–3

Incomplete
Surface colour: 5YR7/1 light grey
Break: wide black core, thin brown reduction zones
Decoration: Horizontally combed on shoulder and lower body, with a wide reserved band at the maximum body diameter. Unusually the reserved band was not burnished.
Heavily wheel ridged in, distinctly piriform.
Previously published: TD XI, 120–121 no. 4; KOPETZKY, *The MB IIB-Corpus of the Hyksos Period at Tell el-Dabᶜa,* 2007, 199 fig. 4.2.

604. 6783G A/V-o/18 planum 1–2 Phase D/2 (88/392) Plate 107

TG	I-b-2	f	W2	–	re	3

pht. 4.5 cm. Wd. 0.6 cm.
Incomplete
Surface colour: 10YR3/1 very dark grey
Break: uniform dark grey
Decoration: Parallel series of incised lines made with a multi-toothed comb, with in the preserved part no reserved bands.
Previously published: TD XI, 126 no. 2.

Type Group L.13.2 Biconical

This is the most common form of Combed Tell el-Yahudiya jugs. Such vessels have a rolled rim, strap handle, a rounded biconial to piriform body and a ring or disc base. The horizontal grooves are separated by a reserved band at the mid-point of the vessel.

605. 6127+6794X A/V-p/18 planum 1–2 + A/V-p/17 surface Phase D/2 (88/402) Plates 108, 152

GP	I-b-2	f	W2	Bd. gef	ox	3	1B

D. 2.8 cm. Nd. 1.7 cm. Bd. 2.0 cm. H. 10.7 cm. Md 8.3 cm. Wd. 0.4 cm.
VI 77.57
Incomplete
Surface colour: 2.5YR5/3 brown; burnished slip 10YR6/4 light red
Break: red core, blackish red oxidation zones
Decoration: Horizontally combed on shoulder and lower body. Reserved zone at mid-point burnished.
Previously published: TD XI, 147 no. 2, pl. xxxiA.

606. 8400 TD H/III-p/18 planum 6 locus 66 Phase D/2 or later. (93/380) Plate 108

GP	I-d	f–vf	W2	–	ox	3	1B

D. 3.7 cm. Nd. 2.0 cm. pht. 12.1 cm. Md 12.3 cm. Wd. 0.4 cm.
Restored from sherds, incomplete
Surface colour: 2.5YR6/6 light red; burnished slip 10R5/6–2.5YR5/6 red
Break: dark grey thin red oxidation zones
Decoration: Combed horizontally on two zones separated by a burnished band 2 cm. wide. Burnished vertically on the neck and handle, horizontally on the rim and on the reserved band at the maximum diameter of the pot.
Previously published: TD X, 82 no. 181.

607. 3402C TD Stray find (80/148) Plates 108, 152

SPI	I-b-2	f	W2	Bd. gef	Re	3	1B

Bd. 2.4 cm. pht. 11.0 cm. Md 10.4 cm. Wd. 0.5 cm.
Restored from sherds, incomplete
Surface colour: 10YR5/3 brown; burnished slip 10YR4/1 dark grey

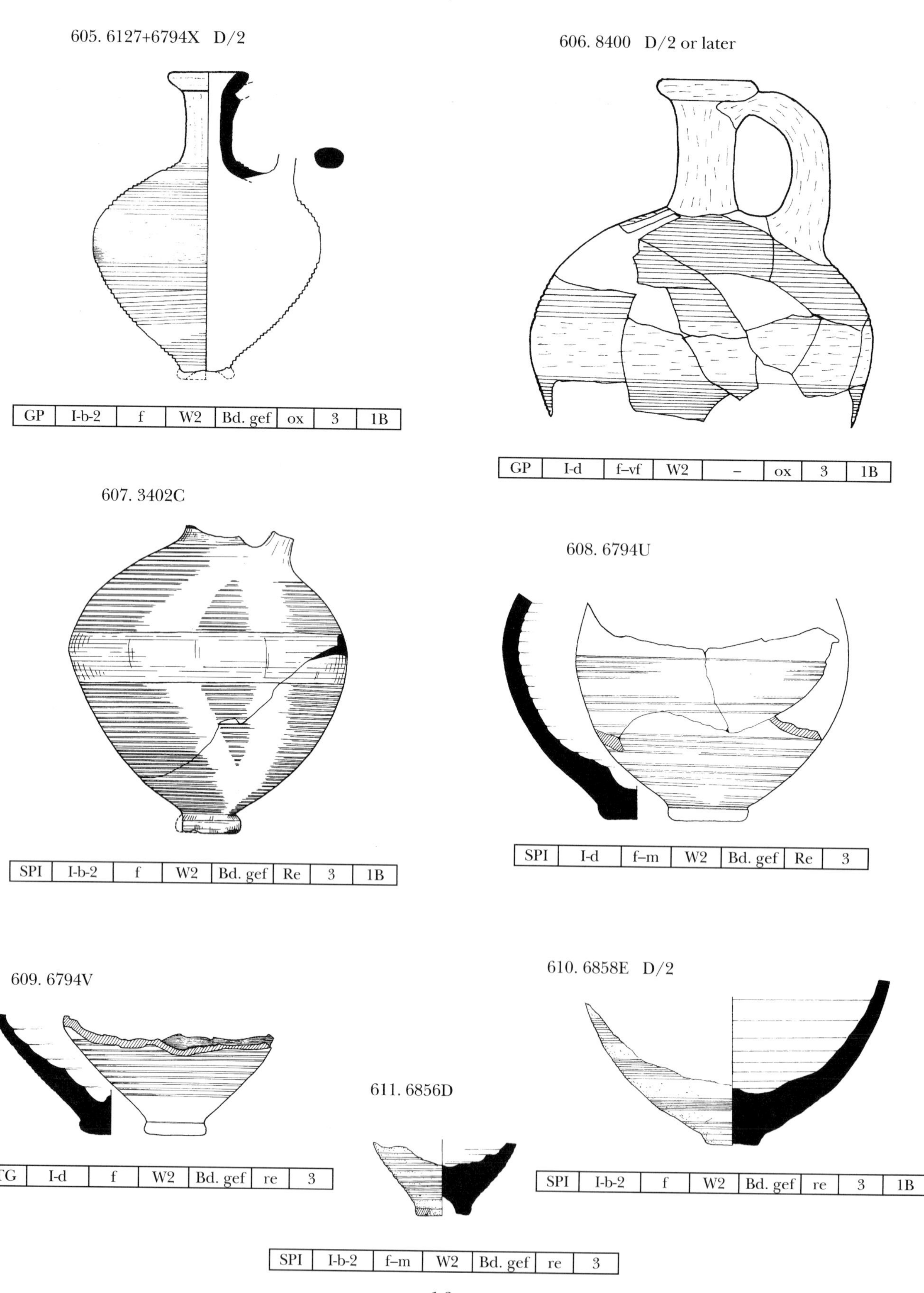

Late Egyptian Type Group L.13.2

Plate 108

Break: uniform dark grey
Decoration: Two zones with horizontal comb impressions.

608. 6794U A/V-p/17 surface (88/067) Plates 108, 153

SPI	I-d	f–m	W2	Bd. gef	Re	3

Bd. 2.0 cm. pht. 8.7 cm. Md 8.3 cm. Wd. 0.6 cm.
Incomplete
Surface colour: 2.5YR4/0 dark grey
Break: light grey in, dark grey out
Decoration: Horizontally combed on shoulder and lower body, with a wide reserved band at the maximum body diameter. Unusually the reserved band was not burnished.
Previously published: TD XI, 217–218 no. 13.

609. 6794V A/V-p/17 surface (88/067) Plate 108

TG	I-d	f	W2	Bd. gef	re	3

Bd. 2.3 cm. pht. 4.3 cm. Wd. 0.9 cm.
Incomplete
Surface colour: 10YR5/2 grey brown
Break: light grey core, dark brown reduction zones
Decoration: Parallel horizontal lines applied with a comb.
Previously published: TD XI, 217 no. 12.

610. 6858E A/V-o/18 planum 2 Phase D/2 (88/267) Plate 108

SPI	I-b-2	f	W2	Bd. gef	re	3	1B

Bd. 2.3 cm. pht. 5.3 cm. Wd. 0.5 cm.
Incomplete
Surface colour: 5YR6/4–6 light reddish brown
Break: red core, grey brown oxidation zones
Decoration: Parallel series of incised lines made with a four-toothed comb at regular intervals around the shoulder and body of the vessel.
Previously published: TD XI, 128, 131 no. 7.

611. 6856D TD A/V-o/18 planum 1–2 surface (88/262) Plate 108

SPI	I-b-2	f–m	W2	Bd. gef	re	3

Bd. 2.0 cm. pht. 2.8 cm. Wd. 0.45 cm.
Incomplete
Surface colour: 7.5YR5.5/3 brown; burnished slip 10YR5/6 light red
Break: uniform grey
Decoration: Parallel series of incised lines made with an eight-toothed comb at regular intervals around the shoulder and body of the vessel.
Previously published: TD XI, 217 no. 11.

612. 6489S TD A/V-p/19 planum 7 Phase E/1 (88/181) Plate 109

TG	I-d	f–vf	W2	–	re	3

pht. 9.0 cm. Md. 17.0 cm. Wd. 0.6 cm.
Incomplete
Surface colour: 10YR.4/4 dark yellowish brown
Break: uniform grey
Decoration: Parallel series of incised lines made with a six-toothed comb at regular intervals around the shoulder and body of the vessel.
Previously published: TD XI, 30–31 no. 12; Kopetzky, *The MB IIB-Corpus of the Hyksos Period at Tell el-Dabʿa*, 2007, 199 fig. 4.3.

Type Group L.13.4 Cylindrical

613. 6857G TD A/V-q/19 planum 2 Phase D/2 (01/079) Plate 109

SPI	I-b-2	m	W2	–	re	3

pht. 8.9 cm. Md. 9.0 cm. Wd. 0.6 cm.
Incomplete
Surface colour: 10YR4/1 dark grey
Break: grey core, brown reduction zones
Decoration: Horizontally combed on the wheel.
Previously published: TD XI, 179 no. 3.

614. 6135J TD A/V-q/19 planum 2 Phase D/2 (94/074) Plate 109

SPI	I-d	f	W2	–	re	3	1B

pht. 6.2 cm. Wd. 0.7 cm
Incomplete
Surface colour: 10YR.4/4 dark yellowish brown; burnished slip 5YR5/1 grey
Break: uniform dark grey brown
Decoration: series of parallel grooves made with a multi-toothed comb.
Previously published: TD XI, 172–173 no. 4.

Miscellaneous L.13 body sherds

615. 1445 Vienna A2991 A/II-n/12 planum 3 Phase E/1 (68/104) Plate 109

SPI	I-b-2	f	W2	–	re	3

Wd. 0.5 cm.
Incomplete
Surface colour: 7.5YR5.5/3 brown; burnished slip 10YR3/1 very dark grey
Break: uniform dark grey
Decoration: Horizontal parallel lines made with a multi-toothed comb separated by a reserved band.
Previously published: TD V, 192, 193.

616. 1606 Vienna AS 3099 A/II-k/11 planum 4 Phase E/1 ? (68/111) Plate 109

TG	I-b-2	f	W2	–	re	3

Wd. 0.5 cm.
Incomplete
Surface colour: 7.5YR5.5/3 brown; burnished slip 10YR3/1 very dark grey
Break: uniform dark grey
Decoration: Horizontal parallel lines made with a multi-toothed comb separated by 2 reserved bands.

617. 6133B2 TD A/V-p/18 planum 2 surface (88/275 or 302) Plate 109

TG	I-b-2	f	W2	–	re	2–3

pht. 3.7 cm. Wd. 0.5 cm.
Incomplete
Surface colour: 5YR5/1 grey
Break: uniform dark grey

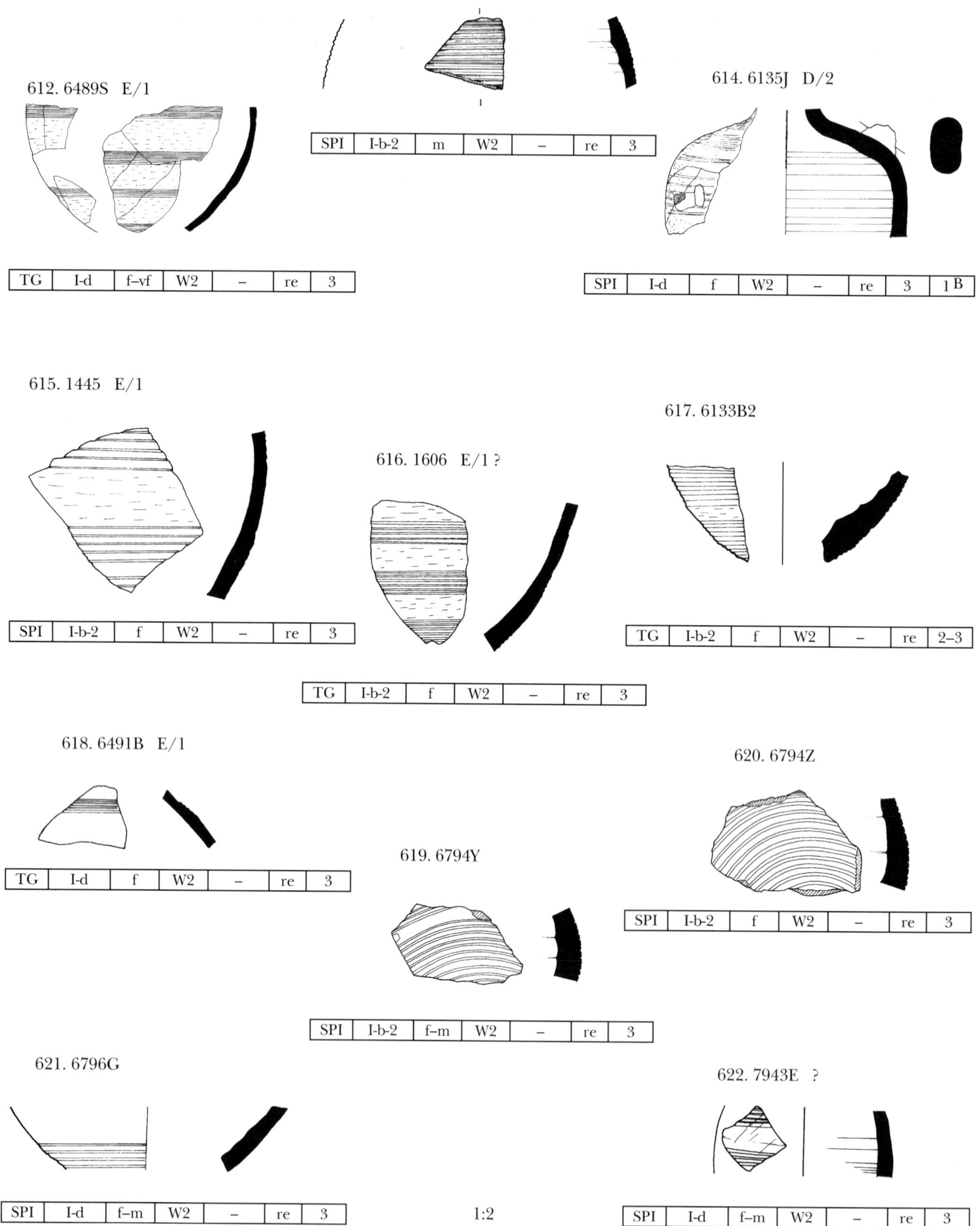

Late Egyptian Type Groups L.13.2, L.13.3, L.13.4 and combed body sherds

Plate 109

Decoration: Horizontal parallel lines made with a multi-toothed comb separated by a reserved band.
Previously published: TD XI, 217 no. 10.

618. 6491B TD A/V-p/19 planum 7 Phase E/1 (88/348) Plate 109

TG	I-d	f	W2	–	re	3

pht. 1.5 cm. Wd. 0.5 cm.
Incomplete
Surface colour: 10YR5/2 greyish brown; burnished slip 7.5YR4/4 dark brown
Break: uniform dark grey
Decoration: One band of incised lines made with a six-toothed comb between two reserved bands.

619. 6794Y TD A/V-p/17 surface (88/067) Plate 109

SPI	I-b-2	f–m	W2	–	re	3

Wd. 0.55 cm.
Incomplete
Surface colour: 5YR7/1 light grey
Break: wide black core, thin brown reduction zones
Decoration: Parallel series of incised lines made with an eight-toothed comb at regular intervals around the shoulder and body of the vessel.
Previously published: TD XI, 217 no. 9.

620. 6794Z TD A/V-p/17 surface (88/067) Plate 109

SPI	I-b-2	f	W2	–	re	3

pht. 3.3 Wd. 0.7 cm.
Incomplete
Surface colour: 7.5YR5.5/3 brown; burnished slip 10YR5/1 grey
Break: dark grey brown core, reddish brown zones
Decoration: Parallel series of incised lines made with a multi-toothed comb.
Previously published: TD XI, 216–217 no. 7.

621. 6796G TD A/V-p/18 planum 1 surface (88/041) Plate 109

SPI	I-d	f–m	W2	–	re	3

pht. 4.0 cm. Wd. 0.6 cm.
Incomplete
Surface colour: 7.5YR5.5/3 brown; burnished slip 10YR4/1 grey
Break: thin mat red core, light grey reduction zones
Decoration: Parallel series of incised lines made with a multi-toothed comb, beneath a reserved band.
Previously published: TD XI, 217 no. 8.

622. 7943E TD A/IV-h/6 planum 1 Phase ? (93/580) Plate 109

SPI	I-d	f–m	W2	–	re	3

Wd. 0.45 cm.
Incomplete
Surface colour: 7.5YR5.5/3 brown; burnished slip 10YR4/1 grey
Break: uniform grey
Decoration: Two bands of parallel grooves separated by a reserved band.

L.14. Late Egyptian XIV (Model Piriform)

Model piriform 2a being approximately 6–8 cms. high with piriform to spherical bodies may be divided into two groups, one having a ring base and the other a button. Like the slender, taller Piriform 2a vessels the decoration invariably consists only of lozenges (gores), usually three or four, filled with a herringbone pattern of incised dots. The comb used for this generally had eight or more points, and the area of incision is usually delineated. Burnishing occurs on the unincised areas.

Type Group L.14.1

Type group L.14.1 comprise those squat piriform vessels with rolled rims, strap handles, piriform to spherical bodies and ring bases. Two decorative schemes are associated with this type comprising four (L.14.1a) or three (L.14.1b) delinated infilled lozenges.

Type Group L.14.1b

623. 2054 Vienna A3384 A/II-o/12 grave 3 Phase D/3 (68/037) Plate 110

SPI	I-d	f–vf	W2	Bd. gef	re	3	1B

D. 2.7 cm. Nd 1.4 cm. Bd. 1.8 cm. H. 8.4 cm. Md. 6.0 cm. Wd. 0.3 cm.
VI 71.42
Incomplete
Surface colour: 10YR5/2 grey brown; burnished slip: 10YR2/1 black
Break: not visible
Decoration: Three lozenges filled with poorly executed horizontal chevrons made with an eight-toothed comb.
Previously published: TD V, 286.

624. 0355 Vienna A1631 A/I-g/3 grave 1 Phase D/3 (66/026) Plates 110, 153

SPI	I-d	f	W2	Bd. gef	re	3	1B

D. 2.5 cm. Nd 1.15 cm. Bd. 1.7 cm. H. 7.5 cm. Md. 4.9 cm. Wd. 0.3 cm.
VI 65.33
Intact
Surface colour: 10YR6/2 grey brown; burnished slip: 10YR5/1 dark grey
Break: not visible
Decoration: Three lozenges filled with poorly executed horizontal chevrons made with an eight-toothed comb.

625. 3532B TD A/II-o/21 planum 2 Phase D/3 (81/310) Plate 110

SPI	I-d	vf	W2	Bd. gef	re	3	1B

Bd. 1.7 cm. pht. 4.6 cm. Md. 4.8 cm. Wd. 0.3 cm.
Incomplete
Surface colour: 2.5Y5/1 grey; burnished slip: 10YR4/1 dark grey
Break: grey core, greyish brown reduction zones
Decoration: Three lozenges infilled with horizontal chevrons, two V-shaped and one ?-shaped made with a twelve-toothed comb.

626. 2321 Vienna A3545 A/II-m/15 grave 3 Phase D/3 (69/110) Plate 110

SPI	I-d	m	W2	Bd. gef	re	3	1B

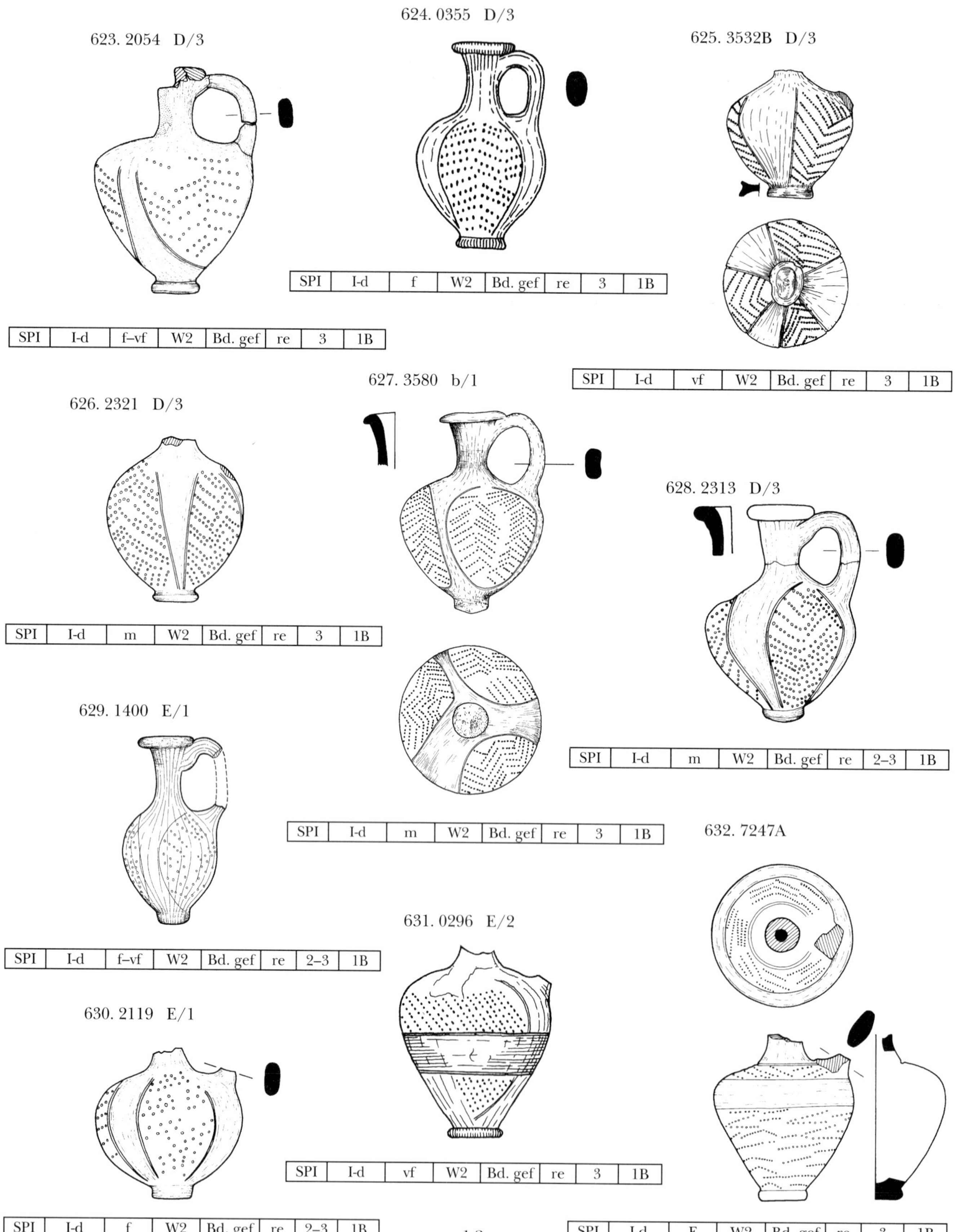

Late Egyptian Type Groups L.14.1b, L.14.2b, L.14.4a, L.14.4b

Plate 110

Nd. 1.2 cm. Bd. 1.7 cm. pht. 6.0 cm. Md. 5.2 cm. Wd. 0.3 cm.
Incomplete
Surface colour: 2.5Y5/1 grey; burnished slip: 10YR4/1 dark grey
Break: grey core, greyish brown reduction zones
Decoration: Three unequal lozenges with zig-zag decoration.
BNL JH325 Egyptian Nile Clay[612]
Previously published: TD XVI, 315, fig. 235, no. 22.

Type Group L.I4.2

Type group L.I4.2 is similar to group L.I4.1, but the jugs of this group have distinct button bases. At present the only decorative scheme associated with these vessels are four (L.I4.2a) or three (L.I4.2b) infilled lozenges.

Type Group L.14.2b

627. 3580 Cairo F/I-i/22 grave 7 Phase b/1 (81/168) Plates 110, 153

SPI	I-d	m	W2	Bd. gef	re	3	1B

D. 2.6 cm. Nd 1.2 cm. Bd. 1.3 cm. H. 7.5 cm. Md. 5.5 cm. Wd. 0.3 cm.
VI 73.33
Intact
Surface colour: 10YR5/1–6/4 grey; burnished slip: 7.5YR4/2 dark brown
Break: not visible
Decoration: Three lozenges filled with poorly executed horizontal chevrons made with an eight-toothed comb.
Previously published: KOPETZKY, *The MB IIB-Corpus of the Hyksos Period at Tell el-Dabᶜa,* 2007, 198 fig. 3.5.

628. 2313 Cairo JE 91711D A/II-m/15 grave 3 Phase D/3 (69/109) Plate 110

SPI	I-d	m	W2	Bd. gef	re	2–3	1B

D. 2.5 cm. Nd 1.2 cm. Bd. 1.6 cm. H. 8.1 cm. Md. 5.9 cm. Wd. 0.35 cm.
VI 72.83
Intact
Surface colour: 10YR5/1–6/4 grey; burnished slip: 7.5YR4/2 dark brown
Break: not visible
Decoration: Three lozenges with zig-zag decoration.
Previously published: TD V, 152; *TD XVI,* 313, fig. 234, no. 10.

629. 1400 Vienna A2953 A/II-l/14 grave 5 Phase E/1 (68/092) Plate 110

SPI	I-d	f–vf	W2	Bd. gef	re	2–3	1B

D. 2.2 cm. Nd 1.1 cm. Bd. 1.2 cm. H. 7.05 cm. Md. 3.2 cm. Wd. 0.3 cm.
VI 45.39
Restored from sherds, complete
Surface colour: 10YR5/3 brown; burnished slip: 10YR4/1 dark grey
Break: light brown core, dark brown reduction zones
Decoration: Three lozenges filled with poorly executed horizontal chevrons made with an eight-toothed comb.
Previously published: TD XVI, 254, fig. 189b, no. 20.

630. 2119 Vienna A3423 A/II-l/16 grave 1 Phase E/1 (69/052) Plate 110

SPI	I-d	f	W2	Bd. gef	re	2–3	1B

Nd. 1.2 cm. Bd. 1.5 cm. pht. 5.5 cm. Md 5.5 cm. Wd. 0.3 cm.
Incomplete
Surface colour: 10YR6/1 grey: burnished slip: 10YR3/1 very dark grey
Break: uniform greyish brown
Decoration: Four lozenges filled with poorly executed horizontal zigzags made with an eight-toothed comb.
BNL JH386 Egyptian Nile Clay[613]
Previously published: TD XVI, 263, fig. 192a, no. 16.

Type Group L.14.4

Type group L.14.4 consists of two incomplete pots from Tell el-Dabᶜa, TD 7247A and TD 296, which although piriform in shape are also decorated in styles usually associated with Late Egyptian biconical vessels in which a reserved zone runs around the mid-point. Above and below this reserved band are standing and pendant triangles (TD 296), or rows of dots made with an eight-toothed comb (TD 7297A). Burnishing occurs only on the neck and reserved zone.

Type Group L.14.4a

631. 0296 Vienna A2259 A/II-l/12 planum 3 Phase E/2 (66/028) Plates 110, 153

SPI	I-d	vf	W2	Bd. gef	re	3	1B

Nd. 1.2 cm. Bd. 2.8 cm. pht. 7.1 cm. Md 5.8 cm. Wd. 0.3 cm.
Incomplete
Surface colour: 10YR6/1 light grey; burnished slip: 2.5YR3/1 very dark grey
Break: uniform grey
Decoration: Frieze of standing triangles above a frieze of pendant triangles separated from each other by a reserved band. Triangles infilled with striations made with a mulit-toothed comb.

Type Group L.14.4b

632. 7247A TD Ezbet Rushdi stray find (89/098)
Plates 110, 154

SPI	I-d	F	W2	Bd. gef	re	3	1B

Nd. 1.4 cm. Bd. 1.85 cm. pht. 6.1 cm. Md 5.35 cm. Wd. 0.3 cm.
Restored from sherds, incomplete
Surface colour: 5YR6/6 reddish yellow; burnished slip: 5YR3/1 very dark grey

[612] P. McGOVERN, *The Foreign Relations of the Hyksos,* Oxford, 2000, 130 no. JH325.

[613] P. McGOVERN, *The Foreign Relations of the Hyksos,* Oxford, 2000, 134 no. JH386.

633. 3389F

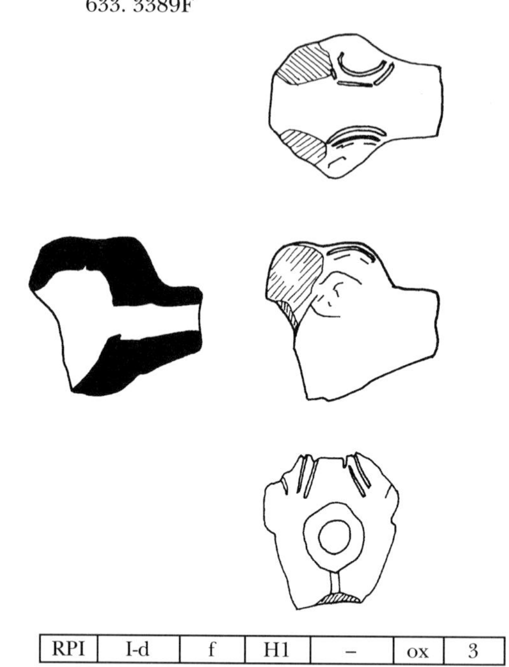

RPI	I-d	f	H1	–	ox	3

634. 9018Y a/2

SPI	I-d	f–vf	W+H	–	re	4

1:2

Late Egyptian Type Groups L.15.1, L.15..2

Plate 111

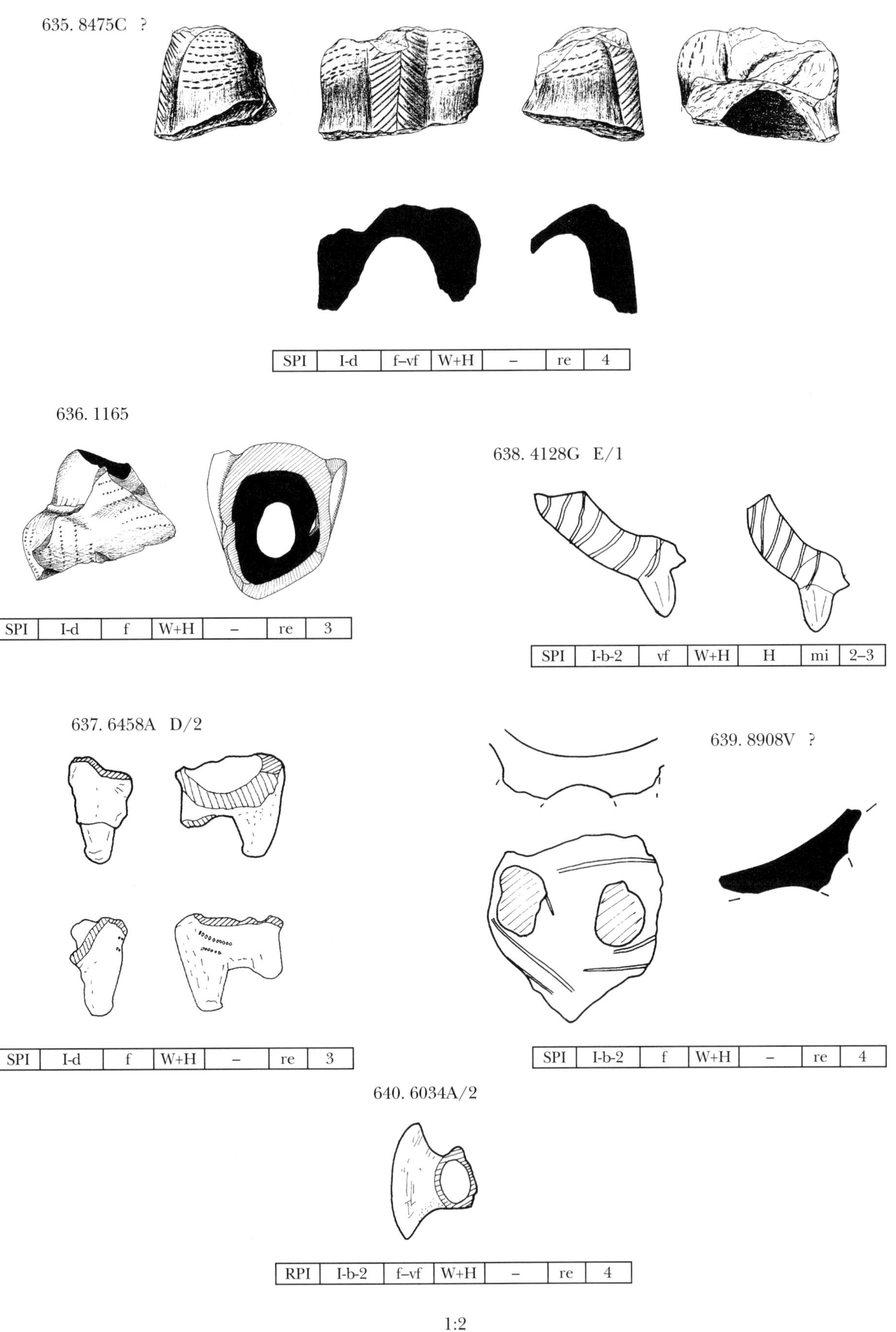

1:2

Late Egyptian Type Group L.15.2

Plate 112

Break: uniform grey
Decoration: Horizontal and oblique lines applied with an eight-toothed comb above and below a horizontally burnished reserved band at the mid-point.

L.15. Late Egyptian XV (Late Egyptian Figural Jugs)

Type Group L.15.1 Ducks

Ducks are represented at Tell el Dabᶜa only by the incomplete TD 3389F.

633. 3389F TD F/I-i/20–21 surface debris (80/143) Plate 111

RPI	I-d	f	H1	–	ox	3

pht. 3.7 × 4.0 × 4.5 cm. Wd. 0.3 cm.
Incomplete
Surface colour: 7.5YR6/4 light brown; burnished slip: 5YR4/2 dark reddish grey
Break: uniform grey brown
Decoration: Incised lines emphasizing the eyes and eyebrows.

Type Group L.15.2 Hawks

Type group L.15.2 is represented by eight incomplete pieces, all of which clearly derive from the typical hawk vessel type.

634. 9018Y TD F/II-r/23 planum 1 L81/6 + L81/12 Phase a/2 (09/047) Plates 111, 154

SPI	I-d	f–vf	W+H	–	re	4

pht. 4.7 cm. Wd. 0.35 cm.
Incomplete
Surface colour: 10YR2–3/1 vey dark grey; burnished slip: 10YR4/2 dark grey brown
Break: uniform black
Decoration: Herringbone pattern on chest; wings infilled with gashes made with a single pointed tool. Vertically burnished.

635. 8475C TD Khatana E/I/B planum ? Phase ? (95/054) Plates 112, 155

SPI	I-d	f–vf	W+H	–	re	4

pht. 4.7 cm. Wd. 0.35 cm.
Incomplete
Surface colour: 10YR2–3/1 vey dark grey; burnished slip: 10YR4/2 dark grey brown
Break: uniform black
Decoration: Herringbone pattern on chest; wings infilled with gashes made with a single pointed tool. Vertically burnished.

636. 1165 Vienna A2796 A/II-k/9 planum 0–1 surface (68/001) Plate 112

SPI	I-d	f	W+H	–	re	3

pht. 4.3 cm. Md. 5.1 cm. Wd. 0.3 cm.
Incomplete
Surface colour: 2.5Y5/1 grey; burnished slip: 2.5Y5/1 grey
Break: uniform black
Decoration: Impressed with a five-toothed comb

637. 6458A TD A/II-i/11 planum 6 Phase D/2 (87/096) Plate 112

SPI	I-d	f	W+H	–	re	3

pht. 1.7 cm. Wd. 0.3 cm.
Incomplete
Surface colour: 2.5Y5/1 grey; burnished slip: 2.5Y5/1 grey
Break: uniform black
Decoration: Incised lines on body.

638. 4128G TD A/II-n/19 planum 2–3 Phase E/1 (01/079) Plate 112

SPI	I-b-2	vf	W+H	H	mi	2–3

pht. 3.2 cm. Wd. 0.3 cm.
Incomplete, one leg and part of the wing preserved
Surface colour: 5YR5/4 light red brown; burnished slip: light reddish brown
Break: wide grey core, thin reddish brown oxidation zones
Decoration: Incised lines on body.
BNL JH900 Egyptian Nile Clay[614]
Previously published: Kopetzky, *The MB IIB-Corpus of the Hyksos Period at Tell el-Dabᶜa*, 2007, 200 fig. 6.6.

639. 8908V TD H/III-t/14 planum 1–2 Phase ? (99/145) Plate 112

SPI	I-b-2	f	W+H	–	re	4

pht. 1.3 cm. Wd. 0.35 cm.
Incomplete
Surface colour: 7.5YR6/2 pinkish grey
Break: black core, red and brown oxidation zone
Decoration: Incised lines on underside.

640. 6034A2 TD F/I-o/21 grave 4 intrusive within grave 4 unstratified (87/216) Plate 112

RPI	I-b-2	f–vf	W+H	–	re	4

pht. 1.3 cm. Wd. 0.35 cm.
Incomplete
Surface colour: 10R5/6 red; burnished slip: not preserved
Break: uniform dark grey

Type Group L.15.3 Fishes

At least five Tell el-Yahudiya fish vessels have been found at Tell el-Dabᶜa.

641. 7354 TD F/I-q/24 planum 1 Phase b/1–a/2 (90/116) Plates 113, 155

SPI	I-d	f–vf	W+H	H	re	4	1B

D. 3.2 cm. Nd. 1.4 cm. H. 12.8 cm. Md. 6.0 cm. Wd. 0.35 cm.
Incomplete
Surface colour: 10YR5/1 grey; burnished slip: 10YR3/1 v dark grey

[614] P. McGovern, *The Foreign Relations of the Hyksos*, Oxford, 2000, 152 no. JH900.

641. 7354 b/1–a/2

SPI	I-d	f–vf	W+H	H	re	4	1B

642. 5511 D/2

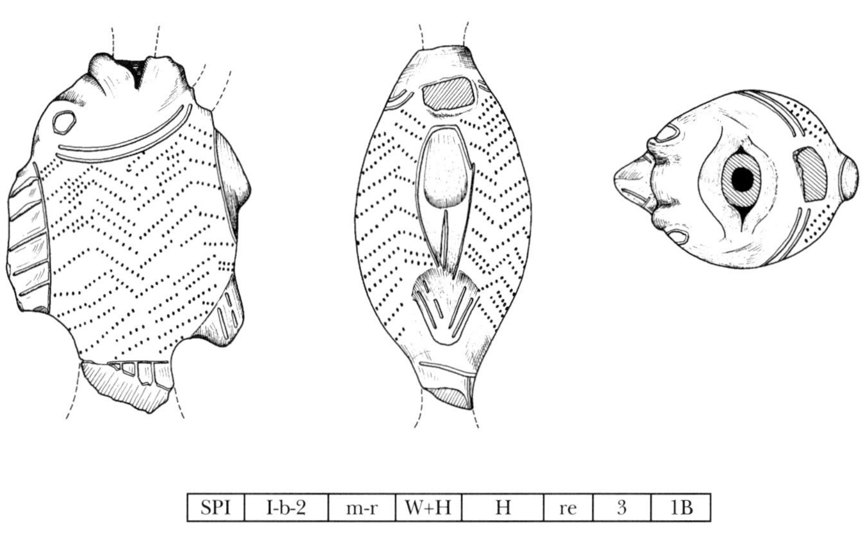

SPI	I-b-2	m-r	W+H	H	re	3	1B

1:2

Late Egyptian Type Groups L.15.3

Plate 113

Break: uniform dark grey
Decoration: Eyes, gills, dorsal and caudal fins outlined by incised lines. Scales indicated by a cross-hatched pattern.
Previously published: PuF 234 nr 289 erroneously dated to the Thirteenth Dynasty; KOPETZKY., *The MB IIB-Corpus of the Hyksos Period at Tell el-Dabᶜa*, 2007, 200 fig. 6.2.

642. 5511 TD A/II-k/9 planum 8–9 Phase D/2 (85/377) Plate 113

SPI	I-b-2	m-r	W+H	Bd. H	re	3	1B

pht. 9.6 cm. Md. 6.8 cm. Wd. 0.35 cm.
Incomplete
Surface colour: 10YR5/1 grey; burnished slip: 10YR3/1 v dark grey
Break: thin red core, thin grey reduction zones
Decoration: Eyes, gills, dorsal and caudal fins outlined by incised lines. Zigzags on body made with a ten-toothed comb.
Previously published: KOPETZKY, *The MB IIB-Corpus of the Hyksos Period at Tell el-Dabᶜa*, 2007, 200 fig. 6.4; *TD XIX* 129, fig. 59, 384, fig 233.85d.

643. 6987 TD F/I-l/23 grave 6 Phase b/1 (88/243) Plates 114, 155

RPI	I-d	f–vf	W+H	Bd. H	mi	3	2R

pht. 10.9 cm. Nd. 3.6 cm. Md. 6.8 cm. Wd. 0.5 cm.
Incomplete
Surface colour: 2.5YR5/1 reddish grey; burnished slip: 10R3/6 dark red
Break: dark grey core, light grey reduction zones
Decoration: Eyes, gills, dorsal and caudal fins outlined by incised lines. Decoration on body impressed with a finger nail.
Previously published: KOPETZKY, *The MB IIB-Corpus of the Hyksos Period at Tell el-Dabᶜa*, 2007, 200 fig. 6.3.

644. 1627 Vienna A3111 A/II-m/12 grave 9 Phase E/2 (68/097) Plate 114

SPI	I-d	f	W+H	–	re	2

pht. 9.3 cm. Wd. 0.3 cm.
Incomplete
Surface colour: 10YR5/1–3 grey brown; burnished slip: 7.5YR5/3 brown
Break: uniform grey
Decoration: Herring-bone pattern impressed on both sides of the body.
Previously published: TD V, 123, 125; KOPETZKY., *The MB IIB-Corpus of the Hyksos Period at Tell el-Dabᶜa*, 2007, 200 fig. 6.5.

645. 0273 Vienna A2247 A/I-g/4 planum 2 Phase D/2 or later (66/017) Plate 114

SPI	I-d	f	W+H	Bd. H	re	3

pht. 1.3 cm. Wd. 0.35 cm.
Incomplete
Surface colour: 2.5Y4/1 vey dark grey; burnished slip: not preserved
Break: uniform dark grey
Decoration: Eyes and gills (?) outlined by incised lines. Dotted decoration on body made with an eight toothed comb.

L.15.5 Cows (?)

646. 9018X TD F/II-r/22+23 planum 1 L81/1 + L81/6 + L81/12 Phase a/2 (09/028) Plates 115, 156

SPI	I-d	f–vf	W+H	Bd. H	re	4

pht. 4.7 cm. Wd. 0.35 cm.
Incomplete
Surface colour: 10YR2–3/1 vey dark grey; burnished slip: 10YR4/2 dark grey brown
Break: uniform black
Decoration: Delineated band around the base of the neck, infilled with a ten-toothed comb. Delineated circles on body, infilled with a ten-toothed comb.

Miscellaneous sherds from Late Figural Vessels

In addition to the main groups L.14.1–5, several body sherds of other figural vessels have also been recovered at Tell el-Dabᶜa. These, however, are too small for the fauna represented to be recognised.

647. 1550 Vienna A1742 A/II-m/14 planum 2 Phase D/2 (68/087) Plates 115, 154

SPI	I-d	f	W+H	–	re	3

pht. 7.1 cm. Wd. 0.4 cm.
Incomplete
Surface colour: 10YR6/3 pale brown; 10YR2/1 black
Break: red core, dark grey reduction zones
Decoration: Dotted decoration made with an eight-toothed comb.

648. 2344 Vienna A3563 A/II-m/15 grave 3 Phase D/3–2 (69/106) Plate 116

SPI	I-d	f–vf	H1	–	re	3

pht. 2.5 cm. Wd. 0.3 cm.
Incomplete
Surface colour: 2.5Y5/1 grey; burnished slip: 2.5Y5/1 grey
Break: uniform black
Decoration: Decoration on the back of the neck (?) made with a multi-toothed comb.

649. 0831 Vienna AS 1809 A/II-m/10 planum 4–5 Phase ? (67/139) Plate 116

SPI	I-d	f	W+H	–	re	3

pht. 1.3 cm. Wd. 0.35 cm.
Incomplete
Surface colour: 2.5Y4/1 vey dark grey; burnished slip: not preserved
Break: uniform dark grey
Decoration: Decoration added with a five-toothed comb.

650. 0939 Cairo ? A/II-k/9 planum 0–1 surface (68/001) Plates 116, 156

SPI	I-d	f	W2	–	re	3	1B

Nd. 1.3 cm. pht. 4.2 cm. Wd. 0.3 cm.
Incomplete
Surface colour: 10YR4/1 grey brown; burnished slip: 10YR2–3/1 very dark grey
Break: uniform grey
Decoration: Oblique lines of dots impressed with a twelve-toothed comb.

643. 6987 b/1

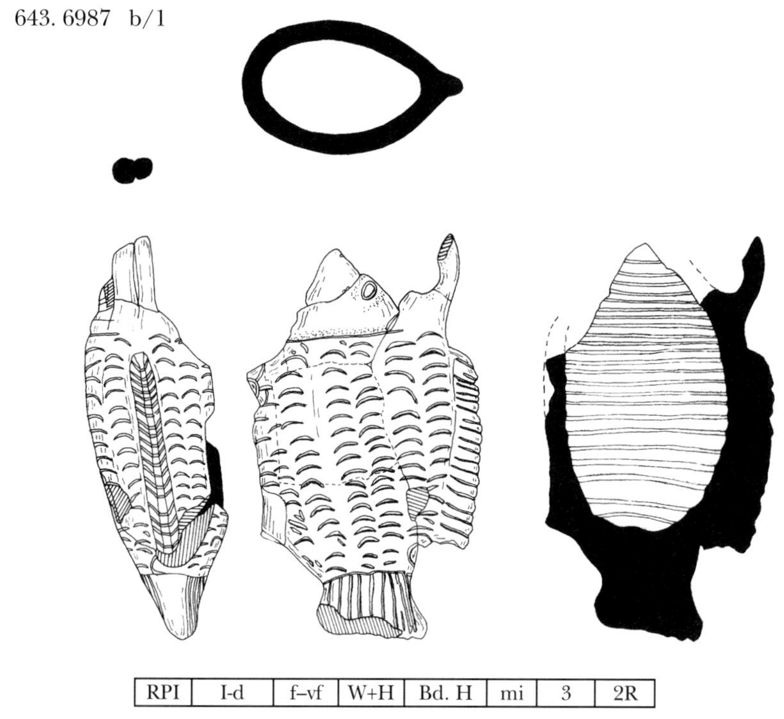

RPI	I-d	f–vf	W+H	Bd. H	mi	3	2R

644. 1627 E/2

645. 0273 D/2 or later

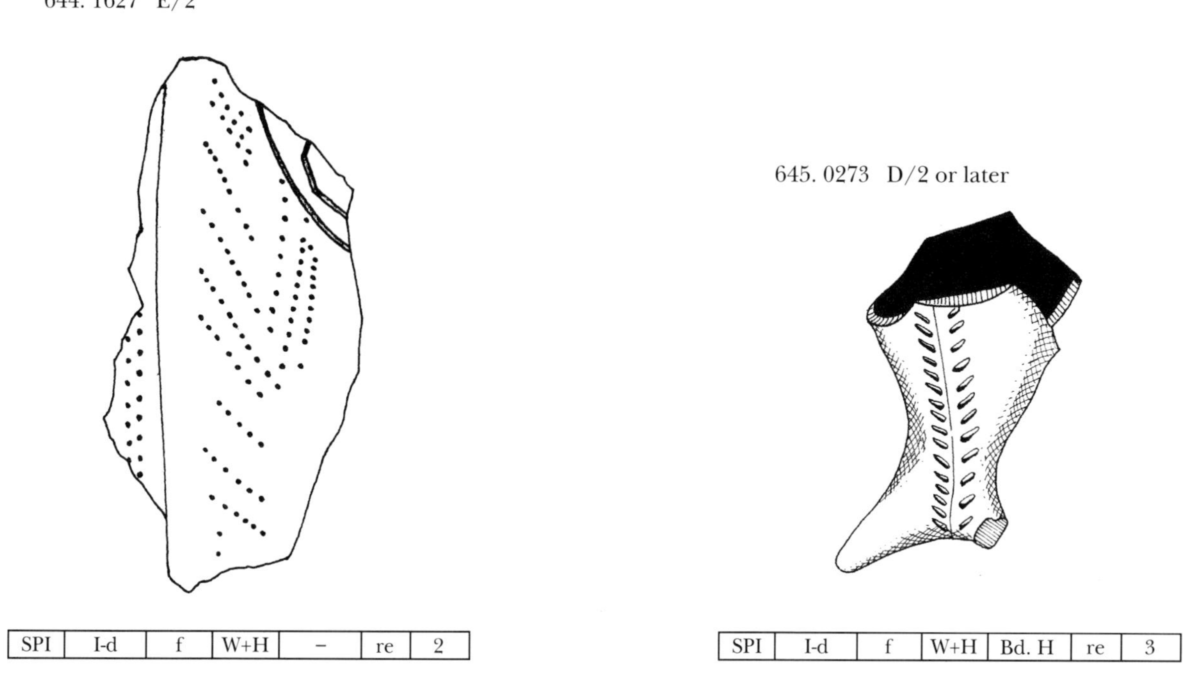

SPI	I-d	f	W+H	–	re	2

SPI	I-d	f	W+H	Bd. H	re	3

1:2

Late Egyptian Type Groups L.15.3

Plate 114

646. 9018X a/2

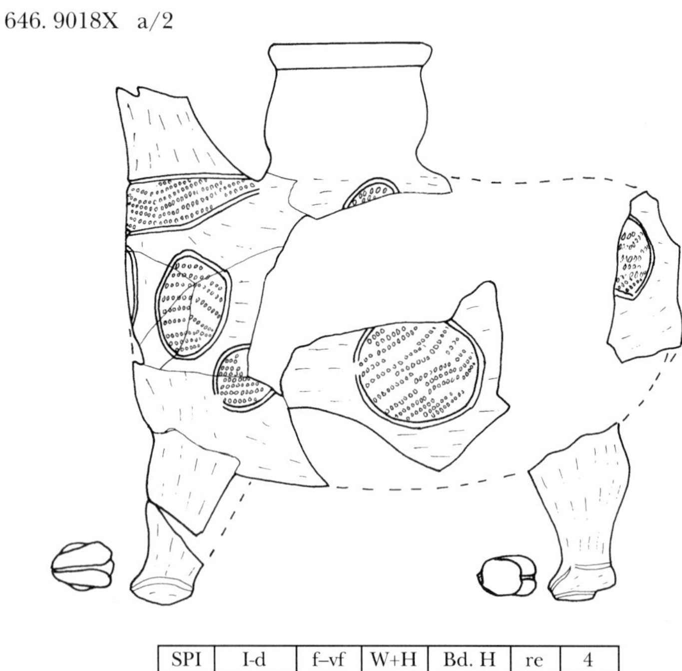

SPI	I-d	f–vf	W+H	Bd. H	re	4

647. 1550 D/2

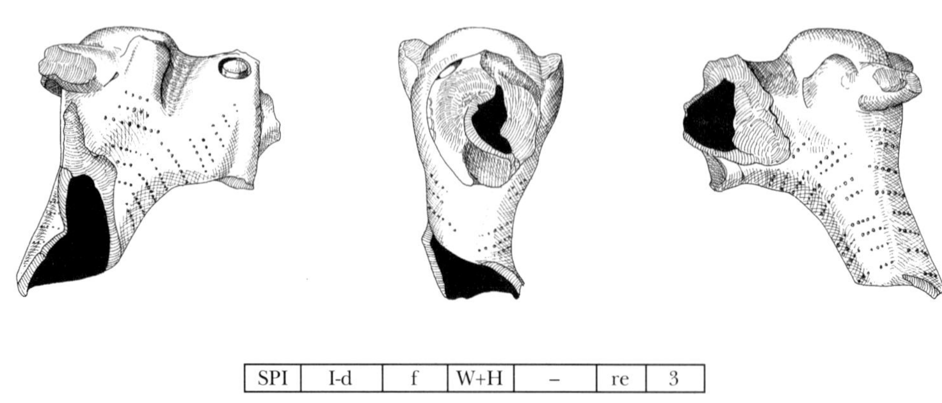

SPI	I-d	f	W+H	–	re	3

1:2

Late Egyptian Type Groups L.15.5 and miscellaneous

Plate 115

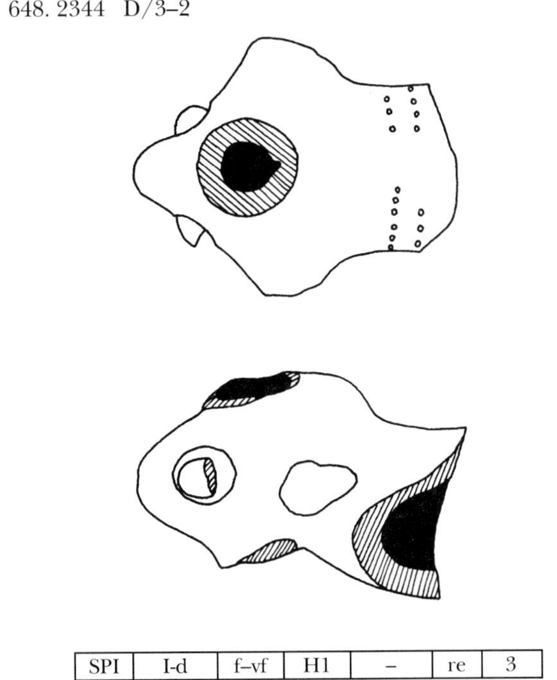

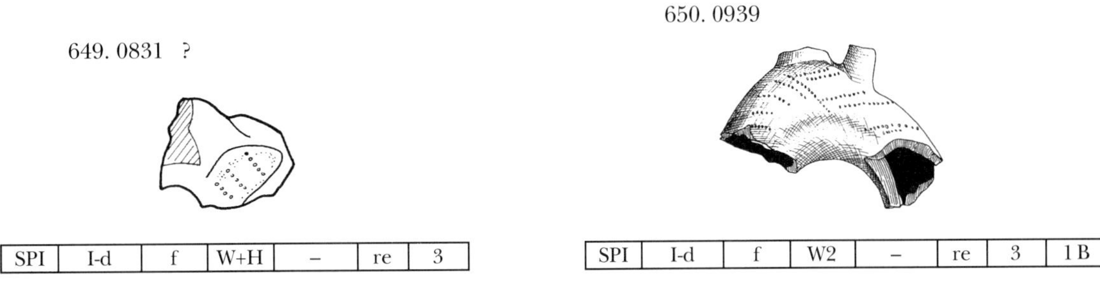

1:2

Late Egyptian miscellaneous figural vessels

Plate 116

Type Group M.1 (Piriform 2 hybrids)

Type group M.1 clearly owes its origins to the Piriform 2a vessels of the Late Egyptian Group (L.1). However neutron activation analysis of such vessels shows them to have been made of Palestinian clays.[615] Such vessels, which are known from Jericho[616] and Tell Ajjul,[617] have rolled rims; piriform bodies, and like the Egyptian vessels which inspired them, infilled lozenge decoration. In contrast to the Egyptian vessels, however, this type always has a double handle, and usually a button or offset disc base.

[615] Kaplan, *Tell el-Yahudiyeh Ware*, 231, Piriform 2b.
[616] Birmingham City Museum 1032.52. Kenyon, *PEQ* 1952, pl. 22, fig. 1; Oxford Ashmolean 1954.576. Kenyon, *Jericho I*, 315–30, fig. 122.14; Jerusalem, Rockefeller Museum V.588. Kaplan, *Tell el-Yahudiyeh Ware*, fig. 61f.
[617] Jerusalem, Rockefeller Museum, 32.2088. Petrie, *Ancient Gaza II*, pl. xxxiv 60M6.

651. 1962 E/2–1

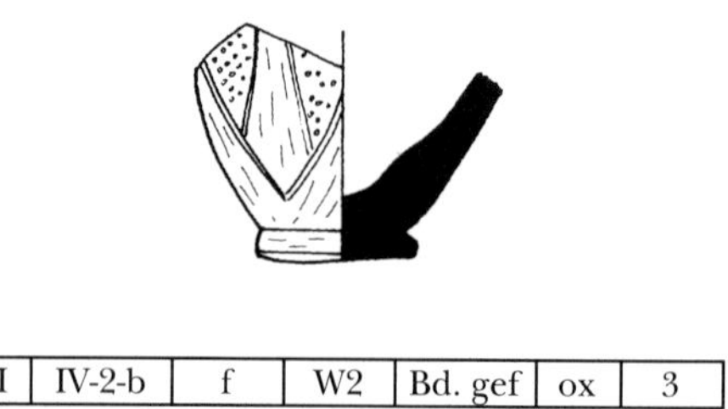

SPI	IV-2-b	f	W2	Bd. gef	ox	3

652. 0067 D/3

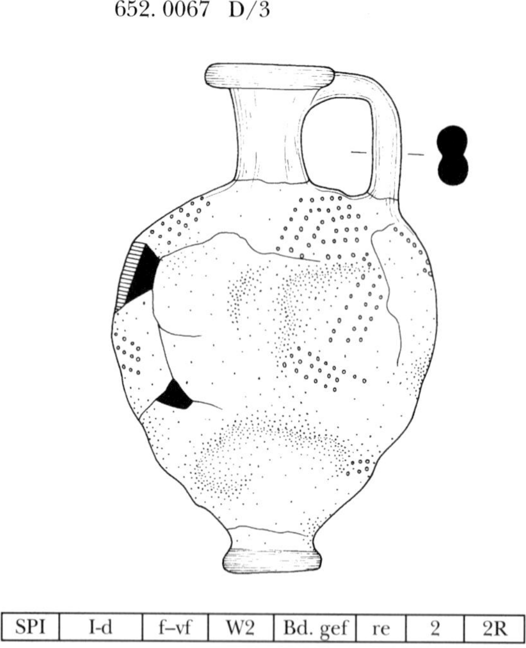

SPI	I-d	f–vf	W2	Bd. gef	re	2	2R

653. 3434 E/1–D/3

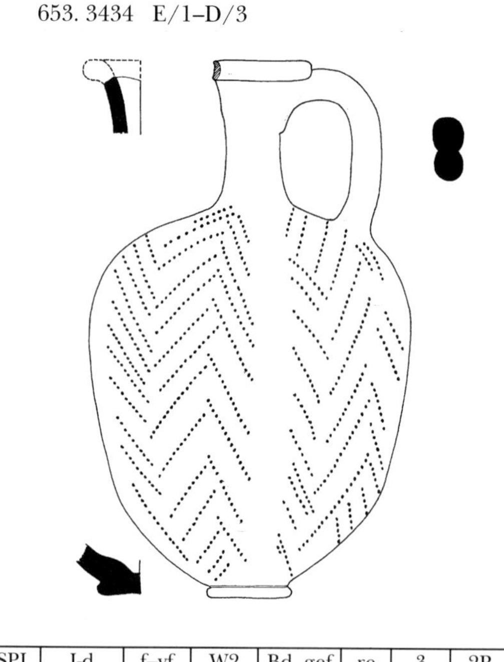

SPI	I-d	f–vf	W2	Bd. gef	re	3	2R

1:2

Type Group M.1–2 (Hybrids)

Plate 116

651. 1962 Vienna A3334 A/II-m/12 grave 10 Phase E/2–1 (69/013) Plate 117

SPI	IV-2-b	f	W2	Bd. gef	ox	3

Bd. 2.5 cm. pht. 3.6 cm. Md. 5.6 cm. Wd. 0.9 cm.
Incomplete
Surface colour: 5YR7/6 reddish yellow; burnished slip: 10YR3/1 very dark grey
Break: yellowish brown core, reddish yellow oxidation zones
Decoration: Lozenge decoration impressed with a multi-toothed comb.
Previously published: TD V, 163, 164.

Type Group M.2 (Piriform 2b hybrids)

By contrast the two vessels TD 67 and TD 3434 comprise Piriform 2b vessels with rolled rims, double handles and ring bases. Both are decorated with undelineated infilled lozenges. Both, however are made of Nile clay and are evident copies of Late Palestinan forms.

652. 0067 Vienna A2172 A/II-l/12 grave 1 Phase D/3 (66/013) Plates 117, 156

SPI	I-d	f–vf	W2	Bd. gef	re	2	2R

D. 3.5 cm. Nd 1.62 cm. Bd. 2.5 cm. H. 14.0 cm. Md. 8.7 cm. Wd. 0.65 cm.
VI 62.14
Intact
Surface colour: 10YR4/2 grey brown; burnished slip: 10YR3/1 very dark grey
Break: dark grey core, brownish reduction zones

Decoration: Undelineated lozenges infilled with chevrons made with an eight-toothed comb; surface poorly preserved.
BNL JH547 Nile clay
Previously published: TD V, 250–51.

653. 3434 Cairo A/II-p/21 grave 4 Phase E/1–D/3 (81/116) Plate 117

SPI	I-d	f–vf	W2	Bd. gef	re	3	2R

D. 3.2 cm. Nd 1.4 cm. Bd. 2.2 cm. H. 14.3 cm. Md. 7.1 cm. Wd. 0.4 cm.
VI 49.65
Restored from sherds, complete
Surface colour 2.5Y5/1 grey; burnished slip: 2.5Y2.5/1 black
Break: grey core, red brown and grey reduction zones
Decoration: Undelineated lozenges infilled with horizontal zigzags made with an eighteen-toothed comb; surface poorly preserved.

Vessels belonging to The Handmade Globular Group

Type Group N.1

At present only one vessel can be attributed to this group, Tell el-Dabᶜa TD 8698, from a grave dated to Phase E/3. With a cut-away spout, incisions at the base of the neck and double handle, it is clearly an early vessel, and although no NAA analysis has yet been carried out on this vessel, visual observation indicates that it is made of a Nile clay. Three horizontal zones of decoration are found on the vessel extending from immediately below the neck to the lower body. The first zone is decorated with standing triangles which are themselves delineated by incised lines; the second band comprises a zigzag again delineated by incised lines, and finally the lower band consists solely of groups of three incised lines arranged in a zigzag pattern.

654. 8698 TD A/II-p/14 locus 286 grave 13 Phase E/3 (98/064) Plates 118, 157

BPI	I-d	f	H1	Bd. gesp	re	2–3	2R

D. 1.8 × 2.8 cm Nd. 1.3 cm. Bd. 3.2 cm. H. 11.1 cm. Md. 6.4 cm. Wd. 0.3 cm.
VI 57.65
Intact
Surface colour: 10YR4/4 very yellow brown; burnished slip 10YR3/1 very dark grey
Break: uniform grey
Decoration: Three incised lines at base of neck. Upper zone of five irregular sized standing triangles infilled with a four-toothed comb. Middle zone of wavy zigzags infilled with two lines of impressed dots made with a four toothed comb. Third zone of standing triangles framed by three parallel lines.
Comment: It is not clear whether this vessel is handmade or wheel made.
Previously published: TD XVI, 216, fig. 136, no. 5.

Type Group N.2.1

Type Group N.2.1 consists of hand made globular jugs with slightly everted or kettle rims and double handles, which may be sub-divided into three sub-groups N.2.1 a–c by the decorative styles. In N.2.1a the vessel has an incised line at the height of the base of the handle, thence vertical incised lines running down towards the base; N.2.1b, in which the decoration consists of two bands of upright triangles; in N.2.1c an upper band of upright triangles and a lower band consisting of groups of three incised lines arranged in a zigzag pattern.

Type Group N.2.1a

655. 7486F TD A/IV-h/4 grave 11 Phase F ? (91/207) Plate 118

SPI	I-d	f	H1	Bd. H	mi	3	2R

pht. 2.2 cm. Wd. 0.4 cm.
Incomplete
Surface colour: 10YR4/4 very yellow brown; burnished slip 5YR4/1–5/6 dark grey
Break: light brown in, dark brown out
Decoration: not discernible.

Type group N.2.1b

656. 4168 TD F/I-i/22 grave 34 Phase c (82/116) Plates 118, 157

RPI	I-d	vf	H1	Bd. gesp	ox	3	2R

D. 2.6 cm Nd. 1.4 cm. H. 12.8 cm. Md 8.2 cm. Wd. 0.3 cm.
VI 64.06
Restored from sherds, incomplete
Surface colour: 5YR6/4 light red brown; burnished slip 10R4/6 red
Break: grey core, brown reduction zones
Decoration: Thin band at base of neck, and two bands of sytanding triangles, each framed with a double frame line. Incised dots made with a single-pointed tool.

657. 8785B TD A/II-p/14 locus 253 grave 10 Phase E/3 (98/267) Plate 118

SPI	I-d	f–m	H1	Bd. gesp	re	2	2R

D. 2.3 cm Nd. 1.3 cm. H. 8.9 cm. Md 5.8 cm. Wd. 0.3 cm.
VI 65.16
Restored from sherds, incomplete
Surface colour: 10YR5/3 brown; burnished slip 10YR3/1 very dark grey
Break: uniform light greyish brown
Decoration: Upper band of five standing triangles and lower band of eight rectangles (only four preserved), each delineated by two frame lines and infilled with a six-toothed comb. Handle protrudes through vessel wall.
Previously published: TD XVI, 207, fig. 125, no. 1.

To group N.2.1b should probably be assigned TD 4043 from F/I i/22 grave 12, which was found in a fragmentary state and was not drawn.

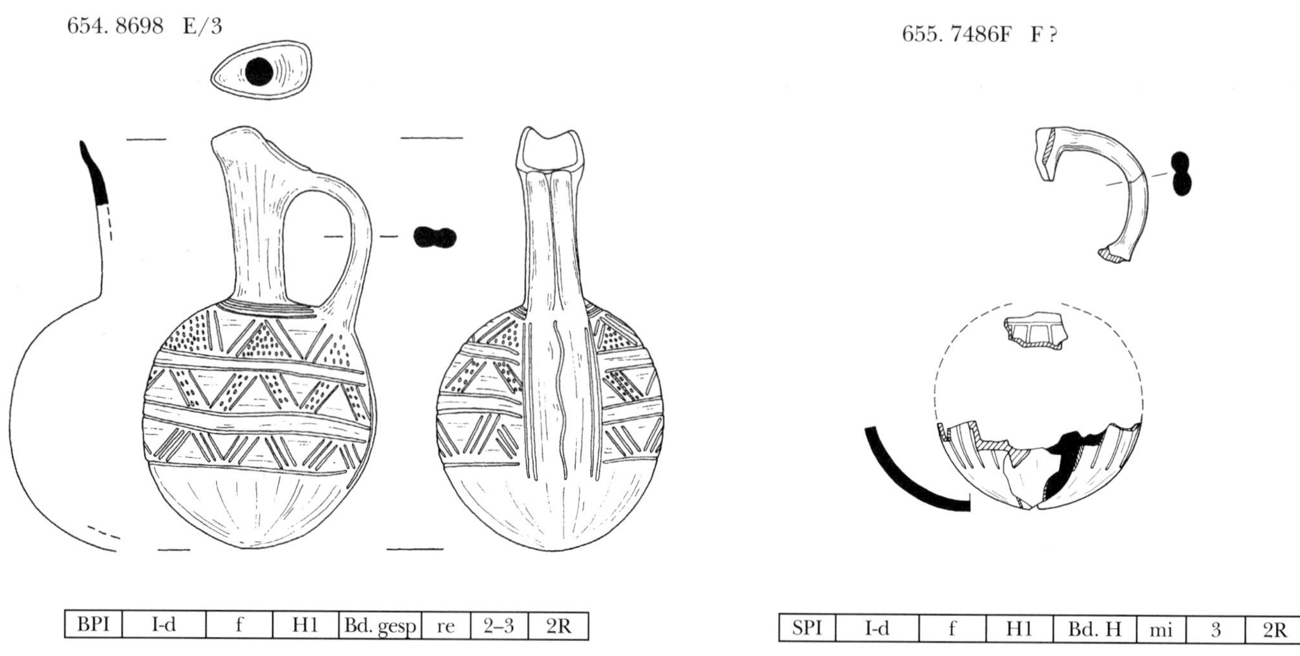

BPI	I-d	f	H1	Bd. gesp	re	2–3	2R

SPI	I-d	f	H1	Bd. H	mi	3	2R

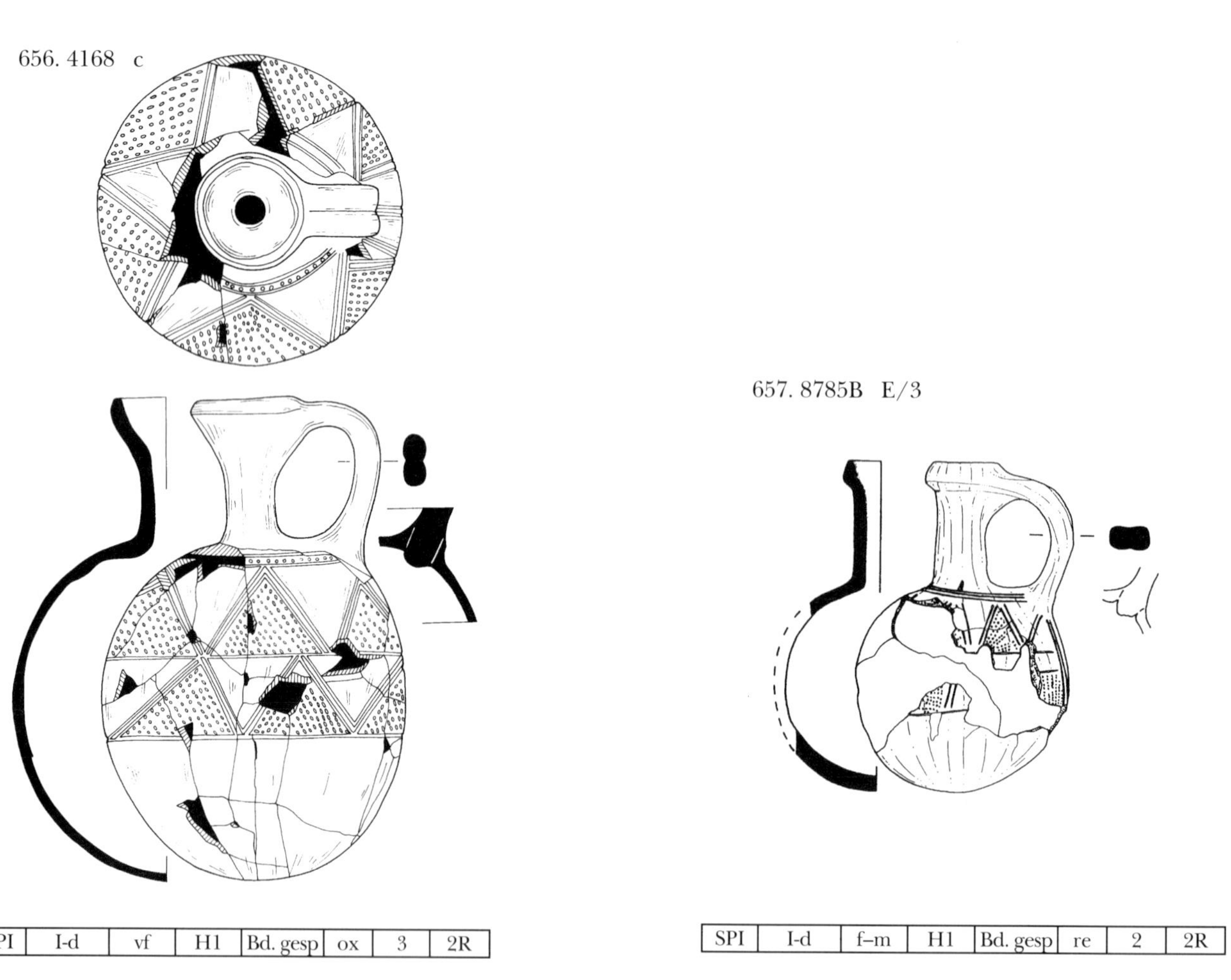

RPI	I-d	vf	H1	Bd. gesp	ox	3	2R

SPI	I-d	f–m	H1	Bd. gesp	re	2	2R

1:2

Handmade Globular Type Groups N.1, N.2.1a, N.2.1b

Plate 118

Type Group N.2.1c

658. 4166 TD F/I-i/22 grave 34 Phase c (82/115) Plates 119, 157

SPI	I-d	vf	H1	Bd. gesp	re	3	2R

D. 1.8 cm Nd. 1.1 cm. H. 7.8 cm. Md 5.0 cm. Wd. 0.25 cm.
VI 66.66
Restored from sherds, complete
Surface colour: 7.5YR5/4 light brown; burnished slip 7.5YR5/4 light brown
Break: not visible
Decoration: On upper body two muster zones and three incised lines at base of neck. Upper zone consists of standing triangles bordered by three incised lines. The lower zone comprises a zigzag made from three incised lines.

659. 4167 TD F/I-i/22 grave 34 Phase c (82/115) Plate 119

SPI	I-d	vf	H1	Bd. gesp	re	3	2R

D. 2.2 cm Nd. 1.2 cm. H. 8.4 cm. Md 5.6 cm. Wd. 0.2 cm.
VI 66.66
Restored from sherds, complete
Surface colour: 7.5YR5/4 light brown; burnished slip 7.5YR5/4 light brown
Break: not visible
Decoration: On upper body two muster zones and three incised lines at base of neck. Upper zone consists of standing triangles bordered by three incised lines. The lower zone comprises a zigzag made from three incised lines.

660. 1782 Vienna A1695 A/II-m/10 planum 6 grave 8 Phase F (68/148) Plates 119, 157

BPI	I-d	f	H1	Bd. gesp	re	3	2R

D. 2.3 cm Nd. 1.2 cm. H. 8.1 cm. Md 5.2 cm. Wd. 0.4 cm.
VI 64.19
Intact
Surface colour: 7.5YR5/4 light brown; burnished slip 5YR4/3–5/2 red brown
Break: not visible
Decoration: On upper body two muster zones and three incised lines at base of neck. Upper zone consists of standing triangles bordered by three incised lines. The lower zone comprises a zigzag made from three incised lines.
Previously published: TD V, 66, 67

661. 4438 F/I-k/20 grave 13 Phase b/3–2 (83/085) Plate 119

BPI	I-d	f–m	H1	Bd. gesp	re	3	2R

D. 2.5 cm Nd. 1.3 cm. H. 9.4 cm. Md 5.7 cm. Wd. 0.35 cm.
VI 60.63
Incomplete
Surface colour: 7.5YR5/4 light brown; burnished slip 5YR4/3–5/2 red brown
Break: not visible
Decoration: On upper body two muster zones and three incised lines at base of neck. Upper zone consists of standing triangles bordered by three incised lines. The lower zone comprises a zigzag made from three incised lines.

662. 8819A TD A/II-p/14 locus 286 grave 13 Phase E/3 (98/063) Plate 119

SPI	I-d	f	H1	Bd. gesp	re	3	2R

D. 2.3 cm Nd. 1.1 cm. pht. 8.3 cm. Md 6.0 cm. Wd. 0.3 cm.
Incomplete
Surface colour: 7.5YR4/2–5/2 brown; burnished slip 10YR4/2 v dark grey
Break: uniform grey brown
Decoration: On upper body two muster zones and three incised lines at base of neck. Upper zone consists of standing triangles bordered by three incised lines. The lower zone comprises a zigzag made from three incised lines.
Previously published: TD XVI, 216, fig. 136, no. 4.

Type Group N.3

Type Group N.3 comprises similar vessels to type group N.2, but in place of a double handle, have a single strap handle. Vessels attributed to group N.3 have two decorative schemes N.3.1a, in which the decoration consists of two zones of alternating standing and pendant triangles; and N.3.1b which has a row of alternating standing and pendant triangles and a row of pendant triangles below.

Type Group N.3.1a

663. 3641 Vienna A3930 F/I-i/22 planum 2 grave 30 Phase c-b/3 ? (81/398) Plate 120

SPI	I-d	f	H1	Bd. gesp	re	3	1B

D. 2.3 cm Nd. 2.0 cm. H. 8.3 cm. Md 5.2 cm. Wd. 0.2 cm.
VI 62.65
Intact
Surface colour: 5YR6/3 light red brown; burnished slip 2.5YR4/4 reddish brown
Break: uniform greyish brown
Decoration: Two zones of alternating standing and hanging triangles separated by reserved bands. The triangles are infilled with oblique lines made with a twelve-toothed comb.

664. 6052 F/I-o/21 grave 5 Phase b/3 (87/217)
Plates 120, 158

SPI	I-d	m	H1	Bd. gesp	re	3	1B

D. 1.95 cm Nd. 1.25 cm. H. 9.0 cm. Md 5.7 cm. Wd. 0.2 cm.
VI 63.33
Intact
Surface colour: 5YR6/3 light red brown; burnished slip 2.5YRN/2 black
Break: uniform grey
Decoration: Two zones of alternating standing and hanging triangles separated by reserved bands. The triangles are infilled with oblique lines made with an eight-toothed comb.

665. 6053 F/I-o/21 grave 5 Phase b/3 (87/088) Plate 120

SPI	I-d	f–m	H1	Bd. gesp	re	2–3	1B

D. 2.4 cm Nd. 1.3 cm. pht. 9.2 cm. Md 5.9 cm. Wd. 0.2 cm.
Restored from sherds, incomplete
Surface colour: 5YR6/3 light red brown; burnished slip 7.5YR4/0 dark grey
Break: uniform grey
Decoration: Two zones of alternating standing and hanging triangles separated by reserved bands. The triangles are infilled with oblique lines made with a ten-toothed comb.

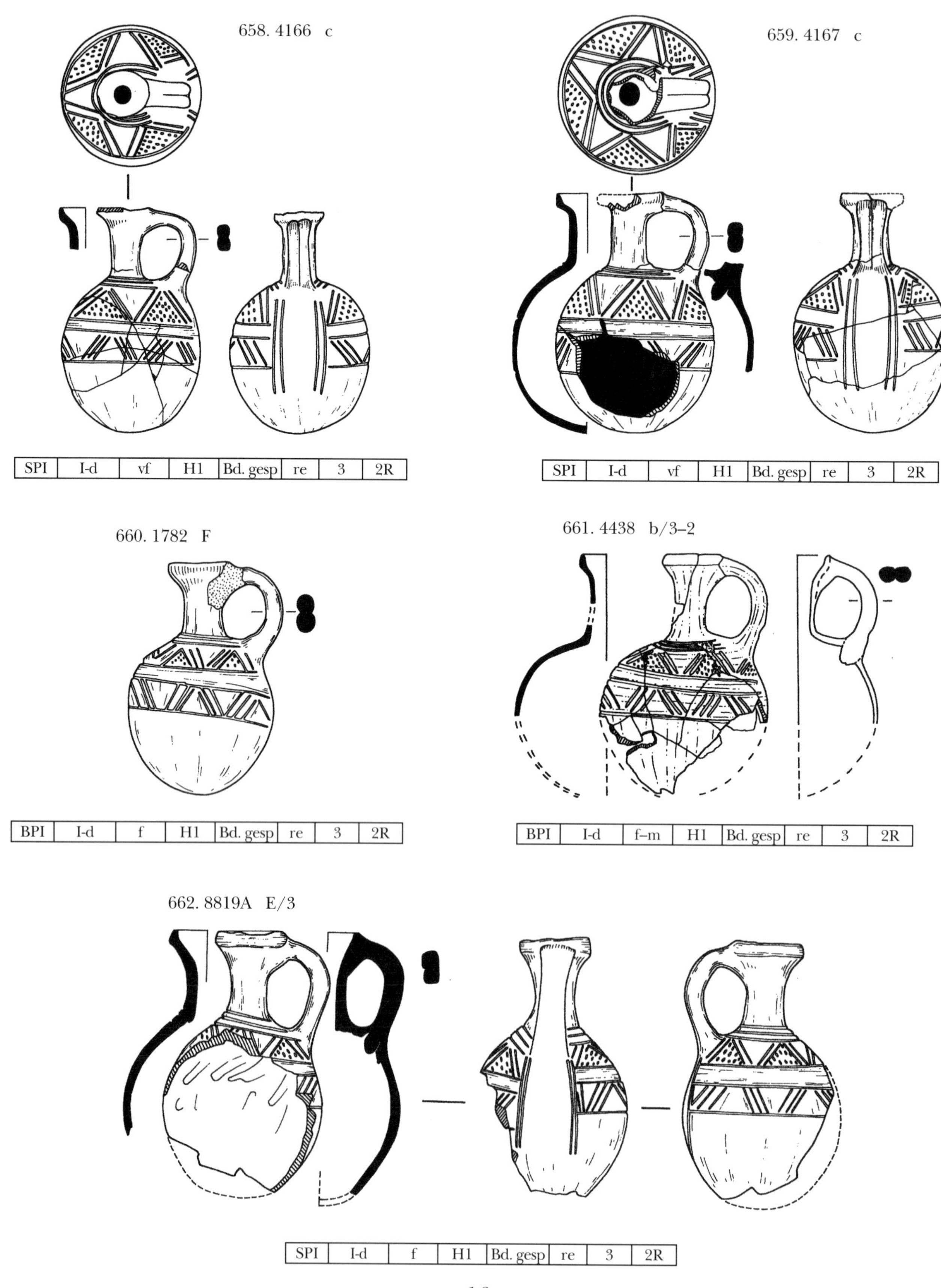

658. 4166 c

SPI	I-d	vf	H1	Bd. gesp	re	3	2R

659. 4167 c

SPI	I-d	vf	H1	Bd. gesp	re	3	2R

660. 1782 F

BPI	I-d	f	H1	Bd. gesp	re	3	2R

661. 4438 b/3–2

BPI	I-d	f–m	H1	Bd. gesp	re	3	2R

662. 8819A E/3

SPI	I-d	f	H1	Bd. gesp	re	3	2R

1:2

Handmade Globular Type Group N.2.1c

Plate 119

663. 3641 c–b/3.?

664. 6052 b/3

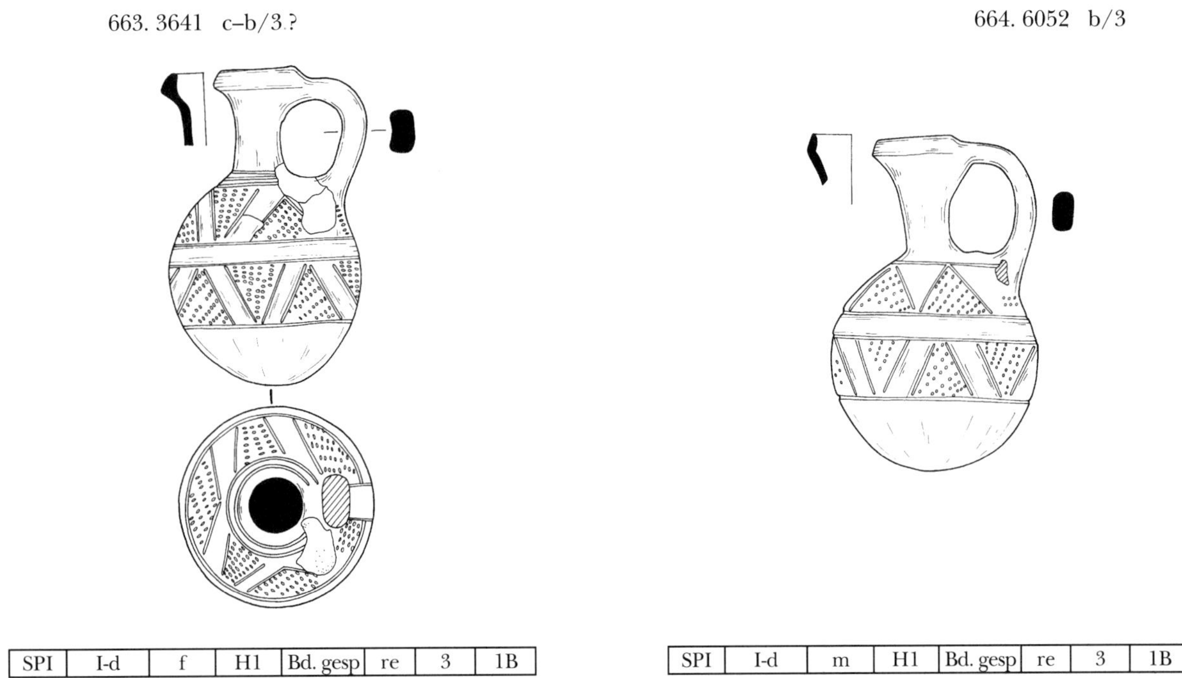

SPI	I-d	f	H1	Bd. gesp	re	3	1B

SPI	I-d	m	H1	Bd. gesp	re	3	1B

665. 6053 b/3

666. 4060A b/2

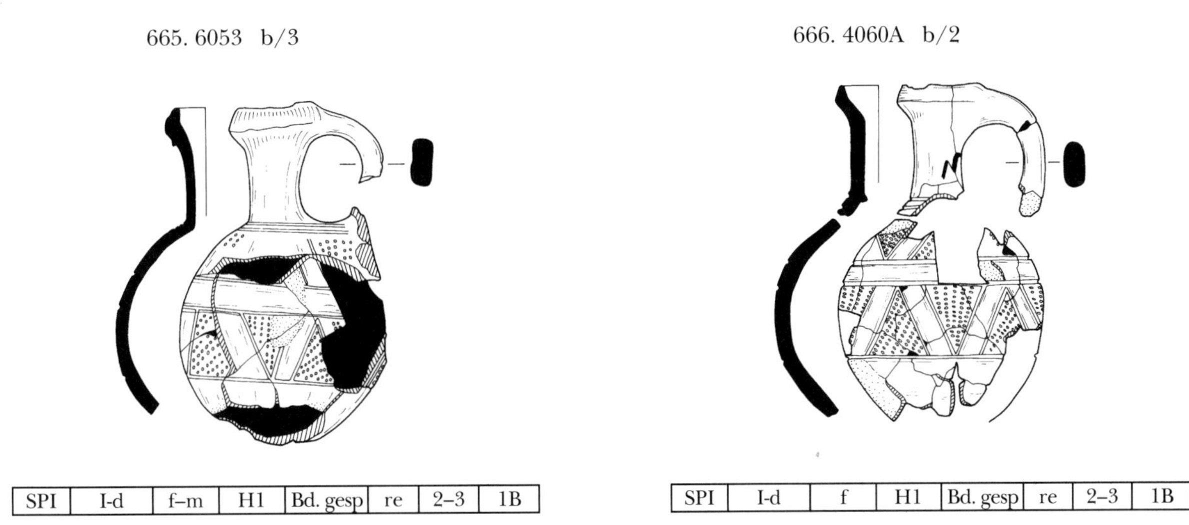

SPI	I-d	f–m	H1	Bd. gesp	re	2–3	1B

SPI	I-d	f	H1	Bd. gesp	re	2–3	1B

1:2

Handmade Globular Type Groups N.2.1c–N.3.1a

Plate 120

666. 4060A F/I-l/20 planum 1 grave 31 Phase b/2 (86/127) Plate 120

SPI	I-d	f	H1	Bd. gesp	re	2–3	1B

D. 2.4 cm Nd. 1.3 cm. pht. 9.0 cm. Md 5.6 cm. Wd. 0.4 cm.
Restored from sherds, incomplete
Surface colour: 5YR6/3 light red brown; burnished slip 7.5YR4/0 dark grey
Break: uniform grey
Decoration: Two zones of alternating standing and hanging triangles separated by reserved bands. the triangles are infilled with oblique lines made with a twelve-toothed comb.

667. 7486E TD A/IV-h/4 grave 11 Phase F ? (91/212) Plates 121, 158

SPI	I-d	m	H1	Bd. gesp	re	3	2R

pht. 6.6 cm. Md 6.4 cm. Wd. 0.35 cm.
Restored from sherds, incomplete
Surface colour: 5YR6/3 light red brown; burnished slip 5YR5/1–3 grey
Break: dark grey core, light grey oxidation zones
Handle does not protrude through vessel wall
Decoration: Horizontal band on shoulder and a row of four unequal standing triangles separated from each other by two parallel lines. The shoulder band and standing triangles infilled by a ten-toothed comb.

668. 7486C TD A/IV-h/4 grave 11 Phase F ? (91/213) Plate 121

SPI	I-d	f	H1	Bd. gesp	mi	2	2R

pht. 6.2 cm. Md 5.5 cm. Wd. 0.35 cm.
Restored from sherds, incomplete
Surface colour: 5YR6/3 light red brown; burnished slip 7.5YR6/2–4 pink
Break: reddish brown in, grey out
Decoration: made with an eight-toothed comb in oblique lines.

Type Group N.3.1b

669. 1771 Vienna A3193 A/II-m/10 planum 6 burial 8 Phase F (68/146) Plates 121, 158

BPI	I-d	f–vf	H1	Bd. gesp	re	2–3	1B

D. 2.5 cm. Nd. 1.4 cm. H. 9.5 cm.. Md 5.8 cm. Wd. 0.3 cm.
VI 61.05
Restored from sherds, incomplete
Surface colour: 5YR6/3 light red brown; burnished slip 10YR3/1 very dark grey
Break: uniform very dark grey
Handle through vessel wall
Decoration: Band of alternating standing and pendant triangles on shoulder, and a frieze of pendant triangles on the body. The triangles are filled with an eight-toothed comb.
Previously published: TD V, 66–68.

670. 1781 Vienna A3202 A/II-m/10 planum 6 burial 8 Phase F (68/148) Plate 121

BPI	I-d	f–vf	H1	Bd. gesp	re	2–3	1B

pht. 5.0 cm. 6.2 cm. Md 6.0 cm. Wd. 0.3 cm.
Restored from sherds, incomplete
Surface colour: 5YR6/3 light red brown; burnished slip 5YR4/2 dark red grey
Break: grey brown core, dark grey reduction zones
Decoration: Frieze of pendant triangles on lower body, infilled with a six toothed comb.
Previously published: TD V, 66, 67.

Type Group N.4

Type group N.4 consists of globular jugs, which in contrast to jugs of type group N.2 have much smaller bodies in comparison to their total height. They have an upright rim and double handle which comes from the rim to a point low down on the shoulder. Four decorative styles are associated with this type: N.4.1a in which a band of decoration is wrapped around the vessel; N.4.1b which consists of one zone of intersecting standing and pendant triangles separated by a reserved zigzag; N.4.1c which has a horizontal band filled with vertical dots above and a row of standing triangles below; and N.4.1d which has two rows of standing triangles.

Type Group N.4.1a

671. 7462 TD A/IV-h/7 grave 7 Phase F-E/3 (91/384) Plates 121, 158

SPI	I-d	f–m	H1	Bd. gesp	re	3	2R

D. 2.0 cm Nd. 1.4 cm. H. 6.9 cm. Md 4.45 cm. Wd. 0.3 cm.
VI 64.49
Incomplete
Surface colour: 7.5YR4/2–5/2 brown; burnished slip 5YR4/1 dark grey
Break: not visible
Decoration: Five incised lines at base of neck and then a band of diagonal striations made with an eight-toothed comb. This is divided, by a reserved zone, from a frieze of two alternating standing and pendant traiangles, somewhat carelessly executed, infilled with dots made with an eight-toothed comb.
Previously published: PuF 229 nr. 276.

672. 7486 TD A/IV-h/4 grave 11 Phase F ? (91/387) Plate 122

BPI	I-d	f	H1	Bd. gesp	re	2–3	2R

D. 2.3 cm Nd. 1.3 cm. H. 6.2 cm. Md 3.8 cm. Wd. 0.3 cm.
VI 61.29
Intact
Surface colour: 7.5YR4/2–5/2 brown; burnished slip 5YR5/4 reddish brown
Break: not visible
Decoration: Four incised lines made at the base of the neck. Two bands of vertical lines made with a nine-toothed comb.

673. 8856A TD A/II-p/14 grave 2 Phase E/2 (98/086) Plate 122

BPI	I-d	f	H1	Bd. gesp	mi	2	2R

D. 2.2 cm Nd. 1.4 cm. H. 6.0 cm. Md 3.43 cm. Wd. 0.3 cm.
VI 57.16
Incomplete
Surface colour: 10YR6/4 light yellow brown; burnished slip 10YR6/4

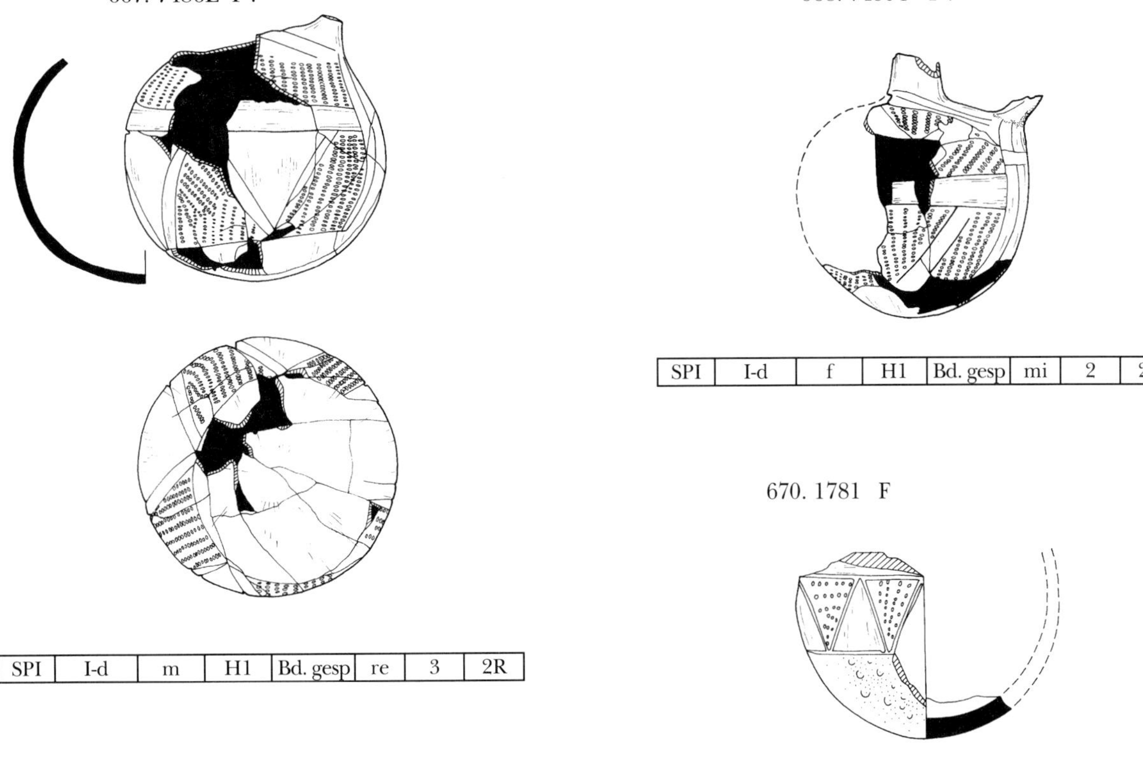

667. 7486E F ?

SPI	I-d	m	H1	Bd. gesp	re	3	2R

668. 7486C F ?

SPI	I-d	f	H1	Bd. gesp	mi	2	2R

670. 1781 F

BPI	I-d	f–vf	H1	Bd. gesp	re	2–3	1B

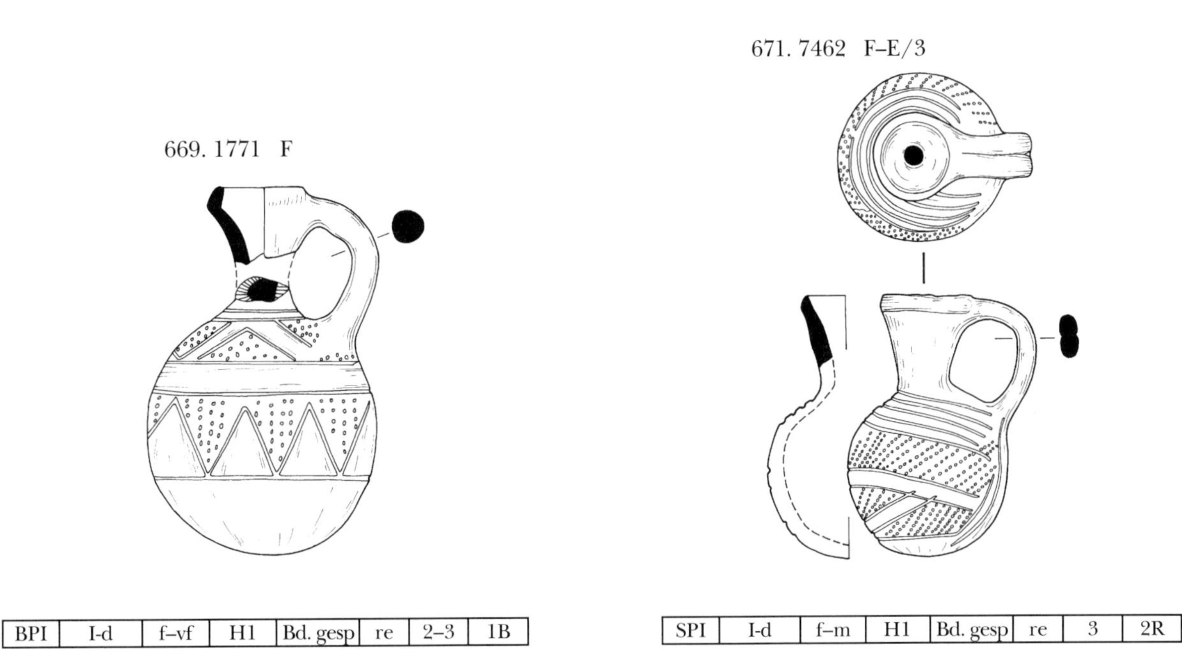

669. 1771 F

BPI	I-d	f–vf	H1	Bd. gesp	re	2–3	1B

671. 7462 F–E/3

SPI	I-d	f–m	H1	Bd. gesp	re	3	2R

1:2

Handmade Globular Type Groups N.3.1a, b, N.4.1a

Plate 121

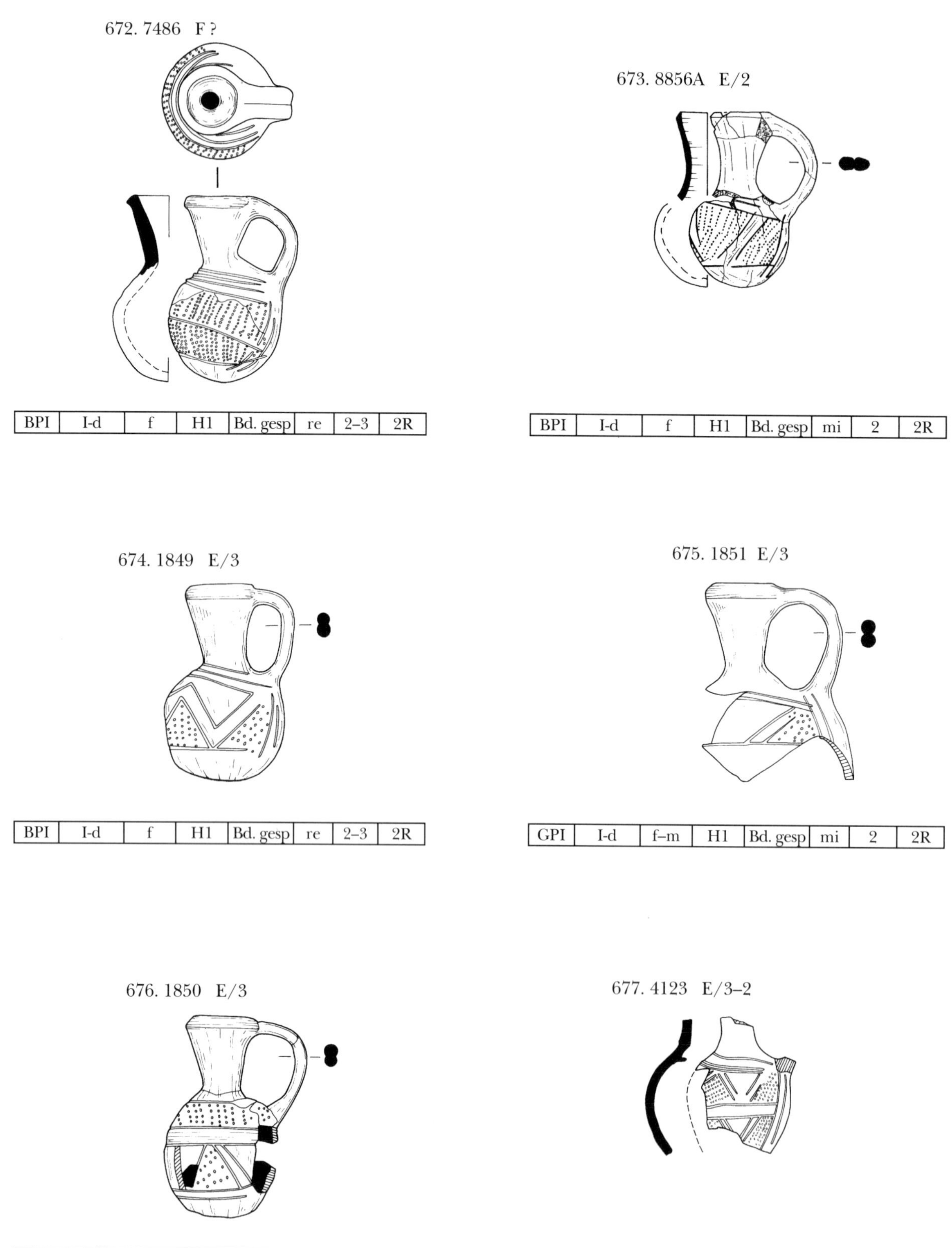

1:2

Handmade Globular Type Groups N.4.1a–d

Plate 122

Break: uniform 10YR6/4 light yellow brown
Decoration: One band of alternating unequal three standing and two pendant triangles filled with oblique lines made with an eight-toothed comb. Incised vertical lines under handle.
Previously published: TD XVI, 239, fig. 170, no. 2.

Type Group N.4.1b

674. 1849 Cairo JE 91180 A/II-n/13 planum 6–7 grave 8 Phase E/3 (68/168) Plates 122, 159

BPI	I-d	f	H1	Bd. gesp	re	2–3	2R

D. 2.2 cm Nd. 1.2 cm. H. 6.6 cm. Md 4.2 cm. Wd. 0.3 cm.
VI 63.63
Intact
Surface colour: 5YR6/3 light red brown; burnished slip 5YR4/3 reddish brown
Break: not visible
Decoration: Three incised lines at the base of the neck. Frieze of four double-framed standing triangles infilled with a six-toothed comb.
Previously published: Bietak, *MDAIK* 26, pl. 21c; Kaplan, *Tell el-Yahudiyeh Ware*, fig. 16b; *TD V*, 89.

675. 1851 Vienna A3254 A/II-n/13 planum 6–7 grave 8 Phase E/3 (68/200) Plate 122

GPI	I-d	f–m	H1	Bd. gesp	mi	2	2R

D. 2.8 cm Nd. 1.3 cm. pht. 7.4 cm. Md 7.2 cm. Wd. 0.3 cm.
Incomplete
Surface colour: 10YR5/3 brown; burnished slip 2.5YR4/4 red brown
Break: brown core, grey brown oxidation zones
Handle not pushed through vessel wall
Decoration: consists of one preserved standing triangle infilled with dots made with a single-pointed tool.
BNL JH313 Egyptian Nile Clay[618]
Previously published: TD V, 89.

Type Group N.4.1c

676. 1850 Vienna A3253 A/II-n/13 planum 6–7 grave 8 Phase E/3 (68/168) Plates 122, 159

RPI	I-d	f	H1	Bd. gesp	mi	2	2R

D. 2.4 cm Nd. 1.3 cm. H. 6.8 cm. Md 4.0 cm. Wd. 0.3 cm.
VI 58.82
Intact
Surface colour: 5YR6/3 light red brown; burnished slip 2.5YR4/4 reddish brown
Break: brown core, grey brown oxidation zones
Handle does not go through vessel wall.
Decoration: Band on shoulder filled with vertical striations made with a five-toothed comb. Below a frieze of standing triangles infilled with dots masde with a five-toothed comb.
BNL JH312 Egyptian Nile Clay[619]
Previously published: TD V, 89.

Type Group N.4.1d

677. 4123 TD A/II-l/17 planum 4–5 Phase E/3–2 (82/161) Plates 122, 159

RPI	I-d	f	H1	–	mi	2	2R

Nd. 1.3 cm. pht. 4.2 cm. Md 4.0 cm. Wd. 0.2 cm.
Incomplete
Surface colour: 5YR6/3 light red brown; burnished slip 2.5YR4/4 reddish brown
Break: brown core, grey brown oxidation zones
Handle does not go through vessel wall.
Decoration: Two rows of double-framed standing triangles filled with oblique lines made with an eight-toothed comb. Three incised lines below handle.

Type Group N.5

Type Group N.5 is formed by at least three globular jugs, known from Tell el-Dab^c^a which are evidently Egyptian in shape (cf. above group N.3), but bear one band of impressed decoration which certainly owes its inspiration to the Palestinian style. Whether this group originated in the Levant is not clear since a preliminary visual analysis would attribute TD 3642 to a Palestinian clay, whilst the others are seemingly made of a Nile clay. A slightly similar jug, TD 6042, has a horizontal band around the upper belly with a zigzag pattern above.

678. 3642 Vienna A3931 F/I-i/22 grave 30 Phase c (82/013) Plates 123, 159

SPI	IV	f	H1	Bd. gesp	re	3	2R

D. 2.0 cm. Nd 1.25 cm. H. 8.7 cm. Md. 5.4 cm. Wd. 0.3 cm.
VI 62.06
Intact
Surface colour: 2.5Y5/1 grey; burnished slip: 2.5YRN/2 black
Break: not visible
Decoration: Three incised lines at base of neck. One horizontal band of verticlal striations running around the pot at the base of the shoulder. Dots made with a five-toothed comb.

679. 5427 TD A/II-k/17 grave 30 burial 1 Phase F (85/269) Plate 123

SPI	I-d	m	H1	Bd. gesp	re	3	2R

D. 2.4 cm. Nd 1.25 cm. H. 9.4 cm. Md. 6.0 cm. Wd. 0.35 cm.
VI 63.82
Intact
Surface colour: 7.5Y5–4/2 brown; burnished slip: 10YR2/1 black
Break: not visible
Decoration: One ornamental band infilled with lines from upper left to lower right made with a five-toothed comb.
Previously published: TD XVI, 146, fig. 84b, no. 18.

[618] P. McGovern, *The Foreign Relations of the Hyksos*, Oxford, 2000, 124 no. JH313.

[619] P. McGovern, *The Foreign Relations of the Hyksos*, Oxford, 2000, 129 no. JH312.

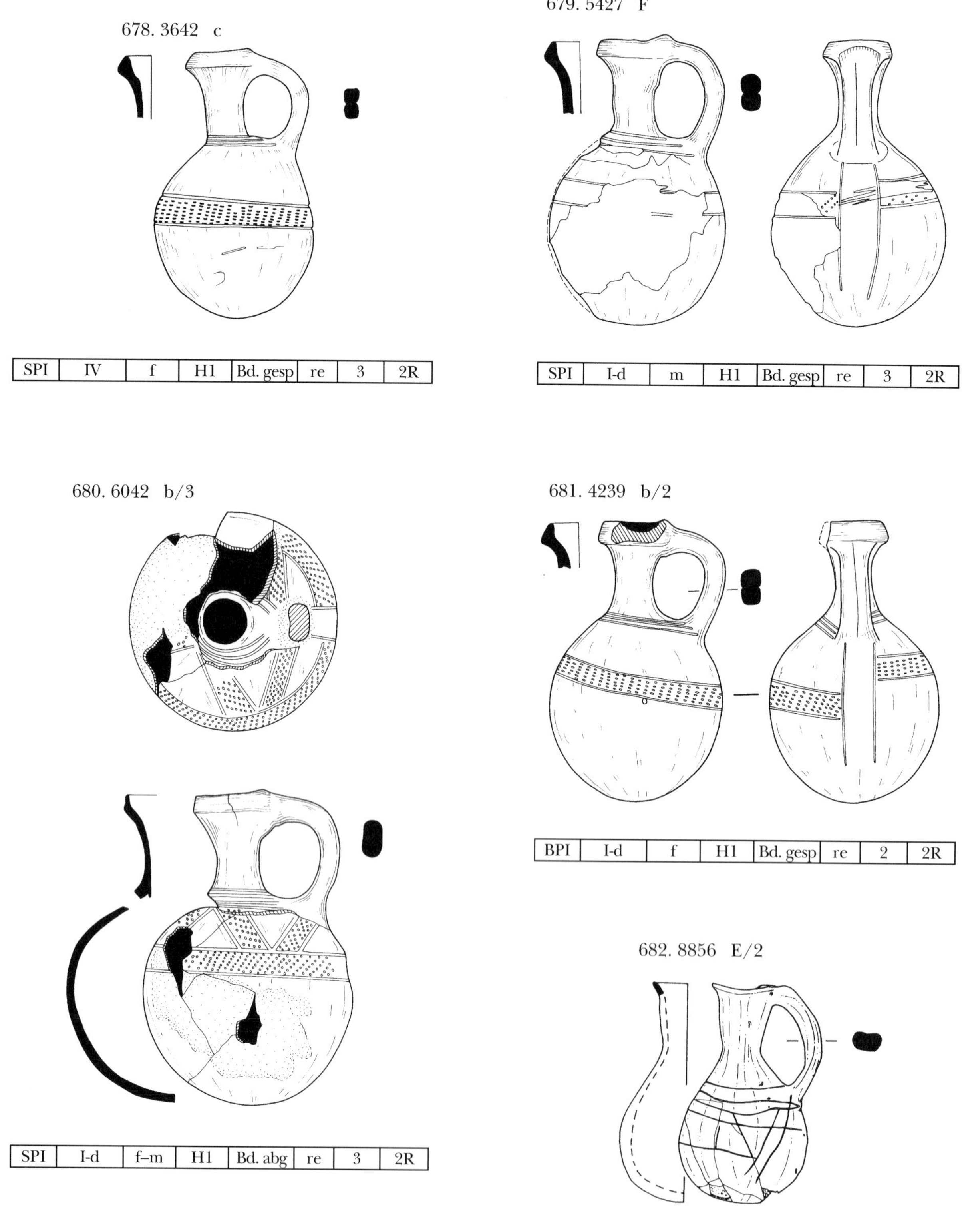

1:2

Handmade Globular Type Groups N.5, N.6

Plate 123

680. 6042 TD F/I-o/21 grave 5 Phase b/3 (87/071)
Plates 123, 160

SPI	I-d	f–m	H1	Bd. abg	re	3	2R

D. 2.2 cm. Nd 1.35 cm. Bd. 1.6 cm. H. 10.3 cm. Md. 7.2 cm. Wd. 0.3 cm.
VI 69.90
Restored from sherds, complete
Surface colour: 2.5Y5/1 grey; burnished slip: 2.5YRN/2 black
Break: light grey core, dark grey reduction zones
Decoration: Three incised lines at the base of the neck. Frieze of striations slanting from top right to bottom left at base of shoulder. Sloping bands extend from the base of the neck to the lower frieze giving the effect of alternating standing and pendant triangles. The bands and frieze are decorated with dots made with a six-toothed comb.

681. 4239 TD F/I-i/23 grave 32 Phase b/2 (82/189)
Plates 123, 160

BPI	I-d	f	H1	Bd. gesp	re	2	2R

D. 2.5 cm. Nd 1.3 cm. H. 9.2 cm. Md. 5.8 cm. Wd. 0.3 cm.
VI 63.04
Intact
Surface colour: 10YR4/1 grey; burnished slip: 10YR2/1 black
Break: not visible
Decoration: Three incised lines at base of neck. One horizontal band of verticlal striations running around the pot at the base of the shoulder. Dots made with a five-toothed comb.
BNL JH830 most similar to Egyptian Nile Clay.[620]

Type Group N.6

Type Group N.6 is known through a single example found at Tell el-Dabca, TD 8856, which is a handmade globular jug with everted rim, strap handle and a simple decoration consisting of horizontal and oblique lines

682. 8856 TD A/II-p/14 grave 2 Phase E/2 (98/086)
Plates 123, 160

SPI	I-d	f	H1	Bd. H	mi	3	1B

D. 2.15 cm. Nd. 1.4 cm. H. 7.4 cm. Wd. 0.2 cm.
Incomplete
Surface colour: 10YR5/2 greyish brown; burnished slip 10YR4/4 dark reddish brown
Break: wide dark grey core, thin red and brown reduction zones
Decoration: Five horizontal lines incised around body with seven irregularly spaced curving vertical lines
Previously published: TD XVI, 239, fig. 169, no. 1.

Type Group N.7

Type Group N.7 is also known through only one vessel, Tell el-Dabca, TD 8665, which has a thickened rolled rim, double handle and a trilobal body, decorated with incised lines.

683. 8665 TD A/II-p/14 locus 273 grave 12 Phase E/3 (97/370) Plates 124, 160

SPI	I-d	f–m	H1	Bd. H	re	3	2R

D. 1.2 cm Nd. 1.05 cm. H. 7.8 cm. Wd. 0.3 cm.
Intact
Surface colour: 10YR4/4 very yellow brown; burnished slip 5YR5/2 dark grey
Break: not visible
Decoration: Consists of parallel lines in twelve vertical zones.
Previously published: TD XVI, 213, fig. 131, no. 4.

Type Group N.9

Vessels of Type Group N.9 comprise squat piriform jugs with rolled rims, double handles and ring bases, known from a single, poorly preserved example from Tell el-Dabca (TD 5934). The preserved decoration comprises a rishi pattern around the neck.

684. 5934 TD A/II-n/19 grave 4 Phase E/1 (84/162)
Plates 124, 161

SPI	I-d	f	W2	Bd. gef	re	2	2R

D. 2.8 cm. Nd. 1.8 cm. Bd. 2.0 cm. H. 7.3 cm. Md 6.4 cm. Wd. 0.3 cm.
Restored from sherds, complete
Surface colour: 10YR5/3 brown; burnished slip 10YR4/1 dark grey
Break: uniform dark grey
Decoration: Poorly preserved but it appears to show overlapping petals. Surface eroded off below the shoulder.

Handmade Globular, type uncertain

685. 6386A TD F/I-m/18 grave 13 Phase ? (87/094)
Plate 124

RPI	I-d	f	H1	–	mi	3

pht. 2.0 cm. Md 5.5 cm. Wd. 0.35 cm.
Incomplete
Surface colour: 5YR6/3 light red brown; burnished slip 2.5YR4/4 reddish brown
Break: brown core, grey brown oxidation zones
Decoration: Two (?) rows of standing triangles (only one preserved) filled with vertical lines made with an eight-toothed comb. cf. TD 4123.

Jars

Whilst most known Tell el-Yahudiya style vessels are jugs, a small number of jars are also known, of which the most complete is a vessel from Hama Phase H.[621] Other incomplete, and later, vessels are known from

[620] P. McGovern, *The Foreign Relations of the Hyksos,* Oxford, 2000, 149 no. JH867.

[621] E. Fugmann, *Hama II. Fouilles et recherches 1931–38,* fig. 139b/5 B 265; Kopetzky, *op. cit.* 178.

683. 8665 E/3

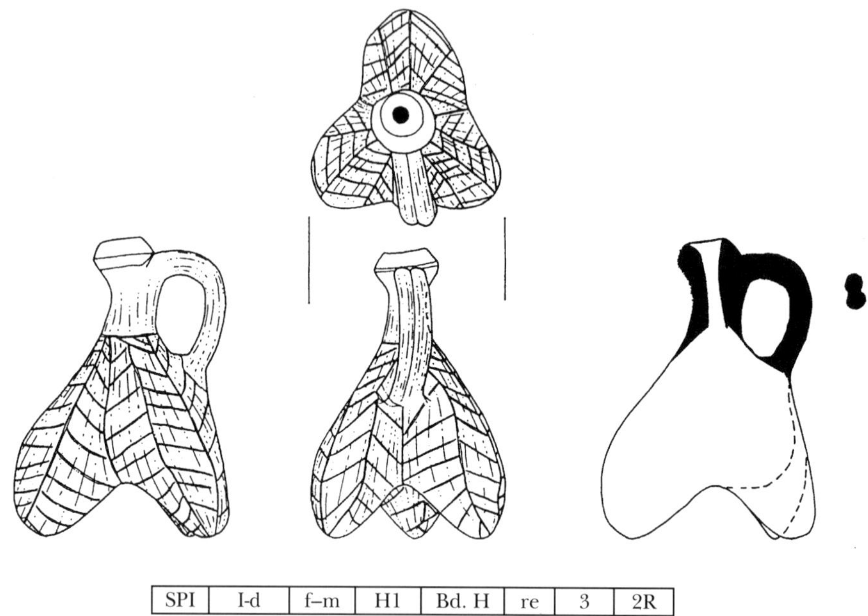

SPI	I-d	f–m	H1	Bd. H	re	3	2R

684. 5934 E/1

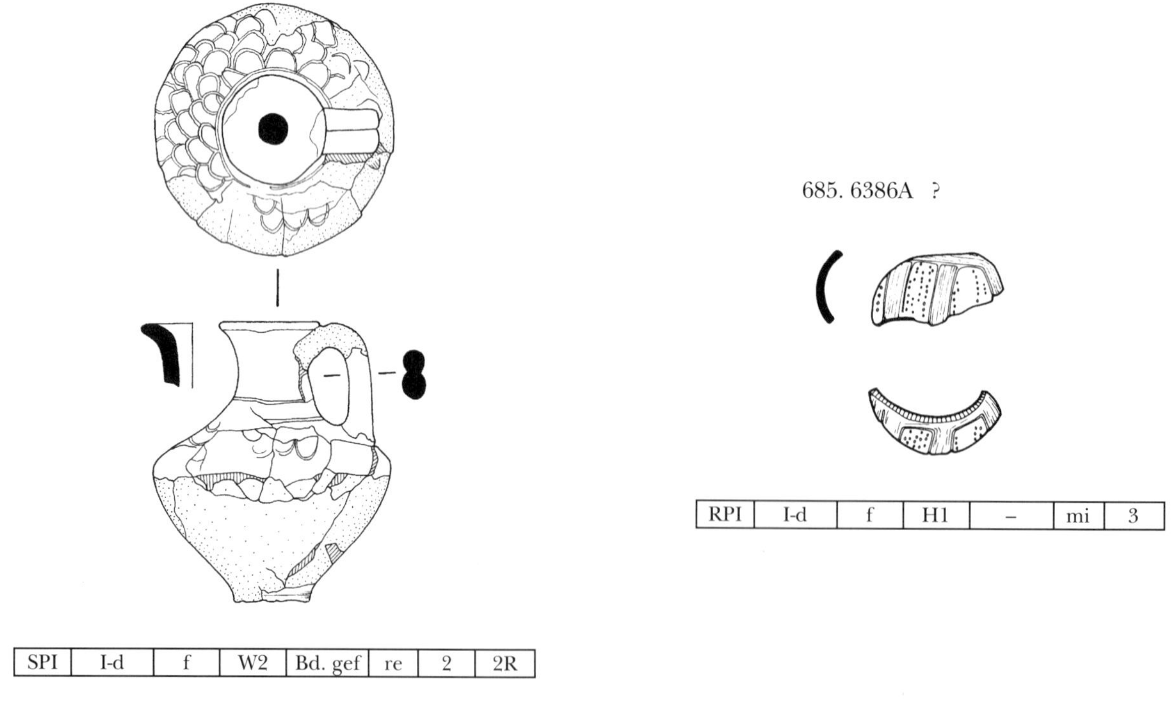

SPI	I-d	f	W2	Bd. gef	re	2	2R

685. 6386A ?

RPI	I-d	f	H1	–	mi	3

1:2

Handmade Globular Type Groups N.7, N.9 and a miscellaneous sherd

Plate 124

Tell el-Dabᶜa. Of these the earlier two were imported from southern Palestine, whilst the latest example was clearly locally made.

Type Group O

686. 4138E TD A/II-l/17 planum 6 Phase F or E/3 (82/374) Plates 125, 161

SPI	IV-2	f	W2	–	re	3

D. 10.0 cm. pht. 2.0 cm. Wd. 0.35 cm.
Incomplete
Surface colour: 7.5YR4.5/4 brown; burnished slip 2.5YR4/6 red
Break: uniform brown
Decoration: Three incised plant designs.
BNL 905: South Palestine
Previously published: Kopetzky, Gefässe im Tell el-Yahudiya Stil, in: E. Cerny, I. Hein, H. Hunger, D. Melmann, A. Schwab (eds.), *Timelines. Studies in Honour of Manfred Bietak*, II, 2006, 181.

687. 3415B TD F/I-j/22 planum 1 Phase b/1–a/2 (81/075) Plates 125, 161

SPI	IV-2	vf	W2	–	re	3

D. 3.5 cm. pht. 4.4 cm. Wd. 0.3 cm.
Incomplete
Surface colour: 10YR5/1 grey; burnished slip 10YR2/1 black
Break: dark grey core, brown reduction zones
Decoration: Three vertical incised plant designs.
BNL: South Palestine.
Previously published: Kopetzky, Gefässe im Tell el-Yahudiya Stil, in: E. Cerny, I. Hein, H. Hunger, D. Melmann, A. Schwab (eds.), *Timelines. Studies in Honour of Manfred Bietak*, II, 2006, 183; Kopetzky, *The MB IIB-Corpus of the Hyksos Period at Tell el-Dabᶜa*, 2007, 199 fig. 4.7.

688. 9026K TD F/II-r/22 L81 Phase a/2 (09/119) Plates 126, 161

SPI	I-b-2	f	W2	–	re	3

pht. 5.1 cm. Md. 14.6 cm. Wd. 0.45 cm.
Incomplete
Surface colour: 5YR4/1 dark grey; all traces of burnishing have been lost
Break: grey core, brown and grey reduction zones
Decoration: Part of a lotus flower.

Open Vessels

Open vessels decorated in typical Tell el-Yahudiya technique are rare. Several fragments of open vessels have come to light at Tell el-Dabᶜa. These are most often decorated with running spirals, incised triangles, and in one case lotus flowers.

Type Group P.1.2

Type group P.1.2 is known from the rim sherd Tell el-Dabᶜa, TD 9026H, which evidently derives from a dish with modeled rim, two, or four handles, and presumably a ring base, although only a rim sherd which bears a handle scar is preserved.

689. 9026H TD F/II-r/22 L81 Phase a/2 (09/119) Plates 126, 162

SPI	I-d	f	W2	–	re	3

D. 24.4 cm. pht. 2.5 cm. Md. 25.2 cm. Wd. 0.7 cm.
Incomplete
Surface colour: 5YR4/1 dark grey; all traces of burnishing have been lost
Break: black core, brown and grey reduction zones
Decoration: Not clear, possibly part of a lotus plant.

Type Group P.2

As yet type group O2 which consists of open vessels, possibly ring-based cups, are the most common. They are usually decorated with spirals and examples have been found at both Tell el-Dabᶜa and Lisht (?).

690. 4506F TD F/I-k/23 planum 0–1 Phase b/2–1 ? (83/141) Plates 126, 162

SPI	I-d	f	W2	–	re	3

pht. 3.5 cm. Md. 5.0 cm. Wd. 0.7 cm.
Incomplete
Surface colour: 10YR5.5/1 grey; burnished slip 10YR4/1 dark grey
Break: very dak grey core, light brown reduction zone
Decoration: Zigzag on rim, running spirals above mid-point.
BNL JH830 Egyptian Nile Clay[622]
Previously published: McGovern, *The Foreign Relations of the Hyksos*, Oxford, 2000, 107 pl. 9d; Kopetzky, Gefässe im Tell el-Yahudiya Stil, in: E. Cerny, I. Hein, H. Hunger, D. Melmann, A. Schwab (eds.), *Timelines. Studies in Honour of Manfred Bietak*, II, 2006, 178.

691. 2510A = 8104H TD A/II-l/14 planum 4–5 Phase F-E/3 (93/631) Plates 126, 163

SPI	I-b-2	f	W2	–	re	3

D. 12.0 cm. pht. 3.5. cm. Wd. 0.4 cm.
Incomplete
Surface colour: 10YR5.5/1 grey; burnished slip 5YR5/4 reddish brown
Break: red core, bluish grey reduction zones
Decoration: One hand drawn spiral preserved on exterior. Wavy line on top of rim, both this line and the spiral are infilled with white pigment.
Previously published: Kopetzky, Gefässe im Tell el-Yahudiya Stil, in: E. Cerny, I. Hein, H. Hunger, D. Melmann, A. Schwab (eds.), *Timelines. Studies in Honour of Manfred Bietak*, II, 2006, 178.

692. 2765 Cairo A/II-o/18 planum ? Phase E/3 ? (79/051) Plate 126

SPI	IV-2	vf	W2	–	re	3–4

[622] P. McGovern, *The Foreign Relations of the Hyksos*, Oxford, 2000, 147 no. JH830.

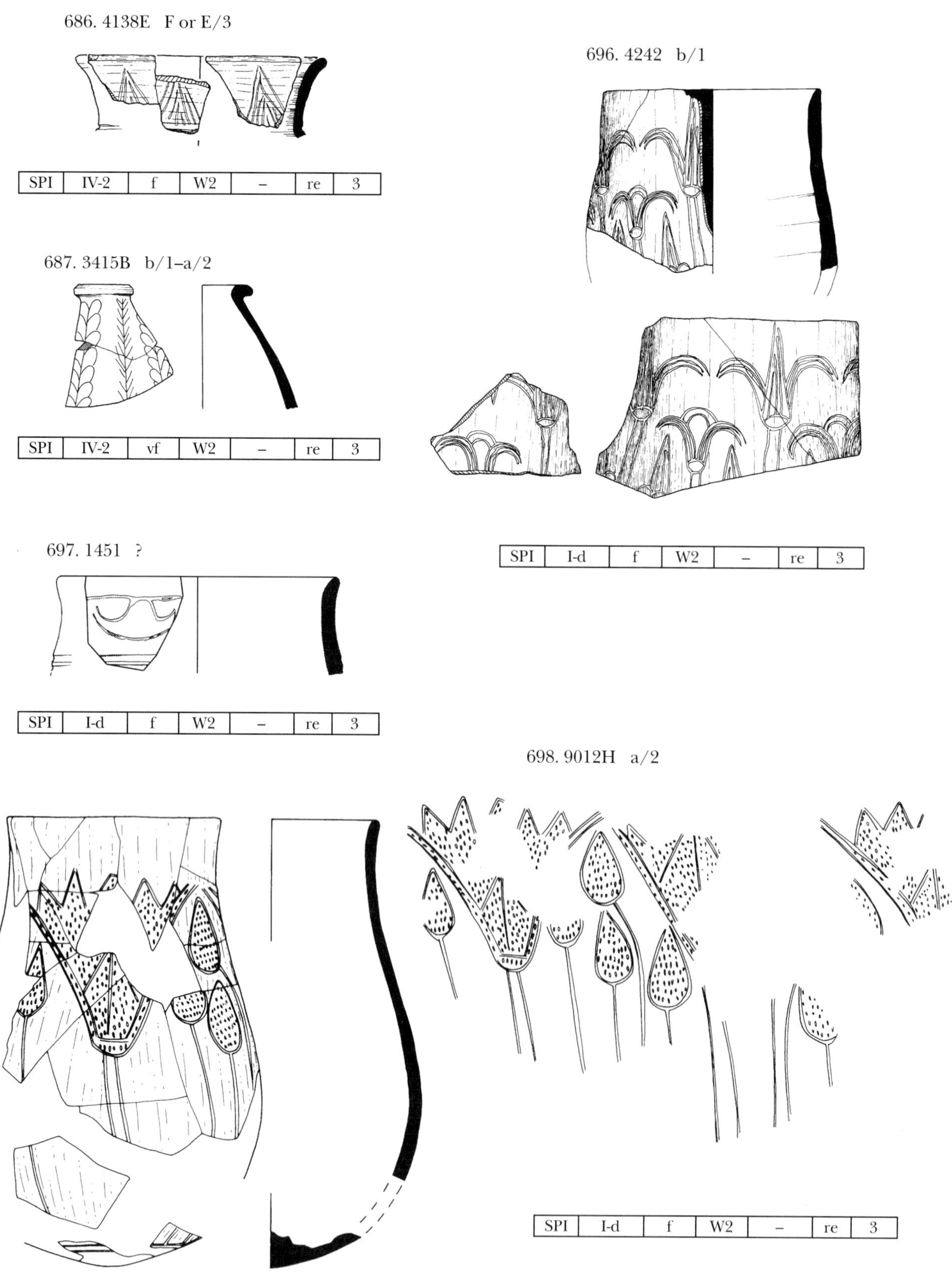

1:2

Late Egyptian Type Groups O, P.4, P.5

Plate 125

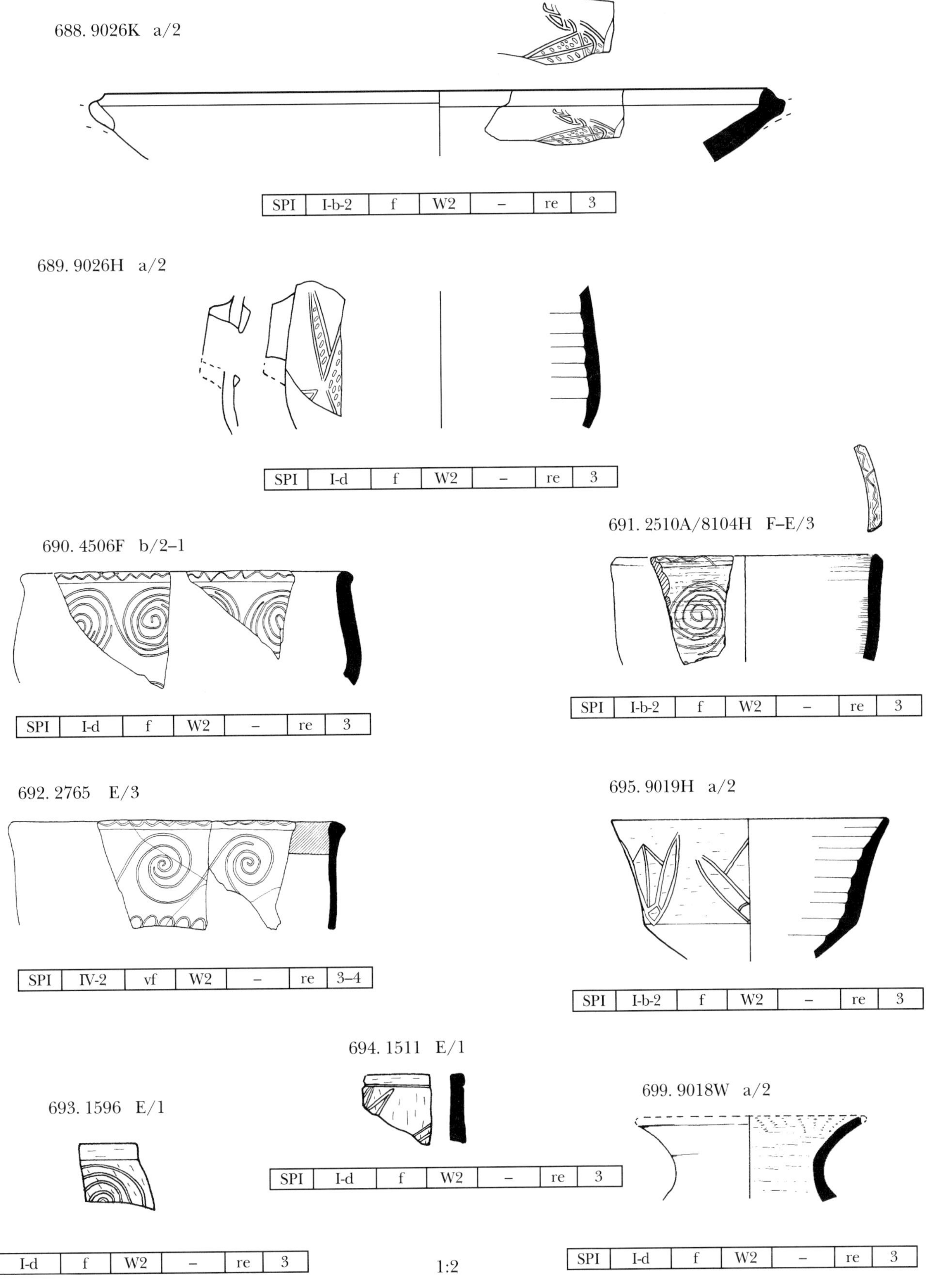

Late Egyptian Type Groups O, P.1, P.2 and Q

Plate 126

D. 9.0 cm. pht. 3.7 cm. Wd. 0.27–0.34 cm.
Incomplete
Surface colour: 10YR3–4/1 dark brown; burnished slip 5YR5/4 dark grey
Break: uniform grey
Decoration: Zigzag on rim, running spirals above mid-point.
Previously published: KOPETZKY, Gefässe im Tell el-Yahudiya Stil, in: E. CERNY, I. HEIN, H. HUNGER, D. MELMANN, A. SCHWAB (eds.), *Timelines. Studies in Honour of Manfred Bietak*, II, 2006, 178.

693. 1596 Vienna A3089 A/II-l/14 planum 2–3 Phase E/1 (68/111) Plate 126

SPI	I-d	f	W2	–	re	3

pht. 2.0 cm. Wd. 0.3 cm.
Incomplete
Surface colour: 10YR5.5/1 grey; burnished slip 10YR4/1 dark grey
Break: uniform grey
Decoration: Spiral.
Previously published: KOPETZKY, Gefässe im Tell el-Yahudiya Stil, in: E. CERNY, I. HEIN, H. HUNGER, D. MELMANN, A. SCHWAB (eds.), *Timelines. Studies in Honour of Manfred Bietak*, II, 2006, 179.

694. 1511 Cairo A/II-n14 planum 1–2 Phase E/1 (68/109) Plate 126

SPI	I-d	f	W2	–	re	3

pht. 2.4 cm. Wd. 0.3 cm.
Incomplete
Surface colour: 10YR5.5/1 grey; burnished slip 10YR4/1 dark grey
Break: uniform grey
Decoration: Incised lotus (?).
Previously published: KOPETZKY, Gefässe im Tell el-Yahudiya Stil, in: E. CERNY, I. HEIN, H. HUNGER, D. MELMANN, A. SCHWAB (eds.), *Timelines. Studies in Honour of Manfred Bietak*, II, 2006, 181.

695. 9019H TD F/II-r/23 L81/6 Phase a/2 (08/096) Plate 126

SPI	I-b-2	f	W2	–	re	3

D. 10.1 cm. pht. 4.7 cm. Md. 10.1 cm. Wd. 0.4 cm.
Restored from sherds, incomplete
Surface colour: 2.5Y/1 gray; burnish 10YR3/2 very dark gray brown
Break: dark grey core, light grey re zones
Decoration: Five incised lotus flowers running around the upper exterior. No burnishing on the inner surface.

Type Group P.4

Type group P.4 is recognised through an incomplete cup from Tell el-Dab^ca, TD 4242. It resembles contemporary Egyptian cups and is decorated with stylised lotus flowers.

696. 4242 TD F/I-i/23 grave 32 Phase b/1 (81/530) Plates 125, 162

SPI	I-d	f	W2	–	re	3

D. 7.6 cm. pht. 6.2 cm. Md. 8.8 cm. Wd. 0.3 cm.
Incomplete
Surface colour: 10YR5.5/1 grey; burnished slip 10YR2/1 black
Break: uniform grey
Decoration: Incised lotus plants.
Previously published: KOPETZKY, Gefässe im Tell el-Yahudiya Stil, in: E. CERNY, I. HEIN, H. HUNGER, D. MELMANN, A. SCHWAB (eds.), *Timelines. Studies in Honour of Manfred Bietak*, II, 2006, 182.

Possibly belonging to this group is also the fragment TD 1451

697. 1451 (Vienna A2995) A/II-n/12 planum 3 Phase ? (68/103) Plate 125

SPI	I-d	f	W2	–	re	3

D. 10.0 cm. pht. 3.2 cm. Wd. 0.5 cm.
Incomplete
Surface colour: 10YR5.5/1 grey; burnished slip 10YR4/3 brown
Break: uniform grey
Decoration: Part of an incised lotus plant (?).
Previously published: KOPETZKY, Gefässe im Tell el-Yahudiya Stil, in: E. CERNY, I. HEIN, H. HUNGER, D. MELMANN, A. SCHWAB (eds.), *Timelines. Studies in Honour of Manfred Bietak*, II, 2006, 182.

Type Group P.5

Type group P.5 is known from an incomplete beaker from Tell el-Dab^ca, TD 9012H. It resembles contemporary Egyptian beakers and is decorated with stylised lotus flowers, decorated in typical Tell el-Yahudiya technique.

698. 9012H TD F/II-r/22 planum 1 L81/1 Phase a/2 (06/567) Plates 125, 163

SPI	I-d	f	W2	–	re	3

D. 7.6 cm. pht. 6.2 cm. Md. 8.8 cm. Wd. 0.3 cm.
Incomplete
Surface colour: 10YR5.5/1 grey; burnished slip 10YR2/1 black
Break: uniform grey
Decoration: Incised lotus flowers and buds, infilled decoration made with a five-toothed comb.

RINGSTANDS

The fragment, TD 9018W, from Khatana pit complex L81, is possibly part of a ringstand. It is burnished on the interior, and on the inner rim are a series of incised vertical lines made with a ten-toothed comb. Since however it is incomplete, the possibility that this piece is actually the neck of an unknown jug type cannot be discounted.

Type Group Q

699. 9018W TD F/II-r/22 planum 1 L81/6 Phase a/2 (09/119) Plates 126, 163

SPI	I-d	f	W2	–	re	3

D. 7.6 cm. pht. 6.2 cm. Md. 8.8 cm. Wd. 0.3 cm.
Incomplete
Surface colour: 10YR5.5/1 grey; burnished slip 10YR2/1 black
Break: uniform grey
Decoration: Impressed dots on the inner rim made with a multi-toothed comb.

Concordance of Tell el-Dab^{c}a Inventory Numbers and Catalogue Numbers

Inv no.	Cat no.
0021A	330
0021B	379
0028	443
0039B	381
0047	465
0049C	525
0050	241
0051	300
0054	324
0060	246
0067	652
0131	252
0142	294
0143	269
0144	267
0145	257
0146	268
0147	292
0148	380
0149	304
0150	566
0154	285
0166	348
0167	565
0170	173
0171	368
0172	357
0173	360
0174	421
0175	471
0176	470
0177	469
0178	425
0179	472
0180	431
0181	473
0182	424
0183	422
0184	218
0185	316
0186	263
0187	274
0188	561
0192	196
0193	319
0212	594
0213	275
0214	191
0226	590
0227	601
0228	597
0230	244
0231	336
0244	591
0246	388
0261	492
0273	645
0279	506
0288	251
0296	631
0299	476
0352	321
0354	229
0355	624
0360	276
0361	447
0367	333
0368	296
0369	235
0370	297
0371	270
0373	437
0382	192
0383	299
0384	345
0385	284
0388	427
0389	281
0390	302
0391	313
0402	279
0451	311
0454	457
0456	456
0457	462
0458	463
0459	359
0469	480
0498	598
0522	286
0525	354
0536	468
0537	216
0607	573
0777	374
0781	420
0792	293
0831	649
0835	568
0836	179
0837	297
0858	426
0860	429
0861	307
0864	298
0865	249
0866	352
0867	423
0868	454
0869	261
0874	367
0875	339
0876	183
0877	200
0879A	209
0883	022
0884	559
0885	178
0886	464
0888	358
0895	355
0899	280
0900	382
0939	650
1122	121
1123	054
1165	636
1192	500
1250	558
1251	317
1260	340
1263	341
1269	570
1276	318
1289	224
1328	099
1345	228
1350	461
1358	353
1359	204
1360	309
1361	214
1378	202
1379	433
1382	386
1385	176
1386	346
1389	195
1390	560
1392	282
1394	362
1396	199
1398	264
1400	629
1403	343
1405	385
1409	384
1410	174
1423	409
1430	438
1431	455
1445	615
1451	697
1468A	516
1468B	532
1498	308
1499	237
1500	236

Inv no.	Cat no.
1511	694
1520	389
1550	647
1558	132
1575	502
1587	127
1596	693
1606	616
1608	417
1609	021
1610	021
1611	021
1627	644
1630	122
1674	167
1675	055
1676	057
1679	058
1717	458
1724	511
1734	021
1758	066
1759	067
1760	071
1762	069
1769	060
1771	669
1781	670
1782	660
1785	073
1786	061
1810	109
1833	077
1839	076
1841	074
1842	059
1849	674
1850	676
1851	675
1856	315
1886	031
1895	387
1917	356
1923	242
1924	225
1925	383
1926	227
1927	363
1935	210
1962	651
1963	219
1986A	448
2016	564
2045	170
2054	623
2055	392
2065	576
2068	017
2093	556
2095A	434
2095C	537
2106	295
2111	430
2115	312
2116	466
2117	230
2119	630
2120	250
2124	233
2126	289
2129	277
2130	259
2132	231
2135	323
2136	439
2137	350
2138	334
2139	266
2141	331
2142	338
2143	205
2144	222
2153	234
2154	184
2156	301
2162	207
2164	291
2274	365
2275	344
2276	185
2277	223
2278	289
2308	449
2309	459
2309B	452
2310	349
2313	628
2314	181
2315	180
2316	238
2317	194
2318	288
2319	428
2320	595
2321	626
2322	440
2323	175
2327	260
2328	248
2329	255
2330	243
2331	265
2332	450
2333	451
2334	460
2335	215
2341	303
2344	648
2432	262
2439	273
2510A	691
2510C	098
2518	007
2519	008
2583D	592
2668	372
2702	403
2765	692
2938	226
2939	411
2940	404
2941	405
2942	406
2945	410
2954	201
3007	283
3010	290
3012	297
3013	351
3014	272
3026	347
3028	068
3050	335
3051	481
3052	393
3058K	533
3072	258
3077	407
3077A	408
3116A	002
3139	013
3145	030
3179B	106
3180C	082
3241D1	108
3241D2	112
3241E	111
3254C	101
3269A	168
3274L1	515
3280C	310
3283	023
3301C	063
3339	126
3346	166
3360C	124
3368	554
3389F	633
3400	549
3401	397
3401A	399
3402C	607
3415B	687
3417	494
3423A	376
3425	567
3434	653
3438	593
3442	038
3445H	092
3453A	545
3453B	326
3454	271
3454C	578
3509A	306
3516	188

Inv no.	Cat no.	Inv no.	Cat no.	Inv no.	Cat no.
3517	240	4518	035	6127	605
3518	320	4523	419	6128E	512
3519	203	4539	034	6128F1	509
3520	247	4759E	133	6128F2	474
3521	256	4805	213	6128G	602
3522	254	4838A	037	6128I	600
3532B	625	4902	190	6133B2	617
3532C	093	4903	187	6135	486
3545	123	4904	337	6135G	544
3545A	113	4964A	100	6135H	495
3571	239	4964B	036	6135J	614
3574	245	5210	394	6136E	587
3577	366	5228N	080	6138C	009
3578	220	5228R	583	6173	014
3580	627	5230N	496	6386A	685
3583	221	5250A	004	6386C	517
3583C	579	5351	436	6449D	401
3641	663	5415	193	6451E	531
3642	678	5416	562	6451H	586
3653A	056	5417	342	6457A	130
3956	028	5419	563	6458A	637
3963	402	5420	361	6466B	484
3966	557	5427	679	6466C	493
4043[a]		5436	029	6466D	508
4060A	666	5444	569	6466E	523
4097A	079	5511	642	6466F	524
4121	198	5588	011	6466J1	526
4121B	322	5645	010	6466J2	539
4123	677	5759	253	6466J3	526
4127C	129	5763	278	6466J4	484
4128G	638	5764	177	6466J5	493
4138E	686	5774	432	6466J6	540
4151B	133	5794	232	6489R	490
4164C	325	5795	033	6489S	612
4164D	329	5823	087	6489T	602
4166	658	5925A	513	6491B	618
4167	659	5927B	482	6500D	507
4168	656	5928A	442	6500F	581
4211	003	5934	684	6500G	528
4238	075	5935	078	6500H	538
4239	682	5971E	001	6500L	475
4240	041	5985C	070	6500X	488
4241	040	5987B	505	6783F	588
4242	696	6023D	172	6783G	604
4266A	032	6030	314	6791C	527
4287B	035	6034A	416	6794U	608
4297E	091	6034A2	640	6794V	609
4297F	096	6042	680	6794X	605
4305E	097	6044	065	6794Y	619
4411B	419	6052	664	6794Z	620
4435	072	6053	665	6796F	520
4436A	024	6084	305	6796G	621
4438	661	6089A	327	6806B	491
4465F	015	6089B	328	6807	483
4468C	396	6095B	572	6807D	485
4501	018	6095B2	541	6809H	211
4506A	504	6117	377	6809J	542
4506F	690	6120A	498	6813	444

[a] See above page 531.

Inv no.	Cat no.
6839A	478
6846B	378
6856C	521
6856D	611
6857G	613
6858A	596
6858E	610
6987	643
7021D	095
7025B	555
7044L	085
7046G	026
7056A	020
7056B	418
7062L	208
7065D	550
7067F	005
7149F	110
7150	373
7239	550
7247A	632
7249	575
7347C	131
7351O	090
7354	641
7373E	128
7383D	552
7440C	064
7441B	062
7461	115
7462	151
7463	120
7476	039
7483	116
7484	118
7485	117
7486	672
7486C	668
7486E	667
7486F	655
7490	369
7498	027
7505A	006
7508	045
7509	043
7510	049
7511	048
7512	047
7513	042
7514	044
7515	051
7516	052
7516A	046
7516B	050
7518	119
7540C	019
7595C	012
7596W	088
7597K	086
7597N	105
7597O	081
7598A	102
7651	395
7931	182
7932A	364
7932B	375
7940M	599
7942F	083
7942Y	107
7943E	622
8104H	691
8166G	499
8168C	536
8168G	551
8204F	571
8205P	501
8346C	114
8396B	206
8396C	510
8400	606
8436U	497
8441B	089
8441D	084
8442R	025
8446L	487
8446M	582
8446N	489
8450S	535
8470B	016
8470C	103
8470D	104
8475C	635
8477W	530
8478E	534
8478R	529
8665	683
8668	548
8670	390
8671	398
8672	415
8674	391
8675	412
8677	217
8682	400
8684	053
8692	370
8698	654
8702	414
8704	546
8732U	522
8781B	186
8781D	547
8782	415
8785B	657
8793F	574
8802	371
8819A	662
8826	453
8856	682
8856A	673
8875B	477
8887B	584
8892D	519
8904B	518
8908B	514
8908C	503
8908T	441
8908U	212
8908V	639
8912E	580
8912J	543
8942D	094
8942G	479
8942Q	125
8943G	446
8971R	171
8990R	553
8992R	467
8997L	577
8997M	435
9009Z	445
9012H	698
9012M	589
9018W	699
9018X	646
9018Y	634
9019H	695
9019Z	585
9026G-1	135
9026G-2	137
9026G-3	140
9026G-4	143
9026G-5	136
9026G-6	144
9026G-7	142
9026G-8	150
9026G-9	139
9026G-10	134
9026G-11	163
9026G-12	141
9026G-13	145
9026G-14	147
9026G-15	146
9026G-16	148
9026G-17	152
9026G-18	149
9026G-19	155
9026G-20	154
9026G-21	153
9026G-22	156
9026G-23	157
9026G-24	158
9026G-25	159
9026G-26	160
9026G-27	161
9026G-28	138
9026G-29	151
9026G-30	166
9026G-31	164
9026G-32	165
9026G-33	162
9026H	689
9026K	688
9180	332

VI. Conclusions

Chronology

When the vessels presented in the typology (Part Two) and the jugs from Tell el-Dabᶜa listed in the catalogue (Part Three) are reviewed a number of chronological conclusions come to mind. Kaplan has already recognised the difficulty of correlating the chronological positions of the Tell el-Yahudiya ware in the Levant and in Egypt. Her conclusion that the earliest vessels appeared in Egypt, and that the earliest examples found in the Levant were exported there from Egypt is not only unconvincing, but untrue. From a typological point of view the most archaic attributes on Tell el-Yahudiya jugs can be observed on those found at ᶜAfula. In general they are brown, rather than black, have an ovoid body, a small slightly set-off base, a long narrow neck with a ridged swelling under the rim, incisions at the base of the neck and often just above the base, and bipartite or even tripartite handles which typically slope outwards on their upper part and join the body near the base of the neck. Similar vessels in plain red or brown burnished wares are common on Levantine sites during the late MB IIA period. Moreover it can be seen that some of the earliest vessels in evident Tell el-Yahudiya style, found at Megiddo, – two bowls from tombs 5202 and 5171[623] – belong in Gerstenblith's Phase 3,[624] which is equal to stratum G at Tell Beit Mirsim[625] and Aphek Palace II/Phase 3;[626] a jar from Ashkelon, which derives from the Ashkelon Phase 13 'Moat deposit', dates to the same period as strata G/4 – G/1–3 at Tell el-Dabᶜa, which is equivalent to the later MB IIA;[627] whilst a vessel from Hama stratum H3 also dates to the late MBIIA.[628]

With the exception of the ᶜAfula finds, the find circumstances of all other primeval ovoid Tell el-Yahudiya jugs, our Branch A (= Kaplan's Ovoid 2) from the Levant is not known, and are thus not definitely datable. However, the earliest Tell el-Yahudiya jugs so far found at Tell el-Dabᶜa belong to this primeval Ovoid group. One of them, TD 4211, (above cat no. 3), has a bell rim in the ᶜAfula style and, according to neutron activation analysis was made of a Levantine clay. The fragment was retrieved from a palace of Phase d/1 (= G/4), and this Tell el-Dabᶜa example has a good parallel in a fragment found at Byblos.[629] The position of the handle attachment on the shoulder close to the very slim neck of the Byblos example is in agreement to the piece from Tell el-Dabᶜa. Unfortunately no analysis of the clay from which the Byblite jug was manufactured has been undertaken, but from the published description it is unlikely to be Nile clay. This Byblos vessel also relates to TD 5250A, (above cat no. 4), another shoulder fragment from Tell el-Dabᶜa with a handle attached near to the base of the neck. It was found in a Phase G/1–3 dump which thus provides a *terminus ante quem*, and according to NAA analysis is not of Egyptian manufacture, though its exact origin could not be determined. The same is true for another fragment of a brown burnished vessel, TD 5971E, (above cat. no.1) found in Phase d/2, which also seems to derive from an ovoid vessel of the Primeval Group, with an especially fine fabric and an extremely thin wall. At this stage it is noticeable that every vessel is a unique production, and that the white-filled circular

---

[623] G. Loud, *Megiddo II*, Chicago, 1948, pls. 9.10 and 14.35.

[624] P. Gerstenblith, *The Levant at the Beginning of the Middle Bronze Age*, 1983, 27.

[625] P. Gerstenblith, *The Levant at the Beginning of the Middle Bronze Age*, 1983, 106.

[626] Cf. the pottery forms from these tombs and Gerstenblith's Phase 3 with M. Kochavi and E. Yadin, Typological analysis of the MB IIA Pottery from Aphek according to its Stratigraphic Provenance, in: M. Bietak (ed.), *The Middle Bronze Age in the Levant*, 2002, 219–225.

[627] K. Kopetzky, Gefässe in Tell el-Yahudiya Stil, in: E. Cerny, I. Hein, H. Hunger, D. Melmann, A. Schwab (eds.), *Timelines. Studies in Honour of Manfred Bietak*, II, Leuven, 2006, 177.

[628] Hama H3 is equivalent to Ebla IIIA2, Inner Syria MBI, which is equal to the late MBIIA in Palestine. Cf. L. Nigro, The MB Pottery Horizon of Tell Mardikh/Ancient Ebla, in: M. Bietak (ed.), *The Middle Bronze Age in the Levant*, 2002, 306.

[629] Beirut, American University 4906, 4908, Merrillees, *Levant* 10, 1978, figs. 1, 2. Cf. Bietak, 1989a, 9.

impressions are made, somewhat laboriously with a pointed tool such as an awl.

Since these earliest vessels have been found at Afula, Megiddo, Hama and Tell el-Dabᶜa, it is perhaps possible that the ware evolved independently, although the fact that those Tell el-Dabᶜa examples which have been subjected to neutron activation analysis, were all made of Levantine clays suggest that the ware first appeared in the northern Levant. From there it was dispersed to inner Syria, Palestine, Egypt and Cyprus. Whilst not much is known about the development of Tell el-Yahudiya pottery in inner Syria, it is noticeable that those vessels produced in the northern Levant (present day Lebanon and northern Israel), differed from that produced in the southern Levant, so that it is possible to speak of a Levantine (our Branch C) and a Palestinian or Canaanite style (our Branch B). Whilst the earliest vessels produced in the southern Levant favoured a chequer-board or triangular decoration (our type groups B.1–B.2), this was soon replaced by a preference for a simple banded style (our groups B.3–B.4). At first three or four decorative bands were added to each vessel, each band being filled with a series of straight, or oblique lines made with a comb. Later examples tend to be decorated with only one or two bands, often now infilled with rows of chevrons (cf. our groups D.1, D.2, D.3, D.4, D.5, D.6 and D.7). During the MBIIB the shape of the jugs also evolves from a pronounced ovoid (Kaplan's Ovoid 1, and Ovoid 5) shape to a distinctly piriform one (Kaplan's Piriform 3). Whilst it is sometimes difficult to distinguish between ovoid and piriform vessels when only sherds are present, Stager and Voss point out that at Ashkelon ovoid vessels tended to be thicker walled than the piriform vessels.[630] Finally at the end of the MBIIB period a distinctly cylindrical type (Kaplan's Cylindrical 2) also makes its appearance, cf. Fig. 252.

In the northern Levant, during the later stages of the MBIIA and early MBIIB, there is a preference for piriform (Kaplan's Ovoid 3–4) or biconical shapes. They tend to have four horizontal zones of decoration comprising triangles, rectangles, spirals and wavy lines but no chequer board or horizontal band patterns such as are found on contemporary Early Palestinian vessels.

Trade connections between the Levant and Egypt during the early Thirteenth Dynasty led to the importation, and copying, of Early Levantine Tell el-Yahudiya Ware within Egypt. At first the true Levantine vessels and their Egyptian copies were very similar and the term Levanto-Egyptian can be applied to these early examples (cf. our Branch I). The classic type of Levanto-Egyptian Tell el-Yahudiya Ware, contemporary with the late MB IIA in the Levant and the late Thirteenth Dynasty in Egypt, invariably has a piriform shape (Kaplan's Piriform 1, Merillees' El-Lisht Ware). Such Piriform 1 jugs may have ring bases, convex or concave button bases, bipartite or tripartite, sometimes five-stranded handles, and, usually, an inverted kettle rim; however towards the end of the Thirteenth Dynasty, strap handles and rolled rims appear, which then become typical for the Piriform 2a juglets of the Hyksos Period (cf. below). Whilst Kaplan places the emphasis of her classification system on form, stratigraphic excavations at Tell el-Dabᶜa show that the ornamental schemes found on these Piriform 1 jugs, can often be more meaningful as a classification tool. Over time not only do these jugs tend to become smaller but there is also a trend in the reduction of four to two, and in some cases, one decorative zone. The earliest vessels, those with four zones of decoration may be termed Piriform 1a. They are produced of Levantine clays and seem to originate from the central Levant between Byblos and Kabri, and are closely related to the Early Levantine group.

Not surprisingly, however, most of the MB IIA Tell el-Yahudiya vessels found at Tell el-Dabᶜa belong in the Levanto-Egyptian group (Group I). The majority of such jugs have a piriform shape, but are flattened to various degrees which may, on the one hand be only slightly distinguished from the ovoid shapes, but may also, on the other hand, be so flat that the shoulder breaks nearly in a sharp rounded angle towards the body. The variation of piriform shaped jugs is large. The early piriform jugs, group I.1 (Piriform 1a), which date to the time of the Thirteenth Dynasty may have ring bases, convex or concave button bases, bipartite or tripartite, sometimes five-stranded handles, and usually an inverted kettle rim: however towards the end of the Thirteenth Dynasty, strap handles and rolled rims appear, which become typical for the Piriform 2 juglets of the Hyksos Period. The Piriform 1 jug (termed "El Lisht" ware by Merrillees), is well represented in diminishing sizes from Phase G to the beginning of Phase E/2. True MB IIA imports recovered at Tell el-Dabᶜa include the fragmentary TD 1734, (cat no. 21), from

[630] Cf. below page 560.

a context datable to Phase G. Although incomplete it probably originally had four zones of decoration, an upper large one of rectangles, followed by a frieze of pendant triangles, a band of swimming fish and a lower zone of connected standing and pendant triangles. Such vessels are rare, but TD 1734 may be compared with other jugs which have kettle rims, a tripartite handle joining at the neck below the rim, incisions at the neck, ring bases and four zones of decoration. At present examples of such vessels are known only through an incomplete vessel from Sin el-Fil,[631] and another from Egypt, site unknown, the latter made of a Nile clay.[632] The Sin el-Fil vessel is decorated with four zones of spirals, a motif which reappears in the second zone of the Egyptian vessel, though the other zones comprising standing triangles – top and bottom zone, with the third zone consisting of squares. Another imported type, group I.2, (Piriform Ib), found at Tell el-Dabᶜa has a kettle rim, a double handle joining at the neck below the rim, incisions at the neck, ring bases and three zones of decoration. This type group first appears in Phase G/1–3, continuing into Phase F, and with this type one begins to see more standardization in the styles of decoration. Of these, the most common, and the only one found at Tell el-Dabᶜa, has an uppermost zone consisting of standing triangles, a central zone of rectangles and a lower zone of pendant triangles found on vessels from Sin el-Fil,[633] Tell el-Dabᶜa vessels TD 3956, catalogue. no. 28), and TD 5436 (made of Nile Clay, catalogue no. 29) plus various sherds, all of which are datable to strata G–F, Lisht in the tomb of Senwosretankh,[634] Buhen,[635] and Arpera in Cyprus.[636] Jugs with only two zones of decoration, group I.3 (Piriform 1c) first appear in Phase F–E/3 and continue into Phase E/2 with most examples being found in Phase E/2. The decoration found on these vessels almost always comprises an upper band of standing triangles and a lower one of pendant triangles. Piriform Id vessels, group I.4 are perhaps to be dated as early as Phase F, but this is not certain since the known examples, from Arpera[637] Ras Shamra,[638] and Byblos[639] cannot be precisely dated: however the only examples of the contemporary I.5 vessels, found at Tell el-Dabᶜa, TD 1674 and TD 3269A, above catalogue numbers 57 and 58, date to Phase F. Whilst the dating of the non TD vessels is not certain however, what is clear is that those jugs of groups I.4 and I.5 with standing rectangles come from the Levant, whilst those with five to seven vertical decorative stripes or lozenges tend to be produced of Nile clay and are the forerunners of the entirely Egyptian Piriform 2a jugs (our Branch L.1). These early Piriform jugs were also exported to Cyprus, where they may have influenced the development of Cypriot Black Slip II and III wares. One of the more interesting types of these early piriform jugs are those with naturalistic designs which have been found in such diverse places as Toumba tou Skourou, Tell el-Ghassil, Ashkelon, Tell el-Dabᶜa, Lisht and Thebes.

During the MBIIB period = the Egyptian Second Intermediate Period, these Levanto-Egyptian types developed into a particularly Egyptian style, and it is perhaps not surprising that most of these late Egyptian (our Branch L) have been found in the Hyksos dominated Eastern Delta. Although disputed it seems more than likely that the forerunners of the Hyksos originally migrated to the Eastern Delta from the northern Levant, and evidently brought their own (Levantine) pottery styles with them, which explains the large amount of Middle Bronze influence found in Hyksos pottery.[640] Belonging to this Levantine pottery style was the Levanto-Egyptian Tell el-Yahudiya Ware which, over time, developed, within the Eastern Delta into the myriad shapes seen in our group L, which first appear in Tell el-Dabᶜa Phase E/3. At first these groups are Piriform, having developed most

---

[631] CHÉHAB, Tombe phénicienne de Sin el-Fil, in: *Mélanges syriens offerts à René Dussaud*, 1939, 806, fig. 6a.

[632] Oxford Ashmolean 1896–1908.C.96. PETRIE, 1890, pl. xx. 199–200, MERRILLEES, *Trade and Transcendance in the Bronze Age Levant*, 1974, 67, fig. 59. NAA analysis, KAPLAN, *Tell el-Yahudiyeh Ware*, 230, UU21.

[633] CHÉHAB, Tombe phénicienne de Sin el-Fil, in: *Mélanges syriens offerts à René Dussaud*, 1939, 806 fig. 5c.

[634] Cairo JE 60263. Merrillees, *Trade and Transcendance in the Bronze Age Levant*, 59, fig. 48.

[635] Philadelphia UM E.10765. RANDALL-MACIVER and WOOLLEY, *Buhen*, 1911, 201–202, pl. 49.

[636] Nicosia, Cyprus Museum. MERRILLEES, *Trade and Transcendance in the Bronze Age Levant*, 49, figs. 31.14, 38.

[637] Nicosia, Cyprus Museum. MERRILLEES, *Trade and Transcendance*, 49, figs. 31, 39. KAPLAN, *Tell el-Yahudiyeh Ware*, fig. 41c NAA analysis. KAPLAN, *Tell el-Yahudiyeh Ware*, 229 no. CM15.

[638] Paris Louvre AO 15735. SCHAEFFER, *Syria* 14, 1933, 110, fig. 10.7, KAPLAN, *Tell el-Yahudiyeh Ware*, fig. 42a

[639] MONTET, *Byblos et l'Egypte*, 119, 244, pl. 146, KAPLAN, *Tell el-Yahudiyeh Ware*, fig. 62b.

[640] BIETAK, *BASOR* 281, 1991, 27–72; REDMOUNT, *JMA* 8.2, 1995, 61–89; HOLLADAY, *The Eastern Nile Delta During the Hyksos and Pre-Hyksos Periods*, 1997, 183–252: ASTON, *TD XII*, 392–393.

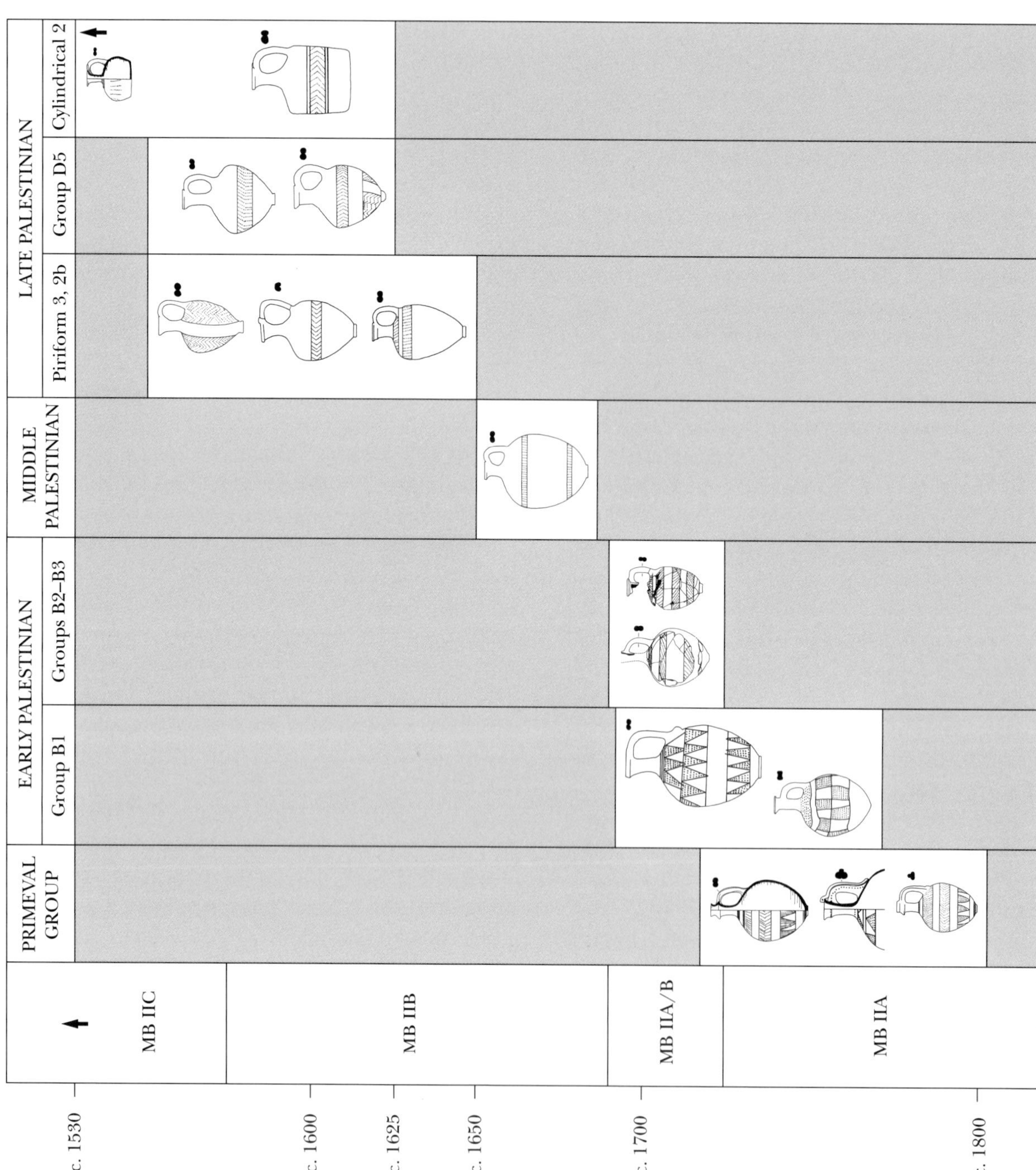

Fig. 252 Palestinian Tell el-Yahudiya jug chronology

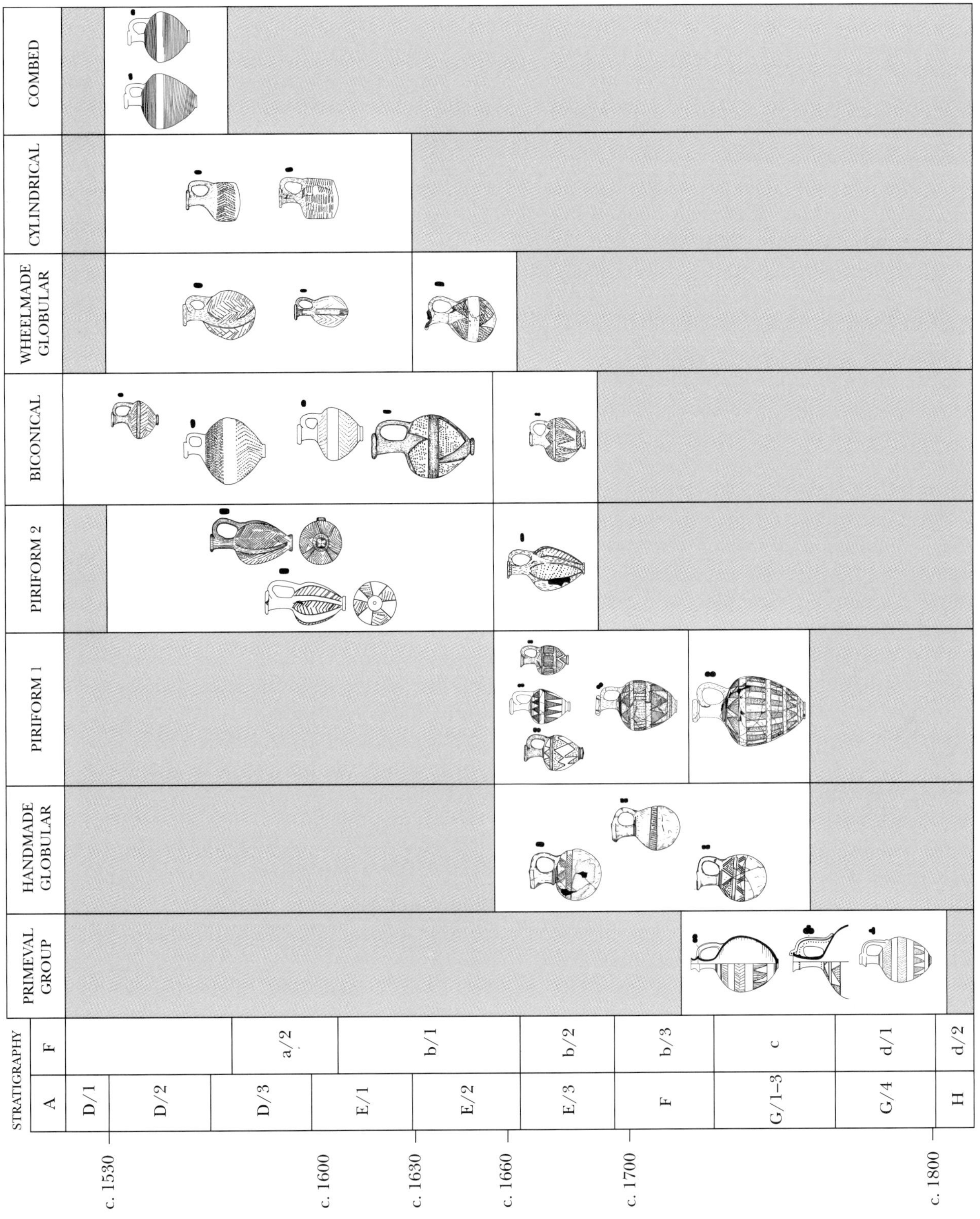

Fig. 253 Tell el-Yahudiya jug chronology as revealed at Tell el-Dabʿa

likely from type groups I.3, I.4 and I.5, Kaplan's Piriform 2a, our type group L.1. This is soon followed however by the ovoid and biconical types (our groups L.2–L.4), and the decoration is usually in two zones comprising an upper zone of standing triangles, and a lower one of pendant triangles. During Phase E/2 the earliest wheel-made globular jugs (our groups L.9.1–2) appear, and as befits their early date are decorated with zones of standing and pendant triangles. During Phase E/1, when the L.1 (piriform 2a) jugs become common, being usually decorated with three or four lozenges, the wheel made globular jugs are also more often than not decorated with similar lozenges. It is also during Phase E/1 that the quadrilobal and Late Egyptian Cylindrical (Kaplan's Cylindrical 1) jugs also appear. Sometime during E/2 the typical Late Egyptian biconical types, Type groups L.5–L.8 (Kaplan's Biconical 1) also appear.

On Cyprus the importation of the Piriform vessels of the Levanto-Egyptian type (Kaplan's Piriform 1) may have inspired the production of the handmade globular vessels, our branch N, which appear in Tell el-Dab^ca from strata G/1–3 to E/3. In terms of their manufacturing techniques, being handmade and having their handles pushed through the vessel wall, these handmade globular vessels are certainly Cypriote inspired, though no examples have yet been found on Cyprus.

During the latest phase of the Hyksos Period, Tell el-Yahudiya ware developed its final decorative phase, a series of incised grooves running horizontally around the body of the vessel, our Type Groups L.13.1–4, the grooving almost certainly being made on the wheel. Whilst they were undoubtedly made in Egypt, the vagaries of archaeological excavation are such that most of the extant complete examples were found in Cyprus. All main forms of Late Tell el-Yahudiya ware, – piriform, biconical, wheel-made globular and biconical were all decorated in this way.

Finally it simply remains to discuss the question of when Tell el-Yahudiya ware ceased to be produced. In a review of Cypriot imports found in Palestine, Oren has categorically denied that Tell el-Yahudiya ware continued into the Eighteenth Dynasty, giving good reasons as to why a number of supposed Eighteenth Dynasty contexts containing such wares could also be earlier.[641] Eriksson, however points to the two tombs Abydos D114 and Abydos E10, both of which undeniably contain material which dates as late as Tuthmosis III, as evidence for the fact that Tell el-Yahudiya ware continued well into the early Eighteenth Dynasty.[642] The problem with both those contexts is that it can not stated with any certainty as to whether the Tell el-Yahudiya vessels concerned were not old ones at their time of deposition, as is certainly the case with a wheel-made globular vessel found in a Twentieth–Twenty-first Dynasty coffin at Saqqara.[643] However, recent excavations at Ezbet Helmi (Tell el-Dab^ca) have produced Tell el-Yahudiya sherds in contexts datable, on ceramic evidence, to the early Eighteenth Dynasty. Whilst such sherds could be residual, it is probably significant that *all* such sherds derive from biconical jars of our groups L.5–L.8 which is suggestive of the fact that the biconical type (Kaplan's Biconical 1) did indeed continue to be produced during the early years of the Eighteenth Dynasty.

Such a date for the latest production of Tell el-Yahudiya ware is also suggested by the cylindrical vessel found in a LB I tomb at Jatt.[644] Leaving aside this particular vessel, which is unique, and thus cannot be dated, no (other) Middle Bronze Age pot was found in the tomb. Thus, although the possibility that this vessel was an old one at the time of deposition cannot be ruled out, it is also possible that it was produced during the Late Bronze I.

The combined Tell el-Dab^ca evidence can be combined to show the typological development shown in Fig. 253.

Decorative Styles as Revealed by the Tell el-Dab^ca Sequence

In terms of dating, the methods and styles of decoration utilised on Tell el-Yahudiya vessels are also very significant. The earliest Tell el-Yahudiya jugs were decorated by means of a single awl; each 'dot' being painstakingly made one at a time. However, sometime during the Thirteenth Dynasty the use of a multi-toothed comb became normal. In Palestine the

641 E. Oren, Cypriot Imports in the Palestinian Late Bronze I Context, *Opuscula Atheniensia* 9, 1969, 136–137.

642 Eriksson, *The Creative Independance of Late Bronze Age Cyprus*, 2007, 172–173. She makes heavy use of the two tombs Abydos D114 and Abydos E10, both of which undeniably contain material which dates as late as Tuthmosis III; however, it can not be ascertained whether the Tell el-Yahudiya vessels found in these tombs were not old ones at their time of deposition.

643 D. Aston, The Pottery, in: M.J. Raven, *The Tomb of Iurudef. A Memphite Official in the Reign of Ramesses II*, London, 1991, 45, pl. 53, no. 71.

644 Yanni, 2000, 53, 69 fig. 6.

use of banded decoration cvery quickly became the norm, and this banded style continued through the MB IIA to MB IIC periods. To the north and south, however, the Levanto-Egyptian branch tended, from a very early stage to favour a frieze of standing triangles on the shouklder and a band of pendant triangles as the lowermost frieze, regardless of how many other zones of decoration divided these two. In the piriform 1a and piriform 1b types the intervening zones usually comprised rows of rectangles. With the evolution of the piriform 1c, which first appeared at Tell el-Dab^ca in phase F only the two zones of standing and pendant triangles still survived. This style of decoration remained extremely popular throughout Phases F to E/1 on all types of Late Egyptian jugs with sporadic examples still occuring on the larger biconical and wheel-made globular jugs in Phases D/3–D/2. During Phase E/1, however the use of lozenges or gores became very normal with the rise in popularity of both the piriform 2a and the wheel-made globular vessels. On these vessels this style of lozenge decoration continued until the demise of both types during Phase D/2. Phase E/1 also saw the introduction of Kaplan's classic Biconical 1 (our type group L.5) with bands of vertical chevrons or oblique lines on both the shoulder and lower body. Vertical chevrons were also utilised on the cylindrical jugs of Phases D/3 and D/2.

Very rarely, horizontal rows were made by holding a multi-toothed comb horizontally against the vessel wall, a style of decoration which occurs on some of the earliest Late Egyptian cylindrical vessels (Phase E/1) and the latest biconical vessels in Phase D/2 and/or later. From Phase G/1–3 to Phase D/3, all decorative elements, with the exception of those found on Late Egyptian cylindrical jugs, be they rectangles, standing and pendant traingles, lozenges or rows of vertical chevrons, the decorated areas were clearly delineated with incised lines, though in the case of a number of the biconical vessels, these incised lines only marked the lower edge of the upper band of decoration and the upper limit of the lower band of decoration. During Phase D/3, however, the decorated areas were sometimes not defined by an incised line though this particular style was never very common.

As noted above the use of grooved (or combed) decoration also came into fashion during Phase E/1. At first, this consisisted of distinct bands of lines made with a multi-toothed comb with broad undecorated areas between them, (cf. cat. nos. 602, 612 and 616). If vessel 6858E, cat. no. 610, found in Phase D/2, were not an old one at time of deposition, then this style may have continued into Phase D/2. However, all other datable pieces with this style of decoration found at Tell el-Dab^ca are assigned to Phase E/1. No grooved (or combed) vessels found at Tell el-Dab^ca can be assigned to Phase D/3, but by Phase D/2 this style of decoration has undergone a marked change. All vessels, whether they are piriform, biconical wheel-made globular, or cylindrical, are decorated with continuous bands of grooves, although the first three types usually have a small reserved band without decoration at the mid-point of the vessel.

Function

Although Tell el-Yahudiya ware has been discussed by various authors (cf. above part one of this monograph), their precise function has never been explained. Åstrom suggested the small size and the narrow necks of the jugs are indicative of the fact that the contents must have been precious liquids, not intended to evaporate easily, such as perfumed oils, or ointments, if not opium, meant to be used in small quantities,[645] and this interpretation was followed, almost word for word, by Kaplan.[646] In this both authors go somewhat further than Amiran who wrote that "it would be too hasty to suggest that the Tell el-Yahudiya juglets were containers for poppy-seed or the other coveted product of the poppy to be distributed in the markets of the MB IIA and B periods."[647] Both Åstrom and Kaplan, however, were clearly influenced by Merrillees who had suggested that jugs of Cypriot Base Ring ware, which when stood on their head resemble a poppy, had been used for such a purpose.[648] One of the early Ovoid (TD 5971E, cat. no. 1) and one of the hand-made globular Tell el-Yahudiya jugs found at Tell el-Dab^ca (TD 7486F, cat. no. 655), bear incised vertical lines which might be representations of the incisions made in an opium poppy, but they are the only two. Investigations into the contents of Tell el-Yahudiya jugs from Tell el-

645 Åstrom, *Three Tell el-Yahudiyeh Juglets in the Thera Museum*, 418.

646 Kaplan, *Tell el-Yahudiyeh Ware*, 123.

647 Amiran, *Israel Museum News* 10, 41.

648 Merrillees, *Antiquity* 36, 1962, 287–292; idem, *Trade and Transcendance*, 32–40. The presence of opiates in the Cypriot Base Ring ware has since been confirmed by several analyses. See, however, Germer, 1981, 125–129.

Dab^{c}a by R. Rottländer have identified a mixture based on animal and plant fat (most probably grain), but no narcotic substances (see below, 621–624). At Tell el-Dab^{c}a there is a general decrease over time in the size of juglets deposited in tombs, which suggests either a rise in the cost of the contents or a preference for smaller quantities. However, whilst it is certain that the jugs must have contained some sort of liquid, the Tell el-Yahudiya style must also have been appreciated for its aesthetic appeal since a small number of figural vessels and open forms are also known in this ware.

It is noticeable that most of the early Tell el-Yahudiya jugs from Tell el-Dab^{c}a, when found in situ, come from graves or temples. Fragments from settlement strata may derive from plundered graves, and although we cannot exclude a profane use, it seems that the Tell el-Yahudiya jugs had a cultic function connected with funerary beliefs. Since most of the cultic finds and funerary features from Tell el-Dab^{c}a have a much stronger Middle Bronze tradition than the features and material culture of everyday life, this again indicates a Levantine origin for the Tell el-Yahudiya ware. In the Hyksos period when Tell el-Yahudiya ware becomes more numerous, the distribution evidence changes in that now, whilst small juglets continued to be placed in tombs, larger vessels of the same type are now found principally in settlement strata.

V. A View from the North

Whilst the last two sections of this book have concentrated on the Tell el-Yahudiya ware found at Tell el-Dab^ca, and thus is representative of that type of pottery found in the Egyptian Eastern Delta, we are fortunate to balance this with material found to the north east. In a series of three short essays, Lawrence Stager and Ross Voss, Aren Maier and Robert Mullins, and Hanan Charaf, in combination with Mary Ownby present the Tell el-Yahudiya pottery found at Ashkelon, Beth Shan and Tell Arqa respectively. Since the material from all three sites covers the entire Middle Bronze Age, this gives an introduction to the typical early forms, and their development into the Late Palestinian, and at Arqa, possibly the Late Syrian forms, absent from the Tell el-Dab^ca corpus.

A Sequence of Tell el Yahudiya Ware from Ashkelon

Lawrence E. Stager and Ross J. Voss

Introduction

The Leon Levy Expedition to Ashkelon has excavated Middle Bronze Age cultural remains in six different fields of the tell (Grids 1, 2, 3, 9, 38 and 50). Tell el Yahudiya Ware has been found in three of these: Grids 2, 38 and 50, at some distance from each other, and in diverse cultural contexts. These include four successive gates and a final rampart construction (Grid 2 Phases 14–10);[1] an intramural necropolis with MB IIB and MB IIC burials (Grid 50); and an outdoor courtyard with domestic installations dating to the MB IIC period (Grid 38). Each of these grids exhibits variable durations of Middle Bronze Age occupation, but no single grid has produced a complete sequence of Tell el Yahudiya Ware. In order to present the entire range of this pottery each grid will be surveyed in the chronological order in which this pottery appears, from earliest to latest. The four gates in Grid 2 provide the best stratified contexts and so will serve as the primary cross-reference for Ashkelon's intra-site Tell el Yahudiya Ware. For external comparisons, the site of Tell el Dab^ca (Avaris) in the eastern Nile Delta will be the primary reference. The Ashkelon typology is based on a type series first formulated by Kaplan and further refined by Bietak.[2]

The Ashkelon corpus of Tell el Yahudiya Ware is relatively small in volume but diverse in type, permitting an unprecedented degree of synchronization between the well stratified sequence of ceramic types at Ashkelon and the typological sequence with absolute dates proposed for Tell el Dab^ca.[3] Tell el Yahudiya Ware serves as just one strong link in a long chain of ceramic types which bind these two great cities together.

The context of Ashkelon's Tell el Yahudiya Ware will be presented in chronological order. The equivalent examples from Tell el Daba will be cross-referenced in order to test the ceramic sequence established for each site.

[1] R. Voss, A Sequence of Four Middle Bronze Gates in Ashkelon, in: M. Bietak (ed.), *The Middle Bronze Age in the Levant. Proceedings of an International Conference on MB IIA Ceramic Material, Vienna, 24th–26th of January 2001*, (Vienna, 2002), 379–384; L. Stager, The MBIIA Ceramic Sequence at Tel Ashkelon and its implications for the "Port Power" Model of Trade in M. Bietak (ed.), *The Middle Bronze Age in the Levant*, Vienna, 2002, 353–362.

[2] See above pages 45–54, and Part II in this book.

[3] M. Bietak, K. Kopetzky, L. Stager and R. Voss, Synchronisation of Stratigraphies: Ashkelon and Tell el-Dab^ca, *Ä&L*, 18, 2008, 49–60.

The Ashkelon Tell el Yahudiya Ware

The earliest Tell el Yahudiya Ware appears in Grid 2, Phase 14. The pottery of brown to red-brown clay is usually slipped and often burnished to a high luster. In Phases 13 and 12 the fabric and surface treatment become more varied. Clays may be brown or gray-brown depending upon the type of juglet (Ovoid or Piriform); the surface may be slipped or unslipped, with burnished and unburnished zones. In Phases 11 and 10 the clay colour may be dark gray or black; the black or dark gray coloured vessels are invariably Egyptian imports. In each type series there is a certain degree of overlap from phase to phase.

In addition to clay colour, other ceramic characteristics such as surface decoration, vessel thickness, and the degree of slip and burnish are important diagnostic features. These individual elements are especially helpful when the sherd is too small to identify a type based on surface decoration alone. For example, clay colour and wall thickness are helpful in distinguishing Ovoid 1 (Kaplan's Ovoid 2) from Piriform 1 (in this volume Group I) juglets. The ovoid vessels have thicker walls, and are invariably slipped and highly burnished. In the following description a list of figures will be presented by phase with the thickness of the bodies, Munsell colour, and surface treatment provided.

Grid 2: Phase 14 = Gate 1 (ca. 1800–1750 BC)

The Tell el Yahudiya Ware found in Gate 1 (Phase 14) and in the Phase 14 Moat Deposit (MD) constitutes a very small portion of the pottery recovered from these phases.[4] Its presence, however, is of great significance, since it documents the earliest appearance of Tell el Yahudiya Ware in the southern Levant.

In Square 76 one sherd of Tell el Yahudiya Ware (Fig. 1 No. 1) was found inside the chamber of Gate 1, in a bedding layer of gray-brown silt (Layer 193). It was sealed under Street 192, composed of compressed black ash. The thin wall, unfilled diagonal stippling, and brown burnished surface are indicative of a Piriform 1a (in this volume I.1) juglet.

In front of the gate another juglet fragment (No. 2) was recovered from Street 16. This street was also made of compacted black ash. The sherd has an irregular brown burnished surface with large chalk-filled punctations set diagonally to the wheel marks, which suggests that this, too, is a Piriform 1a (I.1) juglet. The earliest parallels from Tell el-Dab^ca appear in Phase G/1–3.[5] The presence of Piriform 1a (I1) juglet fragments in Phase 14 might indicate that this vessel type appears earlier in Ashkelon.

Grid 2: Phase 14; Moat Deposit (MD)

A large collection of Tell el Yahudiya Ware was found in Moat 21 located at the base of the MB IIA rampart in Square 56. It was necessary to bury the moat under several layers of dump deposits (Layers 16, 28) in order to make way for an expanded rampart (Glacis #2). The enlarged rampart extended over the inner lip of Moat 21, which was sealed under another street of compressed ash (F13, F239). Layer 17 was composed of black ash, an intentional lining of the sandstone moat, and belongs to its construction in Phase 14. Forty-one Tell el Yahudiya Ware jug and juglet bodies, and one unique everted rim bowl fragment (No. 17), with a chalk-filled incised band and chalk-filled punctations, came from this layer. A thin layer of crushed sandstone (Layer 16) covered the ash, and a scree of rubble (Layer 28) from the rebuilt Gate 2, in turn, covered the crushed sandstone.

The size and diversity of MD requires a group by group analysis.

A. MD Layer 17: Ovoid I Group

Twelve pieces of Tell el Yahudiya Ware were decorated with incised running spiral patterns (Fig. 1 nos. 3 and 5). Six other pieces were decorated with incised running crenellations (Fig. 1 no. 4). Among these, two partially restored pieces exhibit double rows of spiral decoration connected by streamers (Fig. 1 no. 5). One of these sherds links both the spiral and crenellation motif (Fig. 1 nos. 3–4). It is evident that both motifs appear together on the same jug and therefore are part of the overall design. Although the base and rim of this partially restored vessel are missing, it is clear that the decorative scheme was laid out in four zones over the body of the vessel.

[4] Originally this moat deposit was designated Phase 14/13, when we thought it was part of the moat fill representing the end phase of Gate 1 and preparation for building Gate 2 (Phase 13). Further examination indicated that the ash was an intentional lining of the sandstone moat and belongs to its construction in Phase 14.

[5] D. Aston, Ceramic Imports at Tell el-Dab^ca during the Middle Bronze IIA, in: M. Bietak (ed.), *The Middle Bronze Age in the Levant. Proceedings of an International Conference on MB IIA Ceramic Material, Vienna, 24th–26th of January 2001*, Vienna, 2002, 52–53 fig. 17.6–7.

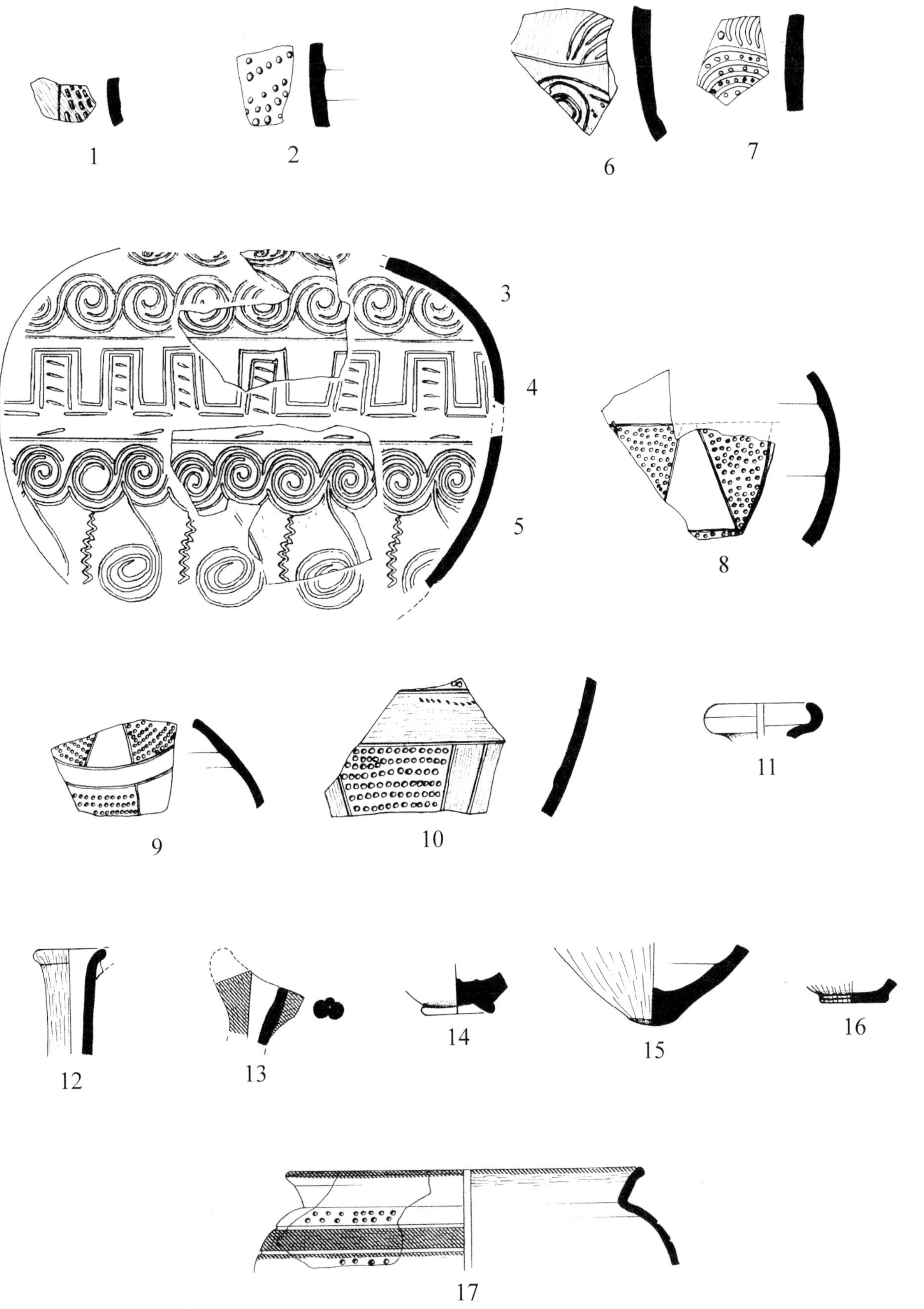

Fig. 1 Tell el-Yahudiya Ware from Ashkelon Phase 14 (1:2)

The neck of the vessel, found on street 13 (RN 90; fig. 2 no. 20) in Phase 13, was seen to join with the rest of the jug by Karin Kopetzky. This fragment displays a running spiral suspended from an incised band or collar filled with tiny chalk-filled punctations. The upper shoulder contains two rows of running spirals beneath which is a central band of framed crenellations. Each crenellation contains several incised rungs. Below the crenellations is another row of running spirals attached to streamers, which separate counter-spirals hanging from the spirals above. This division into four (or five) horizontal zones is one of the hallmarks of the Ovoid 1 form.[6] One sherd from an Ovoid 1 juglet has a spiral with a papyrus branch next to it (Fig. 1 no. 6). Another smaller sherd is difficult to interpret but may be a spreading palm frond (Fig. 1 no. 7). The characteristic slip is dark brown, sometimes shading to a reddish tint, with punctations on the branches. A possible parallel can be seen on the lower part of a red slipped juglet, TD 5588 found in Tell el-Dabᶜa Phase F (above, page 343, cat. no. 11).[7]

All of these Ovoid 1 fragments have a lustrous slip and are highly burnished. The partial restoration of the vessel with the running spirals and crenellations is the finest example from Ashkelon. (There are nine other sherds with spirals and five with crenellations, all non-joining pieces, which belong to this partially restored jug.) In Tell el-Dabᶜa the Ovoid 1 form first appears in Phase G/4 and continues through G/1–3.[8]

B. MD Layer 17: Piriform 1a (I1) Group

A total of 21 Tell el Yahudiya sherds from MD belong to Piriform 1a (I.1) juglets. These fragments exhibit incised horizontal and vertical bands usually combined with triangular, or rectilinear chalk-filled punctations (Fig. 1 nos. 8–10). The punctations can be large dots or stipples. This group is distinct from the Ovoid 1 group in several ways: the slip and burnish on this group is more varied, with the brown slip shading to gray-brown; many of the sherds lack the high luster seen in the Ovoid 1 group, and the slip is often reserved or missing altogether; and the Piriform 1a (I.1) sherds are consistently thinner in section then the Ovoid 1 group. At Tell el-Dabᶜa the Piriform 1a (I.1) group does not appear before G/1–3.[9] In Ashkelon the probable local production of Piriform 1a (I.1) juglets and their appearance in Gate 1 (Phase 14) raises the possibility that this form precedes its introduction into Tell el-Dabᶜa.

C. MD Layer 17: Rims

MD contained a small number of juglet rims of gray-brown fabric. These include two inverted (kettle) rim fragments (Fig. 1 no. 11); two cut-away rims with pinched mouths (Fig. 1 no. 13); three open funnel mouths (Fig. 1 no. 12) and one rolled "tire" rim (RN 881). The simple collarette rim, called a "bell" rim at Tell el-Dabᶜa, and usually associated with the Ovoid 1 type juglet, was not present in MD. The so-called kettle rims are typical of Piriform 1a (I.1) juglets. Cut-away rims are usually associated with brown polished juglets lacking incised or stippled decoration. Candlestick rims are found on Tell el Yahudiya Ware juglets at Tell el- Dabᶜa Phase F.[10] The two candlestick rims from MD have a buff fabric with a red slip. In general, while juglet rims possess some diagnostic features, their fragmentary condition often limits their usefulness in identifying specific types.

D. L17: Bases

There is a wide range of juglet bases in slipped and burnished gray-brown fabric from MD. These include five ring bases (RN 503, 515, 592, 778, 869; cf. No. 14); four stub bases (RN 112, 186, 161, 506; cf. No. 15); and three disk bases (RN 28, 384, 761; cf. No. 16). Only one ring base fragment (RN 28) was large enough to indicate stippled decoration, and it belongs to a Piriform 1a (I.1) juglet. In general, stub bases are associated with brown polished juglets with cut-away rims, as seen in Tell el-Dabᶜa Phase G/1–3;[11] the disk base is most often found on Ovoid 1 jugs, for example Tell el-Dabᶜa G/1–3;[12] and the ring base is

---

[6] D. Aston, Ceramic Imports at Tell el-Dabᶜa during the Middle Bronze IIA, 2002, 51–52.

[7] D. Aston, Ceramic Imports at Tell el-Dabᶜa during the Middle Bronze IIA, 2002, 52 fig. 17.4.

[8] M. Bietak, The Center of Hyksos Rule: Avaris (Tell el Dabᶜa), in: E.D. Oren (ed.), *The Hyksos: New Historical and Archaeological Perspectives*, Philadelphia, 1997, 92–93, figs. 4.4 and 4.5; D. Aston, Ceramic Imports at Tell el-Dabᶜa during the Middle Bronze IIA, 2002, 49–50 fig. 14; cf. also *TD XII*, 122–155.

[9] Cf. this volume pages 347, 552.

[10] D. Aston, Ceramic Imports at Tell el-Dabᶜa during the Middle Bronze IIA, 2002, 50–52, figs. 14, 17.; cf. also *TD XII*, 126–136.

[11] D. Aston, Ceramic Imports at Tell el-Dabᶜa during the Middle Bronze IIA, 2002, fig. 14. 1, 3.

[12] D. Aston, Ceramic Imports at Tell el-Dabᶜa during the Middle Bronze IIA, 2002, fig. 17.5, cf. above page 341, cat. nos. 7–8.

usually found on Piriform 1a (I.1) juglets, for example Tell el- Dab^ca Phase G.[13]

E. MD Layer 17: Handles

MD contained a total of nine juglet handle fragments in brown fabric and polished surface. Five of these are double-stranded and four are single-stranded.

These nine handles, together with the eight rims and twelve bases, delimit the total number of Tell el Yahudiya and brown polished jug/juglet diagnostics present in MD. These modest numbers are an accurate reflection of the prized nature of this ware and its rare contents.

F. MD Layer 17: Undecorated Brown Slipped and Burnished Bodies

In addition to the decorated juglet bodies from Layer 17, there were another 68 sherds that had no incising or punctated decoration. These sherds, however, have brown slip and were highly burnished. Some of the sherds probably belong to Tell el Yahudiya ware juglets but others may be simply highly burnished brown slipped juglets (usually with cut-away mouths) that lack incised decoration. This type of juglet is well represented at Tell el-Dab^ca and at Tell Kabri.[14]

G. MD Layer 17: Provenance

Petrographic analysis on two Tell el Yahudiya Ware sherds from MD (No. 4 and RN 240 [not illustrated]) has shown that they are of Negev coastal clay.[15] Since the majority of the sherds share the same brown clay and slip, these are presumably of local manufacture. If this holds true, then Ashkelon must be considered an early centre of production and distribution of both the Ovoid 1 and Piriform 1a (I.1) juglets, and the commodities contained in them.

Grid 2: The Phase 13 = Gate 2 (ca. 1750–1710 BC)

MD was sealed by Street 13 = 239 running parallel with Glacis #2. This street, leading up from the sea, skirted the lower edge of the rampart and made a right turn towards the city gate. Corridor walls flanked a plaza in front of the stone arched façade of Gate 2. Fragments of several Tell el Yahudiya vessels were recovered from the makeup of the street. In Square 55 three pieces of a very delicate miniature juglet (RN 284; Fig. 2 no. 18), with tiny chalk-filled punctations, were found lying on the surface of Street 239. The pieces are so small that it is difficult to identify the form: the narrow diagonal band on the shoulder is similar to handmade Globular 1 juglets from Phase G/1–3 in Tell el- Dab^ca; the Ashkelon piece, however, is wheel made and must theerfore be something else.

In Square 56 an unslipped miniature cylindrical juglet (RN 104; Fig. 2 no. 19) was found in the make-up of Street 13. This unique vessel was unslipped and unburnished and is made of pink sandy clay. It was decorated with hatched triangles filled with stippled decoration.

The last fragment from Street 13 (RN 89, 91; Fig. 2 no. 21) has what may be flower petals and is another Ovoid 1 type. Fig. 2 numbers 20 and 21 were submitted for petrographic analysis and found to be made of Negev coastal clay and, therefore, locally made in or near Ashkelon.[16]

Grid 2: The Rampart

In Square 87 one Tell el Yahudiya Ware body sherd (RN 1; Fig. 2 no. 22) was found in Layer 100 of rampart fill, which protected the second or third story of Gate 2. This gray-brown and highly burnished sherd has the tip of a stippled triangle and therefore is part of a Piriform 1a (I.1) juglet.

Grid 2: Phase 12 = Gate 3 (ca. 1710–1650 BC)

Gate 3 was founded in the transitional MB IIA/B period. In Ashkelon most of the pottery from Phase 12 comes from the trenches and fills associated with the foundation of this gate. Unfortunately, the interior of the gate and the street leading up to it were stripped away when Gate 4 (Phase 11) was carved inside of it. Very little material culture contemporary with the use of Gate 3 was preserved. The lifespan of the gate could be determined, however, by dating the latest pottery found in the gate foundations and the date of the latest pottery found in the foundations of Gate 4. The pottery spans the working life of thc gate, from transitional MB IIA/B until near the end of MB IIB; at Tell el-Dab^ca this corresponds to Phases F through E/1.

Fragments of Tell el Yahudiya Ware were recovered from the following Phase 12 foundation layers:

[13] D. Aston, Ceramic Imports at Tell el-Dab^ca during the Middle Bronze IIA, 2002, fig. 17.6, 7, cf. above pages 345, 347, cat. nos. 21, 28.

[14] D. Aston, Ceramic Imports at Tell el-Dab^ca during the Middle Bronze IIA, 2002, 49 fig.14; A. Kempinski, *Tel Kabri: The 1986–1993 Excavation Seasons,* Tel Aviv, 2002, 80–81.

[15] Y. Goren and A. Cohen-Weinberger, pers.comm.

[16] Y. Goren and A. Cohen-Weinberger, pers.comm.

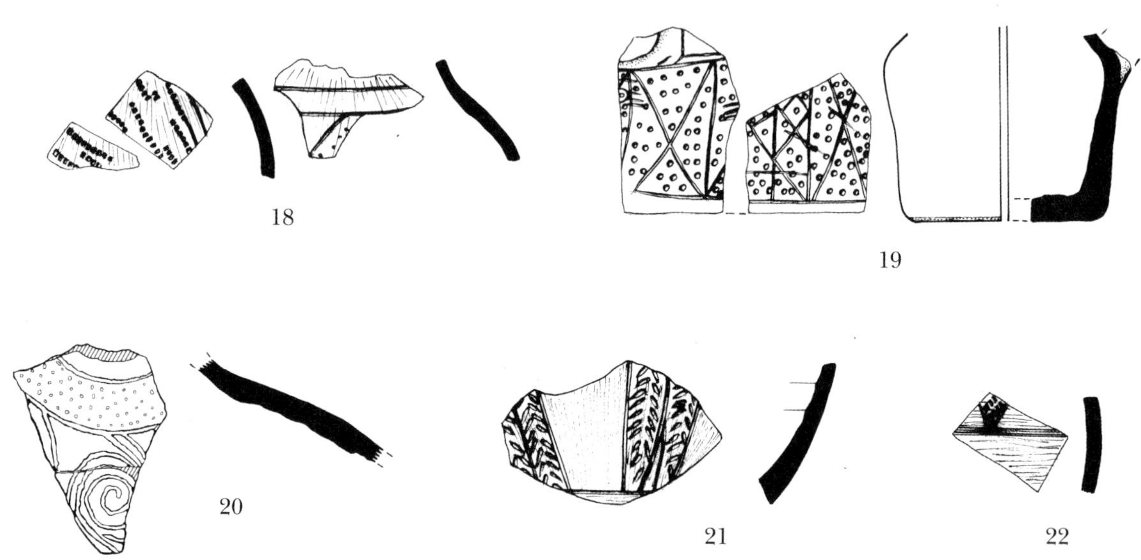

Phase 13

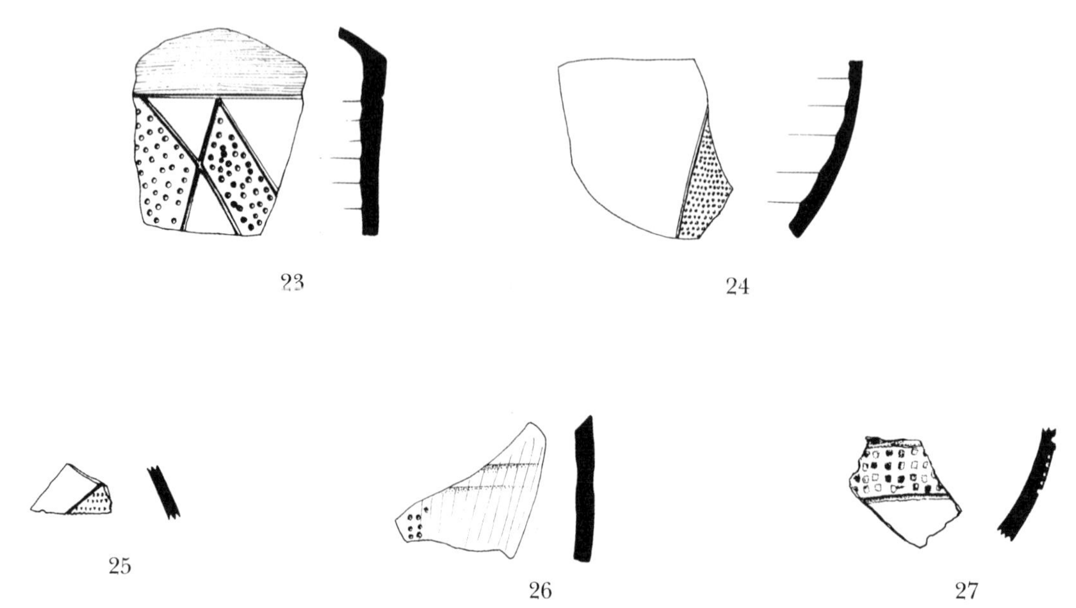

Phase 12

Fig. 2 Tell el-Yahudiya Ware from Ashkelon Phases 13 and 12 (1:2)

In Square 34 a foundation fill (Layer 240) supported part of the lower gate.[17] It yielded the body of a small cylindrical juglet (RN 1; Fig. 2 no. 23) made of gray clay with a brownish-gray burnished surface.

In Square 67 the exterior corridor of the Phase 13 gate was partially buried by a layer of compacted black ash (Layer 7). It contained a juglet body (RN 27; Fig. 2 no.24) made of gray-brown clay with a reddish-brown burnished surface. A small diagonal field of tiny chalk-filled punctations seems to be part of a pendent triangle. The relatively thick body, shape, and surface treatment are suggestive of an Ovoid 1a juglet.

In Squares 84 and 85 the interior of Gate 2 was buried under a series of fills. The first fill consisted of ash, silt and sand (Layer 43) thrown over the Phase 13 street. This layer contained a Piriform 1a (I1) juglet fragment made of gray-brown clay (RN 20; Fig. 2 no. 25). The brown burnished surface has an unburnished field of tiny unfilled punctations set in a triangle.

The next covering layer was composed of compressed black ash (Layer 40). It contained an Ovoid 1a juglet fragment (RN 52; Fig. 2 no. 26) made of brown clay and dark brown burnished surface. A small field of unburnished chalk-filled stiples, at the edge of the sherd, was part of a triangle.

Finally, in a layer of crushed yellow sandstone (Layer 38) there was a possible Ovoid 1a juglet fragment (RN 3; Fig. 2 no. 27) made of brown clay. The sherd has a brown burnished surface with a horizontal band with large chalk-filled punctations.

All the Tell el Yahudiya bodies found in the Phase 12 foundation fills are early examples of this ware. They were in circulation up until the close of Gate 2. Ovoid 1a, Piriform 1a (I1) and Cylindrical juglets were present. Based on their brown colour, their brownish-gray fabric, and surface treatment, we believe they are of local manufacture.

Grid 50: Tomb Deposits (contemporary with Phase 12 = Gate 3)

On the south side of the tell a necropolis was hewn out of the sandstone ridge overlooking the sea. The chamber tombs were in use from the transitional phase of MB IIA/B through the end of the MB IIC period, with continual use throughout most of the Late Bronze Age. This use by generation after generation of family and lineage burials means that the tomb deposits are rarely from closed contexts. This is of less importance in the case of the Tell el Yahudiya ware, however, because these vessels fall exclusively within the Middle Bronze Age period. Several chamber tombs contained a number of complete and nearly complete Tell el Yahudiya Ware vessels. These display discrete typological features which fall within fairly narrow chronological ranges when indexed to the Tell el-Dab^{c}a sequence of Tell el Yahudiya Ware.

The collection of Tell el Yahudiya Ware from the tombs is later than Gates 1 and 2 (Phases 14 and 13). The tomb deposits are of great importance because they continue the sequence of Tell el Yahudiya Ware mostly missing from Gate 3 and Phase 12, thereby filling the gap in the Grid 2 stratified sequence.

The most important aspect of the tomb collection is that it contains a wide variety of forms, documenting the evolution of this pottery from transitional MB IIA/B through the end of the MB IIC period. The Tell el Yahudiya Ware found in Phase 11=Gate 4 and the Phase 10 rampart augments the corpus from the tombs and provides a valuable stratigraphic control for bracketing the date of the Tell el Yahudiya Ware from the tombs. A couple of fragments that appear in the last MB IIC layers of Grid 38 provide additional supplementary evidence.

In the following description the Tell el Yahudiya Ware from the tomb deposits will be presented chronologically starting with the earliest vessels and proceeding to the latest.

A. Chamber Tomb 5: Grid 50.Square 48.Layer 487

In Chamber Tomb 5 a cache of Tell el Yahudiya juglets (RN 46, 47 [= Fig. 3 no. 28], 48, and 93 [= Fig. 3 no. 29] was found clustered in the lowest layer (Layer 487) of the east niche, and covered by washed-in sand and silt. A Piriform 1b (in this volume I2) juglet (RN 47; Fig. 3 no. 28) was missing its handle, neck, rim and base. The handle scar indicates that it was double-stranded. The fabric of the vessel is of coarse brown clay with sand and occasional chalk inclusions indicative of local manufacture. The surface colour is reddish brown with two burnished horizontal bands dividing the vessel into three registers of burnished and unburnished standing and pendent triangles, one of the hallmarks of Piriform 1b (I2) juglets. There are parallels in Tell el-Dab^{c}a Phases F and E/3 (cf. this volume 144–152). The shape, colour and quality of the slip on this

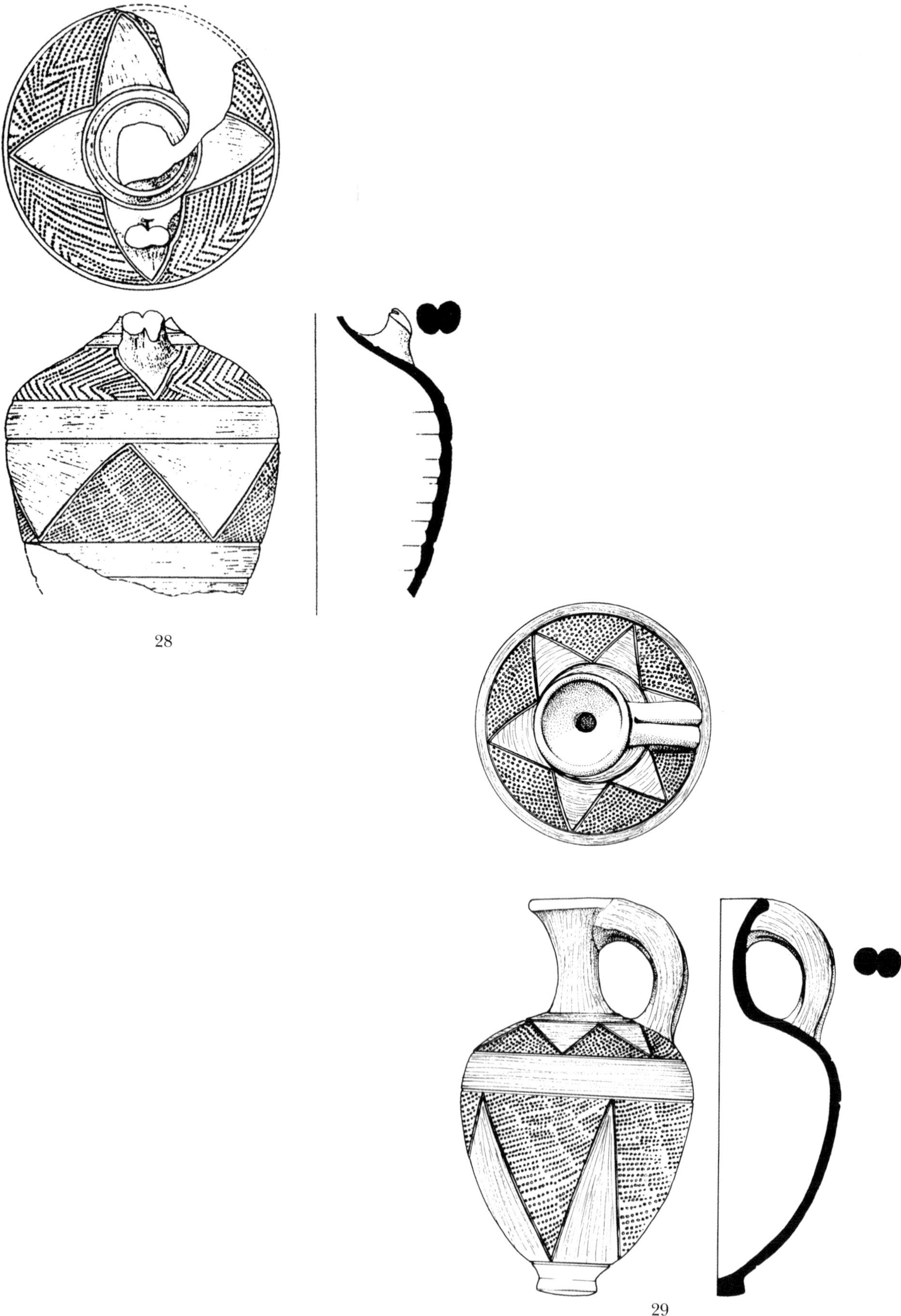

Fig. 3 Tell el-Yahudiya Ware from Ashkelon Phase 12 Chamber Tomb 5

tomb vessel are similar to fragments found in the foundation fills of Gate 3. Together, the form and decorative scheme of the vessel indicate a date in the transitional phase of MB IIA/B.

The next vessel (RN 93; Fig. 3 no. 29) is a Piriform 1c (in this volume I3.2a) juglet made of coarse rust-brown sandy clay with a double-stranded handle. The clay is so friable that much of the slip has slaked off. A single horizontal band at the shoulder separates two registers of burnished and unburnished standing and pendent triangles; this is the characteristic attribute of Piriform 1c (I3) juglets. The rim has a simple funnel mouth; the bottom of the vessel, a button base. A close, though not exact, parallel is found in Tell el-Dabᶜa TD 1833 from Phase E/3 (above page 367, cat. no. 77). At Tell el-Dabᶜa Piriform 1b (I2) and 1c (I3) juglets are contemporary, and the same appears to be the case at Ashkelon since, as found in this burial niche, Fig. 3 nos. 28 and 29 overlap in time. The juglet has the classic form of early MB IIB Tell el Yahudiya Ware (cf. Tell el-Dabᶜa Phase E/3).

The other two vessels in the cache belong to later types and these will be described with reference to Phase 11 and Gate 4.

B. Chamber Tomb 11: Grid 50: Square 47

Chamber 11 was filled with a layer of washed-in sand (Layer 315) covering several large stones from the collapsed ceiling. A number of disturbed burial deposits were found at the bottom of this layer, which contained MB and LB pottery. Five Tell el Yahudiya Ware vessels were found (RN 33[= Fig. 7 no. 36], 41, 45 [= Fig. 4 no. 30], 53 and 46 [= Fig. 7 no. 38]), two of which were zoomorphic pieces. The most extraordinary vessel in the tomb was a zoomorphic juglet in the shape of the Horus falcon (RN 45; Fig. 4 no. 30). This bird vessel was made of gray-brown clay and the entire body has a polished gray surface. The double-stranded handle is attached to the back of the head between which there is a hole for liquids to be poured into the pitcher. Another smaller hole opens just below the beak for the liquid to be poured out. The breast is decorated with an open lotus, or water lily, blossom with two closed buds on either side. Unfortunately the rear portion of the bird was not preserved. The colour of the fabric and the slip are typical of the early Tell el Yahudiya Ware from Ashkelon. This piece was probably made no later than the transitional MB IIA/B period but was deposited as a tomb offering in MB IIB. Petrographic analysis of the clay indicates it was made of Negev coastal clay and therefore it is of local provenance.[18]

The next vessel (RN 53; Fig. 4 no. 31) is a Piriform 1c (I3) juglet, and missing its neck, rim and handle (cf. Fig. 5 no.32). The vessel has a concave disk base and is made of grayish- brown clay. One partially preserved papyrus stem and spray spring from between burnished lotus petals, with triangular panels of chalk-filled punctations in between. Vessels with the lotus motif appear in Tell el-Daba Phase E/3 and continue into E/2 (cf. above pages 376–382). Other Tell el-Yahudiya vessels from Chamber Tomb 11 will be discussed with the Phase 11 material.

C. Chamber Tomb 7: Grid 50: Square 47

The upper level of Chamber 7 was filled with stones from the collapse of the tomb ceiling and washed-in brown silt and yellow sand (Layer 311). Three partially complete Tell el Yahudiya Ware juglets (RN 19 [= Fig. 7 no. 37], 35 [= Fig. 5 no. 32], and 110 [= Fig. 5 no. 33]) were found along the side of the chamber in a mixed deposit containing MB and LB pottery.

One of these vessels (Fig. 5 no. 32) is a Piriform 1c (I3.1d) juglet, missing its neck, rim and handle. It has a concave disk base. It is made of coarse soft gray clay and most of its gray-brown slip has worn away. A horizontal band at the shoulder divides the decorative scheme into an upper zone of framed standing and pendent triangles and a lower zone of five individual papyrus stalks that spring out of an open lotus blossom from the base of the juglet. Without the handle it is difficult to say if this piece is of Palestinian origin, but the gray-brown slip suggests that it may be of local manufacture. Vessels with floral patterns were produced just before the Hyksos period in early MB IIB, or Phase E/3 in Tell el-Dabᶜa. The closest types in form and decoration are found in Tell el-Dabᶜa Phase E/2 with a chronological range extending from ca. 1660–1630 BC.[19]

Another unique vessel (Fig. 5 no. 33) is a Piriform 1d (in this volume, I4.1d) juglet, missing its neck and rim, but preserving one section of its double-stranded handle. This large vessel is made of coarse brown clay with numerous inclusions of sand

[17] R. Voss, *A Sequence of Four Middle Bronze Gates in Ashkelon*, 2002, 383.

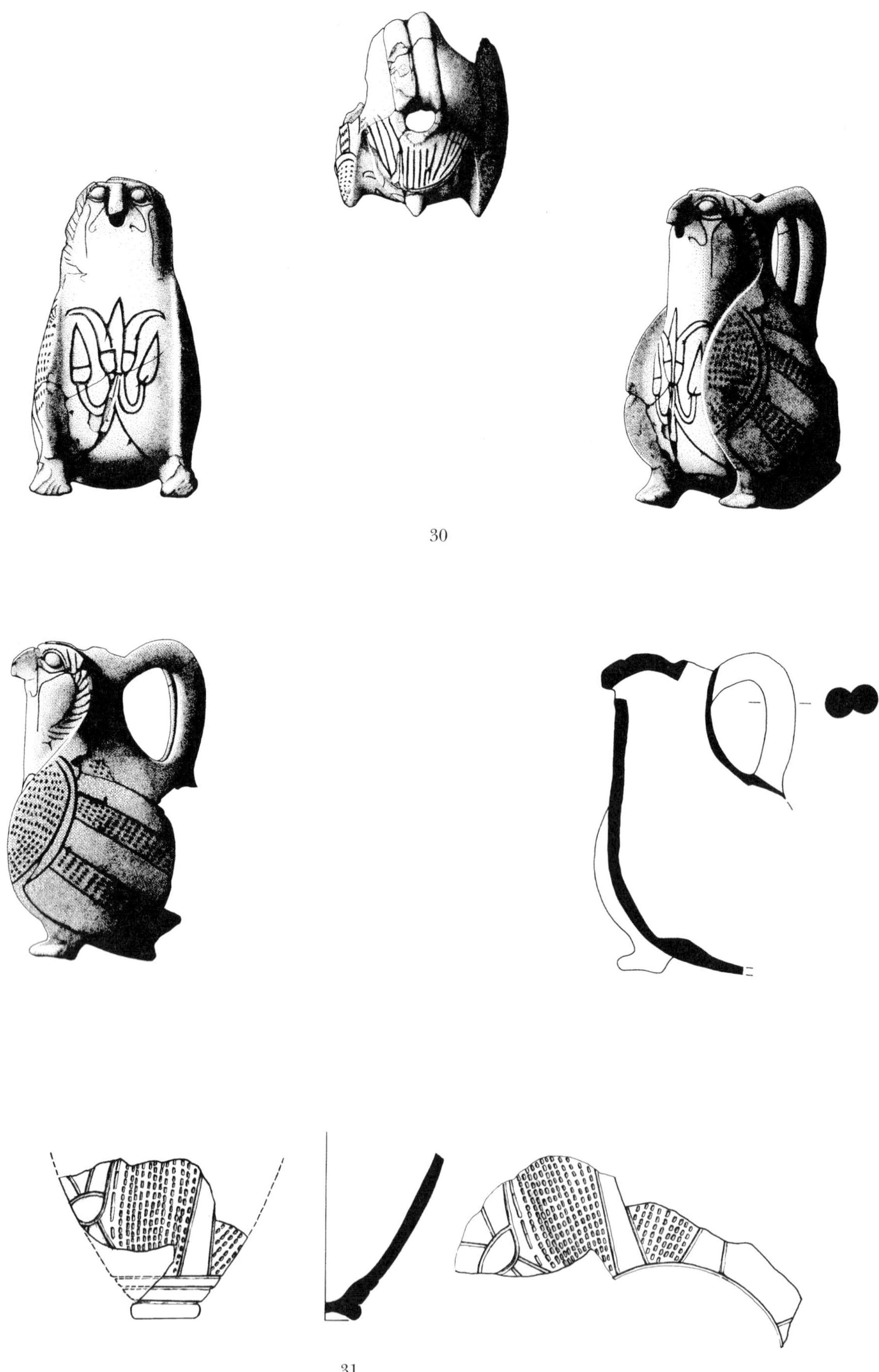

Fig. 4 Tell el-Yahudiya Ware from Ashkelon Phase 12 Chamber Tomb 11 (1:2)

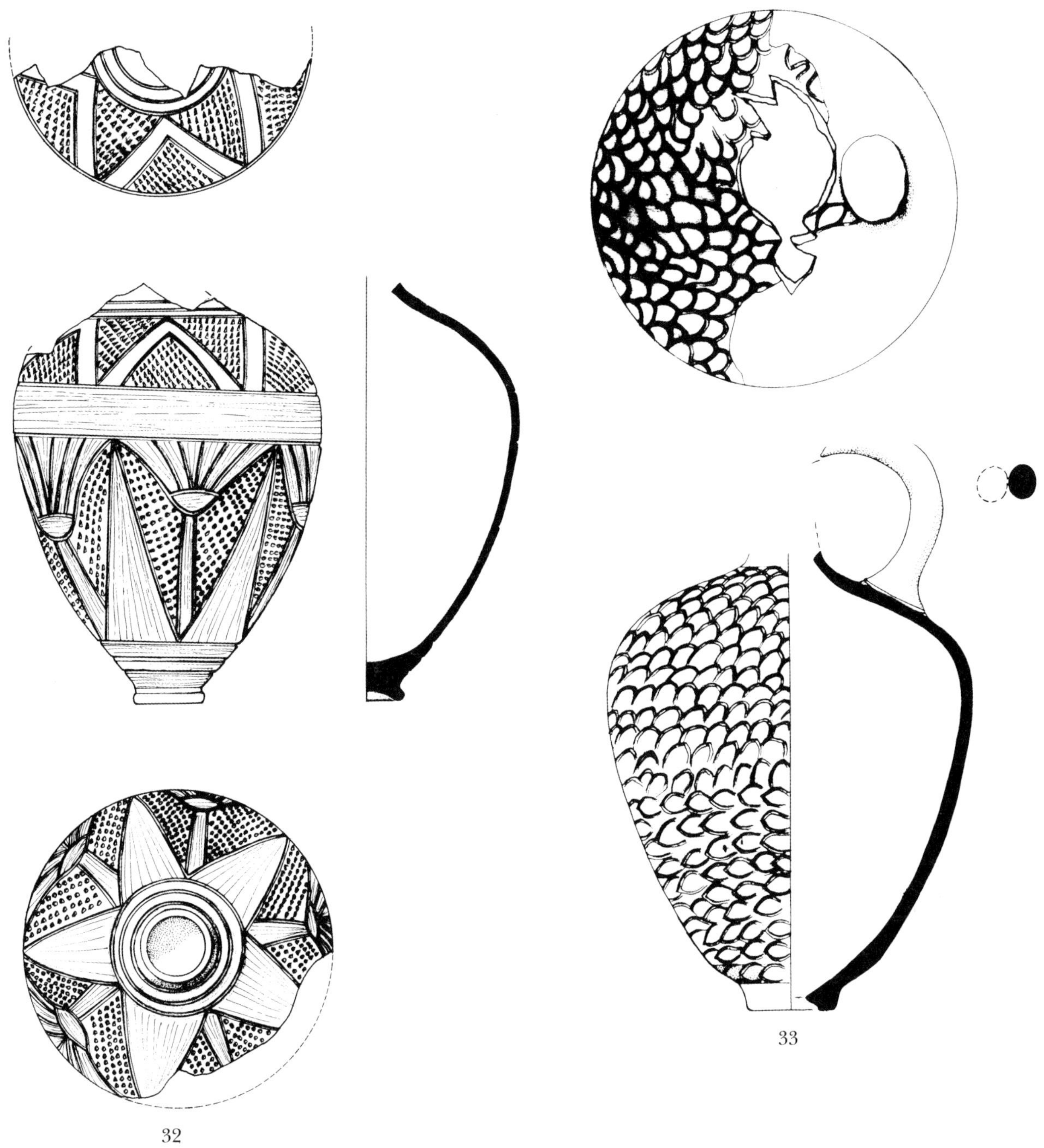

Fig. 5 Tell el-Yahudiya Ware from Ashkelon Phase 12 Chamber Tomb 7 (1:2)

and crushed pottery. The friable nature of the clay has caused flaking of the richly burnished surface, which was covered entirely by a pattern of scales or scallops. The scales run in two directions: from the neck and shoulder to the midpoint of the vessel the scales run in diagonal rows and point up; on the lower half of the juglet, the scales run in horizontal rows pointing left. Finally, there is no evidence that the incised scales were filled with chalk. The bottom of the vessel, which has largely broken away, had a large flat button base. This type of base is a feature of Piriform 1b (I2), 1c (I3) and 1d (I4) vessels beginning in Tell el-Daba Phase F and continuing through E/3.[20]

[18] Y. Goren and A. Cohen-Weinberger, pers.comm.

Grid 50: Tomb Deposits (contemporary with Phase 11 and Gate 4)

The latest series of Tell el Yahudiya Ware from the tombs clusters near the end of the MB IIB period. These later examples are of varied provenances with a significant component of Egyptian imports. The Egyptian wares have a black to gray-black core and similar surface colour, characteristic of Nile clay. The brown and gray-brown Ashkelon clays now make up less than half the assemblage. The appearance of Egyptian-made Tell el Yahudiya Ware is an important new development appearing in Ashkelon Gate 4, the Sanctuary of the Silver Calf, Grid 50 chamber tombs, and in the courtyard deposits of Grid 38.

A. Chamber Tomb 5: Grid 50. Square 48. Layer 487

Returning to Chamber 5, the third Tell el Yahudiya ware vessel found there is a Biconical 1 juglet made of black clay (RN 46; Fig. 6 no. 34, in this volume type group L.2.2). It has a strap handle and a concave disk base. A central burnished band divides the juglet into two zones of decoration. The upper register contains large standing triangles bordered by burnished triangular strips. The triangles are filled with a stippled chevron pattern running horizontally. The lower register has large pendent triangles also bordered by burnished triangular strips but the triangles are filled with a stippled chevron pattern set vertically. This Egyptian vessel, according to Goren and Cohen-Weinberger (personal communication) fits comfortably in Tell el-Dab^ca Phase E/2.[21] It would appear that, in the transition from Daba E/2 to E/1, the decoration of the biconical juglets was simplified by the enlargement of the standing and pendent triangles and the loss of burnished frames around them.

The next vessel from Chamber 5 is a Piriform 2a (in this book type group L.1) juglet (RN 48; Fig. 6 no. 35) made of dark gray clay. It has a strap handle and concave disk base. The decoration consists of four burnished vertical strips separating four elliptical zones of vertical stippled chevrons. This type of juglet first appears at Tell el-Dab^ca in the transition from Phase E/2 to E/1. There are numerous examples in E/1, where it appears to be the dominant form of Tell el Yahuduyah Ware. (cf above Part Three, cat. nos. 201–413).

The last vessel from Chamber 5 is a Piriform 2b (in this book, type group M.1) juglet (RN 164; Fig. 6 no. 40) fragment made of brown clay. The rim, neck, handle and base are missing but the preserved decoration on the body consists of vertical burnished strips separating two elliptical zones filled with vertical lines of unfilled punctations. This probably locally produced piece lacks the vertical rows of stacked chevrons typical of Egyptian Piriform 2a juglets, which may be a pattern unique to local or Levantine examples.

B. Chamber Tomb 11: Grid 50. Square 47. Layer 315

In Chamber Tomb 11 a Biconical 1 (L.2.2) juglet was found in Layer 315 (RN 33; Fig. 7 no. 36). The vessel is made of black clay and has a strap handle and concave disk base with central nipple. Petrographic analysis has established that it is Egyptian.[22] It has a central burnished band which divides the vessel into an upper zone of standing triangles filled with stippled chevrons running horizontally and a lower zone of pendent triangles filled with stippled chevrons running vertically. The earliest example from Tell el-Dab^ca appears in the transition from Phase E/2–E/1.[23]

The next vessel from Layer 315 is the bottom half of a Biconical 3 (in this book type group L.5) juglet (RN 46; Fig. 7 no. 38). The foot is missing but the decoration consists of an uninterrupted series of diagonal unfilled punctations below a horizontal burnished band. The closest parallel from Tell el-Dab^ca appears in transitional Phase E/2–E/1 and the latest example is in Phase D/3.[24] The dark gray clay suggests that this vessel is of Egyptian provenance.

C. Chamber Tomb 7: Grid 50. Square 47. Layer 311

In Chamber Tomb 7 a Piriform 2a (L.1.2) juglet was found in Layer 311 (RN 19; Fig. 7 no. 37). It is made of dark gray clay; its neck, rim and handle are missing. The remaining stub indicates that it had a strap handle. The juglet has a concave disk base with a nipple (in this book "bulb base") in the centre. Four vertical burnished ribbons divide four elliptical zones of vertical stippled chevrons. This is another Egyptian vessel[25] with many parallels in Tell el-Dab^ca starting in Phase E/1 and continuing through Phases E/1 through D/3 (cf. above pages 435–438, cat. nos. 332–338).

[19] Following Bietak's latest dating for this phase.
[20] Bietak 1991: figs. 33.3–5, 34.2, and 48.2.
[21] Bietak 1991: fig. 118; Bietak 1996: pl. 23B.
[22] Y. Goren and A. Cohen-Weinberger, pers.comm.

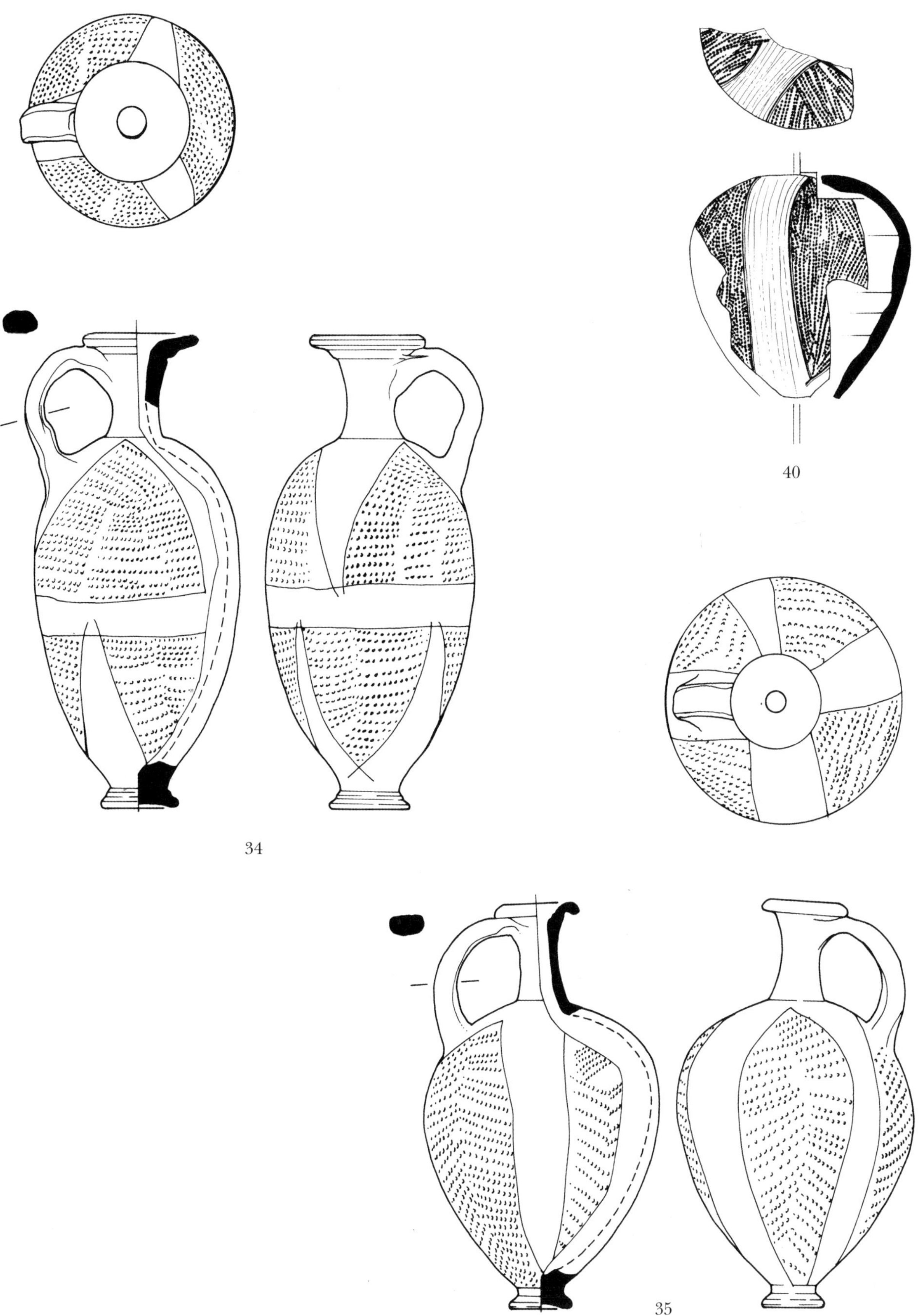

Fig. 6 Tell el-Yahudiya Ware from Ashkelon Phase 11 Chamber Tomb 5 (1:2)

Layer 311 filled the upper part of Chamber Tomb 7. It was a layer of washed- in yellow-brown silt and sand, in which was found the upper shoulder of a squat Biconical 3 (L5) juglet (RN 2; Fig. 7 no. 39). The vessel is made of dark gray clay and has a burnished horizontal band above which rises a radiating field of unfilled stippled decoration. Based on the clay colour and decoration this is another Egyptian vessel. The earliest parallels from Tell el-Dabᶜa are found in the transition from Phase E/2–E/1 and continue as late as D/2.[26]

D. Grid 2: Gate 4 (Footgate) and the Sanctuary of the Silver Calf

In Phase 11 (Square 55) a modest single chambered mudbrick gate opened onto a fan shaped corridor that led down the outer slope of the rampart to a nine meter wide terrace. This terrace supported an extramural building in which was found a ceramic shrine containing a silver-plated bronze calf.[27]

In Room #5 of the Sanctuary, the body of a Tell el Yahudiya juglet (RN 2; Fig. 7 no. 41) was found on the beaten earth Floor 164. The sherd is made of gray clay with a darker black surface decorated with a stippled chevron pattern running horizontally. This Egyptian-made fragment, according to Goren and Cohen-Weinberger (personal communication), preserves a tiny sliver of burnish at its thickest point, probably near the neck of the vessel. The decoration appears to belong to a Biconical 3 (L5) juglet. As noted above, this type of vessel appears in Tell el-Dabᶜa between transitional Phases E/2–E/1 and D/2.[28]

In Square 85 one Tell el Yahudiya juglet fragment (RN 1; No. 42) was found in a layer of debris (Layer 99) dumped on the Mudbrick Floor 103 of the footgate. The sherd is made of dark gray clay. The surface preserves part of a chevron pattern that may belong to a Piriform 2a (L1) juglet.

These last two fragments from Phase 11 belong to types that appear no earlier in Tell el-Dabᶜa than the transition from Phase E/2–E/1 (c. 1630 BC), near the end of the MB IIB period, nor later than Tell el-Dabca Phase D/3 (c. 1600–1570 BC).

Grid 50: Tomb Deposits (contemporary with the Phase 10 Rampart)

The latest tomb deposits of the Middle Bronze Age fall within the MB IIC period. A large number and variety of vessels from this period were found in these tombs but just two of these vessels were Tell el Yahudiya Ware juglets.

A. Chamber Tomb 11: Grid 50. Square 47. Layer 315

The latest Tell el Yahudiya Ware vessel found in Chamber Tomb 11 was the bottom half of a Piriform 2b (M1) juglet (RN 20; Fig. 8 no. 43). It is dark gray in colour and has a concave disk base. The decoration consists of three vertical burnished bands separating three panels of unfilled vertically stacked chevrons.

B. Chamber Tomb 5: Grid 50. Square 48. Layer 530

At the bottom of Chamber Tomb 5, in a layer of silt and sand (Layer 530), the rim, neck and double-stranded handle of a probable Globular 2 juglet (RN 1287; Fig. 8 no. 44) was found. The vessel was made of brown clay and the decoration on the shoulder consisted of an unfilled incised collar encircling the neck. Inside the collar are square segments divided by vertical lines unfilled punctations.

C. Grid 2: The Phase 10 Rampart

In Square 55 the Calf Sanctuary was buried under a layer of rampart fill (Layer 132), from which a body fragment from a possible Globular Tell el Yahudiya juglet of type group L9.6 was recovered (RN 74; Fig. 8 no. 45). The sherd comes from near the base of the vessel, which is thickened and flattened. It is made of gray-brown clay, with two burnished intersecting bands dividing the decoration into two fields of stippled pendent triangles. The clay colour, decoration, and glossy surface are indicative of a locally made vessel. Possible parallels may be found in Tell el-Dabᶜa Phase D/2 (cf. above cat. nos. 584–588).

In Square 76, Corridor 22 and Street 117 from Phase 11 were covered by a massive fill consisting of various layers of mudbrick debris, sand, silt, and clay (Layers 141, 140, and 139). Layer 141, composed of compact dark brown clay, contained some human skeletal remains (Feature 142), probably dumped in the corridor after the robbing of Tomb 13 of Phase 11. The shoulder of a Biconical (in this book type group L5) juglet (RN 1; Fig. 8 no. 46) was covered by this layer. The piece was made of gray-brown clay with brown burnished surface and was probably locally made. The decoration consists of a burnished hori-

[23] Bietak 1991: fig. 118; Bietak 1996: Plate 23B.

[24] Bietak 1991: fig. 129.3, 227; Bietak 1996: pl. 23C.

[25] Y. Goren and A. Cohen-Weinberger, pers. comm.

[26] Bietak 1991: fig. 120.3–6, 142.3–12; Bietak 1996: pl. 23C

Fig. 7 Tell el-Yahudiya Ware from Ashkelon Phase 11 (1:2)

zontal band above which is a herringbone pattern of unfilled punctations, running horizontally. At Tell el-Dab^ca this type, type group L5.3, represents a mature MB IIB form that continues into early MB IIC spanning Phases E/2–E/1, E/1 and D/3. (above pages 463–478) This juglet was originally used in Phase 11 and discarded in the earliest fill layer that buried the corridor leading up to the Gate 4 (the Footgate).

Another piece of Tell el Yahudiya Ware (RN 20; Fig. 8 no. 47) was discovered in Square 67 in Philistine Rampart 4, the earliest of the Iron Age fortifications. The Philistine rampart overlay the last Middle Bronze Age rampart (Phase 10); probably the juglet fragment derived from the earlier rampart fill (Layer 6). The dark gray clay is probably of Egyptian origin. The decoration preserved on the shoulder of the fragment consists of an uninterrupted zone of horizontal chevrons, which is indicative of a Biconical 3 (L5) vessel. Parallels appear in Tell el-Dab^ca Phases E/2, E/1 and D/3, with the latest examples possibly continuing into the early Eighteenth Dynasty (cf. above page 556).

Two of the three pieces of Tell el Yahudiya Ware found in the Phase 10 rampart date to the MB IIC period. If the Biconical (L5) juglets appear no later than the end of Phase D/2, then the date of the burial of the Footgate and Calf Sanctuary whould be approximately 1590–1560 BC, following Bietak.[29]

D. Grid 38: The Courtyard and the Silo

In Square 53 a very small fragment of a Tell el Yahudiya Ware juglet (RN 8; Fig. 8 no. 48) was found in a layer of ash in mudbrick-lined Silo 95. The sherd is made of gray-brown clay indicative of possible local manufacture. The small bit of surface decoration appears to contain a horizontal burnished band with diagonal stippling above (part of a horizontal chevron pattern). This design suggests that the sherd was part of a Biconical (L5) juglet. Again, in Tell el-Dab^ca this form appears as late as at least at the end of Phase D/2.[30] The contents of the silo are of exceptional importance for dating the last phase of the Middle Bronze Age in Ashkelon. In addition to the Tell el Yahudiya fragment there were also an Egyptian *zir* (RN 3), two Proto-White Slip bowl rim fragments (RN 19, 20), and three non-joining bodies of a Chocolate-on-White Ware vessel (RN 18).

In Square 54 a small Tell el Yahudiya juglet fragment (RN 5; Fig. 8 no. 49) lay on a beaten earth Surface 87. The sherd is made of black clay of Egyptian provenance and has a stippled chevron pattern set horizontally. Since the wheel lines and the direction of the chevrons are aligned, the sherd probably was part of a Biconical (L5) juglet, which appears at Tell el-Dab^ca in transitional Phase E/2–E/1 and continues as late as Phase D/2.

The Floor 87 and the Silo 95 represent the latest Middle Bronze Age occupational horizon in Ashkelon. The two Biconical (RN 5, 8) juglet fragments, therefore, belong to the latest Tell el Yahudiya Ware vessels found on the site and thus mark the end of a long tradition.

Acknowledgments

The authors are extremely grateful to Adam Aja, Michael Press, and Peter Rufo for their superlative assistance in preparing this manuscript and its illustrations.

[27] Stager 2006.

[28] Bietak 1991: fig. 120, 137, 140, 142, 236, and 269.

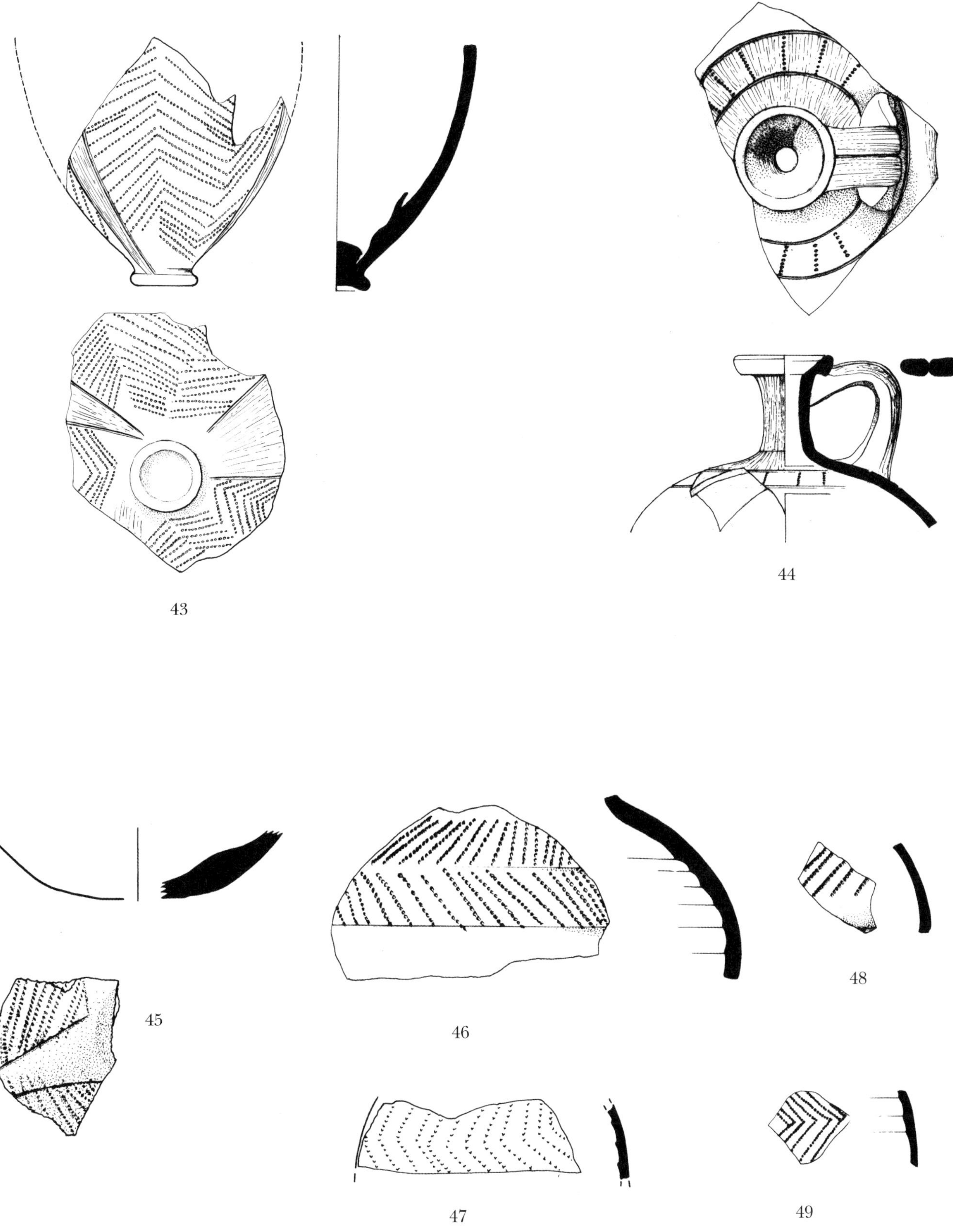

Fig. 8 Tell el-Yahudiya Ware from Ashkelon Phase 10 (1:2)

The Tell el-Yahudiya Ware from Tel Beth-Shean

Aren M. Maeir and Robert A. Mullins

Introduction

The purpose of this paper is to discuss the Tell el-Yahudiya Ware found during excavations at Tel Beth-Shean.[1] However, before we delve into this rather limited corpus, we will begin with a brief introduction to the site and to the relevant Middle Bronze Age IIB remains.

Beth-Shean (Tell el-Husn) is best known as an Egyptian outpost during the New Kingdom Period.[2] The site is strategically located in the Beth Shean Valley at the juncture of the Jezreel and Jordan Valleys (Fig. 1; Levant Grid 1977.2124). This fertile region, part of the 6,000 km long Syro-African Rift, has witnessed a long history of habitation since late Neolithic times where dozens of sites from a variety of peri-

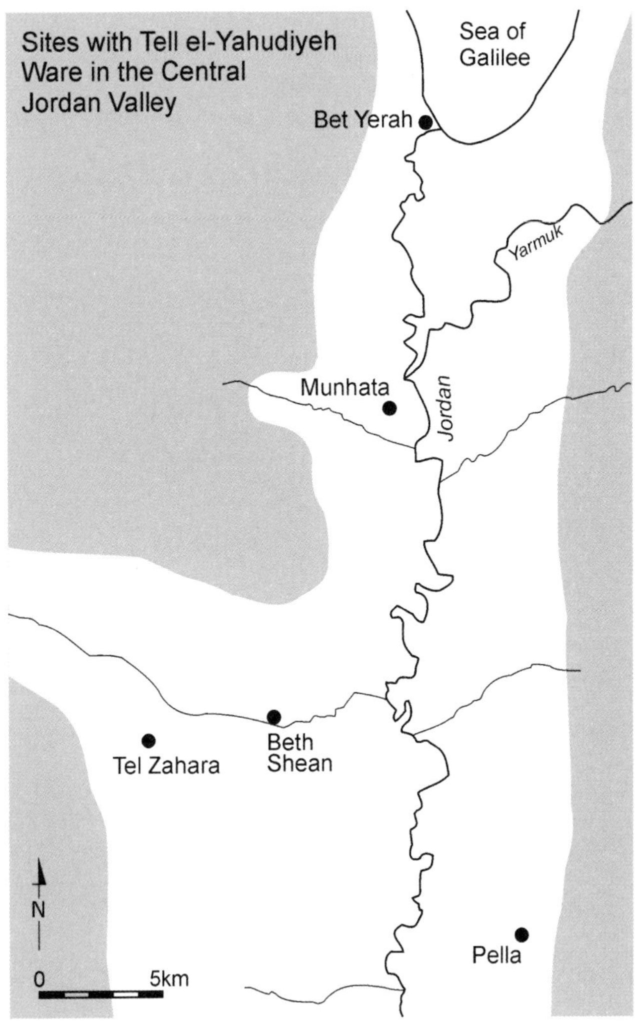

Fig. 1 Sites with Tell el-Yahudiya Pottery in the Central Jordan Valley

---

1 The authors would like to thank A. Mazar, who directed the Hebrew University excavations at Beth-Shean for permission to publish the finds and for his assistance in this process. Additional thanks go to J. Yellin, J. Rosenberg and M. Schiffer. Portions of this research have appeared in the doctoral dissertations of the two authors (A.M. Maeir, *The Material Culture of the Central and Northern Jordan Valley in the Middle Bronze Age II: Pottery and Settlement Pattern*, unpubl. Ph.D. thesis, Jerusalem, 1997; R.A. Mullins, *Beth Shean during the Eighteenth Dynasty: From Canaanite Settlement to Egyptian Garrison*, unpubl. Ph.D. thesis, Jerusalem, 2002), which were carried out under A. Mazar's supervision.

2 The first undisputed reference to Beth-Shean is as *bt š'ir* in a topographic list of Tuthmosis III on the walls of the Karnak temple (D.B. Redford, *Egypt, Canaan, and Israel in Ancient Times,* 1992, 156–60; Y. Aharoni, *The Land of the Bible: A Historical Geography*, 2nd ed., 1979: 156–166, especially 163; J. Simons, *Handbook for the Study of Egyptian Topographical Lists Relating to Western Asia*, 1937: 27–44). The site is mentioned again in the 14th century as *bit ša-a-ni* in Amarna Letter 289:20 (W.L. Moran, *The Amarna Letters,* 1992: 332–33; Y. Aharoni, *The Land of the Bible*, 1979: 171–176; J.B. Pritchard, *Ancient Near Eastern Texts Relating to the Old Testament*, 3rd edition with supplement, 1969, 489). In 1993, a clay cylinder from the Amarna period bearing Akkadian signs was found by workers clearing part of the old University Museum dumps at the foot of the tell. The cylinder contains a message from Tagi to Labᶜayu, two rebellious rulers known from Amarna Letters 252–254, 264–266, 289 (W. Horowitz, An Inscribed Clay Cylinder from Amarna Age Beth Shean, *IEJ* 46, 1996, 208–18, see also Y. Goren, I. Finkelstein and N. Na'aman, *Inscribed in Clay: Provenance Study of the Amarna Letters and other Ancient Near Eastern Texts*, 2004, 267–269. During the 13th century BC, Beth-Shean appears in topographic lists of Seti I (Y. Aharoni, *The Land of the Bible*, 1979, 178) and in *Papyrus Anastasi I* (J.B. Pritchard, *Ancient Near Eastern Texts*, 1969, 477). Three stelae found in a later stratigraphic context by the University Museum excavators date to this period. Two are attributed to Seti I (J.B. Pritchard, *Ancient Near Eastern Texts*, 1969, 253, 255; A. Rowe, *The Topography and History of Beth-Shan*, 1930, 24–29, pl. 41, and the third to Year 9 of Ramesses II (J.B. Pritchard, *Ancient Near Eastern Texts*, 1969, 255; A. Rowe, *The Topography and History of Beth-Shan*, 1930, 33–36, pl. 46). The Ramesses stele mentions a campaign that probably passed by way of Beth-Shean (Y. Aharoni, *The Land of the Bible*, 1979, 182).

Fig. 2 Plan of Tel Beth Shean and the Principal Areas of Excavation

ods dot the landscape.[3] One period of rich occupation was during the Middle Bronze Age, an aspect of which is the focus of this particular study.

Beth-Shean occupies a naturally high hill on the southern banks of Nahal Harod (Nahr Jalud). The surface area of the mound is ca. 4 hectares (10 acres), not unusual for a town of this period, though recent excavations by the Hebrew University of Jerusalem in Areas G and L have demonstrated that settlements from the Middle Bronze Age, Late Bronze Age and

[3] E. Orni and E. Efrat, *Geography of Israel.* 3rd ed., 1980; F. Bender, *Geology of Jordan*, 1974; A. Maeir, *The Material Culture of the Central and Northern Jordan Valley in the Middle Bronze Age II: Pottery and Settlement Pattern*, unpubl. Ph.D. thesis, Jerusalem, 1997, A. Maeir, *"In the Midst of the Jordan": The Jordan Valley during the Middle Bronze Age (ca. 2000–1500 BCE). Archaeological and Historical Correlates*, Vienna, 2010.

Iron Age I were all limited to the highest point of the tell in the south and did not exceed 2 hectares (5 acres) in extent (Fig. 2).[4]

It also seems from the excavations that Beth-Shean was unfortified throughout the Bronze and Iron Ages. This is quite surprising when one considers that most sites in the Levant were protected by city walls during the latter part of Middle Bronze Age. Either the defenses disappeared, or Beth-Shean was a small, unfortified town at this time with the main city of the region located at Tel Rehov (Tell es-Sarem) ca. 6 km/3.5 mi to the south.[5]

Excavations were first conducted at the site by the University of Pennsylvania Museum (hereafter, the University Museum) in 1921–1933.[6] For a brief season in 1983, and then again in 1989–1996, the Institute of Archaeology of the Hebrew University of Jerusalem carried out renewed work on the tell, focusing attention on its settlement history during the Early, Middle, and Late Bronze Ages, as well as during Iron Age I–II.[7]

Three excavation areas particularly relevant to this study are Areas R and G, as well as FitzGerald's deep cut at the southeastern corner of the mound. Area M is located in a portion of this sounding (Fig. 2).

Summary of the Middle Bronze Age stratigraphy

During the last three seasons of excavation in 1930–1933, G.M. FitzGerald revealed three main strata of the Middle Bronze Age-Levels XI, XB and XA. These three appear to be equivalent to Strata R-5, R-4 and R-3 as excavated by the Hebrew University.[8]

Area R, below the central courtyard of Level IX as excavated by A. Rowe in 1927–1928, was dominated in Strata R-5 (Level XIA) and R-4 (Level XB) by a large oval-shaped feature intentionally dug by the inhabitants for a yet to be determined purpose (Figs. 3, 4). Over time, structures built around the "crater" collapsed into it as the edges receded. Three sherds of Tell el-Yahudiya Ware (Fig. 5:6–8) were found in sloping layers related to the Oval Crater.

Significantly, most of the pottery from the initial stage of Middle Bronze Age settlement in Stratum R-5 (Level XIA) does not predate the 17th century BC. The apparent lack of stratified MB IIA or transitional MB IIA/MB IIB pottery in all the areas excavated to date may indicate a gap in habitation on the mound from the end of the Intermediate Bronze Age (EB IV) until renewed settlement takes place in the 17th century.[9]

---

4 Area L produced Middle Bronze Age burials (Stratum L-3) below Byzantine (Stratum L-2) and Early Islamic (Stratum L-1) remains. In Area G was found part of a room dating to the latter part of the Middle Bronze Age. The pottery assemblage included examples of Chocolate-on-White Ware and the body fragment of a Tell el-Yahudiya ware jug/juglet (Fig. 5:5).

5 One possible explanation for this phenomenon has been put forth by B. Arubas. He argues that the Roman builders of Scythopolis severed the sides of the tell to make room for the network of main streets, effectively removing any traces of the city walls. Even so, it is still possible that the inhabitants of Beth-Shean regarded the height of the tell to be sufficient for defense.

6 A. Rowe, *The Topography and History of Beth-Shan*, 1930; A. Rowe, *The Four Canaanite Temples of Beth-Shan, Part I: The Temples and Cult Objects*, 1940; and G.M. FitzGerald, *The Four Canaanite Temples of Beth-Shan. The Pottery*; G.M. FitzGerald, *Beth-Shan Excavations 1921–1923: The Arab and Byzantine Levels;* G.M. FitzGerald, *A Sixth Century Monastery at Beth-Shan*, 1939, began writing a series of final reports, but the onset of World War II brought this to a halt. In 1966, F. W. James, *The Iron Age at Beth Shan: A Study of Levels VI–IV*, published a volume on the Iron Age, and in 1973, E. Oren published the Northern Cemetery (E. Oren, *The Northern Cemetery of Beth Shan*). More recently, F. James and P. McGovern (*The Late Bronze Egyptian Garrison at Beth Shan: A Study of Levels VII and VIII*, 1993) have published Levels VIII–VII, and E. Braun (*Early Beth Shan (Strata XIX–XIII): G.M. FitzGerald's Deep Cut on the Tell*, 2004) on the Early Bronze Age remains from FitzGerald's deep sounding.

7 Y. Yadin and S. Geva, *Investigations at Beth Shean, the Early Iron Age Strata*, Qedem 23, 1986; A. Mazar, Four Thousand Years of History at Tel Beth-Shean: An Account of the Renewed Excavations, *Biblical Archaeologist* 60, 1997, 62–76; A. Mazar, *Excavations at Tel Beth-Shean, 1989–1996, vol. I, From the New Kingdom to the Medieval Period*, 2006; A. Mazar and R. Mullins, *Excavations at Tel Beth-Shean, 1989–1996, vol. II, The Middle and Late Bronze Age Strata in Area R*, Jerusalem, 2007.

8 Level XI produced a mixture of EB III–MB II remains: A. Mazar and N. Panitz-Cohen, *Excavations at Tel Beth-Shean, 1989–1996, vol. III, The 13th and 11th Century BCE in Area N and S*, Jerusalem, 2009. Subsequent study by the Hebrew University has shown that this stratum should be divided into Level XIB (EB III) and Level XIA (MB II). In this paper, any further reference to the earliest period of MB II occupation will be according to the revised designation as Level XIA, equivalent to Hebrew University Stratum R-5.

9 The only MB IIA found at Beth-Shean to date comes from Tomb 92 in the Northern Cemetery, E. Oren, A Middle Bronze I Warrior Tomb at Beth-Shan, *ZDPV* 87, 1971, 109–39; E. Oren, *The Northern Cemetery of Beth Shan*, 1973, 61–67. A few burials on the tell produced early MBIIA/B or early MBIIB material (see the discussion in A. Maeir, *The Material Culture of the Central and Northern Jordan Valley in the Middle Bronze Age II: Pottery and Settlement Pattern*, unpubl. Ph.D. thesis, Jerusalem, 1997, 67; A. Maeir, The Middle Bronze Age II Pottery, in: A. Mazar, and R. Mullins (eds.), *Excavations at Tel Beth-Shean, 1989–1996, vol. II, The Middle and Late Bronze Age Strata in Area R*, Jerusalem, 2007, 296–298, but it remains uncertain whether or not these burials were related to permanent settlement on the mound during MB IIA and most of MB IIB.

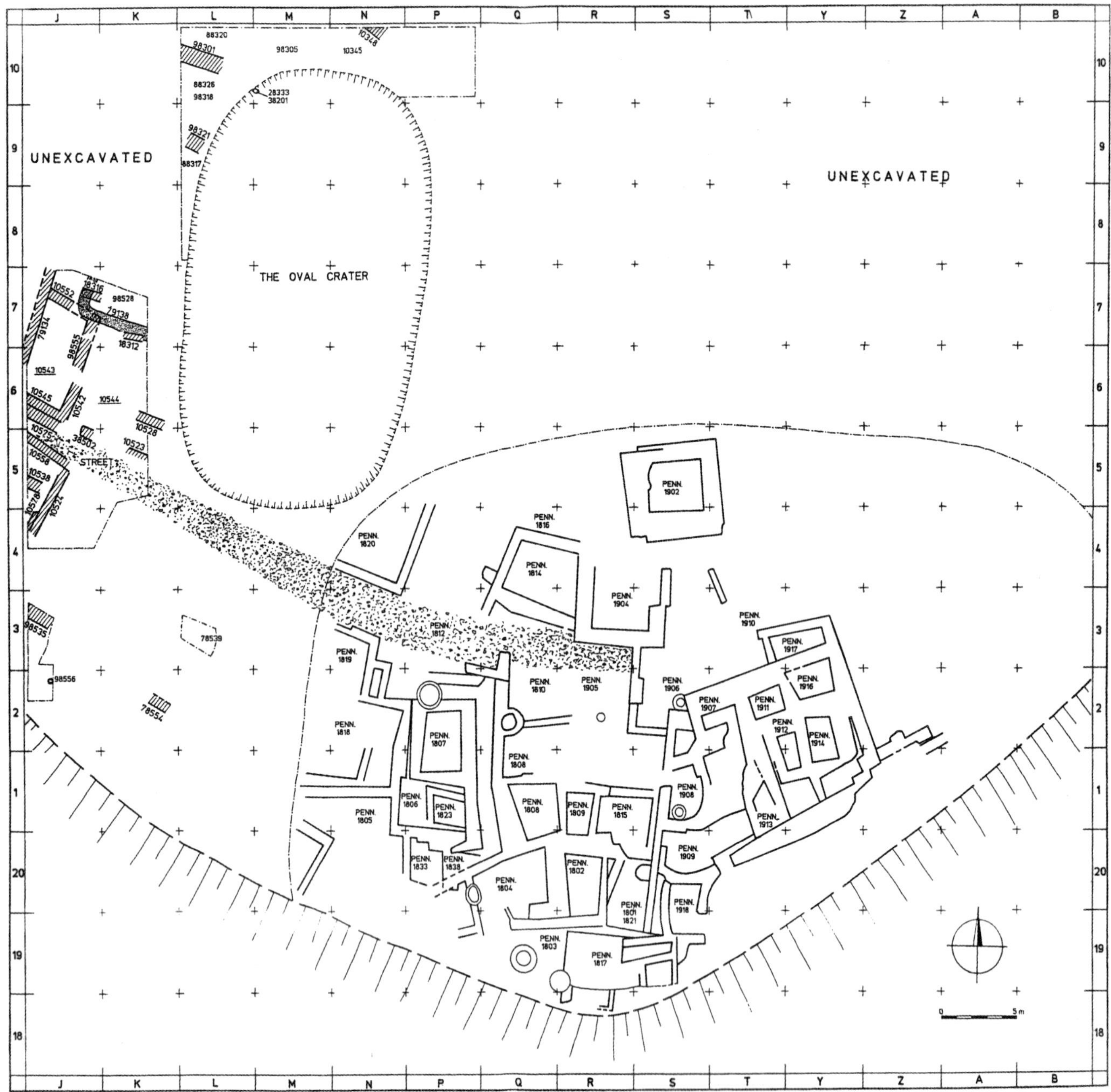

Fig. 3 Plan of Tel Beth-Shean, Hebrew University Stratum R-5 combined with University Museum Level XIA

For the remainder of the period, the Middle Bronze Age town developed in a natural and progressive way until the last settlement of Stratum R-3 (Level XA) ended sometime during the second half of the 16th century BCE.

FitzGerald began his work in 1931 by removing the foundations of Level IX buildings from the Late Bronze Age in order to expose the Level XA settlement below.[10] In the process, he encountered the base of a Tell el-Yahudiya juglet (Fig. 5:4) and a few rooms that appeared to belong to a "higher and later stratum." Unsure as to how he should relate these rooms to features he had already removed in Level IX, or was beginning to encounter in Level XA, FitzGerald tentatively called this phase "Below IX" or "Below Thothmes III". The latter designation was in reference to A. Rowe's

[10] G.M. FitzGerald, Excavations at Beth-Shan in 1931, *PEQFStatement* (July), 1932, 138–148.

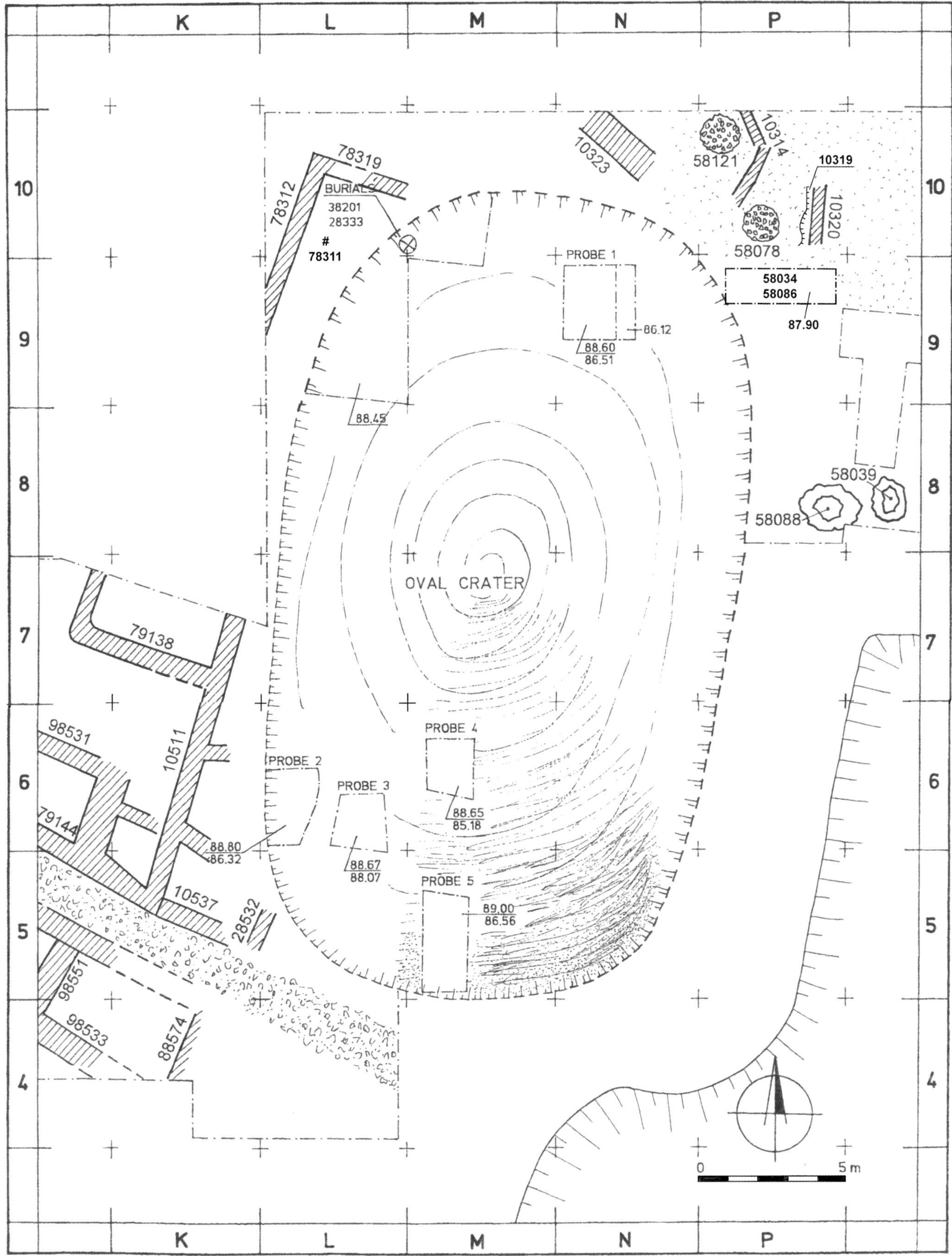

Fig. 4 Plan of Tel Beth-Shean, Hebrew University Stratum R-4

excavations of Level IX, where the Mekal Temple and its precinct were dated to the mid-15th century BCE on the basis of two scarabs of Thutmosis III.[11]

The large difference in date between Level IX (mid-15th century) and Level XA (late 16th century) raised the possibility of a settlement gap of a century or more, even though subsequent study of the pottery indicated that occupation must have continued without interruption.[12]

Renewed work at the site by the Hebrew University in 1989 proved that Level IX of the University Museum (our Stratum R-1) actually existed in two phases (Strata R-1b and R-1a), spanning around a century and a half from Late Bronze Age IB–IIA (ca. 1450–1300 BC).[13] We can now revise the stratigraphy of Level IX to reflect this change: Level IXB (= Stratum R-1b) and Level IXA (= Stratum R-1a).

We also discovered new evidence for the initial stage of the Late Bronze Age (LB IA, ca. 1550/00–1450 BC) in the form of a modest Canaanite temple attributed to Stratum R-2 below the central courtyard of Level IX. This discovery effectively eliminated any possibility of a settlement gap and provided solid evidence for continuity between the Middle and Late Bronze Ages.

In short, the University Museum excavators missed two phases of LB I (Strata R-2 and R1-b). Given the limited extent of Stratum R-2 occupation, Stratum R-1b (Level IXB) is the most likely candidate for FitzGerald's "Below IX" or "Below Thothmes III" level.

Summary of the Middle Bronze Age pottery

The rich and well stratified pottery assemblage from the occupation levels and burials indicates a gradual development during the Middle Bronze Age II.[14] The pottery is typical of north-central Palestine at this time, including a relatively common spectrum of local types.

Stratum R-5 included a few red-slipped juglets. Of special interest in this regard are two infant jar burials (Loci 28333 and 38201) which had been placed into the sides of the Oval Crater early in Stratum R-5 (Fig. 3, Sq. L/10). These vessels become much less common by the time of Strata R-4 and R-3 when Chocolate-on-White Ware and the delicate White Ware (seen primarily in bowl forms) become common. A few examples of the painted "Red, White, and Blue Ware" vessels were also found.[15] Notable is the absence of Cypriot Bichrome Wheelmade Ware at Beth-Shean.[16]

Considering that imported pottery is rare in the Middle Bronze Age, any exceptions are worth noting. Three imports came from Egypt: a drop-shaped pottery bottle found in an early Middle Bronze Age IIB burial, an Egyptian Tell el-Yahudiya black juglet in a transitional early to late Middle Bronze Age IIB context (Fig. 5:2), and a red-slipped closed carinated vessel known during the late Second Intermediate Period and the Early Eighteenth Dynasty in Upper Egypt.

The latter, found in a Stratum R-3 installation along with examples of Chocolate-on-White Ware, provides an important correlation between the end of the Middle Bronze Age in Palestine and the late Second Intermediate Period, as well as perhaps the beginning of the Eighteenth Dynasty in Egypt.

The sole Cypriot import, a White-Painted V feeding bottle, came from inside a storage jar found in the destruction of Stratum R-3 (Level XA) Building 78523.

The Corpus

The Tell el-Yahudiya corpus presented below not only includes finds from the tell excavated by the University Museum and Hebrew University, but also from

---

[11] A. Rowe, *The Topography and History of Beth-Shan*, 1930; A. Rowe, *The Four Canaanite Temples of Beth-Shan, Part I: The Temples and Cult Objects*, 1940.

[12] G.E. Wright, The Four Canaanite Temples of Beth-Shan, Part I, by A. Rowe, *AJA* 45, 1941, 483–485.

[13] Coinciding with the establishment of the Stratum R-1b/Level IXB settlement is the earliest stratified Egyptian-style pottery of the Late Bronze Age; in particular, types characteristic of the mid-18th Dynasty and the time of Tuthmosis III (R. Mullins, *Beth Shean during the Eighteenth Dynasty: From Canaanite Settlement to Egyptian Garrison*, unpubl. Ph.D. thesis, Jerusalem, 2002, 44, 291–294; R. Mullins, The Late Bronze Age Pottery, in: A. Mazar, and R. Mullins (eds.), *Excavations at Tel Beth-Shean, 1989–1996, vol. II, The Middle and Late Bronze Age Strata in Area R*, Jerusalem, 2007, 440–450.

[14] A. Maeir, *The Material Culture of the Central and Northern Jordan Valley in the Middle Bronze Age II: Pottery and Settlement Pattern*, unpubl. Ph.D. thesis, Jerusalem, 1997, 67; A. Maeir, The Middle Bronze Age II Pottery, in: A. Mazar and R. Mullins (eds.), *Excavations at Tel Beth-Shean, 1989–1996, vol. II, The Middle and Late Bronze Age Strata in Area R*, Jerusalem, 2007.

[15] A. Maeir, Red, White and Blue Ware: A Little-Known Group of Painted Pottery of the Middle Bronze II Period, in: E. Oren, and S. Ahituv (eds.), *Aharon Kempinski Memorial Volume. Studies in Archaeology and Related Disciplines*, Beersheva 15, 2002, 228–240.

[16] Two body sherds from the Late Bronze Age levels may belong to the local Palestinian variety of Bichrome Wheelmade Ware (R. Mullins, *Beth Shean during the Eighteenth Dynasty: From Canaanite Settlement to Egyptian Garrison*, unpubl. Ph.D. thesis, Jerusalem, 2002, 44, 291–294; R. Mullins, The Late Bronze Age Pottery, in: A. Mazar and R. Mullins, *Excavations at Tel Beth-Shean, 1989–1996, vol. II, The Middle and Late Bronze Age Strata in Area R*, Jerusalem, 2007, pls. 69:11; 79:9.

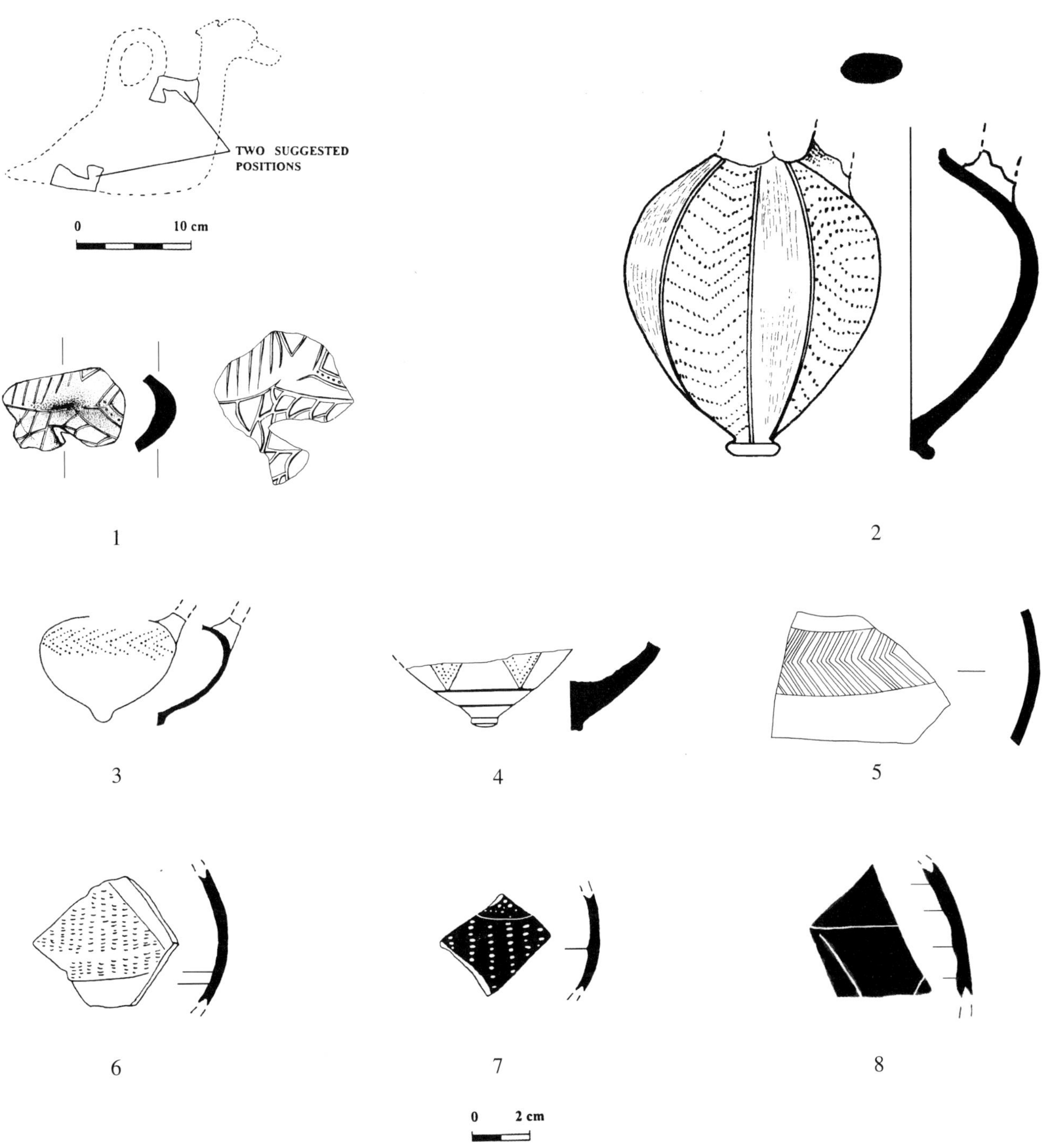

Fig.	Reg. No.	Locus	Square	Stratum	Definition
5:1	783065	78311	L/10	R-4a	Pink plaster floor
5:2	103165	10319	P/10	R-4b	Foundation trench?
5:3	31-11-587	1918	S/19-20	XIA	Room
5:4	31-11-90	"Below Thothmes III"	–	Level IXB?	Unclear context
5:5	284069	28426	C-20	G-3	Makeup of pebble floor 28425
5:6	580105/6	58034	P/9	R-4–R-3	Pink plaster surface
5:7	580275/16	58034	P/9	R-4–R-3	Pink plaster surface
5:8	580329/21	58086	P/9	R-5–R-4	Sloping layers of the Oval Crater

Fig. 5 Tell el-Yahudiya Ware from Tel Beth-Shean

Middle Bronze Age II sites in the Central Jordan Valley that were surveyed as part of the Beth-Shean regional project (Fig. 1).[17]

Only a few examples of Tell el-Yahudiya Ware were found at Beth-Shean.[18] Two fragmentary juglets were found by the University Museum (Fig. 5:3–4) and six vessels and/or sherds by the Hebrew University (Fig. 5:1–2, 5–8).

The limited appearance of Tell el- Yahudiya Ware in Middle Bronze Age II levels at Beth-Shean is probably due to chronological factors more than functional ones. As shown in a number of previous studies, Tell el-Yahudiya Ware became progressively rarer towards the end of Middle Bronze Age IIB. While later examples are known, the *floruit* of this ware is from the late Middle Bronze Age IIA until the middle phase of Middle Bronze Age IIB.[19] Since, as earlier mentioned, the majority of Middle Bronze Age IIB remains at Beth-Shean belong to the terminal phase of the period, one can only expect a limited amount of Tell el-Yahudiya Ware.

The pieces found by the Hebrew University were all made from similarly well-levigated, well-fired clays. Fig. 5:7 was made from very pale brown clay, while the rest had gray-colored fabrics. The decorative zone was usually delineated (Fig. 5:2, 4–8); one was non-delineated (Fig. 5:3). All had some of the original chalk in the punctures or in the incised lines. Burnishing was done by hand and usually limited to the non-decorated zones. Fig. 5:2, 5 had distinctive dark gray or black slips that were highly burnished to a polish in the non-decorated parts. Fig. 5:6–8 were either burnished on the plain clay exterior or on a largely effaced dark gray slip. The thin, even walls of these sherds, as well as the distinctive wheel marks on the interiors, indicate that the original vessels had been expertly wheel-thrown.

Bird-shaped (ornithomorphic) vessel (Fig. 5:1)

Hebrew University excavations. Reg. No. 783065, Locus 78311, Stratum R-4a.[20]

Two small fragments decorated in Tell el-Yahudiya Ware style belong to a unique type of vessel. The pieces were found on the floor of a building at the northwestern corner of the Oval Crater (Fig. 4, Sq. L/10). Only a few burnish lines were detected. The sherds were gray in those places where there was no burnishing and dark gray where burnished. The decoration consisted of incised lines and "scale-like" incisions filled-in with chalk. While the inside of the vessel had wheel marks, the fragment is clearly non-symmetrical. It therefore appears that this piece belonged to a zoomorphic, bird-shaped vessel of the Tell el-Yahudiya Ware class.

The only parallels found to date are somewhat similar bird-shaped vessels from Egypt, usually interpreted as ducks (cf. above page 288, type L.15.1). Examples come from Qurneh and Thebes,[21] as well as from Lisht.[22] Recently, a falcon-shaped vessel was reported in a Middle Bronze Age IIB context at Ashkelon.[23]

While these vessels are not identical to the example from Beth-Shean, they are quite reminiscent.[24] Moreover, only this type of vessel has the peculiar scale-like decoration that was apparently intended to represent feathers.

---

17 A. Maeir, *The Material Culture of the Central and Northern Jordan Valley in the Middle Bronze Age II: Pottery and Settlement Pattern*, unpubl. Ph.D. thesis, Jerusalem, 1997, A. Maeir, *"In the Midst of the Jordan": The Jordan Valley during the Middle Bronze Age (ca. 2000–1500 BCE) - Archaeological and Historical Correlates*, Vienna, 2010.

18 A brief discussion of the Tell el-Yahudiya Ware from Beth-Shean can also be found in A. Maeir, The Middle Bronze Age II Pottery, in: A. Mazar and R. Mullins (eds.), *Excavations at Tel Beth-Shean, 1989–1996, vol. II, The Middle and Late Bronze Age Strata in Area R*, Jerusalem, 2007: 289–291.

19 *E.g.* M. Kaplan, *The Origin and Distribution of Tell el Yahudiya Ware*, 1980; Id., Tell el-Jahudiyeh-Keramik, *LÄ VI*, 335–348; M. Bietak, Archäologischer befund und historische interpretation am beispiel der Tell el-Yahudiya-ware, in: S. Schoske (ed.), *Akten des vierten Internationalen Ägyptologen-Kongresses, München 1985, Band 2.* SAK, Beihefte Band 2, Hamburg, 1989, 7–34.

20 A. Maeir, *The Material Culture of the Central and Northern Jordan Valley in the Middle Bronze Age II: Pottery and Settlement Pattern*, unpubl. Ph.D. thesis, 1997, pl. 33:2; A. Maeir, The Middle Bronze Age II Pottery, in: A. Mazar and R. Mullins (eds.), *Excavations at Tel Beth-Shean, 1989–1996, vol. II, The Middle and Late Bronze Age Strata in Area R*, Jerusalem, 2007, pl. 30:19.

21 M. Kaplan, *The Origin and Distribution of Tell el Yahudiya Ware*, 1980, 321–322, figs. 122:a, 123:c and references there, above page 288.

22 R. Merrillees, *Trade and Transcendence in the Bronze Age Levant*, 1974: 58–59, fig. 43; P.E. McGovern, J. Bourriau, G. Harbottle and S.J. Allen, The Archaeological Origin and Significance of the Dolphin Vase as Determined by Neutron Activation Analysis, *BASOR* 296, 1994, 40–41, fig. 5c, above page 288.

23 L. Stager, The MB IIA Ceramic Sequence at Tel Ashkelon and Its Implications for the "Port Power" Model of Trade, in: M. Bietak (ed.), *The Middle Bronze Age in the Levant: Proceedings of an International Conference on MB IIA Ceramic Material, Vienna, 24th–26th of January 2001*, Vienna, 2002, 357, fig. 16, above page 567 cat. no. 30.

24 The suggested reconstruction in Fig. 5:1 is based on M. Kaplan, *The Origin and Distribution of Tell el Yahudiya Ware*, 1980, 321, fig. 123:c.

Most of the bird-shaped vessels come from Egyptian contexts. This might indicate another Egyptian import to late Middle Bronze Age IIB Beth-Shean, though Stager believes that the bird-shaped vessel from Ashkelon, and perchance the vessel from Beth-Shean, are local Palestinian products.[25]

Finally, other ornithomorphic vessels from Middle Bronze Age IIB contexts appear in the southern Levant. The one from Megiddo belongs to a very different class of pottery (not Tell el-Yahudiya) due to its shape and decoration.[26] Ornithomorphic vessels not belonging to the Tell el-Yahudiya Ware group have also been reported from the terminal Middle Bronze Age IIB phase at Jericho.[27]

Juglet (Fig. 5:2)

Hebrew University excavations. Reg. No. 103165, Locus 10319, Stratum R-4b (Maeir 1997a: pl. 34:10; 2007: pl. 10:19).[27a]

This vessel has a distinct shape and decoration. It was discovered in Stratum R-4b, but in an unclear context that may have been a foundation trench for a structural wall dating to the same phase (Fig. 4, Sq. P/10).

This rather rotund piriform vessel has rounded, though somewhat pronounced shoulders, the remains of the join of a single strap handle on its shoulder, and a well-defined ring base. The body is covered by a dark gray slip. The decoration consists of eight alternating, punctured and non-punctured, vertical segmented zones. Only the plain zones were highly burnished, except in places where the burnish strokes lapsed over the vertical demarcation line. Some of the holes still contained chalk.

It's conspicuous shape and decoration puts it within a distinct group of Tell el-Yahudiya Ware: Kaplan's *Piriform 2a* type[28] or following Bietak's 1989 finetuning, *Piriform 2a mit vier Segmentmusterzonen* type; in this book Late Egyptian group L.1.3b.

On the basis of Kaplan's and Bietak's typological and archaeometric analyses, this type of juglet is of Egyptian origin. In such a case, the Beth-Shean vessel may represent an additional Egyptian import to Beth-Shean. Bietak has already noted that while originating in Egypt, this type of vessel was part of the trade between Egypt and the southern Levant during the late Middle Bronze Age IIB.[29]

The late Middle Bronze Age IIB date of the Beth-Shean juglet reinforces the typological/chronological sequence first suggested by Kaplan and elaborated upon by Bietak *pace* Ward and Dever.[30] Moreover, the Egyptian origin of this vessel was corroborated by Instrumental Neutron Activation Analysis (hereafter, INAA, Fig. 6).[31]

Small, globular juglet (Fig. 5:3)

University Museum excavations. Reg. No. 31-11-587; Locus 1918; Level XIA.[32]

---

[25] L. Stager, The MB IIA Ceramic Sequence at Tel Ashkelon and Its Implications for the "Port Power" Model of Trade, in: M. Bietak (ed.), *The Middle Bronze Age in the Levant: Proceedings of an International Conference on MB IIA Ceramic Material, Vienna, 24th–26th of January 2001*, Vienna, 2002, 357. The Beth-Shean vessel has not been subjected to Neutron Activation Analysis or Petrography; however, P.E. McGovern, J. Bourriau, G. Harbottle and S.J. Allen, The Archaeological Origin and Significance of the Dolphin Vase as Determined by Neutron Activation Analysis, *BASOR* 296, 1994, 40–41, fig. 5c, demonstrated an Egyptian provenience for one of the bird-shaped vessels from Lisht, even though it lacked the scale-like decoration.

[26] G. Loud, *Megiddo II: Seasons of 1935–39*, 1948, pl. 247:1.

[27] K. Kenyon, *Excavations at Jericho, vol. II: The Tombs Excavated in 1955–58*, 1965, 401–402, fig. 162; K. Kenyon, *Excavations at Jericho, vol. III: The Architecture and Stratigraphy of the Tell*, 1981, fig. 13:15.

[27a] A. Maeir, *The Material Culture of the Central and Northern Jordan Valley in the Middle Bronze Age II: Pottery and Settlement Pattern*, unpubl. Ph.D. thesis, Jerusalem, 1997, pl. 34:10; A. Maeir, The Middle Bronze Age Pottery, in: A. Mazar and R. Mullins (eds.), *Excavations at Tel Beth-Shean, 1989-1996, vol. II, The Middle and Late Bronze Age Strata in Area R*, Jerusalem, 2007, pl. 10:19.

[28] M. Kaplan, *The Origin and Distribution of Tell el Yahudiya Ware*, 1980: 21–22, figs. 46–61.

[29] M. Bietak, Archäologischer befund und historische interpretation am beispiel der Tell el-Yahudiya-Ware, in: S. Schoske (ed.), *Akten des vierten Internationalen Ägyptologen-Kongresses, München 1985, Band 2*, 1989, 16.

[30] M. Kaplan, *The Origin and Distribution of Tell el Yahudiya Ware*, 1980, and elaborated upon by M. Bietak, Archäologischer befund und historische interpretation am beispiel der Tell el-Yahudiya-ware, in: S. Schoske (ed.), *Akten des vierten Internationalen Ägyptologen-Kongresses, München 1985, Band 2*, 1989, 20, Abb. 2; *pace* W.A. Ward and W.G. Dever, *Studies on Scarab Seals III: Scarab Typology and Archaeological Context: An Essay on Middle Bronze Age Chronology*, 1994, 82–86.

[31] A. Maeir, *The Material Culture of the Central and Northern Jordan Valley in the Middle Bronze Age II: Pottery and Settlement Pattern*, unpubl. Ph.D. thesis, Jerusalem, 1997, 171; A. Maeir and J. Yellin, Instrumental Neutron Activation Analysis of Selected Pottery from Tel Beth-Shean and the Central Jordan Valley, in: A. Mazar, and R. Mullins (eds.), *Excavations at Tel Beth-Shean, 1989–1996, vol. II, The Middle and Late Bronze Age Strata in Area R*, Jerusalem, 2007, 554–571.

This vessel, in this book type group D.7, is an unusual specimen previously discussed by Kaplan and classified as a local type.[33] Though she believes it belonged to a rare "miniature" type, which is followed in this volume cf. above page 128, the non-delineated chevron decoration clearly relates it to Kaplan's *Piriform 3* type, typical of the late Middle Bronze Age IIB in the Levant.[34] As indicated by the INAA analyses, most of the Tell el-Yahudiya Ware from Beth-Shean appears to be of local Levantine provenience, displaying a chemical signature similar to the material from Afula.[35]

The origin of this juglet in Room 1918 of Level XIA (Stratum R-5) relates it to the earliest phase of stratified Middle Bronze Age occupation on the mound (Fig. 3, Sq. S/19–20). Given the presence of some red slipped and burnished juglets in a Stratum R-5 infant burial (see above, p. 582), it may be possible to relate this vessel to the stratum in which it was found; otherwise, the juglet may have been an heirloom.

Juglet base (Fig. 5:4)

University Museum excavations. Reg. No. 31-11-90, "Below Thothmes III level."[36]

This appears to be an earlier type of Tell el-Yahudiya Ware. The inverted triangles and incised horizontal decoration, as well as the distinct button base, places it in Kaplan's *ovoid type* or Bietak's *frühe palästinensische Gruppe*;[37] in this book groups A–B. These classificatory groups are typical of the *early* stages of the Tell el-Yahudiya Ware, and as conclusively demonstrated typologically and archaeometrically, were produced in the southern Levant.

Probably the best parallels to this fragment come from the relatively well-dated Tell el-Yahudiya Ware juglets found in the potter's pit at Afula and dating to the late Middle Bronze Age IIA/early Middle Bronze Age IIB.[38] If so, this may indicate Middle Bronze Age IIA–B activity at Beth-Shean prior to the establishment of the stratified Middle Bronze Age II levels (Strata R-5, R-4, R-3). A number of burials from the earlier University Museum expedition and the more recent Hebrew University project contained some earlier Middle Bronze Age II pottery (see above, n. 8). Since these burials were not always stratigraphically related to the late Middle Bronze Age II occupation, it is possible that some come from earlier activity on the tell. If so, then this juglet may originate from this timeframe. Alternatively, it may have been an heirloom brought by one of the earliest Middle Bronze Age IIB settlers during the 17th century BC.

The archaeological context is not helpful with regard to this juglet because the sherd came from the "Below Thothmes III" phase. As pointed out earlier, this is most probably an LB I phase that dates to the 15th century BC. At best the sherd might be attributed to Level XA, but even this would place it at the end of the Middle Bronze Age sequence.

The Beth-Shean fragment is probably related to other examples found in the Central Jordan Valley, Beth Yerah,[39] and Munhata – all very similar to the Afula juglets.[40] These examples might be products of the Afula workshop, indicating a pattern of trade between the Jezreel Valley and the central and northern Central Jordan Valley.

---

[32] A. Maeir, *The Material Culture of the Central and Northern Jordan Valley in the Middle Bronze Age II: Pottery and Settlement Pattern*, unpubl. Ph.D. thesis, Jerusalem, 1997, plan IV, pl. 34.6.

[33] M. Kaplan, *The Origin and Distribution of Tell el Yahudiya Ware*, 1980, 28–29, fig. 117c.

[34] M. Kaplan, *The Origin and Distribution of Tell el Yahudiya Ware*, 1980, 63, 72.

[35] A. Maeir, *The Material Culture of the Central and Northern Jordan Valley in the Middle Bronze Age II: Pottery and Settlement Pattern*, unpubl. Ph.D. thesis Jerusalem, 1997, 171–72; A. Maeir and J. Yellin, Instrumental Neutron Activation Analysis of Selected Pottery from Tel Beth-Shean and the Central Jordan Valley, in: A. Mazar and R. Mullins (eds.), *Excavations at Tel Beth-Shean, 1989–1996, vol. II, The Middle and Late Bronze Age Strata in Area R.* 2007, 562.

[36] A. Maeir, *The Material Culture of the Central and Northern Jordan Valley in the Middle Bronze Age II: Pottery and Settlement Pattern*, unpubl. Ph.D. thesis, Jerusalem, 1997, pl. 34.7.

[37] See, though, Ward's and Dever's reservations on these typological/chronological frameworks.- W.A. Ward and W.G. Dever, *Studies on Scarab Seals III: Scarab Typology and Archaeological Context: An Essay on Middle Bronze Age Chronology*, 1994, 82–86.

[38] U. Zevulun, Tell el-Yahudiya Juglets from a Potter's Refuse Pit at Afula, *EI* 21, 1990, 174–190.

[39] One such vessel was published previously (R. Amiran, *Ancient Pottery of the Holy Land*, 1969, pl. 30; M. Kaplan, *The Origin and Distribution of Tell el Yahudiya Ware*, 1980, fig. 110:b), but see U. Zevulun, Tell el-Yahudiya Juglets from a Potter's Refuse Pit at Afula, *EI* 21, 1990, 189, n. 36, who observes that the vessel was wrongly attributed by both of the above researchers to Afula). The other is an unpubl. vessel, very similar to the first, which is in the storerooms of the Israel Antiquities Authority (IAA).

[40] U. Zevulun, Tell el-Yahudiya Juglets from a Potter's Refuse Pit at Afula, *EI* 21, 1990, 184, n. 36, 39.

Body fragment of a large juglet or small jug with a delineated, incised herringbone pattern (Fig. 5:5)

Hebrew University excavations. Reg. No. 284069, Locus 28426, Stratum G-3.[41]

This sherd was found in Area G in the makeup of a pebbled floor at the northeastern corner of a poorly preserved room formed by two mudbrick walls (Fig. 2). The pottery from Stratum G–3 dates to the latter part of the Middle Bronze Age II (see above, n. 4).

The fragment is of interest for several reasons. First of all, it appears to be part of a larger size juglet or a small to medium size jug, somewhat larger than the other Tell el-Yahudiya fragments from Beth-Shean. The incised herring bone decoration is made by a continuous incision, which is unusual as well, since similar decorations that we are aware of were made according to the pointillé method.

Although exact parallels could not be found, one can note a jug with a pointillé herring bone decoration from Jericho Tomb 19.[42] Kenyon placed this tomb in "Group III," indicating a mid-to-late Middle Bronze Age IIB date.[43] This would fit in well with the finds from Beth-Shean.

Body fragments of juglets (Fig. 5:6–8)

Hebrew University excavations. Reg. No. 580105/6 [Fig. 5:6] and 580275/16 [Fig. 5:7] from Locus 58034, Strata R-4–R-3[43a] (1997a, pl. 34:8, 9); Reg. No. 580329/21 [Fig. 5:8] from Locus 58086, Strata R-5–R-4.

Loci 58034 and 58086 are superimposed layers of earth identified in a narrow trench dug in the northeastern corner of the Oval Crater (Fig. 4, Sq. P/9). Both layers sloped towards the Oval Crater. Locus 58034 consisted of at least three pink plaster surfaces attributed to Strata R-4–R-3. Layer 58086 below it clearly related to the Oval Crater and was attributed to Strata R-5–R-4, the earlier Middle Bronze Age II phases at Beth-Shean.

Due to their small size it is hard to determine their exact type and dating. If the vessels were slipped, it has largely disappeared on the surviving fragments. Fig. 5:6 has a few burnish strokes that survived on the plain zone in the upper right with some lapse into the punctured zone. Fig. 5:7, 8 were apparently burnished over the entire body, though only a few strokes are actually visible.

The triangular decorations on Fig. 5:6, 8 are quite common in various Tell el-Yahudiya vessels; however, the completely black decoration inside and outside the triangle of Fig. 5:8, as well as the lack of thc pointillé decoration inside the triangle, is quite atypical.

Juglet with basket handle (not illustrated)

Central Jordan Valley Survey

An out of the ordinary Tell el-Yahudiya Ware juglet with a basket handle (a *situla*) was found by N. Zori at Tel Zahara (Fig. 1). Though unpublished, and its whereabouts presently unknown, its preliminary description and the drawing in the IAA archives substantiate that it is indeed an unusual shape. The only vessel that is even vaguely related to it is a handleless Tell el-Yahudiya Ware juglet/bottle from Ugarit.[44]

The appearance of basket handled jugs can be dated from late Middle Bronze Age IIA to early Middle Bronze Age IIB.[45] This may indicate that the vessel from Tel Zahara was contemporary with the Tell el-Yahudiya Ware production centre at Afula mentioned previously.

Finally, it is worthwhile noting that several Tell el-Yahudiya Ware sherds have been reported from later Middle Bronze Age IIB contexts at Pella as well.[46]

---

41 A. Maeir, The Middle Bronze Age II Pottery, in: A. Mazar and R. Mullins (eds.), *Excavations at Tel Beth-Shean, 1989–1996, vol. II, The Middle and Late Bronze Age Strata in Area R*, Jerusalem, 2007: pl. 37:14.

42 K. Kenyon, *Excavations at Jericho, vol. II: The Tombs Excavated in 1955–58*, 1965, 375, fig. 186:4; M. Kaplan, *The Origin and Distribution of Tell el Yahudiya Ware*, fig. 83:a.

43 K. Kenyon, *Excavations at Jericho, Vol. II: The Tombs Excavated in 1955–58*, 1965, 377.

43a A. Maeir, *The Material Culture of the Central and Northern Jordan Valley in the Middle Bronze Age II: Pottery and Settlement Pattern*, unpubl. Ph.D. thesis, Jerusalem, 1997, pl. 34:8, 9).

44 C.F.A. Schaeffer, *Ugaritica I: Études relatives aux découvertes de Ras Shamra*, 1939, 63, fig. 53:g; R. Amiran, *Ancient Pottery of the Holy Land*, 1969, fig. 36:27; M. Kaplan, *The Origin and Distribution of Tell el Yahudiya Ware*, 1980, 27–28, 317, fig. 115b.

45 See A. Maeir, T.1181, Area L, Hazor: A Multiple Interment Burial Cave of the MBIIa/b Period, in: A. Ben Tor, and R. Bonfil (eds.), *Hazor V: An Account of the Fifth Season of Excavation, 1968*, 1997, 301 for the discussion of this type with regards to Tomb 1181 at Hazor.

46 R.H. Smith, *Pella of the Decapolis, vol. I: The 1967 Season of the College of Wooster Expedition to Pella*, 1973, 202, pl. 40:707; A.G. Walmsley, P.G. Macumber, P.C. Edwards, S.J. Bourke, and P.M. Watson, The Eleventh and Twelfth Seasons of Excavations at Pella (Tabaqat Fahl) 1989–1990, *ADAJ*, 37, 1993, 180, fig. 14; S. Bourke, R. Sparks and M. Schroder, Pella in the Middle Bronze Age, in: P. Fischer (ed.) *The Chronology of the Jordan Valley during the Middle and Late Bronze Ages: Pella, Tell Abu al-Kharaz and Tell Deir Alla*, 2006, 49, figs. 41–42.

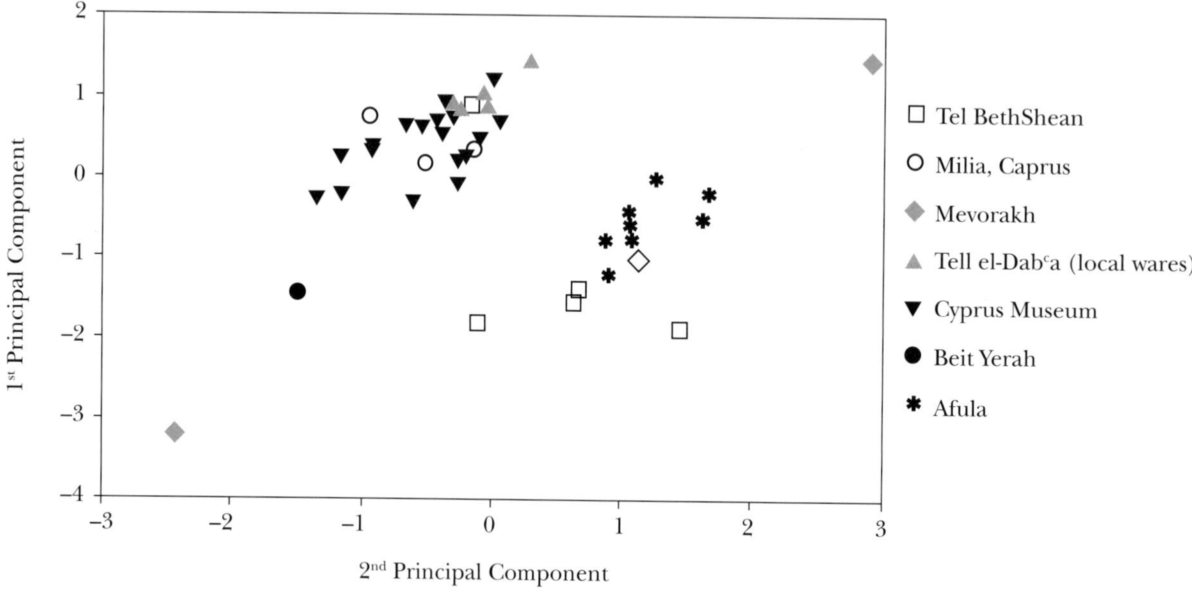

Fig. 6 Principal Component Analysis graph of the Instrumental Neutron Activation Analysis (INAA) of the Tell el-Yahudiyeh Ware from Beth-Shean and its vicinity, compared to examples of Tell el-Yahudiyeh Ware from various sites in the Ancient Near East

Provenience

As part of a larger provenience project on the Middle Bronze Age II ceramics from the Jordan Valley,[47] some Tell el-Yahudiya vessels/sherds from Tel Beth-Shean and the Central Jordan Valley were examined by INAA. Although a detailed discussion has been presented elsewhere,[48] a brief summary of the relevant points are warranted in the context of the present study.

As previously noted, from a typological standpoint, most Tell el-Yahudiya examples from Beth-Shean appear to be local (Palestinian) types. The only exceptions are the fragmentary zoomorphic vessel (Fig. 5:1) and the piriform juglet (Fig. 5:2). In both cases, we believe them to be of Egyptian origin.[49]

Five of the Tell el-Yahudiya vessels/sherds from Beth-Shean were chosen to be analyzed by INAA. Four were "local" types; the fifth (Fig. 5:2) was an Egyptian-type juglet. In addition, a Tell el-Yahudiya juglet from Beth Yerah was sampled.

The INAA results, Fig. 6, were quite distinct. The vessels that appeared to be typologically local plotted very closely to the compositions of the Tell el-Yahudiya production center at Afula. The Egyptian-style Tell el-Yahudiya juglet from Beth-Shean fell nicely within a grouping of Egyptian Tell el-Yahudiya vessels from Cyprus, local Egyptian wares from Tell ed-Dab^ca,[50] and various Egyptian samples analyzed in Berkeley.[51] Sig-

---

47 A. Maeir, *The Material Culture of the Central and Northern Jordan Valley in the Middle Bronze Age II: Pottery and Settlement Pattern*, unpubl. Ph.D. thesis, Jerusalem 1997, 152–180; A. Maeir and J. Yellin, Instrumental Neutron Activation Analysis of Selected Pottery from Tel Beth-Shean and the Central Jordan Valley, in: A. Mazar and R. Mullins (eds.), *Excavations at Tel Beth-Shean, 1989–1996, vol. II, The Middle and Late Bronze Age Strata in Area R*, Jerusalem, 2007, 554–571.

48 A. Maeir and J. Yellin, Instrumental Neutron Activation Analysis of Selected Pottery from Tel Beth-Shean and the Central Jordan Valley, in: A. Mazar and R. Mullins (eds.), *Excavations at Tel Beth-Shean, 1989–1996, vol. II, The Middle and Late Bronze Age Strata in Area R*, Jerusalem, 2007, 554–571.

49 A. Maeir and J. Yellin, Instrumental Neutron Activation Analysis of Selected Pottery from Tel Beth-Shean and the Central Jordan Valley, in: A Mazar and R. Mullins (eds.), *Excavations at Tel Beth-Shean, 1989–1996, vol. II, The Middle and Late Bronze Age Strata in Area R*, Jerusalem, 2007: 562.

50 M. Artzy and F. Asaro, Origin of Tell el-Yahudiya Ware Found in Cyprus, *Report of the Department of Antiquities of Cyprus*, 1979, 135–150; A.B. Knapp and J.F. Cherry, *Provenience Studies and Bronze Age Cyprus: Production, Exchange and Politico-Economic Exchange*, 1994.

51 I. Perlman and F. Asaro, Pottery Analysis by Neutron Activation. *Archaeometry*, 11, 1969, 21–52; J. Yellin, T. Dothan and B. Gould, The Origin of Late Bronze White Burnished Slip Wares from Deir el-Balah, *IEJ* 40, 1990, 257–261.

nificantly, these results do not support the claim of McGovern that Egyptian Tell el-Yahudiya vessels were not imported to the Levant.[52]

The single sample from Beth Yerah did not group with any of the other compositions. This sample, in addition to two outliers from Tell Mevorakh obtained from previous analyses,[53] demonstrates quite clearly that Tell el-Yahudiya Ware was produced at more than one location in the southern Levant during Middle Bronze Age II.[54]

Summary

Typologically, save for one vessel, all are distinctly local types. This is corroborated by INAA, which demonstrated that four of the vessels were local and quite similar to the chemical profile of the Middle Bronze Age II at Afula. The juglet, typologically identified as being of Egyptian origin, was shown to have an Egyptian chemical profile, thus corroborating the typological definition.

Even though we are dealing with a rather limited corpus of Tell el-Yahudiya vessels we can nevertheless draw some important conclusions. First, the pottery sheds important light on aspects of trade and contact during Middle Bronze Age II. Second, there were several production centers for Tell el-Yahudiya Ware in the Middle Bronze Age II Levant. Third, Tell el-Yahudiya Ware of Egyptian origin reached the Levant during the Middle Bronze Age IIB, not only at sites along the southern coastal plain (such as Ashkelon), but at inland sites as well.

If one also considers the Egyptian "carinated vessel" found in a late Middle Bronze Age II context at Beth-Shean,[55] we have additional evidence for intense trade relations between various parts of Egypt and the extensive regions in the Levant until the very end of the Middle Bronze Age II, even continuing into the early New Kingdom.[56]

---

52 P.E. McGovern, *The Foreign Relations of the "Hyksos": A Neutron Activation Study of Middle Bronze Age Pottery from the Eastern Mediterranean*, 2000, 73; see also L. Stager, The MB IIA Ceramic Sequence at Tel Ashkelon and Its Implications for the "Port Power" Model of Trade, in: M. Bietak (ed.), *The Middle Bronze Age in the Levant: Proceedings of an International Conference on MB IIA Ceramic Material, Vienna, 24th–26th of January 2001*, 2002, 357; L. Stager, J. Schloen, D. Master, M. Press and A. Aja, Part Four: Stratigraphic Overview, in: L. Stager, J. Schloen and D. Master (eds.), *Ashkelon I: Introduction and Overview (1985–2006)*, 2008, 227, figs. 14.22–23 for Egyptian (and local) Tell el-Yahudiya Ware at Middle Bronze Age IIB Ashkelon.

53 J. Yellin, Provenance of Selected LBA and MBA Pottery from Tel Mevorakh by Instrumental Neutron Activation Analysis, 87–103 in: *Excavations at Tel Mevorakh (1973–1976). Part Two: The Bronze Age*, 1984; A.B. Knapp and J.F. Cherry, *Provenience Studies and Bronze Age Cyprus: Production, Exchange and Politico-Economic Exchange*, 1994.

54 E.g. L. Stager, The MB IIA Ceramic Sequence at Tel Ashkelon and Its Implications for the "Port Power" Model of Trade, in: M. Bietak (ed.), *The Middle Bronze Age in the Levant: Proceedings of an International Conference on MB IIA Ceramic Material, Vienna, 24th–26th of January 2001*, 2002, 357; L. Stager, J. Schloen, D. Master, M. Press and A. Aja, Part Four: Stratigraphic Overview, in: L. Stager, J. Schloen and D. Master (eds.), *Ashkelon I: Introduction and Overview (1985–2006)*, 2008, 227.

55 A. Maeir, *The Material Culture of the Central and Northern Jordan Valley in the Middle Bronze Age II: Pottery and Settlement Pattern*, unpubl. Ph.D. thesis, Jerusalem, 1997, pl. 41:13; A. Maeir, The Middle Bronze Age II Pottery, in: A. Mazar and R. Mullins (eds.), *Excavations at Tel Beth-Shean, 1989–1996, vol. II, The Middle and Late Bronze Age Strata in Area R*, Jerusalem, 2007, pl. 27:13.

56 The exact dating of the Egyptian carinated vessel is of some importance (A. Maeir, The Middle Bronze Age II Pottery, in: A. Mazar and R. Mullins (eds.), *Excavations at Tel Beth-Shean, 1989–1996, vol. II, The Middle and Late Bronze Age Strata in Area R*, Jerusalem, 2007, 279–82). If it is to be dated to the early New Kingdom, this would indicate that the late MB II Stratum R-3 existed, at least in part, during the New Kingdom Period. This would be excellent evidence for an overlap, at least in parts of Canaan, between the late MB II and the early New Kingdom (R. Mullins, *Beth Shean during the Eighteenth Dynasty: From Canaanite Settlement to Egyptian Garrison*, unpubl. Ph.D. thesis, Jerusalem, 2002, 32).

The Tell el-Yahudiya Ware from Tell Arqa

Hanan Charaf and Mary Ownby

The site of Tell Arqa in northern Lebanon has yielded 23 objects of the Tell el-Yahudiya Ware.[1] This amount is quite modest compared to other imported wares such as the Cypriot White Painted V–VI found on this site.[2] Out of the 23 Tell el-Yahudiya items found, only four come from secure contexts (Table 1). The rest were found in open *loci* from the Middle and Late Bronze Ages.[3] In order to fully appreciate the importance and variety of this ware found at Arqa, it is necessary to discuss not only the stylistical significance of the Tell el-Yahudiya objects, but also the results of the petrographical analysis used to determine their possible provenances.

The corpus of the Yahudiya Ware from Arqa

Hanan Charaf

The corpus of the Tell el-Yahudiya Ware found at Arqa comprises 23 objects found during the various seasons of excavations on the tell.[4] Two belong to Level 14, eleven to Level 13, five to Level 12, one to Level 11. The remaining four sherds come from unstratified *loci*. The majority of the Tell el-Yahudiya Ware belongs to Level 13, corresponding to the time-frame when the Yahudiya Ware witnessed a *floruit* in production and trade.[5]

This assemblage is exclusively comprised of closed shapes (jugs and juglets) of different sizes. Many types are present with a predominance of the piriform shapes. No cylindrical vessel such as those belonging to the Late Palestinian VI group was found amongst the Yahudiya items.

All of the Arqa vessels were made on a fast wheel as witnessed by the fine wheel marks on the interior and the uniformity of the thin walls. Unfortunately, except for part of jug 08/420.001 (Fig. 3:2), no necks or rims were preserved, and only three bases were identified (Fig. 2:4–6). The rest of the corpus is formed by body sherds with nine belonging to upper parts of pots and ten to lower parts (Figs. 1–3).

At least ten items belong to large jugs over 10 cm in height. This type of jug is usually considered to be earlier in date, at least at Tell el-Dabᶜa.[6] At Arqa, however, both small and large sizes co-existed at the end of Level 14/beginning of Level 13. The base 93/814.007 (Fig. 2:4) belongs to a small juglet, while jug 93/894.005 (Fig. 1:6) is part of a larger vessel.

The Tell el-Yahudiya pieces found at Tell Arqa are made in varied but well-fired fabrics ranging from dark brown to greenish beige colours. Figs. 1:3–6, 9, 11, 12 and 3:1, 2 are made in grey clay, Figs. 1:8; 2:1, 3–5 in dark red clay, Figs. 1: 1,7; 2:2 and Fig. 2:9 in brown clay, Fig. 1:2, 10 in dark orange clay, and Fig. 2:7, 8 in bright orange clay. The last piece was made from a light beige greenish sandy fabric (Fig. 2:6). Some of these fabrics are tempered with white and dark grits (mostly basalt) indicating a local (Tell Arqa) or regional (Akkar Plain) provenance, while

---

[1] We would like to thank J.P. Thalmann for kindly allowing me to study and publish the Tell el-Yahudiya Ware from Arqa. Hanan Charaf would like also to thank K. Kopetzky for fruitful discussions on this ware and to M. Bietak for his continuous encouragements and trust. Study of the Arqa corpus was funded by a SCIEM grant. Drawings were done as always by R. Antonios.

[2] H. Charaf-Mullins, Les céramiques importées de l'Ouest, in: J.P. Thalmann, *Tell Arqa – I. Les niveaux de l'âge de Bronze*, Beyrouth, 2006, 173–192.

[3] For a discussion of the stratigraphy of these periods see J.P. Thalmann, *Tell Arqa – I. Les niveaux de l'âge de Bronze*. BAH 177, Institut Français du Proche-Orient, Beyrouth, 2006:33–83).

[4] A list of 22 Tell el-Yahudiya objects was published in an article in 2009 (H. Charaf, Arqa and its regional connections Redux, *BAAL* Hors-Série VI, 2009, 295–310). A new piece (fig. 3:2) was found during the 2009 season of excavations, bringing the total number of Yahudiya pieces at Arqa to 23.

[5] M. Bietak, The Centre of Hyksos rule: Avaris (Tell el-Dabᶜa), in: E. Oren (ed.), *The Hyksos: new historical and archaeological perspectives*, University of Pennsylvania, Philadelphia, 1997, 87–139.

[6] K. Kopetzky, The MB IIB corpus of the Hyksos Period at Tell el-Dabᶜa, in: M. Bietak and E. Czerny (eds.), *The Bronze Age in Lebanon. Studies on the Archaeology and Chronology of Lebanon, Syria and Egypt*, Wien, 2008, 197. She cautions, though, that this might be a local phenomenon particular to Tell el-Dabᶜa.

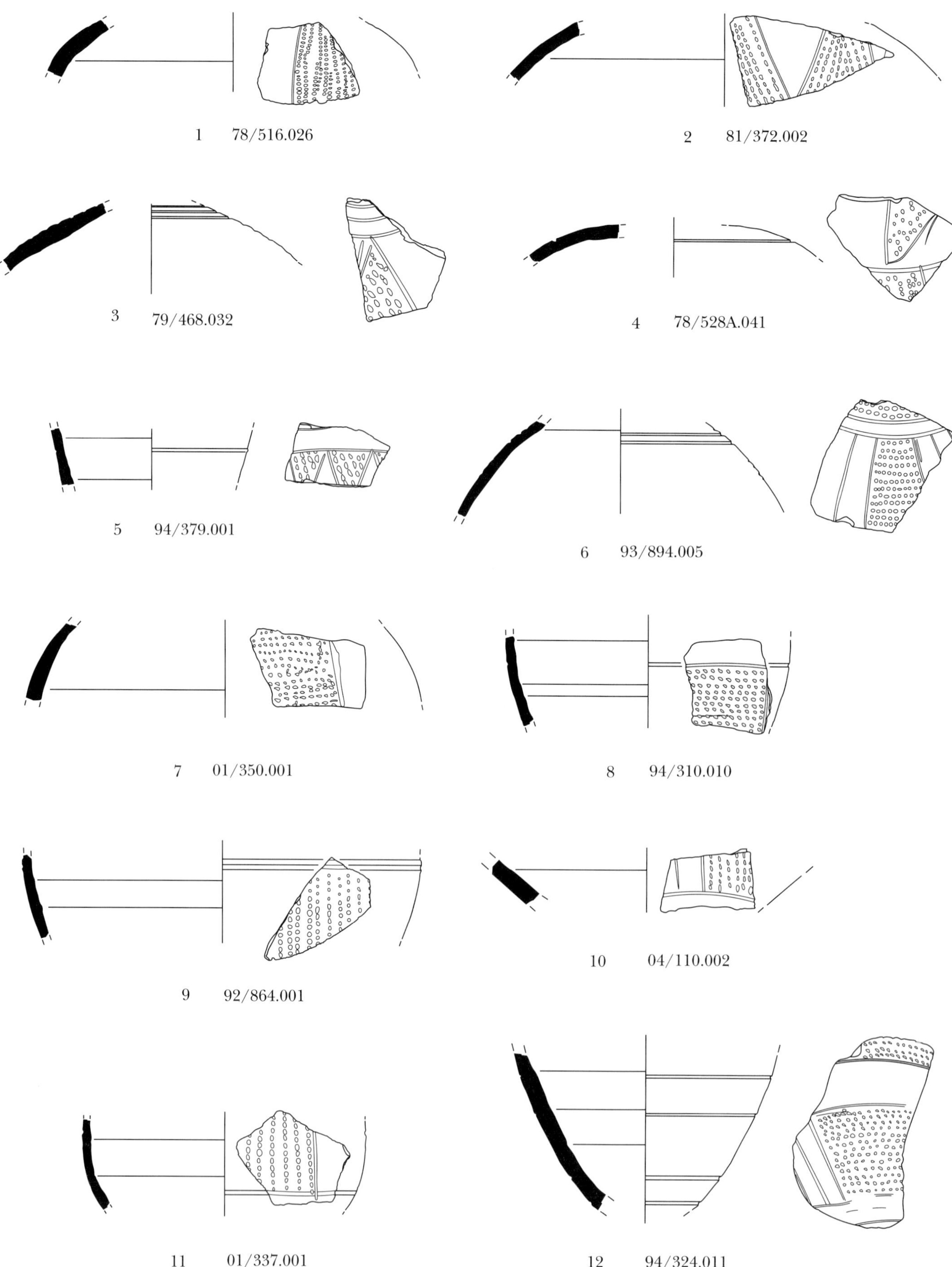

Fig. 1 Tell el-Yahudiya Ware from Tell Arqa (1:2)

others have substantial amounts of sand in them and some iron oxides attesting to other Lebanese origins. A preliminary petrographic analysis on these objects was conducted by Mary Ownby who identified at least five petrographical groups. For the full results of her research see below.

The majority of the vessels display surface colors of either charcoal black (11 items, Figs. 1:2, 3, 5, 6, 8, 10, 12; 2:2–4, 6) or dark brown (8 items, Figs. 1:1, 7, 9, 11, 2:1, 5, 9; 3:1). A small percentage has dark grey (2 items, Figs. 1:4 and 3:2) or orange (2 items, Fig. 2:7, 8) surfaces. One of these vessels (Fig. 1:4) is made at Arqa as demonstrated by Ownby. Yahudiya Ware made in the Northern Levant is not exceptional; in Syria, the site of Mishrifeh-Qatna has yielded a large pot decorated with straight and wavy lines, but in a crude style found in *niveau IV/ensemble b* dated by the excavators to the end of the MB I–MB II.[7] This Qatna vase, however, is not normative in its decoration just like some of the Tell Arqa sherds (Fig. 2:7, 8).

All of the Arqa Tell el-Yahudiya objects are hand burnished. Where it was possible to observe it as some surfaces were worn off, the burnishing covered the plain and the incrusted zones. This pattern is similar to the one covering piriform jugs of Kaplan Type 1 (also known as el-Lisht Ware jugs)[8] and earlier examples from Tell el-Dabᶜa.[9] Some Arqa vessels (Figs. 1:5, 8, 10; 2:2–5) are carefully burnished to a polish, while others (Fig. 2:7, 8) are covered with vertical stroke burnishing, a characteristic typical of both local and general northern Levantine MB pottery. Burnishing was executed either directly on the clay surface (Fig. 3:2) or on a thin layer of slip (Fig. 2:6).

All decorated panels were delineated with grooves and filled with tiny punctures encrusted with white chalk. Most of the time, the chalk has disappeared leaving hollow holes and lines. Generally, the incised lines were also incrusted, although on the jug 01/350.002 (Fig. 3:1), lines are shallow and appear to have been left without any incrustation. The incrusted motif was always executed with lines or groups of dots oriented in the same direction. No chevron or herringbone motif such as that found on later jugs from Egypt, Palestine, and Cyprus was found.

Geometric designs are the most prominent type in the Arqa repertoire. Only two pieces (Fig. 2:8, 9) display floral motifs (lotus flowers) clearly inspired from Egypt. In Lebanon, only five other sites in addition to Arqa have yielded naturalistic decorations: vessels with bird depictions at Ardé in the north,[10] Tell el-Burak[11] and Sidon[12] in the south, and Tell el-Ghassil in the Bekaa Valley,[13] as well as an ichtyomorphic vessel and a jug with lotus flowers at Byblos.[14]

Since the majority of the Yahudiya vessels at Arqa are fragmentary, it was considered more meaningful to discuss those vessels according to their decoration instead of their shape.

---

7 M. Al-Maqdissi/M. Badawi, III. Rapport préliminaire sur la sixième campagne des fouilles syriennes à Mishrifeh/Qatna, in: M. Al-Maqdissi, M. Luciani, D. Morandi Bonacossi, M. Novák and P. Pfälzner (eds.), *Excavating Qatna*, Documents d'Archéologie Syrienne IV, Damascus, 2002, 25–62, fig. 56.

8 M. Kaplan, *The origin and distribution of Tell el-Yahudiya Ware*, 1980, 19.

9 K. Kopetzky, The MB IIB corpus of the Hyksos Period at Tell el-Dabᶜa, 2008: 197. This stands in contrast to the material from the Hyksos period, which is only burnished on the plain zones. Jugs with incised but not incrusted patterns from Stratum E/1 onwards are also entirely burnished (p. 198).

10 H. Salame-Sarkis, Chronique archéologique du Liban-Nord. II: 1973–1974, *Bulletin du Musée de Beyrouth* XXVI, 1973, 91–102, fig. 1 and pl. X: figs. 1, 2. A series of ducks (?) are etched on the shoulder of this jug.

11 J. Kamlah, H. Sader, The Tell el-Burak archaeological project. Preliminary report on the 2002 and 2003 seasons", *BAAL* 7, 2003, 161. Mention of this vase first appeared in this article. It was also studied by D. Kamel, *The Middle Bronze Age Tomb of Tell el-Burak- Lebanon, unpublished* MA thesis, American University of Beirut, 2005, pl. IV, and K. Badreshany, *The Middle Bronze Age pottery of Tell el-Burak*, unpublished MA thesis, American University of Beirut. 2005, figs. 8, 19. This vessel is dark brown in color and of an unusual shape: a tall open tankard with a smooth body carination and a ring base. The decoration consists of five birds with a festoon frieze on the base of the neck and a crosshatched frieze on the lower body. This type of open vessel belongs to the Branch O of the proposed typology here. The accompanying funeral material consists of piriform juglets (some are red slipped and burnished) and bone inlays. Naturalistic Tell el-Yahudiya vessels are almost all made in Egypt and date to late 13th Dynasty/Second Intermediate Period. In light of the other objects found in the Burak tomb this range of dates fits perfectly.

12 Claude Doumet-Serhal, personal communication.

13 L. Badre, Tell el-Ghassil: Tomb 1, in: *Archéologie au Levant. Recueil à la mémoire de R. Saïdah*, Lyon, 1982, 123–132, fig. 7.

14 Respectively, P. Montet, *Byblos et l'Egypte. Quatre campagnes de fouilles 1921–1924.* Paris, 1928, pl. CXLV:910 and M. Dunand, *Fouilles de Byblos, Tome II, 1933–1938.* Atlas, Paris, 1950, pl. CCXI:13199 (photo); M. Dunand, *Fouilles de Byblos, Tome II, 1933–1938,* Texte, Paris, 1958, fig. 675 (drawing), *Levée* XIV.

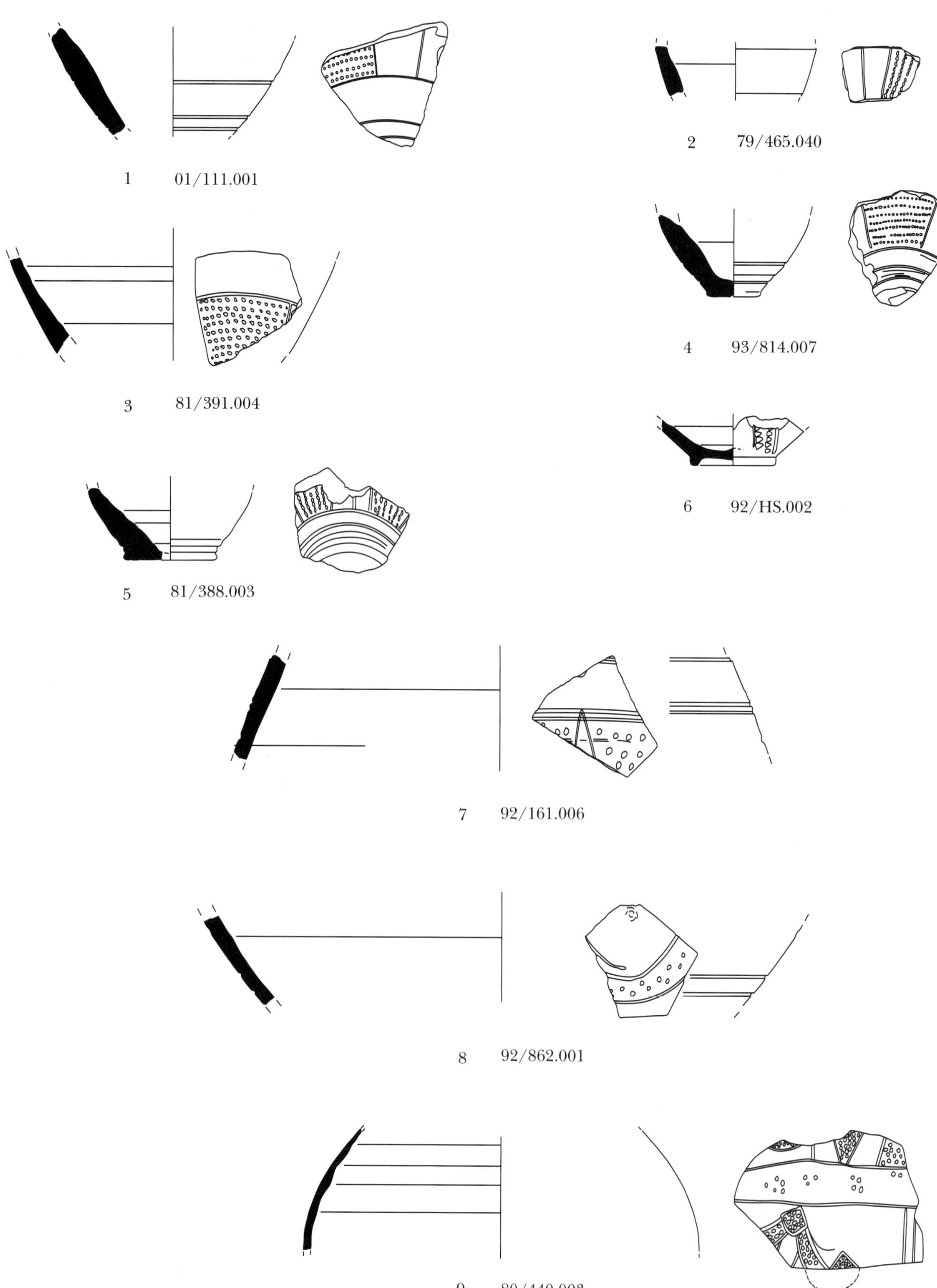

Fig. 2 Tell el-Yahudiya Ware from Tell Arqa (1:2)

Jugs with floral motifs (Fig. 2:8, 9)

A body fragment of a jug made of finely levigated brown marl clay tempered with limestone and quartz was found in an unstratified locus (Fig. 2:9). Its provenance is most probably Tell Arqa or its vicinity. This jug has a round slanting shoulder and very thin walls. The decoration is mostly worn off but still shows two rows of inverted lotus flowers separated by a large band filled with incrusted dots. The lotus flower on the upper row is flanked by a geometric shape (either a triangle or rhomboid) filled with incised dots, while the lower row lotus flower is framed by two vertical incised lines. The size of this vessel prevents us from ascribing it to a precise typology within the Branch J group. Lotus flowers which are an Egyptian motif *par excellence* were also found on a jug from the *Tombeaux de particuliers* at Byblos.[15] These three tombs yielded EB IV ceramics such as one-handled cups, but the bulk of their material dates to the end of the MB I/beginning of the MB II. Another jug found in *Levées* XI to XV at Byblos displays a stemmed lotus flower framed by two vertical bands of reserved lozenges.[16] The lotus flower motif is also attested on local ceramics at Tell Arqa. A cylindrical closed pot from Tomb 13.68 of Level 13 found together with a Cypriot jug of the *White Painted IV-VI Cross Line Style* displays a row of lotus flowers.[17] This *pyxis* is made in local fine reddish clay tempered with basalt and the surface is burnished vertically. Its unique shape *sans* motif has parallels at Ugarit,[18] and at Tell el-Dabᶜa.[19]

The lower part of a large vessel found in an early locus of Level 13 shows a wavy band rendering perhaps a lotus flower (Fig. 2:8) and is not dissimilar in this regard to a jug found at Jericho decorated on its shoulder with a delineated wavy band filled with spaced dots.[20] The Arqa jug is made in bright orange clay rich in iron oxides, indicating a possible origin in Byblos or in its vicinity. The vessel is covered in stroke vertical burnishing just like similar objects from the local MB assemblage.

Jugs with geometric motifs (Figs. 1:1–12; 2:1–7; 3:1,2)

More than 95% of the Tell el-Yahudiya pottery found at Tell Arqa display geometric decoration ranging from triangles to rhomboids to rectangles. All these motifs are common within the known Yahudiya repertoire.

Jugs with triangle motifs (Figs. 1:1–5; 2:7; 3:2)

The seven jugs that display triangle motifs come from different *loci* spanning levels 14 to 12. This style of motif comprised of standing or pendant triangles is regarded as of northern Levantine origin (see above Part Two, page 142).

Inverted triangles

Fig. 2:7 is the upper portion of a large vessel (jug?) covered with two pending inverted triangles filled with dots and framed on the top by three incised lines. The decoration is typical of the Tell el-Yahudiya Ware, even though the punctured dots are spaced unlike the normal Yahudiya Ware where the dots are closer to each other. A similar style of puncturing is present on a possible Tell el-Yahudiya vessel from an MB II tomb at Mtouneh in Syria.[21] This Arqa vessel is made in bright orange clay identical to that of Fig. 2:8 and is fired hard. It is also covered with the same stroke vertical burnishing. Judging by the fabric and the decorative style, these two pieces were probably manufactured by the same potter or workshop. But while Fig. 2:7 was found in an open locus attributed to the transition between Level 13 and 12, Fig. 2:8 comes from a context of the early phase of Level 13. The manufacture (minus the puncturing) of these two pots are strikingly similar to a jug published by Nigro under the category of "Orange Burnished Ware"[22] which originated, according to him, in the Ebla-Qatna region. Indeed, their peculiar technique of burnishing (although not limited to inner Syria) and the firing fit the description of the "Orange Burnished Ware" which Nigro dates to MB IIA (1850–1700 B.C.). If the Arqa vessels originated

[15] P. Montet, *Byblos et l'Egypte. Quatre campagnes de fouilles 1921–1924*, 1928, pl. CXLVIII: 918.

[16] M. Dunand, *Fouilles de Byblos, Tome II, 1933–1938*, Texte, 1958, fig. 675.

[17] J.P. Thalmann, *Tell Arqa – I. Les niveaux de l'âge de Bronze*, 2006, pl. 102:17,18)

[18] C.F.A. Schaeffer, Corpus céramique de Ras-Shamra, in: C.F.A. Schaeffer, *Ugaritica II*, Paris, 1949, fig. 106:15.

[19] P. Fuscaldo, *Tell el-Dabᶜa X. The Palace District of Avaris: The pottery of the Hyksos Period and the New Kingdom (Areas H/III and H/IV)*, Wien, 2000, fig. 41.

[20] M. Kaplan, *The origin and distribution of Tell el-Yahudiya Ware*, 1980, fig. 132:f.

[21] M. al-Maqdissi, *Le Bronze Moyen du Levant septentrional. Etude céramologique*, unpublished PhD dissertation, University of Paris I-Sorbonne, Paris, 1994, pl. 30:222.

[22] L. Nigro, The Smith and the King of Ebla, in: M. Bietak (ed.), *The Synchronisation of Civilisations in the Eastern Mediterranean in the Second Millennium B.C. II*, Wien, 2003, 345–363, fig. 24.

indeed in Byblos, they were produced at a time of increased relations between Ebla and Byblos as demonstrated by Nigro in 2003.

Two other jugs (Figs. 1:5; 3:2) display horizontal framed inverted small triangles filled with incrusted punctures neatly disposed in a row. Both of these vessels are made in grey wares that originate in coastal Lebanon, probably in or around the area of Tripoli. The preserved decoration of jug 08/420.001 (Fig. 3:2) found in one of the earliest pits of Level 14 is formed by two rows of small triangles disposed in an inverted position on the shoulder and on the lower body framing panels of rectangles (?) framed themselves by rows (?) of two incised vertical lines. This decoration is quite close (except for the triangles that are standing at Byblos) to one jug found in the *Tombeaux de particuliers* at Byblos and to a jug found in 2010 in Tomb 736 at Tell Fadous (H. Genz, personal communication).[23] Neutron Activation Analysis shows that this latter jug was made with Egyptian Nile clay[24] while the Arqa one originated in Lebanon. The Arqa and Byblos jugs are different in shape: the Byblos jug is piriform and has a double strand handle attached to the rim, while the Arqa jug is of the squat ovoid shape with a double loop arched handle positioned on the shoulder. This is a shape similar to other local vessels from Arqa found in the same level[25] and to the "Orange Burnished Ware" jug mentioned above. However, this type of ovoid rounded jug with narrow neck and double loop handle on the shoulder is not very common at Arqa until level 13. The decoration on the Arqa jug can be related to the Levanto-Egyptian-Type Group 12.1 according to the typology presented in this volume (above page 144, Fig. 87) but the shape is similar to jugs of the Early Levantine VII-Groups H1.1–H1.2 (Figs. 34–35), and is classified in this volume as type group I1.1

The jug on Fig. 1:5 has the inverted triangle decoration on its lower part; its surface is black and burnished to a luster. The preserved vessel shows triangles framed by an incised line. Maybe the entire jug would have had another row of standing triangles touching the tips of the inverted one just like on jugs from tombs at Sin el-Fil[26] and Ugarit,[27] or separated by a horizontal band just like on a juglet found in a fill dated to the MB I from Yoqne'am.[28] A fragment with a hanging triangle was found at Tell el-Ghassil in the Bekaa Valley.[29] It is made in black clay and burnished on the outer surface.[30] It was found in Level X dated to the MB IIB or to 1775/1750–1650/1640 BC according to Doumet-Serhal's absolute chronology. Unfortunately, the section and orientation of the sherd was not published, so one has to assume that the drawing reflects the true disposition of the triangle, i.e. inverted and not standing.

Fig. 1:4 belongs to the shoulder of a jug (?), defined in this volume as type group I1.2 found in an early locus of Level 13 and made in a local grey fabric with a dark grey surface. The stance of the shoulder which is almost horizontal instead of slanting could belong to a jug similar to that of Fig. 3:2 or to a highly-carinated piriform jug. A hanging triangle decorates this shoulder, but it is executed in a sloppy way. The register below the triangle shows part of a geometrical shape that could be either a rectangle or a rhomboid. Hanging inverted triangles arranged in two registers are a type of decoration found for example on an ovoid jug at Dhibin in Southern Syria.[31]

Standing triangles

Three jugs display standing triangles on their shoulder. Jug 79/468.032 (Fig. 1:3) has a standing triangle surmounted by three parallel horizontal incised lines, while 81/372.002 (Fig. 1:2) shows two large adjoining standing triangles part of a motif running around the

[23] P. Montet, *Byblos et l'Egypte. Quatre campagnes de fouilles 1921–1924*, 1928, pl. CXLVIII:915.

[24] M. Kaplan, *The origin and distribution of Tell el-Yahudiya Ware*, 1980, 229.

[25] J.P. Thalmann, *Tell Arqa – I. Les niveaux de l'âge de Bronze*, 2006, pl. 85:17.

[26] M. Chehab, Tombe phénicienne de Sin el-Fil, in: *Mélanges offerts à M. R. Dussaud*, vol. II, Paris, 1939, 806, fig. 5:b..

[27] R. Amiran, *Ancient Pottery of the Holy Land*, 1969, pl. 36:26.

[28] A. Livneh, The Pottery of the Middle Bronze Age, in: A. Ben-Tor, D. Ben-Ami and A. Livneh (eds.), *Yoqn'eam III. The Middle and Late Bronze Ages*, Jerusalem, 2005, fig. II.34:13, Stratum XXIV.

[29] C. Doumet-Serhal, *Les fouilles de Tell el-Ghassil de 1972 à 1974, Etude du matériel*, Beyrouth, 1996, pl. 58:1.

[30] C. Doumet-Serhal, *Les fouilles de Tell el-Ghassil de 1972 à 1974*, 1996, 166.

[31] F. Braemer and M. al-Maqdissi, La céramique du Bronze moyen dans la Syrie du Sud, in: M. Al-Maqdissi, V. Matoïan and C. Nicolle (eds.), *Céramique de l'âge du Bronze en Syrie I. La Syrie du Sud et la vallée de l'Oronte*, Beyrouth, 2002, pl. XX-B:116. This jug which was published first in Al-Maqdissi, 1994, pl. 24:191 has a double stranded handle and a red-grayish burnished surface. This tomb contained another Tell el-Yahudiya jug and typical vessels of the MB II.

shoulder. Unfortunately, the neck is missing but it is not impossible that the base also bore three incised lines. Such decoration (incised lines on the base of the neck and standing triangles on the upper body) is very common on Levanto-Egyptian II jugs from the Piriform 1b, I.2.2 group (jugs with three decorative areas on the body) and Levanto-Egyptian III of the Piriform 1c, I.3.1 group (jugs with two decorative zones). It is found on the jug mentioned above from the *Tombeaux de particuliers* at Byblos,[32] on three jugs from the Sin el-Fil tomb,[33] and one jug from a tomb at Tell el-Dabᶜa dated to the beginning of the Hyksos period.[34] A fragment found inside the monumental entrance of the MB complex at Beirut[35] together with EB IV and MB II mixed ceramics bears also a quite similar decoration. Two of three Tell el-Yahudiya sherds found at Tell Hizzin in the Bekaa Valley display triangle motifs.[36] Unfortunately, their stratigraphic location is unknown.

A shoulder made at Arqa decorated with part of a triangle filled with vertical dotted lines (78/516.026, Fig. 1:1) could belong to a piriform jug covered either with a series of incised standing triangles similar to Fig. 1:2 and to jugs of the I2 or I3 types, or with segmented zones formed by alternating non-punctured and dotted lozenges each stretching from the shoulder to the base such on Levanto-Egyptian IV, Group I4 jugs. A perfect example of the latter type was found at Byblos in the *Tombeaux de particuliers*.[37]

Jugs with rectangle or square motifs (Fig. 1:7–11)

Rectangles or squares are another motif used profusely on Tell el-Yahudiya vessels. Usually they cover the mid-body or the part of the body below the carination, and are arranged in rows with alternating non-punctured rectangles. The entire body could have either been covered with similar rows, or with rows of pendant or standing triangles or rhomboids. The artists used these basic geometric shapes to create a varied spectrum of decorations. Unfortunately, we don't have enough of a part of a vase at Arqa to display the different styles. However, at least four sherds from our assemblage have fragments of what could have been rectangles.

Vases 94/310.010, 92/864.001, 04/110.002 and 01/337.001 (Fig. 1:8–11) are most probably piriform jugs with rectangles incised on their lower body. These rectangles are framed on all sides by two grooves. Two of these jugs (Fig. 1:9,11) originate in Northern Palestine or in an area of Lebanon close to the border, while the other two (Fig. 1:8,10) are made from southern Lebanese clays. Jugs with incised and filled rectangles covering most of the body were found in Lebanon in tombs at Tell Fadous in the north[38] and Kafer ed-Djarra in the south.[39] They belong to the Early Levantine V- Type Group F3 typology.

Jugs with rhomboid and rectangular motifs
(Figs. 1:6, 12; 2:1–5)

A very popular combination of motif on jugs found in the Levant consists of rectangles on the maximum diameter and the lower body flanked on the base and the shoulder by rhomboids. This decoration is present on jug 94/324.011 (Fig. 1:12) and has an identical parallel at Byblos.[40] The other jugs figured on Fig. 2:1, 2, 4 and 5 have all either rhomboids or long rectangles on the lower body near the base, similar to Levanto–Egyptian jugs of the Piriform 1c type. This type of jugs whose decoration is formed of only two registers filled with rectangles is believed to have originated in the area around Byblos. However, petrographic analysis done on these five jugs indicates that they are all made in similar clays originating from coastal Lebanon possibly in the southern region.

---

32 P. Montet, *Byblos et l'Egypte. Quatre campagnes de fouilles 1921–1924*, 1928, pl. CXLVIII:915.

33 M. Chehab, Tombe phénicienne de Sin el-Fil, in: *Mélanges offerts à M. R. Dussaud*, Vol. II, 1939, 806, fig. 5:a–c.

34 M. Bietak, *Tell el-Dabᶜa V, Ein Friedhofsbezirk der Mittleren Bronzezeitkultur mit Totentempel und Siedlungsschichten*, Wien, 1991, fig. 80:3, Tomb m/12.

35 L. Badre, Bey 003 Preliminary report. Excavations of the American University of Beirut Museum 1993–1996, *BAAL* 2, 1997, fig. 12:13. The drawing orientation is presumably wrong and should be rotated 90° clockwise.

36 H. Genz, H. Sader, personal communication. I would like to thank H. Genz and H. Sader for sending me pictures of the Yahudiya sherds and for allowing me to quote them here.

37 P. Montet, *Byblos et l'Egypte*, 1928, pl. CXLVI: 914.

38 H. Genz, H. Sader, Excavations at Tell Fadous-Kfarabida: Preliminary Report on the 2008 Season of Excavations, *BAAL* 12, in press. I would like to express my thanks to H. Genz for sharing with me the photo of the jug and for allowing me to quote it here. A thorough study of the tomb in which this jug was found appears in H. Genz, S. el-Zaatari, C. Çakirlar, K. Badreshany, and S. Riehl, A Middle Bronze Age Burial from Tell Fadous-Kfarabida, Lebanon, *Ä&L* 20, 2010, 183–206.

39 G. Contenau, Mission archéologique de Sidon (1914), *Syria* 1, 1920, fig. 33:e; Kaplan, *The origin and distribution of Tell el-Yahudiya Ware*, 1980, fig. 30a.

40 M. Dunand, *Fouilles de Byblos, Tome I, 1926–1932*, Planches, Paris, 1937, pl. CLXIII: 3489; 1939, fig. 169: 2854, *Levée* IX.

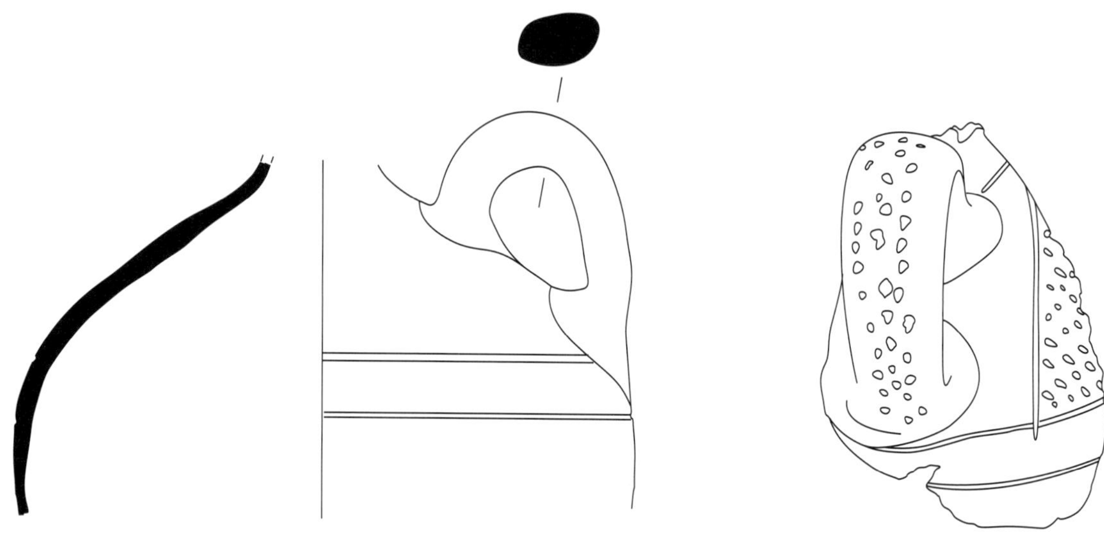

1 01/350.002

2 08/420.001

Fig. 3 Tell el-Yahudiya Ware from Tell Arqa (1:2)

The upper body could have been decorated with multiple variations: standing triangles topped by rhomboids such as at Byblos,[41] or rectangles such as on the jug from Kafer ed-Djarra (see above). The large jug 93/894.005 (Fig. 1:6) found in an open locus from Level 14 has rhomboids on the shoulder alternated with non-punctured panels filled with one or two vertical incised lines. All traces of white chalk have disappeared from the surface. The carefully executed burnishing also covers the punctured areas. The large amount of sand present in the clay matrix indicates a coastal Lebanese origin similar to the other five jugs cited above.

Jugs with miscellaneous motifs (Fig. 2:6)

Even though the majority of the decorations of Tell el-Yahudiya Ware is rendered with grooves and pricked dots, a very small group displays decorations of incised triangular points made with the tip of a thin bar tool (probably similar to the one used for making cuneiform signs). One base incised with such a decoration was found at Arqa on the top soil (92/HS.002, Fig. 2:6). The ring type base is covered with a thick black slip and is carefully vertically burnished. Two parallel vertical lines made with incised triangular points are delineated on each side with two grooves. Kaplan published a sherd found in a survey at Tell es-Saᶜdiyeh in Jordan covered with a similar decoration.[42] The Neogene clay is, as described above, greenish-beige in color and is heavily tempered with *Terra Rossa* suggesting possibly an origin near or at the site of Ardé in the north. It is, so far, the only Yahudiya Ware from Arqa manufactured with this type of clay.

Unidentified motifs (Fig. 3:1)

During the season of excavations in 2001 the fragment of a large jug was discovered in a fill from Level 13 (01/350.002, Fig. 3:1). The clay from which this jug was made is marl with *Terra Rossa* additions. Ownby thinks that this type of clay (Group 3 of her typology) was either available near the river Arqa or at the site of Ardé located some 20 km south-east of Arqa. The loop handle placed on the slanting shoulder imitates MB II jugs and is similar to jug Fig. 3:2. However, the thick handle is a single one punctured with holes filled with white chalk. This particularity hints to a local production or imitation of some Early Levantine I Type Group E.2 jugs, and is here defined as type group I.1.2 in this volume. One can assume that the little preserved decoration on the shoulder shows a triangle or a rhomboid. Faint traces of burnishing indicate that the vessel was burnished.

Distribution of the Tell el-Yahudiya Ware in Lebanon

Most of the 23 Tell el-Yahudiya vessels from Tell Arqa are piriform jugs that belong to Levanto-Egyptian types. While six are of small sizes, the rest belong to rather larger shapes. One of the earliest items found at Arqa (in Level 14 dated to the MBI) is of an Early Levantine type similar to those found in inland Syria. Moreover, two fragments made in orangey clay most probably belong to the "Orange Burnished Ware" present in the Ebla-Qatna region. The decoration adorning the Arqa vessels is normative and belongs to a repertoire well-known from the Northern Levant: pending and standing triangles as well as rectangles and rhomboids. The fragmentary state of the Arqa vessels prevents one from establishing a more elaborate decorative analysis, but it seems that most of the vessels' decorations were divided in at least three registers, putting them into the Levanto-Egyptian II or III typological groups. Levanto-Egyptian groups are the most attested in Lebanon, especially Group Type I2, where three zones on the jug are decorated with standing and pending triangles (Arqa, Byblos, Sin el-Fil, and perhaps also Beirut, Tell el-Ghassil, and Tell Hizzin in the Bekaa). Another piriform jug (Type I2.1b) belonging to the Levanto-Egyptian II group, but with an unusual décor of spirals, appears at Sin el-Fil.[43] Other Levanto-Egyptian groups (Groups III and IV) are represented respectively by piriform 1c jugs with two registers decorated with standing and pending triangles found in tombs from Byblos[44] and Sin el-Fil,[45] and by piriform 1d jugs decorated with vertical incised bands such as at Byblos.[46] Another group, Early Levantine V, similar to the Levanto-Egyptian I group, is attested in the south of Lebanon, in the tomb of Kafer ed-Djarra. The earliest Levanto-Egypt-

[41] M. Dunand, *Fouilles de Byblos, Tome II, 1933–1938,* Texte, 1958, fig. 583, no. 12396, *Levée* XII.

[42] M. Kaplan, *The origin and distribution of Tell el-Yahudiya Ware,* 1980, fig. 132: m.

[43] M. Chehab, Les tombes phéniciennes. Majdalouna, *Bulletin du Musée de Beyrouth* IV, 1940, fig. 6a.

[44] P. Montet, *Byblos et l'Egypte,* 1928, pl. CXLVI: 917.

[45] M. Chehab, Tombe phénicienne de Sin el-Fil, in: *Mélanges offerts à M. R. Dussaud,* vol. II,1939, fig. 5a.

[46] P. Montet, *Byblos et l'Egypte,* 1928, pl. CXLVI: 914.

Object No	Level	Sub-level	Locus description	Type of locus
78/516.026	13	13B	Leveling under Floor 12/II in area 13.04	Open
78/528A.041	13	13E	Area 13.04	Open
79/465.040	Unstratified		Trial sounding done in square AK20 South	Open
79/468.032	Unstratified		Trial sounding done in square AK20 South	Open
80/440.003	Unstratified			Open
81/372.002	12	12A	Leveling over Floor 12/I in area 12.18 South	Open
81/388.003	12	12C	Canalisation 12.16a	Closed
81/391.004	13	13	Areas 13.06 and 13.15	Open
92/HS.002	Unstratified			Open
92/161.006	12/13	12/13	Leveling under Level 13 in square AM21.IV Southwest	Open
92/862.001	13	13 (early)	Leveling to the north of Tomb 12.67 under Room 12.12 in square AL21.III	Open
92/864.001	13	13 (early)	Leveling under Locus 92/862 in square AL21.III	Open
93/814.007	14/13	14/13	Leveling in square AL21 South	Open
93/894.005	14	14 (R)	Leveling in square AL20:b/5. Contaminated by Levels 13 and 12	Open
94/310.010	13	13'	Pit	Closed
94/324.011	13	13' (early)	Pit 13.41	Closed
94/379.001	12	12C/D	Area 12.23 Southeast	Open
01/111.001	13/12	13/12	Beginning of the birkeh in contact with Level 12	Open
01/337.001	13	13	Leveling	Open
01/350.001	13	13	Leveling of ash layer	Open
01/350.002	13	13	Leveling of ash layer	Open
04/110.002	11	11	Leveling over Floor 12/II in Area 11.50	Open
08/420.001	14	14'	Bottom of pit below skeletons	Closed

Table 1 Stratigraphic provenance of the Tell el-Yahudiya Ware from Tell Arqa

ian occurrences appeared around the area of Byblos with Levanto-Egyptian I-piriform 1a type jugs found on the tell and further north at Tell Fadous in a tomb dated by Genz to late MB I.[47] Byblos also yielded the only Lebanese examples of Ovoid and Early Levantine IV jugs and some Early Palestinian V bowls belonging to the "Palestinian Figural Vases" types. It is unknown whether these bowls were made locally or imported from Palestine. Ovoid jugs (of Branch A - the Primeval group) are the most archaic Tell el-Yahudiya examples and are known from the firing kiln at Afula. This seems to strengthen the idea put forth in this manuscript that the earliest Tell el-Yahudiya ware appeared in other regions of the Levant, particularly in the area around Byblos.

While sites in northern Lebanon (Tell Arqa and Tell Fadous) and in the Bekaa valley (Tell Hizzin and Tell el-Ghassil) seem to have stuck mainly to the Levanto-Egyptian repertoire, southern sites such as Majdalouna (and perhaps also Sidon) yielded a Yahudiya vase belonging to the Middle Palestinian III-Type Group C3.[48] This peculiar type, characterized by a decoration made of bands and small concentric circles, was also found further north in a tomb from Sin el-Fil[49] near Beirut which also contained jugs of the Levanto-Egyptian II and III types (see above). Late Palestinian VI cylindrical jugs, very popular in Palestine during the MB IIC/III period, are so far completely absent from southern as well as northern Lebanese sites.

Vessels with naturalistic designs belonging to Branch J groups were found in tombs at Tell el-Ghassil in the Bekaa, as well as on the coast at Arqa, Ardé, Byblos, and Sidon. Unusual open vessels belonging to

[47] H. Genz, S. el-Zaatari, C. Çakirlar, K. Badreshany, and S. Riehl, A Middle Bronze Age Burial from Tell Fadous-Kfarabida, Lebanon, *Ä&L* 20, 2010, 183–206.

[48] M. Chehab, Les tombes phéniciennes. Majdalouna, *Bulletin du Musée de Beyrouth* IV, 1940, fig. 3a.

[49] M. Chehab, Tombe phénicienne de Sin el-Fil, in: *Mélanges offerts à M. R. Dussaud*, vol. II, 1939, fig. 6b.

Branch P are extremely rare; only two examples were found in a tomb dated to the MB II at Tell el-Burak.

Conclusions

The Tell el-Yahudiya vases from Tell Arqa shed precious light onto the inter-regional connections that this site enjoyed during the MB period. The majority of the pots (10 out of 23 items) belong to clays (Group 5) from coastal Lebanon rich in quartz. Only further analysis will indicate if they belong to southern sites just like Group 6 (2 items). Nine vessels were manufactured in Northern Lebanon: only three (Group 4) may have really originated in Arqa itself, while two (Group 3) were either made at Arqa or further south at Ardé. One item, an outlier, was made at Ardé itself attesting to this important site mentioned in the Amarna texts and believed to be the birthplace of Abdi-Aširta, ruler of the Hapiru.[50] Three items (Group 2) were made in the area around Tripoli. Two sherds made in an orangey fabric could have been produced at Byblos. These results prove that while architectural remains and ceramic productions indicate relative autarkic subsistence at Arqa, the site still enjoyed the benefits of a trade network passing through the Homs gap. Ceramic vessels from the Akkar Plain reached places as far as Tell el-Dabᶜa and Qatna, two major hubs during the MB period. The earliest occurrence of Tell el-Yahudiya Ware at Arqa appears in a pit dated to an early phase of the MBI. It was made either at Arqa or at Ardé strengthening the thesis that the northern part of present-day Lebanon was one of the first production centers in the Levant. Investigating further the Tell el-Yahudiya occurrences in Lebanon by submitting the available material to petrographic analysis will help better understand the involvement of Arqa and other sites in the production and circulation of this commodity locally (towards Qatna/Ebla region and towards the south) and regionally (towards Egypt and possibly Cyprus).

Petrographic Analysis of Tell el-Yahudiya Samples from Tell Arqa

Mary Ownby

Introduction

The results of recent excavations carried out at Tell Arqa have revealed that this site participated in international trade in the Middle Bronze Age. The discovery of two Marl C jars at Tell Arqa, indicates that Egyptian goods or people were coming to the site.[51] These vessels have also been found at the sites of Sidon, Byblos, Akko, Tel Ifshar, and Ashkelon.[52] This may be due to their use by sailors or government traders on missions to the Levant, or acquisition by Levantine traders at Egyptian ports.

Evidence for commodities from Tell Arqa arriving in Egypt comes from the discovery of Middle Bronze Age Canaanite jars found at the sites of Tell el-Dabᶜa and Memphis.[53] Petrographic analysis of Canaanite jars from these sites has identified a number of examples that were made of Neogene marl clay with basaltic inclusions. Both the clay and type of basalt suggest the Akkar Plain is their provenance (see below). This is confirmed by the similarity in appearance of Neogene marl and basalt fragments in an Amarna Letter sent from the site of Iraqata, identified as Tell Arqa.[54]

---

[50] Goren, Y, Finkelstein, I. and Na'aman, N, *Inscribed in clay: petrographic investigation of the Amarna Tablets,* Tel Aviv, 2004.

[51] K. Kopetzky, Pottery from Tell Arqa Found in Egypt and Its Chronological Contexts, *AHL*, 26–27, 2007/2008, 23.

[52] B. Bader, The Egyptian jars from Sidon in their Egyptian context: a preliminary report, *AHL*, 18, 2003, 31–37, I. Forstner-Müller and K. Kopetzky, An Upper Egyptian Import at Sidon, *AHL*, 24, 2006, 60–62; I. Forstner-Müller, K. Kopetzky, and C. Doumet-Serhal, Egyptian Pottery of the Late 12th and early 13th Dynasty from Sidon, *AHL*, 24, 2006, 52–59; D. Griffiths and M. Ownby, Assessing the Occurrence of Egyptian Marl C Ceramics in Middle Bronze Age Sidon, *AHL*, 24, 2006, 63–77; M. Dunand, Rapport Préliminaire sur les fouilles de Byblos en 1963, *Bulletin du Musée de Beyrouth*, 17, 1964, 32; E.S. Marcus, E. Porath, R. Schiestl, A. Seiler, and S.M. Paley, The Middle Kingdom Egyptian Pottery from Middle Bronze Age IIa Tel Ifshar, *Ä&L*, 18, 2008, 203–219; L. Stager, The MB IIA Ceramic Sequence at Tel Ashkelon and Its Implications for the "Port Power" Model of Trade, in: M. Bietak (ed.), *The Middle Bronze Age in the Levant, Proceedings of an International Conference on MB IIA Ceramic Material, Vienna, 24th–26th of January 2001,* 2002, 359; M. Bietak, K. Kopetzky, L. Stager and R. Voss, Synchronisation of Stratigraphies: Ashkelon and Tell el-Dabᶜa, *Ä&L* 18, 2008, 52.

[53] A. Cohen-Weinberger and Y. Goren, Levantine-Egyptian Interactions During the 12th to the 15th Dynasties based on the Petrography of the Canaanite Pottery from Tell el-Dabᶜa, *Ä&L* 14, 2004, 69–100; M. Ownby and J. Bourriau, The movement of Middle Bronze Age transport jars: a provenance study based on petrographic and chemical analysis of Canaanite jars from Memphis, Egypt, in: P. Quinn (ed.), *Interpreting Silent Artefacts: Petrographic Approaches to Archaeological Ceramics,* 2009, 173–188.

[54] Y. Goren, I. Finkelstein and N. Na'aman, *Inscribed in Clay, Provenance Study of the Amarna Tablets,* 2004.

As Tell Arqa was a large, prosperous site in the Middle Bronze Age, the Canaanite jars are likely to have come from this site or within its vicinity. These discoveries suggest that Tell Arqa may have participated in international trade networks during the Middle Bronze Age. In order to confirm and clarify this impression, petrographic analysis was undertaken to examine Tell el-Yahudiya vessels that are known to have moved throughout the Eastern Mediterranean in the Middle Bronze Age.

Samples and Methodology

Twenty-two samples of Tell el-Yahudiya Ware were taken for analysis, mostly deriving from the Middle Bronze II level (Table 2). Prior to petrographic analysis, each sample was described macroscopically at 25x magnification with a stereoscope. This provided a fabric description (i.e size and amount of sand, plant remains, and limestone; other inclusions; sorting; porosity; hardness; wall thickness; surface and break colour). These descriptions are designed to assist in relating the petrographic data to the visual appearance of the fabrics in the field (see Appendix for *macroscopic descriptions*). This will allow future samples to be provisionally assigned to one of the petrographic groups designated below (see below for fabric images).

For petrographic analysis, a single thin section was made from each sample and analyzed employing standard procedures.[55] For each sample the colour of the section in plane and cross polarized light was noted, along with the frequency of inclusions and their sorting. The mineral grains were identified and information was recorded on their size range and the shape range for the quartz and limestone inclusions. Finally, the clay type was specified and additional comments were made on firing temperature (i.e. low = 700–800°C) and processing

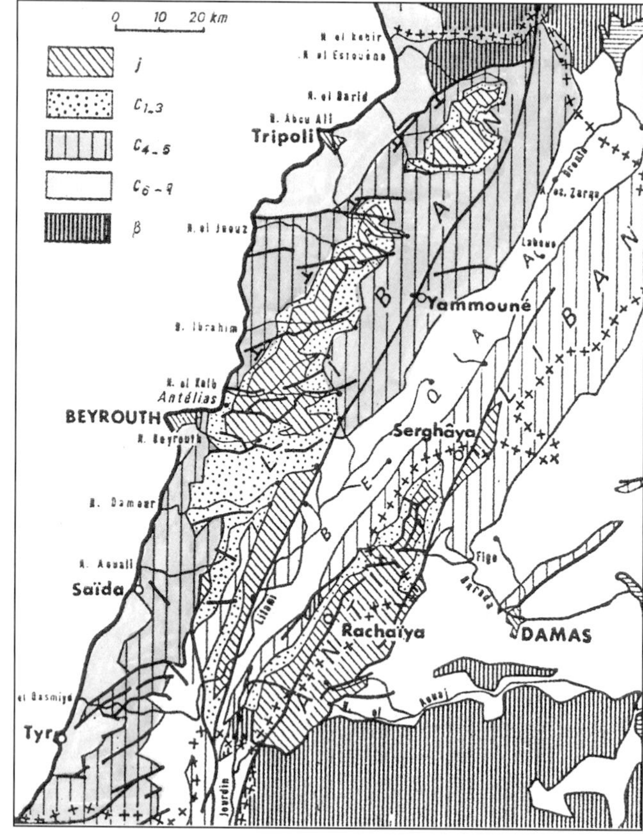

Fig. 4 Simplified Geological Map of Lebanon (from Dubertret 1970: fig. 1) J = Jurassic, C1–3 = Lower Cretaceous (Aptian-Albian), C4–5 = Upper Cretaceous (Cenomanian-Turonian), C6–q = Senonian to Quaternary (including Eocene), B= Basaltic

(see Appendix I for microscopic descriptions and Appendix II for thin section images). The information from the clay and inclusion types was related to soil and geological maps from the Levantine region.[56] This enabled the identification of geographic regions where the clay and mineral types were present. The analysis resulted in the designation of

[55] See I.K. Whitbread, A Proposal for the Systematic Description of Thin Sections towards the Study of Ancient Ceramic Technology, in: Y. Maniatis (ed.), *Archaeometry: Proceedings of the 25th International Symposium,* 1989, 127–138; I.K. Whitbread, *Greek transport amphorae: a petrological and archaeological study,* 1995, 365–396.

[56] Y. Bartov, Geological Photomap of Israel and Adjacent Areas, 1:750,000, 2nd ed., 1994; Y. Dan, Z. Raz, D.H. Yaalon, and H. Koyumdjisky, 1975, *Soil Map of Israel, 1:500,000*; L. Dubertret, *Carte géologique au 50.000e Feuille de Beyrouth*; L. Dubertret, *Carte géologique au 50.000e Feuille de Saida,* 1949; L. Dubertret, *Liban, Syrie et bordure des pays voisins,* 1962; L. Dubertret, Liban, Syrie, et bordure des pays voisins, *Notes et mémoires sur le Moyen-Orient* 8, 1966, 251–358, L. Dubertret, Géologie et Peuplement au Liban, in: J. Besancon (ed.), *Hannon: revue libanaise de geographie,* vol. V, 1970, 11–20; L. Dubertret, Introduction a la Carte Géologique a 1/50,000e du Liban, *Notes et mémoires sur le Moyen-Orient* 13, 1974, 345–403; L. Dubertret and R. Wetzel, *Carte géologique au 50.000e Feuille de Batroun,* 194; M. Ilaiwi, *Soil Map of Arab Countries, Soil Map of Syria and Lebanon,* 1985; A. Sneh, Y. Bartov, and M. Rosensaft, *Geological Map of Israel, 1:200,000, Sheet 1,* 1998; A. Sneh, Y. Bartov, and M. Rosensaft, *Geological Map of Israel, 1:200,000, Sheet 2,* 1998; R. Wetzel, *Carte géologique au 50.000e Feuille de Tripoli,* 1945.

Samples	Date[57]	Group	Postulated Provenance
78/516.026	MB II	4	northern Lebanon
78/528A.041	MB II	4	northern Lebanon
79/465.040	Unstrat	5	Lebanon
79/468.032	Unstrat	3	northern Lebanon
80/440.003	Unstrat	4	northern Lebanon
81/372.002	LB I	5	Lebanon
81/388.003	LB I	5	Lebanon
81/391.004	MB II	5	Lebanon
92/HS.002	Unstrat	outlier	northern Lebanon
92/161.006	MB II/LB I	1	northern Lebanon
92/861.001	NA	1	northern Lebanon
92/864.001	MB II	6	southern Levant
93/814.007	MB I/MB II	5	Lebanon
93/894.005	MB I	5	Lebanon
94/310.010	MB II	5	Lebanon
94/324.011	MB II	5	Lebanon
94/379.001	LB I	2	northern Lebanon
01/118.018	NA	6	southern Levant
01/337.001	MB II	6	southern Levant
01/350.001	MB II	2	northern Lebanon
01/350.002	MB II	3	northern Lebanon
04/110.002	LB II	5	Lebanon
04/111.001	NA	5	Lebanon
08/420.001	MB I	2	northern Lebanon

Table 2 List of Samples

six petrographic groups, and one outlier, that were assigned an interpreted provenance (Table 2). The petrographic results were related to the vessel decoration of the samples to examine any relationships between provenance and design. However, as the recovered sherds are small, any relationships are provisional and links between vessel form and provenance are more difficult to establish.

Results

Group 1

The first group was produced from an iron-rich shale clay with inclusions of quartz, plagioclase, limestone, geode quartz, serpentine, and igneous rock fragments of quartz and plagioclase. The samples were all low fired (700–800°C) and the appearance of the matrix suggests little refinement or temper addition to the raw materials. Therefore, most of the constituents are probably natural to the clay suggesting a clay deposit in an igneous area. While Tell Arqa is located east of a region containing basaltic deposits, igneous geology can also be found in the Aptian section of the Lower Cretaceous outcrops, called the *basalte crétacé*.[58] This volcanic complex consists of deposits with iron-rich clay, iron-rich oolites, and basalts. Such outcrops are common in the Mount Lebanon area, but can be found in other areas, such as the Mount Hermon region and rarely in the Anti-Lebanon.[59] However, the presence of geode quartz,

[57] See contribution by H. Charaf above.

[58] R. Greenberg and N. Porat, A Third Millennium Levantine pottery Production Center: typology, petrography, and provenance of the Metallic Ware of northern Israel and adjacent regions, *BASOR* 301, 1996, 5–24; Y. Goren, The Southern Levant in the Early Bronze Age IV: the petrographic perspective, *BASOR* 303, 1996, 33–72; Y. Goren I. Finkelstein and N. Na'aman, *Inscribed in Clay, Provenance Study of the Amarna Tablets*, 2004, 104–105.

[59] L. Dubertret, *Liban, Syrie et bordure des pays voisins*, 1962.

common in the Lebanese Cenomanian-Turonian deposits, suggests the Mount Lebanon region is more likely the raw material source.[60] Thus, a region where both Lower and Upper Cretaceous deposits are weathering to form an iron-rich shale clay with igneous and sedimentary inclusions is the location of production. Such an area significantly outcrops in the Lebanese mountains north of Beirut and can be found to the south of Tell Arqa/east of Tripoli and also southeast of Tripoli.[61] Therefore, the interpreted provenance is northern Lebanon, with Byblos and the area east of Tripoli as likely possibilities.

A single Tell el-Yahudiya juglet (dated to the late 13th Dynasty) analyzed by Cohen-Weinberger and Goren[62] was produced of material derived from Lower Cretaceous deposits[63]. The suggested provenance is located closer to Byblos, and indicates a comparison between this sample and the Tell Arqa samples would be instructive. If Byblos is indeed the production location, this would fit with known ceramic connections between Tell Arqa and this important site.[64] This vessel was of a piriform 1b/c (type group I2-I3) shape. A Tell el-Yahudiya piriform juglet from Tel Kabri also belongs to this group.[65] Together with the Tell Arqa samples, these four sherds appear to indicate production of Tell el-Yahudiya juglets, possibly of piriform shape, in the northern Lebanese region.

As the ceramic material from the site is still being processed, there was only one drawing available from the two samples in this group. Sample 92/161.006 shows a horizontal decoration band with punctures.

Group 2

Group 2 samples were made from a rendzina clay derived from the weathering of limestone outcrops due to the Mediterranean climate.[66] Quartz, geode quartz, chalcedony, chert, limestone, calcite, silt-size plagioclase grains, and weathered basalt fragments were present. The inclusions appear natural to the clay, suggesting a rendzina formed near a weathering igneous area as the source of the raw materials. However, a mollusc shell fragment in sample 94/379.001 and a bioclast (calcified oceanic organism, probably *Amphiroa sp.*) in sample 01/350.001 suggest the location of production was along a river near the Mediterranean Sea. This river would drain an area with igneous geology that is located in Lebanon based on the geode quartz (Cenomanian-Turonian outcrops) and chalcedony (Senonian /Upper Cretaceous or Lower Eocene outcrops) inclusions.[67] Once again, the area around Tripoli is a likely provenance. This region features rendzina clays and several rivers that drain the Lower Cretaceous and Jurassic basalt deposits located inland.[68] However, areas south to Beirut also have small drainages that could potentially receive weathered basalts from inland.

The Nahr el-ᶜArqa near Tell Arqa drains a region of Pliocene age basalts weathered to different degrees. However, these inclusions are typically more coarsely crystalline than the basalt fragments in the Group 2 samples. This is supported by the petrographic analysis of LBA Amarna Letters sent from Irqata.[69] The results showed that letters from this area contained basalt inclusions that had been weathered to various degrees, along with loose iddingsite and olivine grains from the basalt fragments. Therefore, the lack of coarsely crystalline basalt inclusions may indicate these samples are more likely to have been produced near the Lower Cretaceous outcrops. Furthermore, rendzina clay is not as common in this area

---

60 L. Dubertet, Liban, Syrie, et bordure des pays voisins. *Notes et mémoires sur le Moyen-Orient* 8, 1966: 308–309; L. Dubertret, Introduction a la Carte Géologique a 1/50,000e du Liban. *Notes et mémoires sur le Moyen-Orient* 13, 1974, 376, 378.

61 R. Wetzel, *Carte géologique au 50.000e Feuille de Tripoli,* 1945.

62 A. Cohen-Weinberger and Y. Goren, Levantine-Egyptian Interactions During the 12th to the 15th Dynasties based on the Petrography of the Canaanite Pottery from Tell el-Dabᶜa, *Ä&L* 14, 2004, 75–76, 96.

63 This sample was also subjected to Neutron Activation Analysis by McGovern – P. McGovern, T*he Foreign Relations of the "Hyksos". A neutron activation study of Middle Bronze Age pottery from the Eastern Mediterranean*, 2000, 137, who was unable to assign a certain provenance based on the results.

64 J.P. Thalmann, Tell Arqa et Byblos, Essai de correlation, in: M. Bietak and E. Czerny (eds.), *The Bronze Age in the Lebanon. Studies on the Archaeology and Chronology of Lebanon, Syria, and Egypt*, 2008, 61–78.

65 Y. Goren, and A. Cohen-Weinberger, Petrographic Analyses of Selected Wares, in: A. Kempinski (ed.), *Tel Kabri: the 1986–1993 excavation seasons.* 2002, 442.

66 M. Wieder and D. Adan-Bayewitz, Soil Parent Materials and the Pottery of Roman Galilee: A Comparative Study. *Geoarchaeology*, 17, 2002, 412.

67 Z.R. Beydoun, The Levantine countries: the geology of Syria and Lebanon (maritime regions), in: A.E.M. Nairn, W.H. Kanes and F.G. Stehli (eds.), *The ocean basins and margins. 4A: The eastern Mediterranean*, 1977, 322, 329, 332–333.

68 M. Ilaiwi, *Soil Map of Arab Countries, Soil Map of Syria and Lebanon,* 1985.

69 Y. Goren, I. Finkelstein and N. Na'aman, *Inscribed in Clay, Provenance Study of the Amarna Tablets*, 2004, 108, 114–115, 122.

where Neogene clays are more dominant. Therefore, the interpreted provenance is northern Lebanon. These samples were found in strata dated from the MB I to the LB I suggesting that this production location was long-lived.

The manufacture of these vessels appears to have consisted of utilizing a clay with little modification. Sample 94/379.001 contained a plant remain, but this is not necessarily indicative of intentional temper. The increased amount of quartz inclusions in 08/420.001 could either indicate a small addition of sand or the selection of a clay with larger and more common quartz grains. The firing temperature was low, i.e. 700–800°C. The decorative scheme of sample 01/350.001 features a rectangular area with punctate decoration. Sample 94/379.001 has upside down triangles with punctures that have lost their white filling.

Group 3

Samples in Group 3 were made from a foraminiferous marl with *Terra Rossa* as an addition. *Terra Rossa* is an iron-rich clay/soil with prevalent silt-sized quartz grains that was commonly added to more calcareous clays to make them more workable.[70] The inclusions in the samples comprised silt-sized plagioclase, limestone, foraminifers, geode quartz, and chert. Most of the inclusions appear natural to the clay, with the exception of the large and angular chert grains. These may have been intentionally added; a practice noted for MBA Canaanite jars assigned a provenance near Tell Arqa, which also had a *Terra Rossa* addition.[71] The firing temperature was between 700–800°C.

The similarity of inclusions in these samples to those in Group 2 suggests they were probably produced in the same area. The geode quartz inclusions further support a location in Lebanon. Foraminifers of *Globigerina* and *Globigerinoides* are present, which may indicate a Neogene source for the clay, possibly near Tell Arde to the east of Tripoli.[72] Neogene clay is also found in the region of Tell Arqa. However, the presence of only detrital plagioclase grains may rule out this area where the large Pliocene basalt complexes are likely to have produced a sand/clay mix with inclusions of pyroxenes and olivines, also deriving from igneous inclusions. However, the area around Tell Arqa cannot be excluded as the Nahr el-ᶜArqa may have produced a Neogene clay with lose silt-sized inclusions of plagioclase that was utilized to manufacture Tell el-Yahudiya vessels. More information on the locally available resources is needed to clarify whether these vessels could have been produced at Tell Arqa, especially given the similarity in technology to the MBA Canaanite jars. Knowledge of local raw materials may also indicate that the Group 2 samples produced from a rendzina clay were made near Tell Arqa. Based on the current available information, the samples in Group 3 are assigned an interpreted provenance of northern Lebanon.

Sample 79/468.032 features a triangle with punctate decoration and a plain horizontal band above and below this area. The second sample, 01/350.002, is a single-strand handle with a rectangular area filled with punctures.

Group 4

The foraminifers (*Ammonia, Bulimina, Globigerina, Globigerinoides*) in the Group 4 samples indicate that the clay is a Neogene marl. *Terra Rossa* was added to the marl clay. Other inclusions of quartz, geode quartz, and limestone are natural to the clay and the vessels were low fired (700–800°C). As Neogene marls are commonly found in the region around Tell Arqa, along with geode quartz and chert in local outcrops, this may suggest these vessels were produced at the site. Comparison to MBA Canaanite jars assigned to this provenance, based on the basalt inclusions, revealed very similar clays.[73] However, the lack of basalt grains or detrital inclusions of pyroxenes and plagioclase from them may indicate either the clay is from an area located away from the Neogene igneous outcrops or basaltic sand was added to the MBA Canaanite jars. Along with the

---

70 M. Wieder and D. Adan-Bayewitz, Soil Parent Materials and the Pottery of Roman Galilee: A Comparative Study. *Geoarchaeology*, 17, 2002, 395–397.

71 M. Ownby, *Canaanite Jars from Memphis as Evidence for Trade and Political Relationships in the Middle Bronze Age,* Unpublished PhD thesis, University of Cambridge, 2010, 131.

72 L. Dubertret, *Liban, Syrie et bordure des pays voisins,* 1962; Z.R. Beydoun, The Levantine countries: the geology of Syria and Lebanon (maritime regions), in: A.E.M. Nairn, W.H. Kanes and F.G. Stehli (eds.), *The ocean basins and margins. 4A: The eastern Mediterranean,* 1977, 333–335; Y. Goren, I. Finkelstein and N. Na'aman, *Inscribed in Clay, Provenance Study of the Amarna Tablets,* 2004, 105, 114.

73 M. Ownby, *Canaanite Jars from Memphis as Evidence for Trade and Political Relationships in the Middle Bronze Age,* unpublished PhD thesis, University of Cambridge, 2010, 129–132.

previous two petrographic groups, the lack of direct information on how various outcrops in the region of Tell Arqa interact precludes a precise provenance. The Neogene marl clay provides the best indicator for the provenance of samples in this group. Thus, the interpreted provenance is northern Lebanon, possibly in the Tell Arqa area.

Examination of drawings from the three samples revealed that two have a similar design scheme with shapes filled with punctuate decoration (78/528A.041 and 80/440.003), while the third, 78/516.026, has several vertical rows of filled in punctures in a single rectangular area.

Group 5

Group 5 held the largest number of samples, which were made from a rendzina clay with the addition of *Terra Rossa*. Inclusions of limestone, geode quartz, chalcedony, chert, pyroxenes, and serpentine appeared natural to the clay, but the common, mostly angular quartz grains are likely to have been temper. This suggests a provenance near a quartz-rich sand close to its original outcrops, while the geode quartz, chalcedony, and chert are typical for the Lebanese mountains. There are numerous large and small rivers that flow from the Lebanese mountains towards the Mediterranean Sea. However, the pyroxenes and serpentine inclusions may indicate a source near igneous outcrops that are eroding; particularly as the serpentines in sample 81/391.004 resembles those in Group 1 assigned to the Lower Cretaceous deposits. On the other hand, the macroscopic similarity between 81/388.003 and 81/391.004 in this group with material from Sidon, may suggest a possible provenance in southern Lebanon.[74] Therefore, due to the mostly sedimentary inclusions and widespread distribution of rendzina clays,[75] the interpreted provenance is Lebanon.

As this group includes the largest number of samples, it would suggest a prolific production centre. Furthermore, the manufacture of the vessels was more involved with the addition of quartz sand and *Terra Rossa* to the clay. The firing temperature was low, 700–800°C, as with the other Tell el-Yahudiya samples. The decoration of the ten samples suggests that this group features both horizontal and vertical punctate designs in rectangular spaces as well as triangles filled with punctures. Samples from this group date from the earliest to the latest Middle Bronze Age strata, although the sample with a triangle design is dated to the latest phase.

Group 6

Samples in Group 6 consisted of a *Hamra* clay with large and prevalent limestone inclusions and some quartz grains. Other inclusions comprised chert, geode quartz, K-feldspars, and eroded foraminifers. *Hamra* is an iron-rich clay that develops within the kukar ridges, cemented ancient sand dunes, prevalent along the coast of Palestine.[76] In particular, this soil is common along the northern Palestinian coast (Dan *et al.* 1975). This may suggest the provenance is in this region. However, sample 01/118.008 contains inclusions more typical of the Lebanese mountains, indicating an area closer to Lebanon is possible as the site of production. Thus, the interpreted provenance is the southern Levant.

The production method for these samples involved the addition of limestone, and possibly quartz, to the *Hamra* clay. The vessels were fired to between 700–800°C. The decoration of two samples (92/864.001 and 01/337.001) features vertical rows of punctures and both samples date to the Middle Bronze II.

Outlier

A single sample could not be assigned to one of the groups. It was made from a Neogene clay with a large quantity of *Terra Rossa* added. The sample contained inclusions of quartz, limestone, chert, chalcedony, and serpentine. Most of the inclusions are natural to the clay, suggesting only the addition of *Terra Rossa* was a part of the manufacturing process. The sample was low fired, i.e. 700–800°C. The serpentine fragments in this sample bear a general resemblance to those in the Group 1 samples, while the clay is slightly different to that used for samples in Group 4. This may indicate a provenance in the area east of Tripoli (Tell Arde vicinity) near the Neogene clay deposits but also within the distribution of the Lower Creta-

[74] H. Charaf, personal communication.

[75] M. Ilaiwi, *Soil Map of Arab Countries, Soil Map of Syria and Lebanon*, 1985.

[76] G. Gvirtzman, M. Netser and E. Katsav, Last-Glacial to Holocene kurkar ridges, hamra soils, and dune fields in the coastal belt of central Israel, *Israel Journal of Earth Sciences*, 47, 1998, 29–46; N. Porat, A.G. Wintle and M Ritte, Mode and timing of kurkar and hamra formation, central coastal plain, Israel, *Israel Journal of Earth Sciences*, 53, 2004, 13–25.

ceous outcrops. The presence of Neogene clay, and chert and chalcedony inclusions, allows for the interpreted provenance to be proposed as northern Lebanon.

The small size of this sample precludes a strong association between provenance and design, although it is clear the sherd features a rectangular area with two rows of punctures.

Discussion

The analysis of Tell el-Yahudiya samples from Tell Arqa aimed to further investigate the international contacts of this site. The results showed that most of the vessels were produced in northern Lebanon, close to the western coast. It is likely that a number of the samples were produced near Tell Arqa (Groups 2, 3, and 4) in addition to some coming from other areas of the Levant. As the site was large and prosperous in the MBA it would seem plausible that they would produce some of their own Tell el-Yahudiya vessels. This may have been done with raw materials acquired to the south and southeast of the site. More research into the availability of clay and tempering resources in the areas of Tell Arqa, Tripoli and Byblos is needed to confirm this possibility and clarify these initial provenance assignments.

Nevertheless, what is surprising is that none of the vessels were produced from clays with coastal sand temper. This was noted for a majority of the MBA Canaanite jars produced in Lebanon.[77] The utilization of beach sand indicates these large transport jars were produced near the port, probably for direct exportation of commodities such as resin and oil.[78] The Tell el-Yahudiya vessels do not show such technological choices, which may suggest that they were produced at areas other than the ports. This could be at sites further inland or the potters selected raw materials that were not available on the coast. Possibly the jugs and juglets were produced near where the commodity they may have carried was manufactured. Overall, the lack of technological connection between the Tell el-Yahudiya vessels and the Canaanite jars suggests that they were probably carrying different goods and may have been a part of separate trade networks.

When the petrographic data is related to the decoration and archaeological context of the Tell el-Yahudiya samples, it becomes clear that many of the areas produced vessels with comparable decoration. However, samples dated towards the end of the Middle Bronze Age feature triangles filled with punctures, while the earlier samples typically have rectangles with punctures. As these samples are small, this hypothesis is tentative. Additional information is needed on the relationship between decoration and vessel form, although the Arqa samples appear to come mostly from piriform and ovoid vessels. Finally, some of the areas producing Tell el-Yahudiya vessels exported them to Tell Arqa throughout the Middle Bronze II period.

Conclusion

The results of the current study indicate that there are a number of production locations for these samples. While most seem to be within proximity to Tell Arqa, others are likely to be further afield. Along with the results from petrographic analyses of Tell el-Yahudiya from Tell el-Dab^ca and Tel Kabri, this suggests many areas produced these vessels for local consumption and some exportation. The two piriform vessels from Tell el-Dabᶜa were produced near Byblos and in the northwestern Negev,[79] while four juglets from Tel Kabri were manufactured along the northern Levantine coast.[80] The discovery of a manufacturing centre at Afula also confirms that these vessels were made at numerous sites.[81] While these results support the compositional work conducted on Tell el-Yahudiya ware, primarily Neutron Activation Analy-

[77] A. Cohen-Weinberger and Y. Goren, Levantine-Egyptian Interactions During the 12th to the 15th Dynasties based on the Petrography of the Canaanite Pottery from Tell el-Dabᶜa, *Ä&L* 14, 2004, 73–74, 77–78; M. Ownby and J. Bourriau, The movement of Middle Bronze Age transport jars: a provenance study based on petrographic and chemical analysis of Canaanite jars from Memphis, Egypt, in: P. Quinn (ed.), *Interpreting Silent Artefacts: Petrographic Approaches to Archaeological Ceramics.* 2009, 178–181.

[78] M. Serpico, J. Bourriau, L. Smith, Y. Goren, B. Stern and C. Heron, 2003, Commodities and Containers: A Project to Study Canaanite Amphorae Imported into Egypt during the New Kingdom, in: M. Bietak (ed.), *The Synchronization of Civilizations in the Eastern Mediterranean in the Second Millennium B.C. II*, 365–376.

[79] A. Cohen-Weinberger and Y. Goren, Levantine-Egyptian Interactions During the 12th to the 15th Dynasties based on the Petrography of the Canaanite Pottery from Tell el-Dabᶜa, *Ä&L* 14, 2004, 93, 96.

[80] Y. Goren and A. Cohen-Weinberger, Petrographic Analyses of Selected Wares; in: A. Kempinski (ed.), *Tel Kabri: the 1986–1993 excavation seasons,* 2002, 442.

[81] U. Zevulun Tell el-Yahudiyah Juglets from a Potter's Refuse Pit at Afula, *EI* 21, 1990, 174–190.

sis,[82] which suggested multiple production locations, the petrographic data provides a clearer understanding of provenance differences and manufacturing technology.

The role of Tell Arqa in intraregional trade has been clarified and the site is likely to have played a significant part in MBA interregional trade as well. Its position in the Akkar Plain, giving direct access between the Mediterranean coast and the city-states on the Orontes undoubtedly facilitated its involvement in trade. In any discussion of Middle Bronze Age trade in the Eastern Mediterranean, this site should feature more prominently. Further research on Tell el-Yahudiya ware will hopefully clarify their provenances and continue the very important integration of petrographic data, vessel form, and decoration. Ultimately, the goal is to be able to examine the movement of these vessels by relating their form and decoration to known production regions and gain much additional information on Middle Bronze Age trade in the Eastern Mediterranean.

Acknowledgements

The samples in this study were provided by J.-P. Thalmann and H. Charaf. Valuable discussion and images/figures of the ceramic material was kindly offered by H. Charaf. K. Kopetzky is gratefully acknowledged for having suggested I examine this material and selecting the samples. This analysis was made possible through the generosity of Dr. Charles French who granted permission for the sections to be made and analyzed at the McBurney Laboratory for Geoarchaeology at the University of Cambridge. Mineralogical advice on the sections was provided by Y. Goren and P. LaPorta.

Appendix: Macroscopic and Microscopic Descriptions, Sherd and Thin Section Images

Macroscopic images are at 10× magnification, microscopic images are at 40× magnification, scale bar = 1mm
The first microscopic image is in plane polarized light (PPL), the second in cross polarized light (XPL)

Sample Number: 78/516.026

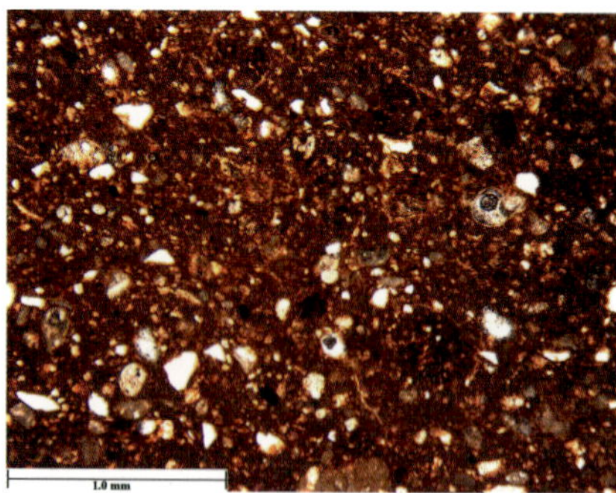
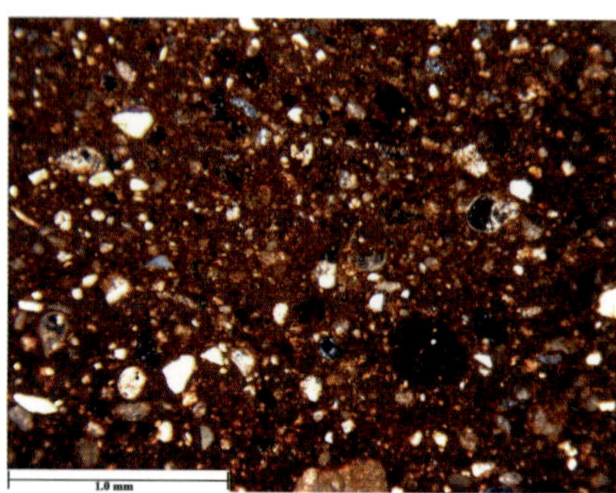

Macroscopic Description
Inclusions: sand – fine [1], medium [1]; limestone – fine [2], medium [1], coarse [1]; red-brown rock particles – fine [1]; microfossils. Poor sorting, medium porosity, medium hard structure. Vessel wall – 5 mm. Break colour: interior zone yellowish brown, exterior zone yellowish red. Surfaces: interior surface dark greyish brown, exterior surface very dark grey.
Microscopic Description
Colour PPL: light red-brown
Colour XPL: medium red-brown
Frequency of Inclusions (estimated): 10%
Sorting: poor

[82] M. Artzy and F. Asaro, Origin of Tell el-Yahudiyah Ware found in Cyprus, *Report of the Department of Antiquities Cyprus*, 1979, 135–150; M. Kaplan, *The Origin and Distribution of Tell el-Yahudiyeh Ware*, 1980; M. Kaplan, G. Harbottle and E. Sayre, Multi-Disciplinary Analysis of Tell el Yahudiyeh Ware, *Archaeometry*, 24, 1982, 127–14; P. McGovern, *The Foreign Relations of the "Hyksos". A neutron activation study of Middle Bronze Age pottery from the Eastern Mediterranean*, 2000.

Size Range: very fine to coarse (0.0625 – 1mm)
Shape Range: subangular to angular (quartz), rounded to subangular (limestone)
Main Inclusions: quartz, limestone (micritic and sparry), foraminifers (*Globigerina, Globigerinoides?, Bolivina?*), iron oxides, opaques, and chert
Additional Inclusions Present: K-feldspar, geode quartz, and pyroxenes
Comments: Neogene marl with *terra rossa*, low firing temperature

Sample Number: 78/528A.041

Macroscopic Description
Inclusions: sand – fine [1], medium [1], coarse [1]; limestone – fine [1], medium [1], coarse [1]; red-brown rock particles – fine [1]; black rock particles – fine [1]. Poor sorting, dense porosity, medium hard structure. Vessel wall – 5 mm. Break colour: interior zone grey, exterior zone brown. Surfaces: interior surface light brownish grey, exterior surface very dark grey.
Microscopic Description
Colour PPL: light brown
Colour XPL: medium brown
Frequency of Inclusions (estimated): 5%
Sorting: poor
Size Range: very fine to medium (0.0625 – 0.5mm)
Shape Range: subangular to angular (quartz), rounded to subangular (limestone)
Main Inclusions: quartz, limestone (micritic and sparry), foraminifers (*Ammonia, Globigerina, Globigerinoides?*), iron oxides, and opaques
Additional Inclusions Present: calcite
Comments: Neogene marl possibly with *terra rossa*, low firing temperature

Sample Number: 79/465.040

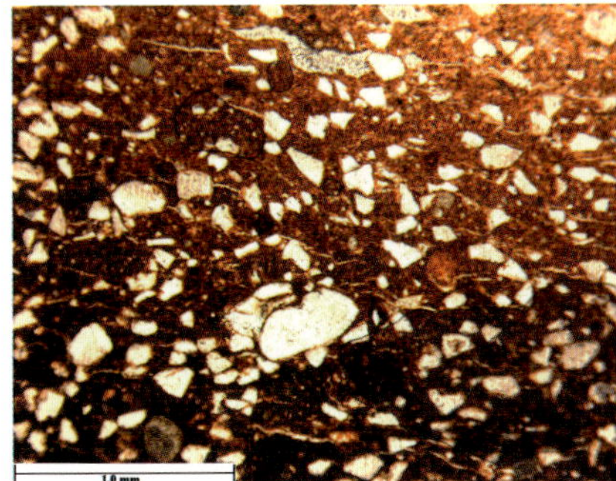

Macroscopic Description
Inclusions: sand – fine [3], medium [2]; limestone – fine [1], medium [1]; red-brown rock particles – fine [1], medium [1]; black rock particles – fine [1], medium [1]. Good sorting, medium porosity, medium hard structure. Vessel wall – 5 mm. Break colour: interior zone red, exterior zone dark brown. Surfaces: interior surface brown, exterior surface very dark brown.
Microscopic Description
Colour PPL: medium red

Colour XPL: medium red
Frequency of Inclusions (estimated): 20%
Sorting: fair
Size Range: very fine to fine (0.0625 – 0.25mm)
Shape Range: subrounded to angular (quartz), subrounded (limestone)
Main Inclusions: quartz, iron oxides, and opaques
Additional Inclusions Present: limestone (micritic) and chert
Comments: rendzina with *terra rossa* and quartz temper, low firing temperature

Sample Number: 79/468.032

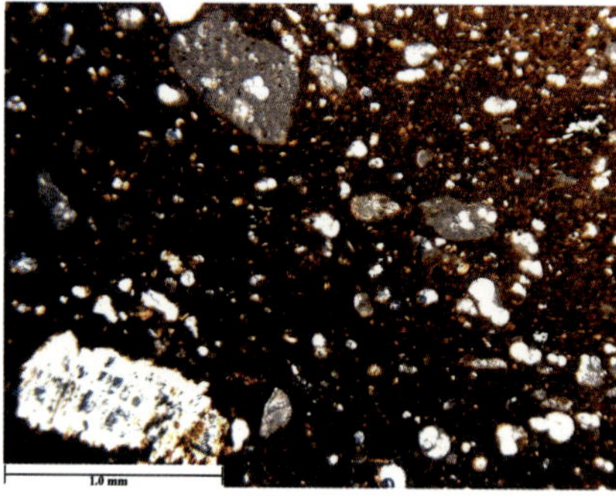
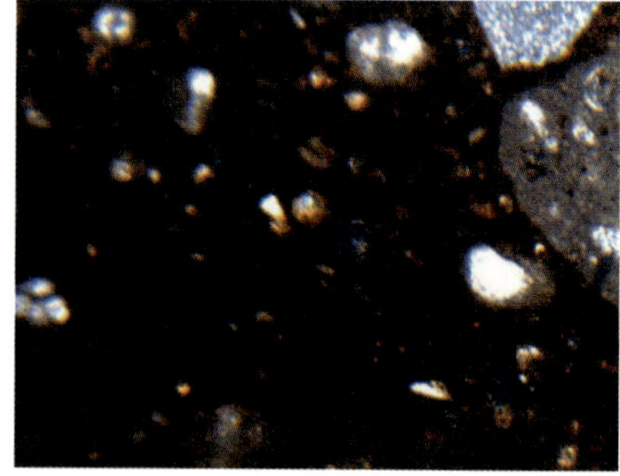

Macroscopic Description
Inclusions: sand – fine [1], medium [1]; limestone – fine [2], medium [2], coarse [1]; red-brown rock particles – fine [1]; black rock particles – fine [1], medium [1], coarse [1]; microfossils. Poor sorting, medium porosity, medium hard structure. Vessel wall – 6 mm. Break colour: interior zone brown, exterior zone reddish brown. Surfaces: interior surface brown, exterior surface very dark brown.
Microscopic Description
Colour PPL: medium reddish-brown
Colour XPL: medium reddish-brown
Frequency of Inclusions (estimated): 5%
Sorting: poor
Size Range: very fine to coarse (0.0625 – 1 mm)
Shape Range: subrounded to angular (quartz), rounded to subangular (limestone)
Main Inclusions: limestone (foraminiferous, micritic, and sparry), foraminifers (*Globigerina, Globigerinoides*), iron oxides, opaques, geode quartz, and chert
Additional Inclusions Present: quartz, calcite, and pyroxenes
Comments: foraminiferous marl with *terra rossa*, low firing temperature

Sample Number: 80/440.003

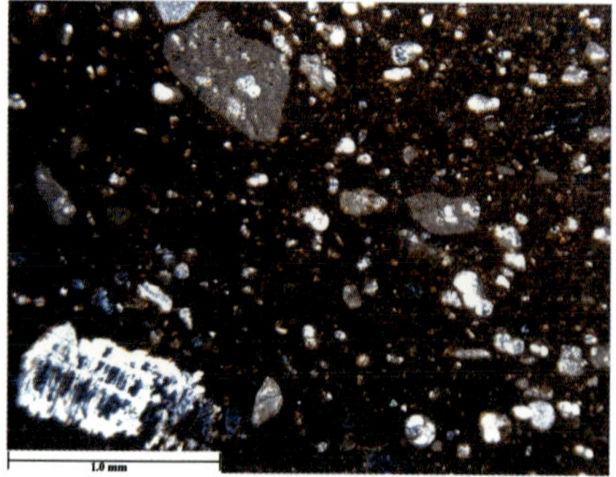
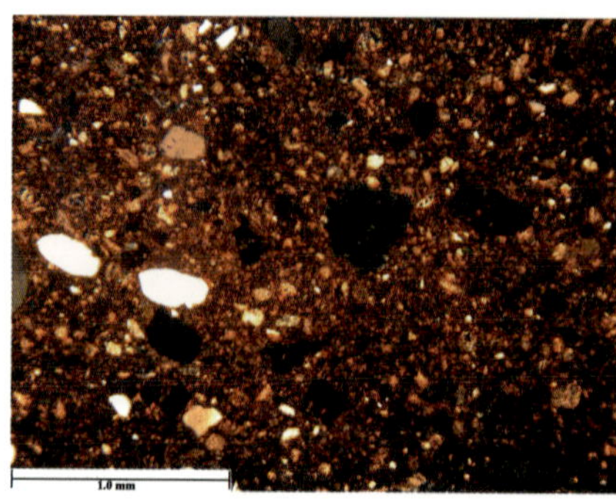

Macroscopic Description
Inclusions: sand – fine [2], medium [2], coarse [1]; limestone – fine [1], medium [1]; red-brown rock particles – fine [1], medium [1], coarse [1]; black rock particles – fine [1], medium [1]; microfossils. Fair sorting, medium porosity, medium hard structure. Vessel wall – 3 mm. Break colour: interior zone brown, exterior zone red. Surfaces: interior surface brown, exterior surface brown.

Microscopic Description
Colour PPL: light reddish brown
Colour XPL: medium reddish brown
Frequency of Inclusions (estimated): 10%
Sorting: poor
Size Range: very fine to medium (0.0625 – 0.5mm)
Shape Range: subrounded to angular (quartz), rounded to subangular (limestone)
Main Inclusions: quartz, limestone (micritic and sparry), foraminifers (*Bulimina, Globigerina, Globigerinoides, Brizalina?*), iron oxides, and opaques
Additional Inclusions Present: polycrystalline quartz, calcite, pyroxenes, olivine?, volcanic glass?
Comments: Neogene marl with *terra rossa,* low firing temperature

Sample Number: 81/372.002

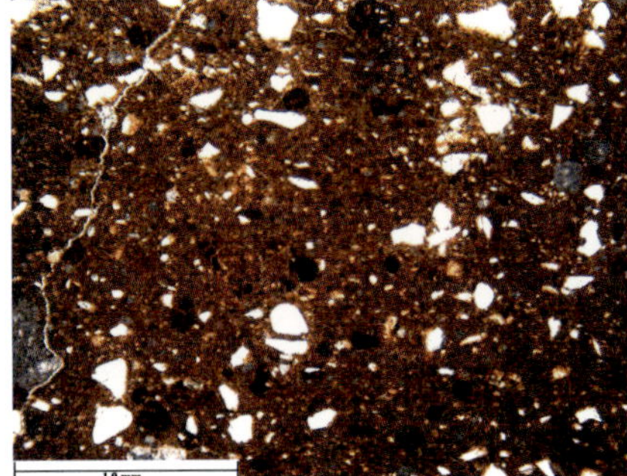
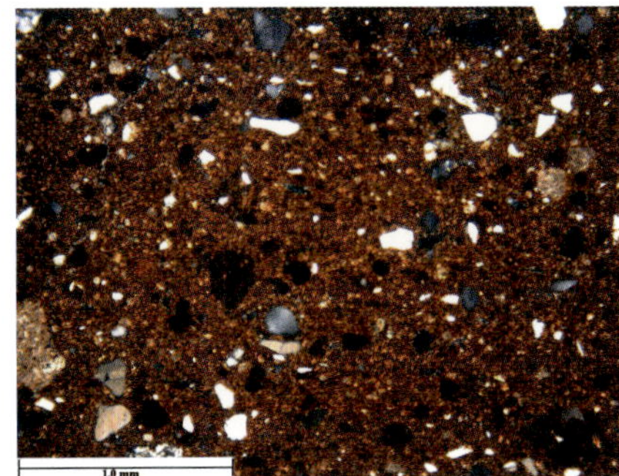

Macroscopic Description
Inclusions: sand – fine [2], medium [2], coarse [1]; limestone – fine [1], medium [1]; red-brown rock particles – fine [1], medium [1]; black rock particles – fine [1]. Fair sorting, medium porosity, medium hard structure. Vessel wall – 4 mm. Break colour: no zones yellowish red. Surfaces: interior surface yellowish red, exterior surface brown.
Microscopic Description
Colour PPL: medium reddish tan
Colour XPL: medium reddish tan
Frequency of Inclusions (estimated): 15%
Sorting: poor
Size Range: very fine to medium (0.0625 – 0.5mm)
Shape Range: subrounded to angular (quartz), rounded to subrounded (limestone)
Main Inclusions: quartz, limestone (micritic), iron oxides, and opaques
Additional Inclusions Present: geode quartz and serpentine
Comments: rendzina with *terra rossa* and quartz temper, low firing temperature

Sample Number: 81/388.003

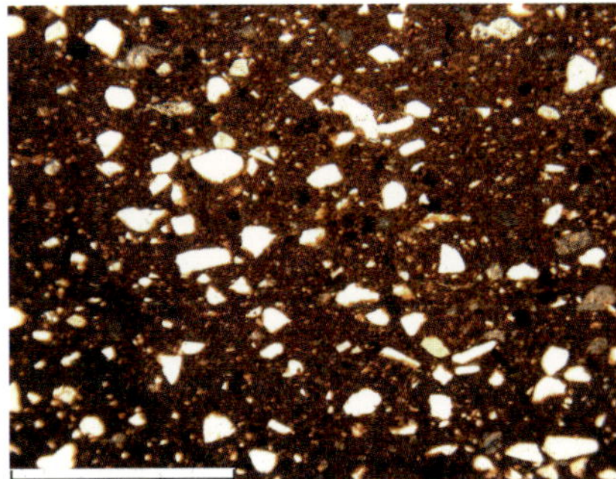

Macroscopic Description
Inclusions: sand – fine [2], medium [1]; limestone – fine [1], medium [1]; red-brown rock particles – fine [1], medium [1], coarse [1]; black rock particles – fine [1]. Fair sorting, medium porosity, medium hard structure. Vessel wall – 7 mm. Break colour: no zones yellowish red. Surfaces: interior surface yellowish red, exterior surface dark brown.

Microscopic Description
Colour PPL: medium reddish tan
Colour XPL: medium reddish tan
Frequency of Inclusions (estimated): 15%
Sorting: poor
Size Range: very fine to medium (0.0625 – 0.5mm)
Shape Range: subrounded to angular (quartz), rounded to subrounded (limestone)
Main Inclusions: quartz, limestone (micritic), iron oxides, and opaques
Additional Inclusions Present: geode quartz, pyroxenes, and serpentine
Comments: rendzina with *terra rossa* and quartz temper, low firing temperature

Sample Number: 81/391.004

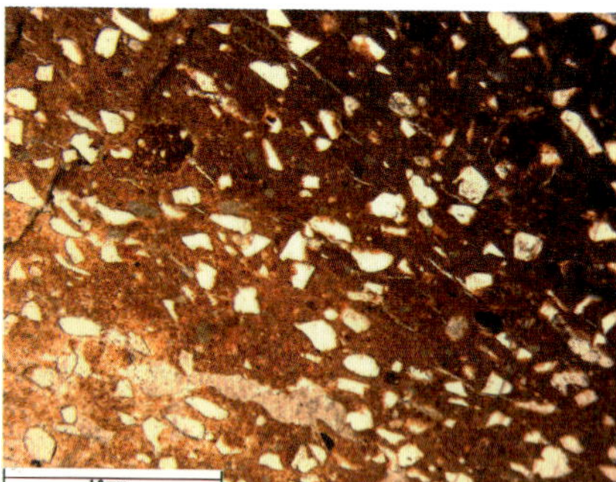
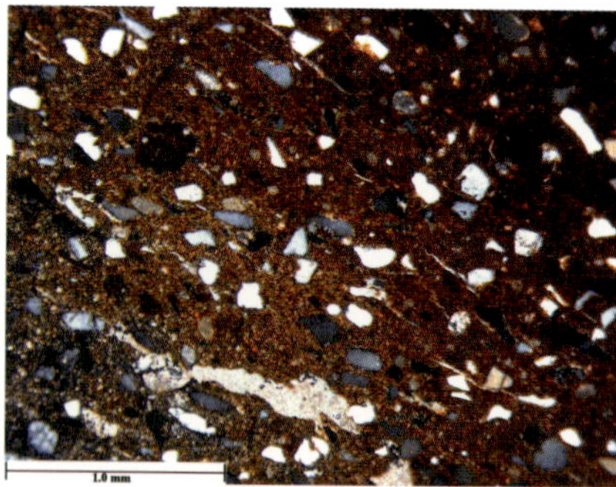

Macroscopic Description
Inclusions: sand – fine [3], medium [1], coarse [1]; limestone – fine [1], medium [1]; red-brown rock particles – fine [1], medium [1]; black rock particles – fine [1], medium [1]. Fair sorting, medium porosity, medium hard structure. Vessel wall – 5 mm. Break colour: no zones yellowish red. Surfaces: interior surface yellowish brown, exterior surface very dark brown.
Microscopic Description
Colour PPL: medium reddish tan
Colour XPL: medium reddish tan
Frequency of Inclusions (estimated): 20%
Sorting: fair
Size Range: very fine to medium (0.0625 – 0.5mm)
Shape Range: subrounded to angular (quartz), rounded to subrounded (limestone)
Main Inclusions: quartz, limestone (micritic), iron oxides, and opaques
Additional Inclusions Present: pyroxenes and serpentine
Comments: rendzina with *terra rossa* and quartz temper, low firing temperature

Sample Number: 92/HS.002

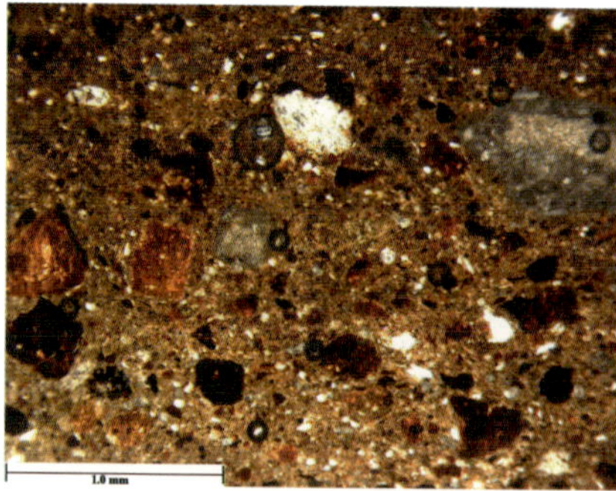
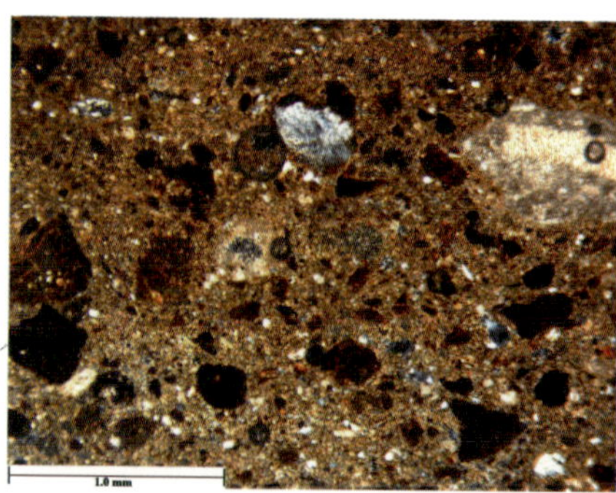

Macroscopic Description
Inclusions: sand – fine [1], medium [1], coarse [1]; limestone – fine [1], medium [1]; red-brown rock particles – fine [2], medium [2], coarse [1]; black rock particles – fine [1], medium [1]. Poor sorting, dense porosity, medium hard structure. Vessel wall – 6 mm. Break colour: interior zone brown, exterior zone yellowish red. Sur-

faces: interior surface grey, exterior surface very dark brown.

Microscopic Description

Colour PPL: medium tan

Colour XPL: medium tan

Frequency of Inclusions (estimated): 5%

Sorting: poor

Size Range: very fine to coarse (0.0625 – 1mm)

Shape Range: subrounded to angular (quartz), subrounded (limestone)

Main Inclusions: quartz, limestone (micritic and sparry), iron oxides, geode quartz, and serpentine

Additional Inclusions Present: calcite and chert

Comments: Neogene marl with *terra rossa* (very much), low firing temperature

Sample Number: 92/161.006

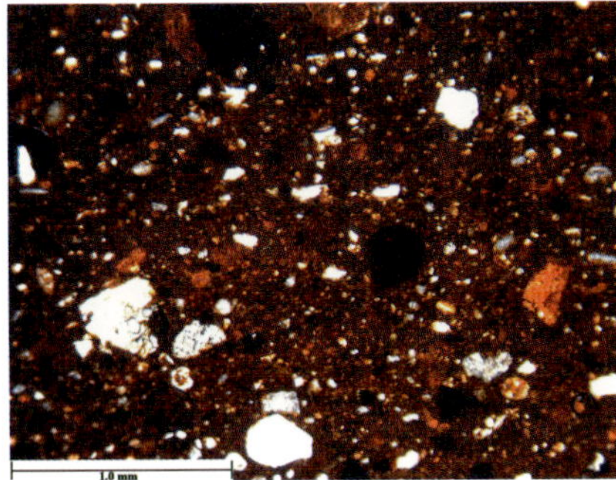
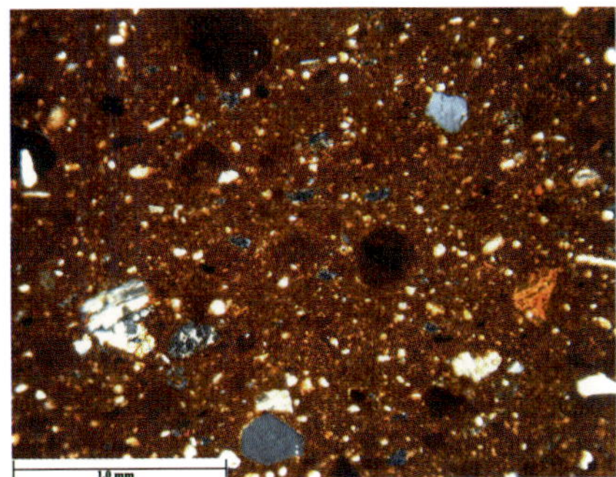

Macroscopic Description

Inclusions: sand – fine [1], medium [1]; limestone – fine [1], medium [1], coarse [1]; red-brown rock particles – fine [2], medium [2], coarse [1]; black rock particles – fine [1], medium [2], coarse [1]. Fair sorting, medium porosity, medium hard structure. Vessel wall – 7 mm. Break colour: no zones red. Surfaces: interior surface red, exterior surface red.

Microscopic Description

Colour PPL: light red

Colour XPL: medium red

Frequency of Inclusions (estimated): 5%

Sorting: poor

Size Range: very fine to coarse (0.0625 – 1mm)

Shape Range: subrounded to angular (quartz), subrounded to subangular (limestone)

Main Inclusions: quartz, plagioclase, limestone (micritic), iron oxides, opaques, geode quartz, and serpentine

Additional Inclusions Present: iron-rich inclusions, igneous rock fragments, calcite, chalcedony, and pyroxenes

Comments: iron rich shale with serpentine and igneous inclusions, low firing temperature

Sample Number: 92/861.001

Macroscopic Description

Inclusions: sand – fine [1], medium [1]; limestone – fine [1], medium [1]; red-brown rock particles – fine [2], medium [1]; black rock particles – fine [1]; microfossils. Fair sorting, dense porosity, medium hard structure.

Vessel wall – 6 mm. Break colour: no zones red. Surfaces: interior surface red, exterior surface red.
Microscopic Description
Colour PPL: light red
Colour XPL: medium red
Frequency of Inclusions (estimated): 5%
Sorting: poor
Size Range: very fine to coarse (0.0625 – 1mm)
Shape Range: subrounded to angular (quartz), subrounded to subangular (limestone)
Main Inclusions: quartz, plagioclase, limestone (micritic), iron oxides, opaques, and serpentine
Additional Inclusions Present: iron-rich inclusions, igneous rock fragments, calcite, geode quartz, and pyroxenes
Comments: iron rich shale with serpentine and igneous inclusions, low firing temperature

Sample Number: 92/864.001

Macroscopic Description
Inclusions: sand – fine [2], medium [1]; limestone – fine [2], medium [2]; black rock particles – fine [1], medium [1]. Fair sorting, medium porosity, medium hard structure. Vessel wall – 4 mm. Break colour: no zones greyish brown. Surfaces: interior surface yellowish brown, exterior surface greyish brown.
Microscopic Description
Colour PPL: dark brown
Colour XPL: very dark brown
Frequency of Inclusions (estimated): 10%
Sorting: poor
Size Range: very fine to medium (0.0625 – 0.5mm)
Shape Range: subrounded to angular (quartz), rounded to subangular (limestone)
Main Inclusions: quartz, limestone (micritic and sparry), eroded foraminifers, iron oxides, and opaques
Additional Inclusions Present: clay pellets and chert
Comments: hamra with quartz and large limestone, low firing temperature

Sample Number: 93/814.007

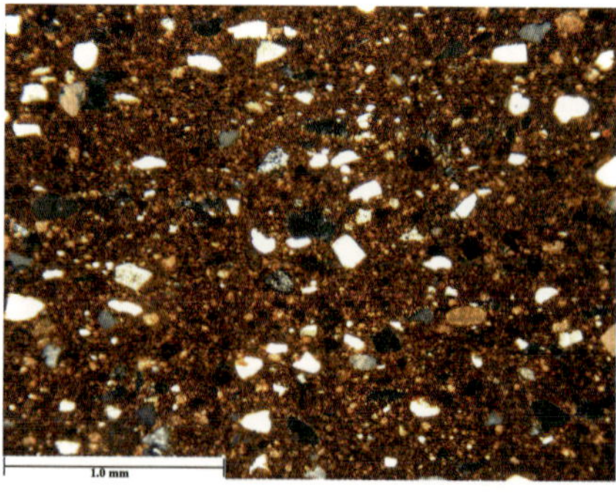

Macroscopic Description
Inclusions: sand – fine [2], medium [1], coarse [1]; limestone – fine [1], medium [1]; black rock particles – fine [1]. Fair sorting, medium porosity, medium hard structure. Vessel wall – 7 mm. Break colour: core very dark grey, outer zones brown. Surfaces: interior surface brown, exterior surface yellowish brown.

Microscopic Description
Colour PPL: medium reddish tan
Colour XPL: medium reddish tan
Frequency of Inclusions (estimated): 20%
Sorting: fair
Size Range: very fine to medium (0.0625 – 0.5mm)
Shape Range: subrounded to very angular (quartz), rounded to subrounded (limestone)
Main Inclusions: quartz, limestone (micritic), iron oxides, and opaques
Additional Inclusions Present: chalcedony, geode quartz, pyroxenes, serpentine, and volcanic glass?
Comments: rendzina clay with *terra rossa* and quartz temper, low firing temperature

Sample Number: 93/894.005

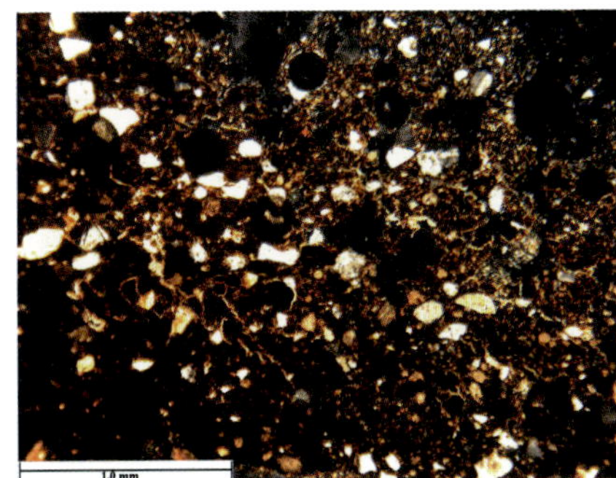

Macroscopic Description
Inclusions: sand – fine [2]; limestone – fine [1]; red-brown rock particles – fine [1]; black rock particles – fine [1]. Good sorting, medium porosity, medium hard structure. Vessel wall – 4 mm. Break colour: no zones brown. Surfaces: interior surface brown, exterior surface dark brown.
Microscopic Description
Colour PPL: dark reddish tan
Colour XPL: very dark reddish tan
Frequency of Inclusions (estimated): 20%
Sorting: fair
Size Range: very fine to medium (0.0625 – 0.5mm)
Shape Range: subrounded to angular (quartz), subrounded (limestone)
Main Inclusions: quartz, limestone (micritic), iron oxides, and opaques
Additional Inclusions Present: geode quartz and serpentine
Comments: rendzina with *terra rossa* and quartz temper, low firing temperature

Sample Number: 94/310.010

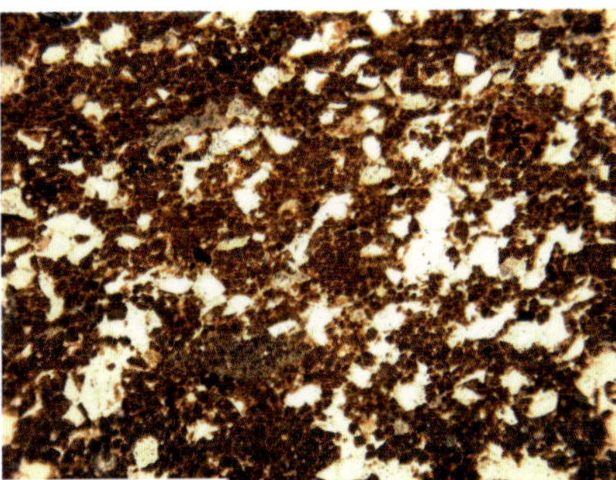
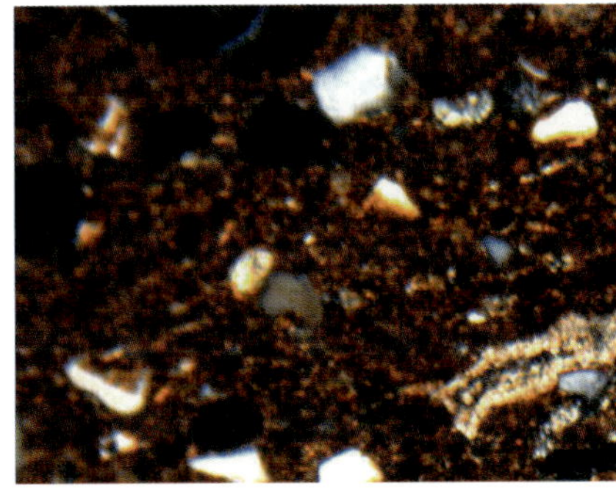

Macroscopic Description
Inclusions: sand – fine [3], medium [1]; limestone – fine [1], medium [1], coarse [1]; red-brown rock particles – fine [1]; black rock particles – fine [1]. Poor sorting, medium porosity, medium hard structure. Vessel wall – 4 mm. Break colour: no zones yellowish red. Surfaces: interior surface yellowish brown, exterior surface very dark brown.

Microscopic Description
Colour PPL: medium reddish tan
Colour XPL: medium reddish tan
Frequency of Inclusions (estimated): 20%
Sorting: fair
Size Range: very fine to coarse (0.0625 – 1mm)
Shape Range: subrounded to angular (quartz), rounded to subrounded (limestone)
Main Inclusions: quartz, limestone (micritic), iron oxides, and opaques
Additional Inclusions Present: geode quartz and serpentines
Comments: rendzina with *terra rossa* and quartz temper, low firing temperature

Sample Number: 94/324.011

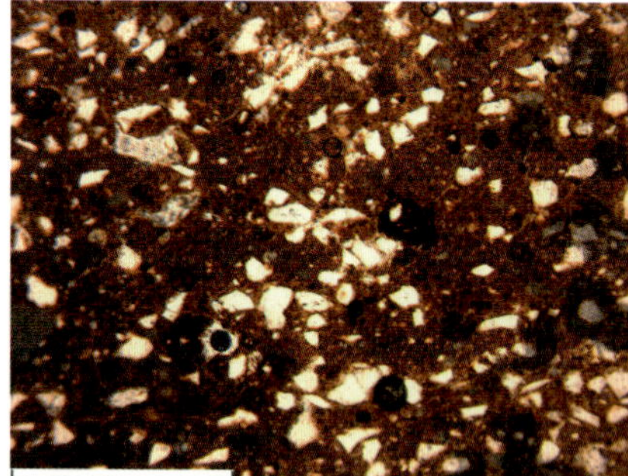

Macroscopic Description
Inclusions: sand – fine [2], medium [1]; limestone – fine [1], medium [1], coarse [1]; red-brown rock particles – fine [1]; black rock particles – fine [1]. Fair sorting, medium porosity, medium hard structure. Vessel wall – 5 mm. Break colour: no zones yellowish red. Surfaces: interior surface reddish yellow, exterior surface very dark grey.
Microscopic Description
Colour PPL: medium reddish tan
Colour XPL: medium reddish tan
Frequency of Inclusions (estimated): 20%
Sorting: fair
Size Range: very fine to coarse (0.0625 – 1mm)
Shape Range: subrounded to angular (quartz), rounded to subrounded (limestone)
Main Inclusions: quartz, limestone (micritic), iron oxides, and opaques
Additional Inclusions Present: geode quartz, pyroxenes, and serpentine
Comments: rendzina with *terra rossa* and quartz temper, low firing temperature

Sample Number: 94/379.001

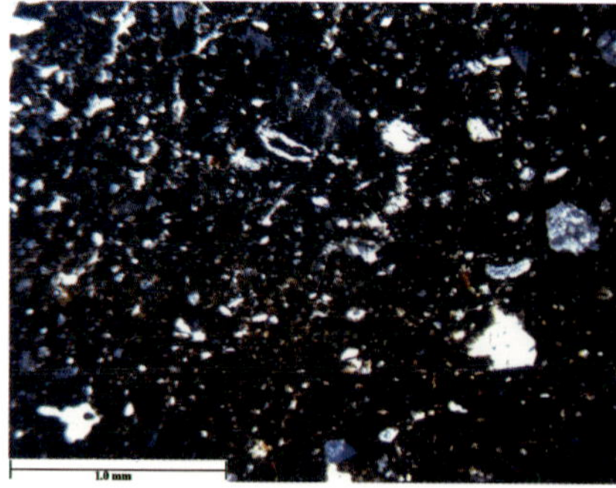
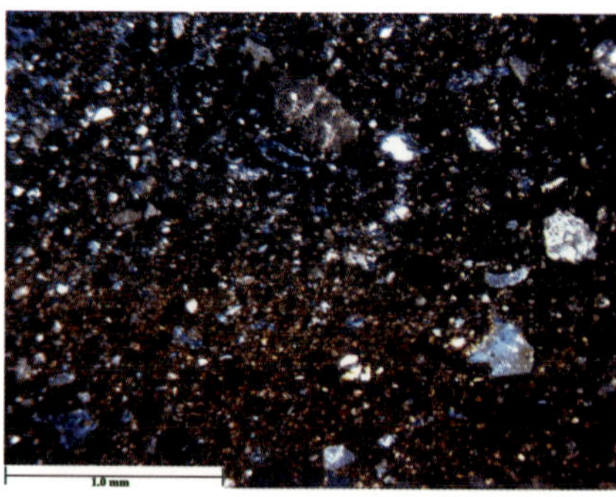

Macroscopic Description
Inclusions: sand – fine [2], medium [1], coarse [1]; plant remains – fine [1]; limestone – fine [1]; red-brown rock particles – fine [1], medium [1]; black rock particles – fine [1]. Fair sorting, medium porosity, medium hard structure. Vessel wall – 4 mm. Break colour: interior zone dark brown, exterior zone reddish brown. Surfaces: interior surface greyish brown, exterior surface dark brown.

Microscopic Description
Colour PPL: medium brown
Colour XPL: medium brown
Frequency of Inclusions (estimated): 5%
Sorting: poor
Size Range: very fine to medium (0.0625 – 0.5mm)
Shape Range: subrounded to angular (quartz), subrouned to subangular (limestone)
Main Inclusions: quartz, plagioclase, limestone (micritic and sparry), iron oxides, and opaques
Additional Inclusions Present: chert, geode quartz, burnt plant remain, shell, serpentine, and weathered volcanic rock fragment
Comments: rendzina no temper, low firing temperature

Sample Number: 01/118.018

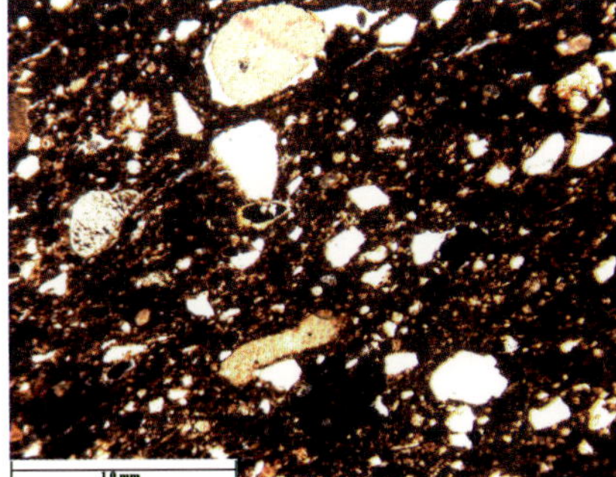
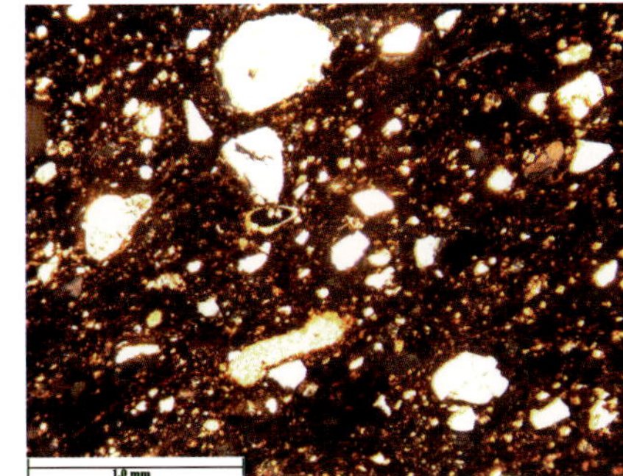

Macroscopic Description
Inclusions: sand – fine [1], medium [1]; limestone – fine [1], medium [1], coarse [1]; red-brown rock particles – fine [1], medium [1], coarse [1]; black rock particles – fine [2], medium [1], coarse [1]. Poor sorting, medium porosity, medium hard structure. Vessel wall – 12 mm. Break colour: interior zone dark yellowish brown, exterior zone red. Surfaces: interior surface brown, exterior surface red.
Microscopic Description
Colour PPL: dark brown to dark red
Colour XPL: very dark brown to very dark red
Frequency of Inclusions (estimated): 10%
Sorting: poor
Size Range: very fine to very coarse (0.0625 – 2mm)
Shape Range: subangular to angular (quartz), rounded to subrouned (limestone)
Main Inclusions: quartz, polycrystalline quartz, K-feldspars, limestone (micritic and sparry), eroded foraminifers, iron oxides, and opaques
Additional Inclusions Present: clay pellets, geode quartz, and chert
Comments: hamra with quartz and large limestone, low firing temperature

Sample Number: 01/337.001

Macroscopic Description
Inclusions: sand – fine [2], medium [1], coarse [1]; limestone – fine [2], medium [2], coarse [1]; red-brown rock

particles – fine [1], medium [1]; black rock particles – fine [2], medium [1]. Poor sorting, medium porosity, medium hard structure. Vessel wall – 4 mm. Break colour: interior zone grey, exterior zone red. Surfaces: interior surface grey, exterior surface brown.

Microscopic Description

Colour PPL: dark brown to dark red

Colour XPL: very dark brown to very dark red

Frequency of Inclusions (estimated): 10%

Sorting: poor

Size Range: very fine to coarse (0.0625 – 1mm)

Shape Range: subangular to angular (quartz), rounded to subrouned (limestone)

Main Inclusions: quartz, polycrystalline quartz, K-feldspars, limestone (micritic and sparry), eroded foraminifers, iron oxides, and opaques

Additional Inclusions Present: clay pellets and chert, chlorite?

Comments: hamra with quartz and large limestone, low firing temperature

Sample Number: 01/350.001

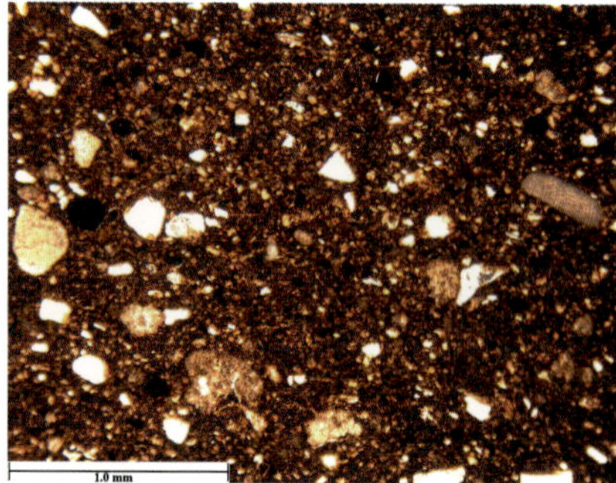

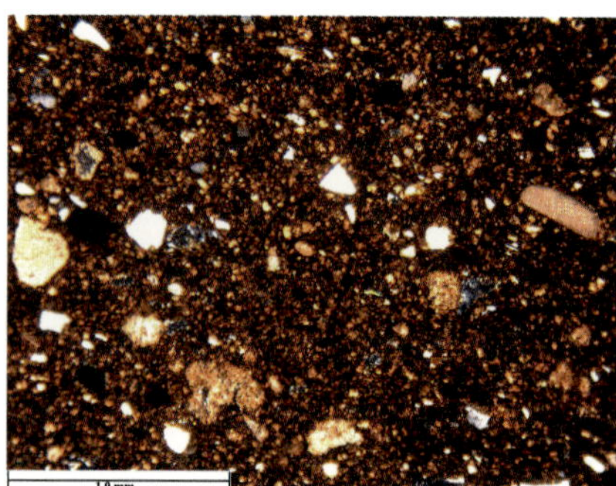

Macroscopic Description

Inclusions: sand – fine [1], medium [1], coarse [1]; plant remains – fine [1]; limestone – fine [1]; black rock particles – fine [1], medium [1]. Fair sorting, medium porosity, medium hard structure. Vessel wall – 6 mm. Break colour: interior zone greyish brown, exterior zone brown. Surfaces: interior surface brown, exterior surface dark brown.

Microscopic Description

Colour PPL: medium brown

Colour XPL: medium brown

Frequency of Inclusions (estimated): 5%

Sorting: poor

Size Range: very fine to coarse (0.0625 – 1mm)

Shape Range: subrounded to angular (quartz), subrounded to subangular (limestone)

Main Inclusions: quartz, plagioclase, limestone (micritic and sparry), calcite, iron oxides, opaques, and pyroxenes

Additional Inclusions Present: weathered volcanic rock fragment, one bioclast (Amphiroa?), and plant remains?

Comments: rendzina no temper, low firing temperature

Sample Number: 01/350.002

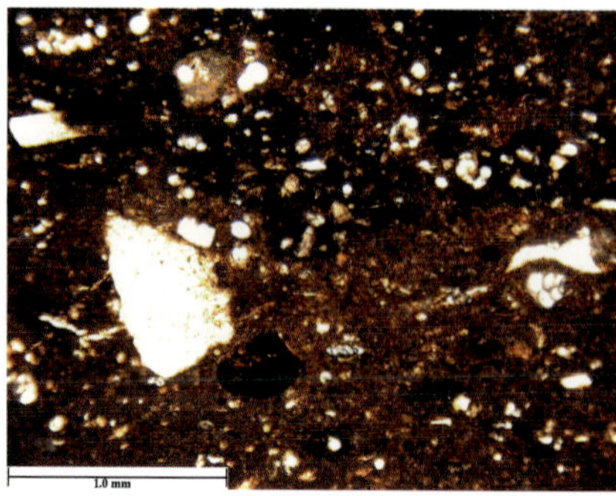

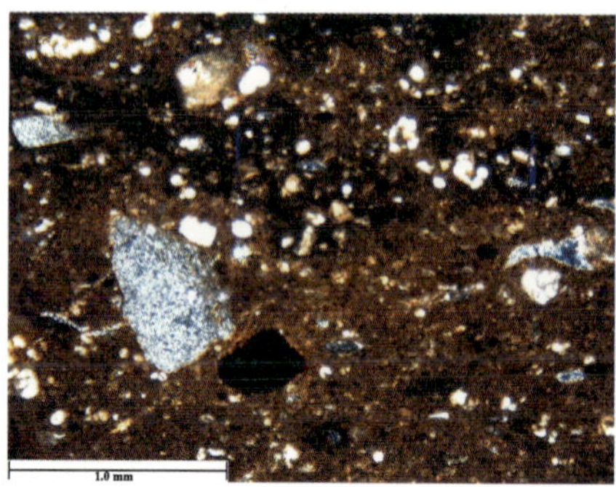

Macroscopic Description
Inclusions: sand – fine [1], medium [1]; limestone – fine [2], medium [1], coarse [1]; red-brown rock particles – coarse [1]; black rock particles – fine [1], medium [1], coarse [1]. Poor sorting, medium porosity, medium hard structure. Vessel wall – 7 mm. Break colour: interior zone dark grey, exterior zone greyish brown. Surfaces: interior surface dark grey, exterior surface dark greyish brown.
Microscopic Description
Colour PPL: medium reddish brown
Colour XPL: dark reddish brown
Frequency of Inclusions (estimated): 5%
Sorting: poor
Size Range: very fine to very coarse (0.0625 – 2mm)
Shape Range: subrounded to subangular (quartz), subrounded to subangular (limestone)
Main Inclusions: limestone (foraminiferous, micritic, and sparry), calcite, foraminfers (*Globigerina, Globigerinoides, Bulimina?*), iron oxides, opaques, and chert
Additional Inclusions Present: quartz, clay pellets, and burnt shell?
Comments: foraminiferous marl with *terra rossa*, low firing temperature

Sample Number: 04/110.002

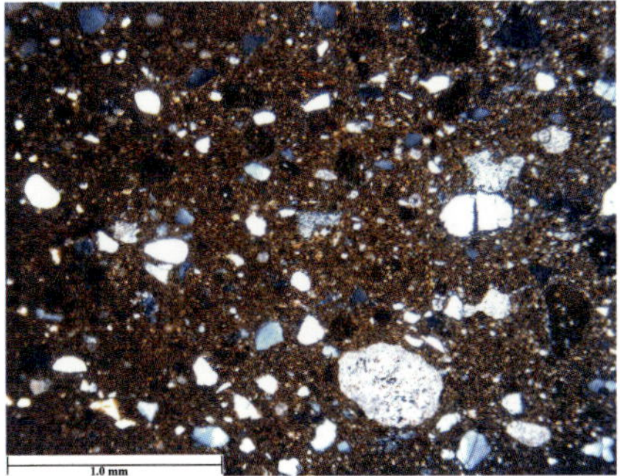

Macroscopic Description
Inclusions: sand – fine [2], medium [1]; limestone – fine [1], medium [1]; red-brown rock particles – fine [2], medium [1]; black rock particles – fine [1]. Good sorting, medium porosity, medium hard structure. Vessel wall – 6 mm. Break colour: no zones yellowish red. Surfaces: interior surface yellowish red, exterior surface reddish brown.
Microscopic Description
Colour PPL: medium reddish tan
Colour XPL: medium reddish tan
Frequency of Inclusions (estimated): 20%
Sorting: fair
Size Range: very fine to medium (0.0625 – 0.5mm)
Shape Range: subrounded to angular (quartz), rounded to subrounded (limestone)
Main Inclusions: quartz, limestone (micritic), iron oxides, and opaques
Additional Inclusions Present: iron-rich oolite, chert, pyroxenes, and serpentine
Comments: rendzina with *terra rossa* and quartz temper, low firing temperature

Sample Number: 04/111.001

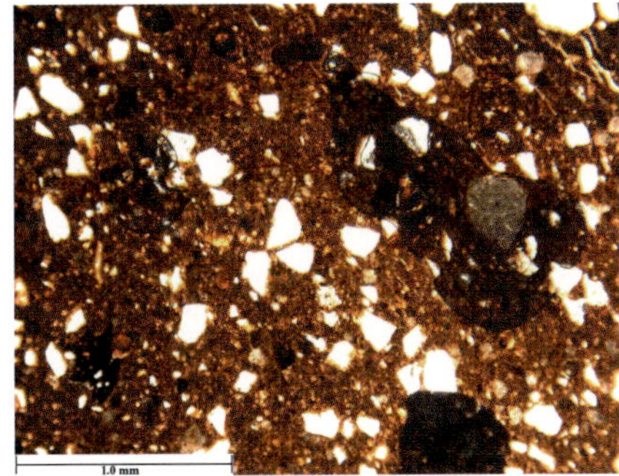

Macroscopic Description
Inclusions: sand – fine [3], medium [1]; limestone – fine [1], medium [1]; red-brown rock particles – fine [1], medium [1]; black rock particles – fine [1], medium [1]. Good sorting, medium porosity, medium hard structure. Vessel wall – 8 mm. Break colour: interior zone brown, exterior zone red. Surfaces: interior surface brown, exterior surface very dark brown.
Microscopic Description
Colour PPL: medium reddish tan
Colour XPL: medium reddish tan
Frequency of Inclusions (estimated): 20%
Sorting: fair
Size Range: very fine to medium (0.0625 – 0.5mm)
Shape Range: subrounded to angular (quartz), rounded to subrounded (limestone)
Main Inclusions: quartz, limestone (micritic), iron oxides, and opaques
Additional Inclusions Present: geode quartz, pyroxenes, and serpentine
Comments: rendzina with *terra rossa* and quartz temper, low firing temperature

Sample Number: 08/420.001

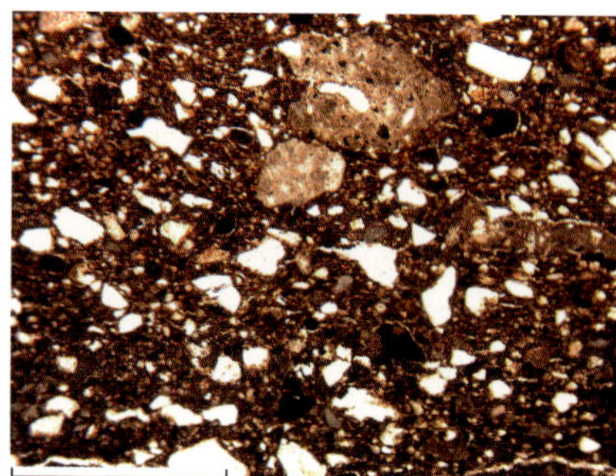
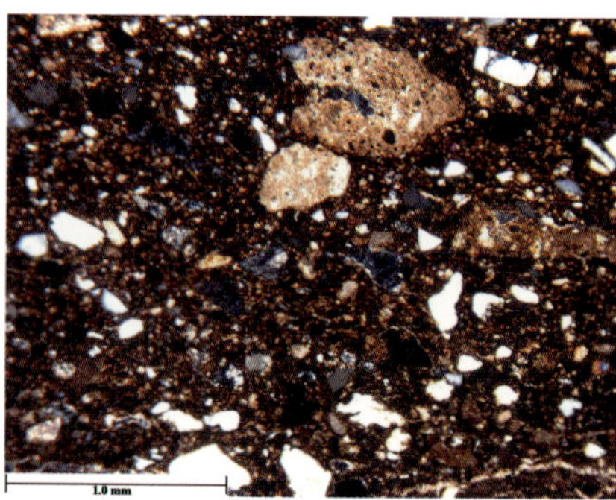

Macroscopic Description
Inclusions: sand – fine [2], medium [1]; plant remains – fine [1]; limestone – fine [2]; red-brown rock particles – fine [1]; black rock particles – fine [2]. Fair sorting, medium porosity, medium hard structure. Vessel wall – 4 mm. Break colour: no zones greyish brown. Surfaces: interior surface yellowish brown, exterior surface brown.
Microscopic Description
Colour PPL: medium brown
Colour XPL: medium brown
Frequency of Inclusions (estimated): 10%
Sorting: poor
Size Range: very fine to coarse (0.0625 – 1mm)
Shape Range: subrounded to angular (quartz), subrounded to subangular (limestone)
Main Inclusions: quartz, plagioclase, limestone (micritic and sparry), calcite, foraminifers (*Bulimina?*), opaques, geode quartz, chert, chalcedony, and pyroxenes
Additional Inclusions Present: igneous rock fragment
Comments: rendzina with possible quartz temper, low firing temperature

VI. Contents Analyses of Tell el-Yahudiya Vessels

The following study on chemical analyses of contents remaining in Tell el-Yahudiya jugs and other containers from Tell el-Dab^{c}a was submitted on 14th of April 1986. It was reappraised and approved by the author on 26th of January 2011.

Laborbericht

Rolf Rottländer

Von der Grabung in Tell el-Dab^{c}a erhielten wir von Herrn Prof. M. Bietak, Kairo, 14 Proben von Gefäßen, die dem Mittleren Reich angehören, zur Untersuchung. Die Proben wurden extrahiert und das erhaltene Rohfett wurde umgeestert, um die für die gaschromatographischen Trennungen benötigten Fettsäuremethylester zu erhalten. Außerdem wurde auf Dünnschichtplatten eine Trennung zum Nachweis von Cholesterin durchgeführt.

Labor-Nr. 979: Probe A/II-n/19, Grab Nr. 5 aus einer kanaanäischen Amphore Außenbeigabe 2, Bauschicht absolut E/1, krustenartige Masse
Cholesterin: schwach positiv; nur wenig Fett vorhanden (Rohfettmenge 18,79 mg)

Das Fett ist sehr stark zersetzt. Cholesterin deutet auf die Anwesenheit von Tierfett hin. Weil aber kein Tierfett mehr (oder auch nur gleich viel) Linolsäure als Ölsäure hat, muss neben dem Tierfett ursprünglich ein Pflanzenfett als Hauptmenge vorgelegen haben. Die große Menge Palmitoleinsäure ist als Abbaustufe einer Fettsäure mit 18 C-Atomen zu interpretieren. Da Linolsäure leichter als Ölsäure abgebaut wird, Linolsäure aber immer noch stärker als die Ölsäure vertreten ist, muss die Palmitoleinsäure wohl auf ehemalige Linolsäure zurückgeführt werden. Eine so stark veränderte Zusammensetzung lässt sich aber nicht mehr scharf identifizieren. Als Fette mit viel Linolsäure und wenig Stearinsäure kommen die Samenfette von: Eichel, Haselnuss, Walnuss und den Getreidearten infrage. Da in Ägypten Bäume und Sträucher nur spärlich vertreten waren, liegt *Getreidefett* nahe.

Zuordnung wegen der starken Fettzersetzung *unsicher*.

Zu dieser Probe sollte man darauf hinweisen, dass wir in einer römischen Amphore wider Erwarten Mehl identifiziert haben. Bei der Bierbereitung, die möglich erscheint, gerät natürlich das Samenöl des Braugetreides, sei es Weizen oder Gerste, mit in das Produkt, wobei es nicht weiter verändert wird. Wenn also Getreidefett gefunden wurde, ist das mit dem Befund „Bier" durchaus verträglich, nur dass eben das Bier als solches nicht nachweisbar ist. Opiate entfallen.

Labor-Nr. 980: Probe F/I-i/22, Grab 33, Beigabe Nr. 1 einer Infans I – Embryobestattung, ausgeschlemmter Inhalt eines großen Tell el-Yahudiya-Kruges. Es wurde dabei destilliertes Wasser verwendet. Str. b/2–3
Cholesterin: schwach positiv; (Rohfettmenge 5,00 mg)

Das Fett dieser probe ist weniger zersetzt als das Fett der Probe 979, dennoch wird Zersetzung wegen des hohen Anteils von Palmitoleinsäure und des Gehalts an Myristinsäure deutlich. Alleinige Anwesenheit von Pflanzenfett scheidet sowohl wegen des Cholesteringehaltes als auch wegen des Anteils von 16 % Stearinsäure aus, was für Pflanzen zu hoch ist. Auf der anderen Seite ist ein Anteil von 17 % Linolsäure für ein Tierfett zu hoch. Daher liegt ein Gemisch von Pflanzen- und Tierfett vor.

Wenn auch für Ägypten eine gewisse Wahrscheinlichkeit dafür besteht, dass ein höherer Anteil Linolsäure auf *Getreide* zurückgeführt werden kann, so ist damit eine sichere Zuordnung noch nicht gegeben.

Auffällig ist der Anteil von Arachinsäure, der uns an sich nur vom Mohn, *Mensch* (hier am Stärksten und von der Elefantenhaut her bekannt ist. Allerdings *reicht* auch dieser Befund *nicht für* eine sichere *Zuordnung aus.* Zur Probe, Labor-Nr. 980, haben wir noch weitere Versuche angestellt. Wir beschafften und Morphin und haben in der Probe gezielt danach gesucht. Der Befunde jedoch war negativ, sodass „Mohn" nicht zu erhärten ist. Andererseits ist unbekannt, wie lange sich Opiate unzersetzt halten.

Labor-Nr. 981: Probe F/I-i/22, Grab 34, Fund Nr. 6 aus rotpoliertem Krug; Str. c/1
Cholesterin: schwach positiv; (Rohfettmenge 2,76 mg)

Auch hier liegt ein zersetztes Fett vor, wie aus dem Myristinsäuregehalt und dem hohen Anteil Palmitoleinsäure deutlich wird. Wenn auch der geringe

Gehalt an Erucasäure zeigt, dass ein schwacher Anteil an *Cruciferen*-Samenfett ursprünglich vorhanden war, so ist doch die Hauptmenge des Fetts Tierfett, wie der hohe Anteil an Stearinsäure (rund 13 %) und der sehr geringe Anteil an Linolsäure zeigt, der ebenso wie der Anteil Linolensäure auf das Cruciferenfett zurückzuführen ist.

Als die Tierfett-Komponente scheiden die Fette von Bison, Geflügel, Hammel, Mensch, Pferd, Rind und Ziege aus. Die größte Ähnlichkeit haben wir mit zwei gealterten Fetten gefunden: Knochenfett eines subrezenten *Rehs* und Knochenfett eines römischen *Hausschweins* (rezentes Hausschwein ist wenig wahrscheinlich).

Wegen der Vermischung und teilweisen Zersetzung des Fettes ist eine *absolut sichere* Zuordnung *nicht* möglich, doch ist die Wahrscheinlichkeit der Zuordnung höher als bei den beiden anderen proben. Ob aus ökologischen Gründen Reh ausgeschlossen werden kann, entzieht sich meiner Kenntnis. Wenn für Labor-Nr. 981 Schweinefett in den Bereich der Wahrscheinlichkeit rückt, und Cruciferenfett sicher ist, so sollte das keinesfalls im Widerspruch mit der Zweckbestimmung „Droge" stehen, da auch heute noch Salbenanreibungen auf Schweinefettbasis mit anderen Samenölen (z.B. ist mir Ringelblume bekannt) vom Volke benutzt werden. Kompliziertere Fettgemische lassen sich ohnehin nicht mehr in die Komponenten zerlegen. Eine Suche nach Morphin verlief negativ.

Labor-Nr. 1658: Probe Nr. 73, Krug rotpoliert (Rohfettmenge 2,69 mg)
GC 6046 N‘, 6078 F“, Cholesterin positiv

Labor-Nr. 1661: Probe Nr. 79, bemalter Krug (Rohfettmenge 8,07 mg)
GC 6052 N‘, 6083 F“, Cholesterin deutlich positiv

Labor-Nr. 1664: Probe Nr. 97, Krug braunpoliert (Rohfettmenge 31,88 mg)
GC 6099 N‘, 6088 F“, Cholesterin positiv

Labor-Nr. 1665: Probe Nr. 98, Krug braunpoliert-inkrustiert (Rohfettmenge 12,77 mg)
GC 6057 N‘, 6089“, Cholesterin deutlich positiv

Im Kurvenverlauf haben diese Proben große Ähnlichkeiten, weswegen sie zusammen behandelt werden. Sie stammen alle aus Krügen. In Probe 1658 war ein gelber Farbstoff zu sehen, der allerdings nicht löslich ist. Andererseits ergab sich aus den Proben 1664 und 1665 ein gelber Farbstoff.

Darüber hinaus unterscheiden sich die Proben 1658 und 1661 dadurch von den beiden anderen, dass sie Cetylalkohol enthalten, der für Fische charakteristisch ist. Trotz dieses Umstandes und trotz des mehr oder minder deutlichen Cholesterinnachweises liegt Tierfett nur mit gewissem Anteil vor. Der hohe Stearinsäureanteil (C 18) ist nämlich teilweise auf eine Fettzersetzung zurückzuführen. Der Anteil von Linolsäure (C 18-2) um 10 % oder etwas geringer jedenfalls zeigt einen Anteil Pflanzenfett. Da Linolsäure der gegen Zersetzung empfindlichste Anteil der vorliegenden Fettsäuren ist, muss gerade ihr Anteil vorher höher gewesen sein. Wahrscheinlich ist mit einem Teil Getreidefett zu rechnen. Ob der untergeordnete Anteil Fischfett eine spätere Kontamination ist, d.h. ob er während der Bodenlagerung in die Proben geriet, oder ob er mit Fischen (oder Meereskrustaceen) vom Menschen in die Probe gebracht wurde, lässt sich von der Analyse her nicht entscheiden, sondern ergibt sich eventuell aus dem Kontext.

Labor-Nr. 1667: Probe Nr. 46, Amphore (Weinrelikt oder Olivenölrelikt ? auch Bier nicht ausgeschlossen) (Rohfettmenge 3,04 mg)
GC 6098 N‘, 6091 F“, Cholesterin deutliche positiv

Es handelt sich um die Füllung einer Amphore. Der sehr hohe Anteil von Stearinsäure (C 18) bei 22 % würde auf Wiederkäuerfett schließen lassen, wenn nicht ein Rest Linolsäure (C 18-2) ehemals vorhandenes Pflanzenfett und damit stärkere Zersetzung andeuten würde. Nach Würdigung der Umstände hat demnach die Amphore Olivenöl, jedoch weder Wein noch Bier enthalten.

Labor-Nr. 1660: Probe Nr. 78, bemalter Krug (Rohfettmenge 3,04 mg)

GC 6051 N‘ , 6082 F“ , Cholesterin deutlich positiv

Labor-Nr. 1662: Probe Nr. 95, Krug rotpoliert (Rohfettmenge 7,50 mg)
GC 6055 N‘, 6084 F“, Cholesterin positiv

Bei diesen Proben handelt es sich um Inhalte aus Krügen. Zwar ist der generelle Kurvenverlauf gleich, doch bestehen auch Unterschiede: Probe 1660 enthält Cetylalkohol, also Fischfett, Probe 1662 einen löslichen gelben Farbstoff, den wir auch in anderen Proben angetroffen haben. Stearinsäure (C 18) etwas über 10 % zeigt an, dass Tierfett nur untergeordnet vorhanden sein kann; Linolsäure (C 18-2) zeigt, dass Pflanzenfett vorhanden sein muss, allerdings vermengt. Ein Anteil Olivenöl unter dem Pflanzen fett ist nicht auszuschließen.

Labor-Nr. 1663: Probe Nr. 96, Krug schwarzpoliert inkrustiert (Rohfettmenge 15, 59 mg)
GC 6056 N' , 6087 F" , Cholesterin positiv

Die Probe stammt aus einem schwarz polierten Krug mit Inkrustation. Auch in ihr wurde der gelbe Farbstoff angetroffen. Reste von Linolsäure (C 18-2) fanden sich nicht. Der Anteil Ölsäure (C 18-1) ist mir 21 % gering. Dementsprechend zeigt ein Anteil von 22 % Palmitoleinsäure eine intensive Fettumwandlung an. Der Anteil Stearinsäure ist vergleichsweise tief, sodass auf ein pflanzliches fett als ehemalige Hauptkomponente rückzuschließen ist. Olivenöl ist nicht auszuschließen.

Labor-Nr. 1666: probe Nr. 143, Krug schwarzpoliert (Rohfettmenge 19,10 mg)
GC 6060 N' , 6090 F" , Cholesterin positiv

Auch diese Fettprobe aus einem schwarzpolierten Krug enthält den löslichen gelben Farbstoff. Die Probe weicht von den voraufgehenden durch einen Gehalt von knapp 10 % Behensäure (C 22) ab. Diese Säure kommt in Senföl, Erdnussöl, Leberöl und Rapsöl vor.

Senf- und Rapsöl scheiden hier aus, weil Erucasäure (C 22-1) fehlt, die in allen Cruciferen anzutreffen ist. Die Zusammensetzung ist mit einem zersetzten Erdnussöl verträglich, während Leberöl ausscheidet, weil es keine entsprechenden Anteile Linolsäure (C 18-2) enthält.

Labor-Nr. 1657: Probe Nr. 7, aus großem Tell el-Yahudiya-Krug (Rohfettmenge 5,65 mg)
GC 6044 N', 6077 F", Cholesterin positiv

Stearinsäure (C 18) ist noch stärker als Ölsäure (C 18-1) vertreten, Linol- und Linolensäure fehlen. Absolut den größten Anteil hat Palmitinsäure (C 16) mit 42 %. Dies sind Charakteristika eines sehr stark zersetzten fettes. Hier liegt wegen Palmitoleinsäure (C 16-1) und Margarinsäure (C 17) wahrscheinlich ein Tierfett vor. Weil aber der Stearinsäureanteil (C 18) wegen der starken Zersetzung in seiner Höhe nicht aussagekräftig ist, kann das Tierfett nicht näher spezifiziert werden.

Labor-Nr. 1659: Probe Nr. 76 (Rohfettmenge 11,12 mg)
GC 6050 N', 6081 F", Cholesterin deutlich positiv

Die Probe ist der voraufgehenden Probe 1657 ähnlich und auch ähnlich stark zersetzt, allerdings ließ sich Cetylalkohol nachweisen. Damit ist Fischfett als Fettbestandteil erkannt.

Die Identifikation des gelben Farbstoffs soll nicht heißen, dass die Substanz intentionell zum Färben gedient hat; die gelbe Farbe kann accidentiell sein) bereitet größerer Schwierigkeiten. Wir haben bisher eine UV-Spektrum, visuelles Spektrum, IR-Spektrum und Massenspektrum angefertigt respektive anfertigen lassen. Vom Doerner-Institut, München, erhielten wir eine Computer-Wahrscheinlichkeitsliste, die nichts erbrachte. Das Molekulargewicht liegt bei 410. Die farbaktive Gruppe ist eine $R_3C - CO - CO - CR_3$ – Konfiguration. Nach IR-Spektrum und Massenspektrum sollte ein aromatischer Kern vorhanden sein. Die Farbsubstanz ist in all den Proben, in denen wir sie fanden, einheitlich. Es handelt sich nur um *einen* Stoff, wie durch Gas- und Dünnschichtchromatographie erwiesen. Weitere Säure- oder Alkoholfunktionen liegen nicht vor. Damit wissen wir allerdings noch nicht positiv, um welches Molekül es sich handelt. Auf 22 Substanzen respektive Pflanzenfarbstoffe haben wir mit negativem Ergebnis geprüft (Tabelle 1).

Unsere Botaniker wissen nichts Weiteres. Moderne Synthesefarbstoffe sollten wohl ausscheiden. Die aufgefundenen Fette lassen keine eingeengtere Zuordnung zu, als bei der jeweiligen Beschreibung angegeben, wie z.B. Olivenöl

Bei Getreidefett muss man natürlich außer an Getreide selbst an Bier denken.

Wo vermengte Fette vorliegen, muss man in der Regel davon ausgehen, dass die Gefäße auch wechselnde Füllungen gehabt haben. Das macht den Befund natürlich in dem Sinne undeutlich, als dass man nicht eine einzige Quelle für das Fett angeben kann.

Alizarin	Curcuma	Genista tinctoria (Färberginster)	
Berberize	Fluorescin	Genista Lydia	
Bier	Gelbwurz (Curry)	Henna	
Hundskamille	Kreuzdorn-Beeren	Labkraut, Wald-Sumach	
Ilex	Kreuzdorn-Blätter	Morin	Wau (Färber- , Reseda)
Johanniskraut	Labkraut, gemeines	Safran	Wein
Zwiebel			

Tabelle 1

Literaturhinweis

R. Rottländer, Der Speisezettel der Steinzeitbauern war erstaunlich reichhaltig, *Umschau* 79 (1979) H 23, 752–753.

– Zum Phosphatgehalt keramischer Scherben. *Archaeophysika* 7 (1980) 87–94.

– Investigations into the fat residues of the bones of the Caune de l'Arago at Tautavel, *Prétirage* zum *Colloque de Tautavel* 1981, 677–678.

– New results of food identification by fat analysis, *Proceedings of the 22nd Symposium on Archaeometry,* Bradford 1982, 218–233.

– Investigations chimiques sur les graisses en Archéologie. Traduit et condense par F. Poplin, *Nouvelles de l'Archéologie,* Printemps 1983 No. 11, 38–43.

– Chemische Analyse prähistorischer Gefäßinhalte, *Enzyklopädie Naturwissenschaft und Technik,* Jahresband 1983, 72–80.

– Chemical investigation of potsherds oft he Heuneburg, upper Danube, *Proceedings of the 1984 Archaeometry meeting,* Washington 1984.

– Nachweis und Identifizierung von archäologischen Fetten. Fette, Seifen, *Anstrichmittel* 87 (1985) H. 8, 314–317.

– Gefäßinhaltsuntersuchungen an ausgewählten Typen römischer Keramik vom Magdalensberg, Kärnten, in: H. Vetters, G. Piccottini (Hrsg.), Die *Ausgrabungen auf dem Magdalensberg 1975–1979,* Klagenfurt 1986, 433–445.

– Untersuchungen auf Fettreste an Sedimentproben der Grabung Felsställe, in: C.J. Kind (Hrsg.) 1984: *Das Felsställe,* Teil 2 (1987).

– Die Resultate der Anwendung der modernen Fettanalytik auf die prähistorische Forschung, *Archaeophysika* 12 (1991) 1–354.

– Chemische Untersuchungen an keramischen Funden von der Heuneburg, Obere Donau, *Fundberichte aus Schwaben* 10 (1995) 19–27.

– Laborbericht über die Fettuntersuchungen der Grabung in Tell el-Dab^ca, Ägypten.

– Laborbericht über Fettuntersuchungen der Grabung Rosenhof, Holstein.

R. Rottländer, M. Bluke, Chemische Untersuchungen an Michelsberger Scherben, *Archaeophysika* 7 (1980) 71–86.

R. Rottländer, J. Hahn, Ein Magdalénien-Siedlungshorizont aus dem Helga-Abri, Stadt Schelklingen, Alb-Donau-Kreis, *Archäologische Ausgrabungen in Baden-Württemberg* 1981, 21–26.

R. Rottländer, I. Hartke, Scientific examination of urns of the type with the little cups attached, *Revue d'Archéométrie, Szpllement* 1981, Vol. III, 251–254.

R. Rottländer, H. Müller-Beck, (Hrsg.), Untersuchung von Gefäßinhalten durch Fettanalysen. Ein Symposionsbericht, *Archaeologica Venatoria* 6, Tübingen 1983, 13 ff.

R. Rottländer, H. Schlichtherle, Food identification by analysis of samples from archaeological sites, *Archaeophysika* 10 (1978) 260–267.

– Untersuchung von Gefäßinhalten. Eine kurze kommentierte Bibliografie, *Beihefte Bonner Jahrbücher, Archaeophysika* 7 (1980) 61–70.

– Analyse frühgeschichtlicher Gefäßinhalte, *Die Naturwissenschaften* 70 (1983) H1, 33–38.

PLATES

1. 5971E

4. 5250A

6. 7505A

7. 2518

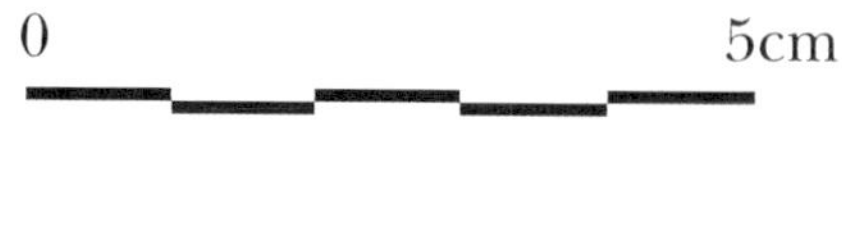

10. 5645

11. 5588

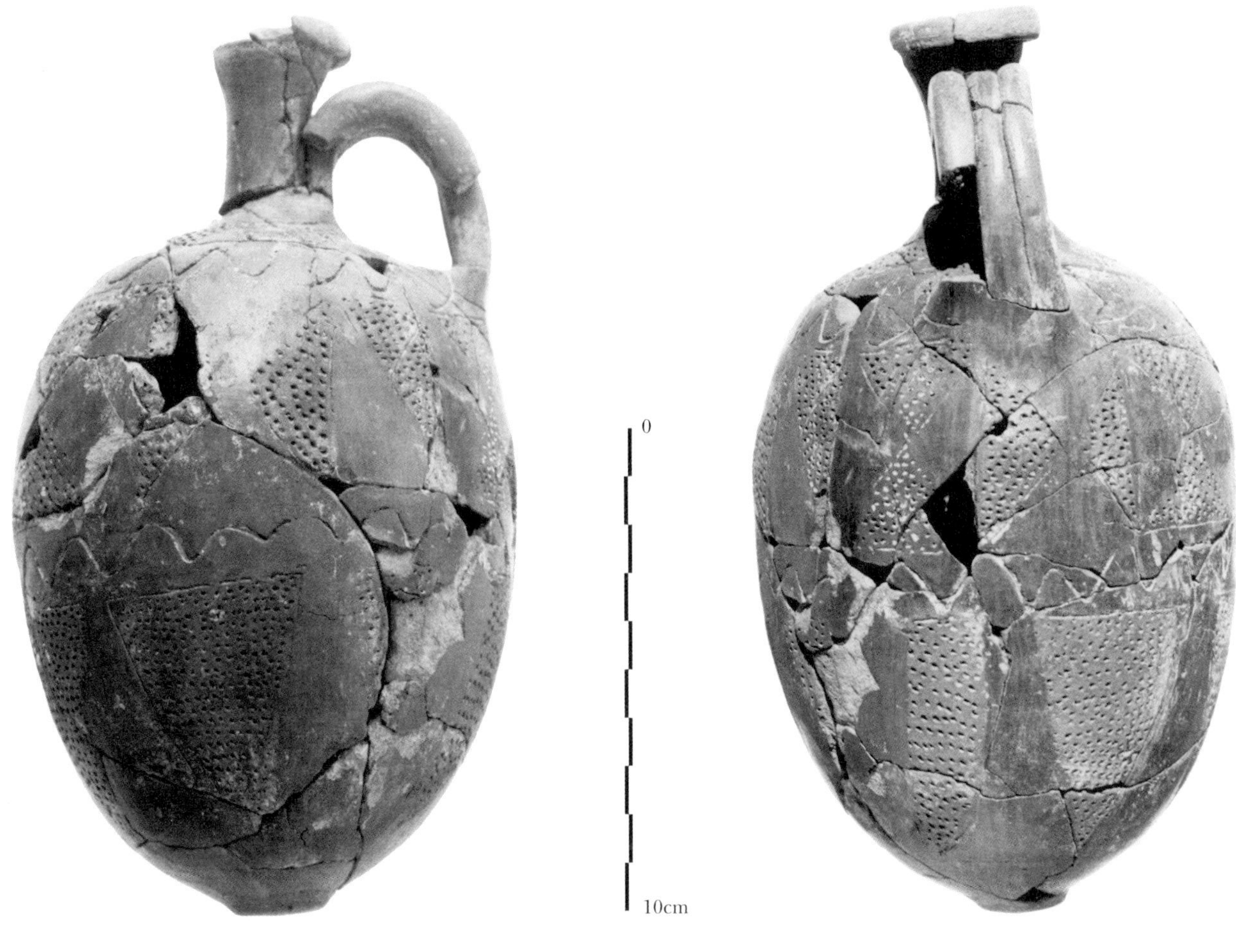

13. 3139

14. 6173

17. 2068

18. 4501

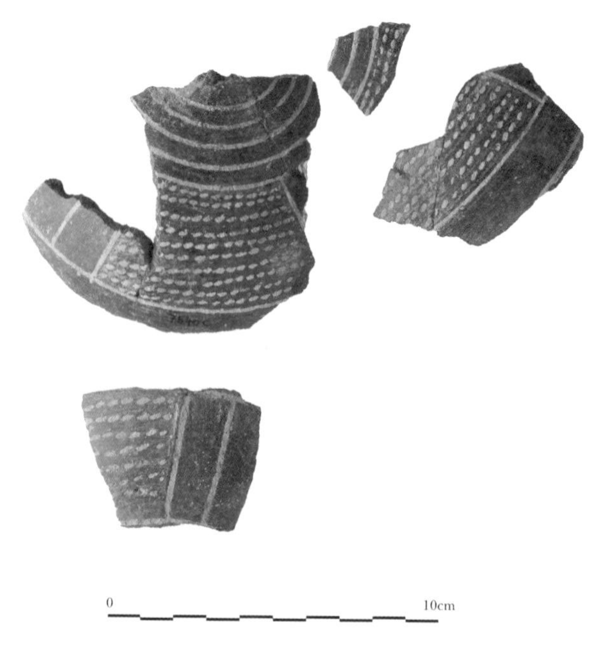

19. 7540C

21. 1609+1610+1611+1734

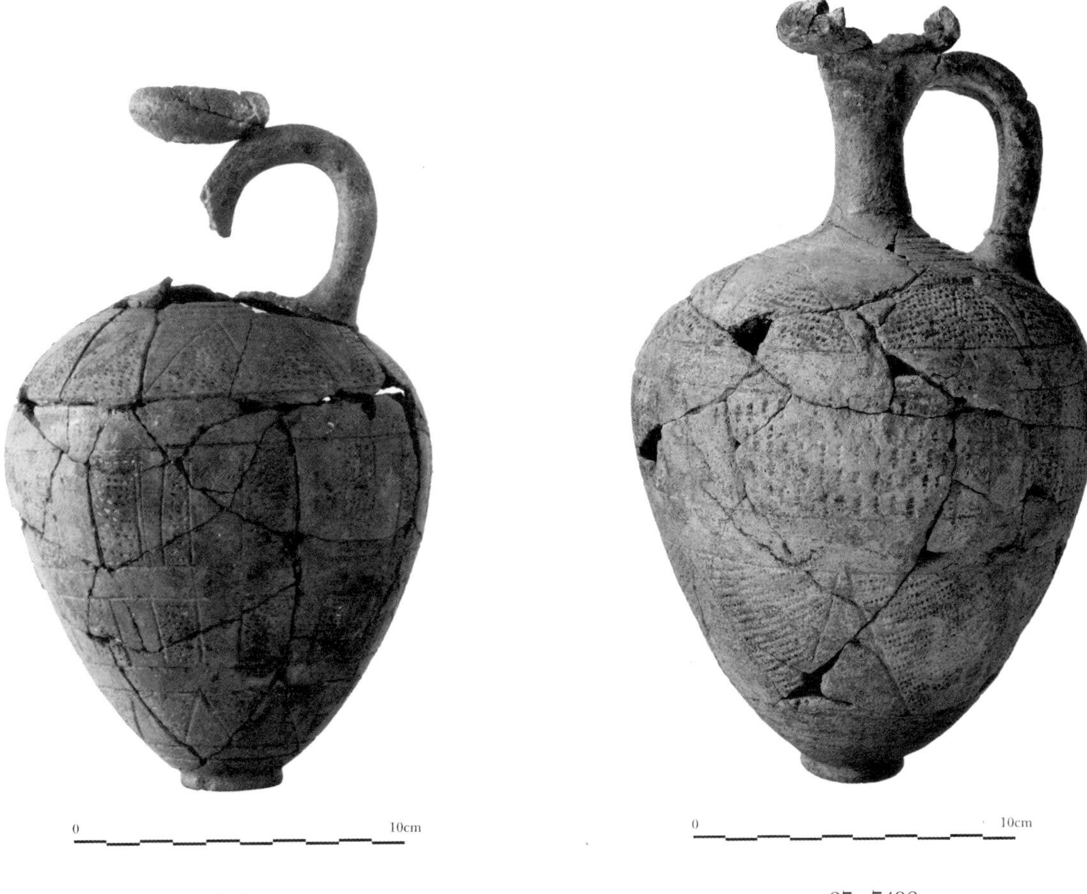

23. 3283

27. 7498

33. 5795

40. 4241

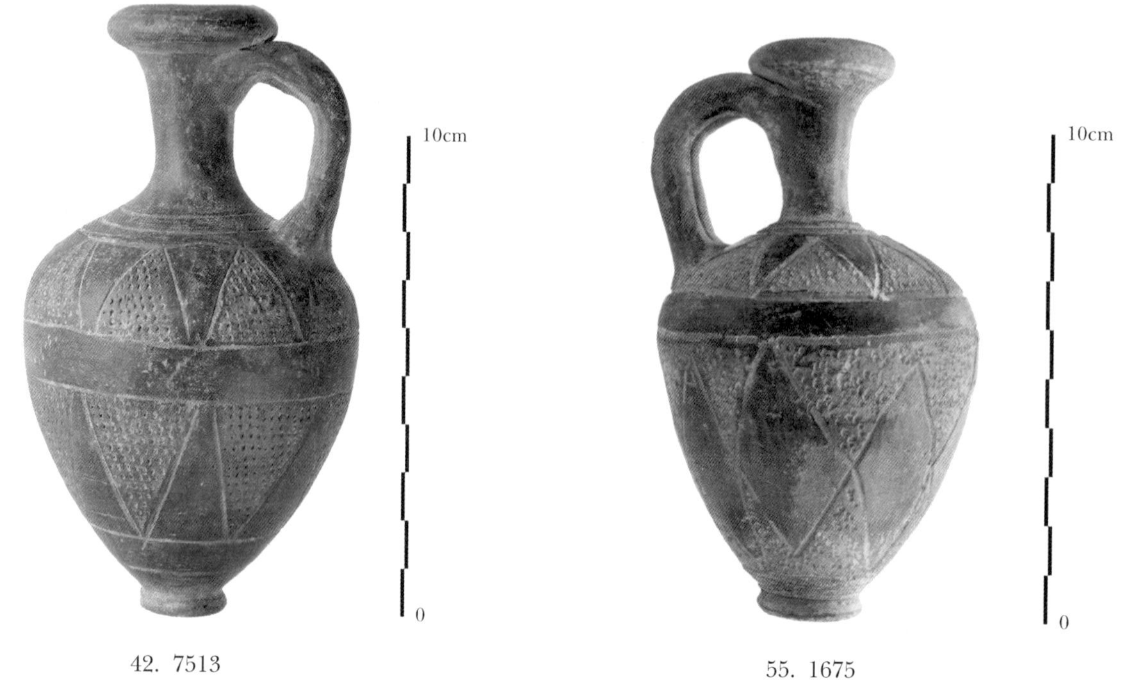

42. 7513

55. 1675

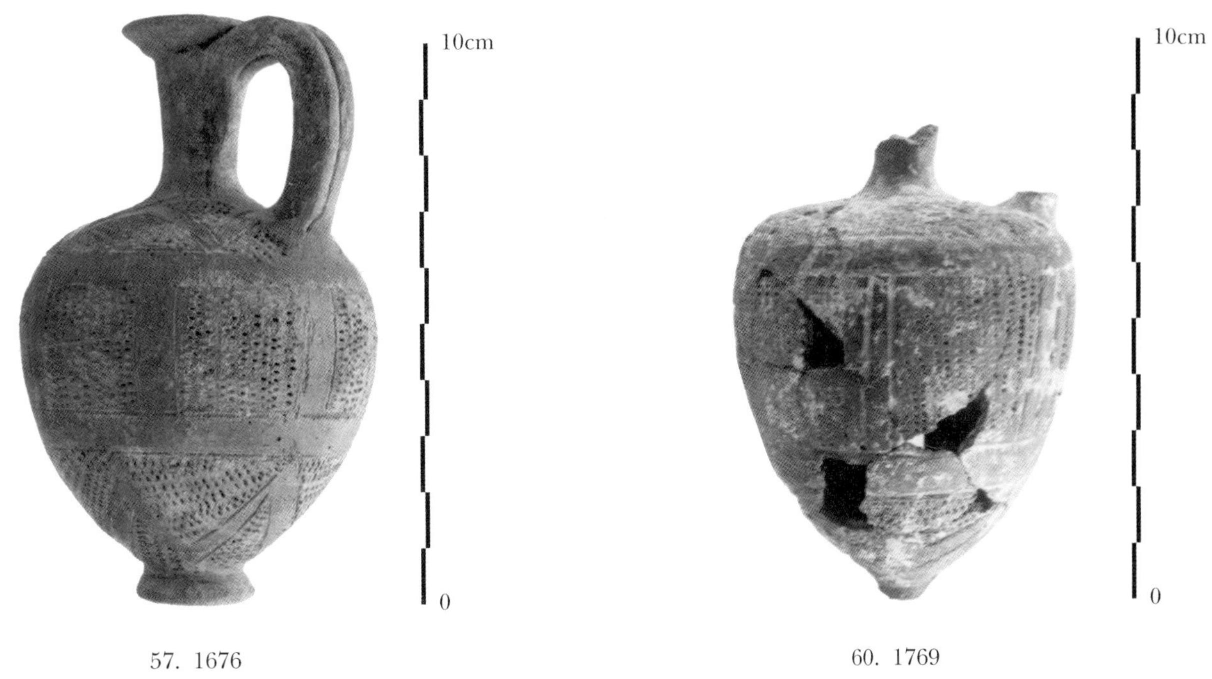

57. 1676

60. 1769

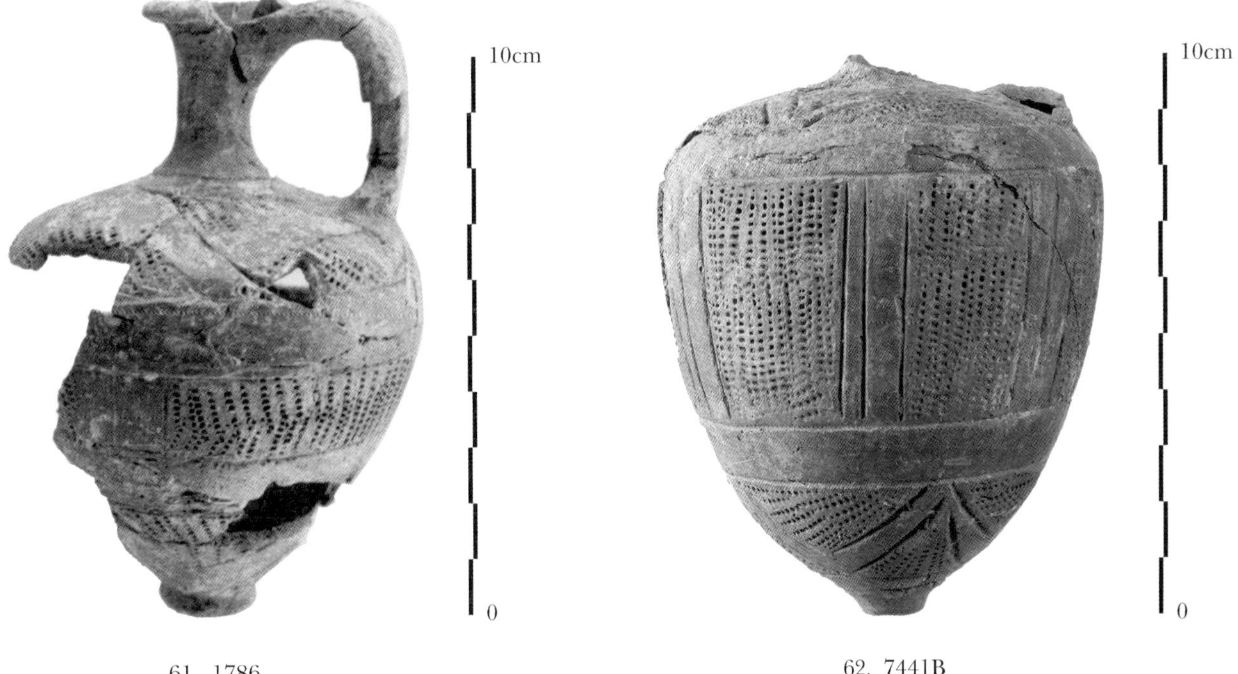

61. 1786

62. 7441B

66. 1758

72. 4435

74. 1841

76. 1839

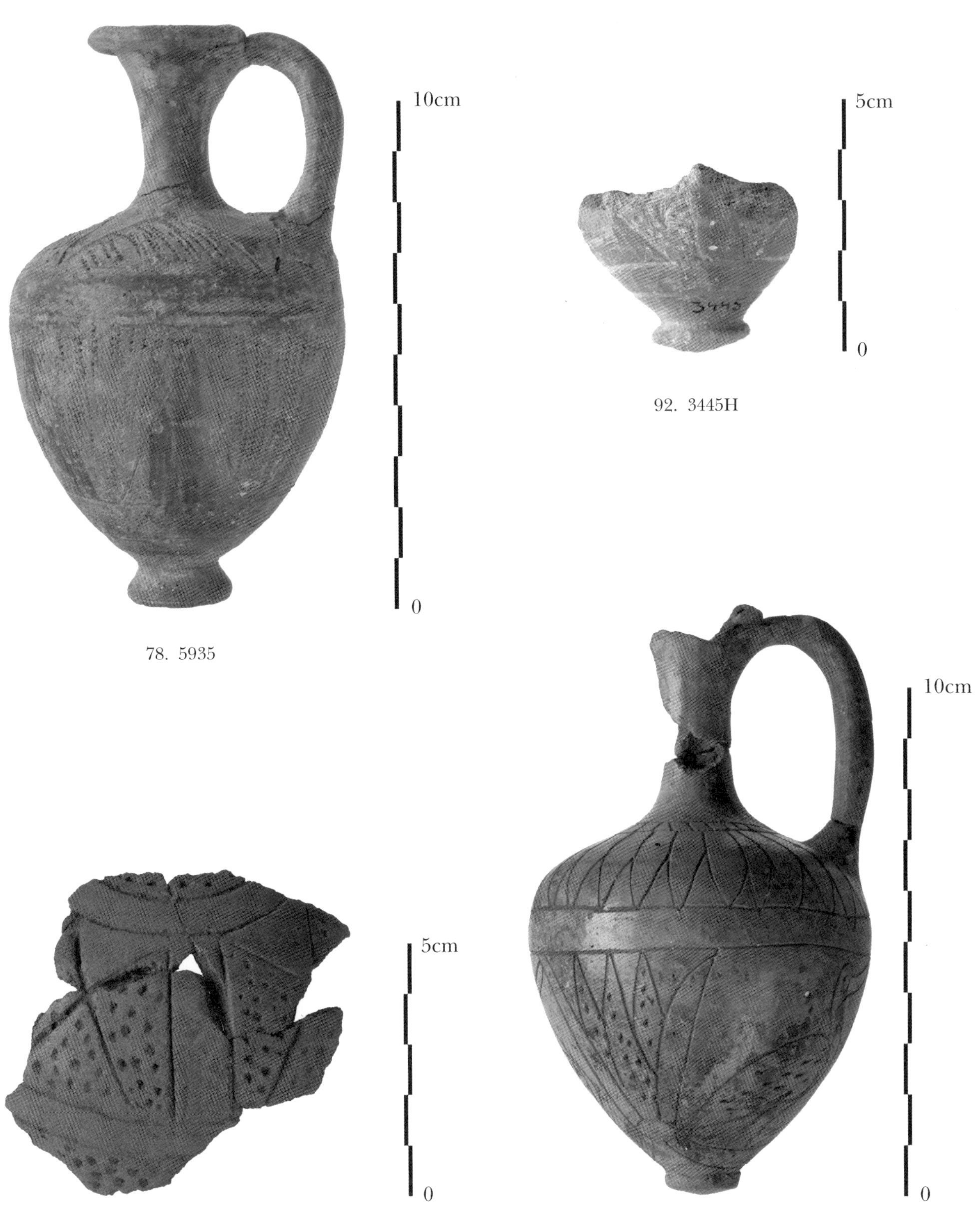

78. 5935

92. 3445H

105. 7597N

117. 7485

115. 7461

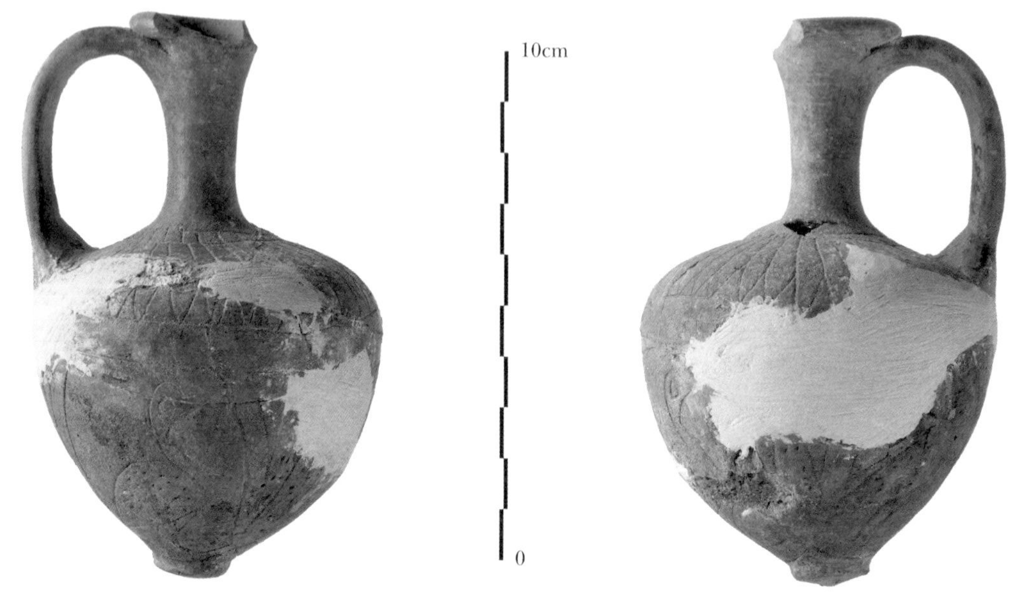

116. 7483

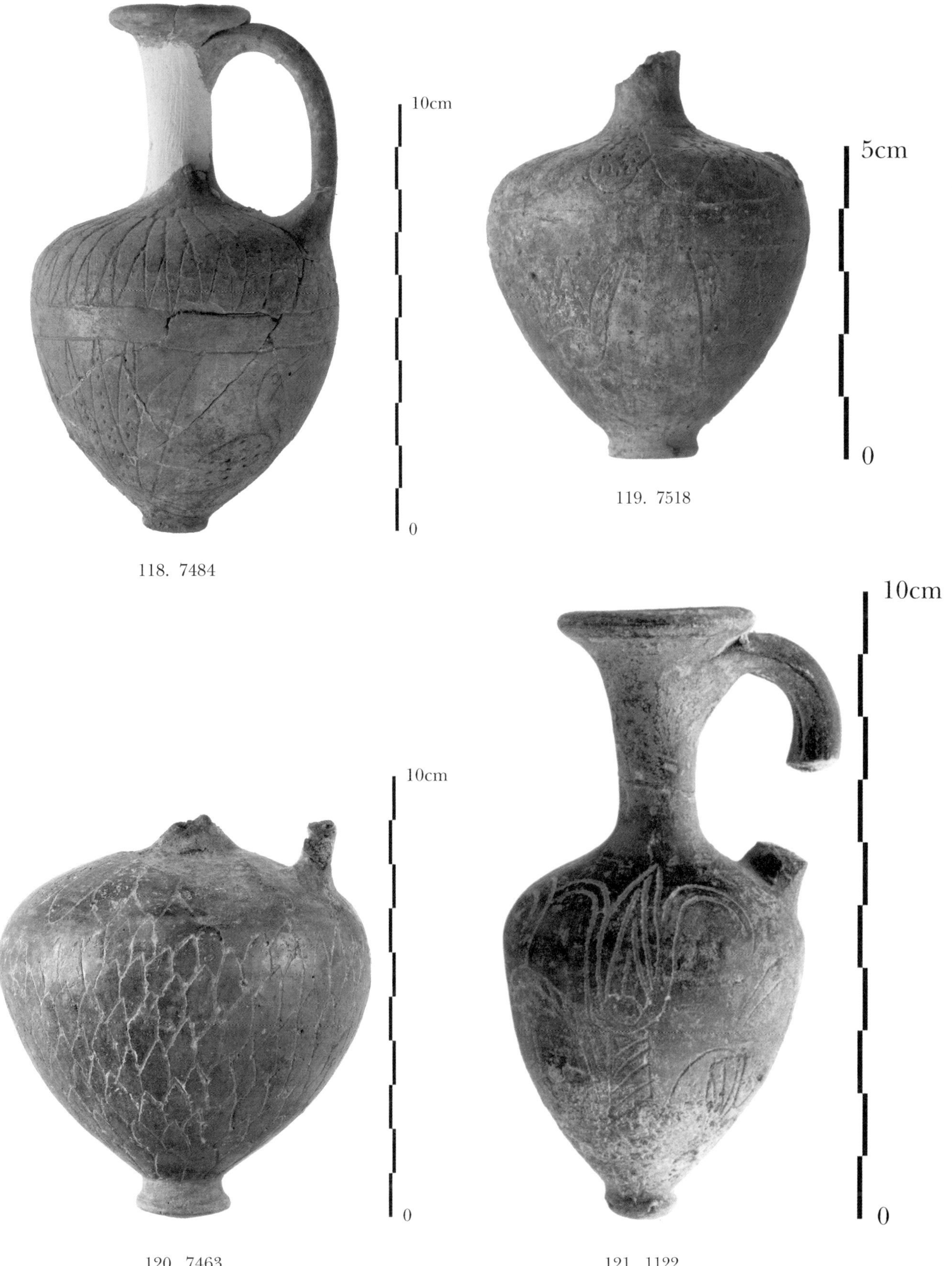

118. 7484

119. 7518

120. 7463

121. 1122

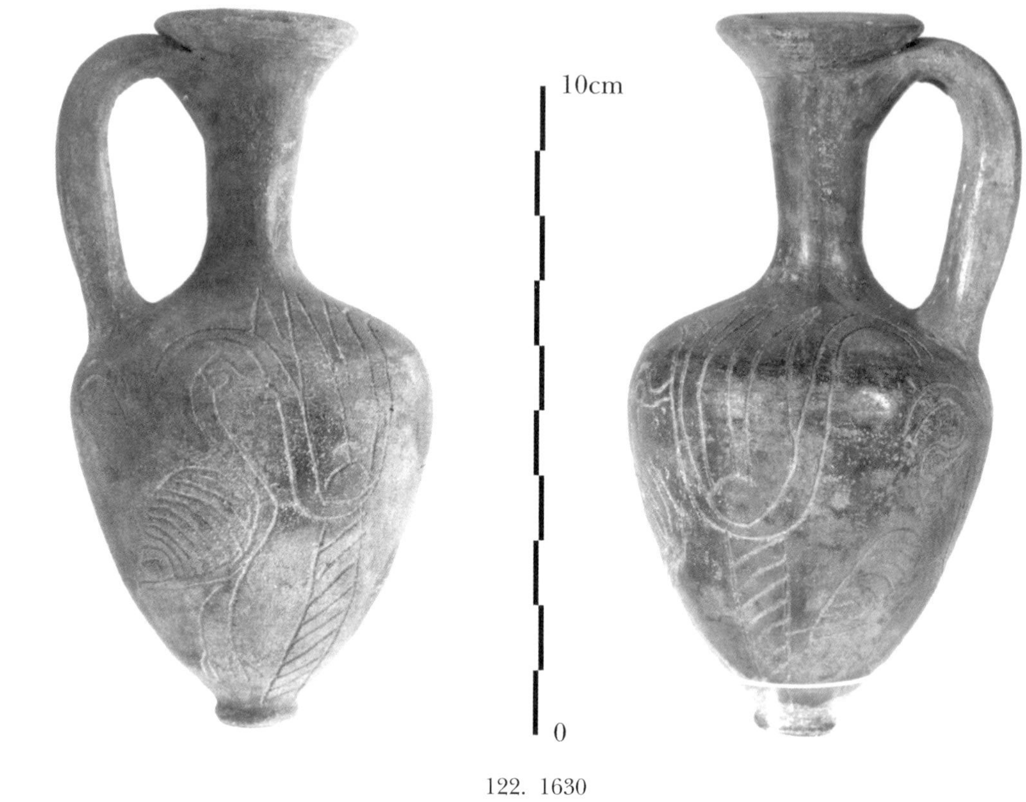

122. 1630

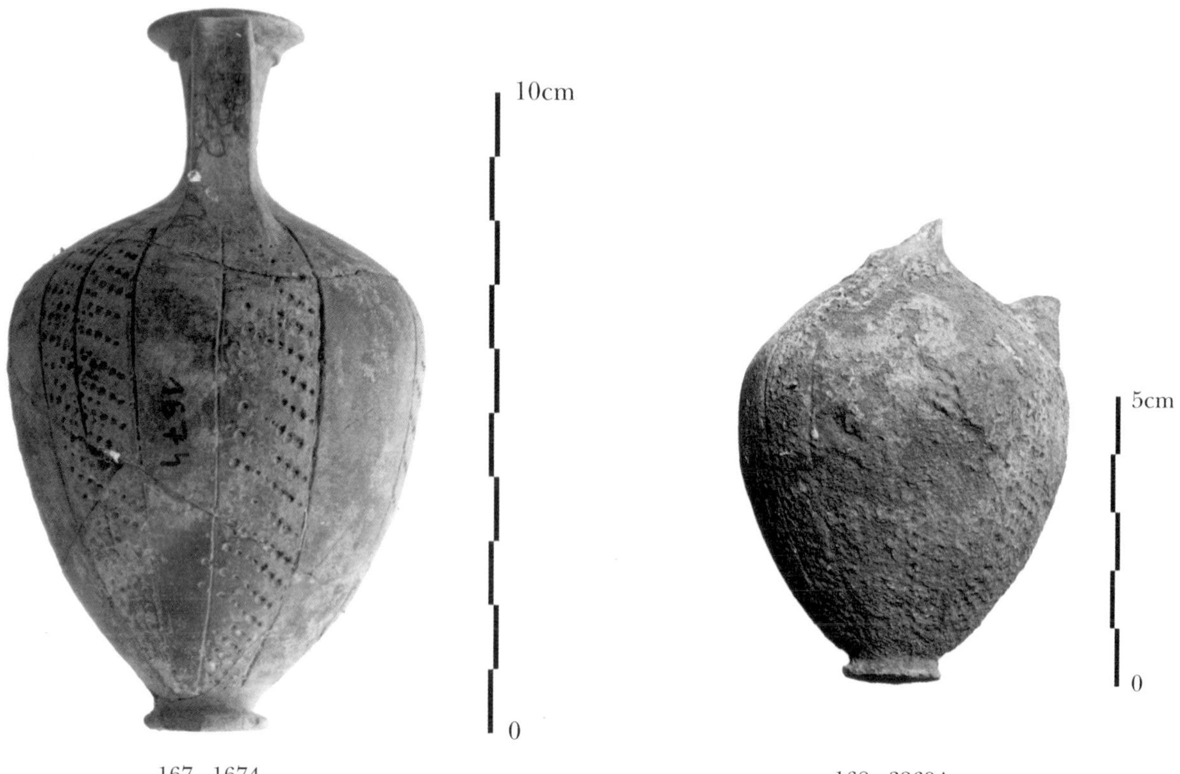

167. 1674

168. 3269A

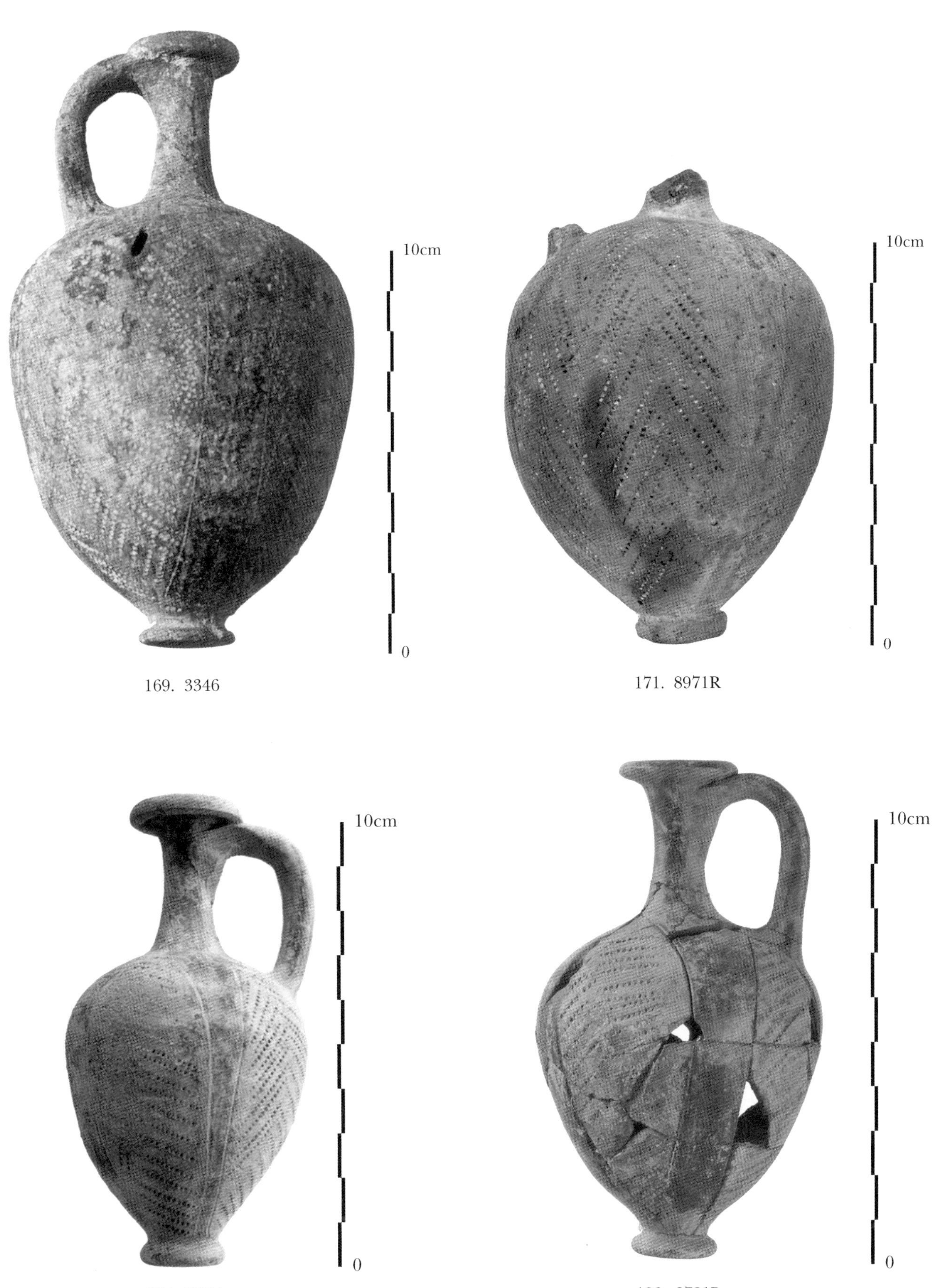

169. 3346

171. 8971R

184. 2154

186. 8781B

232. 5794

270. 0371

278. 5763

291. 2164

332. 9180

339. 0875

342. 5417

344. 2275

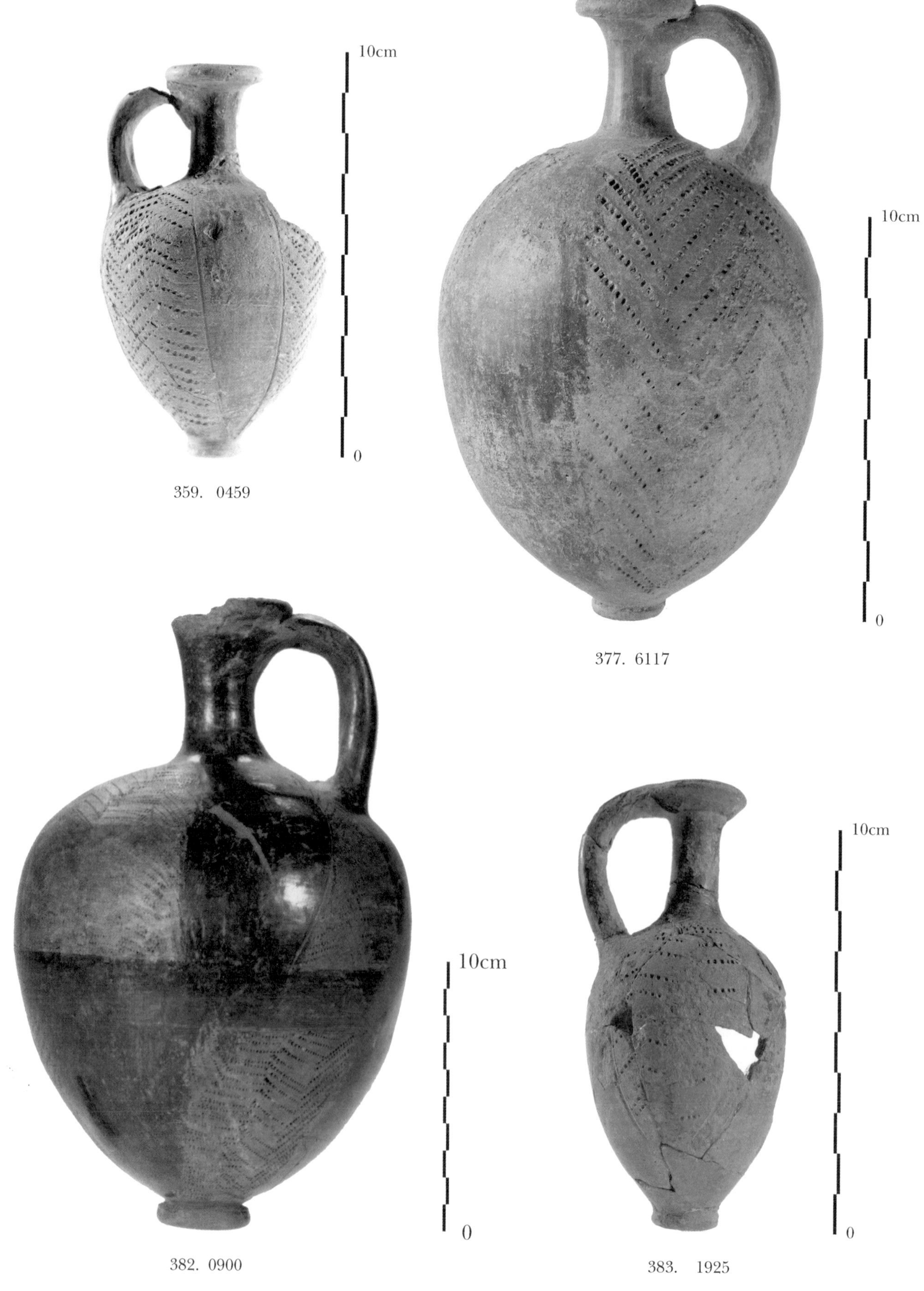

359. 0459

377. 6117

382. 0900

383. 1925

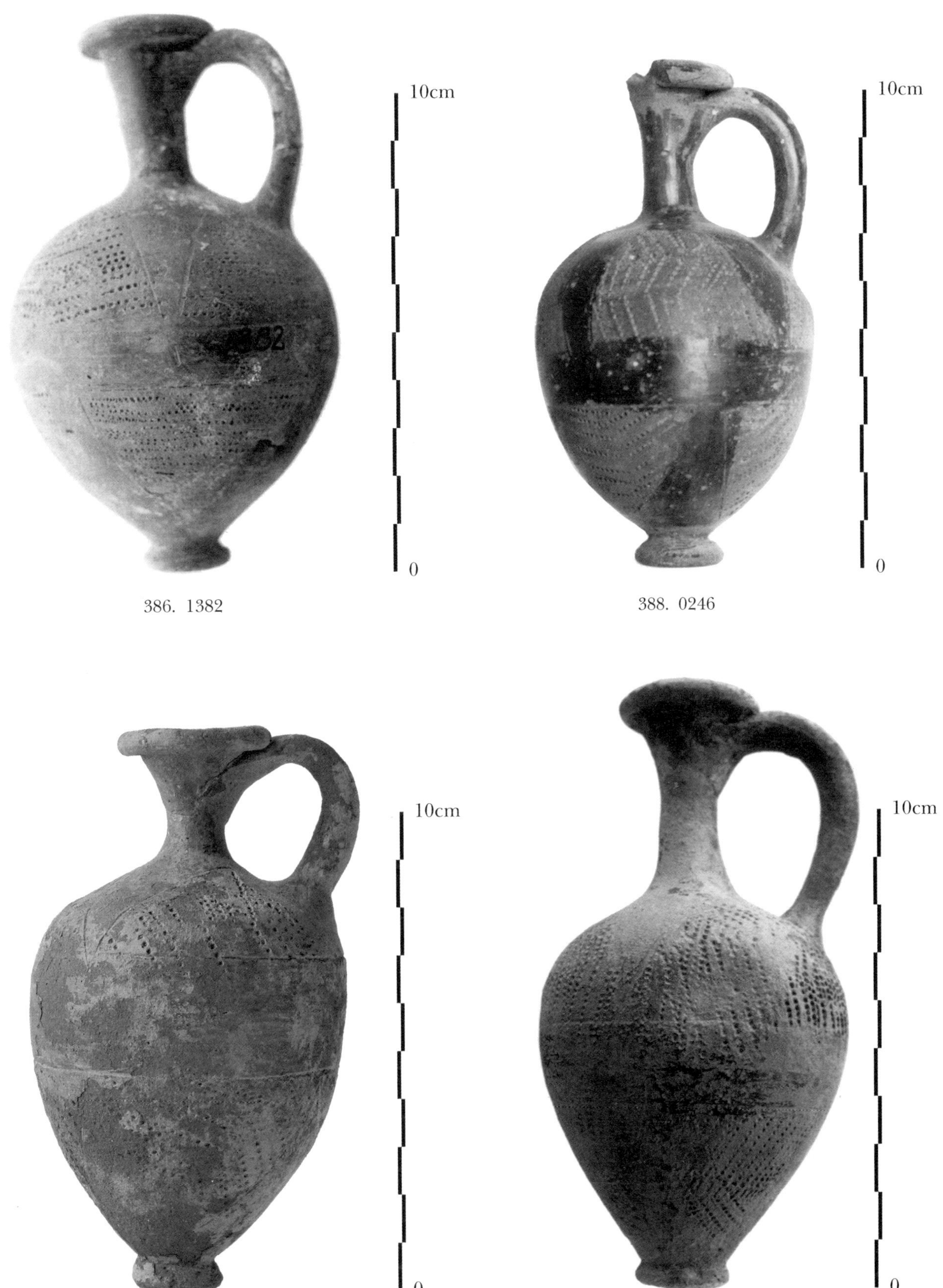

386. 1382

388. 0246

391. 8674

392. 2055

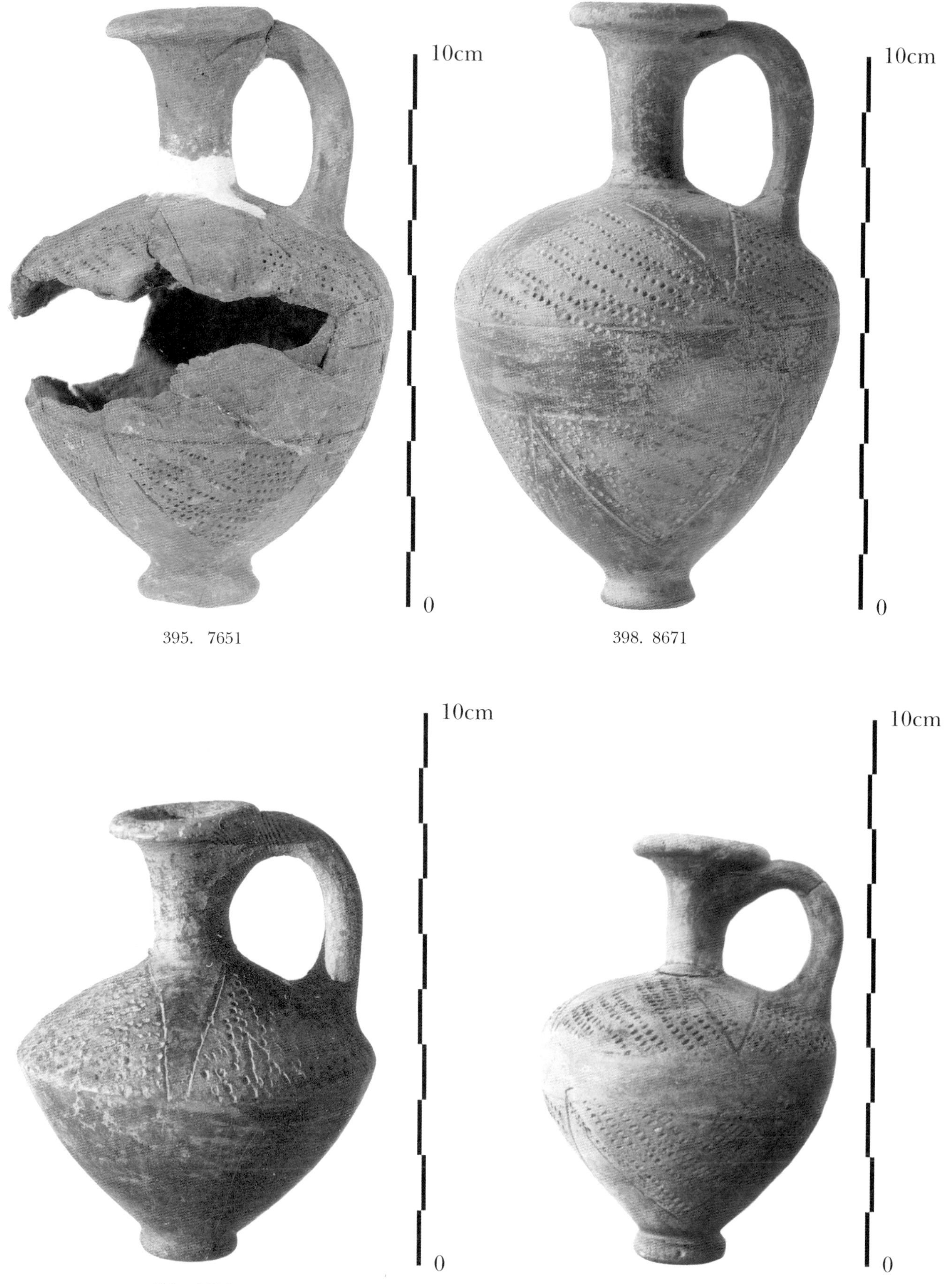

395. 7651

398. 8671

403. 2702

411. 2939

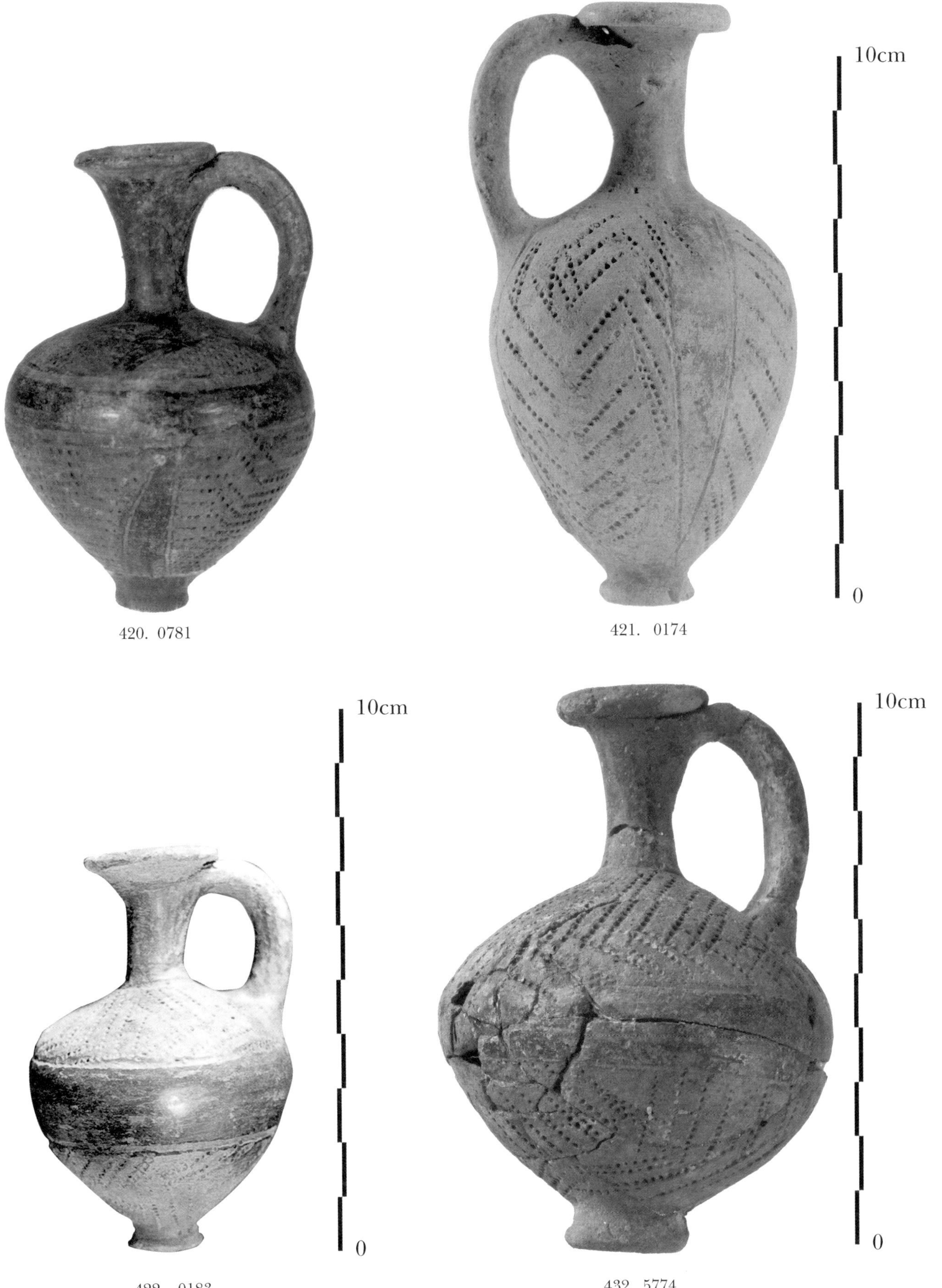

420. 0781

421. 0174

422. 0183

432. 5774

Plate 146

440. 2322

443. 0028

450. 2332

451. 2333

453. 8826

455. 1431

470. 0176

476. 0299

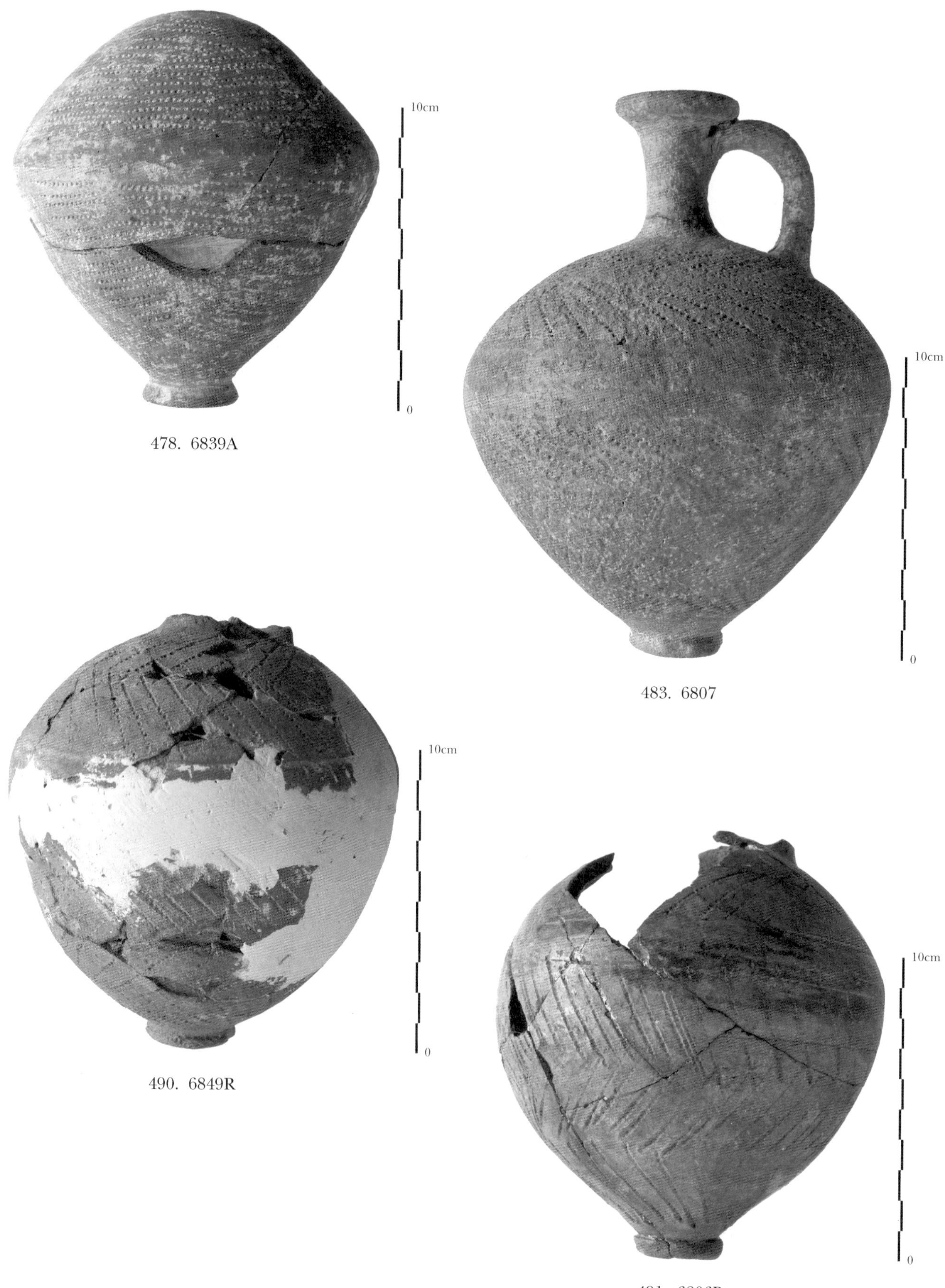

478. 6839A

483. 6807

490. 6849R

491. 6806B

492. 0261

494. 3417

546. 8704

552. 7383D

554. 3368

556. 2093

566. 0150

568. 0835

584. 8887B

0 10cm

589. 9012M

0 10cm

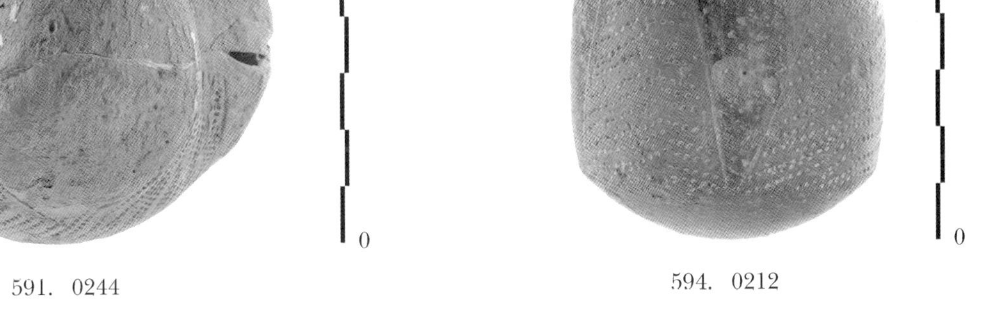

10cm

0

591. 0244

10cm

0

594. 0212

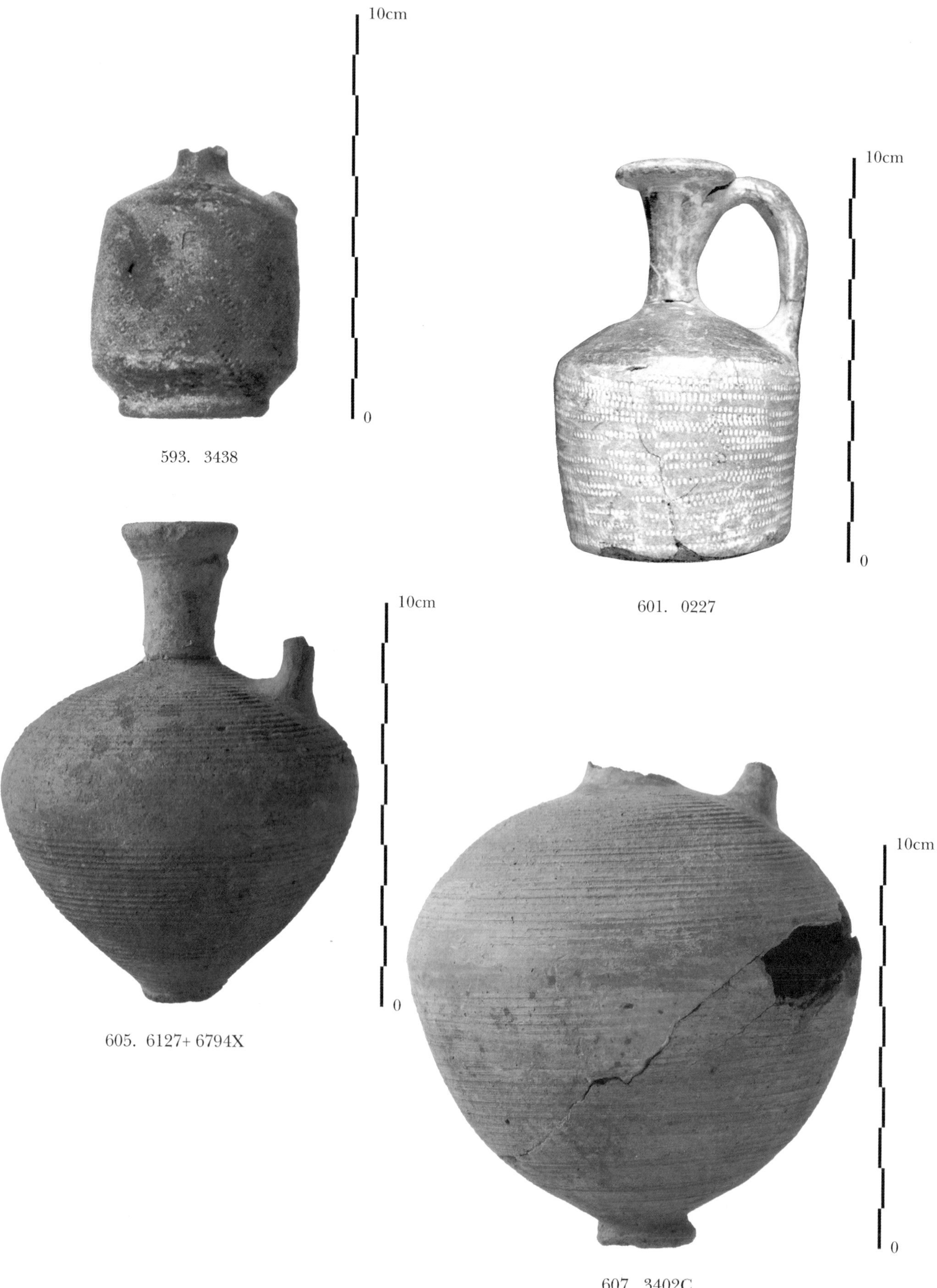

593. 3438

601. 0227

605. 6127+ 6794X

607. 3402C

608. 6794U

624. 0355

627. 3580

631. 0296

632. 7247A

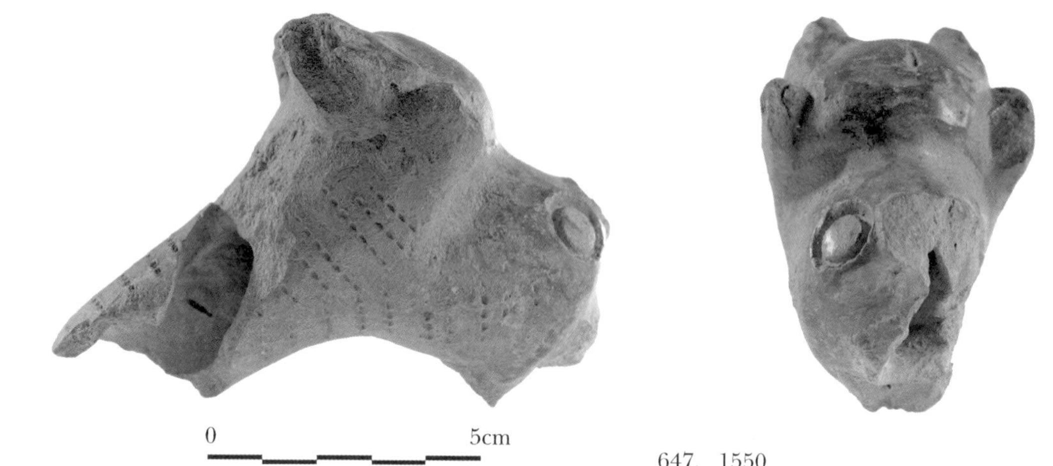

647. 1550

634. 9018Y

635. 8475C

10cm
0

641. 7354

10cm
0

643. 6987

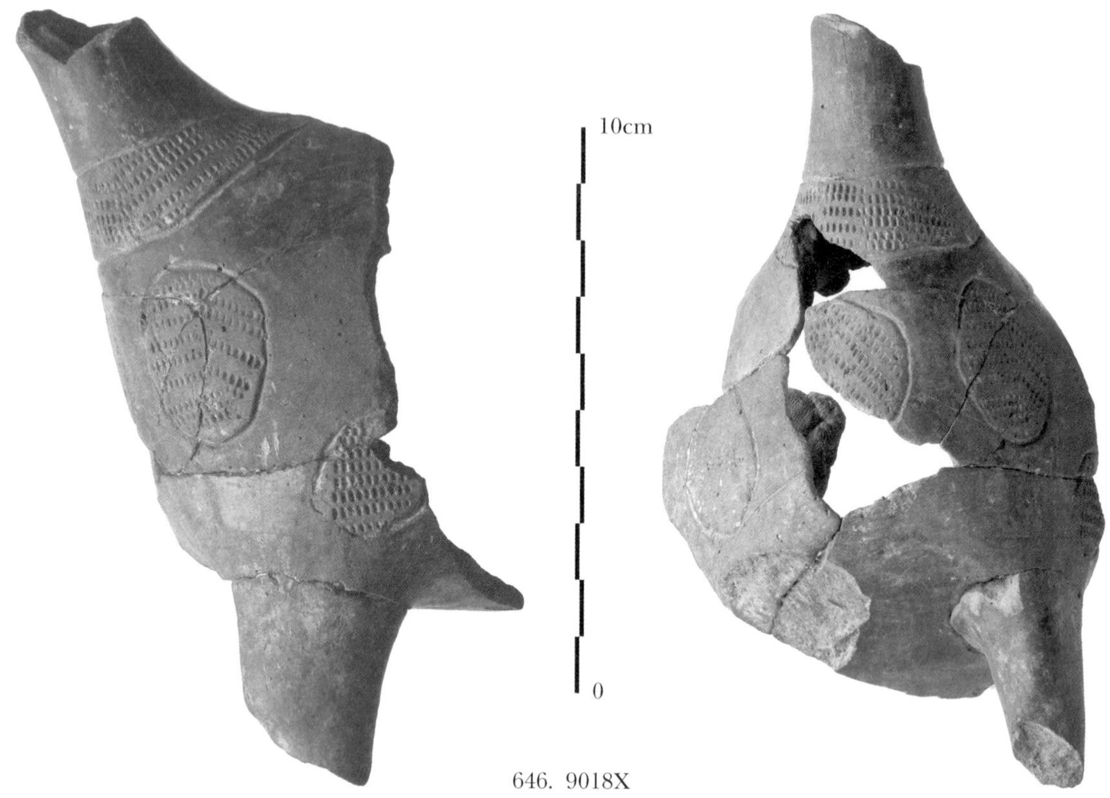

646. 9018X

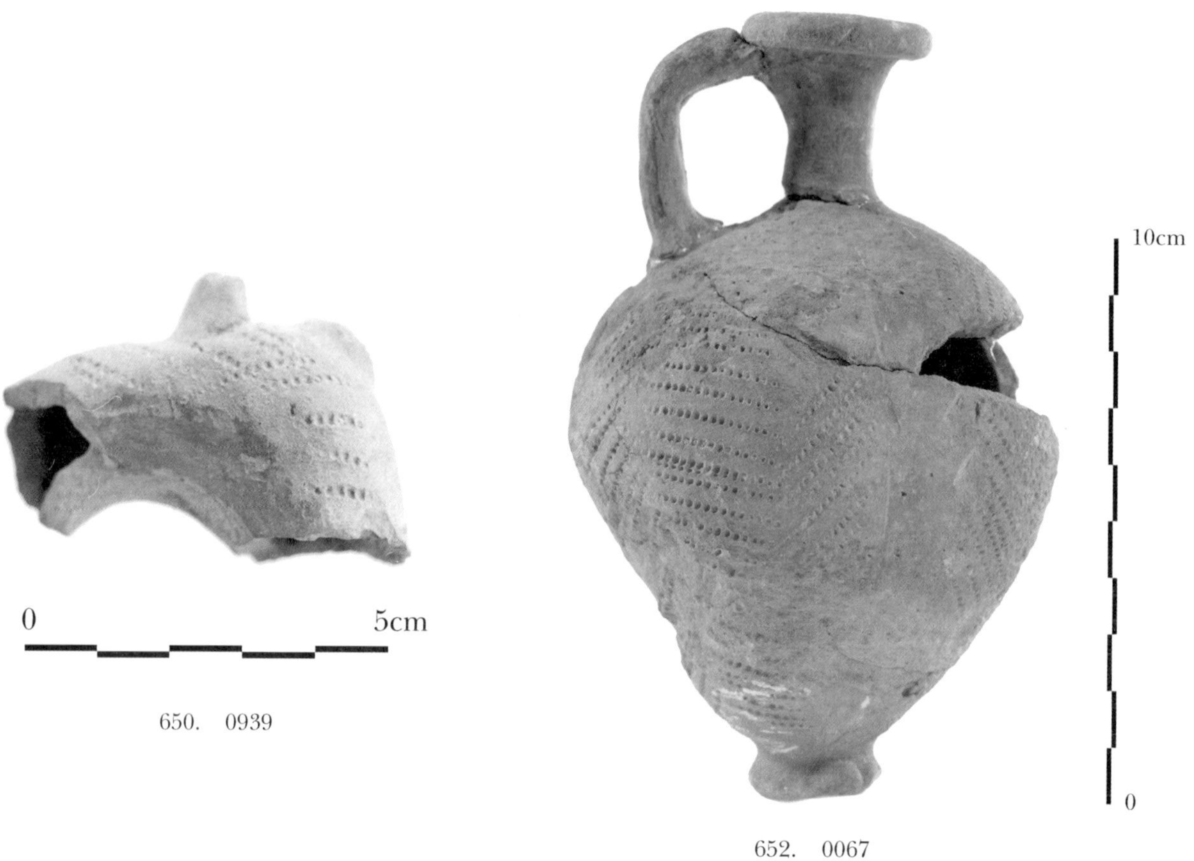

650. 0939

652. 0067

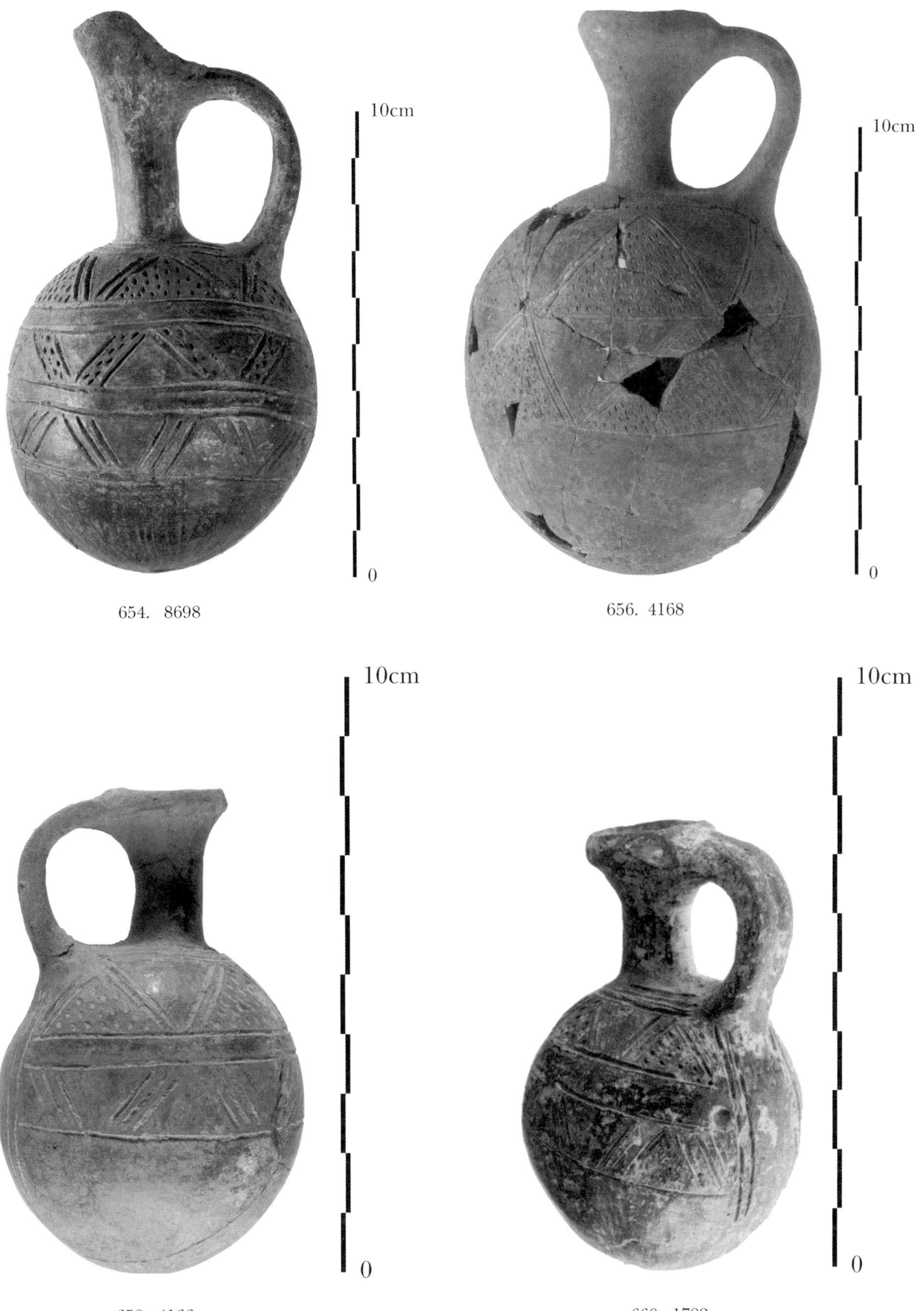

654. 8698

656. 4168

658. 4166

660. 1782

664. 6052 667. 7486E

669. 1771 671 7462

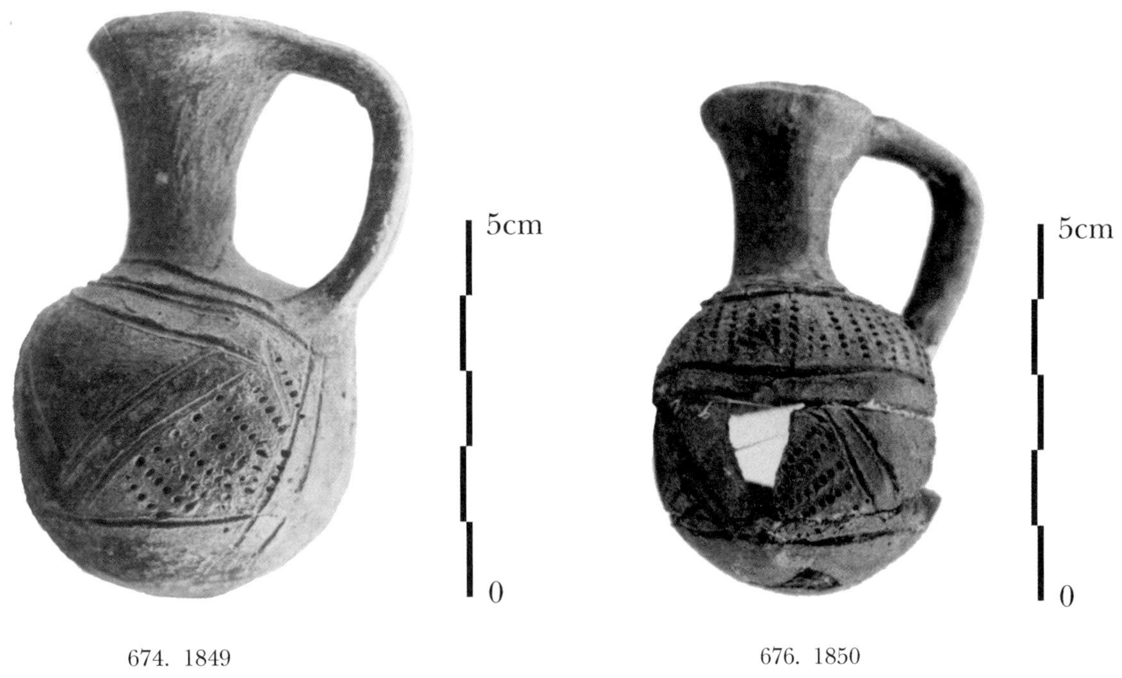

674. 1849

676. 1850

677. 4123

678. 3642

680. 6042

681. 4239

682. 8856

683. 8865

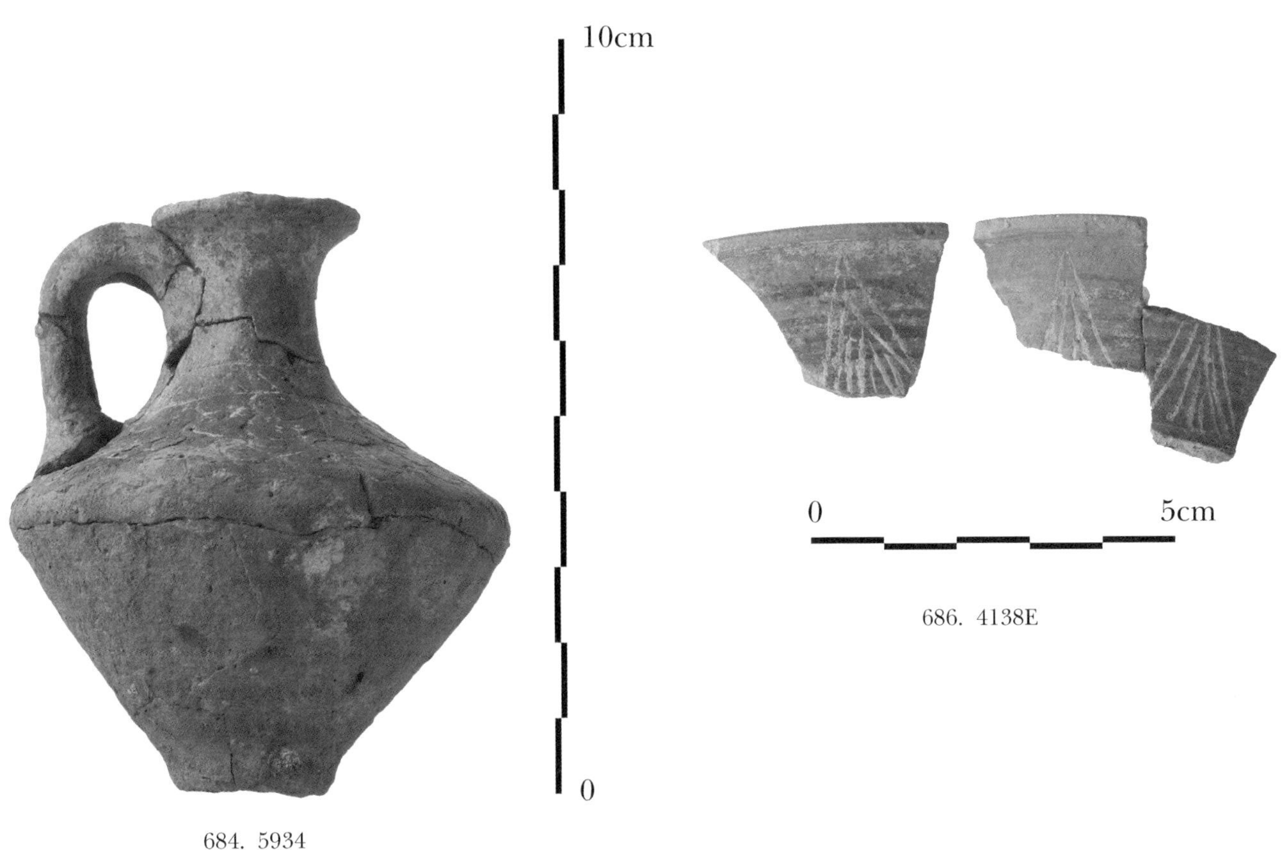

684. 5934

686. 4138E

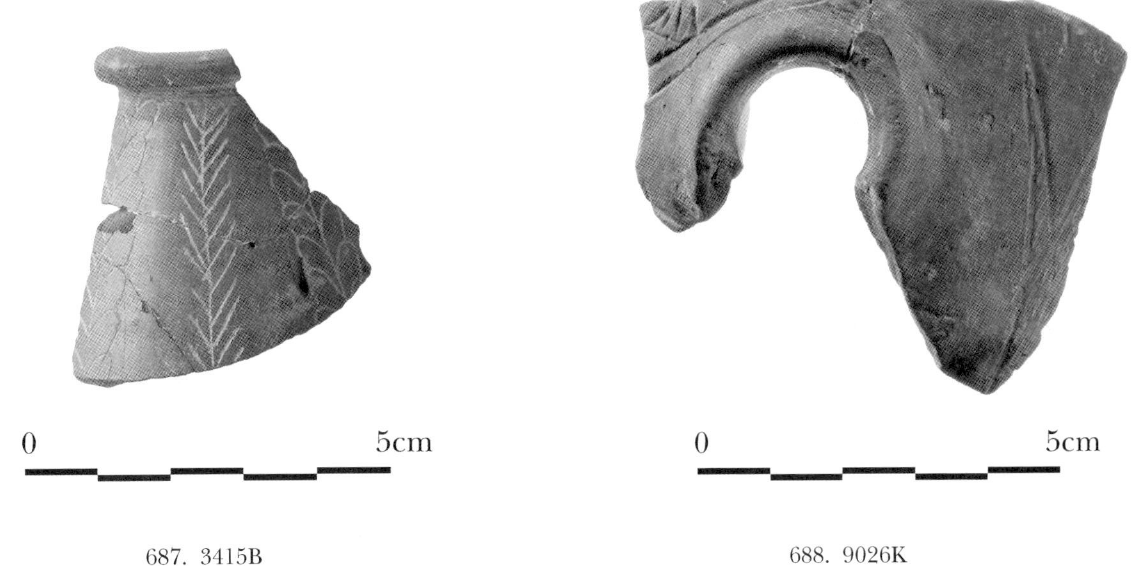

687. 3415B

688. 9026K

689. 9026H

690. 4506F

696. 4242

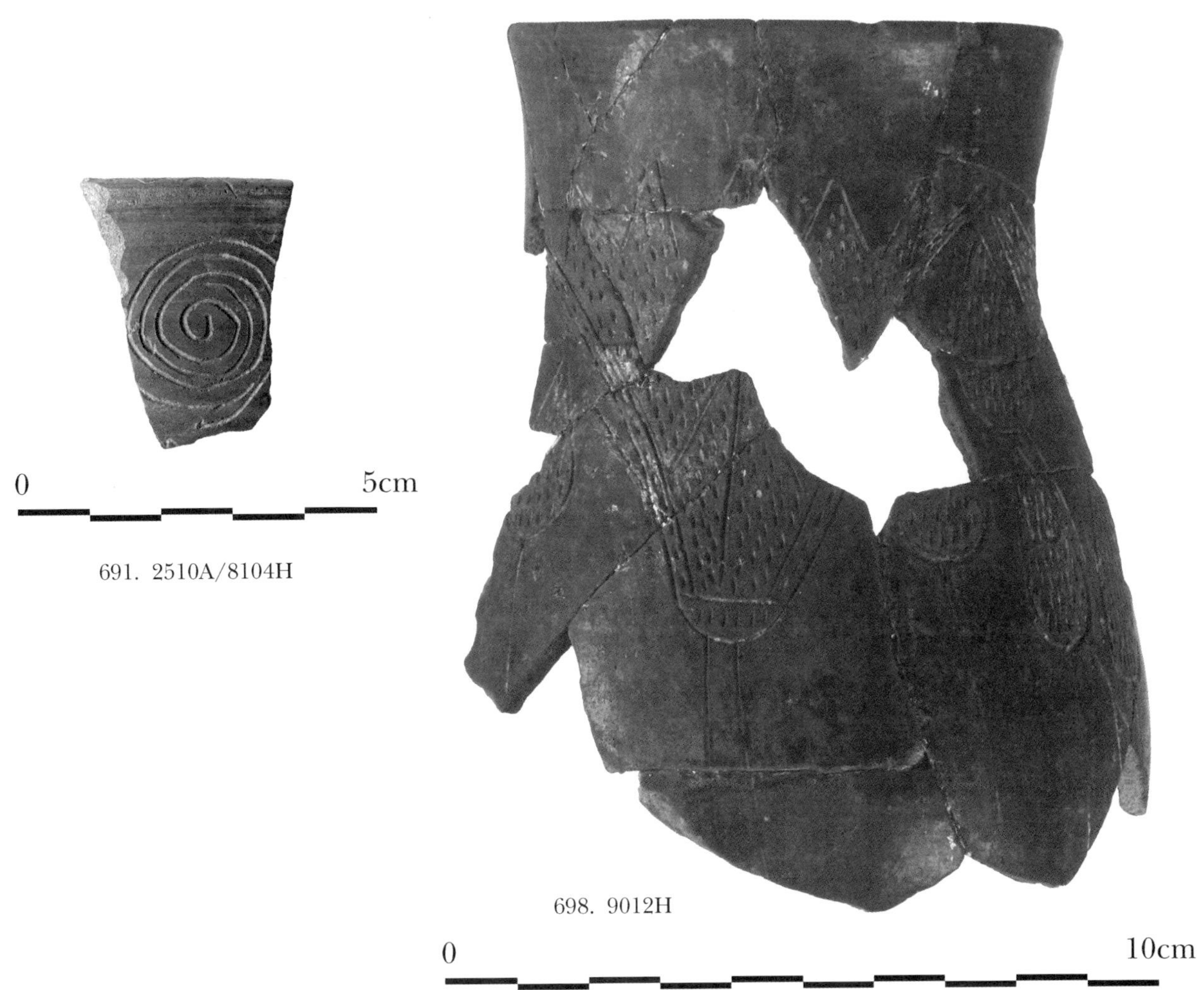

691. 2510A/8104H

698. 9012H

699. 9018W

Bibliography

Adam S., Recent Discoveries in the Eastern Delta, *ASAE* 55, 1958, 308–310.

– Report on the excavations of the Department of Antiquities at Ezbet Rushdi, *ASAE* 56, 1959, 207–226.

Aharoni, Y., *The Land of the Bible: A Historical Geography*. 2nd ed., London 1979.

Albright W.F., The Excavations at Ascalon, *BASOR* 6, 1922, 11–18.

– *Tell Beit Mirsim I: The Bronze Age Pottery of the First Three Campaigns*, Harvard 1933.

– *Tell Beit Mirsim Ia: The Bronze Age Pottery of the Fourth Campaign*, Harvard 1933.

– North-west Semitic Names in a List of Egyptian Slaves from the Eighteenth Century BC., *JAOS* 74 (1954), 222–233.

Amiran R., Tell el-Yahudiyeh Ware in Syria, *IEJ* 7, 1957, 93–97.

– *Ancient Pottery of the Holy Land*, Jerusalem 1969.

– A Fruit-Like Juglet and Some Notes on the Tell el-Yahudieh Style, *Israel Museum News* 10, 1975, 40–48.

Arnold Do., Wandbild und Scherbenbefund. Zur Topfertechnik der alten Ägypter vom Beginn der pharaonischen Zeit bis zu den Hyksos, *MDAIK* 32, 1976, 1–34.

– Zur Keramik aus den Taltempelbereich der Pyramide Amenemhets III. in Dahschur, *MDAIK* 33, 1977, 21–26.

– Techniques and Traditions of Manufacture in the Pottery of Ancient Egypt, Fascicle 1 in: Do. Arnold and J. Bourriau (eds.), *An Introduction to Ancient Egyptian Pottery*, Mainz 1993, 5–141.

Arnold Do., Arnold F., and Allen S., Canaanite Imports at Lisht, the Middle Kingdom Capital of Egypt, *Ä&L* 5, 1995, 13–32.

Artzy M., and Asaro F., Origin of Tell el-Yahudiyah Ware found in Cyprus, *RDAC* 1979, 135–150.

Aston, D.A.,The Pottery, in: Raven M.J., *The Tomb of Iurudef. A Memphite Official in the Reign of Ramesses II*, (EES, Excavation memoir 57) London/Leiden 1991, 47–54.

– Ceramic Imports at Tell el-Dabᶜa during the Middle Bronze IIA, in: M. Bietak (ed.), *The Middle Bronze Age in the Levant. Proceedings of an International Conference on MB IIA Ceramic Material, Vienna 24th–26th of January 2001*, Vienna 2002, 43–87.

– *Tell el-Dabᶜa XII: A Corpus of Late Middle Kingdom and Second Intermediate Period Pottery*, Vienna 2004.

– A History of Tell el-Yahudieh Typology, in: M. Bietak and E. Czerny (eds.), *The Bronze Age in the Lebanon, The Bronze Age in the Lebanon. Studies on the Archaeology and Chronology of Lebanon, Syria and Egypt*, Contributions to the Chronology of the Eastern Mediterranean 17, Vienna 2008, 165–194.

Åström, P., *The Middle Cypriote Bronze Age*, Lund 1957; reprinted as *SCE* IV.1b, Lund 1972.

– Pictorial Motifs in the Middle Cypriote Bronze Age, in: C.F.A. Schaeffer (ed.), *Alasia* I, Paris 1971, 7–14.

– Three Tell el-Yahudiyeh Juglets in the Thera Museum, in: *Acts of the Ist International Scientific Congress on the Volcano of Thera* , Athens 1971, 415–421.

Bader, B., The Egyptian Jars from Sidon in their Egyptian Context: a preliminary report, *AHL*, 18, 2003, 31–37.

– *Tell el-Dabᶜa XIX. Auaris und Memphis im Mittleren Reich und in der Hyksoszeit. Vergleichsanalyse der materiellen Kultur*, Vienna 2009.

Badre, L. Tell el-Ghassil: Tomb 1, in: *Archéologie au Levant. Recueil à la mémoire de R. Saïdah*, Colloques de la Maison de l'Orient Méditerranéen 12, Lyon, 1982, 123–132.

– Bey 003 Preliminary report. Excavations of the American University of Beirut Museum 1993–1996, *Bulletin d'Architecture et d'Archéologie Libanaises* 2, 1997, 6–94.

Badreshany, K., *The Middle Bronze Age Pottery of Tell el-Burak*, unpublished MA thesis, American University of Beyruth 2005.

Bagatti, B., *Excavations at Nazareth I. From the beginning to the XIIth Century*, Jerusalem 1969.

Bartov, Y., *Geological Photomap of Israel and Adjacent Areas, 1:750,000, 2nd ed.*, Jerusalem 1994.

Beck, P.A., The Pottery of the MBIIA at Tel Aphek, *Tel Aviv* 2, 1975, 45–75,

– Area A. Middle Bronze IIA Pottery 173–238, in M. Kochavi, P. Beck, E. Yadin, (eds.), *Aphek-Antipatris I. Excavation of Areas A and B. The 1972–1976 Seasons*, (Tel Aviv University Monographs 19), Tel Aviv 2000.

– The Middle Bronze Age IIA Pottery Repertoire. A Comparative Study, in: M. Kochavi, P. Beck, E. Yadin, (eds.), *Aphek-Antipatris I. Excavation of Areas A and B. The 1972–1976 Seasons*, Tel Aviv 2000, 239–254.

Ben-Arieh, S., *Bronze and Iron Age Tombs at Tell Beit Mirsim*, Israel Antiquities Authority Reports 23, Jerusalem 2004.

Bender, F., *Geology of Jordan*, Berlin 1974.

Ben Dor, I., A Middle Bronze Age Temple at Nahariyah, *QDAP* 14, 1950, 1–41.

Beydoun, Z.R., The Levantine countries: the geology of Syria and Lebanon (maritime regions), in: A.E.M. Nairn, W.H. Kanes, and F.G. Stehli (eds.), *The Ocean Basins and Margins. 4A: The Eastern Mediterranean*, New York - London 1977, 319–353.

Bietak; M., Bericht über die erste Grabungskampagne auf Tell ed-Dabᶜa im Ostdelta Ägyptens im Sommer 1966, *Bustan* 9.1, 1968, 20–24.

– Vorläufiger Bericht über die erste und zweite Kampagne der österreichisten Ausgrabungen auf Tell ed-Dabᶜa im Ostdelta Ägyptens (1966, 1967), *MDAIK* 23, 1968, 79–114.

– Vorläufiger Bericht über die dritte Kampagne der österreichischen Ausgrabungen auf Tell ed-Dab^{c}a im Ostdelta Ägyptens (1968), *MDAIK* 26, 1970, 15–42.

– Avaris and Piramesse, Archaeological Exploration in the Eastern Nile Delta, *Proceedings of the British Academy* 65, 1979, 225–290.

– Die Hauptstadt der Hyksos und die Ramsesstadt, *Antike Welt* 6, 1975, 28–43.

– Tell el-Jahudije Keramik, *LÄ* VI, 1986, 335–348.

– *Archaeological Exploration in the Eastern Nile Delta,*^{2} Oxford 1986.

– Archäologischer Befund und Historische Interpretation am Beispiel der Tell el-Yahudiyeh-ware, in: S. Schoske (ed.), *Akten des 4. Internationalen Ägyptologenkongresses 1985,* BSAK 2, Hamburg 1989, 7–34.

– The Concept of Eternity in Ancient Egypt and the Bronze Age World: An Archaeological Approach, *Eretz Israel* 21, 1990, 10*–17*.

– Egypt and Canaan during the Middle Bronze Age, *BASOR* 281, 1991, 27–72.

– *Tell el-Dab^{c}a V: Ein Friedhofsbezirk der Mittleren Bronzezeitkultur mit Totentempel und Siedlungsschichten Teil I,* Vienna 1991.

– *Avaris, The Capital of the Hyksos. Recent Excavations at Tell el Dab^{c}a,* London 1996.

– The Center of Hyksos Rule: Avaris (Tell el Dab^{c}a), in: E.D. Oren (ed.), *The Hyksos, New Historical and Archaeological Perspectives,* University Museum Monograph 96, Philadelphia 1997, 87–128.

– Relative and Absolute Chronology of the Middle Bronze Age. Comments on the Present state of Research, in: M. Bietak (ed.), *The Middle Bronze Age in the Levant. Proceedings of an International Conference on MB IIA Ceramic Material. Vienna 24th–26th of January 2001,* Contributions to the Chronology of the Eastern Mediterranean 3, Vienna 2002, 29–42.

– Near Eastern Sanctuaries in the Eastern Nile Delta, *Bulletin d'Architecture et d'Archéologie Libanaises Hors Série VI,* Beyrouth 2009, 209–228.

Bietak, M., Forstner-Müller I., Mlinar C., The Beginning of the Hyksos Period at Tell el-Dab^{c}a: A Subtle Change in Material Culture, in: P. Fischer (ed.), *Contributions to the Archaeology and History of the Bronze and Early Iron Ages in the Eastern Mediterranean. Studies in Honour of Paul Åström,* Vienna 2001, 171–181.

Bietak, M., and Hein, I., *Pharaonen und Fremde., Dynastien im Dunkel,* Exhibition Catalogue, Vienna 1994.

Bietak, M., Kopetzky, K., Stager, L.E., Voss, R., Synchronisation of Stratigraphies: Ashkelon and Tell el-Dab^{c}a, *Ä&L,* 18, 2008, 49–60.

Bietak, M., and Kopetzky, K., The Dolphin Jug: A Typological and Chronological Assessment, in: J.D. Schloen (ed.), *Exploring the Longue Durée. Essays in Honor of Lawrence E. Stager,* Winona Lake 2009, 17–34.

Von Bissing, F.W., Review of G.M. Engberg, The Hyksos Reconsidered, *AfO* 14, 1944, 84–86.

Bonnet, H., Zur Herkunft der sogenannten Tell el-Jahudiye-Vasen, *ZÄS* 59, 1924, 119–130.

Bourke, S., Sparks, R., Schroder, M., Pella in the Middle Bronze Age, in: P. Fischer, (ed.), *The Chronology of the Jordan Valley During the Middle and Late Bronze Ages: Pella, Tell Abu al-Kharaz and Tell Deir Alla,* Contributions to the Chronology of the Eastern Mediterranean 12, Vienna 2006, 9–58.

Bourriau, J., Review of J. van Seters, The Hyksos. A New Investigation, *JNES* 28, 1969, 129–133.

– The Dolphin Vase from Lisht, in: P. der Manuelian (ed.), *Studies in Honor of William Kelly Simpson,* I, Boston 1996, 101–116.

Braemer, F., and al-Maqdissi, M., La céramique du Bronze moyen dans la Syrie du Sud, in: M. Maqdissi, V. Matoïan, C. Nicolle, *Céramique de l'age du Bronze en Syrie, vol. I, La Syrie du Sud et la vallée de l'Oronte,* Beyrouth 2002, 23–50.

Braun, E., *Early Beth Shan (Strata XIX–XIII): G.M. FitzGerald's Deep Cut on the Tell,* Philadelphia 2004.

Brink, E.C.M. van den, *Tombs and Burial Customs at Tell el-Dab^{c}a,* Beiträge zur Ägyptologie 4, Vienna 1982.

Brunton, G., *Mostagedda,* London 1937.

Buchholz, H.G., and Karageorghis, V., *Prehistoric Greece and Cyprus,* London 1973.

Charaf, H., Arqa and its regional connections Redux, *Bulletin d'Architecture et d'Archéologie Libanaises Hors-Série VI,* 2009, 295–310.

Charaf-Mullins, H., Les céramiques importées de l'Ouest, in: J.P. Thalmann, *Tell Arqa – I. Les niveaux de l'âge de Bronze,* Bibliothèque archéologique et historique 177, Beyrouth 2006, 173–192.

Chehab, M., Tombe phénicienne de Sin el-Fil, in: *Mélanges syriens offerts à René Dussaud,* Paris 1939, 803–810.

– Tombes phéniciennes, Majdalouna, *Bulletin du Musée de Beyrouth* 4, 1940, 37–53.

Cohen-Weinberger, A. and Goren, Y., Levantine-Egyptian Interactions During the 12th to the 15th Dynasties based on the Petrography of the Canaanite Pottery from Tell el-Dab^{c}a, *Ä&L* 14, 2004, 69–100.

Contenau, G., Mission archéologique à Sidon, *Syria* 1, 1920, 108–154.

Dan, Y., Raz, Z., Yaalon, D.H., Koyumdjisky, H., *Soil Map of Israel, 1:500,000,* Jerusalem: Survey of Israel, 1975.

Debono, F., Rapport de cloture sur les resultants et études des objets du sondage à l'est du lac sacré de Karnak, *Cahiers de Karnak* 8, 1982–1985, Paris 1987, 121–131.

Doumet-Serhal, C., Le Bronze Moyen IIB/C et le Bronze Récent I au Liban: l'evidence de Tell el Ghassil, *Berytus* 42, 1995/96, 37–70.

– *Les fouilles de Tell el-Ghassil de 1972 à 1974, étude du matérial,* Bibliothèque archéologique et historique 146, Beyrouth 1996.

Dubertret, L., *Carte géologique au 50.000^{e} Feuille de Beyrouth,* Beyrouth 1945.

– *Carte géologique au 50.000^{e} Feuille de Saida,* Beyrouth 1949.

– *Liban, Syrie et bordure des pays voisins,* Paris 1962.

– Liban, Syrie, et bordure des pays voisins, *Notes et mémoires sur le Moyen-Orient* 8, 1966, 251–358.

– Géologie et Peuplement au Liban, in: J. Besancon (ed.), *Hannon: revue libanaise de geographie, vol. V,* Beyrouth 1970, 11–20.

– Introduction a la Carte Géologique a 1/50,000^{e} du Liban, *Notes et mémoires sur le Moyen-Orient* 13, 1974, 345–403.

Dubertret, L., and Wetzel, R., *Carte géologique au 50.000^{e} Feuille de Batroun,* Beirut 1945.

Dunand, M., *Fouilles de Byblos,* I, (plates), Paris 1937.

– *Fouilles de Byblos,* I, (text), Paris 1939.

– *Fouilles de Byblos,* II, Paris 1958.

– Rapport Préliminaire sur les fouilles de Byblos en 1963, *Bulletin du Musée de Beyrouth* 17, 1964, 29–35.

Dussaud, R., Observations sur la céramique du IIe Millénaire avant notre ère, *Syria* 9, 1928, 131–150.

Engberg, R.M., *The Hyksos Reconsidered,* Chicago 1939.

Engelbach, R.E., *Harageh,* BSAE 28, London 1923.

Epstein, C., Middle Bronze Age Tombs at Kefar Szold and Ginosar, *ᶜAtiqot* (Hebrew Series) 7, 1974, 13–39.

Eriksson, K.O., *The Creative Independance of Late Bronze Age Cyprus,* Contributions to the Chronology of the Eastern Mediterranean 10, Vienna 2007.

Exhibition catalogue, *25 ans de découvertes archéologiques sur les chantiers de l'IFAO, 1981–2006,* Cairo 2007.

FitzGerald, G.M., *The Four Canaanite Temples of Beth-Shan. The Pottery,* vol. II, part II, Philadelphia 1930.

– *Beth-Shan Excavations 1921–1923: The Arab and Byzantine Levels,* volume III, Philadelphia 1931.

– Excavations at Beth-Shan in 1931. *Palestine Exploration Fund Quarterly Statement* (July, 1932), 138–148.

– Excavations at Beth-Shan in 1933. *Palestine Exploration Fund Quarterly Statement* (January 1934), 123–134.

– *A Sixth Century Monastery at Beth-Shan,* vol. IV, Philadelphia 1939.

Forstner-Müller, I., Vorbericht der Grabung im Areal A/II in Tell el-Dabᶜa, *Ä&L* 11, 2001, 197–220.

– Tombs and burial customs at tell el-Dabᶜa in Area A/II at the end of the MBIIA Period (Stratum F), in: M. Bietak, (ed.), *The Middle Bronze Age in the Levant,* Contributions to the Chronology of the Eastern Mediterranean 3, Vienna 2002, 163–184.

– *Tell el-Dabᶜa XVI. Die Gräber des Areal A/II von Tell el-Dabᶜa,* Vienna 2008.

Forstner-Müller, I., and Kopetzky, K., An Upper Egyptian Import at Sidon, *AHL* 24, 2006, 60–62.

Forstner-Müller, I., Kopetzky, K., Doumet-Serhal, C., Egyptian Pottery of the Late 12th and early 13th Dynasty from Sidon, *AHL,* 24, 2006, 52–59.

Fuscaldo, P., *Tell el-Dabᶜa X. The Palace District of Avaris: The Pottery of the Hyksos Period and the New Kingdom (Areas H/III and H/VI), Part I, Locus 66,* Vienna 2000.

Garstang, J., *El Arabeh,* London 1901.

– Jericho. City and Necropolis I, *LAAA* 19, 1932, 3–22, 35–44.

– Jericho. City and Necropolis II, *LAAA* 20, 1933, 3–42.

– Jericho. City and Necropolis III, *LAAA* 21, 1934, 99–136.

Genz, H. and Sader, H., Excavations at Tell Fadous-Kfarabida: Preliminary Report on the 2008 Season of Excavations, *Bulletin d'Architecture et d'Archéologie Libanaises* 12, in press.

– Tell Hizzin: Digging up New Material from an Old Excavation, *Bulletin d'Architecture et d'Archéologie Libanaises* 12, in press.

Genz, H., el-Zaatari, S., Çakirlar, C., Badreshany, K., Riehl, S., A Middle Bronze Age Burial from Tell Fadous-Kfarabida, Lebanon, *Ä&L* 20, 2010, 183–205.

Germer, R., *Flora des pharaonischen Ägypten,* SDAIK 14, Mainz 1981.

Gerstenblith, P., *The Levant at the Beginning of the Middle Bronze Age,* 1983.

Glanville, S.R.K., Egyptian Theriomorphic vessels in the British Museum, *JEA* 12, 1926, 52–69.

Goren, Y., The Southern Levant in the Early Bronze Age IV: the petrographic perspective, *BASOR* 303, 1996, 33–72.

Goren, Y. and Cohen-Weinberger, A., Petrographic Analyses of Selected Wares, in: A. Kempinski, (ed.), *Tel Kabri: The 1986–1993 Excavation Seasons,* Tel Aviv 2002, 435–442.

Goren, Y., Finkelstein, I. Na'aman, N., *Inscribed in Clay: Provenance Study of the Amarna Letters and other Ancient Near Eastern Texts,* Monograph Series 23, Tel Aviv 2004.

Grant, E., Beth Shemesh, *AASOR* 9, 1928, 1–15.

– *Beth Shemesh,* Haverford 1929.

– *Rumeilah: Being Ain Shems Excavations III,* Haverford 1934.

Grant, E. and Wright, G.E., *Ains Shems V,* Haverford 1939.

Greenberg, R., Horwitz, L.K., Lernau, O., Mienis, H.K., Khalaily, H., Marder, O., A Sounding at Tel Naᶜama in the Hula Valley,*ᶜAtiqot* 35, 1998, 9–35.

Greenberg, R. and Porat, N., A Third Millennium Levantine Pottery Production Center: typology, petrography, and provenance of the Metallic Ware of northern Israel and adjacent regions, *BASOR* 301, 1996, 5–24.

Griffith, F.Ll., *The Antiquities of Tell el-Yahudiyeh,* EEF Excavation Memoire 7, London 1890.

Griffiths, D., and Ownby, M., Assessing the Occurrence of Egyptian Marl C Ceramics in Middle Bronze Age Sidon, *Archaeology and History in Lebanon* 24, 2006, 63–77.

Guy, P.L.O., and Engberg, R.M, *Megiddo Tombs,* Chicago 1938.

Gvirtzman, G., Netser, M., Katsav, E., Last-Glacial to Holocene kurkar ridges, hamra soils, and dune fields in the coastal belt of central Israel, *Israel Journal of Earth Sciences* 47, 1998, 29–46.

Hall, H.R., *The Oldest Civilization of Greece,* London 1901.

Harding, G.L., Four Tomb Groups from Jordan, *Palestine Exploration Fund Annual* 6, 1953.

Hassan, S., *Excavations at Giza II,* Cairo 1936.

HEIN, I., and JÁNOSI, P, *Tell el-Dabᶜa XI. Areal A/V. Siedlungsrelikte der späten Hyksoszeit,* Vienna 2004.

HOLLADAY, J.S., jr., *Cities of the Delta III. Tell el-Maskhuta,* ARCE Reports 6, Undena 1982.

– The Eastern Nile Delta During the Hyksos and Pre-Hyksos Periods: Toward a Systematic/ Socioeconomic Understanding, in: E.D. OREN (ed.), *The Hyksos, New Historical and Archaeological Perspectives,* University Museum Monograph 96, Philadelphia 1997, 183–252.

HOROWITZ, W., An Inscribed Clay Cylinder from Amarna Age Beth Shean, *Israel Exploration Journal* 46, 1996, 208–218.

ILAIWI, M., *Soil Map of Arab Countries. Soil Map of Syria and Lebanon,* Damascus 1985.

ILIFFE, J.H., Pottery from Ras el ᶜAin, *QDAP* 5, 1936, 111–126.

INGHOLT, H., *Rapport préliminaire sur sept campagnes des fouilles à Hama en Syrie (1932–38),* Copenhagen 1940.

JAMES, F.W., *The Iron Age at Beth Shan: A Study of Levels VI–IV,* Philadelphia 1966.

JAMES, F.W., and MCGOVERN, P.E., *The Late Bronze Egyptian Garrison at Beth Shan: A Study of Levels VII and VIII,* Philadelphia 1993.

JUNKER, H., *Der Nubische Ursprung der sogenannten Tell el-Jahudiye Vasen,* Vienna 1921.

KAMEL, D., *The Middle Bronze Age Tomb of Tell el-Burak- Lebanon,* Unpublished MA thesis, American University of Beyrouth 2005.

KAMLAH, J., and SADER, H., The Tell el-Burak archaeological project. Preliminary report on the 2002 and 2003 seasons, *Bulletin d'Architecture et d'Archéologie Libanaises* 7, 2003, 145–173.

KAPLAN, J., A Cemetery of the Bronze Age discovered near Tel Aviv Harbor, *ᶜAtiqot* 1, 1955.

KAPLAN, M.F., *The Origin and Distribution of Tell el-Yahudiyeh Ware,* Gothenburg 1980.

KAPLAN, M.F., HARBOTTLE, G., SAYRE, E.V., Multi-disciplinary Analysis of Tell el-Yahudiyeh Ware, *Archaeometry* 24, 1982, 127–142.

– Tell el-Yahudiyeh Ware: A Re-evaluation, in: P.M. RICE (ed.), *Pots and Potters: Current Approaches in Ceramic Typology,* Monographs of the Institute of Archaeology, 25, Los Angeles 1984, 227–241.

KARAGEORGHIS, V., *Nouveaux documents pour l'étude du bronze récente à Chypre,* Nicosia 1965.

KEMP, B.J., and MERRILLEES, R.S., *Minoan Pottery in Second Millenium Egypt,* Mainz 1980.

KEMPINSKI, A., A Syrian Cylinder Seal from Tomb 984 at Tel Kabri, in: M. J. MELLINK, E. PORADA, and T. ÖZGÜÇ (eds.), *Aspects of Art and Iconography: Anatolia and its Neighbors. Studies in Honor of Nimet Özgüç,* Ankara 1993, 333–338.

– *Tel Kabri: The 1986–1993 Excavation Seasons,* Tel Aviv 2002.

KENYON, K.M., Excavations at Jericho, 1952, *PEQ* 1952, 62–82.

– *Excavations at Jericho I. The Tombs excavated in 1952–54,* London 1960.

– *Excavations at Jericho II. The Tombs excavated in 1955–58,* London 1965.

– *Excavations at Jericho III. The Architecture and Stratigraphy of the Tell.,* London 1981.

KENYON, K.M., and HOLLAND, T., *Excavations at Jericho. Volume Four. The Pottery Type Series and Other Finds,* Oxford 1982.

KNAPP, A.B., and CHERRY, J.F, *Provenience Studies and Bronze Age Cyprus: Production, Exchange and Politico-Economic Exchange,* Monographs in World Prehistory 21, Madison, WI 1994.

KOCHAVI, M., and YADIN, E., Typological analysis of the MB IIA Pottery from Aphek according to its Stratigraphic Provenance, in: M. BIETAK (ed.), *The Middle Bronze Age in the Levant,* Contributions to the Chronology of the Eastern Mediterranean 3, Vienna 2002, 189–225.

KOPETZKY, K., Gefässe in Tell el-Yahudiya Stil, in: E. CERNY, I. HEIN, H. HUNGER, D. MELMANN, A. SCHWAB (eds.), *Timelines. Studies in Honour of Manfred Bietak,* II, Leuven 2006, 177–186.

– The MB IIB-Corpus of the Hyksos Period at Tell el-Dabᶜa, in: M. BIETAK and E. CZERNY (eds.), *The Bronze Age in the Lebanon. Studies on the Archaeology and Chronology of Lebanon, Syria and Egypt,* Contributions to the Chronology of the Eastern Mediterranean 17, Vienna 2008, 195–241.

– 2007/2008. Pottery from Tell Arqa Found in Egypt and Its Chronological Contexts, *AHL* 26–27, 2007/2008, 17–58.

LACOVARA, P., An Incised Vase from Kerma, *JNES* 44, 1985, 211–16.

LIVNEH, A., The Pottery of the Middle Bronze Age, in: A. BEN-TOR, D. BEN-AMI and A. LIVNEH (eds.), *Yoqnᶜeam III. The Middle and Late Bronze Ages,* Jerusalem 2005, 41–138.

LOAT, W.L.S., *Gurob,* BSAE 10, London 1905.

LOUD, G., *Megiddo II. Seasons of 1935–1938,* Oriental Institute Publications 62, Chicago 1948.

LUFT, U., Asiatics in Illahun, A Preliminary Report, in: *Atti VI Congresso Internazionale di Egittologia* II, Turin 1993, 291–297.

MACALISTER, R.A.S., *The Excavations at Gezer 1902–1905 and 1907–1909,* London 1912.

MACE, A.C., The Egyptian Expedition, 1920–1921, *BMMA* 16, Nov. 1921, 5–19.

MAEIR, A.M., *The Material Culture of the Central and Northern Jordan Valley in the Middle Bronze Age II: Pottery and Settlement Pattern,* unpublished Ph.D. thesis, University of Jerusalem 1997.

– T.1181, Area L, Hazor: A Multiple Interment Burial Cave of the MBIIa/b Period, in: A. BEN TOR and R. BONFIL (eds.), *Hazor V: An Account of the Fifth Season of Excavation, 1968,* Jerusalem 1997, 295–340.

– Red, White and Blue Ware: A Little-Known Group of Painted Pottery of the Middle Bronze II Period, in: E.D. OREN and S. AHITUV (eds.), *Aharon Kempinski Memorial Volume,* Studies in Archaeology and Related Disciplines 15, Beersheva 2002, 228–240.

– The Middle Bronze Age II Pottery, in: A. MAZAR and R. MULLINS (eds.), *Excavations at Tel Beth-Shean, 1989–1996. Volume II. The Middle and Late Bronze Age Strata in Area R,* Jerusalem 2007, 242–389.

– *"In the Midst of the Jordan": The Jordan Valley during the Middle Bronze Age (ca. 2000–1500 BCE). Archaeological and Historical Correlates,* Contributions to the Chronology of the Eastern Mediterranean 26, Vienna 2010.

MAEIR, A., and YELLIN, J., Instrumental Neutron Activation Analysis of Selected Pottery from Tel Beth-Shean and the Central Jordan Valley, in: A. MAZAR and R. MULLINS (eds.), *Excavations at Tel Beth-Shean, 1989–1996. Volume II. The Middle and Late Bronze Age Strata in Area R,* Jerusalem 2007, 554–571.

AL-MAQDISSI, M., Rapport préliminaire des travaux archéologiques dans la lisère orientale du Leja I. Le site de Mtouné (in Arabic), *AAAS* 37–38, 1987–88, 63–73.

– Chronique des activités archéologiques en Syrie, *Syria* 70, 1993, 443–576.

– *Le Bronze Moyen du Levant septentrional. Etude céramologique,* Unpublished PhD dissertation, University of Paris I-Sorbonne, Paris 1994.

AL-MAQDISSI, M., and BADAWI, M., III. Rapport préliminaire sur la sixième campagne des fouilles syriennes à Mishrifeh/Qatna, in: M. AL-MAQDISSI, M. LUCIANI, D. MORANDI BONACOSSI, M. NOVÁK and P. PFÄLZNER (eds.), *Excavating Qatna,* Documents d'Archéologie Syrienne 4, Damascus 2002, 25–62.

MAZAR, A., Four Thousand Years of History at Tel Beth-Shean: An Account of the Renewed Excavations, *Biblical Archaeologist* 60, 1997, 62–76.

MAZAR, A. (ed.), *Excavations at Tel Beth-Shean, 1989–1996. Volume I. From the New Kingdom to the Medieval Period,* Jerusalem 2006.

MAZAR, A. and MULLINS, R. (eds.), *Excavations at Tel Beth-Shean, 1989–1996. Volume II. The Middle and Late Bronze Age Strata in Area R,* Jerusalem 2007.

MCEWAN, C.W., The Syrian Expedition of the Oriental Institute, *AJA* 41, 1937, 8–16.

MCGOVERN, P.E., *The Foreign Relations of the "Hyksos". A Neutron Activation Study of Middle Bronze Age Pottery from the Eastern Mediterranean,* British Archaeological Reports International Series 888, Oxford 2000.

MCGOVERN, P., BOURRIAU, J., HARBOTTLE, G., ALLEN, S., The Archaeological Origin and Significance of the Dolphin Vase determined by Neutron Activation Analysis, *BASOR* 296, 1994, 31–41.

MERRILLEES, R.S., Opium Trade in the Bronze Age Levant, *Antiquity* 36, 1962, 287–292.

– Some Notes on Tell el-Yahudiyeh Ware, *Levant* 6, 1974, 193–195.

– *Trade and Transcendance in the Bronze Age Levant,* Gothenburg1974.

– El-Lisht and Tell el-Yahudiyeh Ware in the Archaeological Museum of the American University of Beyrouth, *Levant* 10, 1978, 75–98.

– Late Cypriote Pottery from Byblos "Necropole K", *RDAC* 1983, 181–192.

– Chronological Conundrums: Cypriot and Levantine Imports from Thera, in: D.A. WARBURTON, (ed.), *Time's Up. Dating the Minoan Eruption of Santorini,* Monographs of the Danish Institute at Athens 10, Athens 2009, 247–251.

– *The Ethnic Implications of Tell el-Yahudieh Ware for the History of the Middle to Late Bronze Age in Cyprus,* in print.

MONTET, P., *Byblos et l'Égypte, Quatre campagnes de fouilles 1921–1924,* Bibliothèque archéologique et historique 11, Paris 1928.

MORAN, W.L., *The Amarna Letters,* Baltimore, 1992.

MÜLLER V., *Opfergruben der Mittleren Bronzezeit in Tell el-Dab^ca,* unpublished Ph.D. thesis, University of Göttingen 1996.

– Offering Deposits at Tell el-Dab^ca, in: C.J. EYRE, (ed.), *Proceedings of the Seventh International Congress of Egyptologists,* OLA 82, Leuven 1998, 793–803.

– Bestand und Deutung der Opferdepots bei Tempeln in Wohnhausbereichen und Gräbern der Zweiten Zwischenzeit in Tell el-Dab^ca, in: H. WILLEMS (ed.), *Social Aspects of Funerary Culture in the Egyptian Old and Middle Kingdoms,* OLA 103, Leuven 2001, 175–204.

– Offering Practices in the Temple Courts of Tell el-Dab^ca and the Levant, in: M. BIETAK, (ed.), *The Middle Bronze Age in the Levant,* Contributions to the Chronology of the Eastern Mediterranean 3, Vienna 2002, 269–295.

– *Tell el-Dab^ca XVII. Opferdeponierungen in der Hyksoshauptstadt Auaris (Tell el-Dab^ca) vom späten Mittleren Reich bis zum frühen Neuen Reich,* Vienna 2008.

MULLINS, R. A., *Beth Shean during the Eighteenth Dynasty: From Canaanite Settlement to Egyptian Garrison.* Unpublished Ph.D. Jerusalem 2002.

– The Late Bronze Age Pottery, in: A. MAZAR and R. MULLINS (eds.), *Excavations at Tel Beth-Shean, 1989–1996. Volume II. The Middle and Late Bronze Age Strata in Area R,* Jerusalem 2007, 390–547.

MURRAY, A.S., *Handbook of Greek Archaeology,* London 1892.

MURRAY, A.S., SMITH, A.H., WALTERS, H.B., *Excavations in Cyprus,* London 1900.

MYRES, J.L., Excavations in Cyprus, 1894, *JHS* 17, 1897, 134–173.

– *Handbook of the Cessnola Collection of Antiquities from Cyprus,* New York, 1914.

NAVILLE, E., *The Shrine of Saft el-Henneh and the Land of Goshen,* London 1887.

– *The Mound of the Jew,* London 1890.

NEGBI, O., Cypriote Imitations of Tell el-Yahudiyeh Ware from Toumba Tou Skoura, *AJA* 82, 1978, 137–149.

NIGRO, L., The MB Pottery Horizon of Tell Mardikh/Ancient Ebla, in: M. BIETAK (ED.), *The Middle Bronze Age in the Levant,* Contributions to the Chronology of the Eastern Mediterranean 3, Vienna 2002, 297–328.

– The Smith and the King of Ebla. Tell el-Yahudiyeh ware, Metallic Wares and the Ceramic technology of Middle

Bronze Syria, in: M. Bietak (ed.), *The Synchronisation of Civilisations in the Eastern Mediterranean in the Second Millennium II*, Contributions to the Chronology of the Eastern Mediterranean 4, Vienna 2003, 345–363.

Oren, E.D., Cypriot Imports in the Palestinian Late Bronze I Context, *Opuscula Atheniensia* 9, 1969,

– A Middle Bronze I Warrior Tomb at Beth-Shan, *Zeitschrift des Deutschen Palästina-Vereins* 87, 109–139.

– *The Northern Cemetery of Beth Shan*, Philadelphia and Leiden.

– The "Kingdom of Sharuhen" and the Hyksos Kingdom, in: E.D. Oren (ed.), *The Hyksos, New Historical and Archaeological Perspectives*, University Museum Monograph 96, Philadelphia 253–283.

Orni, E., and Efrat, E., *Geography of Israel.* 3rd ed., Jerusalem 1980.

Ory, J., Excavations at Ras el 'Ain, *QDAP* 5, 1936, 111–112.

– Excavations at Ras el-Ain II, *QDAP* 6, 1937, 99–120.

– A Middle Bronze Age Tomb at El-Jisr, *QDAP* 12, 1946, 31–42.

– A Bronze Age Cemetery at Dhahrat el-Humraiya, *QDAP* 13, 1948, 75–89.

Otto, H., Studien zur Keramik der mittleren Bronzezeit in Palästina, *ZDMG* 61, 1938, 147–276.

Ownby, M., *Canaanite Jars from Memphis as Evidence for Trade and Political Relationships in the Middle Bronze Age*, unpublished Ph.D. thesis, University of Cambridge, 2010.

Ownby, M., and Bourriau, J., The movement of Middle Bronze Age transport jars: a provenance study based on petrographic and chemical analysis of Canaanite jars from Memphis, Egypt, in: P. Quinn (ed.), *Interpreting Silent Artefacts: Petrographic Approaches to Archaeological Ceramics*, Oxford 2009, 173–188.

Payne, J., Ashmolean Museum. Bomford Appeal Acquisition, 1971, *Burlington Magazine* June 1972, 399.

Peet, T.E., *The Cemeteries of Abydos II*, EEF Excavation Memoire 34, London 1913.

Peet, T.E. and Loat, W.L.S, *The Cemeteries of Abydos III*, EEF Excavation Memoire 35, London 1914.

Perlman, I. and Asaro, F., Pottery Analysis by Neutron Activation, *Archaeometry* 11, 1969, 21–52.

Perrot, J., Nouvelles découvertes en Israël, *Syria* 29, 1952, 294–306.

Petrie, W.M.F., The Egyptian Bases of Greek History, *JHS* 11, 1890, 271–277.

– *Kahun, Gurob and Hawara*, London 1890.

– *Illahun, Kahun and Gurob*, London 1891.

– *Diospolis Parva, The Cemeteries of Abadiyeh and Hu*, EEF Excavation Memoire 20, London 1901.

– *Hyksos and Israelite Cities*, BSAE 12, London 1906.

– *Gizeh and Rifeh*, BSAE 13, London 1907.

– *Qurneh*, BSAE 15, London 1909.

– *Ancient Gaza I*, BSAE 53, London 1930.

– *Ancient Gaza II*, BSAE 54, London 1932.

– *Ancient Gaza III*, BSAE 55, London 1933.

– *Ancient Gaza IV*, BSAE 56 London 1934.

– *City of Shepherd Kings*, BSAE 64, London 1952.

Petrie, W.M.F. and Brunton, G., *Sedment II*, BSAE 35, London 1924.

Pézard, M., *Qadesh: Mission archéologique à Tell Nebi Mend*, Paris 1931.

Phytian-Adams, W.J., Report on the Stratification of Askalon, *Palestine Exploration Fund Quarterly Statement* 55, 1923, 60–84.

Porat, N., Wintle, A.G., Ritte, M., Mode and timing of kurkar and hamra formation, central coastal plain, Israel, *Israel Journal of Earth Sciences* 53, 2004, 13–25.

Posener, G., Les Asiatiques en Égypte sous les XIIe et XIIIe dynasties, *Syria* 34 (1957), 145–163.

Prag, K., A Tell el-Yahudiyeh Style Vase in the Manchester Museum, *Levant* 5, 1973, 128–131.

– A Tell el-Yahudiyeh Ware Fish Vase: An Additional Note, *Levant* 6, 1974, 192.

Pritchard, J.B., The Bronze Age Cemetery at *Gibeon*, Philadelphia 1963.

– *Ancient Near Eastern Texts Relating to the Old Testament.* 3rd edition with supplement, Princeton 1969.

Quirke, S.G.J., *The administration of Egypt in the Late Middle Kingdom: The Hieratic Documents*, Malden 1990.

Randall-MacIver, D., and Mace, A.C, *El Amrah and Abydos 1899–1901*, London 1902.

Randall-MacIver, D., and Woolle,y C.L., *Buhen*, Philadelphia 1911.

Redford, D.B., Mendes & Environs in the Middle Kingdom, in P. der Manuelian (ed.), *Studies in Honor of William Kelly Simpson* II, Boston 1996, 680–682.

– *Egypt, Canaan, and Israel in Ancient Times.* Princeton, 1992.

Redmount, C.A., *On an Egyptian/Asiatic Frontier: An Archaeological History of the Wadi Tumilat*, unpublished Ph.D. thesis, University of Chicago 1989.

– Pots and Peoples in the Egyptian Delta: Tell el-Maskhuta and the Hyksos, *JMA* 8.2, 1995, 61–89.

Reisner, G.A., Excavations at Kerma – Hepzefa, Prince of Assiut and Governor of the Sudan, *BMFA* 13 no. 80, Dec. 1915, 73–83.

– *Excavations at Kerma IV-V*, Cambridge Mass., 1923.

Rowe, A., *The Topography and History of Beth-Shan*, Palestine Section of the University Museum, vol. I. Philadelphia 1930.

– *The Four Canaanite Temples of Beth-Shan, Part I: The Temples and Cult Objects*, Palestine Section of the University Museum, vol. II. Philadelphia 1940.

Salame-Sarkis, H., Chronique archéologique du Liban-Nord. II: 1973–1974, *Bulletin du Musée de Beyrouth* 26, 1973, 91–102.

Saller, S.J, *Excavations at Bethany*, Jerusalem 1957.

Save-Söderbergh, T., *Ägypten und Nubien*, Lund 1941.

– The Hyksos Rule in Egypt, *JEA* 37, 1951, 53–71.

SCHAEFFER, C.F.A, Les fouilles de Minet el-Beida et de Ras Shamra. Quatrième campagne (1932). Rapport sommaire, *Syria* 14, 1933, 93–127.

– *Missions en Chypre*, Paris 1936.

– Les fouilles de Ras Shamra-Ugarit. Neuvième campagne (1937). Rapport sommaire, *Syria* 19, 1938, 213–344.

– *Ugaritica* I, *Études relatives aux découvertes de Ras Shamra*, Mission de Ras Shamra Tome III, Paris 1939.

– Corpus céramique de Ras-Shamra, in: C.F.A. SCHAEFFER, *Ugaritica II*, Paris 131–301.

SCHNEIDER, T., 1998, *Ausländer in Ägypten während des Mittleren Reiches und der Hyksoszeit. Die ausländischen Könige*, ÄAT 42/1, Wiesbaden 1998.

– *Ausländer in Ägypten während des Mittleren Reiches und der Hyksoszeit. Die ausländische Bevölkerung*, ÄAT 42/2, Wiesbaden 2003.

SCHIESTL, R., *Tell el-Dabᶜa XVIII. Die Palastnekropole von Tell el-Dabᶜa. Die Gräber des Areals F/I der Straten d/2 und d/1*, Vienna 2009.

SEIDEL, M., Gefäß in Form einer Fliege in: A. EGGEBRECHT (ed.), *Pelizaeus Museum, Hildesheim*, Mainz 1993, 49 no. 40.

SELLIN, E., *Tell Taᶜanek*, Vienna 1904.

SELLIN, E., and WATZINGER, C., *Jericho*, Leipzig 1913.

SERPICO, M., BOURRIAU, J., SMITH, L., GOREN, Y., STERN, B., HERON, C., Commodities and Containers: A Project to Study Canaanite Amphorae Imported into Egypt during the New Kingdom, in: M. BIETAK (ed.), *The Synchronization of Civilizations in the Eastern Mediterranean in the Second Millennium B.C. II*, Contributions to the Chronology of the Eastern Mediterranean 4, Vienna 2003, 365–376.

SHIPTON, G.M., *Notes on the Megiddo Pottery of Strata VI–XX*, Chicago 1939.

SIMONS, J., *Handbook for the Study of Egyptian Topographical Lists Relating to Western Asia*, Leiden 1937.

SLIWA, J., Die Siedlung des Mittleren Reiches bei Qasr el-Sagha, Grabungsbericht 1987 und 1988, *MDAIK* 48, 1992, 177–191.

SMITH, R.H., *Pella of the Decapolis. Volume I: The 1967 Season of the College of Wooster Expedition to Pella*, London 1973.

SMITH, W.S., *Interconnections in the Ancient Near East*, New Haven 1965.

– *The Art and Architecture of Ancient Egypt*, Baltimore 1965.

SNEH, A., BARTOV, Y., ROSENSAFT, M., *Geological Map of Israel, 1:200,000, Sheet 1*, Jerusalem 1988.

– *Geological Map of Israel, 1:200,000, Sheet 2*, Jerusalem 1988.

STAGER, L.E., The MBIIA Ceramic Sequence at Tel Ashkelon and its implications for the "Port Power" Model of Trade in: M. BIETAK (ed.), *The Middle Bronze Age in the Levant*, Contributions to the Chronology of the Eastern Mediterranean 3, Vienna 2002, 353–362.

– The House of the Silver Calf of Ashkelon, in: E. CERNY, I. HEIN, H. HUNGER, D. MELMANN, A. SCHWAB (eds.), *Timelines. Studies in Honour of Manfred Bietak*, II, OLA 149.2, Leuven 2006, 403–410.

STAGER, L.E., SCHLOEN, J., MASTER, D., PRESS, M., AJA, A., Part Four: Stratigraphic Overview. in: L.E. STAGER, J. SCHLOEN, and D. MASTER (eds.), *Ashkelon I: Introduction and Overview (1985–2006)*, Harvard Semitic Museum Publications, Final Reports of the Leon Levy Expedition to Ashkelon, Winona Lake 2008, 212–323.

STEINDORFF, G., *Aniba* I–II, Hamburg, 1937.

SUKENIK, E.L., Archaeological Investigation at ᶜAffula, *Journal of the Palestine Oriental Society* 41, 1948, 1–79.

TARAQJI, A.F., Tell Sakka, *Syria* 70, 1993, 453–56.

– Nouvelles découvertes sur les relations avec l'Égypte à Tel Sakka et à Keswé dans la region de Damas, *BSFE* 144, 1999, 27–43.

THALMANN, J.P., *Tell Arqa – I. Les niveaux de l'âge de Bronze*, Bibliothèque archéologique et historique 177, Beyrouth 2006.

– Tell Arqa et Byblos, Essai de correlation, in: M. BIETAK and E. CZERNY (eds.), *The Bronze Age in the Lebanon. Studies on the Archaeology and Chronology of Lebanon, Syria, and Egypt*, Contributions to the Chronology of the Eastern Mediterranean 17, Vienna 2008, 61–78.

TUFNELL, O., *Lachish IV. The Bronze Age*, London 1958.

VAN SETERS, J, *The Hyksos: A New Investigation*, New Haven 1966.

VERCOUTTER, J., Excavations at Mirgissa II, *Kush* 13, 1965, 62–73.

– Mirgissa II, Les Nécropoles, Paris 1975.

VERMEULE, E., *Toumba tou Skourou. The Mound of Darkness: A Bronze Age Town on Morphou Bay, Cyprus*, Boston, 1974.

VON DER OSTEN, H.H., *Svenska Syrienexpedition I: die Grabung von Tell es-Salihiyeh*, Lund 1956.

VOSS, R.J., A Sequence of Four Middle Bronze Gates in Ashkelon, in: M. BIETAK (ed.), *The Middle Bronze Age in the Levant. Proceedings of an International Conference on MB IIA Ceramic Material, Vienna 24th–26th of January 2001*, Contributions to the Chronology of the Eastern Mediterranean 3, Vienna 2002, 379–384.

WALMSLEY, A.G., MACUMBER, P.G., EDWARDS, P.C., BOURKE, S.J., WATSON, P.M., The Eleventh and Twelfth Seasons of Excavations at Pella (Tabaqat Fahl) 1989–1990, *Annual of the Department of Antiquities of Jordan* 37, 1993, 165–240.

WARD, W.A., and DEVER, W.G., *Studies on Scarab Seals III: Scarab Typology and Archaeological Context: An Essay on Middle Bronze Age Chronology*, San Antonio, 1994.

WEIGALL, A.E.P., Upper Egyptian Notes, *ASAE* 9, 1908, 105–112.

WEINSTEIN, J., Review of R.S. Merrillees, Trade and Transcendance in the Bronze Age Levant, *JARCE* 14, 1977, 111–114.

WELCH, F.B., The Influence of the Aegean Civilisation on South Palestine, *ABSA* 6, 1900, 117–24.

WESTHOLM, A., Some Late Cypriote Tombs at Milia, *QDAP* 8, 1939, 1–20.

WILLIAMS, B.B., Archaeology and Historical Problems of the Second Intermediate Period, unpublished Ph.D Dissertation, University of Chicago 1975.

WINKLER, E.M. and WILFING, H., *Tell el-Dabᶜa VI, Anthropologische Untersuchungen an den Skelettresten der Kampagnen 1966–1969, 1975–1980, 1985*, Vienna 1991.

WINLOCK, H.E., The Museum's excavations at Thebes, *BMMA* 18, 1923, 11–23.

WRIGHT, G.E., The Four Canaanite temples of Beth-Shan, Part I, by A. Rowe, *American Journal of Archaeology* 45, 1941, 483–85.

YADIN, Y., AHARONI Y., AMIRAN, R., DOTHAN, T., DUNAYEVSKY, I., PERROT, J., *Hazor I. An Account of the First Season of Excavations 1955*, Jerusalem 1958.

YADIN, Y. and GEVA, S., *Investigations at Beth Shean, the Early Iron Age Strata*, Qedem 23. Monographs of the Institute of Archaeology, Jerusalem 1986.

YANNI E., A Late Bronze Age Tomb at Jatt, *ᶜAtiqot* 40, 2000, 49–82.

YELLIN J., Provenance of Selected LBA and MBA Pottery from Tel Mevorakh by Instrumental Neutron Activation Analysis, in: *Excavations at Tel Mevorakh (1973–1976). Part Two: The Bronze Age*, Qedem 18. Monographs of the Institute of Archaeology, Jerusalem 1984, 87–103.

YELLIN, J., DOTHAN, T., GOULD, B., The Origin of Late Bronze White Burnished Slip Wares from Deir el-Balah, *Israel Exploration Journal* 40, 1990, 257–261.

YON, M., *Manuel de céramique chypriote I,* Lyons, 1976.

ZEVULUN, U., Tell el-Yahudiyah Juglets from a Potter's Refuse Pit at Afula, *Eretz Israel* 21, 1990, 174–190.

Index

Notes

Notes

UNTERSUCHUNGEN DER ZWEIGSTELLE KAIRO DES ÖSTERREICHISCHEN ARCHÄOLOGISCHEN INSTITUTS

Herausgegeben in Verbindung mit der Kommission für Ägypten und Levante der Österreichischen Akademie der Wissenschaften von MANFRED BIETAK

Band I — MANFRED BIETAK, *Tell el-Dab^ca II. Der Fundort im Rahmen einer archäologisch-geographischen Untersuchung über das ägyptische Ostdelta.* Wien 1975.

Band II — LABIB HABACHI, *Tell el-Dab^ca and Qantir I. The Site and its Connection with Avaris and Piramesse.* Aus dem Nachlaß herausgegeben von EVA MARIA ENGEL. Unter Mitarbeit von PETER JÁNOSI und CHRISTA MLINAR. Wien 2001.

Band III — JOACHIM BOESSNECK, *Tell el-Dab^ca III. Die Tierknochenfunde 1966–1969.* Wien 1976.

Band IV — MANFRED BIETAK und ELFRIEDE REISER-HASLAUER, *Das Grab des ^cAnch-Hor, Obersthofmeister der Gottesgemahlin Nitokris* (mit einem Beitrag von ERHART GRAEFE). Wien 1978.

Band V — MANFRED BIETAK und ELFRIEDE REISER-HASLAUER, *Das Grab des ^cAnch-Hor, Obersthofmeister der Gottesgemahlin Nitokris. Teil II* (mit Beiträgen von JOACHIM BOESSNECK, ANGELA VON DEN DRIESCH, JAN QAEGEBEUR, HELGA LIESE–KLEIBER und HELMUT SCHLICHTHERLE). Wien 1982.

Band VI — DIETHELM EIGNER, *Die monumentalen Grabbauten der Spätzeit in der Thebanischen Nekropole* (mit einem Beitrag von JOSEF DORNER). Wien 1984.

Band VII — MANFRED BIETAK, *Tell el-Dab^ca IV. Stratigraphie und Chronologie* (in Vorbereitung).

Band VIII — MANFRED BIETAK, unter Mitarbeit von CHRISTA MLINAR und ANGELA SCHWAB, *Tell el-Dab^ca V. Ein Friedhofsbezirk der Mittleren Bronzezeit mit Totentempel und Siedlungsschichten.* Wien 1991.

Band IX — EIKE M. WINKLER und HARALD WILFLING, *Tell el-Dab^ca VI. Anthropologische Untersuchungen an den Skelettresten der Kampagnen 1966–69, 1975–80, 1985.* Wien 1991.

Band X — JOACHIM BOESSNECK und ANGELA VON DEN DRIESCH, *Tell el-Dab^ca VII. Tiere und historische Umwelt im Nordost-Delta im 2. Jahrtausend anhand der Knochenfunde der Ausgrabungen 1975–1986.* Wien 1992.

Band XI — KARL KROMER, *Nezlet Batran. Eine Mastaba aus dem Alten Reich bei Giseh (Ägypten). Österreichische Ausgrabungen 1981–1983.* Wien 1991.

Band XII — DAVID A. ASTON, MANFRED BIETAK, *Tell el-Dab^ca VIII. The Classification and Chronology of Tell el-Yahudiya Ware.* With contributions by Aren Maeir, Robert Mullins, Lawrence E. Stager, Ross Voss, Hanan Charaf and Mary Ownby. Ausgrabungen in Tell el-Dab^ca, Manfred Bietak (Hrsg.). Wien 2012.

Band XIII — PETER JÁNOSI, *Die Pyramidenanlagen der Königinnen. Untersuchungen zu einem Grabtyp des Alten und Mittleren Reiches.* Wien 1996.

Band XIV — MANFRED BIETAK (Hrg.), *Haus und Palast im Alten Ägypten. Internationales Symposium 8. bis 11. April 1992 in Kairo.* Wien 1996.

Band XV — ERNST CZERNY, *Tell el-Dab^ca IX. Eine Plansiedlung des frühen Mittleren Reiches.* Wien 1999.

Band XVI — PERLA FUSCALDO, *Tell el-Dab^ca X. The Palace District of Avaris, The Pottery of the Hyksos Period and the New Kingdom (Areas H/III and H/VI), Part I. Locus 66.* Wien 2000.

Band XVII — SUSANNA CONSTANZE HEINZ, *Die Feldzugsdarstellungen des Neuen Reiches – Eine Bildanalyse.* Wien 2001.

Band XVIII — MANFRED BIETAK (Ed.), *Archaische Griechische Tempel und Altägypten, Internationales Kolloquium am 28. November 1997 im Institut für Ägyptologie der Universität Wien.* Mit Beiträgen von DIETER ARNOLD, ANTON BAMMER, ELISABETH GEBHARD, GERHARD HAENY, HERMANN KIENAST, NANNO MARINATOS, ERIK ØSTBY und ULRICH SINN, Wien 2001.

Band XIX — BETTINA BADER, *Tell el-Dab^ca XIII. Typologie und Chronologie der Mergel C-Ton Keramik. Materialien zum Binnenhandel des Mittleren Reiches und der zweiten Zwischenzeit.* Wien 2001.

Band XX — MANFRED BIETAK und MARIO SCHWARZ (Eds.), *Krieg und Sieg. Narrative Wanddarstellungen von Altägypten bis ins Mittelalter, Interdisziplinäres Kolloquium, 29.–30. Juli 1997 im Schloß Haindorf, Langenlois.* Wien 2002.

Band XXI — IRMGARD HEIN und PETER JÁNOSI, *Tell el-Dab^ca XI, Areal A/V, Siedlungsrelikte der späten Hyksoszeit.* Mit Beiträgen von K. KOPETZKY, L.C. MAGUIRE, C. MLINAR, G. PHILIP, A. TILLMANN, U. THANHEISER, K. GROSSCHMIDT. Wien 2004.

Band XXII — NADIA EL-SHOHOUMI, *Der Tod im Leben. Eine vergleichende Analyse altägyptischer und rezenter ägyptischer Totenbräuche. Eine phänomenologische Studie.* Wien 2004.

Band XXIII — DAVID ASTON in collaboration with MANFRED BIETAK, and with the assistance of BETTINA BADER, IRENE FORSTNER-MÜLLER and ROBERT SCHIESTL, *Tell el-Dab^ca XII. A Corpus of Late Middle Kingdom and Second Intermediate Period Pottery.* Volume I: Text; Volume II: Plates Wien 2004.

VERLAG DER ÖSTERREICHISCHEN AKADEMIE DER WISSENSCHAFTEN

Band XXIV PETER JÁNOSI, *Giza in der 4. Dynastie. Die Baugeschichte und Belegung einer Nekropole des Alten Reiches, Band I, Die Mastabas der Kernfriedhöfe und die Felsgräber.* Wien 2005.

Band XXV PETER JÁNOSI (Ed.), *Structure and Significance. Thoughts on Ancient Egyptian Architecture.* Wien 2005.

Band XXVI GRAHAM PHILIP, *Tell el-Dabᶜa XV. Metalwork and Metalworking Evidence of the Late Middle Kingdom and the Second Intermediate Period.* Wien 2006.

Band XXVII MANFRED BIETAK, NANNÓ MARINATOS and CLAIRY PALIVOU, *Taureador Scenes in Tell el Dabᶜa (Avaris) and Knossos* (with a contribution by Ann Brysbaert). Wien 2007.

Band XXVIII IRENE FORSTNER-MÜLLER, *Tell el-Dabᶜa XVI. Die Gräber des Areals A/II von Tell el-Dabᶜa.* Ausgrabungen in Tell el-Dabᶜa, Manfred Bietak (Hrsg.). Wien 2008.

Band XXIX VERA MÜLLER, *Tell el-Dabᶜa XVII. Opferdeponierungen in der Hyksoshauptstadt Auaris (Tell el-Dabᶜa) vom späten Mittleren Reich bis zum frühen Neuen Reich. Teil I: Katalog der Befunde und Funde; Teil II: Auswertung und Deutung der Befunde und Funde.* Ausgrabungen in Tell el-Dabᶜa, Manfred Bietak (Hrsg.). Wien 2008.

Band XXX ROBERT SCHIESTL, *Tell el-Dabᶜa XVIII. Die Palastnekropole von Tell el-Dabᶜa. Die Gräber des Areals F/I der Straten d/2 und d/1.* Ausgrabungen in Tell el-Dabᶜa, Manfred Bietak (Hrsg.). Wien 2009.

Band XXXI BETTINA BADER, *Tell el-Dabᶜa XIX. Auaris und Memphis im Mittleren Reich und in der Hyksoszeit. Vergleichsanalyse der materiellen Kultur.* Ausgrabungen in Tell el-Dabᶜa, Manfred Bietak (Hrsg.). Wien 2009.

Band XXXII KARIN KOPETZKY, *Tell el-Dabᶜa XX. Die Chronologie der Siedlungskeramik der Zweiten Zwischenzeit aus Tell el- Dabᶜa. Teil I: Auswertung und Datierung; Teil II: Abbildungen und Tabellen.* Ausgrabungen in Tell el-Dabᶜa, Manfred Bietak (Hrsg.). Wien 2010.

Band XXXIII LOUISE C. MAGUIRE, *Tell el-Dabᶜa XXI. The Cypriot Pottery and its Circulation in the Levant.* Ausgrabungen in Tell el-Dabᶜa, Manfred Bietak (Hrsg.). Wien 2009.

Band XXXIV JULIA BUDKA, *Bestattungsbrauchtum und Friedhofsstruktur im Asasif. Eine Untersuchung der spätzeitlichen Befunde anhand der Ergebnisse der österreichischen Ausgrabungen in den Jahren 1969–1977, Band I: Topographie, Architektur und Funde.* Wien 2010.

Band XXXV M. BIETAK, E. CZERNY, I. FORSTNER-MÜLLER (Eds.), *Cities and Urbanism in Ancient Egypt. Papers from a Workshop in November 2006 at the Austrian Academy of Sciences.* Wien 2010.

Band XXXVI PERLA FUSCALDO, *Tell el-Dabᶜa X/2. The Palace District of Avaris. The Pottery of the Hyksos Period and the New Kingdom (Areas H/III and H/VI), Part II: Two execration Pits and a Foundation Deposit.* Wien 2010.

forthcoming ERNST CZERNY, *Tell el-Dabᶜa XXII. „Der Mund der beiden Wege". Die Siedlung und der Tempelbezirk des Mittleren Reiches von Ezbet Ruschdi.* Ausgrabungen in Tell el-Dabᶜa, Manfred Bietak (Hrsg.).

forthcoming TINE BAGH, *Tell el-Dabᶜa XXIII. Levantine Painted Ware from Egypt and the Levant.*

CONTRIBUTIONS TO THE ARCHAEOLOGY OF EGYPT & THE LEVANT

Herausgegeben von MANFRED BIETAK

forthcoming ANGELIKA LOHWASSER, *Aspekte der napatanischen Gesellschaft. Archäologisches Inventar und funeräre Praxis im Friedhof von Sanam – Perspektiven einer kulturhistorischen Interpretation.*

VERLAG DER ÖSTERREICHISCHEN AKADEMIE DER WISSENSCHAFTEN

CONTRIBUTIONS TO THE CHRONOLOGY OF THE EASTERN MEDITERRANEAN

Edited by MANFRED BIETAK and HERMANN HUNGER

VERLAG DER ÖSTERREICHISCHEN AKADEMIE DER WISSENSCHAFTEN

Volume XXV	Francis Breyer, *Ägypten und Anatolien. Politische, kulturelle und sprachliche Kontakte zwischen dem Niltal und Kleinasien im 2. Jahrtausend v. Chr.* Vienna 2010.
Volume XXVI	Aren Maeir, *In the Midst of the Jordan (Jos 4:10): The Jordan Valley During the Middle Bronze Age (circa 2000–1500 BCE) – Archaeological and Historical Correlates.* Vienna 2010.
Volume XXVII	Walter Gauss, Evangelia Kiriatzi, *Pottery Production and Supply at Bronze Age Kolonna, Aegina: An Integrated Archaeological and Scientific Study of a Ceramic Landscap.* With contributions by Myrto Georgakopoulou, Areti Pentedeka, Bartlomiej Lis, Ian K. Whitbread, Yiannis Iliopoulos, Ägina Kolonna, Forschungen und Ergebnisse 5. Vienna 2011.
forthcoming	Robert Schiestl, Anne Seiler (eds.), *Handbook of the Pottery of the Egyptian Middle Kingdom* Volume I: *The Corpus Volume,* Volume II: *The Regional Volume.*
forthcoming	Gudrun Klebinder-Gauss, *Keramik aus klassischen Kontexten im Apollon-Heiligtum von Ägina-Kolonna. Lokale Produktion und Importe,* Ägina Kolonna, Forschungen und Ergebnisse 6.
forthcoming	Louise C. Maguire, *Painting Practices in White Painted and White Slip Wares.*
forthcoming	Celia Bergoffen, *Late Cypriot Pottery in Southern Canaan.*
forthcoming	Kathryn O. Eriksson, *Cypriot Bronze Age White Painted V and VI Wares. Problems of Chronology and First Appearances.*
forthcoming	Irmgard Hein, *Craftsmanship in Red and Black: The Manual of Cypriot Bichrome Wheelmade Ware.*
forthcoming	Katharina Pruckner, *Äginetische Keramik der Schachtgräberzeit. Bichrom und vollständig bemalte Keramik aus dem Brunnen SH B1/06 in Ägina Kolonna,* Ägina Kolonna, Forschungen und Ergebnisse 7.
forthcoming	Felix Höflmayer, *Die Synchronisierung der minoischen Alt- und Neupalastzeit mit der ägyptischen Chronologie.*

BERICHTE DES ÖSTERREICHISCHEN NATIONALKOMITEES DER UNESCO-AKTION FÜR DIE RETTUNG DER NUBISCHEN ALTERTÜMER

Herausgegeben von der Kommission für Ägypten und Levante der Österreichischen Akademie der Wissenschaften durch Manfred Bietak

Band I	Manfred Bietak und Reinhold Engelmayer, *Eine frühdynastische Abri-Siedlung mit Felsbildern aus Sayala – Nubien.* Wien 1963. Österreichische Akademie der Wissenschaften, Phil.-hist. Klasse, Denkschriften, Bd. 82.
Band II	Reinhold Engelmayer, *Die Felsgravierungen im Distrikt Sayala – Nubien. Teil I: Die Schiffsdarstellungen.* Wien 1965. Denkschriften, Bd. 90.
Band III	Manfred Bietak, *Ausgrabungen in Sayala – Nubien 1961–1965. Denkmäler der C-Gruppe und der Pan-Gräber-Kultur* (mit Beiträgen von Kurt Bauer, Karl W. Butzer, Wilherlm Ehgartner und Johann Jungwirth). Wien 1966. Denkschriften, Bd. 92.
Band IV	Karl Kromer, *Römische Weinstuben in Sayala (Unternubien).* Wien 1967. Denkschriften, Bd. 95.
Band V	Manfred Bietak, *Studien zur Chronologie der nubischen C-Gruppe. Ein Beitrag zur Frühgeschichte Unternubiens zwischen 2200 und 1550 v. Chr.* Wien 1968. Denkschriften, Bd. 97.
Band VI	Fathi Afifi Bedawi, *Die römischen Gräberfelder von Sayala Nubien.* Wien 1976s. Denkschriften, Bd. 126.
Band VII	Eugen Strouhal und Johann Jungwirth, *Die anthropologische Untersuchung der C-Gruppen- und Pan-Gräber-Skelette aus Sayala, Ägyptisch-Nubien.* Wien 1984. Denkschriften, Bd. 176.
Band VIII	Manfred Bietak und Mario Schwarz, *Nag^{c} el-Scheima, eine befestigte christliche Siedlung, und andere christliche Denkmäler in Sayala – Nubien.* Wien 1987. Denkschriften, Bd. 191.
Band IX	Manfred Bietak und Mario Schwarz, *Nag^{c} el-Scheima. Teil II. Die Grabungsergebnisse aus der Sicht neuerer Forschungen.* Wien 1998. Denkschriften, Bd. 255.

In Vorbereitung:

Eugen Strouhal und Erich Neuwirth, *Die anthropologische Untersuchung der spätrömischen-frühbyzantinischen Skelette aus Sayala, Ägyptisch-Nubien.*

Eugen Strouhal und Erich Neuwirth, *Die anthropologische Untersuchung der christlichen Skelette aus Sayala, Ägyptisch-Nubien.*

VERLAG DER ÖSTERREICHISCHEN AKADEMIE DER WISSENSCHAFTEN